Revit® Essentials for Architecture

covers Version 2021 and beyond

by: Paul F. Aubin

with Foreword by: Harlan Brumm

G3B PRESS

The Aubin Academy

Revit® Essentials for Architecture

covers Version 2021 and beyond

By: Paul F. Aubin

© 2020 Paul F. Aubin

ALL RIGHTS RESERVED. No part of this work covered by the copyright herein may be reproduced, transmitted stored or used in any form or by any means graphic, electronic, or mechanical including but not limited to photocopying, recording, scanning, digitizing, taping, Web distribution, information networks, or information storage and retrieval systems, except as permitted under Section 107 or 108 of the 1976 United States Copyright Act, without the prior written permission of the publisher.

Autodesk, the Autodesk logo, AutoCAD, Autodesk® AEC Collection, Autodesk® Navisworks®, Autodesk® Revit® and Autodesk® Revit LT™, are registered trademarks or trademarks of Autodesk, Inc., and/or its subsidiaries and/or affiliates in the USA and/or other countries.

ISBN-13 print: 978-0-578-73106-3

G3B Press
c/o Paul F. Aubin Consulting Services, Inc.
P.O. Box 223
Oak Lawn, IL 60454
USA

To learn more about titles by G3B Press, the book's author and other offerings by Paul F Aubin Consulting Services, Inc. please visit: **paulaubin.com**. Updates are posted to the articles section of the site. Please use Contact page to send email to the author.

Notice to the Reader

Publisher does not warrant or guarantee any of the products described herein or perform any independent analysis in connection with any of the product information contained herein. Publisher does not assume, and expressly disclaims, any obligation to obtain and include information other than that provided to it by the manufacturer. The reader is expressly warned to consider and adopt all safety precautions that might be indicated by the activities described herein and to avoid all potential hazards. By following the instructions contained herein, the reader willingly assumes all risks in connection with such instructions. The publisher makes no representations or warranties of any kind, including but not limited to, the warranties of fitness for particular purpose or merchantability, nor are any such representations implied with respect to the material set forth herein, and the publisher takes no responsibility with respect to such material. The publisher shall not be liable for any special, consequential, or exemplary damages resulting, in whole or part, from the readers' use of, or reliance upon, this material.

This book is independent of Autodesk, Inc., and is not authorized by, endorsed by, sponsored by, affiliated with, or otherwise approved by Autodesk, Inc. The views expressed herein are solely those of the authors/presenters and are not those of Autodesk, Inc., its officers, directors, subsidiaries, affiliates, business partners, or customers.

Disclosure: This book contains links to external resources by the same author. Those may contain affiliate links and the author will be compensated if you make a purchase after clicking on the included links.[†]

• The Aubin Academy •

Contents

Foreword	v
Preface	vii
Section I: Introduction and Methodology	1
Chapter 1: Quick Start Overview	3
Chapter 2: Conceptual Underpinnings of Revit	39
Chapter 3: Revit User Interface	63
Section II: Creating the Building Model	85
Chapter 4: Creating a Building Layout	87
Chapter 5: Setting Up Project Levels and Views	147
Chapter 6: Column Grids and Structural Layout	205
Chapter 7: Groups and Links	249
Chapter 8: Vertical Circulation	301
Chapter 9: Floors and Roofs	361
Chapter 10: Developing the Exterior Skin	405
Chapter 11: Families and the Family Editor	463
Section III: Construction Documents	547
Chapter 12: Detailing and Annotation	549
Chapter 13: Working with Schedules, Tags and Data	595
Chapter 14: Ceiling Plans and Interior Elevations	647
Chapter 15: Printing and Output	669
Chapter 16: Worksharing	681
Section IV: Conceptual Massing and Rendering	707
Chapter 17: Conceptual Massing	709
Chapter 18: Rendering and Presentation	755
Appendix	779
Endnotes	779
Index	781

• Revit Essentials for Architecture •

• The Aubin Academy •

Foreword

Teaching has always been a passion of mine. I started teaching AutoCAD in high school – taking over an entire class of high school kids from the actual teacher (not sure that was a great idea on his part). One summer, as a side gig, I taught architects and engineers for a reseller. It is one of the main reasons I joined Autodesk. The chance to support customers and teach them new ways of use technology was too good to pass up.

13 years ago, very early in my career at Autodesk, I had the opportunity to meet Paul at my first Autodesk University in Las Vegas. Even then, Paul was considered a first-rate instructor. I remember how awesome it felt to attend one of his classes and get the chance to learn from him, see him present and engage with the attendees, and experience a true master at work. Seeing how he could motivate, teach complex topics, and handle difficult questions was eye opening. It inspired me to be better and work harder so I could stand next to Paul.

Over the years, I have gotten a chance to call Paul a friend. He is not just a great speaker, book author, and teacher, but also person and family man. To this day, I am grateful for the opportunity to work with him.

When he asked me to write this forward, there was no hesitation at all. I knew instantly that this updated book would be thorough, honest, and tell you the facts, information, and insights you need to be successful with Revit.

As the Product Manager for Architecture at Autodesk, I get to see a lot content, a lot of books, videos, blogs posts, forums posts, that get written and shared every day. Not all content is created equal. It takes time and effort to test, check, and validate the best ways to complete tasks and workflows. Paul does that. He spends the time needed to truly understand the subject. He asks the right questions and is always looking to further his knowledge so that he can help you be better. He also practices what he preaches – he puts his suggestions into practice with clients and projects around the world. He tells you the facts: the good, the bad, and even the ugly.

Learning Revit is not just about learning a new piece of software. It requires learning a new process and adopting new ways of thinking about architecture practice and design. BIM does not just result in a 3D model and more coordinated documents; it can take you down a path of delivering better buildings for your clients and even for the world. It is not for the faint of heart to go down this path. You need strength of conviction and a will to take on the challenge. It will challenge you - and you will need to learn to think differently about how you design buildings. The payoff is worth the effort.

In this book, Paul shows you how to use Revit to be successful on any BIM project. Even more importantly, he shares the methods, workflows, and best practices that help you along your BIM journey to deliver the best building projects you can. Paul's Architecture and teaching experience means that you will learn how to use Revit for Architecture in the best possible ways and make clear the context and reasons why his recommendations will lead to optimal outcomes. Learning Revit is more than just following tutorials and learning picks and clicks, but also the rationale behind the ways of working. Paul helps you understand the concepts and practices just as much as the tools and functionality.

There is no doubt that this book will be an amazing reference along your journey with Revit and your first BIM projects. Paul's advice will help you while you hold this book in your hands, but it will also stick with you long after you put it down as well.

Since my early days with the Revit team, Paul's books and classes were always the first ones I recommended to new learners of Revit and BIM. That is no different today. There is simply no one more suited to the task. Learning Revit is worth the investment and there is no better teacher than Paul.

Harlan Brumm

Senior Product Manager – Architecture, Autodesk

Preface

WELCOME

Within the pages of this book you will find a comprehensive introduction to the methods, philosophy, and procedures of the Autodesk® Revit® software and its use for architecture. Revit is an advanced and powerful building design and documentation software package. By following the detailed tutorials contained in this book, you will become immersed in its workings and functionality.

WHO SHOULD READ THIS BOOK?

The primary audience for this book is users new to Revit. However, it is also appropriate for existing Revit users who wish to expand their knowledge. Revit includes tools for most major building design disciplines including: Architecture, Structure, and MEP. There are also tools tailored toward Construction, Fabrication and site work. Folks in the Interiors and Landscape Architecture disciplines also find success using Revit. Revit ships as a stand-alone package or as part of a collection. The functionality of Revit is the same in both offerings. There is also a limited version called: Autodesk® Revit® LT. This book focuses on the architectural features of Revit. If you are a practitioner of another discipline, you can still find value in these pages, but please keep in mind that there will be very limited coverage of tools outside of the architectural tool set. You are also able to follow along in most lessons using Revit LT. However, some features covered in this book are not available in Revit LT. Those will be pointed out in the text as appropriate.

Basic knowledge of the Windows operating system and basic use of a mouse and keyboard are assumed to follow the lessons in this book. However, no prior computer-aided design software knowledge is required. If part of your job requires that you design buildings, produce architectural construction documentation, design drawings, facilities layouts, or interior design studies and documentation, then this book is intended for you. Architects, interior designers, design build professionals, facilities planners, and building industry CAD professionals will benefit from the information contained within. Prior knowledge and familiarity with architectural practice, procedures, and terminology are assumed.

FEATURES IN THIS EDITION

Revit Essentials for Architecture combines a straightforward, reader-friendly style with detailed project-focused exercises that encourage you to learn by doing. Readers will gain practical, firsthand experience with the powerful and popular Autodesk® Revit® software; purpose-built for Building Information Modeling (BIM), which industry leading architects and building design professionals are using to move beyond traditional Computer Aided Design (CAD) and drafting to manage complex projects, foster collaboration and boost productivity. With tools for early schematic design and planning, detailed design development studies and tools to create complete sets of deliverables including traditional construction document sets and digital output, Revit offers the modern architect everything they need to be successful in today's competitive market.

Within these pages you will find a concise manual focused squarely on the rationale and practicality of creating architectural projects within the BIM paradigm. The emphasis is on proven best practice procedures rather than a series of independent commands and tools. The goal of each lesson is to help readers complete building design projects successfully. You will find equal emphasis on "why" individual tools and features are used, not just "how" to perform the picks and clicks.

The text and exercises seek to give the reader a clear sense of the value of the tools, while remaining focused on practical examples from architectural practice. Revit Essentials for Architecture provides resources designed to shorten your learning curve, raise your comfort level, and, most importantly, give you real-life, tested, and practical advice on the usage of the software to create architectural Building Information Models.

Features:

- Thorough coverage of the essential skills required to use Revit to create building design projects including: modeling tools, setting up views, composing sheets, working with design options, linked files and team collaboration with worksharing.

- The author combines his extensive experience as an educator and architectural professional with a straightforward, engaging writing style, making even complex material easier for readers to master and apply to real projects.

- Practical, project-focused exercises encourage readers to "learn by doing," giving them a deeper understanding of the BIM process and the tools and techniques used to complete it.

- BIM Manager tips throughout the text offer readers practical insights on what is required to manage building information modeling in a modern architectural setting.

- Dataset files are available for download from the author's website. Files are provided for each chapter, so you can skip to just the topics you need or follow the lessons from start to finish.

- Dataset and instructions in the text are provided in both imperial and metric units.

- Check your progress by comparing your results to the completed versions provided in each chapter's downloadable dataset.

- Use the book with Autodesk® Revit®, or Autodesk® Revit® LT software.

WHAT YOU WILL FIND INSIDE

Section I of this book focuses on the underlying theory and user interface of Revit. This section is intended to get you acquainted with the software and put you in the proper mindset. Section II relies heavily on tutorial-based exercises to present the process of creating a building model in Revit, relying on the software's powerful Building Information Modeling (BIM) functionality. Two projects are developed concurrently throughout the tutorial section: one residential and one commercial. Detailed explanations are included throughout the tutorials to identify clearly why each step is employed. Annotation and other features specific to construction documentation are covered in Section III. Section IV includes coverage of the conceptual modeling features and rendering.

• The Aubin Academy •

WHAT YOU WON'T FIND INSIDE

This book is not a command reference. This book approaches the subject of learning Revit by both exposing conceptual aspects of the software and extensive tutorial coverage. No attempt is made to give a comprehensive explanation of every command or every method available to execute commands. Instead, explanations cover broad topics of how to perform various tasks in Revit, with specific examples coming from architectural practice. The focus of most of the material in this book is the design development and construction documentation phases of architectural design. Some conceptual design and presentation tools are also explored.

STYLE CONVENTIONS

Style Conventions used in this text are as follows:

Text:	Revit for Architecture
Step-by-step tutorials:	Perform these steps.
Menu picks:	**Save As > Project**
On screen input:	For the length input: **10'-0"** [**3000**].
Ribbon Tabs:	On the Architecture tab, on the Build panel, click the Wall tool
File and Directory names:	*C:\REA_8ed_I\Chapter10\Sample File.rvt*

When files are noted in the text, their names will be listed including file extensions (e.g. ".rvt"). If you do not see extensions listed on your system, you will need to enable them in Windows Explorer. To do so, open Windows Explorer, click on the View tab, and then check: "File name extensions".

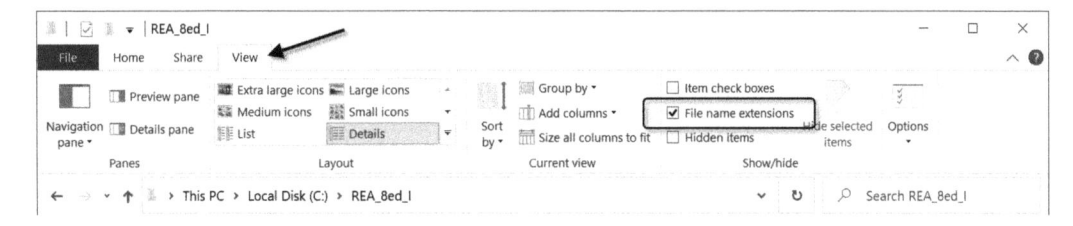

UNITS

This book references both imperial and metric units. Symbol names, scales, references, and measurements are given first in imperial units, and are then followed by the metric equivalent in square brackets[ ]. For example:

When there are two versions of the same file, they will appear like this within the text: *Curtain Wall Dbl Glass.rfa* [*M_Curtain Wall Dbl Glass.rfa*].

When the scale varies, a note like this will appear: 1/8"=1'-0" [1:100].

If a measurement must be input, the values will appear like this: **5'-6"** [**1650**].

Please note that in many cases, the closest logical corresponding metric value has been chosen, rather than a "direct" mathematical translation. For instance, 10'-0" in imperial units translates to: 3048 millimeters. However, a value of: 3000 will be used in most cases as a more logical value.

The downloadable dataset is included in both imperial and metric units. This includes all referenced files unless noted otherwise. See the "Download the Book Dataset" topic on page xi below for information on how to install the dataset in your preferred choice of units.

HOW TO USE THIS BOOK

The order of chapters has been carefully thought out with the intention of following a logical flow and architectural process. If you are relatively new to Revit, it is recommended that you complete the entire book in order. However, if there are certain chapters that do not pertain to the type of work performed by you or your firm, feel free to skip those topics. But bear in mind that not every procedure will be repeated in every chapter. For the best experience, it is recommended that you read the entire book, cover to cover. For example, the early chapters cover the detailed procedures for drawing walls, step-by-step with each click. Later chapters may simply say, "Draw a wall from this point to this," without detailing exactly how to draw a wall. Most importantly, even after you have completed your initial pass of the tutorials in this book, keep your copy of Revit Essentials for Architecture handy, as it will remain a valuable resource in the weeks and months to come.

COMPUTER HARDWARE

If Revit is your primary production application, you will want to consider maximizing your hardware to boost performance. Two important considerations are your processor and the amount of random-access memory (RAM). Computer systems today have multi-core processors. This essentially means the system has several processors working in tandem on the same chip. 8-core systems are considered a practical minimum for Revit, and it is not unusual to see machines in use with many more. The primary benefit of higher core counts (and higher RAM capacity) is the generally smoother running of more than one application or Revit session at a time, which is very typical in AEC working groups.

The amount of memory your system has will have a more direct impact on Revit performance. In practice, general Revit usage and basic models will require a minimum of 16GB of RAM. But because of the relatively low price of RAM and how you must install it in pairs, it makes sense to go with 32GB as a baseline minimum. Go for 64GB if you regularly deal with models larger than 400MB and 128GB if you work with models of 1GB or more. Note that the amount of memory is dependent on the CPU platform you have; typical desktops may be limited to a maximum of 64GB; working with larger models will necessitate moving to a more powerful computing platform, e.g. a Xeon Workstation, Intel High-End Desktop, Or AMD Threadripper-based system which can support 128GB.

Another important consideration is your storage subsystem. Today, solid state drives (SSDs) are typically standard. 1TB drives are the most popular size to accommodate all your programs and data files. Even on a corporate network with project files residing on the server, Revit creates local copies on workshare enabled projects, so you need a large amount of free space available. Revit files can be very large and saving local files can take a while if your storage system is not up to par. Installing a second drive dedicated to Revit and other BIM applications can reap large performance rewards. Finally, consider your video card. Oddly enough Revit does not require a very high-end investment is this area. Revit runs very well with medium level cards and performance does not appreciably scale up with very expensive high-end cards. However, faster graphics cards will allow you to work in more complex 3D views with more complex geometry using shaded or realistic view modes. And if your other applications that you use alongside Revit require higher end cards, they can certainly be worth the investment.

DOWNLOAD THE BOOK DATASET

Files used in the tutorials throughout this book are available for download at: **paulaubin.com**. Most chapters include files required to begin the lesson and often a completed version is provided as well that you can use to check your work. This means that you will be able to load the files for a given chapter and begin working regardless of whether you completed the chapter before it or not. The dataset is provided as a single downloadable self-executing WinZip file. The files will unzip by default into a folder on your *C:* drive named: *REA_8ed_I* [*REA_8ed_M*] by default, but you can install the files to a different location (such as *My Documents*) if you prefer. Inside this folder will be a folder for each chapter. Please note that in some cases such as the *Chapter03* folder there are no Revit files. In such cases, a text document is included to explain that this folder was left empty intentionally. To download and install the dataset, do the following:

1. In your web browser, visit: **paulaubin.com**.
2. Click on the **Books** link at the top.
3. Click on the link for the book whose files you wish to access.

    Downloads will be listed in the "Downloads" section of the page.
4. There may be more than one item to download. Click each item you wish to download and follow any instructions of your browser to complete the download.
5. Run the self-executing WinZip (EXE) file to unzip the files to your hard drive.

> **NOTE:** Please note that the accompanying dataset *only* contains the Revit files (RVT, RFA), and other related resource files (DWG, TXT), necessary to complete the tutorial lessons in this book. The provided dataset does *not* contain the Autodesk® Revit® software. Please contact your local Autodesk reseller if you need to purchase a copy. A 30-day trial is available for download from **autodesk.com**.

If you wish to install both the imperial and metric datasets, simply download and unzip both files. Installation requires approximately 1.7 GB of disk space (double this if you install both).

CURRENT RELEASE AND BEYOND...

With the rapid pace of software development, it is not always possible to provide a new edition of the book with every new release of the software. Furthermore, since significant changes to the core functionality of Revit happen infrequently and many of the new features released annually are often focused on up and coming areas in the building industry (and therefore outside of the focus of this book), in many cases a new release of the software does not automatically necessitate an update to the book's lessons. Therefore, you are encouraged to check this book's page at **paulaubin.com** when a new version of Revit is released to see what if any impact (if any) it will have on your existing edition of Revit Essentials for Architecture. It is expected that relevant new features can often be covered with an addendum rather than a full book revision. Instructions on how to access such addenda, when and if they become available, will be posted to the website.

WE WANT TO HEAR FROM YOU

We welcome your comments and suggestions regarding Revit Essentials for Architecture. Please forward your comments and questions to:

G3B Press
c/o Paul F. Aubin Consulting Services, Inc.
P.O. Box 223
Oak Lawn, IL 60454

Or submit comments via the web form at: **paulaubin.com/contact**.

ABOUT THE AUTHOR

Paul F. Aubin is the author of many book titles on Revit including his "deep dive" into the Revit family editor: Renaissance Revit. He has also authored dozens of Revit video training titles on **LinkedIn Learning**[†] covering all levels of Revit, Dynamo and ReCap. Paul is an independent architectural consultant providing content creation, implementation, and training services to architectural firms worldwide. His career of over 30 years, includes experience in design, production, BIM management, coaching, reality capture, and training. Paul is an active member of the Autodesk user community and has been a top-rated speaker at Autodesk University (AU) and other industry conferences for many years. Paul is an associate member of the American Institute of Architects (AIA), an Autodesk Expert Elite, the founder of **ChiNamo**: the Chicago Dynamo users' group and is a member of the board of directors for the **Volterra-Detroit Foundation**. He lives in Chicago with his wife and their three children are beginning their careers in cities around the country.

Follow Paul on:

@paulfaubin

linkedin.com/in/paulaubin

Contact Paul directly at:

paulaubin.com/contact

Learn more about additional books and video training authored by Paul F Aubin, as well as services and training offered by Paul F Aubin Consulting Services, Inc.[‡]

PAUL F. AUBIN
CONSULTING SERVICES

www.paulaubin.com

DEDICATION

This book is dedicated to my family.

• The Aubin Academy •

ACKNOWLEDGMENTS

I would like to take a moment to extend my appreciation for the people who have provided assistance and support to the writing of this book. This is the eighth edition of this book and with some many editions, the list of people to thanks has grown quite considerably. In order to save space and more importantly to avoid the risk of forgetting someone, I would simply like to extend my thanks to all of those professionals and friends who have provided me with support, advice and/or made contributions to this and my other projects through the years. To the many who have contributed passages, served as editors, proofread, given advice, helped me figure out formulas and modeling challenges, and recommended the book to their colleagues and friends, you have my heartfelt thanks.

I am ever grateful for blessings I have received from my many friends and family. Finally, I am most grateful for the constant love and support of my wife, Martha, and our three wonderful children.

CREDITS:

Technical Editor: Desirée Mackey, PE, SE, Design Technology Practice Leader at GEI Consultants, Co-Founder at BD Mackey Consulting

Foreword: Harlan Brumm, Senior Product Manager – Architecture, Autodesk

Layout Consultation: Nigel French – nigelfrench graphic design ltd.

Cover Design: Michael Brumm

Cover Rendering and Figures: Paul F. Aubin

SECTION I

Introduction and Methodology

INTRODUCTION

This section introduces the methodology of Revit. The concept of "Building Information Modeling" (BIM) is introduced and defined as are many other important topics and concepts. Within this section you will gain valuable experience using Revit by exploring its interface and be presented with its overall conceptual underpinnings.

SECTION I is organized as follows:

Chapter 1: Quick Start Overview
Chapter 2: Conceptual Underpinnings of Revit
Chapter 3: Revit User Interface

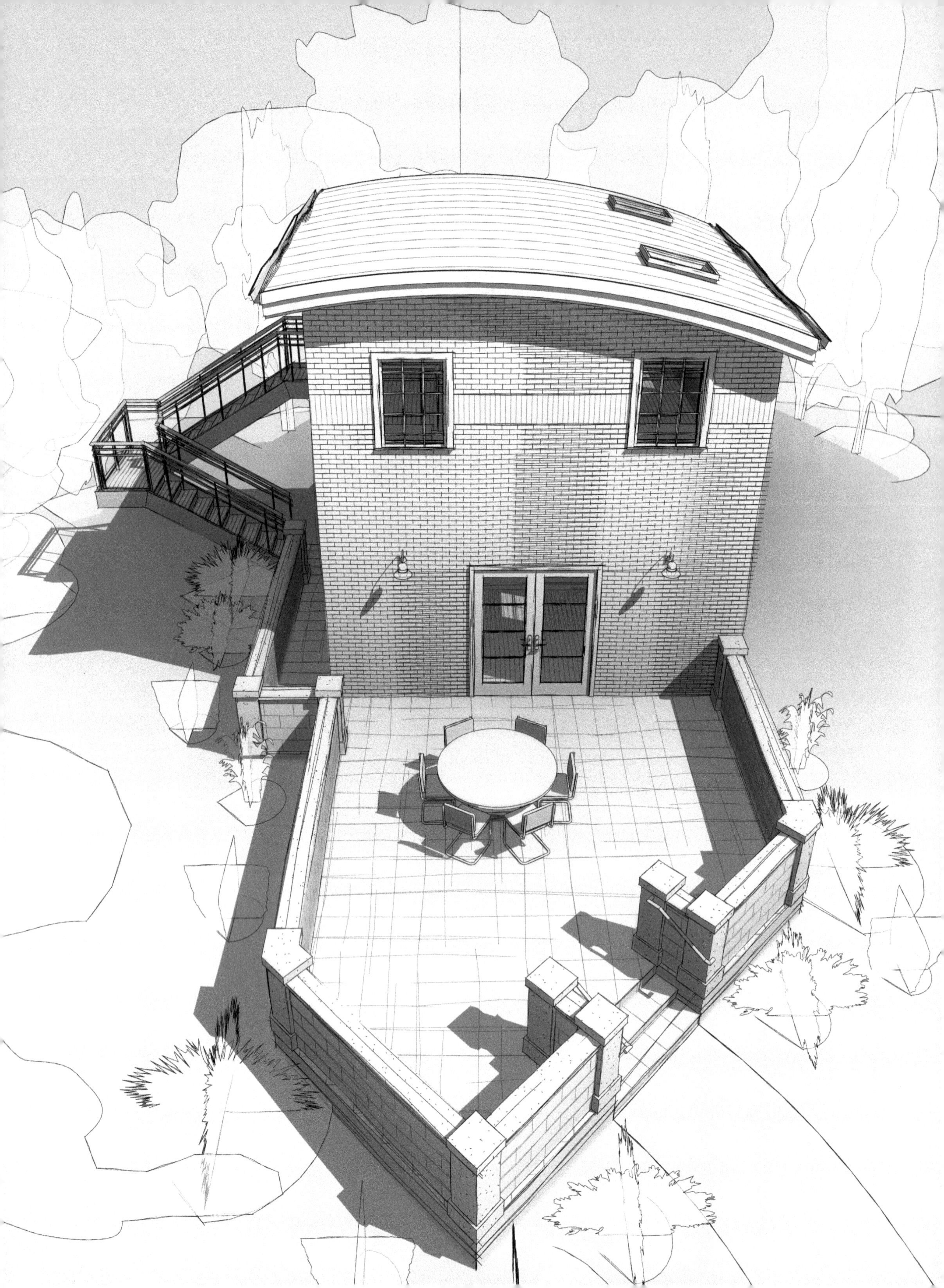

CHAPTER 1
Quick Start Overview

INTRODUCTION

This chapter provides a simple quick start tutorial designed to give you a brief tour of some of the most common elements and features of Autodesk® Revit®. You should be able to complete the entire exercise in single sitting. But feel free to save your progress at any time if you need a break.

OBJECTIVES

At the completion of this tutorial, you will have experienced a first-hand look at what Revit has to offer. In this chapter you will:

- Experience an overview of the software
- Create your first Revit model
- Receive a first-hand glimpse of many Revit tools and methods
- Get comfortable with the Revit interface

CREATE A SMALL BUILDING

For this tutorial, we will take a "whirlwind" tour of the architectural tools in Revit. All the tools covered in the following steps use simple, and often default, settings. The chapters that follow cover each of these tools and settings in more detail. So, don't worry if a topic is not covered in depth at this point. Think of this chapter as something akin to warm-up exercises before a full workout.

INSTALL THE DATASET FILES AND OPEN A PROJECT

The lessons that follow require the dataset files included for download with this book. If you have already downloaded and installed the files, skip to step 3 to begin. If you need to install the files, start at step 1.

1. If you have not already done so, download the dataset files accompanying this book.

    Refer to the "Download the Book Dataset" topic on page xi in the Preface for instructions on downloading and installing the book's dataset files.

2. Launch Autodesk® Revit®.

4 | Chapter 1

> **TIP:** You can click in the search field next to the Windows Start button and then begin typing: **Revit** in the search field. Alternatively, you can press the WINDOWS key on the keyboard to show the start menu and activate search. After a few letters, Revit will appear in the search results. (If you have more than one version installed, please choose Revit 2021 or later).

3. On the Home screen, beneath Models, click the Open button.

⇨ In the "Open" dialog box, browse to the location where you installed the dataset files, and then double-click the *Chapter01* folder.

⇨ Within this folder, double-click select the *Pavilion.rvt* file and then click the Open button (see Figure 1.1).

Alternatively, can double-click the file.

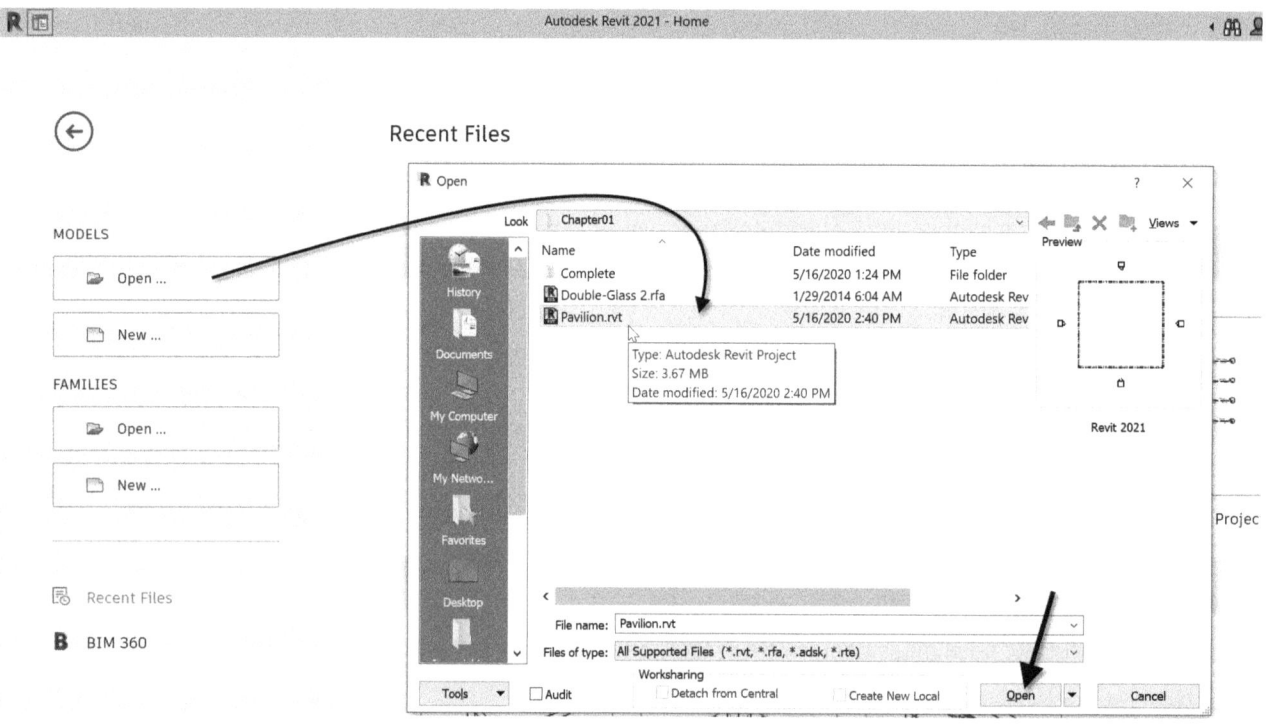

FIGURE 1.1 *Open the pavilion project to get started*

> **NOTE:** In this quick start tutorial, only one project has been provided and it uses Imperial units. The remainder of the book provides a Metric dataset as well.

The project will open in Revit with the *Level 1* floor plan view visible on screen. This project has been started already and contains a Property Line element (dashed square) in the middle of the screen. There is also a toposurface terrain model element in this file that represents the site for the building (you will learn about toposurface elements in Chapter 5 and Chapter 7). Let's start by displaying this item so we know where to place the walls of our building.

BEGIN A NEW MODEL

To get started, we need to begin with the basics: walls, doors, and windows. These elements are the basic building blocks of any architectural model. Adding these elements in Revit is simple and straight forward.

Typically, on the left side of the screen, running vertically is a panel named: **Project Browser**. (If you do not see Project Browser on your screen, you can open it by going to the View tab, click the User Interface drop down button and then check Project Browser). Project Browser lists several representations of our project including views (drawings), schedules (tabular lists), and sheets (drawings on title block borders). Four floor plan views are provided here: *Level 1*, *Level 2*, *Roof*, and *Site*. The *Level 1* first floor plan view is bold indicating that it is the currently active view and open onscreen. We can use the Project Browser to open other views. (An annotated overview of the Revit interface is shown in Figure 3.2 in Chapter 3 which covers the user interface in detail.)

CREATE AN UNDERLAY

We can display any of the other plans as an underlay to the current view to help us coordinate elements at different levels. Let's try the *Site* plan.

1. On the Project Browser, double-click to open the *Site* plan view.

   Notice that the *Site* plan view opens in its own tab at the top of the view area (just below the ribbon). You will now have two tabs open: *Level 1* and *Site*. These tabs make it easy to switch back to any open view. Also notice that the *Site* view includes site contours and a shape in the middle of the plan. This shape is a Building Pad element and represents the building's footprint and its entrance patio.

   ⇨ Click back on the *Level 1* tab to return to the first floor plan view. (Alternatively, on the Project Browser, double-click *Level 1* to return to the first floor plan view).

Also on the left side of the screen, above the Project Browser is the Properties palette. (If yours is not displayed, open it from the View tab, User Interface drop down). Near the top of the palette, on a small drop down menu it should read: "Floor Plan: Level 1." This indicates that we are seeing the properties of the first floor plan view (see the left side of Figure 1.2).

FIGURE 1.2 *Edit the Properties of the Level 1 floor plan view and assign an underlay*

2. On the Properties palette, within the "Underlay" grouping locate the "Range: Base Level" property.

   ⇨ Click on this value (currently "None") and from the pop-up menu that appears, choose **Site** (see the middle of Figure 1.2).

   ⇨ Click Apply to see the results (see the right side of Figure 1.2).

> **NOTE:** Alternatively, you can simply move your mouse away from the Properties palette and changes will be applied automatically.

Notice that only the patio and building footprint outline appeared. This is because the Topography category is turned off in the *Level 1* plan view. Notice also that the outline appears in halftone gray as well. This reinforces visually that this is simply an underlay; much like underlays in traditional hand drafting.

• Revit Essentials for Architecture •

6 | Chapter 1

CREATE WALLS

We begin our building model with some simple walls. Along the top of the screen is located a collection of icons and tools organized on tabs called the "ribbon." The "Architecture" tab should currently be active.

1. On the ribbon, click the Architecture tab (if not already active) and then click the Wall tool (click the top half of the button. If you click the drop down instead, choose: **Wall: Architectural**) (see item 1 in Figure 1.3).

    A "Modify | Place Wall" tab appears on the ribbon (tinted green) with several options and tools available.

    ⇨ On the Draw panel (right side of the ribbon), click the rectangle icon (item 2).

Just beneath the ribbon, running horizontally across the screen, additional settings appear (this area is called the "Options Bar").

⇨ From the "Location Line" list on the Options Bar, choose: **Finish Face: Exterior** (item 3).

In addition to the ribbon and the Options Bar, you can also find pertinent settings on the Properties palette allowing you to interact with and change the settings of the walls as you draw them. For example, at the top of the Properties palette, a drop down list appears (known as the Type Selector) which currently reads: Basic Wall Generic – 8".

⇨ Verify that the Type Selector, shows: **Generic -8"** (item 4).

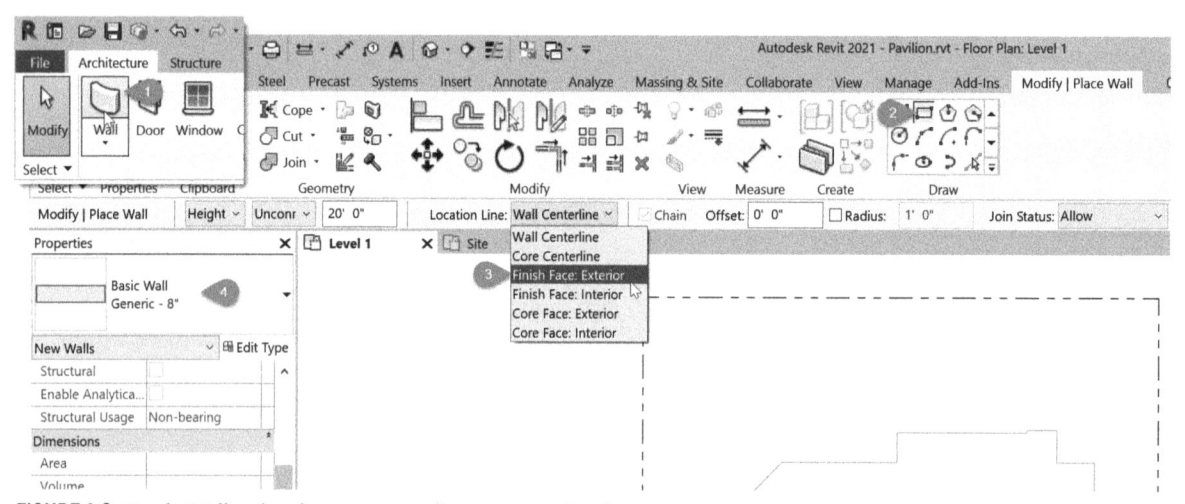

FIGURE 1.3 *Set the Wall tool to draw generic walls in a rectangular shape*

If necessary, you can roll the wheel on your mouse up a little to zoom in closer.

2. With the mouse pointer (now shaped like a cross hair) click the lower right corner of the gray shape on screen (use the small magenta square to snap to the endpoint) (see the left side of Figure 1.4).

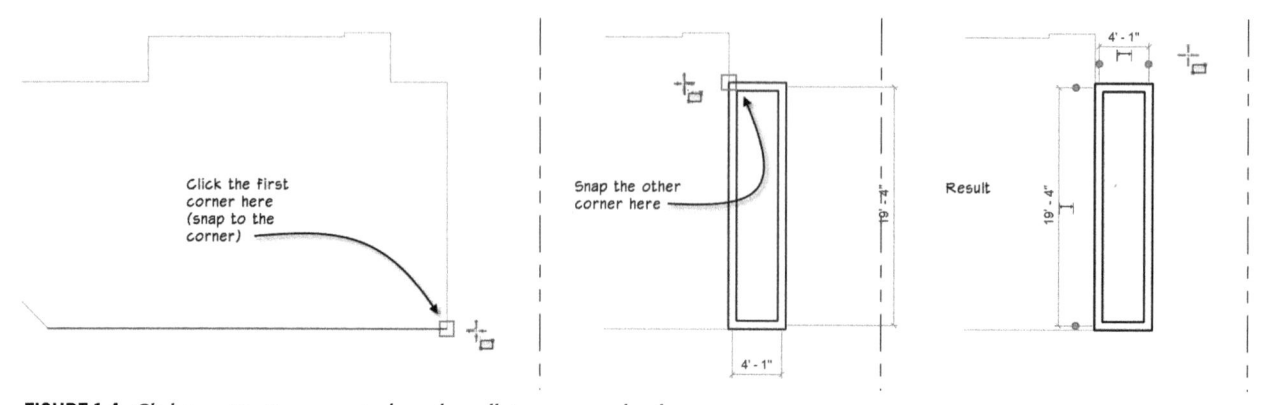

FIGURE 1.4 *Click two opposite corners to draw the walls in a rectangular shape*

⇨ Pick the Endpoint of the short horizontal edge indicated in the middle of Figure 1.4.

• The Aubin Academy •

The result is shown on the right side of Figure 1.4.

You will now have four walls onscreen. However, the space they define is very narrow. We can easily adjust this. Before we can manipulate the walls, however, we must cancel the current wall creation command. (If you don't, anywhere you click will begin creating another wall).

3. On the ribbon, on the far left, click the Modify tool (or press the ESC key twice).

> **NOTE:** Either method can be used anytime to cancel the current command and return to the Modify (selection pointer) tool. You can also access Cancel on the right-click menu. In Revit there is always one active tool. The default tool is the "Modify" tool, which is really just the standard mouse selection pointer.

4. Click on the vertical wall on the left to select it.

   Objects selected onscreen will appear shaded in color. This is light blue by default. The selection colors can be changed in Options if desired.

   ⇨ On the temporary dimension that appears, click directly on the blue text (see the left side of Figure 1.5).

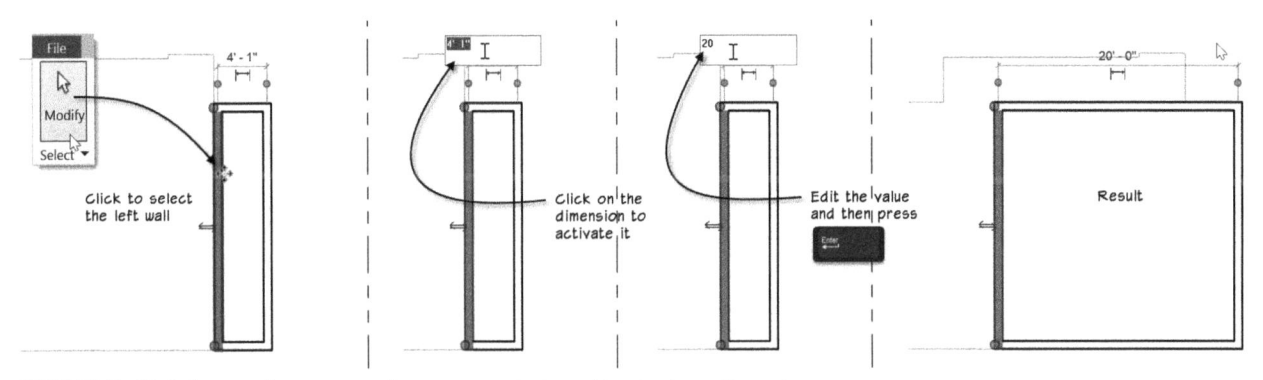

FIGURE 1.5 *Click the text of a temporary dimension to edit it resulting in the wall's moving*

⇨ In the text field that appears, type: **20** and then press ENTER (see the right side of Figure 1.5).

Notice that the wall moved to a new location, a distance equal to the value we input, and that the two horizontal walls stretched with it to remain connected. Please note that when you edit this way, the selected element moves (a wall in this case). The dimensions that we used for this edit are referred to as "temporary dimensions."

5. On the Architecture tab of the ribbon, click the Wall tool again.

   ⇨ From the "Location Line" list, choose: **Wall Centerline**.

   ⇨ On the Properties palette, from the Type Selector choose: **Generic -5"**.

6. Draw a vertical wall from top to bottom of the room, dividing it approximately into thirds (see Figure 1.6).

> **NOTE:** The exact dimensions are unimportant at this point, we will move the wall next.

8 | Chapter 1

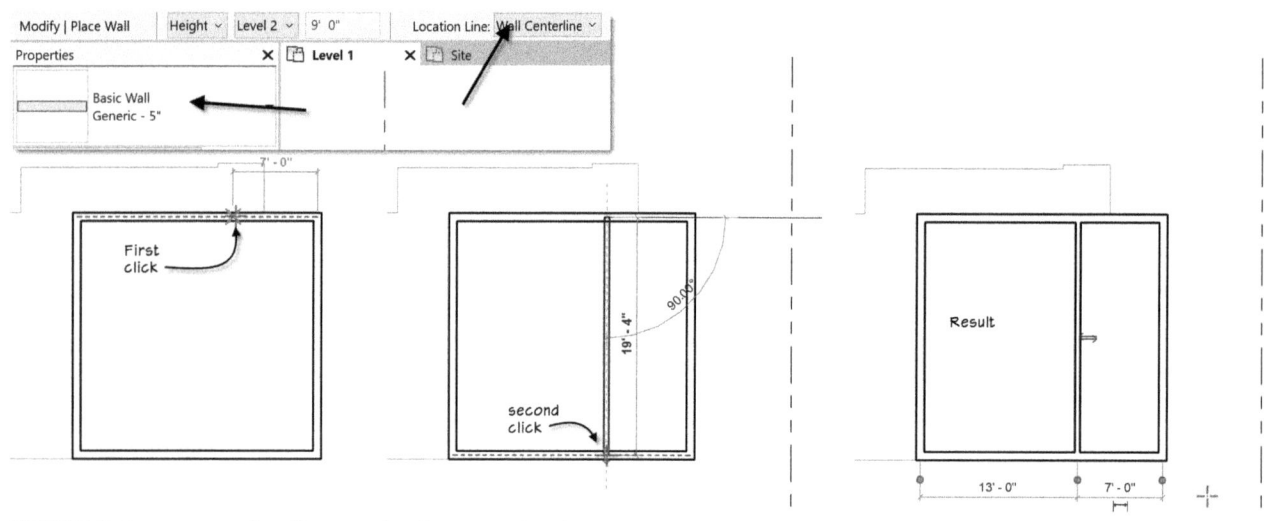

FIGURE 1.6 *Draw a vertical wall in a random location within the space*

- On the ribbon, click the Modify tool or press the ESC key twice.

7. Select the wall you just drew.

   A temporary dimension will appear between this wall and its neighbors. (It may appear above or below the wall; it will depend on how closely you are zoomed in or out).

8. Beneath the temporary dimension, click the small icon (that looks like a little dimension) to make the dimension permanent (see the left side of Figure 1.7).

- On the ribbon, click the Modify tool or press the ESC key twice.

Now that the dimension is permanent, notice that it remains onscreen even when the wall is no longer selected.

9. Click to select the dimension.

- Click the small "EQ" (Toggle Dimension Equality) icon beneath the dimension (see the middle of Figure 1.7).

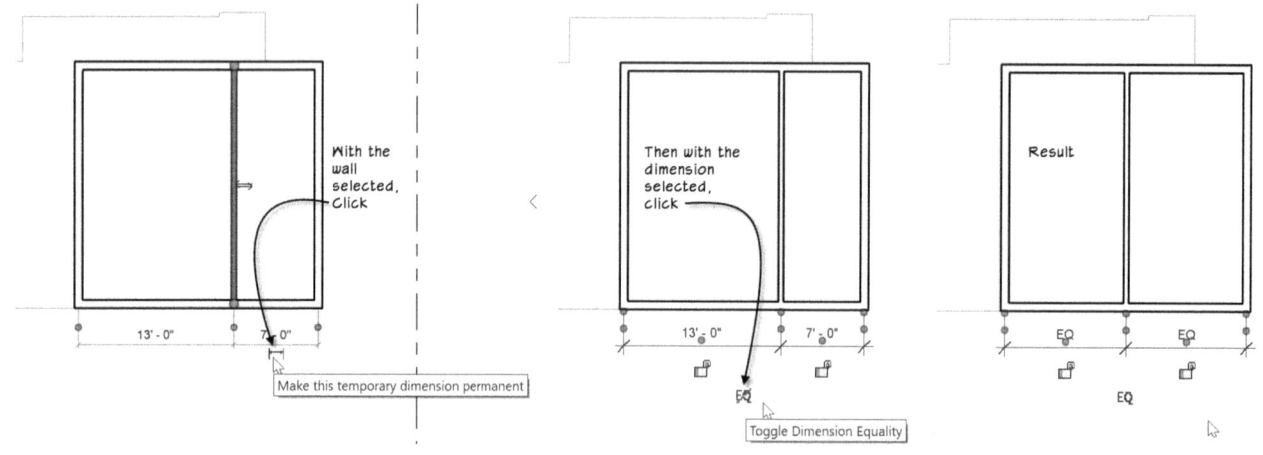

FIGURE 1.7 *Toggle the Dimension Equality and watch the middle wall move to become centered*

> **NOTE:** This icon is part of the Revit constraint system. The constraint system is used to "lock-in" design intent. This notion is an integral part of the underlying concepts inherent to Revit.

10. From the File menu choose: **Save**.

It is important to remember to save every so often to preserve your work. Revit is configured by default to remind you to save at regular intervals; but it will *not* automatically save. You can edit the reminder interval to a duration of

• The Aubin Academy •

your choosing (**File** menu > **Options**); but when the message asking you to save appears, you should always heed the suggestion and choose the "Save the project" option to perform a save (see Figure 1.8).

```
Project Not Saved Recently                    ×
You have not saved your project recently.
What do you want to do?

→ Save the project
→ Save the project and set reminder intervals
→ Do not save and set reminder intervals

                                      Cancel
```

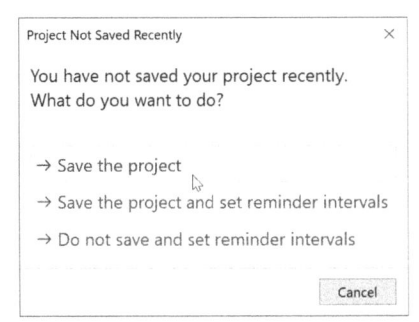

FIGURE 1.8 *Revit will remind you to save at regular intervals*

> **NOTE:** You can find more information and tutorials on working with walls in Chapter 4.

INSERT DOORS AND WINDOWS

Now that we have a few walls, let's add some openings. Revit has both doors and windows that work essentially the same way. Let's take a look.

1. On the Architecture tab of the ribbon, click the Door tool.

A tab labeled Modify | Place Door will appear to the right of the other ribbon tabs. This tab is tinted in a green color like we saw for walls. This is referred to as a contextual tab. Such tabs appear whenever you create a new element or select an existing element for editing.

   ⇨ On the Modify | Place Door tab, click the Tag on Placement button. (It will highlight in blue)

   Accept all the remaining defaults. Move the pointer near the top horizontal wall to begin door placement.

Move the mouse around without clicking it yet. Notice how the door follows the cursor and stays attached to the wall as it does. If you move the mouse away from the wall, the door will disappear. This is because elements such as doors are "hosted" elements. The door will be "hosted" by the wall. In other words, it is not possible to place a door freestanding without a wall host. Also notice that moving the mouse from one side of the wall to the other will flip the door in or out relative to the wall. (You can also press the SPACEBAR to flip the door "hand" before placement.) The gray underlay we added previously indicates a patio shape to the left of the plan and wrapping around the top. Our first door will be out to that passageway along the top.

2. Position the mouse on the top wall near the right side of the passageway so it swings out and click (see Figure 1.9).

10 | Chapter 1

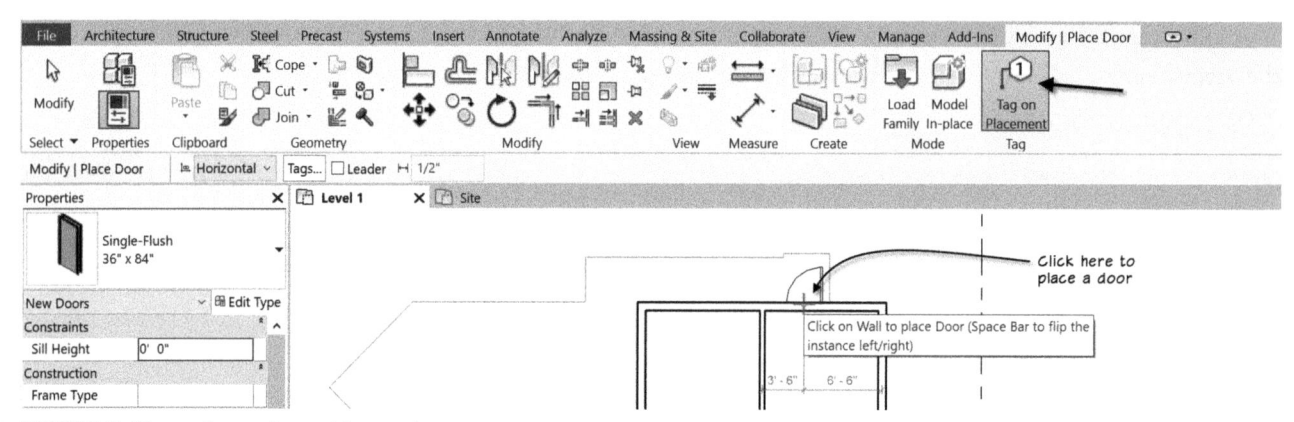

FIGURE 1.9 *Place a door to the outside near the passageway*

3. Place another near the top of the interior vertical wall.

   Notice that door tags have automatically appeared, and the numbers have filled in sequentially. This is because we toggled on the "Tag on Placement" option above. We will learn more about tags later.

Sometimes after placing a door, it is not positioned or oriented correctly. Just like the walls above, we can select a door, and then edit its temporary dimensions to move it to the desired location. There are also small flip control icons on the door to control its orientation.

4. Click the Flip control to change the interior door's orientation (see Figure 1.10).

   Repeat if desired on the other door. You can also tap the SPACEBAR to flip it.

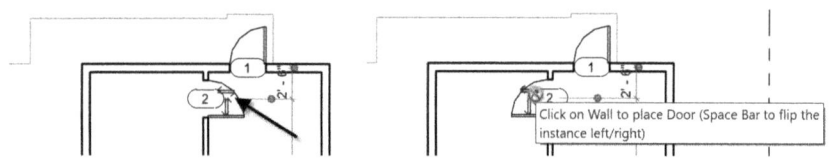

FIGURE 1.10 *Doors number sequentially; use the flip controls to change door orientation*

Adding windows works the same way as adding doors.

5. On the ribbon, click the Architecture tab and then click the Window tool. (No need to cancel the door command first).

   ⇨ Turn on Tag on Placement and accept the remaining defaults.

   ⇨ Move the pointer over the top horizontal wall and then move slightly up then down.

Again, notice how this controls the placement orientation of the window. As with the door, you can always flip it later if necessary. The side of the wall you pick will determine which side the "exterior" side of the window faces.

6. Place windows in the top and bottom horizontal walls only (see Figure 1.11).

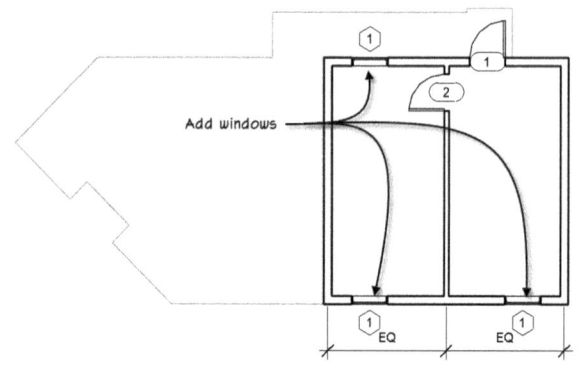

FIGURE 1.11 *Place windows in the horizontal walls*

• The Aubin Academy •

Quick Start Overview | 11

Let's place one more door in the wall at the left. For this door we will use a different style of door (called a "family" in Revit) and to do so, (since it is not currently contained in this project) we will load it from an external library.

7. On the Architecture tab of the ribbon, click the Door tool.
   ⇨ On the Modify | Place Door tab, to the right on the Mode panel, click the Load Family button.
   ⇨ Navigate to the folder where you installed the book dataset files.
   ⇨ From there, double-click the *Chapter01* subfolder.
   ⇨ Select *Door-Exterior-Double-Full Glass-Wood_Clad.rfa* and then click Open (or simply double-click it).

This action loads the door component into the currently active project making it available to place in the model. (This door family file is a copy of one provided with the content included in the Imperial install of the product.)

8. Place the door in the center of the left wall swinging out. Use the temporary dimensions to assist you in placement (see Figure 1.12).

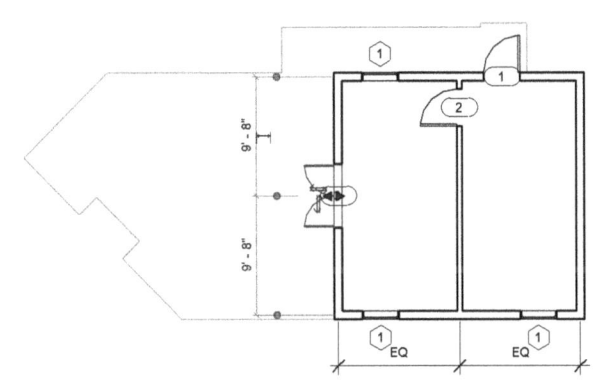

FIGURE 1.12 *Load and place a double entry door*

   ⇨ On the ribbon, click the Modify tool or press the ESC key twice.

9. Save the project.

> **NOTE:** You can find more information and tutorials on working with doors and windows in Chapter 4.

WORKING IN OTHER VIEWS

In Revit, we are not limited to just floor plans, we can work in many types of views. Our project includes elevation and ceiling plan views already. We can also add section views and three-dimensional (3D) views. Many other view types are also available and discussed in future chapters. One thing to keep in mind is that all these views representing the project are taken from the same Revit model; they are *not* separate drawings.

VIEW THE MODEL IN 3D

Opening a 3D view will give us a good overall look at the model. Look at your Project Browser; currently we have just three view categories: *Floor Plans, Ceiling Plans* and *Elevations*.

1. On the Quick Access Toolbar (at the top left-hand corner of the application frame), click the Default 3D View button (it looks like a small bird house) (shown in the upper left corner of Figure 1.13 below).

   This creates a new view called: *{3D}* and places it in a new category on Project Browser called: *3D Views*.

This is the default 3D view in Revit. You can modify it as you like or create others from it. We will use this one for our tutorial but make some simple adjustments to its vantage point. Notice that the *{3D}* view is an isometric view

• Revit Essentials for Architecture •

of our building model. We can see the walls, doors, and windows we added from a bird's eye vantage point. We also see the Toposurface terrain model that was included in this project at the start and some dashed lines representing the levels in the model. You can change the vantage point of a 3D view interactively on screen.

> **NOTE:** If you do not see any walls, check the discipline of your view. Make sure that no elements are selected (press ESC twice), then on the Properties palette, set the Discipline to: **Architectural**.

On the right side of the screen, locate the small Navigation Bar.

2. On the Navigation Bar, click the Steering Wheels icon. (You can also press F8).

A "steering wheel" control will appear on screen and follow the position of your cursor. Several types of 3D navigation are possible with this steering wheel.

Position the steering wheel over the middle of the model.

3. Move your mouse to the left side of the steering wheel over the Orbit option and then click and drag the mouse in the view window to spin the model around interactively.

⇨ Drag side-to-side to move around the building.

⇨ Drag up or down to change height of the vantage point.

4. Spin the model around so that the front double door is visible (see Figure 1.13).

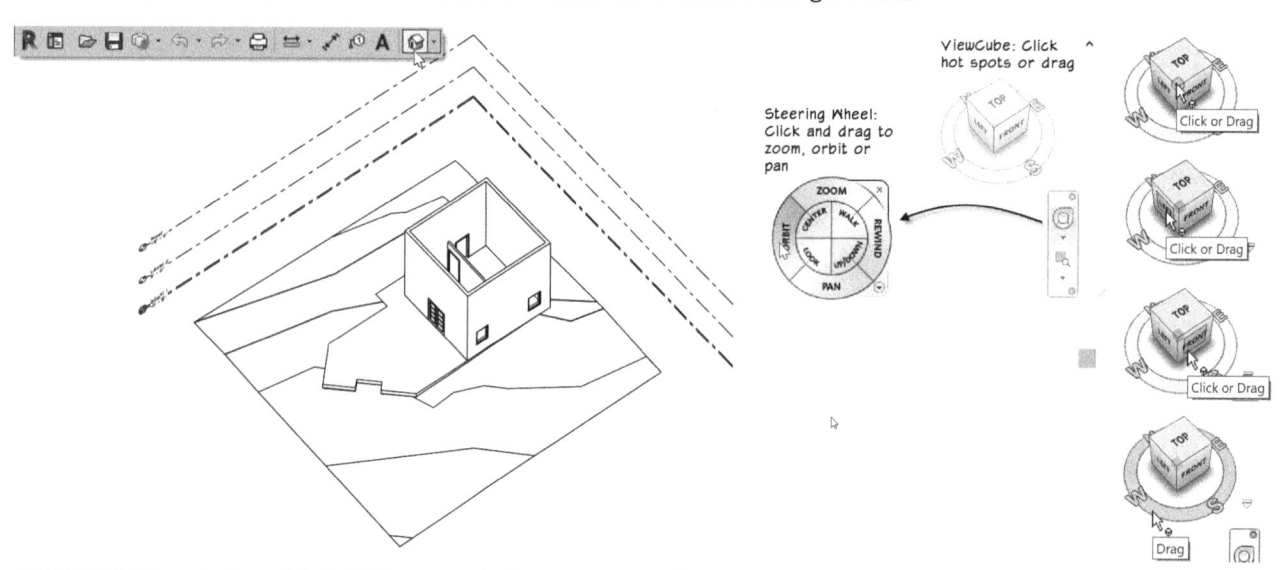

FIGURE 1.13 *Dynamically modify the {3D} view window's vantage point and orientation*

Several other options are possible. For now, just try Orbit, Zoom, and Pan. To use each option, click and drag. Another option is the ViewCube in the upper right corner of the screen. You can click several hot spots on the ViewCube to orient the model to that position. You can drag the ViewCube as another way to orbit.

> **TIP:** You can also spin the model by holding down the SHIFT key and dragging with the middle wheel or right mouse button on your mouse or simply click and drag the ViewCube.

5. On the ribbon, click the Modify tool or press the ESC key.

CREATE A SECTION VIEW

Let's create a section view to help us understand the relationships built into our model as we make some simple edits.

1. On the Project Browser, double-click to open the *Level 1* floor plan view
   (or just click its already open tab at the top of the window).

   ⇨ On the ribbon, click the View tab and then click the Section tool.

2. Click to the left of the double door.

   ⇨ Move the pointer through the model to the right keeping the section line horizontal.

   ⇨ Click outside the model to the right to complete the section line (see Figure 1.14).

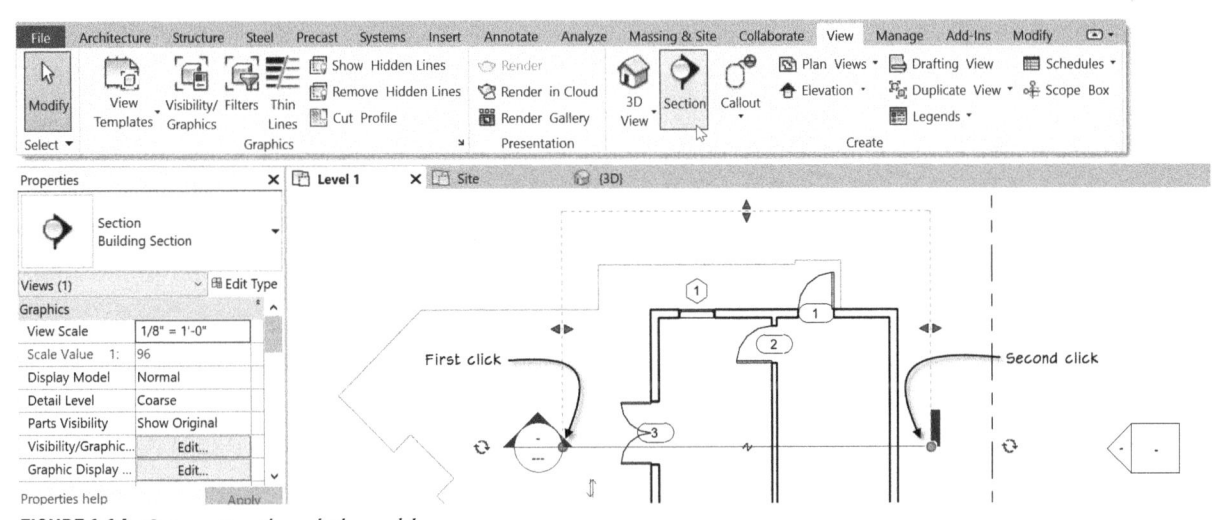

FIGURE 1.14 *Cut a section through the model*

A section line, with a section head and tail will appear. Three blue dashed lines with drag handles will also appear. The section head will be light blue (by default) indicating that it is selected.

3. Click next to the section line in the empty white area of the view
   background being careful not to click on any geometry.

> **TIP:** This is a quick way to deselect the selected element(s). You can also just press the ESC key.

Notice that the Section Head now turns dark blue. It is no longer selected, but the dark blue color indicates that it is an interactive element. In this case, it has a linked view associated with it and acts as a "hyperlink" to the associated section view. In the Project Browser, notice that there is now a *Sections* category included in the list. As we saw with the 3D View above, Revit automatically creates such branches in the Project Browser as needed.

4. Double-click the dark blue Section Head to open the associated view.

   You should now see the *Section1* view on screen. (As an alternative, you can select the section object in plan, right-click and choose: **Go To View** or just open it from Project Browser).

5. On the Project Browser, double-click to open the *West* Elevation view.

We now have five views open. You will see these as tabs across the top of the view area. Your ribbon should still be on the View tab.

6. Hover over the tab of the *Floor Plan: Site* view. Click the small X that appears to close it.

7. On the View tab, from the Windows panel, click the Tile Views button (see Figure 1.15).

14 | Chapter 1

⇨ On the right-hand side of any viewport, click the flyout beneath the zoom tool and choose: **Zoom All to Fit** (alternatively, on the keyboard, type the letters **ZA**).

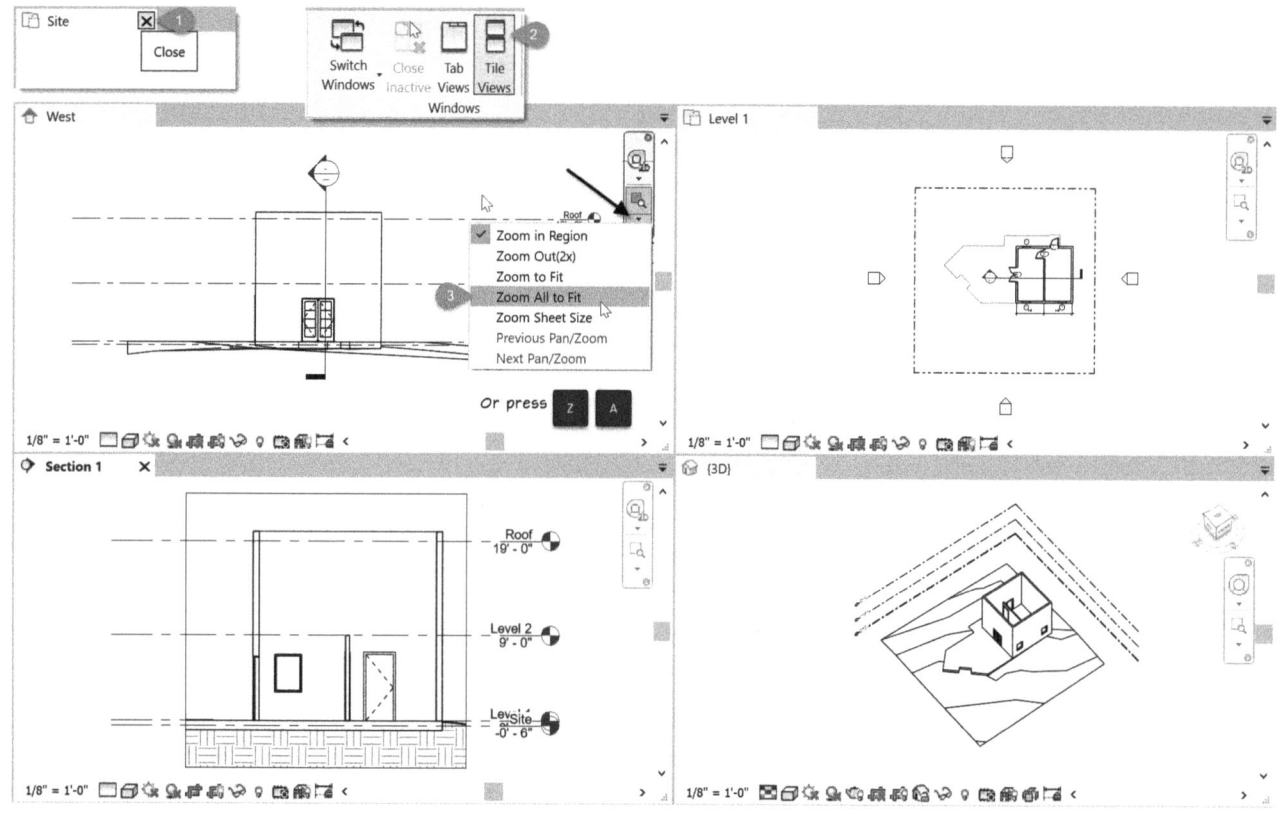

FIGURE 1.15 *Tile the views on screen to view them all at once; close the Site plan and zoom all to fit*

TIP: You can find more information and tutorials on working with views in Chapter 5.

EDIT IN ANY VIEW

When you edit your model, you may perform the edits in any view. Changes will automatically be applied to all views. This is the power of the Revit platform! You are describing a single virtual building model or Building Information Model (BIM) (see Chapter 2 for complete details) which you can view or edit in many ways. Regardless of where you make the edit—plan, section, elevation, 3D, or even schedules, all views are coordinated. These graphical and tabular views are just different ways of portraying the data within the single BIM.

EDITING LEVELS

With our current screen configuration, look at the elevation and section views. This project has been set up to have two stories plus a roof. Our walls on the exterior currently go right past the second floor level. Let's adjust this.

1. Click in the *Level 1* floor plan view window, to make it active. (Its title will appear slightly bolder than the other tabs).

⇨ If you want to zoom in a little closer, roll the wheel on your mouse.

Place your mouse pointer (the Modify tool) over one of the exterior walls.

Notice the way that it highlights under the cursor. (If you move the mouse away without clicking, the wall will no longer highlight.) This is called "pre-selection highlight" or just "pre-highlight" and is a useful aid in proper selection.

• The Aubin Academy •

Quick Start Overview | 15

⇨ Pre-highlight one exterior wall—do not click yet.

⇨ Press the TAB key (just press it, don't hold it down)

Notice how all the exterior walls now pre-highlight. This is called a chain selection.

⇨ Click the left mouse button to select the pre-highlighted elements.

REMEMBER: Highlight, TAB, and then click.

Notice how all four exterior walls are now shaded light blue in all open views. They are also a little transparent in the views other than plan. The Properties palette should be visible onscreen. By default, it is on the left side of the screen docked above the Project Browser. If you do not see the Properties palette, on the green colored Modify | Walls tab of the ribbon (which appeared when we selected the walls) click the Properties tool. Make sure you only click the tool if the Properties palette is not currently displayed. Clicking it when it is displayed will hide it.

2. On the Properties palette, from the "Top Constraint" list, choose: **Up to level: Roof** and then click Apply (see Figure 1.16).

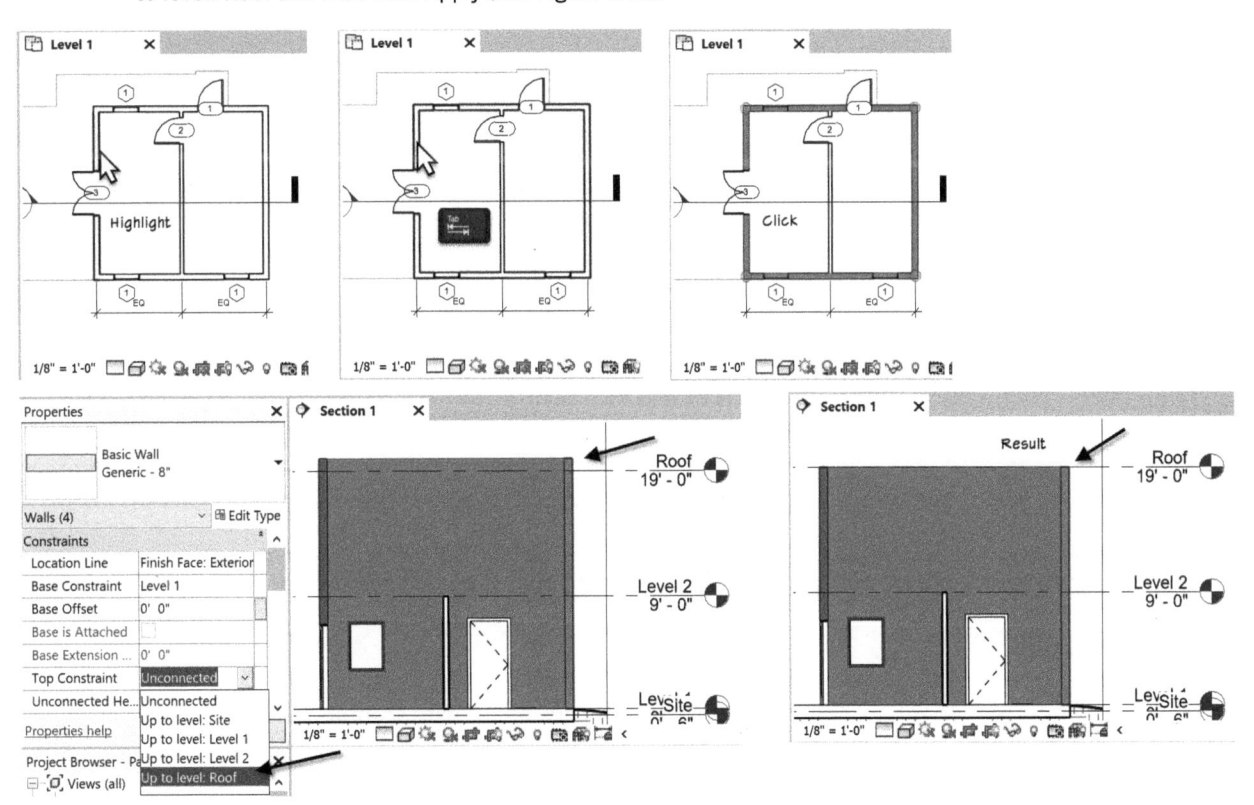

FIGURE 1.16 *Use the Properties palette to edit the height constraint of the selected walls*

Notice how the walls attach to the Roof level. You can see this best in the elevation and section views. If we were to change the height of the Roof level, the walls would also adjust accordingly. Let's try that.

Click anywhere in the West elevation view.

3. Click to select the Roof level line.

Notice the temporary dimensions that appear.

⇨ Zoom In Region to get a better look if you need to (right-click to access **Zoom In Region**, or use the Navigation Bar to access it). Drag a rectangular region on screen to indicate which portion of the view to zoom in on. (Or just roll the wheel).

• Revit Essentials for Architecture •

16 | Chapter 1

Like the walls and other elements drawn so far, we can edit the blue dimension value to move the Level lines to a new location. We will move both Level 2 and the Roof level; starting with the Roof.

⇨ Click the blue text of the temporary dimension between Level 2 and
Roof, type **11** and then press ENTER (see Figure 1.17).

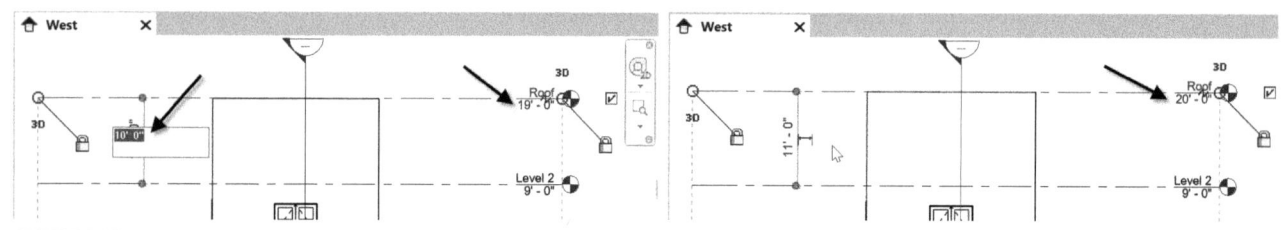

FIGURE 1.17 *Move the Level line with the temporary dimension*

> **NOTE:** Be sure to use the temporary dimension between Level 2 and Roof. If you edit the height of the Roof level directly (the height shown on the level head symbol), you will need to type: **20** instead. The height on the Level shows its height from zero.

Notice that not only does the Roof level line move, but since we constrained the walls to the Roof level, the top edge of the walls adjusts as well!

4. Select Level 2.

⇨ Click the blue text of the temporary dimension between Level 1 and Level 2, type: **10** and then press ENTER.

Notice that this moves Level 2 relative to Level 1, and the distance between Level 2 and the Roof has changed as well. This is because only the item that is selected will move, and in this case, we only had Level 2 selected. This change also only affected the level. It had no impact on the exterior walls. This is because none of the exterior walls have their Top Constraint set to Level 2. However, if you look at the section, you will see that interior wall was affected by this change.

> **NOTE:** You can find more information and tutorials on working with walls in Chapter 4 and with levels in Chapter 5.

MODIFY A WINDOW

Let's edit a window next. Again, we can edit in whatever view is convenient with confidence that the edit will appear in all appropriate views automatically.

1. Spin the 3D model view to show the north wall.

You can hold down the SHIFT key and drag with the middle wheel button on your mouse or click the small corner hot spot on the top surface on the ViewCube.

2. Select the window on the north wall. (You can select it in any view—try plan).

⇨ Click on the title bar of the 3D view, then of the section view.

Not only is the window highlighted light blue (indicating that it is selected) in all views, but in each of these views where it is visible, the temporary dimensions appear when the view is made active.

3. Edit the temporary dimension values to move the window. Click on the dimension text, type any number (a little bigger or smaller than the current number is fine), and then press ENTER.

• The Aubin Academy •

Notice how the window moves instantly in all views. When using Revit, you will never have to worry about chasing down a change in several different views to be certain that it has been coordinated everywhere. This will boost productivity and help reduce the number of costly change orders.

⇨ Move additional windows in the same way if you wish.

At this point you may wish to line up the window on the north wall across the plan with the one on the south. You can do this and have Revit maintain the relationship with the Align tool.

Work in the plan view.

4. On the ribbon, on the Modify | Windows tab, on the Modify panel, click the Align tool.

You first indicate the point of reference (what you want to align to). We'll use the window we just moved.

⇨ Click near the center of the window you just moved (the one with the position you like) to set the point of alignment.

⇨ Click near the center of the opposite window (the one you want to move) to align it to the reference point.

⇨ Click the lock icon to constrain the alignment of the two windows together (see Figure 1.18).

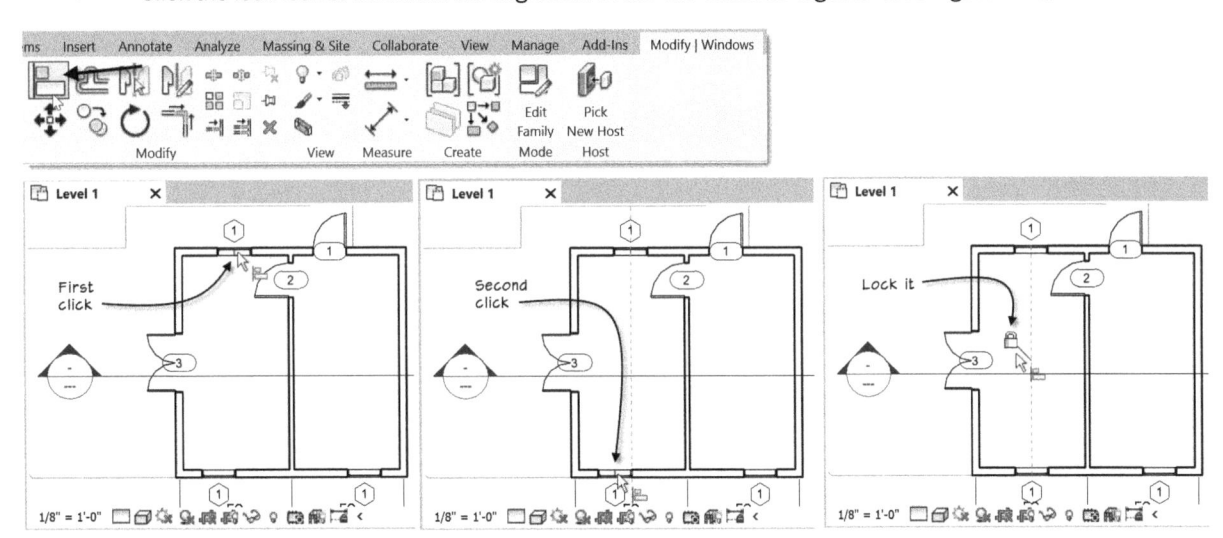

FIGURE 1.18 *Use the Align tool to line up two objects with each other*

5. On the ribbon, click the Modify tool or press the ESC key twice.

If you now move either window, they will move together. Try it!

ADD OPENINGS ON THE SECOND FLOOR

Now let's add some fenestration on the second floor.

1. Click anywhere in the floor plan view. On the Project Browser, double-click to open the *Level 2* floor plan view.

   Notice how the new view opens as a tab in this tile. You can switch between the two plans by clicking their tabs.

Following the above procedures, add windows and a door to Level 2 as shown in Figure 1.19.

TIP: You can use the temporary dimensions to help you in placing the openings in logical locations.

18 | Chapter 1

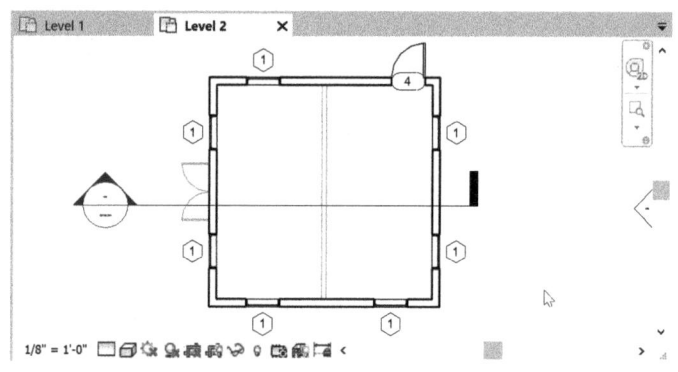

FIGURE 1.19 *Add doors and windows to Level 2*

Fine-tune the placement of any of these openings and feel free to repeat the alignment procedure on any of the pairs of windows as well.

2. Save the model.

COMPLETING THE MODEL

Our project is coming along. Let's keep going and add some more geometry to enclose it with a floor and roof and refine the walls a little.

ADD A FLOOR

The second floor of our building will have an interior balcony on the right overlooking the space to the left.

Work in the *Level 2* floor plan view.

1. On the ribbon, click the Architecture tab and then click the Floor tool.

Floor is a "split button" tool. This means that the top half of the button performs the most common command or action. If you click the lower half of the button, a pop-up menu appears with several alternate choices for the tool. In this case, the default top half of the button gives us the Floor tool we need. Split buttons and other interface conventions are discussed in more detail in Chapter 3.

When you click the Floor tool, the floor plan will turn gray placing the drawing editor into "Sketch mode." The ribbon will also change to show a Modify | Create Floor Boundary tab. Sketch mode is a special two-dimensional drawing mode used when the element that you are creating has a shape that Revit cannot easily "guess." In this case, it would not be possible for Revit to assume the size and shape of the floor that we want, so instead, we will sketch it. This is easy to do, given that we already have several walls and can use them for the basis of the sketch.

On the Draw panel of the ribbon (on the right), the "Boundary Line" and "Pick Walls" icons will already be enabled (selected and tinted blue).

2. Click one of the horizontal exterior walls, then the other.

⇨ Click the vertical exterior wall on the right.

Notice that with each wall you click a magenta sketch line will appear on the wall. Also notice that the sketch lines will appear on either the inside face of the wall or the outside face depending on which side of the first wall you clicked. Notice also that the right side corners automatically formed clean corners to one another. If the sketch lines appear on the outside face of a wall, click the double arrow flip control (appearing on one of the sketch lines) to reposition the sketch line to the other face. Repeat as required to locate all three sketch lines on the inside face as indicated on the left of Figure 1.20.

• The Aubin Academy •

NOTE: The first sketch line you click will have two smaller parallel lines next to it. You can ignore those for this exercise. They indicate the "direction" of the floor when it is made from a directional material such as corrugated deck or precast joists.

The floor will only cover the right half of the plan, so for the last wall, we will use the vertical one in the center on the plan rather than the exterior one on the left.

⇨ Click on the vertical wall in the center (see the middle of Figure 1.20).

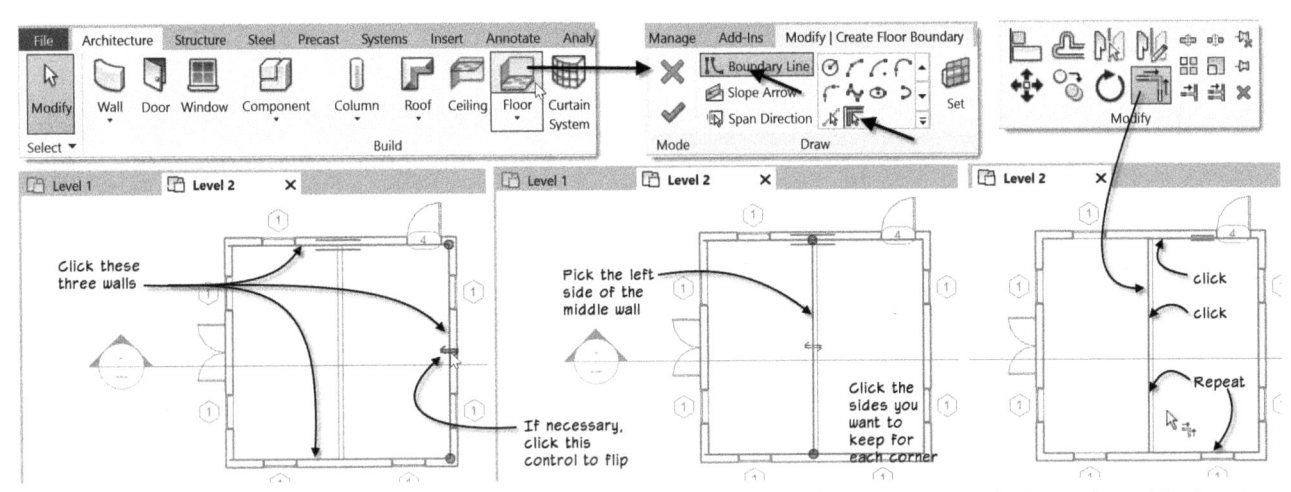

FIGURE 1.20 *Create floor sketch lines from the existing walls and use Trim/Extend to clean it up (Sketch lines in the figure enhanced for clarity)*

3. On the Modify panel, click the Trim/Extend to Corner tool.

⇨ Click the vertical sketch line in the center of the plan, and then click the right side of the horizontal line at the top.

NOTE: When using the Trim/Extend tool you always select the portion of the lines that you want to keep.

⇨ Repeat by clicking the vertical again, then the right side of the horizontal one on the bottom (see the right side of Figure 1.20).

You cannot finish the sketch if it does not form a closed shape. In this case, we created a closed rectangle. It doesn't matter what the shape is, but all corners must be closed (joined) to one another. If your sketch is not closed and you try to finish, you will receive a warning dialog. Click the Continue button and look for any issues in the sketch.

4. On the ribbon, click the Finish Edit Mode (Green checkmark) button.

⇨ In the first dialog that appears, click the Attach button, then click Yes in the next one (see the right side of Figure 1.21).

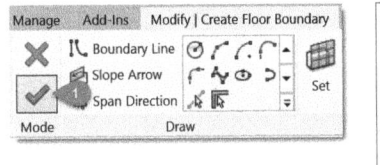

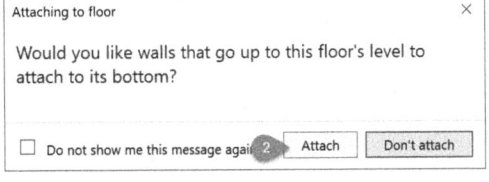

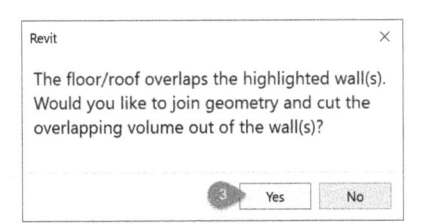

FIGURE 1.21 *Finish the Sketch and then attach the floor and walls and join the geometry*

5. Switch to the {3D} view. If necessary, on the Project Browser, double-click it to open it.

⇨ Spin the model around and angle down to see the new floor.

20 | Chapter 1

You can also study it in the section view (see Figure 1.22). The first question (Attach) establishes a relationship between the short wall in the middle of the plan by attaching it to the underside of the floor. The other message (Join Geometry) establishes a relationship between the floor and the three exterior walls by allowing the floor to cut into the walls making it represent a platform framing style construction.

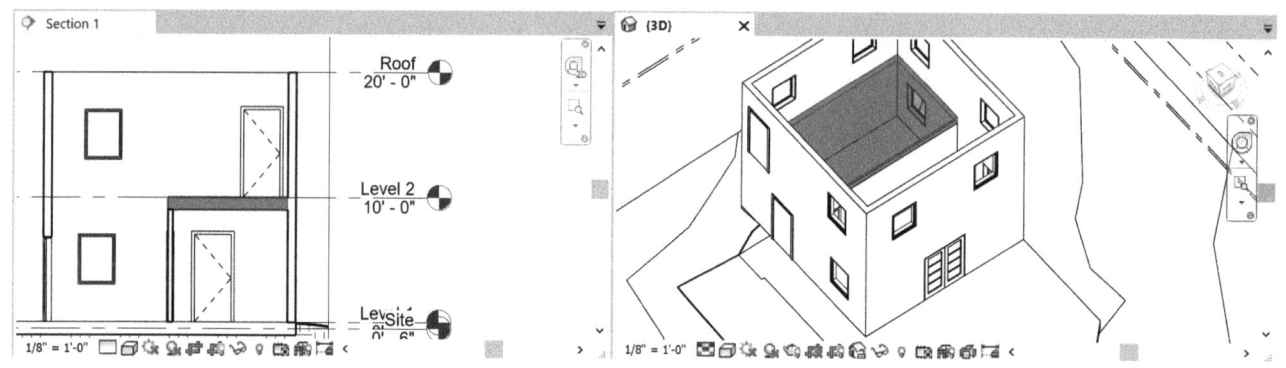

FIGURE 1.22 *Study the new floor in the {3D} and Section 1 views*

> **NOTE:** You can find more information and tutorials on working with floors in Chapter 6.

ADD A ROOF

We can sketch a roof in much the way as we sketched the floor. There are a few roof techniques available. If you want a shed, gable or hip roof, use the "Roof by Footprint" option. We will see examples of some of these forms in Chapter 9. For this exercise, we will make a curved sweeping shape using the "Roof by Extrusion" option.

1. Click the *West* elevation tab. Or if necessary, open it from the Project Browser.

> **NOTE:** North is toward the top of the screen in plan view. Therefore, the top elevation mark symbol is the North elevation, the bottom one is South, the right one is East, and the left one is West. From a plan view, you can double-click the triangle portion of the marker to open the associated elevation in a similar fashion to the way we opened the section above.

2. On the Architecture tab of the ribbon, click the drop down arrow on the Roof tool.
   ⇨ From the drop down menu that appears, choose: **Roof by Extrusion**.

With roof by extrusion, we sketch a simple 2D shape that will be used to form the roof's profile. The roof will extrude this shape along the length of the building. Since we are working in an elevation, Revit needs us to establish the plane in which we wish to sketch our roof profile. This is known as the "Work Plane."

3. In the "Work Plane" dialog, accept the defaults (Pick a plane) and click OK.

   If you look at the bottom of the screen on the Status Bar, the prompt reads: "Pick a vertical plane."

   ⇨ Click the wall facing us (see Figure 1.23). Do this by clicking near the edge of the wall.

> **TIP:** To click the face of the wall, or any plane in Revit, you need to position the Pick Plane tool over the edge of the element. The perimeter of the plane will pre-highlight indicating which plane will be selected when you click.

• The Aubin Academy •

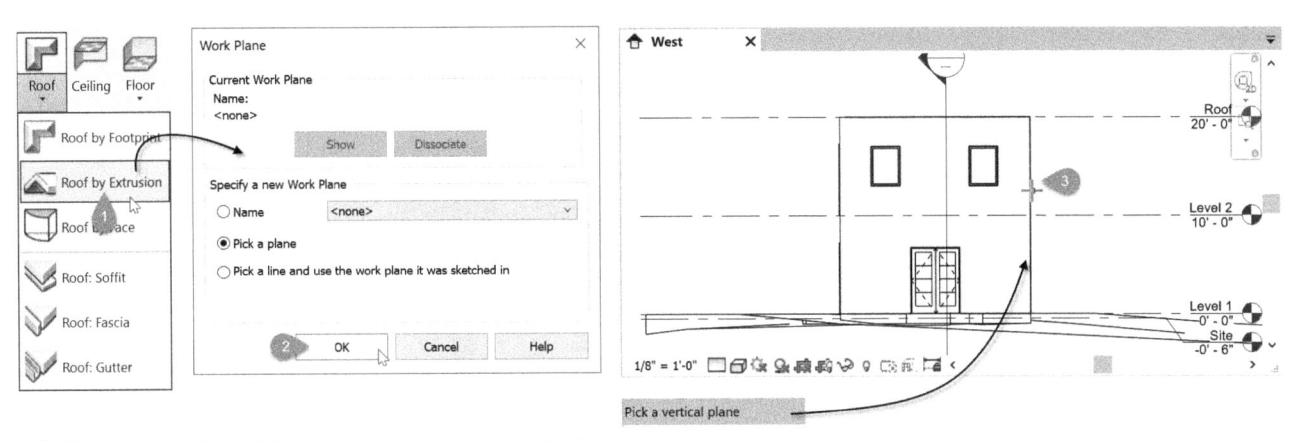

FIGURE 1.23 *Click the wall facing the view to set it as a work plane*

> In the "Roof Reference Level and Offset" dialog that appears, verify that the Level is set to Roof with a 0 offset (this is the default) and then click OK.

We are placed into sketch mode (like the floor element above). We will now create a curved shape for the roof. On the ribbon, the Modify | Create Extrusion Roof Profile tab appears, and on the Draw panel, the Line tool should already be active. Let's switch to an arc instead.

4. On the Draw Panel, directly beneath the Line tool, click the Start-End-Radius Arc tool.
   > Click the first point of the arc at the top left corner of the wall (see the left side of Figure 1.24).
   > Set the next point about 6° below the right top corner (zoom in if necessary) (see the middle of Figure 1.24).

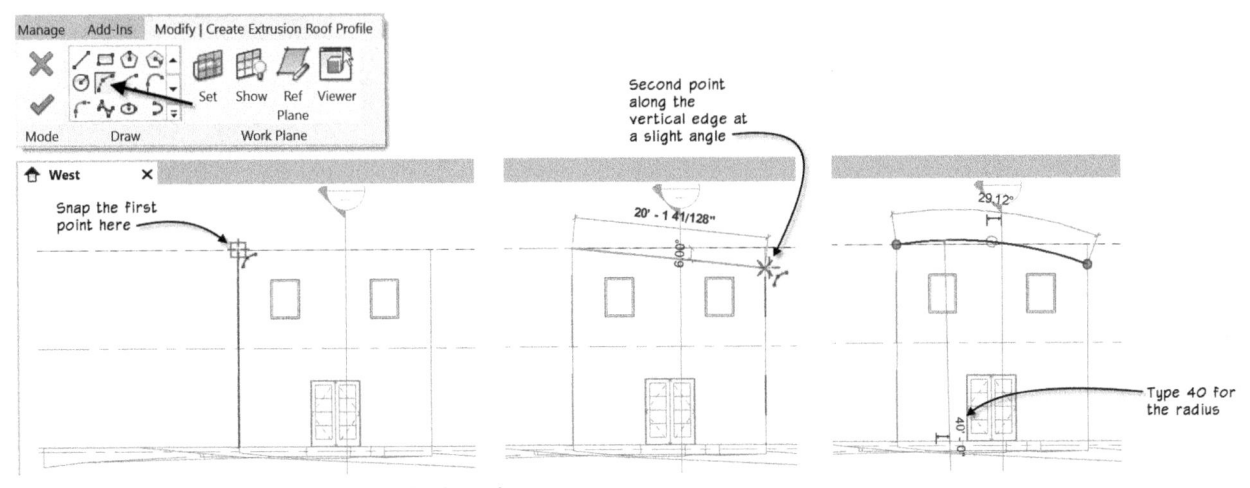

FIGURE 1.24 *Create a three-point arc shape for the roof extrusion*

The final point determines the radius, which we can click by eye onscreen, or we can simply type it in.
   > Some trial and error reveals a value of 40 works well. Type: **40** and then press ENTER.

5. On the ribbon, click the Finish Edit Mode (green checkmark) button.
6. Switch to the {3D} view.

The roof automatically spanned over the entire building model. However, its eaves are flush with the walls and the walls pass through the roof. Let's add an overhang to the roof and then we will fix the walls.

The roof should still be selected; if it is not, click on it now.

Notice the small arrow handles pointing away from the roof on two ends of the extrusion.

7. Click and drag each of these handles slightly away from the walls to create an overhang (see Figure 1.25).

• Revit Essentials for Architecture •

22 | Chapter 1

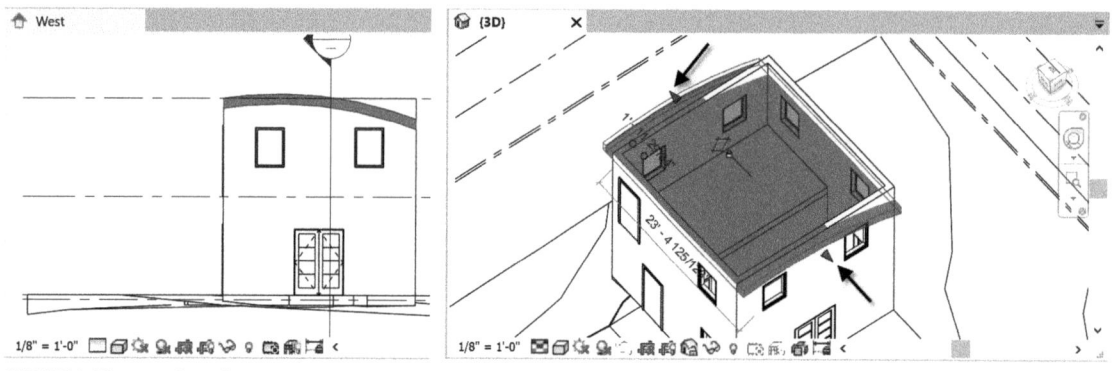

FIGURE 1.25 *Stretch roof extrusion handles to make overhangs*

The previous edit was simple because we were changing the overall length of the extrusion. To add overhangs in the other direction, we can edit the sketch.

   8.   With the roof still selected, on the Modify | Roofs tab, on the Mode panel, click the Edit Profile button.

The sketch line will reappear, and the roof will temporarily disappear. You can switch back to the elevation view or edit the sketch directly in 3D. Remember, you can edit in any view and the change will occur in all views.

   ⇨   Drag the ends of the line away from the walls slightly as shown in Figure 1.26.

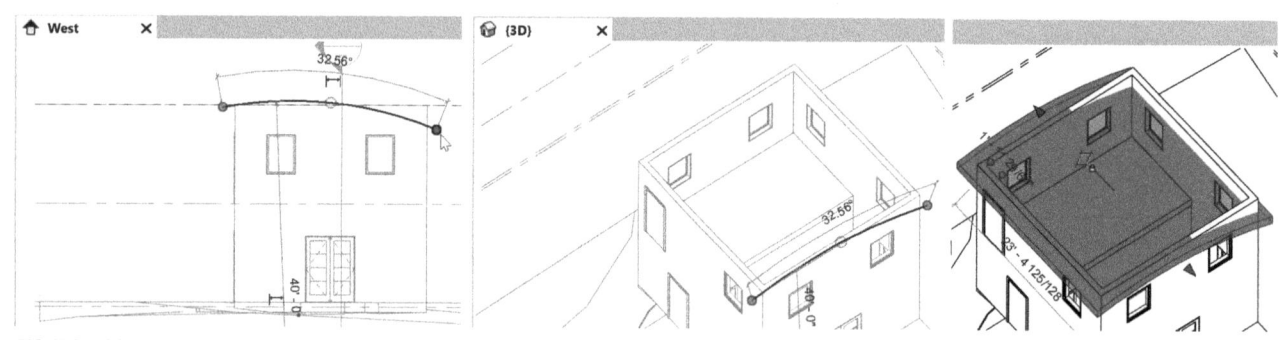

FIGURE 1.26 *Edit the sketch line to re-shape the roof to include overhangs*

   9.   On the ribbon, click the Finish Roof button.

   10. Use the TAB select method above to chain-select all the exterior walls. You can do this in any view including the {3D} view.

   ⇨   On the Modify | Walls tab of the ribbon, on the Modify Wall panel, click the Attach Top/Base button.

   ⇨   Click any edge of the roof (see Figure 1.27).

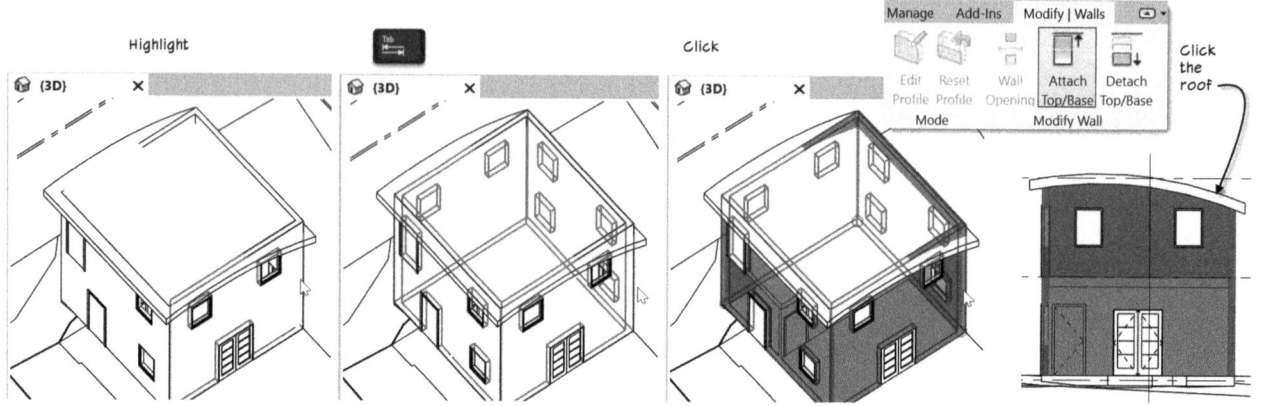

FIGURE 1.27 *Attach the walls to the roof*

• The Aubin Academy •

Quick Start Overview | 23

> **NOTE:** If you edit the shape of the roof, the walls will remain attached. Try it out if you like. Select the roof. On the ribbon click the Edit Profile button and change the shape of the arc. Finish the sketch to see the change to the roof shape and how the walls remain attached. Undo any change before continuing.

11. Save the model.

> **NOTE:** You can find more information and tutorials on working with roofs in Chapter 9.

ADD A STAIR

We have no way to reach our second floor balcony now. Let's add a Stair.

1. Return to the *Level 1* floor plan view. Click the tab if it is still open, otherwise double-click its name on Project Browser.

> **TIP:** When you open a new view from Project Browser, it will add a new tab to the current tile. If your views are all maximized (full screen), all of your tabs will be grouped together, but if you previously tiled the views (like we did above), then you want to remember to click into the tile where you want to open the view to make that tile active before you double-click another view on Project Browser. Doing so will open the new view in the active tile. However, if you forget to do this, you can grab the tab and drag it away from the tile to "tear it off" of the frame. This makes it a floating window. You can leave it floating if you wish, or you can drag it to a different tile to dock it where you want it. Pay attention to the blue highlighting while dragging before you release your mouse. This indicates whether it will add to an existing tile or make a new one. You can also reset your entire workspace by clicking the Tab Views button on the View tab. This will return you to a single tile with all open views as tabs within this tile. More information on user interface is found in Chapter 3.

⇨ On the Architecture tab of the ribbon, on the Circulation panel, click the Stair tool.

The Modify | Create Stair tab will appear on the ribbon. The Stair will go to the north (top) side of the building. There is a little bump out on the existing patio for this purpose.

⇨ Click at the midpoint (triangle symbol) of the patio bump out and drag straight up (see Figure 1.28).

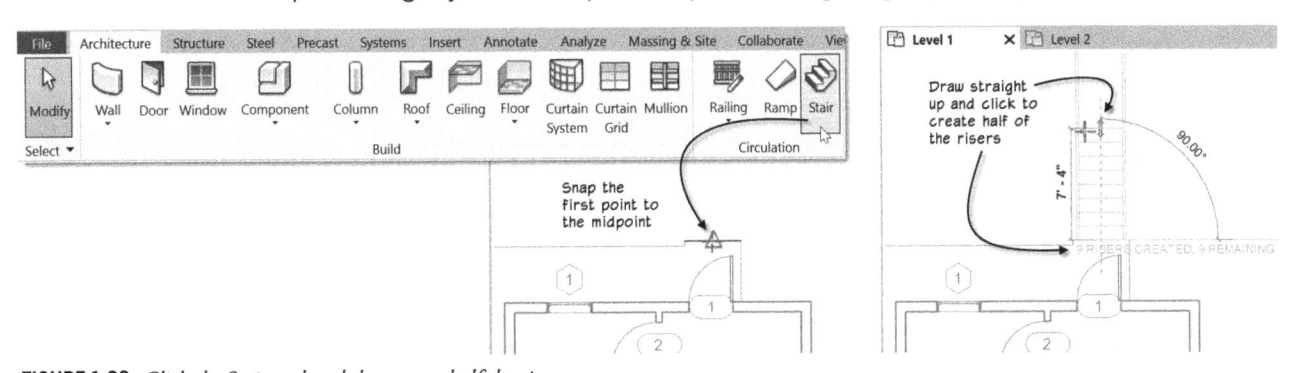

FIGURE 1.28 *Click the Stair tool and then create half the risers*

A small label in gray text will appear on screen indicating how many risers have been created and how many remain. Revit calculates this based on the settings built into the Stair element and its type. For more information on Stairs, please refer to Chapter 8.

2. Drag straight up until the gray label reads "9 Risers created, 9 remaining" and then click to create the first 9 risers.
3. Click a point next to the first run of stairs at the location indicated on the left side of Figure 1.29.

• Revit Essentials for Architecture •

24 | Chapter 1

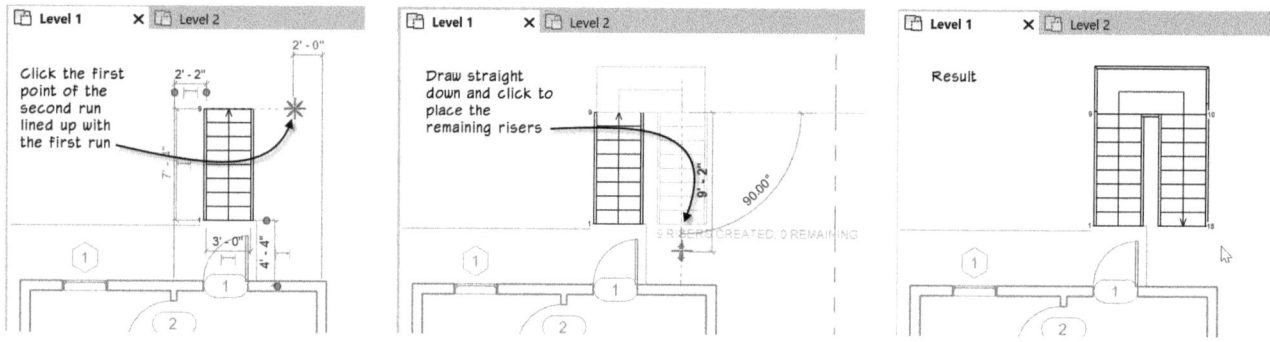

FIGURE 1.29 *Create a second run using up the remaining risers*

⇨ Drag straight down until the message indicates that zero risers remain and then click to create the remaining risers.

This will give us the basic Stair, but it will not "hook up" with the second floor. We need to add a landing at the top.

    4.   On the ribbon, click the Landing tool, then click the Create Sketch icon.

⇨ On the Draw panel, click the Rectangle icon.

⇨ Snap one corner of the rectangle to the Stair run and the other corner to the face of the building.

If necessary, use Align to ensure that the sketch lines match the inside edges of the Stair run (see Figure 1.30).

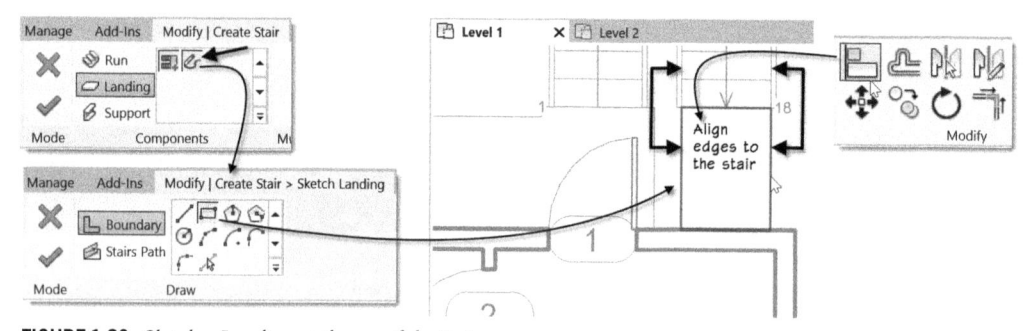

FIGURE 1.30 *Sketch a Landing at the top of the Stair run*

If it becomes necessary to use the Align tool, first click the inside edge of the Stair as the alignment reference, then click the sketch line as the object to align.

    5.   Click the Finish Edit Mode (green checkmark) button.

The new Landing will appear with Supports on three sides. We don't need the Support at the face of the building, so we can simply delete that one.

    6.   Select the Support at the building wall and delete it (see the left side of Figure 1.31).

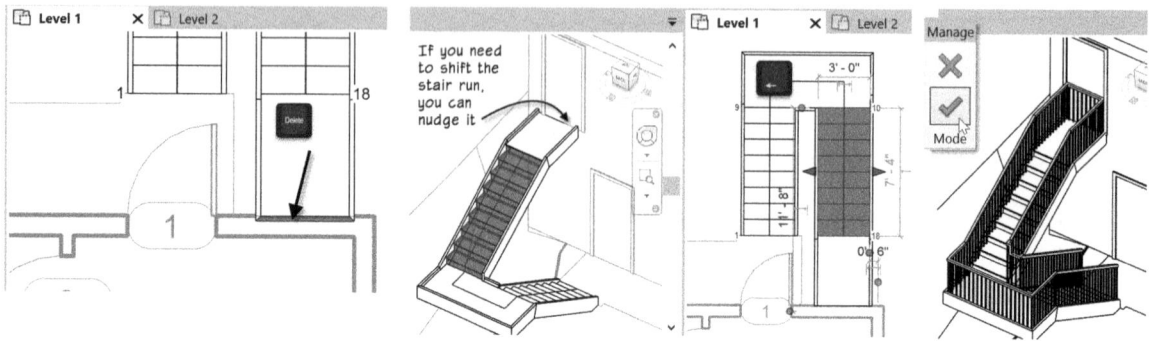

FIGURE 1.31 *Delete the unneeded Support*

    If you look in the {3D} view, your stair might not line up properly with door on the second floor. Simply select the upper run (in plan or 3D) and nudge it a little. To nudge, press the arrows on your keyboard.

• The Aubin Academy •

7. On the ribbon, click the Finish Edit Mode button to complete the stair (see the right side of Figure 1.31).

The new stair will appear complete with railings. However, even though we deleted the unneeded Support, we still ended up with the railing wrapping around that edge. We'll take care of that next. You might assume that we can solve this in a similar way to the previous edit and simply edit the railing and delete the unneeded segment. However, in Revit each railing must be a single path. So, if tried this, it will generate a warning and not allow us to continue. So instead, we need to edit the existing railing and then create a new one for the other side. The simplest way to do this is to copy the existing railing and then edit each copy.

8. In the {3D} view, (click its tab, or open it from Project Browser if you closed it) select the railing (see item 1 in Figure 1.32).

   ⇨ On the Modify | Railings tab, on the Clipboard panel click the Copy to Clipboard tool (or press CTRL + C (item 2).

   ⇨ Click the dropdown menu on the Paste tool and choose: **Aligned to Same Place** (item 3).

   We now have two identical railings in the same spot. The one you just pasted is still selected, so we can edit it directly.

9. On the Modify | Railings tab, on the Mode panel, click the Edit Path button (item 4).

   For this step, it will be easier to work in a floor plan. Just click into one of your open floor plan tabs. We need to delete just part of the path.

   ⇨ Place your mouse point beneath the doorway at the right run of the stair approximately in the middle, but below the (item 5).

   ⇨ Click and hold down your mouse and drag up and to the left until you have surrounded the sketch lines in the middle of the railing only (see item 6). Release the mouse to make the selection.

   This method of selection is referred to as a "crossing window" selection. You can learn more about selection in Chapter 3. The Properties palette should indicate that the selection is <Sketch> (5) (see item 7). This means that the selection includes 5 sketch lines. The quantity is the number in parenthesis and gives important and useful feedback about your selections.

10. Delete the selection and then on the ribbon click the Finish Edit Mode button (see item 8 in Figure 1.32).

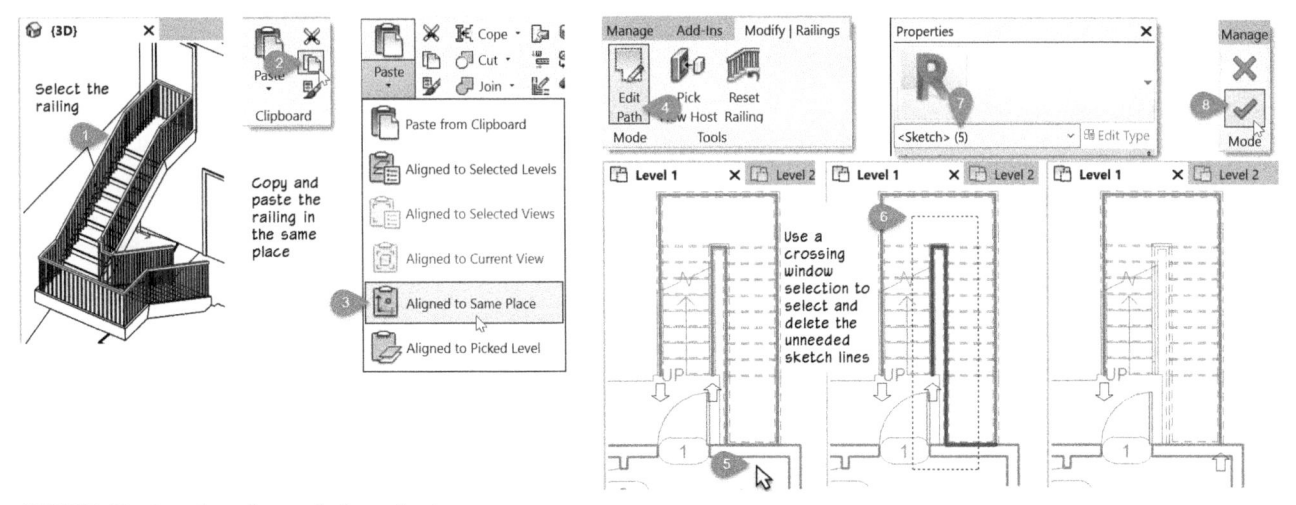

FIGURE 1.32 *Copy the railing and edit its sketch*

It will not look much different, but if you look carefully, you will see that the currently selected railing applies only around the outer edge of the stair. So now we just need to edit the other copy in the reverse configuration.

11. Select the other copy of the railing (click near the middle of the stair to select it).

    ⇨ On the ribbon, click the Edit Path button again.

• Revit Essentials for Architecture •

26 | Chapter 1

⇨ Using similar technique as before select and delete the unneeded sketch lines; however, select the opposite sketch lines this time.

⇨ Click outside and below the railing to the right, and the drag to the left and up to cross through the sketch lines of the right-hand run. Do not include the middle sketch lines selected (and deleted) above.

⇨ Delete these. Then make another crossing selection to select the remaining outside sketch lines again avoiding the middle ones. Delete them.

12. On the ribbon, click the Finish Edit Mode button.

We now have two separate railings: one on the inside edge of the stair and one on the outside edge and the railing across the doorway is no longer there.

> **NOTE:** You can find more information and tutorials on working with Stairs and Railings in Chapter 8.

CREATE A CUSTOM WALL TYPE

To refine our basic model, let's make a quick modification to the exterior walls. Let's see what our building would look like if we added brick veneer.

1. In the *{3D}* view, right-click one of the exterior walls and choose: **Select All Instances** > **Visible in View**.

⇨ On the Properties palette (confirm that the filter list reads: Walls (4) indicating that the selection includes 4 walls.

⇨ To the right of this, click the Edit Type button.

2. In the "Type Properties" dialog, click the Duplicate button. In the dialog that appears, type: **Wall w Brick Veneer** and then click OK once (see Figure 1.33).

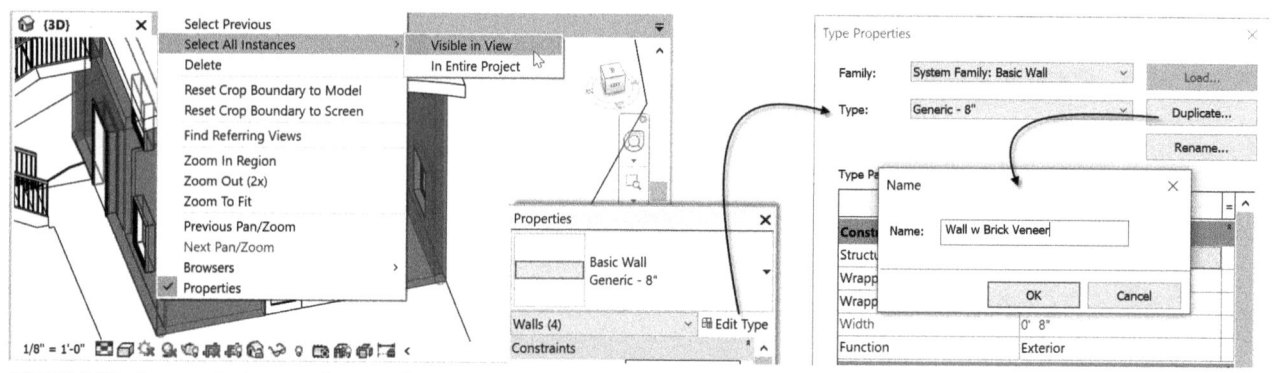

FIGURE 1.33 *Create a duplicate wall type and give it a descriptive name*

We now have a new wall type. Next, we will edit its structure to add the Brick veneer.

3. Remaining in the "Type Properties" dialog, click the Edit button next to Structure.

⇨ In the Thickness column next to Structure [1], type: **0 4** (that is zero SPACE four) and then press ENTER (see item 1 in Figure 1.34).

4. In the middle of the dialog, click the Insert button (item 2) and then click the Up button (item 3).

This will add a new layer and then move it to the top of the list.

⇨ In the Thickness column for item 1, type: **0 4** (that is zero SPACE four) and then press ENTER (item 4).

⇨ Change the Function of item 1 (which is the new layer) to: **Finish 1 [4]** (it's for exterior finishes) (item 5).

5. Click in the Material column and then click the small browse button (item 6) to open the "Material Browser" dialog.

From the list of materials on the left, choose: Brick, Common (item 7) and then click OK (item 8).

⇨ Click OK twice to complete the wall type (item 9).

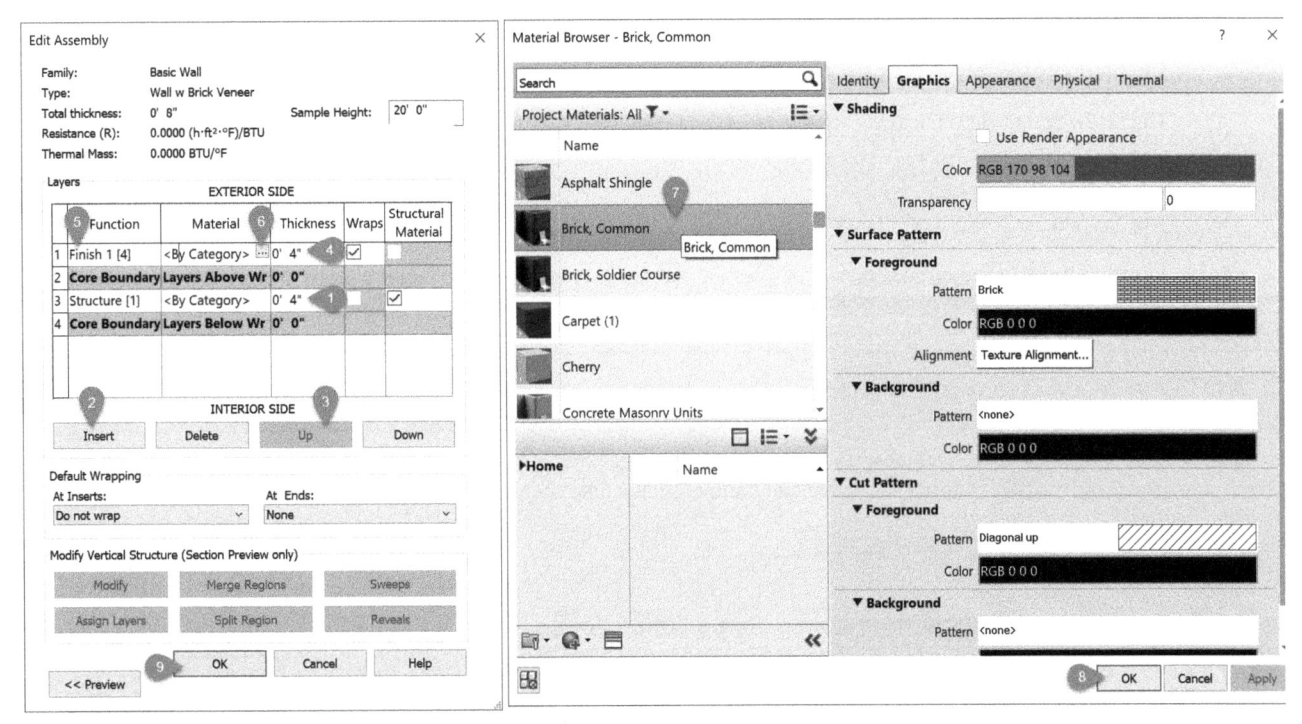

FIGURE 1.34 *Insert new wall layers and configure the materials*

6. In the *{3D}* view, from the View Control Bar, choose: **Shaded** for the Visual Style pop-up and then zoom in on the brick.

You can also try the others like Consistent Colors and Realistic. To see the brick in plan or section views, you must change the level of detail to: Medium or Fine. There is a control for this also on the View Control Bar between the Visual Style pop-up that we edited here and the Scale list (see Figure 1.35).

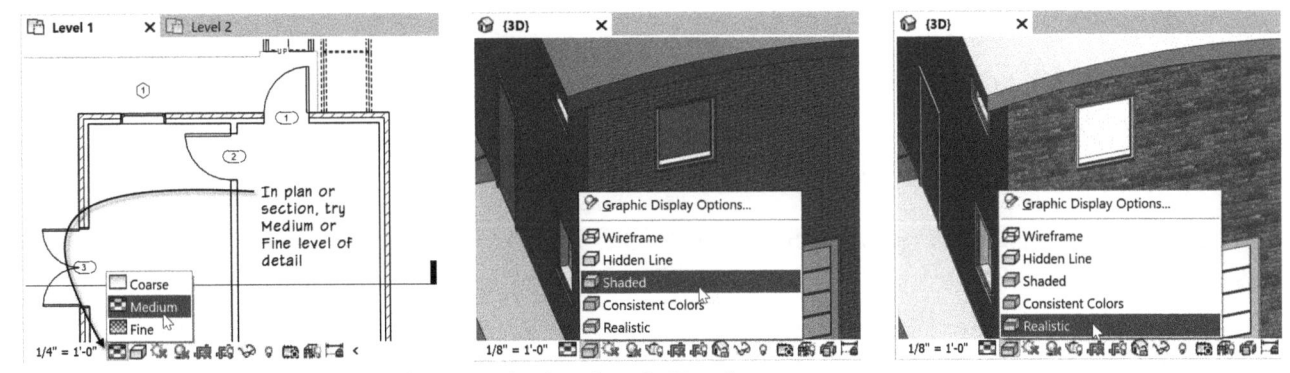

FIGURE 1.35 *Use the View Control Bar to change Visual Style and Level of Detail*

We could add many more embellishments like railings on the patio and second floor balcony, adjustments to the windows and roof eaves, and additional materials to name a few. For now, we'll shift our attention to some construction documentation items like door and window schedules, dimensions and some sheets for printing.

7. Save the project.

CREATE A SCHEDULE

We can create automated schedules of most element categories in Revit. All we need to do is generate a Schedule view which, while not graphical like the plan, section, and elevation views, it dynamically reports the items in the

28 | Chapter 1

building model. Using a schedule you can view information related to the model and even edit it directly from a schedule view. Let's do a simple example to get a feel for it.

1. On the Project Browser, right-click Schedules/Quantities and choose: **New Schedule/ Quantities**.

   The "New Schedule" dialog will appear.

   ⇨ From the "Category" list, choose: Doors and then click OK.

   The "Schedule Properties" dialog will appear.

2. In the "Schedule Properties" dialog, on the "Fields" tab, in the "Available Fields" list, click: "Mark" and then click the Add button in the middle of the dialog.

> **NOTE:** "Mark" is the door's number field.

   ⇨ Repeat for the following Fields: Level, Width, Height, Family and Type, and Comments (see Figure 1.36). (Alternatively, you can double-click a field name to add it).

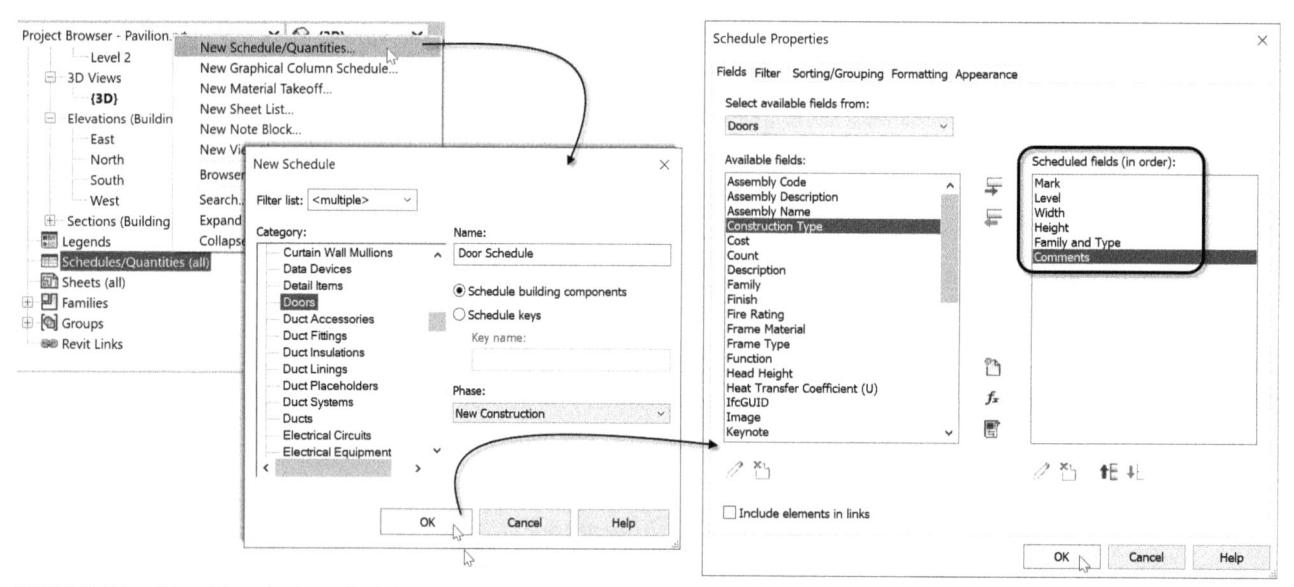

FIGURE 1.36 *Add Fields to the door schedule*

3. Click OK to create the Schedule.

A Schedule view will appear onscreen as a tab in the active tile. The Schedule view appears much like a spreadsheet. Let's close some of the other views and then tile at the Schedule next to one of the floor plans.

4. If you still have the windows tiled on screen, move your mouse over the other tabs, and when the X appears, click it to close all other views except the *schedule* and the *Level 1* floor plan.

   ⇨ Zoom in on the plan view.

5. In the *Door Schedule* view, click on door number 3.

The row will highlight in the Schedule and the door itself will highlight in the plan.

   ⇨ Highlight the value in the Mark field, type: **5**, and then press ENTER.

   Notice that the value changes in the door tag on the floor plan as well. The selection has moved down one line in the schedule and door 4 is now selected.

6. Select door 2 in the schedule, click in the family and type column in the schedule and then choose: **Single-Flush: 30"** × **80"** from the pop-up list (see Figure 1.37).

• The Aubin Academy •

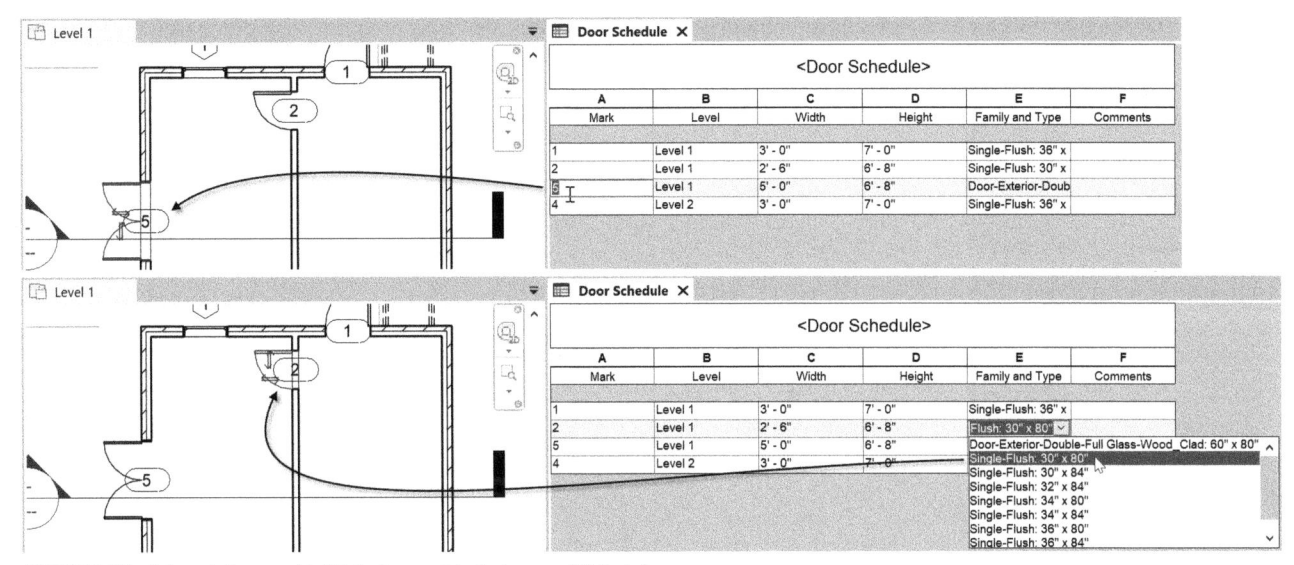

FIGURE 1.37 *Selected elements highlight in graphical views and Schedules*

Notice that the size of the door changes in both the Schedule and the floor plan. This is the correct way to change the size of a door since most doors use "type-based" parameters to control their width. To illustrate this point, try an experiment. Click in the width column for door 1. In the Width field, change the value to: **2**. A message will appear stating that: "This change will be applied to all elements of type Single-Flush: 36" × 84"." This means that all doors of this type will be affected when you click OK. Go ahead and click OK to see this. If you open the second floor, you will see that the door here is also 2'-0". This is likely not the desired result, particularly since the family and type value still indicates that the name of this door is Single-Flush: 36"×84", which is likely to foster some confusion. This topic will be discussed in more detail in later chapters. For now, it suffices to say that if you wish to change the width or height of the door, you should choose a different door family and/or type instead rather than simply edit the dimensions directly in the schedule (unless you really want to edit *all* doors at once). Be sure to undo the change to the single doors before continuing.

7. Click in the schedule view to make it the active window.
   - On the View tab, click the Schedules drop down and then choose: **Schedules/Quantities**.

   This is an alternative way to create a new schedule.

   - In the "New Schedule" dialog, from the "Category" list, scroll to the bottom, choose: **Windows** and then click OK.
   - In the "Schedule Properties" dialog, on the "Fields" tab, add the Type Mark, Level, Family and Type, Width, Height, and Count fields.

8. Click the Sorting/Grouping tab.
   - For "Sort by," choose: **Level** and then check the "Header" check box.
   - For "Then by," choose: **Family and Type**.

9. At the bottom of the dialog, check the "Grand totals" check box and clear the "Itemize every instance" check box.
   - Click OK to create the Schedule (see the left side of Figure 1.38).
   - Click in the first line item in the schedule.

   Notice that this line item represents three windows on Level 1 and consequently, all three are selected in the plan view.

10. In the *Level 1* floor plan view, add windows to the right wall. Choose a different size than the ones already used in the model.

• Revit Essentials for Architecture •

30 | Chapter 1

Notice that the new windows appear immediately in the Schedule. Since we used a different type (size) the new ones appear on their own line item in the schedule (see the right side of Figure 1.38).

If you wish to make any other modifications to the windows in the model, you can watch them adjust accordingly in the schedule.

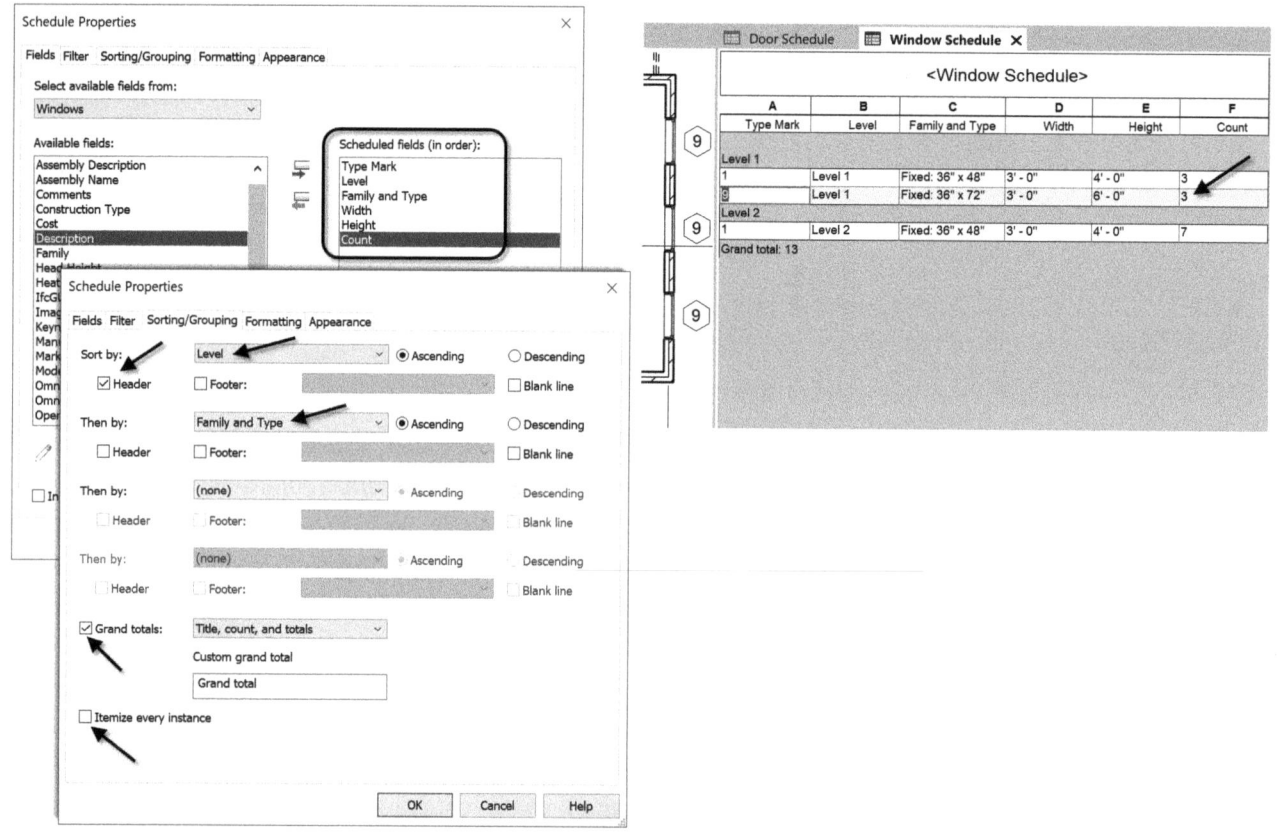

FIGURE 1.38 *Configure the Window Schedule to sort and total the windows in the project by Level*

11. Save the model.

> **NOTE:** You can find more information and tutorials on working with Schedules in Chapter 13.

PREPARING OUTPUT

At some point in your project, you will need to output your designs and produce some form of deliverable. This could be a collection of printed drawings or a PDF. In Revit you use "sheet" views for this purpose. These views emulate the final paper output and allow us to compose the completed sheets formatted the way we wish, complete with title blocks.

ADD A SHEET

While it is possible to directly print the views we already have, we will get more polished and professional results by creating sheet views. A sheet can contain one or several views. Sheets are at full size, that is, the scale is 1:1. Graphical views added to sheets can be at different scales. The exact composition is up to you and your office standards.

1. Close both schedule views.
2. On the ribbon, click the View tab and then on the Sheet Composition panel, click the Sheet tool.

• The Aubin Academy •

⇨ In the "New Sheet" dialog accept the defaults and then click OK.

A blank sheet view with a title block appears. (Beneath the Sheets branch of the Project Browser, you can also expand the branch to see the new sheet listed.) There is currently only one title block choice available, but you can load other title block borders in your own projects. You can even create your own custom title block including your company logo, information, and other standard graphical elements (see the "Create a Custom Title Block Family" topic on page 193 in Chapter 5 for more information).

The new sheet is ready to receive views. We have a few ways to do this. Right-click the sheet view name on the Project Browser and choose: **Add View**. A dialog will appear listing all available views, or simply drag and drop the desired view from Project Browser to the sheet onscreen. We'll use drag and drop here.

3. From the Project Browser, drag the *Level 1* floor plan view over the Sheet area and release. Click to place it on the sheet.

After you drop, an outline of the view will appear attached to the cursor. This is called the viewport boundary and it automatically sizes itself to the extents of the dragged view's contents. You can use this to place it on the sheet where desired.

⇨ Position the view in the upper left corner of the sheet and then click to place it.

⇨ Repeat the drag and drop process for each of the remaining floor plans.

4. Drag each of the Schedule views to the sheet as well (see Figure 1.39).

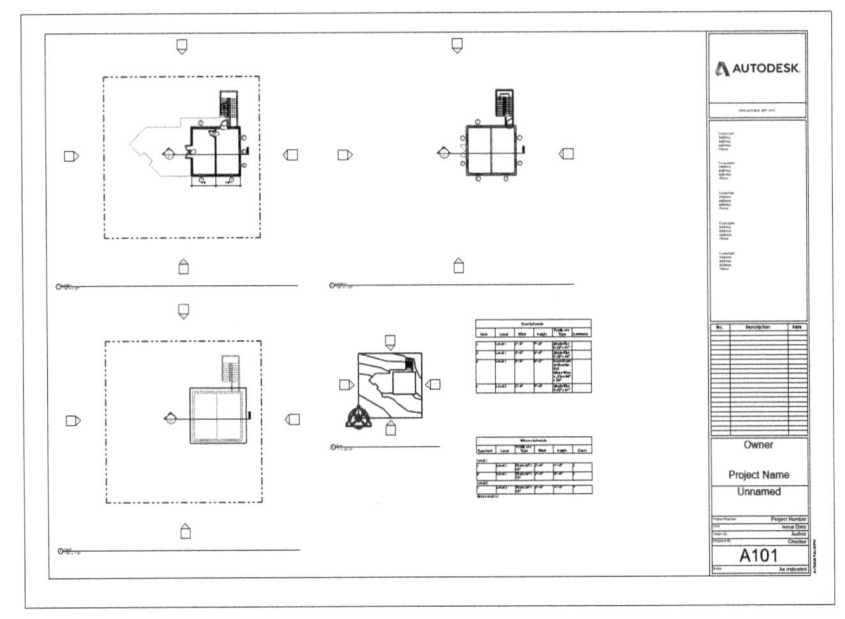

FIGURE 1.39 *Drag all the plans and schedules to the sheet view and position them*

If you need to re-position a view after you drag it, you can click on it directly on the sheet, and then drag it again to move it or use the arrow keys on your keyboard to nudge it slightly. When you add the Site plan, notice that it is a little smaller than the others. Each view has its own scale setting that is used when it is added to a sheet. A view title appears beneath each view as you place it.

5. Repeat the entire process to create another sheet and add the elevations and section views.

Suppose that you wish to change the scale of a view after it is added. For instance, after adding all the elevations and the section view to this new sheet, you may wish to enlarge the Section view.

6. Select the Section view on the sheet, right-click and choose: **Activate View**.

• Revit Essentials for Architecture •

This makes the view editable as if you had opened it from the Project Browser and edited the original section view.

> Look for the Properties palette on your screen (it is docked above the Project Browser by default). If you closed it, right-click in the Section view and choose: **Properties**.

7. On the Properties palette, beneath the "graphics" grouping, change the "View Scale" to: **¼" = 1'-0"** and then click the Apply button.

⇨ Right-click in the view again and choose: **Deactivate View**.

Reposition the view as required.

Notice that the change in scale only affected the graphics of the view. The graphics of the model elements such as walls, doors, and windows enlarged but the text and annotations remained the same size, relative to the sheet & title block. You may also notice that the title bar may no longer match the viewport. You can click on the viewport to access round grips at either end of the title bar to change its length. If you want to move the entire title bar, do *not* click the viewport first. Rather click on the title bar directly and then drag it.

If you look at the right corner of the title blocks or at the sheets listed on the Project Browser, you will notice that logical numbers have been automatically assigned, but the names of the two sheets are "Unnamed." You can rename (or renumber) the sheets by selecting the title block and then click on the blue text of the title or number to edit it. An alternative method is to right-click the sheet on the Project Browser and choose: **Rename**.

8. Zoom in on the view titles beneath the elevations.

Notice that each drawing has been automatically numbered sequentially.

Switch back to the other sheet (A101).

Notice that the section marks and elevation marks in the floor plan views correctly reflect the numbers of elevations and sections on sheet A102 (see Figure 1.40).

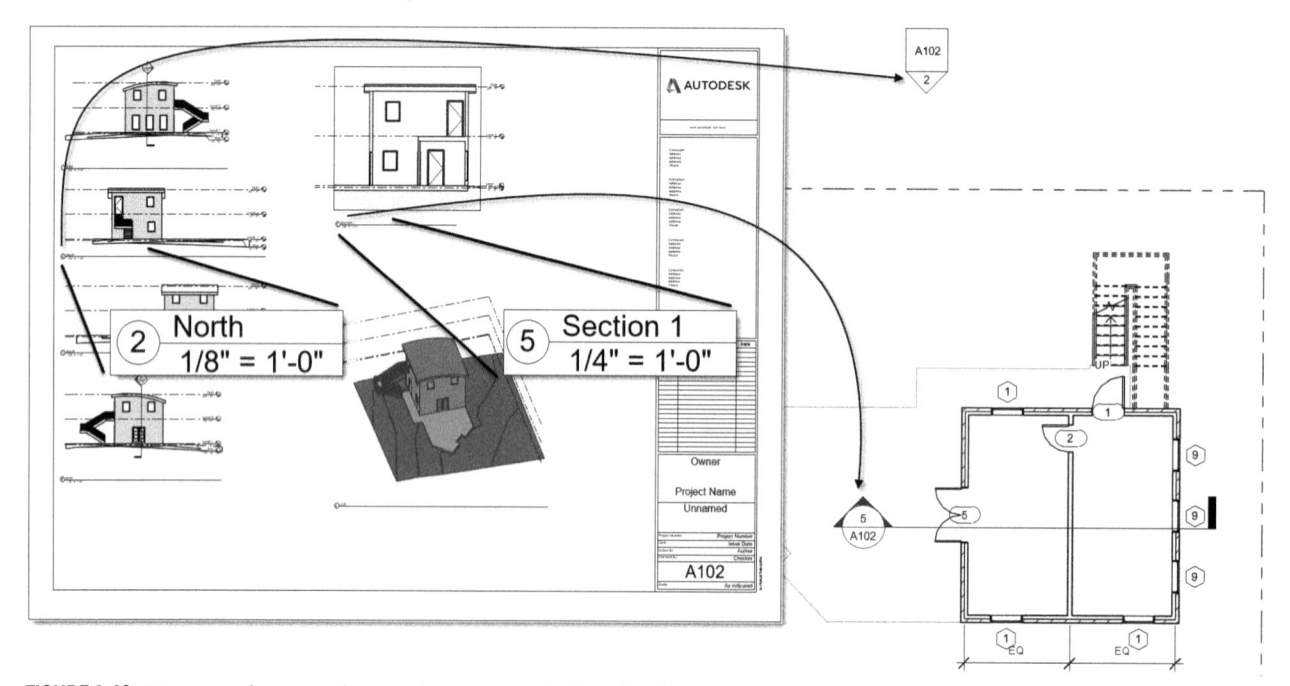

FIGURE 1.40 *View tag references and view titles are automatically updated*

9. Perform any other edits and do some exploring.

ADD DIMENSIONS

Typically, when you issue sheets, you also need to include some dimensions on the plans and other views. We have a few basic dimensions on the plan already, but let's add a few more to clarify the design a bit.

1. On the Project Browser, double-click on the *Level 1* floor plan view to open it.
   ⇨ On the Annotate tab, on the Dimension panel, click the Aligned tool.
   ⇨ On the Options Bar, choose: **Wall Faces** from the first drop down list.
2. In the plan window, click on the outside face of the top horizontal wall (see item 1 in Figure 1.41).
   ⇨ Move the mouse down and then click at the center of the double door (item 2).
   ⇨ Continue down and then click the outside face of the bottom horizontal wall (item 3).
3. Move the pointer outside the building to the left and click in an empty space to place the dimension (item 4).

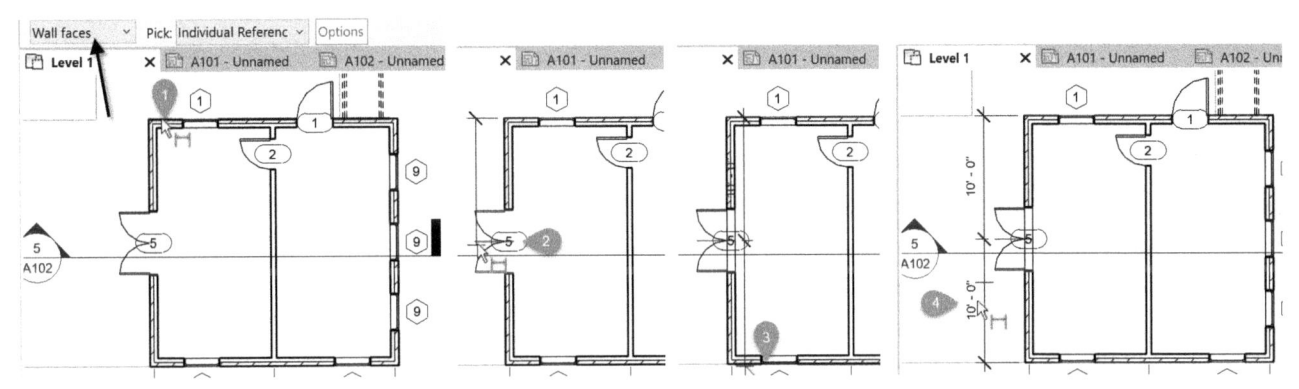

FIGURE 1.41 *Add dimensions by picking individual elements*

Compare this dimension to the equal one at the bottom of the plan. Using the Wall Faces option allows us to dimension to exactly the points we desire. Let's add another dimension across the top wall using a slightly different technique.

If you canceled the command, on the Annotate tab, on the Dimension panel, click the Aligned tool again.

4. On the Options Bar, from the Pick drop down list, choose: **Entire Walls** from the second drop down list.
   ⇨ Next to the drop down, click the small Options button.
   ⇨ Check the Openings check box, choose the Widths option, and then click OK.
5. Select the top horizontal wall, move the mouse up, and click in an empty space to place the dimension (see Figure 1.42).

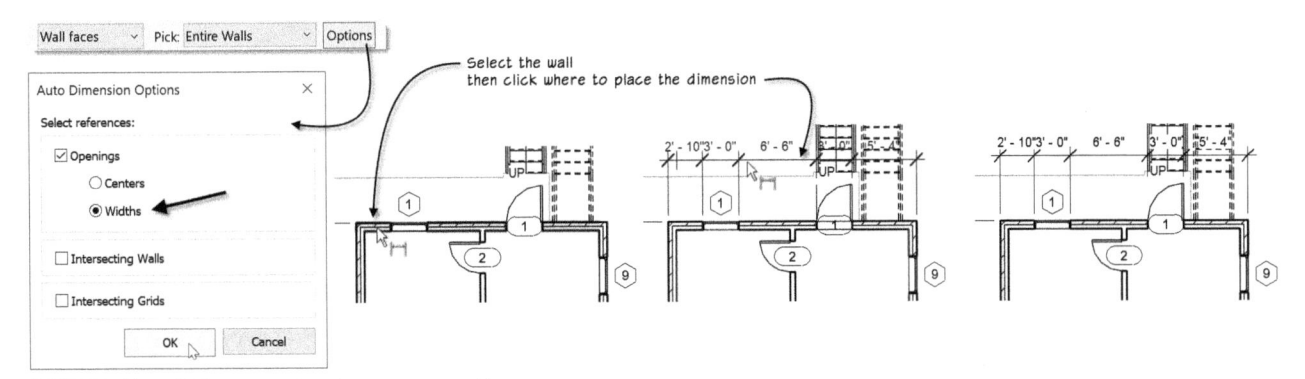

FIGURE 1.42 *Add dimensions by selecting entire walls*

Notice how this adds a complete string of dimensions including the openings in the wall in a single step!

34 | Chapter 1

Feel free to experiment further before continuing. Also note that you can select elements in the model and use these newly placed dimensions to adjust their locations just like you can with temporary dimensions. For example, you can select the window and edit the dimension value to move it onto a proper brick dimension. Give it a try. Also notice that when you return to the Sheet, all these dimensions appear on the corresponding view. Remember, edits in one view appear in all appropriate locations in Revit—no separate update process is necessary!

OUTPUT

Feel free to print your two sheets out to your printer or plotter. Or you can create a digital plot instead by printing to a PDF file. To create a PDF file, you need to have a PDF printer installed such as Adobe Acrobat or Bluebeam. Most computers have one. Check with your IT support personnel for more information. File menu

SOLAR STUDIES

Giving you tools for producing traditional document sets and plotting are key strengths of the Revit software package. However, there is so much more that Revit can do. Schedules can be used to quantify elements in the model and assist professionals in cost estimating, reducing waste, and coordinating data with other applications outside of Revit. If you work with consultants who also use Revit for MEP or Structural engineering, the models you produce in Revit can be used to facilitate clash-detection studies and help catch conflicts before they become costly change orders in the field. Revit can even help us study how our building will interact with its environment by enabling us to create very accurate shadow studies. In our final exercise in this Revit quick tour, let's take a brief look at the Sun Path feature.

1. On the Project Browser, double-click to open the {3D} view.

⇨ Orbit the model around so that you can see the Stairs and front door. (You can click the North-West corner of the ViewCube).

2. On the View Control Bar at the bottom of the view window, click the Sun Path icon and choose: **Sun Path On**.

The "Sun Path -Sun Not Displayed" dialog will appear. This message tells us that we need to adjust some settings for the Sun to appear.

⇨ In the "Sun Path -Sun Not Displayed" dialog, choose the "Use the specified project location, date and time instead" option.

⇨ Next to the Sun Path icon, click the Shadows icon (see Figure 1.43).

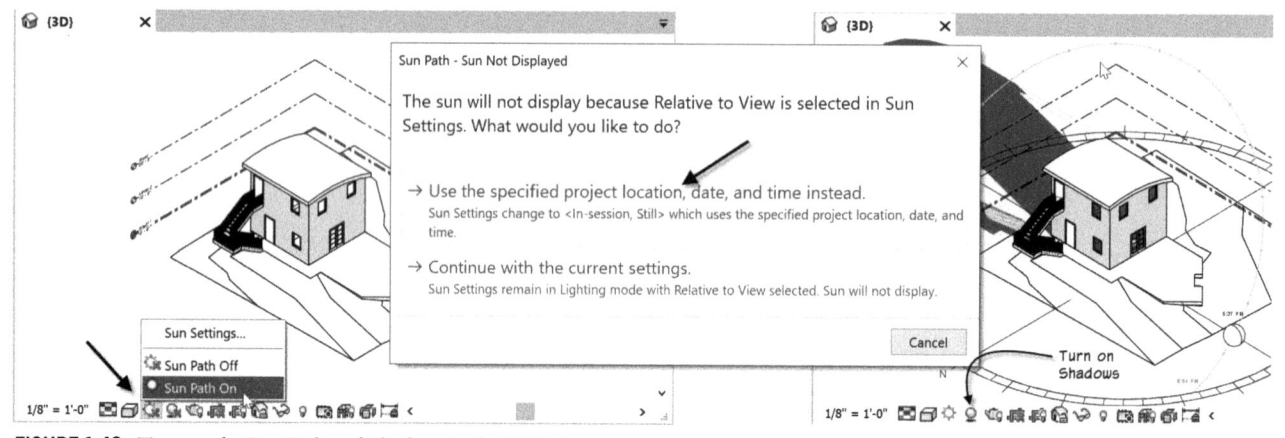

FIGURE 1.43 *Turn on the Sun Path and Shadows in the {3D} view*

A circular compass will appear surrounding the model and a long shadow will appear behind the building. We can change a few settings and have Revit display shadows using the project's location in the world and the actual position of the Sun.

3. Click the Sun Path icon again and choose: **Sun Settings**.

   Position the "Sun Settings" dialog next to the 3D view window. Several presets are available.

4. Click on Summer Solstice and then click Apply.

   ⇨ Change the time to 1:00 PM and then click Apply (see Figure 1.44).

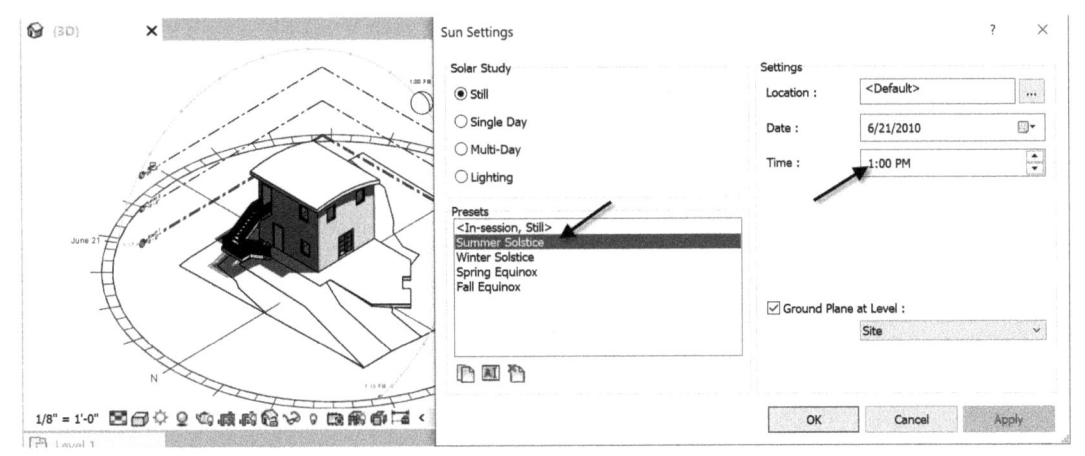

FIGURE 1.44 *Choose Summer Solstice and 1:00 PM*

Notice that the shadow shifts as you make these changes. This tool is completely interactive. You can click on the Sun icon in the view window and drag it to alternate positions. When you drag, a yellow-shaded area (called the Total Sun Area) will appear representing the Sun's total movements throughout the year for your project's geographic location. You can drag the Sun along the yellow arc to change the time of day, or along the Analemma (figure-8 shaped path) to change the month. There are also text labels indicating both the date and time of day that you can click on and manipulate as an alternate way to change the Sun's position and alter the shadows accordingly. You can find more detail on features of the Sun path in the online Help. Let's try one more variation.

5. Return to the "Sun Settings" dialog.

   ⇨ Beneath Solar Study, choose Single Day.

   ⇨ Check the box for Sunrise to sunset.

   ⇨ From the Time Interval list, choose: **15 Minutes**.

6. Uncheck the "Ground Plane at Level" check box and then click OK (see Figure 1.45).

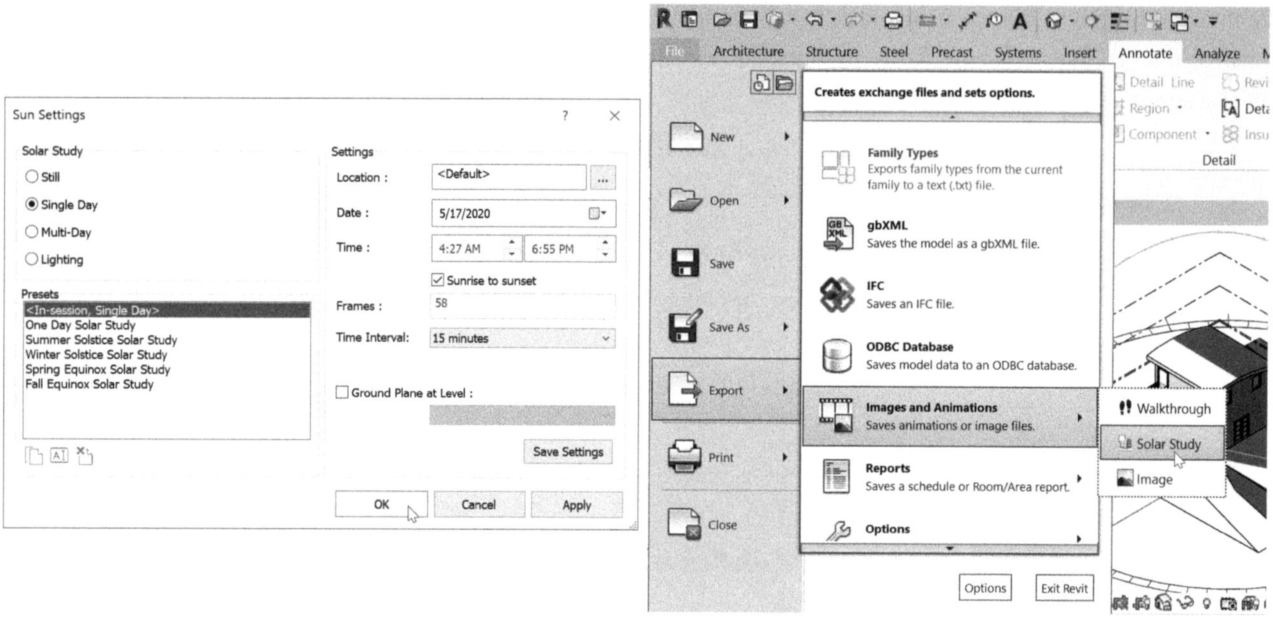

36 | Chapter 1

FIGURE 1.45 *Configure a single day solar study from early morning to early evening*

These settings tell Revit that we want to study how the Sun moves across the sky from morning to evening on a single date. Now let's create an AVI file of the results.

7. From the File menu, choose: **Export** > **Images and Animations** > **Solar Study**.

⇨ Change the Frames/Sec to 5 and then click OK.

8. In the "Export Animated Solar Study" dialog, choose a folder where you wish to save the file, accept the suggested file name and then click Save.

⇨ Click OK in the next dialog to complete the export.

9. In Windows Explorer, browse to the location where you saved the AVI and double-click it.

The animation file will open in whatever media player you have installed on your system. You will see the shadows move across the ground as the day goes by! A sample of the file is provided in the *Chapter01\Complete* folder. Feel free to experiment further with any of the settings and export another file if you like.

10. Save and close the project.

Congratulations! You have completed your first Revit project! Your journey into Revit and Building Information Modeling awaits you in the coming chapters.

• The Aubin Academy •

SUMMARY

- ☑ Getting started with Revit is easy—click a tool on the ribbon and place the item in the view window.

- ☑ Walls, Doors, and other elements interact with each other as you place them in the model.

- ☑ Relationships and constraints are maintained automatically as you work. You can even "lock in" design intent if you choose.

- ☑ Build or edit your model from any view and changes are fully coordinated in all views. Edits cannot get out of sync!

- ☑ Views include graphical representations like plans and sections and non-graphical tabular representations like schedules.

- ☑ Sheets are special views designed for composing a title block layout and printing.

- ☑ Drag and drop to add views to sheets.

- ☑ All view references are fully coordinated on the views and sheets.

- ☑ You can print physical sheets or export the sheets to a PDF.

- ☑ Create fully interactive solar studies using the sun path feature.

CHAPTER 2
Conceptual Underpinnings of Revit

INTRODUCTION

Autodesk® Revit® is an advanced software package for architects and other professionals involved in the design, documentation, and construction of buildings. It facilitates the creation of a "Building Information Model" (BIM) in which plans, sections, elevations, 3D models, quantities, and other data are fully coordinated and can be readily manipulated, accessed and shared in a variety of meaningful ways. From the BIM database, one can perform design tasks, query quantities and takeoffs, and generate drawing sheets for construction documentation needs. The advantages of this approach are many. From a production point of view, it means less time drafting and coordinating building data, because all drawings and reports come from the same source model. If the model changes, all "views," whether floor plans, sections, elevations, or schedules reflect the change immediately. To work effectively in such an environment, it is important to understand a bit about what it means to create and work within a Building Information Model. This is the primary goal of this chapter.

OBJECTIVES

In this chapter, we will explore the meaning of Building Information Modeling and take a high-level look at the architectural features in the Revit software package. Working in a provided dataset, you will learn how to view a single model in many ways that serve a variety of architectural drawing and documentation needs. Topics in this chapter include:

- Building Information Modeling
- The fully coordinated nature of a Revit project file
- The basics of Revit architectural elements
- An introduction to Revit families and types
- Core concepts within the context of a project

BUILDING INFORMATION MODELING

Building Information Model(ing) "BIM," is frequently assumed to be synonymous with simply generating a three-dimensional (3D) model of a building—whether that model has any useful non-graphical information or not, and regardless of the level to which the 3D model is detailed. There is much more to BIM than that. Building Information Modeling remains an evolving concept; one that will continue to change as the capabilities of technology and our own ability to manipulate technology improve. However, there are some key aspects that are well established and can be compiled into a working definition.

3D models are certainly important in BIM; in many ways critically so. However, the emphasis really belongs on the "I"—Information in BIM. That information can be either graphical (3D or even 2D) or non-graphical; either contained directly in the building model or accessible from the building model through linked data that is stored elsewhere. When you practice BIM, you are making a model which is a full description of a building—not just a 3D model. A data model is just as valid a model as a geometric model. (This is not a new concept in Architecture: consider the existing requirement in most jurisdictions of both a set of drawings *and* a written specification to complete a construction documents package.) Despite the importance of these distinctions, when we think of a Building Information Model, a three-dimensional geometric model of the building is often what comes to mind. So, the first step to fully understanding BIM is to realize that "BIM" and "3D Model" are not the same thing.

In simple terms, a Building Information Model is a complete representation or depiction of a building that aids in its design, construction and potentially ongoing management. Such representation will often employ any combination of 3D graphics, 2D abstractions, and/or non-graphical data as required for conveying full intent. The coordination and delivery of information and intent is the most important goal in BIM. To be considered BIM, all deliverables should be fully coordinated and the BIM itself should provide a platform for meaningful computation on the data contained within the BIM.

REVIT KEY CONCEPTS

So now that you've got a good idea of the BIM concept you may be wondering how it specifically relates to Revit. Even more importantly, you may also be wondering how BIM will improve the way you work. Throughout the course of this book, and even more as you begin working with Revit on your own projects, you will gain comfort and familiarity with key Revit concepts. In this topic, we will identify and describe some of the most important Revit concepts, including Revit elements, families & types, and editing modes.

ONE PROJECT FILE—EVERYTHING RELATES

In a Revit project (which is often contained within a single model file), you will notice that no matter the location within the project where you perform your work, no matter what kind of view you are working in, all changes occur immediately in all views, and all elements retain their relationships with each other. This is one of the most significant benefits to using Revit. You can make a change in any view (plan, section, elevation or schedule) with complete confidence that the change is instantly reflected throughout the entire project file in all other views.

> **NOTE:** Changes to "Drafting" views occur only in the edited view. Drafting views by definition are not linked to the model directly. These concepts are discussed in Chapter 12.

The most talked about examples of this kind of behavior usually have to do with the "physical" aspects of your building project. If you move a door in a plan view, for example, the same door will also move wherever it appears in an interior elevation or perspective view. Another equally important example is in the "informational" aspects of that door. If you go into a schedule view where that door is listed and change it from wood door to a glass door, not only could this affect calculations, quantities or costs for that door directly in the schedule, but also the change will be reflected in all graphical views—for example, in shaded views, the door will now appear transparent. Likewise, if this data is linked to cost estimation or green building calculations, the change to a glass door type will have other important impacts as well. This is a good example of how the "I" in BIM often deserves equal or even more emphasis than the "M."

Another important aspect of Revit is the Project Browser. Every view, family and group are clearly listed and organized in the Project Browser. The advantage of this is that all pieces of the project are always accessible and neatly organized. It is not possible for a team member to accidentally save project data in the wrong folder or location. Views and other elements in a project automatically appear in the correct location on the Project Browser.

REVIT ELEMENTS

In Revit you create a virtual representation (or model) of your project, using various types of elements. An element in Revit is simply a discrete building block or piece of data like an object or drawing sheet. The four most common types of elements are Model elements (walls, doors, roofs), Datum elements (levels, grids, reference planes), View elements (plans, sections, schedules), and Annotation elements (tags, text, dimensions). Your graphical model primarily contains model elements. Model elements graphically represent "real" items in your building. View elements enable you to display, study, and edit the model in depictions that represent traditional architectural drawing types. All views automatically appear in logical categories in the Project Browser tree. Specific architectural scale, level of detail, and other display characteristics are the province of views. Views can be placed on sheets and plotted (to paper or PDF) to produce presentation drawings or drawing sets. To prepare views of your Revit model to appear on and print from sheets, annotation elements such as text, dimensions, and tags are used to notate and clarify the information shown (see Figure 2.1).

There are several kinds of elements. Each represents something fundamental to your project.

REVIT ELEMENTS

MODEL Elements

HOST Elements
Built-in-place construction

FLOORS
WALLS
ROOFS
CEILINGS
STAIRS
RAMPS

COMPONENT Elements
Everything else In your model

DOORS
WINDOWS
FURNITURE
SPECIALTY ITEMS

VIEW-SPECIFIC Elements

VIEW Elements
The way you see and interact with things in Revit. Views interact with all other elements.

FLOOR PLANS
CEILING PLANS
3D VIEW
ELEVATION
SECTIONS
SCHEDULES

DATUM Elements
Non-physical items used to establish project context.

LEVELS
COLUMN GRIDS
REFERENCE PLANES

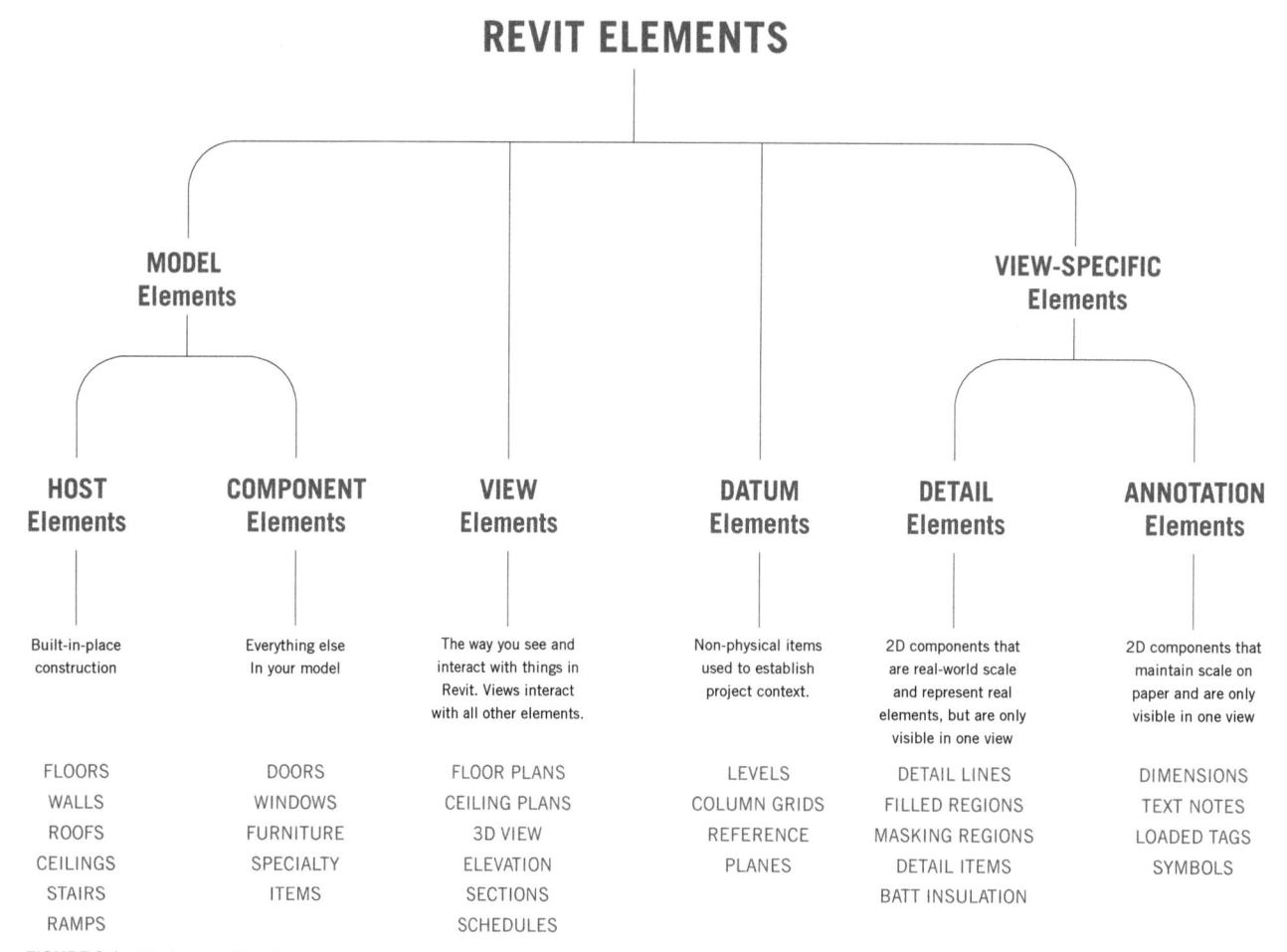

DETAIL Elements
2D components that are real-world scale and represent real elements, but are only visible in one view

DETAIL LINES
FILLED REGIONS
MASKING REGIONS
DETAIL ITEMS
BATT INSULATION

ANNOTATION Elements
2D components that maintain scale on paper and are only visible in one view

DIMENSIONS
TEXT NOTES
LOADED TAGS
SYMBOLS

FIGURE 2.1 *Understanding Revit elements*

Annotation elements are fundamentally different than model elements in that they belong to the view in which they are added and appear only in that view. Model elements appear in all views in which they logically should appear. (A door placed in plan will appear also in elevation, but a door tag placed in plan will not appear automatically in elevation). Datum elements establish planes of reference in three-dimensional space. They are useful for establishing benchmarks, context and working planes for your project's geometry.

MODEL ELEMENTS

You can think of model elements as the items you use to describe the physical aspects of your building project. These elements can be separated into two sub-categories (as shown in Figure 2.1)—Host Elements and Component Elements. To use an analogy, hosts represent items that are typically constructed in place at the job site like walls and roofs. Component elements are delivered and installed in the building like doors and furniture. The figure shows further examples of each of these element types. For the purpose of our discussion here, let's consider the most common element of each category: a wall (host) and a door (component) (see Table 2.A).

TABLE 2.A *Comparing host and component elements*

Host Elements (for example: Walls)	Component Elements (for example: Doors)
Here are the similarities:	
Both categories include families	
Basic Wall	Single-Flush
Families can have multiple types	
Generic – 4" Brick	30" × 84"
Exterior – Brick on CMU	36" × 80"
Here are the differences:	
Their Basic Role in Projects	
Define spaces and enclosures	Modify/detail spaces and enclosures
Their relationship in hosting	
Can host components (A wall can host a door)	Does not typically host other model elements and often must be hosted (A door is hosted by a wall)
They are saved in different places	
Saved in project files (transferred to new projects)	Saved in RFA (family) files (loaded into new projects)

The primary concept to understand about model elements is that they are the elements that you use to create a (virtual) physical model that depicts your building, and these same elements are the ones that appear within any of the views of your project.

When adding a wall to your project, you start by deciding the type of wall you are creating and in what location the wall should appear. Determining how the lines and patterns that represent that wall will look on a drawing is handled automatically by the software. In this way, you are constructing a model of the required walls rather than drafting a specific representation of them as you might in manual or CAD drafting.

To get a complete listing of all the model elements available in Revit, and how they will appear graphically in your project, click the Manage tab on the ribbon and then click the Object Styles button. In the "Object Styles" dialog box study the list on the "Model Objects" tab (see Figure 2.2).

44 | Chapter 2

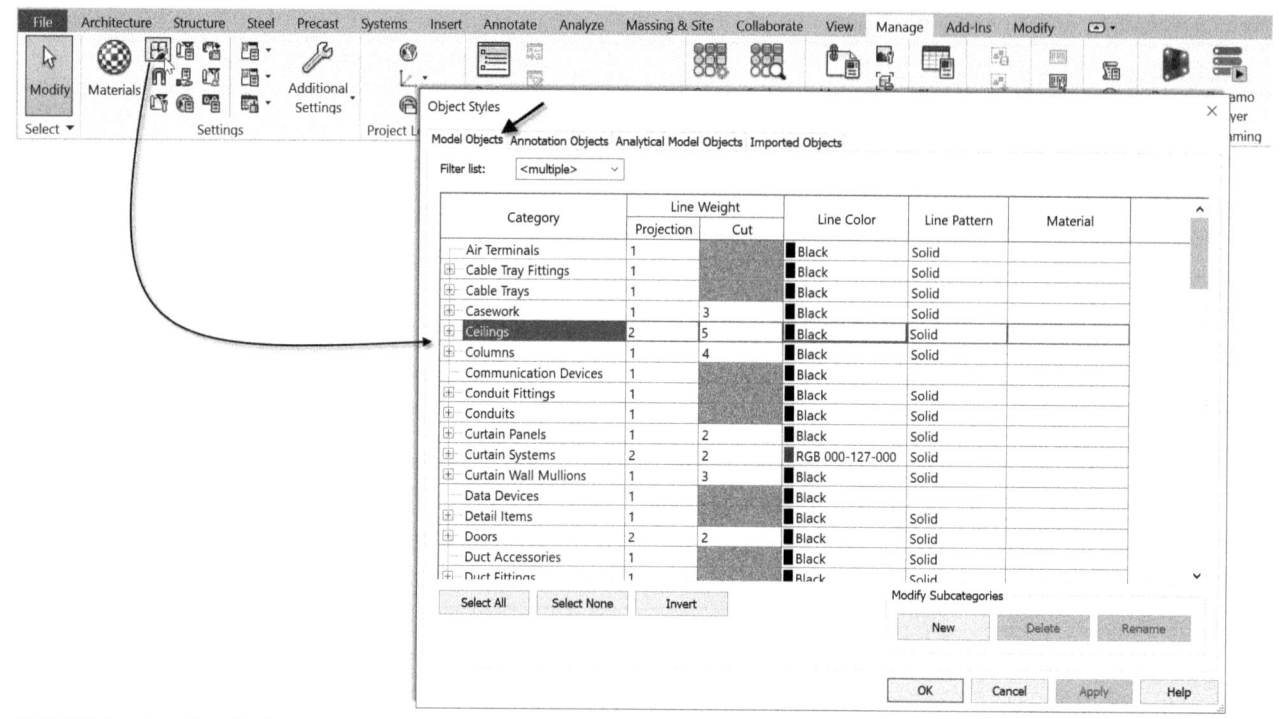

FIGURE 2.2 *A list of model elements appears in the "Object Styles" dialog*

DATUM ELEMENTS

Datum elements include Levels, Grids and Reference Planes. Each shares a common purpose of helping you establish a frame of reference for the geometry in your building projects. Levels represent horizontal planes cutting through the building at each floor level. They literally represent building levels. Levels are added from section, elevation or 3D views. Grids are vertical planes used to represent column grid lines (see Figure 2.3). The intersection of two grids typically indicates the location of a column in plan views. Grids are seen in plan, elevation, and section views. Reference planes are used for more generic purposes. When you wish to establish a reference benchmark that is neither a level nor a grid, use a reference plane. Reference planes can be added to any orthographic view. Of the three datum elements, only levels can appear in 3D views. You will learn more about levels in Chapter 5, grids in Chapter 6, and reference planes in Chapter 11.

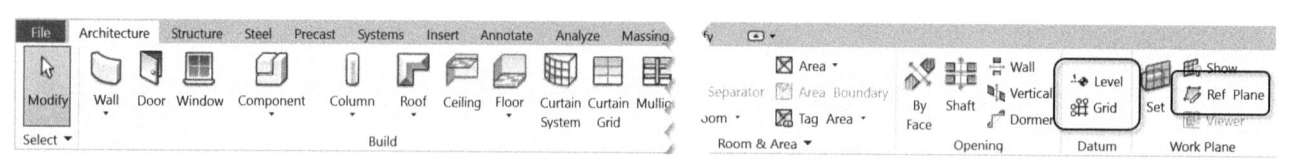

FIGURE 2.3 *Datum elements include levels, grids, and reference planes available on the Architecture tab of the ribbon*

VIEW-SPECIFIC ELEMENTS (ANNOTATION AND DETAIL ELEMENTS)

If you return to Figure 2.1, you will see that the view-specific elements branch contains two sub-branches. The first sub-branch is annotation elements and the other is details. View-specific elements appear only in the view(s) in which they are added. This makes their behavior unique in relation to the other types of Revit elements. Annotation elements include all the text and other descriptive architectural symbology that is required on drawings to explain and clarify the intent of the graphics. This includes tags, dimensions, and symbols. They automatically adjust to the scale assigned to the view. In some cases, annotation elements can be used to manipulate the objects from within the view where they are placed. Dimensions are one such example. But the dimension itself, while capable of "driving" the geometry, appears only in the view to which it is added. We saw a simple example of this behavior in the previous chapter and will see plenty of other examples of dimensions used to manipulate model geometry in the lessons that follow.

To get a complete listing of all of the annotation elements and see how they will appear graphically in your project, open the "Object Styles" dialog box again (shown above in Figure 2.2) and this time study the list on the "Annotation Objects" tab.

Detail elements (also called detail items and detail components) also display in only the view in which they are drawn, but they are full-scale 2D elements used to represent actual model items. Detail elements are the closest thing to what you might consider "drafting" in Revit. They rarely cause changes in other views, or to the project model. Detail elements are used to show model elements in a level of detail that would be impractical to model in live model views. For example, we would not build each brick and mortar joint in a brick wall, or the screws and other fasteners used to hold construction components together. Such items are just as "real" as the overall building forms such as walls, floors, and roofs, but building them would adversely affect computer performance without adding any real benefit to our efforts in the project. Detail elements provide us a means to create fully articulated construction documents coordinated with our overall virtual model in a way that conserves computer resources and adheres to traditional architectural visual communication. The Revit detailing process is covered in Chapter 12.

VIEW ELEMENTS

As you develop your project in Revit, you will work with and create several views. Every Revit project begins with at least some views already in the Project Browser. The specific views that are available are a function of the template project from which the project is created. (A project template provides the framework and settings for a new project. More information on project templates is available in Chapter 5).

To open and work in a view, you simply double-click its name in the Project Browser. Views are available for every architectural drawing type traditionally included in architectural documentation sets. Like the drawings they represent, views allow you to interface with your model and edit its contents and composition within a context like plan, elevation, or section. Unlike traditional drawings, (as mentioned above) an edit in one view is instantly reflected in all appropriate views throughout the project.

Multiple Views-One Model—Imagine two friends living on opposite sides of the same street. Let's assume that the street runs north-south and that one friend lives on the west side of the street while the other lives on the east side. One day, both friends were looking out their window at the same time, as a car was passing by on the street below. The car was traveling from the south to the north. Which way would the friends say that the car was driving relative to their respective vantage points? The friend in the house on the west side of the street would describe the car as traveling from his right to his left, while the friend on the east side would say the car traveled from her left to her right. Which friend was correct? What if both friends snapped a photo at the same time? The two photos would show a different "view" of the same car and its travel pattern. Upon comparing photos with one another, would the two friends describe the respective scenes as two different cars? Or would they rather describe them as two different ways of seeing the same car? Two different "views."

This hypothetical scenario illustrates how project views work in Revit. When working in Revit, we frequently switch from view to view to edit and create elements; and although the specific graphics displayed on screen may vary (like showing the driver or passenger side of the car in the scenario above), they convey aspects of the same model. Therefore, the specific view in which you make an edit is irrelevant. A change to the model occurs in only one place—the model. You can study the change from any number of vantage points as represented in the various views available to you in the Project Browser. To see the various view types available in Revit, you can look at the Create panel on the View tab (see Figure 2.4).

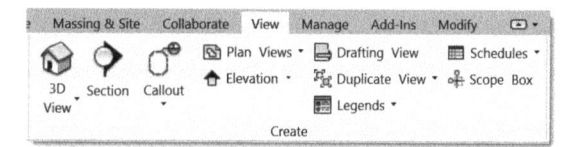

FIGURE 2.4 *Use the View tab to see the view types available*

> **NOTE:** Revit includes both graphical views like plans, sections, and elevations and tabular views like schedules and material takeoffs. Both types provide the means to study and manipulate models. Examples occur throughout the coming chapters.

COMPONENTS, MODEL LINES, AND DETAIL LINES

Most elements in Revit are purpose-built elements that have obvious functions based upon their namesakes like wall, door, room tag, and section. The function of each of these elements is easily inferred from their respective names. However, there are also more generic tools in the software as well. These tools include items like components, text, and lines. A component is a model element including several categories. They can be furniture, fixtures, site elements and several other items that are placed in models. Use the component tool to place any element that does not have its own dedicated button.

Text and lines on the other hand can be either model or annotation elements. The same distinction (discussed above) between model and annotation applies to these elements as well—model text and model lines are used to represent real items in the model. For instance, if you want to create signage you create it with model text. If instead you wanted to callout some information about an item in a view, such as indicating the spacing of joists, or some general notes, you would use the text tool. This text would appear only in the view it was created. Model lines might be employed to create inlaid patterns on walls or floors or to represent control joints on a masonry wall or other items that you don't find necessary to model three-dimensionally, but still want to see in more than one view.

While the creation process and graphical appearance on screen of model and detail lines may appear very similar and therefore make it difficult to distinguish them from one another, they are in fact very different. For example, if you draw a floor pattern using model lines, it will appear in all appropriate views like the floor plan view and a 3D view of the space. Model lines added to the surface of a wall would appear in both elevation and section views as if you painted these lines on the surfaces of the model.

On the other hand, detail lines, like other annotation, will appear in only the view in which it is added. Adding a detail line is like drawing on a piece of trace covering the view of your project and will not be added physically to your building model. It is treated like other annotations as a simple embellishment to that view only. The most common use of such embellishment would be on enlarged details created from the model. Rather than meticulously model components that would only be practical to show in large scale drawings of a design, detail lines (and other similar drafted elements) can be employed to represent those elements that would otherwise take too much time and effort to model throughout and would also add unnecessary overhead to the model without a commensurate amount of useful benefit. Such items might include building paper in a wall or roof section, nails, screws or other fasteners, reinforcing, flashing or even moldings and trim in some cases. It would certainly be possible to model any of these elements, but in most cases, the additional overhead and effort required to model them would not be justified. Understanding what not to model is perhaps even more important than knowing what or how to model.

This is a very important issue and understanding it is critical to understanding BIM and using Revit in the most efficient and practical manner.

If necessary, you can select any model line and convert it to a detail line and vice versa. To do so, simply select the line and then, on the context ribbon tab that appears, click the Convert Lines button. Revit will automatically convert the line to the other type (see Figure 2.5).

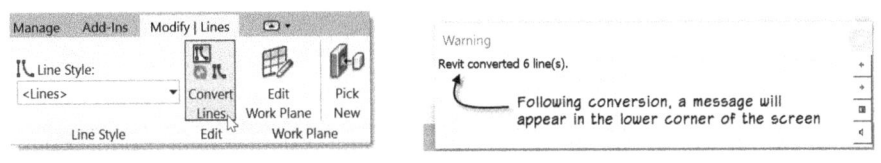

FIGURE 2.5 *Model lines can be converted to detail lines and vice versa*

FAMILIES & TYPES

One of the most common terms in Revit is the term "Family." A family in Revit is an object designated for a particular purpose that has a specific collection of parameters and behaviors. Within the limits established by the family and its parameters, a potentially endless number of "Types" can be spawned. Types are named variations in the family and its parameters. Where a family establishes the physical form and a set of available variable parameters, a type is a specific version of the family with actual values for each parameter. The term "Family" was selected to characterize objects in Revit that have an inherited-property relationship and comes from the notion of a parent-child relationship.

To illustrate how this concept works in Revit, we will look at some common categories of families and describe how they are created and used in a project. You will notice these follow along similar lines as the element hierarchy covered above, with an additional element classification called: "System Families."

MODEL ELEMENT FAMILIES

Everything in the Revit software belongs to a category and a family. Each of the element types shown in Figure 2.1 above has a corresponding family classification. Recall that the model element branch includes both host and component elements. This means that we have both host families and component families. The most common example of a host family is the wall family. The organization of elements follows a hierarchical progression from global (category) to specific (instance) parameters and can be referred to as a "Family Tree." Table 2.B is an example of a wall family tree:

TABLE 2.B *Family tree examples—Sample wall family tree*

Element Category	Walls
↳ Family/System Family	↳ Basic Wall
↳ Type	↳ Exterior – Brick on CMU
↳ Instance	↳ Specific wall(s) selectable in the project

You can also see the hierarchy interactively in a Revit project. To do so, expand the *Families* branch of the Project Browser. A wall family tree is illustrated here (see Figure 2.6).

48 | Chapter 2

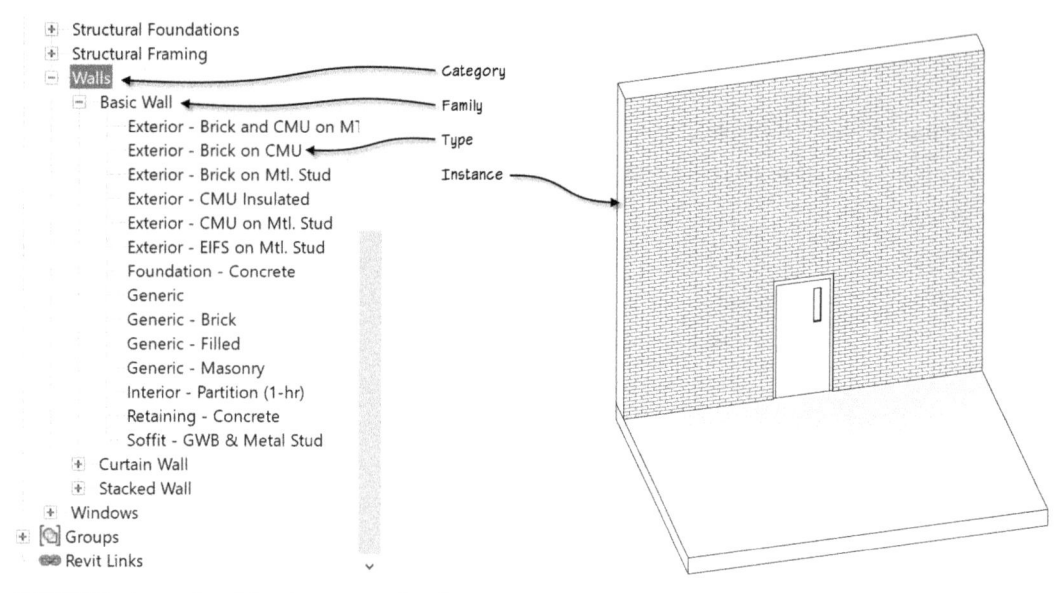

```
  Structural Foundations
  Structural Framing                    ← Category
  Walls
    Basic Wall                          ← Family
      Exterior - Brick and CMU on Mt
      Exterior - Brick on CMU           ← Type
      Exterior - Brick on Mtl. Stud
      Exterior - CMU Insulated          Instance
      Exterior - CMU on Mtl. Stud
      Exterior - EIFS on Mtl. Stud
      Foundation - Concrete
      Generic
      Generic - Brick
      Generic - Filled
      Generic - Masonry
      Interior - Partition (1-hr)
      Retaining - Concrete
      Soffit - GWB & Metal Stud
    Curtain Wall
    Stacked Wall
  Windows
  Groups
  Revit Links
```

FIGURE 2.6 *A typical wall family tree viewed in the Project Browser*

Walls are system families (see below). System families are hard-coded into the software and cannot be created or edited by the user. There are many kinds of system families, but system families that are also model elements (like walls) can also be referred to as host families. Host elements represent "built in place" construction. This means they can control the location and orientation of hosted elements attached to them (like the door shown in the figure). While we cannot add or remove system families, we can add, edit, or delete the types associated with system families. If the wall type that you wish to use is not present in the current project, you can either duplicate and modify a similar type that is resident in the file or transfer one from another project. Wall types and other host element types always live in project files. Component families, on the other hand, represent items that are purchased and installed in a project (not assembled in place). Perhaps the most common component element family is a door family. Table 2.C is an example of a door family tree:

TABLE 2.C *Family tree examples—Sample door family tree*

Element Category	Doors
↳ Family/System Family	↳ Single-Flush
↳ Type	↳ 34" × 80"
↳ Instance	↳ Specific instance of a door selectable in the project

A door family tree is illustrated here (see Figure 2.7).

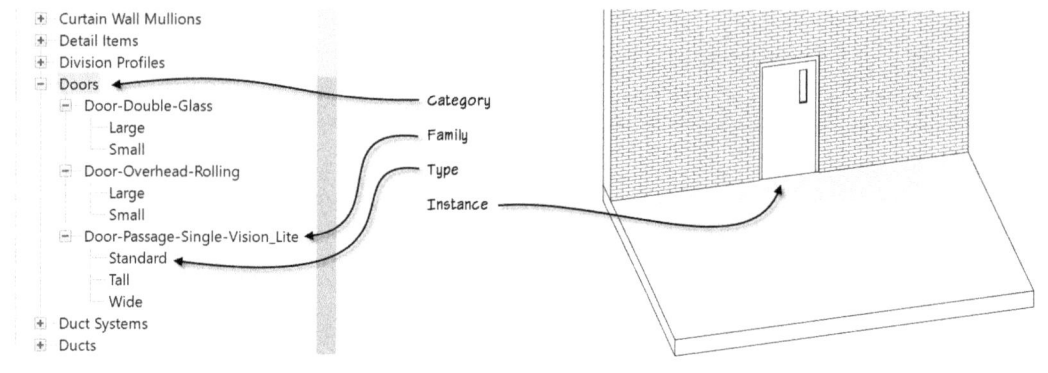

```
  Curtain Wall Mullions
  Detail Items
  Division Profiles
  Doors                                 ← Category
    Door-Double-Glass
      Large                             ← Family
      Small
    Door-Overhead-Rolling               ← Type
      Large
      Small                             Instance
    Door-Passage-Single-Vision_Lite
      Standard
      Tall
      Wide
  Duct Systems
  Ducts
```

FIGURE 2.7 *A typical door family tree viewed in the Project Browser*

Unlike system (host) families, component families do not have to be resident in the project file before you can use them. You can load component families from external family (RFA) files (as such, they are also referred to as "Loadable Families"). Loading a component family will typically load all types associated with that family into the current project (unless the family file has a "Type Catalog" associated with it like Structural shapes—see the online Help and Chapter 6 for more information). You can also create new types within the project just as you can with host families or by editing the family file. Barring these subtle differences, host and component families are like one another. There are other less subtle differences as well, but for now those remain out of the scope of the current discussion. Families will be covered in more detail throughout the coming chapters, and Chapter 11 is devoted entirely to the topic of families and the Family Editor.

ANNOTATION FAMILIES

Annotation families are like model families in that they are also objects that have a specific collection of parameters and behaviors. However, those parameters and behaviors are specific to annotation rather than the model. For example, there are families for dimensions, text, tags, and datum elements. You can see most annotation families loaded in your project by expanding the Annotation Symbols branch in the Project Browser (see Figure 2.8).

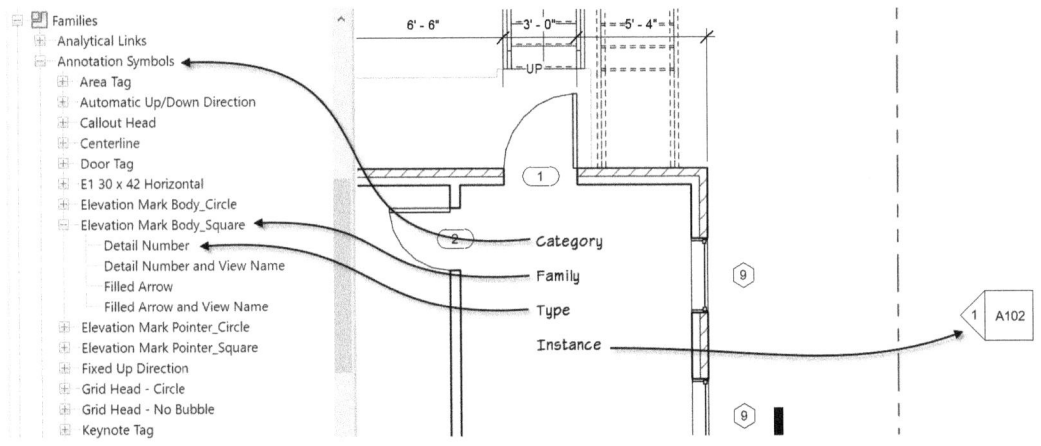

FIGURE 2.8 *Annotation element families appear beneath Families > Annotation Symbols on the Project Browser*

Many annotation families serve special purposes in a project. A title block for instance is a special kind of annotation family that is used when you create a sheet view. It can include text fields, called labels that automatically report project data and can also contain company logos and other graphics. Some annotation families, like level heads, section heads, and elevation heads are typically associated directly to some other view in the project and provide a means to navigate from one view to another. For example, add a section line in a plan view to indicate where the section is cut. Double-click the section head to open the associated section view. Tags usually contain a symbol created from simple geometry and a label that reports a specific parameter or parameters from an associated object. Examples include the door number, room number, or area of a room. Some are simple symbols that you can add to any view. One such example is the centerline symbol included in the default template.

SYSTEM FAMILIES

In general terms, a system family is any family that is built into the Revit software by the programmers and fundamental behavior or features cannot be altered or reconfigured by users. We can only interact with what they've provided. Many of the elements on which we have already commented are system families such as walls, roofs, text, and dimensions. System families include more than just annotation and model elements. All aspects of the software are organized hierarchically into a category and family structure. Families even include items designed to help organize the way we work with the software. Such is the case with the browser organization system family. Look at the Project Browser. At the top is a heading labeled "Views (all)" (see Figure 2.9).

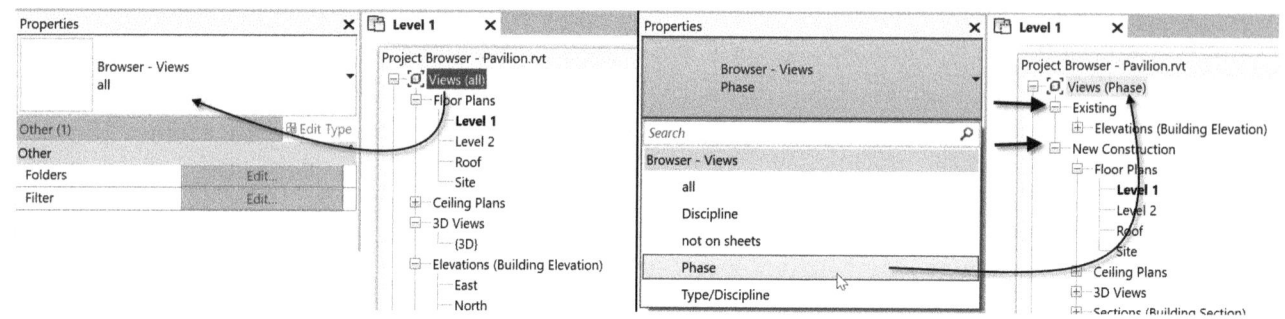

FIGURE 2.9 *Even the organization of the Project Browser is governed by a family*

In the parenthesis, (all) is a type associated with the browser organization system family. Like most families, the browser family includes other types. You can select a different one on the Properties palette (see the right side of Figure 2.9). Many of the other types available are quite useful depending on the kind of project on which you are working and/or the phase or composition of the design team.

Changing the browser organization can help you find a specific view you need on large projects with many views. For example, if you are working in a project that will have many phases (existing, foundations, new construction, etc.), the Phase organization type can be helpful. Discipline organization will sort the views by various disciplines like Architectural, Structural, or Mechanical. Not on sheets will hide all the views that have already been added to a sheet in the project, thus showing only those views not currently on a sheet. This is a handy way to be sure you don't forget to include an important view on a sheet in your document set.

EXPLORE AN EXISTING PROJECT

We have covered a lot of important concepts in this chapter so far. However, we have only discussed these topics in the abstract. If you did the tutorial in Chapter 1, you have had some hands-on exposure to the basics of the software. To help reinforce and solidify the concepts presented there and here, let's open and explore a simple file provided with the book's dataset files. We will still be discussing topics at a high level in this exercise but having a project open as a backdrop will make the concepts easier to understand.

INSTALL THE DATASET FILES AND OPEN A PROJECT

The lessons that follow require the dataset files included for download with this book. If you have already downloaded and installed the files, skip to step 3 to begin. If you need to install the files, start at step 1.

1. If you have not already done so, download the dataset files accompanying this book.

    Refer to the "Download the Book Dataset" topic on page xi in the Preface for instructions on downloading and installing the book's dataset files.

2. Launch Autodesk® Revit®.

3. On the Home screen, beneath Models, click the Open button. (You can also find Open on the Quick Access Toolbar at the top left corner of the screen).

> **NOTE:** For this brief tutorial, units do not play a crucial role in the exercise. Therefore, the provided file is in imperial units. For the remainder of the book, Metric datasets are provided as well for most lessons.

⇨ In the "Open" dialog box, browse to the *Chapter02* folder.

⇨ Double-click *Chapter02.rvt* to open the project. You can also select it and then click the Open button.

The project will open in displaying a sheet with an overhead 3D view.

The dataset for this chapter provided courtesy of Mark Schmieding, FAIA.

GETTING ACQUAINTED WITH THE PROJECT

For this tutorial, we will explore a series of sheet views included in the project. A sheet view is a special kind of view that emulates a sheet of paper from which drawing sets can be printed to output devices. Sheet views typically include a title block which contains project and drawing information. Revit remembers the last view that was open when the project was saved. In this case, it is a three-dimensional aerial view of this small one-floor project for a youth center. It includes offices, exam and counseling rooms, a multipurpose room, and media rooms. Let's take a closer look (see Figure 2.10).

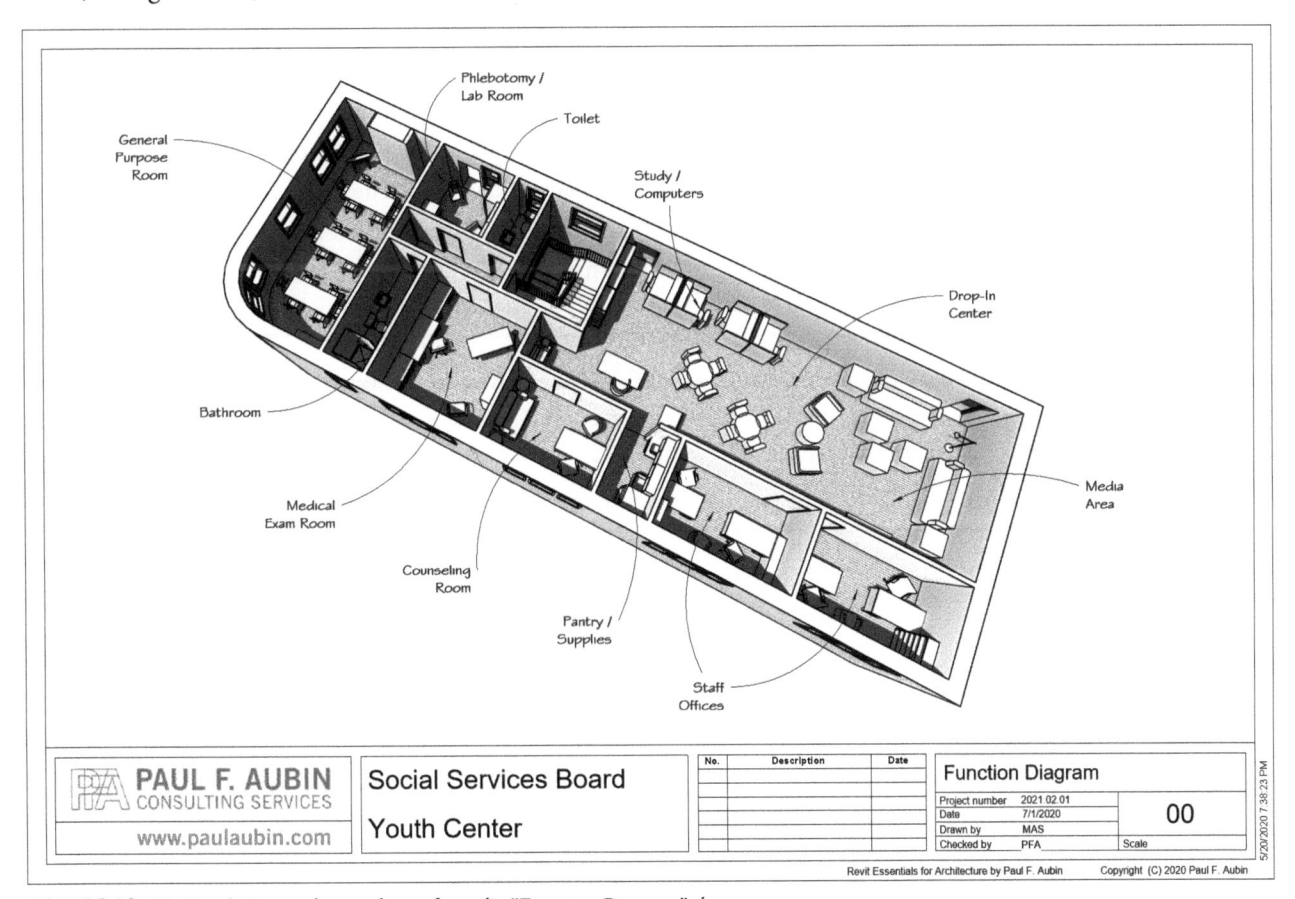

FIGURE 2.10 *The Youth Center dataset shown from the "Function Diagram" sheet*

VIEW NAVIGATION

You can use the wheel on your mouse to zoom in and out in any view. You can hold the wheel in and drag to pan the screen. If you are working on a laptop and don't have a wheel mouse, you can use the commands on the Navigation Bar (located by default in the upper right corner of the view window) to navigate in any view. Depending on the kind of view active on screen, you will have access to differing tools on the Navigation Bar (see Figure 2.11). Among these are the Steering Wheel, the Zoom pop-up, and the ViewCube. The ViewCube and 3D steering wheel appear in 3D views.

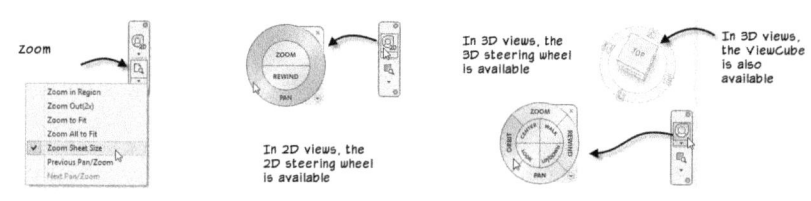

FIGURE 2.11 *Zoom the sheet to Sheet Size and pan around to see it as it will print. Pan with the wheel mouse or the steering wheel*

> **NOTE:** Revit includes 3D connexion device support. If you have one of these devices connected to your computer, you can use it to navigate in 2D and 3D views. Additional icons will appear on the Navigation Bar indicating that the device is detected and available for use in Revit. Learn more at: **3dconnexion.com**.

The zoom pop-up offers many ways to zoom the current window. Most of these commands will be available in all kinds of views, like: **Zoom To Fit** (which fits the screen to the extent of the model) and: **Zoom In Region** (which allows you to drag a rectangular region on screen to magnify that area). We also have the handy: **Zoom Sheet Size** available. This command zooms a view to a size comparable on screen to the actual size it will appear when printed. Since Revit displays line weights and other graphics accurately on screen, this can give you a good preview of how the sheet will look when printed (with today's high resolution monitors, this is a good approximation). Each of the zoom commands has a command shortcut that you can execute via the keyboard. These shortcuts are two characters and you simply type both characters in succession to execute the appropriate command. For example, to issue Zoom to Fit, you can simply type: ZF. All of the zoom shortcuts are shown in Table 2.D.

TABLE 2.D *Keyboard shortcuts for Zoom commands*

Zoom Command	Keyboard Shortcut
Zoom in Region	ZR
Zoom Out (2x)	ZO
Zoom to Fit	ZF
Zoom All to Fit	ZA
Zoom Sheet Size	ZS
Previous Pan/Zoom	ZP

1. From the Zoom pop-up on the Navigation Bar, choose: **Zoom in Region**.

    You can also type ZR to issue this command. If Zoom in Region is already selected (a checkmark appears next to it) then simply click the zoom icon to execute the command.

    ⇨ Drag a rectangular region around the upper left corner of the drawing.

2. Hold in the wheel on the mouse and drag around to pan the model.

    If you prefer, you can use the scroll bars instead.

The image you see on screen is the view named: *Large Overview*. It is in the *3D Views* branch of the Project Browser. It has been added to the current sheet and displays in a "Viewport".

3. Zoom back out. The easiest way is to choose: **Zoom to Fit** from the Zoom pop-up menu (shortcut: ZF).

The Steering Wheel offers an alternative to wheel mouse navigation with such commands as dynamic zoom and pan. Click the Steering Wheel icon to make it appear. In this case, since we have a sheet active, only the two-dimensional commands will appear. (This is true even though a 3D view is placed on the sheet; the sheet itself is still two-dimensional).

   4.   Click on the Steering Wheel icon (the tool tip will read "2D Wheel").

Each function works the same way. Place your mouse on the area of the wheel for the function you want. It will highlight as your cursor passes over it. You are also simultaneously moving the wheel around the screen with the movement of your mouse, so it takes some practice. Click and drag with the mouse to begin the function. For example, if you wish to zoom, move the wheel to the area of the screen that you wish to center your zoom on, move the pointer over the Zoom part of the wheel, click and hold down the mouse and begin to drag. Dragging up zooms in, dragging down zooms out. Varying the speed of your dragging varies the speed of the zooming. Release the mouse button to stop zooming and make the wheel reappear to change functions. Pan works the same way except that panning occurs in the direction that you drag (see Figure 2.12).

FIGURE 2.12 *Steering wheels offer many view navigation functions. Drag on the part of the wheel labeled for the function you want to use*

As you perform several zooms and pans, they are stored in memory. You can use the Rewind function to back up through previous zooms and pans in a visual way. Move your mouse pointer over the Rewind function, click and hold down. A ribbon of thumbnail previews will appear, each representing a previous zoom or pan. Drag to the left to highlight previous zooms and pans, drag back to the right to move forward. Release the mouse to stop rewinding or forwarding. When you are done with the wheel, click the small close box ("X") in the upper right corner of the wheel or press ESC.

   5.   When finished experimenting with Steering Wheel, close it to continue.

UNDERSTANDING SCREEN TOOL TIPS

You can get feedback on the elements onscreen as your mouse passes over them.

   1.   Zoom to Fit. (In addition to the methods already covered, you can right-click to access common zoom commands like Zoom to Fit.

   ⇨   Move your mouse pointer into the middle of the screen and pause it there—pause over the drawing, (not a text note).

        Do not click the mouse.

Notice how a rectangular border highlights around the 3D image. As you pause the mouse, an onscreen tool tip should appear as well. In this case, this tip will read: Viewports : Viewport : No Title (see Figure 2.13).

> **NOTE:** The same information appears in the status line at the bottom left corner of the Revit interface.

54 | Chapter 2

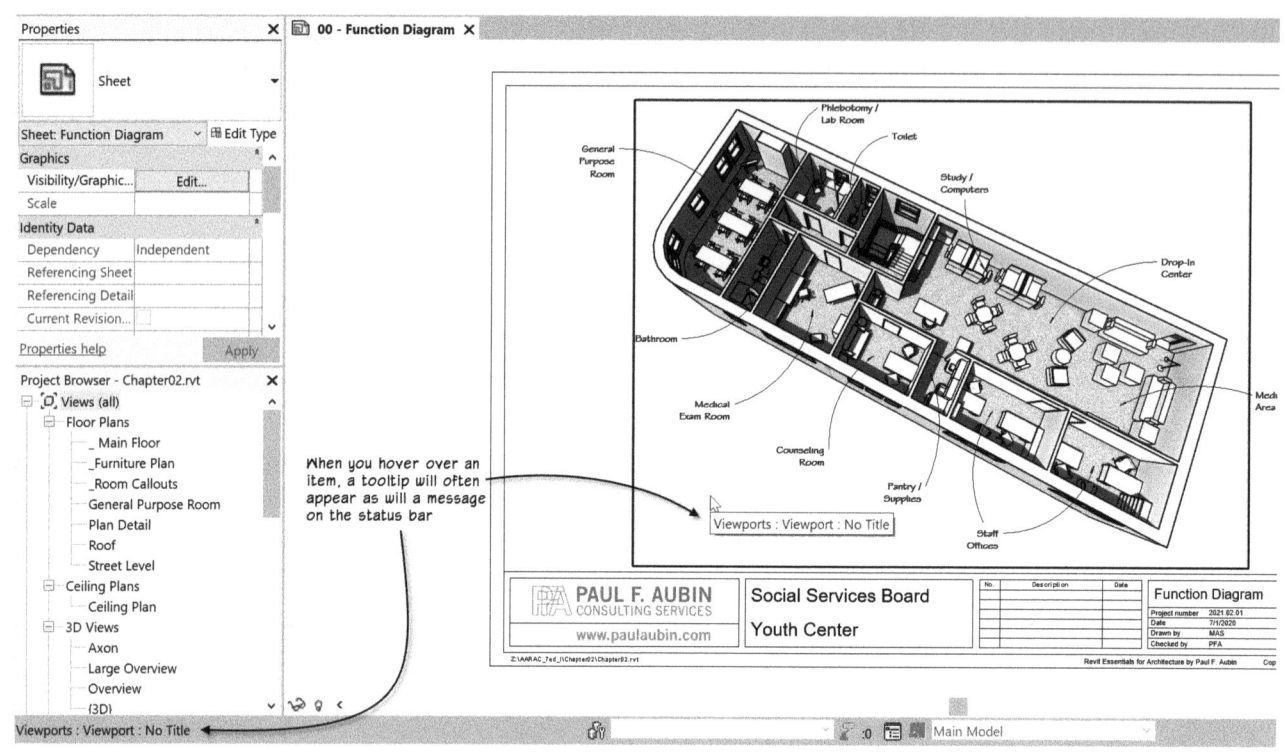

FIGURE 2.13 *Tool Tips will indicate the element category, family, and type*

The tool tip conveys three bits of information about the element highlighted—its **Category : Family name: Type name**. So, in this case, the element category is "Viewports," the family is "Viewport" and the type is "No Title."

   2.   Now hover the pointer over a piece of text but do not click.

This is called "Pre-highlighting." The tool tip for a piece of text will read—Text Notes : Text : 3D Notes. Here, Text Notes is the category, Text is the family and 3D Notes is the type. Since the 3D view is a viewport containing one of our project views, you do not see the elements within the model pre-highlighting. However, you can choose to "Activate" the viewport and that will give you access to the building model elements shown within the view. Editing them from a viewport is no different than opening the view from the Project Browser and editing them there; the results are the same view either way. Let's take a look.

   3.   Pre-highlight the viewport, and then click to select it this time.

   ⇨   On the Modify | Viewports ribbon, click the Activate View button (you can double-click inside the viewport as well).

Notice that the sheet title block and the text labels have grayed out. While they are still visible, this graying effect indicates that they are currently inactive and that you are now working inside the viewport.

   4.   Move the mouse around the model.

      Notice that the elements within the model now pre-highlight.

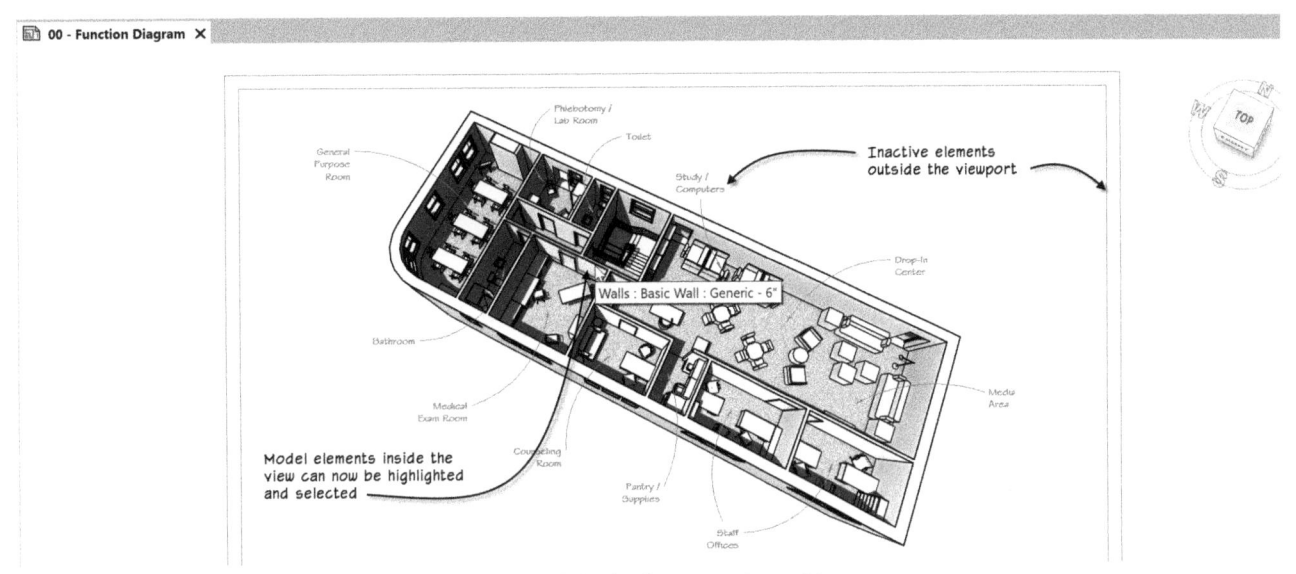

FIGURE 2.14 *Once the viewport is activated, you can pre-highlight the elements in the model*

We will not actually edit any model objects in this view but do take notice of the tool tips. The interior partitions, for example, display as: Walls : Basic Wall : Generic - 6". The category is: Walls, the family is: Basic Wall and the type is: Generic - 6" (see Figure 2.14).

> Feel free to select objects if you like, but don't edit anything. If you accidentally move or change an element, click the undo icon on the Quick Access Toolbar (QAT) at the top left corner of the Revit interface. Or press CTRL + Z.

You may also notice that with the three-dimensional view now active, in addition to the Navigation Bar, the ViewCube is also displayed. The ViewCube is a 3D navigational tool available in all Autodesk products. Clicking on any of the labeled sides of the cube will orient the view to that direction such as top, front, or right. There are also several active regions between faces that will orient the view at an angle between the two adjacent faces. For example, click the edge between front and right to orient the view to the southeast. Click the corner between three faces to orient the view to an axonometric orientation. You can also click and drag any edge of the cube to orbit the model in real-time. Feel free to experiment with the ViewCube to get the hang of it (see Figure 2.15).

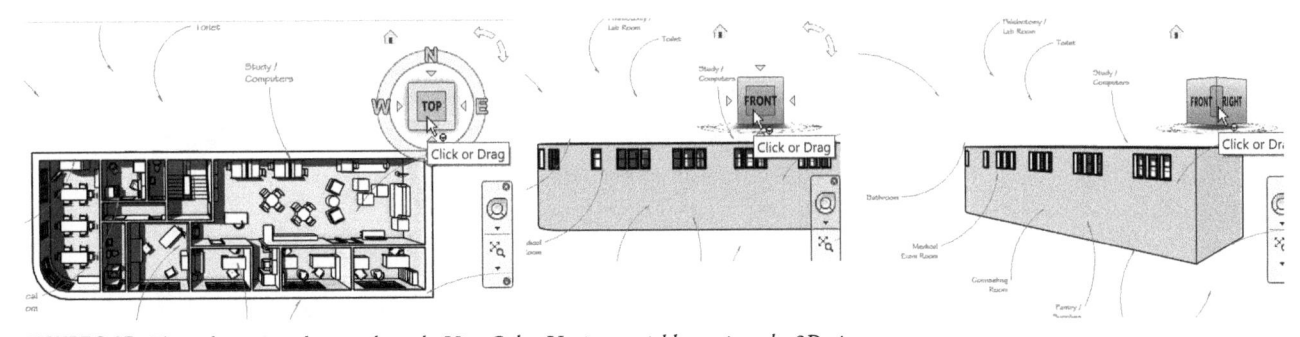

FIGURE 2.15 *Three-dimensional views show the ViewCube. Use it to quickly reorient the 3D view*

In addition to the ViewCube, the Steering Wheel has more options in a three-dimensional view. You can orbit the view, change the center of rotation, move the vantage point up and down, and walk and look around the model. Consult the online help for more information on these options and the many ways you can customize the Steering Wheels to suit your preferences.

    5.   Feel free to experiment with the ViewCube and the 3D Steering Wheel in this 3D view.

    ⇨   Before continuing, reset the view back to its original state.

56 | Chapter 2

To do this, click the Steering Wheel, and then use the Rewind tool or right-click on the Steering Wheel and choose: **Undo View Orientation Changes**.

6. When you are done exploring in the model, right-click in the Viewport again and choose: **Deactivate View**.

This returns you to the sheet and the elements in the view are no longer selectable.

VIEWS AND DETAILING

Earlier we discussed how model and annotation elements were handled in distinct ways. Continuing in this file, let's explore the difference between model and view-specific/annotation elements a bit further.

1. On the Project Browser, beneath the *Views (all)* branch, double-click to open the: *_Main Floor* plan view.

This is the basic floor plan view for this project.

2. On the Project Browser, double-click to open the *_Room Callouts* plan view.

This plan is very similar to the *_Main Floor* view except that it also includes callouts around the General Purpose Room on the left and some elevation and section markers. A sheet has been provided showing each of these views.

3. On the Project Browser, beneath the *Sheets (all)* branch, double-click to open the *05 – Room Callout* sheet view.

Notice how the only visual difference here is that the plan appears on a title block sheet in this view.

4. On the Project Browser, double-click to open the *02 – Floor Plan* sheet view.

This is the sheet presentation of the *_Main Floor* plan view. In other words, this sheet composes the *_Main Floor* plan view on a title block for printing. You can easily see which views appear on a sheet in the Project Browser.

5. On the Project Browser, beneath the *Sheets* branch, expand the tree (click the small plus (+) sign) beneath the *01 – Shaded Plan* sheet.

⇨ Double-click the sheet to open it (see Figure 2.16).

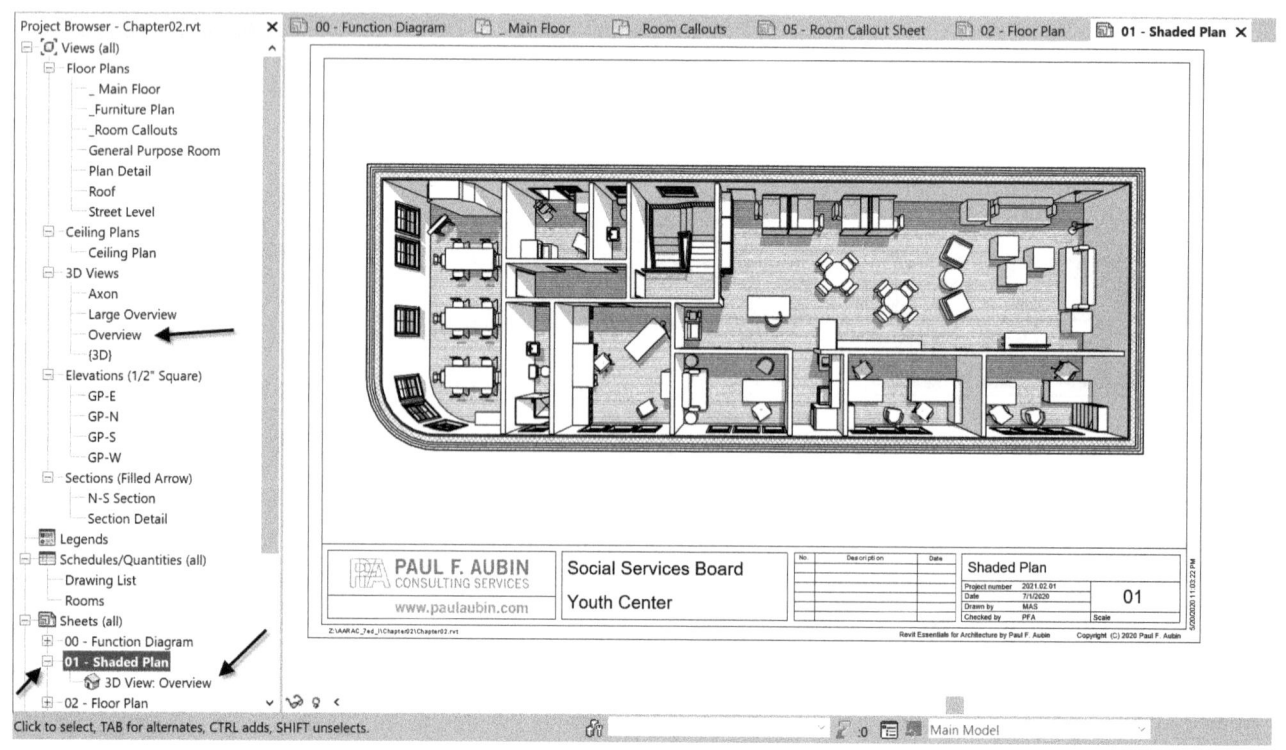

FIGURE 2.16 *Expand the sheet entries in the Project Browser to see the views they contain*

This provides an easy way to see which views are inserted on sheets. Another useful tool (noted above) gives us a way to see which views have not yet been placed on sheets.

6. On the Project Browser, scroll to the top and select the *Views (all)* branch.

   ⇨ On the Properties palette, from the Type Selector (drop down list at the top), choose: **not on sheets** (similar to Figure 2.9 above).

Notice that the list of views on the Project Browser now shows only those views that are not yet assigned to a sheet. In this project, there are only a couple views not placed on sheets. Expand each sub-group to see.

7. Make sure that "Views (not on sheets)" is selected, and then on the Properties palette, change back to: **all**.

This sets the default browser organization back to showing all views regardless of their placement on sheets.

8. On the Project Browser, double-click to return to the *_Main Floor* plan view. Or just click its tab if it is still open.

Suppose that we needed to create another floor plan that was similar to this one, but that was to convey a different type of information on the printed sheet or that we were planning to use simply as a convenient place in which to edit the model with no intention of adding it to a sheet. To achieve either goal, we simply duplicate an existing view.

9. On the Project Browser, right-click the *_Main Floor* plan view and choose: **Duplicate View > Duplicate**.

A new floor plan view named: *_Main Floor Copy 1* will appear and become active. Notice that none of the room labels or dimensions were copied in this operation. This might be useful if you were creating a "working" view. A "working" view is intended as a view in which you manipulate the model only and do not plan to add to a sheet for printing. Bear in mind that nothing prevents the working view from being used on a sheet; rather it is simply not intended for that purpose by our project team. If we want to duplicate the view, including the tags and dimensions, we choose a different command.

10. On the Project Browser, right-click the original *_Main Floor* plan view again and choose: **Duplicate View > Duplicate with Detailing**.

> **NOTE:** "Duplicate with Detailing" is short for "Duplicate with view-specific detailing elements and annotation elements." Remember that the "detailing" is being copied, while the model elements are simply being viewed.

A new floor plan view named: *_Main Floor Copy 2* will appear and become active. Notice that this copy includes copies of the room tags and dimensions.

   ⇨ Right-click *_Main Floor Copy 2* and choose: **Rename**.

   ⇨ Type: **Area Diagram** and then press ENTER.

11. With the CTRL key held down, select each of the dimensions in the view (five total).

   ⇨ Press the DELETE key.

We do not need dimensions for the new view we are creating. However, there is no way to duplicate only the room tags and not the dimensions, so simply deleting them achieves the desired result. But the critical thing to remember here is that the dimensions still exist in the original *_Main Floor* view. We only deleted the copied ones here.

12. On the Annotate tab of the ribbon, on the Color Fill panel, click the Color Fill Legend tool.

    A small square with a tag will appear attached to the cursor.

   ⇨ Click a point above the plan to place the Color Scheme Legend.

58 | Chapter 2

⇨ In the dialog that appears, for Space Type, choose: Rooms and then click OK.

As you can see, the Scheme 1 color scheme color codes each room based on its name. The legend itself is currently overlapping the plan. To make it fit better, we can resize and/or move it.

13. Click on the Color Fill Legend and then drag the small round Control at the bottom up to make the legend two columns (see Figure 2.17).

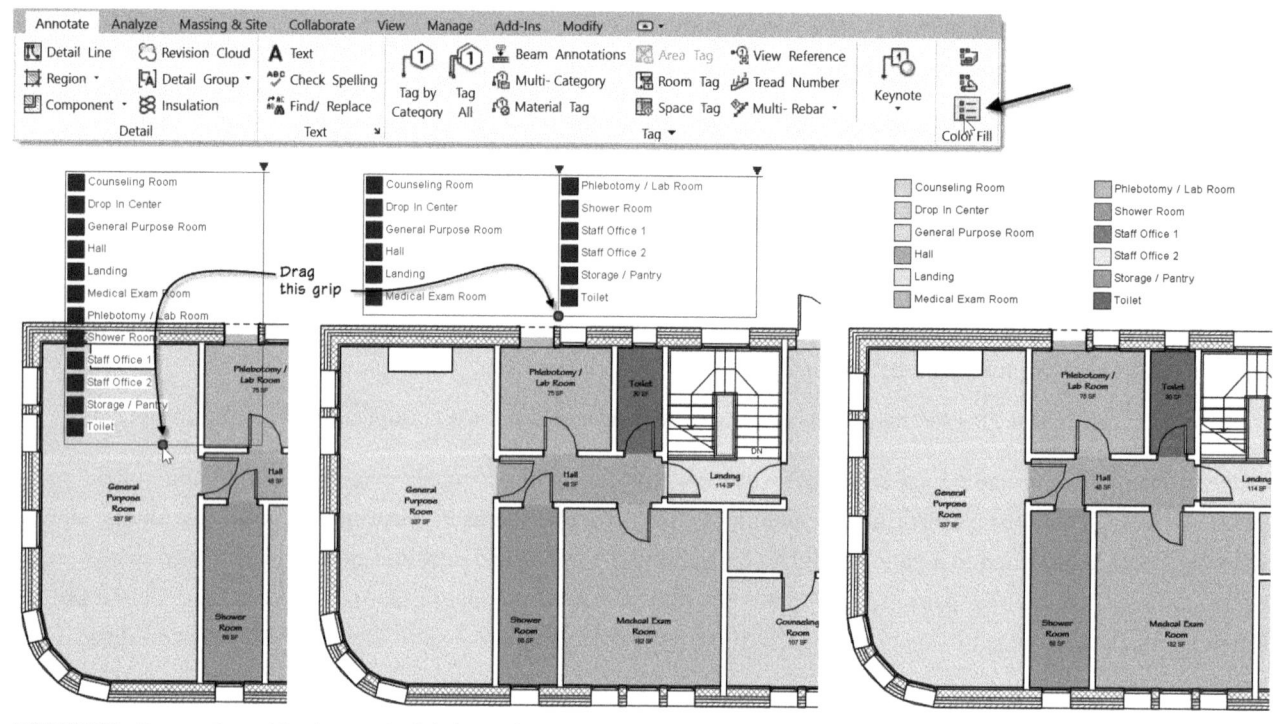

FIGURE 2.17 *Create a Legend for the new shaded plan and then resize the legend*

14. On the Project Browser, double-click to open the *04 – Area Diagram* sheet view.

A sheet appears on screen, which does not yet have a drawing on it. Let's add our new shaded plan to this sheet.

⇨ On the Project Browser, right-click the 04 – Area Diagram sheet and choose: **Add View**.

⇨ From the "Views" dialog, choose: **Floor Plan: Area Diagram** view and then click the Add View to Sheet button.

⇨ Click to place the view on the sheet.

Notice that the view is a little too big for the sheet. We can adjust the scale of the view and it will update automatically on the sheet.

15. On the Project Browser, select the: *Area Diagram* view.

⇨ On the Properties palette, from the View Scale list, choose: **1/8"=1'-0"** (see Figure 2.18).

• The Aubin Academy •

Conceptual Underpinnings of Revit | 59

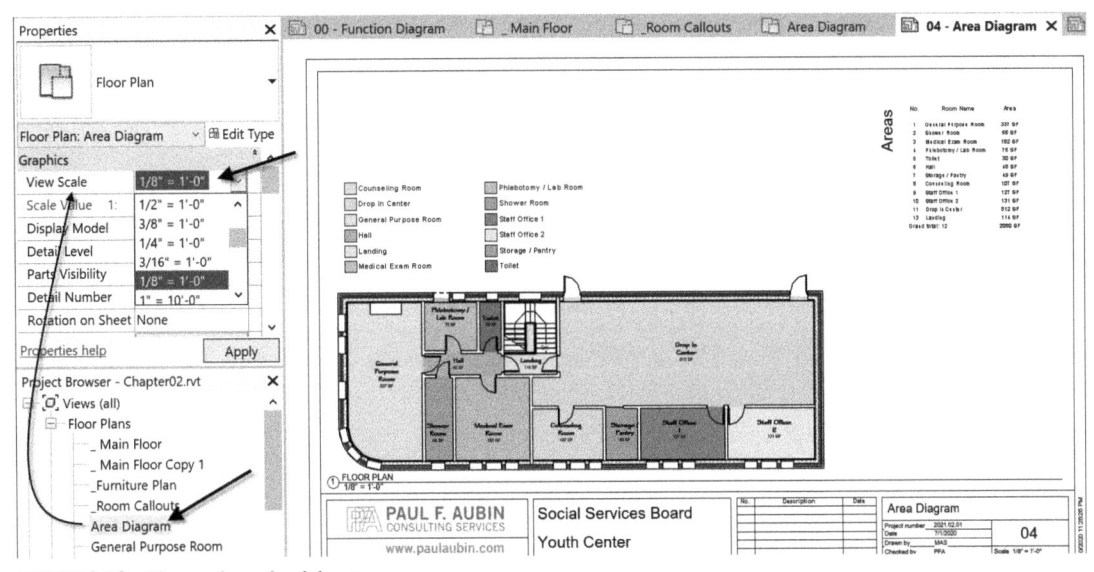

FIGURE 2.18 *Change the scale of the view*

You should see the change on the sheet immediately. If necessary, you can move the viewport around to make a nicer composition on the sheet.

You should also look at the *_Furniture Plan* floor plan view and the *03– Layout Plan* sheet next. In this view and sheet, you will notice that the plan is displayed with furniture. Therefore, creating plans with and without detailing (text and other annotation) is not the only way to vary the specifics of what we see. We can also control the visibility of each type of element in any Revit view. The visibility settings are a parameter of the view itself. This is how we can choose to display the furniture in the *_Furniture Plan* view and not display it in the *_Main Floor* view. On the View tab of the ribbon, on the Graphics panel, you can choose the Visibility/ Graphics tool (VG). This will display a dialog listing all element categories and enables you to turn on and off these categories within the current view. While we will discuss the specifics of this process in later chapters, the important point for this exercise is that this sort of control is possible and extremely useful. If you wish to explore the "Visibility/Graphics Overrides" dialog, please feel free to do so. Simply undo your changes before continuing with the lesson.

EDIT IN ANY VIEW

Perhaps the most powerful feature of Revit is the ability to edit in any view and see the results instantly in all views.

1. On the Project Browser, double-click to open the *06 – General Purpose Room* sheet view. Then on the View tab, on the Windows panel, click the Close Inactive button.

This closes all the other tabs. As you can see from this simple exercise, it is easy to end up with many open view tabs. Using this tool every so often helps keep a tidy workspace and preserves computer resources. The 06 sheet we have open shows a plan and four interior elevations. All these views show the General Purpose Room.

2. Select the plan view on the left, right-click and choose: **Activate View** (or double-click on the viewport).

3. On the Architecture tab of the ribbon click the Window tool.

   ⇨ Click a point on the exterior wall on the left to add a new window (see Figure 2.19).

• Revit Essentials for Architecture •

60 | Chapter 2

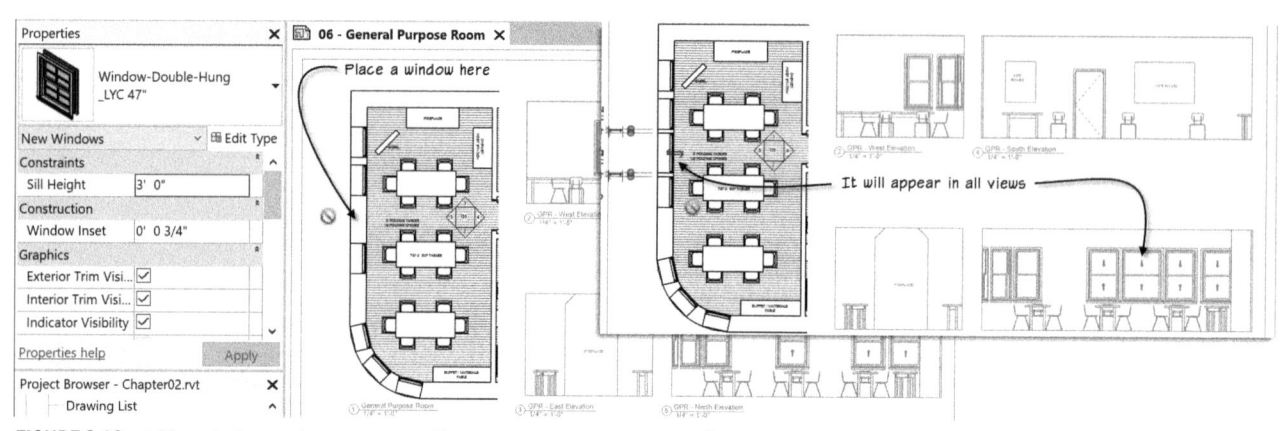

FIGURE 2.19 *Add a window and it appears in all appropriate views automatically*

Notice that the window appears immediately in the north elevation (detail 5 on the sheet).

    4.   Right-click in the plan view again and choose: **Deactivate View**.

EXPLORE A DETAIL VIEW

As we have noted above, a detail view is a little different than the other views. Typically it will include a live view of the model—usually a callout of some part of a section or plan—and various types of annotation and other graphical embellishments drawn on top. One such detail view has been included in this sample dataset.

    1.   On the Project Browser, expand (click the plus [+] sign) the *07 – Building Details* sheet view.

    Beneath this sheet is a listing of three views that are already placed on the sheet.

    ⇨   Beneath the *07 – Building Details* sheet view entry, double-click to open the: *Section : Section Detail* view.

    2.   Pre-highlight some of the elements in this view (see Figure 2.20).

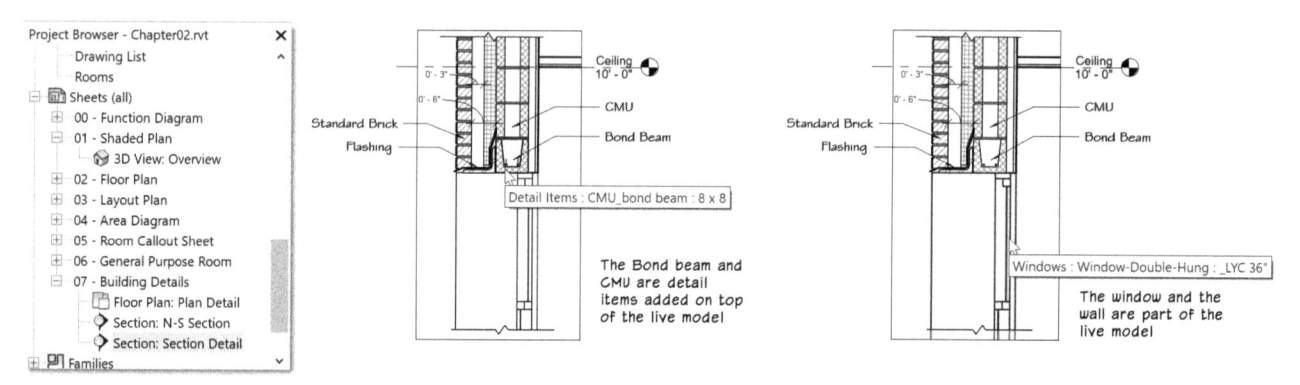

FIGURE 2.20 *Explore a detail view—Note the combination of detail and model elements*

Notice that the detail view contains both model elements (which would appear in all views) and detail elements (which appear only in this view). Even though the detail elements represent items like concrete blocks, brick, flashing, and bond beams, the level of detail required in a construction detail is much higher than that required in nearly any other view. Therefore, these types of items are typically drawn as detail elements on top of the model view geometry to keep overhead low and reduce the amount of time and effort required to build your overall model. An even easier way to see this is to change the way the model displays on the Properties palette.

    3.   Make sure that nothing is selected (press ESC). On the Properties palette, next to Display Model, choose: **Halftone**.

    Notice how the elements that are parts of the 3D model now display grayed out.

    ⇨   Set it to: **Do not display** next.

• The Aubin Academy •

This time the model disappears and only the detailing remains.

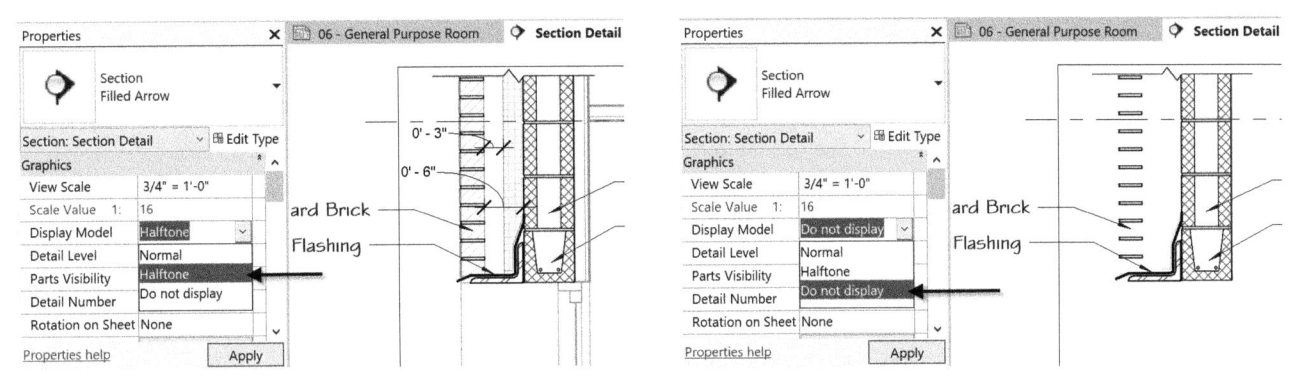

FIGURE 2.21 *Change the display properties of detailing to see the difference between model and detailing more clearly*

Complete coverage of the detailing procedure can be found in Chapter 12. Continue to explore in this dataset as much as you wish to get a better feel of how the various elements and views in a Revit project interact. Close Revit when you are finished exploring. You do not need to save the file.

SUMMARY

- ☑ Building Information Modeling (BIM) is the process of creating an accurate representation of the building including its form, functions, and systems from which detailed and accurate information can be extracted.

- ☑ Using BIM successfully requires a firm understanding of the concepts and techniques enabling its use.

- ☑ All items in Revit belong to predefined categories.

- ☑ All Revit elements belong to families.

- ☑ There are system families and component (loadable) families. Within each of these we have both model and annotation elements.

- ☑ Model system families can also be host to other component (loadable) families.

- ☑ All views show the same source data stored in a single source model. If changes are made in one view, the change is immediately available in all other views.

- ☑ Model elements are those items that represent real building components and are visible in all views.

- ☑ Annotation or drafting elements appear only in the view to which they are added and include notes, dimensions, and detail embellishments.

CHAPTER 3
Revit User Interface

INTRODUCTION

This chapter is designed to acquaint you with the user interface and work environment of Autodesk® Revit®. The Revit user interface is logically organized and easy to learn. In this chapter, we will explore its major features. Many features of the interface follow standard Microsoft Windows™ conventions. Some aspects of the user interface are unique to Revit. In this overview, our goal is to make you comfortable with interacting with and receiving feedback from your Revit software.

OBJECTIVES

To get you quickly acquainted with the Revit user interface, topics we will explore include:

- An overview of the Revit user interface
- Interface terminology
- Working with the Ribbon, Quick Access Toolbar, and the Options Bar

UNIT CONVENTIONS

Throughout this book, imperial units and files will be listed first, followed by metric in brackets, for example, imperial [metric]. Imperial dimensions throughout this text appear in the "Feet and Inch" format for clarity. However, when typing imperial values into Revit, neither the foot symbol (') (when typing whole feet) nor the hyphen separating the feet from inches (when typing both) is required. Therefore, to type values of whole feet, simply type the number. To type values of both feet and inches, type the number of feet with the foot symbol (') followed immediately by the number of inches; the inch symbol is not required when preceded by a number of feet. You can also separate feet from inches with a space (press the SPACEBAR) and omit the unit symbol. When typing only inches, the inch (") symbol is required unless you preface the value with a leading 0' or 0 SPACEBAR. Consult Table 3.A for input examples.

• Revit Essentials for Architecture •

TABLE 3.A *Acceptable Imperial Units Input Formats*

Value Required	Type This:
Four feet	**4** or **48"**
Six inches	**.5** or **6"** or **0'6** or **0 6** (zero SPACEBAR six)
Five feet six inches	**5.5** or **5'6** or **66"** or **5 6** (five SPACEBAR six)
Four feet six and three eighths inches	**4.53125** or **4'6.375** or **4'6 3/8** or **54.375"** or **4 6.375** (4 SPACEBAR 6.375) or **4 6 3/8** (4 SPACEBAR 6 SPACEBAR 3/8)

> **NOTE:** Dimensions throughout this text are given in the "Feet and Inch" format for clarity. However, feel free to enter dimension values in whatever of the above acceptable formats you prefer. Eliminating the inch or foot marks where possible reduces keystrokes and is recommended despite their inclusion in this text.

If using the metric dataset, all values in this text are in millimeters (unless noted otherwise) and can be typed in directly with no unit designation required.

> **NOTE:** Regardless of the default units setting in a project file, you can always type numbers in the other measuring system and Revit will automatically convert them. For example, if working in an Imperial file, you can type in: 4000mm and Revit will convert the distance automatically to: 13'-1 123/256". Likewise, if working in a Metric file, typing in a value of: 10' returns a value of 3048.0mm. Use ' for feet, " for inches, mm for millimeters, cm for centimeters and m for meters.

HOME SCREEN

When you first launch Revit, the "Home Screen" screen will appear (see Figure 3.1). This is like a welcome page that offers you options to open or create Revit files. In the "Models" area on the left, you can use the Open button to open an existing Revit project. Use the New button to create a new Revit project from a template. Similar buttons appear for the "Families" area. Open existing family files to edit content in your library and create new ones to add to your library. Families will be discussed in detail in Chapter 11. Several of your recently opened files will appear with preview icons to the right. You can simply click the preview image to re-open that file. In this book we will open only locally stored files. But if your firm has access to BIM 360 (a cloud-based service for storing and collaborating on design files) you can click the BIM 360 link on the left to access cloud models. This toggles the right-hand side of the screen to the BIM 360 interface from the Recent Files interface. We will be using Recent Files here.

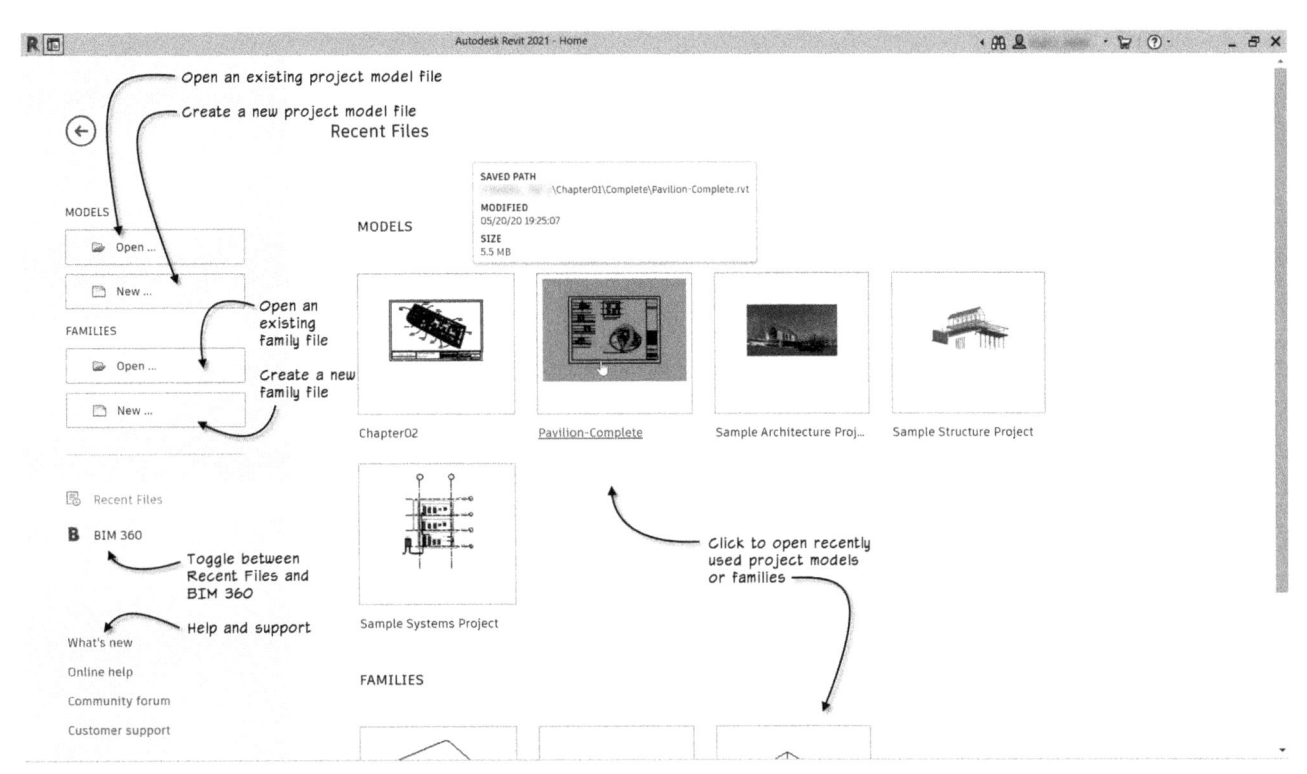

FIGURE 3.1 *The Home screen greets you when you launch Revit*

On the bottom left, you will find links to "What's New," the help system, and other online resources.

UNDERSTANDING THE USER INTERFACE

Revit offers a clean and streamlined work environment designed to put the tools and features that you need to use most often within easy reach. In addition to the many onscreen tools and controls, many of the most common tools also have keyboard shortcuts. The topic of shortcuts will be explored below. Figure 3.2 shows the Revit screen with each of the major interface elements labeled for your reference. Open any model to see this interface.

66 | Chapter 3

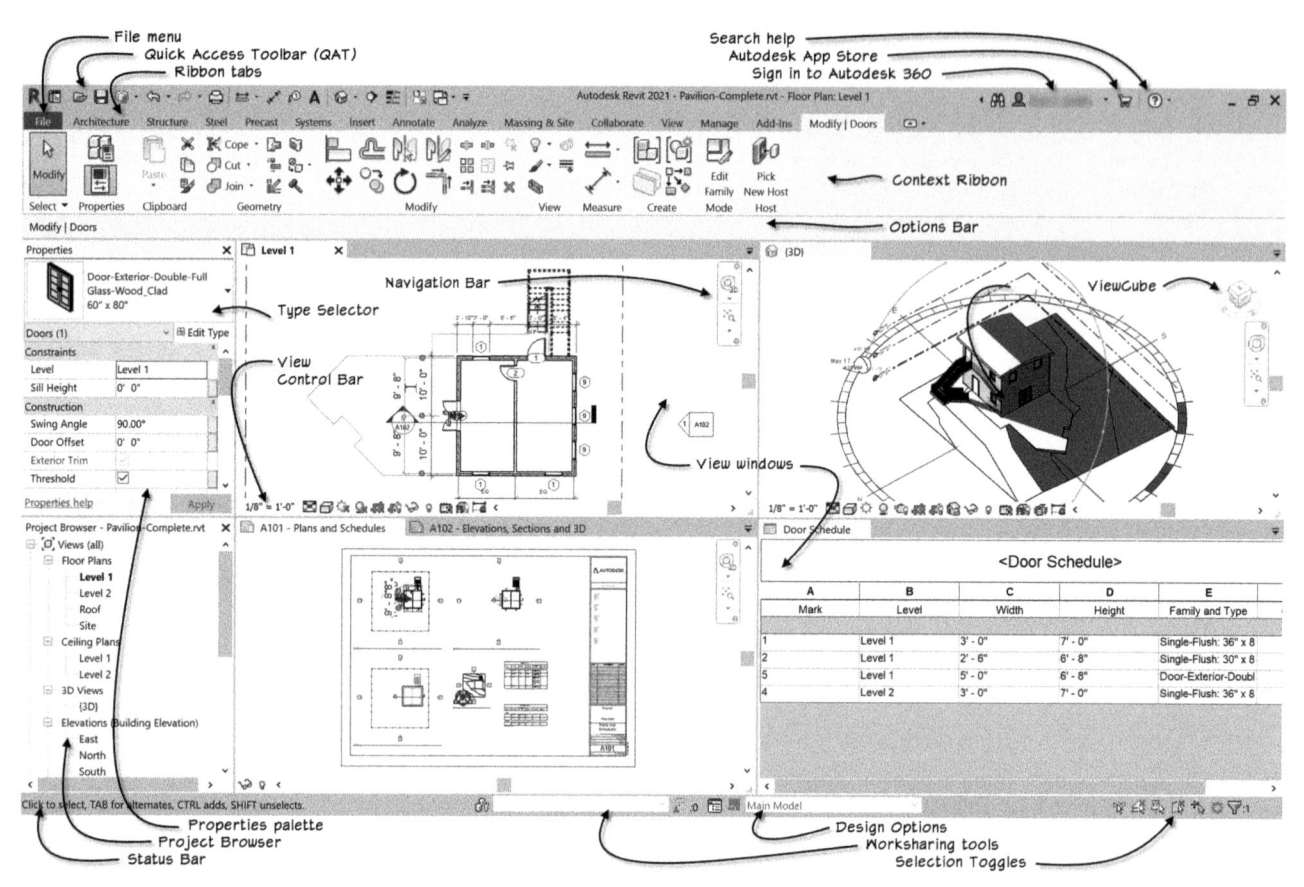

FIGURE 3.2 *The Revit User Interface*

There are many elements to the Revit interface. The ribbon is the tabbed panel across the top of the screen that includes all the software's buttons and controls. This ribbon adjusts to present tools to you in context with the task you are performing. Above the ribbon, in the top left corner of the application frame is the File menu and the Quick Access Toolbar (QAT). At the top right are the standard Windows minimize, maximize, and close icons, accompanied immediately to the left by the help, app store and login information for your Autodesk account. The status bar occupies the bottom edge of the application frame. On the left side of the screen (usually docked/attached) are the Project Browser and the Properties palette stacked atop one another. The Properties palette allows immediate and ongoing access to the properties of any view or selected element in your Revit environment. The Project Browser can be thought of as the "table of contents" for your Revit project. It reveals all the various representations of your project data—referred to in Revit as "Views." Views in Revit can be graphical (drawings, sketches, diagrams) or non-graphical (schedules, legends, takeoffs) and offer the means to both query your project (output) and to manipulate and edit it (input). The Project Browser also lists the families, groups, and linked files that reside in the project. When you open one or more of these views, they occupy view windows that can be tiled or tabbed. Finally, stretched across the top of the screen just beneath the ribbon is the Options Bar. Options appear in this space as you work depending on the item or tool you have selected. (All of these items are labeled in Figure 3.2). Take some time to acquaint yourself with the various user interface elements. You can also right-click many items to see additional context-sensitive menus. Do not choose any right-click menu commands or click any buttons currently. You can simply click away from the menu to close it or press the ESC key.

FILE MENU

The File menu contains standard file management commands like New, Open, Save, and Print. If this is your first time launching Revit, the right side of the File menu will be empty. But as you open and close files, the list of recent files will begin to populate. Revit remembers the last several files you had opened and shows them here. You can even click the pushpin icon to permanently "pin" a particular file to the menu, making it easier to load next time (see the left side of Figure 3.3).

Many items on the File menu have sub-menus. Sub-menus on each item list the various file formats that can be opened or created. For example, a Revit project file contains all the work you do on your building projects. It is the primary file type in Revit and has an RVT file extension. A Revit family file has an RFA extension and each family file contains a single piece of Revit content that can be loaded and used in one or more projects. When creating new Revit files, separate options are offered for Conceptual Mass, Annotations, and Title Blocks. While these are all family files and will use the RFA extension, each is typically created from different template files and settings (see the right side of Figure 3.3).

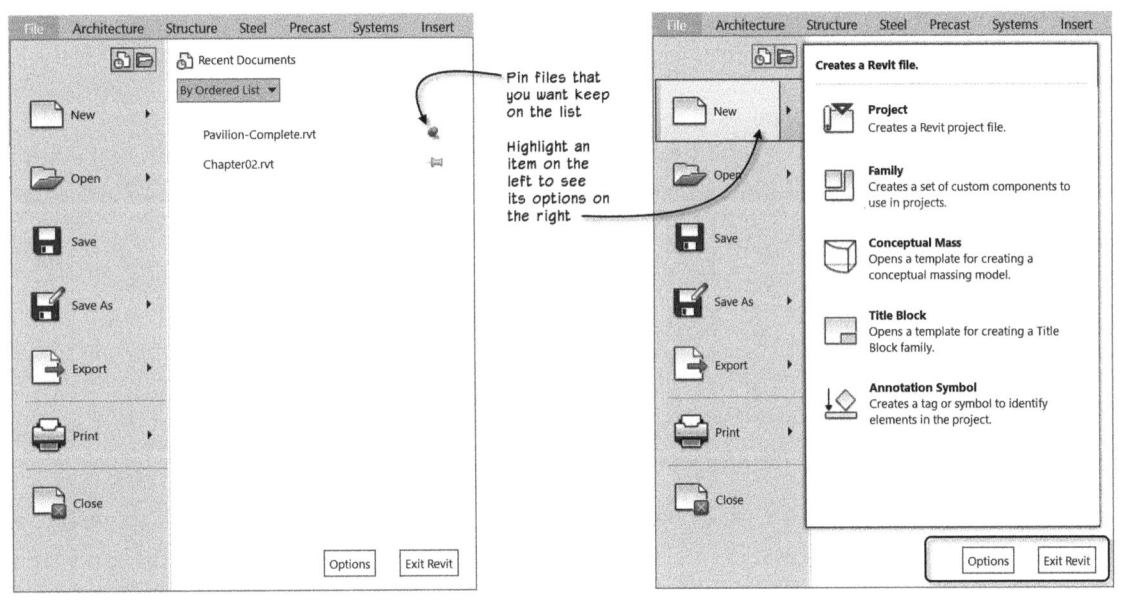

FIGURE 3.3 *The File menu*

On the Save As sub-menu, options will be available based on the current file you have loaded. For example, you cannot save a project file (RVT) as a family file (RFA). Therefore, the **Save As > Family** option is grayed out when you are in a project. However, you can save a project as a new project template. Project Templates have an RTE extension and are discussed in the next chapter. In addition to the options for saving, Revit files can be exported to a number of industry standard formats, such as DWG (AutoCAD drawing file), DGN (MicroStation drawing file), and IFC (Industry Foundation Classes).

> **NOTE:** Some additional considerations regarding opening and saving files come into play when working in a team project. Teams projects are those that have "Worksharing" enabled and are opened, managed and saved a little differently. Please refer to Chapter 16 for more information.

At the bottom of the File menu two buttons appear: Options and Exit Revit. Upon exiting, Revit will prompt you to save any unsaved work. Use the Options button to open the "Options" dialog. This dialog has many program preferences that you can configure. Most of the out-of-the-box settings are suitable for the beginner. There may be some items that you or your CAD/BIM Manager will want to adjust. Refer to the "Selection Toggles" topic on page 81 below and the online help for more information.

QUICK ACCESS TOOLBAR

The Quick Access Toolbar (QAT) as its name implies is a location for commonly used tools to which you wish to have easy and "quick access." The default QAT includes many common tools such as: Open, Save, Synchronize with Central, Undo, Redo, Close Hidden Windows, and Switch Windows (see Figure 3.4). You can add buttons to the QAT with the menu on the right end of the QAT itself. For example, the New command is not part of the default QAT. Simply choose it from the pop-up menu to add it. At the bottom of this menu, you can also choose the Customize Quick Access Toolbar command to open a dialog with more options. In this dialog, you can rearrange tools on the QAT, add separators, and remove commands. For other commands not included on the list, locate them on the ribbon (see the next topic), right-click the tool, and choose: **Add to Quick Access Toolbar**.

FIGURE 3.4 *The Quick Access Toolbar*

RIBBONS

You issue commands in Revit by clicking their tools on the ribbon. The ribbon includes a series of tabs that appear just beneath the QAT. Each tab is separated into one or more panels. Each panel contains one or more tools (see Figure 3.5).

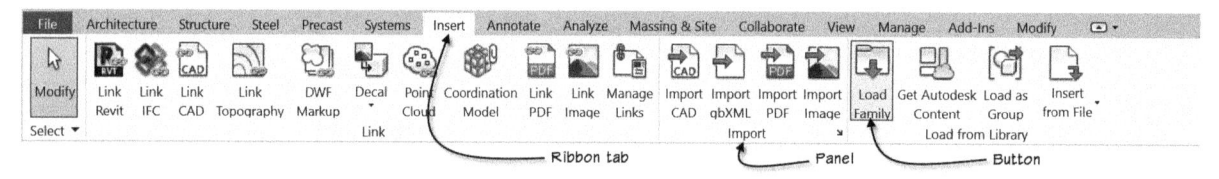

FIGURE 3.5 *The ribbon contains many tabs with tools grouped into panels (Insert tab shown)*

To navigate the ribbon, click a tab, locate the panel and tool you need, and then just click the tool to execute a command. When tutorial instructions are given in this text, you will be directed first to the tab, then the panel, and finally the tool. For example, instructions to execute the Load Family tool might look something like this:

1. On the Insert tab of the ribbon, on the Load from Library panel, click the Load Family button.

In the context of the exercise, when it is obvious which tab or panel, the description might be shortened to something like:

On the Load from Library panel, click the Load Family tool.

Or just:

Click the Load from Library tool.

You can vary the tabs that are displayed on the ribbon in the "Options" dialog. To do so, from the File menu, choose: **Options**. In the "Options" dialog, on the User Interface tab, check or uncheck the tabs you wish to hide and show in your interface. This feature is only available in the full version of Revit (part of the AEC Collection). In Revit LT, the tabs are fixed.

> **NOTE:** The ribbon interface adjusts dynamically with your screen resolution. Images in this book were captured at a screen resolution of 2560 pixels wide with text size set to 175%. In most cases, this shows the full ribbon panels and buttons. In some cases, longer ribbon tabs (like Architecture, View and Manage, et al) may be truncated which reduces the size and/or orientation of some of the buttons. What you see onscreen on your own system may also vary from images in this text depending on your screen resolution and if you have the Revit window maximized.

CONTEXTUAL RIBBON TABS

In addition to the default ribbon tabs, certain actions you perform in the software will cause other ribbon tabs to appear. These "contextual" ribbon tabs contain tools and commands specific to the item you are creating or editing. Contextual tabs will often be attached to the standard Modify tab. For example, if you select a wall element in the model, a Modify | Walls contextual ribbon tab will appear. If you execute the floor tool and begin creating a floor element, a Modify | Create Floor Boundary tab will appear with the tools and options required to enable you to sketch a floor. In both cases, the standard Modify tab and its tools will remain on the left side of the ribbon (see Figure 3.6). By default, when you complete a command, Revit will return to the previous tab you were on prior to the start of the modify command.

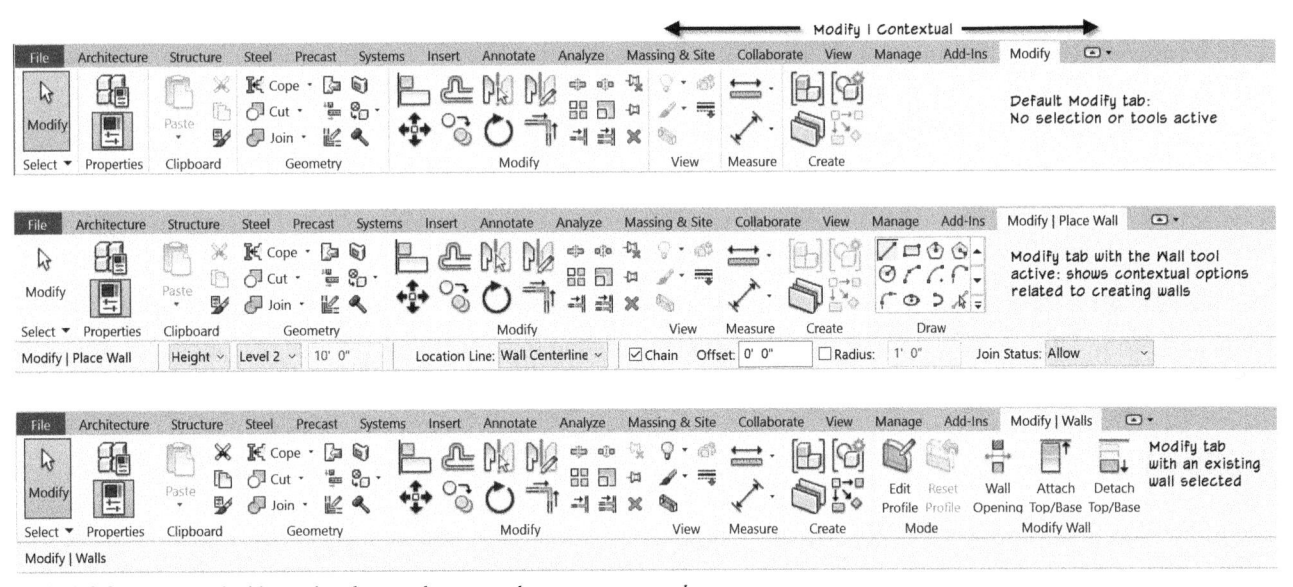

FIGURE 3.6 *Contextual ribbon tabs adjust to the active selection or command*

> **NOTE:** Please note that if you install any third-party add-on applications, you may also get additional tabs on your ribbon.

PANELS

Ribbons are segregated into panels to further classify and group the various tools. If you use the tools on a panel frequently, you can "tear off" the entire panel. This makes the panel into a floating toolbar on your screen. You can drag such a floating panel anywhere you like, even to a secondary monitor if you have one attached to your system. If you "tear off" any panels, Revit will remember the custom locations of the panels the next time you launch the application. If you tear off a panel and later wish to restore it, simply move your mouse over the floating panel. This will make gray bars appear on each side. On the left side, there is a drag bar that you can use to drag the panel around your screen to a new location. On the right side, there is a small icon that if clicked will restore the panel to its original ribbon tab and location (see the top of Figure 3.7).

> **NOTE:** Feel free to tear off panels if you wish; however, all instructions in the tutorials that follow assume that panels are in their default locations on the ribbon tabs and refer to them as such.

> **BIM Manager Note:** You can reset the QAT and all the custom positions of ribbon panels by deleting the *UIState.dat* file on your system. The default location of this file is: *C:\Users\<USERNAME>\AppData\Roaming\Autodesk\Revit\Autodesk Revit 2021\ENU*.

On the panel title bar (bottom edge of the panel), most panels simply show the name of the panel. In some cases, however, they will display an arrow indicating that the panel is expandable (see the bottom left side of Figure 3.7). Click the panel title to expand the panel and reveal hidden tools.

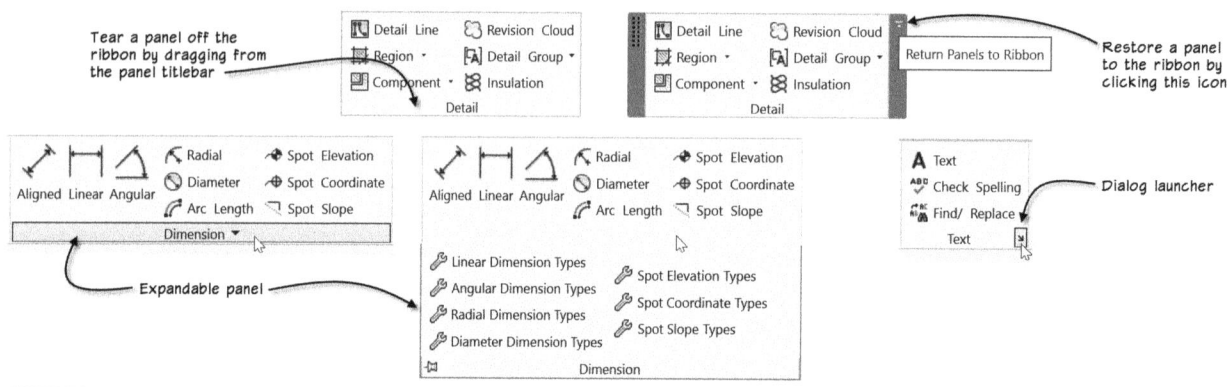

FIGURE 3.7 *Torn off panel (top), expanded panel (bottom left) and dialog launcher icon (bottom right)*

You may also see a small diagonal arrow icon on the right side of the panel title on some panels. This is a "Dialog Launcher" icon. Clicking an icon such as this will open a dialog that usually allows you to configure options or settings (see the bottom right side of Figure 3.7).

RIBBON VIEW STATE

The ribbon has four viewing states. The default state shows the complete ribbon and panels. A portion of the top of the screen is reserved for the ribbon. Click the tabs to switch which tools display, but the same amount of screen space is used regardless of the current tab. This mode makes it easiest to see the tools but uses more precious screen space (see Figure 3.8).

Three alternative states are available that use less screen space. The small icon to the right of the Modify tab is used to toggle to the next state. Click it once to switch to the next state. Each time you click it will toggle to another state. Alternatively, if there is a state you want, you can click the small drop down menu next to the icon to open a menu and select the state you want.

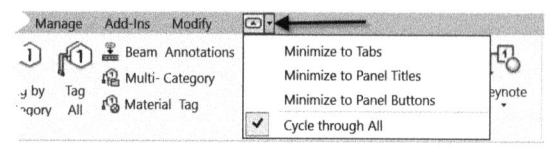

FIGURE 3.8 *Cycle through several minimized ribbon options*

Feel free to try any of the three minimized ribbon states, but the instructions and figures throughout this text use the full ribbon display mode. Adjust accordingly if you choose to use one of the minimized modes.

> **NOTE:** Double-clicking a ribbon tab will cycle to the next display mode. If your ribbon configuration seems to have changed unexpectedly, it is likely that you inadvertently double-clicked a tab.

TOOLS

Ribbon panels contain tools. These tools will appear using one of three types of buttons: Buttons, Drop-down buttons, and Split buttons. Examples of each type of button can be seen on most ribbon tabs. On the Architecture tab, examples of a button are the Door and Window tools (see the left of Figure 3.9). Clicking a button simply invokes that tool. On the Model panel, the Model Group tool is an example of a drop down button. In this case, if you click the tool, a drop down list will appear showing the various options for the tool (see the middle of Figure 3.9).

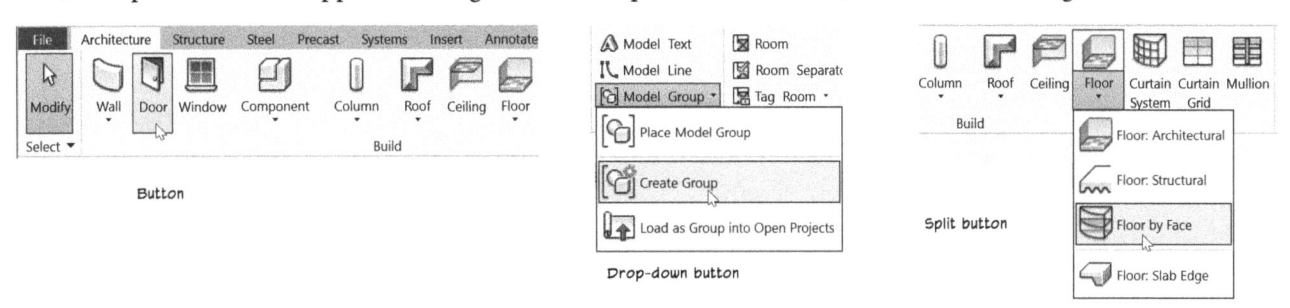

FIGURE 3.9 *Examples of each kind of button on the ribbon*

Split buttons can be either vertical or horizontal. They appear like the other buttons until you pass your mouse over them, at which point it will be clear that only part of the button highlights under the mouse. The portion of the button with the small pop-up indicator (small triangle) behaves like a drop down button. The other side behaves like a normal button. On the Architecture tab, the Wall, Roof, and Floor tools are examples of split buttons (see the right side of Figure 3.9).

Some tools will appear grayed out if the command is not available in the current context. For instance, if you have a sheet view active on screen, most tools such as Wall, Door, or Roof on the Architecture tab will not be available. If you are in a plan view, you cannot click the Level tool. There are plenty of other examples; walls cannot be drawn in an elevation view and you cannot render unless you are in a 3D view. If a tool you want to use is grayed out, try opening a different view and try again.

USER INTERFACE OPTIONS

Several aspects of the user interface have customizable options. We have already discussed tearing off ribbon panels, right-clicking tools to add to the QAT and opening the "Options" dialog to hide and show ribbon tabs in the full version of Revit. In addition, you can customize other settings for the user interface as well. To open the "Options" dialog, from the File menu, click the Options button (shown on the right side of Figure 3.3 above). Click the User Interface tab on the left. Some settings are straight forward such as "active theme." Revit offers a choice of Dark or Light choose the one you prefer. Some of the other settings like enabling the Recent Files list or displaying contextual tab on selection are best left enabled (which is the default).

72 | Chapter 3

> **NOTE:** As noted above, you can use this dialog to customize which ribbon tabs will display. When you launch Revit for the first time, you may have seen a wizard guiding you through the customization of your interface. Revit calls this setting up your workspace. Based on your answers to a few questions, it will suggest which ribbon tabs to hide and show. You can always decline the suggestion and visit this tab of the Options dialog later to change the settings any time.

Tooltip assistance is very handy. When you pause your mouse over tools, a tooltip usually appears. Tooltips give you the name of a tool, its keyboard shortcut (in parenthesis), a short description, a long description, and often a descriptive image or even a short animation. Tooltip assistance can be configured to different levels of information. The Normal option will first display the minimal tip then after a few moments, the more detailed tip will appear. This is the default and recommended setting (see Figure 3.10).

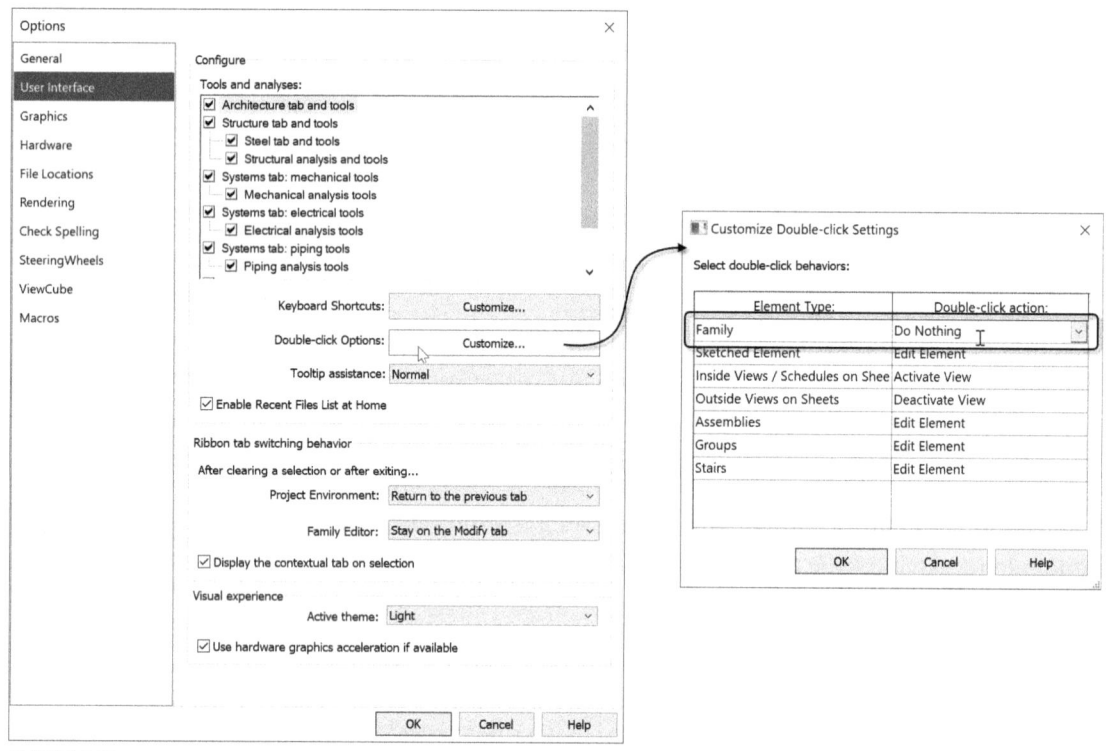

FIGURE 3.10 *Configure preferences for your user interface in the "Options" dialog*

Double-click options displays a dialog that allows you customize what happens when you double-click certain elements onscreen. For each item listed you can choose between various options ranging from edit the element to do nothing. It is recommended that you accept most defaults accept the item for family. For family setting it to Do Nothing is a better choice for most users. It can be disconcerting to accidentally double-click a family or tag and find yourself in the family editor without warning.

KEYBOARD SHORTCUTS

Keyboard shortcuts provide a way to execute commands without first locating them on the ribbon. They are simple keystroke combinations that can be typed as an alternative way to issue a command. To use a keyboard shortcut, simply type the two letters on the keyboard in succession. You do NOT press ENTER following the keystrokes. When you view the tooltips for commands on the ribbon, the keyboard shortcut for the command (if it has one) will appear in parenthesis next to the command name (see Figure 3.11). Tooltip assistance can be a useful way to learn the keyboard shortcuts for your most frequently used tools and commands. In general, once you learn the shortcuts, they will usually be the fastest way to issue commands.

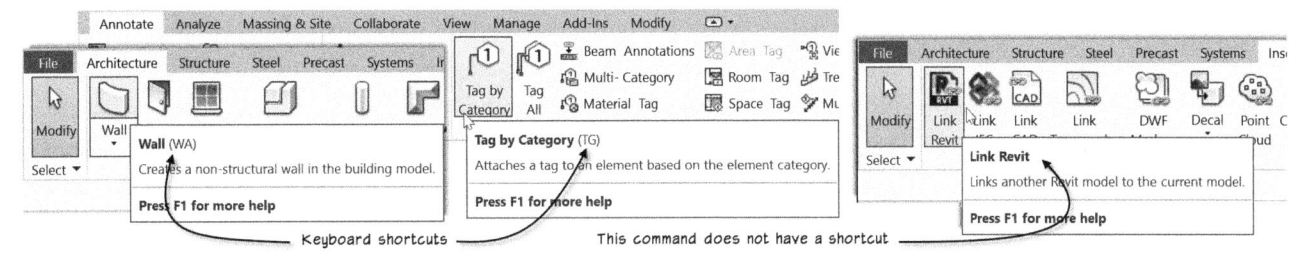

FIGURE 3.11 *Many common commands have keyboard shortcuts*

You can easily modify the existing keyboard shortcuts and add shortcuts to commands that do not already have them. To do this, click the Customize button on the User Interface tab of the "Options" dialog (you can also find it on the User Interface drop down button on the View tab or keyboard shortcuts even has a shortcut of its own: just type KS). In the "Keyboard Shortcuts" dialog, you can scroll through all the currently assigned shortcuts. In some cases, like the Properties command, there will be more than one shortcut. All work the same, so choose the one you prefer. If you wish to add a new shortcut, locate the desired command and select it in the list. Next, type the desired shortcut in the "Press new keys" field and then click the Assign button. If you wish to edit an existing shortcut, first select and then remove it, then assign a new one. Be careful not to assign a shortcut to a command that is already in use. Revit will allow duplicates and will cycle through them when you type the shortcut. But it is a nicer experience to avoid this.

PROJECT BROWSER

When you open a Revit project file, its contents will be displayed in the Project Browser. Think of the Project Browser as the table of contents for your project. It is the primary organizational tool for a Revit project. It is typically docked on the left side of the screen but you can also tear it off and place it anywhere you like, even on a second monitor if you have one attached (see the left side of Figure 3.12).

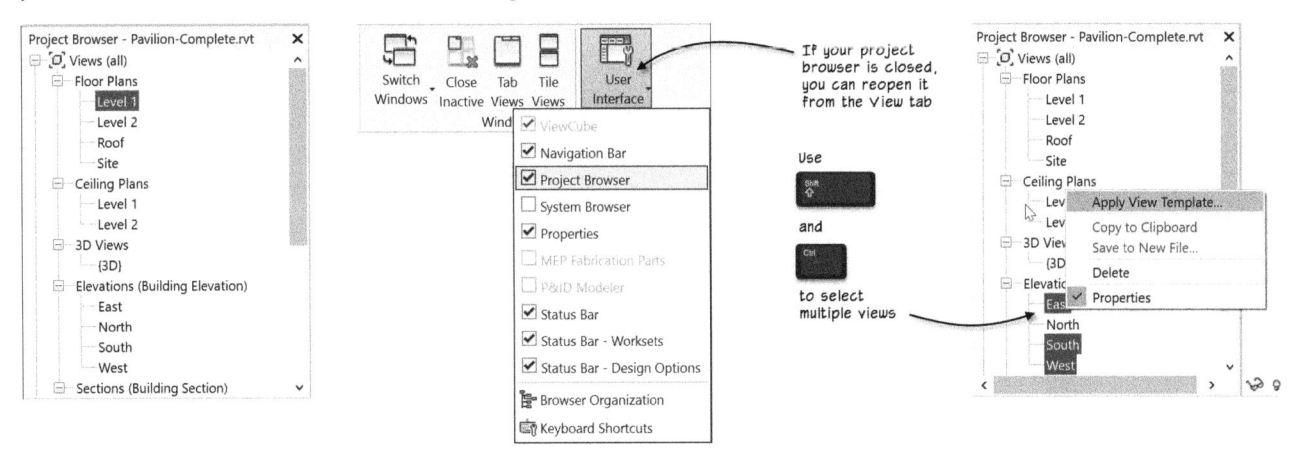

FIGURE 3.12 *The Project Browser*

The name of the currently active view will appear bold in the Project Browser. You can open any view by simply double-clicking on its name in the Project Browser. This is the most common function of the Project Browser. In addition, you can right-click views in the browser to access commands specific to that item. To select multiple views, select the first view, then hold down the CTRL key and select additional views. You can also use the SHIFT key to select everything between any two items. Once you have more than one view selected, you may right-click on any of the highlighted view names to access a menu that will apply to the entire selection of views. This might be useful if you wish to make a global change such as applying a View Template to several views at once (see the right side of Figure 3.12).

You can re-size and move the Project Browser depending on your screen resolution and space needs. Changes you make to the size and location of the Project Browser will be retained when you close Revit and launch a new session—even moving it to a secondary monitor! While it is possible to close the Project Browser, it is not recommended. Since the Project Browser is the primary means of interacting with and navigating between your project's views, closing it makes these functions difficult and inefficient. Should you inadvertently close the Project Browser, you can restore it by clicking View tab and then clicking on the User Interface drop down button. A pop-up menu will appear from which you can select the Project Browser option to redisplay it (see the middle of Figure 3.12).

Views are listed at the top in the *Views*, *Legends*, *Schedule/Quantities*, and *Sheets* branches. In the previous chapter, we explored this part of the Project Browser and its organization options. Please refer to that discussion for more details. To interact directly with elements within your model from the Project Browser, you will work within the *Families*, *Groups*, and the *Revit Links* branches of the Project Browser tree. Every family, group, and Revit file link in a project is listed among these items. We will be exploring all these branches in the upcoming chapters.

Right-click options are sometimes available on each branch and sub-branch of the Project Browser. Please take a moment to right-click on each item and study the menus and commands that are available. One such item is Search. In large projects with many views and/or families, this will prove very helpful to locate items. When you choose the Search option, a dialog will display where you can input your query. Next and Previous buttons allow you to move through each instance.

Another important aspect of the Project Browser is its presentation of the project's sheets. Although sheets are technically classified as views in Revit, they have some unique properties not shared by other views. They are also presented in their own branch of the Project Browser. Expand the *Sheets* branch to see the sheet views in your project. Since sheets can have other views placed on them, a plus (+) will appear next to the sheet name. Expanding this will reveal the names of the views that have been placed upon the sheet. A sheet appearing in the Project Browser without a plus or minus sign indicates that the sheet does not yet contain references to any other views. (The dataset from Chapter 2 provides a good example of each condition.) Like other views, you can open a sheet view by double-clicking on its name in the Project Browser. In addition, you can open referenced views placed on sheets by double-clicking their names beneath the expanded sheet name. Conversely, if you right-click a view on the Views branch, you can choose to open its sheet if it is placed on a sheet or find the views that refer to it. Schedule views and legends placed on sheets also appear indented beneath their sheet names as well.

PROPERTIES PALETTE AND THE TYPE SELECTOR

The Properties palette is another important interface element that will stay onscreen as you work and does not need to be closed to continue working. You simply interact with the properties you wish to edit and either click the Apply button or simply shift focus away from the palette to accept the changes and continue working. This makes work more fluid with fewer disruptions from having to go in and out of dialog boxes.

You can edit element properties on the palette both when you are creating new elements and when you select existing elements. Like the Project Browser, the Properties palette can be docked or floating. By default, it appears docked on the left side of the screen above the Project Browser. If nothing is selected, the Properties palette will show the instance properties of the active view (see the left side of Figure 3.13). Every element in Revit, from model elements like walls and floors, to annotation elements like text and tags, and even views themselves can be edited via this palette. All the settings shown on the Properties palette will be instance properties. This means that the settings affect just the current selection of elements (or the new element being created). Most elements also have type properties. Editing the type properties affects all elements in the model sharing that type (whether they are selected or not). To access type properties, click the Edit Type button at the top right of the Properties palette (see item 1 in Figure 3.13). If your selection includes elements of different kinds, use the filter drop down on the Properties palette to focus on objects of the same category (item 2). After choosing a category from the filter list, the category name and its quantity will appear on the list instead (item 3).

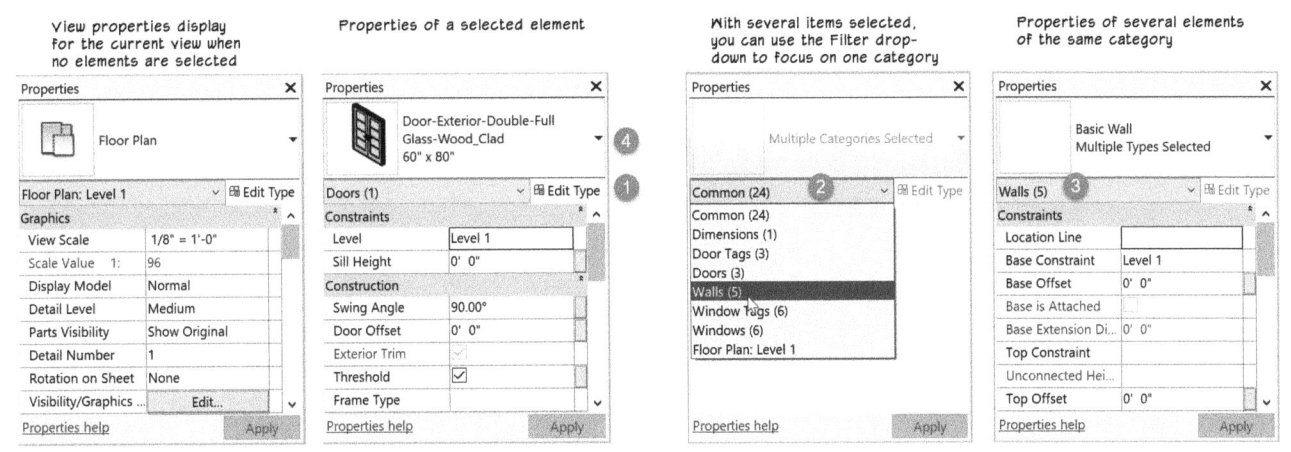

FIGURE 3.13 *The Properties palette can edit instance properties of elements or views. Click Edit Type to access type properties*

At the top of the Properties palette, we have the Type Selector. The Type Selector is a drop down list of types available in your project for the kind of item you are creating or editing (item 4). Families have at least one but can have several types. Think of a type as a "saved variation" of a family. For example, a double flush door might have several standard size configurations. Each such variation would be saved (within the family) as a separate type that we could select from the Type Selector list. Whenever you create elements, you will choose an appropriate type from this list. You can also use the Type Selector to change the type of elements already in the model. Simply select an element and then choose a different type from the list.

> **NOTE:** If you prefer, you can right-click the Type Selector and clone it to the QAT or the Modify tab of the ribbon. Feel free to use these options if you like, but instructions throughout this text will assume that you are accessing the Type Selector from its default location atop the Properties palette.

You will interact with both the Type Selector and Properties palette when creating or modifying elements. When you are creating an element, you first choose the tool for the item you wish to create on the ribbon. Next choose a type from the Type Selector and if necessary, edit other properties on the Properties palette. If you are modifying an existing element, simply select the element (or elements) and then choose the desired type from the Type Selector and/or modify the desired parameters on the Properties palette. If you wish to modify all elements of a type globally across the entire project, click the Edit Type button instead.

When you select multiple elements, if they all share the same type, the Type Selector will display the name. If the selection of items is the same category of element (all doors, for example) but are not currently the same type, then the Type Selector will remain active, but will display a message reading "Multiple Types Selected" (see the right side of Figure 3.13) or "Multiple Families Selected." If you select multiple elements and the Type Selector reports "Multiple Categories Selected," this indicates that you have made a selection of dissimilar elements (like a wall and a door), and you cannot make changes to them together using the Type Selector. You may be able to edit other Properties, but the options available on the Properties palette will be limited only to those properties that the selection of elements shares.

OPTIONS BAR

The Options Bar runs horizontally across the screen and is located directly below the ribbon and displays options available for elements you are creating. On occasion, some options will also display for existing elements you have selected as well (see Figure 3.14).

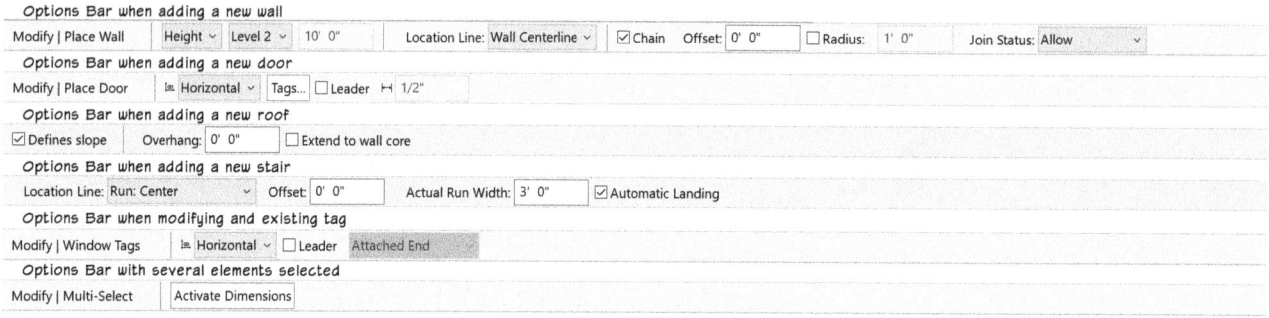

Options Bar when adding a new wall
Modify	Place Wall	Height	Level 2	10' 0"	Location Line: Wall Centerline	☑ Chain	Offset: 0' 0"	☐ Radius: 1' 0"	Join Status: Allow
Options Bar when adding a new door
Modify	Place Door	Horizontal	Tags...	☐ Leader	1/2"
Options Bar when adding a new roof
☑ Defines slope	Overhang: 0' 0"	☐ Extend to wall core
Options Bar when adding a new stair
Location Line: Run: Center	Offset: 0' 0"	Actual Run Width: 3' 0"	☑ Automatic Landing
Options Bar when modifying and existing tag
Modify	Window Tags	Horizontal	☐ Leader	Attached End
Options Bar with several elements selected
Modify	Multi-Select	Activate Dimensions

FIGURE 3.14 *Examples of the Options Bar when creating or editing various model elements*

You will interact with the Options Bar regularly as you work in Revit. In many cases, you will configure settings on the Options Bar, the contextual ribbon and/or the Properties palette as you interact with a command.

THE CANVAS (VIEW WINDOW DISPLAY AREA)

The most interactive portion of the interface is the canvas area where you work with the views of your building model. When you open a view, it appears in a window in the canvas area. At least one view window must be open to work in a project. You can however open several views for a project at one time. They will appear as tabs across the top of the canvas area. You can also tile (type WT) or cascade (type WC) the windows onscreen. These commands are also on the View tab. If you have many views open at once, tiling can make the actual windows very small and hard to work with. To prevent this, you can restore them back to tabs within a single tile (use the Tab Views tool on the View tab for this or type TW). Be sure to close unneeded windows when you no longer need them. An easy way to do this is to use the Close Inactive tool on the View tab or QAT.

STATUS BAR

The Status Bar is the gray bar along the bottom edge of the Revit application frame. If you glance down at the Status Bar, you will notice a constant readout of feedback appears there. In some cases, the information provides prompts and clues as to what actions are required within a command; in other cases, the feedback may simply describe an action taking place or describe an element beneath the cursor. We saw examples of this in Chapter 2 in Figure 2.13.

In addition to the Status messages, the Status Bar includes two other optional controls: Status Bar – Worksets and the Status Bar – Design Options. These two controls provide shortcuts to these two Revit features. Worksets is the collection of tools that enable multiple users to access the same Revit model simultaneously. You can learn more about them in Chapter 16. Design Options provides a mechanism to consider alternative design schemes in the same Revit model. See the "Design Options" topic on page 392 in Chapter 9 for more information.

VIEW CONTROL BAR

Every graphical view window has a View Control Bar located at the bottom edge of its window (see Figure 3.2 above). The View Control bar serves two purposes—it displays at a glance the most common view settings of the window and provides a simple and convenient way to change them if required.

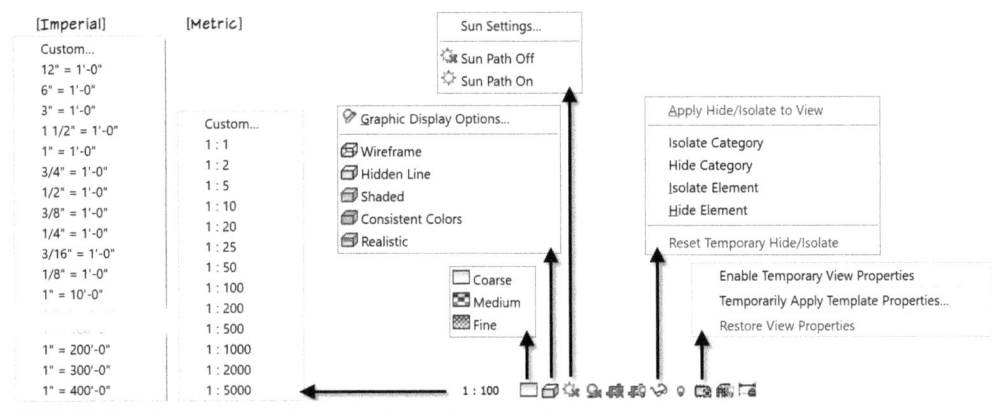

FIGURE 3.15 *The View Control Bar provides quick access to the most common view settings*

Many of the settings are also accessible from the Properties palette. To access these settings in Properties, make sure no elements are selected, and then look at the Properties palette. Most of the settings change the view in some way. For example, the scale pop-up will change the plot scale of the view. This will have an immediate effect on the size of all view-specific elements in the view and will also affect the intensity of line weights. The level of detail pop-up has three options: coarse, medium and fine. This setting can be used to show more detail or less detail in the view. Families in your model must support the feature for any difference to be seen. Many of the out-of-the-box families have two or three levels of detail triggered by this setting. For example, the steel families used to create structural framing and columns can display single line graphics in coarse and fully articulated structural steel shapes complete with filleted corners in fine.

Use the visual style pop-up to switch the display of the active view from hidden line to shaded to even realistic or ray trace in 3D views. There are many toggle icons including: shadows on and off, crop region enabled and disabled, crop region visible and invisible, reveal hidden elements, display analytical model and reveal constraints mode. Each of these controls you simply click to toggle the mode on or off.

The Temporary Hide/Isolate (looks like sunglasses) command can be used to hide elements temporarily. To use the temporary Hide/Isolate tools, select an element or elements in the model and then click the Hide/Isolate icon and choose an option. The Hide Element option temporarily makes the selected element(s) invisible. The Isolate Element option leaves the selected elements visible and hides everything else. There are also options to hide or isolate the entire category of objects based upon the category of objects you have selected. For example, if you select a door in the model and then choose Hide Category, all doors in the view will temporarily hide. When you use the temporary Hide/Isolate command, a cyan border will appear around the current view window with a label in the upper left corner until the mode is disabled. The important thing to know about using the Temporary Hide/Isolate function in a view is that the changes it makes to the view window will not be saved outside the current work session. If you wish to make the Hide/Isolate settings permanent, select the Temporary Hide/Isolate icon and choose: **Apply Hide/Isolate to View** from the pop-up.

SELECTION METHODS

Before elements can be modified in Revit, they must be selected. There are various methods used to select elements and it is worth taking the time to master them all. As you move the cursor around a view window, you will notice that any elements available for selection will temporarily highlight while under the cursor—this is known as "pre-highlighting." The purpose of pre-highlighting is to preview what will be selected if you click the mouse so that you know you have the correct item. This is particularly helpful when working in a complex model with many elements close together. Use pre-highlighting (and often the TAB key—see below) as a tool to assist you in accurate selection.

• Revit Essentials for Architecture •

SELECTION BY CLICKING

The simplest way to select an element is to click on it. When you select an element, it will display in the selection color (light blue by default) on screen—this indicates that the element(s) is selected. Once selected, an element will remain selected until you deselect it. You can deselect elements in a few ways: selecting another element will automatically deselect the current selection set (unless you hold down the CTRL key) and become the new selection set. You can deselect all elements without creating a new selection set by clicking on a blank portion of the screen (where there are no elements) or by pressing the ESC key. (You can also click the Modify tool on the ribbon).

To add or remove elements from the current selection set:

- Hold the CTRL key down while clicking on another element. The new element will be added to the current selection set.

- Hold the SHIFT key down while clicking on a selected element to remove the element from the current selection set (it will no longer be highlighted in the selection color).

- Hold both the CTRL and SHIFT key down to toggle the current selection—if it is selected, this will deselect and vice versa. If you do this while making a selection box (next topic) it will reverse the selection; anything selected will be deselected and vice-versa.

> **TIP:** If you accidentally pick an object without holding down the CTRL key (or if you accidentally click in the white space), you will lose your selection set (which will be replaced with only the one element just picked or nothing if you click in white space). You can restore your previous selection set by right-clicking in the view window and then choosing: **Select Previous**. You can also select previous by holding down the CTRL key and then pressing the LEFT ARROW key. Either action will restore your previous selection without having to start all over again.

Selected elements also appear shaded and semi-transparent. Selection and pre-selection colors and other settings can be customized in the "Options" dialog on the Graphics tab.

SELECTION BOXES

Even with the CTRL and SHIFT keys, making selections of multiple elements can be time consuming if you only click elements. A faster and more efficient way to create a large selection set is by using a selection box. To create a selection box with the Modify tool, click and hold down with the left mouse button next to an element, drag a rectangular box around the elements you wish to select. Elements will pre-highlight as you make the selection box.

The direction in which you drag the selection box determines which specific elements are selected. If you create your selection box by dragging from left to right on the screen, the edge of the selection box will appear solid as you drag and only elements completely within the box will be selected. If you create your selection box by dragging from right to left on the screen instead, the edges of the selection box will appear dashed and any element completely or partially included in the box will be selected (see Figure 3.16).

Revit User Interface | 79

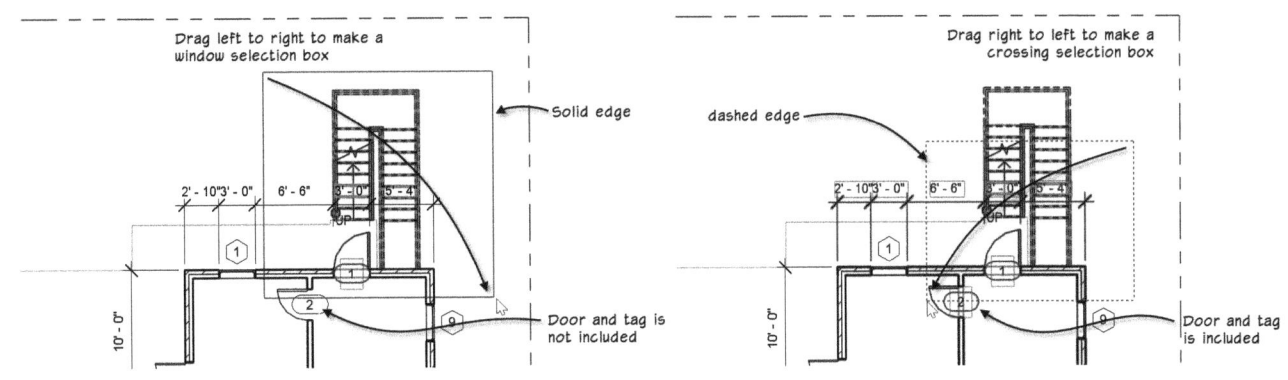

FIGURE 3.16 *Selection boxes vary with the direction you drag*

You can always combine methods—first create a selection box, and then use the CTRL and SHIFT keys to add and remove from the basic selection by clicking or dragging additional selection boxes.

FILTER SELECTION

Another approach to building a large selection set is to deliberately select too many elements and then use the Filter tool to remove categories you don't need from the selection. The Filter selection tool is located on the Status Bar and on the ribbon. Remember, when using the Filter selection tool, you always start with a selection that includes *more* than the items you want, and you then filter out the undesired elements by category (see Figure 3.17).

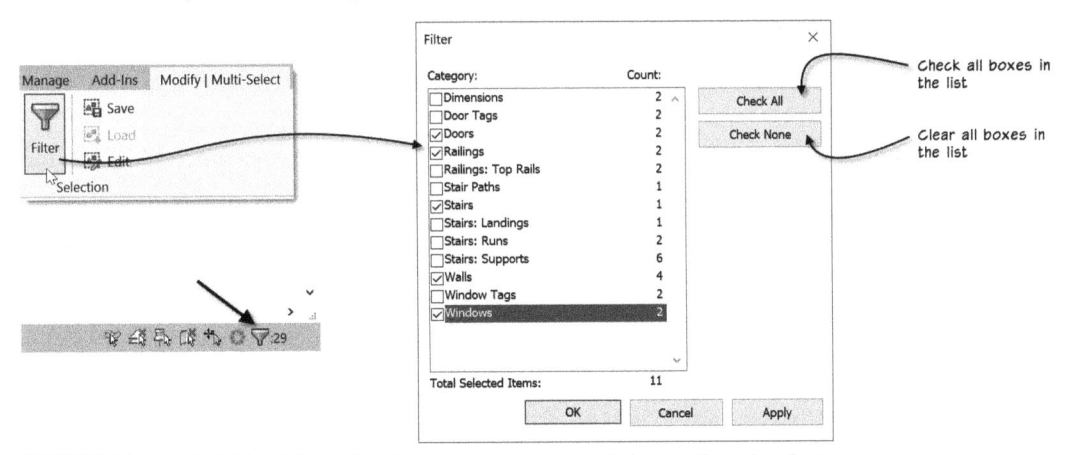

FIGURE 3.17 *Use the "Filter Selection" dialog to remove categories of elements from the selection set*

Once again, you can continue to add and remove from the selection that results from the filter using any of the other methods discussed.

RIGHT-CLICK SELECTION METHODS

You can access a few useful selection methods on the right-click menu. The first was mentioned in a tip above. If you wish to reselect the same selection again, right-click and choose: **Select Previous**. This will restore the previous selection. It will only go back the one previous selection.

You can also use the right-click to select items like the one you already have selected. To do this, first select an element or simply pre-highlight it and then right-click. Choose one of two commands:

> **Select All Instances > Visible in View**—selects all elements within the current view only that share the same family and type as the selected element. For this to work, a single selection is necessary. The command will be grayed out for

multiple selections. So, for example, if you right-click on a wall, you can use this command to select all walls like the one selected within the current view.

Select All Instances > In Entire Project—works exactly like the Visible in View option, except it selects elements throughout the entire model! Use this with care as you will be selecting both elements you can see onscreen in the current view and potentially many more that are not currently visible but occur elsewhere in the model.

Another command on the right-click menu is: **Create Similar**. This is not a selection command but is similar in concept to the commands noted here. With this command, you will be creating a new element that has the same family, type and other settings as the one you selected to start.

THE ALMIGHTY TAB KEY

You will find that the TAB key is probably the most used and most useful of all the modifier keys on the keyboard when working in Revit. As mentioned in the previous topic, being able to quickly add or remove from a selection set can greatly increase your efficiency during a work session. In general, you can think of the TAB key as a "toggle switch," allowing you to cycle through potential selections. When you attempt to pre-highlight an element on screen, sometimes a neighboring element will pre-highlight instead. No matter how subtly you move your mouse to capture the desired element, it often proves difficult or impossible to highlight the right one. The TAB key provides the solution to this situation.

> **TIP:** "When in doubt, press TAB."

While there are dozens of examples of using the TAB key in a Revit session, a few examples are presented here that will give you an idea of where using the TAB key proves most handy.

TAB **to Pre-Highlight Elements for Selection**—When the Modify tool (to select), or any other tool with built-in selection bias like the Dimension, Split, or Align tools, (just to name a few) is near two or more elements, you can use the TAB key to pre-highlight each element in succession (cycle through) before you click to make your selection. Each time you press TAB, a different element will pre-highlight until all items have been cycled through. Once you have tabbed through all elements, the cycling will repeat (see Figure 3.18).

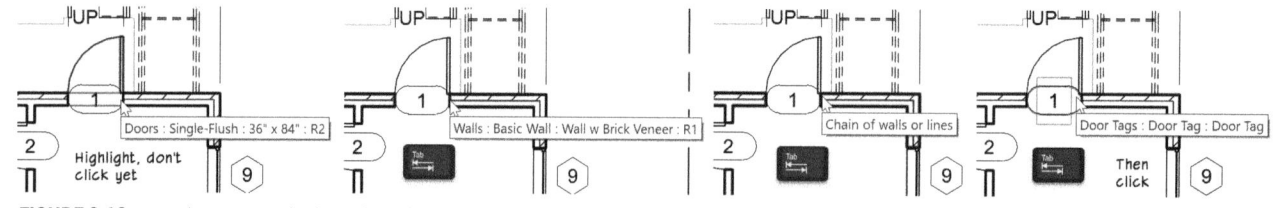

FIGURE 3.18 *Use the* **TAB** *to cycle through and pre-highlight nearby elements*

When the element that you wish to select is pre-highlighted, click the mouse as normal to select it. This is important. Do not forget to click once the items you want to select are highlighted. If you don't, when you move your mouse nothing will be selected, and you will have start over.

TAB **During Dimensioning**—When you are using existing geometry for reference points such as when adding dimensions, using the align command or tracing a background, you can use the TAB key to cycle through possible reference points (see Figure 3.19).

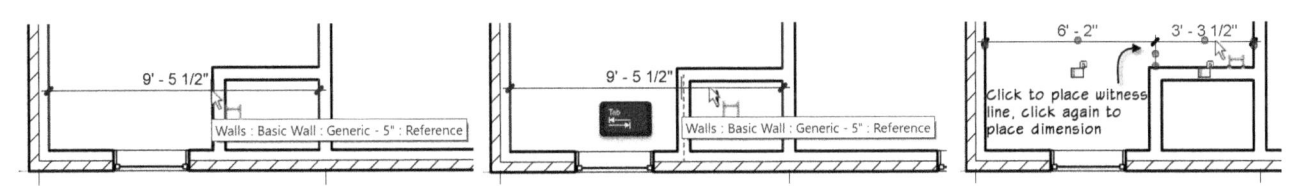

FIGURE 3.19 *Use the* TAB *to cycle through dimension reference points*

TAB **for Chain Selection**—Chain selection is a very powerful feature of Revit. Chain selection works with walls or lines. Like an actual chain, chain selection highlights all the walls or lines that touch one another end to end. To make a chain selection, you first pre-highlight a single wall or line. Next you press the TAB key and in so doing, any walls or lines that form a chain (i.e., are located end-to-end) with that wall or line are pre-highlighted together. Finally, you click the mouse to make the selection with a single mouse-click (see Figure 3.20). Don't forget to click when the chain pre-highlights. If you don't click, when you move your mouse away nothing will be selected. Remember: **Highlight,** TAB**, then click**.

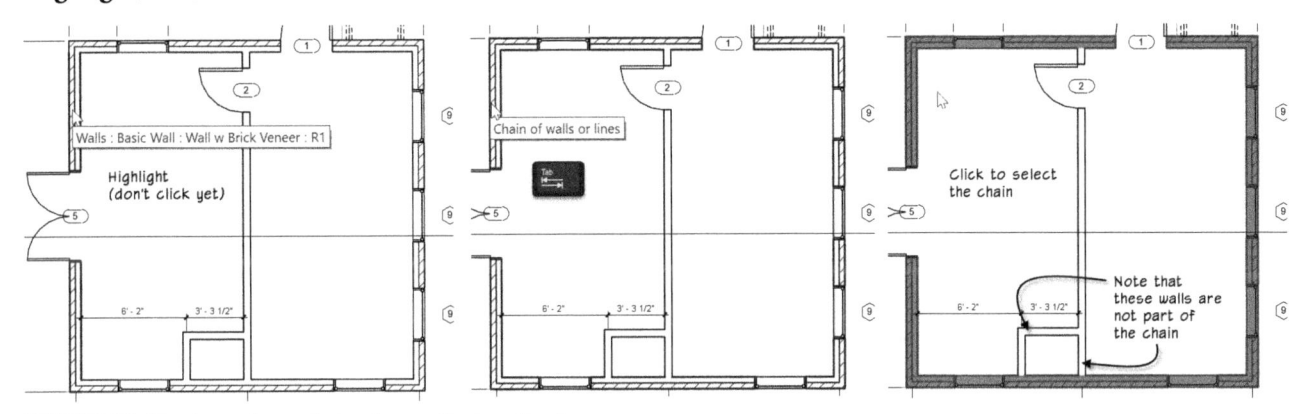

FIGURE 3.20 *Use the* TAB *key to chain select a collection of walls*

Notice in the figure that only the outer walls—the ones touching end to end—were selected. The inner walls, even though they "touch" were not selected. A chain is very specific. They *must* touch endpoint to endpoint.

There is also a "partial" chain. To use this, select the first element you want selected. Highlight the last item you want, and then press TAB to highlight all the elements in the chain in between. Click to select the partial chain.

There are dozens of additional ways to use the TAB key in Revit. One of the easiest things to do is simply try tabbing in various situations while you work in the software. Other examples will be presented throughout this book in the tutorials that follow. The most important thing to do is practice it so that you are comfortable. Once you get familiar and comfortable with using the TAB key, you'll wonder how you lived without it.

SELECTION TOGGLES

There are several selection modes that you can toggle on and off to control which kinds of elements can be selected and how. These include:

Select links—links are other project (RVT) or drawing (DWG) files that are inserted into your current project and remain connected to the original file. If the original file is changed, the link can be refreshed to display the latest changes in your current project. Links will be discussed in detail in Chapter 7. When you toggle this setting off, you will not be able to select linked files onscreen. Commands that require selecting a link (like coordination review) are not affected, you'll still be able to select the link even if it is off.

Select underlay elements—each floor plan view has an underlay setting that allows you to place any other floor plan in the project as an underlay to the current view. This quite literally emulates the same concept from traditional paper-based drafting where you could place one sheet under the current one and use it for reference as you work. In Revit, when you place an underlay, the elements in the underlain level are live model elements, meaning that you can select and even modify them. In cases where this would be undesirable, toggle this setting to prevent underlay elements visible in the view from being selected. Even though you can't select them with the setting enabled, you will still be able to snap to underlay geometry.

Select pinned elements—the pin position tool (available on the Modify tab, on the Modify panel) allows you to prevent elements from being moved. If you have an element whose location you wish to maintain, you can select it and then click the Pin tool. This is helpful for items that you don't wish to have moved inadvertently. If you toggle this selection mode, not only will the element's position be pinned, but you will not be able to select any pinned elements either. Some hosted elements like curtain wall grids and mullions also use the pin concept to keep them associated with their host element. Such elements will also be prevented from selection when this mode is active. Certain elements are pinned by default. For example: imported DWG files that use Origin to Internal Origin placement, curtain wall grids, etc.

Select element by face—the default selection behavior requires you to select elements by their edges. In cases where you would like to select by the surface instead, use this toggle. For example, the only way to select a floor element in a plan view is if you can see its edges. If the edges are covered by the walls, you would not be able to select the floor. Toggle this mode to allow the selection of elements like floors by clicking on their faces instead (anywhere in the plan). The same is true in 3D views. Sometimes selecting elements by their faces makes 3D selection easier.

Drag elements on selection—when this mode is on, you can select and move an element in a single motion. This can sometimes be undesirable. To prevent both selection and movement in the same action, toggle this mode off.

Selection toggles can be configured in two locations: the Select (expandable) panel on the ribbon just below the Modify tool, and at the lower-right corner of the application frame on the Status Bar (see Figure 3.21).

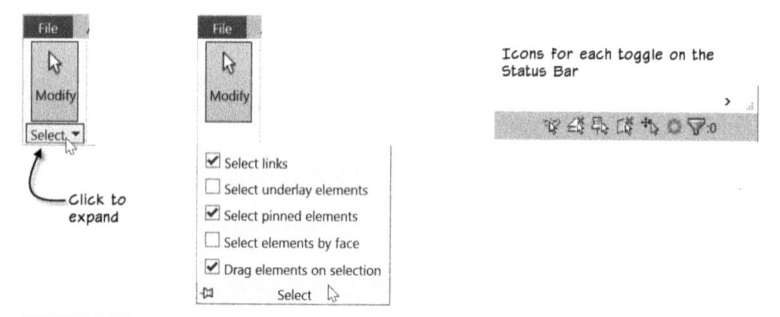

FIGURE 3.21 *Use selection toggles to exclude certain elements from selection*

Each of these modes is a toggle switch which will remain on or off until you change it. The setting is persistent from one session of Revit to the next. So, if you toggle one off, quit Revit and then reopen Revit to continue work tomorrow, the toggles will persist in whatever state (on or off) they were left in. Also, it is important to understand that these settings are part of the Revit application and not part of the project file. This means that each user will be able to set the selection toggles to suite their own preferences without their choices affecting other members of the project team.

TEMPORARY DIMENSIONS

Although you can toggle the reference point used by temporary dimensions using the TAB key (as noted above), it is often more efficient to change the default behavior instead. Defaults for temporary dimensions can be configured for walls, doors, and windows. Depending on your preferences, you can have the temporary dimensions default to either the centers (default) or edges of objects. Click the Manage tab of the ribbon. On the Settings panel, click the Additional Settings dropdown. From the drop down menu that appears, choose: **Temporary Dimensions** (see Figure 3.22).

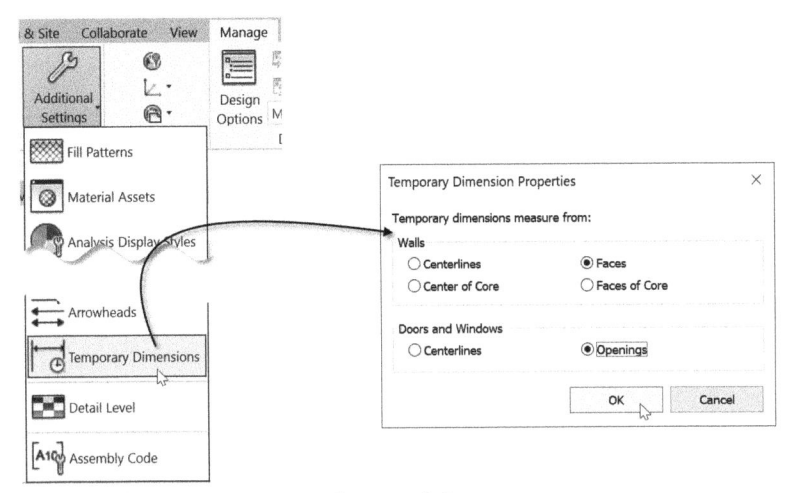

FIGURE 3.22 *Configure temporary dimension behavior*

Choose your preference for both the "Walls" and "Doors and Windows" settings. Revit defaults to centerlines for both. For Walls, you can dimension faces, centerlines, and/or wall cores. For Doors and Windows, choose between centerlines and openings. The author recommends Faces for walls and openings for Doors and Windows. Temporary Dimension settings are saved with the project file. So, you will need to check it in each new project. Many project settings are accessible from both the Additional Settings drop down button and directly on the Manage ribbon. Feel free to look at any of the others.

SNAPS

Revit includes dimension snaps and object snaps. The Snaps button is on the Manage tab on the Settings panel. Dimension snaps adjust with your zoom level on screen. As you zoom out, the snap increment becomes larger. As you zoom in, it becomes smaller. You can customize the increment upon which it adjusts at the top of the dialog for both length and angles. In the middle of the dialog, all the object snap modes are listed. You can turn them on and off to suit your preferences. They are all on by default. You do not need to change anything in this dialog but do become familiar with all the items it contains. Make note of the keyboard shortcuts next to each object snap. (These are two character codes in parenthesis). As you work on your models, you can type these shortcuts as needed to force Revit to use an object snap. This amounts to an override that lasts for the next click of the mouse.

SUMMARY

- ☑ The user interface of Revit uses many common Windows conventions and some unique ones as well.

- ☑ The ribbon along the top of the screen contains several tools organized into tabs.

- ☑ Each ribbon tab is divided into panels.

- ☑ Tools come in three varieties: buttons, drop down buttons, and split buttons.

- ☑ The Options Bar changes to reflect the current tool or command.

- ☑ One or more views of the project can be opened at one time in the workspace (canvas) area. They can be tiled, tabbed, or cascaded.

- ☑ The Project Browser, along the left side by default, contains all the views of the project as well as the families, groups, and linked files.

- ☑ Project Browser is like a "table of contents" for your project.

- ☑ Manipulate the display settings of the active view with the View Control Bar.

- ☑ The Status Bar along the bottom of the screen shows prompts for the current command.

- ☑ Select elements with the modify tool (mouse pointer), use the CTRL key to add to the selection set, and the SHIFT key to remove from the selection set or hold down both to reverse the selection.

- ☑ Drag left to right to select all elements within the selection box (window), right to left to select all those in contact with the dashed box (crossing).

- ☑ The TAB key is used to cycle through potential selections when more than one is possible.

- ☑ Use the TAB key to "chain" select walls or lines. (A chain is walls or lines touching end to end.)

- ☑ Configure settings "Temporary Dimensions" dialog to suit your personal preferences.

- ☑ Selection toggles exclude certain items from selection such as links, pinned elements and underlays.

SECTION II

Creating the Building Model

INTRODUCTION

The first step toward reaping the benefits of Building Information Modeling (BIM) is to construct a building model in the software. The tools provided for this purpose in Autodesk® Revit® are many and varied. In this section we will explore the many building modeling tools available such as walls, doors, windows, columns, beams, stairs, railings, roofs, floors, and curtain walls. In Chapter 11, we will take a detailed look at Revit family components and the Family Editor.

SECTION II is organized as follows:

Chapter 4: Creating a Building Layout

Chapter 5: Setting Up Project Levels and Views

Chapter 6: Column Grids and Structural Layout

Chapter 7: Groups and Links

Chapter 8: Vertical Circulation

Chapter 9: Floors and Roofs

Chapter 10: Developing the Exterior Skin

Chapter 11: Families and the Family Editor

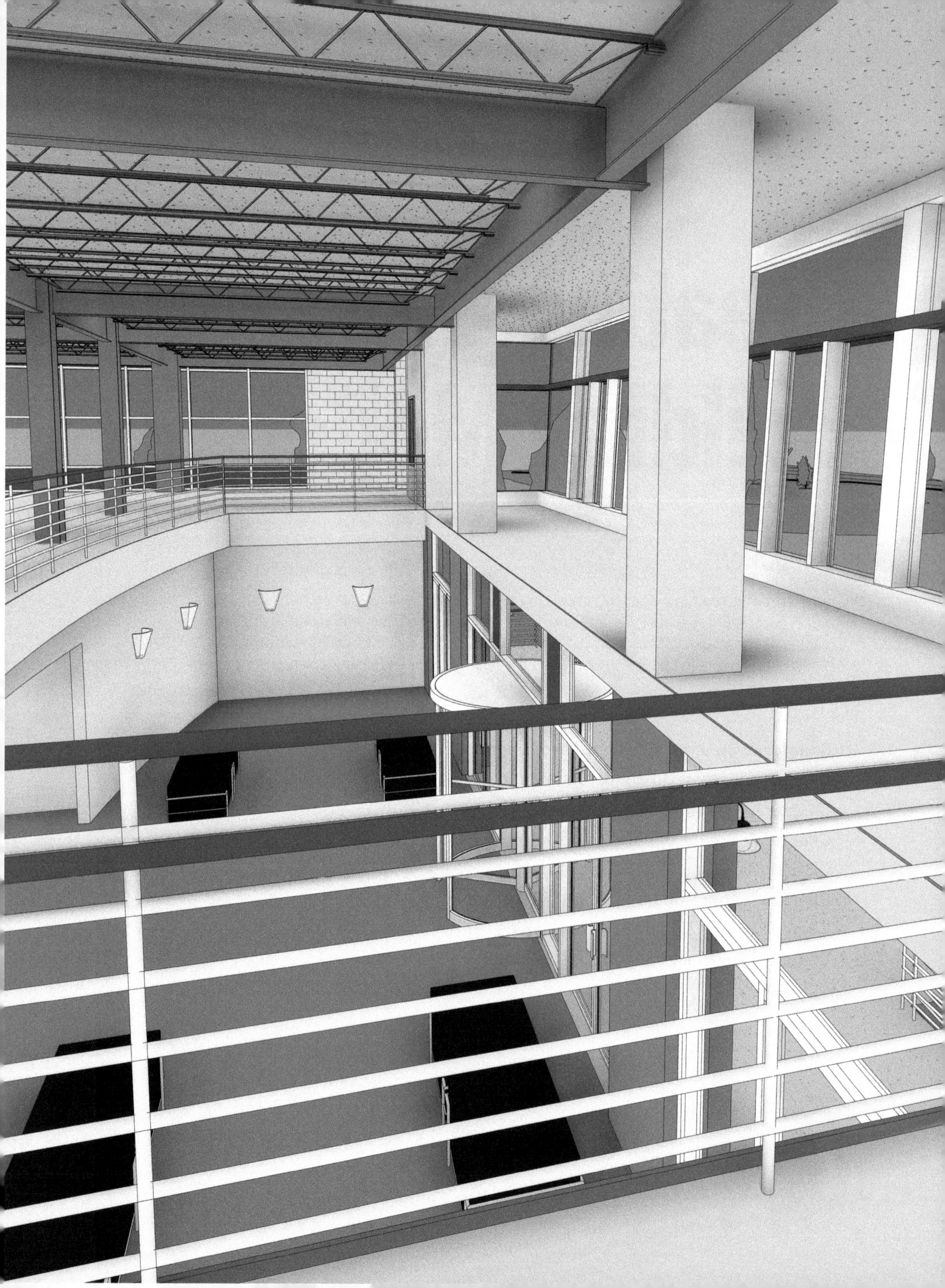

CHAPTER 4
Creating a Building Layout

INTRODUCTION

The first few chapters were intended to get you comfortable with the conceptual underpinnings of Autodesk® Revit®. Now that you have the correct mind-set and a level of comfort with the user interface, get ready to roll up your sleeves—it is time to begin creating our first model. Most of our attention in this book is given to the design development and construction documentation phases. The tutorial exercises in this book will explore two building types concurrently, starting at different points in the project cycle. This will give a sense of the multiple ways you can approach the design process while also keeping some variety in the lessons. Don't feel limited to the techniques covered here. The aim of the tutorials is to showcase common workflows. But exploration is highly encouraged and in so doing, you may discover equally valid ways to achieve the same end results.

In this book we start our models directly in the Revit project environment beginning with wall layout. However, Revit also includes a complete conceptual modeling environment where you can design your building form as a series of masses and forms. Massing studies can then become the basis for a building design as your project moves from conceptual design to design development. The conceptual design environment offers an excellent way to perform conceptual design studies during the early schematic design phases of the project. While we will not begin our projects in this chapter with conceptual massing, if you would like to learn more, you can find an introduction to the conceptual environment in Chapter 17.

OBJECTIVES

Throughout the course of the hands-on tutorials in this chapter, we will lay out the existing conditions for a small residential renovation project. We will explore the various techniques for adding and modifying walls, doors, and windows. In addition, we will add plumbing fixtures and other elements to make the layout more complete. After completing this chapter, you will know how to:

- Add and modify walls and work with Temporary Dimensions
- Explore wall properties
- Add and modify doors and windows
- Assign Phasing parameters to model components
- Add plumbing fixtures and other "Components" to the model
- Build an in-place family

88 | Chapter 4

WORKING WITH WALLS

Since walls are the basic building blocks of any building, we will start with them. We will create a new temporary project and sketch some walls to get comfortable with the various options. Later we will create one of the actual projects that will be used throughout the rest of the book.

CREATE A NEW PROJECT

We will begin our work in a new project created from the default architectural template file. The lessons that follow require the dataset files included for download with this book. Refer to the "Download the Book Dataset" topic on page xi in the Preface for instructions on downloading and installing the book's dataset files if you still need to do so.

1. Launch Autodesk® Revit®.

    The Home screen should appear. Let's be sure that we are starting from the out-of-the-box default architectural template.

2. In the Models area, click the New button.

3. In the "New Project" dialog, in the "Template file" area, be sure that the **Imperial-Architectural Template** [**Metric-Architectural Template**] appears on the drop down list.

    If you need to, click the Browse button to locate the template file.

    The default template location for the Imperial template file is:

    C:\ProgramData\Autodesk\RVT 2021\Templates\English-Imperial\default.rte

    The default template file name and location for the Metric template file is:

    [C:\ProgramData\Autodesk\RVT 2021\Templates\English\DefaultMetric.rte]

> **NOTE:** If you are in a country for which your version of Revit does not include these template files, they have both been provided with the book's dataset files. Please browse to the *Templates* folder in the location where you installed the dataset files to locate them. See the Preface for more information on the dataset files.

4. In the "Create New" area, verify that the Project radio button is selected and then click OK (see Figure 4.1).

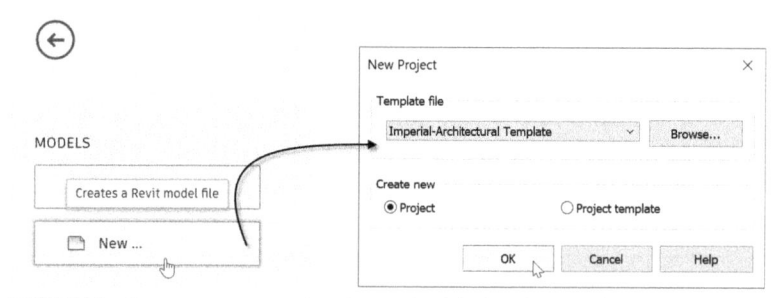

FIGURE 4.1 *Create a new project based upon the default architectural template file*

To configure the default template file and the other fields that show on the template file list, open the File menu and click the Options button. Click the File Locations tab on the left and then edit the list of Project template files. You can click the plus sign icon to add templates to the list, click the minus sign to remove templates from the list and use the move rows up and down icons to reorder the list. Changes will show in the drop down list the next time you create a new file.

• The Aubin Academy •

GETTING STARTED WITH WALLS

Most building objects are found on the Architecture tab of the ribbon. As discussed in the previous chapter, the ribbon (which is the primary interface for nearly all Revit commands) can be shown in four formats: The full ribbon, minimized to buttons, minimized to panel titles and minimized to tabs. While you may prefer to use one of the minimized options, instructions and images throughout this text will assume you are using the full ribbon (see the "Ribbon View State" topic on page 70 in Chapter 3 for more details.) Beneath the ribbon is a small space called the Options Bar (see the "Options Bar" topic on page 76 in Chapter 3) utilized by certain commands and functions. We will begin by working with walls. You can add walls point by point or enable the "Chain" option to create them in series (each segment beginning where the previous one ended). Walls will "join" automatically with intersecting walls at corners and intersections. Walls have many parameters such as length, height, and type; can have custom shapes and profiles; and can receive (i.e., host) doors and windows and automatically create openings for them.

1. On the Architecture tab of the ribbon, on the Build panel, click the Wall tool (or press WA) (see Figure 4.2).

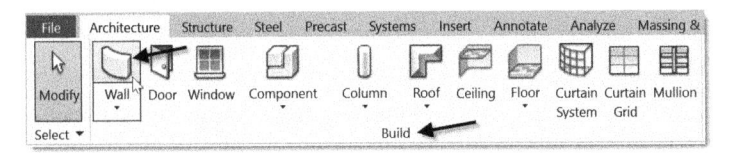

FIGURE 4.2 *The Wall tool on the Architecture tab of the ribbon*

Several things will happen onscreen: The "Modify | Place Wall" tab will appear on the ribbon, several settings will appear on the Options Bar, the Properties palette will change to reflect the wall you are drawing, the pointer will change to a crosshair cursor and the Status Bar prompt will read: "Click to enter wall start point."

The following list explains the major fields and controls that you can manipulate while adding a wall. You can find these items on the Properties palette, on the Options Bar or both (see Figure 4.3).

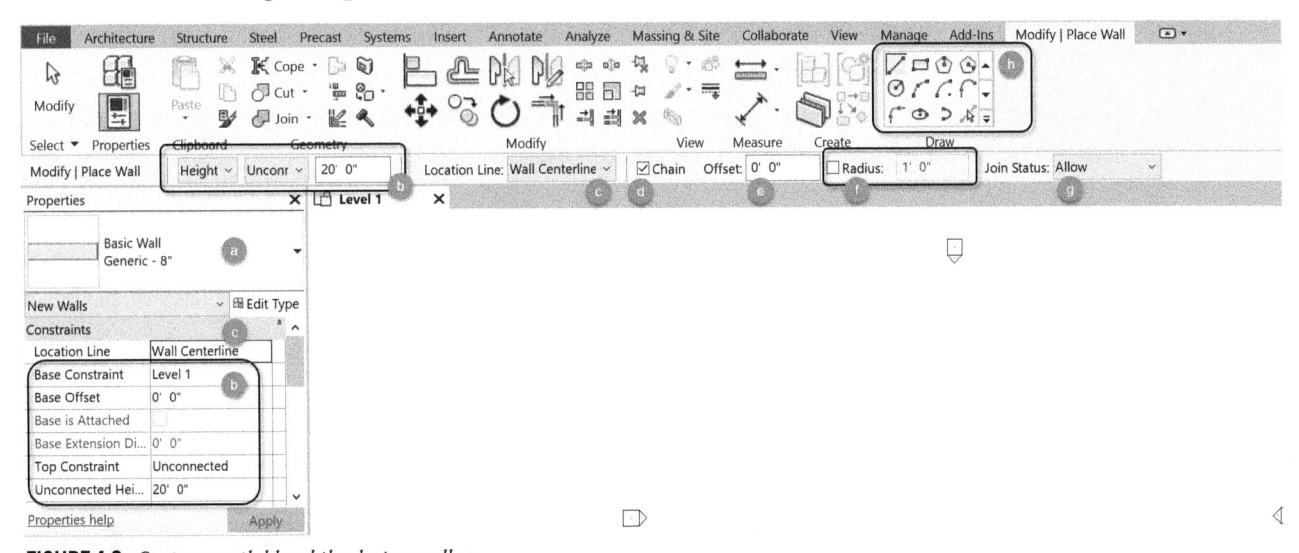

FIGURE 4.3 *Options available while placing walls*

    a. **Type Selector**—Use this drop down to choose from a list of types (wall types in this case) in the current file. The specific list is populated by the template we used to create the project. Always choose a type from this list before configuring other options.

> **BIM Manager Note:** Walls are a system family. System families have built-in parameters predefined within the software that are not editable by the end user. (They typically represent building components that are constructed on-site like walls, floors or roofs as opposed to those created in a factory or shop and delivered to the site and installed like doors and light fixtures.) System family instances cannot be edited outside of the Project Editor. Furthermore, the system family itself cannot be renamed, deleted, or edited. System families do have types like component families. User edits are permitted to the system family's types. Changes to types apply to all instances throughout the model. If you maintain a custom office standard template file, you can include your custom types within this file so that users will have access to them in each new project created from that template.

b. **Height**—There are two options for Height; a drop down list of parametric height options and a text field (available when "Unconnected" height is chosen). When you choose "Unconnected" you can simply type in a fixed height for the wall. The heights of walls can also be connected to the project's levels instead. (Our project created from the default template has two levels: Level 1 and Level 2.)

c. **Location Line**—A point within the width of the wall that is used as a reference. Choices include: Wall Centerline, Interior and Exterior Finish Faces and several "Core" options. The core of the wall will be discussed in detail in later chapters. Location line can be helpful in placement but is most important when changing a wall to a type with a different thickness. It is also useful when flipping the direction of the wall.

d. **Chain**—This option creates walls in a sequence automatically joined end to end. If you deselect the Chain option, you will need to indicate the start and end points of each wall segment you draw. With Chain enabled, the end of your first wall will automatically become the start point of the next wall and so on. This option is selected by default.

e. **Offset**—Use this field to input a numerical value. The walls you create will be placed parallel (offset) to the points you click at a distance equal to this value.

f. **Radius**—This option can be used to create rounded corner joins as walls are created. Place a checkmark in the box before the Radius field becomes available. Input the desired radius in the field.

g. **Join Status**—Choices here are: Allow and Disallow. By default, all walls join to one another as you create them. If you want to disable this behavior, choose Disallow.

h. **Draw tools**—Walls can be drawn in a variety of shapes or created from existing model components. Choose to draw walls line by line, as a rectangle, circle, arc, etc. The Pick Lines option will allow you to pick existing linework on screen and create walls from those lines. The Pick Faces option is similar except that it creates walls from the faces of 3D geometry. Straight line is the default.

Now that we have an overview of the available options, let's see some of them in practice.

2. At the top of the Properties palette, from the Type Selector, choose: **Generic -8"** [**Generic – 200mm**].

> **TIP:** If the Properties palette is not open onscreen, you can open it in a variety of ways. You can right-click and choose: **Properties** or click the Properties tool on the ribbon or type the keyboard shortcut: PP or CTRL + 1.

Verify that the "Line" icon is selected in the Draw panel. Accept the defaults for all remaining options.

3. Click anywhere on screen to place the first point of the wall.

⇨ Move your mouse to the right, keep it horizontal, but don't click yet.

Creating a Building Layout | 91

Notice the dimension on screen as you move the mouse. As you move your pointer, this dimension automatically snaps to whole unit increments. Depending on the size and resolution of your screen, the exact increment may vary. For example, if you are using Imperial units, the increment defaults to: 4'-0" and the increment for Metric defaults to: 1000mm. Examples are shown in Figure 4.4.

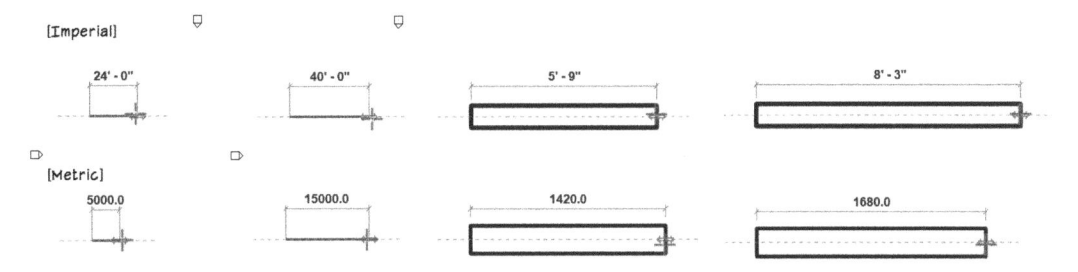

FIGURE 4.4 *The dimension increment varies with the level of zoom (The exact values on your screen may not match the figure)*

As you zoom in, the increment of the dimension will reduce. Depending on the unit type you are using, you may need to zoom in or out to see this. This is easy to do with the wheel. Simply roll the wheel up or down to zoom in or out. If you zoom off screen, keep the command active, press and hold the wheel button in and then drag. This will pan the screen. You can also access zoom commands on the Steering Wheel (F8) or the right-click menu.

4. Roll the wheel of your mouse to zoom in or out and watch the effect on the snap increments.

5. Click to set the other point of the wall. (Keep it horizontal for now, but the length is unimportant.)

    A single wall segment will be created.

Often you will want to create more than one wall segment, each beginning where the previous one ended. You can achieve this with the "Chain" option on the Options Bar. Chain should be checked by default.

6. On the Options Bar, verify that there is a checkmark in the "Chain" check box to enable this option.

    ⇨ Click any point on screen to begin placing the next wall.

    ⇨ Click two more points at any locations on screen (see Figure 4.5).

    Notice that the corners where each pair of walls meet has formed a clean intersection (called a "Wall Join").

FIGURE 4.5 *Use the Chain option to create continuous wall segments*

7. Remaining in the wall command, on the Draw panel click the Tangent End Arc icon.

The Tangent End Arc tool continues the wall in a tangential relationship to the previous segment. Other Arc options are also available.

⇨ Move the pointer in any direction and click to place the end point of the Arc.

8. Add another segment if you wish.

9. To finish adding walls, click the Modify tool on the Selection panel of the ribbon or press the ESC key twice (see Figure 4.6).

• Revit Essentials for Architecture •

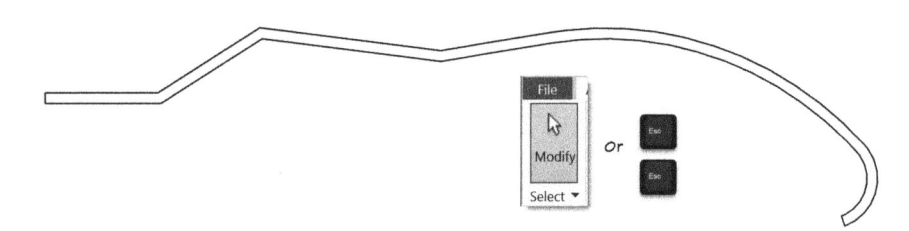

FIGURE 4.6 *To complete a command use the Modify tool or the* ESC *key*

Think of these few walls as a simple "warm up" exercise. Drawing them helped us explore some of the basic wall options. However, these walls have been placed a bit too randomly to be useful. Let's delete them now and create some new ones.

USING A CROSSING SELECTION BOX

Before we can delete the existing walls, we need to select them. There are many ways to select objects in Revit. Several methods were explored in the "Selection Methods" topic on page 77 in Chapter 3. As we saw in that topic, a convenient way to select multiple objects at one time is with the Window and Crossing selection methods. In either technique, you create a box by dragging from a corner diagonally to an opposite corner. To create a window selection, click and drag from left to right. To make a crossing selection, click and drag the opposite direction—from right to left. A window selection selects only those items surrounded by the box, while a Crossing selects anything touched by or within the box. This was discussed briefly in Chapter 3. Let's review it now.

1. Click a point below and to the right of the walls you have on screen.

   ⇨ Hold down the mouse button and drag up and to the left far enough to touch all objects with the dashed (Crossing) selection box (you can see an example in Figure 3.16 in Chapter 3).

   Just be careful not to select the elevation symbols.

   ⇨ When all the walls highlight, release the mouse button.

All the walls will turn blue to indicate that they are now selected. Once you have a selection of objects, you can manipulate their properties, move, rotate, or mirror them (notice that these and other tools appear on a Modify | Walls tab of the ribbon. You can also delete them.

2. Press the DELETE key on your keyboard to delete the walls. (You can also click the small red "X" icon on the Modify | Walls tab.)

ADDING WALLS WITH THE RECTANGLE OPTION

When you draw walls, tools are available to create walls that form closed geometric shapes like rectangles, circles, and polygons. Often using these is the quickest way to lay out such shapes. Let's try the rectangle option now.

1. On the Architecture tab of the ribbon, click the Wall tool (or type WA).

   ⇨ Verify that **Generic -8"** [**Generic – 200mm**] is chosen for the element type.

   ⇨ Accept the defaults for Height and Location Line and then click the Rectangle shape icon on the Draw panel (see Figure 4.7).

Creating a Building Layout | 93

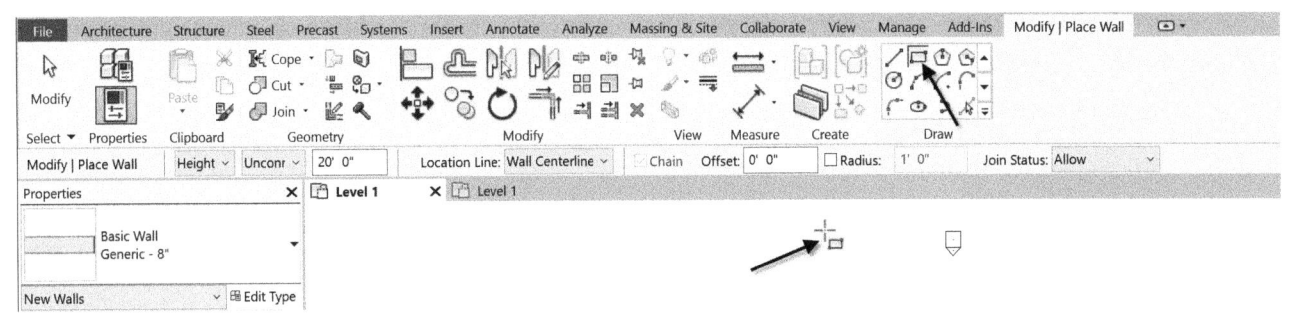

FIGURE 4.7 *Using the rectangle draw option for walls*

Our project contains four elevation markers. Let's zoom the screen to fit these to the screen so they are visible.

2. On the keyboard, type ZF (or right-click and choose: **Zoom To Fit**).

> **NOTE:** If you prefer, you can also choose: **Zoom To Fit** from the Zoom tool on the Navigation Bar. However, where available, the keyboard shortcuts like the one suggested in the previous step are usually quicker once you learn them. Shortcuts for zoom commands are listed in Table 2.D in Chapter 2.

The mouse pointer will show a small rectangle next to it indicating that we are in rectangle drawing mode.

3. Click a point within the upper left region of the space surrounded by the elevation markers.

    ⇨ Move the mouse down and to the right and watch the values of the dimensions.

    ⇨ Click a point (click only once) in the lower right region of the space surrounded by the elevation markers.

Notice that the Temporary Dimensions continue to display on the walls just drawn. Furthermore, these dimensions appear in blue. The blue color indicates that their values may be edited dynamically; or put another way, blue typically means "interactive."

4. Click directly on the blue numerical value of the horizontal dimension.

    The value will become an editable text field.

    ⇨ Type a new value into this field and then press ENTER. (The exact value is unimportant—see Figure 4.8).

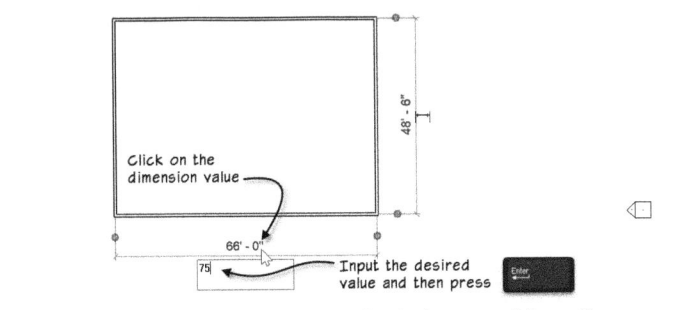

FIGURE 4.8 *Use the Temporary Dimensions to edit the locations of the walls*

> **NOTE:** The value on your screen will most likely vary from that shown in the figure.

5. The Wall command is still active. Using the same technique, draw another rectangle overlapping the first.

Notice that the Temporary Dimensions now reference points from the first rectangle to points on the new one. You can edit these values in the same way that we edited the ones above. You can also move the witness lines of the dimensions to gain more control over their exact locations. We will explore this technique below. If you wish, try some of the other sketch shapes like circle or polygon. In the case of the polygon, additional controls will appear on the Options Bar to control the quantity of sides.

6. When you are finished exploring walls, from the File menu choose: **Close** to close the current project.

7. When prompted to save, choose No.

CREATE AN EXISTING CONDITIONS LAYOUT

Now that we have practiced adding a few walls and seen some of the options available while doing so, let's begin creating an actual model. In this book we will follow two projects from the early schematic phase through to the construction document phase. We will start with the first floor existing conditions for our residential project. The residential project is an 800 SF [75 m2] residential addition. This project will require a little bit of demolition and new construction and will require plans, sections, elevations, details, and schedules. In this project we will explore the Phasing tools—Demolition, Existing and New Construction will be articulated later in the tutorial. This will give us the required separation between construction phases of the project. The completed files for this chapter are available in the *Chapter04\Complete* folder. You can open the completed version at any time to compare it to your progress.

CREATE A NEW RESIDENTIAL PROJECT

We will use the same template file that we used above to begin our residential model.

1. Create a new project file using the default Architectural Template file as we did in the "Create a New Project" topic on page 88 above.

Be sure that the *Level 1* floor plan view is open onscreen. You can see this indicated in bold (under *Views (all) > Floor Plans*) on the Project Browser and in the tab name at the top of the canvas.

2. On the Architecture tab of the ribbon, click the Wall tool (shown in F 4.2 above).

⇨ From the Type Selector (at the top of the Properties palette), choose **Generic -12"** [**Generic – 300mm**].

⇨ For Height choose: **Unconnected** and set the value to: **18'-0"** [**5500**].

> **TIP:** You can do this on the Options Bar or the Properties palette. If you are using Imperial units, simply type: **18** and then press enter. No unit symbol or zero inches is necessary. Also note that to enter a value like: **18'-2 1/2"** you can type it in several ways. For example, you can type: **18' 2 1/2"** or **18' 2.5"** or **18 2 1/2** or **18 2.5** or **18.20833**. Refer to the "Unit Conventions" Chapter 3 for more information.

⇨ For the Location Line, choose: **Finish Face: Exterior** and then click the Rectangle sketch icon (see Figure 4.9).

Creating a Building Layout | 95

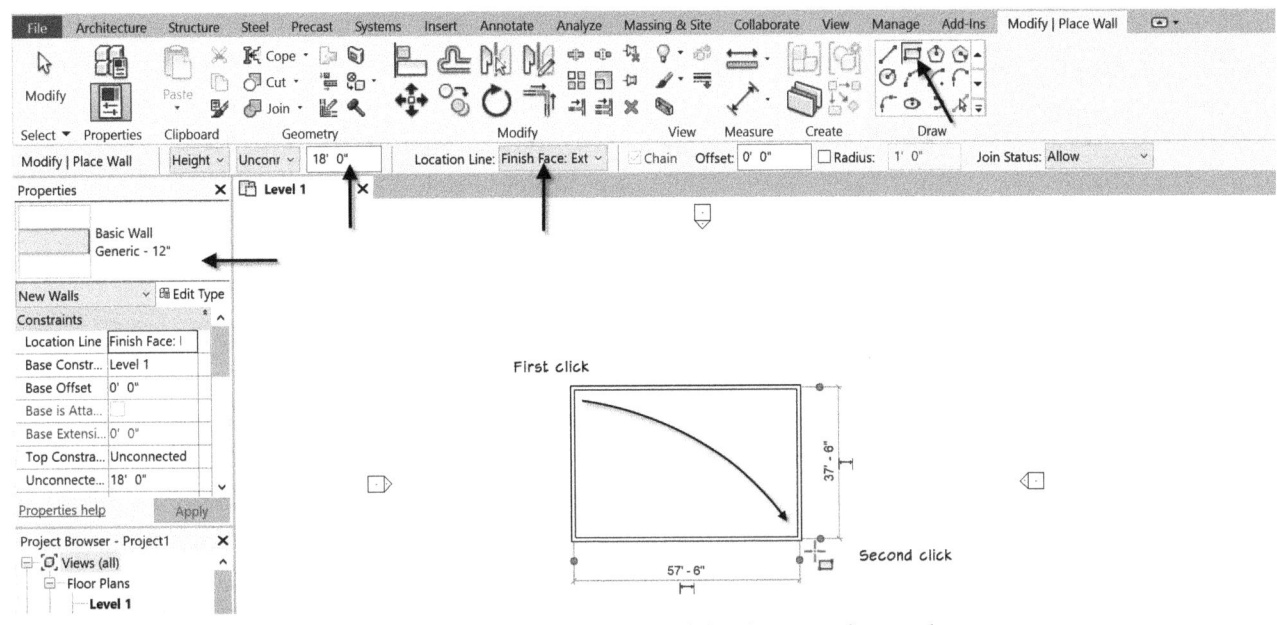

FIGURE 4.9 *Set the Options for the exterior walls of the residential project and then draw a simple rectangle*

3. Click two opposite corners on screen within the space bounded by the elevation markers (the exact size is not important for initial placement).

Notice that even though we have chosen a location line of finish face: exterior, the temporary dimensions still have witness lines at the centerlines of the walls. This is simply a default behavior independent of the wall's individual location line setting. If you want to input a value for the dimension based upon the face of the walls, you can simply move the witness lines.

4. Click on the small blue circle handle on one of the horizontal dimension's witness lines.

   Zoom into the small blue circle to see this well. Notice that the witness line moves to one of the wall faces. If you click it again, it will move again, this time to the opposite face. One more click returns it to the centerline (see Figure 4.10).

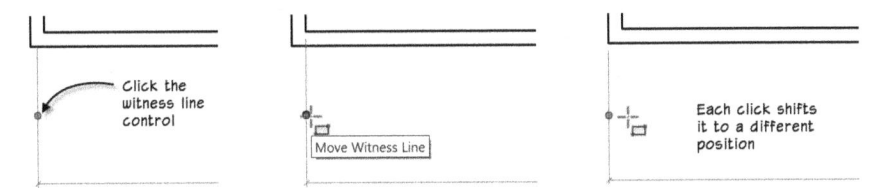

FIGURE 4.10 *Move the witness lines of the temporary dimension*

5. Repeat the process of clicking the witness line shape handle (of the horizontal dimension) until both sides reference the outside edges of the rectangle.

   ⇨ Click the blue numeric value of the horizontal dimension, input: **33'-0"** [**10000**] and then press ENTER.

6. Repeat this process on the vertical dimension making the outside face to face dimension equal to: **24'-0"** [**7300**] (see Figure 4.11).

• Revit Essentials for Architecture •

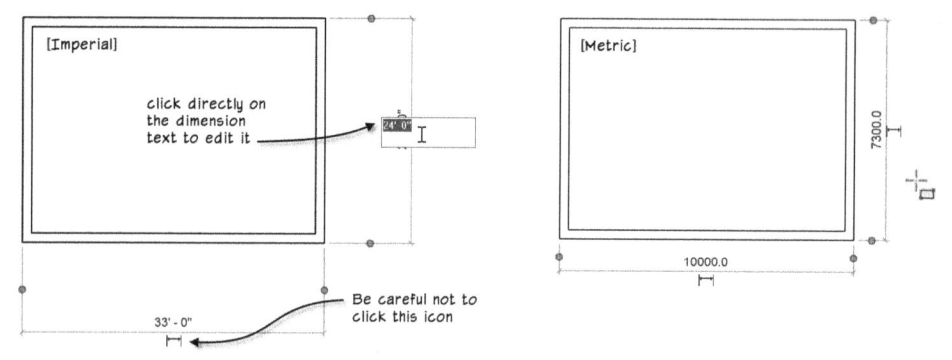

FIGURE 4.11 *Edit the size of the rectangle to match the desired outside dimensions*

> **CAUTION:** Be careful not to click the small "permanent" dimension icon when editing the dimension values. Clicking this icon will make the temporary dimension a "permanent dimension" (it will remain in the current view even after the associated wall is deselected). If this happens, simply select the permanent dimension thus created and delete it.

> **TIP:** If your witness lines are in the wrong locations when you edit the temporary dimension, simply repeat the process to move the witness lines and then repeat the dimension edit process to correct it.

7. On the Select panel, click the Modify tool, or press ESC twice to complete the operation.

You should now have four walls in a rectangular configuration measuring 33'-0" x 24'-0" [10000 × 7300] outside dimensions.

> **NOTE:** If you need to modify the dimensions after deselecting them, you can reselect any wall and the Temporary Dimensions will reappear. However, you will need to select one wall at a time to make edits. Select one wall, edit witness lines if required, and then type in your desired distance in the Temporary Dimension. Repeat in the other direction. Also, keep in mind that the element you select is the one that will move when editing the dimensions.

8. From the File menu, choose: **Save As>Project**.
   ⇨ In the "Save As" dialog, navigate to your *Documents* folder, your Desktop or some other preferred location.
   ⇨ For the File name, type: **04 Residential** and then click the Save button.

USING OFFSET

Let's begin adding the interior partitions. There are several techniques that we could employ to do this. In this sequence, we will use the Offset tool. The Offset tool moves or copies the selected objects parallel to the original by an amount that you input.

1. On the Modify tab of the ribbon, click the Offset tool (or press OF).

The Options Bar for offset has two modes: Graphical and Numerical. When you choose Graphical, the numeric input field is disabled, and you use a temporary dimension on screen to indicate the distance of the offset. When you choose the Numerical option, you input the offset distance first, and then use the pointer on screen to indicate the side of the offset. In both cases, you can enable the "Copy" check box, which will create a copy of the object as it offsets. If you disable this option, the object you offset will be moved parallel to itself by the amount you indicate.

⇨ On the Options Bar, verify that Numerical is chosen (if it is not, choose it now).

⇨ In the Offset field on the Options Bar, input: **12'-5 1/2"** [**3794**] and verify that "Copy" is selected.

If working in imperial units, type: **12 5 1/2** (that is **12** SPACE **5** SPACE **1/2**). The mouse pointer will change to an Offset cursor and the Status Bar will prompt for a selection.

2. In the model canvas move the Offset cursor over the upper edge of the bottom horizontal wall.

A dashed line will appear indicating the location of the offset. If you move your mouse up and down this line will shift up and down as well (see Figure 4.12).

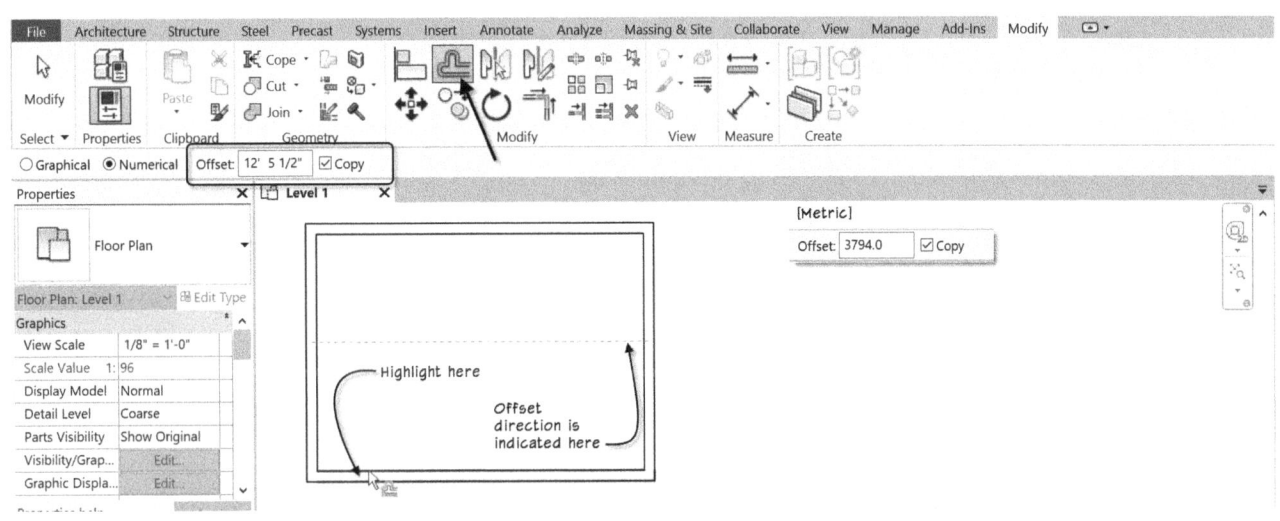

FIGURE 4.12 *Offsetting a new wall*

3. When the dashed line appears above the wall (inside the house) click the mouse. A new wall will appear inside the house.

> **TIP:** As in most places in Revit, if you press the TAB key, the pre-highlighted selection will cycle to the next available option. In this case, all four walls will pre-highlight and the offset result would be a concentric ring inside or outside the building. Go ahead and try it if you like. Press the TAB key once, and then move the pointer to indicate outside or inside. The dashed line will indicate a rectangle now instead of a single edge. If you click to create the walls, be sure to undo (Quick Access Toolbar) after this experimentation.

4. Click the Modify tool or press the ESC key twice to complete the operation.

USING COPY

Copy is like offset except it can copy in any direction, not just parallel. The copy tool lets you select one or more elements and then copy them to a new location. You click two points onscreen to indicate where you want the copies to end up (the distance from the original).

1. Select the vertical wall on the left.

   A Modify | Walls tab will appear on the ribbon.

   ⇨ On the Modify panel, click the Copy tool (or press CO).

98 | Chapter 4

> **NOTE:** Many editing tools in Revit allow you to first click the tool and then select the element(s) that you wish to edit. In this case, you would click the Copy tool on the Modify tab first. Then following the prompt on the Status Bar, you would select the walls (or other elements) you wish to copy. When using this method you must PRESS enter (or right-click) to complete the selection process. The rest of the command sequence would be the same.

When using the Copy tool, you input the distance of the offset (between the original and copy) directly on the screen by clicking two points. At the Status Bar, a prompt reads "Click to enter move start point."

2. Click a point anywhere on screen. (The exact start point is not important in this case, but for convenience, you can click directly on the wall).

⇨ Begin moving the wall to the right (don't click yet), type: **12'-8 1/2"** [**3818**] and then press ENTER to finish (see Figure 4.13).

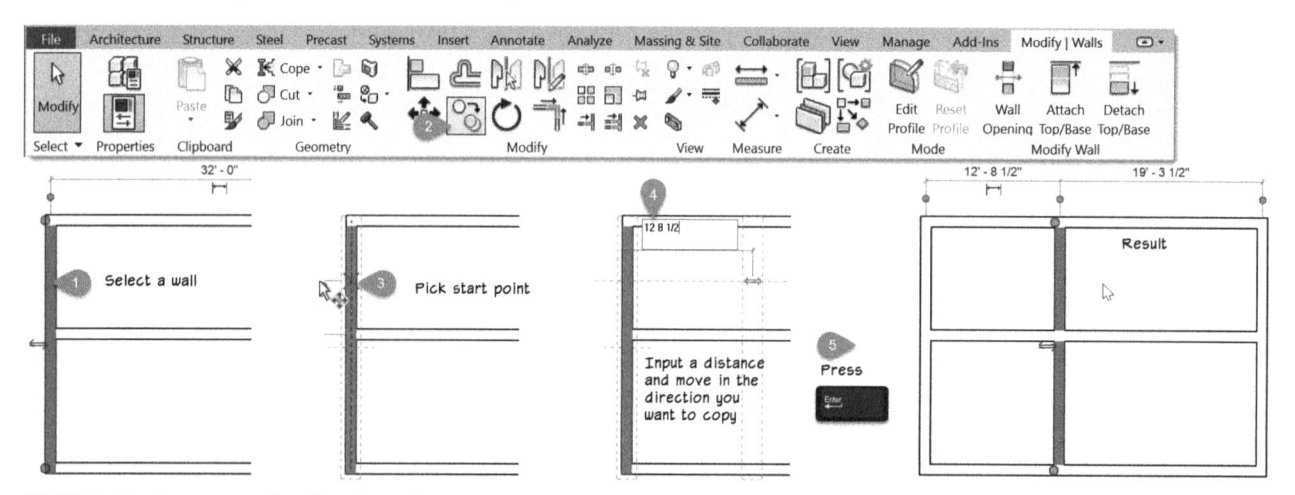

FIGURE 4.13 *Copy a vertical wall to the inside*

3. On the Select panel, click the Modify tool or press the ESC key twice.

⇨ Save your project.

EDITING PARAMETERS

One of the features that makes Revit such a powerful tool is the ability to easily change an object's parameters at any time, as design needs change. Let's look at modifying some of the walls as we continue with the layout of the first floor existing conditions for the residential project.

1. Select the two internal walls created in the previous steps.

To select the two walls, you can hold down the CTRL key and click each of the walls one at a time, or you can click just inside the house near the lower right corner and then drag up and to the left until both walls highlight (see Figure 4.14).

Creating a Building Layout | 99

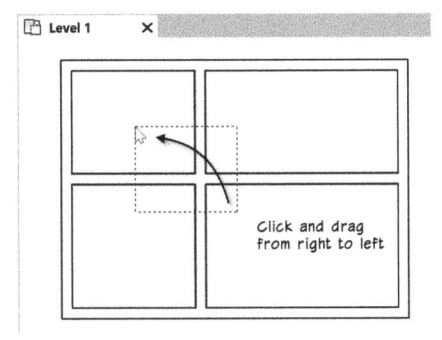

FIGURE 4.14 *Select the interior walls using a crossing selection*

> **NOTE:** The Properties palette should be open onscreen already. (The default location is docked to the left side of the Revit application frame.) If it is not, there are several methods to open it: click the Properties tool on the Modify tab of the ribbon, type the shortcut: PP, press CTRL + 1 or right-click and choose: **Properties**.

2. On the Properties palette, beneath the Constraints grouping, for the Location Line, choose: **Wall Centerline**.

⇨ From the Type Selector (at the top), choose: **Generic – 5"** [**Interior - 135mm Partition (2-hr)**] (see Figure 4.15).

> **TIP:** To make this change, click in the Location Line field, and then click the small down arrow that appears to choose the: **Wall Centerline** option from the popup menu.

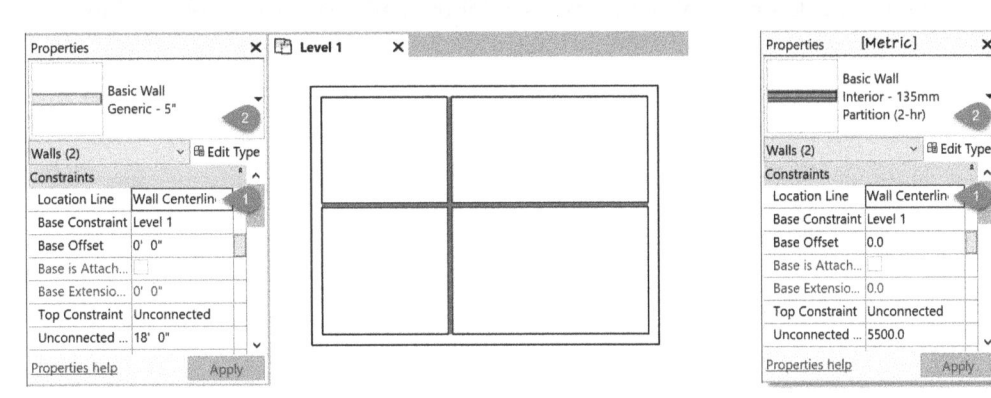

FIGURE 4.15 *Change the parameters of the interior walls on the Properties palette*

To apply such a change, you either click the Apply button on the Properties palette, or simply shift focus away from the palette by moving your mouse away from the palette. This will apply the change automatically.

3. Apply the changes and notice the change to the thickness of the walls.

ADJUST LOCATION WITH TEMPORARY DIMENSIONS

In the "Create a New Residential Project" topic on page 94 above, we learned to use the temporary dimensions and the handles on the witness lines to edit the location of walls. We can use the same technique to verify our room size now.

1. Click on the interior vertical wall.

The temporary dimensions will appear indicating its current location relative to the other walls. However, depending on the settings of your system, the dimensions may be from the centerlines. The desired size of the room that we are verifying are to the inside faces of the walls (as you might expect from field dimensions). Click the "Move Witness

• Revit Essentials for Architecture •

100 | Chapter 4

Line" grip controls as shown above in Figure 4.10 to move the witness lines to the inside faces of one of the rooms. You can repeat to verify other rooms. This is effective but slow. To speed things up, we can also change the default behavior of the dimensions from now on so that they show to the inside faces instead of walls instead. We do this with the temporary dimensions command.

> **NOTE:** Revit will remember the modified location of witness lines during your work session. To try it out, select a wall and edit the witness line of a Temporary Dimension as indicated above in the "Create a New Residential Project" topic on page 94. Deselect the wall. Reselect the same wall and notice that the witness lines remember the modified location. However, this only applies in the current work session. When you close the project and reopen, they will reset to their defaults.

2. On the Manage tab of the ribbon, on the Settings panel, click the Additional Settings drop down button and choose: **Temporary Dimensions**.

⇨ In the walls area, click Faces and then click OK (this is shown in Figure 3.22 in Chapter 3).

3. Click the vertical interior wall again.

The dimension from the inside face of the left exterior wall to the inside face of the selected wall should be 12'-0" [3600.3] (yours may not match exactly, not to worry we will be adjusting it next).

4. Click on the horizontal interior wall.

This time, the dimension from the inside face of the bottom exterior wall to the inside face of the selected wall should read 11'-9" [3576.3]. So, this gives us a quick way to check the distances for the walls that we have placed. However, despite best efforts to transfer field measurements to our building model, errors can creep into our calculations. The first distance we measured (the horizontal distance between the two vertical walls) is incorrect based on our field notes. Fortunately, errors like this are very easy to correct in Revit.

5. Select the interior vertical wall and then click directly on the activated blue text of the left-hand dimension.

⇨ Input the correct value: **11'-6"** [**3500**] (see Figure 4.16).

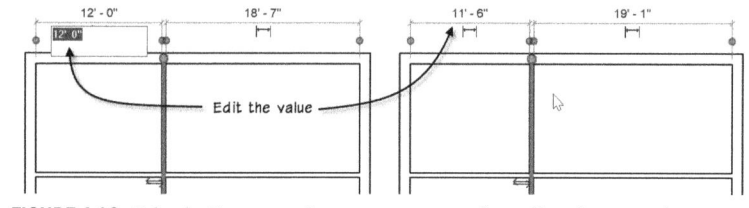

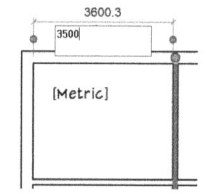

FIGURE 4.16 *Edit the Temporary Dimension to move the wall to the correct location*

6. Save the project.

> **TIP:** If you find the text size of the Temporary Dimensions difficult to read, open the File menu and choose Options. On the Graphics tab, in the "Temporary Dimension Text Appearance" area, choose a larger size value from the drop down and then click OK.

SKETCH THEN MODIFY

The offset and copy techniques covered above are effective ways to add new walls based upon walls already existing in the model. In many cases, however, it is easier to sketch the new walls and then use the temporary dimensions to position them correctly. We can refer to this as: "sketch then modify." Let's try that technique next.

Creating a Building Layout | 101

1. On the Architecture tab of the ribbon, click the Wall tool.

   ⇨ From the Type Selector (on the Properties palette), choose: **Generic – 5"** [**135mm Partition (2-hr)**].

   On the Draw panel, verify that the Line icon is chosen. For Location Line, verify that it is: **Wall Centerline**.

2. Move the mouse over the exterior vertical wall on the left.

Notice that the centerline of the wall highlights and a Temporary Dimension appears.

3. Move the mouse slightly until the value of the dimension above the interior horizontal wall is about 4'-0" [1200] and then click to set the first point.

4. Move the pointer horizontally to the right and click to set the second point just past the middle of the plan (see Figure 4.17).

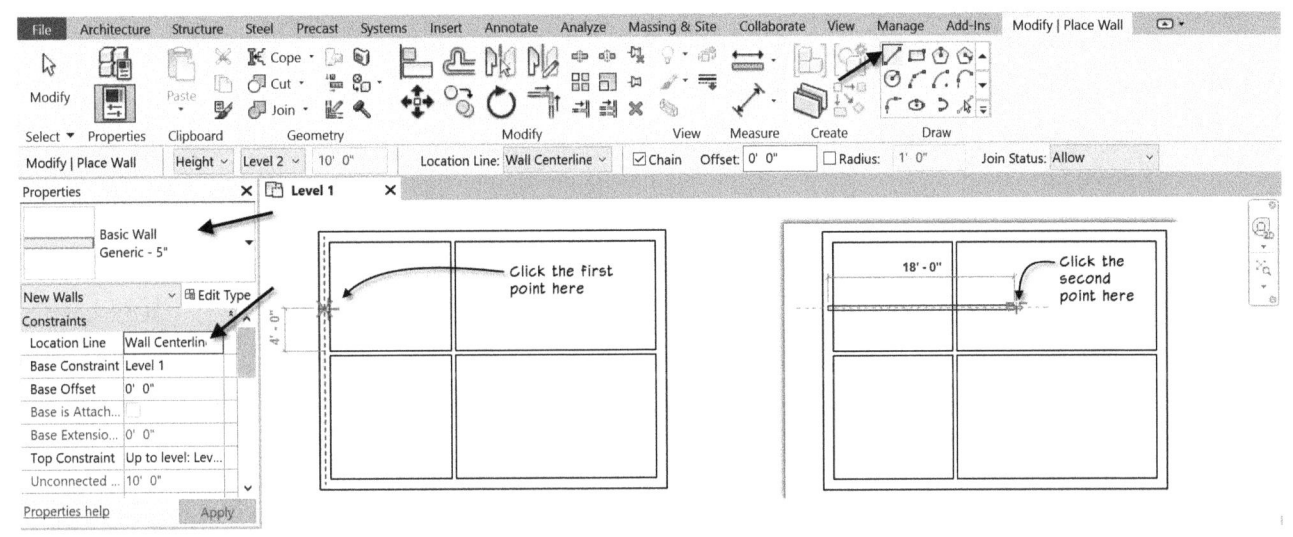

FIGURE 4.17 *Sketch a wall segment above the horizontal interior wall*

NOTE: The exact locations of both clicks are not critical since we will use Temporary Dimensions to edit them next. Use the figure to achieve approximate placement.

5. Click the Modify tool or press ESC twice to complete the command and then click to select the wall just created. Several Temporary Dimensions will appear on screen.

   ⇨ Click the blue text of the Temporary Dimension between the new wall that you just created and the other horizontal interior wall (it currently reads: 3'-9 1/2" [1132.3]).

6. Type: **3'-10"** [**1170**] and then press ENTER (see Figure 4.18).

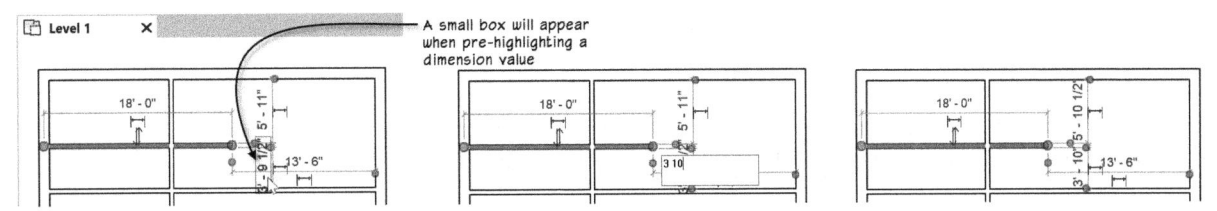

FIGURE 4.18 *Sketch a horizontal wall and use temporary dimensions to fine-tune its placement*

7. Using the same process, create a vertical wall approximately 3'-0" [900] to the left of the existing interior vertical wall.

   ⇨ Start at the lower exterior wall and draw up until it intersects with the upper horizontal interior wall (the one drawn in the last step).

   ⇨ Using the Temporary Dimensions, edit the face to face distance between the two walls to be: **2'-6"** [**750**] (see Figure 4.19).

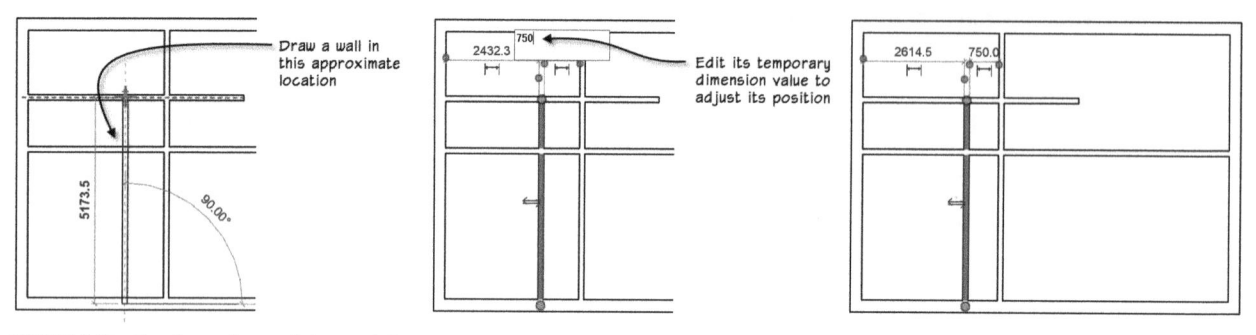

FIGURE 4.19 *Sketch another wall (vertical this time) and use Temporary Dimensions to fine-tune its placement*

8. Select the vertical interior wall that you just completed (the one on the left).

   At each end of the wall is a small round blue grip handle.

   ⇨ Click and drag the handle at the bottom upward.

   ⇨ Using the temporary guidelines that appear, drag up and snap to the horizontal wall (see Figure 4.20).

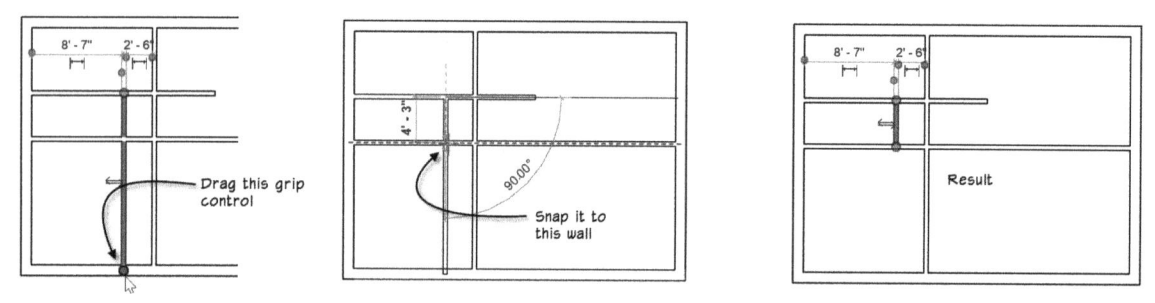

FIGURE 4.20 *Drag the wall end handle up to the intersection with the horizontal wall*

TRIM AND EXTEND

While the control handles are quick and easy, another common way to perform such an edit is using the Trim and Extend tools. (The layout of the Modify panel varies slightly in Revit LT).

1. On the Modify tab of the ribbon, click the Trim/Extend to Corner tool (or press TR).

The Trim/Extend to Corner tool will create a clean corner from the two segments by either lengthening or shortening the selected segments.

2. Click the vertical wall that was just edited with the shape handle.

> **NOTE:** Pay attention to the prompt at the Status Bar, in this case instructing you to select the first wall that you want to Trim or Extend. Please note that you are further prompted to select the "part that you wish to keep."

   ⇨ Next click the horizontal wall to the right of the intersection (see Figure 4.21).

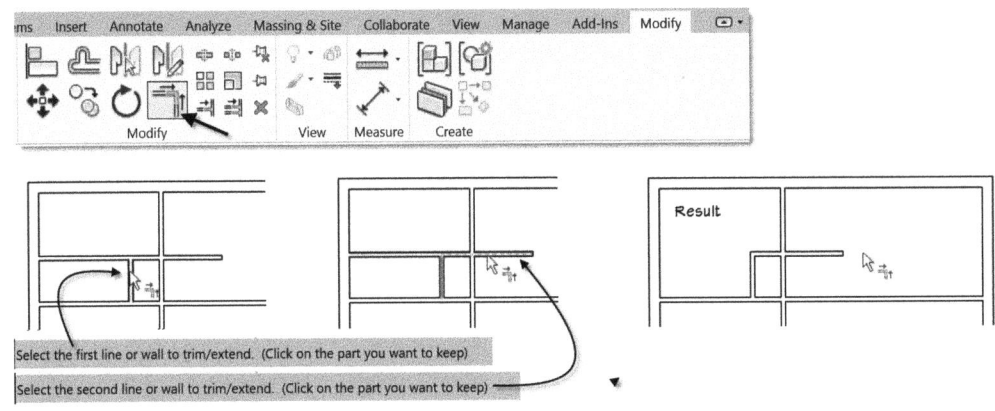

FIGURE 4.21 *Using Trim to create the closet corner*

3. Click the Modify tool or press the ESC key twice.

USING THE PICK LINES MODE

Let's continue adding to our wall layout by using a technique that combines features of some of the previous techniques. We will add walls using the Wall tool and its "Pick Lines" mode. We will use this in conjunction with its built-in Offset option on the Options Bar to place the wall close to where we need it.

1. On the Architecture tab of the ribbon, click the Wall tool.

    On the Type Selector, verify that the type is set to: **Generic – 5"** [**Interior - 135mm Partition (2-hr)**].

    ⇨ On the Draw panel, click the Pick Lines icon to activate this mode.

    Verify that the Location Line is: **Wall Centerline**.

2. On the Options Bar, in the Offset field, type: **6'-0"** [**1800**].

> **NOTE:** There are two number fields on the Options Bar. Be sure to input in the Offset field, not Height.

3. Move the mouse next to the right side of the interior vertical wall in the middle of the plan.

    The right face of the wall will pre-highlight.

    ⇨ Be sure that the temporary guideline indicates a new wall to the right (if it is to the left, move the mouse slightly) and then click.

4. Click the Modify tool or press the ESC key twice.

5. Select the new wall and edit the dimension between this wall and the one from which it was offset to: **6'-6"** [**1983**] (see Figure 4.22).

104 | Chapter 4

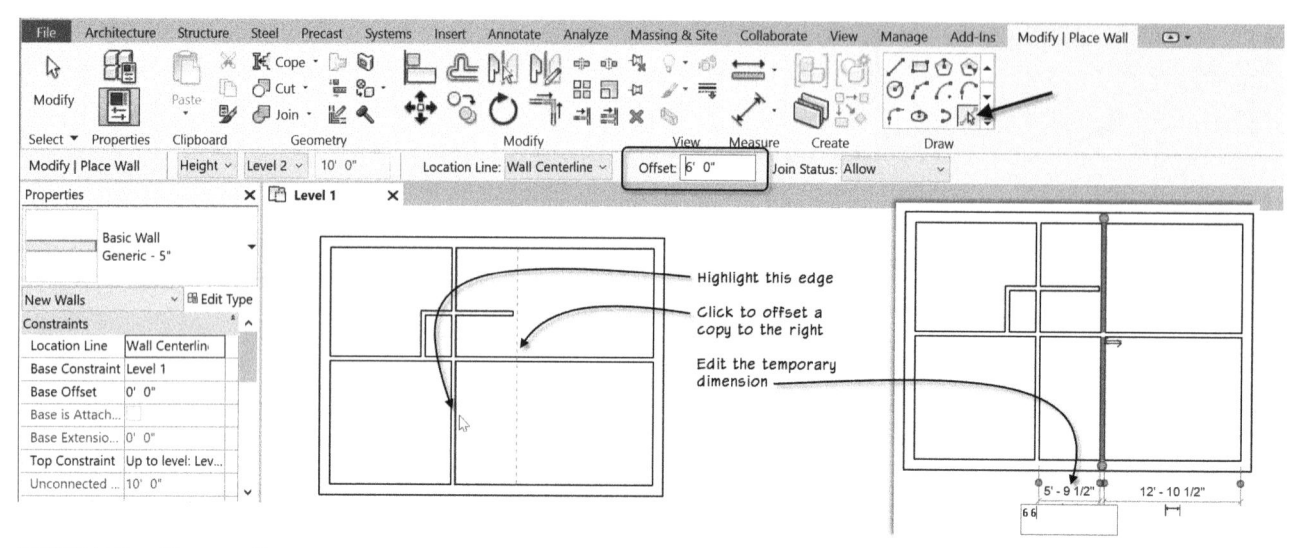

FIGURE 4.22 *Adding a wall using the Pick Lines mode*

In this case we used two steps: first offsetting to an approximate amount and then using the Temporary Dimensions to fine-tune the result precisely. If you want to calculate the exact offset to use instead of editing the Temporary Dimension, you can do so. The offset value will be measured from the line you pick to the Location Line of the new wall—in this case wall centerline. Therefore, half of the wall's width would have to be added to the dimension. Despite the relative ease of this calculation, it is typically easier to place the wall close and then edit the dimension to the exact value as we have done here. We can refer to this approach as: "sketch then modify."

TRIM/EXTEND SINGLE ELEMENT MODE

Let's modify a few more wall segments using the Trim/Extend Single Element tool.

1. On the Modify tab of the ribbon, click the Trim/Extend Single Element tool.

In this mode you first select the element to use as a boundary and then the click the wall or line you wish to extend or trim to the selected boundary. Once again, we'll be clicking the part we want to keep.

> **TIP:** Remember to read the prompts on the Status Bar.

2. Click the vertical interior wall on the right as the boundary (the one we just created—it doesn't matter which face, left or right).
3. Click the short horizontal wall at the top to extend (see the top row of panels in Figure 4.23).

Creating a Building Layout | 105

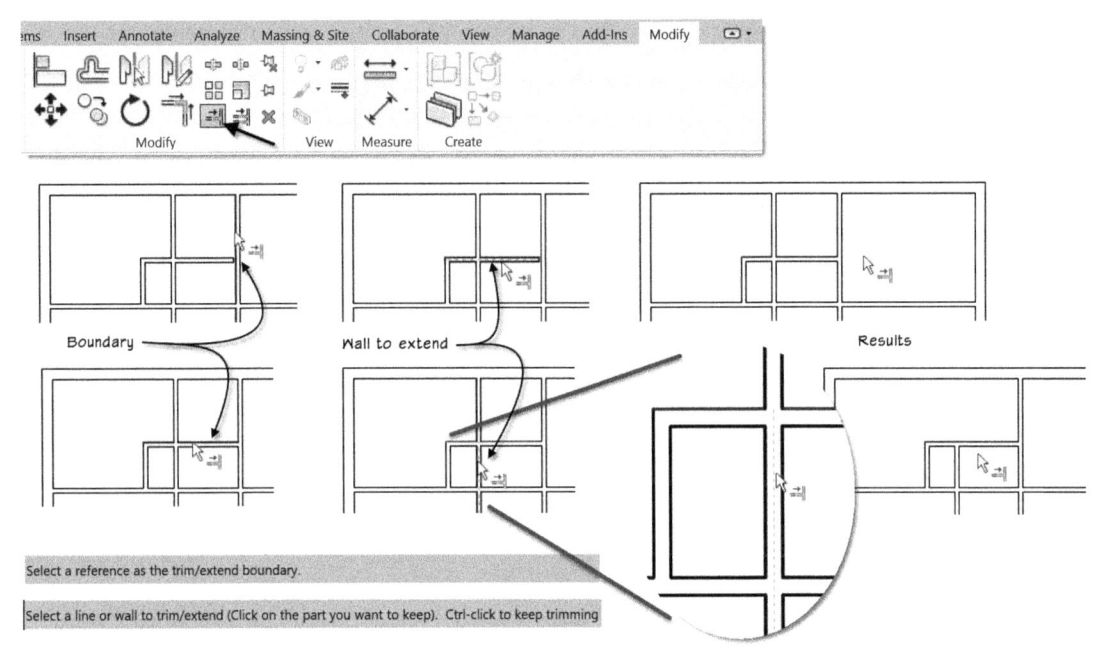

FIGURE 4.23 *Use the Trim/Extend Single Element to create "T" Intersections*

4. Remain in the command and use the same technique to trim away the vertical wall at the top of the closet (see the bottom row of panels in Figure 4.23).

   Remember to click the piece you want to keep—read the Status Bar.

5. Click the Modify tool or press the ESC key twice.

USING THE SPLIT AND MOVE TOOLS

The layout is coming along. Next let's focus on the stair hallway in the middle of the plan.

1. On the Modify tab, click the Split Element tool (or press SL).

   ⇨ Place the cursor (shaped like a knife) over the long horizontal wall in the middle of the plan where it intersects the left vertical wall in the middle.

   ⇨ The horizontal wall should highlight. If it does not, press the TAB key a few times until it does.

2. When the horizontal wall is highlighted and small vertical line appears at the cursor, click the mouse to split the wall (see Figure 4.24).

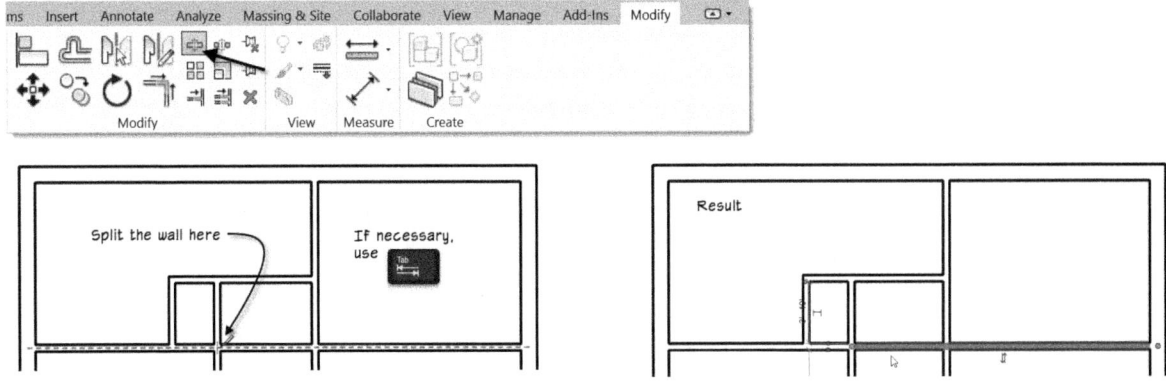

FIGURE 4.24 *Split the horizontal wall in the middle into two segments*

3. Click the Modify tool or press the ESC key twice.

4. Click to select the right side of the wall we just split.

• Revit Essentials for Architecture •

106 | Chapter 4

Notice how the wall is now two segments. Use Split anytime you need to break a single wall into two parts.

5. With the wall selected, on the Modify | Walls tab click the Move tool (or press MV).

⇨ Pick a start point on screen, anywhere on the wall.

6. Begin moving the mouse up (do not click) and then type: **0 10 [250]** and press ENTER (see Figure 4.25).

NOTE: If you are working in Imperial units, the input is zero SPACEBAR ten. You can also type: **10"** instead.

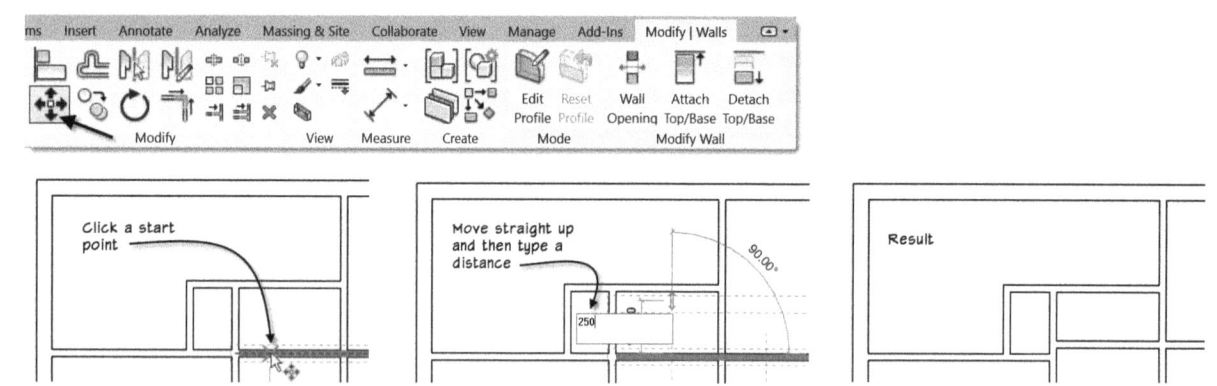

FIGURE 4.25 *Move the split portion of the wall up*

7. Select the vertical wall on the left (the one intersecting where we just split) and then click the Copy tool on the Modify | Walls tab.

⇨ Pick a start point on the selected wall and then move to the right.

⇨ Move the mouse to the right, type: **3'-6" [1078]** and then press ENTER.

The middle space will now be divided in half.

TIP: You can begin moving the mouse to the right, type the desired value, and then press ENTER. Or use any other technique covered so far. The dimension given in the previous step is a center-to-center distance.

8. Verify that the face to face dimension between the new wall and the original is: 3'-1" [942]; if it is not, edit the Temporary Dimensions (see the left panel of Figure 4.26).

9. Using the middle panel of Figure 4.26 as a guide, Trim the two new walls to form a corner as shown.

10. Using the right panel of Figure 4.26 as a guide, drag the shape handle up and then edit the Temporary Dimension to: **8'-3" [2500]**.

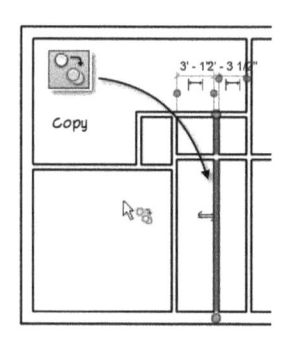

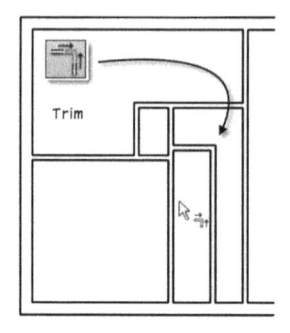

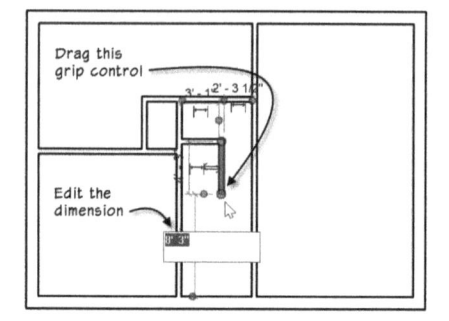

FIGURE 4.26 *Copy, trim, and edit walls for the hallway stairs*

11. Save your Project.

CREATE SIMILAR

At the top middle of the plan is a small half-bath. Let's sketch these walls to complete the wall layout of our first floor existing conditions. As an alternative to the Wall tool, you can create a new wall that matches an existing one.

1. Select one of the interior walls on screen. On the Create panel of the ribbon, click the Create Similar button.

This will run the Wall command with the settings matched from the selected wall. Verify the wall type and other settings and note that then match the selected wall.

2. Working at the top middle of the plan, sketch two wall segments to create a small half-bath.

3. Edit the Temporary Dimensions to make the inside clear dimensions of the half bath: 4'-4" [1300] × 3'-6" [1050] (see Figure 4.27).

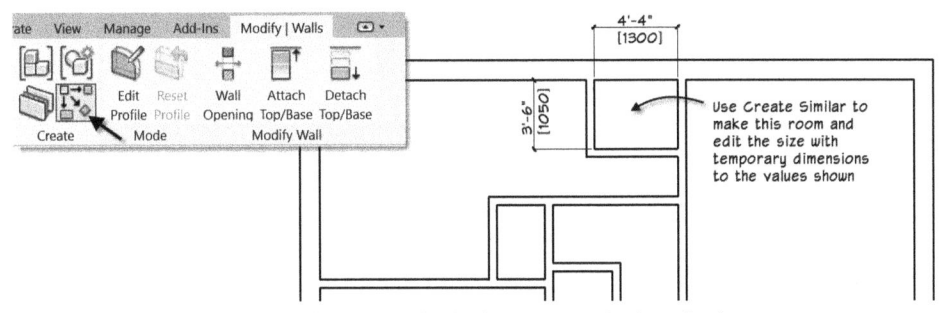

FIGURE 4.27 *Sketch the small half-bath and edit the dimensions to the desired values*

HINT: Remember: Select the wall that you want to move before editing a Temporary Dimension. The highlighted wall will move relative to the non-selected wall.

4. Extend the vertical wall in the middle of the stair hallway up to the half-bath (see the left side of Figure 4.28).

5. Use the Split tool with the "Delete Inner Segment" option on the Options Bar to remove the small piece of wall shown in the middle panel of Figure 4.28.

6. Use the Trim/Extend to Corner tool to complete the layout as shown in the right panel of Figure 4.28.

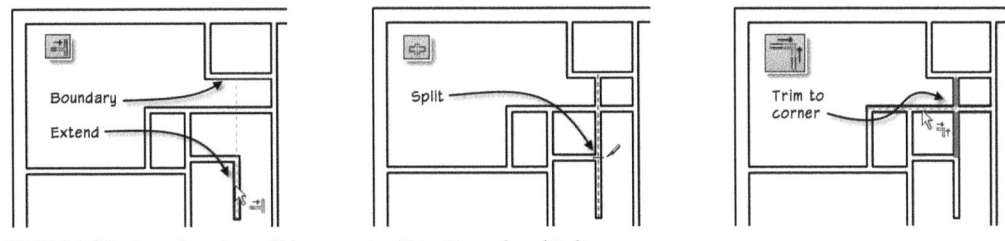

FIGURE 4.28 *Complete the wall layout using Trim/Extend and Split*

Figure 4.29 shows the completed wall layout for the residential project's first floor existing conditions. There is still plenty of work to do but use the illustration to check your work before you continue. Do not add any dimensions. They are provided in the figure to help you check your work. If a wall is in the wrong location, you can select it, and then modify the temporary dimension to fix it.

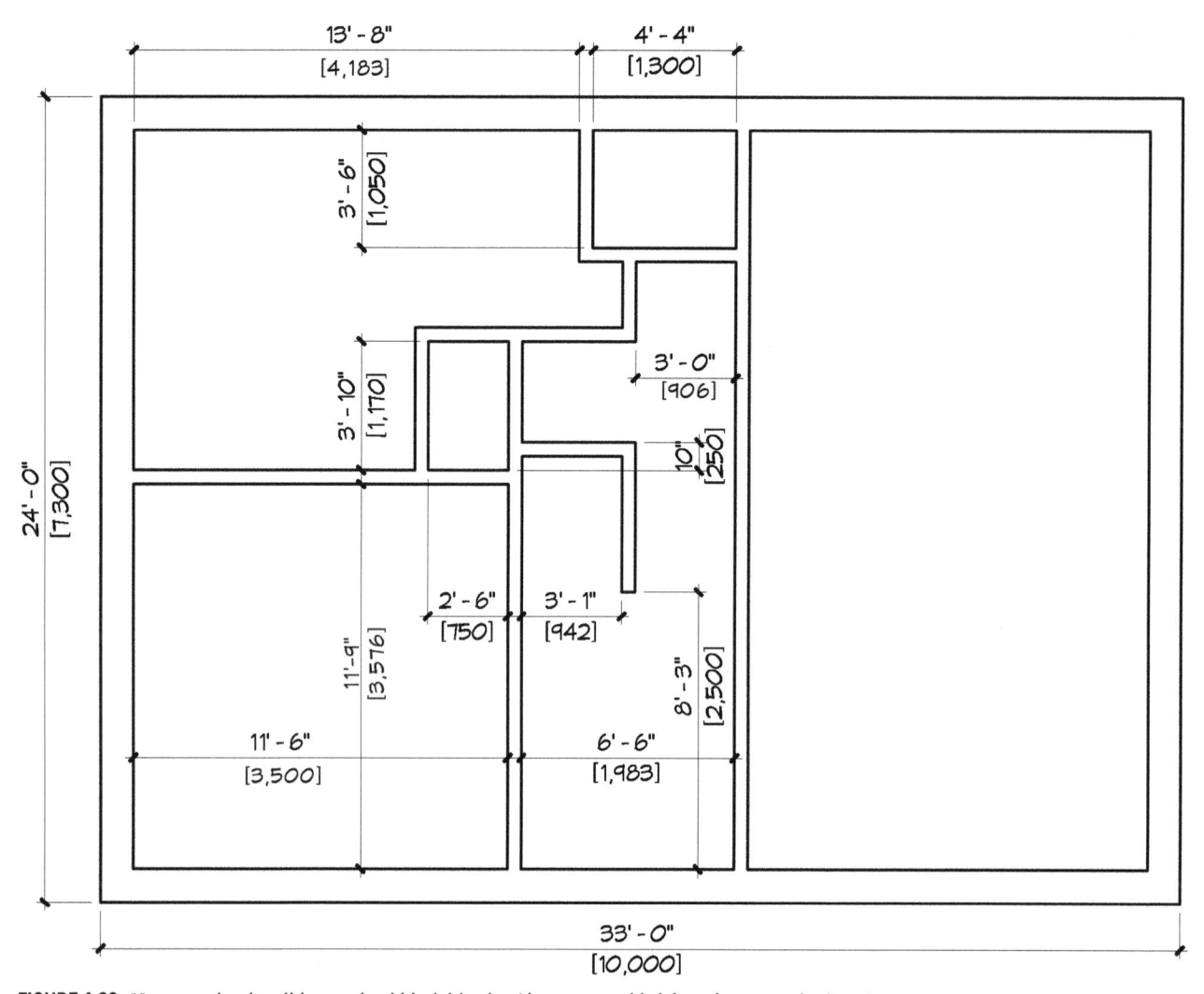

FIGURE 4.29 *Your completed wall layout should look like this (dimensions added for reference in the figure)*

7. Save the Project.

WORKING WITH PHASING

We have completed the layout of existing walls on the first floor of the house. Assigning the walls to a construction phase will help us distinguish them as existing construction as the project progresses. Revit includes robust Phasing tools allowing us to designate these walls as existing construction quickly and easily. Every element in the model has two phasing parameters: "Phase Created" and "Phase Demolished."

In this way you can track the "life span" of any element in the model. In the case of the walls that we have drawn here, all of them are existing construction and none will be demolished yet. We will be demolishing some of the windows and doors later in the chapter.

ASSIGN ELEMENTS TO A CONSTRUCTION PHASE

Each view in your project has a current phase assignment. Newly created elements automatically inherit this current phase from the view at the time of creation. So, in this case, the current phase (from the default template that we used to begin the project) is the **New Construction** phase. Therefore, all the walls currently belong to this phase as well. It is easy to change this assignment.

1. Using a window selection, select all the walls in the model.

    To do this, click and drag to surround all walls but be sure not to select the elevation markers.

The drop down filter list near the top of the Properties palette should read: **Walls (14)** (shown at the top left of Figure 4.30). If instead it says Common with a different quantity, make your selection again and be sure to include just the walls.

> **TIP:** It is a good idea to get in the habit of checking the quantity of selected items on the Properties palette before you perform any changes. If the quantity reads an amount that is unexpected, you can investigate first before making any changes. The quantity also appears at the bottom-right corner of the screen next to the filter icon.

2. On the Properties palette, scroll down and locate the Phasing grouping.
    ⇨ From "Phase Created," choose: **Existing**.
    ⇨ For the "Phase Demolished," verify that: **None** is chosen and then Apply (see Figure 4.30).

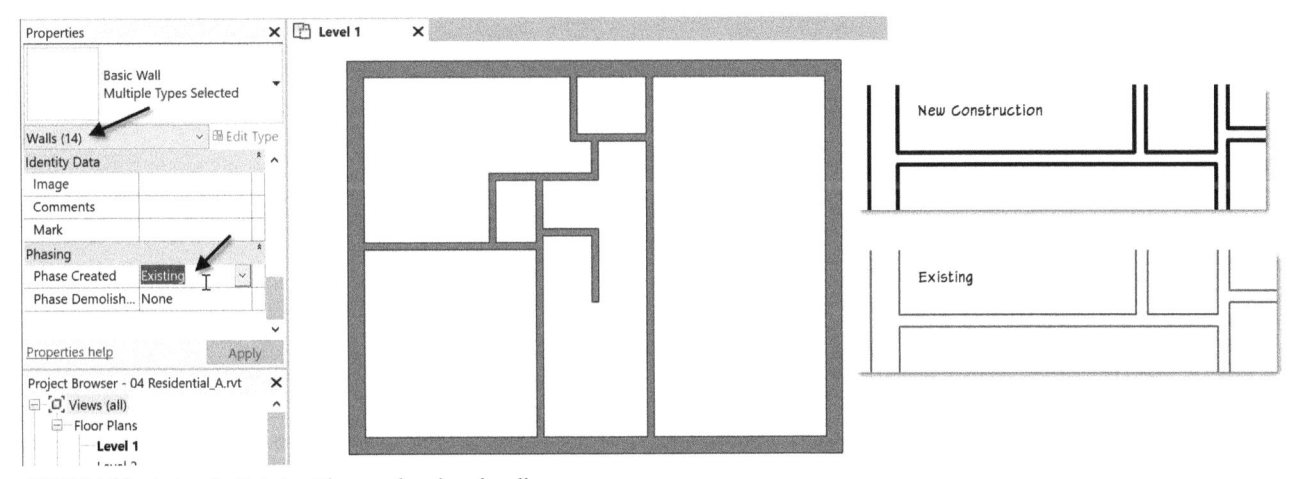

FIGURE 4.30 *Assign the Existing Phase to the selected walls*

3. Click in empty white space to deselect all the walls to see the change.

The walls will display in a lighter line weight and will also be colored gray. This indicates that they are existing construction (this is shown on the right side of the figure). Assigning a phase to an element automatically assigns a graphic override to it.

4. Save the project.

EXPLORING PHASING PROPERTIES

At this time, it is appropriate to explore Phasing a bit deeper to get a full understanding of the tools available. Many of the changes we are about to make are not required by our residential project, therefore we will save a copy of the project in which to experiment and then reopen the original when we finish exploring. Make sure you have saved the project as instructed in the previous step. This will ensure that we can reopen the original file in its current state.

1. From the File menu, choose: **Save As > Project**.
    ⇨ Name the project: **04 Residential_Temp.rvt** and then click Save.
2. On the Architecture tab click the Wall tool.
3. Accept all the default settings and draw a single wall segment anywhere in the

110 | Chapter 4

model but joining or crossing one or more of the existing walls.

⇨ Click the Modify tool or press the ESC key twice.

Notice that the new wall came in as New Construction. Notice also that it did join with the existing wall(s). Elements you create automatically use the current phase assigned to the view. In this case, while we changed the phase of the walls to Existing, the Level 1 floor plan view is still assigned to New Construction. Therefore, all newly drawn elements will default to New Construction as well (see the left side of Figure 4.31).

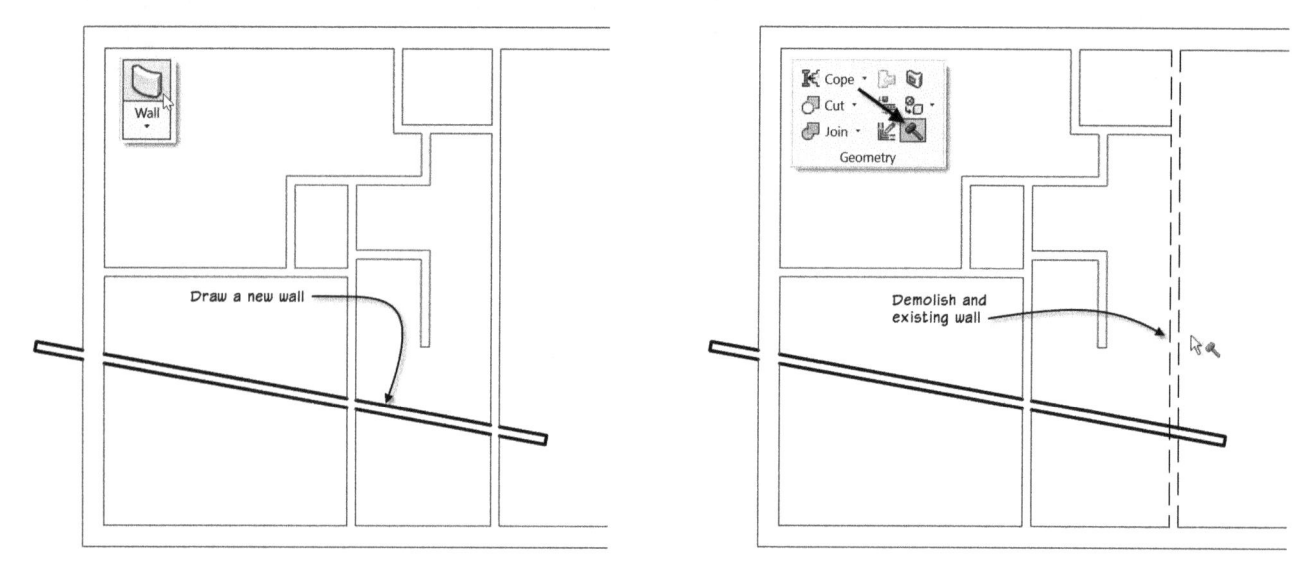

FIGURE 4.31 *Newly created objects inherit the phase set to the active view*

4. On the Modify tab, on the Geometry panel click the demolish tool.

⇨ Using the demolish cursor, select an existing wall to demolish. Click the Modify tool (or ESC twice) to finish (see the right side of Figure 4.31).

Alternatively, select the existing wall and then on the Properties palette locate the Phase Demolished list, and choose: **New Construction**. Notice that the wall is now displayed using a dashed line style.

5. Select a different existing (phase) wall.

⇨ On the Properties palette, from the Phase Demolished list, choose: **Existing**.

The demolish tool cannot be used for this edit.

Notice that this time, the wall has disappeared. This is because each view (*Level 1* floor plan in this case) has a "Phase" and "Phase Filter" setting that control the display of elements within the view. To understand why the wall disappeared, let's change the current phase of the *Level 1* floor plan view to Existing and see how the display of elements changes.

6. Click in empty to space to make sure that there are no elements selected (or press ESC twice) and look carefully at the Properties palette.

Notice that the palette still has many active parameters. Look carefully at the top of the palette; the Type Selector reads "Floor Plan" just beneath it the filter drop down list reads: Floor Plan: Level 1. This tells us that instead of seeing the properties of a selected element, the palette is now displaying the properties of the view itself: "Level 1" in this case. To Revit both objects and views have properties we can manipulate. (For more information on this concept, you can review the "Properties Palette and the Type Selector" topic on page 74 and Figure 3.13 in Chapter 3). As you can see, like our walls above, in a "Phasing" grouping at the bottom of the palette views also have two phasing parameters.

7. Beneath the Phasing grouping, for Phase, choose: **Existing** (see Figure 4.32).

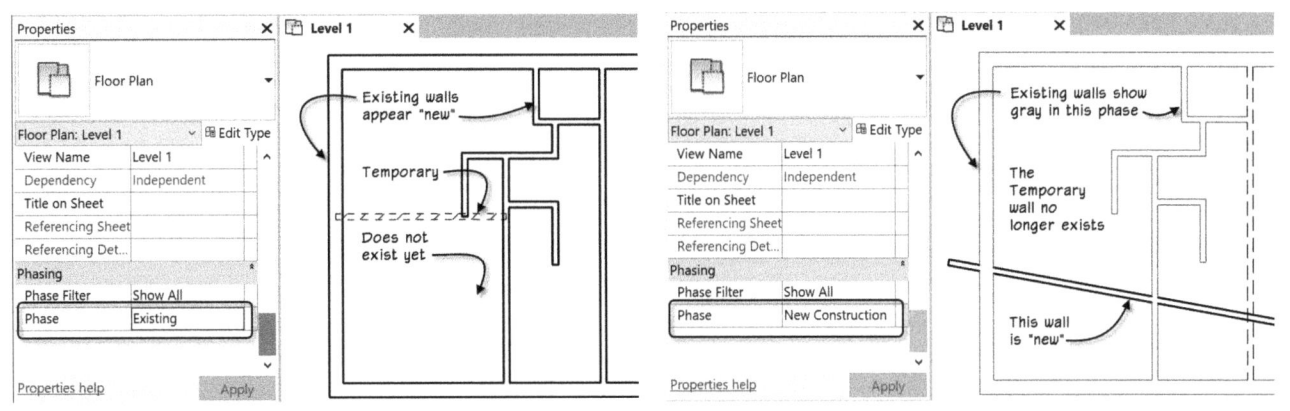

FIGURE 4.32 *Change the current phase of a view and study the results on the elements shown*

This change makes the "Existing" phase the current phase for the *Level 1* view. Therefore, the view will now show only items that existed in that phase. This means that no elements assigned to the New Construction phase will show (because they do not yet exist during the Existing phase time period). The wall that we specified as demolished in New Construction will now appear solid again because during the Existing phase, it was not yet demolished. Furthermore, all the previously light gray walls now appear bold and black. That is because relative to the current phase (Existing), they are (were) new. Phasing essentially gives us a timeline with which to view our projects. When you set a view to a different phase, the relative "definition" of "Existing," "New," and "Demolished" shift accordingly. Finally, the wall that we set to "demolished" in the Existing Phase now appears again, but it is dashed and cross hatched. This style indicates "temporary" construction, which occurs when an element is both created and demolished within the same phase. Examples of temporary elements are temporary dust walls, construction barrier, or possibly furniture that is relocated to a temporary space.

While we can create as many phases as we need for a particular project, Revit gives us four conditions (Phase Status) that can be used to describe (and graphically convey) an element at any point in time. These are built into the software. You can edit their display characteristics, but you cannot delete them or add more. The four states are "Existing," "New," "Demolished," and "Temporary."

    8.   Draw another wall.

    ⇨   Select the new wall and study its phasing Properties.

Notice that the newly drawn wall was automatically assigned to the Existing phase. Any elements that we draw will automatically be added to the current phase of the view. We will make use of this technique below when we add doors and windows.

In addition to the current Phase setting, we can also assign a "Phase Filter" in the Properties palette. A Phase Filter does not change the active phase; rather it changes which elements display and how they appear in the current view based on their phase "lifespan" designations. By default, all views are set to "Show All." Several Phase Filters are included in the default templates from which our project was created. To see some of these, be sure to deselect all elements so that you see the view's settings on the Properties palette. Scroll down and you will see the Phase Filter drop down for the current view. For example, if you choose: **None**, all elements will display (from all phases) and their graphics will display the same regardless of phase setting. This is not very useful for printing, but helpful if you want to try to find missing elements. There are several other possibilities available; some might be easier to grasp with more than the two default phases. Keep in mind as you explore further, that the Phase Filter and Phase setting work together. For example, if you choose Show Complete for the Phase Filter and leave the Phase of the view set to Existing, you will see different results than if you set the Phase back to New Construction. Give it a try. Show Complete displays how the project will look at the completion of the current phase. This means that all elements will appear bold and no demolition will be displayed. Another example is "Show Previous Phase." This will make everything disappear if the current phase is set to Existing since there is currently no phase before Existing in the current project. However, if you change the Phase to New Construction it would show only the items that are left remaining (not demolished) from the Existing phase.

You can control the settings of these overrides as well as edit and add phases in the "Phasing" dialog. To open this dialog, click the Manage tab and on the Phasing panel, click the Phases button. Feel free to explore this dialog now if you wish. A good example of a typical task that you could perform in this dialog would be to set up phases of construction in a large project. For example, you could create a "Foundations and Caissons" phase, "Phase 1" and "Phase 2 New Construction" phases. For our residential project, the out-of-the-box phases of "Existing" and "New Construction" are sufficient. So, feel free to experiment here in this temporary version of our project, but when we return to the original, we will use the two default phases only.

When you are finished experimenting with Phasing, return to the previously saved residential project file.

9. From the File menu, choose: Close (or press CTRL + W).

⇨ When prompted save the file.

10. From the File menu, choose: *04 Residential* from the Recent Documents list to re-open it.

The wall layout should look like it did in Figure 4.30 above with all walls assigned to the Existing phase. If you prefer, a version of the project file in the correct state is provided for your convenience in the *Chapter04* folder. The file is named: *04 Residential-Walls.rvt* [*04 Residential_M-Walls.rvt*].

WORKING WITH DOORS AND WINDOWS

Continuing with our layout of the residential existing conditions, let's add some doors and windows. Doors and windows automatically interact with walls when inserted to create the opening and attach themselves to the wall in an intelligent way. Doors and windows cannot be placed free-standing in a Revit model. They must be inserted in an appropriate host wall.

ADD A DOOR

Doors are "wall-hosted" elements. This means that doors must be placed within walls. Like walls, doors have both type and instance parameters. Changing an instance property affects the door (or doors) currently selected. Changing a type property affects all doors of that type whether selected or not. This project has one door family currently loaded named: *Single Flush* [*M_Single-Flush*]. This family has several types.

1. Be sure that the *Level 1* view of the Residential project is open and then zoom out to see the entire plan layout. You can do this with the mouse wheel (just double-click the wheel) or the commands on the Navigation Bar.

2. On the Architecture tab, click the Door tool (or press DR) (see Figure 4.33).

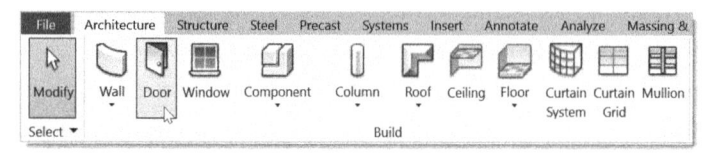

FIGURE 4.33 *The Door tool on the Architecture tab*

Much like the Wall tool, when you click the Door tool, a context tab is appended to the Modify tab, some options appear on the Options Bar and the Properties palette also shows relevant settings. The Status Bar prompt will read: "Click on a Wall to place Door."

3. From the Type Selector (on the Properties palette), choose: **36" x 80"** [**0915 × 2032mm**].

The following list explains the major fields and controls shown on the ribbon, Options Bar and Properties palette when you are adding a door (see Figure 4.34).

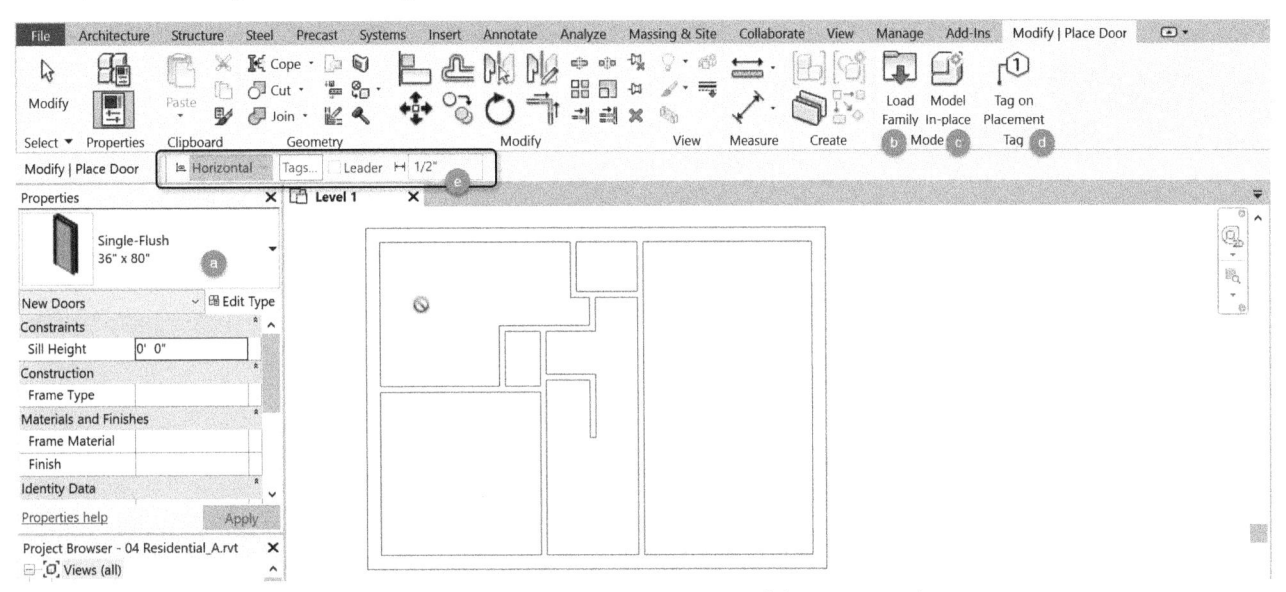

FIGURE 4.34 *Choose your options for adding doors on the ribbon, the Options Bar and the Properties palette*

    a. **Type Selector (change element type)**—Use this drop down to choose from a list of door families and types in the current file. The specific list is populated by the door families that are already loaded into the template we used to create the project. Always choose a type from this list before configuring other options on the Properties palette. If the family you want is not on the list, you can use the Load Family button (item b) to load additional families and types from an external library.

    b. **Load Family**—Use this button to browse external libraries and load other families and types not already available in the current project. "Libraries" are simply folders on your hard drive or network server that contain family (RFA) files.

    c. **Model In-place**—Use this button to create a custom in-place family. In-place families are meant to be used only once and typically represent a custom condition that relies heavily on surrounding project context. It would be rare to create an in-place door family. A more common example is showcased below, in the "Create A Unique Element" topic on page 136 where we will build a custom fireplace. Fortunately, many door families are included with the software and many more are available online on various Revit-themed web sites. Simply do a web search for "Revit door families," and you are bound to come up with plenty of options. The Family Editor (for creating regular component families) will be explored in Chapter 11.

    d. **Tag on Placement**—This button is a toggle setting. When selected (highlighted blue) Revit will add a tag to each door as they are added to the project (see the "Insert Doors and Windows" topic on page 9 in Chapter 1 for an example). Even if you deselect this option, you can still add tags to doors later. It is toggled off by default.

    e. **Options Bar Tag Options**—When "Tag on Placement" is selected, several options are available to control how the tags behave. The first controls the orientation of the Tag. Choose either horizontal or vertical. Next is the Tags button. This displays a dialog where you can choose which tag to use. You can select from tags that are already loaded in the project or use the Load Family button within the dialog to load additional

114 | Chapter 4

ones. The Leader check box adds a leader line to the tags and offsets the tag away from the host object. The leader length field sets how long the leader is.

As you move your mouse pointer around on screen, a door will only appear when you move the pointer over a wall. If you are unhappy with the direction of the door swing, press the SPACEBAR to flip it *before* you click to place the door. (This is noted on the Status Bar—you remembered to look there, right?)

Verify that the Tag on Placement option is disabled. (Remember, this is a toggle; each time you click it turns on or off).

4. Move the mouse to the horizontal exterior wall at the top right side of the plan.

⇨ Position the door roughly in the center of the large room on the right and then click the mouse (see Figure 4.35).

As with walls, Temporary Dimensions will guide your placement.

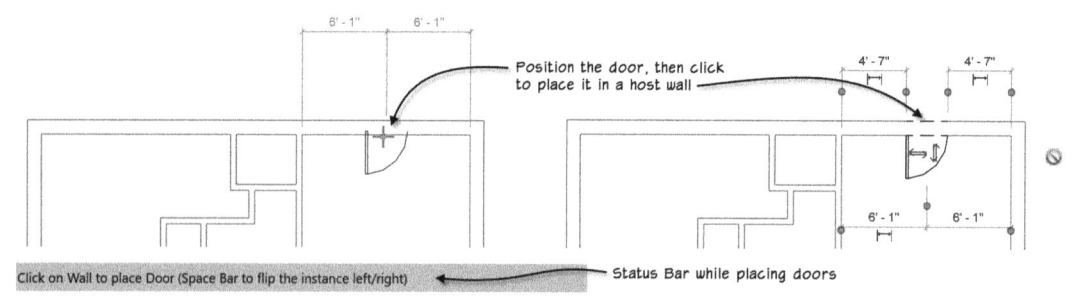

FIGURE 4.35 *Click to place the first door*

Notice that the door cuts a hole in the wall. However, notice that the hole in the wall is filled with dashed lines. This is Phasing at work again. At the start of this segment, we returned to the saved copy of the file, which had the *Level 1* floor plan view's phase set to "New Construction." Therefore, Revit is showing this door as being a new door placed into an existing wall. This requires the opening for the door to be shown as demolition while the door appears as new construction. This is a useful feature, but in this case, it is not what we want.

5. Click the Modify tool or press the ESC key twice.

CHANGE THE PHASE FILTER

Let's try repeating the Phase Filter exercise above to see the different ways that this condition will display in each phase.

Make sure that there are no elements selected; on the Properties palette, make sure that *Floor Plan: Level 1* is listed at the top.

1. Beneath the Phasing grouping, for the Phase Filter, choose: **Show Previous** + **Demo** (see the left side of Figure 4.36).

With this phase filter active, you only see the previous phase and any demolition. Which is consistent with a traditional "demo plan." In this case, the only demolition is the opening for the door.

2. Change the Phase Filter again and this time choose: **Show Previous** + **New** (see the middle of Figure 4.36).

This phase filter hides the demo, but clearly articulates the phase in which each object was created.

3. Change the Phase Filter again and this time choose: **Show Complete** (see the right side of Figure 4.36).

This filter shows what the view would look like when the current phase is complete. Showing the view this way, the articulation between phases is no longer important so the graphics no longer reveal when elements were created. This is like what might be done on an "as-built" plan.

• The Aubin Academy •

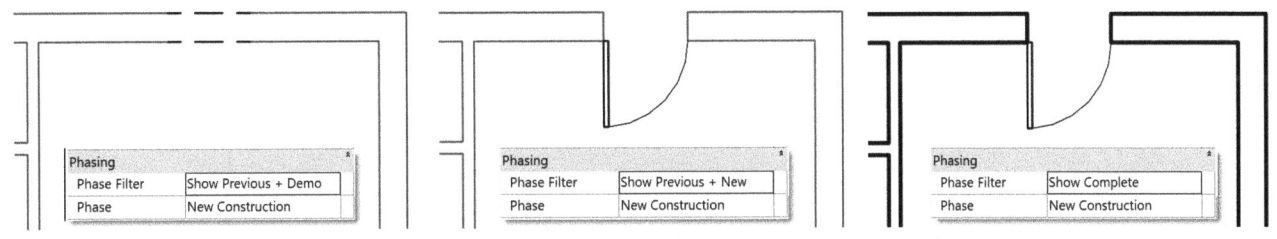

FIGURE 4.36 *Change the Phase Filter to view the model at different points in time relative to the current Phase*

    4.   On the Properties palette, for the Phase Filter choose: **Show All** to reset.

The power and potential of the Phasing parameters was seen when we explored these options with just walls. Now that we have added a door, we can truly see the full potential of these tools. If this door truly were a new door being added to these existing walls, all these graphical behaviors would be managed for us automatically by Revit simply by assigning the door to the New Construction phase. It turns out that this door is an existing door. Therefore, we need to change its phase parameter to make it (and the host wall) display properly.

    5.   Select the door in the model.

          Notice that the Properties palette now displays the properties of the selected door.

    6.   Beneath the Phasing grouping, from the Phase Created, list choose: **Existing**.

    7.   Deselect the door by clicking in the white background of the Canvas area to see the change.

The door now displays the same as the wall in which it is inserted, and the dashed demolition lines no longer display. This is because the door and wall now belong to the same phase, therefore there is no demolition required. Since we are going to add several more existing doors, let's change the view's active phase to Existing (as we did above) to save us the trouble of having to edit the phase property of the doors (and windows that we will add below) later on.

    8.   On the Properties palette, be sure that the properties of the floor plan view are displayed and then for the Phase choose: **Existing**.

The walls will turn bolder to reflect this change.

> **NOTE:** A typical set of construction documents requires existing conditions, demolition, and new construction drawings. In Revit this is easily achieved by duplicating the views (plans, sections and/or elevations, even schedules) and editing the views' Phase and Phase Filter parameters to display the correct data (see the "Create an Existing Conditions View" topic on page 309 in Chapter 8 for an example of this.

PLACE A DOOR WITH TEMPORARY DIMENSIONS

Let's add several more existing doors to our model. For the next several doors, it will be easier to place them if the Temporary Dimensions are set to the openings rather than the centers. (This is like the change we made for walls above).

    1.   On the Manage tab of the ribbon, on the Settings panel, click the Additional Settings drop down button.

    ⇨   Choose: **Temporary Dimensions**.

    2.   In the "Temporary Dimension Properties" dialog, in the doors and windows area, choose Openings and then click OK (the dialog is pictured in Figure 3.22 in Chapter 3).

> **NOTE:** This setting is already configured with this option in the metric file, so this change is only necessary if you are working in Imperial units.

116 | Chapter 4

3. On the Architecture tab, click the Door tool.

⇨ From the Type Selector, choose: **30"x80"** [**0762 × 2032mm**].

⇨ Verify that "Tag on Placement" is not selected.

Move the cursor to the upper left corner of the plan and position it so that the door is being added to the topmost horizontal exterior wall.

⇨ When the Temporary Dimension shows: 2'-0" [600] from the upper left corner, click the mouse to place the door.

As before, the temporary dimensions will remain on screen until you cancel the command or place another door.

4. Edit the Temporary Dimension on the left, type: **2'-4"** [**762**] and then press ENTER.

The door will shift the indicated amount (see Figure 4.37).

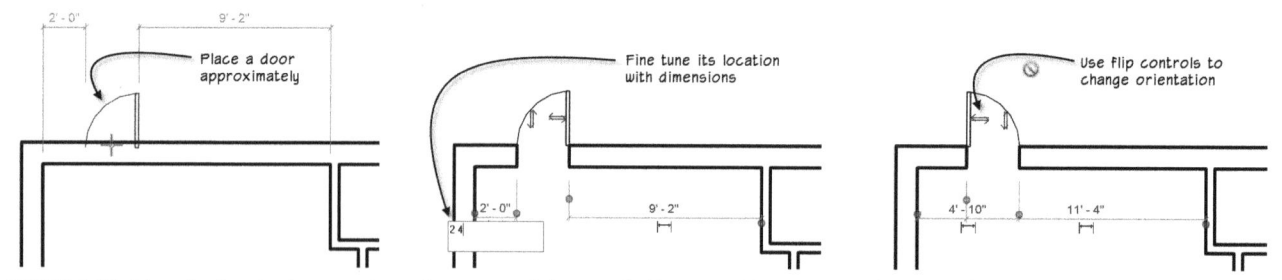

FIGURE 4.37 *Place the door in the approximate location, and then use the Temporary Dimensions to fine-tune placement*

Notice there are two sets of small arrow handles, one group horizontal and the other vertical. Use these handles to flip the door swing if needed. You can also move the mouse slightly in and out of the room as you are placing a new door and tap the SPACEBAR to flip it side to side. Use the flip arrow control handles *after* you place the door.

5. Click the flip controls on the door to swing it into the plan as indicated.

LOAD A DOOR FAMILY

The next door that we are going to add is a bi-fold door for the small closet in the middle of the plan. There is no bi-fold family available in the current project. Therefore, we will need to load a bi-fold door family and its types.

1. You should still be in the door command. If you have canceled it, click the Door tool again.

As noted, if you open the Type Selector, there is only the Single Flush family (shown as a gray bar with a small icon image of the family) and its types (the items listed beneath the gray bar) loaded.

⇨ On the Modify | Place Door tab, on the Mode panel, click the Load Family button (see item b in Figure 4.34 above).

2. Browse to the location where you installed the book's dataset files.

3. Double-click the *Chapter04* folder, choose: *Bifold-2 Panel.rfa* [*M_Bifold-2 Panel.rfa*] and then click Open.

There will be a pause while Revit loads the family.

> **TIP:** If at any time during these steps a Save Reminder appears, click the Save the Project option. It is rarely a good idea to cancel the save reminder. Saving your work regularly is important.

4. Open the Type Selector.

Notice that there are now two families shown on the list, each with its own types indented beneath (see Figure 4.38).

• The Aubin Academy •

Creating a Building Layout | 117

⇨ Choose: **Bifold-2 Panel : 30" x 80"** [**M_Bifold-2 Panel : 0762 × 2032mm**].

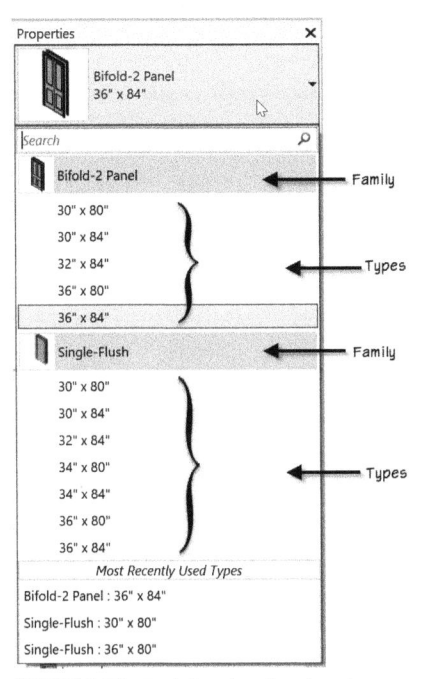

FIGURE 4.38 *Each family is listed with an icon preview and its types indented beneath*

5. Move the pointer over the left vertical wall of the closet in the middle of the plan.

⇨ Using the Temporary Dimensions, get the door centered on the vertical wall.

Do NOT click the mouse to place the door yet.

⇨ Slowly move the mouse left to the right.

Notice that you can control whether the door swings into or out of the closet with the mouse, but not which side of the opening (up or down in this case) that it swings. Take note of the Status Bar. There it notes that you can use the SPACEBAR to flip the swing.

6. Press the SPACEBAR to flip the swing.

⇨ Press it again to flip back (see Figure 4.39).

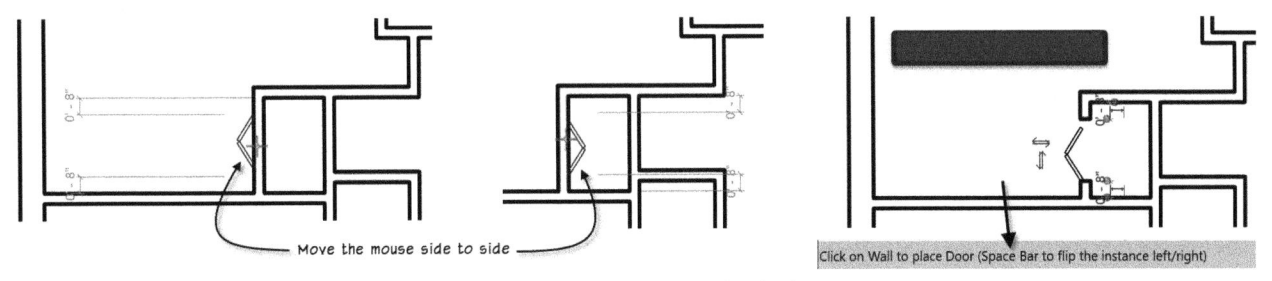

FIGURE 4.39 *Move the mouse to control door placement, and press the* **SPACEBAR** *to flip the door*

7. When the door opens to the lower portion of the wall, click the mouse.

Don't worry if you added the door with the wrong swing. We can easily edit it after the door is placed. To do so, simply click the flip control handles or select it and press the SPACEBAR again.

8. Click the Modify tool or press the ESC key twice.

9. Save your project.

• Revit Essentials for Architecture •

CHANGE THE DOOR SIZE

Door size is governed by a door's type. If you wish to change the size of door in your model, simply choose a different type. If you wish to use a size that is not on the list, you must either edit an existing door type or create a new type with a different size. Here we simply choose a different size, the process to create a new size is covered below.

1. Select the door in the top right of the plan.

    ⇨ On the Properties palette, from the Type Selector, choose a new size, such as:
    Single-Flush : 34" x 80" [**M_Single-Flush : 0864 x 2032mm**].

2. Click next to the drawing in an empty space to deselect the door (or press ESC).

You can edit other instances or type parameters for the selected element (door in this case) on the Properties palette as well. For example, we used this technique above to set the Phase Created parameter of our first door. You could input the Frame Material or Finish. (These are just text fields and will accept any input typed in. To change the actual materials represented in a shaded or rendered view the corresponding type properties should be modified.) You could adjust the Sill or Head height of the door, which would shift its position vertically in elevation.

EDIT DOOR PLACEMENT WITH DIMENSIONS

We have seen several examples so far of the use of Temporary Dimensions to control the placement of elements in the model. We can also create permanent dimensions, which give us even greater flexibility and control over element placement.

1. Select the door in the top left side of the plan.

Two Temporary Dimensions will appear; one on either side—take notice of the small blue icon that looks like a dimension itself just below the dimension line (see the left side of Figure 4.40).

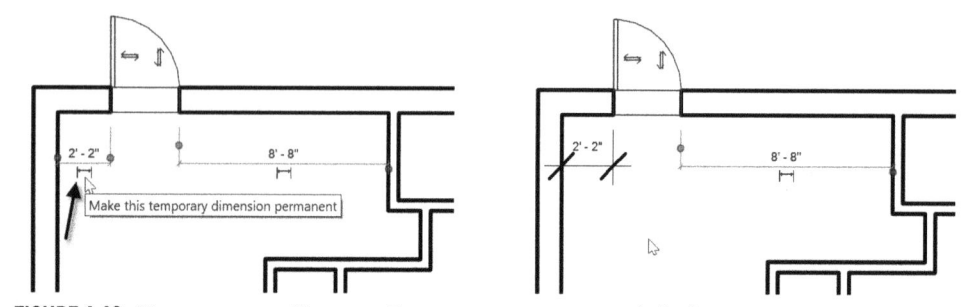

FIGURE 4.40 *You can convert a Temporary Dimension to permanent with the dimension icon*

2. On the left side dimension, click this icon to make the dimension permanent (see the right side of Figure 4.40).

When you do this, a permanent dimension will appear. It will be colored black. Various colors are used in Revit to indicate various states of selection and/or if the element is editable. Table 4.A gives a summary of the common colors and what they signify:

> **NOTE:** Selection color can be customized. On the File menu, click the Options button. On the Graphics tab of the "Options" dialog, change the colors to suit your preference. Element colors can be customized in the "Object Styles" dialog (Manage tab, Settings panel, Object Styles Button).

TABLE 4.A *Colors used in the Revit interface*

Color	Signifies
Black	The element is not selected, nor active for editing.
Outlined in Blue	The element is pre-highlighted (caused by the mouse passing over it, or the TAB key being used to cycle to the element).
Light Blue	The element is selected.
Dark Blue	The element is interactive (for example, Temporary Dimension text, shape handles, and view tags like sections and elevations).
Orange	Alert color. Indicates an element with an error or warning.
Magenta	Used for sketch lines in sketch-based elements such as floors, roofs, and railings.

When you make the Temporary Dimension permanent, the new dimension appears in black. However, the text stays dark blue if the associated element (the door in this case) remains selected. The new permanent dimension is a new element in the current view (*Level 1*). To access the options of the new permanent dimension, we must select it instead of the door.

3. Click on the new permanent dimension (Click the black lines, not the blue text).

The door will deselect (turning black) and the permanent dimension will select (turning light blue) instead.

4. Click the small padlock icon beneath the dimension (see the left side of Figure 4.41).

The padlock icon will "close" to indicate that the dimension is now constrained.

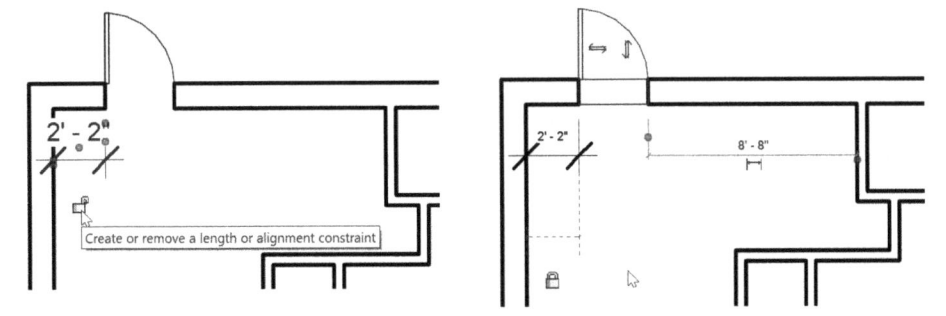

FIGURE 4.41 *Apply a constraint to the door position using the padlock on the permanent dimension*

> **NOTE:** The following examples would be more appropriate in a New Construction model since it is unlikely that we would need to maintain constraints in an existing layout. These tools are covered here merely for the educational value, not as a recommendation of their usage for existing conditions plans.

5. Click on the door to select it.

The permanent dimension will deselect (turning black) and the door will select (turning light blue) instead.

• Revit Essentials for Architecture •

Notice the padlock icon that displays beneath the dimension (see the right side of Figure 4.41). If you click on the dimension value and attempt to edit, it will not work. The only way that you could edit the value would be to first remove the constraint. You can do this by clicking the closed padlock icon. Let's test our new constraint with a quick experiment. We will undo it when we are finished.

6. Select the left vertical exterior wall.

7. Move the pointer over the selected wall (the pointer changes to a small move cursor), click and drag the wall to the left. The exact amount is not important.

Notice that the wall moved, and the door also moved and maintained its distance to the wall.

⇨ Undo the change. (Click the Undo icon on the QAT or press CTRL + Z.)

8. Try the same experiment with the right vertical exterior wall. Move it to the right.

Notice that the door on that side did not move. It has no constraints applied to it.

⇨ Undo the change.

> **NOTE:** Dimensions are annotation elements. Therefore, they are "view-specific"—meaning that they appear only in the view in which they are added. Walls and doors on the other hand are model elements and appear in all views in which they would normally be seen. However, although the display of dimensions is view specific, their constraints are not. If the dimension is locked, the constraint is enforced throughout the model, even if the dimension is not displayed in the current view. Or even if you delete the dimension without removing the constraint. To help you locate existing constraints in your model, there is a display mode that temporarily reveals constraints in the view. This is shown in the next topic.

APPLYING AN EQUALITY CONSTRAINT

Let's apply another kind of constraint to a different door. The door that we have on the right should be centered in the room. We can add a permanent dimension with an equality constraint to maintain this relationship automatically for us. If your door is already centered in that room, you might want to move it a little before we start so that you can see the result of the equality constraint more clearly.

1. On the Annotate tab, on the Dimension panel, click the Aligned dimension tool (or press DI).

We are going to place the dimension directly this time because we want more control over the specific witness lines. When you place a dimension, pre-highlight the elements that you wish to dimension. If the wrong element pre-highlights, use the TAB key to cycle to the one you want.

2. Move the mouse pointer over the inside face of the right exterior vertical wall.

Most likely, the wall centerline will pre-highlight, not the edge. If the inside edge highlights, then go ahead and click to select it. Otherwise, use the TAB key to highlight an alternate selection first.

3. Press TAB. (Repeat if necessary) until the inner face of the wall pre-highlights and then click to select it (see Figure 4.42).

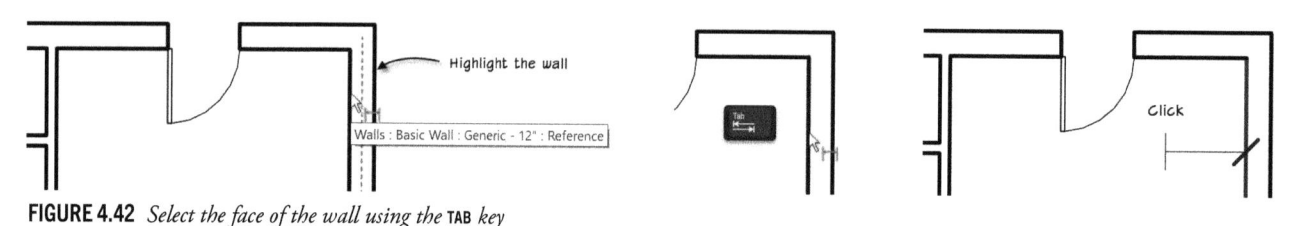

FIGURE 4.42 *Select the face of the wall using the* TAB *key*

A dimension requires at least two witness lines. An equality dimension must have at least three. We will add the door next, then the opposite wall.

- ⇨ Move your pointer over the door.

    By moving around over the door, you should be able to highlight left, right and center without the need to TAB.

4. Highlight the center of the door and then click to add this witness line.
5. Using the TAB key method again, highlight and then click the inside face of the vertical wall on the other side of this room (see the left side of Figure 4.43).

You should now have three witness lines. To place the dimension, click anywhere in the blank white space of the room. Be sure not to click on any geometry or Revit will try to add or remove witness lines to that geometry.

6. Click in empty white space to place the dimension.

Notice the small "EQ" icon with a line though it (see the middle of Figure 4.43). This indicates that the permanent dimension is not set to maintain an equal distance. If you click this icon, you enable the equality constraint and force the elements attached to the dimension to remain equally spaced.

7. Click the EQ icon to enable the equal constraint.

Notice that the Dimension Equality toggle icon no longer has the slash through it (see the right side of Figure 4.43). If your door was not previously centered, it will move to the center now.

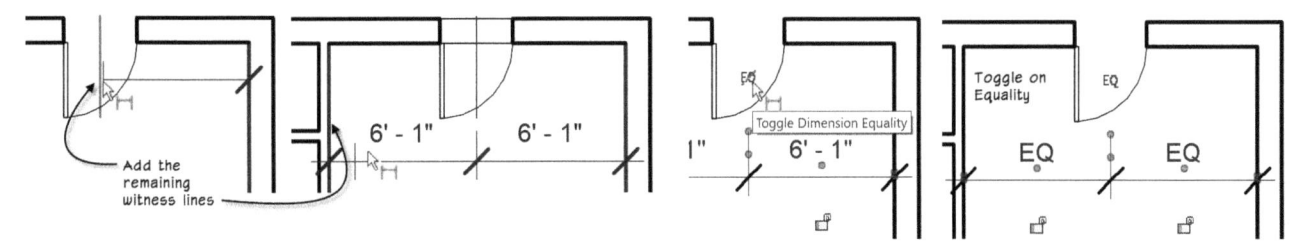

FIGURE 4.43 *Toggle on the dimension equality constraint*

- ⇨ Click Modify or press ESC twice to exit the dimension command.

8. Repeat the experiment above and move the exterior wall.

Notice that the door remains constrained to the center of the room.

- ⇨ Undo the wall move.

WORKING WITH EXISTING CONSTRAINTS

Once again, this sort of constraint is not necessary in an existing conditions plan, but the procedure can be applied anytime you need three or more elements to be equally spaced. If you want to use this technique to center elements and then delete the dimension, you can do this. When you do, Revit will display a warning asking if you want to maintain the constraint.

1. Select the equality dimension onscreen.

- ⇨ Delete it using the icon on the Modify tab or press the DELETE key on the keyboard.

A dialog will display with three options. The message in the dialog indicates that it is possible to delete the dimension but maintain the constraint. In other words, if you click OK, the dimension element is deleted, but the door will continue to be constrained equally between the two walls. If you click Unconstrain, it will also remove the constraint. In which case, if one of the walls or the door later moves, the others will not stay equally spaced.

122 | Chapter 4

2. In the dialog, click OK to delete the dimension but keep the constraint (see Figure 4.44).

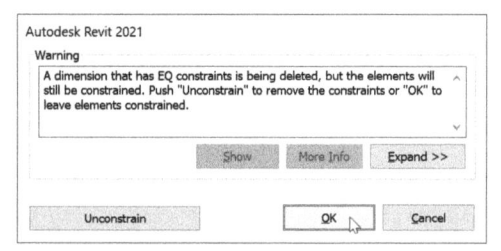

FIGURE 4.44 *Deleting a constraining dimension does not automatically remove the constraint*

If you select either wall or the door, a small EQ icon will appear and some dashed lines to indicate that they are still constrained, but it is subtle. A better option is to use the "Reveal Constraints" mode to see where all the constraints are in an interactive temporary display.

3. On the View Control Bar (at the bottom of the view window), click the Reveal Constraints icon (see the left side of Figure 4.45).

   Constraints appear in a dark red color.

   ⇨ Select the equality constraint.

   ⇨ Either click the EQ to remove it, or simply delete the selected dimension (see the right side of Figure 4.45).

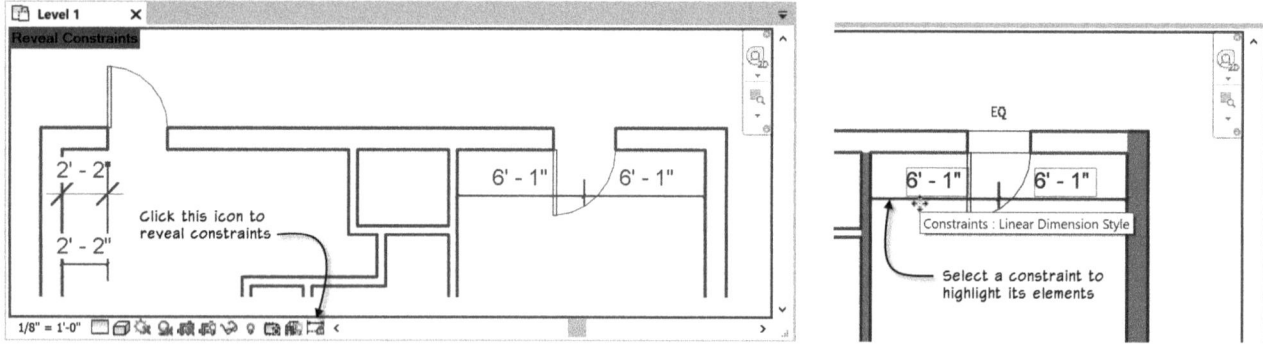

FIGURE 4.45 *Reveal constraints to modify and remove hidden constraints*

4. Click the Reveal Constraints mode icon again to disable the mode.
5. Save the Project (or press ctrl + S).

ADD A NEW DOOR SIZE

The existing door to the small half-bath at the top of the plan need to be quite small. This size required is not available in our current list of door types. Since it is the same door family, we will simply create a new type with the desired size. To do this, we need to choose one of the existing types of this family, duplicate it, and then edit the size parameters of the duplicated type.

1. On Architecture tab, click the Door tool.

   ⇨ From the Type Selector, choose Single Flush: **30" x 80"** [M_Single-Flush : 0762 × 2032mm].

   Don't place it yet.

2. Directly beneath the Type Selector, click the Edit Type button (see the left side of Figure 4.46).

The "Type Properties" dialog will appear. At the top you can see that the family is: Single Flush [M_Single-Flush] and the type is: 30" x 80" [0762 3 2032mm] (see the left side of Figure 4.46). The family list includes all the door families loaded in the current project. This currently includes only the Single Flush and Bi-fold families. Next to

• The Aubin Academy •

the family list is the Load button. You can use this button to load additional families from external libraries as we did above. The type list includes all the types available for the selected family. If you scan that list, you will not find the size we need which is: 28" x 80" [0710 × 2032mm]. Next to the Type list is the Duplicate button. You use this button to create a copy of the currently selected type. This is how you make a new size. Duplicate an existing one and edit it. Let's do that now.

3. Next to the Type list, click the Duplicate button (or press ALT + D).

A new "Name" dialog will appear suggesting the name: Single Flush: 30" x 80" (2) [M_Single-Flush : 0762 × 2032mm (2)]. It is a good idea to change this name. Let's follow the convention established with the out-of-the-box families and name this type after its size.

4. Change the name to: **28" x 80"** [**0710 x 2032mm**] and then click OK (see the middle of Figure 4.46).

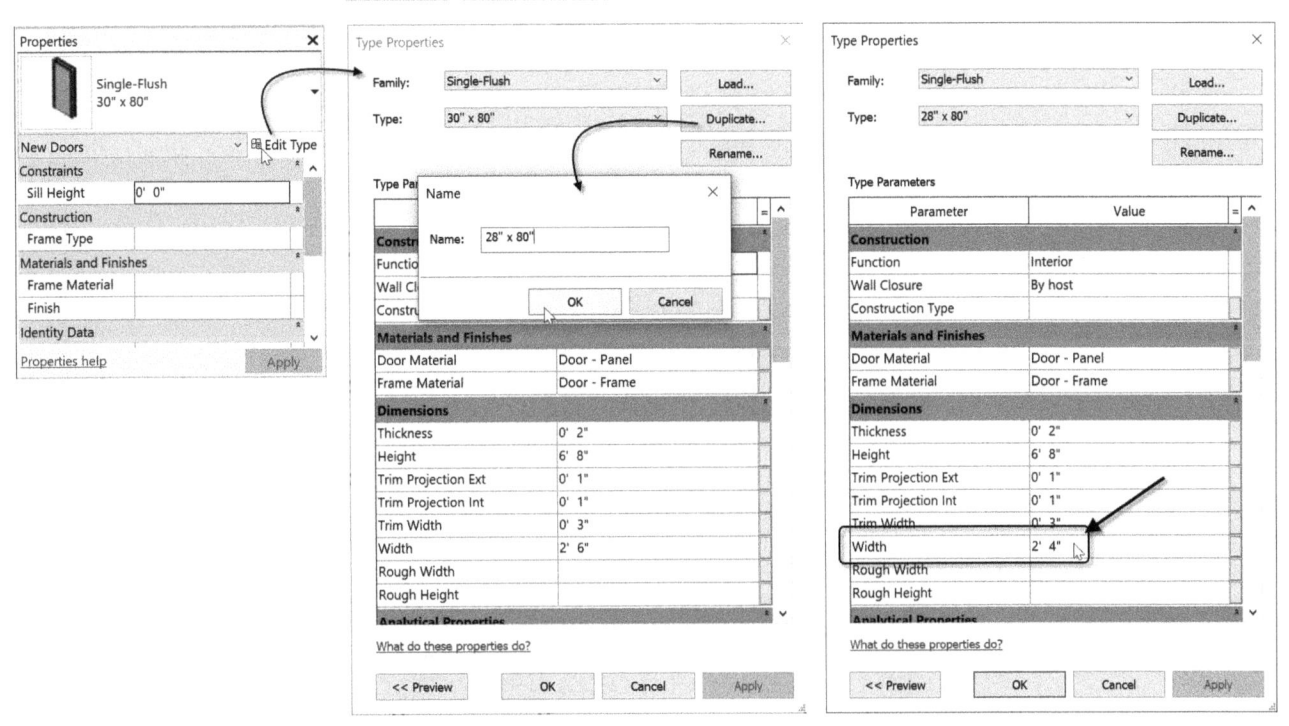

FIGURE 4.46 *Create a new type by duplicating an existing one*

Now that we have created and named a new type, we simply edit it to size we need.

5. Beneath the Dimensions grouping, for Width, type: **2'-4"** [**710**] and then click OK (see the right side of Figure 4.46).

We are now ready to add a door using our new door type.

6. Add a door to the small half-bath at the top of the plan.

⇨ Use the SPACEBAR to swing the door in and to the right (see Figure 4.47).

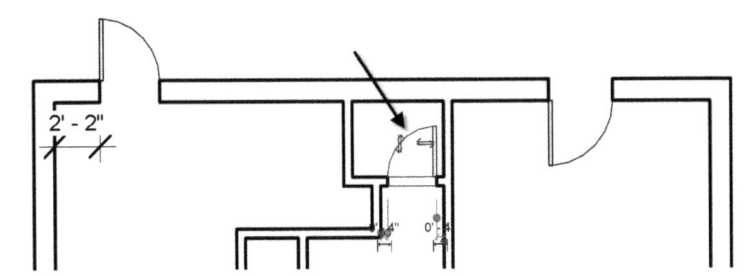

FIGURE 4.47 *Add a door in the new type to the half-bath*

• Revit Essentials for Architecture •

124 | Chapter 4

ADD THE REMAINING DOORS

1. Using Figure 4.48 as a guide and the techniques covered above, place the remaining doors in the plan.

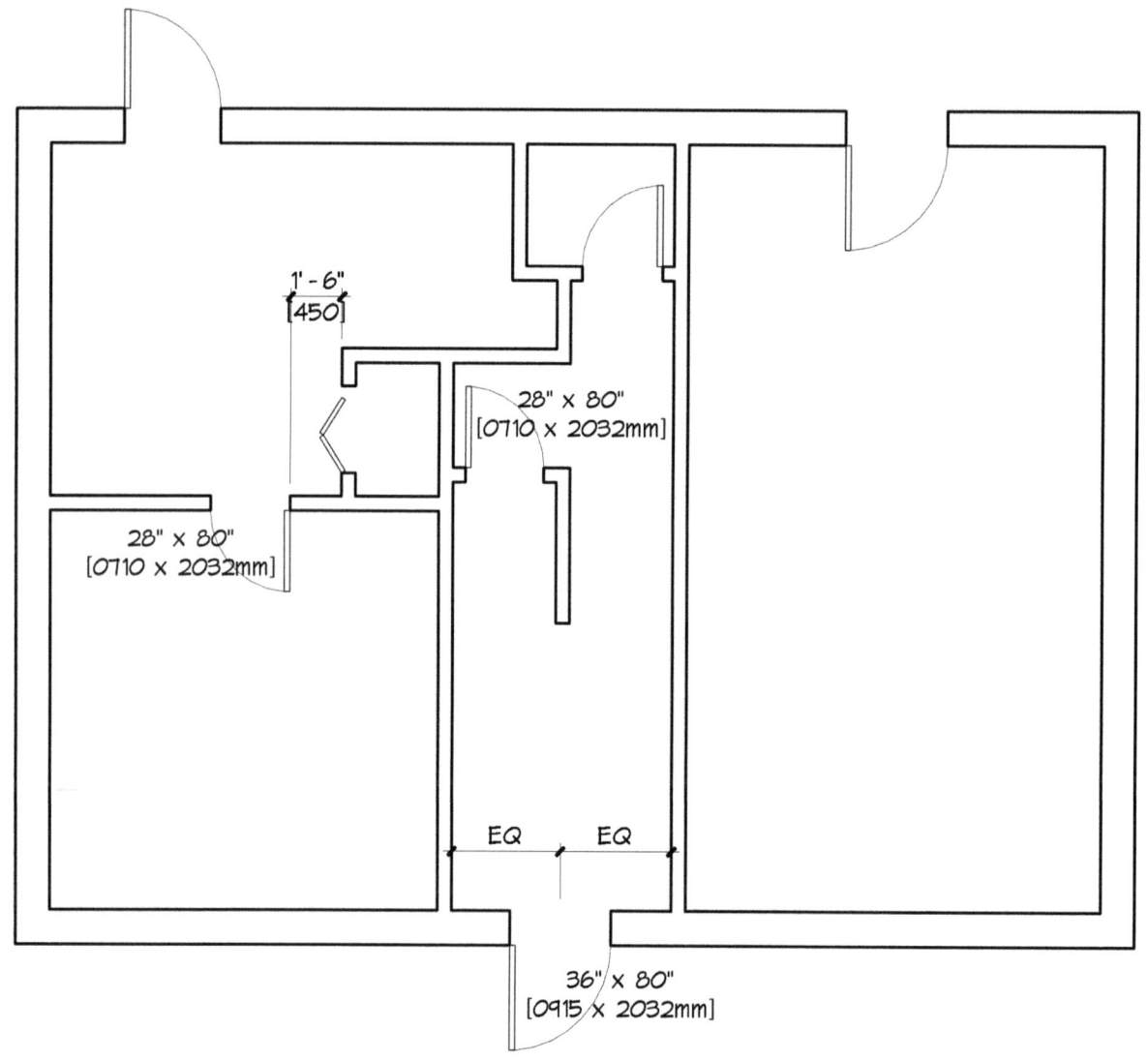

FIGURE 4.48 *Add the remaining doors as shown*

> **HINT:** For a quick way to add doors of the same type (with similar parameters) you can select a door, right-click, and choose: **Create Similar** (or use the Create Similar button on the ribbon or press CS).

2. Save the project.

ADD WINDOWS

Working with windows is nearly identical to working with doors. Many of the parameters are the same, and placement and manipulation of windows works the same as with doors.

1. On the Architecture tab, click the Window tool (or press WN).

All the options for placing windows match those of doors. For detailed descriptions of each of these options, see Figure 4.34 above and the accompanying descriptions.. The size that we need is not included on the list. So, as we did above for the door, we will create a new Double Hung window type.

2. From the Type Selector, choose: **Window-Double Hung: 30" x 46"** [**M_Window-Double Hung: 750 × 1200mm**].

⇨ On the Properties palette, right beneath the Type Selector, click the Edit Type button.

⇨ Next to the Type list, click the Duplicate button (or press ALT + D).

⇨ Change the name to: **36" x 54"** [**915 x 1422mm**] and then click OK.

3. Beneath the Dimensions grouping, for Height, input: **4'-6"** [**1422**] and then click OK.

4. Repeat the duplicate process and create two new window types:

⇨ **36" x 32"** [**0915 x 0800mm**]

⇨ **24" x 32"** [**0600 x 0800mm**]

On the ribbon, be sure that the Tag on Placement button is deselected.

5. Using Figure 4.49 as a guide and the techniques covered above, place the windows as indicated.

Use the new types that you just created for all these windows.

Note that the window in the lower left corner is placed at the midpoint of the room as is the one in the half bath. The temporary dimensions should automatically snap to a centered configuration as you move the mouse nearby. This can also be done easily by making a permanent dimension as above and then clicking the EQ constraint.

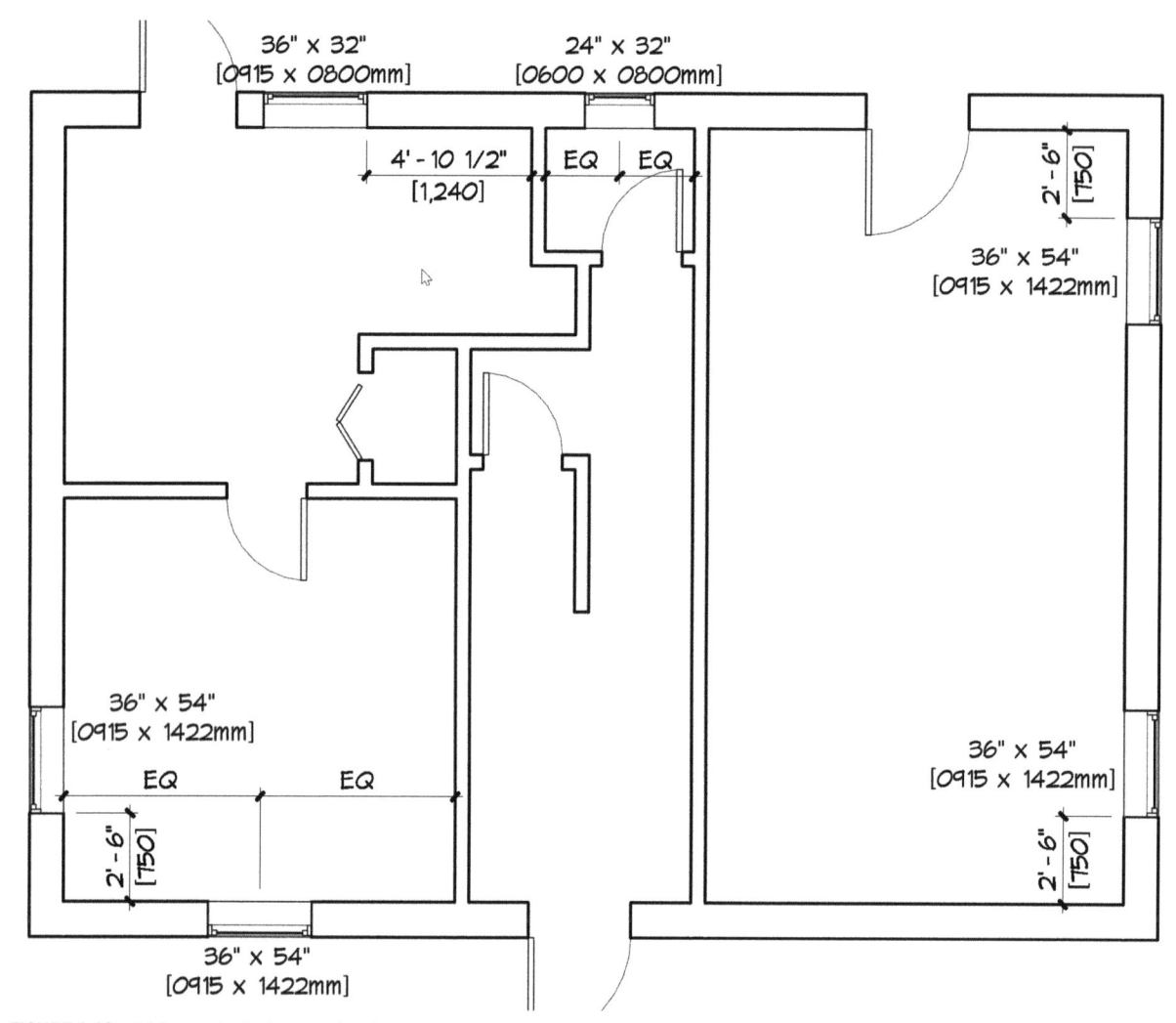

FIGURE 4.49 *Add several windows to the plan*

6. Save the project.

ADD CASED OPENINGS

There are several passages between the hallway and the neighboring rooms that are simply openings in the walls. You place these the same way as doors or windows, and in fact, they are doors. The element includes a hole in the wall (and sometimes the casing), but no door panel.

1. On the Architecture tab, click the Door tool.

2. On the Modify | Place Component tab, on the Mode panel, click the Load Family button.

 ⇨ In the "Load Family" dialog, on the left-hand side, click the Imperial Library [Metric Library] shortcut icon.

 ⇨ Double-click the *Doors* folder, choose: *Door-Opening.rfa* [*M_Door-Opening.rfa*] and then click Open.

> **NOTE:** If your installation of Revit does not have these library folders, copies of the designated family file are included in the *Chapter04* folder. Feel free to load them from there instead.

3. From the Type Selector, choose: **Door-Opening : 30" x 80"** [**M_Door-Opening : 0762 × 2032mm**].

 ⇨ Using Figure 4.50 as a guide, place four Openings in the locations indicated.

Creating a Building Layout | 127

> **TIP:** Use the temporary dimensions to place them 6" [150] from the intersection with the other walls. The horizontal opening at the top should be centered.

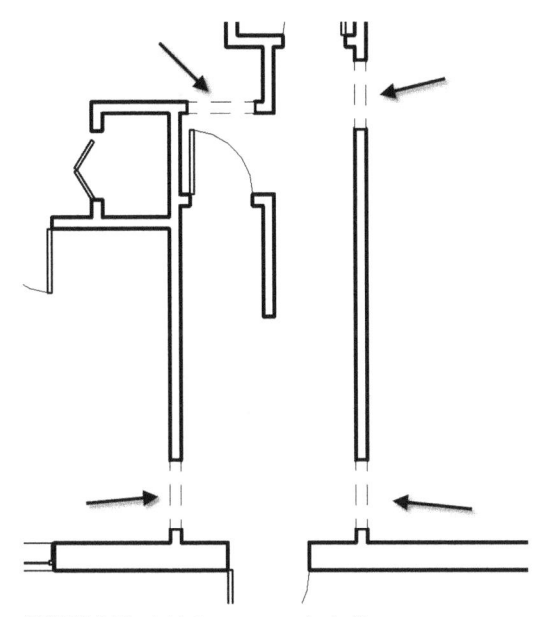

FIGURE 4.50 *Add Openings to the hallway*

After placement, you can click on a Cased Opening and move it or edit it just like the other doors and windows.

LOAD A CUSTOM FAMILY

There is one additional window in the existing house that we need to add. In the front of the house in the living room (right side at the bottom) is a picture window comprised of a fixed window flanked by two double-hung units. We could add this as three windows simply enough. However, it is better to use a single family that contains the three windows. To save time, this configuration of three windows has been preassembled and saved as a family file and included in the *Chapter04* folder. In this sequence, we will load this family into our current project and add it to the front of the existing house. A short exercise showing how to create such a window is presented later in Chapter 11.

1. On the Architecture tab, click the Window tool.
2. On the Modify | Place Window tab, on the Mode panel, click the Load Family button.
   ⇨ In the "Load Family" dialog, browse to the location where you installed the dataset files and open the *Chapter04* folder.
   ⇨ Choose *Existing Living Room Front Window.rfa* and then click Open.

Use the same family for both imperial and metric. Rather than provide two separate families, this family contains both metric and imperial types.

   ⇨ From the Type Selector, choose: **(2) 2'-0" x 4'-8" DH + 4'-0" x 4'-8" FX [(2) 0600 x 1400mm DH + 1200 x 1400mm FX]**
3. Add the window to the bottom horizontal wall in the room at the right (see Figure 4.51).

128 | Chapter 4

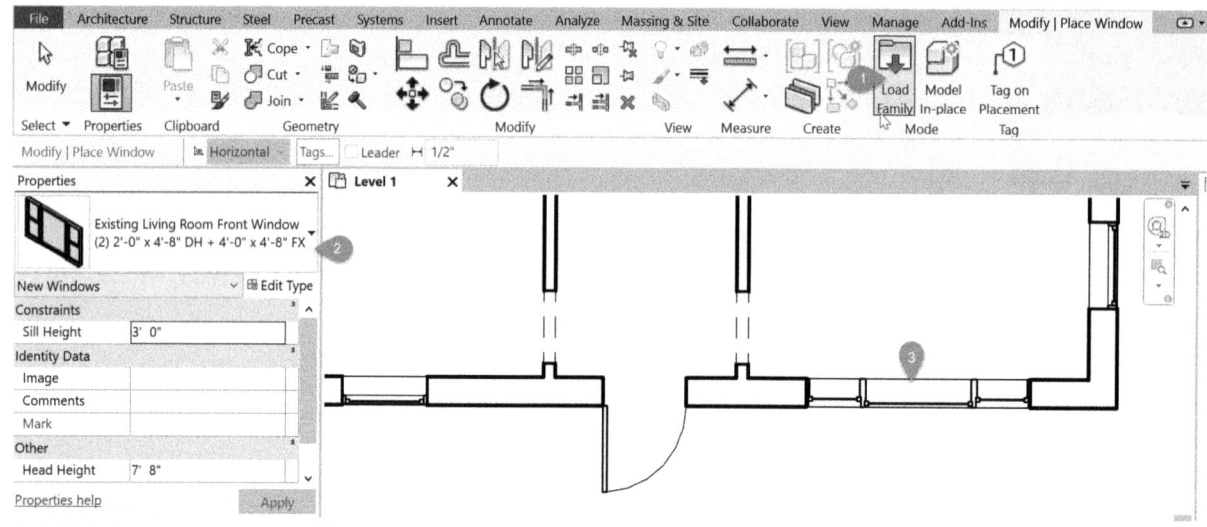

FIGURE 4.51 *Create an instance of the imported family at the front of the house*

4. Click Modify or press ESC twice.

5. Save the project.

MODIFYING DOOR SIZE AND TYPE

Modifying doors and windows is easy. We have already covered most of the basic techniques above. It turns out that the door in the top right of the plan (the first one we added) is supposed to be a double door. Furthermore, it is a French door leading out to an existing patio. Let's make this edit to our model.

1. Select the Single Hinged door at the top right corner of the plan (the first one we added).

   ⇨ Open the Type Selector and scroll through the choices.

There are three door families currently available in the model. The single hinged, the cased opening and the bifold. Note that there are no double doors currently available.

2. On the Insert tab, on the Load from Library panel, click the Load Family button.

Accessing the Load Family button from the Insert tab is an alternative to the approach used above from within the door tool. It simply loads the family into the project and makes it available for use without placing an instance in the model. It is a good option for the task at hand since the door we want to change already exists in the model.

3. In the "Load Family" dialog, on the left-hand side, click the Imperial Library [Metric Library] shortcut icon, double-click the *Doors\Residential* folder, choose: *Door-Exterior-Double-Full Glass-Wood_Clad* [*M_Door-Exterior-Double-Full Glass-Wood_Clad.rfa*] and then click Open.

When choosing this family, next will display the "Specify Types" dialog. Some families have many types saved within them. You can select a single type or multiple types in this dialog. This allows us to select only those types we need without unnecessarily loading types we don't need.

> **NOTE:** Should you later need additional types, you can repeat the steps here to load the same family and redisplay the type catalog and then choose additional sizes. Note that you can choose multiple sizes at once using the SHIFT and CTRL keys.

⇨ In the "Specify Types" dialog, select: **68" x 80"** [**1700 × 2100mm**] and then click OK.

• The Aubin Academy •

Nothing more will happen. Once again, the Load Family command on the Insert tab *only* loads the family. It does not place an instance.

4. Select the Single Hinged door at the top right corner of the plan (the first one we added).

⇨ Open the Type Selector, again, and notice that we now have the double door that we just loaded as an option.

⇨ Choose: **Door-Exterior-Double-Full Glass-Wood_Clad : 68" x 80"** [**M_Door-Exterior-Double-Full Glass-Wood_Clad : 1700 × 2100mm**].

> **NOTE:** You can use this technique for windows and other elements as well.

The new door type has replaced the previous one and remains nicely centered since we added the equality constraint to this door earlier. In plan view, it is not obvious what effect choosing a glass door family had. To see the glass, we will have to view the model in 3D.

VIEWING THE MODEL IN 3D

All the work we have done on this model so far has been within a single floor plan view. However, as we saw in previous chapters, you can add or edit elements in any view you wish and then view them or edit them in elevation, section, and/or three-dimensional views. Let's have a look at how the model is shaping up in the third dimension.

1. On the View tab (or QAT), click the Default 3D View icon. (Choose Default 3D, not Camera or Walkthrough).

A new view will appear on screen named: *{3D}*. This name is assigned automatically to the default 3D view in Revit. The default 3D view is an axonometric of the complete building model looking from the southeast. This view appears in the Project Browser beneath the *3D Views* category. From the default view, we can see the ganged window that we added above in the front of the house. Even though the graphics in the floor plan view for the middle window were slightly different than the two flanking windows, from the 3D vantage point it is now very clear that the middle window is fixed while the two flanking ones are double-hung.

You can dynamically pan and/or zoom any view as we have already seen in previous chapters. In a 3D view, you can "orbit" the view. When you do this, you can change the angle and height from which we are viewing the model and spin it in all three dimensions (see Figure 4.52).

130 | Chapter 4

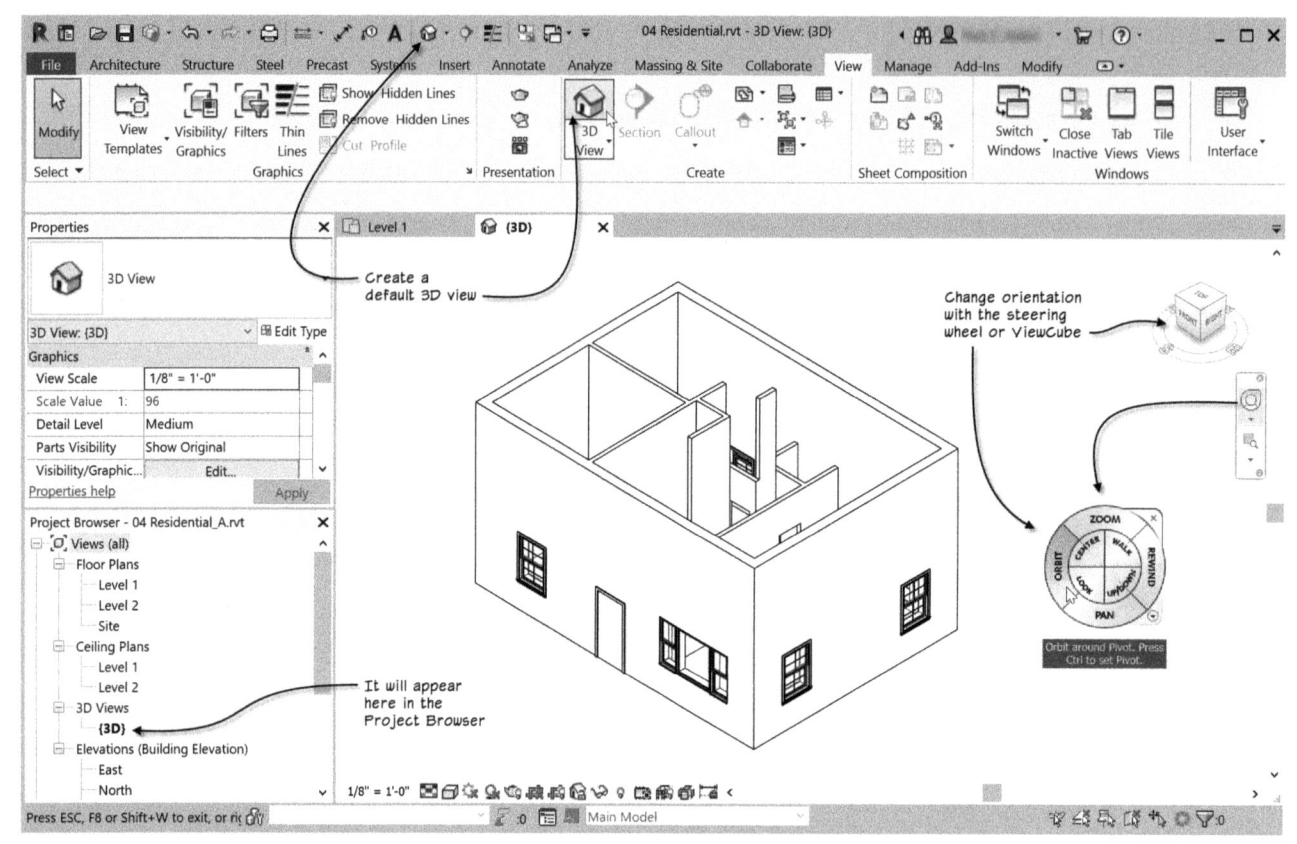

FIGURE 4.52 *Display the Default 3D view and manipulate it dynamically with the Steering Wheel*

2. In the 3D view window on the Navigation Bar, click the Steering Wheel icon (or press F8).

Note that the Steering Wheel appears on screen and follows the movement of the cursor. The Steering Wheel has several controls. Among them are: Pan, Zoom, and Orbit. We explored several of these back er 2. By now you should already be comfortable with panning and zooming. Orbit is only available in a 3D view. Let's give Orbit a try in our 3D view.

3. Move your mouse pointer over the Orbit portion of the Steering Wheel; click and hold down the mouse button and then drag to orbit.

    The pointer will change to an orbit icon to indicate that this mode is active. A Pivot point icon will also appear on screen.

In the middle of the Steering Wheel, move your mouse pointer over the Center portion; click and drag over the model to relocate the pivot point. In the Orbit mode, drag side to side to rotate the model and drag up or down to tilt the vantage point up or down. There are a few other options as well like Look and Up/Down. Give them a try.

4. Orbit the model around so that you can see the back of the house.

⇨ Pan and Zoom to fine-tune the view to your liking.

5. On the View Control Bar (bottom left corner of each view window) click the Model Graphic Style icon and choose: **Shaded** from the pop-up menu that appears (see Figure 4.53).

• The Aubin Academy •

Creating a Building Layout | 131

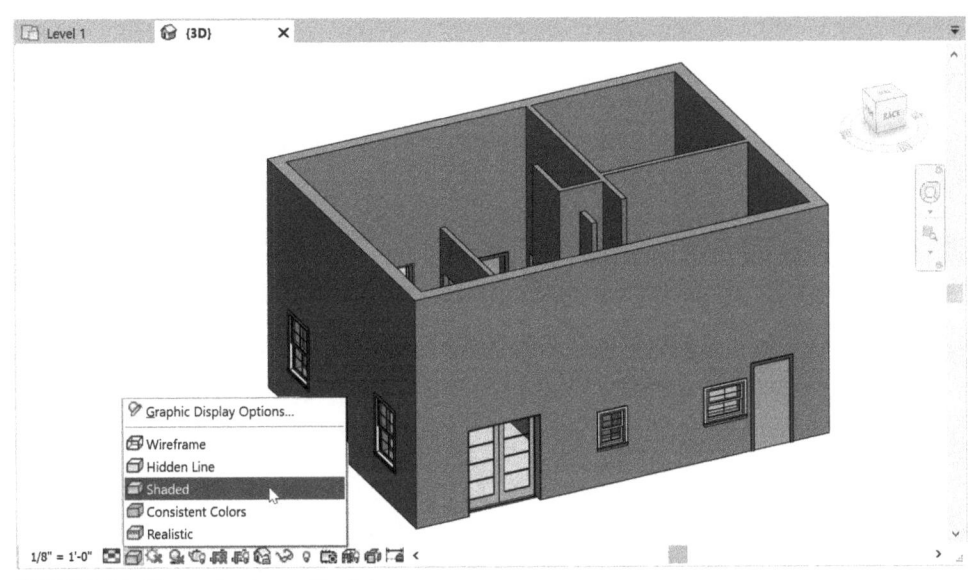

FIGURE 4.53 *Change the view to Shaded*

> **TIP:** The dynamic viewing functions can also be performed with a wheel mouse and the CTRL and SHIFT keys. Drag with the mouse wheel held down to pan, hold down the CTRL key and drag with the wheel, or simply roll the wheel to zoom. Hold down the SHIFT key and drag with the wheel to orbit. Your specific mouse and mouse driver will determine the exact behavior. Mouse drivers by many manufacturers allow customization of specific button functions. 3D Connexion devices are also supported. If you have one installed a special icon for it will appear on the Navigation Bar.

There are several other display modes on the Visual Style pop-up. Feel free to explore them if you like, but until we add materials to our model, the other modes like Realistic and Ray Trace will not be very impressive.

> **TIP:** The keyboard shortcut for Shaded is SD. The keyboard shortcut for Hidden Line is: HL.

The default three-dimensional view: {3D} is always available. You could certainly use this view exclusively and simply orbit, scroll, and zoom the view as needed each time you displayed it. However, once you get a 3D view displaying just the way you like, you are encouraged to save the view. The new view will be added to the Project Browser beneath the *3D Views* category along with any other 3D views your project has.

6. Make any adjustments to the 3D view that you like.

⇨ Right-click the name *{3D}* beneath 3D Views on the Project Browser and choose: **Rename**.

⇨ Give the new view a unique name such as: **Rear Existing French Door** and then click OK.

At this point, if you click the Default 3D view icon again, the default {3D} view will be created anew. If you click the 3D view icon and the {3D} view already exists, it will open this existing one instead of creating a new one.

EDIT IN ANY VIEW

From our explorations in 3D, you may have noticed that many of the interior walls are the wrong height. We can correct this easily. If you can't see this clearly, try orbiting the model to tilt it down or simply select one of the exterior walls. Elements selected in a 3D view will display transparently while the element is selected.

1. Close your *Rear Existing French Door* view and then click the Default 3D view icon to create a new {3D} view.

• Revit Essentials for Architecture •

132 | Chapter 4

⇨ On the View tab, on the Windows panel, click the Window Tile icon (or press WT).

2. Orbit the view down slightly so that you can clearly see the heights of the interior partitions.

Remember, in addition to the techniques already covered, you can orbit 3D views by dragging the ViewCube.

⇨ On the Navigation Bar, click the zoom drop down and then choose: **Zoom All to Fit** (or simple press ZA)

3. Activate the View: *Floor Plan: Level 1* by clicking on its view tab.

⇨ Create a crossing selection window within the building. Drag from right to left to select all interior walls.

Be sure to select only the interior walls and not any of the exterior ones. Do not worry about selecting doors and Openings. We will remove them from the selection next. All of the selected elements will highlight in light blue in both views (see Figure 4.54).

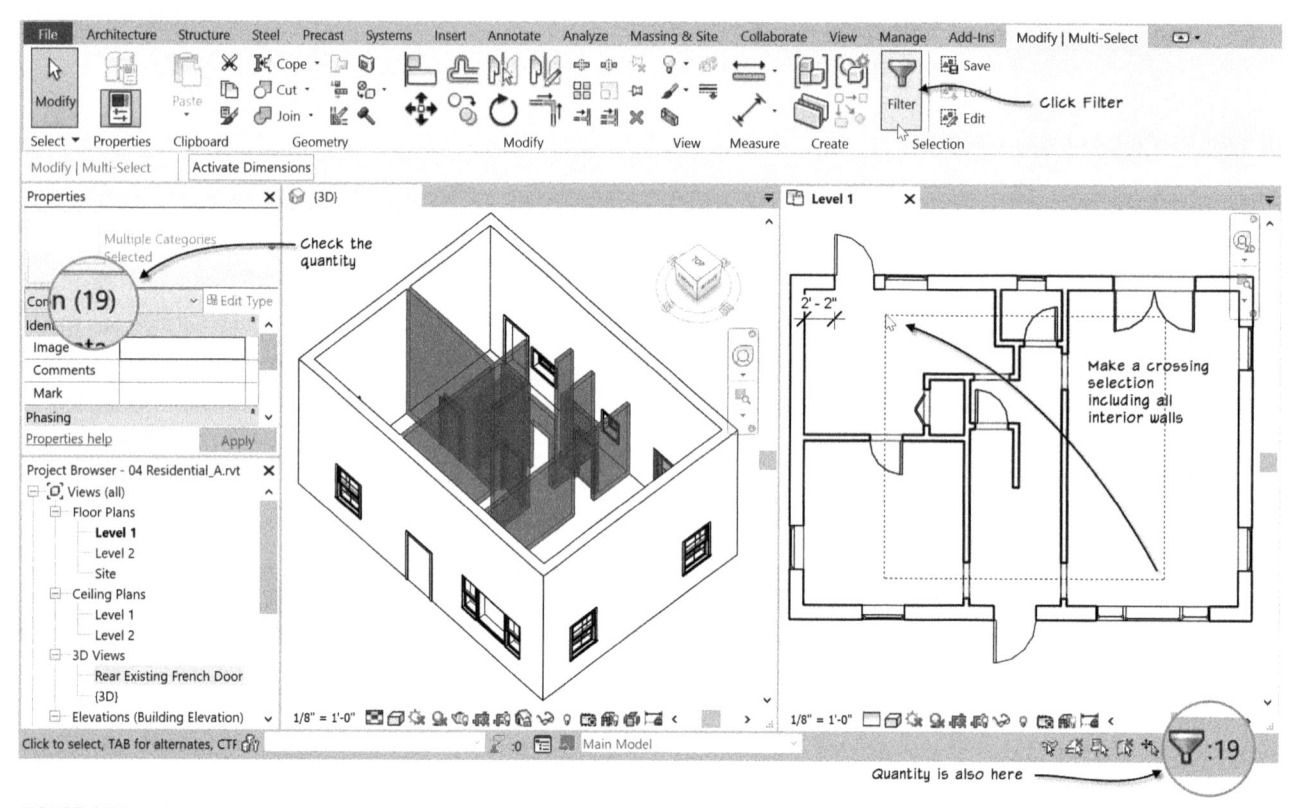

FIGURE 4.54 *Select all interior walls*

4. On the ribbon (or bottom right corner of the application frame) click the Filter button.

NOTE: The quantity of selected elements will appear next to the Filter icon on the Status Bar at the lower-right and on the Properties palette. Your quantity may vary from the one shown.

5. In the "Filter" dialog, click the Check None button, then check only walls and then click OK (see Figure 4.55).

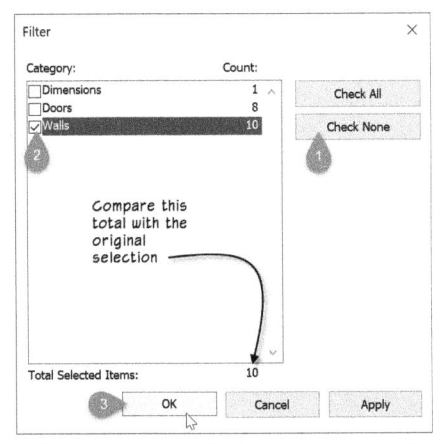

FIGURE 4.55 *Now only the interior walls will be highlighted*

⇨ On the Properties palette, beneath the Constraints grouping, for "Top Constraint," click in the empty cell to the right, click the drop down arrow, choose: **Up to level: Level 2** and then click Apply (see Figure 4.56).

> **NOTE:** In this case the field next to Top Constraint is empty because the values for the elements in the selection vary. In some cases a field might be empty because there is no value. There is really no way to tell the difference except by paying close attention to how many elements you have selected. If there is more than one element in your selection, use caution when editing "blank" values.

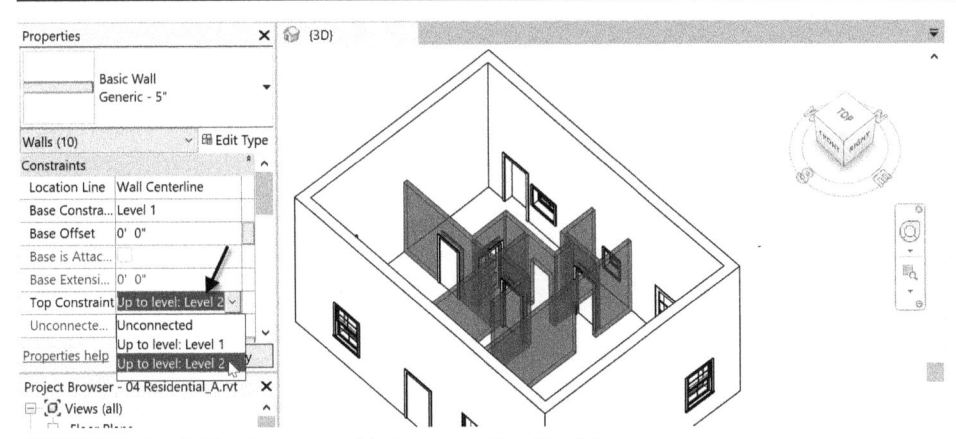

FIGURE 4.56 *Set the Top Constraint of the interior walls to Level 2*

Note that even though we made the change from a 2D floor plan view, the edit appeared in the 3D view immediately. In Revit, every view is always up to date. There is no need to coordinate or refresh anything. Regardless of the view you are working in, all edits apply directly to the model. You simply choose the most convenient and logical view in which to work and Revit takes care of the rest.

In this exercise, we have constrained the top of the interior walls to the height of the second floor. It turns out that the default template from which we started our project included two levels. However, the height of those levels does not match the existing conditions of our residential project. We will adjust the height of the levels, and in so doing, all these interior partitions will automatically adjust with the level height. This is the primary reason to apply such a constraint in the first place.

6. Click on the {3D} tab to make it active.

⇨ Zoom out and pan as required so that you can see the level heads outside the building model.

7. Click on Level 2 to select it.

134 | Chapter 4

⇨ Click again directly on the blue dimension text beneath the Level 2 label.

The text will highlight—ready to receive input.

⇨ Change the value to: **9'-0" [2700]** and then press ENTER (see Figure 4.57).

Notice the immediate change to all the interior walls in the 3D view.

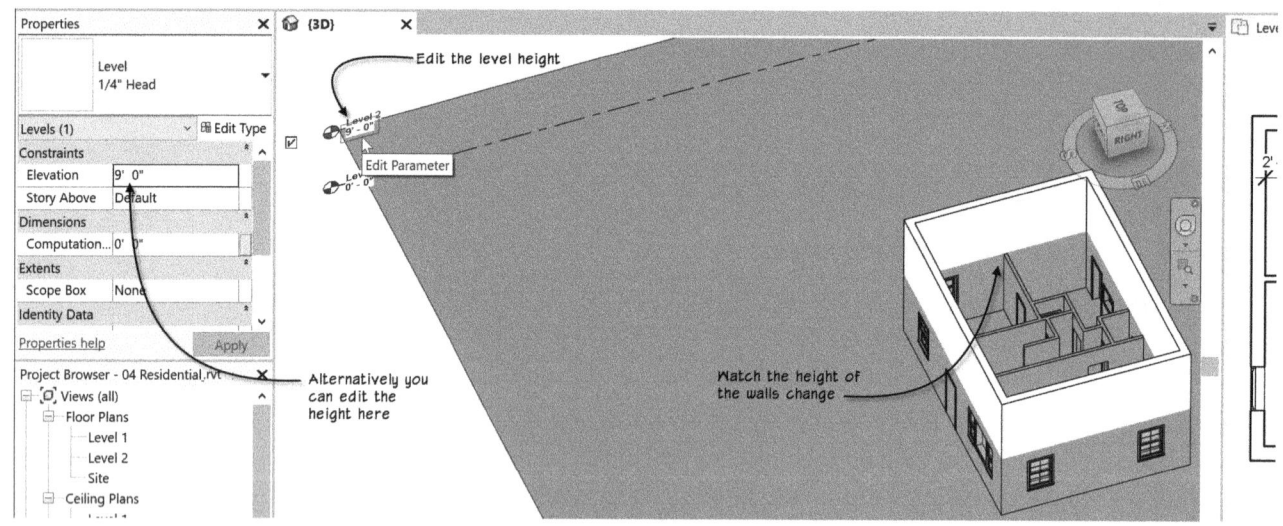

FIGURE 4.57 *Adjust the height of Level 2 and see the immediate effect on the interior walls*

8. Hover over the {3D} view tab and then click the small X to close it. .

⇨ In the remaining tab: *Level 1*, Zoom the window to fit (type ZF).

When you have many open windows, they can all be closed except the current one using this command. This helps keep your interface organized and preserves memory and computer resources.

9. Save your project.

ADDING PLUMBING FIXTURES

The small half-bath in the top of our plan could use some fixtures. The library of components provided with Revit includes a variety of items such as furniture, toilets, trees, parking spaces, equipment, electrical fixture symbols, targets, tags, and much more. All these items are families, and many have special behaviors and parameters appropriate to the object that they represent. In this exercise, we will simply load the families we need and insert them in the model much like we did for the doors, windows, and cased openings above.

ADD COMPONENTS TO THE MODEL

You add Components like plumbing fixtures and furniture in nearly the same way as doors, windows, and Openings. Each family may vary slightly depending on the parameters built into it. However, the overall process is the same: on the Architecture tab click the Component tool, choose an item from the Type Selector or click the Load Family button to access the library. Place the item in your model.

1. On the Architecture tab, click the Component tool (or press CM).

If you open and scroll through the Type Selector, you will note that no plumbing fixture families currently appear on the list. As we did above for doors and windows, we will simply load the items we need from the library.

2. On the Modify | Place Component tab, on the Mode panel, click the Load Family button.

⇨ In the "Open" dialog, on the left-hand side, click the Imperial Library [Metric Library] shortcut icon, double-click the *Plumbing* folder. Next, double-click the *Architectural* folder, then *Fixtures* and finally *Water Closets*.

You will note that there is a domestic and commercial toilet, each with a 2D and a 3D version.

> **BIM Manager Note:** It should be noted that the "3D" plumbing fixtures contain a 2D symbol that appears only in floor plan views and a 3D symbol that appears only in the 3D views. Revit automatically switches between the appropriate representations as needed. Another way to think of such objects is: 2 ½D: meaning somewhere between a 2D representation and a 3D model. When you create a Building Information Model, it is important to recognize techniques such as this and to realize that "Model" does not always mean "3D." Nor does "Model" imply that every facet and screw of an item should be painstakingly represented in graphical form. Always remember to strike a balance between what is conveyed graphically and what is conveyed by other means such as with attached data parameters—this is the "I" in BIM. In many cases, an "Information" model is much more practical and useful to a project team than a "3D" model. There are many types of models. Statisticians and economists refer to their spreadsheets as "models." Meteorologists refer to their predictions and weather simulations as "models." As Architects, we tend to only think "3D" when the word model is mentioned. Learning to embrace BIM means understanding that a model is not always 3D, and that the "I" is just as important as, and sometimes more important than, the "M." A really good BIM will include both a graphical and data model tightly integrated with one another. Model in this context therefore can more accurately be described as a "representation" or a "simulation" of our building project.

3.   Choose *Toilet-Domestic-3D.rfa* [*M_Toilet-Domestic-3D.rfa*] and then click Open.

If you get a warning: "No tag Loaded," simply click No to continue. Like doors and windows above, the Component tool can use Tag on Placement as well. We don't need a tag, so make sure that is off.

⇨   Zoom in on the half-bath at the top of the plan (see the left side of Figure 4.58).

We can change the orientation of the element as we are placing it. The easiest way to do that is to tap the SPACEBAR.

⇨   Tap the SPACEBAR (see the middle of Figure 4.58).

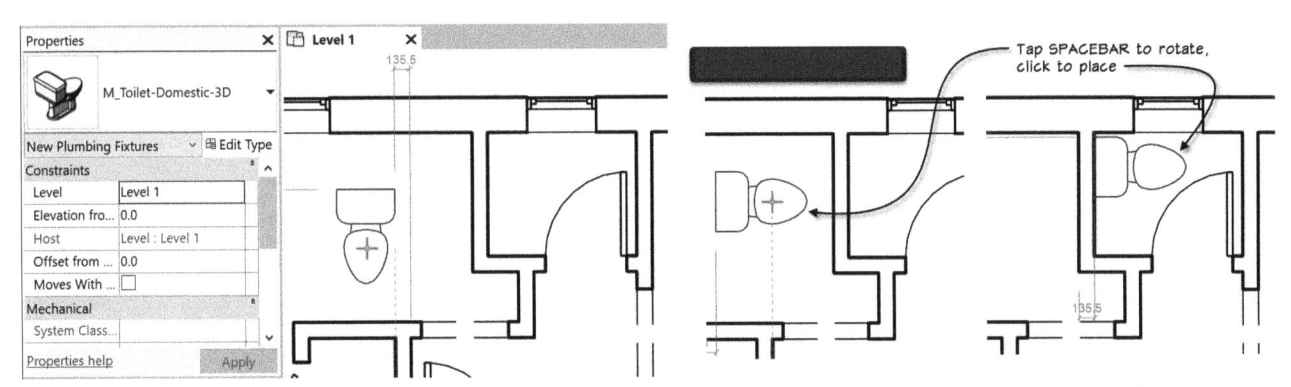

FIGURE 4.58 *The toilet family is wall-hosted, so it automatically attaches to the walls. Use the temporary dimensions to fine-tune placement*

4.   Click a point on the left vertical wall to place the toilet in the model (see the right side of Figure 4.58).

This toilet room is clearly not up to current code! Such is the nature of existing conditions. Just place the toilet very close to the intersection with the exterior wall. We still need room for a small sink.

5.   On the Place Component tab, click the Load Family button again.

⇨   Return to the *Plumbing\Architectural\Fixtures* folder and then double-click the *Sinks* folder.

⇨   Open the *Sink-Single-2D.rfa* [*M_Sink-Single-2D.rfa*] family this time.

Move the pointer around and for this family notice that we are not allowed to place it freestanding like the toilet. This Component is hosted (very similar to doors and windows, except it won't cut a hole in the wall). Move near a wall, and you will see it appear. However, it will be too big for the space that we have available. Sometimes what we find in the field does not meet current building standards. The sink in this existing half-bath is very small.

6. On the Properties palette, click the Edit Type button.

⇨ Next to the Type list, click the Duplicate button (or press ALT + D).

⇨ Change the name to: **18" x 15"** [**450 × 375mm**] and then click OK.

7. Beneath the Dimensions grouping, for "Depth," type: **1'-3"** [**375**].

> **TIP:** Remember, if you are using Imperial units, you can simply type 1 3 with a space between the numbers, and Revit will interpret this as 1'-3".

8. Beneath the Dimensions grouping, for "Width", type: **1'-6"** [**450**] and then click OK.
9. Place the sink next to the toilet. Use the Temporary Dimensions to fine-tune the placement of both the sink and the toilet.

It will be a tight fit. You will need to set the values of the Temporary Dimensions to about 1" [25] between the walls and the Components to get everything to fit.

> **TIP:** You can also select the element and "nudge" it with the arrow keys on your keyboard to move it. The element will move slightly onscreen with each press of the arrow. Zooming will affect how far the nudge goes. To move ten times, hold the SHIFT and then press the arrow keys.

10. Click the Modify tool or press the ESC key twice.
11. Save the project.

CREATE A UNIQUE ELEMENT

The first floor existing conditions plan is nearly finished. We still need to add the fireplace in the living room and stairs in the middle of the plan. While it would be possible (and maybe preferable) to create a fireplace family in the Family Editor and save it in our library for use in any project, this would only make sense if we used the same fireplace design often. If you design a lot of homes that use the same fireplace, this is exactly what you should do. Refer to techniques in Chapter 11 to learn how to create a loadable component family. In this case, we will create the precise fireplace we need for this project directly in-place. This is called an "In-Place Family."

> **IMPORTANT:** In-place families are not designed to be moved, copied, rotated, etc. They are meant to be used only once. If you need to use it more than once within this project or in a different project, a regular loadable component family should be created in the Family Editor, saved to a library and then loaded into your project as needed. The Family Editor will be explored in detail in Chapter 11.

CREATE AN IN-PLACE FAMILY

To get started, we will create a new in-place family and assign it to a predefined category. Revit has a long list of predefined categories. Categories are at the top of the hierarchy discussed in the "Families & Types" topic on page 47 in Chapter 2.

Creating a Building Layout | 137

1. Zoom in on the middle of the right vertical exterior wall. This is where our fireplace will go.
2. On the Architecture tab, click the drop down button on the Component tool and choose: **Model In-Place**.
   ⇨ In the "Family Category and Parameters" dialog, choose: **Generic Models**, and then click OK (see Figure 4.59).

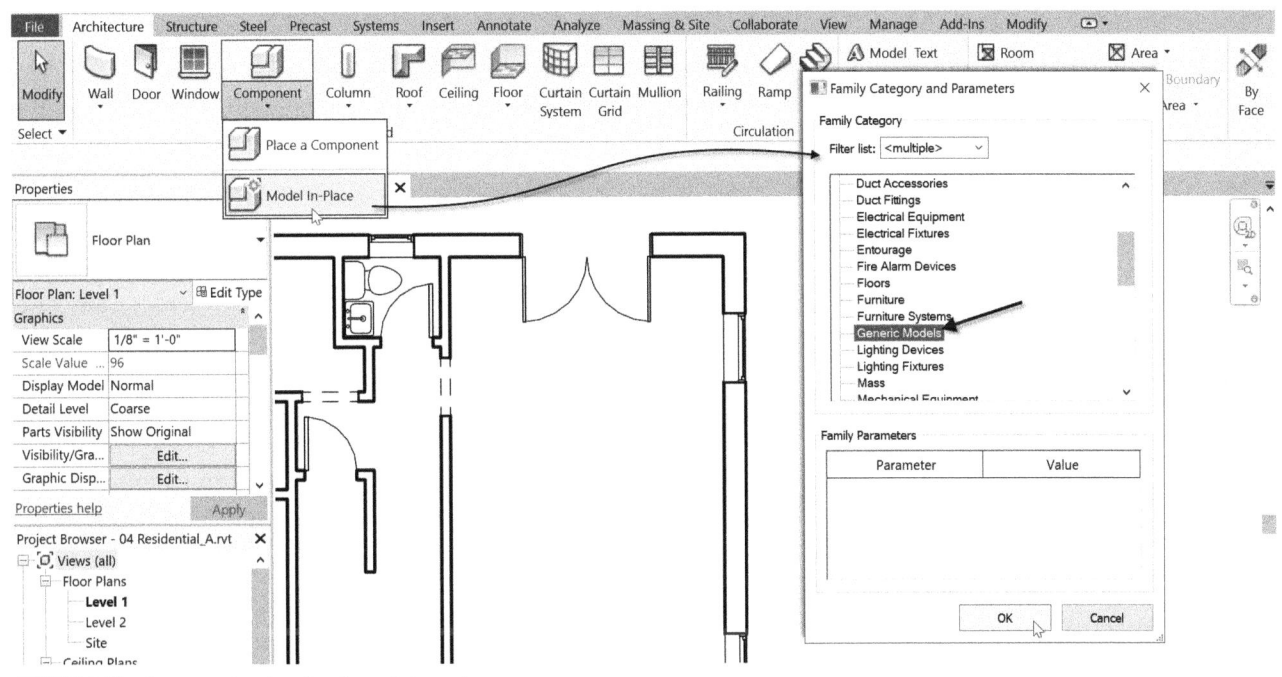

FIGURE 4.59 *Create an in-place family and choose its category*

> **NOTE:** Modeling in-place is not available in Revit LT. If you are using LT, you can create an actual component family and load it instead. From the File menu, choose: **New > Family**. Then choose the *Generic Model.rft* [*Metric Generic Model.rft*] template from the list and then click Open. Add the reference planes as noted below, but instead of measuring them from the existing walls, place them so that the rectangular space they describe is centered on the two reference planes already in the template. Build the rest of the family following the same steps indicated. Save the file when finished as: **Fireplace** and then load it into the project and place it where indicated in the figures below. A version of this family is provided in the *Chapter04\Complete* folder called: *Fireplace for LT.rfa*.

The family category list is a fixed list built into the software. When you create a family, you must assign it one of these categories. The family you create will inherit the characteristics of the category to which it is assigned. In general, when choosing a category, try to select the one that most closely matches the actual object that you are creating. The Construction Specifications Institute (CSI) spec section for fireplaces is Division 10—Specialties (10300 Fireplaces and Stoves), which would tempt us to choose "Specialty Equipment." However, your choice of category does impart certain behaviors to your family. Specialty Equipment is intended more for free-standing equipment items and does not have a "cut" representation. Items like 10340 Manufactured Exterior Specialties, 10500 Lockers or 10670 Storage Shelving are all examples of things that would work well in the Specialty Equipment category. Items in Revit that are "cuttable" interact with the cut plane of floor plan and section views and show bold when cut and lighter when viewed in projection. Since we will want our fireplace to interact with the wall and appear bolder when cut in plan, we need a category that supports cutting.

We get this cutting behavior because we chose the "Generic Models" category above. This is sort of a "catch all" category. You typically choose Generic Models when the item you are modeling does not fit neatly into any of the

• Revit Essentials for Architecture •

138 | Chapter 4

other categories. Generic Models does not impart any specialized parameters that might be available from other more descriptive categories, but aside from the need for interaction with the cut plane, our existing fireplace has no other specialized needs. So Generic Model will work OK here.

⇨ In the "Name" dialog, type: **Existing Fireplace** and then click OK.

You are now in "In-Place family editing" mode. The model will gray out but remain visible for reference. The ribbon tabs will change showing a collection of In-Place family editing tools instead of the usual tools. Take a look at the Create tab for example(see Figure 4.60).

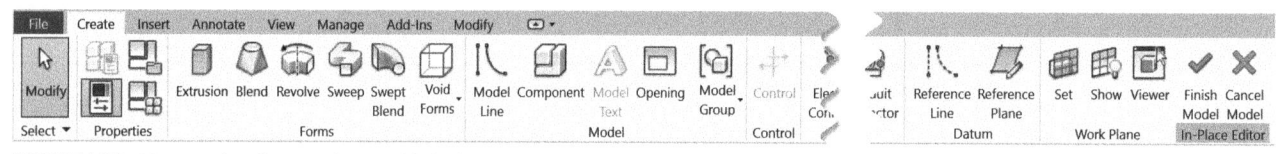

FIGURE 4.60 *The Family Editor mode is enabled when you create a new in-place family*

The Create tab includes many family editing tools. You can create solid and void forms, insert Components, or add connectors. Simply click on the other tabs to access these tools as normal. Note that several tools like walls, doors, and floors are not available in family editing mode. You cannot place (nest) a system family within another family. Also notice that the "In-Place Editor" panel with its Finish and Cancel buttons appears on the right side of the ribbon in all tabs.

ADDING REFERENCE PLANES

When you construct complex geometry, it is often useful to have guidelines to assist in locating elements. Reference planes are used for this purpose in families. You sketch a reference plane like the way you sketch walls or lines. You can snap and constrain other elements to reference planes, making them useful tools for design layout. You can add reference planes in any orthographic view of the model. (Reference planes do not show in 3D.) In this example, we will add them within our In-Place family. When you add them in this way, the reference planes will become part of the In-Place family and will be visible only when editing the In-Place family.

1. On the Create tab, on the Datum panel, click the Reference Plane tool. (Do not click Reference Line; make sure you click Reference Plane).

2. Click a point inside the large room on the right near the exterior wall, just above the lower window.

⇨ Move the pointer horizontally to the right past the exterior wall and then click outside.

The exact locations of either click are not critical so long as you draw horizontally and above the window.
A small reference plane (green dashed line with round blue handles at the ends) will appear.

⇨ Edit the Temporary Dimension from the bottom horizontal wall to: **7'-11"** [**2400**] (see the left side of Figure 4.61).

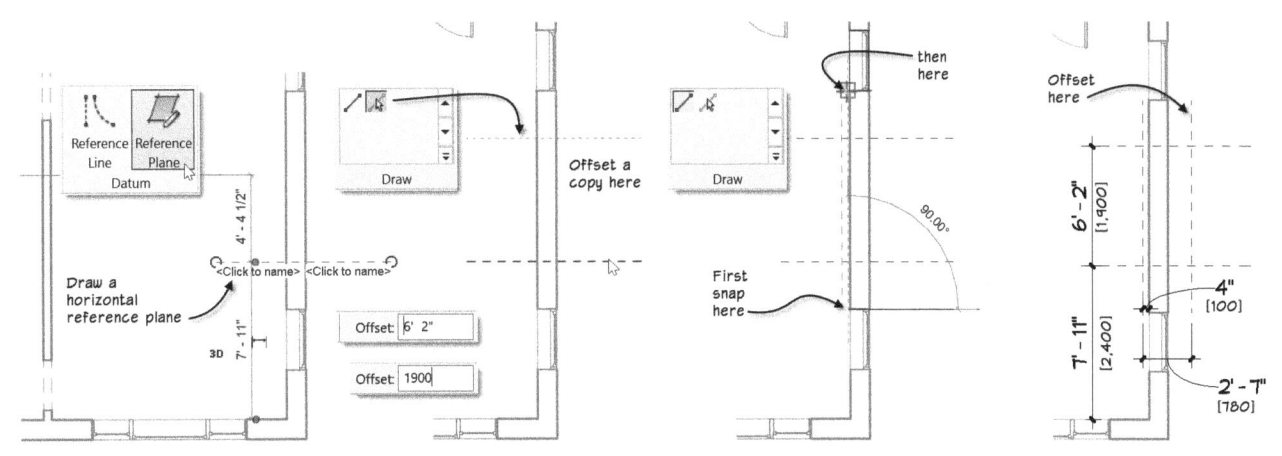

FIGURE 4.61 *Create two horizontal and two vertical reference planes to frame out the fireplace footprint (dimensions for reference only)*

3. On the Modify | Place Reference Plane tab, on the Draw panel click the Pick Lines icon.

    ⇨ On the Options Bar, in the Offset field, type: **6'-2"** [**1900**].

    ⇨ Pre-highlight the first reference plane and move the mouse so that the offset line appears above.

4. Click to create the new reference plane (second panel from the left in Figure 4.61).

Now we'll repeat the process to create two more vertical reference planes. These will frame out the rectangular footprint of the fireplace.

5. On the Draw panel, switch back to the Line icon, and then type: **4"** [**100**] in the Offset field.

    ⇨ Snap to the endpoint of the lower window on the inside edge of the wall.

    ⇨ Snap to the endpoint of the upper window on the inside edge of the wall (third from the left in Figure 4.61).

> **TIP:** The start and end points suggested will make the first reference plane fall to the inside of the house and the second to the outside. If you click the points in the wrong order, do not cancel, simply tap the SPACEBAR to flip the line.

6. Switch back to the Pick Lines tool and then change the Offset to: **2'-7"** [**780**].

    ⇨ Offset the reference plane you just drew to the outside of the house (see the right side of Figure 4.61).

We now have four reference planes that we can use to guide the creation of our fire-place's form. This is common best practice. Complete details on the use of reference planes in families will be discussed in Chapter 11.

CREATE A SOLID FORM

Using our reference planes as a guide, let's create the overall mass of the fireplace.

1. On the Create tab, on the Forms panel, click the Extrusion tool (see the top of Figure 4.62).

    ⇨ On the Options Bar, in the "Depth" field, type: **9'-0"** [**2750**]. (Be sure to set the Depth and not the Offset—Item 1 in Figure 4.62.)

2. On the Draw panel, for the sketch shape, click the Rectangle icon (see item 2 in Figure 4.62).

    ⇨ Snap to the intersection of two of the reference planes and then snap to an opposite intersection to define the rectangular shape (see items 3 and 4 in Figure 4.62).

    ⇨ Close all four padlocks (see item 5 in Figure 4.62).

140 | Chapter 4

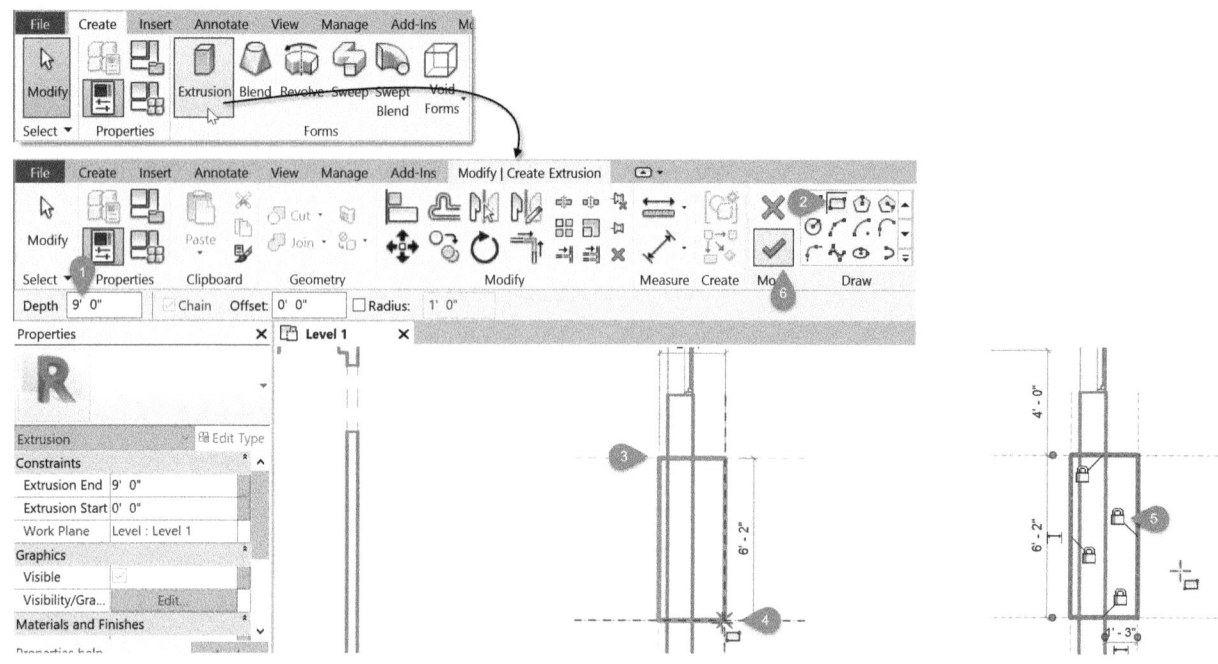

FIGURE 4.62 *Sketch the overall shape of the extrusion*

3. On the Modify | Create Extrusion tab, on the Mode panel, click the Finish button (large green checkmark) (see item 6 in Figure 4.62).

This gives us our basic fireplace mass. We now need to carve out the firebox.

CREATE A VOID FORM

Using the same basic process, we can create a Void form that will carve away from the solid form in our family giving us the firebox opening.

1. On the Create tab, click the Void Forms drop down button and then choose: **Void Extrusion**.

    The Modify | Create Void Extrusion tab will appear with the same Sketch tools as before.

    ⇨ On the Options Bar, in the "Depth" field type: **4'-0"** [**1200**].

2. On the Draw panel, click the Pick Lines icon.

    ⇨ Click the left vertical edge of the solid extrusion (see panel 1 in Figure 4.63).

    A magenta sketch line will appear directly on top of this edge.

3. On the Options Bar, change the Offset value to: **1'-0"** [**300**].

    ⇨ Highlight the right edge of the solid extrusion and move the mouse slightly until the dashed line is within the fireplace structure. When it is, click to create a magenta sketch line (see panel 2 in Figure 4.63).

4. Change the Offset value to: **0** (zero).

    ⇨ On the Draw panel, click the Line icon.

5. Using the temporary dimensions as a guide, click the first point on the left edge a bit down from the top corner and draw it down and to the right at a 20° angle (see panel 3 in Figure 4.63).

    ⇨ Click the Modify tool or press the ESC key twice.

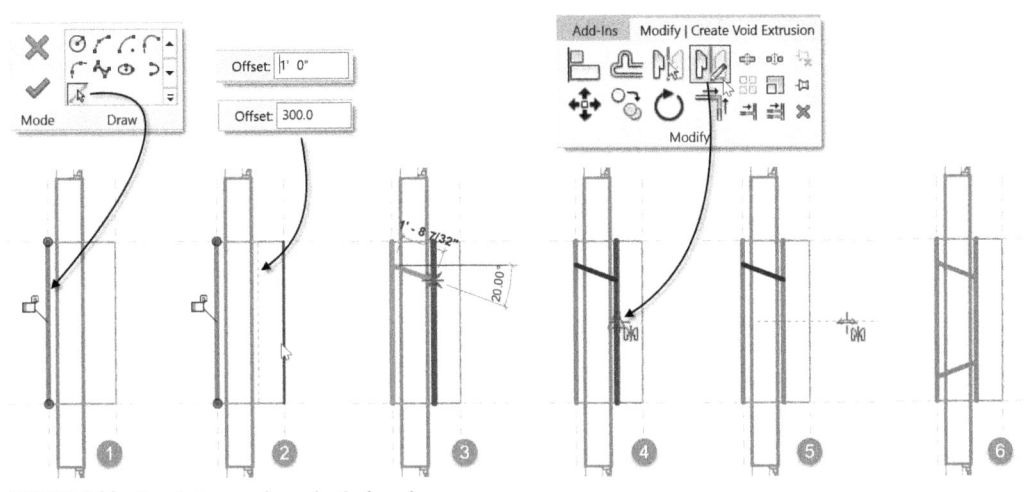

FIGURE 4.63 *Sketch lines to form the firebox shape*

6. Select the 20° line and then on the Modify | Create Void Extrusion tab, click the Mirror Draw Axis tool (or press DM).
   ⇨ Click the midpoint of the vertical sketch line already drawn (see panel 4 in Figure 4.63).
   ⇨ Move the mouse horizontally and click the finish the mirror line (see panel 5 in Figure 4.63).

The result is shown in panel 6. Now we will use the Trim/Extend to Corner tool (the same one we used for walls at the start of the chapter) to clean up the sketch.

7. On the Modify tab, click the Trim/Extend to Corner tool (or Type TR).
   ⇨ Trim all four corners to make an enclosed shape (see Figure 4.64).

> **REMEMBER:** Select the portion of the sketch line that you wish to keep.

8. Click the Modify tool or press the ESC key to finish trimming.

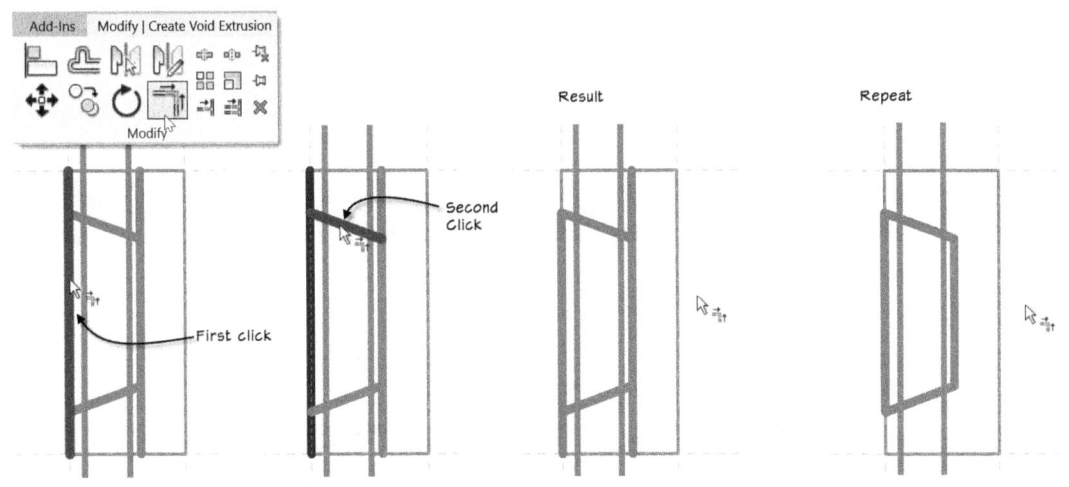

FIGURE 4.64 *Edit the sketch lines to finalize the shape*

9. On the Mode panel, click the Finish Edit Mode button.

While the void is still selected, it will appear solid. However, when you deselect, it will cut away from the previously drawn solid to form the fireplace shape.

10. Click in empty space to deselect the element.
11. On the In-Place Editor panel, click the Finish Model button (big green checkmark).

• Revit Essentials for Architecture •

142 | Chapter 4

This completes the editing of our family and returns us to the project editor mode.

JOIN THE FIREPLACE WITH THE WALL

The Fireplace family is finished but it overlaps the wall. Let's fix this.

1. On the Modify tab, click the Split tool (or type SL).
⇨ On the Options Bar, place a checkmark in the "Delete Inner Segment" check box.
2. Split the exterior vertical wall on both sides of the fireplace (see Figure 4.65).

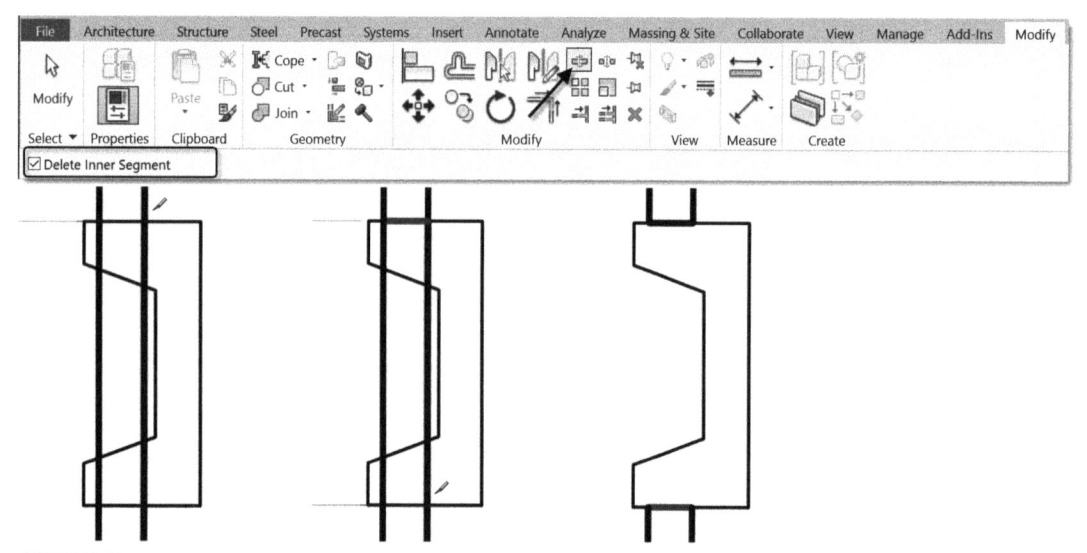

FIGURE 4.65 *Split the exterior wall*

3. Click the Modify tool or press the ESC key twice.

This is close to what we want but let's make one more edit.

4. On the Modify tab, on the Geometry panel, click the Join tool (see the top of Figure 4.65).
⇨ Click one of the exterior walls (the ones we just split).
⇨ Then click the Fireplace to join them (see Figure 4.66).

TIP: Remember to watch the Status Bar for detailed prompts.

5. Repeat for the other wall. Pick the wall then the fireplace.

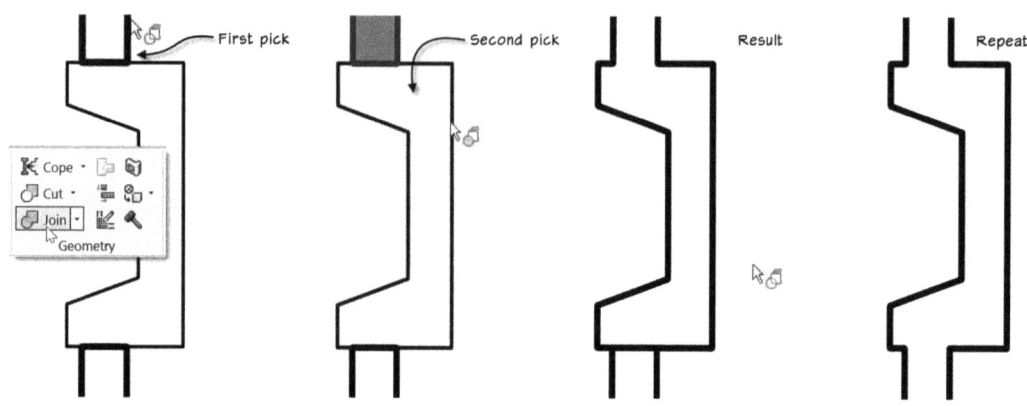

FIGURE 4.66 *Use Join Geometry to join the walls to the Fireplace*

• The Aubin Academy •

Creating a Building Layout | 143

6. Click the Modify tool or press the ESC key twice to cancel the Join command.

7. On the QAT, click the Default 3D view icon.

⇨ Use the techniques covered above and orbit the model around so that you can see the Fireplace.

We modeled the fireplace a bit too short. However, for now we will leave this alone. In later chapters we will address the height of the fireplace as well as how it changes width on the second floor. The fireplace could also use a mantel and a hearth. However, because there will be no new work done in the living room of this project and therefore no sections or elevations are needed of the fireplace, that extra level of detail is unnecessary for this tutorial. What we have created works well for the floor plan. If you wish to try it anyway for the practice, feel free. Select the fireplace, and then on the Modify | Generic Models tab, click the Edit In-Place button. This will return you to the in-place family editor where you can add these accoutrements using additional solids.

RESET THE CURRENT PHASE

Congratulations! Our work on residential project first floor existing conditions layout is complete for now (see Figure 4.67). We still need to add the Stairs to this model. However, Stairs will be covered in a dedicated chapter. Therefore, we will save our layout without the Stairs for now.

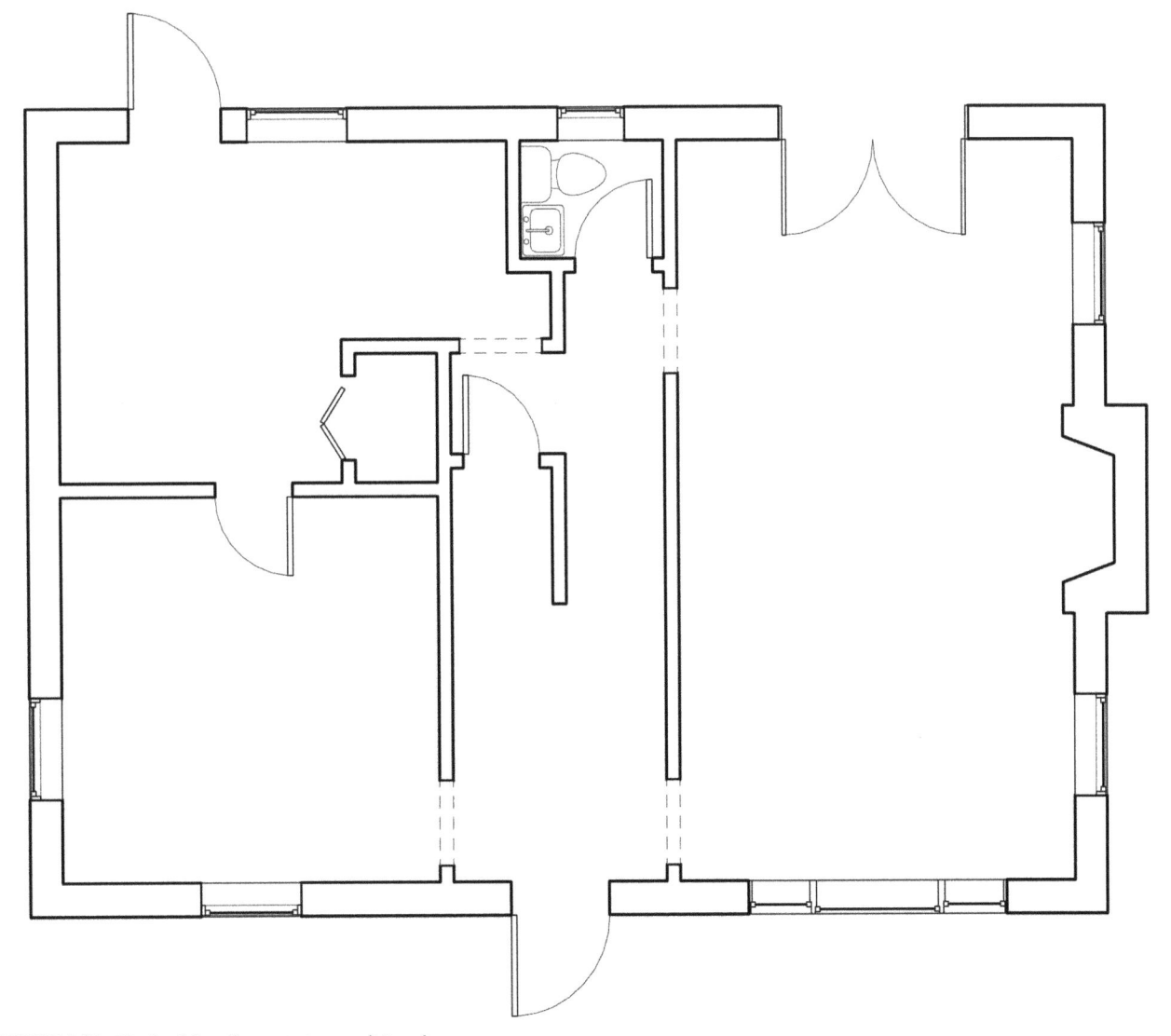

FIGURE 4.67 *The final first floor existing conditions layout*

• Revit Essentials for Architecture •

1. Make sure there are no objects selected. Then on the Properties palette, beneath the Phasing grouping, for "Phase," choose: **New Construction**.

   Verify that "Phase Filter" is set to Show All.

2. Click Apply to see the change.

> **NOTE:** Later in Chapter 7, we will actually duplicate this view and create a permanent Existing Conditions view. For now, we have simply returned the view to its Phase settings at the start of the chapter.

3. Save the project.

SUMMARY

- ☑ To add elements in Revit, choose a tool on the ribbon, choose a type from the Type Selector, set additional options on the Properties palette and Options Bar and then click to add the item in the view window.

- ☑ Walls can be added one segment at a time or chained to draw them end to end.

- ☑ Sketch Walls quickly and then use Temporary Dimensions to fine-tune size and placement precisely.

- ☑ Edit the witness lines of temporary dimensions by clicking or dragging the handles.

- ☑ Permanent dimensions can be used the same as temporary dimensions while the dimensioned elements are selected.

- ☑ Use Trim, Extend, Split, Offset, Move, and Copy to quickly layout a series of Walls.

- ☑ Assign elements to construction Phases to show Existing, Demolition and New Construction.

- ☑ Doors, Windows, and Openings automatically "cut" a hole in, and remain attached to, the receiving host Wall.

- ☑ Add Walls, Doors, and Windows quickly, and modify their properties later.

- ☑ Use temporary and permanent dimensions to fine-tune Door and Window placement.

- ☑ Door, Window, and Component Types can be included with the project template or loaded as needed from library files.

- ☑ Use the component tool to add additional items like plumbing fixtures, furniture, and equipment.

- ☑ It is not always necessary to model all elements three-dimensionally. And even 3D components often incorporate 2D geometry for plan views.

- ☑ View the model interactively in 3D, plan, section, etc. to study and investigate possibilities in the design.

- ☑ Use In-Place Families for unique conditions that must be modeled in context and will not be reused in other projects.

- ☑ Do not use In-Place Families for items that must be reused or placed in several locations or other projects.

- ☑ Edit in any view and see the change immediately in all views.

CHAPTER 5
Setting Up Project Levels and Views

INTRODUCTION

Setting up a new project can involve many steps and some careful decisions. Among the items for consideration are the floor levels, column grids, project settings and, most importantly, the many views your project will require to facilitate editing, querying and publishing project data. The most common use of views is to display your model graphically on screen. However, views are not just for display; views are also used to create and edit data and graphics in the building model. Each task you perform in your building model will occur in one or more views. This means that having the right views in place early in the project will make the entire team's job easier. Equally important is setting up the floor levels in your building. Each significant horizontal datum in the building will be represented by a level in Autodesk® Revit®. Usually you will have a level for each actual building level, but in some cases, there will be additional ones for other important conditions like "top of steel," or "top of footing."

OBJECTIVES

In this chapter, we will explore project templates, levels and views. We will explore many of the out-of-the-box project templates provided with the software. Following this exploration, we will begin our commercial project. We'll add the required floor levels and we'll add some simple geometry to the project for basic context and proceed to explore the many different types of views available in Revit. After completing this chapter, you will know how to:

- Open and explore several project templates
- Create a new project from a template
- Create levels
- Set up preliminary views
- Understand switching between and working with views
- Work with sheet views
- Print a digital cartoon set

> **BIM Manager Note:** There are many other aspects to successful project setup such as column grids, object style settings, project units, project parameters, shared parameters, location of project families and libraries, and worksharing setup. While it is possible to set up all such items before project work begins, in many cases changes to project setup occur as needed in the project timeline. To simulate this reality, basic setup tasks will be performed here with many other related topics being discussed in later chapters.

USING PROJECT TEMPLATES

When you create a new project, the software does not presume to know the type of building you wish to create, how many levels or the kinds of views you intend to use to view and edit it. Every project must have at least one level, and some basic views are common to nearly all projects like floor plans and elevations, but mostly you must create the specific levels and views you need in your projects. To save time and ensure consistency from one project to the next, project templates are available when creating new projects. A project template is simply a Revit project that has been preconfigured to contain the most common and useful views, families, settings (and even levels) required to start a new project. Revit ships with several sample project templates, and you can customize and save your own templates based upon your preferred standards. A project template will help get you started, but since each project is unique, a certain degree of setup is always required. Exploration of common tasks required during project setup is the primary topic of this chapter.

Project template files provide a means to quickly apply project setup information, enforce company standards and project-specific settings and save time. Keep in mind however that template files apply only at the time of project creation and do not remain linked to the template. (It is however possible to "transfer project standards" from one project to another later, as required). A project template is simply a project file preconfigured for a type of building or task that has been saved in the template format. Template files have an RTE extension and are available when you create a new project model file. In addition to the time saved when creating projects, templates help to ensure file consistency and office standards by giving all projects the same starting point. Several pre-made template files are available with the product and are ready to use. However, because office standards and project-specific needs vary, many firms customize default templates to better suit their needs.

> **NOTE:** Templates used in this book include those typically installed in the United States. When you install Revit, you are given the option to install several other templates and content files appropriate to other parts of the world. The exact items you have available may therefore vary from those shown here. If you do not see the default templates (or content items) in your installation, you can go to the Insert tab and click the "Get Autodesk Content" button to download the default templates and libraries.

> **BIM Manager Note:** Revit saves all project data within the project file. This includes families, settings, levels and views. Therefore, template files provide an excellent tool for promoting and maintaining office standards. Frequently used families, title blocks, and other resources can be stored in the template. Less frequently used items can be stored in separate "library" or "warehouse" files on the office network. Loading items on demand when needed can help keep the template file size smaller. While the specific settings and content contained in a template vary from firm to firm, the goal is to include those items that are most frequently needed by most projects.

The best way to demonstrate the importance of using project templates and understand what is included with the software is to create some test projects using some of the provided templates.

Setting Up Project Levels and Views | 149

CREATE A NEW PROJECT WITH THE DEFAULT TEMPLATE

Let's create a new project using the default template (the same one we used in the previous chapter) and explore some of its settings.

1. Launch Autodesk® Revit®.
2. On the Home screen, beneath Projects, click the New button.

The "New Project" dialog includes a drop down list containing the most used project templates. For example, in the default US Imperial installation, the list will include the "Architectural Template" and the "Construction Template" In imperial and metric units. The item labeled "Imperial-Architectural Template" is the standard *default.rte* Revit template file. You can use this choice by simply clicking OK in the dialog. To verify that you have the correct file, or to choose an alternate one, click the Browse button.

⇨ If Imperial-Architectural Template is not listed, click the Browse button. The default template file name and location for the US installation is: (Paths may vary slightly for other regions and previous versions of Windows).

C:\ProgramData\Autodesk\RVT 2021\Templates\English-Imperial\default.rte

C:\ProgramData\Autodesk\RVT 2021\Templates\English\DefaultMetric.rte

3. From this location select the *default.rte* [*DefaultMetric.rte*] template file and then click Open (see Figure 5.1).

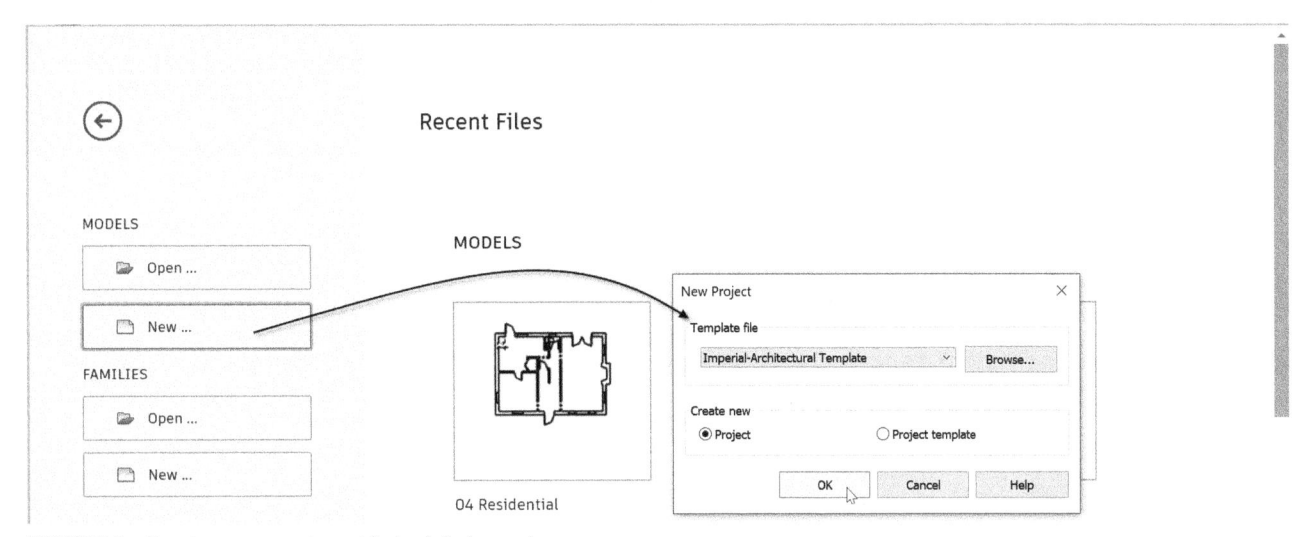

FIGURE 5.1 *Creating a new project with the default template*

> **NOTE:** If your version of Revit does not include the template files cited here, they have been provided with the dataset files. Please browse to the *Templates* folder in the location where you installed the dataset files to locate them.

4. In the "Create New" area, verify that Project is selected and then click OK.

The imperial and metric templates are very similar in composition. Other than units, the only obvious difference is in the shape of the building elevation tags. The imperial file uses a square elevation tag, while the metric template uses a round tag by default (see Figure 5.2).

FIGURE 5.2 *The shape of the Elevation tag varies in the North American and non–North American templates*

• Revit Essentials for Architecture •

> **BIM Manager Note:** You can customize the look of the elevation tags if you wish. To learn more, see the "Loading Custom Elevation Tags" topic on page 173 below or the "Creating Custom Elevation Tags" topic on page 485 in Chapter 11.

Elevation tags are an obvious on-screen difference between the metric and imperial templates. There are some other minor differences as well, but despite these minor differences, the "default" imperial and metric templates are virtually the same. They contain the same starter levels and views. They have the same basic families preloaded, and the other settings are similar but with unit-specific or regional vernacular differences (like "Cast-in-Place" vs. "Cast In Situ," for the concrete materials in the "Material Browser").

5. On the Manage tab, on the Settings panel, click the: Project Units button (or press UN).
   ⇨ Explore the various settings without making any permanent changes.
   ⇨ Click Cancel when finished.

> **BIM Manager Note:** Imperial Units in Revit use feet as the primary unit by default. (Refer to the "Unit Conventions" topic on page 63 in Chapter 3 for more information.) This means that numbers typed without unit designations will be interpreted as feet. If you have experience with AutoCAD, this will take some getting used to as the default unit in AutoCAD is the inch. Using the Project Units command discussed here, you could conceivably change the default of your project template to inches rather than feet. However, on-screen temporary dimensions would display in inches only (no feet). Further, you will also need to adjust the settings of your dimension types if you want them to display both feet and inches. Feel free to experiment with such changes if you wish; realize, however, that a complete emulation of the AutoCAD behavior will be somewhat elusive. Instead, be **patient** as you get used to the "new" default.

6. On the Project Browser, beneath *Views (all)*, examine the contents of: *Floor Plans*, *Ceiling Plans*, and *Elevations (Building Elevation)*.

   There will be three Floor Plan views: *Level 1*, *Level 2*, and *Site*.

   There will be two Ceiling Plan views: *Level 1* and *Level 2*.

   And beneath *Elevations*, there are four elevation views: *East*, *North*, *South*, and *West* (see Figure 5.3).

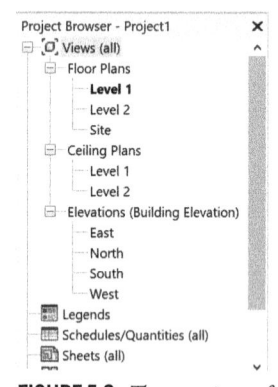

FIGURE 5.3 *There are just a few pre-made plan and elevation views*

7. On the Architecture tab of the ribbon, on the Build panel, click the Wall tool.

> **NOTE:** You need only click the top half of the Wall button to execute the default Wall command. If you click the lower half, you will get a drop down menu from which you will have to choose: **Wall: Architectural**. This is the same command either way, it is just a little quicker to click the top half of the button to avoid the menu. Please refer back to the "Tools" topic on page 71 in Chapter 3 for more information on the kinds of buttons.

Setting Up Project Levels and Views | 151

⇨   On the Properties palette, open the Type Selector.

There will be several wall types available in the project (see Figure 5.4).

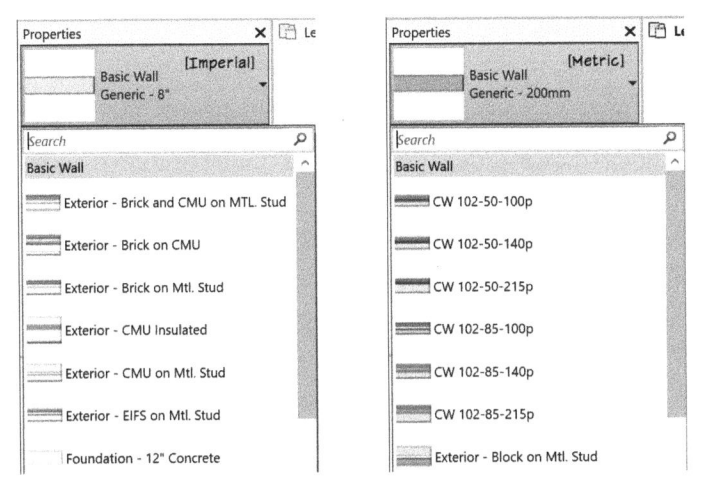

FIGURE 5.4 *Several wall types are present in the project*

> **NOTE:** The list varies slightly between imperial and metric, but as noted above the two lists are largely comparable.

8.   Select any type and draw a short horizontal segment of wall in the middle of the screen.

⇨   On the ribbon, click the Modify tool or press ESC twice.

Section, elevation and level heads are loaded in the project (however, these may vary slightly in imperial and metric).

9.   On the View tab, on the Create panel, click the Section tool.

⇨   Click a point anywhere onscreen below the wall you just drew and then move the mouse in a straight line and click again above the wall (see the left side of Figure 5.5).

Notice the Section Head and the Section Tail that appear.

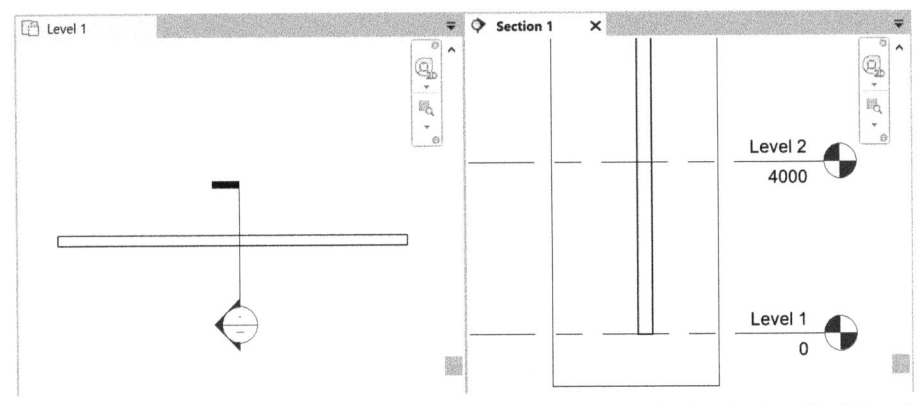

FIGURE 5.5 *Section lines are preconfigured in the template with a section head and tail and levels have level heads*

10.   On the Project Browser, expand: *Sections (Building Section)* and then double-click: *Section 1*.

Take note of the level heads to the right (see the right side of Figure 5.5).

Many other settings can be explored if you wish. If you are interested in building a custom template for your office, you may also like to explore the *Families* branch of the Project Browser and most of the commands on the Settings panel of the Manage tab. Pay particular attention to the Additional Settings drop down and its many settings.

• Revit Essentials for Architecture •

152 | Chapter 5

11. From the File menu, choose: **Close**.
12. When prompted to save changes, click No.

THE CONSTRUCTION TEMPLATE

Let's repeat the exploration process in the provided construction project template.

1. If you are back on the Home screen, click the New button under models.
   Otherwise, from the File menu, choose: **New** > **Project**.

   ⇨ In the "New Project" dialog, in the "Template file" area, choose: Imperial-**Construction Template** [**Metric-Construction Template**] from the drop down list.

   If the Construction template is not shown on the drop down list, the click the Browse button. The dialog should open directly to your default template folder as before. If it does not, browse to the template location listed at the start of the tutorial above. For your convenience, a copy of this template is also provided with the book's dataset files in the *Templates* folder. Select the *Construction-Default.rte* [*Construction-DefaultMetric.rte*] template file and then click Open.

   ⇨ In the "Create New" area, verify that Project is selected and then click OK.

The first thing you should notice about this template is that there are many more views in the Project Browser; particularly beneath the *Schedules/Quantities* branch (see Figure 5.6).

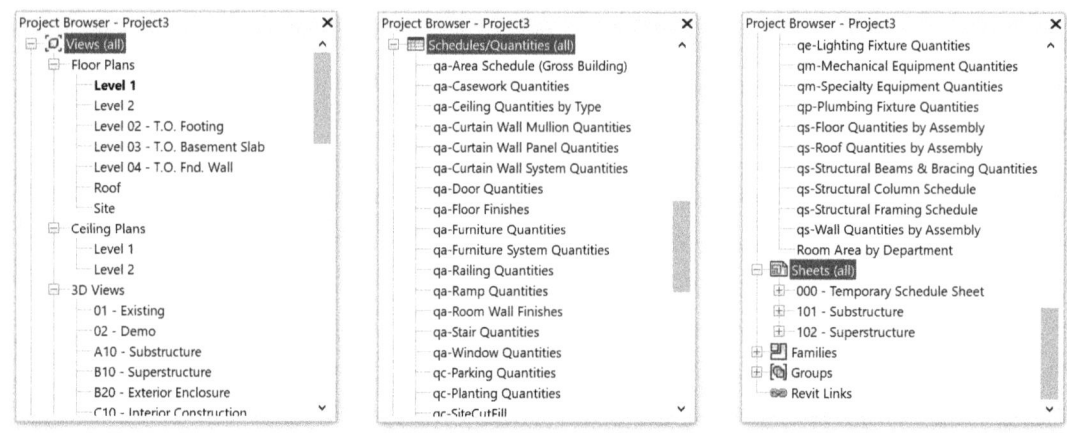

FIGURE 5.6 *The Construction template is preloaded with dozens of schedules and views*

Spend some time in this template exploring the floor plan, ceiling plan, and elevation views like we did above. The same four elevation views are provided here. There are a few additional floor plan views, however, and if you open one of the elevation views, you will notice that there are levels defined for the foundation and footing. The most significant addition to this template, which was not included in the *Default* template, is the inclusion of dozens of schedule views. As you can see from the names of these schedules (which vary between the imperial and metric units versions), you can determine quantities for nearly every element in the project.

2. On the Project Browser, double-click the floor plan View: *Level 1* to make it active.
3. Create a wall anywhere on the screen. Click Modify or press ESC twice when done.
4. On the Project Browser, double-click the: *qs-Wall Quantities by Assembly* [*Wall Quantities by Assembly*] Schedule view to open it (see Figure 5.7).

Setting Up Project Levels and Views | 153

A	B	C	D	E	F	G	H	I	J
Assembly Code	Assembly Description	Wall Assembly	Calculated To Butt-End Dimensions Area	Volume	Length - Center To Center	Width	Wall Type	Description	Comments
B2010	Exterior Walls	Exterior - Brick and CMU on Mtl. Stud	310.00	348.33	31' - 0"	1.16			
Grand total: 1			310.00	348.33					

FIGURE 5.7 *Schedules will populate automatically as elements are added to the model*

Take a little time exploring these schedules now if you like. Add a few more walls or some doors and then open some of the schedules to see how they update. Schedules will be covered in detail in later chapters. The exact list and names of schedules in the imperial and metric templates vary. Therefore, despite your unit preference, you may wish to open both templates and look at each of them.

5. On the Project Browser, expand: *Elevations (Building Elevation)* and then double-click: *East*.

6. Zoom in on the level heads to the right (see Figure 5.8).

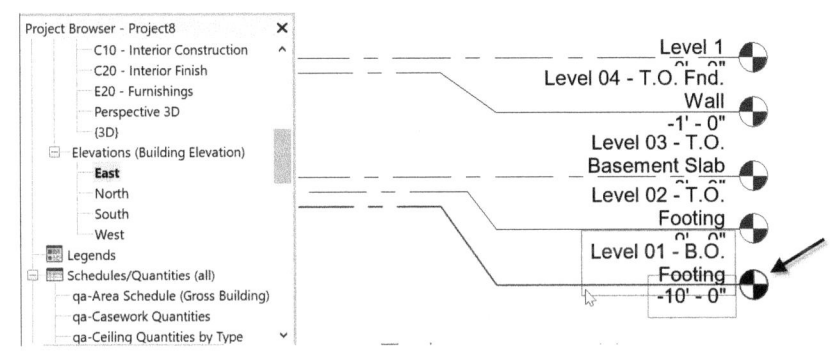

FIGURE 5.8 *Blue level heads indicate an associated floor plan view while black level heads have no plan views*

If you compare the list of floor plan views in the Project Browser with the level heads in the elevation, you will notice that there is no "B.O. Footing" floor plan. Further, the B.O. Footing level head is colored black rather than blue like the others. The color blue on screen indicates interactivity. We have seen this in previous chapters with the temporary dimensions and section heads. Here, when you see a tag like the level heads colored blue, it is also interactive. Double-click on the level head to open the associated floor plan view. Think of it like a hyperlink in a web browser. The same behavior is true with elevation tags and section tags. If the symbol is black, (like the B.O. Footing level here) it means that it is just annotation and there is no associated view.

7. From the File menu, choose: **Close** (or press CTRL + W).

8. When prompted to save changes, click No.

OTHER TEMPLATES

The imperial content contains a *Commercial-Default.rte* and a *Residential-Default.rte* template as well. You can create a project from each of these and explore them the same way. The United States installation also contains some Canadian variations in the *Metric* folder. Even if you do not have imperial templates installed, you can find copies of these templates with the files installed from the dataset files in the *Templates* folder. Revit is available in many languages and regions throughout the world. You may have access to templates not mentioned here depending on your specific version of Revit.

STARTING A PROJECT WITHOUT A TEMPLATE (NOT RECOMMENDED)

After exploring several of the provided templates in the exercise above, you should be getting a sense of the variety of settings and elements that reside in a typical template. If you start a project without one, you are forced to either configure/create all these items on your own manually as needed or import them from other projects or libraries. While it is possible to do this, the amount of extra work that it adds to your project makes it an ill-advised approach to creating a new project.

CREATE YOUR OWN TEMPLATE

Hopefully, you are beginning to see the benefits to starting new projects with a template. There is no compelling reason to begin projects any other way. As you work through the exercises in the coming chapters, you will certainly discover areas where the default templates could be enhanced and improved. Make note of these observations as you go. When you are ready, try your hand at creating your own template file. The basic steps are simple:

1. From the File menu, choose: **New** > **Project**.
    ⇨ Load the existing template that is most like the one you wish to create.
    ⇨ Choose the "Project Template" option in the "New Project" dialog.
2. Edit any settings as you see fit. (Change Settings, add or delete views, load or delete families, etc.)
3. Add, edit, or delete Materials. (Note that every piece of content loaded into a project will bring along its materials in the future, settings in a template are only a starting point).
4. Configure settings on the Manage tab such as units, fill patterns, line styles, objects styles, etc.
5. Also configure the settings from the Additional Settings pop-up menu.
6. When finished configuring, choose: **Save As** > **Template** from the File menu.
    ⇨ From the "Save as type" list, verify that Template Files (*.*rte*) is selected.
7. Be sure to browse to your preferred *Template* folder, type a name for your new template and then click the Save button.

> **BIM Manager Note:** Once you have a standard template in place, it is imperative that all users be required to use it. In some cases, a project will have special needs not addressed by this office standard template. In such cases, project-based derivatives can be created. If you want to learn more about creating templates, visit: linkedin-learning.pxf.io/Aubin and look for the four-part series called: **Revit Templates**. Part one is: Annotation, followed by System Settings, then Views and Sheets and finally Content[§].

SETTING UP A COMMERCIAL PROJECT

Now that we have seen some of the features and benefits of creating projects from templates, let's create an actual project that we will follow (as well as the one started in the last chapter) throughout the remainder of the book. This project is a 30,000 SF [2,800 SM] small commercial office building. The project is mostly core and shell with some build-out occurring on one of the tenant floors. The tutorials that follow walk through the startup of the commercial project and the setup of several views including: plans, elevations, sections, and schedules. At the end of the chapter, we will generate sheet views and print a cartoon set. The completed files for the project are available with the dataset files in the *Chapter05\Complete* folder.

Getting started with the commercial project gives us a nice practical exercise to further the goals of this chapter: namely, the understanding of project templates, levels, and views. Even though we have explored many templates

Setting Up Project Levels and Views | 155

thus far, we'll use the default template for this project. This is because the default template gives a common starting point in both imperial and metric units. We will adjust the project levels to suit the needs of our commercial building and then begin creating views that we will need. In some cases, we will create these items ourselves, and in others we will borrow them from additional templates as appropriate.

It is a good idea to take the opportunity early in the project cycle to develop a digital "cartoon set." Like a traditional paper-based cartoon set, a digital one is simply a collection of preliminary sheets that will allow you to assess the quantity and composition of each of the drawings, schedules, and other deliverables required in the final document package. This will assist the team in allocating resources to the project. Remember, like everything else in Revit, the cartoon set will evolve and update automatically as the project progresses. The goal at this early stage is to assist with planning and gain a jump-start on production.

WORKING WITH LEVELS

Before we start our commercial project, close all files that you currently have open (from the File menu choose: Close or press CTRL + W). If it is easier, you can exit Revit, choose not to save when prompted, and then launch a fresh session. In either case, be sure that all files are closed before proceeding. (You do not need to save anything from the previous exercises).

ADDING AND MODIFYING LEVELS

1. From the Home screen, click the new button, select the Imperial-Architectural Template [Metric-Architectural Template] and then click OK.

    If you don't have the Architectural Template option, recall from above that this is simply the *default.rte* [*DefaultMetric.rte*] template file. If you are in a country for which your version of Revit does not include these template files, they have both been provided with the dataset files in the *Template* folder.

By now we have started a few projects this way, and the familiar *Level 1*, *Level 2*, and *Site* plan views will show on the Project Browser. As our first task in our new commercial project, let's modify and add to the project levels.

A level is a horizontal datum element used to represent each of the actual floor levels or other significant reference heights in the building. Levels are used to organize projects vertically, in the "Z" axis. Typically, you will add a level for each story of the building ("First Floor," "Second Floor," "Roof" etc.) In addition, levels can also be used to define other meaningful horizontal planes such as the "Top of Structure" or the "Top of Footing." We saw examples of this in several of the sample templates. For our commercial project, we need four stories, a roof, and a grade level.

Look at the Architecture tab of the ribbon. Notice that the level tool is grayed out. This is because the currently active view: *Level 1*, is a floor plan view. You cannot add or edit levels in a floor plan view (see the left side of Figure 5.9). To do so, you must switch to an elevation, section or 3D view.

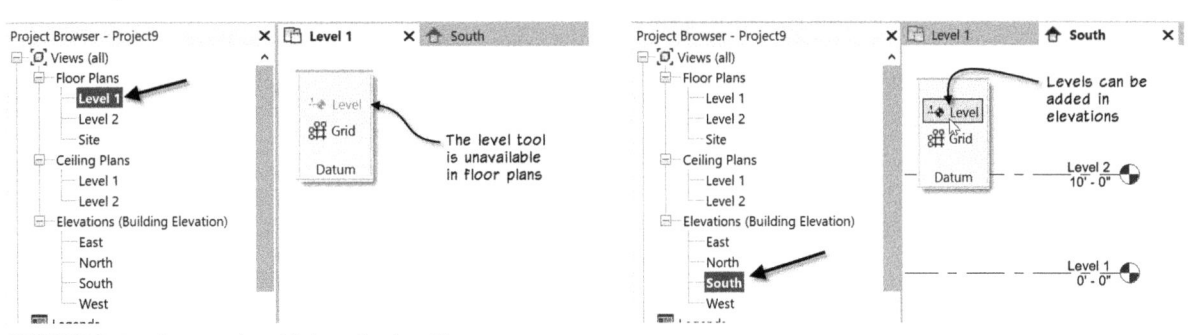

FIGURE 5.9 *Levels cannot be added or edited in Plan views*

2. On the Project Browser, expand *Elevations (Building Elevation)* and then

• Revit Essentials for Architecture •

156 | Chapter 5

double-click: *South* (see the right side of Figure 5.9).

In this view, you can see two existing levels: Level 1 and Level 2.

> **NOTE:** Notice that even though there is a "Site" Floor Plan view in the Project Browser, there is not a "Site" level. The *Site* view is actually associated to: Level 1. In other words, there can be multiple plan views associated with the same level. In addition, as we saw above, you can also have levels that have no associated plan views. We will explore these concepts further below.

3. Zoom in on the level heads at the right side of the screen so that you can see them clearly.

Most elements in Revit will show a tool tip when you pass the mouse over them. Please note that you can change the behavior of these tips in the "Options" dialog from the File menu.

⇨ Move your pointer over the level line to see a tool tip.

⇨ Move your pointer over the level head to see a different tip (see Figure 5.10).

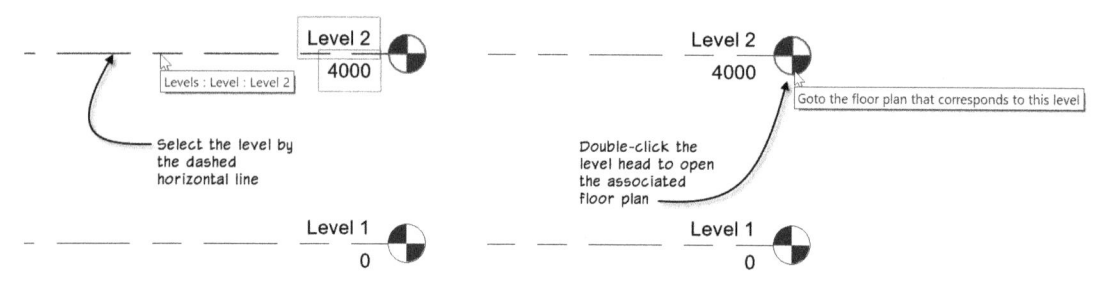

FIGURE 5.10 *Tool tips appear when you highlight elements onscreen*

To select the level, click the dashed level line as shown on the left side of Figure 5.10. To open the associated floor plan view for the level, double-click the blue level head (or right-click and choose: **Go to Floor Plan**) as shown on the right side. If the level head is black, that means that there is no associated view (seen with the construction template above). The level by itself is a datum for documentation and modeling purposes only and should not be confused with the actual plan view, which is one of many ways to view and interact with your Revit model. Levels typically have associated floor plan views, but it is not required that they do so. On the other hand, floor plans *must* be associated to a level. This association cannot be changed! So new levels must always be created from the Level tool or by copying existing levels. Duplicating a floor plan does *not* create a new level!

4. Select Level 2 (click the dashed line, not the level head symbol or the text).

When you select the level, it will highlight in light blue (indicates that it is selected) and several additional drag controls and handles appear. As you move your pointer over each one (don't click them yet; simply hover the pointer over each one), the handle will temporarily highlight and the tool tip will appear (see Figure 5.11).

Moving left to right and top to bottom in Figure 5.11, the following briefly describes each control.

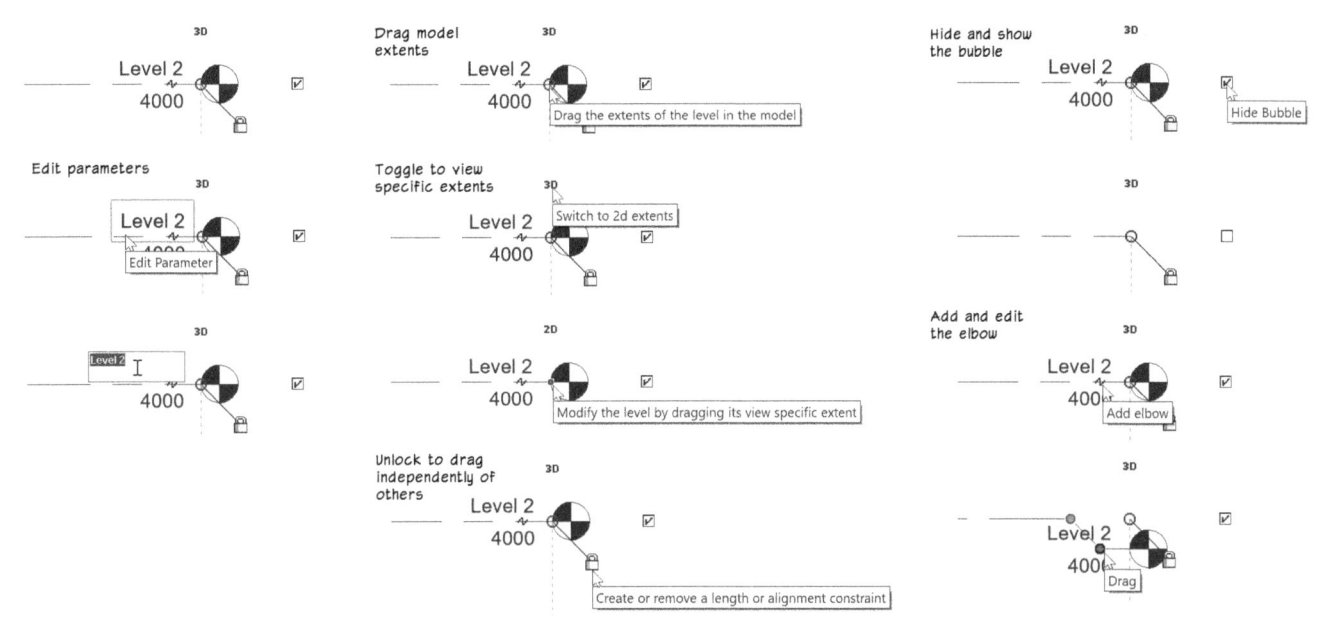

FIGURE 5.11 *Levels have many control handles and drag points*

Edit Parameter—Click the blue text to rename the level or edit its height. If you rename a level, you will be prompted to also rename associated plan views. You can accept or reject this suggestion. This means that the level and its associated views can have different names if you wish.

> **BIM Manager Note:** The height is measured from an "Elevation Base," which is a type parameter of the level system family. The Elevation Base is the zero point from which the level heights are measured. The Elevation Base can be either "Project" or "Shared." With Elevation Base set to Project, the values will be relative to the origin of the project (Level 1 is at zero in the default template). If you choose the "Shared" Elevation Base, values will report relative to a shared origin (in the shared coordinate system). This could be the height at Sea Level or some other appropriate datum height. You can find more information on this topic in the on-line help, and shared coordinates are covered later in Chapter 7.

Modify the Level Drag Control—This round handle is used to drag the extent of the level. If the length or alignment constraint parameter is also active, dragging one level will affect the extent of the other constrained levels as well. Levels are constrained to one another by default.

2D/3D Extents Control—When 3D Extents are enabled, editing the extent of the level line literally changes the size of the datum plane representing the level and affects all other section and elevation views parallel to the current one. If you toggle this to 2D Extents, dragging the extent of the level line affects the graphical representation in the current view only. The open circle changes to a small view specific extent dot control.

Length and Alignment Constraint—This padlock icon is used to constrain the length and extents of one level line to the others nearby. This is useful to keep all your level lines lined up with one another.

Hide/Show Bubble—Use this check box control to hide or show the level head bubble at either end of the level line. This control toggles from hide to show.

Add Elbow—This small "squiggle-shaped" handle creates an elbow in the level line. This is useful when the annotation of two level heads overlap one another in a view. Click this handle to create the elbow, and then drag the resultant drag handles to your liking. This is a graphical effect in the view only. The level datum height is unchanged.

5. Click anywhere next to the level (where there are no objects) to deselect it (or press the ESC key).

158 | Chapter 5

6. On the ribbon, click the Architecture tab and then click the Level tool (on the Datum panel).

⇨ Zoom out so that you can see the entire length of the levels.

⇨ Move the cursor above the left ends of the existing levels.

A temporary dimension will appear with an alignment vector above the top level.

7. When the temporary dimension reads: 12'-0" [3600], click the mouse to set the first point (see the left side of Figure 5.12).

⇨ Move the pointer over to the right side; when an alignment vector appears above the existing level heads, click to set the other point (see the right side of Figure 5.12).

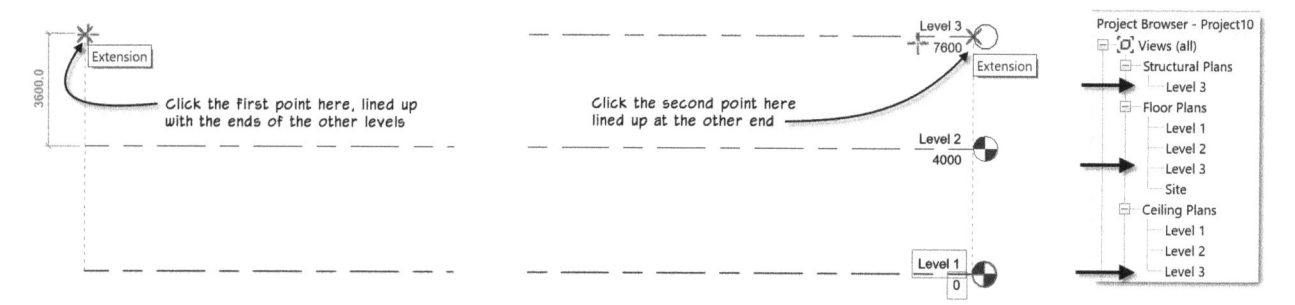

FIGURE 5.12 *Add a level aligned with the existing ones*

TIP: Remember, you can zoom in to change the temporary dimension snap increment if necessary. Also, you can simply type the value that you wish while the temporary dimension is active and then press ENTER to apply it. Finally, like other tools that we have already seen, you can place the level at any dimension and then edit the value of the temporary dimension later to the desired value.

A new level is added. You will also get three new plan views: a *Level 3* floor plan view, a *Level 3* Structural Plan view and a *Level 3* ceiling plan view. If you have Revit LT, you will not get a structural plan (see the right side of Figure 5.12). To control whether adding a new level also creates new plan views, use the "Make Plan view" check box on the Options Bar. Furthermore, if you click the "Plan View Types" button, you can control which type of plan view(s) are created. As noted, in the full version of Revit, a floor plan, a structural plan, and a ceiling plan view are created. We don't need the structural plans, but we can delete it later. Notice also that the "Length and Alignment" constraint is also automatically applied as you add levels if you snap lined up with the ends.

• The Aubin Academy •

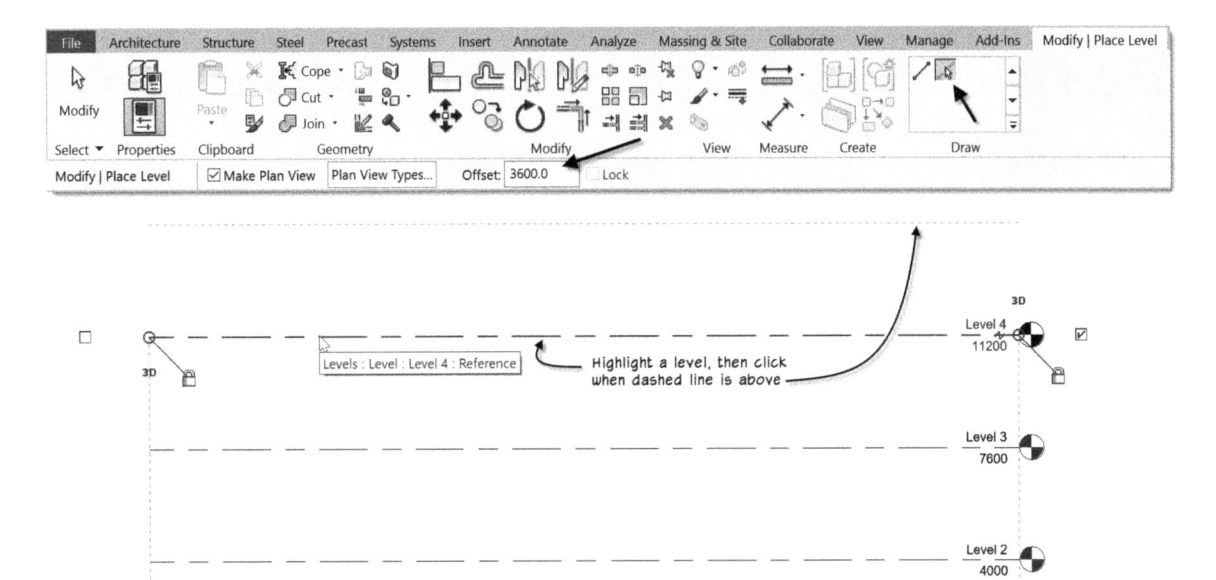

FIGURE 5.13 *As you add new levels, by default new floor plan and ceiling views are created*

The level command should still be active. If you canceled it, click the Level tool on the ribbon to restart it.

8. On the Modify | Place Level tab of the ribbon, on the Draw panel, click the Pick Lines icon.

   ⇨ On the Options Bar, in the Offset field, type: **12'-0"** [**3600**].

   ⇨ Place your mouse pointer over the Level 3 line, and when the dashed offset line appears above, click to create a new Level 4.

9. Repeat once more to create an additional level above Level 4 (shown in Figure 5.13).

You should now have five levels. Our project already has a *Site* plan view. But if you edit its properties, you will see that the associated level is Level 1. There is nothing wrong with that approach, but in our project, we need Level 1 to be raised above the grade level a few feet. Even if this weren't the case, it is sometimes preferable to have dedicated level for the site plan regardless. To do this, we must first delete the existing site plan view and recreate it with a new level. It is not possible to change the associated level of a plan after it is created.

10. On the Project Browser, right-click the *Site* floor plan and choose: **Delete**.

    ⇨ On the ribbon, on the Architecture tab, click the Level tool.

11. On the Options Bar, click the Plan View Types button.

    ⇨ Click on Ceiling Plan and then Structural Plan to deselect them (leave only Floor Plan highlighted) and then click OK.

12. On the Draw panel, click the Pick Lines icon and then in the Offset field on the Options Bar, input: **3'-0"** [**900**].

    ⇨ Offset a level beneath Level 1 (see Figure 5.14).

    ⇨ On the ribbon, click the Modify tool or press the ESC key twice.

160 | Chapter 5

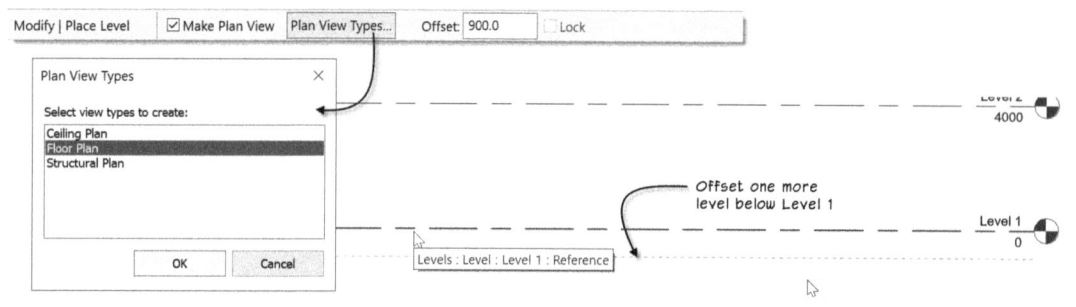

FIGURE 5.14 *Add the final level below Level 1 with only an associated floor plan view*

Note that a new "Level 6" has appeared in only the *Floor Plans* branch of the Project Browser.

> **TIP:** If you forget to click on the Plan View Types button, you can always delete the unwanted view(s) later.

> **BIM MANAGER NOTE:** You can create your levels and plan views at the same time as we did here. You can also remove the option to create plan views completely when new levels are added. You may choose to do this to create datum views to demarcate Top of Steel, Top of Plate, or Bottom of Footing, etc. New plan views can be created and associated to any existing levels at any time. To add a view to an existing level, on the View tab, click the Plan Views drop down and choose: **Floor Plan**. By default, Revit selects the "Do not duplicate existing views" option in the "New Plan" dialog. To create another floor or ceiling plan on a level that already has one, clear this check box. Select the level where you wish to add a plan and select an appropriate scale before clicking OK. If you are creating a duplicate plan, you can also right-click an existing view at any time in the Project Browser and duplicate it directly.

RENAMING LEVELS

We can accept the default level names as they appear, or we can change them to something more suitable for our specific project. The names of levels can be anything that makes sense to the project team typically carrying a name that everyone expects to see in elevation/section documentation. Levels in the model will appear in their correct physical locations; however, in the Project Browser, by default they will sort alphabetically. On larger projects with many levels, it might make sense to use a naming scheme with a numerical prefix such as 01 Level, 02 Level, etc. (In projects with more than 10 stories, you should consider placing a leading zero in the level names so that Level 10 does not inadvertently sort before Level 1). We'll just rename the top and bottom levels in this project to something a bit more descriptive.

> **TIP:** Browser Organization controls which views are shown in the Project Browser and how they are organized. It is possible to modify the default organization to make the plans sort by associated level height instead of alphabetical. An example of customizing the Browser Organization is presented below in the "Working with Browser Organization" topic on page 198.

1. Select Level 5 (the one at the top).

   ⇨ Click on the blue text of the name to edit it. Type: **Roof** for the new name and then press ENTER.

   A dialog will appear asking you if you like to rename the corresponding plan views.

   ⇨ Click Yes to accept the change (see Figure 5.15).

• The Aubin Academy •

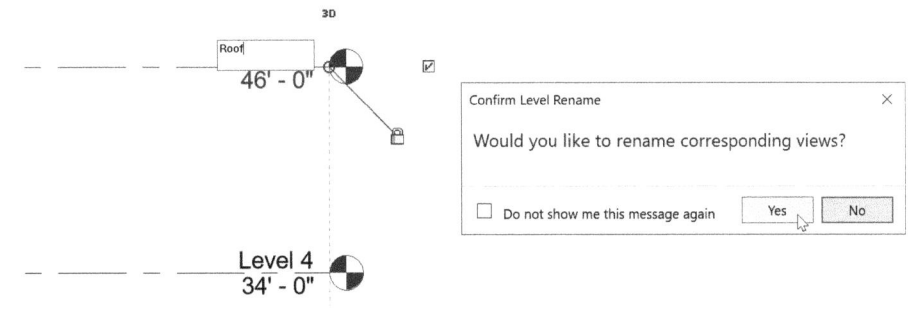

FIGURE 5.15 *Rename the top level to Roof and accept the renaming of corresponding views*

When you choose "Yes" in this dialog, the two associated plan views, *Level 5* floor plan and *Level 5* ceiling plan, become "Roof." Since we don't really need a ceiling plan for the roof, however, let's delete this view.

   2.   On the Project Browser, right-click the *Roof* ceiling plan view and choose: **Delete**.

Notice that on the Project Browser, there is a *Structural Plans* category. If you expand this, you will notice that it contains three plans: *Level 3*, *Level 4*, and *Roof*. These were created when we made the new levels. The Roof structural plan was renamed along with the other plans when we answered "Yes" above. We do not need the structural plans currently. In a future chapter we will set up a separate file for the structural and will add the necessary views at that time. For now, we will simply delete these.

   3.   Select *Level 3* structural plan, hold down the SHIFT key and select the
        Roof structural plan and then press the DELETE key.

        Notice that the *Structural Plans* category disappears when the last view is deleted.

   4.   Select *Level 6* (the one at the bottom). Rename it to: **Street Level**.

   ⇨   In the dialog that appears, answer No this time.

You are not required to name levels and the views the same. In this example, we will find it useful to call out the level on the elevations and sections as "Street Level," but the floor plan associated to this level will be our site plan. Therefore, in this case, it is better to name the level and the plan view separately.

   5.   On the Project Browser, beneath *Floor Plans*, right-click *Level 6* and choose: **Rename**.

   ⇨   Name the view: **Site** and then click OK.

   6.   In the elevation view on screen, double-click the level head symbol for Street Level.

Notice that this opens the *Site* view. So, while the names are no longer the same, they are still linked to one another.

APPLY A VIEW TEMPLATE

When you create a view, certain defaults are automatically applied to it like display settings and scale, for example. Typically, a site plan is drawn at a scale smaller than the default 1/8"=1'-0" [1:100] used here. Further, there are certain object categories that typically do not display on site plans and other less obvious settings as well. While we could manually configure all the various settings needed to make this view a more suitable site plan, we can do this more efficiently by applying a view template. A view template is simply a collection of saved view settings that can be applied to a view in one step. Many view templates are included in the project file already, and you can make your own as well.

   1.   On the Project Browser, double-click on *Site* to open it.

        Take notice of the elevation markers, and the space in the middle between them.

162 | Chapter 5

2. On the Properties palette, make sure that the filter drop down at the top reads "Floor Plan: Site."

⇨ Beneath the Identity Data grouping, click the button next to the View Template setting (currently labeled: <None>).

⇨ In the "Apply View Template" dialog, select Site Plan from the list and then click OK (see Figure 5.16).

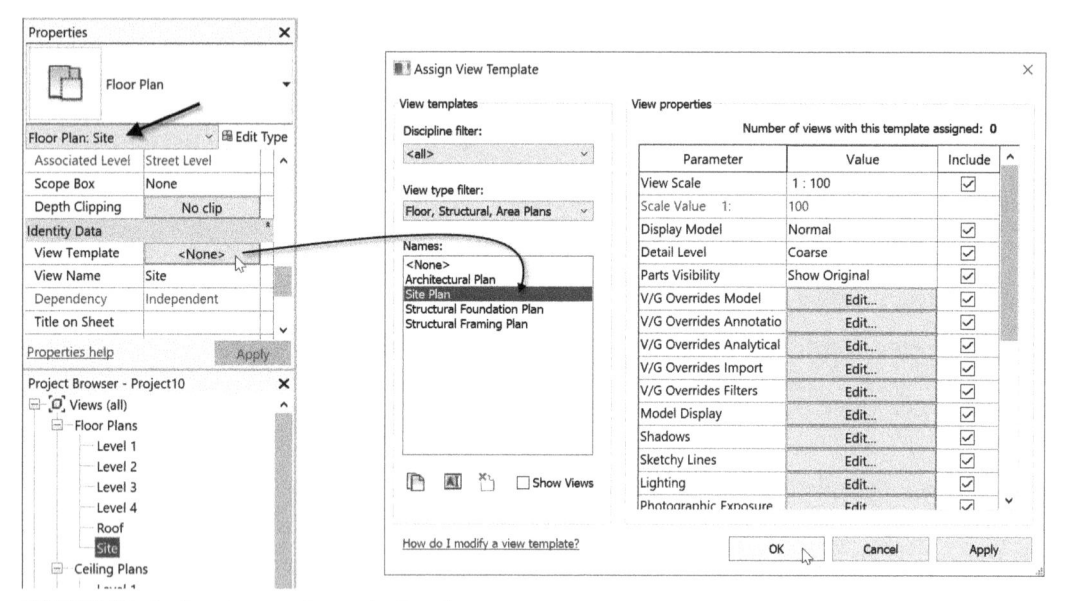

FIGURE 5.16 *Apply a view template to the Site plan view*

The most obvious change will be the increase in size of the elevation tags (in the Imperial file only, the metric file does not change scale). This reflects that the scale of the view has changed. There are other settings that were changed as well. For example, two icons appear in the center of the view. They currently occupy the same location. One is the Project Base Point icon and the other the Survey Point icon. The Project Base Point icon can be used to relocate the project, and the Survey Point can be used to adjust a reference point relative to a linked site file. We will discuss these icons further in Chapter 7. To preserve the work we've done so far, it is a good time to save.

3. From the File menu, choose: **Save**.

⇨ In the "Save As" dialog that appears, browse to the *Chapter05* folder.

⇨ Give the project a name such as: **REA Commercial** and then click the Save button.

CREATE A SIMPLE SITE

Now that we have created and named all our levels, we can move on to adding some basic building elements to our model. Having some simple geometry in the file will make planning views and setting up preliminary sheets easier. Since the site plan is already open, this is a good place to start.

CREATE A TOPOSURFACE

The first thing we need in a site plan is our site! Revit has some simple site design tools that enable us to build a topographical surface upon which our building model can sit. We can also add planting, parking, property lines, and other site accoutrements. You can build a Toposurface in two ways: by manually placing points or by importing site data from external files. In this chapter, we will create a simple surface manually as a temporary ground plane for our project setup. Later in Chapter 7 we'll get into more detail on the Site tools, build a site model and link it into our project replacing the simple site that we are creating here. This one will serve as a temporary stand-in.

1. On the ribbon, click the Massing & Site tab (Site tab if you are using Revit LT).

• The Aubin Academy •

Setting Up Project Levels and Views | 163

2. Click the Toposurface tool.

The Modify | Edit Surface tab will be displayed on the ribbon. The existing items in the view (such as the elevation tags) will gray out. The Place Point tool on the Tools panel should be selected. (If it is not, click it now.)

⇨ On the Options Bar, verify that the Elevation field is set to: **0** (zero).

3. Zoom out slightly and click five points across the top of the screen slightly above the top elevation marker.

⇨ Change the Elevation to **-3'-0"** [**-900**] (negative). Click another set of points horizontally beneath the south elevation marker (see Figure 5.17).

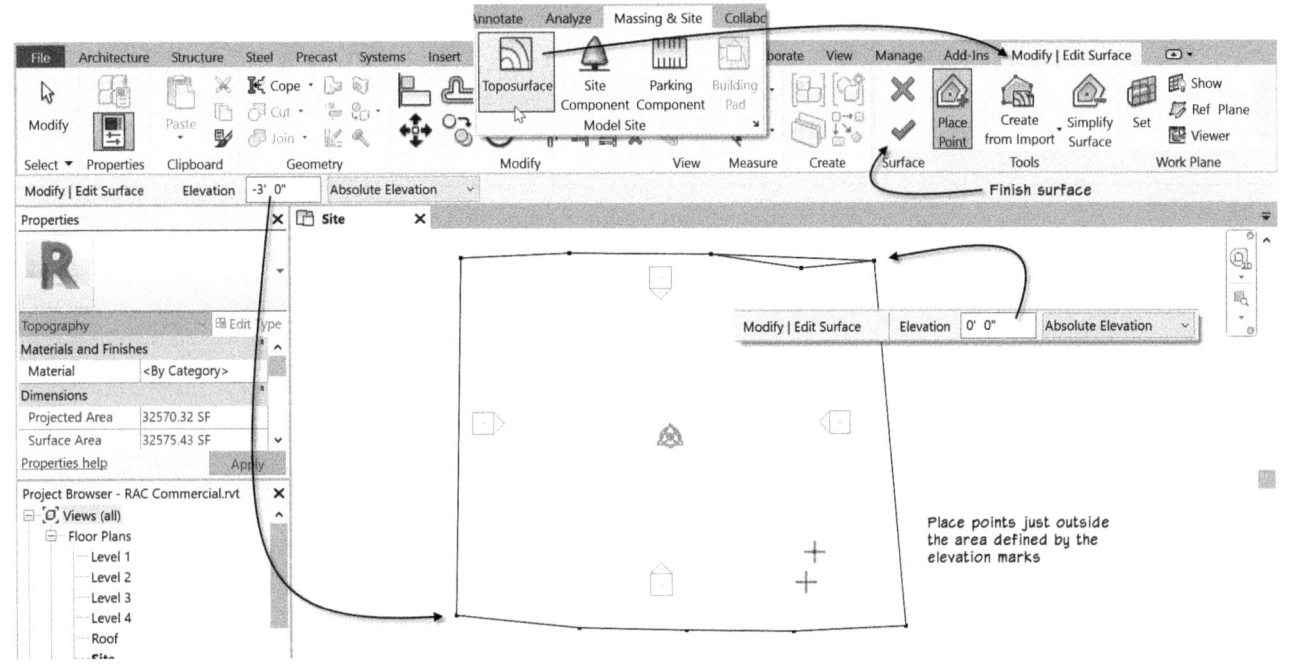

FIGURE 5.17 *Create a Toposurface from sketched points*

Do try to build the surface so that it is larger than the elevation markers all the way around. Do not worry about making it exactly like the figure. If you want to edit any points, click the Modify tool, select the point you want to change and then simply drag them where you like.

4. On the ribbon, click the Finish Surface button (large green checkmark).
5. Open the East elevation view.

Zoom in as necessary and study the results. Notice that the surface appears with a gentle slope and an earth pattern applied where the grade is cut (see Figure 5.18).

• Revit Essentials for Architecture •

164 | Chapter 5

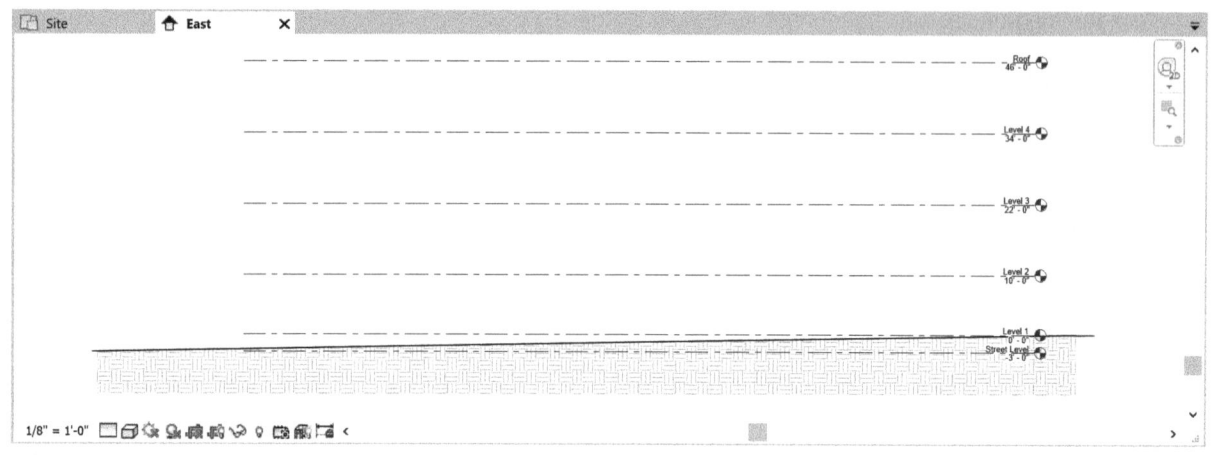

FIGURE 5.18 *Finish the sketch and view the Toposurface in elevation*

> **NOTE:** If you only see the edge of the Toposurface and not the earth hatching, this means that the points you placed above were inside the elevation zone (to the left of the East elevation marker). The hatching only shows when the elevation line actually cuts through the Toposurface (making it essentially a section at that point).

Like any sketch-based object in Revit, you can select the Toposurface at any time and click the Edit Surface button on the ribbon. This will return you to sketch mode where you can select and modify the points from which the topo is derived. You can move the points, change their elevations, add new points, and delete existing points. If you choose to add a new point, you add it at an absolute elevation like the ones we added above, or when editing an existing surface, you can also choose to make them relative to the surface. You will find this on the Options Bar after you click the Place Point tool. Feel free to experiment with this Toposurface before continuing. We will be deleting it in favor of a new one we will create from an imported CAD file later in Chapter 7. So have some fun exploring the options and don't worry about "messing" this one up. We only need some sort of ground plane for now to give our building model a base upon which to sit. The exact shape of the base is not terribly important.

ROUGH OUT THE BUILDING FORM

Since our goal in this chapter continues to be the overall setup of our commercial project, we will take this opportunity to add some simple geometry to the project to suggest building form. The purpose is not to arrive at design solution, but rather to provide enough of a building form to give the various views and sheets that we will establish below some context. The tasks that follow are therefore simple suggestions of project setup workflow. Feel free to vary the steps as appropriate when following the process in setting up your own projects.

ADDING WALLS CONSTRAINED TO LEVELS

To suggest the overall form of our building we'll draw some simple walls. At this early stage of the project, some simple generic walls will be sufficient. As the design evolves the wall types, layout and shapes can be changed and edited to suit our needs.

1. Click the X on the *East* view tab to close this view and return to the *Site* floor plan view tab.
2. On the ribbon, click the Architecture tab and then click the Wall tool (or press WA).
   - ⇨ From the Type Selector, (on the Properties palette) choose: **Basic Wall: Generic -12"** [**Basic Wall: Generic -300mm**].
   - ⇨ On the Modify | Place Wall tab, on the Draw panel, click the rectangle icon.

• The Aubin Academy •

⇨ On the Options Bar, from the Height list, choose: **Roof**.

⇨ For the Location Line, choose: **Finish Face: Exterior** (see Figure 5.19).

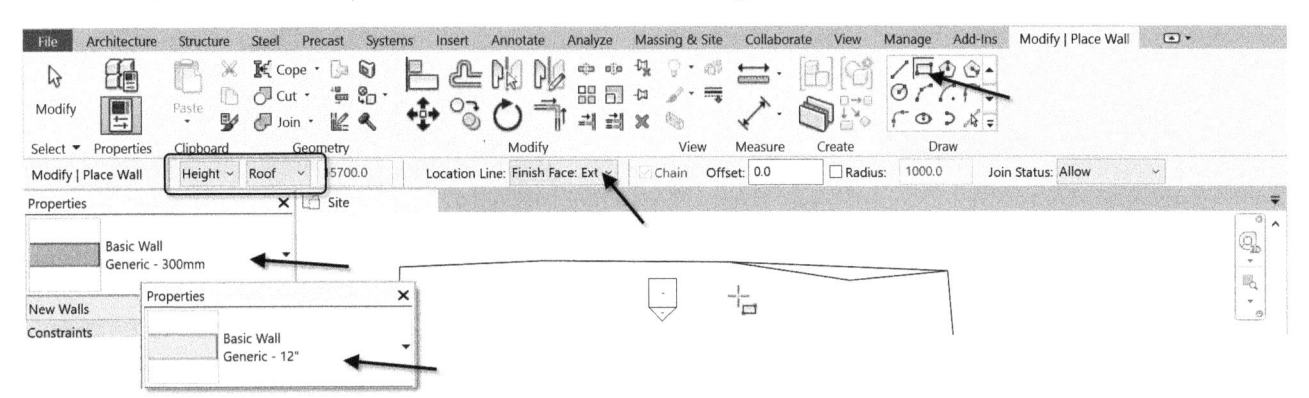

FIGURE 5.19 *Set the options to create new walls*

3. In the view window, click two opposite corners to create a rectangle in the middle of the elevation markers.

   Temporary dimensions will remain on screen.

   ⇨ Edit the horizontal temporary dimension to a value of: **104'-0"** [**31500**].

   ⇨ Edit the vertical temporary dimension to a value of: **64'-0"** [**19200**] (see Figure 5.20).

Make sure the rectangle is roughly centered in the space defined by the elevation markers. If you need to move the walls, select all four walls and then drag them to reposition.

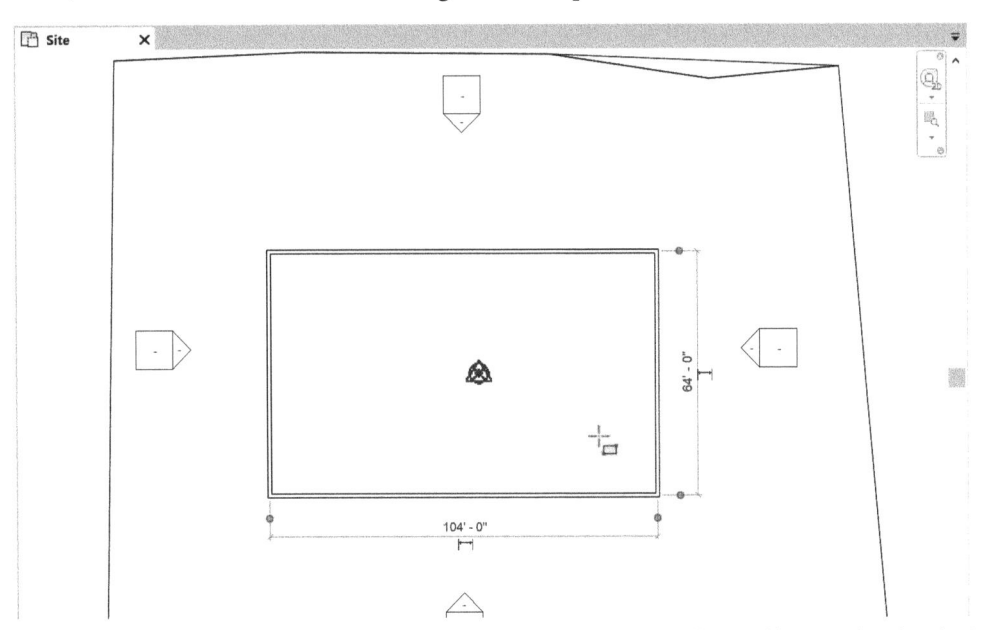

FIGURE 5.20 *Edit the temporary dimensions of the walls and ensure that they fall roughly centered within the elevation markers*

4. On the Project Browser, double-click to open the *East* elevation view.

5. Zoom in near the bottom of the building

Since we drew the walls on the Site Plan view, the bottom edges should meet the Toposurface nicely.

6. On the Quick Access Toolbar (QAT), click the Default 3D View icon (small bird house).

   ⇨ On the View Control Bar, click the Model Graphics Style icon and choose: **Shaded** (or press SH) (see Figure 5.21).

166 | Chapter 5

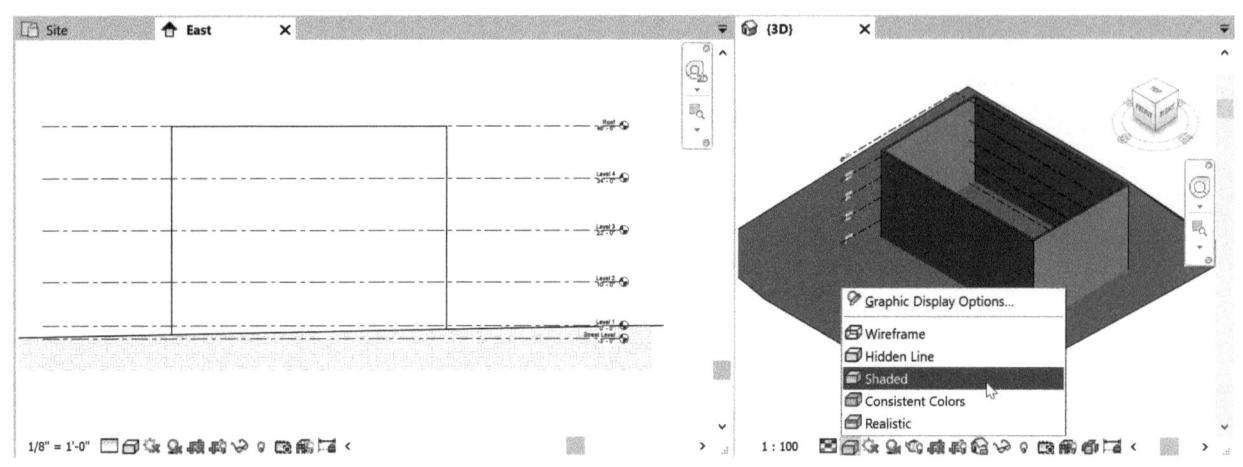

FIGURE 5.21 *Study the model in elevation and 3D to see the results of adding the four walls*

ADD A SIMPLE ROOF

We now have a big hollow box sitting on our terrain. Let's add a simple roof.

1. On the Architecture tab, click the Roof tool. (If you click the drop down arrow on the Roof tool it is: **Roof by Footprint**).

A message will appear requesting that we select the desired level to build the roof. This message appears because we are in a 3D view. Naturally, we will want to create the roof at the Roof level.

2. In the "Lowest Level Notice" dialog, choose: **Roof** from the drop down list and then click Yes (see Figure 5.22).

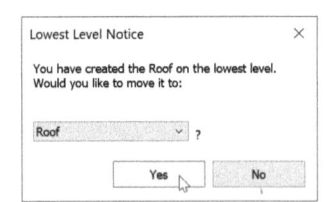

FIGURE 5.22 *When creating a roof in 3D, clarify the desired creation level*

- On the Modify | Create Roof Footprint tab, on the Draw panel, verify that the Boundary Line tool is active and that the Pick Walls icon is selected. (These are both defaults and should already be chosen).

- On the Options Bar, clear the checkmark from the "Defines slope" check box.

3. Using the TAB key, chain select all four walls and then click to create sketch lines (see Figure 5.23).

Setting Up Project Levels and Views | 167

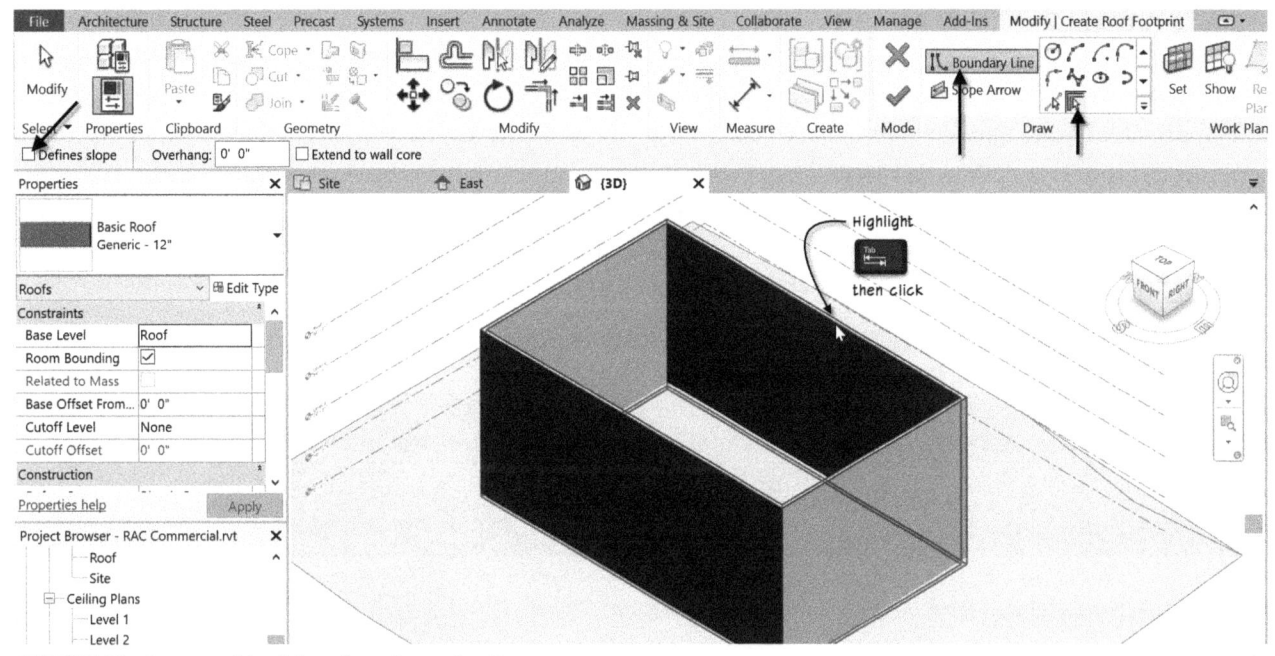

FIGURE 5.23 *Create roof sketch lines for a chain of walls*

4. Zoom in as required and verify that the sketch lines are on the inside edge of the walls. If they are not, click the small flip control to shift the sketch lines.

5. On the ribbon, click the Finish Edit Mode button.

Since we cleared the "Defines slope" check box, you will get a simple flat slab of a roof placed at the top edge of the walls. If you got a hip roof instead, you forgot to clear this check box. Select the roof, and on the ribbon that appears, click the Edit Footprint icon. Select all four sketch lines, and then, on the Options Bar, clear the "Defines Slope" check box. Then click the Finish Edit Mode button.

ADJUST WALL HEIGHT

Our goal at this stage is to create a very rough model that we can use to help set up and understand the views in our project. We don't need to get too concerned with the details of the design at this stage. However, one quick edit to the walls is appropriate. Let's adjust the wall height to suggest a parapet at the roof.

1. Chain select all four walls (pre-highlight one wall, press TAB to chain highlight and then click to select all four).

2. On the Properties palette, for the Top Offset parameter, type: **4'-0"** [**1200**] and then apply (see Figure 5.24).

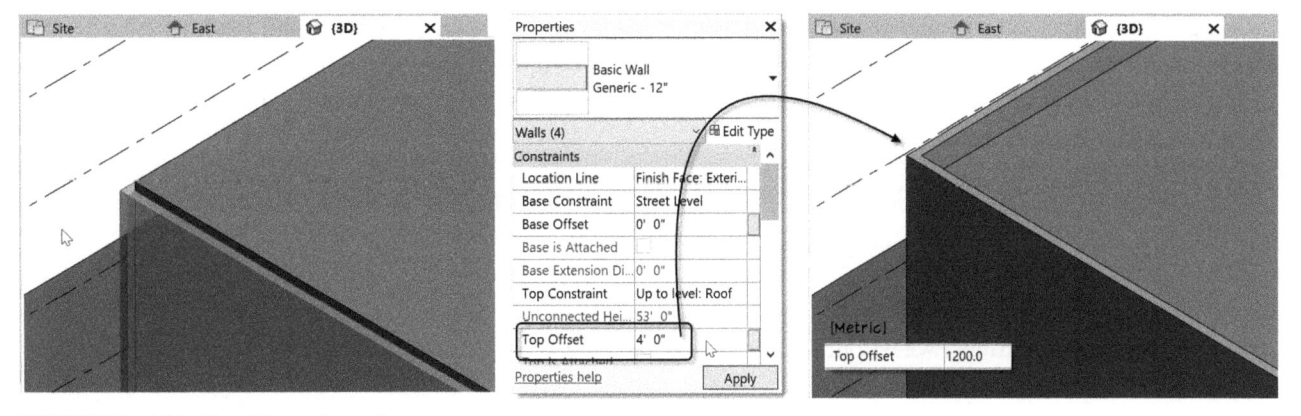

FIGURE 5.24 *Add a Top Offset to the walls to represent a parapet*

3. Save the Project.

• Revit Essentials for Architecture •

SLANTED WALLS

In the coming chapters, the design of both our projects will evolve. At this stage of our commercial project we have little information other than the number of levels, a vague notion of the slope of the site and few ideas of the building's overall form. It is desired that some sort of special treatment be given to the front façade. We don't have the specifics about this treatment yet but at this stage can make a few assumptions. To do this, we will sketch out a few simple walls on the front façade of our building to suggest that some design element will later occur in this location. Let's assume that this feature will occur on the upper floors of the building.

1. On the Project Browser, double-click to open the *Level 2* floor plan view.

> **TIP:** It is very easy to accidentally double-click the *Level 2* ceiling plan instead of the *Level 2* floor plan view. So be sure to pay close attention to the branch of the Project Browser and ensure that the "Level 2" you are double-clicking is beneath *Floor Plans* and not *Ceiling Plans*. To help prevent this, simply collapse the *Ceiling Plans* branch by clicking the small minus (-) sign next to it.

2. On the Architecture tab, click the wall tool (or press WA).

   ⇨ From the Type Selector, choose: **Generic - 8"** [**Generic - 200mm**] and on the Options Bar, for the Height, choose: **Roof**.

   ⇨ Click the first point on the existing wall at the lower portion of the plan, toward the left-hand side (the exact location will be set later) (see item 1 in Figure 5.25).

   ⇨ Move your cursor straight down, type: **8'-0"** [**2400**] and then press ENTER (see item 2).

3. Move to the right horizontally and click a point to the right side.

4. For the last point, move straight up and click on the existing horizontal wall to finish

   ⇨ On the ribbon, click the Modify tool or press the ESC key twice.

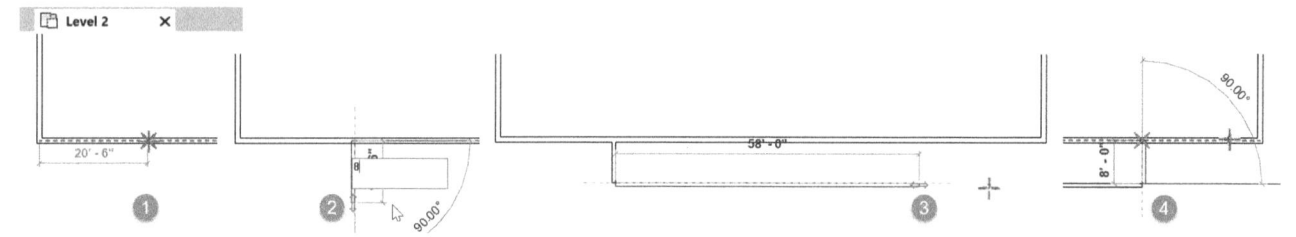

FIGURE 5.25 *Draw three walls to create a simple rectangular form on the front of the building form*

The last walls we drew used the location line setting of: Finish Face: Exterior, so this setting was remembered for these new walls. Also, it is likely that your exterior face is pointing to the inside of the building now. You can tell which side is out by the position of the flip control (double arrow control at the midpoint of a wall). If these double arrows are on the inside, you will want to flip the walls. You can do this one at a time using the grip control, or you can select them all and flip with the SPACEBAR.

5. Select the three walls you just created. (You can use a crossing selection, or a chain selection).

   ⇨ Tap the SPACEBAR to flip the walls.

Recall from the "Temporary Dimensions" topic on page 82 in Chapter 3, that we can change our preferences for temporary dimension settings. We will now adjust the position of the two vertical walls we just added, but it might be easier to do if you adjust your temporary dimension settings first.

6. On the Manage tab, click the Additional Settings dropdown menu and choose: **Temporary Dimensions**.

⇨ For Walls, choose: Faces, for Doors and Windows choose: Openings and then click OK (shown in Figure 3.22 in Chapter 3).

7. Select one of the vertical walls and then edit the temporary dimension to: **20'-0"** [**6000**].

8. Repeat the process on the other side using the same dimension value (see Figure 5.26).

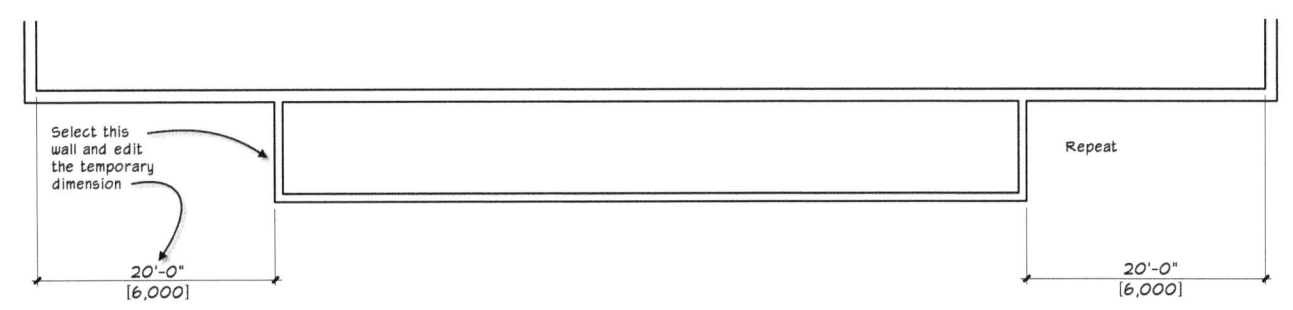

FIGURE 5.26 *Edit the temporary dimensions to move the vertical walls (dimensions in the figure for reference)*

Select the horizontal wall and verify that it is: 8'-0" [2400] from the front face of the building. If it is not, use the temporary dimension to adjust it.

This gives us a simple rectangular footprint for our front façade feature. Now let's make it slightly more interesting using the slanted walls feature.

9. Select the horizontal wall of the front façade feature.

10. On the Properties palette, change the Cross-Section setting to: **Slanted** and then for the Angle From Vertical, input: **10** and Apply (see Figure 5.27).

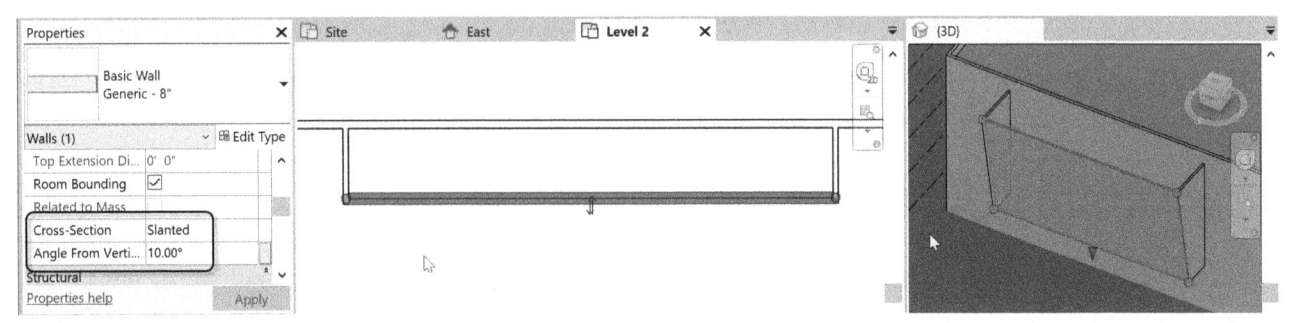

FIGURE 5.27 *Adjust the size of the rectangle using temporary dimensions*

With an angle of 10° the effect is subtle but noticeable. The angle can be positive or negative. Positive angles slope away from the building, while negative ones slope in towards the building. Feel free to try other angles if you like and to apply an angle to the side walls as well. In Figure 5.28, the middle wall is at 10° while the two side walls are at 5°.

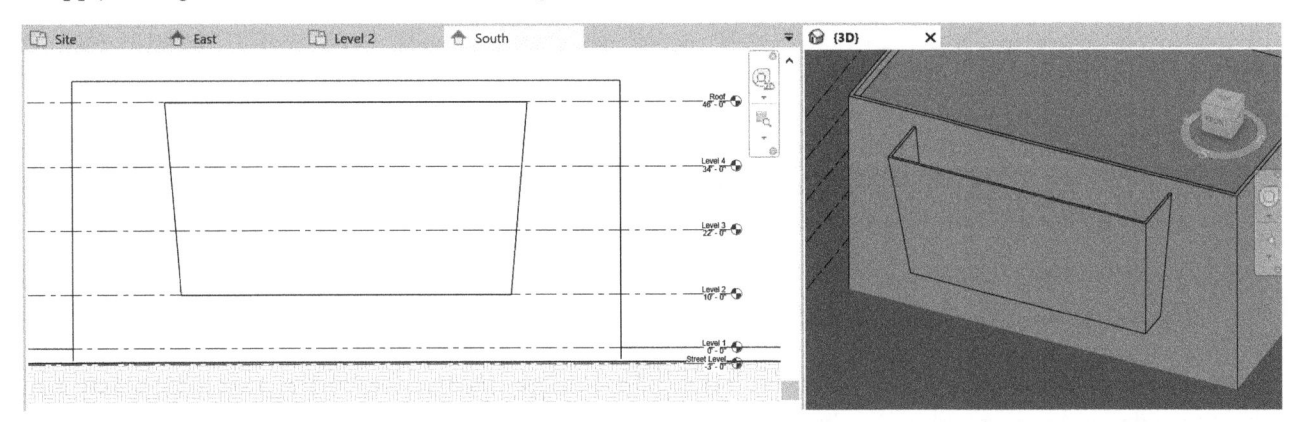

FIGURE 5.28 *Make the walls slanted*

• Revit Essentials for Architecture •

170 | Chapter 5

Let's try seeing what this feature would look like as a curtain wall instead. We can easily swap these walls out with a curtain wall family and type.

11. Select the three walls of the façade feature.
    ⇨ On the Properties palette, from the Type Selector, choose: Curtain Wall:Exterior Glazing.

The walls now become glazing with regular subdivisions both horizontally and vertically. This is more than suitable to suggest that this façade feature will be a glazed treatment of some kind for this preliminary stage of the design. However, we can make one more simple modification.

12. Select the long horizontal curtain wall segment.
    ⇨ On the Properties palette, scroll down beneath Vertical Grid and for the Justification choose: **Center** and then apply (see Figure 5.29).

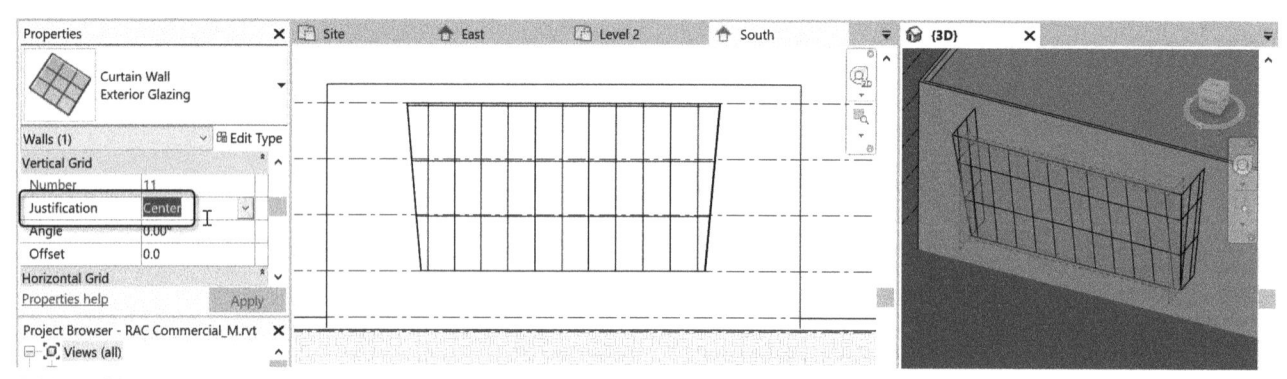

FIGURE 5.29 *Adjust the centering of the grid lines on the front facing curtain wall*

We will continue to refine this design in later chapters. But for this stage of the project, what we have is satisfactory.

13. Save the project.

WORKING WITH ELEVATION VIEWS

The default templates that we used to create our project already included four building elevations. As our project progresses, we can work with these elevations, delete them, and/or add additional ones. Elevation views are vertical slices through the building model cut from a certain point and projected orthographically. Level heads will display automatically in elevation views, and elevation view tags will appear by default in all intersecting plan views to indicate where the elevations are cut. The four default elevation views are sufficient to our needs at this time, but we will make a series of adjustments to fine-tune them.

ADJUSTING ELEVATION TAGS

We have added enough geometry to our model to begin studying the effectiveness of our elevations. As we study them, we can see that it might be beneficial to adjust a few things.

1. On the Project Browser, double-click each elevation view in succession.
    ⇨ Zoom and pan within each elevation to study them carefully.

    If you still have many other views open, you can close the others to reduce the number of open tabs.

As you open each elevation, take note of the edges of the Toposurface. Most of the surface appears in section with a bold top edge and an earth fill pattern beneath. This result is due to the locations of the elevation tags in the plan views. Let's take a closer look at the elevation tags to get a better understanding of their behavior.

2. On the Project Browser, double-click to open the *Level 1* plan view.

⇨ Zoom in on the bottom (South) elevation tag.

⇨ Move the mouse pointer over the tag.

As it highlights onscreen, notice that it is made of two pieces. The elevation tag is the square [round] shape, and the arrow (triangle) portion indicates the viewing direction and extent of the associated elevation view (see the left side of Figure 5.30). In the middle of the figure, you can see how it looks when you select them. A small dash appears within each tag. These are text labels that fill in automatically when the elevation view is placed on a sheet. (An example is shown on the right side of the figure.) We will add sheets later in this chapter, so you do not have to create them now.

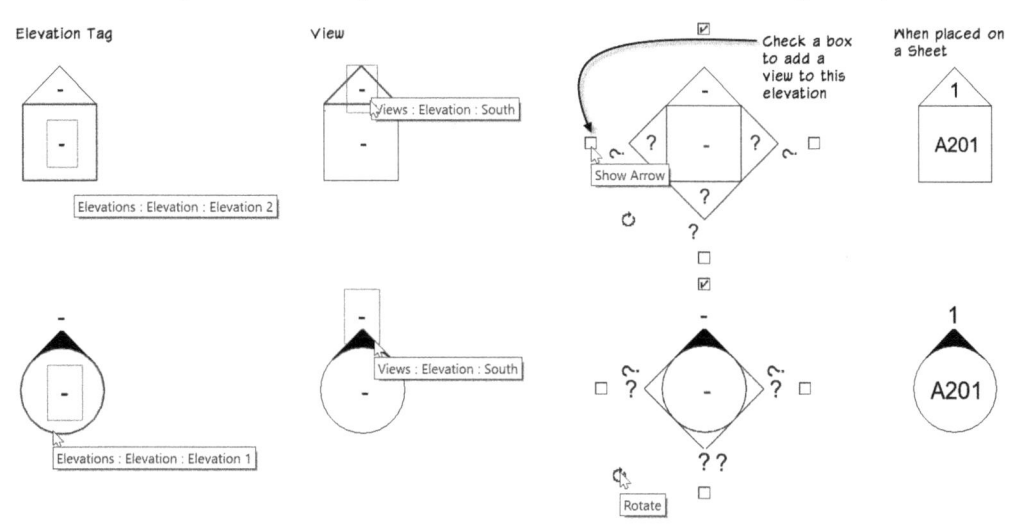

FIGURE 5.30 *Elevation tags and elevation view indicators, (highlighted, selected and on sheets)*

3. Select the Elevation Tag (square in imperial and round in metric).

By default, one elevation arrow is active per elevation tag. Each elevation tag can have up to four elevation arrows and corresponding elevation views. Three additional elevation view Indicator arrows will appear temporarily as long as the Tag is selected (see the middle of Figure 5.30). Small check boxes appear that you can use to add new elevation views. If you remove a check-mark, the associated elevation view will be deleted. A prompt will appear to warn you of this. To test this out, check one of the empty boxes, and then note the addition of a new elevation view on the Project Browser. Remove the checkmark from the same box, and a warning will appear indicating that this new view will be deleted. There is also a rotate handle that appears when the tag is selected. This will rotate the entire elevation tag and all its associated views. As the elevation tag is rotated it will snap to 90° increments and perpendicular to adjacent walls and other geometry. Try it out if you like; just be sure to undo before continuing.

4. Deselect the Elevation Tag and then select the Elevation view Indicator arrow.

When this arrow is selected, it turns blue. You can double-click the blue arrow to open the associated elevation view. First select the arrow, and then double-click it if you want to open the view. Selecting the elevation arrow also reveals a line perpendicular to the direction of the arrow (see Figure 5.31).

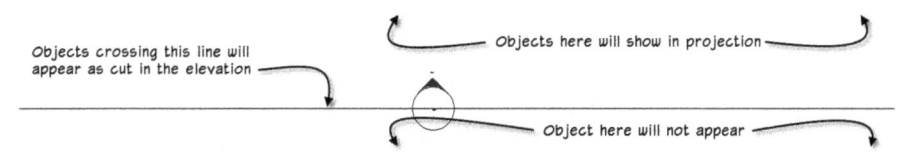

FIGURE 5.31 *Handles and drag controls on the elevation view indicators*

172 | Chapter 5

This line indicates the extent of the cut plane of the elevation view. Objects crossing this line will show as cut like a section. We have seen this above with the Toposurface. Objects behind this line will not be shown in the elevation view. Objects in front of the line appear in projection. Let's explore this.

5. Type ZF on the keyboard, or from the Zoom pop-up on the Navigation Bar, choose: **Zoom to Fit**.

6. Select both parts of the south elevation Tag (the Tag and the arrow for the bottom most one pointing up).

⇨ Drag it to up into the building just above the front façade (see Figure 5.32).

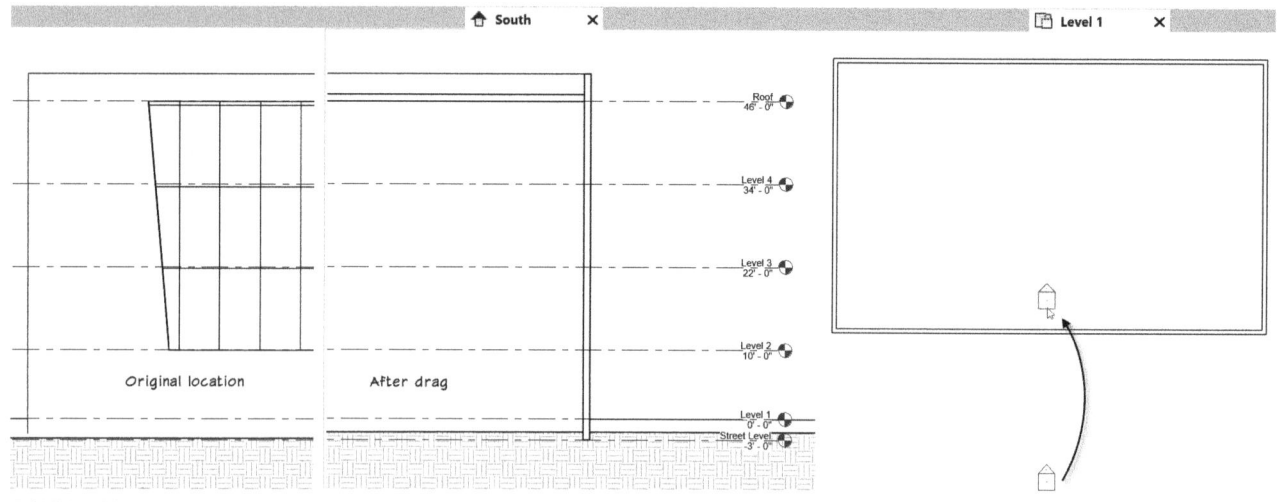

FIGURE 5.32 *Moving the South elevation tag and arrow inside the building results in a section*

If you tile both the plan and elevation views side by side on the screen while performing these steps, you can see the elevation view change instantly as you move the tag around. The easiest way to do this is to tear the tab of one of the views off, then place it next to the other. To tear it off, click and hold down on the tab and then drag it away from the canvas frame. It should pop out as a floating window. You can leave it this way and resize it by stretching the edges. Or you can drag it to one of the edges and a blue shaded area will appear to indicate how it will dock to the frame. When the blue highlighting matches your desired docking configuration, release the mouse. It is also possible to use the window tile (WT) tool, but this will tile all open windows. So, dragging just one view and manually tiling it is a little nicer in this case.

We don't want to keep this change so we will simply undo it.

7. Undo (CTRL + Z) the change or simply move the symbol back to its original location.

While we do not want to make our elevation into a section, but we do want to make some minor adjustments to their locations. When doing so, it is important to note that you must select both parts of the elevation—the tag and the arrow, before moving as we did here. To test this, select only the elevation symbol and drag it again. When you are done, reselect the elevation and note that the section line (where the elevation is cut) remains in its previous location. This is what happens if you do not select both pieces. (Be sure to undo before continuing). This is useful in some situations where the tag is in the way of other geometry. You can move the tag, but not affect where the elevation is cut. So always think about this before moving an elevation. Are you trying to move the cut? Or just the symbol?

8. Move each elevation view tag closer to the building on all four sides. (Select both the elevation tag and the arrow).

> **TIP:** To move the selection slightly onscreen, you can use the arrow keys to "nudge" the selection. Each press of the arrow nudges a little bit. Hold the SHIFT key and nudge to move times ten.

9. Click the Modify tool or press the ESC key.

• The Aubin Academy •

Setting Up Project Levels and Views | 173

LOADING CUSTOM ELEVATION TAGS

You may find that the elevation tag used in the out-of-the-box template does not match your office standard. We can customize the elevation tag to match our standards. To do so, we must build two custom annotation families: one for the arrow and the other for the tag itself, called the "body." Once we have both pieces, we combine them to create the final elevation tag. The Family Editor is the environment in Revit where such customizations occur. Since use of the Family Editor can be complicated and sometimes intimidating, in this lesson, we will dispense with the steps to create the custom elevation tag and simply load one that has been provided for you. If you wish to try your hand at creating it yourself, refer to the "Creating Custom Elevation Tags" topic on page 485 in Chapter 11 for the complete process.

1. On the Insert tab, on the Load from Library panel, click the Load Family button.
   ⇨ In the "Load Family" dialog, browse to the *Chapter05* folder.
   ⇨ Select the *NCS Elevation Tag.rfa* file and then click Open.

This process loads an external Revit family file (RFA) into our current project. This file is an elevation tag drawn to the specifications outlined in the US National CAD Standard (NCS). The next step is to swap out the existing elevation tags in our project with the new one we have just loaded.

2. Select any one of the existing elevation tags onscreen.

Remember the tag is the square [round] part in the middle. The triangular part is the elevation view itself. Be sure to select the tag. On the Type Selector, it will say: Elevation: Building Elevation.

3. On the Properties palette, click the Edit Type button (see item 1 in Figure 5.33).

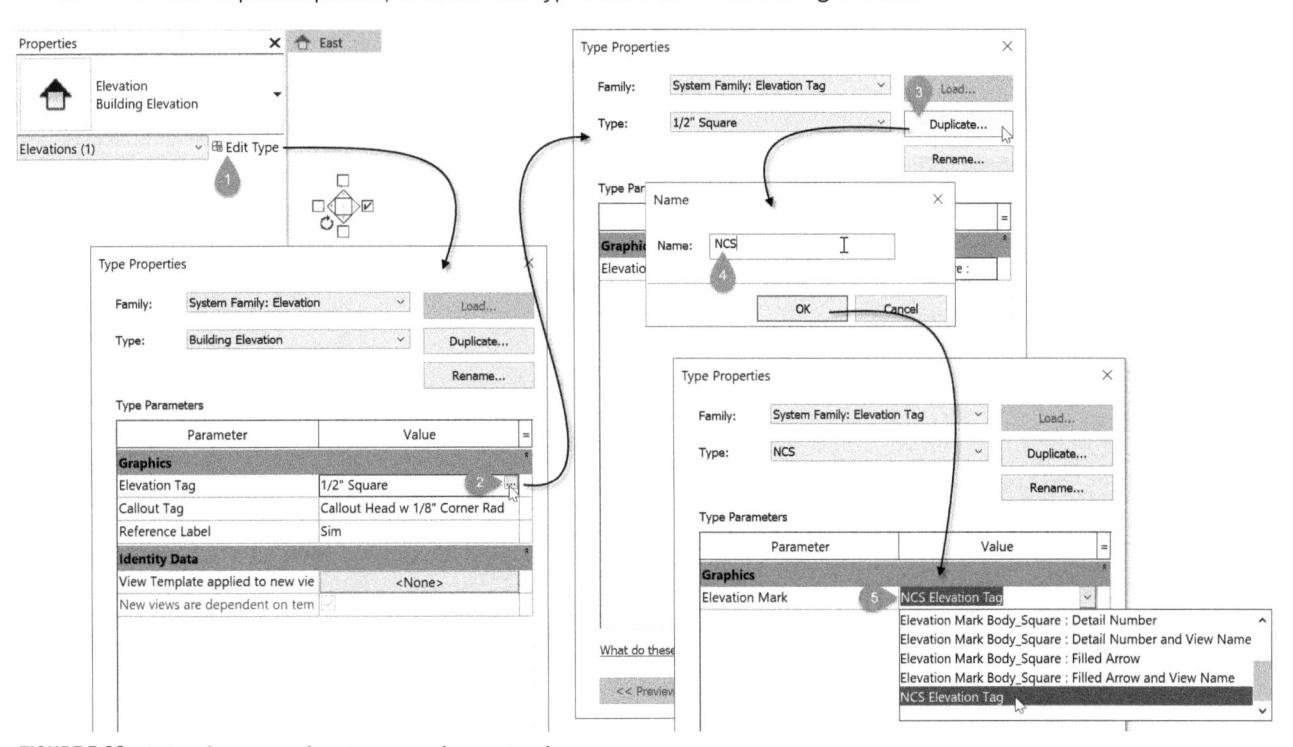

FIGURE 5.33 *Assign the custom elevation tag to the exterior elevations*

4. In the "Graphics" grouping, click in the field next to Elevation Tag and then click the small browse button that appears (item 2).

A second "Type Properties" dialog will open. This one is the properties of the Elevation Tag itself. At the top of the dialog the family and type are shown as drop down lists. Next to the Type are some buttons.

• Revit Essentials for Architecture •

174 | Chapter 5

5. Click the Duplicate button to copy the type (or press ALT + D) (item 3).

⇨ For the name, type: **NCS** and then click OK (item 4).

6. In the "Graphics" grouping, change the Elevation Mark to: **NCS Elevation Tag** (see item 5 in Figure 5.33).

⇨ Click OK to dismiss the dialog, and then click OK again to see the result.

> **BIM MANAGER NOTE:** In this example we modified the "Building Elevation" type to use the custom NCS family. If you prefer, in the first "Type Properties" dialog (item 2 in Figure 5.33), you could duplicate instead to create a new elevation type and preserve the original. The rest of the steps would be the same. When you are finished, you would have to apply this new type to the other three elevations already in the file.

ADJUSTING ELEVATION CROPPING

The elevation views by default do not use or show the crop regions. This means that the view continues to dynamically resize itself as the building geometry grows and shrinks. If you wish to limit the size of the elevation, you can display the crop region and then resize it to crop away the unwanted portion of the view. This is helpful when planning for sheets and printing.

1. Open the *South* elevation view.

Take note of the odd way the edges of the Toposurface displays. It is accurate relative to the position of the elevation but does not give a nice clean edge that would be more desirable in a finished elevation drawing. Adjusting the Crop Region can help.

2. On the View Control Bar, click the Show Crop Region view icon.

    The Crop Region will appear as a long rectangle surrounding the elevation.

3. Select the Crop Region.

⇨ Drag the handles to crop away the unwanted portion of the view (see Figure 5.34).

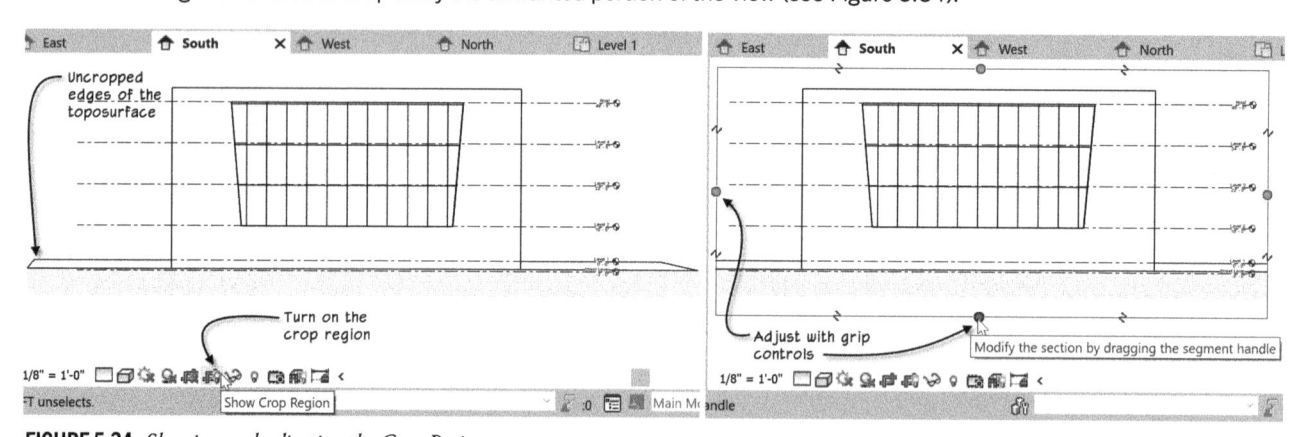

FIGURE 5.34 *Showing and adjusting the Crop Region*

4. Click the Hide Crop Region icon (same icon used to show it).

If you like the results, repeat the process on the North elevation. Otherwise, click the Do Not Crop View icon (to the left of the Show/Hide Crop Region icon) to turn it off and return to the full uncropped view. Please note that the "Crop View" icon toggles to become the "Do Not Crop View" icon after you click it and likewise the "Show Crop Region" icon toggles to become the "Hide Crop Region" icon. When the view is not cropped, all new geometry will appear automatically as the view dynamically adjusts to display the entire model. When it is cropped, items added later that are located outside the crop region will be cropped in the view. For example, later in the book we will add a stair tower to the roof of the building. The current cropping will need to be adjusted at that time to display this feature. Finally, take note of the way the level lines adjust with the crop region. Try dragging the crop region in toward the middle of the building. Notice that the level heads will shorten but remain just outside the edge of the crop region. When the crop region is larger than the extents of the levels (or grids—see the next chapter) they will not extend to meet the crop region.

5. Repeat the cropping process on the other elevations.

Dragging the crop region controls is a quick and easy way to adjust the crop region. You can also select the crop region, and then on the ribbon, click the Size Crop tool. This will open a dialog where you can adjust the width and height numerically. You can use this method to input a value that will fit within the available size within your sheet title block. This is because these numbers are based on final plotted dimensions.

ADJUSTING LEVEL HEADS

Now that we have moved and resized the elevations, all the views will display correctly. However, the level heads still may need adjustment.

1. On the Project Browser, double-click to open the West elevation view (or just click the tab if it is already open).

In some views the levels are a little off-center or a bit too long or short. Enabling Cropping might take care of it, but we can also adjust the extent of the levels by dragging the ends.

2. Click on one of the level lines.

⇨ Click and drag the small hollow circle handle at the end of the level line and stretch it to the desired length (see Figure 5.35).

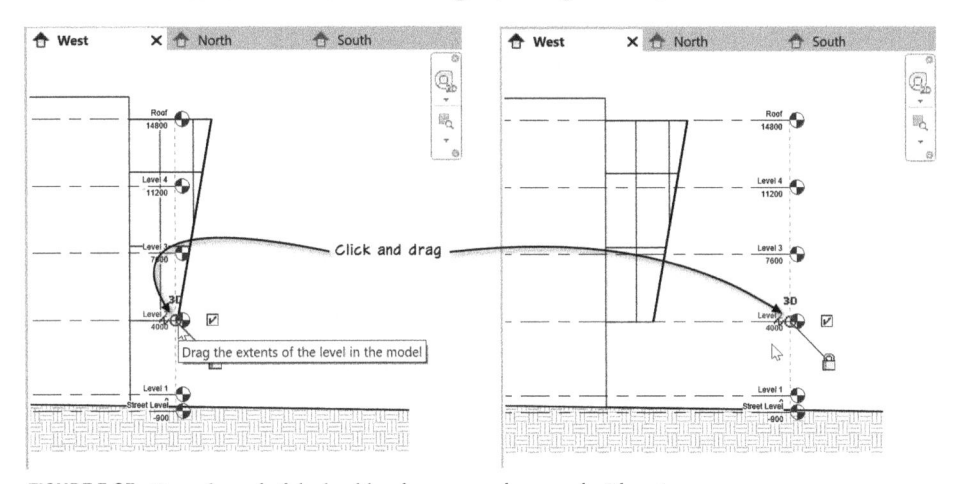

FIGURE 5.35 *Drag the end of the level heads to center them on the Elevation*

Repeat on the other side if necessary.

3. Enable the crop and adjust its size if desired.

The precise amount of the stretch does not matter. You simply want the result to have the level heads comfortably centered on the elevation, with a little room on each side. If you are working in the Metric file, the levels are shorter than the building. Simply stretch them out away from the building in the same way.

4. Perform similar adjustments in the *North* (or *South*) elevation views if necessary.

Notice that you only need to adjust the extents of the levels in two elevation views. Since elevations (like all Revit views) are live views of the model, changes you made in the *West* view can be seen automatically in the *East* view and likewise the changes in the *North* view appear automatically in the *South* and vice versa. You will also notice that when you drag one level line, all of them will adjust together. This is because they are all constrained to one another (see the "Adding and Modifying Levels" topic on page 155 above).

> **NOTE:** Were we to change the extents of the level to 2D, the change would apply only to the view in which it was changed. Further, the same level can have 2D extents enabled in one view and continue to display its 3D extents in other views. Should you have occasion to modify the 2D extents or add or remove elbows for your levels (or grids), you can "push" these changes to other parallel views using the "Propagate Extents" tool. (Select the level in question and then on the Modify | Level tab, click the Propagate Extents tool. Check the view(s) you wish and then click OK). Please note that propagate extents works only on uncropped views.

5. Review all four elevations and make any final adjustments to level extents and view cropping.
6. Save the Project.

> **BIM Manager Note:** An alternative way to set the extents of levels, grids and view crop regions is to use a Scope Box. A Scope box is a three-dimensional box that you sketch in plan and give a height to. Scope boxes have a unique name and can be used to define the extents of any datum element or view. They help control the extents of elements that are assigned to them and provide a convenient way to modify the extents. When you stretch the shape of the scope box, it will in turn adjust all the associated elements. When using a scope box, the shape handle grips on the element (like the open circles on the levels) will be disabled. This means that the only way to adjust the extents of an element assigned to a scope box is to adjust the scope box which will in turn modify all associated elements. The benefit of scope boxes is that you can simultaneously modify the crop regions, levels, and/or grids in many views. If you wish to try a scope box, on the View tab, on the Create panel, click the Scope Box tool. Assign a name and set a height on the Options Bar and then drag out a rectangle in plan. To assign it, select the desired views, levels or grids, and look for the Scope Box property on the Properties palette.

ADD ELBOWS

To fine-tune your elevations a little further, you can add an elbow to the Street Level line. Select the Street level line and then click the Add Elbow handle near the level head. This is pictured above in top middle frame of Figure 5.11. Once you add the elbow, two handles appear that you can use to adjust its position. Move them in such a way as to make the labels more legible. Perform this action on each elevation, or you can do it in the *North* elevation and then use the Propagate Extents tool to push the change to the *South*. Repeat for *West* and *East*.

EDIT LEVEL HEIGHTS

Earlier when we set up all the levels, we neglected to adjust the default height between Level 1 and Level 2. By default, in the Imperial template it is 10'-0" and it is 4000mm in the Metric template. However, for this project, the heights of all four levels should be 12'-0" [3600]. The change was postponed till now so that we can get a sense of the power of some of the simple constraints that we have already built into our model.

1. On the Project Browser, double-click to open the *West* elevation view (or just click its open tab).
2. Select Level 2.

Notice the temporary dimensions that appear. You can certainly edit those values to move the levels to their correct height. However, the problem with that technique is that you must move the levels one at a time. A better approach is to select and move them all together.

3. Select Level 2, Level 3, Level 4, and the Roof level.

> **TIP:** Remember, you can hold down the CTRL key and click each one or drag a window from right to left touching each level you wish to select.

At this point, we could click the Move tool on the Modify tab. This would require us to click a start point and then an end point to indicate the amount we wish to move. To move this way, you would have to calculate the amount of move required. The math required in this case is simple, but in general, temporary dimensions offer a nicer approach. Unfortunately, the temporary dimensions do not appear automatically with a multiple selection such as this. However, we can enable them to appear with the click of a button.

4. On the Options Bar, click the "Activate Dimensions" button.

   ⇨ In the temporary dimension that appears between Level 1 and Level 2, type: **12'-0"** [**3600**] (see Figure 5.36).

   Watch the top edge of the wall as you press ENTER.

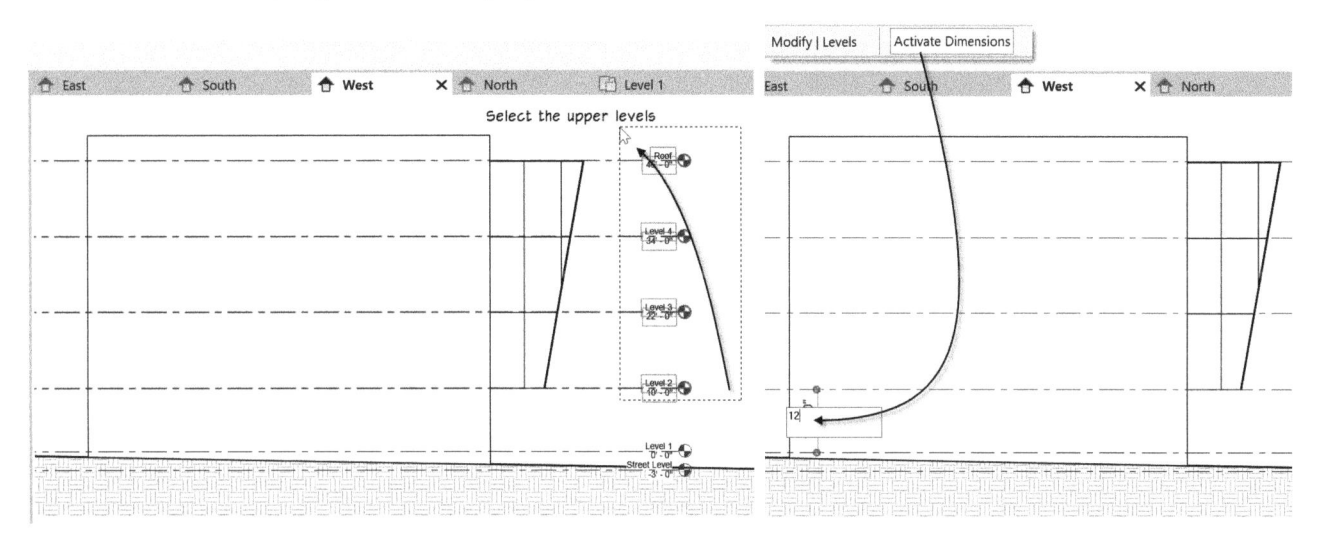

FIGURE 5.36 *Activate Dimensions on a multiple selection to move them together with temporary dimensions*

You should notice that the top edge of the walls move with the levels. This is because earlier, we constrained the tops of the walls to the Roof level. This is another example of the power of the parametric relationships between elements in a Revit model.

CREATING SECTION VIEWS

Unlike elevations, section views are not included in the default template; instead, we create them where needed. Section views are also vertical cuts through the building model and like elevations, level heads will appear in sections. You can create a section from plans or elevations and section heads appear in all intersecting views automatically. Adding Sections to our model is a simple task.

ADD A SECTION

Let's add two building sections, one longitudinal and one transverse through our preliminary building form.

1. On the Project Browser, double-click to open the *Level 1* floor plan view (or simply click that open tab).

178 | Chapter 5

> **TIP:** By now you likely have several views open. To conserve computer resources and clear up visual clutter on screen, you can close inactive views. A quick way to do this on the View tab of the ribbon click the Close Hidden tool. This tool is also located on the QAT.

⇨ On the View tab, click the Close Inactive tool (it is also on the QAT).

2. On the View tab, on the Create panel, click the Section tool (it is also on the QAT).

⇨ Click the first point on the outside left of the building near the middle.

⇨ Move the pointer horizontally to the right and then click the second point outside the building to the right (see Figure 5.37).

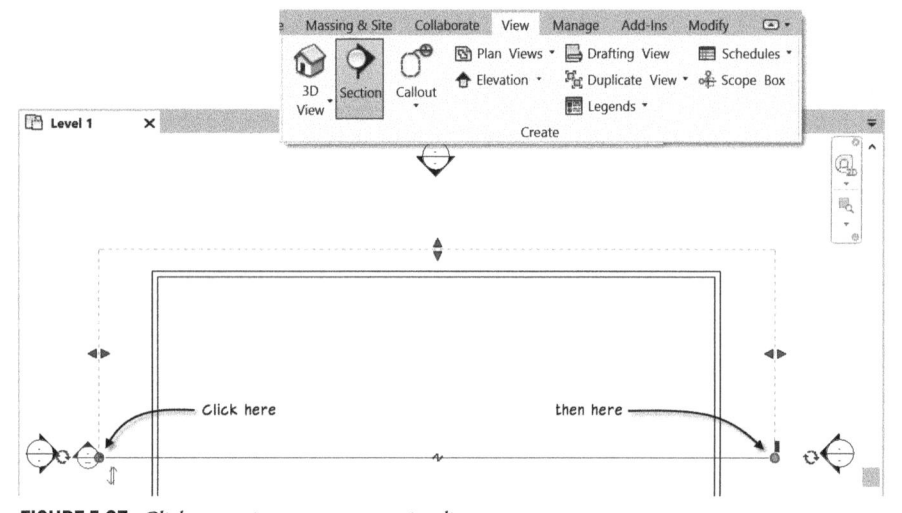

FIGURE 5.37 *Click two points to create a section line*

A section line will appear with several drag controls and handles on it. Like the other tags and symbols that we have seen so far, simply hover the mouse pointer over each control; the handle will temporarily highlight and the tool tip will appear indicating the function (see Figure 5.38). Brief descriptions of each control follow.

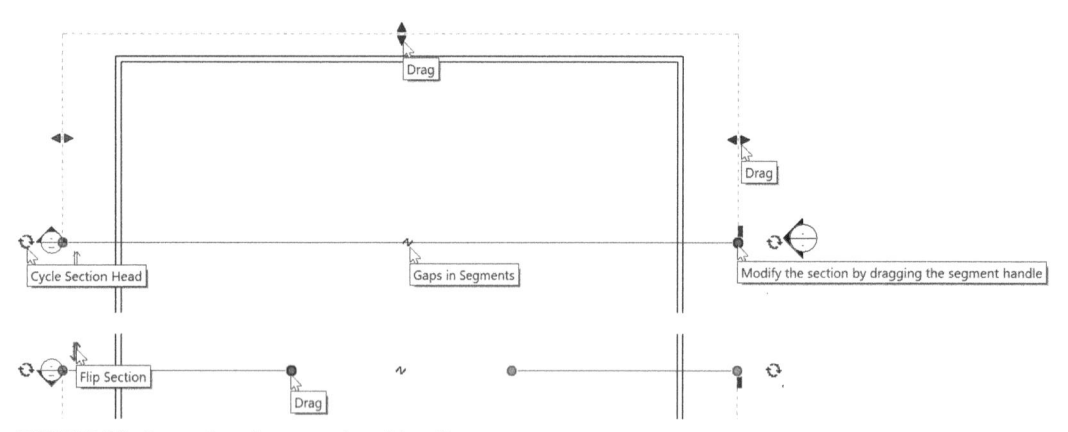

FIGURE 5.38 *Section line drag controls and handles*

Cycle Section Head/Tail—These controls appear at each end; one for the head and another for the tail. Each time you click one of these handles, the section head or tail will cycle to a different symbol from those loaded in the project file.

Flip Section—Click this control to flip the section line and symbols to look the opposite way.

Setting Up Project Levels and Views | 179

Segment Drag Handle—This handle (round dot) appears on each end of the section cut line and controls the length of the section line and moves the section heads with it. Dragging this handle does not change the size of the section crop box.

Drag—Drag Handles appear on three sides of the section crop box. Use them to define the precise extent of the associated section view. If you prefer to set these values numerically, edit the properties of the section.

Gaps in Segments—This control breaks the section line itself and removes the inner segment. You can then drag the exact length of each end segment. This is a graphical display only.

Notice that when you add the section marker, a new "Sections" branch appears in the Project Browser and that an associated Section view appears on this branch.

3. Using the Drag Handles, make any desired adjustments to the extent of the section box or the position of the section heads.

   If you wish, click the "Gaps in Segments" handle to remove the middle section of the Section Line.

4. On the Project Browser, expand *Sections (Building Section)*.

   ⇨ Right-click *Section 1* and choose: **Rename**. (Alternatively, you can do a "slow" double-click. Click, pause slightly, then click again to rename in place).

   ⇨ Type: **Longitudinal** and then click OK.

5. Double-click *Longitudinal* to open the view.

> **TIP:** You can double-click the blue section head in any plan view to jump to the associated section view.

Notice the box that surrounds the section in the view. This is the crop region for this section, and it matches the size of the section box that we created in plan. This is functionally identical to the crop region we manipulated for the elevations above. By default, crop regions are turned on in section views.

6. Repeat the steps above to create a vertical section looking to the right.

   ⇨ Rename the view to: **Transverse**.

Make any additional adjustments that you wish. When you open other views (like plans and elevations), the section lines will appear automatically. You can make the same sort of adjustments to them in each view: add gaps to the line or drag the section head to a different location. These adjustments are view specific. You can also adjust the size of the crop region from any view. This is not view specific. If you adjust the crop region or the location of the section line itself in any view, it will move accordingly in all other views.

7. Save the project.

SCHEDULE VIEWS

We have now created and worked with several types of views. While floor plans, ceiling plans, sections and elevations may be the most common views that our projects will contain, Revit includes many distinct view types. (You can see them all on the View tab.) One of the most powerful view types at our disposal is the schedule view.

A schedule view is not a drawing, but rather a non-graphical view of a collection of related data queried from the model and presented in tabular format. You do not need to "draw" and manually compile your schedules when you work in Revit. Working them up in Excel and importing them in is not required. You simply create a schedule view

180 | Chapter 5

directly in the software by indicating which data fields you wish to include and how you wish it to be formatted and the data required to populate the schedule comes directly from the model itself.

ADD A SCHEDULE VIEW

In this sequence, we will add a few simple schedule views to our project. We will not get into a detailed explanation of scheduling features at this time. Detailed information on schedules is found in Chapter 13.

1. On the Project Browser, locate the *Schedule/Quantities* branch and right-click it.

   ⇨ From the pop-up that appears, choose: **New Schedule/Quantities**.

   ⇨ In the "New Schedule" dialog, choose: Walls from the Category list and then click OK (see Figure 5.39).

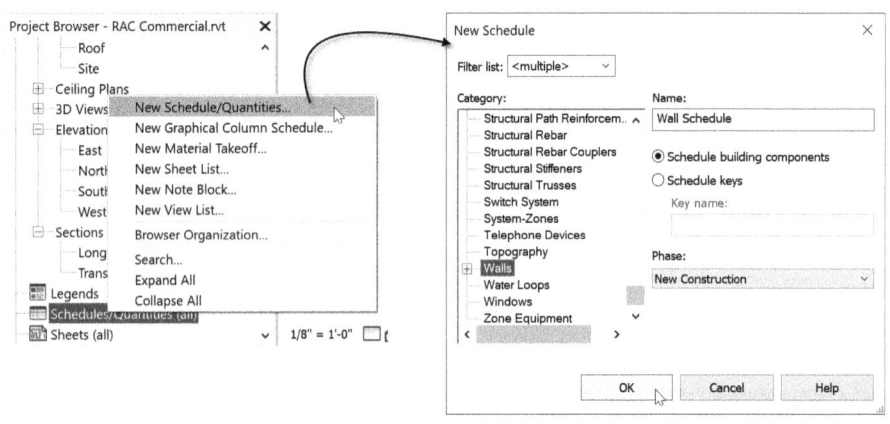

FIGURE 5.39 *Create a new wall schedule*

2. In the "Schedule Properties" dialog, from the Available fields list, select: "Type Mark" and then click the Add parameter button in the middle.

   ⇨ Repeat this process for the "Length," "Width," "Family and Type," and "Comments" fields (see Figure 5.40).

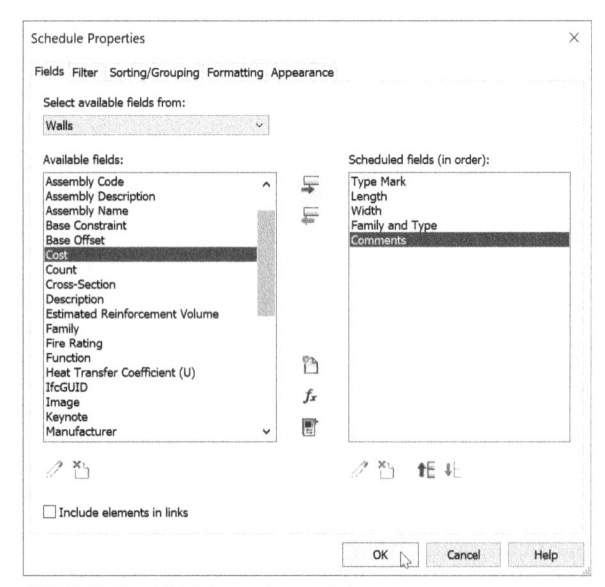

FIGURE 5.40 *Add fields to the schedule*

3. Click OK to complete field selection and open the schedule view.

The *Wall Schedule* view will appear on screen with each of the seven walls that we currently have in our project listed. The walls do not yet have "Type Marks" or "Comments," so these fields are empty. Later, as we edit the data parameters of these walls, these fields will update to reflect the latest information. The schedule view also appears in the

• The Aubin Academy •

Schedules/Quantities branch of the Project Browser (see Figure 5.41). You can open it from there any time just like the other views of the project that we explored above.

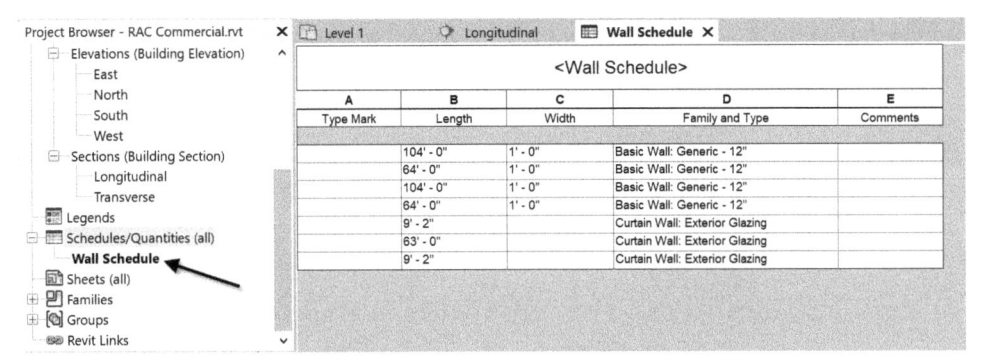

FIGURE 5.41 *The Wall Schedule appears in the Project Browser and opens on screen*

IMPORTING SCHEDULE VIEWS FROM OTHER PROJECTS

When we began this chapter, we opened several out-of-the-box Revit template projects. It was noted above that starting a project from a template was the preferred method of beginning a project. In some cases, you will begin a project with one template and then later realize that a family, type, or view required already exists in another template file or project. Rather than recreate the item, it is easier to borrow the element from the other project. In this topic, we will create a new project from the *Commercial-Default.rte* template file (installed with the out-of-the-box Imperial templates) and borrow some Schedule views from that project to use here.

> **NOTE**: The *Commercial-Default.rte* template file is installed with the out-of-the-box Imperial templates. If you did not install the Imperial templates, or your version of Revit does not give you access to this file, it has been provided for you in the *Templates* folder with the dataset files.

1. From the File menu, choose: **New** > **Project**.
   ⇨ In the "New Project" dialog, in the "Template File" area, click the Browse button.
   ⇨ Browse to the *English-Imperial* folder if not already there.
2. Select the *Commercial-Default.rte* template file, click Open and then click OK.

Many views like those that we have spent time configuring above also appear in this project template and some are unique. Feel free to spend some time exploring, but the schedules will be our focus here.

3. On the Project Browser, expand *Schedules/Quantities*.
   ⇨ Double-click on *Door Schedule*.

Take note of the formatting of the schedule view. Several fields appear, and some columns contain headers. As noted above, we will learn how to build such a schedule in Chapter 13; for now, it will be useful to simply copy this view with all its formatting and headers for use in our project.

4. On the Project Browser, right-click on *Door Schedule* and choose: **Copy to Clipboard**.
   ⇨ Switch back to your project which should still have several tabs open. You can click any one of the open graphical view tabs to switch.

This will return you to your original project so that you can paste the Schedule. Be sure to open a floor plan before pasting. The Paste command will not be available if you open a schedule view first.

5. On the Modify tab, click the Paste tool (or press CTRL+ V). If you get a "Duplicate Types" dialog, click OK to dismiss it.

On the Project Browser, beneath *Schedules/Quantities*, the pasted *Door Schedule* view will appear and it will open automatically. Notice that this Schedule contains all the preformatted columns but lists no doors. This is because our project does not yet contain any doors.

ADD A DOOR TO THE PROJECT

When you add elements to the project, they will automatically appear in all appropriate views—including the Schedule views. Let's add a door to our project to see this.

1. On the Project Browser, double-click to open the *Level 1* floor plan view (or click its open tab).
2. On the ribbon, click the Architecture tab and then click the Door tool (or press DR).
3. On the Modify | Place Door tab, click the Tag on Placement button to toggle it on.
4. Add a door to the middle of the top horizontal wall.
⇨ On the ribbon, click the Modify tool or press the ESC key twice.

   Zoom in to see the door. Note that the door number in the tag reads: 1.

5. On the Project Browser, double-click to open the *Door Schedule* view (You can also click the Door Schedule tab that is already open, but since there are two: one for this project and one for the template we copied from, it is easier to use the Project Browser to ensure you go to the correct view).

   Notice that the door also appears in the Schedule. (If it does not, you might have clicked the wrong view tab).

6. The header for column A in the schedule currently reads: vv. This should say "Mark." Click right on vv and change it to: **Mark**.
7. Click in the door Number field on the Schedule.
⇨ Change the door number to: **101** and then press ENTER.
8. Return to the *Level 1* plan view and confirm that the door tag reflects the new number (see Figure 5.42).

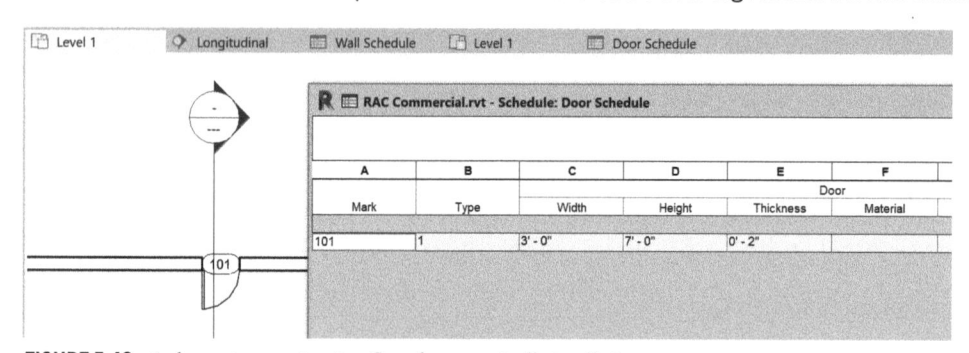

FIGURE 5.42 *A change in any view is reflected automatically in all views*

In Revit, a change made in one view applies in all associated views. You are not changing a graphic representation in a drawing. You are editing the parameters of an element in your building information model. This change must therefore be reflected in all views that show that component of the model—regardless if they are graphical views or tabular views.

9. Return to the other project and repeat the process to copy and paste the other two schedule views (*Room Schedule* and *Window Schedule*) to your *REA Commercial* project.

> **TIP:** You can select both schedules on the Project Browser by selecting the first, then hold the CTRL key, and select the other. Then right-click to access **Copy to Clipboard**.

> **BIM Manager Note:** If you use the same schedule views (or any views) repeatedly from one project to the next, you should create your own project template that already includes the views you require. You can even put them on sheets in that template. In this way, new projects will have these views and sheets immediately upon starting.

> **TIP:** You can switch between open views using the CTRL & TAB keys. Hold down CTRL and then press TAB. Each time you press TAB, you will cycle to another open view.

10. Close the other project without saving it (CTRL + W).
11. Return to the *Level 1* floor plan view tab. On the View tab, click the Close Inactive button.
12. Save your *REA Commercial* project.

SHEET VIEWS AND THE CARTOON SET

A sheet is a special type of view that is intended for publishing your document set—they are views for printing, publishing or sharing. When you create a sheet, you can add a title block to it, configure the print setup to match the paper size and other required printing parameters and then add viewports containing the various views of your project. Since most architectural projects will require printed or PDF output (often at several points) in the life of the project, it is a good idea to set up a set of sheets to create professional looking results. Sheets can be used for physical prints and PDFs.

Project submission time is usually a high-stress endeavor characterized by panic as project team members scramble to assemble the required sheets and output everything required for a submission. This frenzy often occurs at the last minute, which contributes to the stressful environment and often to errors and omissions. One simple way to help alleviate this situation is to create the sheet views early in the project so that they are ready to print at any time. Since all Revit views are live, you can create a sheet with views inserted early in schematics that have very little information on them (like the views we have created here), and over the life of the project, these sheets will reflect all project changes immediately as they occur. This means that you can print a sheet or set of sheets at a moment's notice with complete confidence that the information portrayed on those sheets represents the latest state of the project.

> **BIM Manager Note:** Consider adding several preconfigured sheet views to your office-standard project template. This will ensure consistency from one project to the next and simplify project setup. The *Commercial-Default.rte* template file used above gives a good example of this approach. Take some time to study the sheets included therein to glean ideas for your own templates.

CREATE A FLOOR PLAN SHEET

Let's start with some floor plan sheets.

1. On the Project Browser, right-click Sheets and choose: **New Sheet**.
⇨ In the "New Sheet" dialog, accept the defaults and click OK (see Figure 5.43).

184 | Chapter 5

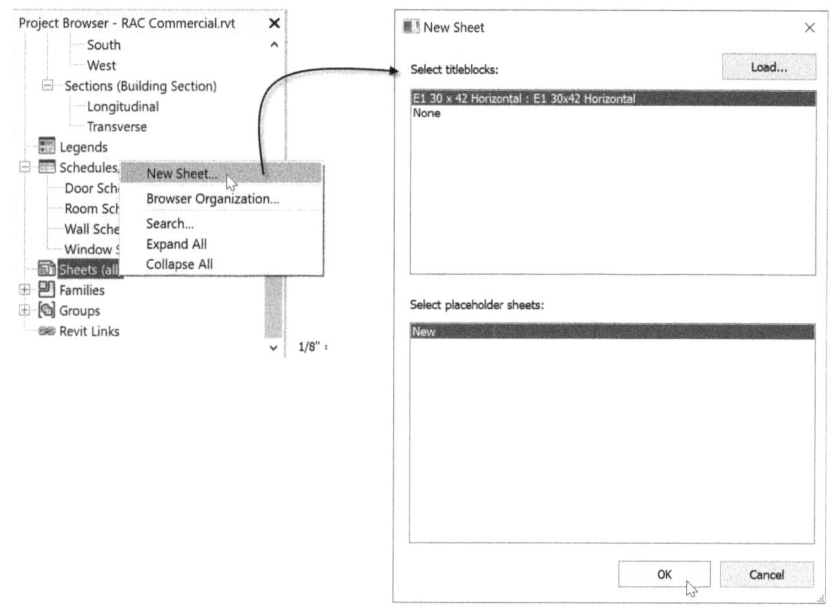

FIGURE 5.43 *Create a new sheet and accept the default title block*

A plus (+) sign will appear next to the Sheets node indicating that a new sheet has been added. The sheet will also open on screen.

2. Expand the *Sheets* branch.

The sheet will have a default name and number that we can change.

⇨ Zoom in on the lower right corner of the title block.

Notice that the title block includes the name and number of the sheet as you would expect.

3. On the Project Browser, right-click on the sheet (currently named A101 -Unnamed) and choose: **Rename**.

⇨ Change the sheet Name to: **Floor Plans**, (leave the number as A101) and then click OK.

Note the change on the title block as well.

> **TIP:** If you prefer, you can rename and re-number Sheets directly in the title block. Click on the title block to highlight it and then click the blue text to edit the value. The result will be the same.

Make sure that the A101 – Floor Plans sheet is open. It should have opened automatically when it was created.

4. Zoom back out.

5. From the Project Browser, drag the *Level 1* floor plan view and drop it on the sheet.

⇨ Click to make the final placement (see Figure 5.44).

• The Aubin Academy •

Setting Up Project Levels and Views | 185

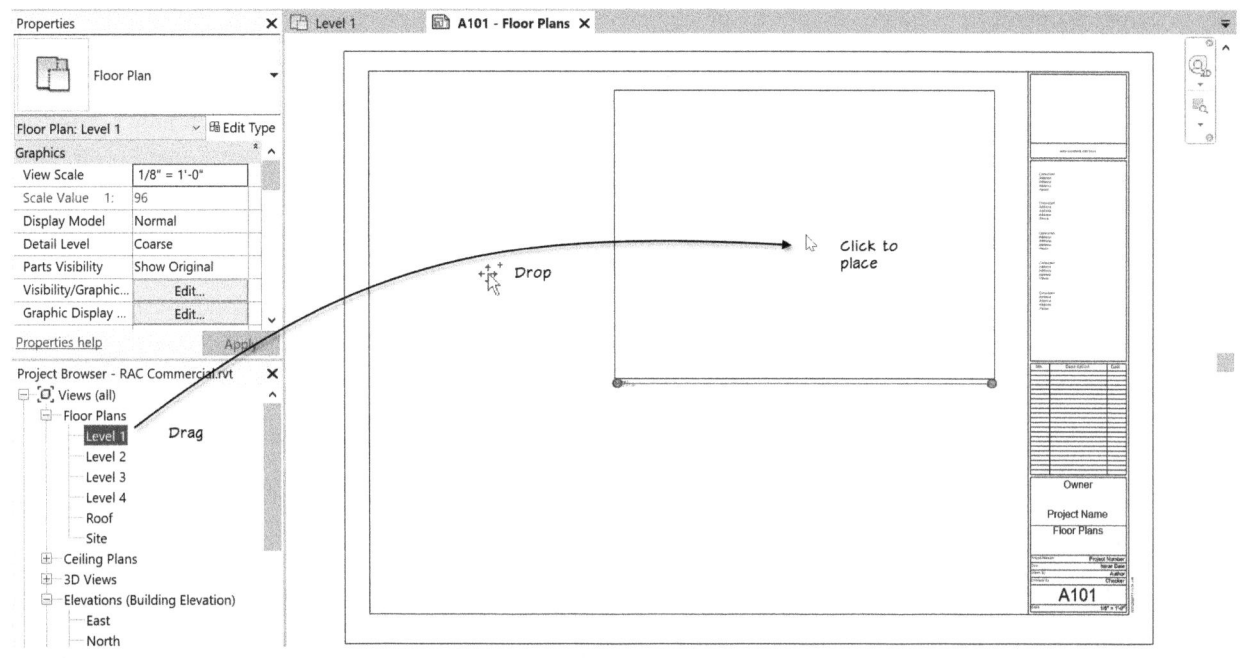

FIGURE 5.44 *Drag the Level 1 floor plan view and drop it on the sheet*

    6.   Zoom in on the view title beneath the floor plan on the sheet.

Notice that the view's name on the sheet is "Level 1." While this is logical, and in some cases desirable, chances are we would like the name of this drawing on the printed sheet to be something else. This is easily changed.

    7.   On the Project Browser, select the *Level 1* floor plan view. (Just select the name on the Project Browser).

    ⇨   On the Properties palette, scroll down to the Identity Data grouping, and then in the "Title on Sheet" parameter field type: **First Floor Plan** (see Figure 5.45).

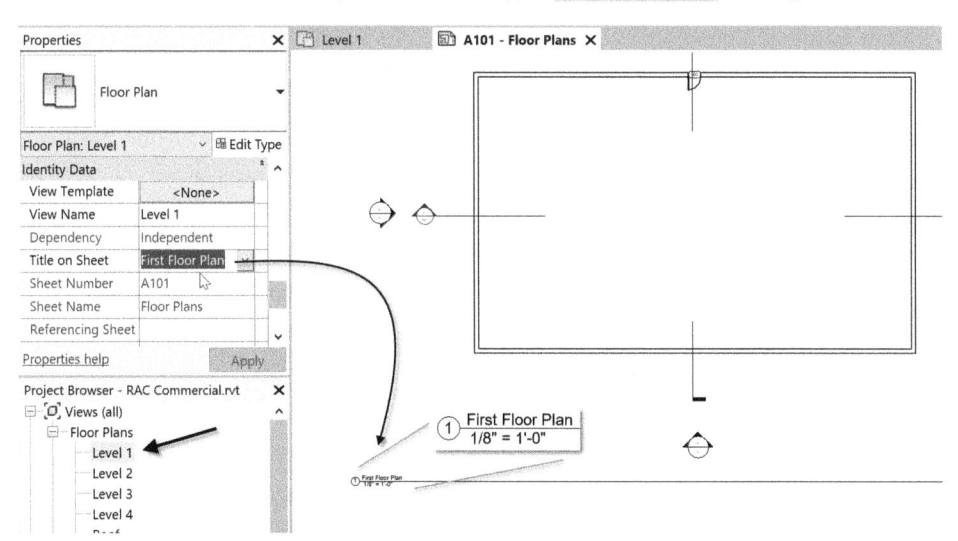

FIGURE 5.45 *Edit the value of the Title on the Sheet*

    8.   Click Apply to complete the change.

Notice the change to the view on the sheet. The Title on Sheet parameter overrides the view name. If you delete the value for Title on Sheet, it will revert to the view name. Also notice that the number in the view title tag has automatically filled in with the number 1. This is because this is the first (and currently only) view on this sheet. Revit will automatically enumerate the annotation of all views as you drag drawings onto sheet views. This will become more apparent when we set up the elevation and section sheets.

• Revit Essentials for Architecture •

186 | Chapter 5

9. Save the project.

Take note of the A101 sheet on the Project Browser. A small plus (+) sign will appear next to a sheet when there are views placed on it. You can click the plus sign to see each view listed beneath the sheet. If you prefer, you can double-click on views from here to open them as an alternative to the *Views (All)* branch we have used up till now.

CREATE A SHEET LIST

Revit makes it easy to create a list of all the drawing sheets in our project. A sheet list will resemble the other schedules that we already have, and it can even be placed on a sheet as a sheet index. Furthermore, it can be used to help us create and edit the sheets in our project. Let's create a sheet list and then use it to add more sheets.

1. On the Project Browser, right-click on the *Schedules/Quantities* branch and choose: **New Sheet List**.

   ⇨ In the "Sheet List Properties" dialog, select Sheet Number and then click the Add parameter icon in the middle.

   ⇨ Add additional fields like Sheet Name, Drawn by, Checked by, Sheet Issue Date and Guide Grid.

> **TIP:** As an alternative to clicking the Add icon, simply double-click the field you want to add.

2. Click the Sorting/Grouping tab.

   ⇨ For Sort by, choose: **Sheet Number** and then click OK.

Fields like drawn by, checked by, and other similar text fields must be edited individually on each sheet. However, one of the benefits of the Sheet List schedule is that you can edit those values directly in the table, which is usually more efficient than doing them individually. Another key advantage to the Sheet List Schedule is that we can use it to create Sheets. Think of it as queuing up list of available sheets, complete with pertinent information filled in and ready to add to the project.

3. On the Modify Schedule/Quantities tab, on the Rows panel, click the Insert Data Row button.

A new row will appear in the Schedule. It will automatically number as sheet A102. Using this method, you can create several "placeholder" sheets and fill in their values in the other columns of the Schedule.

   ⇨ For the name of A102, begin typing: **Floor Plans**. After the first letter or two, Revit will guess the name from your previously input values. You can keep typing, or just choose from the mini pop-up (see Figure 5.46).

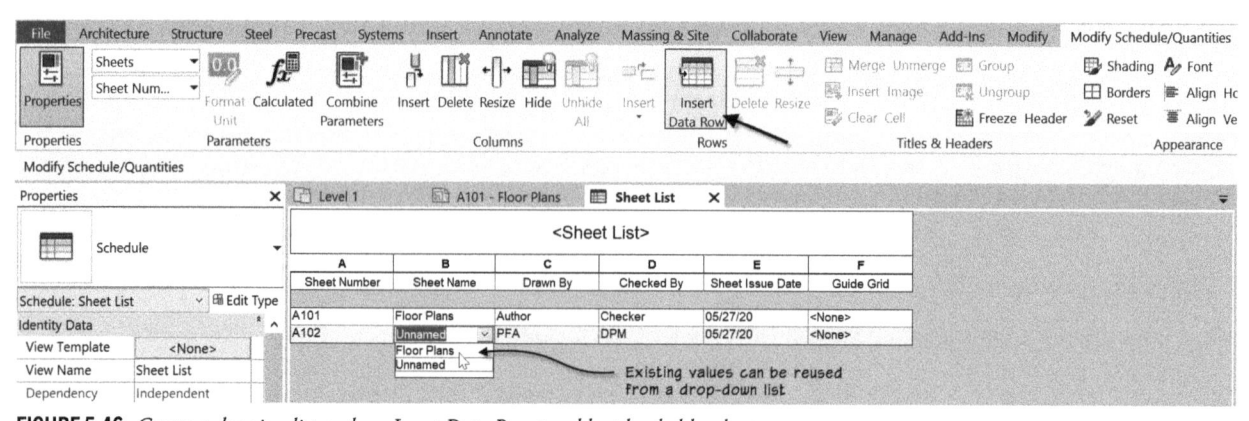

FIGURE 5.46 *Create a drawing list and use Insert Data Row to add a placeholder sheet*

   ⇨ You can input your own initials in the "Drawn By" and "Checked By" fields and input a date for sheet issuance if you like.

Using Table 5.A, we'll set up the rest of the floor and ceiling plan sheets.

• The Aubin Academy •

CREATE THE REMAINING FLOOR PLAN SHEETS

Let's create the remaining floor plan sheets.

1. On the Project Browser, select the *Level 2* floor plan.
   - On the Properties palette, change the "Title on Sheet" parameter to: **Second Floor Plan**.
   - Repeat this process for each view listed in Table 5.A.

> **TIP:** If you prefer to input the Title on Sheet parameter in a schedule, try making a View List. The process is the same as adding a Sheet List and you can you add the Title on Sheet parameter field to the View List. This will enable you to quickly edit it from the Schedule.

2. Repeating the process outlined above, in the Sheet List Schedule, click the Insert Data Row button for each of the sheets listed in the "Drag to Sheet" column of Table 5.A below.
   - Each time you click, check the number in the Sheet Number column and edit as necessary. They will number in sequence, so with a little strategy, you can reduce the amount of renumbering you have to do.
3. Using the values in the table, fill in the sheet names (and other fields if desired).

> **TIP:** To reuse existing values in the Schedule, click the drop down arrow in the text field.

TABLE 5.A *Titles on Sheets for Plan Views*

View Name	Title on Sheet	Drag to Sheet
Floor Plan Views		
Level 2	Second Floor Plan	A102 – Floor Plans
Level 3	Third Floor Plan	A103 – Floor Plans
Level 4	Fourth Floor Plan	A104 – Floor Plans
Roof	Roof Plan	A105 – Roof Plan
Site Plan	Architectural Site Plan	A100 – Architectural Site Plan
Ceiling Plan Views		
Level 1	First Floor Reflected Ceiling Plan	A111 – Reflected Ceiling Plans
Level 2	Second Floor Reflected Ceiling Plan	A112 – Reflected Ceiling Plans
Level 3	Third Floor Reflected Ceiling Plan	A113 – Reflected Ceiling Plans
Level 4	Fourth Floor Reflected Ceiling Plan	A114 – Reflected Ceiling Plans

> **NOTE:** The sheet numbers suggested here are based on the US National CAD Standard recommendations. If you prefer a different sheet numbering scheme, feel free to use it instead.

> **TIP:** If you want to quickly input the Drawn By and Checked By fields, you can make the Sheet List schedule the active tab, then on the Properties palette, click the Edit button next to Sorting/Grouping. In the "Schedule Properties" dialog that appears, set the Sort by to (none) and uncheck "Itemize every instance." When you click OK, you will have a single line item in the schedule. Edit the values for Drawn by and Checked by. Do not edit any other fields as when the schedule is configured this way, you are editing ALL sheets at once. When you are finished, return to Sorting/Grouping and reset to Sort by Number and turn itemize every instance back on.

CREATING SHEET VIEWS FROM PLACEHOLDER SHEETS

We now have nine new placeholder sheets in our sheet list, but if you look at the Project Browser, we still have just the one sheet. The purpose of adding placeholder sheets is that it allows you to configure a list of standard sheets and to input all the fields before you need the sheet in the set. Another useful purpose of placeholder sheets is to allow the addition of consultant sheets to the sheet list without having those sheet views listed in your Project Browser. When you are ready, you simply add a new sheet as we did before, but this time we will be able to choose from the list of available placeholder sheets.

If it is not already, open the Sheet List schedule.

> **NOTE:** On the Modify Schedules/Quantities tab, on the Filter Placeholder Sheets tab, there are three buttons. The default one is: Show. This shows both placeholder and actual sheets in the list. The Hide button hides the placeholders showing only the actual sheets in the list and the Isolate button does the opposite. Try these out before continuing if you wish.

1. On the Modify Schedules/Quantities tab, click the New Sheet button.

    This is the same as right-clicking the *Sheets (all)* branch on the Project Browser as we did above.

    Notice the list of placeholder sheets at the bottom.

2. Select A100 in the list. Hold down the SHIFT key and then select A114 and then click OK (see Figure 5.47).

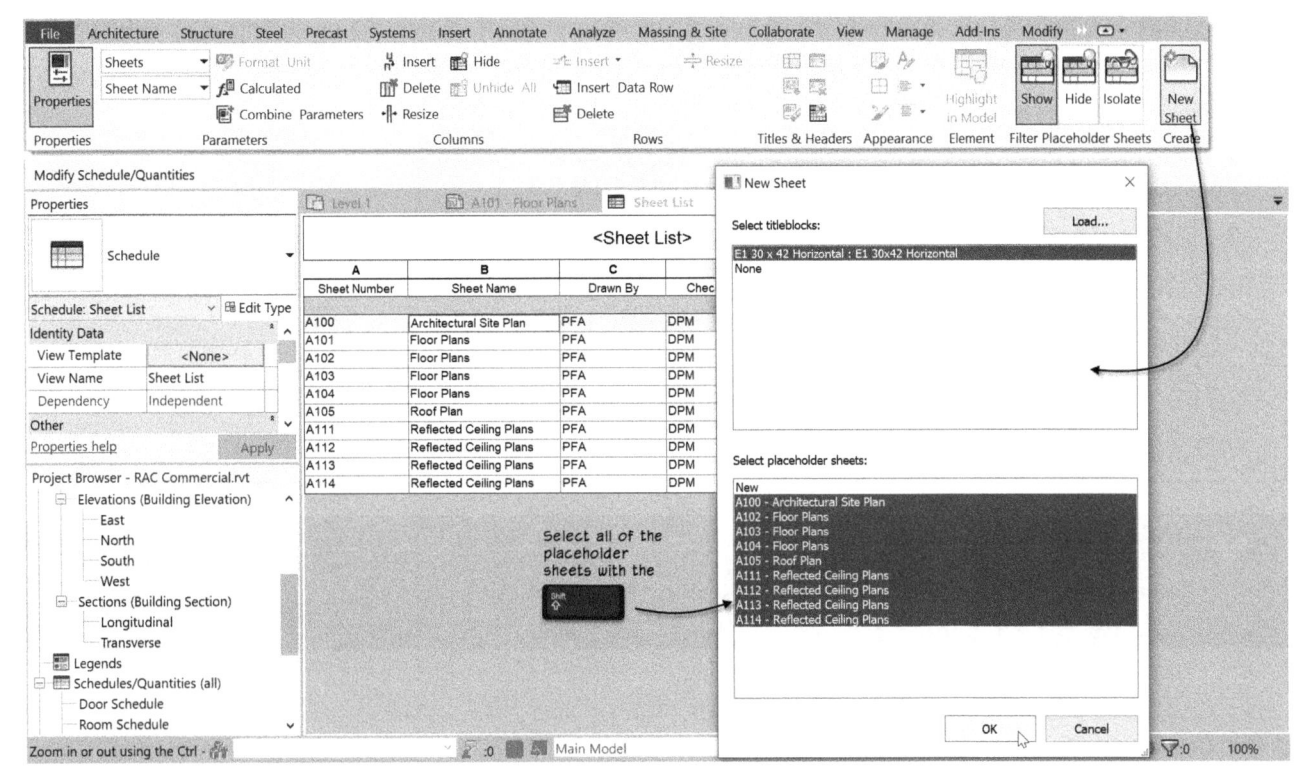

FIGURE 5.47 *Create several sheets at once using placeholder sheets*

Nine new sheets will appear on the Project Browser ready for you to drag and drop views. Zooming in on the title blocks will reveal that all the data input in the Schedule is already filled into the appropriate fields. Now that we have all our plan sheets created, let's add the views to them.

Right now, we will simply drag the views onto the appropriate sheets and place them in approximately the same location. Once we have the Structural Grids in Chapter 6, we can adjust the position of the manually placed views to make sure that they all align with one another using the Guide Grid feature. With the Guide Grid feature you can overlay a grid on top of a title block sheet and use it to keep similar views lined up across multiple sheets. But since it requires the column grids, we will wait till Chapter 6 to explore that feature.

3. Using Table 5.A above as a guide, drag each of the floor and ceiling plan views onto their respective sheets.

⇨ Place each one in the same general area on the sheet.

> **NOTE:** If you are working in the Metric files, the scale of the *Site* plan should be changed before adding to the sheet. To do this, open the *Site* plan view, scroll down and click the button next to View Template and then in the dialog that appears, change the scale to: **1:200**.

4. Save the project.

CREATE ELEVATION AND SECTION SHEETS

We will need a couple of sheets for our building elevations and building sections.

1. Repeating the process outlined above, create the sheet views indicated in Table 5.B

190 | Chapter 5

Two methods were covered above. Create the sheet directly (using the tool on the ribbon or right-click on the *Sheets* branch of the Project Browser) or you can first create placeholder sheets in the Sheet List schedule and then create the sheets from those placeholders. You can use whichever method you prefer here.

2. Repeating the process outlined above, edit the "Title on Sheet" parameter of each of the elevation and section views as indicated in Table 5.B.

3. Drag each of the views to the appropriate Sheets as indicated in Table 5.B.

    As an alternative, you can also place views on sheets using the View button. This is on the View tab, on the Sheet Composition panel.

NOTE: You are only creating three additional sheets here and there are two views being placed on each of these sheets.

TIP: If your elevation or section views are too wide for the sheet, you can use the crop region handles to resize them. The crop region is already on by default for section views. For elevation views, you must repeat the process outlined earlier in the "Adjusting Elevation Cropping" topic on page 174 above to edit.

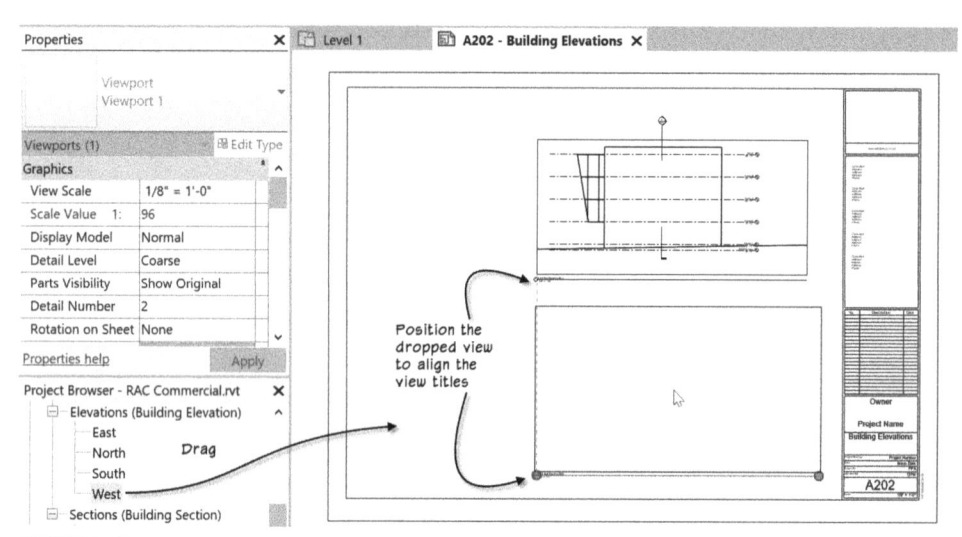

FIGURE 5.48 *Create elevation and section sheets and drag the appropriate views*

When you create your first elevation sheet, you will notice that the second view you drag to the sheet attempts to align automatically with the first as you drag. This will help you keep the sheet neatly organized (see Figure 5.48).

Setting Up Project Levels and Views | 191

TABLE 5.B *Titles on Sheets for Elevation and Section Views*

View Name	Title on Sheet	Drag to Sheet
Elevation Views		
North	North Building Elevation	A201 – Building Elevations
South	South Building Elevation	A201 – Building Elevations
East	East Building Elevation	A202 – Building Elevations
West	West Building Elevation	A202 – Building Elevations
Section Views		
Longitudinal	Longitudinal Building Section	A301 – Building Sections
Transverse	Transverse Building Section	A301 – Building Sections

    4.   Create one more sheet numbered: **A601** and titled: **Schedules**.

⇨   Drag each of the schedule views (except the view and sheet lists) and drop them on this sheet.

For now, just position them so that there is room for them to grow as the project progresses. In some cases, you will notice that the data in columns might wrap to a second line. You can use the small triangular control handles at the top of each column to drag and resize them.

When you have completed these Sheets, take note of the elevation and section tags in the various views. All of the callouts will fill in automatically with their position on the sheet and sheet number (see Figure 5.49).

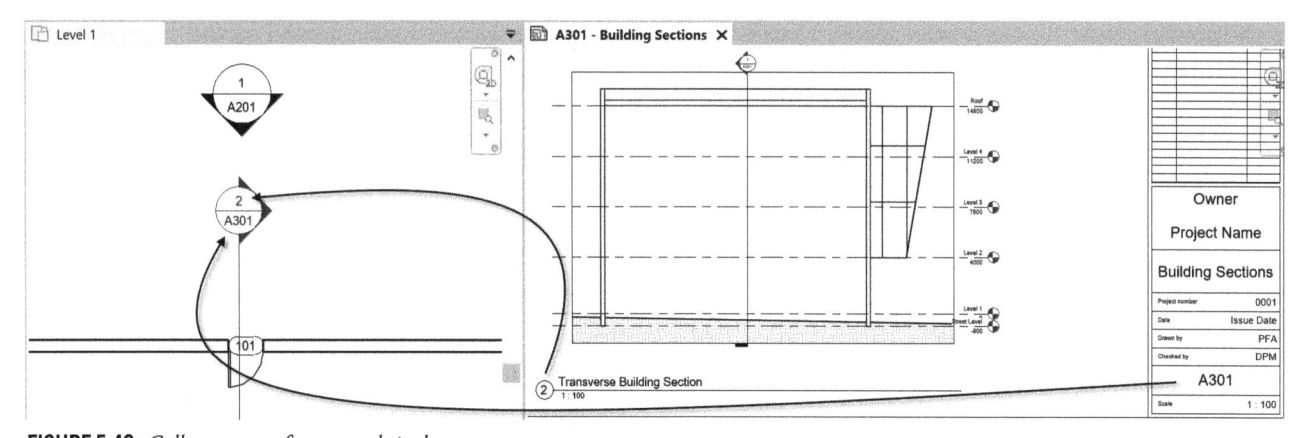

FIGURE 5.49 *Callouts cross reference to their sheets*

ADJUSTING VIEW TITLES

When you drag a view onto a sheet, the viewport automatically creates a view title that spans the width of the viewport. Sometimes you want to adjust the placement and length of this view title. You can also remove them if you don't want them displayed.

    1.   Double-click to open the A301 sheet.

    2.   Click on the upper viewport (this is one of your section views).

192 | Chapter 5

Notice that shape handles appear at each end of the view title. You can use these to resize it.

⇨   Using the shape handle at the right, drag the title to about half of its current width.

3.   Click on the other viewport and repeat.

⇨   Drag the length of the second one to match the first. It should snap automatically (see the left side of Figure 5.50).

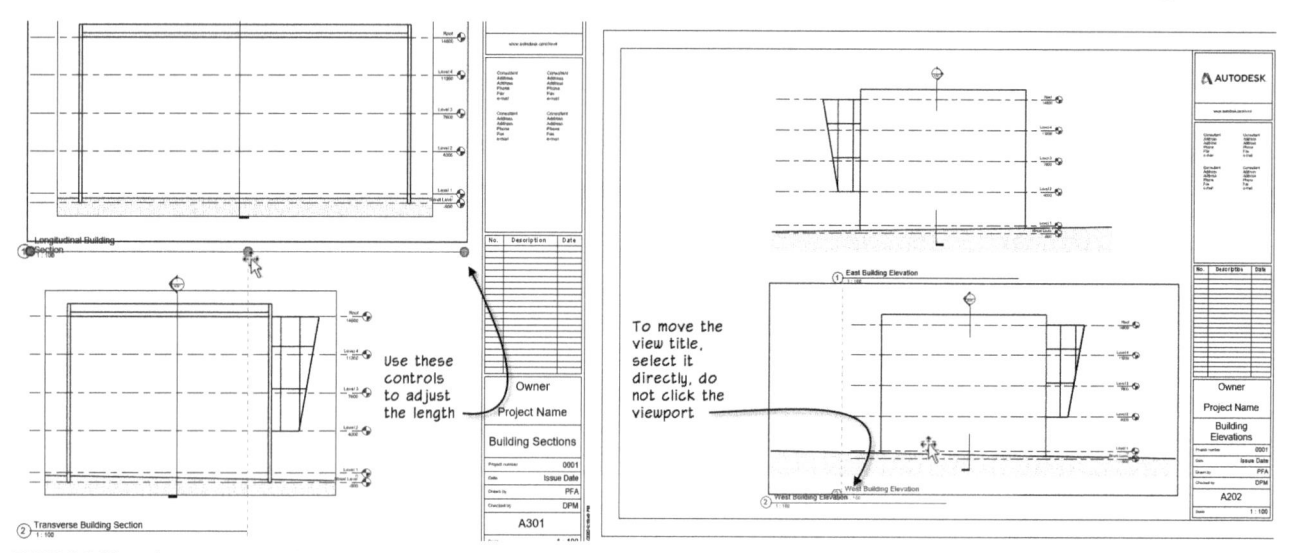

FIGURE 5.50 *Adjusting view title length and moving the view title*

If you want to move a view title without moving the viewport, you must select it separately.

4.   Deselect everything. Click directly on the view title (not on the viewport).

⇨   Drag it where you want it to go (see the right side of Figure 5.50).

> **BIM Manager Note:** In some cases, when you increase the length of the title on the sheet parameter, the title bar under the viewport will wrap the title onto two lines. If you prefer to have it not wrap, you can edit the view title family. To do this, expand the *Families* branch on the Project Browser and then expand *Annotation Symbols*. Right-click on *View Title* [*M_View Title*] and then choose: **Edit**. In the dialog that appears, click Yes. In the Family Editor window that opens, click on the View Name label on screen, and use the Drag handle on the right to make it wider. On the ribbon, click the Load into Projects and Close button. If a dialog appears showing multiple projects, check the box next to your *REA Commercial* project and then click OK. If prompted to save the family, click Yes and choose where you want to save it. In the "Reload Family" dialog, choose the "Override parameter values of existing types" item. Any sheets that previously wrapped the title to two lines should now be displaying on a single line.

MANAGE OPEN VIEWS

At this point, every sheet that we have created is likely still open. You can see which views and sheets are open using the Switch Windows drop down button on the QAT or on the far right of the view tabs. In a project this size, it is probably OK to have several windows open at once; however, as a matter of best practice, it is a good idea to periodically close unused windows. The easiest way to do this is with the Close Inactive tool on the View tab. If you have views tiled onscreen, this command will close all but the active tab in each tile.

1.   If necessary, use the switch windows drop down to choose A101 – Floor Plans from the list (you can also double-click this view on the Project Browser to make it active.

2.   On the View tab of the ribbon (or the QAT), click the Close Hidden icon.

Setting Up Project Levels and Views | 193

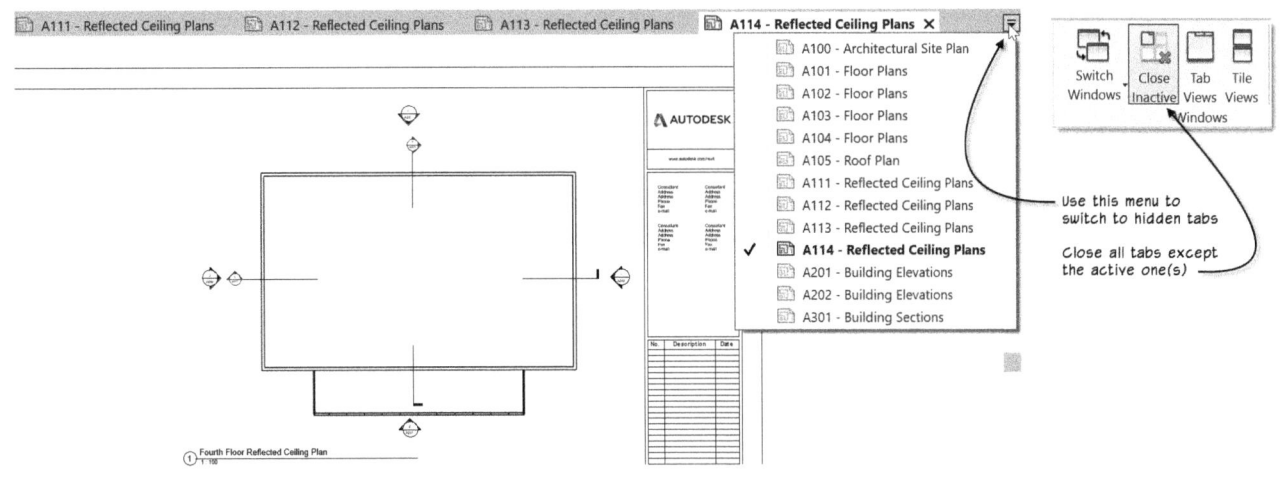

FIGURE 5.51 *Maximize and then close hidden windows*

3. Save the project.

CREATE A CUSTOM TITLE BLOCK FAMILY

The only sheet we still need at this stage is a cover sheet. To create it, we will build a custom title block family. Many times, firms have title blocks already drawn in other CAD programs that they wish to import into Revit. You can do this if you wish. The exact steps will not be covered here. The approach we will use here will be to create a very simple title block family from scratch using Revit tools. You can see what this will look like in Figure 5.54 below.

> **NOTE:** If you prefer to skip this exercise, you can instead load the custom title block family file provided with the dataset files. To do so, skip to the "Create a Cover Sheet" topic on page 196 below.

1. From the File menu, choose: **New > Family**.

   ⇨ In the "New Title Block" dialog, double-click the *Title blocks* folder, select the
   E1 - 42 × 30.rft [A1 metric.rft] template and then click Open.

   The ribbon will change to reflect that we are now in the Family Editor.

2. On the Create tab of the ribbon, click the Line tool.

   ⇨ On the Modify | Place Lines tab, on the Subcategory panel, choose: **<Wide Lines>** from the Style list.

   ⇨ On the Draw panel, click the rectangle icon.

   ⇨ On the Options bar, in the Offset field, type: **3/4"** [**18**].

3. Click the first corner of the rectangle by snapping to the one of the corners of the rectangle already in the file.

   ⇨ After you click the first corner, tap the SPACEBAR to flip the offset to the
   inside and then click the diagonally opposite corner.

The new rectangle will appear 3/4" [18] smaller than the original one due to the offset we used.

   ⇨ On the ribbon, click the Modify tool or press the ESC key twice.

4. Select the bottom line of the rectangle you just drew.

   ⇨ On the Modify | Lines tab, click the Copy button.

   ⇨ Click any start point, move straight up 6" [130] for the second point.

You can use the temporary dimensions or type in the value.

• Revit Essentials for Architecture •

194 | Chapter 5

5. Draw five vertical lines within this space to separate it into a series of boxes (see item 1 in Figure 5.52).

6. On the Modify tab, on the Measure panel, click the Use the Aligned Dimension tool.

   ⇨ Add witness lines starting with the vertical edge on the left side, include each of five vertical lines, and end with the vertical edge on the other side (seven witness lines total) (see item 2 in Figure 5.52).

   ⇨ Click anywhere above the boxes to place the dimension and then click the EQ toggle (see item 3 in Figure 5.52).

   This will space all the lines equally.

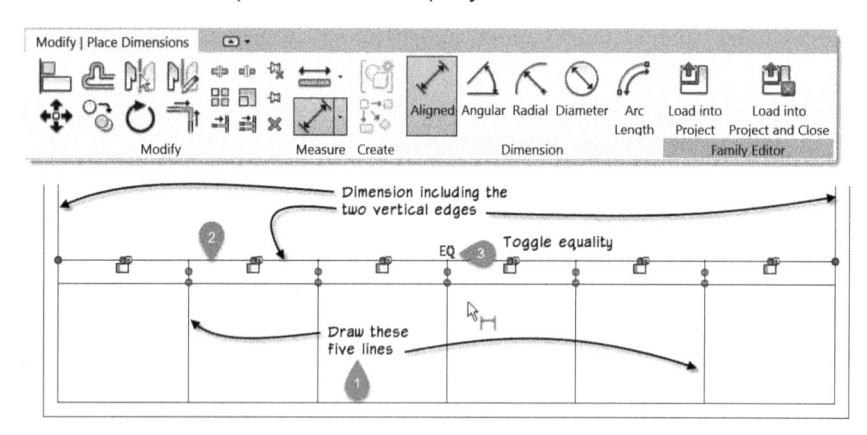

FIGURE 5.52 *Draw a horizontal bar at the bottom and divide it into boxes*

7. On the Create tab of the ribbon, click the Text tool.

8. On the Properties palette, click the Edit Type button and then click the Duplicate button.

   ⇨ Name the new text type: **Title Text** and then click OK.

   ⇨ For the Text Size, type: **1/2"** [**10**].

   ⇨ Select the Bold check box and then click OK.

   Feel free to change the font or other settings if you like.

9. In the first box that you drew above, click a point in the upper left corner to place the text.

   ⇨ Type the following: (press ENTER after each line)

   Consultant Name

   Address 1

   Address 2

   Phone

   ⇨ On the ribbon, click the Modify tool or press the ESC key twice.

10. Copy this block of text to the next box.

    Leave a couple of boxes empty for a company logo and an Architect's seal.

    You can add a new text note to one of them that says: **Drawing Index:** and another that says: **Architect's Seal:**. You might want to use the smaller text size (see Figure 5.53).

• The Aubin Academy •

Setting Up Project Levels and Views | 195

FIGURE 5.53 *Add text blocks for consultants and a location for the Architect's seal*

If you want to import a company logo, click the Insert tab, then click the Image button. Browse to the location of an image file to bring it in. The file must be saved in JPG, JPEG, BMP or PNG image file formats. Once you place the image, use the handle at the corner to resize it.

11. On the Create tab, click the Label tool.

12. Use the same procedure as above to create a new Label Type called:
 Large Titles. Make the text size 1" [25] and Bold.

13. Click OK after creating the Type and then choose the Center icon on the Alignment panel before placing the label.

 ⇨ Click a point near the top middle of the title block.

 ⇨ In the "Edit Label" dialog, double-click **Project Name** to add it to the Label Parameters list and then click OK.

 ⇨ Drag the handles to make the title wider.

14. Create another Label type with smaller text size and add additional centered labels beneath the title such as Project Address and Issue Date (see Figure 5.54).

> **NOTE:** In the "Edit Label" dialog, you can add more than one parameter to a single Label. So for example, Project Address, Project Issue Date, and Client Name can all be added to the same Label. On the far right, check the box in the break column to make each parameter fall on its own line.

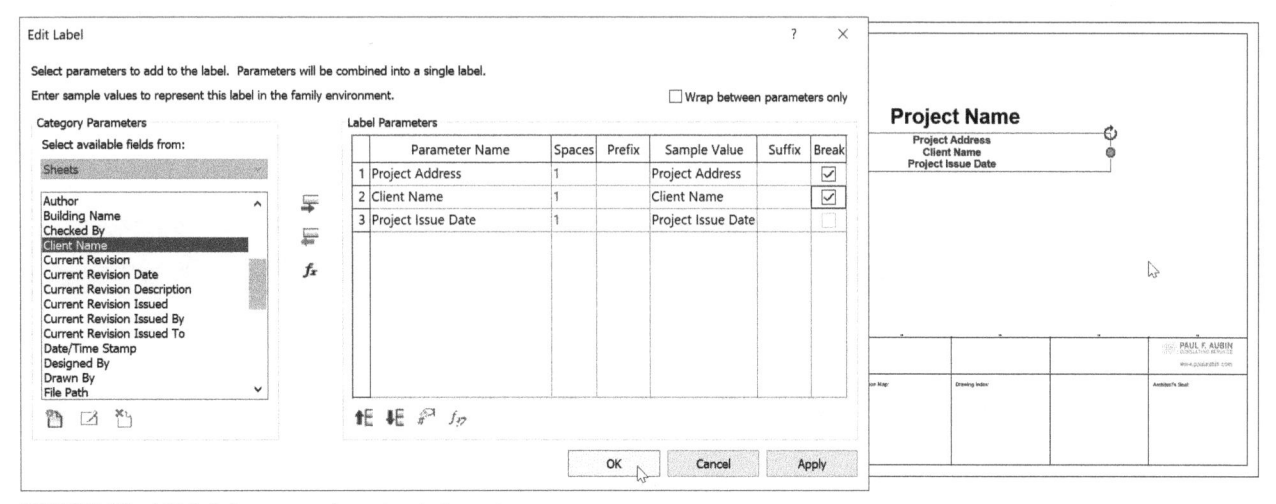

FIGURE 5.54 *Add Labels to report the project information*

Feel free to make any other embellishments you wish. You can draw additional lines and add more labels and text. Use labels when you wish to link the text to project data. When this title block is used in the project, the Project Name, Client Name, Address and Date will automatically fill in. The consultants on the other hand will need to be edited manually in the title block later. While it is possible to make the consultant items link to labels as well, the

196 | Chapter 5

process to do so is beyond the scope of this short tutorial. Consult the online help for more information on creating title blocks and custom shared parameters if you wish to learn more.

15. On the Family Editor panel, click the Load into Project and Close button.

⇨ In the "Save File" dialog that appears, click Yes.

⇨ Save the title block family to the folder of your choice. Name it: **REA E1 30 × 42 Cover Sheet** [**REA A1 Cover Sheet**] and then click Save.

If you get a warning it is OK to ignore it. If you are already in a sheet, it will try to place the title block in the existing sheet. Just press ESC to cancel.

CREATE A COVER SHEET

Now that you have built your own custom title block family for the cover sheet, we can use it in the project and create the cover sheet.

1. On the Project Browser, right-click *Sheets* and choose: **New Sheet**.

⇨ In the "New Sheet" dialog, choose your new cover sheet title block and then click OK.

> **NOTE:** If you decided to skip the title block family creation exercise above, click the Load button and browse to the *Chapter05* folder. Select the *REA E1 30 × 42 Cover Sheet.rfa* [*REA A1 Cover Sheet.rfa*] file and then click Open.

2. On the Project Browser, right-click on the new sheet (currently A602 – Unnamed) and choose: **Rename**.

⇨ Re-number it to: **G100** and rename it to: **Cover**.

Why don't we add a 3D axonometric of the project to our Cover Sheet? We can use the default *{3D}* view, but since it is opened automatically by the Default 3D View tool, it might be better to create a copy of it first to prevent accidental or unintended modifications to the cover sheet.

3. On the Project Browser, expand *3D Views*, right-click the *{3D}* view and choose: **Duplicate View > Duplicate**.

⇨ Rename the view: **Cover Axonometric**.

4. Use the ViewCube and Steering Wheels to adjust the view to a pleasing vantage point.

⇨ Right-click directly on the ViewCube and choose: **Save View**.

> **TIP:** If you have a wheel mouse, hold down the SHIFT key and drag with the wheel to quickly spin the model in 3D.

5. Drag the Cover Axonometric view onto the Cover Sheet and position it.

When you drop the view on the Cover Sheet, it is probably too large for the Sheet. We can easily adjust the scale of a view after it has been placed.

6. On the Project Browser, select the *Cover Axonometric* view.

⇨ On the Properties palette, from the view Scale list, choose a smaller scale.

We also do not want a title under this viewport on the cover. To do this, we need to duplicate the viewport type.

7. Select the viewport on the sheet (click directly on it).

The Properties palette should read Viewport: Viewport 1 on the Type Selector.

Setting Up Project Levels and Views | 197

⇨ On the Properties palette, click the Edit Type button (see Figure 5.55).

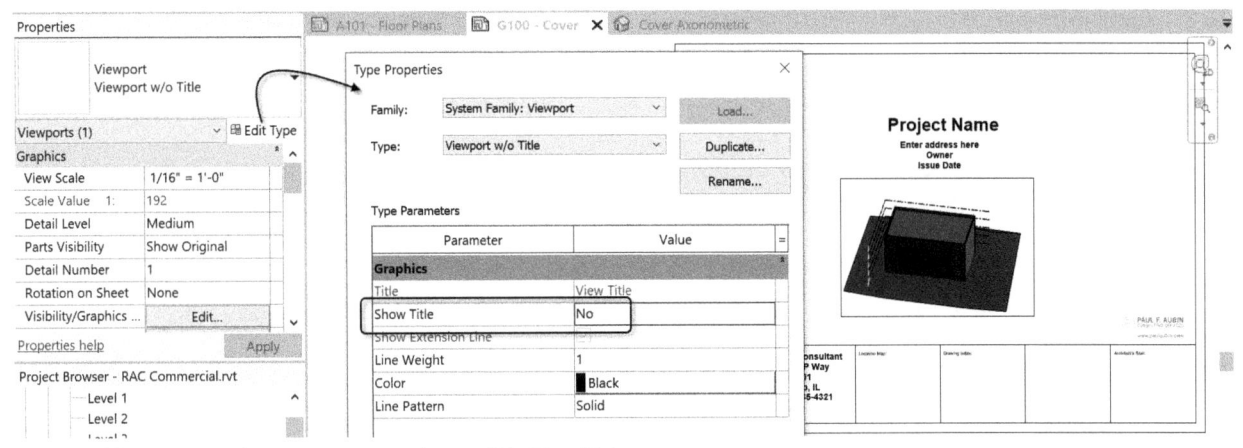

FIGURE 5.55 *Duplicate the Viewport Type and turn off the View Title*

⇨ Click the Duplicate button, name the new type: **Viewport w/o Title** and then click OK.

⇨ For Show Title, choose No and then click OK.

> **NOTE:** If you are using the Metric files, you can use the No Title Type already in the project instead of creating a new one.

8. Reposition the view as necessary.

EDIT PROJECT INFORMATION

When we built the title block family, we created labels that would display the project data such as name and address. You may have noticed that most fields have not yet changed yet. The information that these labels reference is global to the entire project and is stored in a common system family named "Project Information." We can edit its values at any time, and the new values will immediately populate all sheets in the project. Let's take a look.

1. On the Manage tab, click the Project Information button.

⇨ In the "Project Properties" dialog, input values for the various fields (see Figure 5.56).

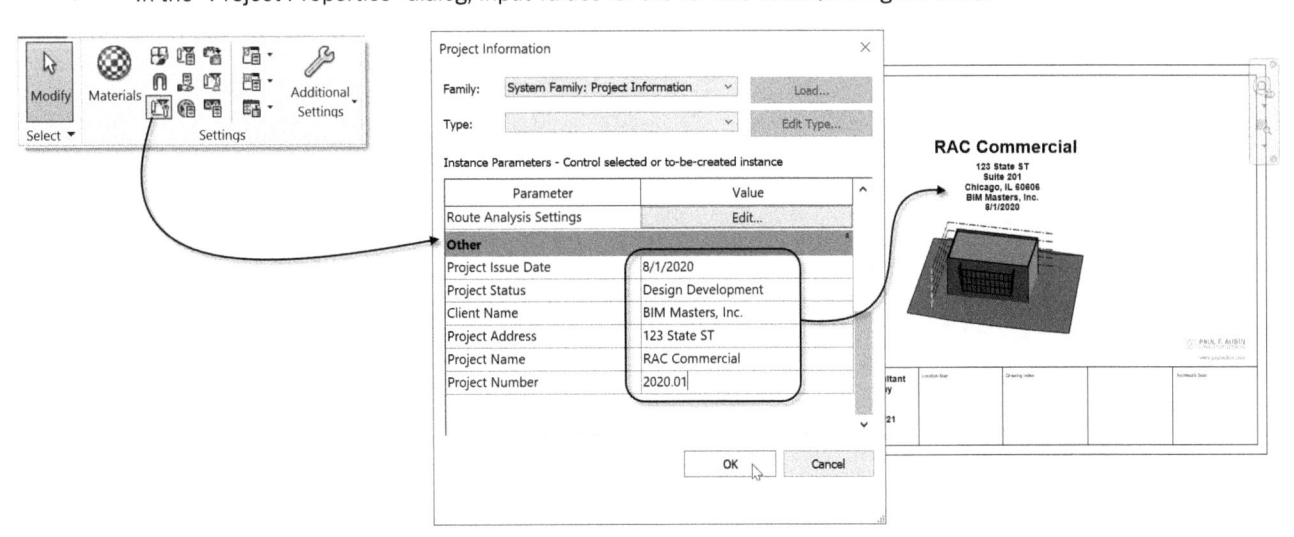

FIGURE 5.56 *Edit Project Information*

2. Open any sheet and view the title block fields.

• Revit Essentials for Architecture •

198 | Chapter 5

Notice the change to the values.

3. Save the project.

ASSIGN A STARTING VIEW

A starting view will open whenever you open the project regardless of which view was active when the project was last saved. In this case, we will use this feature to set our new cover sheet as the starting view for the project.

1. On the Manage tab, on the Manage Project panel, click the Starting View button.
2. In the "Starting View" dialog that appears, choose: **Sheet: G100 – Cover Sheet** and then click OK.
3. Save the project.

To see the effect of this change, you would need to close the project and then reopen it. Feel free to do this now if you wish, or you can simply wait till later to test it out.

WORKING WITH BROWSER ORGANIZATION

As the quantity of views and sheets in your projects increases, you may find it useful to explore other ways to organize your Project Browser. For example, you can choose to hide all views that are already on sheets from the *Views* branch of the Project Browser. You can also customize the choices available.

MODIFY BROWSER ORGANIZATION

As noted above, you can expand the plus sign next to the sheet and then double-click the view indented beneath it to open a view directly. You can also open the sheet first and then right-click the viewport and choose: **Activate View**. This allows you to work directly in the view while maintaining the context of its placement on the sheet for reference.

1. On the Project Browser, scroll to the top and then select: *Views (all)*.
⇨ On the Properties palette, from the Type Selector, choose: **not on sheets**.

This will filter the view list to show only those views that have not yet been placed on sheets. In our case, only the default *{3D}* view will remain (see Figure 5.57).

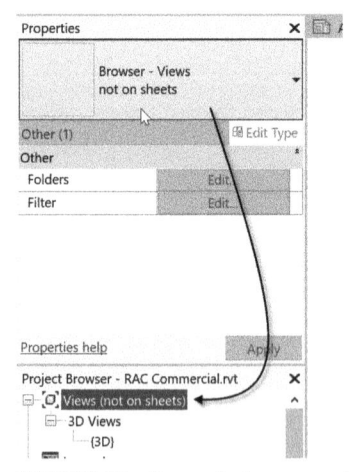

FIGURE 5.57 *Change the browser to display only the views not already on sheets*

There are other browser organization types as well. One sorts by discipline, another by phase, and so on. The not on sheets type gives the most dramatic difference at the current stage of our project.

• The Aubin Academy •

2. Return to the: **Views (all)** organization.

Similar filtering types are available for the *Sheets* branch. To see them, select the *Sheets (All)* branch of the Project Browser and look to the choices on the Type Selector. A good one is: Sheet Prefix.

3. On the Project Browser, select the *Sheets (All)* branch.

⇨ On the Properties palette, from the Type Selector, choose: **Sheet Prefix**.

This organization will give us two groupings, one for the "A" sheets and another for the "G" sheets. Often architects have sheet numbering schemes where the first two or three characters are codes for drawing types. With the NCS-derived numbering scheme suggested above, the first character is the discipline code and the number immediately following it is a drawing type code where 1 equals plans, 2 equals elevations, 3 equals sections, and so on. In this case, it might be useful to filter the list by the first two characters rather than just the first. Using Browser Organization, we can create our own types.

4. On the Project Browser, right-click the *Sheets (Sheet Prefix)* branch and choose: **Browser Organization**.

⇨ In the "Browser Organization" dialog, click the Edit button.

⇨ In the "Browser Organization Properties" dialog, click the Grouping and Sorting tab.

You can sort and group by several items. Only the first one is used in this case. Group by is set to Sheet Number with 1 leading character. We simply need to change this to 2.

⇨ For the first Group by option, change the number of Leading characters to: **2** (see Figure 5.58).

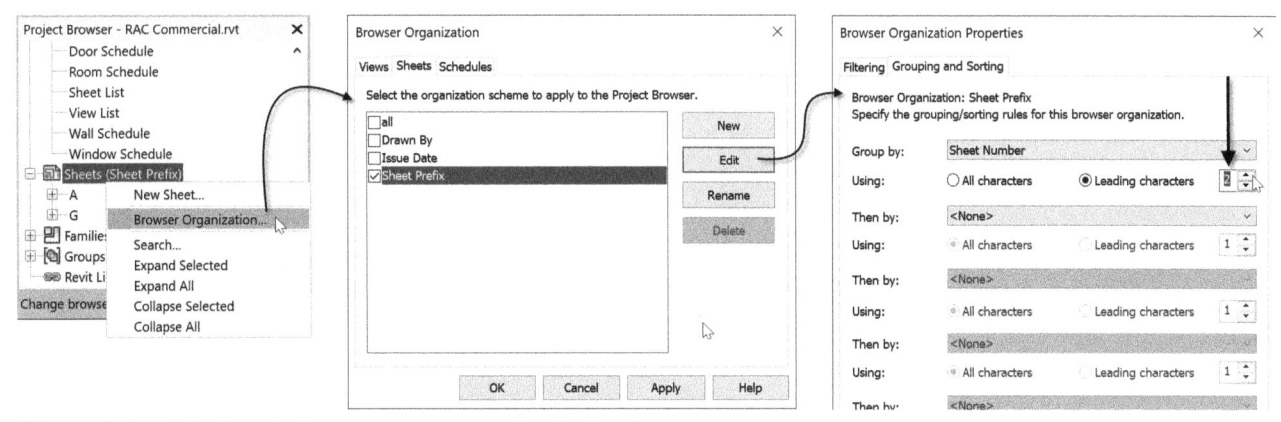

FIGURE 5.58 *Edit the Sheet Prefix organization to group by 2 leading characters*

5. Click OK twice.

Explore the results in the Project Browser. It should look like Figure 5.59.

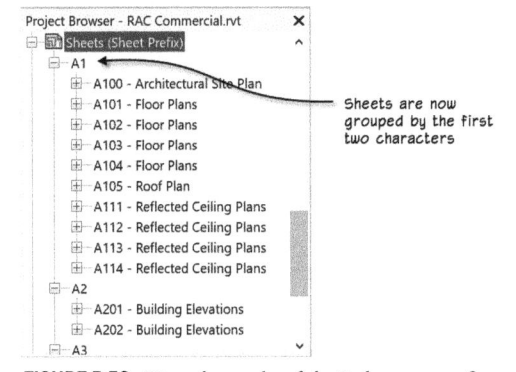

FIGURE 5.59 *View the results of the 2 character prefix*

• Revit Essentials for Architecture •

200 | Chapter 5

This provides a nice organization, but unfortunately the general sheets which should come first appear at the bottom of this alphabetical list. We have no control over this on Browser Organization, but we can do something about the Sheet List.

CREATE A CUSTOM PARAMETER

If we return to the Sheet List that we created above, we will see that all of the latest sheets including the Cover Sheet should now appear on the list.

1. On the Project Browser, beneath *Schedules/Quantities*, double-click the *Sheet List* schedule.

    You can make any modifications to the parameters listed that might be necessary.

You may notice one small problem with our sheet list. While all the "A" sheets sort nicely, our Cover Sheet appears last in the list. This is an unfortunate limitation in the sorting options we have available. Let's look at a work-around solution to address this problem.

2. On the Properties palette, click the Edit button next to Fields.

3. In the "Sheet List Properties" dialog, on the Fields tab, click the New Parameter icon in the middle.

    ⇨ In the "Parameter Properties" dialog, for the Name input: **Sheet Sort Number**.

    ⇨ For the "Type of Parameter" choose: **Number** and then click OK once (see Figure 5.60).

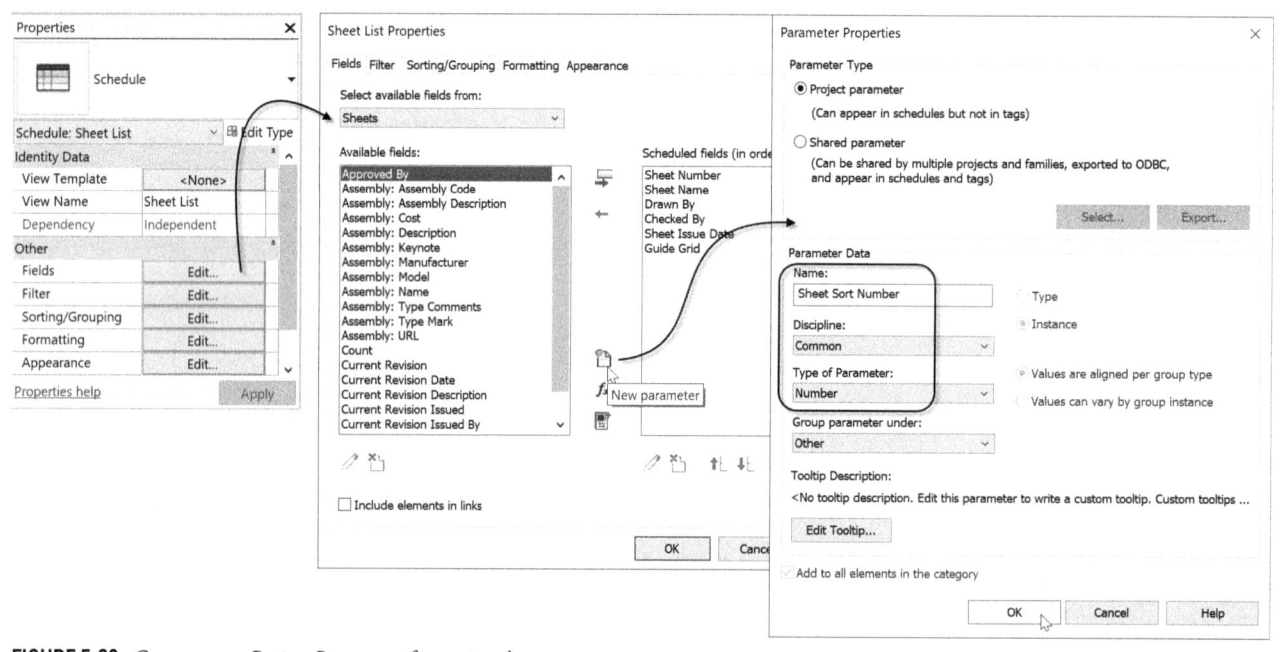

FIGURE 5.60 *Create a new Project Parameter for sorting sheets*

What we have created is a custom parameter that can receive a numeric value. Next, we'll change the sorting of the table to sort on our new field so that sheet G100 can come before sheet A100.

4. Still in the "Sheet List Properties" dialog, click the Sorting/Grouping tab.

    ⇨ Change Sort by to: **Sheet Sort Number** and then select the Descending radio button.

5. For the next sort criterion (next to "Then by"), choose: **Sheet Number** and leave it set to Ascending.

    ⇨ Click OK to finish.

Setting Up Project Levels and Views | 201

An empty Sheet Sort Number column will appear in the table. Simply input numbers into these fields to indicate how you want the sheets to sort. However, since we only needed to force the cover sheet to the top of the list, using two sort criteria as indicated will spare us the effort of inputting values in this field for all sheets. When you sort in ascending order, any blank fields will come first. Therefore, the list currently looks the same. Inputting any value in the cover sheet will force it to the top (since we told the first sort to go in reverse—descending). If you find this "trick" confusing, feel free to input an actual number in the Sheet Sort Number field for every sheet.

6. Input 1 in the Sheet Sort Number field for the G100 sheet (see Figure 5.61).

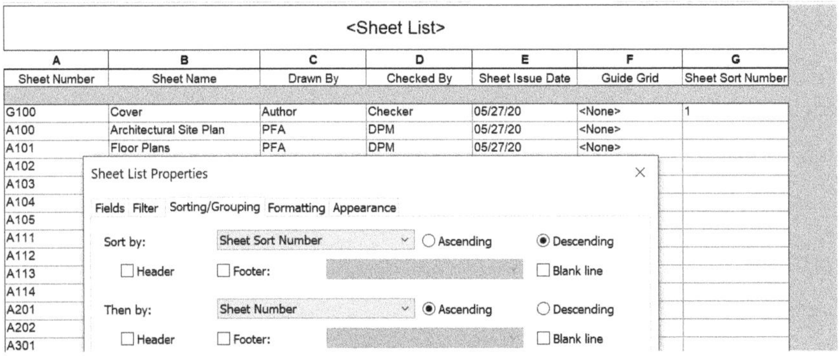

FIGURE 5.61 *Edit the sorting values in the Drawing List table*

7. Save the project.

There are many other ways you can customize the browser organization even further. For example, you can add additional grouping criteria, filter the list and change how the items sort. If you would like to experiment, you can edit browser organization again, and this time, click the New button. Give the new browser organization a name, and then edit the settings. You can also customize the Browser Organization for the Schedules branch as well.

DRAFTING VIEWS

One other type of view bears mention in this discussion: the Drafting view. A drafting view is unlike other views in that it is not linked to anything in the model. The purpose of a drafting view is to create details, diagrams, or sketches that are not easily modeled or that you and your project team have deemed not worth modeling. Remember that Building Information Modeling is as much about information as it is about graphics. In some cases, a simple diagram or some sketched embellishment on a detail is all that is required to convey design intent. In these cases, a drafting view is often appropriate. Drafting views provide a blank sheet of paper suitable for importing legacy CAD details, image files or natively drawn sketches.

While we are not creating any drafting views in this chapter, Chapter 12 is devoted to the subject of detailing. We will have the opportunity to add drafting views to our project at that time. Also you can look back to the "Explore a Detail View" topic on page 60 in Chapter 2 for an example of a drafting view.

PRINTING A DIGITAL CARTOON SET

Going through the upfront process of creating sheet views gives you a few benefits. First, this task can be handled by a single individual early in the project without the pressure of a looming deadline. If one person sets up all the necessary sheets, there is a greater chance for consistency from sheet to sheet in terms of naming and drawing placement. Following this process also gives you a digital cartoon set. Just like the traditional cartoon set, the digital version will help make good decisions about project documentation requirements and the impact on budget and personnel considerations. One extra advantage of the digital cartoon set over the traditional one is that the digital one becomes the real building model and document set! Don't be concerned with the finality that this seems to imply. The model remains completely flexible and editable (as we have seen).

PREPARING FOR OUTPUT

Before you print it is always a good idea to check over your views and sheets one more time and make any final modifications required. In addition to anything you may have missed when going through this chapter, we have one finishing touch to add to our cover sheet. Let's put the sheet list on the cover. However, in its current state, it shows many fields that we may not want to include on the cover sheet index. This is not a problem. We can easily make a duplicate of our sheet list and modify it specifically for the needs of the cover sheet.

1. On the Project Browser, right-click the Sheet List and choose: **Duplicate View** > **Duplicate**.

    Sheet List Copy 1 will appear on the Project Browser.

2. Right-click Sheet List Copy 1 and choose: **Rename**.

    ⇨ Name it: Sheet Index and then click OK.

    ⇨ Rename the original Sheet List and call it: Working Sheet List.

    Make sure that the newly copied *Sheet Index* view is open and active onscreen.

3. Click on the header labeled "C" directly above Drawn By in the schedule.

    This will select the entire column.

4. On the Modify Schedule/Quantities tab, on the Columns panel, click the Delete button.

    ⇨ Repeat for the **Checked By** and **Guide Grid** columns.

5. Select Sheet Custom Sort column.

    ⇨ On the Modify Schedule/Quantities tab, on the Columns panel, click the Hide button.

It is important that you do not delete the Sheet Custom Sort parameter. Doing so would prevent it from being used to sort the list. Therefore, we hid the field instead. Also, don't delete a row in the schedule. This would delete the corresponding sheet from Project Browser.

6. On the Properties palette, click the Edit button next to Appearance.

    ⇨ Uncheck Show Title and then click OK.

7. Open the: *G100 – Cover Sheet*.

    ⇨ Drag the Sheet Index and place it on the sheet.

    ⇨ Adjust the column widths as necessary.

If you added a spot for the sheet index in your custom title block, you can place the index there (see Figure 5.62).

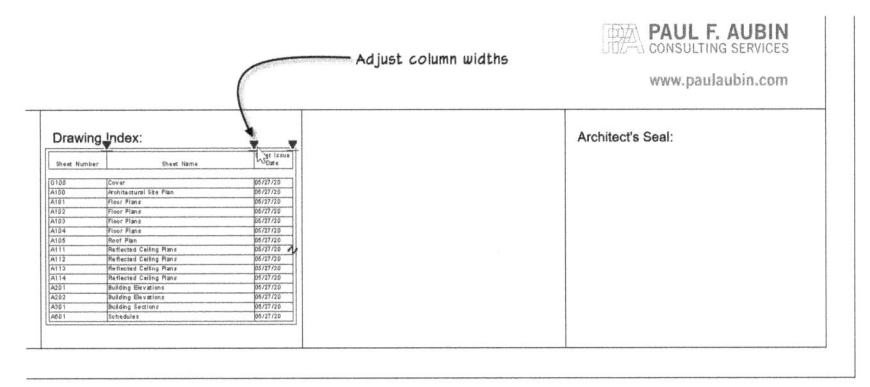

FIGURE 5.62 *Add the Sheet Index to your cover sheet*

CREATE A PDF

As the final task in this chapter, go ahead and plot out the project sheets. You could print to a physical plotter, but to save paper, let's create a PDF instead. The basic steps are outlined here but depending your system and the PDF driver you have installed; the specifics might vary.

Creating a PDF is just like plotting to paper. Choose the Print command from the File menu and then choose a PDF printer. Choose any specific options for your PDF driver like sheet size. Make sure you choose the same size as the sheet you configured in Revit. For the Print Range, choose the Selected views/sheets option to print all sheets at once. Click the Select button and check all sheets.

Under Settings, click the Setup button and verify the sheet size again, set the Zoom to 100% and make sure that Landscape orientation is chosen. Back in the "Print" dialog, in the middle, choose the "Combine multiple selected views/sheets into a single file" option. This will make one PDF file with multiple pages. Click OK to plot the PDF.

A multi-sheet PDF file will be generated that you can open in your PDF program of choice.

SUMMARY

- ☑ Template files provide a means to start new projects with consistent content and setup.

- ☑ All new projects should be created from an agreed upon office template file.

- ☑ Levels establish horizontal datum elements positioned vertically in the Z direction for use as floor levels and other reference points.

- ☑ Wall heights can be constrained to Levels and will thus change height automatically if a Level changes.

- ☑ Views are used to study, create, and manipulate model data.

- ☑ Views can be graphical like plans, sections, and elevations or non-graphical like schedules and drawing lists.

- ☑ Edits made in one view are immediately seen in all appropriate views.

- ☑ Sheets are used to create drawing sets for printing and presentation.

- ☑ You can create your own custom title block to use in your Revit projects.

- ☑ Generate a Drawing List to plan your set or place on your cover page.

- ☑ Before printing to a paper plotter consider generating a digital plot instead

- ☑ PDF files are a popular choice for digital plots; simply plot as normal but choose a PDF plotter instead of a physical one.

- ☑ Choose the option that combines all plotted views into a single PDF for the most convenient file for delivery.

CHAPTER 6
Column Grids and Structural Layout

INTRODUCTION

In this chapter, we will explore the layout of basic structural components. We will begin with the layout of the column grid lines for the commercial project begun in the previous chapter. We will also add columns and framing members to this project and begin to explore strategies related to separating and sharing data among the various disciplines involved in a project team. Finally, we will revisit the residential project to create a foundation plan.

OBJECTIVES

In this chapter, we will begin by adding column grid lines and columns. The goal will be to understand the features and behaviors of grids and columns in Autodesk® Revit®. We will also look at Beams and Joists to complete the framing. Footings will also be explored. After completing this chapter, you will know how to:

- Add and modify column grids
- Add and modify architectural and structural columns
- Load steel shape families
- Create structural framing elements
- Copy elements to levels
- Create foundation wall footings

WORKING WITH GRIDS

In Chapter 2, Figure 2.1 we explored the hierarchy of Revit elements. In the datum elements branch of the hierarchy, we find levels, grids, and reference planes. In the last chapter, we worked with levels. These are horizontal planes (expressed graphically as lines in elevation and section views and as planes in 3D views with level head annotation). They typically define floor levels or stories of the building but can also be used to define other horizontal datum elements such as "top of footing" or "bottom of steel." Grids are very similar to levels in almost every way except that they define vertical planes through the building. The most common use of grids is to define the locations of structural columns in the building. As such, they are typically adorned with grid bubble annotation. Grids are typically added in two directions and their intersections are used to identify unique locations for each column. Like levels and section lines, grids exhibit intelligent annotation characteristics and will appear automatically in all appropriate views such as plans, elevations, and sections at the proper scale and location. The third type of datum, the reference plane, also shares many characteristics of levels and grids, but is more generic in nature and does not have any annotation automatically associated with it. Reference planes will be explored in later chapters.

OPEN A PROJECT

The lessons that follow require the dataset files included for download with this book. Refer to the "Download the Book Dataset" topic on page xi in the Preface for instructions on downloading and installing the book's dataset files if you still need to do so.

1. Launch Autodesk® Revit®.

   ⇨ If you are on the Home screen, you can click the Open button beneath Models. Otherwise, from the File menu, choose **Open** > **Project**. In the "Open" dialog box, browse to the *Chapter06* folder.

   ⇨ Double-click *06 Commercial.rvt* if you wish to work in Imperial units. Double-click *06 Commercial_M.rvt* if you wish to work in Metric units. You can also select it and then click the Open button.

ADD GRID LINES

Let's begin laying out a column grid in this project. A grid is a vertical datum element used mostly to represent column locations and structural framing in the building. Grids help with locating objects in plans and elevations.

1. On the Project Browser, double-click to open the *Level 1* floor plan.

   This view shows the first floor plan as we left it at the end of the previous chapter.

2. On the Architecture tab, on the Datum panel, click the Grid tool (or press GR) (see Figure 6.1).

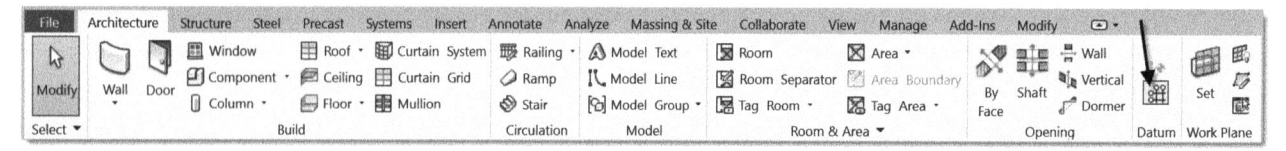

FIGURE 6.1 *The Grid tool on the Architecture tab*

Some common tools appear on Modify tab, on the Draw panel like the Line and Pick Lines icons. Line is the default and allows you to click any two points to specify the extent of the grid line. Grid lines can be drawn at any angle: they can be curved and they can also be multi-segment. You can also create the grid lines based upon existing elements in the model. To do this, use the Pick Lines icon.

3. Accepting the default Line option, click any two points within the building footprint to add a grid line.

   ⇨ On the ribbon, click the Modify tool or press the ESC key twice.

4. Select the grid line you just created.

Notice that many of the same handles and controls appear on the grid line that appeared on the level lines in the previous chapter (see Figure 5.11 in the previous chapter). Place your pointer over each control to see a screen tip indicating its function (see Figure 6.2). Zoom in as required.

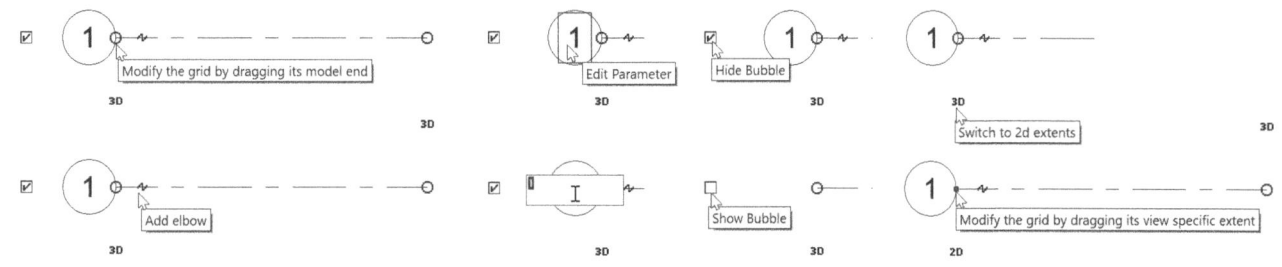

FIGURE 6.2 *Grids have many control handles and drag points*

Moving left to right in Figure 6.2, the following briefly describes each control.

Modify the Grid by dragging its model end—This round handle is used to drag the extent of the grid. If the length or alignment constraint parameter is also active, dragging one grid will affect the extent of the other constrained grid lines as well. Grids are constrained to one another by default. If 2D extents are enabled, this control becomes a small filled dot (shown at the right of the figure).

Add Elbow—This small handle creates an elbow in the grid line. This is useful when the annotation of two grid lines overlap one another in a view. Click this handle to create the elbow, and then drag the resultant drag handles to your liking to make the annotation legible.

Edit Parameter—Click the blue text to re-number the grid line directly in the bubble. Keep in mind that this renames the grid in the same way as renaming it on the Properties palette. Grid labels must be unique.

Hide/Show Bubble—Use this control to hide or show the grid bubble symbol at either end of the line.

2D/3D Extents Toggle—When 3D Extents are enabled, editing the extent of the grid line in one view affects all views in which the grid appears (except views where 2D extents are enabled) and literally changes the extent of the virtual plane representing the grid. If you toggle this to 2D Extents, dragging the extent of the grid line affects only the graphical representation in the current view.

Length and Alignment Constraint (not shown in the figure)—A padlock icon used to constrain the length and extents of one grid line to the others nearby. This is useful to keep all your grid lines lined up with one another.

5. Undo the creation of the grid line (the Undo icon is on the QAT or press CTRL+ Z).

> **NOTE:** You can also delete the grid, but the automatic numbering of the next grid you add will start at number 2 since it is the next number in the sequence. If you undo the grid instead, it returns the starting number to 1.

Sometimes it is easier to use existing geometry to assist in the creation of the grid lines.

6. On the ribbon, click the Grid tool again.
   ⇨ On the Modify | Place Grid tab, on the Draw panel, click the Pick Lines icon.
   ⇨ On the Options bar, in the Offset field, type: **4"** [**100**] and then press ENTER.
   Position the mouse pointer over the inside edge of the bottom horizontal wall.

7. When the dashed line appears on the inside of the building, click to add the grid line (see Figure 6.3).

• Revit Essentials for Architecture •

208 | Chapter 6

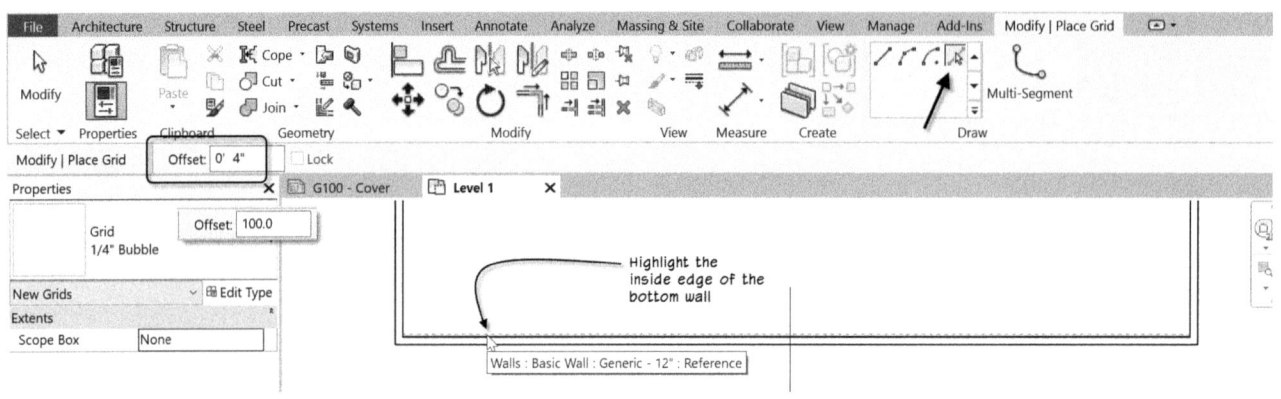

FIGURE 6.3 *Create a grid line based on a picked wall edge*

Depending on whether you deleted the first grid line or used Undo, the number parameter of this grid line may be "1" or it may be "2." If it is 2, we can edit it.

If necessary, click on the grid bubble text parameter (blue text) and then change the value to: **1**.

You should now have grid line 1 offset slightly to the inside edge of the bottom horizontal wall with a bubble on the left. The extent of the grid line matches the length of the wall since we used the wall to create it. Let's stretch it a little longer.

8. Click on the model end handles of grid 1 and stretch each end longer away from the outside edges of the model (see Figure 6.4).

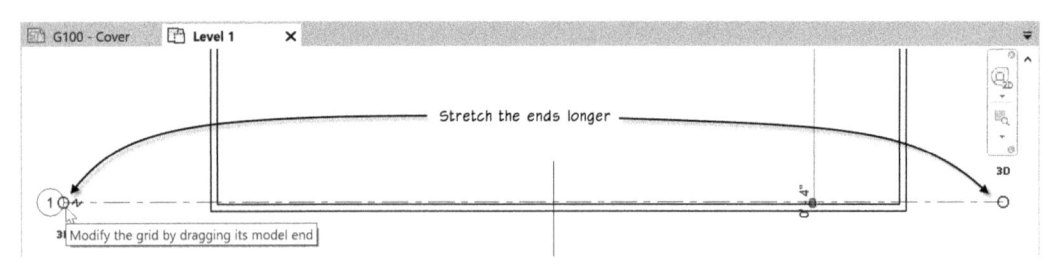

FIGURE 6.4 *Lengthen the grid lines by dragging the model end handles*

You should still be in the Place Grid command. If you canceled the command, click the Grid tool again.

9. On the Draw panel, click the Line icon, and on the Options bar change the Offset to: **20'-0"** [**6000**].

10. Move the pointer over the previous grid line.

⇨ Move your mouse slightly if necessary, until the dashed line is above the previous grid line and then click to place a new one (see Figure 6.5).

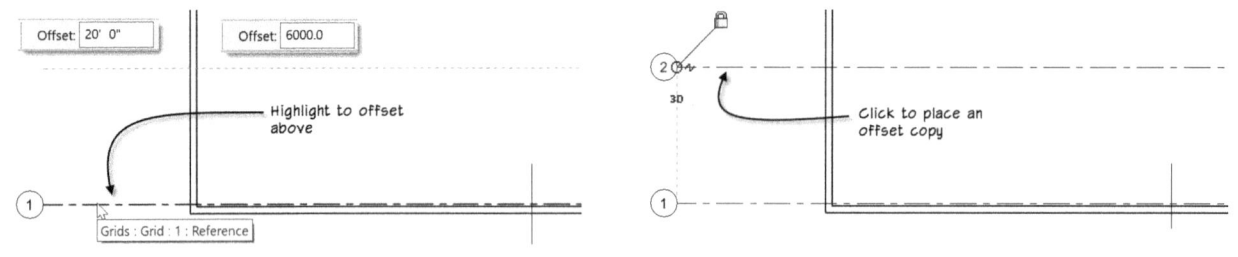

FIGURE 6.5 *Using Pick Lines place a second grid line*

This time, since we stretched the length of the previous grid line, when you use it to pick for the new one, the new grid will match its length instead of the wall. Also notice the closed padlock icon that appears connected to the new grid line at each end. This indicates that the new grid line is constrained to the previous one. Like levels in the previous chapter, if you edit the extent of one grid, they will both change together.

• The Aubin Academy •

At this point, we could continue adding grid lines using the same process. Instead, let's test the alignment constraint and then explore alternate techniques to create the additional grid lines.

11. On the ribbon, click the Modify tool or press the ESC key twice.
12. Select grid line 2.
    ⇨ Using the "Model end" drag handle, drag the bubble horizontally a little bit.

    Notice that both grid bubble 1 and 2 move together.

    Position the bubbles where you want them.
13. Save the project.

COPY GRID LINES

We could draw each additional grid line as noted above using either the Line or Pick Lines tools. We can also copy the existing ones using either the Copy tool or the Array tool. The Copy tool is basically a Move command that moves a copy instead of moving the original. The Array command can create several equally spaced copies in one action. It also has the option to "group and associate" the copies so that the parameters assigned to the array are maintained and remain editable. Let's explore a few options.

1. Select grid line 2.
   ⇨ On the Modify | Grids tab, click the Copy tool (or press CO).

> **TIP:** Be sure to choose Copy on the Modify panel, not Copy on the Clipboard panel.

On the Options bar, there are three available check boxes. The "Disjoin" box is grayed out. ("Constrain" and "Multiple" are not currently selected.)

2. On the Options bar, place checkmarks in both the "Constrain" and "Multiple" check boxes.

The "Constrain" check box limits the movement of the copy in the vertical or horizontal direction and the "Multiple" option makes more than one copy in the same operation.

   ⇨ For the start point, click anywhere on grid 2.
   ⇨ Move the pointer straight up (you don't have to be too careful; this is what Constrain is for).
3. Using the temporary dimensions, place two copies above grid line 2 spaced at: **20'-0"** [**6000**] (see Figure 6.6).

   If you prefer, you can type the distance in, and press ENTER instead of using the onscreen dimensions.

210 | Chapter 6

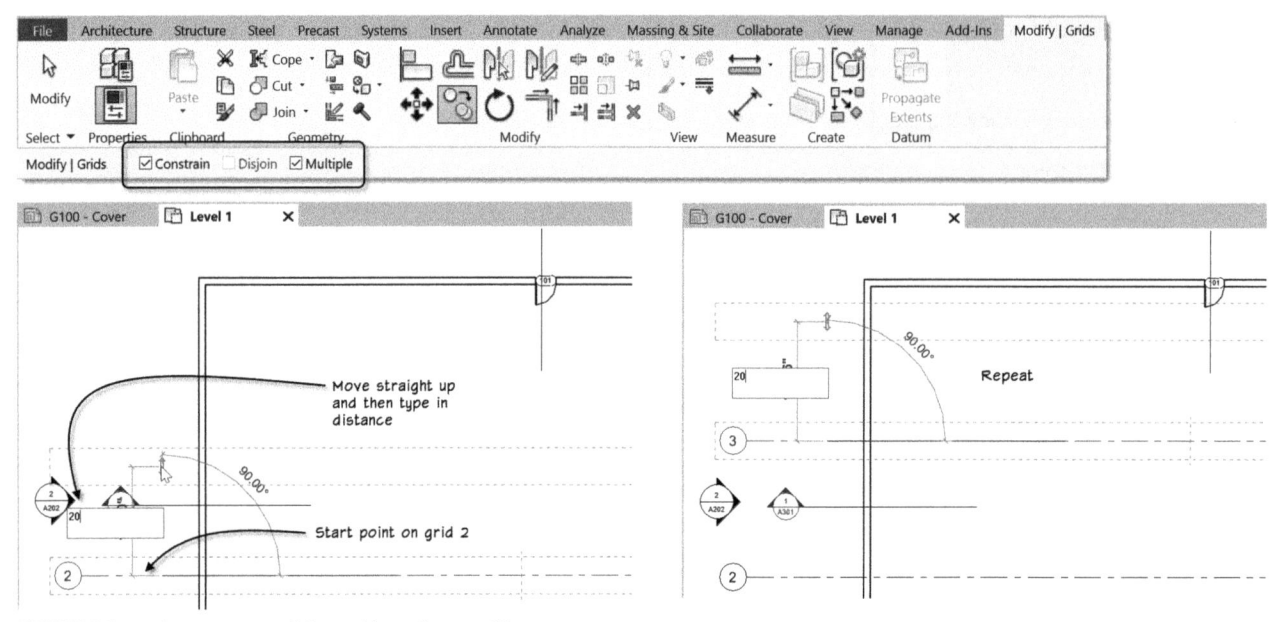

FIGURE 6.6 *Make two copies of the grid line above grid line 2*

    4.   On the ribbon, click the Modify tool or press the ESC key twice.

Notice that the two new grid lines numbered automatically as "3" and "4." Revit will always number the new grid lines in sequence after the last one placed. If you were to delete one grid (grid 4 for example), and then add another grid line, it would automatically number to "5." However, if you were to undo the placement of grid line 4, then the next one would be "4" instead.

    5.   Select either of the new grid lines.

Notice that the temporary dimensions reference the walls and not the other grid lines. If you wish to move them with the temporary dimensions, you can first move the witness lines. You can also use the Move tool if you prefer. Let's move both grid lines up slightly to make the middle bay slightly larger.

    6.   Select grid lines 3 and 4. (You can use the CTRL key or a Crossing selection to do this—be certain to select only the two grid lines.)

    ⇨   On the Options bar, click the Activate Dimensions button.

        The lower witness line references the bottom wall. We want it to reference grid 2 instead.

    ⇨   Highlight the grip on the witness line of the lower dimension and then drag it up to grid 2 (see the left side of Figure 6.7).

    7.   Edit the value of the lower temporary dimension to: **21'-4"** [**6700**] (see the right side of Figure 6.7).

Column Grids and Structural Layout | 211

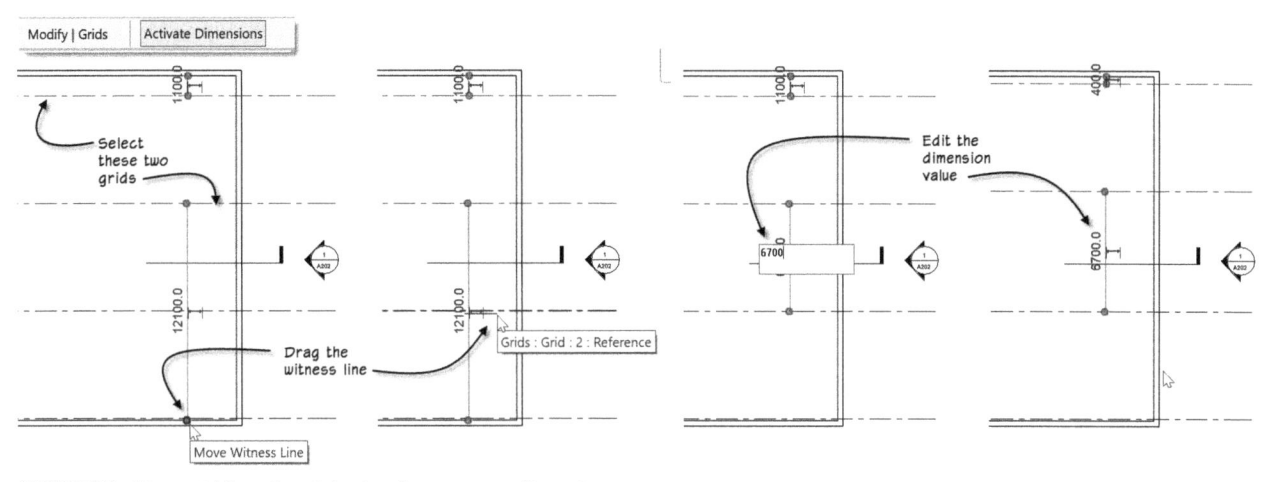

FIGURE 6.7 *Move grid lines 3 and 4 using the temporary dimensions*

- ⇨ On the ribbon, click the Modify tool or press the ESC key twice.
- **8.** On the Architecture tab, click the Grid tool (or press GR).
- ⇨ On the Place Grid tab, click the Pick Lines icon.
- ⇨ On the Options bar, in the Offset field, type: **4"** [**100**] and then press ENTER.
- **9.** Position the pointer so that the light blue dashed line appears at the inside edge of the left vertical wall and then click to add the grid line.
- ⇨ On the ribbon, click the Modify tool or press the ESC key twice.

Notice that this grid line became number 5. For the vertical bays, we want to use letters.

- **10.** Click on the text label of the new vertical grid line.
- ⇨ Edit the bubble designation to: **A**.
- **11.** Adjust its length so that it projects above and below the building footprint (like we did for the others).

ARRAY GRID LINES

To make the rest of the lettered grids, we could draw them or copy them as we have already done. Or we can try the Array command to make several copies that are equally spaced.

    Select grid line A (if not already selected).

- **1.** On the Modify | Grids tab, on the Modify panel, click the Array tool (or press AR).

The Array command has many options. First, you can choose between a linear or radial array on the Options bar. Next there is the "Group and Associate" check box. With this option enabled, all the arrayed items (the original and the copies) will be grouped together. When thus grouped, you can select them later and edit the quantity of items in the array. The remaining items will adjust to match the new quantity either adding or deleting elements in the group. This can be a very powerful and useful functionality that has many applications in building design. This being our first opportunity to explore this tool, we will test it out here with our grid lines. Ultimately, we will want an ungrouped array because the final spacing of our column grid is not equal (as is typical in most buildings), however it will still be educational to explore the "Group and Associate" option of array briefly nonetheless.

- ⇨ On the Options bar, verify that the "Linear" icon is chosen and that "Group and Associate" is selected.

Array is much like the move and copy commands in that it requires you to pick two points on screen to indicate the spacing of the array. We have two options for what these two points can represent in the array: they can be the spacing

212 | Chapter 6

between each element, or the total spacing of the entire array. To set the spacing between each element, choose the "2nd" option next to "Move To." To set the total spacing, choose the "Last" option.

> **TIP:** In this case, the only bad thing about choosing the "Last" option is that the right-most grid line will become grid line B and then the four in the middle lettered sequentially left to right from C to F. You would then need to edit each grid bubble parameter to fix this. Use the "2nd" option to avoid this problem.

⇨ Choose the "2nd" option.

⇨ For the "Number," (which is the quantity) type: **6** and make sure that the "Constrain" box is selected.

The number indicates the total quantity of elements in the final array. This quantity includes the original selection. The "Constrain" option works like the same option in the Copy command (see above) by limiting movement to horizontal and vertical only.

2. Watch the Status bar for prompts. Click the first point anywhere on the selected grid line.

⇨ Move the pointer to the right about: 18'-0" [5400] and then click (see Figure 6.8).

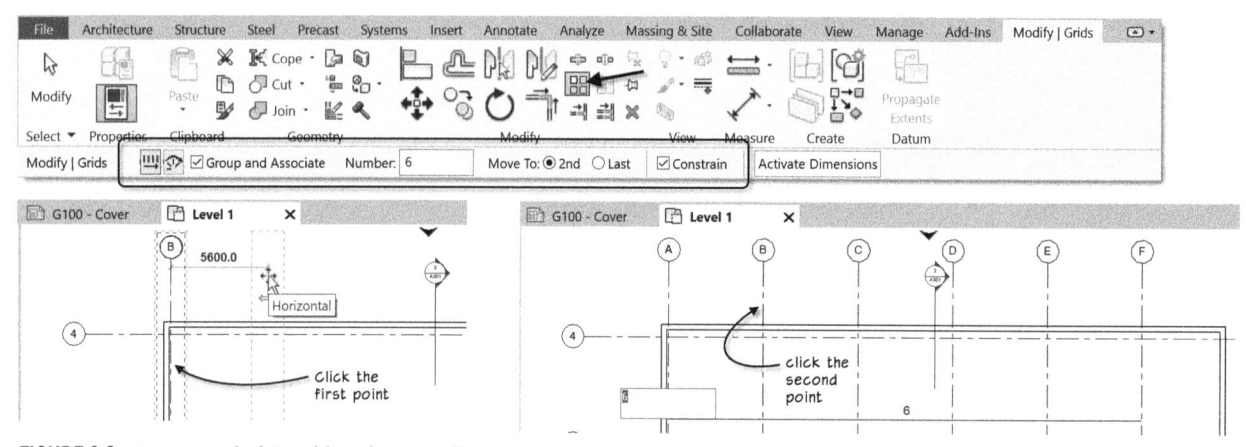

FIGURE 6.8 *Array a total of 6 grid lines horizontally*

The last element of the array is not quite close enough to the inside edge of the right wall. Using the temporary dimensions like we did above, we can adjust it to the exact location we need. Since the array is grouped, all items will adjust to maintain an equal spacing as we do this.

⇨ On the ribbon, click the Modify tool or press the ESC key twice.

3. Select the last item (grid line F on the right).

Notice that a dashed box appears around the grid line. This indicates that the element is part of a group.

4. On the Options bar, click the Activate Dimensions button. You may need to zoom out a bit to see them.

The last grid line (labeled F) needs to be 4" [100] from the inside face of the right wall (like its counterpart on the left).

⇨ Move Witness Lines and edit the temporary dimension value to: **4" [100]** from the inside face of the wall.

> **TIP:** Instead of dragging the Witness Line handle, simply click it. Each time you click, it will shift to a new reference point in the wall. It will cycle from inside to center to outside and then back again.

Column Grids and Structural Layout | 213

> **NOTE:** The wall is 12" [300] thick. So you can place the Witness Lines in any convenient location and take this value into account to achieve the correct location. For example, leaving the witness line in the center, you could type in: 10" [250] as an alternative.

Notice that all the grid lines between A and F adjust with this change and remain equally spaced. This is because of the grouped Array.

   5. Deselect grid line F and then re-select it (click on it again).

A temporary dimension will appear on the arrayed items with a single text parameter that indicates the number of items in the array (see Figure 6.9). You may need to try more than once. It is sometimes hard to see.

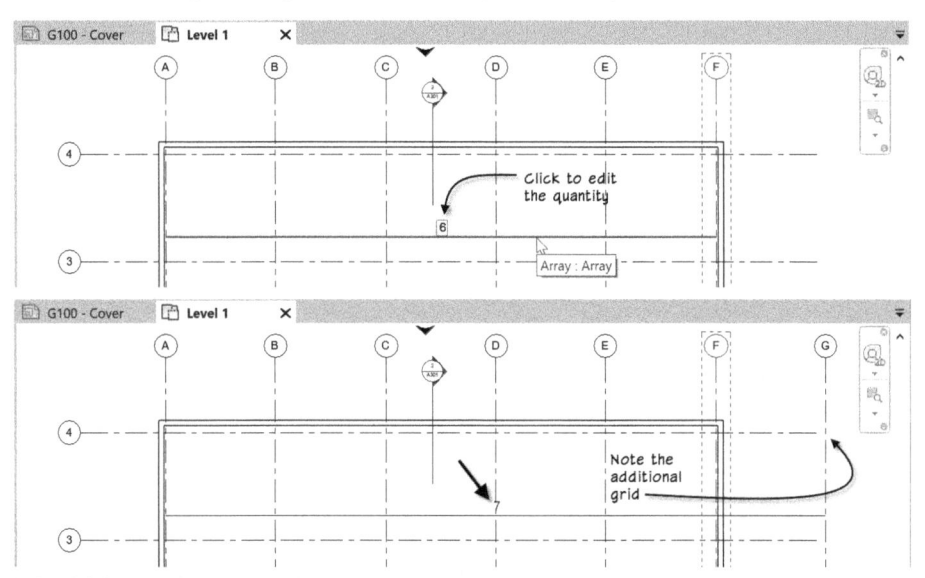

FIGURE 6.9 *Edit the quantity of items in the array with the Edit Text parameter*

   ⇨ Click to select this text parameter. Type in: **7** and then press ENTER.

Notice that a new grid line is added and lettered automatically.

   6. Repeat the process typing: **5** this time.

Notice that the last two grid lines are deleted. Notice also that the spacing between the items remains unchanged. This is because we used the "Move To 2nd" option above to create the array.

   7. Undo twice.

This is the benefit of using the "Group and Associate" parameter when you create the array. However, as we mentioned above, the spacing of our commercial building's column grid is not actually equal. Therefore, we will need to ungroup this array. Before we do, feel free to experiment further with the array. For example, you can select any one of the grid lines and move it. All the others will move accordingly. This can be tricky, as the one you select stays stationary and all the others move relative to it. Be sure to undo after you try this.

When one of the grouped elements is selected, you can also choose the Edit Group button on the ribbon. This will make an Edit Group mode active and a toolbar will appear. In this mode, you can manipulate the elements within the group. When you choose the Finish button, the change is applied to all group instances (all the elements in the array in this case). In this case, appropriate edits might be resizing the grid line or adding or removing the bubble at either end. We will explore groups in more detail in Chapter 7. Be sure to undo any explorations you made returning to 6 grid lines equally spaced and sequentially numbered before continuing.

• Revit Essentials for Architecture •

214 | Chapter 6

DIMENSION THE GRID LINES

Next, we'll ungroup the array. This will allow us to adjust their grid line spacing independently.

1. Select all vertical grid lines—A through F (use the CTRL key or a crossing selection).

    The Modify | Model Groups tab will appear on the ribbon.

    ⇨ On the Modify | Model Groups tab, on the Group panel, click the Ungroup button (or press UG).

The grid lines will now be ungrouped and remain selected. Since they are no longer part of an array, they now move independently of one another. Try a few moves if you like but be sure to undo before continuing. We are going to adjust several grid lines now. This will be easier with some permanent dimensions rather than the temporary dimensions since we can place the witness lines exactly where we want them.

2. On the Modify tab of the ribbon, on the Measure panel, click the Aligned Dimension tool.

    ⇨ Starting with grid line A, click successively on each lettered grid line A–F (see Figure 6.10).

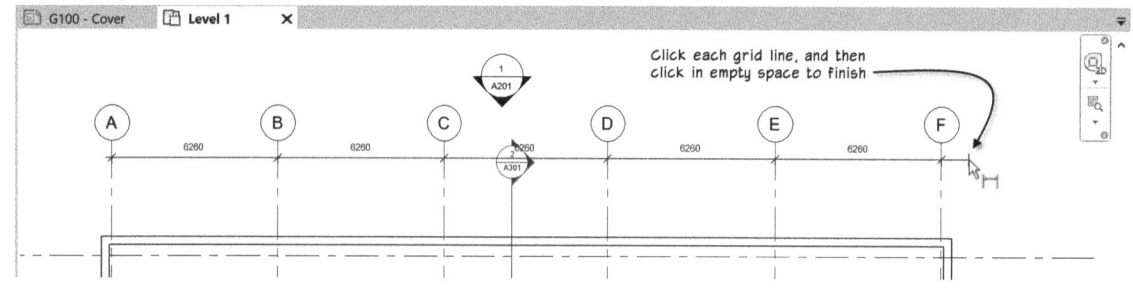

FIGURE 6.10 *Add a dimension string to the lettered grid lines*

3. After you click on grid line F, move the mouse to a spot where you want to place the dimension string and then click in empty space to set the dimension string and end the command.

> **TIP:** Make sure that you click in an empty spot to place the dimension, if you click on another model element, it will add a witness line instead. Keep an eye on the Status Bar for prompts as you work.

⇨ On the ribbon, click the Modify tool or press the ESC key twice.

4. Select grid line B

Notice that now that we have added a string of dimensions, in addition to the normal temporary dimensions we also can edit the dimension values of the string we just added as well.

⇨ Click on the blue dimension text between grid line A and B, type: **22'-2"** [**6740**] and then press ENTER.

Grid line B will move to the right slightly.

5. Select grid line C next and edit the distance between it and B to: **14'-4"** [**4400**].

This time, grid C will move. Remember; always select the element that you wish to move before editing dimension text. Otherwise you will simply move B back in the other direction!

6. Repeat moving left to right for the remaining vertical grid lines as shown in Figure 6.11.

Column Grids and Structural Layout | 215

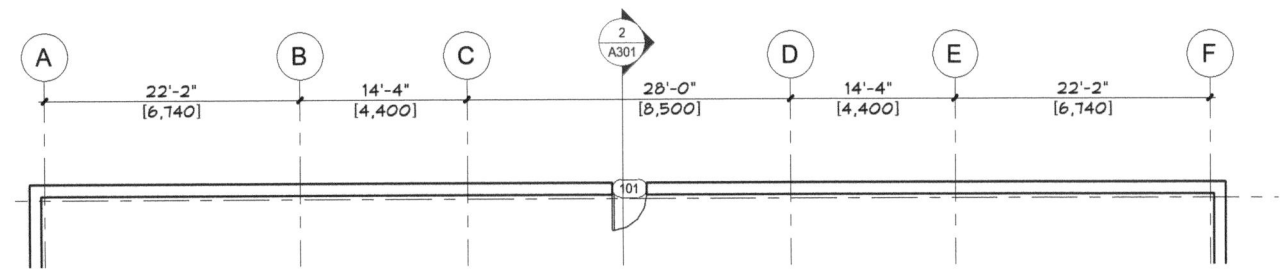

FIGURE 6.11 *Edit dimension values to move grid lines*

Our feature façade on the front of the building (we created sloped walls for this in the last chapter) will require some structural support. We can add a few additional grid lines in the front for these.

7. On the Architecture tab of the ribbon, click the Grid tool (or press GR).
   ⇨ On the Place Grid tab, verify that the Line icon is selected.
8. Move the pointer to the inside of the building above the lower wall and click between grid lines C and D.
   ⇨ Move down past the building and click again to place the bubble.
   The bubble will automatically enumerate as "G."
9. Click in the text parameter of the new bubble and change the value to: **C.3**.
   ⇨ Using the temporary dimensions, move the grid line so that it is: **9'-0" [2700]** from grid line C (see Figure 6.12).

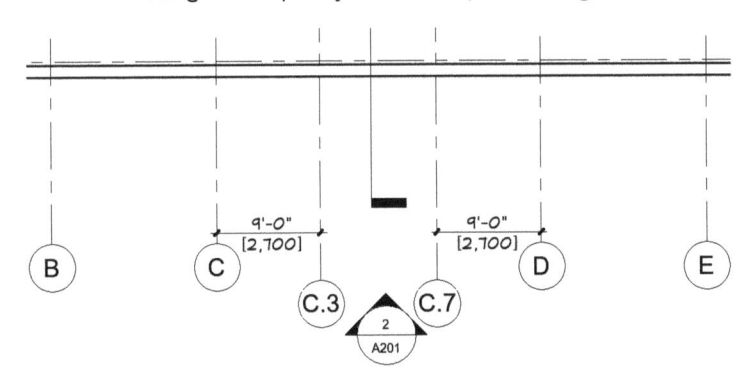

FIGURE 6.12 *Add grid lines at the bottom of the plan for support of the front façade (Grid bubbles B, C, D and E enabled in the figure for clarity)*

10. Add grid line C.7 to the other side of the C-D bay using the same offset (see Figure 6.12).
11. Save the project.

ADD AND EDIT DIMENSIONS

Let's add a dimension string to the numbered grid lines too. When you add a dimension, there are some useful settings on the Options Bar.

1. Start the Aligned Dimension tool (you can find it as before on the Modify tab, Annotation tab or on the QAT or simply type DI).
   ⇨ On the Options Bar, choose: **Wall Faces** from the first drop down list.
   ⇨ From the "Pick" list, choose: **Entire Walls**.
   ⇨ Next to this, click the Options button, check the "Intersecting Grids" option and then click OK.
2. Select the exterior vertical wall at the left. Move to the left and click in empty space to place the dimension.

If you wish to add the exterior walls to the horizontal string we created earlier, you can edit the existing dimension.

• Revit Essentials for Architecture •

3. To do this, select the existing horizontal dimension.
   ⇨ On the Modify | Dimensions ribbon tab, click the Edit Witness Lines button.
   ⇨ Click on geometry that is not already part of the dimension, like the exterior face of the two exterior vertical walls.

They will be added as witness lines. If you click on an existing witness line that is already part of the dimension, it will be removed.

4. To finish, click in empty space (not on any geometry).

VIEWING GRIDS IN OTHER VIEWS

All the work we have done on grid lines so far has been in the *Level 1* floor plan view. However, like other datum elements, grids will automatically appear in all orthographic views. (Grids do not appear in 3D).

1. On the Project Browser, double-click to open the *West* elevation view.

   Notice how the numbered grid bubbles appear here running vertically on the elevation.

2. On the Project Browser, double-click to open the *South* elevation view.

This time only the lettered bubbles appear. Like the plan views, if you drag the end of one grid, the others will stretch as well. If you find the bubbles in the middle to be too close together, you can use the handles to give them an elbow.

3. On the Project Browser, double-click to open the *Longitudinal* section view.

In this view, grid lines C.3 and C.7 do not show since the section is looking toward the north. If the section were looking south, they would appear. If you want to experiment, you can return to the *Level 1* floor plan view, select the section line for the *Longitudinal* section and then click the flip control handle. (Or select the crop region rectangle surrounding the view, right-click and choose: **Flip Section**). Re-open the Longitudinal section view to see that these two grids will then appear. Flip it back before continuing.

Our column grid layout is now complete. We are ready to begin using the intersections between grids to locate our columns. Before we begin that process however, our grid lines can also be used to enhance our sheet layouts. The next topic will look at doing so.

ADD A GUIDE GRID

With the guide grid feature, you can overlay a temporary grid on top of a sheet title block and use it to align similar views across multiple sheets. For example, using this tool, we can make all the floor and ceiling plans appear on the same location from one sheet to the next. Sheets were set up for this project in the previous chapter. At that time, we simply dropped each floor plan view on the sheet in an approximate location. Using the grids we have now added to the project and the guide grid tool, we can align our floor plan sheets with one another precisely.

1. On the Project Browser, double-click to open the *A101 – Floor Plans* sheet.
2. On the View tab, on the Sheet Composition panel, click the Guide Grid tool.
   ⇨ In the "Assign Guide Grid" dialog that appears, type: **Plan Sheets** for the Name and then click OK (see Figure 6.13).

Column Grids and Structural Layout | 217

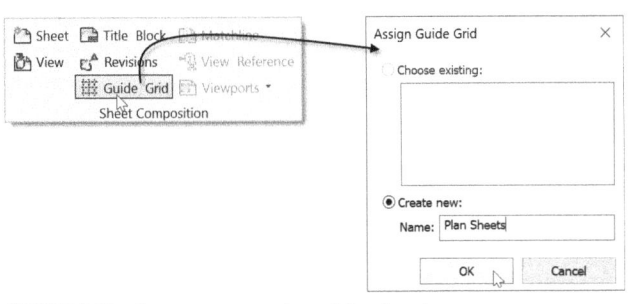

FIGURE 6.13 *Create a new guide grid for plan sheets*

A light blue grid object will appear across the sheet. If you select it, you can modify its grid spacing on the Properties palette and manipulate the overall extents with the control handles on the edges.

3. Select the guide grid onscreen. (Click at the outer edge to select it).

⇨ On the Properties palette, change the Guide Spacing to: **5"** [**125**] and then click Apply.

The grid of blue squares will increase in size, making it easier to work with. It will also be helpful to reduce the size of the overall grid. Each of our plan sheets contains only one plan, so we only need a small portion of the guide grid visible to align them. Reducing the size of the overall grid is another way to make it easier to work with.

4. Using the shape handles at the edges of the guide grid, reduce it until you can see just one intersection (see the left side of Figure 6.14).

   Make sure you are happy with the placement of the plan on this sheet. If not, adjust it now before continuing.

5. On the Modify | Guide Grid tab, click the Move tool (or press MV).

⇨ Uncheck (if necessary) the Constrain check box on the Options Bar.

⇨ For the start point of the move, click on the intersection of the blue lines in the middle of the guide grid.

TIP: If you have trouble snapping to the intersection on the guide grid, type SI first to force Revit to snap to intersection.

6. Snap the second point of the move at the intersection of grids A and 4 (zoom as required) (see Figure 6.14).

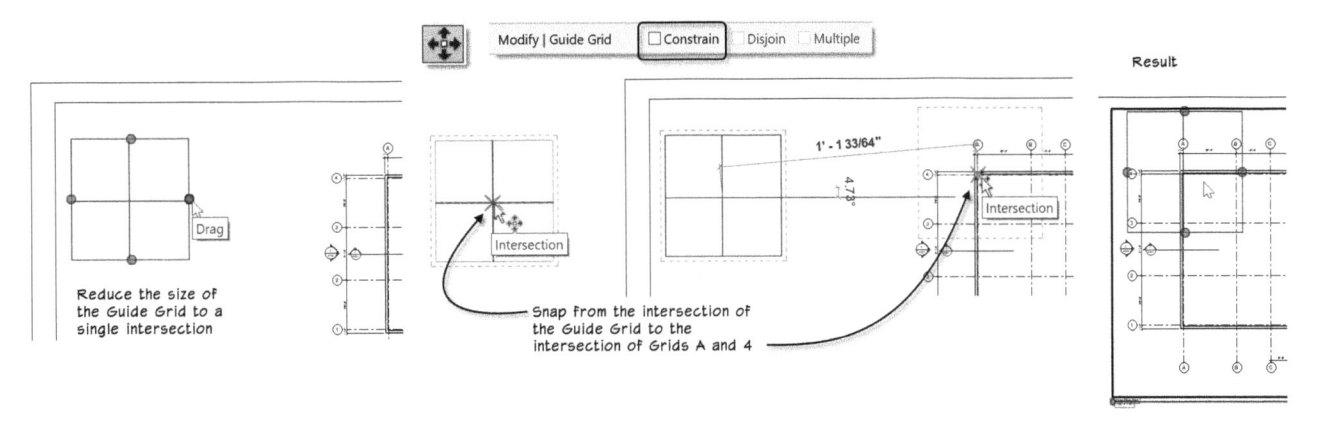

FIGURE 6.14 *Move the guide grid to line up with the plan grid lines*

We now have the guide grid aligned perfectly with the intersection of grids A and 4. The Guide Grid will remember this position relative to the sheet and we can now use it to align other plans to the same position.

7. On the Project Browser, double-click *A102 – Floor Plans*.

⇨ On the Properties palette, scroll to the bottom and in the Other

• Revit Essentials for Architecture •

grouping, from the guide grid list, choose: **Plan Sheets**.

Notice that the same guide grid will now appear on this sheet in the same location. You can now align the viewport in the same way as the previous sheet and the views will thereby be in the same relative location on each sheet.

8. Click anywhere in the viewport to select it.
9. On the Modify | Viewports tab, click the Move tool.
   ⇨ For the first point, click the intersection of grids A and 4 (zoom in as necessary).
   ⇨ For the second point click the intersection in the guide grid.

> **TIP:** To prevent unnecessary zooming, you can drag the viewport randomly out of the way first, and then perform the move command and snap precisely.

10. Open each floor plan and ceiling plan sheet and repeat the process of moving the views to snap to the guide grid.
    ⇨ Remember in each of these moves, that you are moving the viewport to the Guide Grid, *not* the other way around.

> **TIP:** You can also open the *Working Sheet List* Schedule and set the guide grid parameter there as an alternative to using the Properties palette. You can also select several sheets on the Properties palette by using the SHIFT or CTRL keys, and then change the Guide Grid parameter on the Properties palette for the entire selection at once.

You can use levels, grids, reference planes and view crop boundaries to align with guide grids. Unfortunately, you cannot use walls or other model geometry. Therefore, we waited until this chapter to add the guide grid and line up the viewports. If you wish to line up viewports on other kinds of sheet like elevations or sections, you can use the guide grid tool to create another guide grid sized and positioned specifically for elevations and/or sections. You can create as many guide grids as necessary to set up all your sheets.

When you are finished aligning the viewports, you can set the guide grid parameter back to: <None> if you no longer wish them to display onscreen. However, it should be noted that guide grids do not print, so you can leave them displayed indefinitely onscreen without worry that they will appear in final output.

> **TIP:** It can sometimes be helpful to first line up the guide grid with a convenient column grid intersection in the plan and then move both the viewport and guide grid together to your final desired location. This makes it easier to compose the sheet just how you want it.

11. On the Project Browser, double-click to open the *Level 1* floor plan view.
    ⇨ On the View tab of the ribbon, on the Windows panel, click the Close Inactive button.
12. Save the project.

WORKING WITH COLUMNS

Revit is a multi-discipline tool and it includes a complete collection of structural tools. This makes it easy for extended project teams to work together in Revit and seamlessly share models back and forth (if all users are on the same version; for example, 2021). Even if you are not a structural engineer you can use the structural tools to begin the layout of columns and if desired, as well as beams and braces. Like all Revit elements, structural elements remain parametric and editable after they have been added to the model. Therefore, when the structural analysis comes back from the engineer, you can swap in the correct types and sizes to meet the requirements of the design.

> **NOTE:** If you do not see non-architectural tabs like Structure or System in your copy of Revit, you likely have those tabs hidden. When you first install Revit, there is a Workspace wizard that appears and suggests tabs you might want to hide based on your discipline and job role. If you have followed the advice in that wizard and hidden certain tabs, you can always restore them by going to the File menu and choosing: **Options**. In the dialog that appears, click the User Interface tab and check the boxes for the tabs you want to restore.

> **DISCLAIMER:** No structural analysis of any kind has been performed on the designs in this book. The shapes used in this book serve illustration purposes and are not to be construed as a recommendation of structural integrity or an actual design solution.

ADD COLUMNS

Revit includes two types of columns: Architectural Columns and Structural Columns. An Architectural Column provides the location and finished dimensions (including column wrap, furring, finishes, etc.) of a column in an architectural space. The Structural Column is the actual structural material responsible for supporting building loads typically without any enclosure or finish. Examples include steel or concrete columns. Let's look at both kinds.

Continue in the *Level 1* view opened above.

1. On the Architecture tab click the drop down button (bottom half) on the Column tool and choose: **Column: Architectural**.

   ⇨ From the Type Selector, choose: **Rectangular Column: 24" x 24"** [**M_Rectangular Column: 610 × 610mm**].

   ⇨ Move the pointer to the intersection of grid lines A and 4 (upper left corner of the building).

   The pointer will snap to the intersection automatically (see the left side of Figure 6.15).

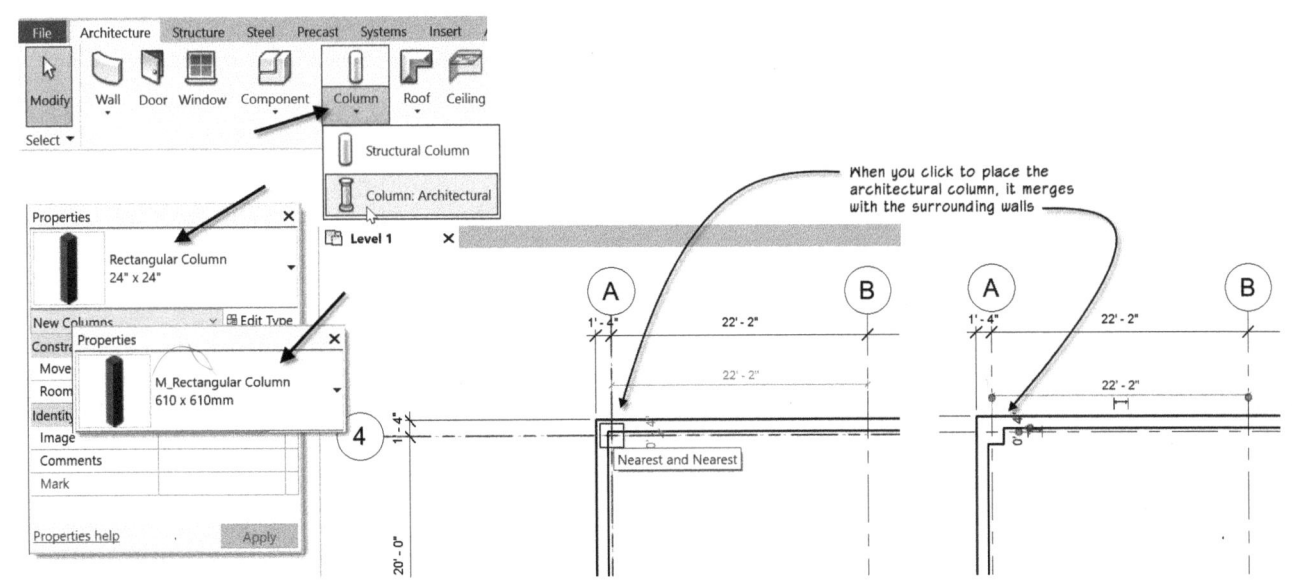

FIGURE 6.15 *Add an architectural column to the A4 grid intersection*

2. Click at the intersection to place the Column (see the right side of Figure 6.15).

220 | Chapter 6

Notice that the architectural column automatically interacts with the walls at the intersection and graphically displays as an integrated column.

3. Continue placing columns at all of the intersections around the perimeter of the building (see Figure 6.16). Do not place columns at the interior intersections.

> **TIP:** You can simply click at each intersection or you can use the Copy tool. If you use Copy, be sure to select "Multiple" on the Options bar and use the TAB key to select a good start point for the copy.

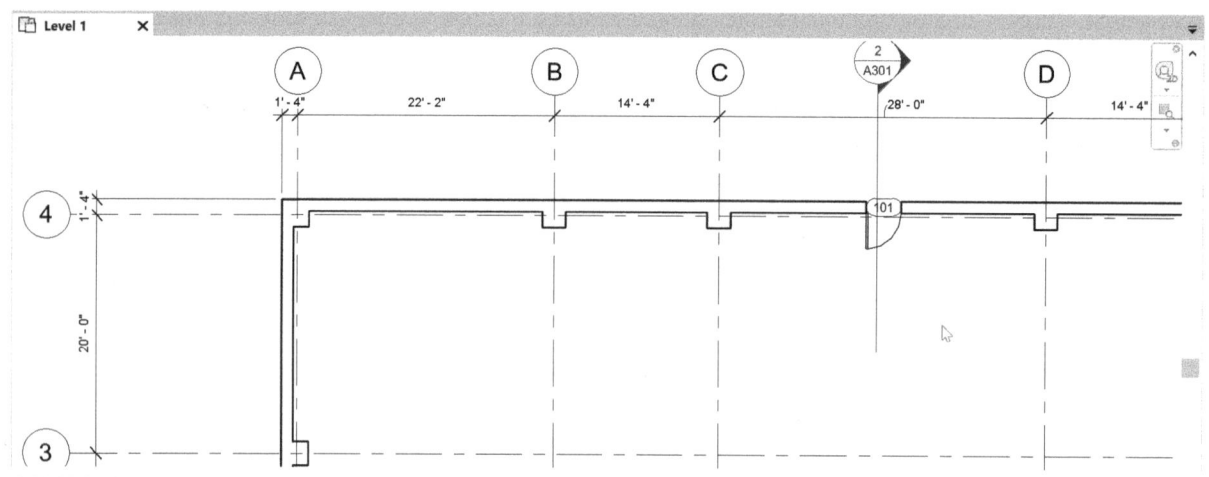

FIGURE 6.16 *Architectural Columns around the perimeter integrate with the walls*

⇨ On the ribbon, click the Modify tool or press the ESC key twice.

Let's try some structural columns next.

4. Click on the drop down button on the Column tool.

⇨ Choose: **Structural Column** from the pop-up (or press CL).

5. Open the Type Selector.

Notice that there are only two structural column types loaded in the current project (there is only one in the metric project). Structural columns, like other component families in Revit can be loaded as needed from external libraries.

6. On the Modify | Place Structural Column tab of the ribbon, click the Load Family button.

Revit will display your default library folder. If it did not go there automatically, you can browse there manually. There are shortcut buttons on the left side of the dialog to assist with this. They are labeled either Imperial Library or Metric Library.

7. Double-click the *Structural Columns* folder, then double-click the *Steel* folder.

⇨ Double-click the *W-Wide Flange-Column.rfa* [*M_W-Wide Flange-Column.rfa*] family file.

The "Specify Types" dialog will appear on screen. This shows a list of industry standard steel-shape sizes in a list that we refer to as a "Type Catalog." Scroll through the list to see all the sizes. You can select one size or multiple items using the SHIFT and CTRL keys. We only need one.

⇨ Scroll in the list, locate and select the: W12x87 [W310x97] size (see Figure 6.17).

8. Click OK to load the family (and type).

Column Grids and Structural Layout | 221

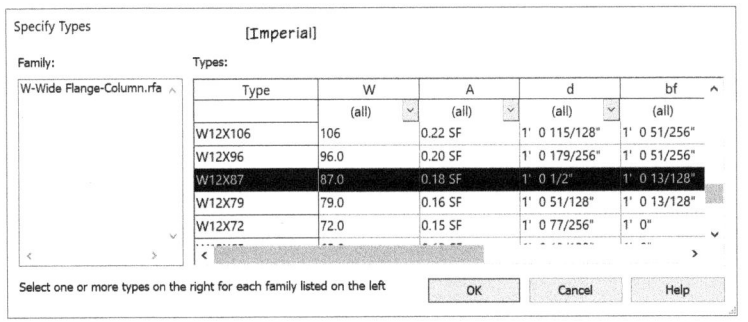

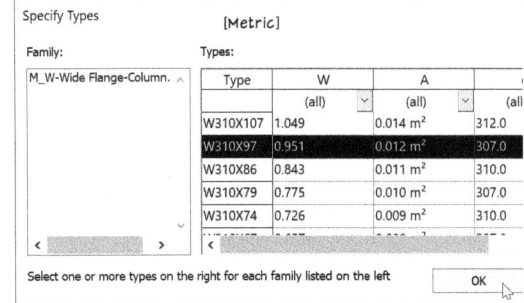

FIGURE 6.17 *Common industry steel shapes are available to load from the family file*

If you are working in the Imperial file, you will get a "Family Already Exists" dialog. Click the "Overwrite the existing version" option. (This is the same family that was already loaded, but we have now loaded another type.)

⇨ If necessary, from the Type Selector, choose the newly loaded: **W12x87** [**W310x97**] type (see item 1 in Figure 6.18).

Structural columns have many of the same parameters as architectural columns—and more. If you move the pointer around the screen before you click, you will note that like the architectural column, the structural column will pre-highlight grid lines and walls as possible hosts. (However, if you insert a structural column at a wall, it will not merge with the wall the same way that the architectural one did.)

In addition to behaviors shared with architectural columns, there are some additional options on the ribbon. For example, the "On Grids" button (on the Multiple panel) allows you to place several structural columns at once on a selection of grid lines, and the "At Columns" button allows you to place a structural column at the location of a selection of architectural columns. Let's give these both a try. But first let's get the height set correctly.

9. On the Options Bar, from the drop down on the left, choose: **Height** (item 2).

> **NOTE:** If you miss this setting, the column height will go down from the current level and generate a warning saying that the object is "not displayed in the current view". If this happens, you can undo and try again.

⇨ On the Modify | Place Structural Column tab, on the Multiple panel, click the "At Grids" button (item 3).

The Modify | Place Structural Columns > At Grid Intersection tab will appear on the ribbon.

10. Click the pointer above grid line 3 and to the right of grid line E and then drag to the left of grid line B and below grid line 2 (item 4).

• Revit Essentials for Architecture •

222 | Chapter 6

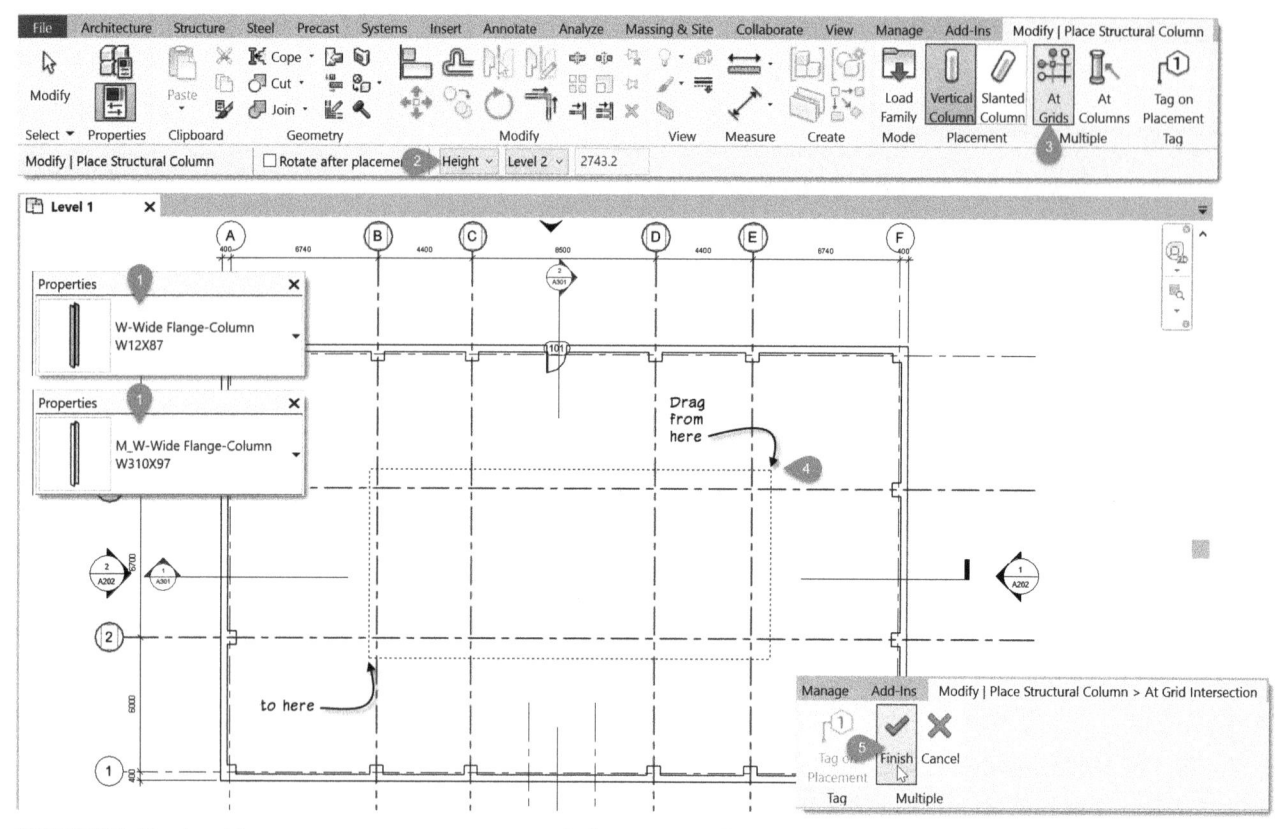

FIGURE 6.18 *Use the grid intersection option to create structural columns at several intersections*

The grid lines will highlight, and several ghosted columns will appear. If you are satisfied with this selection, you click the Finish Selection button on the ribbon. Otherwise, you simply select again until you are satisfied. If you decide not to add the columns, you can click the Cancel button (red "X") on the ribbon.

11. On the ribbon, click the Finish button (item 5).

> **NOTE:** If you get an error that nothing appears in the view, undo and try again making sure you choose: **Height** on the Options Bar instead of Depth.

You will now have a steel column at each grid intersection in the middle of the building. Let's try the "At Columns" option next. In addition, we will also adjust the height of the columns as we add them.

12. On the Options bar, from the right drop down (currently reads Level 2) choose: **Roof**.

This will create a single continuous Structural Column from Level 1 (the current level) up to the Roof.

13. On the Modify | Place Structural Columns tab, click the At Columns button.

⇨ Click and drag a selection window surrounding the entire building to select all the architectural columns.

14. On the ribbon, click the Finish button.

⇨ On the ribbon, click the Modify tool or press the ESC key twice.

Since we are using the "At Columns" option, the selection only sees architectural columns. Furthermore, using either of these multiple placement modes will not place a duplicate column at an intersection that already contains one. So, you don't have to be very careful with your selection windows.

• The Aubin Academy •

EDIT COLUMNS

We now have structural columns at all grid intersections including the ones at the perimeter walls. We can modify columns using many of the same techniques we use for other elements. If you wish to change the type of column, you can select one or more and choose a new type from the Type Selector. You can move, copy, or rotate them. For example, sometimes we need to rotate the flange of the steel.

1. Select all the steel columns in the center of the plan (the ones not enclosed by architectural columns).

    The easiest way to do this is to click and drag from just above and to the left of grids B and 3, and down and to the right of grids E and 2.

    ⇨ Tap the SPACEBAR to rotate them 90 degrees.

We might also want to modify the height. Recall that we changed the height for the ones at the perimeter to span the complete height of the building. We did not do this for the ones in the middle, but we cannot see this in the current plan view. Let's look at the section.

2. On the Project Browser, double-click to open the *Transverse* section view.

UNDERSTANDING LEVEL OF DETAIL

When you switch to this view, you will likely not notice much detail regarding the structural columns. This is because structural elements display at various levels of detail. This allows for simplified graphics in smaller scale drawings, and more detail in larger scale drawings. You can easily modify the default settings for this behavior, or simply adjust the level of detail display for an individual view. For example, Figure 6.19 shows the variation in the three detail levels when viewing Structural elements such as the columns we have in our model. As you can see, the Coarse detail level shows simple linework for the steel shape in plan and a single line for it in section (and elevation). This is the currently active display detail level in both the floor plan and section views in our project. If you switch to Medium or Fine detail level, the graphics for the steel shape will get progressively more detailed in plan. In elevation and section, display is more detailed than Coarse, but the same graphics display for both higher levels of detail (see Figure 6.19).

> **NOTE:** Line weight display adjusts automatically when you vary the scale of the view. Note the change in scale in each panel of the figure and experiment on your own screen to make the medium and high displays more legible. In order to see line weights, you must have Thin Lines toggled off (press TL).

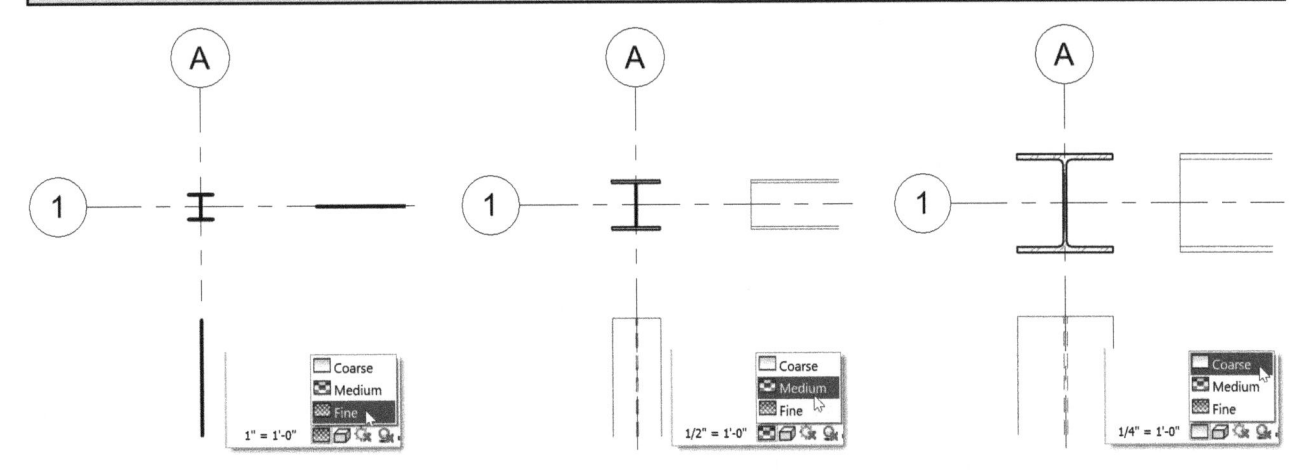

FIGURE 6.19 *Three levels of detail display*

1. In the *Transverse* section view, on the View Control bar, change the Detail Level to: **Medium**.

• Revit Essentials for Architecture •

The Columns will now display with the correct dimensional thickness in the section rather than the diagrammatic single-line display. Zoom around the section as needed to see clearly that the architectural columns stop at Level 2 while the structural ones embedded in them go all the way to the roof. Naturally, it is likely that these columns would be constructed in sections and not be a single continuous four-story-tall column. However, for design purposes, they function in the building as a single continuous column, which is how we will leave them for now. However, in the "Working with Parts" topic on page 225 below, we will look at how we can use the Parts functionality to divide the four-story-tall columns into more realistic components for construction. Regardless, we will leave our architectural columns (which in this project represent the finish materials wrapping the columns) spanning only a single level. Later we will copy these architectural columns to the other floors.

2. Zoom in on grid line 2 or 3 at Level 1. (The middle bay).

⇨ Move your pointer over the Columns and note the screen tips that appear (see Figure 6.20).

TIP: If you have trouble highlighting the overlapping elements, use the TAB key to cycle through adjacent elements.

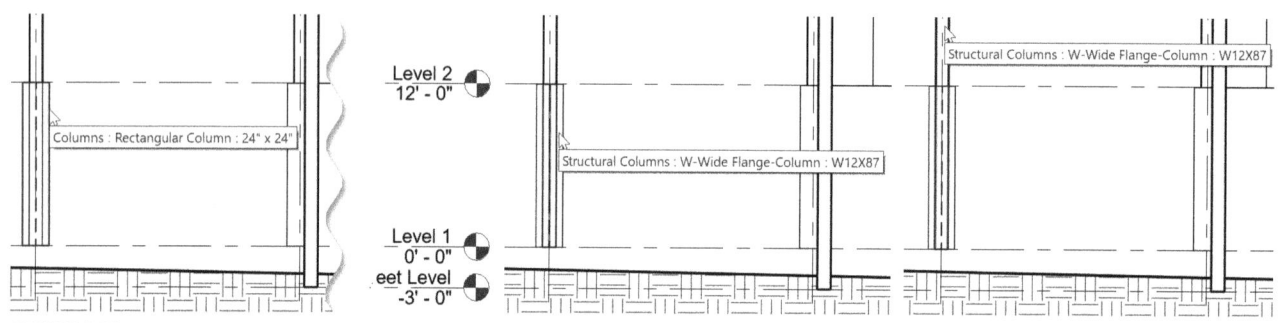

FIGURE 6.20 *In section view, we see columns in the middle of the building at different heights than those beyond*

In our section view, several of the columns are in the same place. Some of these are the shorter ones in the center of the building and the tall ones appear beyond at the perimeter of the building. We can still select the ones we need to edit in this view, or if you prefer, we can return to the *Level 1* plan view and select there. Instead of selecting them directly onscreen, we'll use an option on the right-click menu to select objects by type. This will ensure that we include all the columns in our selection, not just those we can see in the section.

3. Highlight one of the steel Columns (any one, tall or short).

⇨ Right-click and choose: **Select All Instances > In Entire Project**.

Be careful with this command. It literally selects all instances of a family type in the entire project—both seen and unseen. In this case, that is exactly what we want, but in many cases, it may not be. Keep this in mind before using this tool in your work. For example, if you choose to select all instances of a door while working in a plan view, realize that you are also selecting similar doors on other floors of the building! In those cases, it would be safer to use the other option: **Select All Instances > Visible In View**. This option functions the same way by selecting all instances of the selected family and type but limits selection to those you can see in the active view. For our current selection needs, this would exclude those columns that are cropped out of the section view. So, use of the "In Entire Project" option is better for us here.

4. On the Properties palette, for Base Level, choose: **Street Level**.

⇨ For Top Level, choose: **Roof** (see Figure 6.21)

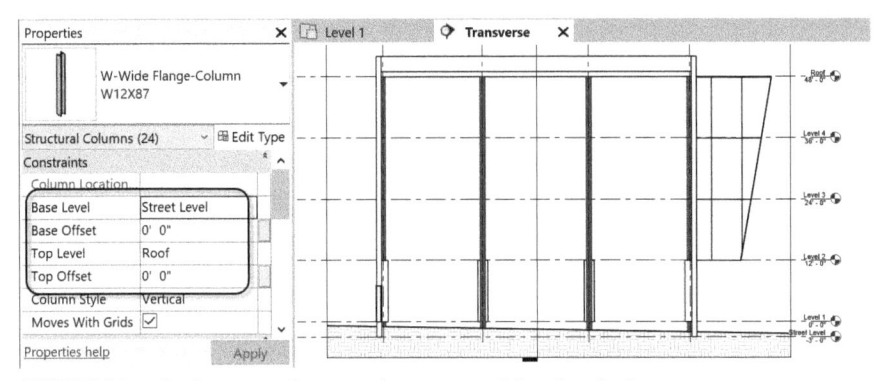

FIGURE 6.21 *Edit the Base and Top Level parameters of the selected columns*

Notice the height of all the steel columns now spans from below the first floor to the roof.

5. On the QAT, click the Default 3D View icon.

6. Click on the roof and then on the View Control bar, from the Hide/Isolate pop-up (icon looks like sunglasses), choose: **Hide Element**.

   Orbit the model as required to get a better look. You can drag the ViewCube, use a steering wheel (or hold down the SHIFT as you drag with the mouse wheel).

You will notice that all steel structural columns were impacted by this change, not just the ones we could see in the section view. This is because as noted above, Select All Instances selects across the entire model, not just the elements visible in the current view.

⇨ When you are finished viewing in 3D, click the Temporary Hide/Isolate icon again and choose: **Reset Temporary Hide/Isolate**.

WORKING WITH PARTS

Revit includes some construction modeling features. Specifically, we have "Parts" and "Assemblies." Parts are used to break up elements in the model into components more representative of how they will be constructed. Assemblies allow a way to group elements in a certain area into a named assembly of components and then create isolated detail drawings of just the assembly. Both features are useful for helping to take a model generated to convey design intent and make it more useful in planning and coordinating construction. These features are not available in Revit LT. If you are using Revit LT, please skip this topic.

CREATE PARTS

There is much we could explore about using both features, but for now, we will perform a simple exercise to take our full height columns and break them into sections more consistent with how they might be constructed. So, for this exercise, we'll keep things simple and assume that the steel columns will be constructed from two sections each about two stories tall. We can leave them full height in the overall model but use the Parts functionality to convey that they are constructed in segments. Let's take a look.

1. On the Project Browser, double-click to open the *Transverse* section view.

   If you have not selected any new elements, you can:

   ⇨ Right-click any steel column and choose: **Select All Instances > In Entire Project** (the quantity on the Properties palette should be 24).

2. On the Modify | Structural Columns tab, on the Create panel, click the Create Parts button (see Figure 6.22).

226 | Chapter 6

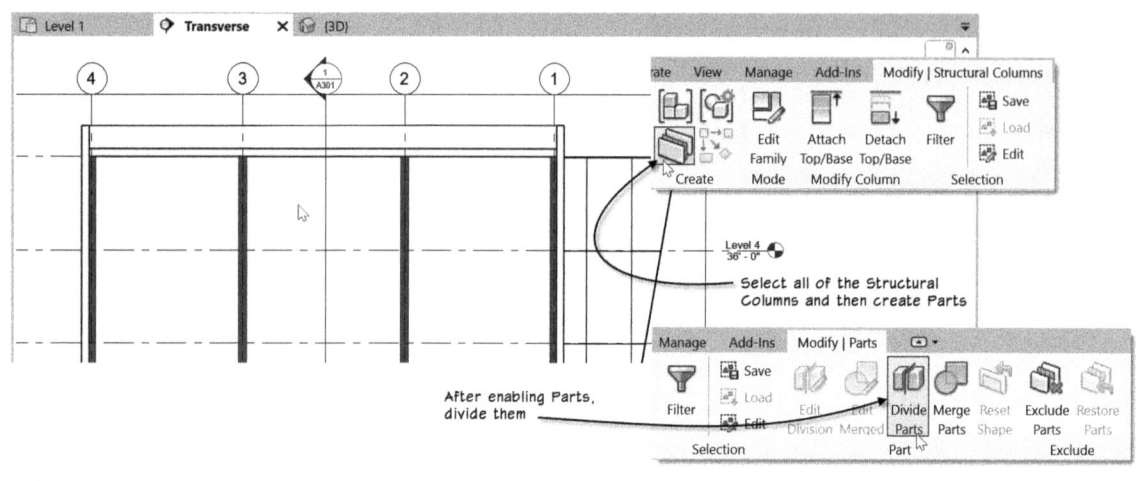

FIGURE 6.22 *Enable Parts for a selection of elements*

The selected elements will now have Parts enabled. All we need to do is show Revit where we want to break our columns into sections using the Divide Parts tool.

3. On the Part panel, click the Divide Parts button (see the bottom of Figure 6.22).

The "Work Plane" dialog will display. This is asking us to designate a plane upon which we will sketch lines or other shapes to divide our Parts. In our case, the most convenient plane to use is one of our grid lines parallel to the view.

⇨ In the "Work Plane" dialog, from the Name list, choose: **Grid D** (see Figure 6.23).

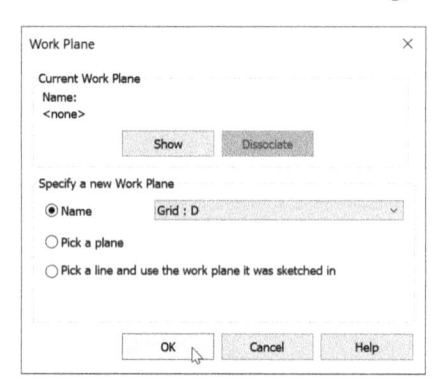

FIGURE 6.23 *Choose a convenient work plane upon which to sketch the division lines*

The Modify | Division tab will now appear on the ribbon. There are two ways that we can divide the Parts. We can use the Edit Sketch button to access all the typical sketch tools like lines, arcs, circles and polygons. Or we can click the Intersecting References button to access a list of eligible reference elements like the levels in our project. We'll use this method since we simply want to divide the columns in half.

4. On the Modify | Division tab, click the Intersecting References button.

⇨ In the "Intersecting Named References" dialog, check Level 3 and then click OK (see Figure 6.24).

• The Aubin Academy •

Column Grids and Structural Layout | 227

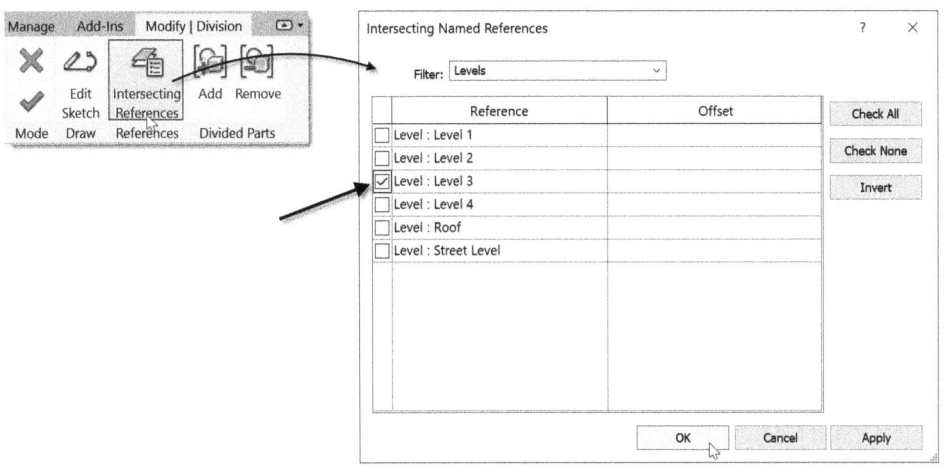

FIGURE 6.24 *Choose Level 3 and then finish the edit*

You will notice that in the "Intersecting Named References" dialog we could select one or more levels. There are also options for grids and reference planes in the Filter list at the top. For our purposes, the levels give us what we need, so we will not use one of those options this time.

5. On the Modify | Division tab, click the Finish Edit Mode button (big green checkmark).

Once you have finished dividing your parts, move your mouse around the columns to pre-highlight them. Notice that only half will highlight at a time and the tooltip will read "Parts." On the Properties palette, you can toggle the display mode to Show Parts, Show Original or both simultaneously. You can see examples in Figure 6.25.

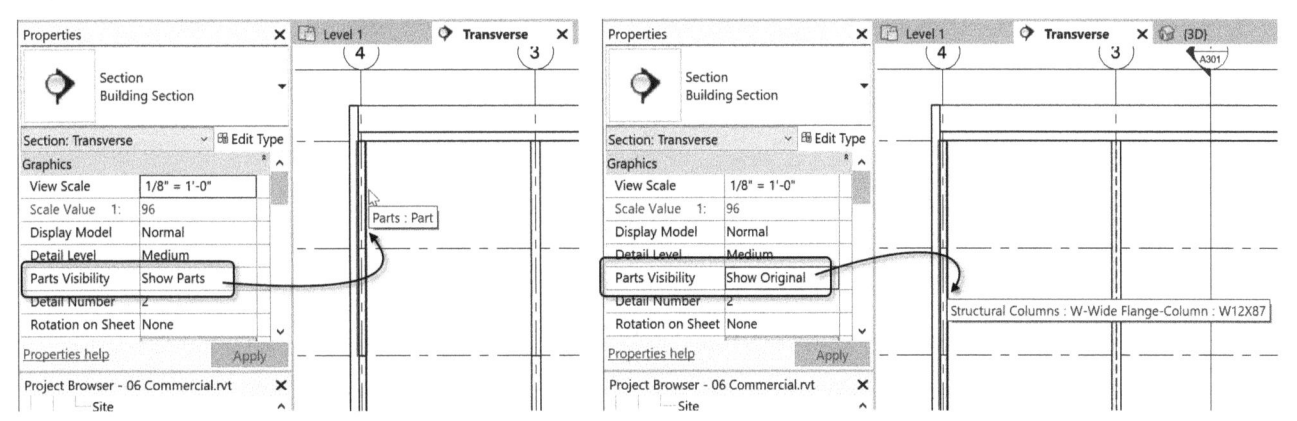

FIGURE 6.25 *The Parts Visibility parameter on the view's Properties palette can show either the original elements or the parts*

6. On the Properties palette, for Parts Visibility, choose: **Show Original** (see the right side of Figure 6.25).

REUSING EXISTING GEOMETRY

Leveraging existing elements is always more efficient than creating new ones. We can copy elements or use various "pick" tools to create new elements from existing ones.

COPY AND PASTE ALIGNED

Let's copy our architectural columns to other floors.

1. On the Project Browser, double-click to open the *Level 3* floor plan view.

• Revit Essentials for Architecture •

228 | Chapter 6

Notice that only the Structural Columns show in this view. The structural columns show because they span multiple levels and therefore intersect this view's cut plane. The architectural columns do not show because they occur on Level 1 and are a single story in height.

2. On the Project Browser, double-click to open the *Level 1* floor plan view (or click its open tab to switch).

We could use the same selection method that we used above to select all the architectural columns, but let's explore another technique this time.

3. Make a window selection (from left to right) surrounding the entire building (don't include the grid lines). (See item 1 in Figure 6.26).

   This will select all visible elements in the building model.

   ⇨ On the Modify | Multi-Select tab of the ribbon, click the Filter button (item 2).

   ⇨ In the "Filter" dialog, click the "Check None" button.

   ⇨ Check *only* the Columns check box and then click OK (item 3).

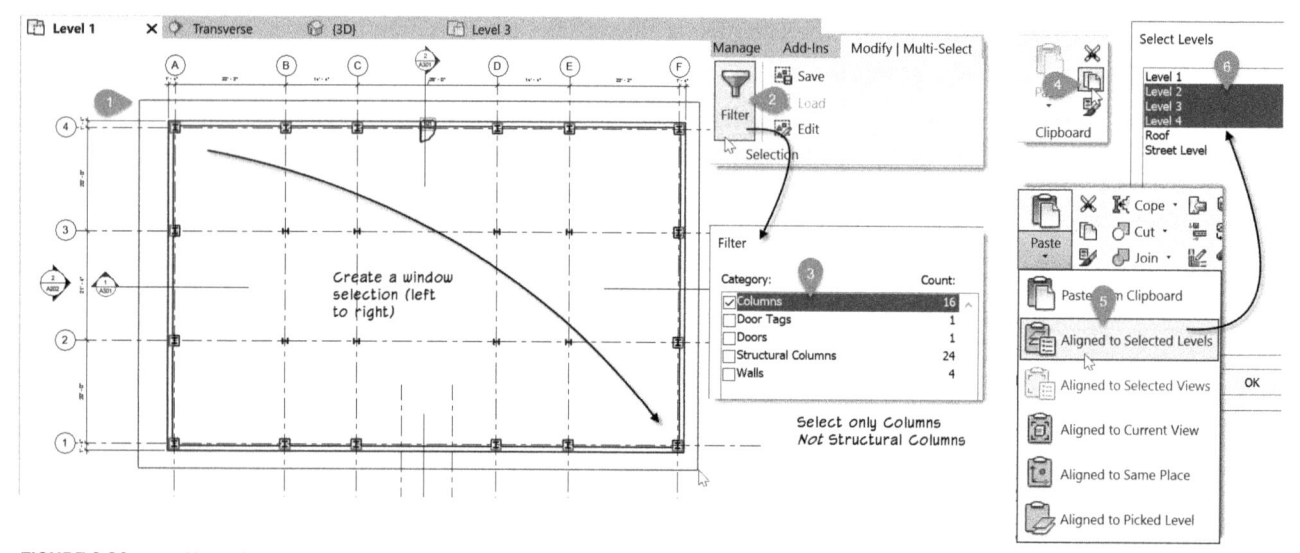

FIGURE 6.26 *Use filter selection to modify a selection and remove unwanted items*

Only the Architectural Columns should now be selected in light blue. (Note that Architectural Columns are referred to in the "Filter" dialog simply as "Columns".)

4. On the Modify | Columns tab of the ribbon on the Clipboard panel, click the Copy to Clipboard tool (or press CTRL + C) (item 4).

   ⇨ On the Clipboard panel, click the drop down button on the Paste tool and then choose: **Aligned to Selected Levels** (item 5).

   ⇨ In the "Select Levels" dialog, select Level 2 and drag down to Level 4.

   This should highlight Levels 2, 3 and 4. You can also select Level 2 first and then use the CTRL key to select levels 3 and 4 as well (item 5).

5. Click OK to complete the paste operation.

6. On the Project Browser, double-click to open the *Transverse* section view (or click its tab if already open).

Notice that the architectural columns have been pasted to the upper levels and remain selected on the top level. Check other views as well if you wish.

   ⇨ On the ribbon, click the Modify tool or press the ESC key twice.

7. Save the project.

• The Aubin Academy •

ADDING STRUCTURAL CORE WALLS

Now that we have a column grid with associated columns, it is a good time to sketch in the building core. To do this, we will use Structural Walls. Structural Walls are essentially the same as other walls except that the "Structural Usage" parameter for them is automatically set to: Bearing and the "Structural" property is checked on. We add structural walls in the same way as other walls.

1. On the Project Browser, double-click to open the *Level 1* floor plan view (or simply click the tab for it if it is already open).

    ⇨ On the View tab, or the QAT, click the Close Inactive button.

    ⇨ Zoom in on the two bays between column grids C and E at the top of the plan (between grid lines 3 and 4).

> **TIP:** Right-click and choose: **Zoom In Region** or type ZR. Zoom In Region is also located on the Navigation bar.

2. On the Architecture tab of the ribbon, click the drop down button on the Wall tool and choose: **Wall: Structural**.

    ⇨ From the Type Selector, from the Basic Wall family types, choose:
    Generic - 8" Masonry [Generic - 225mm Masonry].

    ⇨ On the Options Bar, choose: **Height** from the first pop-up.

    A warning will appear in the lower-right corner. Click anywhere to dismiss this; Revit is simply readjusting the height settings for us, but we are about the modify them anyway

    ⇨ On the Properties palette, set the Location Line to: **Wall Centerline**.

    ⇨ Set the Base Constraint to: **Street Level** and set the Top Constraint to: **Up to level: Roof**.

These settings instruct our structural wall to go the full height of the building from the lowest level to the highest. We will also need the core walls to continue past the roof to allow stair access to the roof. So, let's also add a "Top Offset" parameter. Keep in mind that all these parameters can be edited later as the project progresses and as design needs dictate.

3. For the Top Offset parameter, type: **12'-0" [3600]** (see Figure 6.27).

    Take note of the "Structural Usage" parameter—note that it is set to "Bearing" automatically.

230 | Chapter 6

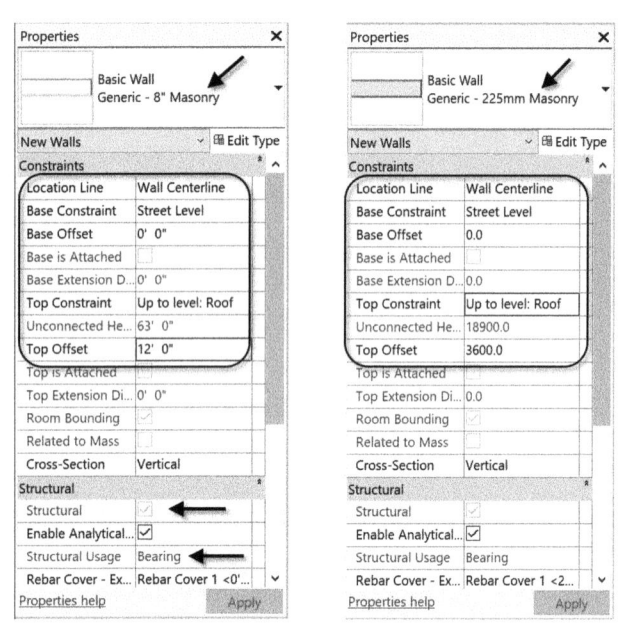

FIGURE 6.27 *Configure the parameters for structural wall the full height of the building*

⇨ Click Apply (or simply shift focus away from the palette) to continue.

4. On the Draw panel, click the Pick Lines icon.

⇨ On the Options bar, in the Offset field, type: **1'-2" [350]** and then press ENTER.

With the Pick Lines option enabled, we will be able to select existing geometry from which to create the walls. The walls will be created at 1'-2" [350] from the selected geometry.

5. Highlight grid line C and when the light dashed offset line appears to the right of the grid line, click the mouse to create the wall.

⇨ Repeat for grid line 3 (horizontal) when the offset line appears below the grid line (see Figure 6.28).

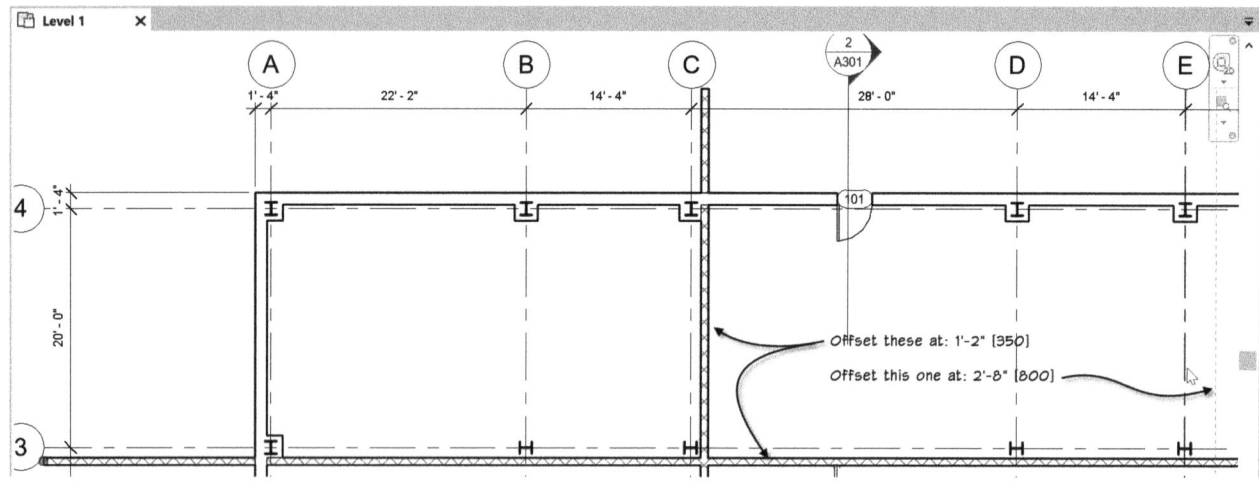

FIGURE 6.28 *Create walls from grid lines using the pick lines option with an offset value*

6. Change the Offset value on the Options Bar to: **2'-8" [800]** and then create one more wall to the right of grid line E.

⇨ On the ribbon, click the Modify tool or press the ESC key twice.

7. On the Modify tab of the ribbon, on the Modify panel, click the Trim/Extend to Corner tool.

8. Trim the two bottom intersections as shown in Figure 6.29 (remember to select the side of the wall that you want to keep).

Column Grids and Structural Layout | 231

9. On the Edit panel, click the Trim/Extend Multiple Elements tool.

⇨ Select the top exterior wall as the boundary.

⇨ Trim the two top intersections to butt into the inside edge of the exterior horizontal wall as shown in Figure 6.29.

Remember to click the side of the wall you want to keep. For more information on the Trim/Extend tool, refer to the tutorials r 4.

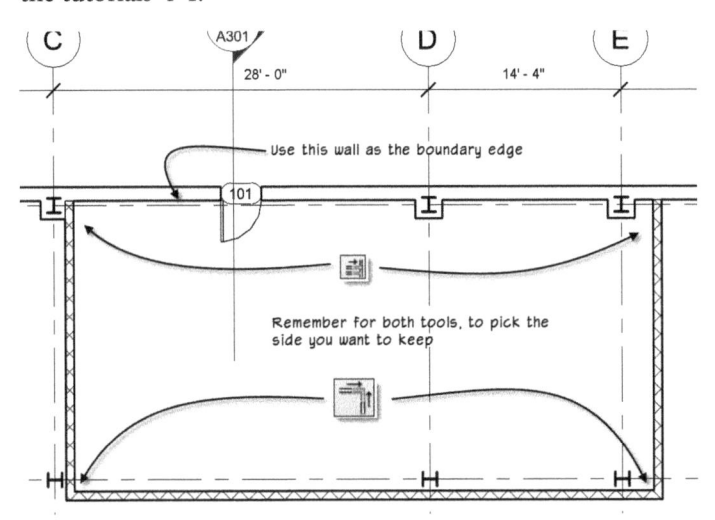

FIGURE 6.29 *Trim the walls to form the core layout*

⇨ On the ribbon, click the Modify tool or press the ESC key twice.

CONVERT A WALL TO A STRUCTURAL WALL

Let's view the model in section to see what we have so far.

1. Double-click the blue Section Head between grid lines C and D.

   The *Transverse* building section view will open.

2. Click on the crop boundary to select it. Click and drag the control handle at the top edge and drag it up enough to see the top of the core walls.

⇨ Select one of the grids and drag the control at the top to stretch the bubbles up a bit (see Figure 6.30).

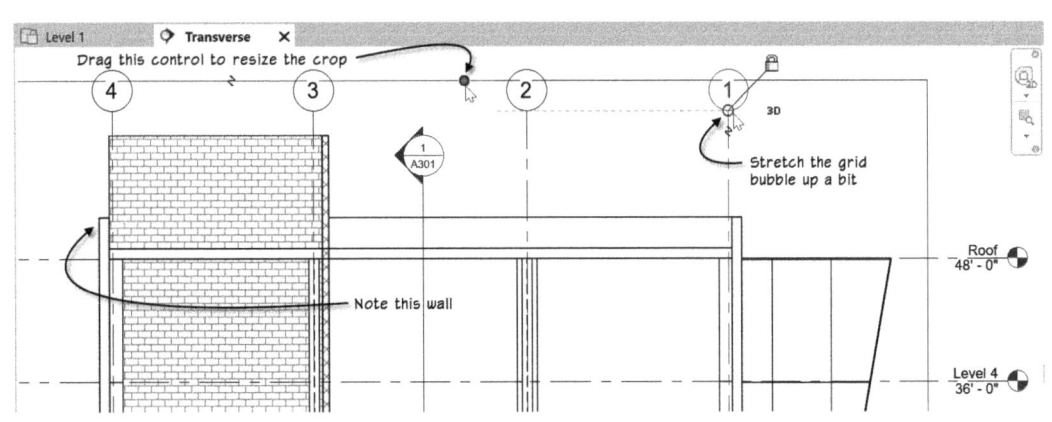

FIGURE 6.30 *Drag the crop boundary large enough to see the top of the new walls*

Notice that the exterior wall on the left only projects to the parapet height. This wall would also need to be part of the core. Let's split this existing wall and then change the middle portion to have its parameters match the rest of the core.

3. Click back on the *Level 1* floor plan view tab to make it active.

• Revit Essentials for Architecture •

232 | Chapter 6

4. On the Modify tab of the ribbon, on the Modify panel, click the Split Element tool (or press SL).

   On the Options Bar, make sure that Delete Inner Segment is *not* checked.

   ⇨ Place the pointer at the intersection of the exterior wall and the core wall at grid C.

   ⇨ When the pointer snaps to the intersection, click the mouse to split the wall.

5. Repeat on the other intersection near grid E (see the left side of Figure 6.31).

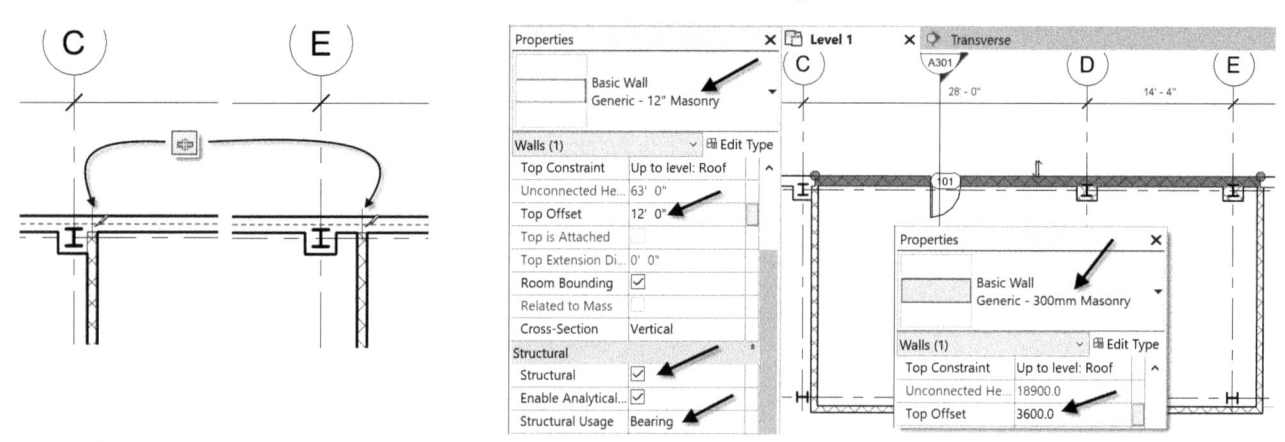

FIGURE 6.31 *Split the upper horizontal wall in two places to form the top wall of the core*

   ⇨ On the ribbon, click the Modify tool or press the ESC key twice.

6. Select the middle horizontal wall segment (created by the splits).

7. On the Properties palette, from the Type Selector, choose: **Generic - 12" Masonry** [**Generic - 300mm Masonry**].

   ⇨ Change the Top Offset to: **12'-0"** [**3600**].

8. Beneath the Structural grouping, check the "Structural" check box and verify that the Structural Usage parameter is set to Bearing and then click Apply (see the right side of Figure 6.31).

EDIT WALL JOINS

Graphically, the wall should now appear as the other core walls do (except that the thickness varies). If you are unhappy with the way the walls clean up at the corners, you can use the Wall Joins tool to edit them.

1. On the Modify tab of the ribbon, on the Geometry panel, click the Wall Joins tool.

   ⇨ Click at the first intersection near grid C.

   A square will appear surrounding the intersection.

2. On the Options bar, click the Next or Previous buttons to see the various solutions.

   ⇨ Repeat as many times as you like. Stop at the one you like. The Edit Joins tool will stay active.

3. Repeat for the other intersection near grid E (see Figure 6.32).

Column Grids and Structural Layout | 233

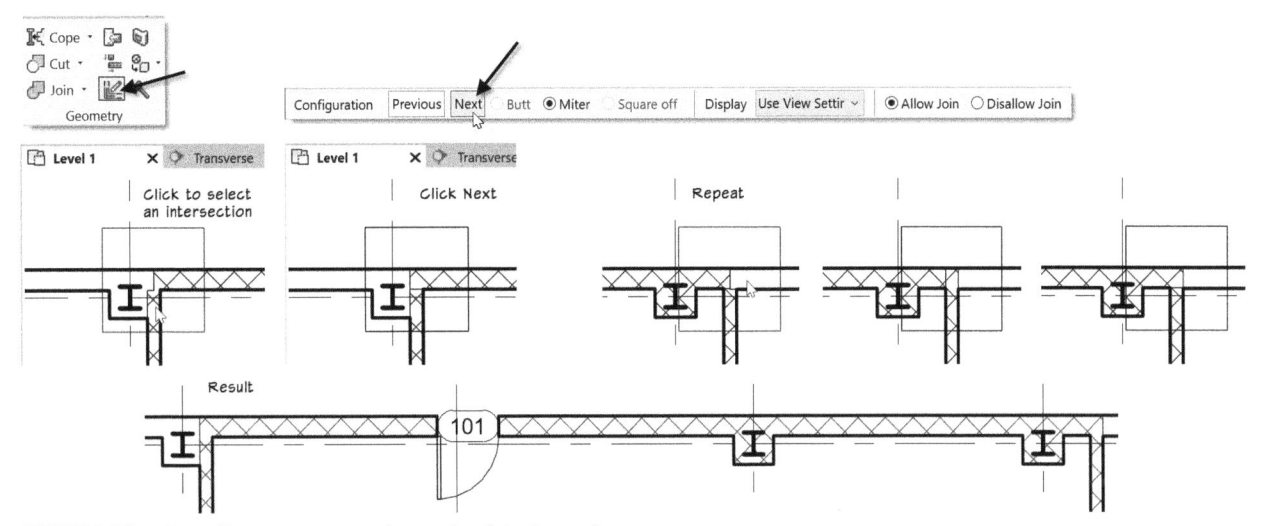

FIGURE 6.32 *Edit Wall Joins to improve the graphical display at the corners*

⇨ When you are finished editing, click the Modify tool or press the ESC key twice.

> **TIP:** In some cases, you can disjoin the walls using the drag handles at the ends instead of Edit Joins. Drag the handles away from the intersection to disconnect the walls from one another. Then use the Trim tool to re-join the walls. Try Edit Joins first. You can also right-click the handle and choose: **Disallow Join**. This prevents the walls from joining at all. This is useful when you want a wall to butt into a curtain wall mullion for example or to accurately convey differences in fire rating conditions. To disallow several walls at once, use a crossing selection or the CTRL key and select several walls at once while in the Edit Wall Joins command. Then choose the Disallow Join option on the Options Bar.

4. Double-click the blue Section Head between grid lines C and D again.

Notice that the outside wall now matches the others in the core.

⇨ Click the Default 3D View icon to open the default *{3D}* view to check your work there as well.

⇨ Open the *Longitudinal* Section and expand the Crop Region there and adjust the height of the grids as well.

5. Save the project.

ADDING FLOORS

The most obvious omission that you might notice in our current sections is the lack of any floor slabs. Adding floors is easy to accomplish. However, even though we want them to display in sections, we will draw them in a plan view. In fact, if you try to create a floor element while an elevation or section is active, you will be prompted to open a plan instead. So, let's do that first.

CREATE A FLOOR FROM WALLS

The easiest way to create a floor is by using the existing walls that bound it.

1. On the Project Browser, double-click to open the *Level 1* floor plan view.
2. Close inactive views.
3. On the Architecture tab of the ribbon, click the Floor tool (if you click the drop down, it is: Floor: Architectural).

On the Modify | Create Floor Boundary tab, on the Draw panel, the Boundary Line and Pick Walls modes should be active already.

• Revit Essentials for Architecture •

234 | Chapter 6

> ⇨ Click first on each of the vertical exterior walls (left and right sides), and then the bottom horizontal one, and only one of the top horizontal ones (see the left side of Figure 6.33).

NOTE: Be sure to click on the inside edges. If you accidentally create sketch lines to the outside edge, use the Flip control at the middle of the sketch line (double arrow) to flip the sketch to the inside.

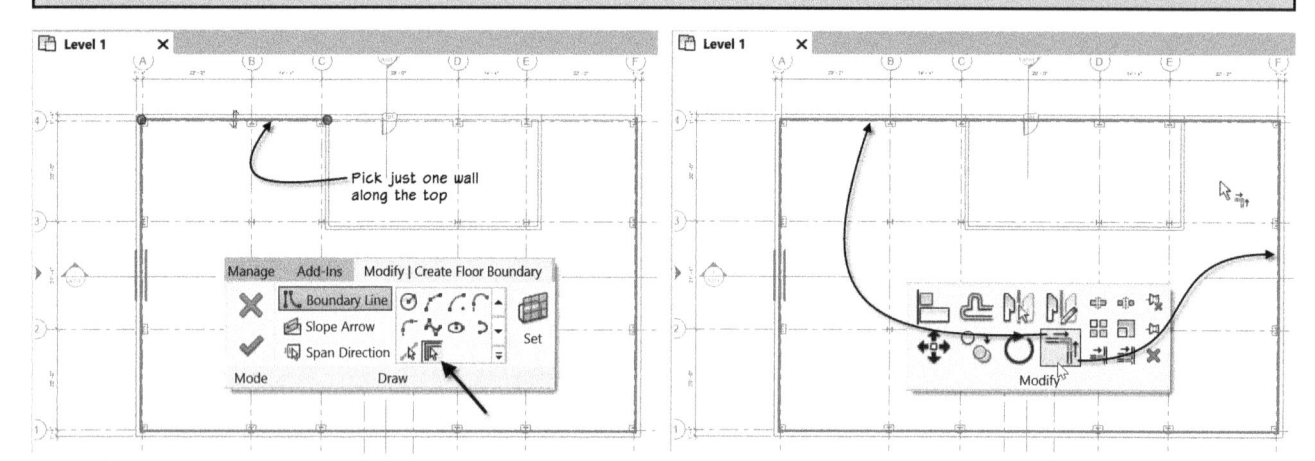

FIGURE 6.33 *Create sketch lines from walls (Sketch lines enhanced for clarity)*

4. Use the Trim/Extend to Corner tool to join the two open sketch lines (see the left side of Figure 6.33).

Above, you were instructed to click the vertical wall on the left first. Notice that this applies a special symbol (two parallel lines) to that sketch line only. This is the Span Direction of the floor. Revit allows you to edit the floor type to apply structural deck to your design. The symbol on this first sketch line indicates the direction of the decking. You can use the Span Direction button on the ribbon to change the span direction to a different sketch line later if required. We will not be doing this in this exercise, but you are welcome to explore this on your own.

5. Click the Finish Edit Mode button (big green checkmark).

A message will appear on screen that reads:

"The floor/roof overlaps the highlighted wall(s). Would you like to join the geometry and cut the overlapping volume out of the Wall(s)?"

If you answer yes to this message, Revit will use the floor volume to cut away the overlapping portion in the various walls. If you answer no, the two elements will remain overlapping and appear unfinished in sections and possibly throw off volume calculations you may later generate.

6. In the dialog that appears, click Yes.

You can always edit the automatic joins later, but in general, it is a good idea to allow Revit to apply joins when prompted at the early stages of design. This automated prompt connects the various building elements in logical ways and does so more efficiently than we can do manually at this stage. As your model becomes more refined and the project progresses beyond design development, you may wish to manage the joins manually. You would use the Join Geometry tool on the Modify tab for this purpose.

COPY FLOOR SLABS TO LEVELS

1. Double-click the blue Section Head between grid lines C and D again.

You can see the new floor slab at Level 1. If you look carefully at the intersections, particularly at the right side, you will see the effect of the join geometry message in the previous topic (zoom in as required).

2. Select the new floor slab element, and then press CTRL + C. Or on the Modify | Floors tab, on the Clipboard panel, you can click the Copy to Clipboard tool

3. On the Modify | Floors ribbon tab, on the Clipboard panel, click the drop down button on the Paste tool and choose: **Aligned to Selected Levels**.

⇨ In the "Select Levels" dialog, select Level 2, Level 3, and Level 4 and then click OK.

> **TIP:** Use the CTRL key to select more than one level, or simply drag through the names.

The other approach you can take to create the upper level floors would be to simply open each plan view and repeat the sketching steps. Naturally, the copy/paste method is a little quicker. However, looking in the section view, you may notice that the upper floors did not automatically join with the walls. There is a Join tool on the Modify tab on the Geometry panel. You can find examples of how to use this tool in Chapter 9. While using the Join tool would give the desired result in this section view, the process can be tedious and would need to be repeated in the *Longitudinal* section as well.

More efficient would be to have Revit prompt us to join automatically again. To be prompted by the message we received in the previous topic, you must create the floor manually or edit the sketch of an existing floor. Since we have copied the floors here, and did not benefit from auto-prompting, we can simply edit the floors, and without making any actual edits to the sketch, click the Finish Edit Mode button on the ribbon. This will trigger Revit to prompt us to join and cut volumes as above. To try this, simply select a pasted floor. On the Modify | Floors tab click the Edit Boundary tool. A "Go To View" dialog will appear (you cannot edit the sketch from a section view), select any floor plan view listed in the dialog and then click the Open View button. Make no changes to the sketch. On the ribbon, click the Finish Edit Mode button. The message we saw above will appear again. Click Yes. Reopen the section and repeat the process on the other floors. You may have to complete a few of the joins on the back wall manually. This process is not required to complete the tutorials in this chapter and is left to the reader as an optional exercise.

CREATE A SHAFT

You should now have a floor slab at each level and we already had a roof at the top. However, these new floor slabs now interrupt our building core. We will need a shaft for the elevators and stairs that will come later. We will add a shaft now using approximate dimensions and then later, in Chapter 8, we will add the vertical circulation elements and fine-tune the size and shape of the shaft to suit the design as required.

1. On the Project Browser, double-click to open the *Level 1* floor plan view (or click its tab to switch).

2. On the Architecture tab, on the Opening panel, click the Shaft tool.

    The Modify | Create Shaft Opening Sketch ribbon tab appears. On the Draw panel, the Boundary Lines and Line modes should be active.

⇨ On the Draw Panel, click the Rectangle icon.

3. Snap to the lower left inside endpoint of the core walls.

⇨ For the other corner, snap to the inside midpoint of the top exterior wall (see Figure 6.34).

236 | Chapter 6

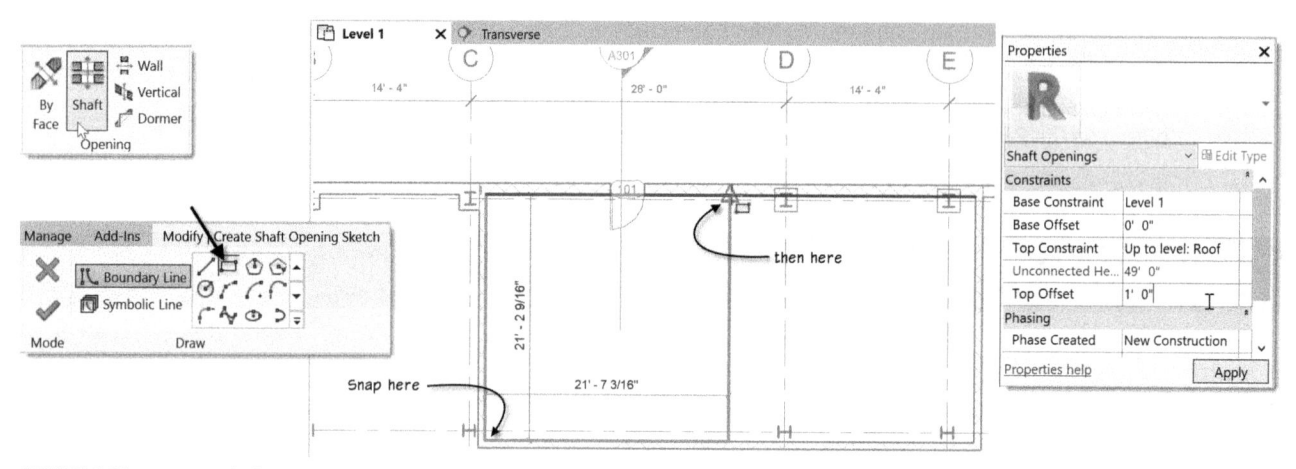

FIGURE 6.34 *Create a shaft opening*

> **NOTE:** If you have difficulty snapping to the Midpoint, snap close to the location shown in the figure instead.

4. On the Properties palette, for the Base Constraint choose: **Level 1** and for the Top Constraint choose: **Up to level: Roof**.

   ⇨ For the Top Offset, type: **1'-0"** [**300**], for the Bottom Offset, type: **0** (zero) and then click Apply.

   ⇨ On the ribbon, click the Finish Edit Mode button and then deselect the Shaft.

5. On the QAT, click the Default 3D View icon.

   ⇨ Hold down the SHIFT key and drag with your wheel button, (or drag the ViewCube or use the Steering Wheel) to orbit the model around so you can see down into the core (see Figure 6.35).

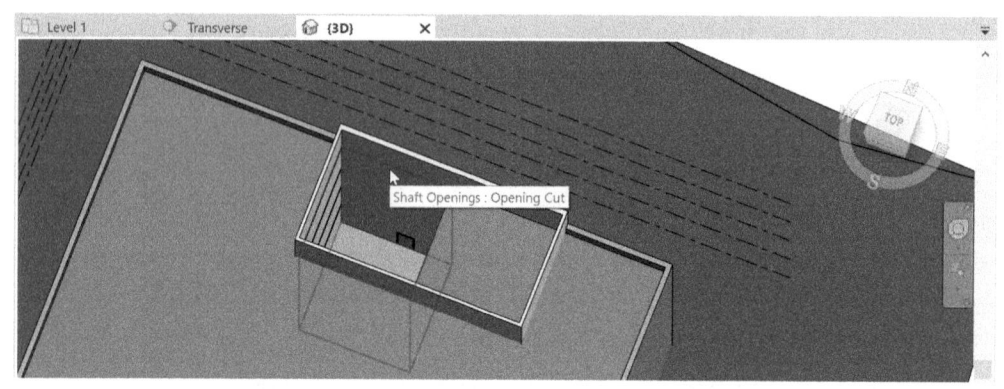

FIGURE 6.35 *The completed shaft cuts through all of the floors and the roof*

You should see the shaft opening cut through all the floors and roof to create a void.

6. On the Project Browser, double-click to open the *Level 1* floor plan view (or click its tab).

7. On the View tab, on the Create panel, click the Section tool.

   ⇨ Create a section (from left to right) through the top portion of the core.

   ⇨ Click anywhere to deselect the section, and then double-click the new Section Head to open the view (see Figure 6.36).

• The Aubin Academy •

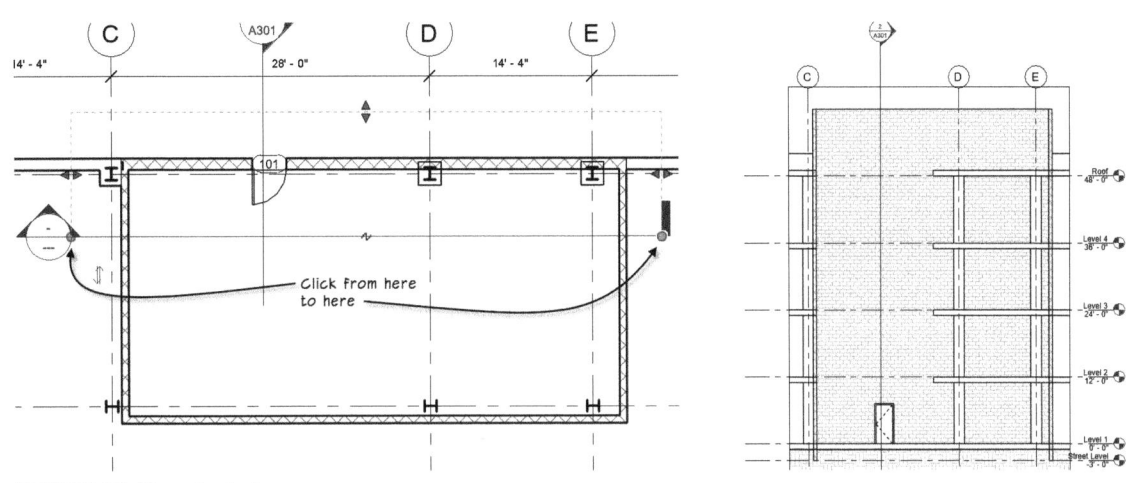

FIGURE 6.36 *View the shaft in a new section view*

Study the way that the shaft has cut the slabs in this and other views.

8. On the Project Browser, beneath *Sections (Building Section)* right-click *Section 1* and choose: **Rename**.

⇨ Name the view: **Section at Building Core** and then click OK.

9. Save the project.

CREATING STRUCTURAL FRAMING

So far, we have explored columns, grids, and floors. In addition to these tools, Revit also includes tools to create beams and braces. If your primary job function is architectural, you may not be responsible for adding these elements to the model. This task might fall on the structural engineers on your team. However, like the columns, even though they will ultimately be sized by the structural engineer, you can add the basic components to your model at any appropriate point in the design process and later re-size and reconfigure them as appropriate based upon your structural engineer's design and analysis. This is accomplished typically by simply selecting the elements and editing the type applied in the Properties palette. It is also a common workflow to simply remove the structural elements you created and replace them with a link to the structural engineer's file when you receive it. We will explore this option in the next chapter. In this topic, we will take a brief look at the structural beam and brace tools available. Feel free to explore beyond what is covered here.

WORKING WITH BEAMS

You can add Beams to your model by sketching, or you can create them automatically based upon a column grid. In this exercise, we will use our grid to create beams.

1. On the Project Browser, double-click to open the *Level 2* floor plan view.
2. On the Structure tab, on the Structure panel, click the Beam tool.

> **NOTE:** If you don't see the Structure tab in your interface, from the File menu, click the Options button and then on the User Interface tab, be sure that Structure tab and tools is checked.

Like the columns above, we will first load a family to use for the beam shape.

3. On the Modify | Place Beam tab, click the Load Family button.

⇨ Double-click the *Structural Framing* folder, and then double-click the *Steel* folder.

238 | Chapter 6

4. Double-click the *W-Wide Flange.rfa* [*M_W-Wide Flange.rfa*] family file.

A list of industry standard steel-shape sizes will appear. Scroll through the list to see all of the sizes (similar to Figure 6.17 8). If your copy of Revit does not have these folders or files, you can find copies in the *Chapter06* folder.

⇨ In the "Specify Types" dialog, select: **W18 x 40** [**W460 x 52**] and then click OK.

In the "Family Already Exists" dialog, click the Overwrite the existing version option to accept the reload.

⇨ From the Type Selector, choose the newly loaded: **W18 x 40** [**W460 x 52**] type.

5. On the Modify | Place Beam tab, click the On Grids button.

Make sure that Tag on Placement is off (not highlighted in blue).

6. Dragging from right to left, select all grid lines.

7. On the Modify | Place Beam > On Grid Lines tab, click the Finish button.

After a short pause, it will appear as though the command is finished, but nothing will appear to have been created. This is because the detail level of our plan view is set to: Coarse.

⇨ On the ribbon, click the Modify tool or press the ESC key twice.

8. On the View Control bar, change the Detail Level to: **Medium**.

Beams will appear at each major grid line between the columns (see the left side of Figure 6.37).

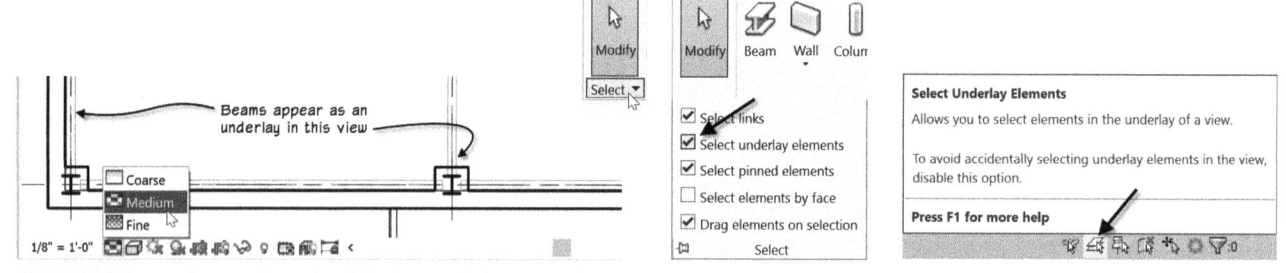

FIGURE 6.37 *Switch to Medium detail level to see the beams in plan*

UNDERSTANDING UNDERLAYS

You will also notice that the beams appear to be light gray rather than bold and black like other elements. This is because they are set lower than level 2 and therefore fall below the view range of our current *Level 2* floor plan. Because of this, they normally would not display. The reason we can see them is that they are being displayed as an underlay. An underlay allows you to show the geometry from another level under the geometry displayed in the current plan. This is helpful when you need to use another level for reference in creating the elements on the current level. You can use any other level (that has a view associated with it) as an underlay. In this case, we are seeing an underlay of Level 1. To configure which level you want as an underlay, be sure that no elements are selected and then look at the properties of the current view on the Properties palette. There you can choose a different level to display as an underlay or set it to None if you no longer want to display it. There is also an option that allows the underlay orientation which can be look down or look up.

It is also important to keep in mind that underlay elements are live model elements and can be selected and modified as long as the "select underlay elements" setting is active. This means we should exercise care when selecting and or making modifications of underlay elements to ensure we don't get unexpected results. If you are unable to highlight or select underlay elements, you must enable their selection.

Several selection toggles are available on the drop down of the Modify tool and as icons in the lower-right corner of the application frame. These are pictured on the right side of Figure 6.37. If you don't wish to accidentally select the underlay elements, simply toggle off the "Select underlay elements" option.

MODIFYING FRAMING ELEMENTS

As noted in the previous topic, the framing occurs just below the current level 2. If you open a section however, you will see that the framing coincides with the floor. Let's lower it a little more to allow room for the floor slab on top of it.

1. On the Project Browser, double-click to open the *Longitudinal* section view.
2. On the View Control bar, change the Detail Level to: **Medium**.
⇨ Zoom in on Level 2 to view one of the beams up close.

It is now clear that the beams appear at the same height as the top of the slab, but below the height of level 2.

3. Pre-highlight one of the Beams.
⇨ Right-click and choose: **Select All Instances > In Entire Project**.
4. On the Properties palette, beneath the Constraints grouping, set the Start Level Offset and the End Level Offset parameters to: **-4"** [**-100**] (negative values).

Adding this negative offset moves the Beams below the level enough to allow the topping slab to cover them. There is an alternative setting on the Properties palette as well. The Z Offset will move the profile of the beam and achieve nearly the same result. Start and End level offsets can be different at each end. The Z offset applies across the entire beam. Right now, the beams are still overlapping the slab. We currently have a generic slab with a larger than required thickness, but in later chapters, we will change the composition of the slab to show more detail and adjust its thickness. When we do, the Beams will already be at the correct elevation.

There are other Beam creation methods and options. You can sketch Beams and create them specifically as Girders, Joists, Purlins, etc. When you use the grid option as we have here, Revit determines the usage automatically. In this case we have Girders. You can view the Structural topic in the online help for more details on this subject.

BEAM SYSTEM PRACTICE

Feel free to experiment further with the various beam options before continuing. For example, there is also a Beam System tool on the Structure tab. With this tool, you create an array of beams within a sketched shape—usually infilling a column bay. You can use the Automatic Beam System option to create the system by just clicking on one of the beams we just created, or you can sketch the shape of the system manually. The shape that you sketch will be filled in with an automatically generated array of beams. Before starting the Beam System routine, load an appropriate beam family such as a bar joist. To do this, click the Insert tab of the ribbon and then click the Load Family button. Browse to the same folder as the girder above. Select a family and type that you want to load, such as a K-Series Bar Joist family. To use the newly loaded bar joist family in the Beam System, choose it on the Options bar. There is also an Elevation parameter on the Properties palette so you can give the system a negative offset relative to the level like we did here for the Girders. It is best to work in plan for these. Give it try!

WORKING WITH BRACES

To complete our preliminary structural layout, let's add a few cross braces at the building core.

1. Return to the *Level 1* floor plan view.

240 | Chapter 6

> **TIP:** If you would like, you can try modeling the brace in a 3D view and use the "3D Snapping" option on the Options Bar to assist.

- On the Structure tab, on the Structure panel, click the Brace tool.
2. On the Modify | Place Brace tab of the ribbon, click the Load Family button.
- Double-click the *Structural Framing* folder, and then double-click the *Steel* folder.
- Double-click the *L-Angle.rfa* [*M_L-Angle.rfa*] family file.

  Once again, a list of industry standard steel-shape sizes will appear. Scroll through the list to see all of the sizes (similar to Figu817 above).

3. From the list, select: **L6 x 6 x 3/8** [**L152 x 152 x 9.5**] and then click OK.
- Verify that: **L6 x 6 x 3/8** [**L152 x 152 x 9.5**] is chosen from the Type Selector.
- On the Options bar, from the "Start" list, choose: **Level 1** and then type: **2'-0"** [**600**] in the offset field next to it.
4. From the "End" list, choose: **Level 2** and type: **-2'-0"** [**-600**] in the offset field.

   Toggle off Tag on Placement if necessary.

5. Snap the start point to the column at grid intersection 3C.
6. Snap the end point to the column at grid intersection 4C.
7. Repeat to create another brace from grid intersection 4D to 4E.

   Feel free to add additional Braces or Beams as desired.

- On the ribbon, click the Modify tool or press the ESC key twice.

As with the Beams, Braces will not appear in Coarse detail level. You can change this in the *Level 1* plan if you wish. Or you can create additional Section views as we did above (see Figure 6.38).

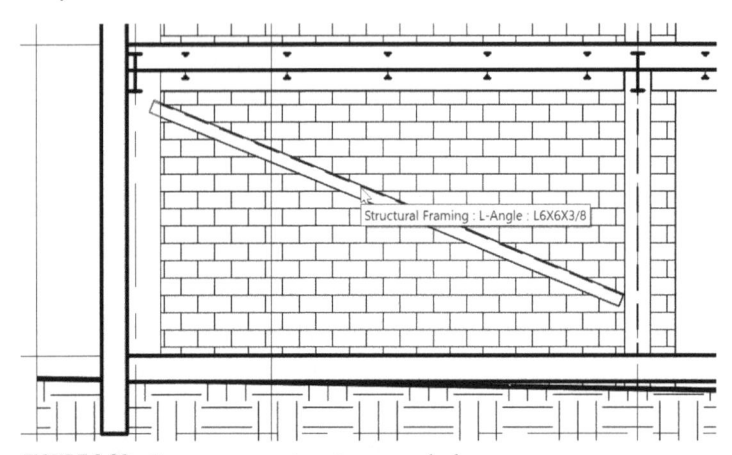

FIGURE 6.38 *Create a new section view to see the braces*

> **TIP:** Get in the habit of naming each new view (like the sections created here) with a good descriptive name. (Follow office standard naming guidelines as appropriate).

Column Grids and Structural Layout | 241

CREATE A NEW MODEL GROUP

The same framing layout will occur on all four floors of the project. We could copy it to each level as we did with the other elements, but let's take advantage of groups to make it easier to edit the framing later. Anytime that you have a repetitive (or "typical") portion of your building design—such as a typical stair, toilet room, or framing layout as in this case—you can use groups to manage them. We saw groups briefly at the start of the chapter with the Array command. In that instance, we ungrouped the array. In this case, we will leave the items grouped. The process is simple. Select the elements, group them, and then insert instances in the model. Whenever you need to make a change, edit any instance of the group. When you are finished editing, the change will apply to all instances of the group across the entire project. This also makes it easier to delete your preliminary structural elements once the structural engineer's model is available.

1. On the QAT, click the Default 3D View icon.
   ⇨ Dragging from right to left, select the entire model.
2. On the Modify | Multi-Select tab (or at the lower right corner of the Application Status bar), click the Filter icon.
   ⇨ In the "Filter" dialog, click the Check None button.
3. Check only the Structural Framing check boxes (there should be two such items) and then click OK.
   Do not include the Structural Columns in the selection.

You may not be able to see the selected elements. It depends on the angle of your 3D view and what other elements obscure them. While it is nice to see the selection for visual confirmation, filtering by only structural framing ensured that the beams and braces are selected. If you do wish to see the selected elements regardless, use the Temporary Hide/Isolate (sunglasses) pop-up and then choose: **Isolate Element**.

4. On the Modify | Structural Framing tab of the ribbon, on the Create panel, click the Create Group icon.
   ⇨ In the "Create Model Group" dialog that appears, type: **Typical Framing** and then click OK (see Figure 6.39).

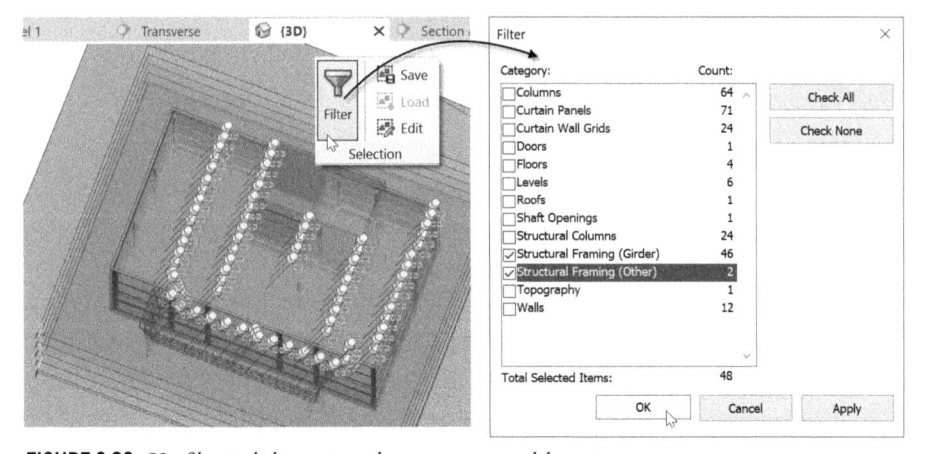

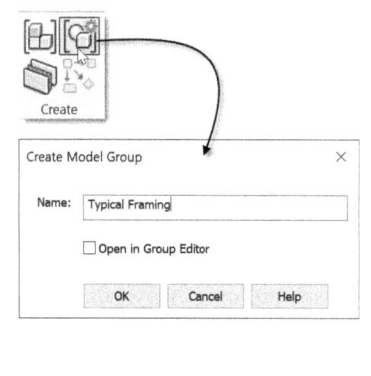

FIGURE 6.39 *Use filter to help create and name a new model group*

5. On the Project Browser, double-click to open the *Level 1* floor plan view.
6. On the Project Browser, expand *Groups* (near the bottom of the list), then expand the *Model* branch.
   Notice that "Typical Framing" is listed in the *Model* category.
7. Right-click on *Typical Framing* and choose: **Select All Instances > In Entire Project**.

Currently there is only one instance of this group in the model, so this just selects that one instance. We could have used any other selection method here as well. Notice the small "L" shaped icon with grip handles and "X" and "Y"

• Revit Essentials for Architecture •

242 | Chapter 6

labels that appears at the center of the group. This indicates the insertion point of the group. Using the handle at the intersection of the two axes, we can relocate the insertion point. The other round handles allow you to rotate the axes. The "X" and "Y" labels allow you to flip the group about either the X or Y-axis. Refer to Chapter 7 for more detailed information on groups.

8. Click and drag the insertion point handle (at the intersection of the "L") and snap it to the intersection of grid lines A and 1.

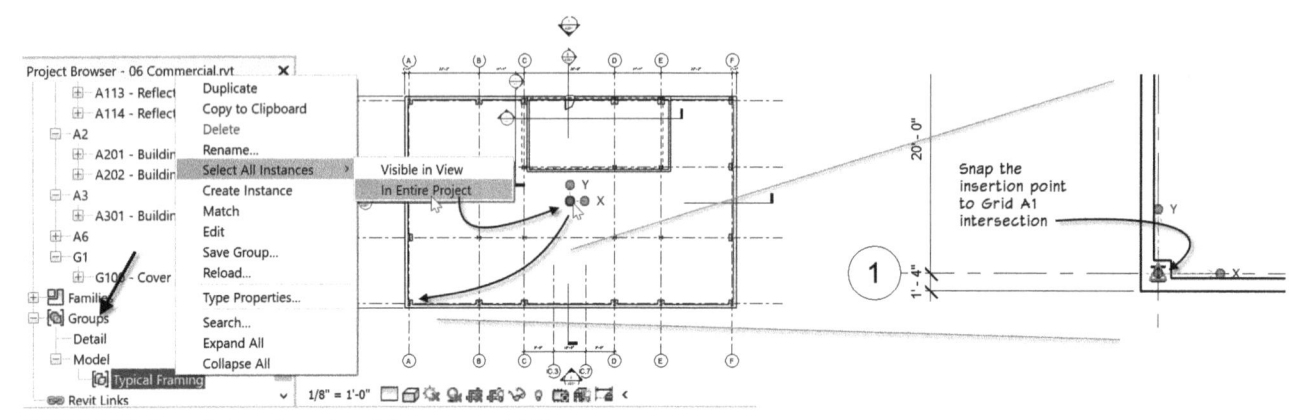

FIGURE 6.40 *Drag the insertion point of the group to grid A1*

> **TIP:** If you have trouble doing this, drag it close first, then zoom in to finish. You can use Temporary Hide/Isolate to hide the column and make snapping to the grids easier. Use Reset Temporary Hide/Isolate to re-display the column when finished.

9. On the Project Browser, double-click to open the *Level 2* plan.

⇨ Right-click the *Typical Framing* group on the Project Browser and choose: **Create Instance**.

⇨ Snap the new group instance to the intersection of grid lines A and 1.

10. Repeat for *Level 3* and *Level 4*.

If you prefer, you can use the Copy and Paste Aligned method showcased elsewhere in this chapter instead.

11. Open any section view to see the result.

EDITING GROUPS

This completes the work on the commercial project for this chapter. You can experiment on your own with the group if you wish. We will not cover the steps in detail now as the next chapter is devoted almost exclusively to working with groups. Therefore, you can undo any changes you make when you are finished, or you can leave them. It is up to you. Please refer to Chapter 7 for detailed information and tutorials on groups and group editing.

1. From the File menu, choose: **Close**. When prompted to save the project, click Yes.

To complete our brief exploration of structural tools in Revit we will have a look at the Footing tools provided. To do this, we will switch to the Residential project begun in Chapter 4. Some new footings are required for the addition on the back of the house. If you wish, after completing the exercise in the Residential project, you can return to the Commercial project and add footings there as well.

Column Grids and Structural Layout | 243

OPEN THE RESIDENTIAL PROJECT

Be sure that the Commercial project has been closed and saved.

1. On the QAT, click the Open icon (or press CTRL + O).
  ⇨ Browse to the *Chapter06* folder.
2. Double-click *06 Residential.rvt* if you wish to work in Imperial units. Double-click *06 Residential Metric.rvt* if you wish to work in Metric units. You can also select it and then click the Open button.

The project will open to a cover sheet showing a 3D view of the model. The *First Floor* view looks like it in Chapter 4 with the exception of some new walls boxing out where the addition will be. The *Second Floor* and *Basement* floor plan views have been provided for you. If you wish to gain some additional practice modeling the elements on these levels yourself, refer to the Appendix (included as a PDF) for exercises covering the layout of these levels.

ADD CONTINUOUS FOOTINGS

You can create three types of footings in Revit: Wall Foundation, Isolated Foundation, and Slab Foundation. A wall foundation is very easy to add and is associated with existing walls. An isolated foundation is a component family that can be inserted anywhere a footing is required, such as a pier footing, pile cap, etc. A slab foundation is a sketch-based element drawn just like a floor element that you can sketch any shape that is required. They are categorized as foundations however, and share characteristics with other types of foundations. Foundation tools are accessed on the Structure tab of the ribbon from the Foundation panel.

1. On the Project Browser, double-click to open the *Basement* floor plan view.
2. On the Structure tab, on the Foundation panel, click the Wall Foundation tool (see Figure 6.41).

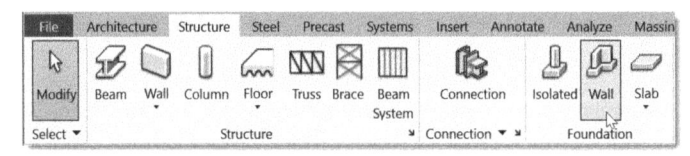

FIGURE 6.41 *Create a Wall Foundation*

  ⇨ From the Type Selector choose: **Bearing Footing - 36" x 12"** [**Bearing Footing -900 × 300**].

   A "Select Wall(s)" prompt will appear on the Status Bar (lower-left corner of the application frame).

We are adding footings only to the new construction. The new construction for the addition is bold and black while the existing construction is gray in color. There are three new construction walls in the addition at the top of the plan.

3. Click the vertical new construction wall on the left of the addition (top left of the plan).

A "Warning" message will appear in the lower right corner of the screen (see Figure 6.42). This is considered an "Ignorable" Warning message in Revit. It indicates a situation to which you should be made aware, but if you choose to ignore it, this condition does not prevent you from continuing your work. In this case, the Foundation that we just added is not visible in the current view because it is placed at the bottom of the wall which is outside the view range of this floor plan. We must perform a few steps to correct this and display the Foundations.

244 | Chapter 6

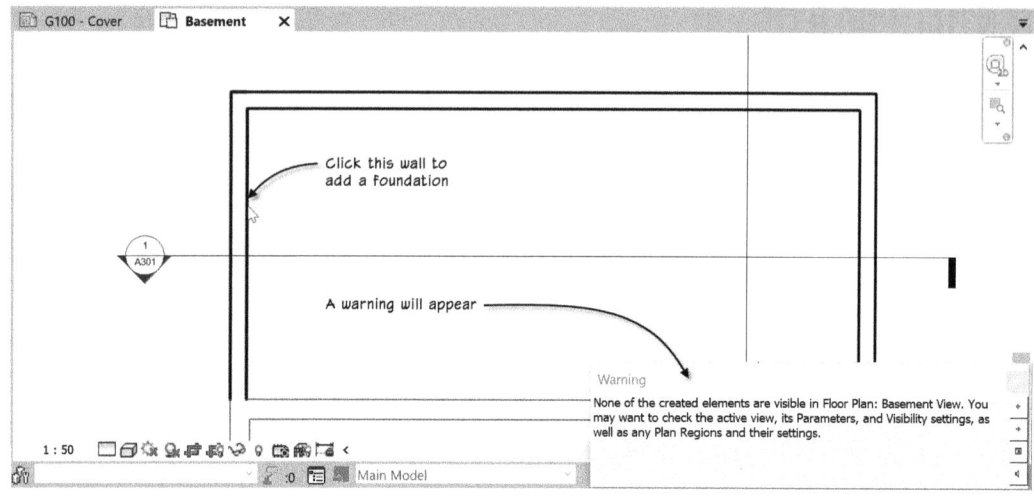

FIGURE 6.42 *Revit "Ignorable" Warning box*

⇨   On the ribbon, click the Modify tool or press the ESC key twice.

ADJUSTING VIEW RANGE

On the Properties palette, make sure the filter drop down list near the top reads: Floor Plan: Basement. This tells us we are editing the view's properties not the properties of a selected object. If it says something else, press ESC.

1.   On the Properties palette, scroll down to the Extents grouping and then click the Edit button next to "View Range."

⇨   In the "View Depth" area, in the Offset field, type: **-2'-0"** [**-600**] (see Figure 6.43).

FIGURE 6.43 *Edit the View Range of the Basement level floor plan*

2.   Click OK to see the results.

We now see the footing, but it is not displaying the way we might expect. Its edges display in a continuous line style and in the Imperial file, it shows a surface pattern for its material (concrete in this case). To fix the line style, we need to understand a little more about the View Range settings. When you make the View Depth lower than the "Bottom" of the Primary Range, the elements falling within the range between Bottom and View Depth use a special Revit Line Style called **<Beyond>**. By default, this style uses a continuous line, with a line weight of 1 so the result is not very apparent in the current view. We can, however, edit this line style and make it use a hidden line pattern which will in turn make geometry within the View Depth range also display as hidden. This can be accomplished globally on the Manage tab > Additional Settings > Line Styles. A change made there will affect the entire project, which may be desirable, but it would only take care of the edge. The surface pattern must be edited separately. Instead, we can edit both the line pattern and the remove the surface pattern by editing the Visibility/Graphic overrides of the Basement plan view.

• The Aubin Academy •

OVERRIDE VISIBILITY/GRAPHICS

It can certainly be appropriate to globally change the definition of the <Beyond> Line Style throughout the entire project. But it is sometimes better to apply a change like the one suggested in the previous topic only to the current view.

1. On the View tab, on the Graphics panel, click the Visibility/Graphic button (or press VG).

    Changes made in this dialog affect *only* the current view (*Basement* in this case).

2. On the Model Categories tab, scroll down and expand the Lines category.

    ⇨ Select the <Beyond> item.

    ⇨ Click the Override button that appears in the Lines column.

3. In the "Line Graphics" dialog, change the Pattern to Hidden and then click OK once and then click the Apply button to see the change in the view window (see the left side of Figure 6.44).

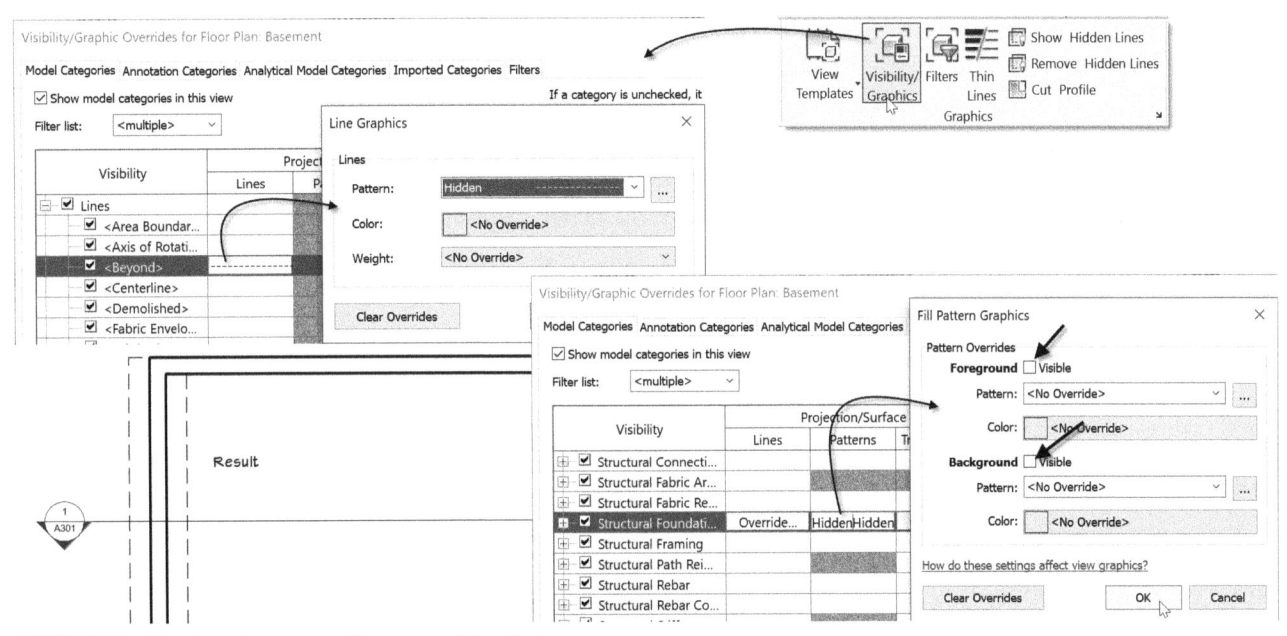

FIGURE 6.44 *Edit the surface pattern for structural foundations*

4. Scroll down and select the Structural Foundations category.

    ⇨ In the Projection/Surface, Patterns column, click the Override button.

    ⇨ Clear the "Visible" check box and then click OK twice (see the right side of Figure 6.44).

These visibility edits apply at the category level for this view. This means that any new foundation elements that you add to this view will display using the same visibility settings.

5. Add two more Footings to the other two walls of the addition.

> **TIP:** Select the footing already in the model and then click the Create Similar tool on the ribbon or type "CS". The Create Similar tool allows you to use the elements visible within the Canvas as an onscreen tool palette.

⇨ On the ribbon, click the Modify tool or press the ESC key twice.

MAKE A STEP FOOTING (EDIT WALL PROFILE)

Like many building model elements in Revit the footings will interact intelligently with the walls to which they are associated. For example, if we edit the profile of the wall to make a step at the bottom, the footing will adjust accordingly.

1. On the Project Browser, double-click to open the *North* elevation view.

In this view, the topography is concealing the foundation walls and footings from view. For now, we will simply hide the terrain so that we can work with the footings and foundations walls.

2. Select the Topo surface, and then on the View Control bar, choose: **Hide Element** from the Temporary Hide/Isolate pop-up icon (looks like sunglasses).

You should now be able to see the footings and walls. Remember that Temporary Hide is limited to this view and work session only.

3. Select the wall facing (parallel) this elevation. (Use TAB if necessary to select it.)
    ⇨ On the Modify | Walls tab of the ribbon, on the Mode panel, click the Edit Profile button.

The Profile is a sketch that defines the elevation shape of the wall. By default, this profile is a simple rectangular shape defined by the length and height of the wall. We can edit the sketch of this profile to create a wall with an alternate shape.

4. Using the Offset tool, offset the bottom edge down: **1'-6" [450]**.
    ⇨ Click the Line icon on the Draw panel and then draw a vertical sketch line at: 11'-0" [3300] from the right side.
5. Using the Trim/Extend to Corner tool, complete the sketch as shown in Figure 6.45.

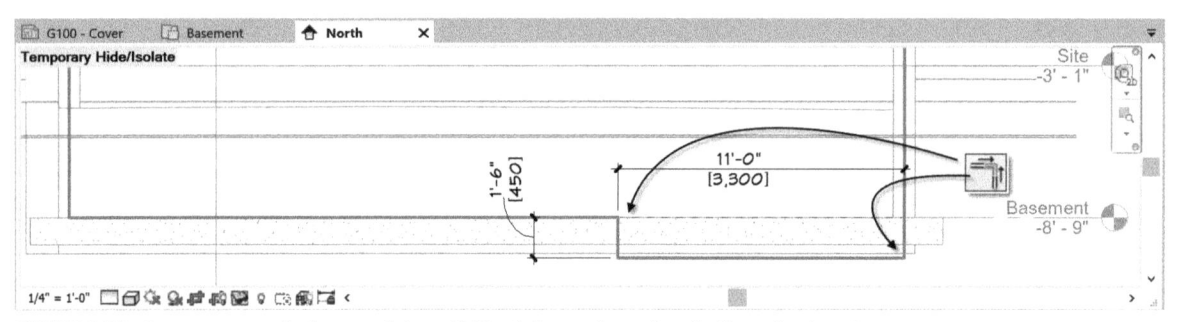

FIGURE 6.45 *Create a step in the bottom of the wall (sketch lines enhanced in the figure for clarity)*

    ⇨ On the ribbon, click the Finish Edit Mode button.

The Footing will automatically adjust to match the new configuration of the wall.

6. Perform similar Steps on the adjoining wall (*West* elevation).

Study the model in various views. Remember that you will need to hide the Toposurface temporarily in other views to see the foundations (see Figure 6.46).

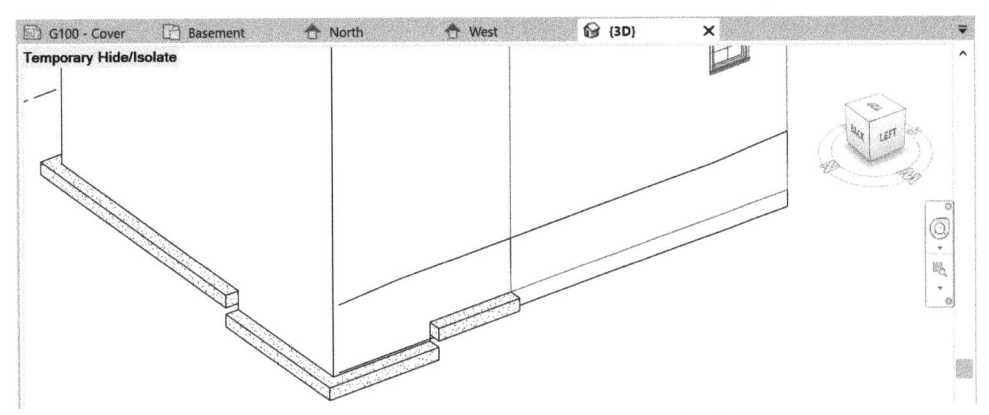

FIGURE 6.46 *The completed foundation in the {3D} view (with the Toposurface hidden)*

There is plenty more that we could do to finish up the foundation of the residential project. We could add existing Footings (remember to work in that phase) or we could add an Isolated Foundation to the chimney and the columns in the basement. We could also add isolated Foundations at each column in the Commercial project. When you choose the Isolated Foundation tool, you will be prompted to load a family for its use. This is left to the reader as an additional exercise. Feel free to experiment in both projects with these and other structural tools.

SUMMARY

- ☑ Grid lines are datum elements that establish column grid intersections.

- ☑ Grid lines share many features with levels and appear automatically in all orthographic views.

- ☑ Structural tools in Revit include Columns, Beams, Beam Systems, Braces, Walls, Slabs and Foundations.

- ☑ Structural Columns represent the actual structural support members of the building.

- ☑ Architectural Columns are typically used to represent the finished column as it would be seen in the building. Use them for Column wraps, etc.

- ☑ Structural walls are walls that have their Structural Usage parameter set to: Bearing and the Structural parameter checked on.

- ☑ Floor slabs can be created by picking the bounding walls as edges.

- ☑ You can create framing layouts and plans using Beams and Braces.

- ☑ Group a collection of elements and reuse it elsewhere in the model. If the group changes, all instances will update.

- ☑ A wall foundation remains associated to host walls.

- ☑ An isolated foundation is a component family that you place in your model.

CHAPTER 7
Groups and Links

INTRODUCTION

In this chapter, we will take a detailed look at groups and linked files. Groups provide a mechanism to standardize typical design elements throughout the project. A group consists of a collection of elements that can be placed into the model as a single unit. You can edit any single instance of the group and the changes will propagate to all instances throughout the model. Groups have many other features as well including the ability to have overrides applied to individual instances. Links are like groups except that the definition of the link is a separate Autodesk® Revit® project. The link maintains a connection to this project and when it changes, you can reload the link to immediately update link instances with those changes.

OBJECTIVES

In this chapter, we will work with both model and detail groups. We will explore how to create groups, modify them and strategies for using them effectively in your projects. After completing this chapter, you will know how to:

- Create groups
- Modify groups
- Override elements in group instances
- Create attached detail groups
- Swap groups with one another
- Work with links
- Convert a group to a link

CREATING GROUPS

The first part of this chapter will deviate from our Commercial and Residential projects to explore groups in a file that will be more suitable to conveying the critical concepts. Later in the chapter, we will return to the Commercial project to put into practice what we have learned about groups and explore links. Groups can be created in any project. Creating them is as simple as selecting elements in your project and then clicking the Create Group button. Groups appear on the Project Browser on their own branch.

OPEN A PROJECT

The lessons that follow require the dataset files included for download with this book. Refer to the "Download the Book Dataset" topic on page xi in the Preface for instructions on downloading and installing the book's dataset files if you still need to do so.

1. Launch Autodesk® Revit®.

⇨ If you are on the Home screen, you can click the Open button beneath Models. Otherwise, from the File menu, choose **Open** > **Project**. In the "Open" dialog box, browse to the *Chapter07* folder.

2. Double-click *Understanding Groups.rvt*. You can also select it and then click the Open button.

> **NOTE:** Please note that for the first part of this chapter, units are immaterial to the lessons covered and as such only one dataset has been provided rather than the customary separate Imperial and Metric datasets of other chapters. Regardless of your unit preference, please open the file indicated here.

WORKING WITH GROUPS

Groups are appropriate for nearly any repetitive (typical) design condition. Hotels, dormitories, apartment complexes, and condominiums give us plenty of opportunities to utilize groups in very effective ways. In this example, we will work with a very simple hotel room layout.

1. On the Project Browser, double-click to open the *Architecture* floor plan.

    This view shows the basic floor plan of a hotel guest room. Walls, doors, windows, and some basic fixtures are included.

2. Double-click to open the *Section 1* section view.

Here you will notice in addition to the items we can see in plan, there is also a multi-height ceiling plane in this model and some furniture items.

⇨ If you wish, open other views to explore the dataset further before continuing (see Figure 7.1).

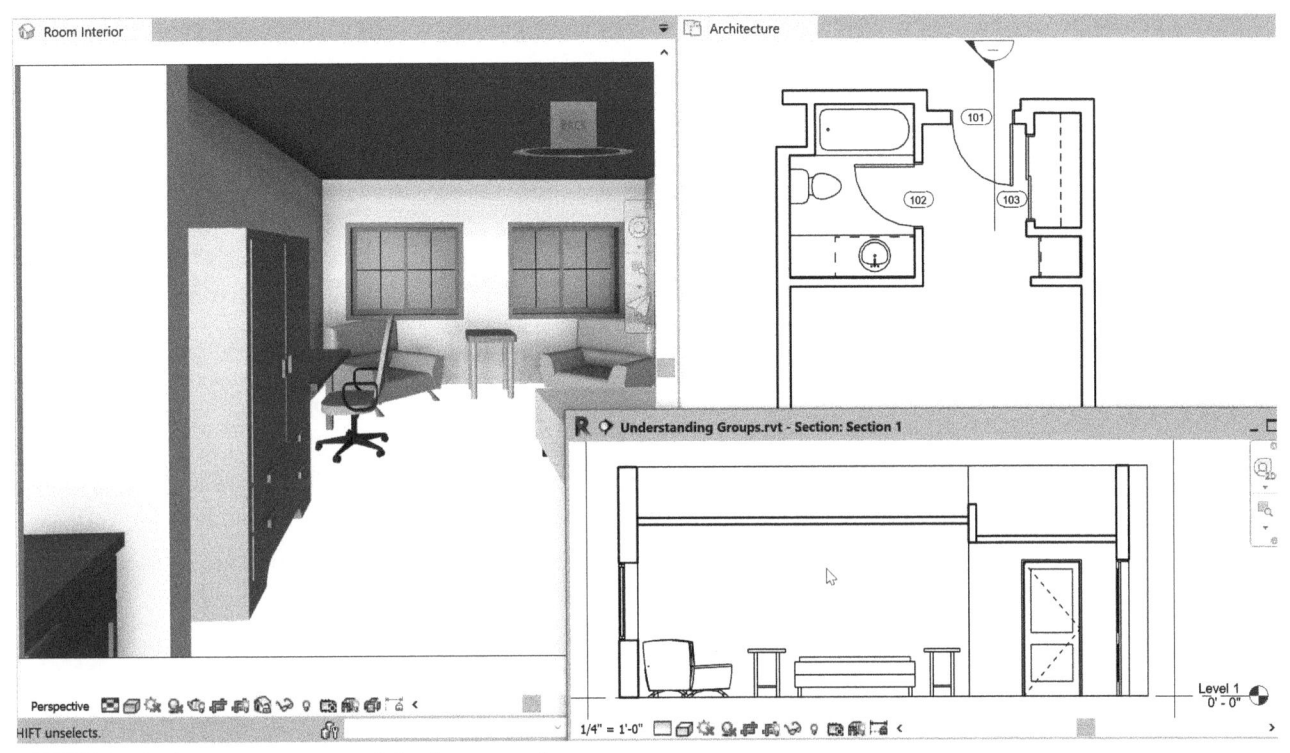

FIGURE 7.1 *The dataset represents a simple hotel guest room layout*

3. Click on the *Architecture* tab to return to this view.

⇨ Close any other open tabs or views.

CREATE A NEW GROUP

Our first task in the process of understanding groups is to create one.

Continue in the *Architecture* floor plan.

1. Using a window selection, select all elements on screen. (Click above and to the right of the model and drag down to the left surrounding all elements.) The Modify | Multi-Select tab will appear on the ribbon.

⇨ On the Create panel, click the Create Group button (or press GP).

An error dialog will appear. When you made your selection window, the elevation and section view tags were included in the selection. View tags cannot be included in a group. Simply clicking OK in this warning will automatically exclude them from the selection set.

⇨ Click OK in the warning dialog to dismiss it.

The "Create Model Group and Attached Detail Group" dialog will appear.

2. In the Model Group Name field, type: **Guest Room A**.

⇨ For the Attached Detail Group name, Input: **Tags** and then click OK (see Figure 7.2).

Since we have selected both model and detail elements, Revit will create two groups. One will be a model group containing the walls, doors, windows, furniture and fixtures. The other will be a detail group that contains the door and window tags.

252 | Chapter 7

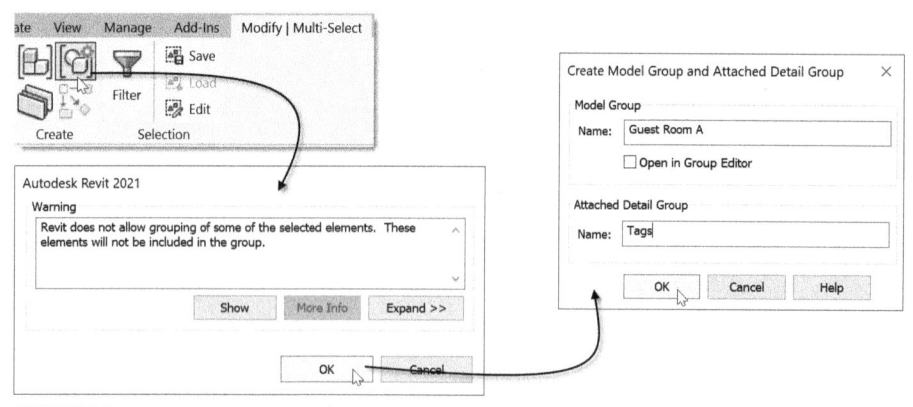

FIGURE 7.2 *Create a new group and give it a name*

It is not possible for detail elements and model elements to be in the same group. The detail group will be an "Attached Detail Group." This means that this detail group is associated to its parent model group. Later, we can have instances of the attached detail group automatically applied to instances of the model group. To see each group, simply move your mouse over them on screen.

   3.   Move your mouse near the edge of one of the walls.

        You will see a dashed box appear around the model group with a screen tip indicating its name.

   4.   Move your mouse over one of the door or window tags.

        You will see a dashed box appear around the detail group with a screen tip indicating its name (see the left side of Figure 7.3).

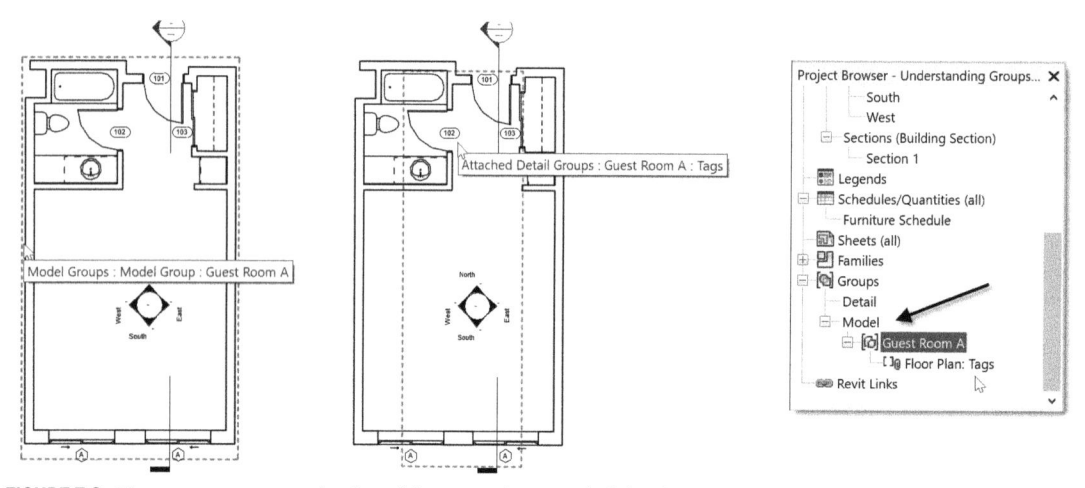

FIGURE 7.3 *Two groups were created—A model group and an attached detail group. Groups appear hierarchically on the Project Browser*

Groups that you create will also appear in the Project Browser.

   5.   On the Project Browser, expand the *Groups* branch. This reveals the *Detail* and *Model* branches.

   ⇨   Expand the *Model* branch.

        You will see the: *Guest Room A* group indented beneath the *Model* branch.

   ⇨   Expand the *Guest Room A* entry to reveal the attached detail group named: *Tags* (see the right side of Figure 7.3).

Each model group you create will appear beneath the: *Groups > Model* branch in the Project Browser. Attached detail groups will always appear beneath the group to which they are attached. If you create a group from detail elements by themselves, without associated model geometry, they will appear beneath the: *Groups > Detail* branch.

• The Aubin Academy •

CREATE A GROUP INSTANCE

Now that we have created a group, we can easily add additional instances of the group in our project. You can do this from the model group button on the Architecture tab or the *Groups* branch of the Project Browser.

1. On the Architecture tab, on the Model panel, click the Model Group drop down and then choose: **Place Model Group**. (Alternatively, on the Project Browser, expand *Groups*, then *Model*, and then right-click *Guest Room A* and choose: **Create Instance**).

   A dashed rectangle will appear on screen with the mouse pointer in the center.

   ⇨ Click on screen to place the new group instance to the left side of the original.

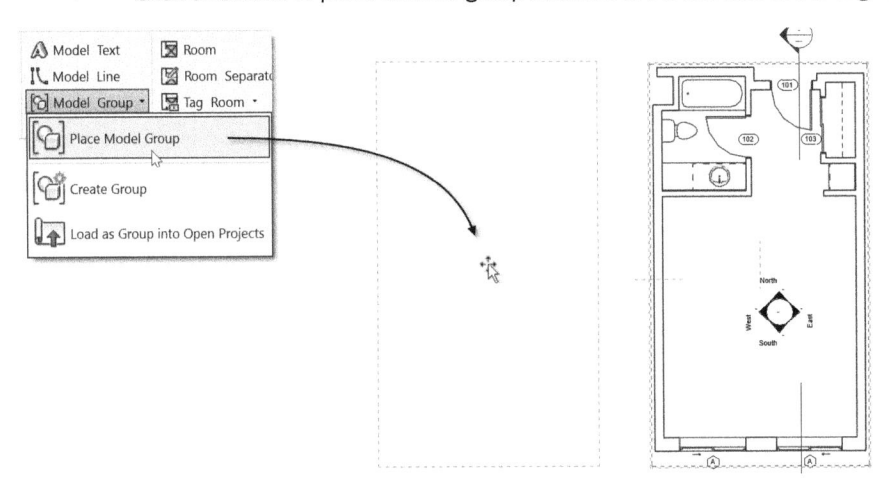

FIGURE 7.4 *Place an instance of the group*

2. On the Modify | Model Groups tab of the ribbon, click the Finish button.

Another guest room will appear. (It does not include any annotation because as we saw above, the annotation is included in a separate detail group. We'll add this below.) When you create a group, the geometric center of the group becomes the insertion point by default. Therefore, when we added this instance; our mouse pointer was positioned in the center of the group. You can move the origin to a more useful location simply by dragging it.

3. Select the group instance that you just created.

   In the center of the group, a blue group origin icon will appear (X and Y axes).

4. Click and drag the round handle at the intersection of the two axes.

   ⇨ Drop the icon on the wall endpoint at the top left corner of the hotel room (see Figure 7.5).

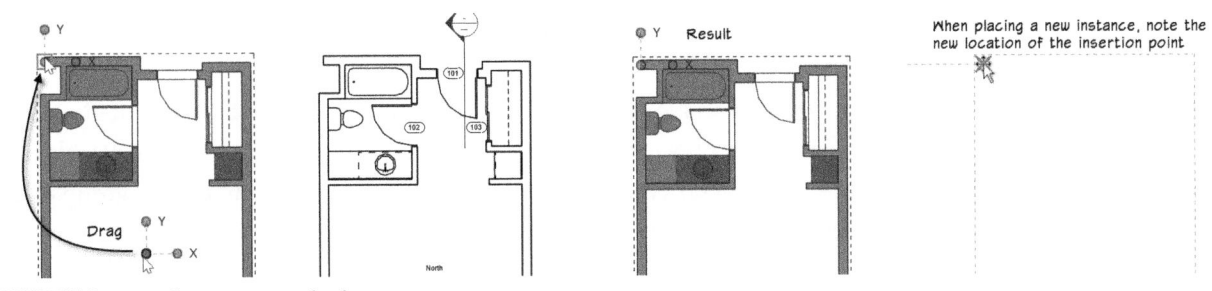

FIGURE 7.5 *Move the group origin by dragging*

5. On the Project Browser, right-click *Guest Room A* again and choose: **Create Instance**. (You can also drag and drop it).

   Notice the location of the mouse pointer relative to the group outline this time.

   ⇨ Click a point to the right of the original to place the new group instance.

• Revit Essentials for Architecture •

254 | Chapter 7

⇨ On the Modify | Model Groups tab of the ribbon, click the Finish button.

If you select the original group instance, you will notice that the insertion point for it is also at the upper left corner as well. Edits you make to one instance of a group apply automatically to all instances.

WORKING WITH ATTACHED DETAIL GROUPS

Look at the original guest room (the one that has tags). Notice that there are three doors, each with its own unique number. On the other hand, the two windows share the same designation of: "A." The default Revit door tags show the instance "Mark" parameter of doors, which is unique for each door while window tags show the "Type Mark" for windows which is the same for all instances of a given type. Keep these observations in mind as we perform the next several steps.

To add tags to the other group instances, we could manually tag each item in the group. A faster method is to use our attached detail group. An attached detail group can automatically be applied to any instance of its parent model group.

1. Select one of the groups (without annotation) on the left or right.

⇨ On the Modify | Model Groups tab of the ribbon, on the group panel, click the attached detail groups button.

2. In the dialog that appears, place a checkmark in the box next to:
Floor Plan: Tags and then click OK (see Figure 7.6).

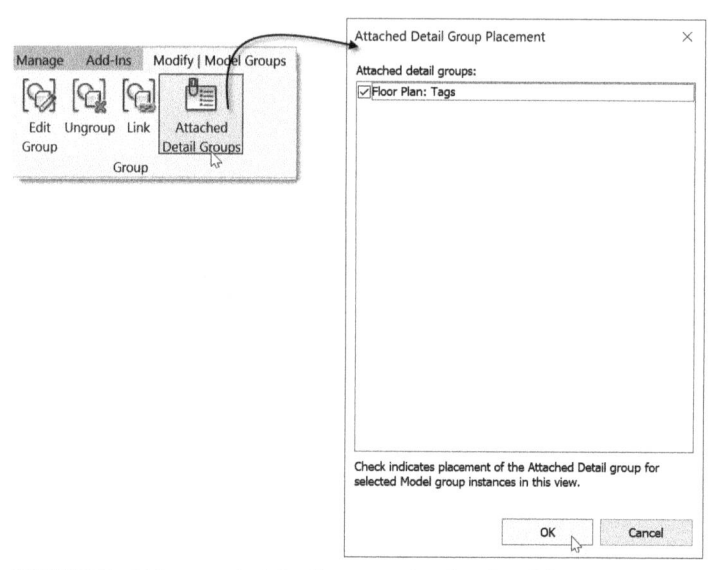

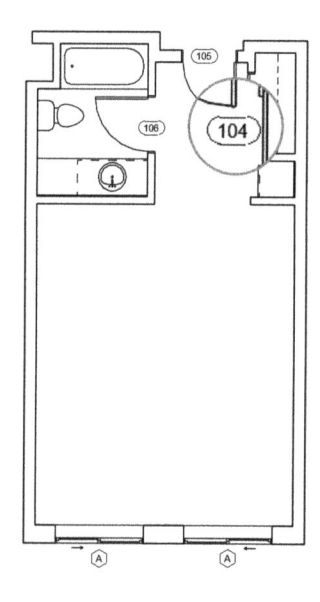

FIGURE 7.6 *Add an attached detail group to the selected model group*

3. Repeat the process to add an attached detail group to the other model group as well.

An instance of the attached detail group will appear. Notice that each of the door tags will have incremented sequentially to show unique numbers. The window tags however will show the same designation that the originals did. Notice that the doors all get assigned unique numbers even though the tags all belong to the same detail group. Tags in Revit (whether in a group or not) always report the values contained in their hosts—doors in this case.

EDITING GROUPS

You can edit a group at any time. When you do, changes you make to the group will be applied to all instances when the edit is complete. This is one of the most powerful benefits of using groups. Furthermore, edits to a model group can also have an automatic impact on any attached detail groups. To understand the value and potential of editing a group, we can start with a very simple modification.

1. Select any one instance of the *Guest Room A* group onscreen.
   ⇨ On the Modify | Model Groups tab of the ribbon, on the Group panel, click the Edit Group button (or press EG).

This enables the Group Edit mode. The background of the canvas area is tinted yellow and the Edit Group panel appears at the upper left corner of the view. The elements that are members of the group remain bold, and all of the other elements on screen become grayed out and cannot be selected or edited, but they can be added to the group as we will see below. For this example, we will make a very simple edit.

2. Select one of the windows in the group you are editing.
   ⇨ From the Type Selector, choose: **Window-Sliding-Double:36"x48"**.

In the group editor, the selected window will immediately reduce in size and the associated tag will change from A to E—even though this tag resides in a separate detail group!

3. On the Edit Group panel (which is floating in the corner of the canvas), click the Finish button (or press FG) (see Figure 7.7).

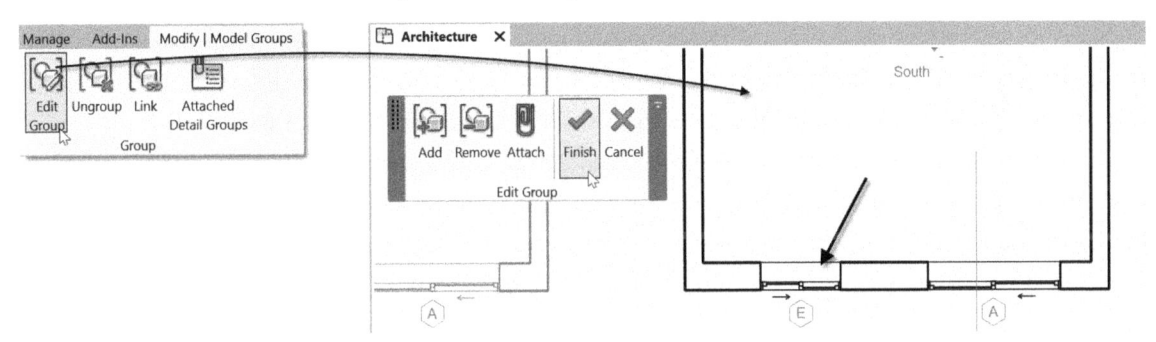

FIGURE 7.7 *Make a change in the Group Editor*

When you have finished, the edit will be applied to all instances of the group. Notice that the attached detail groups update as well. Let's try another edit.

4. Select one instance of the *Guest Room A* group.
   ⇨ On the Modify | Model Groups tab of the ribbon, on the Group panel, click the Edit Group button.
5. Perform the same edit made above to the other window.
6. On the Architecture tab, click the Window tool (or press WN) and then toggle on the Tag on Placement option.
   ⇨ Create a new **Fixed:36"x48"** window in the space between the two existing windows (see the left side of Figure 7.8).

Notice that the window tag is also created, but it comes in grayed out. This is because it is annotation and is therefore automatically excluded from the model group that we are currently editing.

   ⇨ On the Edit Group panel, click the Finish button (or press FG).

The new window configuration will appear in all instances of the group but the tag for the new window will not.

7. Select the window tag for the new window.

Since it is not part of any group, the Tag selects independently as a freestanding element in the project (see the top-right side of Figure 7.8).

256 | Chapter 7

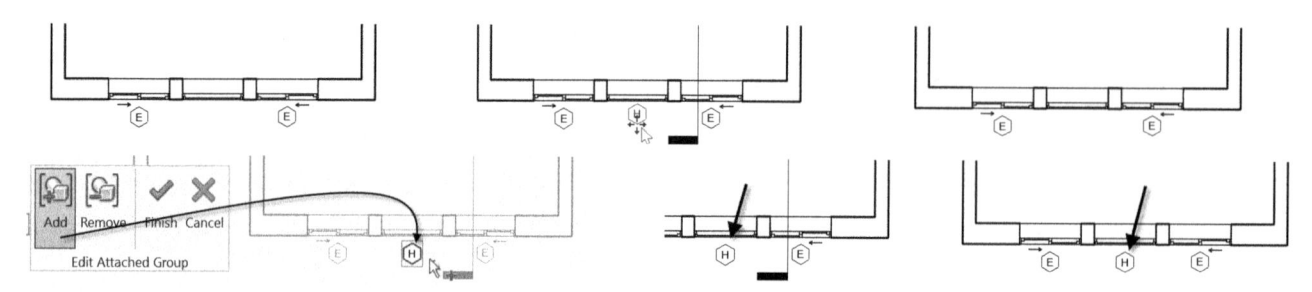

FIGURE 7.8 *Tags for newly added group elements must be added manually to the attached detail group*

8. Select the *Tags* attached detail group (the instance with the stray window tag).

⇨ On the Modify | Attached Detail Groups tab of the ribbon, on the Group panel, click the Edit Group button (or press EG).

9. On the Edit Attached Group floating panel, click the Add to Group button.

⇨ Select the window tag (Tag H) and then click the Finish button (see the bottom-right side of Figure 7.8).

The tag for window type H should now appear in all three instances of the attached detail group. Again, since this tag references a type parameter (the Type Mark), the letter displays the same value in all instances of the attached detail group. We had to manually edit the attached detail group to add the tag; however, if you were to edit the model group again and delete one of the host doors or windows then the tag in the attached detail group would also be deleted automatically even though it is in a different group—you would not have to separately edit the detail group for this. Hosted elements like tags cannot exist without their host.

DUPLICATE AND EDIT A GROUP

Making a variation of a group is simple to do. Once you have two or more variations, you can easily swap them out with one another.

1. Select the instance of the *Guest Room A* model group on the left.

⇨ On the Properties panel of the ribbon, click the Edit Type Properties button (or on the Properties palette, click the Edit Type button).

2. In the "Type Properties" dialog, click the Duplicate button (or press ALT + D).

⇨ In the "Name" dialog, type: **Guest Room B** and then click OK twice (see the left side of Figure 7.9).

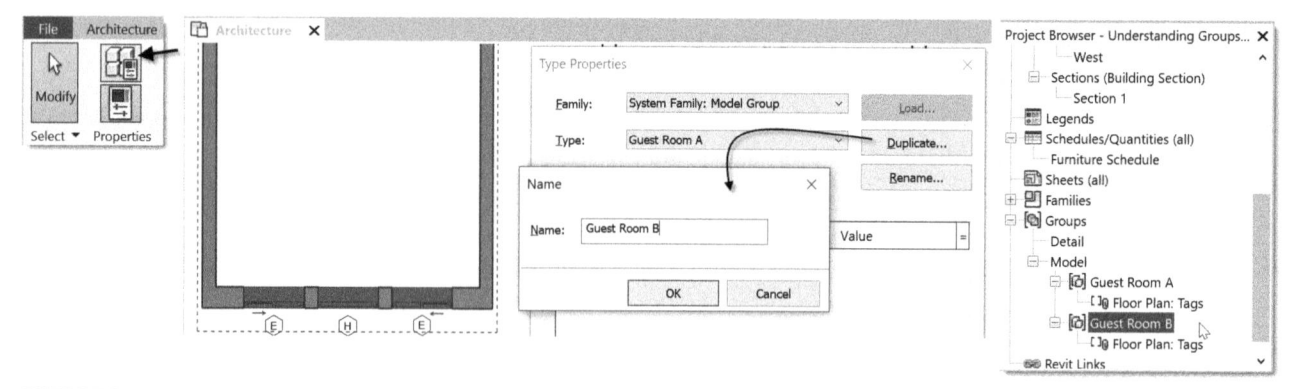

FIGURE 7.9 *Create a duplicate of the model group*

Notice the appearance of *Guest Room B* on the Project Browser. If you expand it, you will see that a copy of the *Tags* attached detail group has also been created and associated to the new model group (see the right side of Figure 7.9).

3. Select the same instance onscreen (now *Guest Room B*).

⇨ On the ribbon, click the Edit Group button.

4. Delete the middle window and make some other obvious change (such as enlarging the bathroom or flipping a door).

⇨ Finish the group (see Figure 7.10).

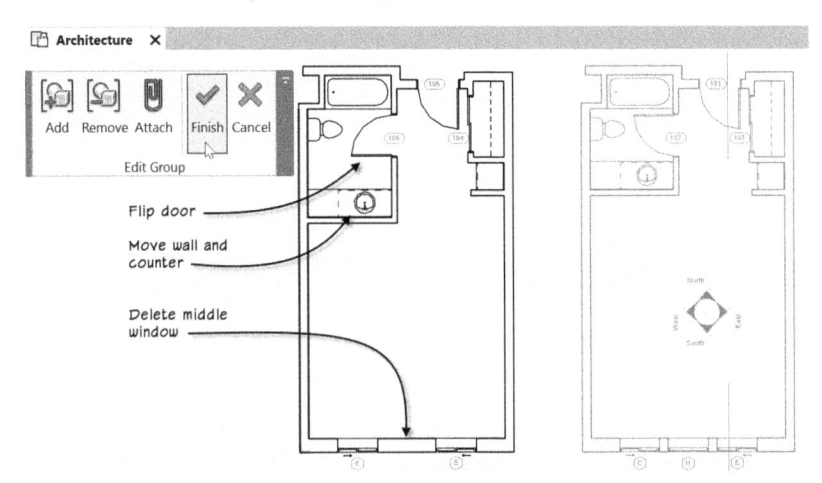

FIGURE 7.10 *Modify model group Guest Room B*

Not surprisingly, the change only affects the currently selected group. This is because it is currently the only instance of *Guest Room B* in the project. At this point, however, we can experiment with swapping group instances and see the ease at which we can switch from one group to another and see another one of the benefits of the attached detail group functionality. Take notice of the names of the attached detail groups on the Project Browser. For both model groups, the attached detail groups have the same name—*Tags*. This is important for the next experiment. If you use the same name for the attached detail groups, they will automatically swap when the parent model groups swap. Let's take a look.

5. Select one instance of the *Guest Room A* group onscreen.

⇨ From the Type Selector, choose: **Guest Room B**.

Since we tried to make the difference between the A and B Guest Rooms obvious, you should be able to spot the changes to the model right away. The most interesting change however is that the attached detail group has changed automatically as well. Since the attached detail groups for each model groups have the same name, Revit can swap them appropriately as well. This behavior works if the name of the attached detail group is the same for each model group.

EXCLUDING GROUP MEMBERS

Situations will often arise during a project where one instance of a group needs to be slightly different from the other instances in the project. In this case, we could certainly repeat the process covered in the previous sequence and duplicate and edit another group. However, doing so could begin to dilute the usefulness of groups and make management of the multiple potential variations cumbersome and time consuming. In scenarios such as this, Revit offers us the ability to create overrides to individual group instances. To illustrate the point, a simple example is appropriate.

Continue from the previous Exercise.

1. Delete the two group instances copied above leaving only the original one (in the middle) and its attached detail group onscreen.

Notice that the attached detail groups are deleted automatically when their hosts are deleted. Make sure the group in the middle is *Guest Room A*. If it is not, select it and change it on the Type Selector.

• Revit Essentials for Architecture •

2. Select the remaining model group instance on screen.

3. On the Modify panel, click the Mirror -Pick Axis button (or press MM).

⇨ For the mirror edge click on the centerline of the vertical wall on the right side of the group (see Figure 7.11).

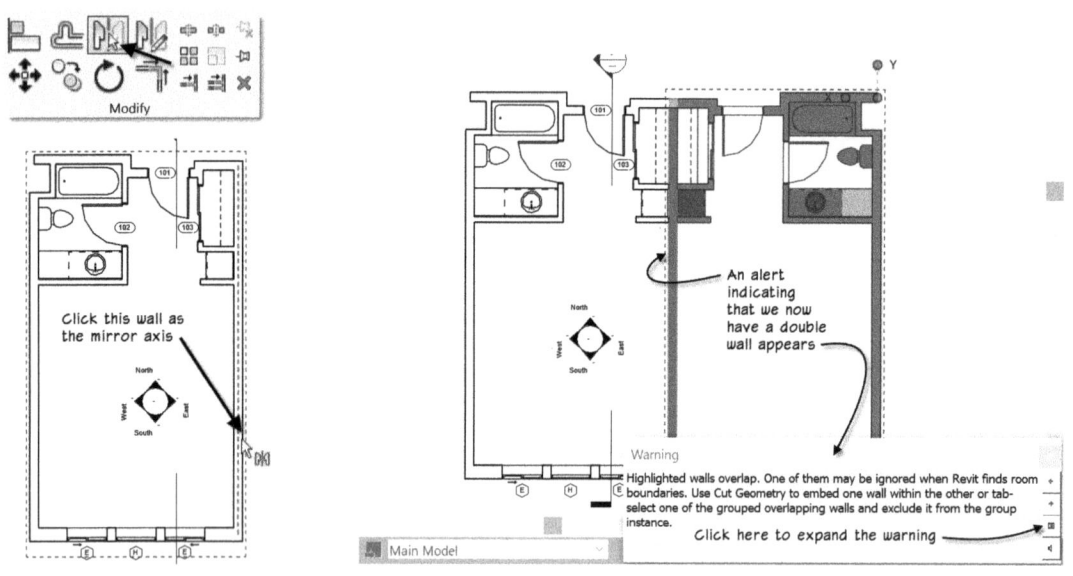

FIGURE 7.11 *Mirror a copy of the Guest Room A group*

When you complete the mirror command, a copy of the group will appear, and a warning dialog will also appear at the bottom right corner of the screen. This warning is not serious and can be ignored. All such "ignorable" warnings will appear in this location on screen and will have a yellow tint to the dialog in which they appear. It is still a good idea to read the warning message as there is some useful information conveyed in them. In this case, Revit is alerting us that we now have two walls overlapping in the same spot. While we can ignore this situation, the message further explains that room boundaries may be affected. If you click anywhere, the message disappears. So, if you missed it, here is the complete text of the warning:

> "Highlighted walls overlap. One of them may be ignored when Revit finds room boundaries. Use Cut Geometry to embed one wall within the other or TAB-select one of the grouped overlapping walls and exclude it from the group instance."

The right side of Figure 7.11 shows the warning message. If you wish, you can expand the warning dialog to get more detailed information. Do this with the small icon on the right side of the warning dialog. If the warning has closed already, on the Manage tab, on the Inquiry panel you can click the Warnings button to access it and any other warnings your project file may have. When you fully expand the error, you can click on each of the overlapping walls to highlight them on screen. The one "on top" will highlight more obviously (see Figure 7.12).

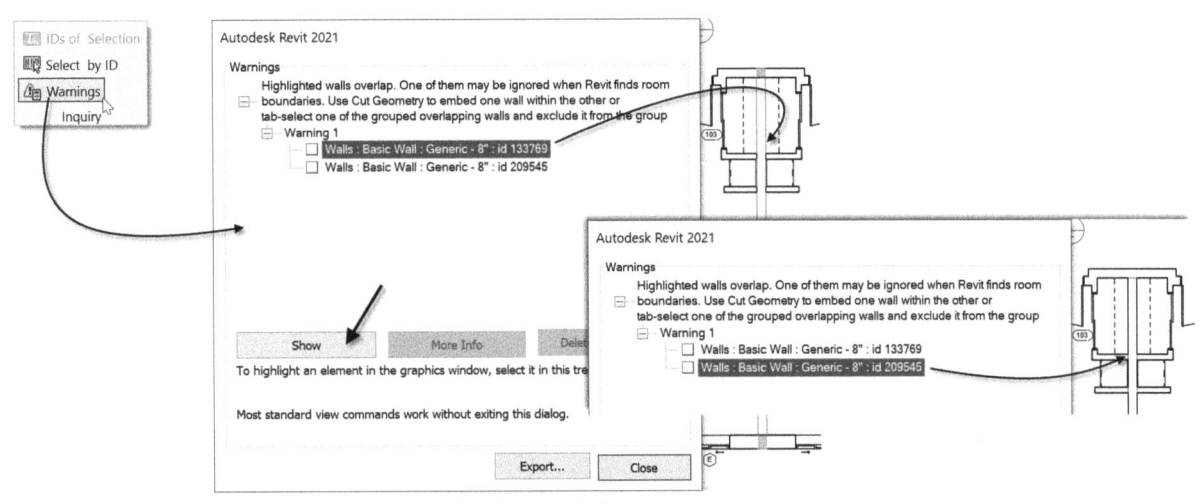

FIGURE 7.12 *Click the Expand icon to see a more detailed error dialog*

If you wish to see the element highlighted in other views, click the Show button. Each time you click Show, it will open another view window and highlight the element in question. When you are done reviewing the warning, click the Close button to dismiss it. If you did click show, make sure you return to the *Architecture* floor plan view and then close the other views.

In addition to potentially having an adverse effect on rooms, you can also see that the overlapping walls do not cleanup very nicely. The solution to both problems is simple: any element in any group can be *excluded* from an individual instance of the group. In this situation, we can exclude the duplicate wall from one of the groups.

   4. Place your mouse over the double wall.

   Notice that the group pre-highlights.

   ⇨ Press the TAB key.

   Notice that the other group pre-highlights.

   ⇨ Press the TAB key again.

   This time, the wall within one of the groups pre-highlights.

   5. Click to select this wall.

> **TIP:** Notice that on the Modify | Walls tab, there is a "Show Related Warnings" icon. This gives you a shortcut to the Review Warnings dialog discussed above, letting you know that there are warnings associated with the selected element.

   ⇨ Click the Group Member icon in the canvas area to exclude this wall from the group (see Figure 7.13).

   ⇨ Deselect the group.

• Revit Essentials for Architecture •

260 | Chapter 7

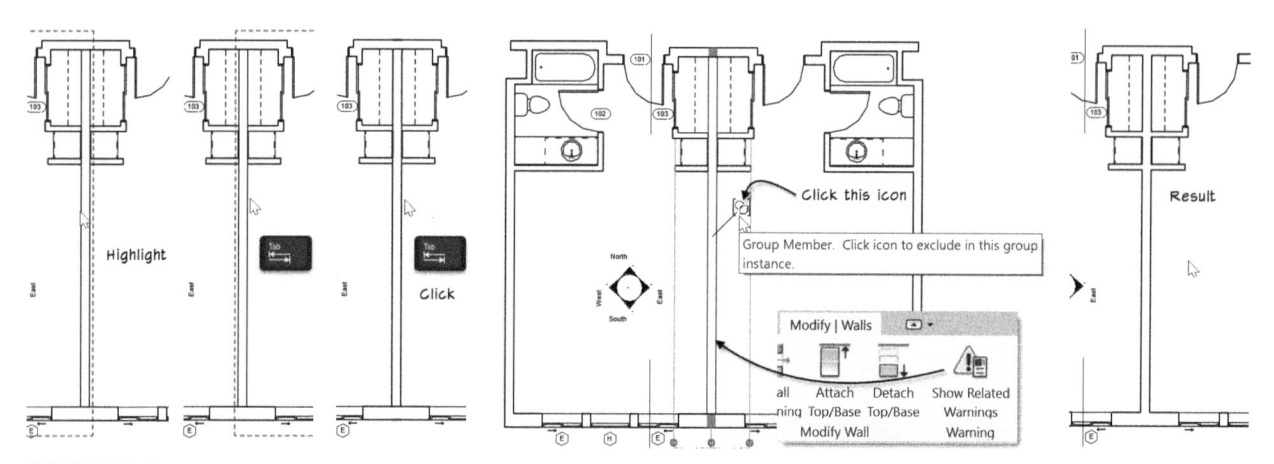

FIGURE 7.13 TAB *into the group, select the wall and then click the icon to exclude it*

Notice that the extra wall has been removed and the cleanup is now correct. It is important to realize that this change is not simply graphical override—Revit has removed one instance of one of the walls. For example, were we to have counted the walls before we started and then re-count them now, there would be one wall fewer in our model. Rather than count the walls, which might prove tricky, let's do a similar experiment using furniture, which is easier to count.

6. On the Project Browser, double-click to open the *Furniture* floor plan view.

    Furniture elements will appear in the original guest room.

7. Select all the furniture elements.

> **TIP:** Use a window selection to select all the furniture and then click the Filter button on the ribbon to remove any unwanted element categories.

⇨ On the ribbon, click the Create Group button (or press GP).

8. In the Create Model Group Name field, type: **King-01**.

9. Using the technique covered in the "Create a Group Instance" topic on page 253 above, drag the origin point to the same location as the Guest Room group.

10. Mirror the furniture group to the other guest room (see Figure 7.14).

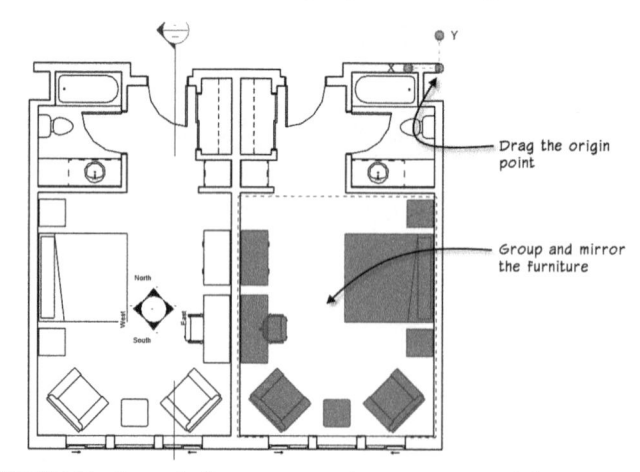

FIGURE 7.14 *Group the furniture, move the origin point, and then mirror a copy*

11. On the Project Browser, beneath *Schedules/Quantities*, double-click to open the *Furniture Schedule* view.

• The Aubin Academy •

Study the table and take note of the totals in the "Count" column. Notice that we currently have 4 Side Chairs (Chair-Viper: Chair). This is impressive; Revit gives us an accurate count even when the items it is counting are inside groups! Let's exclude one chair from a group and see the impact on the schedule.

12. Return to the *Furniture* floor plan.

> **TIP:** **Close the Architecture view, and then** on the View tab, choose: Tile Windows (or press WT) to see both plan and schedule side by side.

13. Using the TAB key, select one of the Side Chairs (bottom of the plan, near the windows).
    ⇨ Click the exclude group member icon to exclude this chair from the group (see Figure 7.15).
    ⇨ Deselect the chair after excluding it to see it disappear.

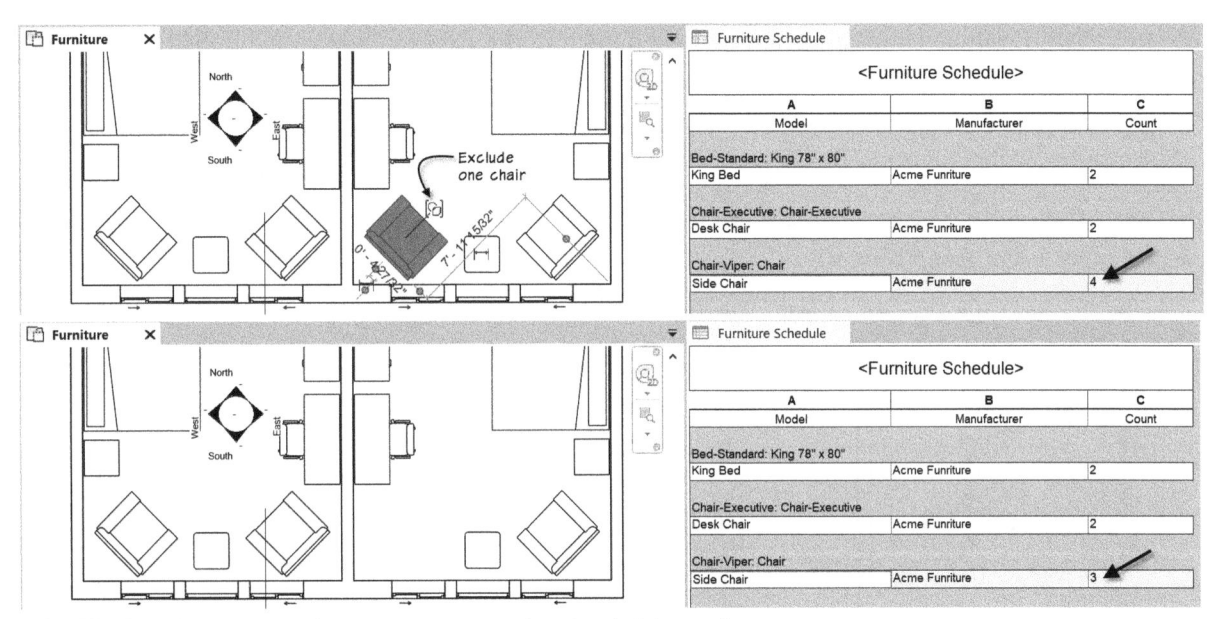

FIGURE 7.15 *Excluding an item from a group removes it from the schedule as well*

Now that is even more impressive; the schedule accurately reflects the quantity shown in the model. This example illustrates that you can use the exclude from groups feature with confidence, as Revit will accurately reflect the exclusions throughout the model.

> **TIP:** If you lose track of which groups have excluded members, when you highlight them onscreen, a message reading: "(members excluded)" will appear on the Status Bar next to the group name. If you select them, a Restore all Excluded Members button will appear on the ribbon.

You should try a few more experiments to become comfortable with the full behavior of this feature. For example, move your mouse over the missing chair and it will pre-highlight as if it were there. In this way, you can TAB back into the group and bring the element back (include it). Be careful when editing a group that has overrides applied. You can edit either instance of the furniture group onscreen. However, if you edit the one with the excluded chair, you will not be able to edit the chair at all. If you instead edit the one without exclusions, you will have the ability to edit all its elements including both chairs. You can even move or otherwise edit the chair that is excluded in one of the other groups. The change will be visible in the group(s) that shows the chair and not visible in any that exclude it. If you like, try some of these experiments now before continuing.

262 | Chapter 7

14. Save the project.

CREATING ATTACHED DETAIL GROUPS FOR EXISTING MODEL GROUPS

The attached detail groups that we made earlier were created at the same time as the host model groups. You can also create them later even after the model group has been created.

1. Return to the *Furniture* floor plan.
2. On the Annotate tab, on the Tag panel, click the Tag by Category button.
   ⇨ On the Options Bar, uncheck the Leader check box.
3. Click on each piece of furniture in the guest room that shows both side chairs.
   ⇨ Click the Modify tool on the ribbon or press the ESC key twice.

As you can see, all the furniture numbers have already been input in this dataset. To learn more about tagging and editing tag parameters, see Chapter 13. You can move the tags around after placement as required.

4. Select all the furniture tags, (right-click and choose: **Select All Instances** > **Visible in View**) and then on the Modify | Furniture Tags tab, click the Create Group button (or press GP).

Notice that Revit displays the "Create Model Group and Attached Detail Group" dialog and automatically recognizes that these tags apply to our group King-01.

⇨ In the attached detail group Name field, type: **Tags** (see Figure 7.16).

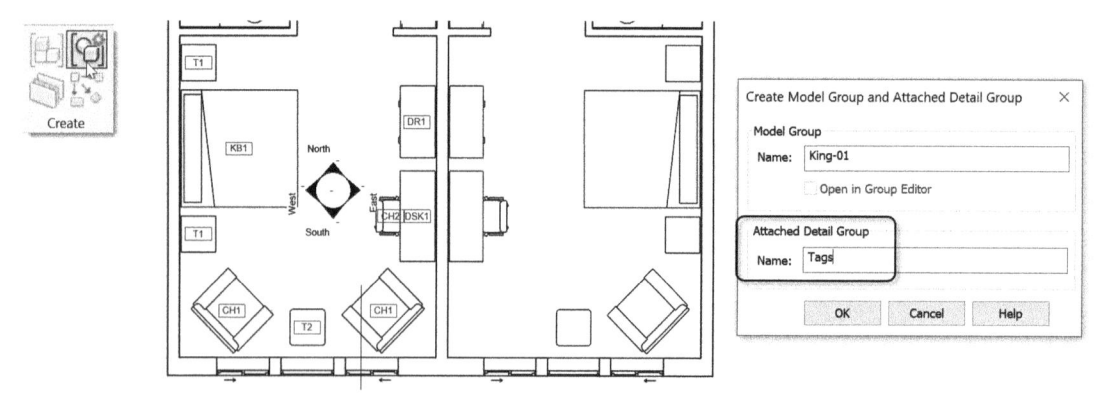

FIGURE 7.16 *Revit will automatically create an attached detail group from tags attached to a model group*

Now that we have an attached detail group for our furniture, we could add it to the other instance of our furniture model group. However, we will do something a little different with it below.

ADDING DETAIL GROUPS TO MIRRORED GROUPS

Attached detail groups can be very useful as we have seen. They do have limitations as well. If we return to the *Architecture* floor plan, we will notice that the mirrored group has no tags.

1. From the Project Browser, re-open the *Architecture* floor plan.
2. Select the mirrored group (on the right side).
   ⇨ On the ribbon, click the Attached Detail Groups button.
   ⇨ In the "Attached Detail Group Placement" dialog, check Floor Plan: Tags and then click OK.

Notice that despite the model group's being mirrored, the detail group remains "right-reading." This is true if you mirror in any direction. Furthermore, you can mirror a selection of both model and detail groups together in the same operation and the detail groups will remain right-reading as the model group mirrors.

   3. Select both model groups and both detail groups (4 elements total). Be careful not to select the section or elevation tags.

   ⇨ On the Modify | Multi-Select ribbon tab, click the Mirror -Draw Axis button (or press DM).

This allows you to sketch the mirror line rather than pick an object. In this case, we will mirror the selection up at a distance above the selection to allow room for a corridor between the rooms.

   4. Using the temporary dimension as a guide, click the first point about 5'-0" above the top walls to indicate the middle of the corridor.

   ⇨ Drag the mouse horizontally and then click again to complete the mirror (see Figure 7.17).

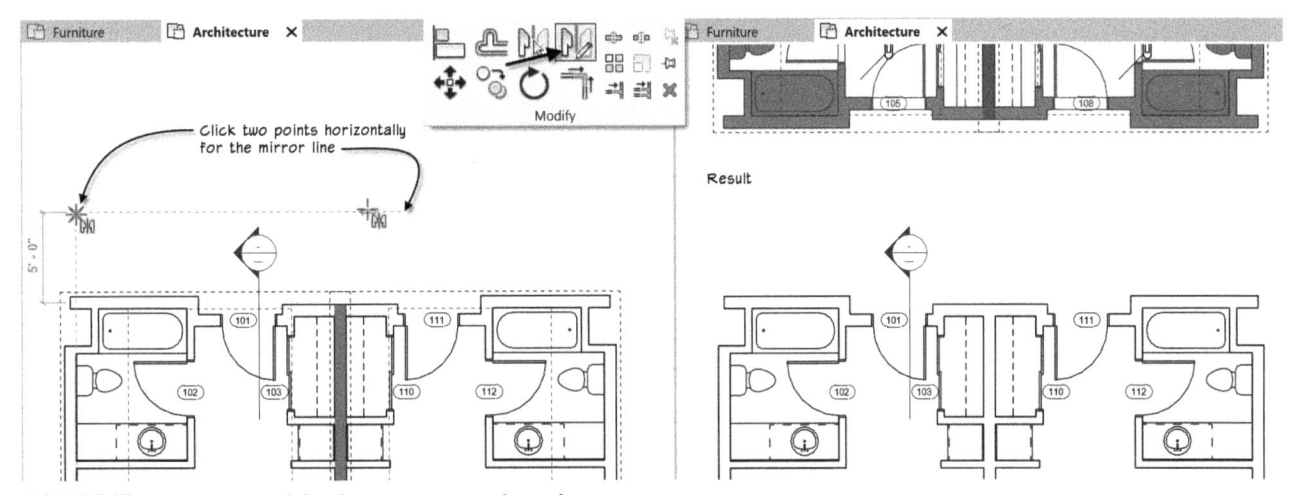

FIGURE 7.17 *Tags in mirrored detail groups remain right reading*

If you zoom in on the new rooms and study the tags, you will see that they are right-reading, yet they each display a unique door number sequentially incremented from where the previous door numbering left off.

   5. Select all groups on screen (4 Model and 4 attached detail groups).

   6. Mirror the selection around the centerline of the right most vertical wall.

   As before, a warning will appear indicating that you have duplicate walls again. Ignore this warning for now.

There are now eight total guest rooms each with its own Tags.

   7. Select the four guest rooms in the middle. (Clicking with the CTRL key is the easiest method of selection in this case.)

   ⇨ From the Type Selector, choose: **Guest Room B**.

As we saw earlier in the chapter, not only does the guest room geometry change, but the attached detail groups update as well. Remember, the attached detail groups swap out as well because they have the same names. If you do not keep the names the same ("Tags" in this case), they will not swap out.

   8. Use the process covered in the "Excluding Group Members" topic on page 257 above to exclude the extra walls.

   9. Save the project.

264 | Chapter 7

DUPLICATE GROUPS ON PROJECT BROWSER

Returning to the *Furniture* view will reveal that while the walls, doors, and windows contained in the duplicated model groups were copied to from additional guest rooms, the furniture was not. This is simply because the furniture is contained in a separate model group. Let's duplicate our furniture group and make an alternate for the other guest room type.

1. On the Project Browser, beneath *Model Groups*, right-click the *King-01* group and choose: **Duplicate**.

    ⇨ Right-click the new copy and choose: **Rename**. Call it: **Queen-01** (see Figure 7.18).

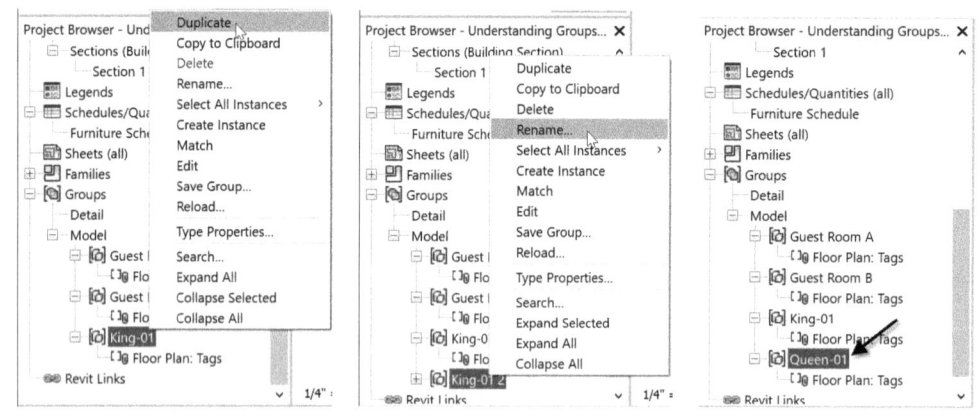

FIGURE 7.18 *Duplicate and rename a group on the Project Browser*

Notice that the *Queen-01* group also has its own attached detail group named: *Tags*.

There are several commands on the right-click menu. Here is a brief description of each:

Duplicate—Creates a copy of the group and adds a number at the end of the name.

Make Element Editable—This command is only active in a project using Worksharing. Worksharing is a process enabling a team of people to work in the same Revit project. See Chapter 16 for more information.

Copy to Clipboard—This copies the group to the clipboard. This is a fast way to use the same group in another project. If you paste it in the same project, it behaves like Duplicate.

Delete—This deletes the group definition from the project. You can only use this command if no instances of the group are inserted in the project. Use with caution.

Rename—Use to assign a new name to a group definition.

Select All Instances > Visible In View—Use this command to select all instances of the group in the current view only.

Select All Instances > In Entire Project—Use this command to select all instances of the group throughout the entire project. Be careful as this command selects all instances on all levels, even the ones that may not show in the current view.

Create Instance—This adds an instance of the group. It will place you in the command ready to click a point to place the group.

Match—Use this command to swap one group with another on screen. The group you right-click will be the "source" and you will be prompted to select the group(s) to which to apply the source definition.

Edit—This command will export the group to a new Revit project and open it for editing. In this way, you can edit a group independently of the current project and save it as its own file outside of the project. To use the group saved this way in a project, click the Insert tab and then on the Load from Library panel, click the Load as Group button and follow the prompts.

Save Group—This command will also export the group to a new Revit project, but it will not automatically open it. You will simply be prompted for the file name and location in which to save it.

Reload—This is a shortcut to the Load as Group button on the Insert tab. Use it to load an external file and replace the internal group definition with the imported file.

Type Properties—Opens the "Type Properties" dialog for the selected group.

A similar list of commands appears when you right-click a detail group.

2. Return to the *Furniture* floor plan.

3. Select the instance of the furniture group with the excluded chair.

   Notice that the excluded chair appears when the group is selected.

   ⇨ On the ribbon, click the Restore All Excluded button (or press RA).

   The previously excluded chair will be restored.

4. With the group still selected, choose: **Queen-01** from the Type Selector.

> **NOTE:** If you skip the "Restore All Excluded" step, the excluded chair will still reappear when swapping groups. Instance-level overrides are not retained when changing types.

5. On the Group panel, click the Edit Group button (or press EG).

   ⇨ Select the bed and from the Type Selector, choose: **Bed-Standard : Queen 60" x 79"**.

6. Delete one of the lounge chairs and move the bed and nightstands down to fit the room better (see the left side of Figure 7.19).

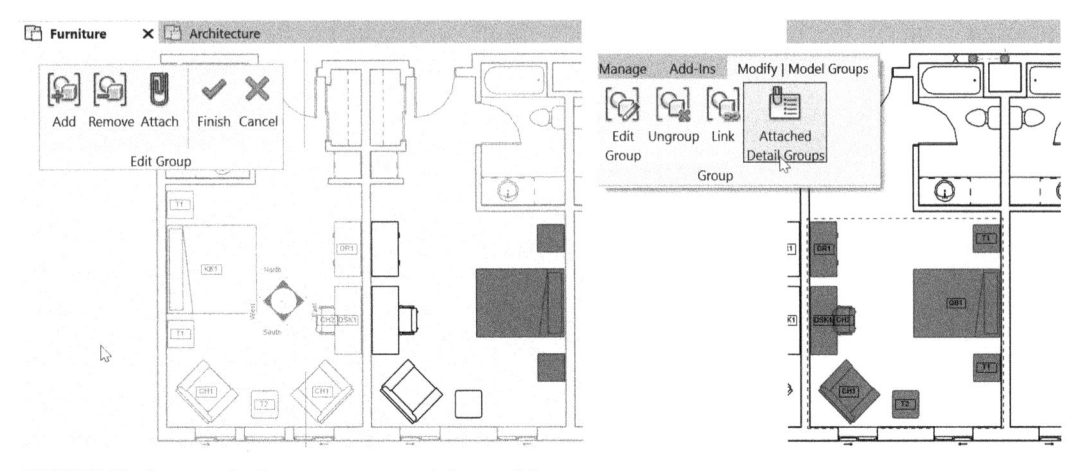

FIGURE 7.19 *Swap in the Queen-01 group and then modify it*

   ⇨ On the Edit Group panel, click the Finish button to complete the edit (or press FG).

7. Select the Queen-01 group onscreen.

   ⇨ On the Group panel, click the Attached Detail Groups button.

   ⇨ In the "Attached Detail Group Placement" dialog, check Floor Plan: Tags and then click OK (see the right side of Figure 7.19).

266 | Chapter 7

Notice that the tags have automatically adjusted to the new furniture layout of the group.

8. Using any of the techniques covered so far; add furniture and model and detail groups to the remaining guest rooms (see Figure 7.20).

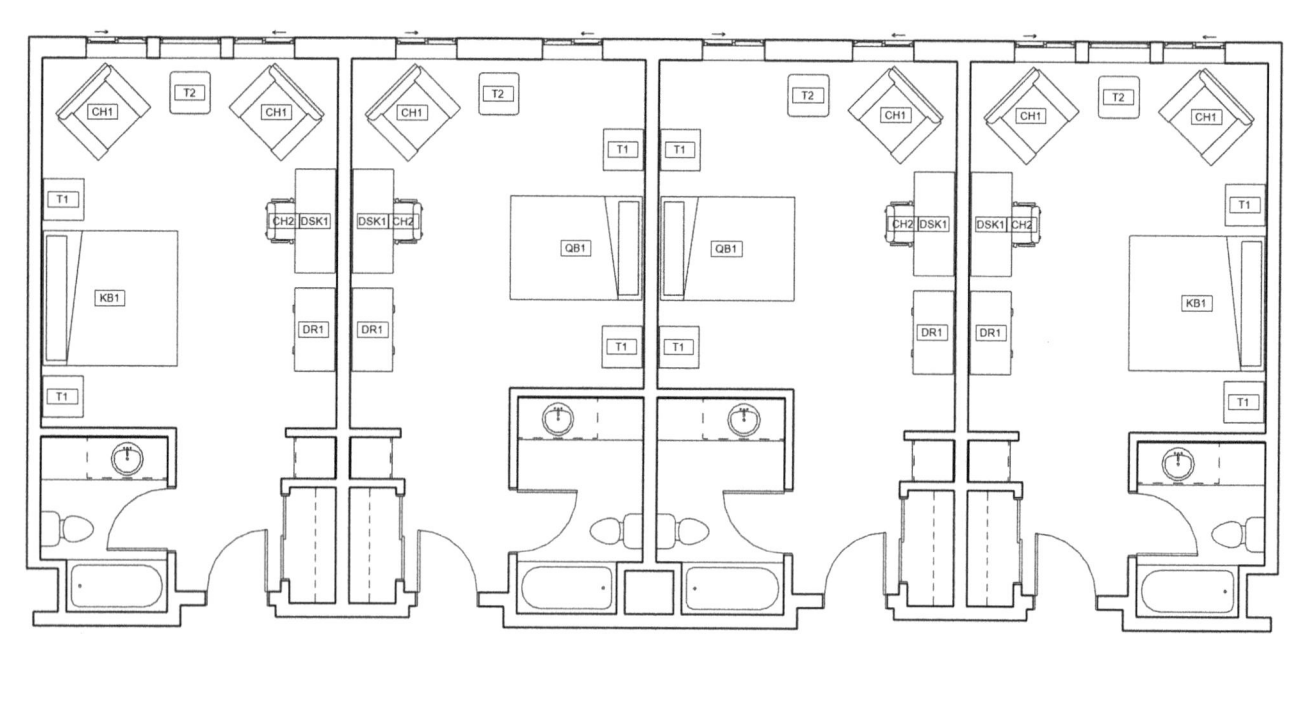

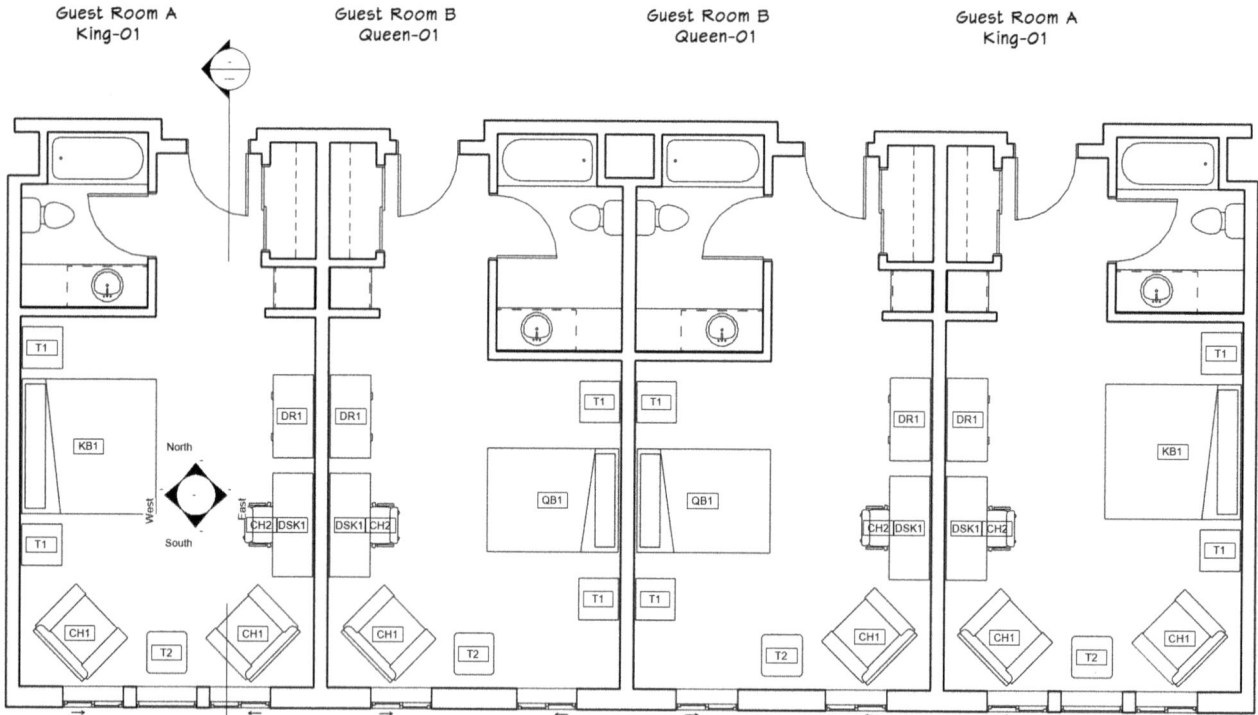

FIGURE 7.20 *Add furniture groups to the remaining rooms*

MAINTAINING GROUPS

As you can see, working with groups so far has made it easier to compose our overall plan layout and quickly replicate a series of similarly configured spaces. After this initial design work, you may be tempted to ungroup your groups to gain more direct access to the elements they contain. While it is certainly possible for you to do this, you may want to

• The Aubin Academy •

consider keeping your groups active well into design development or even CDs. The reason for this is simply because despite our best efforts to minimize them, design changes continue to occur well into the construction document phase and even beyond. Groups can help you make such changes more efficiently.

ADD MISSING ELEMENTS TO GROUPS

While design changes occur for any number of reasons, in this next example, we will consider a change resulting from an oversight during the design phase.

1. On the QAT, click the Default 3D View icon.

Compare the original room that we started with to all the copied versions and notice that the copies do not include the ceiling elements. Since we have been working exclusively in plan views, we did not notice that the ceilings were not included in the original selection set from which the groups were created (see Figure 7.21).

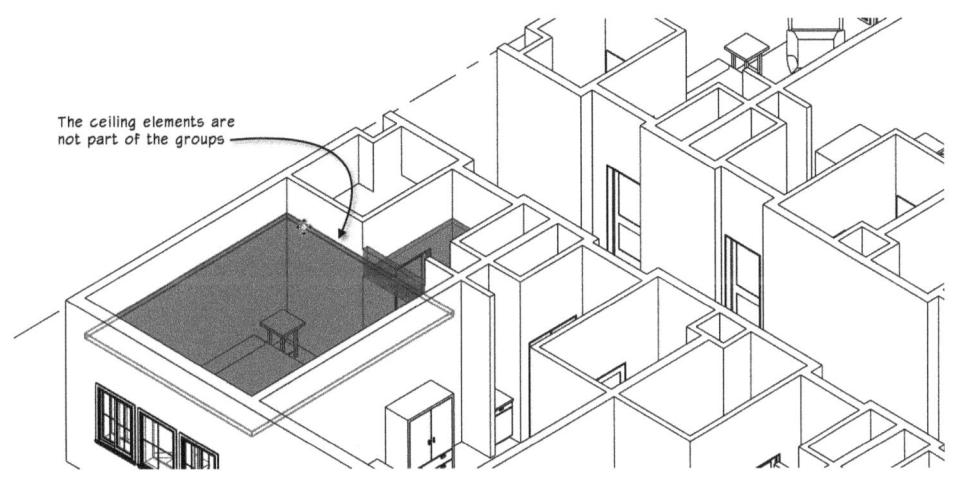

FIGURE 7.21 *Switching to 3D view reveals elements missing from the groups*

The fix for Guest Room A is simple. For Guest Room B there is an extra step. In the original Guest Room A group (shown in the figure) the ceiling elements are positioned in the proper location. All we must do is add those stray ceiling elements to the group and they will appear in all instances of Guest Room A. For Guest Room B, we first need to copy the ceiling elements into position relative to one of our Guest Room B groups and then add them to the group. While the 3D view was useful to identify the problem, a ceiling plan view is the best choice for making the required edits.

2. On the Project Browser, double-click to open the *Level 1* Ceiling Plan.

   ⇨ Zoom in on the original Guest Room A; (it has an interior elevation tag within it), making it easy to locate.

If you compare the elements in the original Guest Room A to the others, you will notice that there is a small wall separating the main guest room from the entry foyer. We'll need to mirror this wall from Guest Room A to Guest Room B to form the boundaries for the ceiling elements.

3. Place your mouse over the wall between the foyer space and the main room and then look at the Status Bar (at the bottom-left corner of the application frame).

   Press TAB if necessary to highlight the wall.

A message will appear reading: **Walls : Basic Wall : Generic 5"**. The format of this message is: Category: Family :Type. All Revit objects appear in this format when pre-highlighted on screen. (See the "Status Bar" topic on page 76 in Chapter 3 for more information) (see the left side of Figure 7.22).

• Revit Essentials for Architecture •

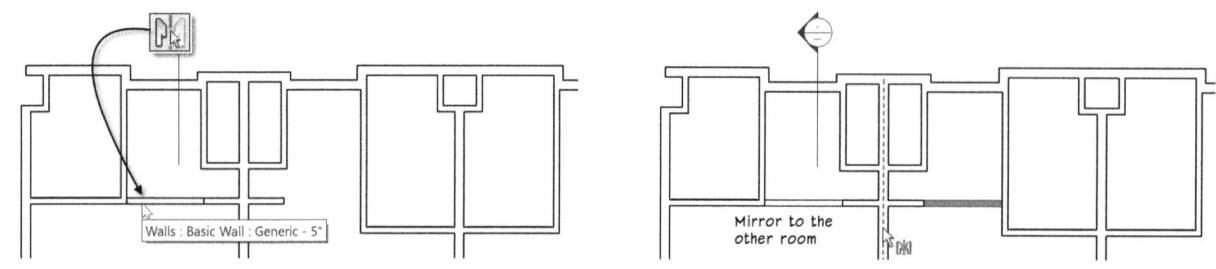

FIGURE 7.22 *The Status Bar reports the category, family, and type of pre-highlighted elements*

4. When the indicated wall between the foyer space and the main room highlights, click it to select it.

If your wall is not in the same location, you may have moved it during the previous exercises. Use the Align tool on the Modify tab to position it back where it was shown in the figure before proceeding.

5. On the ribbon, click the Mirror -Pick Axis button.

⇨ Using the center of the wall between the two guest rooms, mirror the elements to the neighboring room (see the right side of Figure 7.22).

While it would be possible to select and mirror the existing ceiling objects to the other space as well, in this case it will be easier to recreate them since the shapes of the rooms do not match. We are now ready to edit the group.

6. Select the original instance of the Guest Room A group.

⇨ On the Group panel, click the Edit Group button (or press EG).

7. On the floating Edit Group panel, click the Add button (or press AP).

This tool allows us to add items from the main model into the group. When we are finished editing, these elements will appear in all instances of the group.

Move your mouse near the edge of the toilet room in Guest Room A. The ceiling object will pre-highlight.

⇨ Click the ceiling to add it to the group (see Figure 7.23).

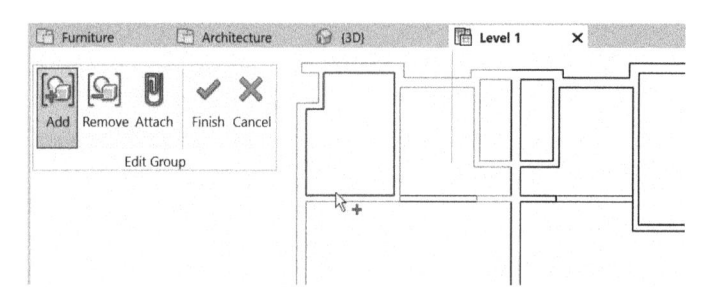

FIGURE 7.23 *Add ceilings and the wall to the group*

8. Repeat for the foyer ceiling, the closet ceiling, and the small wall (the one we mirrored).

9. Finally, add the Ceiling in the main guest room space to the group.

Press the TAB key if necessary to assist in adding any of the elements.

10. Once you have added four ceilings and the wall to the group, click the Finish button on the Edit Group panel (or press FG).

If you return to the {3D} view, you should notice that the four Guest Room A groups now have ceilings. To add ceilings to the Guest Room B groups, we will simply create new ones.

11. In the Ceiling Plan *Level 1*, select the instance of Guest Room B to which we mirrored the small wall above.

12. Click the Edit Group button (or press EG).

⇨ Add the small wall to the group.

⇨ Press the Modify tool to disable the add mode.

13. On the Architecture tab, on the Build panel, click the Ceiling tool.

⇨ From the Type Selector, choose: **Compound Ceiling : GWB on Mtl. Stud**.

⇨ Click inside each enclosed space (toilet room, closet, foyer and main guest room space) to add ceilings.

We can make the ceiling in the guest room taller.

14. Select it and on the Properties palette, change the Height Offset From Level to: **9'-0"**.

15. Click the Finish button on the Edit Group panel when done (or press FG).

If you return to the *{3D}* view, you should now have ceilings in all rooms.

CREATING A NESTED GROUP

As we have seen, most model elements can be added to model groups. We can also make a group that contains other groups. So-called "Nested Groups" can be useful but can also present certain challenges. For example, in the dataset we have open, it might be useful to group all the various guest rooms and their furniture into a single group named something like "**Typical Floor Layout**." This approach may certainly prove valuable at the early stages of design where you stand to gain an advantage from the ease of being able to edit a group instance and have the changes apply across the entire project. However, there are limitations. The most notable is that attached detail groups only work one level deep. Recall that you cannot make a group containing both model and detail groups as members. You will still be able to apply attached detail groups to the nested instances of the model groups, but you will have to use the TAB key to select each instance before placement. With careful planning, you can certainly make a workable solution; the only caution is to plan your strategy carefully before execution.

To create a nested group, you simply select objects (including other groups) and then click the Create Group button as we have done already.

1. On the Project Browser, double-click to open the *Section 1* Building Section view.

2. On the Architecture tab, on the Datum panel, click the Level button (or press LL).

⇨ Using the Pick Lines draw icon, create a Level 12'-6" above the existing Level 1 (see Figure 7.24).

270 | Chapter 7

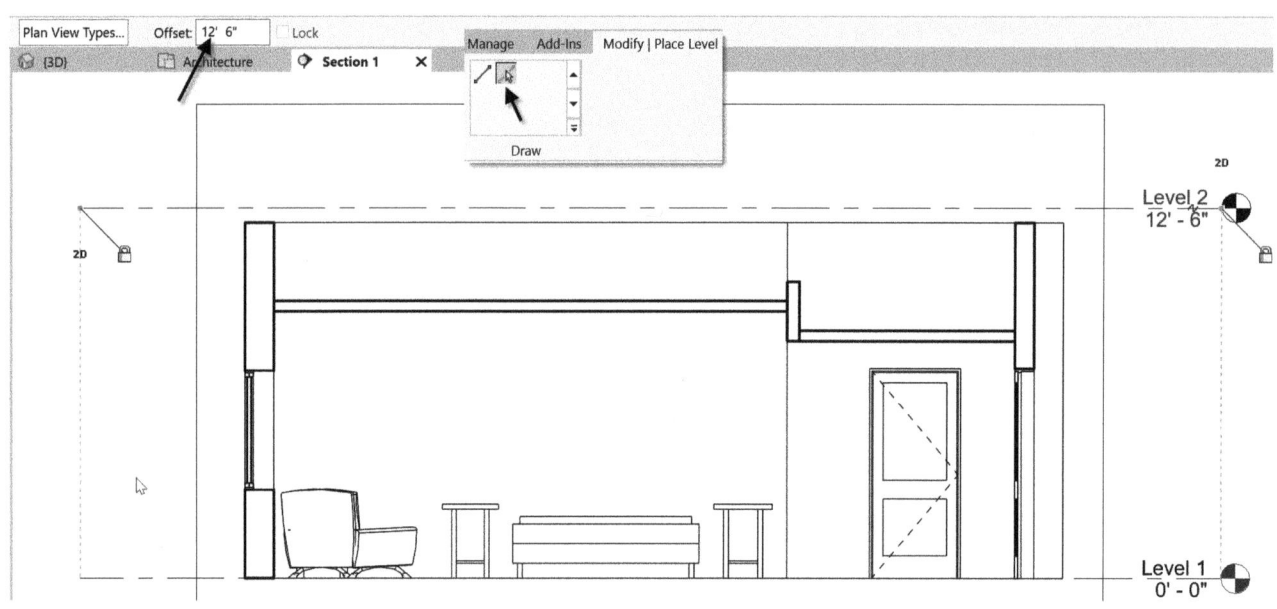

FIGURE 7.24 *Add a new level*

3. Return to the *Architecture* floor plan view.

4. Select all eight model groups on screen. (If you include the section, elevations or detail groups in the selection, Revit will automatically filter these out. Or you can do this yourself with the Filter button).

⇨ On the Modify Model Groups tab, on the Create panel, click the Create Group button.

⇨ Name the group: **Typical Floor Layout** and then click OK.

Take notice of the Project Browser after you complete the group. *Typical Floor Layout* will show *Guest Room A* and *B* indented beneath it. This indicates that these two groups are nested within it (see Figure 7.25).

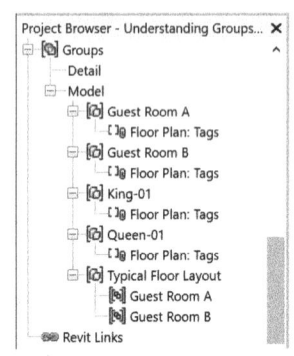

FIGURE 7.25 *Create a group with other groups nested within it*

5. On the Project Browser, double-click to open the *Level 2* floor plan.

This view was created with the new level.

⇨ On the Project Browser, right-click *Typical Floor Layout* and choose: **Create Instance**.

6. Snap to the group origin of the group on the level below and then click the Modify tool (see Figure 7.26). (If it does not snap to the origin, you can try turning on the underlay for the previous level).

⇨ If necessary, click the finish button on the ribbon to complete the paste.

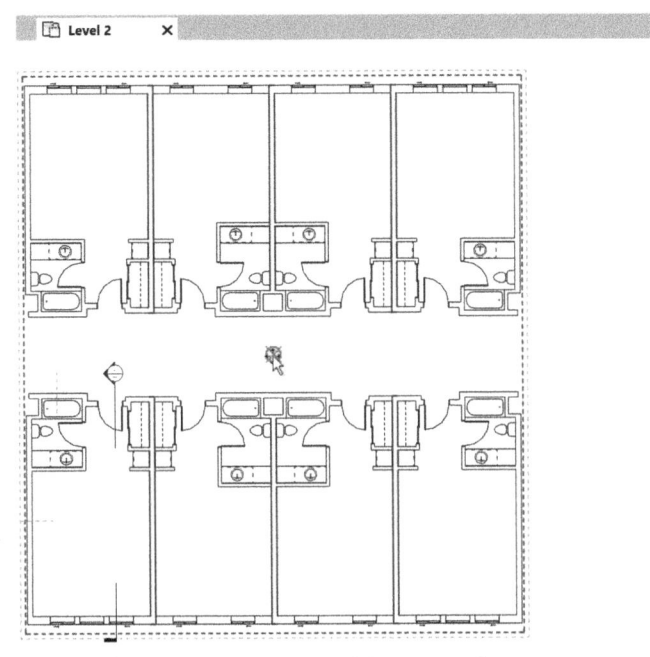

FIGURE 7.26 *Create a new instance of the group at the group origin*

ADDING ATTACHED DETAIL GROUPS TO NESTED GROUPS

If you want to add the *Tags* attached detail groups, you must use the TAB key.

1. Place your mouse over one of the guest rooms.

    Notice that the entire floor layout group pre-highlights.

    ⇨ Press the TAB key.

2. Click to select the nested group instance.

3. Click the Attached Detail Groups button, choose the Floor Plan: Tags group and then click OK (see Figure 7.27).

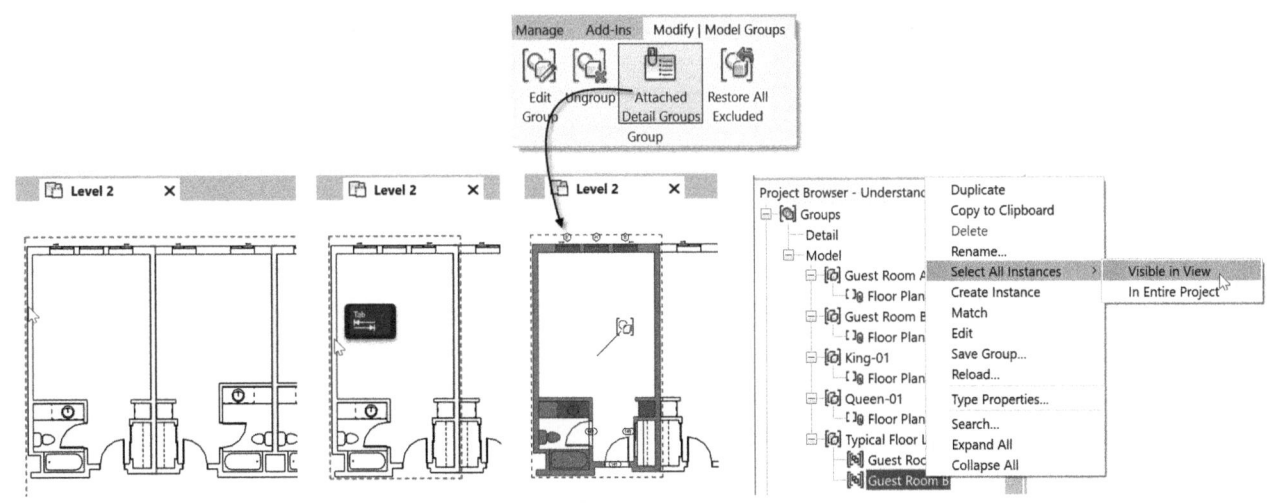

FIGURE 7.27 *Add an attached detail group to the nested model group (using* TAB *to select)*

You can repeat the process on the other groups if you like. However, it will be quicker to use Select All Instances > Visible in View (shown on the right side of the figure) instead. This will select all the nested groups of a type and then when you click the Attached Detail Groups button it will apply to all of them at once. Following any of the procedures covered so far, you can also edit either the nested groups or the overall group and see the results throughout the model and in the attached detail groups. Feel free to experiment further before continuing.

GROUPS AND LINKS

We have explored many techniques and advantages of working with groups so far in this chapter. You can begin to see the many advantages of including groups in your workflow. While working with groups directly in a project can prove a useful strategy for managing typical and repetitive design conditions, it is sometimes even more advantageous to export a group to its own separate file. This can be achieved by saving the group or converting it to a linked file.

SAVING A GROUP TO A FILE

A group can be saved to a separate Revit file. This enables you to work on the group independently of the project. This can be useful if the project is particularly large and/or if you want to have another colleague working on the group at the same time as you or someone else is in the project file. It also allows you to use the group in other projects.

1. On the Project Browser, right-click the *King-01* group and choose: **Save Group**.

   ⇨ In the "Save Group" dialog, browse to the *Chapter07* folder, verify that the "Include attached detail groups as views" check box is selected, and then click Save (see Figure 7.28).

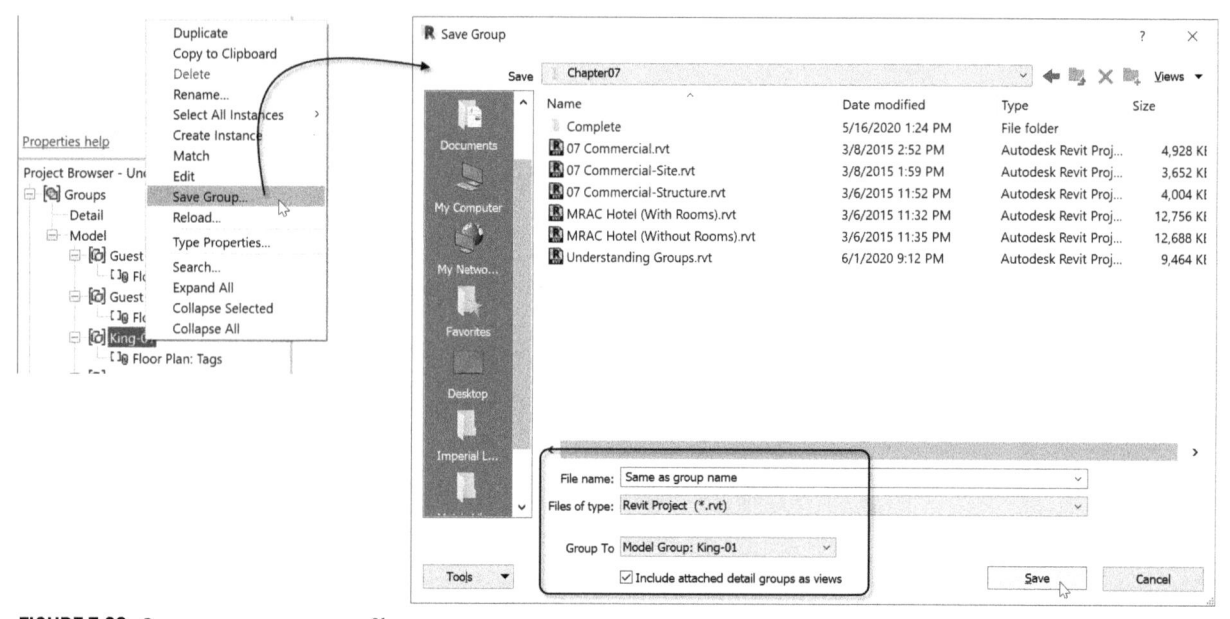

FIGURE 7.28 *Save a group to a separate file*

The file name defaults to the same name as the group: *King-01* in this case. Once the save is complete, you can open the file to study the result.

2. From the *Chapter07* folder, open the *King-01* file.
3. On Project Browser, expand Views.

You should have two floor plan views: *Level 1* and *Tags*. Tags contains the annotation that was in the attached detail group of the same name in the main project. The *Level 1* view contains the model geometry. You can make any edits here that you like. Upon saving those changes, we can reload them back into the main project.

4. In the *Level 1* floor plan view, make a noticeable change to the furniture layout.

   ⇨ Save and close the *King-01* file.

Groups and Links | 273

5. Back in the main project, right-click the *King-01* group on Project Browser again and choose: **Reload**.

⇨ In the dialog that appears, browse to the *Chapter07* folder and select the *King-01* file to reload.

Accept the defaults and click OK in any warnings.

If you are not in a view that shows the furniture, switch to one now to see the results.

CONVERT A GROUP TO A LINKED FILE

Revit also provides the ability to embed other Revit files in your project as Revit links. A linked file provides many of the same advantages as groups but remains a separate project file on your hard drive or server maintaining a live link for easy reloading. In this way, another individual can work in the linked file simultaneously. When the linked file is saved, you can capture the latest changes by reloading the linked file. The process is like the one just outlined, but the path to the link file is saved with the project so that we do not have to browse to each time we reload. Links are not as interactive as groups. The walls within them will not clean up with the walls in the host file for example. And you cannot edit them in the same Revit session without first unloading the link and then opening the file. But they do cut down on file size which can help performance, as well as offer a way to separate architecture from interiors into distinct teams. Worksharing is another option. Worksharing will be covered in Chapter 16.

1. On the Project Browser, double-click to open the *Level 2* floor plan.

⇨ Select the *Typical Floor Layout* group onscreen.

2. On the Group panel, click the Link button (or press LG).

⇨ If a warning appears, click OK.

This warning indicates that elements will be deleted. This is because we had previously applied tags (via an attached detail group) to the original model group. When you convert a group to a link, the annotation cannot remain applied. It is possible to reapply tags to the elements in a link, but this must be done separately. If you wish, you can click the Expand button in the warning to see more information on what will be deleted.

⇨ In the "Convert to Link" dialog, click the "Replace with a new project file" option (see Figure 7.29).

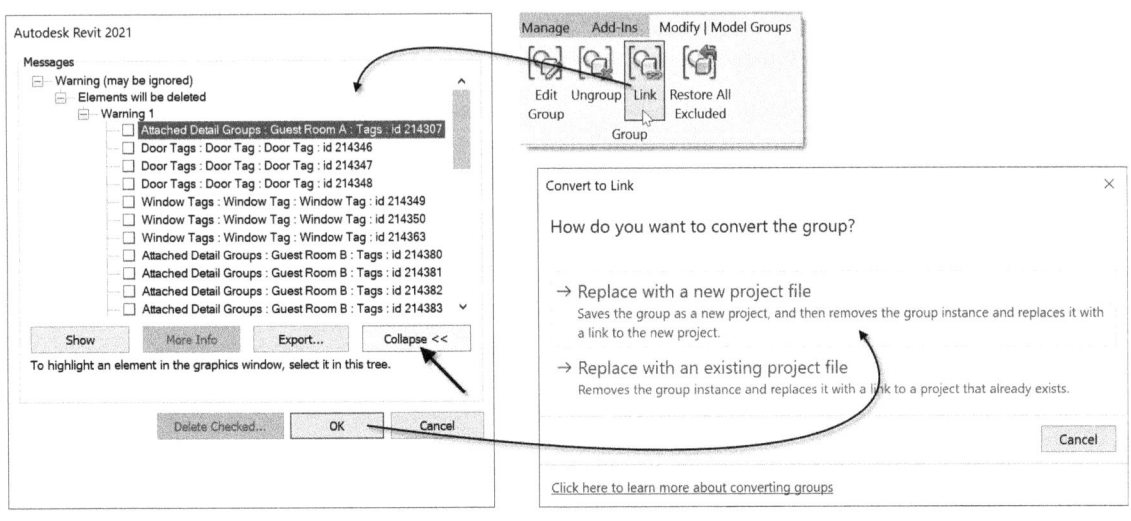

FIGURE 7.29 *Convert the group to a separate linked file*

3. In the "Save Group" dialog, browse again to the *Chapter07* folder, accept the other defaults and then click Save.

The second message allows us to create a new file from the group we are replacing, or to point to an existing file already on our hard drive or server to swap in its place. In this case, creating a new project file was our obvious choice. When

• Revit Essentials for Architecture •

274 | Chapter 7

the conversion is complete, you will see that the newly created file automatically appears in the *Revit Links* branch of the Project Browser (see Figure 7.30). Here you can access features of the linked file via the right-click menu.

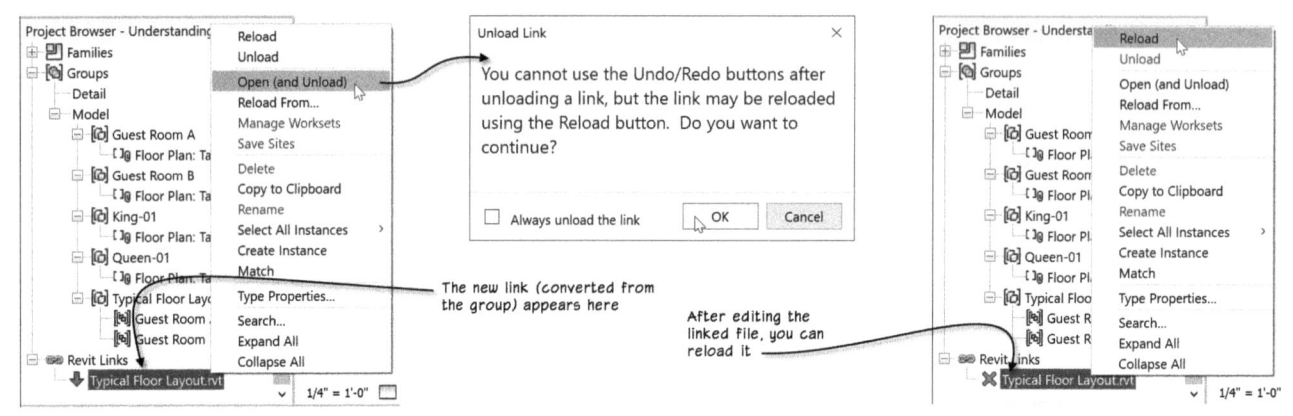

FIGURE 7.30 *Linked Revit files appear in their own branch on the Project Browser*

Feel free to open the linked file, make a few edits, and then re-save and reload the file. When you try to open the linked file, Revit will warn you that it must be unloaded in the current project, and that unloading can't be undone. This is normal. Click Yes to proceed. Once edits are complete in the *Typical Floor Layout.rvt* file and saved, you can close it and back in the *Understanding Groups.rvt* file, right-click the linked file on the Project Browser and choose: **Reload**. You will not need to browse to it again. The path for links is saved with the project. You can also right-click on the *Revit Links* branch of the Project Browser and choose: **Manage Links** to see a dialog listing paths and other information about linked files.

BINDING LINKED FILES (TO GROUPS)

The opposite of converting a group to a linked file is "Bind," which converts a linked file into a group.

1. Select the linked file (it highlights with a solid box around instead the dashed box used by groups).

   ⇨ On the Modify | RVT Links tab, on the Link panel, click the Bind Link button.

2. In the dialog that appears, check Attached Details only and then click OK.

3. In the "Duplicate Group Names" dialog that appears, click Yes.

   ⇨ In the warning that appears, click the Remove the link button (see Figure 7.31).

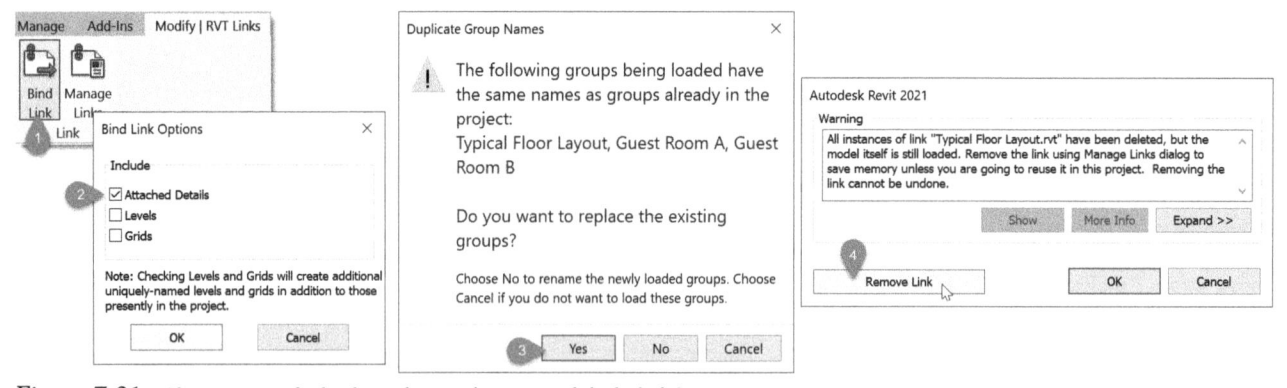

Figure 7.31 *Choose options for levels, grids, nested groups and the link definition*

The Revit link should now be removed and in its place the group that we started with should have been restored. In the message about duplicate groups choosing "Yes" overwrites the existing versions of the nested groups like Guest Room A and B and King-01 and Queen-01. In the final warning dialog, it is possible to click OK to ignore the

• The Aubin Academy •

warning, but this results in the Link's remaining in the "Manage Links" dialog even though we had removed the only instance of it onscreen. If you plan to add a new instance, you can click OK instead.

4. Save the project.

WORKING WITH ROOMS IN GROUPS

When the time comes to add room objects to our project we can choose to add them within the groups or outside the groups. If we add a room to each Guest Room group, they will appear in all instances just like other elements do. We can then tag them inside an attached detail group or individually directly on the floor plan view.

Another approach is to simply add the rooms outside of any groups directly in the project. Since the room object will conform automatically to the shape defined by the walls (both those inside and any that are outside of the groups), either approach is completely valid.

To compare methods, try both approaches in the current project.

1. In the *Architecture* floor plan view, select one of the Guest Room groups (use the TAB key to assist in selection).
   ⇨ Click the Edit Group button on the ribbon.
2. On the Architecture tab, on the Room & Area panel, click the Room button, and then add a Room in the main space within that group.

You will see the room object conform to the shape of the main room plus the entry foyer. If you like you can repeat the process to add additional rooms for the closet and toilet room. However, in some cases, for a hotel room layout such as this, you may not want to have separate rooms for each of these spaces, but might instead prefer a single room that expands to include the closet and toilet rooms within it. Let's look at how to do this."

3. Click the Modify tool on the ribbon or press the ESC key twice.
4. Select the walls that separate the toilet space and closet from the main space (5 total).
   ⇨ On the Properties palette, uncheck "Room Bounding" (see Figure 7.32).

When you apply the change, the room should now ignore the interior walls and fill the entire guest room layout.

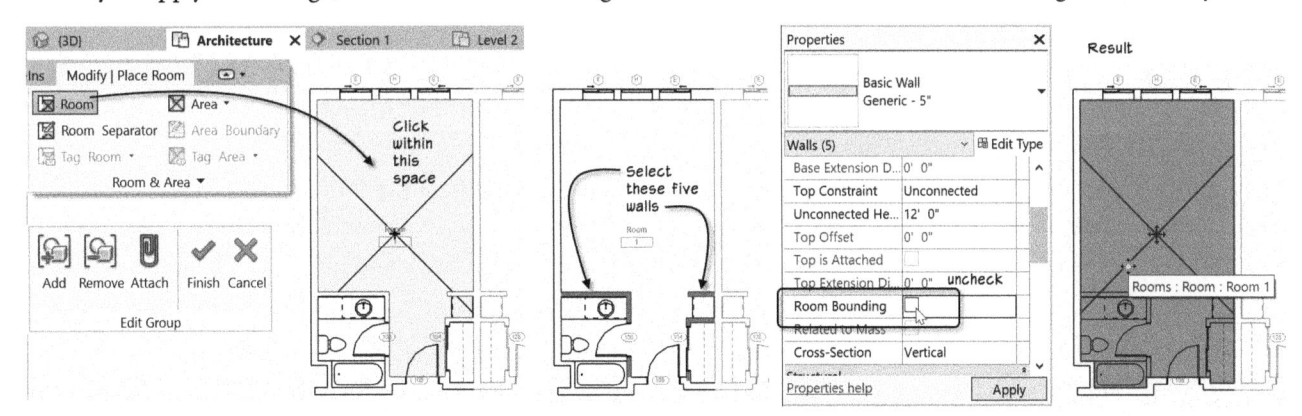

FIGURE 7.32 *Adding rooms to the group and varying the Room Bounding behavior*

When you finish the group, the room will be added to all instances of this group. The room tag will need to be attached separately to the attached detail group as explained in the "Editing Groups" topic on page 242 in Chapter 6. If you wish to try the alternative method, simply exit the edit group mode without preserving the changes and add rooms directly to the project. Notice that they will still see the wall boundaries that reside inside the groups. Tags can also be free-standing or grouped in attached detail groups. If you decide to place the rooms outside the groups, keep in mind that you may still need to edit the groups to adjust the room bounding behavior of the closets and rest rooms.

There are certainly plenty of other equally useful applications of groups including typical toilet room layouts, typical stair tower, office furniture layouts, etc. For example, in the previous chapter we used a simple group to create a typical floor framing condition that was copied to multiple floors in the building. There are almost limitless applications for groups.

For your further experimentation, a larger and more complete dataset like the one utilized in this chapter has been provided. You will find two versions of "REA Hotel" in the *Chapter07* folder. One version named *REA Hotel (Rooms Inside Groups).rvt* has the room objects embedded within the Guest Room groups. The other version *REA Hotel (Rooms Outside Groups).rvt* has the rooms placed directly in the project (not in the groups). You are encouraged to open each of these files and experiment further with all of the techniques covered in this chapter (see Figure 7.33).

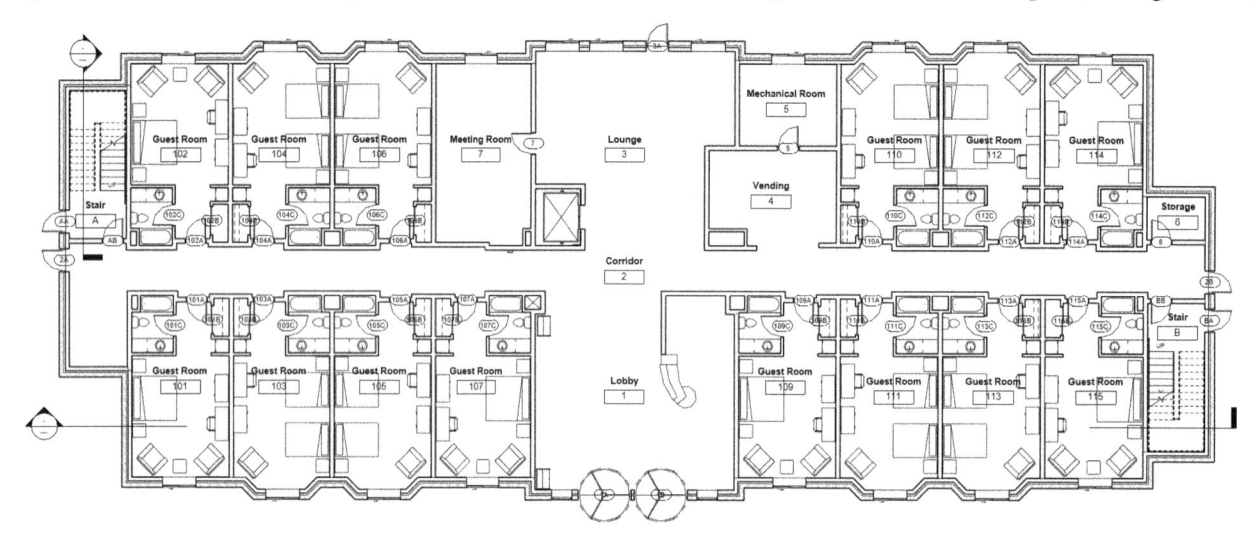

FIGURE 7.33 *The REA Hotel.rvt file is provide for your further experimentation*

LINKED PROJECTS

Throughout the course of this chapter, we have worked in a separate dataset and not re-visited our commercial and residential projects. Groups and linked files can be used in any project, but our residential project has no need for either. However, our commercial project can make use of both. We have already added a group to our commercial project at the end of (for the structural framing) and we can also make use of Linked files for certain aspects of the project as well.

Many firms using Revit take advantage of linked files as a way of splitting up larger projects into more manageable pieces. It is common to see separations made along various disciplines (such as architectural, structural and mechanical) and sometimes between major functional areas of the project (like core, shell, and interiors). These are of course suggestions and each firm and in fact each project can and often will implement some variation of these. To see a practical example, let's return to our commercial project to see how some of these concepts might apply and allow the project to progress.

> **BIM MANAGER NOTE:** Using linked files is only one way in which Revit teams collaborate. The other method involves a toolset called "Worksharing." The process involves the creation of a "Central" model stored on a common network server and individual "Local" files on each team member's workstation. Revit keeps track of changes that each user makes by enabling object locking. Worksets will be discussed more extensively in Chapter 16. If you are working in a team of Revit users, then Worksharing is a must. Please set aside time to read the material included in Chapter 16 before participating in your first team project. Worksets are typically used for internal collaboration by members of the same discipline and linked files are typically used to collaborate with external consultants such as Civil, Structural, MEP and other design firms. However, these are just guidelines and both links and worksharing can be used internally and externally.

LOAD THE COMMERCIAL PROJECT

For this exercise, we return to our commercial project begun in the last two chapters. Be sure that all other projects are saved and closed.

1. On the QAT, click the Open icon (or press CTRL + O).
2. In the "Open" dialog box, browse to the *Chapter07* folder.
   ⇨ Double-click: *07 Commercial.rvt* if you wish to work in Imperial units.
   ⇨ Double-click: *07 Commercial_M.rvt* if you wish to work in Metric units.
   You can also select it and then click the Open button.

The project is in much the same state as we left it at the end of the previous chapter. However, some important changes have been made since we closed it there. For this reason, be certain that you use the new dataset provided for 7 and do not attempt to continue in your own files from the previous chapter. The building still looks the same, but the toposurface is no longer in the file. The geometry for the site was removed and we will now walk through the process of creating a separate Revit project for the site data. Using techniques covered in this chapter, we will then link this new Site project back into the Commercial project.

CREATE AND LINK A SITE PROJECT

Frequently you will receive site plan data from outside firms in AutoCAD DWG or Microstation DGN format. Revit readily imports files saved in either format (and others as well). The linework in those files can be used to create a Toposurface. (In order for this to work correctly, the linework in the file must be drawn at the correct Z-height corresponding to the actual contour level you wish to create.)

> **BIM MANAGER NOTE:** If your Civil Engineer did not draw the contours at their actual elevations, you must open the file in the original application (AutoCAD or Microstation) and move the contour lines to their correct Z heights. If you do not own a copy of the application, you can ask your consultant to do this for you before they send the file. Revit also has support for Civil 3D files via the Link Topography tool. But to use this tool, your project must be on BIM360. BIM360 is a cloud-based collaboration platform offered by Autodesk. The service offers a powerful suite of tools enabling teams to access projects from any location. This is a subscription-based service. To learn more about availability and pricing, contact your Autodesk reseller or visit: **Autodesk.com**. If you want to learn more about using BIM 360 Design (including the connection with Civil 3D), check out the author's course: **BIM 360 Design Essential Training** at **LinkedIn Learning**[†].

Let's import some contour lines from a DWG file and generate a new Toposurface. We will create a new Revit project in which to do this. We could, of course, import the CAD file directly into our Commercial project, but as noted above, it is common "best practice" for such data to be contained in a separate project and then linked back into our project. This makes it easier to coordinate the sometimes different needs and workflows of the different disciplines responsible.

> **NOTE:** If you prefer to skip this exercise, you can instead use the Commercial Site project file provided in the *Chapter07\Complete* folder. To do so, skip to the "Link the Site Project" topic on page 283 below.

1. From the File menu, choose: **New > Project**.

⇨ In the "Template File" area, be sure that default Architectural template file is selected (dialog shown in Figure 5.1 in Chapter 5).

> **NOTE:** If your version of Revit does not include the template files cited here, both have been provided with the dataset files. Please browse to the *Templates* folder in the location where you installed the dataset files to find them.

2. In the "Create New" area, verify that Project is selected and then click OK.

3. Double-click to open the *Site* floor plan view.

LINK THE SITE PLAN CAD FILE

CAD files can be linked into Revit projects just like native Revit projects can. Doing so gives similar benefits. If the original CAD file is modified by your consultant, you will be able to easily reload the changes.

1. On the Insert tab of the ribbon, click the Link CAD button.

⇨ In the "Link CAD Formats" dialog, browse to the *Chapter07* folder.

2. Select (do not double-click) the *Commercial-Site.dwg* [*Commercial-Site_M.dwg*] file (don't click Open yet).

Several options appear at the bottom of the dialog.

Current view only—this check box will import the file into the active Revit view only. This means that the CAD file will not display in any other view. If you recall the "Revit Elements" topic on page 41 in Chapter 2, we learned there that Revit treats model elements differently than annotation elements. Model elements appear in all views while annotation elements appear only in the view in which they are created. When unchecked, this setting treats the linked file like *model* elements. When it is checked, the link will be treated like *annotation* (view specific) elements. This can be useful in some cases, but if you wish to use the imported file to generate a Toposurface, as we do here, it must be treated as model. Therefore, do *not* check this option in this case.

Layers—most CAD files use layers (or levels in DGN files) to organize the geometry they contain. These layers/levels will be maintained in the incoming file. If you wish to import only certain layers in the CAD file, you can choose either the "Specify" or "Visible" options. Visible brings in all layers not turned off or frozen in the saved CAD file. The Specify option will display the list of all layers and let you select the ones you need. The default setting brings in all layers.

Colors—most DWG or DGN files are saved in multiple colors. The options here allow you to control how this color data is handled on import. If the CAD data was drawn in a black background, try the Invert option to make the colors read better.

Import units—Auto-Detect is usually the best option. However, in cases where Revit misinterprets the units in the CAD file, you can designate the proper unit manually.

Lines Slightly Off Axis—This check box is on by default. Sometimes when you import CAD files, the linework can be slightly skewed. This can cause inaccuracies when imported into Revit. This check box will attempt to correct these lines to prevent issues when importing. It is recommended that you use this setting for most files "building scale" or smaller. For larger files like site plans, it is often better to turn this off to prevent Revit from "correcting" geometry that does not require it.

Positioning—there are several options. "Auto -Center to Center" simply matches the geometric center of the imported file to the geometric center of your active Revit view helping to ensure that something will show up when you finish. If the file is a one-time import and you are reasonably certain that you will not need to import additional files, this can be the most convenient option. If the imported file has a known and meaningful origin, the "Auto -Origin to Internal Origin" can be used. When you allow Revit to align the origin of the DWG or DGN file to the Revit model origin, you can later import additional DWG or DGN files based upon the same origin point and be certain that they will automatically align properly with the existing geometry. The only problem with the Origin to Internal Origin option is that your Revit project may not be built to match the origin in the incoming file, or the origin might be far from the model geometry. In this case, you can use one of the other options, adjust and then establish "shared coordinates" (see below) between your project and the link. The benefit of this approach is that it does not force you to adopt the origin of the incoming file at the expense of the host project.

Several manual options are also available allowing you to use the mouse pointer to place the imported file in any location you like. If you intend to move the linked file into the proper position after import, the manual options can prove more convenient.

Place at—controls which level the link is imported to. This is only available when "Current view only" is not checked.

3. Make sure that "Current view only" is not checked.

⇨ For Colors, choose: **Invert**, for Layers choose: **All**, for Import Units leave it set to: **Auto-Detect** And uncheck: Correct lines that are slightly off axis.

4. For Positioning, choose: **Auto – Origin to Internal Origin**, leave Orient to View checked on and Place at set to: **Level 1**, and then click the Open button (see Figure 7.34).

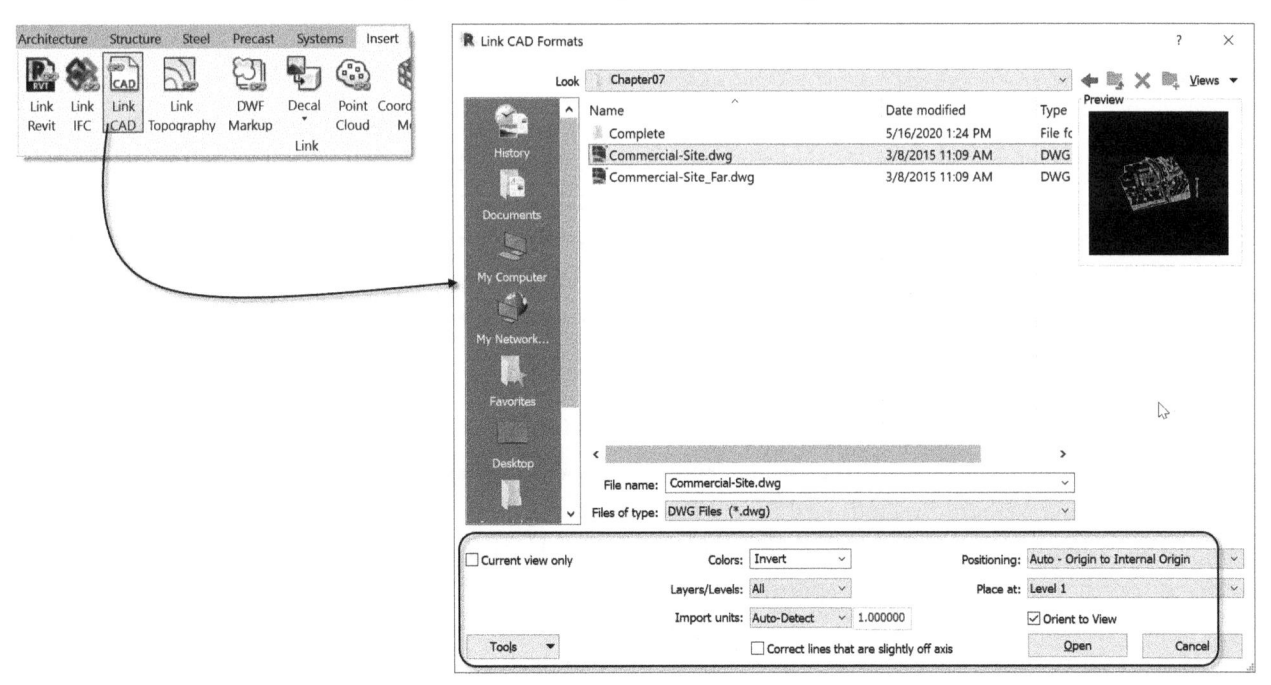

FIGURE 7.34 *Import the site data from a DWG file*

5. From the Navigation Bar, choose: **Zoom to Fit** (or press ZF).

The CAD file has been inserted into the Revit project relative to its own origin point. The Revit origin occurs at the point where the two blue icons in the center of the elevation marks appear onscreen. These icons are called the "Project Base Point" (circular shape) and the "Survey Point" (triangle shape). There is also a third point called: Internal Origin which we will see later.

> **BIM Manager Note:** In this CAD file, the origin is not too far from the site of the building. However, in many real-life projects, the origin can be quite far from the building(s). If the origin of the CAD file is greater than 20 miles [32.18km] away from the geometry in the file, Revit may not be able to use the Origin to Internal Origin option. In such a case, the Center to Center option will be substituted. If this occurs in your projects, you can acquire coordinates from the linked CAD file and leave it positioned at the center. In most cases, this will be preferable over trying to link the file far away from the Revit origin. The steps to acquire coordinates are covered below in the "Saving Shared Coordinates" topic on page 289. The example below acquires coordinates from another Revit file, but you can follow the same procedure to acquire coordinates from a linked CAD file as well. When you do, the Survey Point will move far away from the geometry onscreen. This is because by default it is clipped to the origin and when you acquire the coordinates of the CAD file, the origin will be very far away. In such a case, it is better to unclip the Survey Point before you acquire. This way it will remain unmoved onscreen. However, when you select it, you will note that the coordinates will change to reflect the new coordinates acquired from the linked file. You can then move it to a logical location relative to some benchmark in the civil file such as a street pole, manhole cover, or other fixed benchmark item as appropriate. Unclipping the icons and moving them is also discussed below.
>
> If the geometry in the linked file occupies a space exceeding a 20 miles [32.18km] radius, a warning will display. You will be warned about reduced accuracy when using such a file (see Figure 7.35). In that case it is best if you can open the original file and modify it to fit within the 20 miles [32.18km] radius. Usually this involves zooming to extents and deleting extraneous items that occur far away from the critical geometry.
>
> **FIGURE 7.35** *Revit warns if geometry exceeds a 20 mile distance*
>
> In the *Chapter07* folder, a version of the CAD file whose geometry is very far from the origin has been provided for you to experiment with if you choose. It is called: *Commercial-Site_Far.dwg* [*Commercial-Site_M_Far.dwg*]. Feel free to repeat any of the steps above using this file instead and then follow the acquire procedure as outlined here and compare the difference.

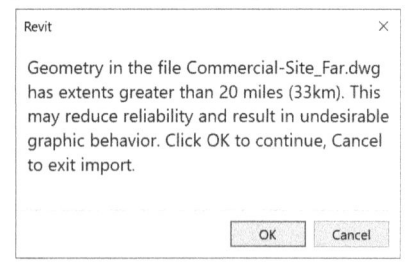

If you zoom in on the CAD file, you will notice labels on the contours and several spot elevations. These labels are in feet [meters]. They tell us the actual height at which each of the contour lines is placed in the CAD file.

6. On the Project Browser, double-click to open the *South* elevation view.

Notice that we have the default Level 1 at 0 and Level 2 at 10'-0" [4000] and that the contour lines from the imported DWG file appear above these levels at the distance indicated by the plan labels we just studied. (You can measure this with the measure tool on the Modify tab if you like). Returning to the *Site* plan view tab, we will note a blue rectangular shape in the file indicating the location of the building. Furthermore, interpolation of the contour labels puts the elevation at the front façade at approximately: **81'-0"** [**24300**]. We will use this number in the elevation view to adjust the height of Level 2. Then we will rename the two levels to something more descriptive for their use here in the site project we are creating.

7. In the *South* elevation view, change the height of Level 2 to: **81'-0"** [**24300**].

Groups and Links | 281

No need to zoom, you can select the level and make this change on the Properties palette.

8. Rename Level 2 to: **Street Level** and rename Level 1 to: **Datum**.

   When prompted about renaming corresponding views, choose: Yes for both.

9. Save the project as: **Commercial-Site**.

10. On the QAT, click the Default 3D View icon.

    ⇨ On the View Control Bar, choose: **Shaded**.

11. Orbit the model.

Notice that the contours in the CAD file are just lines and do not have any surface so no shading appears yet.

BUILD A TOPOSURFACE FROM IMPORTED DATA

Now that we have imported the 3D contour line data from the DWG file, we can use it to create a more accurate Toposurface than the one created from manual points in Chapter 5.

1. On the Massing & Site tab, click the Toposurface button.

   The Modify | Edit Surface tab will appear with the Place Point button active.

2. On the ribbon, click the Create from Import button.

   ⇨ From the pop-up that appears, choose: **Select Import Instance**.

   ⇨ Click anywhere on the imported DWG to select it.

3. In the "Add Points from Selected Layers" dialog, click the "Check None" button.

   ⇨ Place a checkmark in only the "C-Site-Cntr" and the "C-Site-Cntr-Intm" check-boxes to select only those two layers and then click OK (see Figure 7.36).

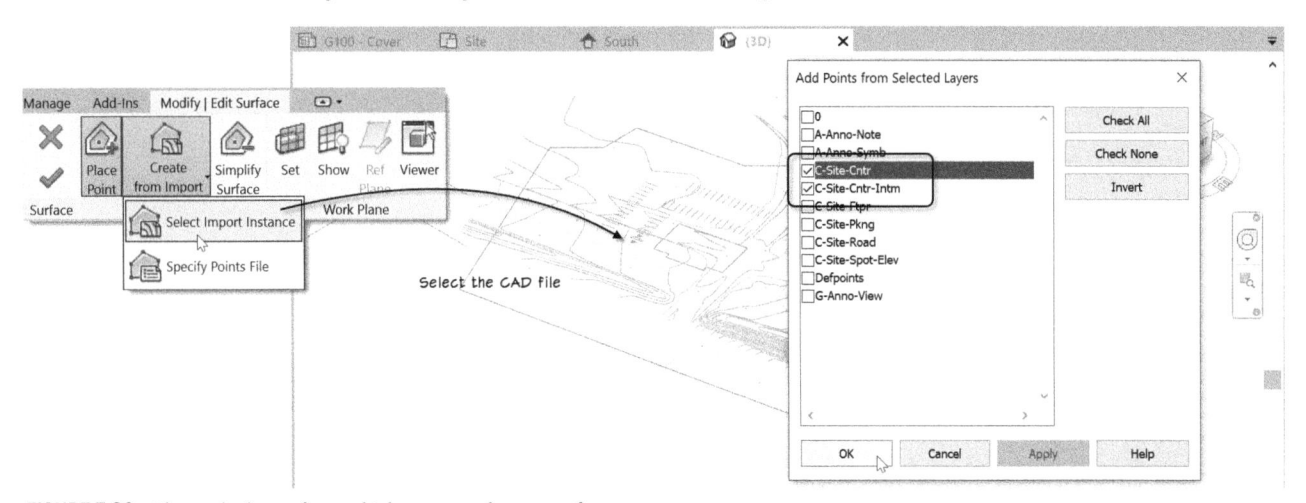

FIGURE 7.36 *Choose the layers from which to create the toposurface*

Several points will be extracted from the geometry on the selected layers, and from those points a Toposurface will be created.

4. On the ribbon, click the Finish Surface button to exit sketch mode and complete the Toposurface.

   ⇨ Orbit the model.

Notice that there is now a three-dimensional surface spread across the contours from the CAD file and the surface is shaded in brown.

282 | Chapter 7

5. On the Project Browser, double-click the *East* elevation view.

If you zoom in, you'll see a sloping profile of the terrain similar to the manual surface we created in Chapter 5. This Toposurface has more points and does a better job suggesting the roads that surround the building site. The manual method of placing individual points that we used in Chapter 5 is effective when you do not have any civil engineering files to import. If you receive a site plan file, it is usually easier to use the linked file. Otherwise, you can quickly create a suitable site for your building model with the point sketching method as well. Either method is appropriate for creating a toposurface in your own projects.

ADD A BUILDING PAD

Let's add a Building Pad. A Building Pad adds a simple slab surface that cuts into the terrain model as appropriate to suggest the required excavation or other prepared surface of construction.

1. Return to the *Site* view tab.

The site plan data imported from the DWG file includes a rectangle that approximates the rough footprint of the building. We can use this to assist us in sketching the Building Pad. However, now the Toposurface is concealing the linked file.

2. On the View Control Bar, click the Visual Style pop-up and choose: **Wireframe** (see item 1 in Figure 7.37).

3. On the Massing & Site tab, click the Building Pad button (item 2).

   ⇨ On the Modify | Create Pad Boundary tab of the ribbon (now in Sketch mode) click the Pick Lines icon (item 3).

4. Position the pointer over one a line of the blue building footprint in the middle of the site (the line should pre-highlight) and then press the TAB key (this should pre-highlight the entire chain).

   ⇨ When all lines of the shape pre-highlight, click the mouse to create sketch lines (item 4).

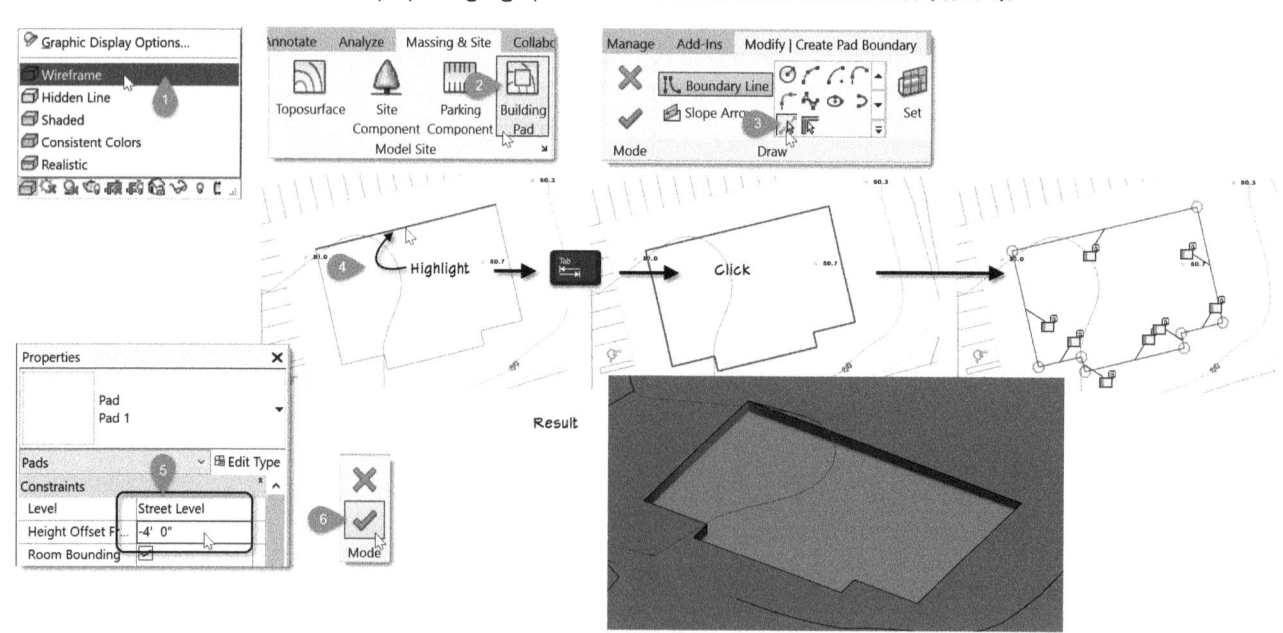

FIGURE 7.37 *Use the TAB key to chain select and create sketch lines*

5. On the Properties palette, change the Level to: **Street Level**.

   ⇨ For the Height Offset From Level parameter, input: **-4'-0"** [**-1200**] (see item 5 in Figure 7.37)

6. On the ribbon, click the Finish Edit Mode button (big green checkmark) (see item 6 in Figure 7.37).

7. Return to the *{3D}* view tab.

Zoom as required to see the Pad and its relationship to the Toposurface.

8. Save the Project.

There is plenty more work that we can do to the Site project. However, for the purposes of preparing the file for linking into the Commercial project (which is the primary goal for it in this chapter) we have completed enough work in the Site file for now. If you wish to go further with the Site project, refer to the Appendix for additional exercises on splitting the surfaces, applying materials and suggestions on adding trees and parking.

9. From the File menu, choose: **Close** (or press CTRL + W)

> **NOTE:** It is important to close the current project before continuing. Revit will not allow you have both a host and a linked project open at the same time in the same session of Revit.

LINK THE SITE PROJECT

Now that we have built a *Site* project, imported contours from the Civil Engineer and created a toposurface, we are ready to link this project into the *Commercial* project. The process of creating a Revit link is nearly identical to the process used in the "Link the Site Plan CAD File" topic on page 278 above. The *Commercial* project file should still be open. If you closed it, please reopen *07 Commercial.rvt* [*07 Commercial Metric.rvt*] now.

1. In the *07 Commercial.rvt* [*07 Commercial Metric.rvt*] project file, on the Project Browser, double-click to open the *Site* plan view.

2. On the Insert tab, on the Link panel, click the Link Revit button.

   ⇨ In the "Import/Link RVT" dialog, choose *Commercial-Site.rvt*, accept the default Auto - Internal Origin to Internal Origin positioning and then click Open.

   If you decided to skip the previous exercise and did not create the *Commercial-Site* file, you can instead link to the *07 Commercial-Site.rvt* [*07 Commercial-Site_M.rvt*] file provided in the *Chapter07* folder.

When the site file is linked in, it does not align with the building properly. It is to the upper left of the building (and if you looked in elevation, it is also at the wrong height). The *Site* project was created from a CAD file using the CAD file's origin. Our building was created in the center of our project template's elevation view markers where the Revit file's Base Point (origin) is located (you can see this origin in the current view as the blue icons in the center of the screen), therefore it is not surprising that things do not line up. While we could have started with the site plan data and built our model to match the orientation of the imported file (True North), it was more convenient to model our building relative to the project template setup with the footprint of the building orthogonal to the screen edges (Project North).

One of the advantages of using linked files is that each model file can maintain its own coordinate system, called Project (or Internal) Coordinates, with its own Base Point (origin) without imposing it on the other files in the project. There is a bit of setup required to synchronize the different models' coordinate systems, but once complete, each model maintains its own internal coordinates (Project Coordinates) and also understands how it relates to the other files (Shared Coordinates).

The basic setup process for establishing shared coordinates is as follows:

- Gather all required project files and decide which one will be "primary." (This is the file from which the others will acquire their coordinates.)
- Link the files.
- Move and rotate linked files as required to establish the correct geographic relationships. (For example, in our case here, move the site file link so that the site data is correctly oriented and located under the building).
- Save Shared Coordinates for each pair of files.

The overall process is straightforward. Let's walk through the process now with our two project files. For step 1, we have two project files, the *Commercial* project and the *Commercial Site*. The "Primary" file in this case will be the *Site* file. By "primary" we just mean that we will "acquire" coordinates from the *Site* file. More detail on acquiring coordinates is found in the "Saving Shared Coordinates" topic on page 289 below. We have already accomplished step 2 by linking the *Site* file in the previous sequence. The next task is to move and rotate the linked file (*Site* project) to match the orientation and location of the host project (*Commercial* project). We can achieve this using the Move and Rotate tools or the Align tool. Let's look at both options.

USING ROTATE AND MOVE

We can use the rotate tool to rotate a link in the same way as any other Revit element.

1. Zoom to fit. Select the linked site file onscreen. (You can click on it anywhere and the entire file will highlight.)
   ⇨ On the Modify | RVT Links tab, click the Rotate button (or press RO).

If you know how much you want to rotate, you can simply type in the angle in the field on the Options Bar and then press ENTER. Otherwise, you can rotate graphically on screen. A small round "center of rotation" control will appear at the middle of the selection. Using this control, you can change the center of the rotation to the desired position. You can either click the center of rotation control directly onscreen and then click the new location, or simply click the Place button on the Options Bar and then click where you would like the center to be. You can even tap the SPACEBAR as a shortcut to clicking the Place button, so there are plenty of ways to change the center of rotation.

2. Click the small blue circle handle indicating the center of rotation onscreen or click the Place button on the Options Bar (see item 1 in Figure 7.38).
   ⇨ Click at the lower-right endpoint of the building footprint to place the center of rotation (item 2).
   ⇨ Move the mouse toward the upper endpoint of the building edge and then click along the line (item 3).
3. Finally, move the mouse to the right. It will snap vertically. When it does, click to finish the rotation (item 4).

The result should be that the building footprint is perfectly orthogonal to the screen as shown in the far right of the figure.

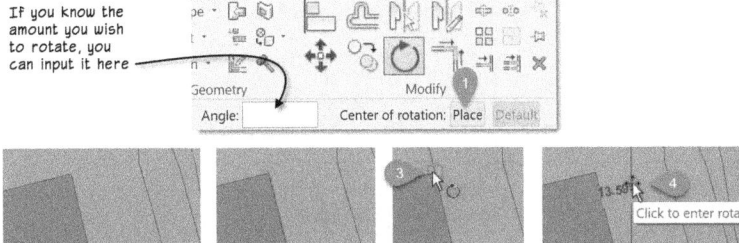

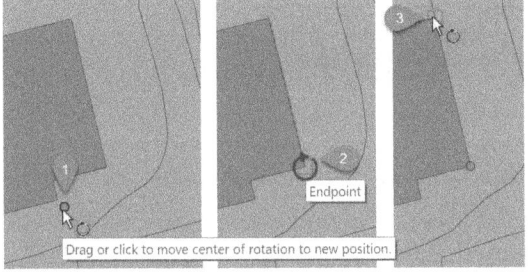

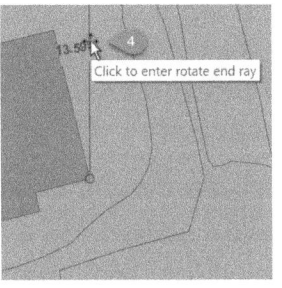

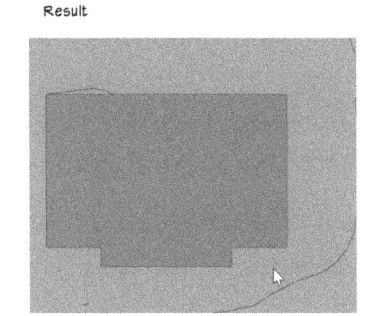

FIGURE 7.38 *Rotate the linked site file to make the building footprint horizontal*

Next, we'll move the file and snap it to our building model.

> The Link should still be selected, if it is not, click to select the linked file again.

4. On the ribbon, click the Move button (or press MV). (Make sure that Constrain on the Options Bar is not checked.)
   ⇨ For the start point, use the same endpoint about which you rotated.
5. For the move end point, snap to the corresponding endpoint on the building model geometry. (You may need to pan or zoom. Use your wheel mouse for this.)

> **TIP:** If you are having trouble snapping to the precise point, move it close, then zoom in and repeat. You can type the shortcut SE to force Revit to snap to an endpoint.

The linked file will remain selected (highlighted in light blue). The footprint of the building should be shaded a little darker helping you determine if it is lined up properly. Repeat move or rotate if necessary to fine tune the position or try the Align command as outlined next.

ALTERNATIVE POSITIONING TECHNIQUE (USING ALIGN)

The Rotate tool is an important tool and you should be sure you are comfortable with the technique for changing the center of rotation. However, there is an easier way to position the linked file with the building model—use the Align tool. If you wish to follow the steps, undo the move and rotation steps from the previous topic (CTRL + Z or the drop down on the QAT). Otherwise, skip to the next topic: "Position the Link Vertically."

1. On the Modify tab, click the Align button (or press AL).
   ⇨ For the alignment reference, click the outside edge of the top horizontal wall of the building model.
   ⇨ Click the top angled edge of the building footprint sketch in the linked file next (see the top of Figure 7.39).
2. Repeat the Align process to align the vertical edge (see the bottom of Figure 7.39).

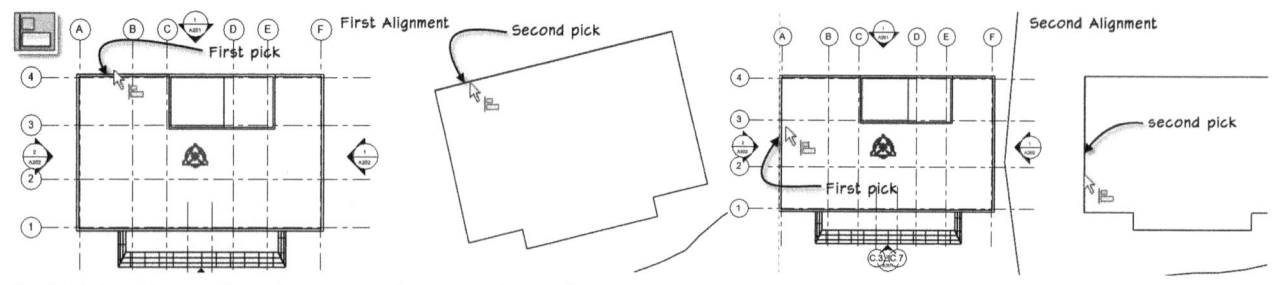

FIGURE 7.39 *Align can be used to rotate and move simultaneously*

Select the linked file when you are finished and as before, it will highlight and turn transparent so that you can visually verify that the alignment is correct. Both methods: using align and using rotate/move achieve the same result. The align method is a bit quicker, but there will be times when rotating and/or moving is preferred. Be sure you are comfortable with both methods before continuing.

POSITION THE LINK VERTICALLY

Finally, if we look at one of the elevation views, it will become clear that there is one more adjustment required. Recall that in the "Link the Site Plan CAD File" topic on page 278 above, we noted that the contour lines near the center of the building are at 81'-0" [24300] We adjusted one of the levels to this height in the *Site* file in preparation for making the vertical adjustment here.

1. Open the *North* elevation view.

Currently we do not see the linked file in this view at all. This is because the elevation view has the crop region enabled. We must temporarily disable it to make the required adjustment.

2. On the View Control Bar, click the Do Not Crop View icon. (The View Control Bar appears in Figure 5.34 in Chapter 5).

    Notice that once you disable the cropping, the linked file appears and the toposurface in that file covers the entire building. Zoom out as necessary.

3. On the Modify tab, click the Align button (or press AL).
    ⇨ For the alignment reference, click on the Street Level line of the building model (in the current project).
    ⇨ For the entity to align, click the Street Level line in the linked file. (You may have to zoom out to find it.)
    Do not click the lock icon.

4. On the ribbon, click the Modify button.

    The Toposurface should now appear at the base of the building model (see Figure 7.40).

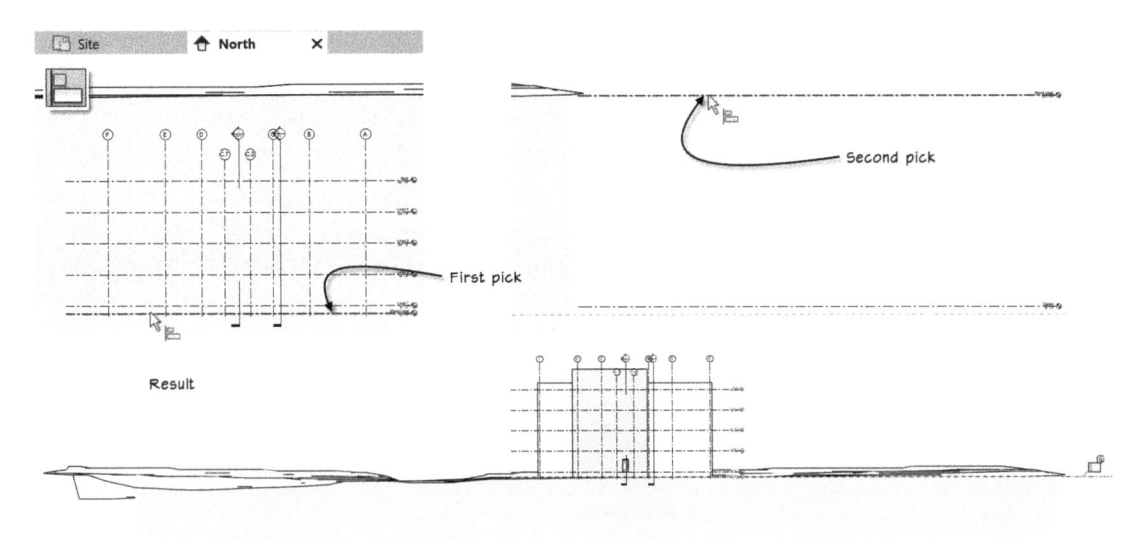

FIGURE 7.40 *Move the link file vertically in the elevation view using the Align tool*

5. On the View Control Bar, click the Crop View icon.

Check all four elevations. If necessary, click the Show Crop Region icon in each elevation, adjust the Crop Region, and then hide the Crop Region again. Finally make sure that the crop is turned on for each elevation.

6. Save the project.

SURVEY POINTS, PROJECT BASE POINTS, AND SHARED COORDINATES

The basic mechanics of linked files have already been discussed in the topics above. As we have seen in the previous sequence, when files authored by different parties are linked together, it is important to establish a common reference point for these files. This will ensure that common physical features maintain their proper geometric relationship and position relative to one another. To help us in maintaining these relationships, Revit projects have the following tools:

Project Base Point—represented by a circular icon, it is a meaningful reference point of the project with respect to the project coordinate system. This coordinate system relates to the project itself, and by default the Project Base Point is at the origin which is in the center of the floor plan view.

Survey Point—represented by a triangular icon, it can be used to identify a known point in the physical world. This might be some benchmark indicated by the Civil Engineer. The Survey Point is useful to correctly locate and orient your building project in another meaningful coordinate system such as the coordinate system used by a civil engineering application. By default, the Survey Point is also at the origin in the center of the floor plan.

Internal Origin—represented by X/Y axis indicator, this icon can be displayed in any view and shows the location of the built-in internal origin point. This point cannot be adjusted. Turning on this indicator is for visual reference only. By default, all the other two points: Project Base Point and Survey Point coincide with the Internal Origin.

Shared Coordinates—reconcile the differences between the current project's coordinate system and the coordinate system used by linked file(s). Setting up a Shared Coordinate system keeps all linked files in the correct relative positions to one another while allowing each to maintain its own internal coordinate systems. This feature is not available in Revit LT. If you are using Revit LT, please skip this topic.

UNDERSTANDING INTERNAL ORIGIN, PROJECT BASE AND SURVEY POINTS

The default template from which we began our *Commercial* project has the Project Base Point and the Survey Point icons displayed in the *Site* plan view. Other views do not display them by default. The Internal Origin marker is hidden in all views. If you wish to see these points in any view, their visibility is easy to control. We'll demonstrate in a plan view.

1. Open the *Level 1* plan view.
2. On the View tab, click the Visibility/Graphics button (or press VG).

    The Internal Origin, Project Base Point and the Survey Point icons are subcategories of the Site category.

3. Scroll down and expand the Site category.

    ⇨ Place a checkmark in the Internal Origin check box and then click Apply (move the dialog out of the way if necessary to see the result) (see Figure 7.41).

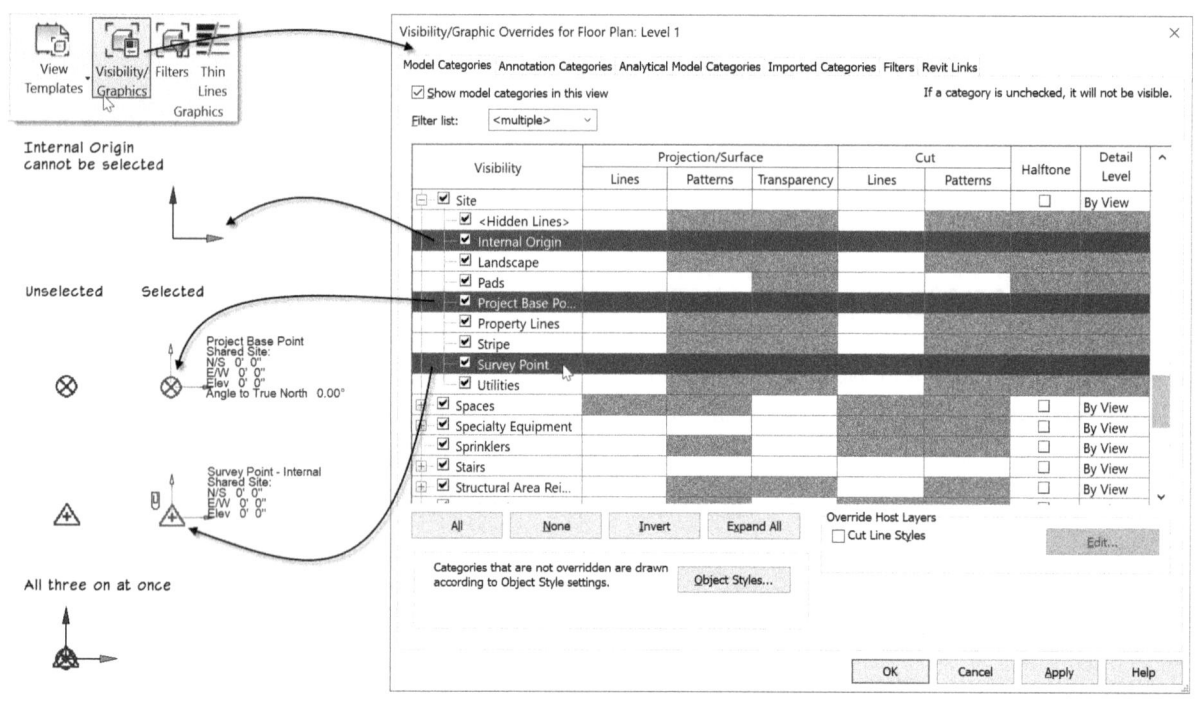

FIGURE 7.41 *Turn on Project Base Point and Survey Point*

⇨ Uncheck the Internal Origin, check the Project Base Point and then click Apply.

⇨ Repeat for the Survey Point.

If you check two or all three of these boxes, the points will appear superimposed on top of each other since in this project, they are all currently in the same location.

Like other display settings, this visibility change must be performed in each view where you wish to have these points display. The Internal Origin appears like and X and Y axis symbol. It is visual only and cannot be selected, nor can you snap to it. The Project Base Point is a round symbol with a cross through the middle. The Survey Point is triangular with a small plus (+) sign in the center. Both points are displayed on the left side of Figure 7.41 as they appear when not selected and when selected. The bottom left of the figure shows what it will appear like if you turn all three on at once.

4. Switch back to the *Site* plan view tab.

    The Project Base and Survey Points are already displayed here. This was the default in the template file we used to start this project.

5. Select the Project Base Point. (Use the TAB key if necessary.)

The coordinates of the point are listed as editable dimensions next to the icon. You can type new values into any of these dimensions. For now, do *not* make any changes. If you do so, it would move the project relative to the Survey point. This would be a physical model-based changed that would be evident in all views, not just the one where these points are visible.

6. Deselect the Project Base Point and select the Survey Point. (Use the TAB key if necessary.)

EDIT A VIEW TEMPLATE

Notice that both points are currently located at the origin (0,0,0). Again, do *not* change the location at this time. Let's turn on the Internal Origin. The trouble is, if you try to use Visibility/Graphics, all the settings will be grayed out and unavailable for edit. This is because back in the "Apply a View Template" topic on page 161 in Chapter 5 we assigned a View Template to the *Site* plan view. When a view template is assigned to the Properties of the view, it takes control of the visibility/graphics (and several other) settings. So, to display the Internal Origin, we must edit the view template applied to this view.

1. Return to the *Site* floor plan view tab.
2. On the Properties palette, scroll down to the View Template setting and then click the button next to it labeled: Site Plan.
   ⇨ In the "Assign View Template" dialog, on the right next to V/G Overrides Model, click the Edit button.
   ⇨ Scroll down to the Site category, expand it and then check the Internal Origin check box.
3. Click OK twice to dismiss both dialogs and return to the view window.

   The Internal Origin marker will now appear superimposed on top of the other two (as shown in the lower left of Figure 7.41 above).

SAVING SHARED COORDINATES

If all we need is for the link of the site to appear here, then we could call the current setup complete. However, if we decide to also link the architectural file to the site file, we will not want to repeat the move, rotate, and/or align steps performed here in that file. Saving a shared location for the file makes each file (the host and the link) aware of the other and what offsets and rotations are required for correct orientation within both files. We only have two files now, but the usefulness of shared coordinates only increases when we have more files involved. When a shared location is saved from the host file, Revit saves this information into the link file. This can be done with any kind of link, including linked CAD files.

1. Continue in the *Site* plan. Select the linked (site) file onscreen.
   ⇨ On the Properties palette, beneath Identity Data, change the Name to: **Site Model** (see item 1 in Figure 7.42).
2. Beneath Other, next to Shared Site, click the: <Not Shared> button (item 2).

The "Share Coordinates" dialog lists two ways that the coordinate systems can be reconciled. The two methods are very similar. In each case, the shared coordinate information must be saved to both the host file and the linked file. Publishing sends the information from the host to the link, while acquiring pulls the information from the link to the host. Technically, either option can work. But it is recommended that you make the file that contains the site data the primary file. This will typically yield the best results and is a common practice. In this case, this means we will want to acquire the coordinates from our site file since we are currently in the *Commercial* (architectural) file. After

290 | Chapter 7

we do so, Revit will save the coordinate information to both files the next time we save the current model. In other words, in addition to saving the current model Revit also writes the Shared Coordinates back to the *Site* model as well.

3. Click the "Acquire the shared coordinate system from" radio button (item 3).
4. At the bottom of the dialog, click the Change button (item 4).

Shared coordinates are stored in a "Shared Site" within the file. Revit projects can have one or more shared sites within them. This is useful when the same building model must be repeated on a site, such as a multi-building campus of condominium buildings. Naming the shared sites descriptively can be helpful. In our case, since we have only one building model, we could simply accept the default location name (Internal). However, it is good practice to get in the habit of renaming the default location so that later you can use this to verify that you have, in fact, reconciled the coordinates. Plus descriptive names tend to be more user friendly.

⇨ In the "Location Weather and Site" dialog, click the Rename button (item 5) and change the name to: **Commercial Site Location** (item 6).

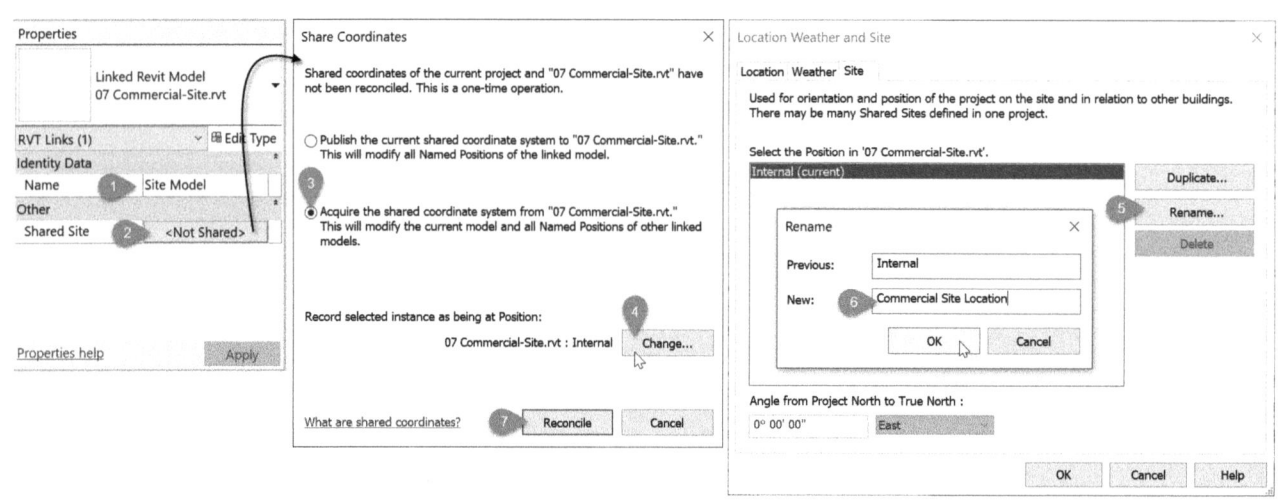

FIGURE 7.42 *Acquire the shared coordinates system and save it to a renamed location*

5. Click OK two times.
⇨ In the "Select Site" dialog, click the Reconcile button (item 7).

On the Properties palette, the Shared Site now says: "Commercial Site." Take notice of the new location of the Survey Point icon (triangular one). You may need to zoom out. Also, it may be concealed by the icons from the linked file. They will be gray in color. If you hover over these icons, you can see the survey point from the current file pre-highlight however (see the left side of Figure 7.43). When we acquired the coordinates of the site project, the survey point moved to mark (identify) the origin of that file which is near the lower-left corner of the site file.

6. Save the project.
⇨ In the "Location Position Changed" dialog, choose the Save option (see the right side of Figure 7.43).

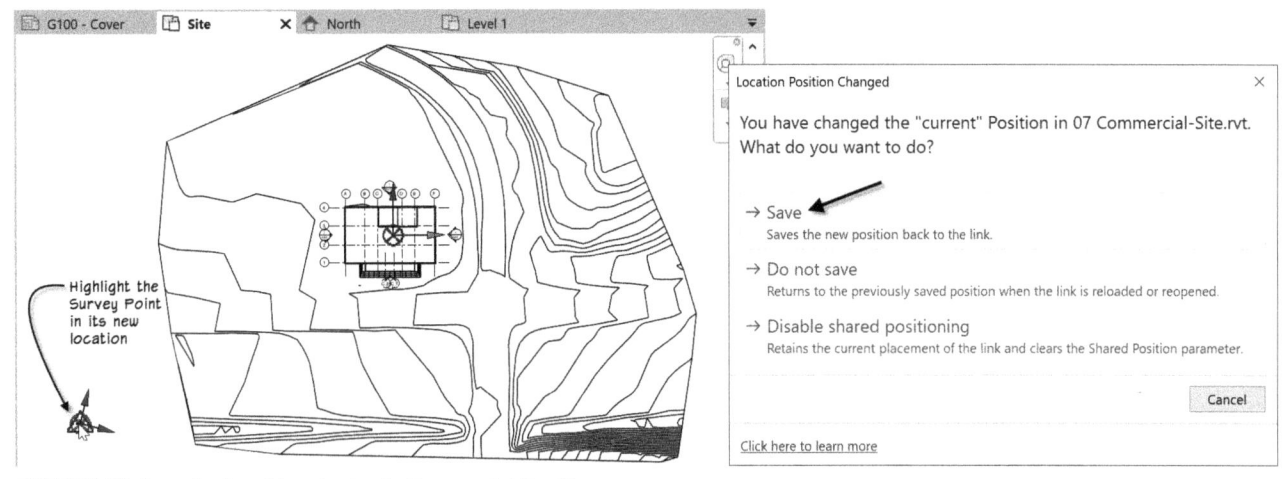

FIGURE 7.43 *Save the shared location in the Commercial Site file*

7. Select the Survey Point icon onscreen.

   Notice that the coordinates read 0,0,0 and that the axes are at a slight angle (see the left side of Figure 7.44).

8. Select the Project Base Point icon onscreen.

   Notice that the coordinates of this point now report relative to the new location of the Survey Point (see the right side of Figure 7.44). These values are easier to read on the Properties palette.

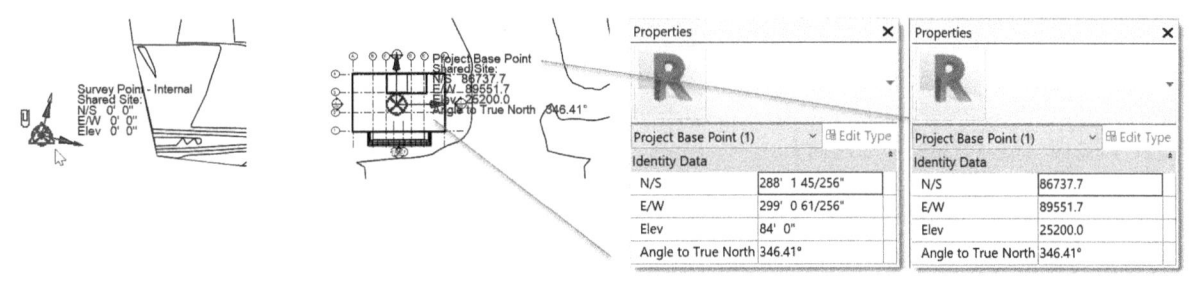

FIGURE 7.44 *Now that coordinates are shared between the host file and the linked file, the Project Base point origin is relative to the Survey Point*

Next to the survey point is paper clip icon. If you move the survey point while it is clipped, the entire linked file will move with it. You are not really moving the survey point but rather the location of the host project relative to the linked file. This would be very similar to the move, rotate and/or align steps performed in the "Link the Site Project" topic on page 283 above. If you unclip the survey point and then move it, you will be changing the position of the survey point only. It would be marking a different location on the shared coordinate system. You would do this if there were a more meaningful benchmark rather than the linked file's origin point. This might be a location designated by your Civil Engineer such as some known benchmark or site feature.

The project base point can also be moved to a more useful location. Simply drag it to your preferred location. You might wish to do this to make the Project Base Point reference a more meaningful point, such as the corner of the building or a grid intersection A1.

9. Select the Project Base Point onscreen.

10. Zoom in as necessary and drag the Project Base point to the intersection of grids 1 and A (see Figure 7.45).

    If necessary, type SI to force snapping to the intersection while dragging.

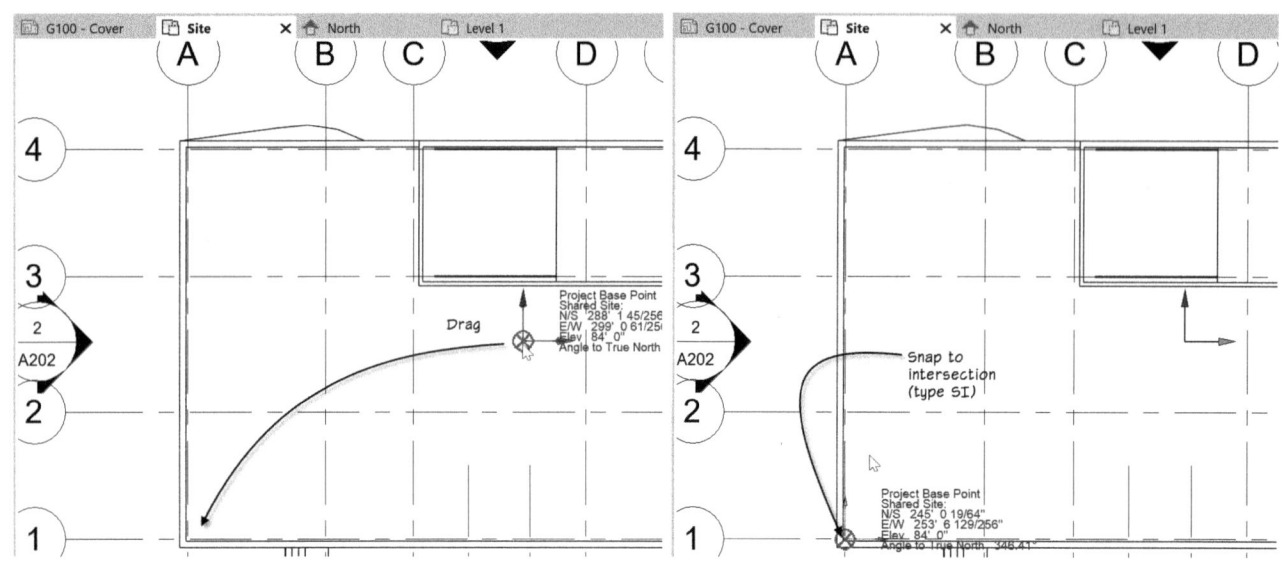

FIGURE 7.45 *Relocate the Project Base point to a more meaningful location*

This change has no impact on the coordinate system, the origin or the position of the two files. It merely relocates the icon to a more useful location for the project team. If you pay attention to the coordinates before and after dragging, you will note that moving the point simply moves it to a different location on the shared coordinate grid and the coordinates which are measured from the Survey point update accordingly.

11. Save the project.

ROTATE A VIEW TO TRUE NORTH

Floor plan views can be oriented either to "Project North" or to "True North." Every plan view has this parameter. True North is the geographic direction of North given to us by the Civil Engineer or Land Surveyor. This is the actual geographical north direction. Project North is typically parallel to the predominant geometry in the building and is oriented for convenience when composing sheets. By default, floor plan views are oriented to Project North. Changing a view to display True North is easy once shared coordinates are set up.

> Continue in the *Site* plan view. Make sure that no objects are selected.

On the Properties palette, beneath Graphics, next to Orientation, notice that the view is currently set to Project North, but that it is grayed out and we cannot change it. This is another setting controlled by the view template (see the "Edit a View Template" topic on page 289 above).

1. On the Properties palette, beneath Identity Data, next to View Template, click the Site Plan button.
⇨ Scroll down and locate the Orientation property. Change it to: **True North** and then click OK.

The view will rotate to make True North point straight up. If you click either the Survey or Project Base points, you will see the new orientation reflected in these icons as well.

2. On the Project Browser, open any other floor plan view, such as *Level 1*.

Notice that the orientation in the other plans is still set to Project North, which is parallel to the predominate building geometry. Each plan view can be set to either Project North or True North as required.

LOCATION WEATHER AND SITE

In the previous sequence we used the "Location Weather and Site" dialog to rename the default "Internal" Site for the linked topography file. Let's look at this dialog again and see what else we can do.

1. On the Manage tab, on the Project Location panel, click the Location button.

On the Location tab, in the "Project Address" field you can input the city, the postal address of the project, or even the exact longitude and latitude and press ENTER. Revit will use an Internet Mapping Service to set your project's location based on your input. You can also drag the icon in the map to fine-tune the position. Setting the location to your actual site address is important to get proper lighting and shadows when performing Solar studies (refer to Chapter 18 for more information), and for calculating heating and cooling loads in MEP design.

2. In the Project Address field, type: **Chicago, IL** and then press ENTER.

   If you prefer, you can input a different address. Try a complete postal address. You can also zoom and pan in the map and drag the red pointer icon that appears.

3. Click the Site tab again.

This is the dialog that we saw above. Notice that even though we renamed the site while saving shared coordinates, it is still listed as "Internal" here. Remember, there are two files: the site we renamed is in the *Commercial Site.rvt* file. We are currently in the *07 Commercial.rvt [07 Commercial Metric.rvt]* project file. As noted above, it can be easier to verify the shared coordinates if you rename the Site to something other than Internal. Also notice the angle from Project North to True North corresponds to the rotation that we have established between the two files.

4. Click on the Rename button and change the name to: **Commercial Building Architecture** and then click OK twice.

LINKING BY SHARED COORDINATES

For each pair of files, you only need to establish the shared coordinates once. In other words, if the person working in the *Commercial Site* project wishes to link the architectural file, they can do so without repeating the steps in the "Saving Shared Coordinates" topic on page 289 above. If you wish to try this, you must first close the *Commercial* project. You cannot have both a host file and a link file open at the same time in the same session of Revit. This feature is not available in Revit LT. If you are using Revit LT, please skip this topic.

1. First save the current project and then close it (CTRL + W).
2. Open the *Commercial Site* project.
   ⇨ Open the *{3D}* view.
3. On the Insert tab, click the Link Revit button. Browse to and select the *07 Commercial.rvt [07 Commercial Metric.rvt]* project file.
   ⇨ Before clicking Open, for Positioning choose: **Auto – By Shared Coordinates** and then click Open to complete the linking.

The Commercial project will appear in exactly the correct spot on the site. If you edit the properties of the linked file, you will see that the Shared Site was assigned to the location named "Commercial Building Architecture".

There are other important features of shared coordinates that are worth your time and exploration. For example, the same linked file can be copied multiple times in a host project and assigned to different shared sites. This is useful in a campus situation with multiple identical buildings on the same site. To do this, you reopen the "Location Weather & Site" dialog, click the Site tab, and Duplicate one of the saved sites rather than renaming it. Each named site can have its own saved coordinates.

• Revit Essentials for Architecture •

294 | Chapter 7

4. If you opened the site project, save and close it now. Then reopen the commercial project before continuing.

CREATE AND LINK A STRUCTURAL PROJECT

Now that we have completed setup of our site model, we will next isolate the structural elements and create a separate linked file from them. This will leave only architectural elements (walls, doors, windows, column enclosures (architectural columns), floors, and roofs) in the *07 Commercial.rvt* [*07 Commercial Metric.rvt*] project file. You may recall that in the previous chapter, we created columns, beams, and braces in our commercial project. These elements and the core walls are the ones that we will separate out to their own structural model. However, some of these elements like the grids and the core walls need to appear in both files. We'll look at a special way to achieve that as well.

CONVERT A GROUP TO A LINK

The task of separating the structural elements into their own file can be accomplished in a few ways. We could create a separate file, and then select the required elements and copy and paste them from our project to the new one. We can also use the techniques already covered in this chapter and isolate the required objects using groups and then convert that group to a link. If you prefer to use copy and paste in the next sequence, feel free to do so. The steps that follow will highlight the approach using groups to reinforce the skills we learned at the start of the chapter.

1. In the *07 Commercial.rvt* [*07 Commercial_M.rvt*] file, on the QAT, click the Default 3D View icon.

    The view named *{3D}* will re-open.

2. Using a window selection, select all elements on screen.

    ⇨ Click the Filter button, deselect everything except Model Groups.

    If there are Structural elements shown, choose those as well, but do *not* include Structural Columns.

At this point, we can go directly to the group step; however, it is often good practice to use the Temporary Hide/Isolate icon (on the View Control Bar) to isolate the selected elements first to be sure you have the desired selection.

3. On the View Control Bar, click the Temporary Hide/Isolate icon and choose: **Isolate Element** from the pop-up.

    You should only have Beams, Braces, and maybe Joists selected on screen.

4. On the ribbon, click the Create Group button (or press GP).

    ⇨ In the "Create Model Group" dialog, type: **Structure** for the Name and then click OK (see Figure 7.46).

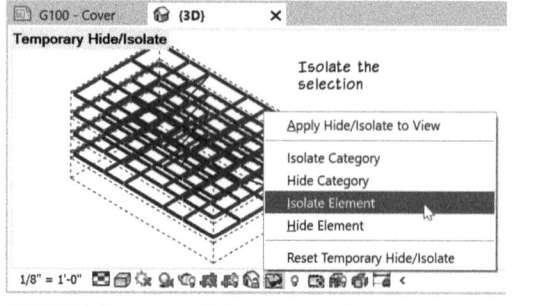

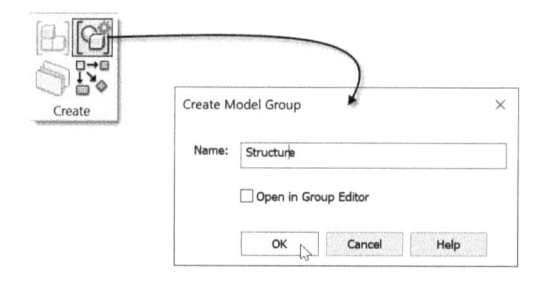

FIGURE 7.46 *Group all the Structural framing*

At this point we have two options: we can simply save the group to a file (as seen in the "Saving a Group to a File" topic on page 272 above) or we can convert it to a link (using the procedure covered in the "Convert a Group to a Linked File" topic on page 273 above). Let's use the link option.

5. With the *Structure* group still selected, on the Group panel of the ribbon, click the Link button.

• The Aubin Academy •

⇨ In the "Convert to Link" dialog that appears, choose the "Replace with a new project file option".

⇨ In the "Save Group" dialog, browse to the *Chapter07* folder and then click Save.

Using this method, we have quickly and efficiently gathered all the structural framing and moved it to a separate linked Revit file. If you were to unload the Link now, none of the Structure would remain in the *07 Commercial.rvt* [*07 Commercial_M.rvt*] project file. At this point we could open the new *Structure.rvt* file and continue the exercise in there. However, one limitation of either the Save to Group or Convert to Link method is that the resulting file is not based on the default Revit template. This means the resulting file has no levels, few annotations, and only the bare minimum of views. As a result, it will prove better in practice to create a new file using your preferred template first, and then insert the newly created file into it as a group. In this way, we can ensure that the Structural file (or any file created this way) benefits from the office standards embedded in a template project. The process would be very similar to the steps covered above in the "Binding Linked Files (to Groups)" topic on page 274.

WORKING WITH COPY/MONITOR

To save a few steps, a file has already been created from the standard template and included with the Chapter 7 files. We'll open this file, make a few preparations and then insert our group into it. The preparations that we need involve copying the levels and grids from our main *Commercial* project over to the *Structural* file. While it is possible to simply copy these items to the structural file using groups or copy and paste, a better approach is the Copy/Monitor tool which is specifically designed for this purpose. The Copy/Monitor tool allows you to copy certain elements (levels, grids, walls, floors, and columns) from a linked file and keep them associated back to the originals. In this way, you can monitor changes as they occur and update the copies to match. This provides a very practical way for project teams to collaborate on shared elements even when they are not physically located in the same office. This feature is not available in Revit LT. If you are using Revit LT, please skip this topic.

1. Save and Close the *07 Commercial.rvt* [*07 Commercial_M.rvt*] project file.

2. From the *Chapter07* folder open the *07 Commercial-Structure.rvt* [*07 Commercial-Structure_M.rvt*] file.

The project will open with the *South* elevation view visible on screen. We had to close the commercial project above because we are about to link it and Revit will not allow you have both projects (the host and the Link) open at the same time in the same Revit session.

3. On the Project Browser, right-click the *Revit Links* branch and choose: **New Link**.

> **NOTE:** This is simply an alternative to the method covered above. If you prefer, you can continue to use the Link Revit button on the Insert tab instead.

⇨ In the "Import/Link RVT" dialog, choose *07 Commercial.rvt* [*07 Commercial_M.rvt*].

⇨ For Positioning, choose: **Auto — Internal Origin to Internal Origin** and then click Open. In the "Nested Links Invisible" dialog that appears, click Close.

> **BIM Manager Note:** The warning simply informs us that the file has links of its own that will not carry through to the current host. If we wanted them to, we could edit the link type in the commercial project to be Attachment rather than Overlay. This is done in the Manage Links dialog. Overlaid reference files are direct links. Attachments can nest several levels deep.

4. On the Collaborate tab, click the Copy/Monitor button and then choose the:
Select Link option from the pop-up (see item 1 in Figure 7.47).

⇨ Select the Commercial project link instance onscreen.

296 | Chapter 7

The Copy/Monitor tab will appear on the ribbon.

5. On the Copy/Monitor tab of the ribbon, click the Copy button (item 2).

⇨ On the Options Bar, click the Multiple check box (item 3).

⇨ Select Levels 1 through 4 and "Roof" in the linked file. (Use the CTRL key or a crossing selection) (item 4).

6. On the Options Bar, click the Finish button(item 5).

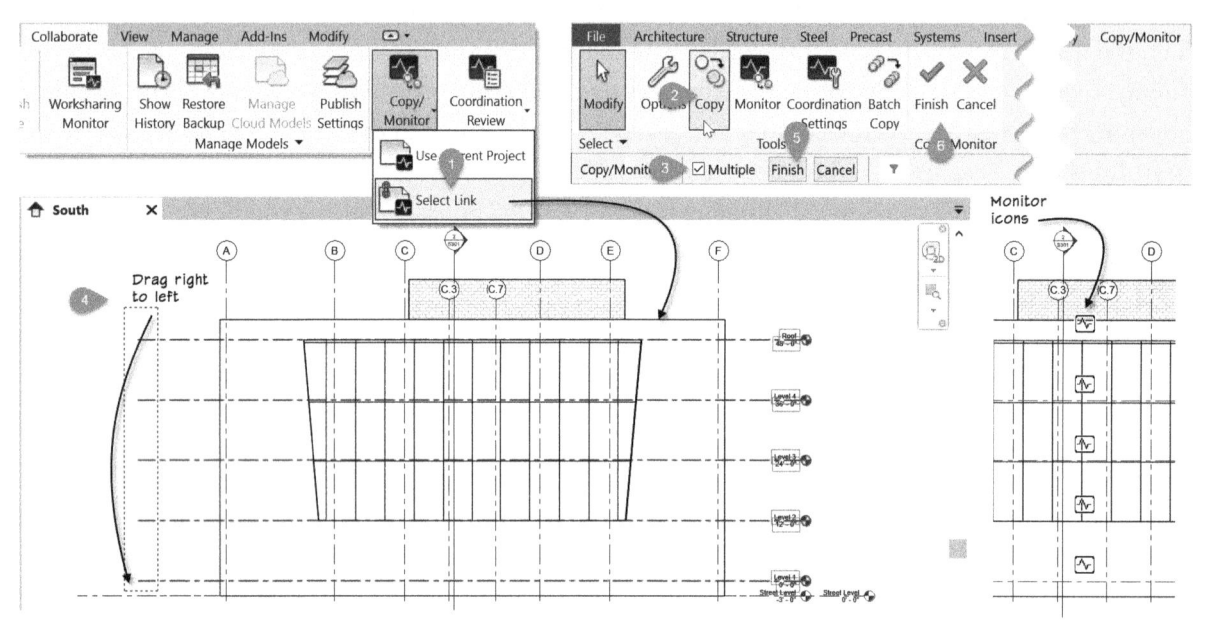

FIGURE 7.47 *Use Copy/Monitor to copy the levels*

Be sure to click the Finish button on the Options Bar, not the one on the ribbon. This finishes selection. The one on the ribbon finishes the command. A small monitor icon will appear next to each monitored item. If a level is changed in the main *Commercial* project, the structural engineer can re-enter the Copy/Monitor mode and use the Coordination tool on the Ribbon to synchronize the changes.

7. Return to the Copy/Monitor tab of the ribbon and then click the Finish button. This finishes the Copy/Monitor mode (item 6).

CREATE STRUCTURAL PLANS

We now have a set of levels in the structural file that match (and are monitoring) the ones in the commercial file. But we have no floor plans.

1. On the View tab, click the Plan Views button. From the pop-up that appears, choose: **Structural Plan**.

⇨ In the dialog that appears, select all the levels except the Street Level and then click OK.

2. On the Project Browser, expand *Structural Plans*, select *Level 1*, hold down the SHIFT key and then select *Roof*.

This will select all the structural plan views.

⇨ Right-click the selected plans and choose: **Apply View Template**.

⇨ Select **Structural Framing Plan** and then click OK.

Having assigned this view template, we now see only structural components. This will make selecting the remaining items for copy/monitor much easier.

• The Aubin Academy •

COPY/MONITOR GRIDS, WALLS AND COLUMNS

Now that we have copied the levels and set up framing plans, we are ready to copy and monitor the remaining structural items.

1. On the Project Browser, double-click to open the *Level 2* structural plan view. If necessary, zoom to fit (type ZF).
2. Use the Copy/Monitor steps above (with the multiple option) to copy all the grids, all the structural (steel) columns and the four core walls.

> **TIP:** Make a crossing window selection, click the small Filter icon on the Options Bar, deselect Columns (Architectural) and Floors and then click OK.

3. Click the Finish button on the Options Bar.
4. On the Copy/Monitor tab of the ribbon click the Finish button.

INSERT A GROUP

To complete our structural model, we'll import the group we created from the framing members above.

1. Return to the *South* elevation view tab.
2. Use Temporary Hide/Isolate to hide the linked model.
3. On the Insert tab, click the Load as Group button.
   - In the "Load File as Group" dialog, browse to the *Chapter07* folder.
   - Select the *Structure.rvt* file and then click Open. (If a message regarding duplicate Types appears, click OK.)

After a short pause, you will note that the *Structure* group is now available on the Project Browser beneath the *Model Groups* branch.

4. On the Project Browser, beneath the *Model Groups* branch, right-click *Structure* and choose: **Create Instance**.
   - To insert it in the correct location, simply type: **0** (zero) and then press ENTER.
   - On the Edit Pasted panel of the ribbon, click the Finish button.
5. On the Project Browser, double-click to open the *Longitudinal* section view.
6. Select the group instance on screen, and then on the ribbon, click the Ungroup button.

We will leave the nested Typical Framing groups alone. So only click Ungroup once. This way, we can still benefit from their being grouped should we need to edit the framing later.

7. Save and close the Structural model.

USING RELOAD FROM TO SWAP A LINK WITH ANOTHER FILE

Now that we have completed the setup of our structural model, we are ready to load it into our main *Commercial* project. Since we already have a link to the *Structural* group created above, the process will involve simply swapping the file referenced by this link. This can be done in the "Manage Links" dialog or on the Project Browser > Revit Links branch.

1. Re-open the *07 Commercial.rvt* [*07 Commercial_M.rvt*] file.
2. On the Insert tab, click the Manage Links button.

298 | Chapter 7

⇨ In the "Manage Links" dialog, be sure that the Revit tab is active.

⇨ Click on the Structure entry at the left. (Click on the name so that row highlights).

⇨ Click the "Reload From" button at the bottom (see Figure 7.48).

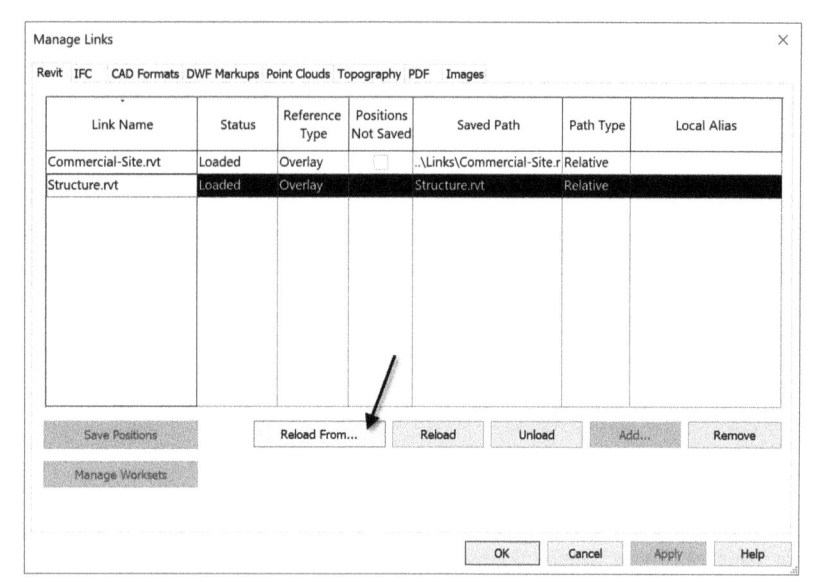

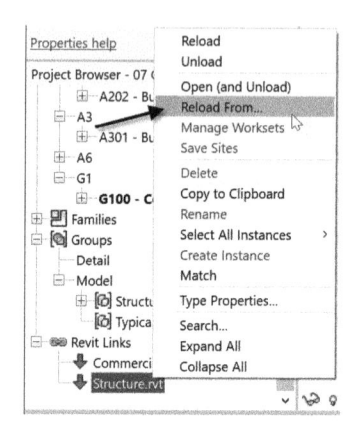

FIGURE 7.48 *The Manage Links dialog—Reload a link from an alternate file and/or location*

3. Select *07 Commercial-Structure.rvt* [*07 Commercial-Structure_M.rvt*] and then click Open.

4. Click OK to close the "Manage Links" dialog.

Alternatively, you can expand the *Revit Links* branch on the Project Browser. Right-click the *Structure* file and choose: Reload From. Browse to the file (see the right side of the figure).

In this example, we used "Reload From" because we wanted to point the linked file to a different project file than the one originally used. In normal circumstances, you will want to use the Reload button that simply loads the latest saved changes from the same RVT file. If you no longer want the Linked file, you can use the Remove button.

> **BIM MANAGER NOTE:** If you try to open a project that is actively linked by the currently open project, Revit will display a warning indicating that the linked file must first be unloaded before it can be opened. In other words, you cannot have both projects open at the same time in the same Revit session. This limitation does not prevent two different users from working simultaneously in each of the projects since each team member will be working on a different computer system. However, if both users are actively changing their respective models, you should save frequently and periodically use the "Manage Links" dialog (or Revit Links branch) to reload the linked project(s).

The best place to see the results of the work we have done here is in one of the section views. Open a section view and select the linked structural file. (Use the TAB key if necessary.) You will see it highlight on screen and be able to clearly see the elements that have been moved and copied to this linked file in comparison to those that remain in the host commercial project.

If you should ever wish to "turn off" a linked file, you can unload it. Do this in the "Manage Links" dialog. When a linked RVT file is unloaded it will not be visible in any view. At a later point in time it can be reloaded and therefore made visible again. Unloading it also has the benefit of removing the data from the computer's memory, which reduces the burden on the computer's resources. If you wish to try it out, follow these steps:

5. On the Insert tab (or the Manage tab), click the Manage Links button.

⇨ Click the Revit tab, select the *07 Commercial-Structure* [*07 Commercial-*

Structure_M] file, and then click the Unload button.

> **NOTE:** Revit will warn you that this cannot be undone. While this is true, all it really means is that the undo command will not work with this action; you can always return to the Manage Links dialog and reload it.

⇨ When asked to confirm, click Yes and then click OK.

> **TIP:** Most functions available in the Manage Links dialog can also be found on the right-click menus on the *Revit Links* branch of the Project Browser.

In the next chapter, we will continue to refine the *Commercial* project and its linked files. For now, however, our work with groups and links in this chapter is complete.

6. Save and close all project files.

SUMMARY

- ☑ Groups offer a powerful means to create and manage typical design conditions and keep all instances of them coordinated throughout the project.

- ☑ Any selection of objects can be grouped. Model element and annotation elements however cannot occupy the same group.

- ☑ When creating a group from a selection of model elements and attached annotation elements (such as tags) the annotation becomes a separate attached detail group.

- ☑ Attached detail groups contain annotation that is linked to the model elements in the corresponding model group.

- ☑ The insertion point of a group can be adjusted by dragging the control on screen. Subsequent instances of the group will insert relative to this location.

- ☑ When you edit any instance of a group, the changes are applied to all instances.

- ☑ Elements can be excluded from individual instances of groups making a unique condition. Changes to the groups still apply to the other elements in the group.

- ☑ Groups can contain other groups creating so-called "nested" groups.

- ☑ Groups can be saved to files thereby becoming independent Revit projects.

- ☑ Groups can be converted to linked Revit projects.

- ☑ A separate Revit project can be linked to your current project. If the external project changes, the link can be updated to reflect the changes.

- ☑ Linked projects can be converted to groups.

- ☑ You can link AutoCAD or Microstation files to Revit projects.

- ☑ Contour lines in linked CAD files can be used to create points in a Revit toposurface element.

- ☑ Maintain proper positioning of linked projects using shared coordinates.

- ☑ Internal Origin, Project Base points and Survey points give onscreen icons for easy understanding of project coordinates.

- ☑ Use Copy/Monitor to copy certain kinds of elements from a linked file and keep the copies coordinated with the original linked file.

- ☑ You can swap instances of groups and links with other groups or links respectively.

CHAPTER 8
Vertical Circulation

INTRODUCTION

In this chapter, we will look at Stairs, Railings, and Ramps. We will explore these elements in both of our projects. The residential project contains existing stairs on the interior and an existing exterior stair at the front entrance. The core of the commercial building will include stairs, railings, and elevators. The exterior entrance plaza leading up to the commercial building calls for stairs, a ramp, and railings.

OBJECTIVES

We will add stairs for the existing conditions of the residential project and lay out the core for the commercial project. Our exploration will include coverage of the stairs, railings, ramps, and elevators. After completing this chapter, you will know how to do the following:

- Add and modify stairs
- Add and modify railings
- Add and modify floors and shafts
- Add and modify ramps
- Add elevators

STAIRS AND RAILINGS

Stairs (like walls) are system families. This means that stair families are predefined in the software and are therefore part of the original template from which our project was built. There are three families representing a few common stair forms: Precast, Monolithic, and Assembled. Stair families include a couple basic types each to get us started. If we want to use a stair type that is not included in the original template, either we have to create a duplicate of one of the existing types within the project, or we have to import a type from another project (Transfer Project Standards or Copy and Paste can be used for this purpose). Stairs, like most Revit elements, have both instance and type parameters. Type parameters include riser and tread relationships, stringer settings, and basic display settings. Width and height parameters and clearances belong directly to the stair object (instance parameters). With the Assembled stair family, each major part of the stair is created from its own parametric system family. We can manipulate these parts using the type dialogs and if necessary, we can convert any portion of a component-based stair to a sketch-based element if further customization is required. Railings are separate elements but the stair element will create railings by default. Railings can also be edited or added independently later. For situations where the railing is not required, we simply delete the auto-created one after we build the stair.

OPEN A PROJECT

The lessons that follow require the dataset files included for download with this book. Refer to the "Download the Book Dataset" topic on page xi in the Preface for instructions on downloading and installing the book's dataset files if you still need to do so.

1. Launch Autodesk® Revit®.
2. If you are on the Home screen, you can click the Open button beneath Models. Otherwise, from the File menu, choose **Open > Project**. In the "Open" dialog box, browse to the *Chapter08* folder.

⇨ Double-click *08 Residential.rvt* if you wish to work in Imperial units.

⇨ Double-click *08 Residential_M.rvt* if you wish to work in Metric units.

You can also select it and then click the Open button.

ADD A STAIR TO THE RESIDENTIAL PLAN

This is the residential project that was begun in Chapter 4. We added some footings to it in Chapter 6, and the second floor existing conditions have also been laid out for you. You can find an additional exercise for the layout of the second floor in the Appendix (available as a PDF). (Feel free to complete that exercise first before continuing if you have not completed it already). In Chapter 4, you may recall that we completed the existing conditions on the first floor without adding any stairs. We will add stairs now to the residential project in a few locations.

1. On the Project Browser, double-click to open the *First Floor* plan view.

We'll start with a very simple Stair—the existing front entrance stairs.

2. Right-click and choose: **Zoom In Region** (or press ZR).

⇨ Click and drag a region around the front door at the bottom of the plan (see Figure 8.1).

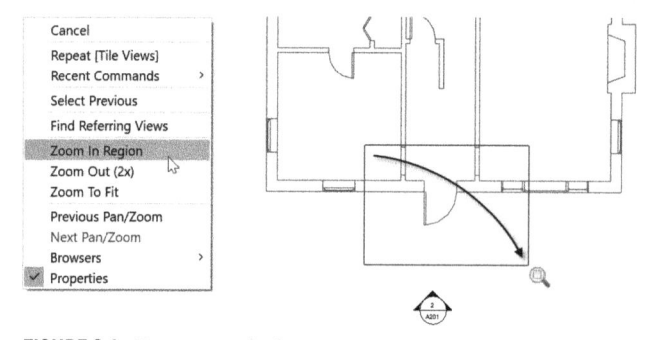

FIGURE 8.1 *Zoom in on the front entrance*

3. On the Architecture tab, on the Circulation panel, click the Stair button.

The view window will gray out and the Modify | Create Stair tab will appear on the ribbon.

Stairs are made of a collection of components. These include: Runs (which contain the treads and risers), Supports, and Landings. Stairs will always have at least one Run, but Supports and Landings are not required. There are three component-based stair families: Assembled Stair, Cast-In-Place Stair, and Precast Stair. The choice of family determines many of the settings for each component, however, like most families, we can customize these by adding new types. Each family includes a default type with settings appropriate to get you started (see Figure 8.2). (The metric template includes a few additional types for the Assembled Stair).

4. From the Type Selector, choose the: **Cast-In-Place Stair:Monolithic Stair** type.

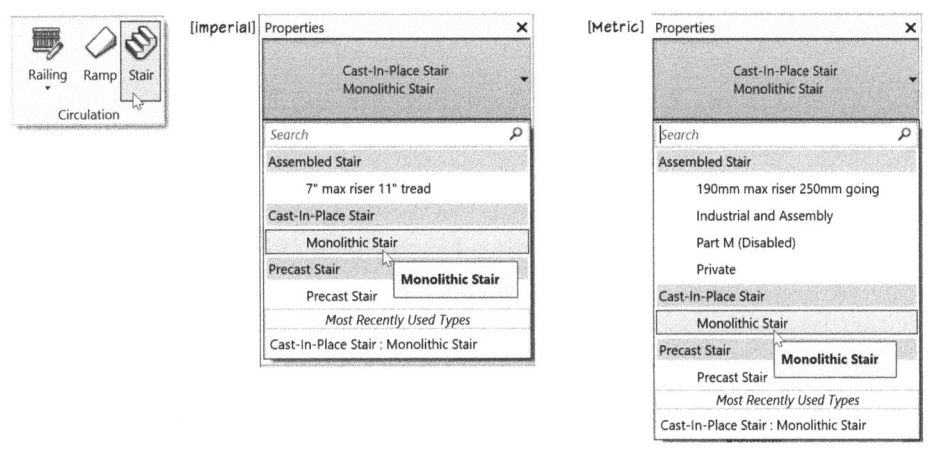

FIGURE 8.2 *Component-based stairs have three system families available from the Type Selector*

On the ribbon, we have Run, Landing, and Support tools. Next to these we have several predefined stair shapes like straight run, spiral, and winders. Also, if you look at the Options Bar, there are settings for: Location Line, Offset, Actual Run Width and Automatic Landing.

⇨ On the Modify | Create Stair tab, let's stick with the Run tool and Straight run shape options (both defaults).

⇨ On the Options Bar, set the "Actual Run Width" to: **4'-0"** [**1200**] and accept the other defaults (see Figure 8.3).

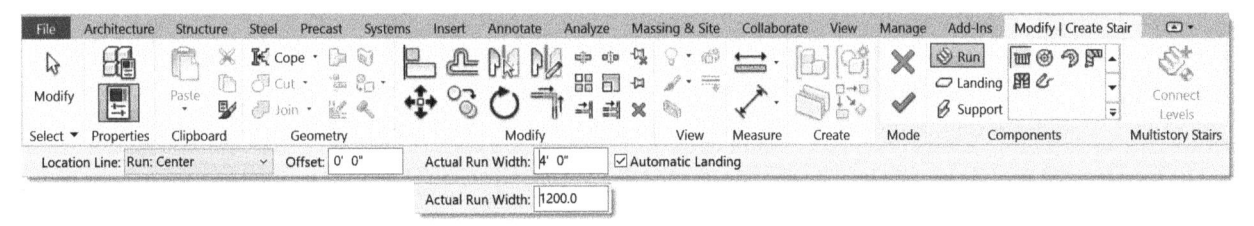

FIGURE 8.3 *Configure the options for the stair*

5. On the Properties palette, beneath the "Constraints" grouping, for the "Base Level" choose: **Site**, and for the "Top Level" choose: **First Floor**.

6. Beneath the "Dimensions" grouping, set the "Desired Number of Risers" to: **6**.

⇨ Beneath the "Phasing" grouping, from the "Phase Created" list, choose: **Existing** (see Figure 8.4).

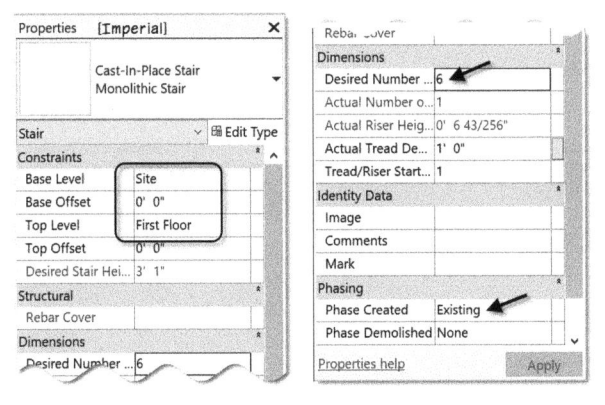

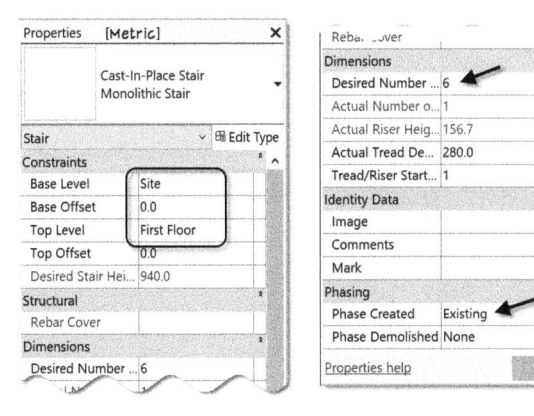

FIGURE 8.4 *Configure the stair properties*

7. Move your pointer near the middle of the front door.

• Revit Essentials for Architecture •

304 | Chapter 8

⇨ Click the mouse to set the first point of the Stair run (see the left side of Figure 8.5).

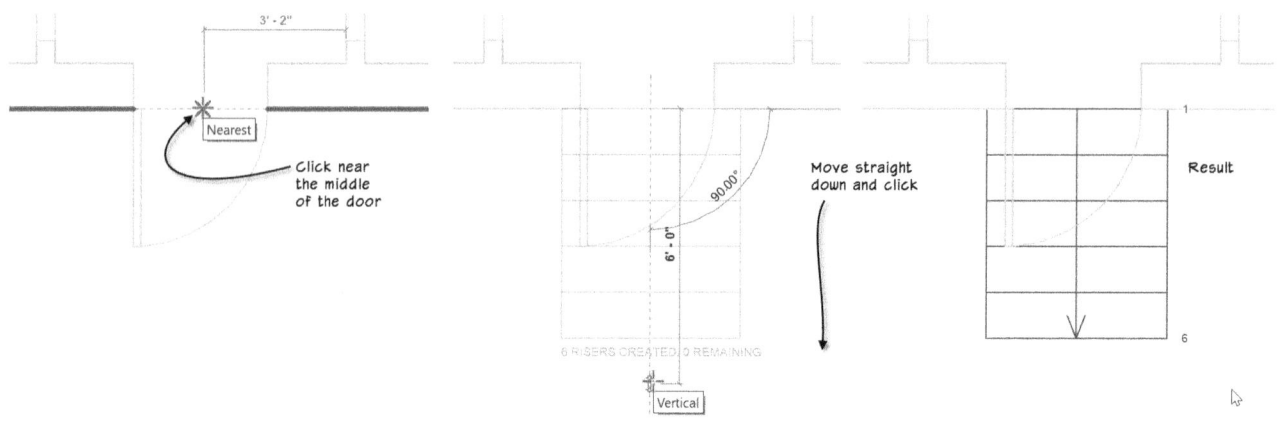

FIGURE 8.5 *Create a straight run of stairs with two clicks*

As you drag the mouse (after the first pick) a note in gray text will appear indicating how many risers you have placed. If you click again before you use up all the risers, you create a landing. In this case, we only have 6 risers and want a straight run, so we will click only one more point.

⇨ Move the pointer straight down and when the number of risers reads "0 Remaining" click the second point (see the middle of Figure 8.5).

The stair run will appear with a number at each end (see the right side of Figure 8.5). When you create the stair, the first point of the run is at the bottom of the run (riser 1 in the figure) and the last point you click is at the top (riser 6 in the figure). So, we will need to flip this stair, but we'll take care of that below. Let's check the railing settings first. When you create a stair, Revit automatically adds a railing, which is a separate element. Most stairs require railings, so Revit adds them automatically to save you time. Use the railing tool (on the ribbon) to choose the railing type you wish it to add, or if you prefer, choose "None" to instruct Revit not to add a railing. If you forget to use this tool to choose a railing, you can always select the railing(s) in the model window and edit or delete them later.

8. On the Tools panel of the ribbon, click the Railing button.

⇨ In the "Railings" dialog, choose: **Handrail – Rectangular [900mm]** accept the default position of Treads and then click OK.

9. On the ribbon, click the Finish Edit Mode button (large green checkmark).

10. On the Project Browser, double-click to open the *East* elevation view.

As we noted above, the stair is oriented the wrong way (see the left side of Figure 8.6). This is easy to fix.

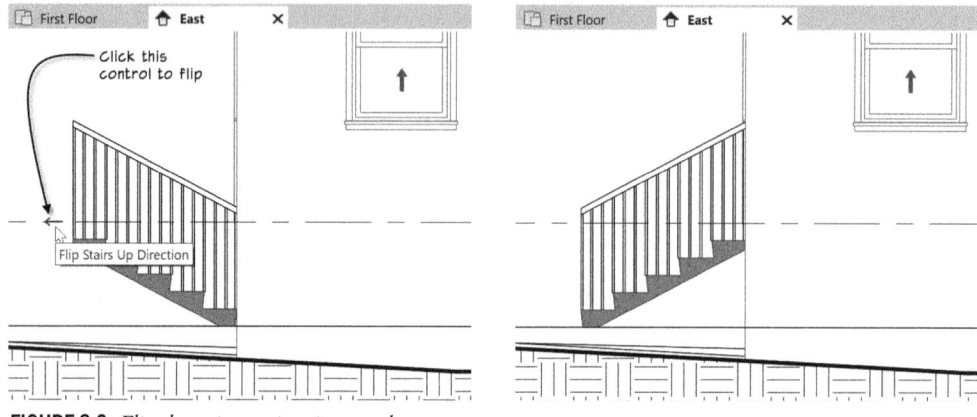

FIGURE 8.6 *Flip the stair to orient it properly*

11. Select the Stair.

• The Aubin Academy •

⇨   Click the small flip control at the top (left) of the Stair (see the right side of Figure 8.6).

You can view it in other views as well, to see that it was created properly. Try any section, elevation, or 3D view for this.

PHASING THE RAILINGS

When you create a stair, railings are created as well. However, even though we assigned the stair to the Existing phase, the railings came in at New Construction. In the future, if you remember to change the phase of the view before you sketch the stair you can prevent this. In this case, we will simply change the phase of the railings.

1.   If not already open, on the Project Browser, double-click to open the *First Floor* plan view.
2.   Select both railings (CTRL click is easiest in this case).
⇨   On the Properties palette, change the Phase Created to: **Existing**.

The railings should now display similarly to the stairs and other geometry in the plan view.

MODIFY A TOPOSURFACE

If you study the stair in an elevation view such as the *East* elevation you will see that the stair does not actually sit on the grade. It appears to "float." We could edit the stair and adjust it accordingly (using Base and Top Offsets), but upon further consideration, it is typically not desirable to have the terrain slope toward the building structure. Therefore, a better approach in this situation would be to adjust the Toposurface to provide better grading.

1.   On the Project Browser, double-click to open the *East* elevation view (see the right side of Figure 8.6 above).
⇨   On the View tab (or the QAT), click the Close Inactive Views button.
⇨   On the Project Browser, double-click to open the *Site* plan view.
⇨   On the View tab, click the Tile Views button (or press WT).
2.   In the *Site* view, select the Topography: Surface element.
⇨   On the Modify | Topography tab, click the Edit Surface button.

If you receive a warning about the possibility of points not being visible due to the current view's clipping, you can ignore it as it will not affect the edits that you need to make.

3.   On the Tools panel, click the Place Point tool.
⇨   On the Options Bar, type: **-3'-1"** [**-940**] (negative numbers) in the Elevation field.
⇨   Snap a point to each of the lower corners of the building and to the two lower corners of the stair.
⇨   Change the Elevation to: **-2'-8"** [**-800**] and then snap two more points at the top of the stairs (see Figure 8.7).

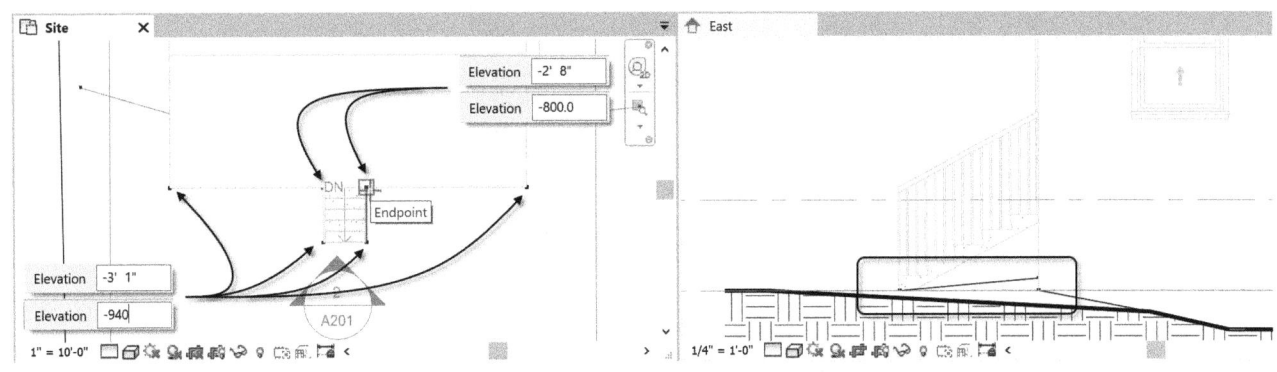

FIGURE 8.7 *Add points along the front of the house and stairs*

• Revit Essentials for Architecture •

4. On the ribbon, click the Finish Surface button (large green checkmark).

Check the results in the *East* elevation view. Zoom in again if necessary. Notice that the stair is now touching the ground instead of floating in space and the terrain now has positive drainage at the front of the house.

5. Save the project.

> **CREATE A GRADED REGION INSTEAD**
>
> In this project, we are still modeling existing construction, so the procedure covered here is appropriate since it is likely that the topography was properly graded in the existing conditions. However, if you wish, you can treat the grading as a new improvement, rather than an existing condition and use the Graded Region tool in this situation instead. The Graded Region tool works with the project's phases by "demolishing" the original toposurface and then creating a new one assigned to the current phase in its place. For this to work properly, your existing toposurface must be assigned to the previous phase. When you edit the grading of the new topography element, Revit is then able to calculate cut and fill volumes in your project.
>
> If you wish to try this, undo the edited points. The toposurface element is already assigned to the Existing phase in the dataset. Click on the Massing & Site tab of the ribbon and then click the Graded Region tool. The "Edit Graded Region" dialog will appear, offering you two options. The first option is useful in situations like this where there is a small amount of new grading. You will get an exact copy of the topography, which you can then edit. The second option is useful when you are doing major site work. In that case, only the perimeter is copied and you re-grade the entire site. Choose the first option and then follow the same steps outlined above in the "Modify a Toposurface" topic on page 305. When you finish the surface, you will have two topography elements: the existing one and a new one with the new grading assigned to the New Construction phase.
>
> To see the cut and fill calculations, select the toposurface element and view its properties. The cut, fill, and Net cut/fill will be listed on the "Other" grouping on the Properties palette. You can also create a Schedule for topography elements and include the cut and fill fields there.

COPY AND DEMOLISH A STAIR

At the back door of the existing house is another stair like the one in the front. However, this one will be demolished to make way for the new addition. Feel free to create a new stair using the procedure covered above. However, another way to create this stair is to copy, rotate, and modify it from the one we just created at the front.

1. On the Project Browser, double-click to open the *First Floor* plan view.
   ⇨ Select the stair.
2. On the Modify tab, click the Copy tool (or press CO).
   ⇨ Click any start point and then click to place the copy near the back of the house within the space of the new addition (this is in the upper portion of the plan; use an approximate location for now).

   Notice that the railings will also be copied automatically.
3. With the stair still selected, click the flip control.
4. Move the stair so that it touches the house centered on the existing back door (see Figure 8.8).

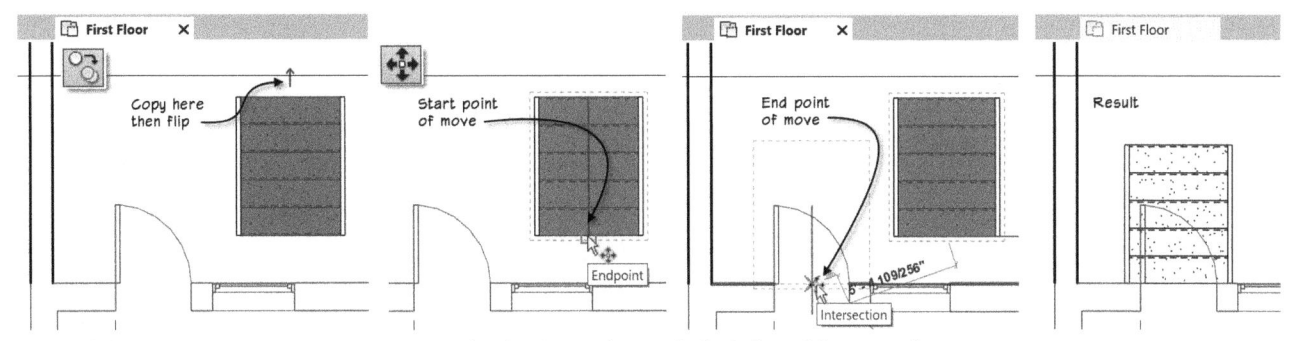

FIGURE 8.8 *Copy, flip, and then move the stair (and railings) into place at the back door of the existing house*

⇨ Click the Modify tool on the ribbon or press the ESC key twice.

You can use other methods to achieve the same result. For example, we could have used object snaps when copying the stair to snap it directly into the correct place, and then use the flip control as we did above to flip the stair instead of rotating it. You can also do the rotation first with the "Copy" option on the Options Bar to copy and rotate it in one step in the original location, and then move the copy to the new location with object snaps. The exact procedure you follow is not important if you arrive at the desired result.

5. Double-click the blue vertical section head (cutting vertically through the new addition) or open the *Transverse* section view from the Project Browser.

You will note, similarly to above, that the stair floats above the terrain at the back of the existing house. This is because the grade slopes from the front of the house down toward the back. So, by the time we reach the back of the house, the stair requires a few additional risers.

6. In the Transverse section view, on the View Control bar, click the Visual Style pop-up and choose: Wireframe (see the left side of Figure 8.9).

7. On the Modify tab, on the Measure panel, click the Measure Between Two References tool.

⇨ Snap to the bottom corner of the stair for the first point.

⇨ Click on the terrain directly below the stair for the second point (see the right side of Figure 8.9).

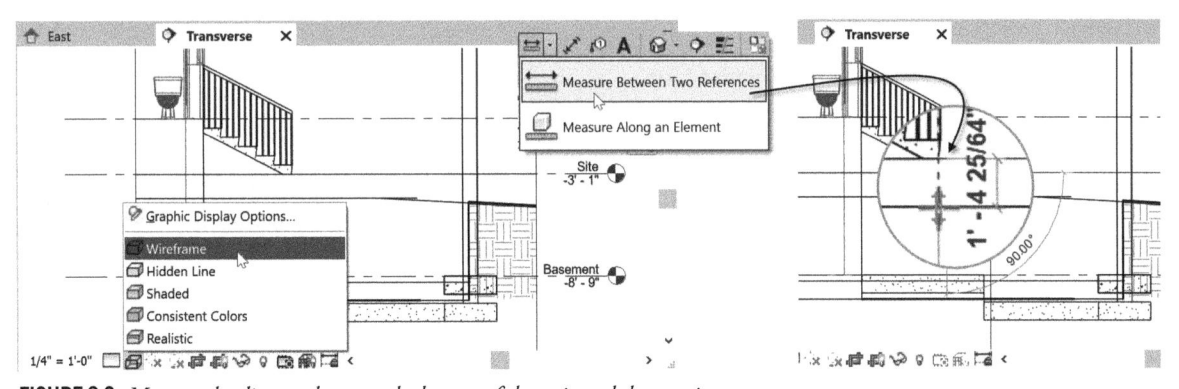

FIGURE 8.9 *Measure the distance between the bottom of the stair and the terrain*

The distance rounded off should be about: 1'-4" [410]. We will use this value to adjust the stair height.

⇨ Click the Modify tool or press the ESC key twice to cancel the measure tool.

8. Remaining in the section view, select the stair.

⇨ On the Properties palette, In the Base Offset field, type: **-1'-4"** [**-410**] and then apply.

A warning will appear. We can click OK to dismiss this. It is informing us that our stair no longer has enough risers to reach the desired top level. We will fix this next (see Figure 8.10).

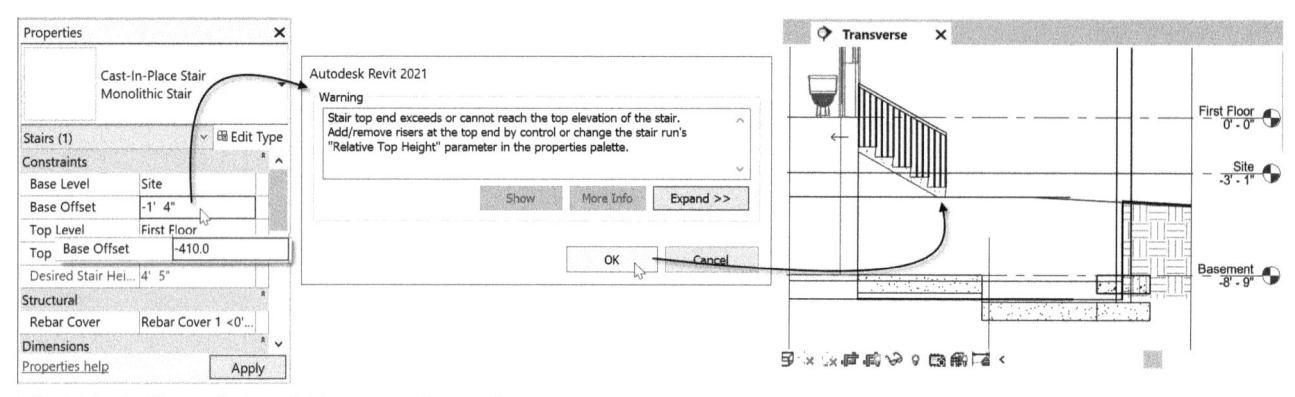

FIGURE 8.10 *Change the Base Offset to move the stair down*

9. On the Modify | Stairs tab, click the Edit Stairs button.

⇨ Select the stair run. Drag the small round control at the top of the stair to the left to add two risers (see the left side of Figure 8.11).

10. Move the stair run back to the face of the wall. You can use the Move or Align tools, or edit the temporary dimension (see the middle of Figure 8.11).

⇨ When you click the Finish Edit Mode button (large green checkmark) the railings will adjust to the edited stair (see the right side of Figure 8.11).

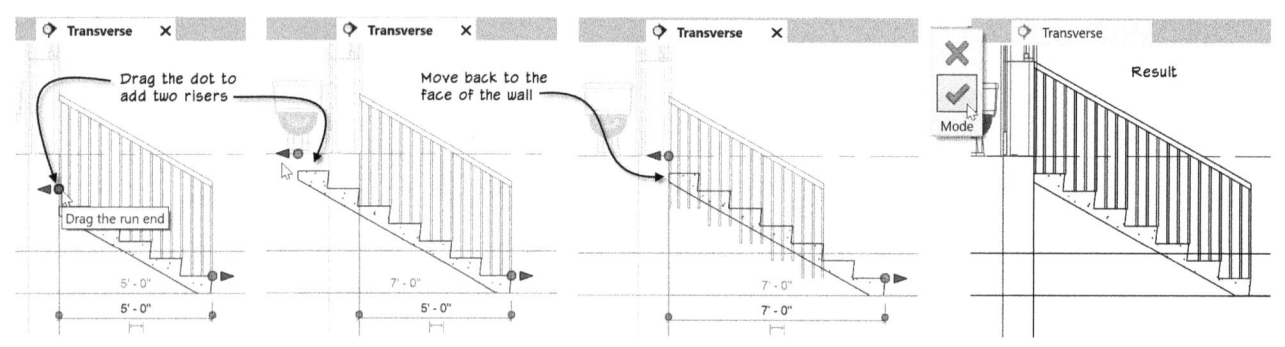

FIGURE 8.11 *Add two new risers to the stair*

The section view is still set to wireframe.

⇨ You can reset the section view back to: **Hidden Line**.

The stair is now configured properly, but when you select it or its railings, you will notice that its phase is New Construction. When you create a new element, either using a creation tool or copying as we did here, the new item takes on the phase of the view you are working in. So, we need to adjust this and then we also want to demolish it.

11. In the *First Floor* plan view, using the CTRL key select both railings and the stair.

⇨ On the Properties palette, change the Phase Created to: **Existing**.

12. On the Modify tab, on the Geometry panel, click the Demolish tool (icon looks like a hammer).

⇨ Click on the stair and each of the railings to mark them as demolished in the current phase. (You can do this in any view.)

> **NOTE:** As an alternative, you can also select the stair and railings, edit their Properties, and then change the "Phase Demolished" setting to: **New Construction**.

⇨ Click the Modify tool or press the ESC key twice.

> **NOTE:** Be sure that the "Phase Created" of the stair and railings is also set to Existing, otherwise, when you demolish them, they will become "Temporary" construction. In Revit, temporary construction are elements that are created and demolished in the same phase.

The stair and railings will turn dashed to indicate that they are to be demolished.

CREATE AN EXISTING CONDITIONS VIEW

The next stair that we will build is the main stair in the existing house. Before we do, let's explore a technique to make working with phases a bit simpler. In Chapter 4, we temporarily changed the current Phase of the *First Floor* plan view (named *Level 1* in that chapter) to "Existing" to add all of the existing construction. At the end of the lesson, we set the Phase back to "New Construction." We could repeat that process here as well. As an alternative approach, it is easier to maintain two first floor plan views—one set permanently to the Existing phase, and the other set to the New Construction phase. In this way, you can simply open the view for the phase in which you wish to work. This will prevent much of the manual phase assignments like we have done on the stairs so far.

1. On the Project Browser, right-click the *First Floor* plan view and choose: **Duplicate View > Duplicate**.

    There are three duplicate options on the submenu, make sure you are choosing the first one: Duplicate.

    ⇨ Right-click the new *First Floor Copy 1* view and choose: **Rename** (you can also select it on the Browser and then press F2).

    ⇨ For the new Name type: **First Floor Existing Conditions** and then click OK.

    The *First Floor Existing Conditions* view should have opened automatically (it should be bold on the Project Browser). If it did not, double-click to open it now.

    Make sure there is nothing selected. The Type Selector on the Properties palette should read "Floor Plan."

2. On the Properties palette, scroll down and from the Phase list choose: **Existing**.

This will set the current phase of the copied view to: Existing. This means that any elements we add while working in this view will be assigned to the Existing construction phase automatically. Creating this view is not required, but sometimes it is easier than remembering to set the Phase parameter of each object we create or changing the Phase of the view back and forth. With Existing set as the current Phase, notice that the rear stair is no longer dashed. It is still set to be demolished (in the future), but since we are now viewing the plan as it looks during the Existing phase, these stairs are not yet demolished at this point in time. The walls of the addition have also disappeared. Again, during the Existing phase, those walls do not yet exist. Remember, as we saw in Chapter 4, when you set a view to a different phase, the relative definition of "Existing," "New" and "Demolished" shift accordingly. All the geometry in this view also turns bold, as now (the Existing phase), these items were new.

3. Double-click to open the *First Floor* plan view.

Notice that this view, still set to New Construction phase, continues to show all the new construction walls and shows them bold. The existing construction is still grayed out and the rear stair shows as demolished.

4. Switch back to the *First Floor Existing Conditions* plan view tab.

    ⇨ On the View tab, click the Tab Views button (or press TW) and then press the Close Inactive Views button.

5. Save the project.

310 | Chapter 8

CREATE A STRAIGHT INTERIOR STAIR

The existing interior stair is also a simple straight-run stair going from the first to the second floor. However, there are a few custom details on the first few treads and some railing treatments that will make the stair a bit more interesting. We will begin in like the other, but then customize it to add the required details.

Working in our newly created *First Floor Existing Conditions* plan view, Zoom and Pan to the middle of the existing house layout.

1. On the Architecture tab, on the Circulation panel, click the Stair tool.

It is always best to start with the type you want to use. For the last stair we used the monolithic family, this time we will use the Assembled Stair family. Where the monolithic family is a single element, the assembled stair is constructed from various components. These include supports, runs and landings.

2. On the Properties palette, from the Type Selector, choose: **7" max riser 11" tread** [**190mm max riser 250mm going**] (see item 1 in Figure 8.12).

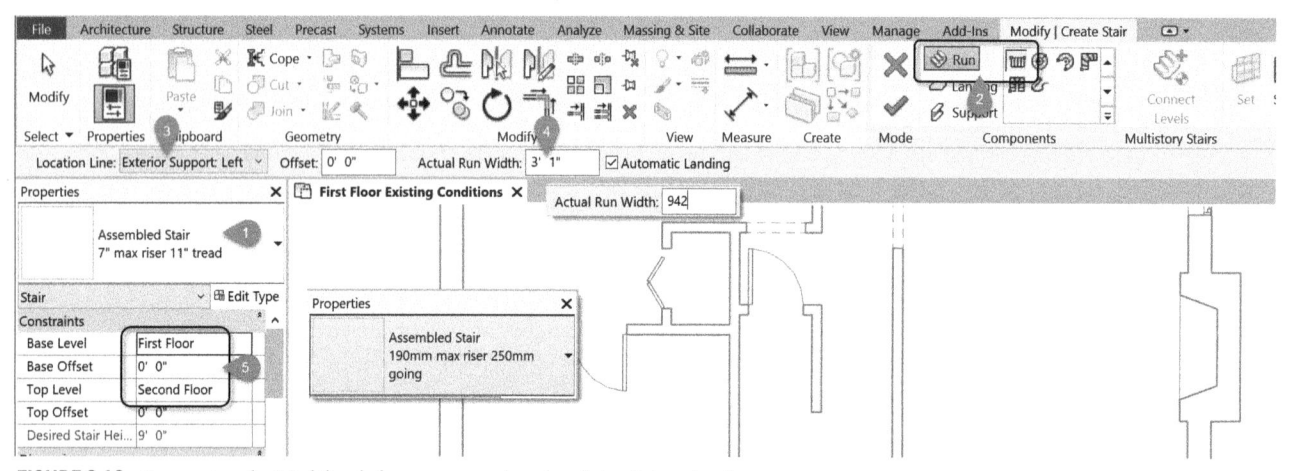

FIGURE 8.12 *Comparing the Modify tab for component-based and sketch-based stairs*

3. On the Modify | Create Stair tab, on the Components panel, verify that the Run tool is selected and that Straight icon is also selected (item 2).

⇨ On the Options Bar, for the Location Line, choose: **Exterior Support: Left** (item 3).

⇨ Set the Actual Run Width to: **3'-1"** [**942**] (item 4).

⇨ On the Properties palette, verify that the "Base Level" is set to: **First Floor** and the "Top Level" is: **Second Floor** (item 5).

The stair we are going to draw is in the middle of the plan above the house's front door. We will use the wall on the left of the front door to help us locate the stair.

4. Highlight the inside edge of the wall to left of the stair corridor. When the temporary dimension reads: 3'-6" [1200], click the first point of the stair run (see the left side of Figure 8.13).

⇨ Move the pointer straight up far enough to place all of the risers in a single run and then click again (see the right side of Figure 8.13).

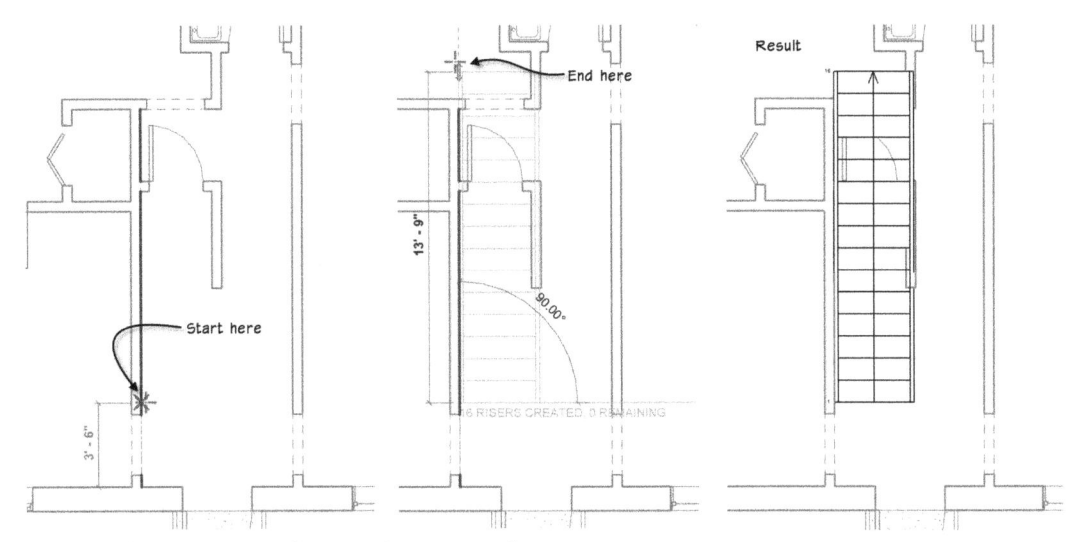

FIGURE 8.13 *Place the stair adjacent to the existing wall*

> **NOTE:** In the metric file, a warning will display stating that the Actual Run Width is less than the minimum. This warning can be safely ignored. Simply click anywhere onscreen to dismiss it.

As you can see, the stair is too long for the space. The parameters configured above were all "instance" parameters. Instance parameters apply directly to each individual object in the model. Take note of the settings in the Dimensions area. Here we have settings to control the size of the treads and risers. Notice that our stair currently has 16 [15] risers and a tread depth of: 11" [250]. Since the stairs existing in this house were built before current building code requirements were in place, we need smaller treads and taller risers than the defaults used here.

5. On the Properties palette, change the Actual Tread Depth value to: **8" [240]** and then click Apply.

    An error will appear stating: "The Actual Tread Depth of stair is less than the Minimum Tread Depth specified in the stair type."

Each stair type includes rules that determine the slope of the stair. These are usually based on local building codes. Therefore, we are seeing some warnings appear. We could simply edit the type and change the settings to make them less restrictive, but since this is a special case stair matching existing conditions, it will be better to make a duplicate type first. In this way, we preserve the existing type for use on other stairs while creating a variation suited to the stair we are currently creating. Fortunately, you will note that this error message has an OK button and does not force us to cancel or undo our changes. Therefore, we can ignore this warning for now and continue. We'll clear it up in the next sequence.

   ⇨ Click OK to dismiss this warning.

6. On the Manage tab, on the Inquiry panel, take note of the Warnings button.

When you dismiss warnings without taking any action to resolve them, they will remain in the project. On the Manage tab you can see when there are unresolved warnings whenever the Warnings button is available (see the top of Figure 8.14). In this case, when we perform the steps in the next topic, it will also have the effect of resolving the warning for us.

312 | Chapter 8

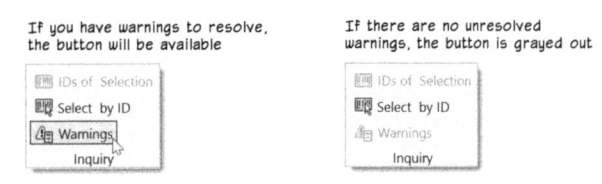

FIGURE 8.14 *Ignored warnings remain until resolved.*

> **BIM MANAGER NOTE:** It should be noted that while it is possible to ignore this and many other errors in Revit, you should always try to minimize the quantity of unresolved warnings. If you allow many warnings to pile up unresolved, it can begin to slow performance in your models. On the Manage tab, on the Inquiry tab, click the Warnings button to review any unresolved warnings. If you click it now, you will see the warning we just dismissed. In practice it is a good habit to check the "Warnings" dialog on a regular basis and do what you can to resolve them.

CREATE A NEW STAIR TYPE

In this sequence, we will create a new stair type and edit the parameters to help it conform to the existing conditions. This will involve applying less stringent tread and riser rules on our stair to allow for a steeper slope.

1. On the Properties palette, click the Edit Type button.
2. Click the Duplicate button (or press ALT + D).
   ⇨ In the "Name" dialog, type: **Existing House Stair** and then click OK (see the left side of Figure 8.15).

If you scroll through the list, you will see that there are many settings we can configure. Let's start by getting the slope of the stair within the range of our existing conditions. You have two ways to do this. You can use the stair calculator, or you can set the minimum tread depth and maximum riser height instead. If your building code establishes the slope based on a proportion of the risers to the treads, you can click the Edit button next to "Calculation Rules." For our purposes here, we will not use the stair calculator and instead will simply set the tread and riser proportion we need based on existing field conditions.

3. In the "Calculation Rules" grouping, for the "Maximum Riser Height" **12"** [**300**].
   ⇨ For "Minimum Tread Depth" type: **8"** [**200**] (for the metric file, change the Minimum Run Width to: **900** (see the right side of Figure 8.15).

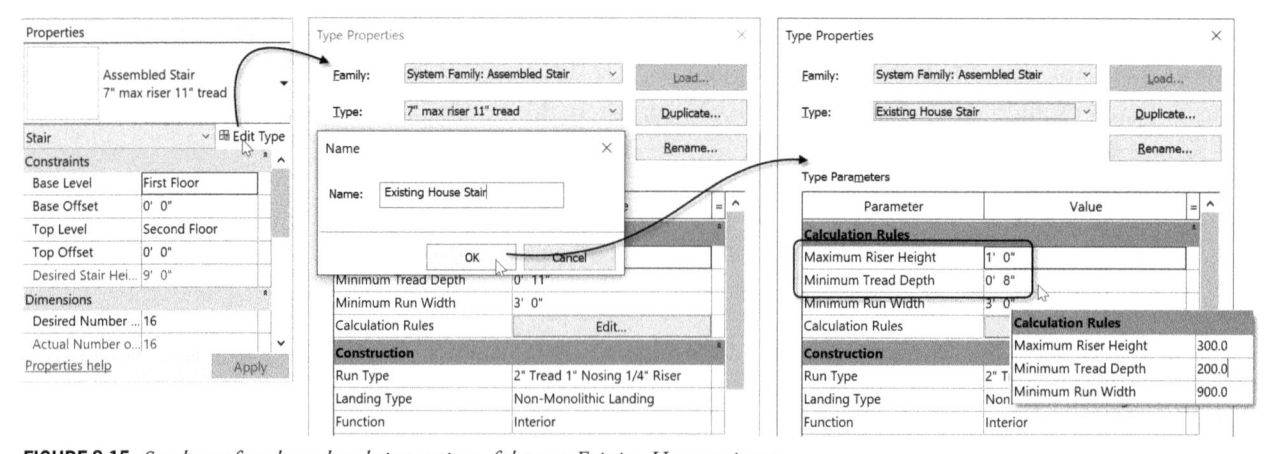

FIGURE 8.15 *Set the preferred tread and riser settings of the new Existing House stair type*

4. Click OK to accept the values.

You will not see any obvious result from this change. However, a change has occurred behind the scenes. The warning that we previously ignored is now resolved.

• The Aubin Academy •

On the Manage tab, on the Inquiry panel, notice that the Warnings button is now grayed out (see the bottom of Figure 8.14).

5. On the Properties palette, beneath the "Dimensions" grouping, set the Desired Number of Risers to: **14** and verify that the Actual Tread Depth value is: **8" [200]**.

We are close to having the stair we need now, but since the original stair we created had a different slope, the Actual Number of Risers is more than the Desired Number. You can also see this in the model canvas with a note that appears near the top of stair (see the left side of Figure 8.16). We can adjust the stair directly on screen with the control handle grips.

6. Click on the stair Run onscreen. (Make sure to select the Run and not the Supports).

⇨ Drag the round shape handle at the top straight down two treads (one in the metric file) (see Figure 8.16).

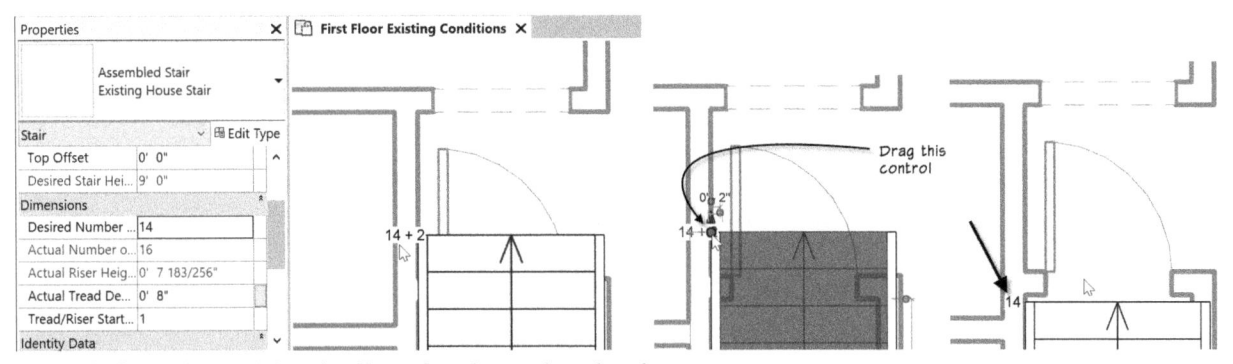

FIGURE 8.16 *Use the round shape handle to adjust the actual number of risers*

Notice that the indicator in canvas on the stair and in the Actual Number of Riser field on the Properties palette now read 14. Also notice that the stair now fits the available space.

7. On the ribbon, click the Finish Edit Mode button.

The stair object will appear in the space between the two walls in the center of the plan. Notice that a cut line appears automatically. Also, we get an arrow and label pointing up. We will add the stair going down to the basement later.

EDIT THE STAIR TYPE

When you look at the stair we created, it appears to be too wide; part of it overlaps the neighboring walls. This overlap are the supports of the stair. The Assembled Stair family contains one or more Run, Support and Landing components. Each component is controlled by its own family and type. This stair naturally has no landings, but as we can see, it does currently have a support on each side. We will need to make some adjustments to the stair type we created above to address how these supports behave.

1. Select the stair.

The filter drop down on Properties should read: **Stairs (1)**. (if it says Railings, try again).

⇨ On the Properties palette, click the Edit Type button.

2. Beneath the "Supports" grouping, for the Right Support, choose: Carriage (Open).

⇨ Repeat for the Left Support.

A Carriage (Open) support is notched in the shape of the treads and risers (saw tooth shape) and supports the treads from underneath. The Stringer (Closed) support occurs at the edges of the stair with the treads and risers spanning in between. A typical wooden stair would use a Carriage (Open) support, while a steel pan stair would typically use a Stringer (Closed) support. Illustrations of several of stringer settings are shown in Figure 8.17. As you can see on the right side of the figure, you can offset Carriage (Open) supports using the Right Lateral Offset and Left Lateral Offset parameters. You can also add one or more middle supports. These must be of the carriage type. Feel free to experiment with these settings if you like, but for our stair here, we do not need middle supports and we can leave the offsets at zero.

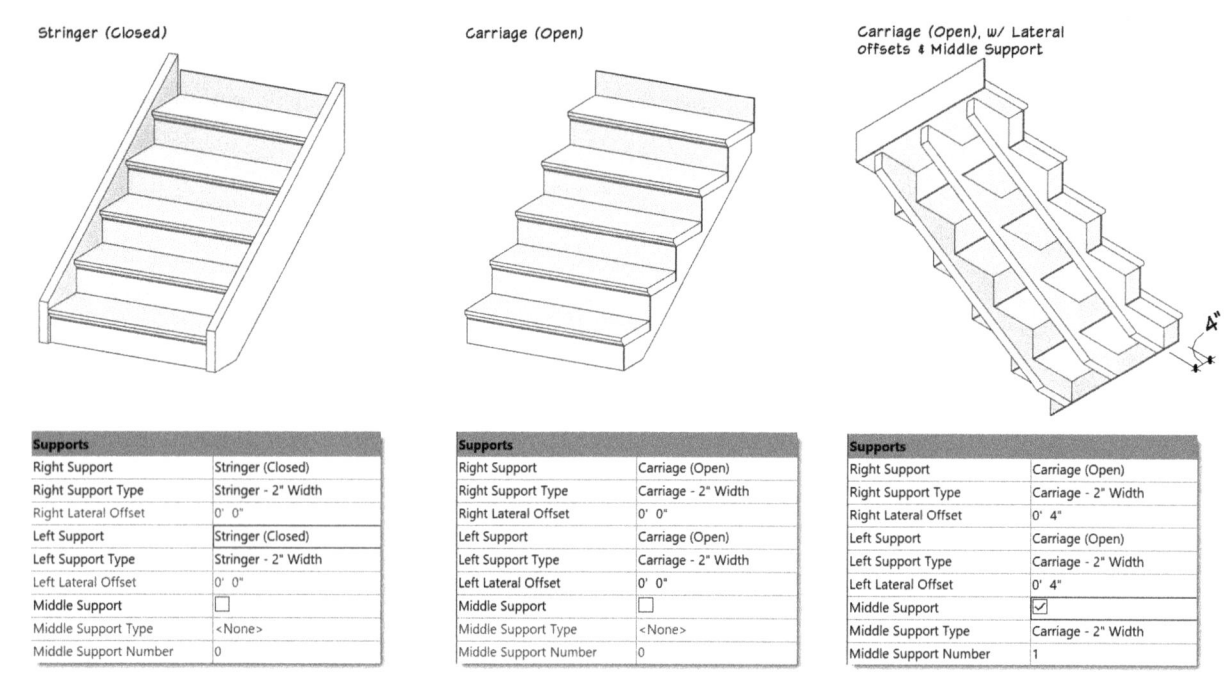

FIGURE 8.17 *Understanding support types*

Notice that when you choose a different type of support, it automatically changes the system family and type assigned to that support (Right Support Type and Left Support Type fields). Also if you want to edit the dimensions of the support material such as the height and thickness, you can click in either of the Right Support Type and Left Support Type fields and then click the small browser button to access the "Type Properties" dialog for that support type. In this case, we will leave those settings as they are.

3. Click OK to apply the changes and return to the model.

You will note that the stair has reduced in width and now fits within the walls better.

CREATE A SECTION VIEW

To help us with the next several steps, it will be useful to have a section through the stairs. You can create sections quickly with just two clicks anytime you want to get a better look at some portion of your model.

1. On the ribbon, click the View tab and then on the Create panel, click the Section tool (this tool is also on the QAT).
⇨ Create a section line running vertically through the stair. (Click from bottom to top.)
2. Deselect the Section Line (click away from it) and then double-click the Section Head to open the associated view (you can also right-click the section line and choose: **Go to View**).

The section shows both our stair and its railing beyond.

3. On the Project Browser, right-click the *Section 1* view and choose: **Rename**.
⇨ Call it: **Section at Existing Stair** and then click OK.
4. Open the section and tile the plan and section windows (type WT or use the tool on the View tab).

If you have other windows open, close all except the *Section at Existing Stair* and the *First Floor Existing Conditions* views and then tile again. If you built a graded region above, it will be showing in section. You can select it and then on the View Control Bar, click the Temporary Hide/Isolate pop-up and choose: **Hide Element**.

CREATE THE "DOWN" STAIR

In addition to the stair we have added here, the house also has an existing stair going down to the basement. The simplest way to create this one is with copy and paste.

1. Select the stair.
2. On the Modify | Stairs tab, on the Clipboard panel, click the Copy tool (or press CTRL + c).
    ⇨ On the Clipboard panel, click the Paste Aligned drop down button and then choose: **Aligned to Selected Levels**.
    ⇨ In the "Select Levels" dialog, choose: Basement and then click OK (see the left side of Figure 8.18).

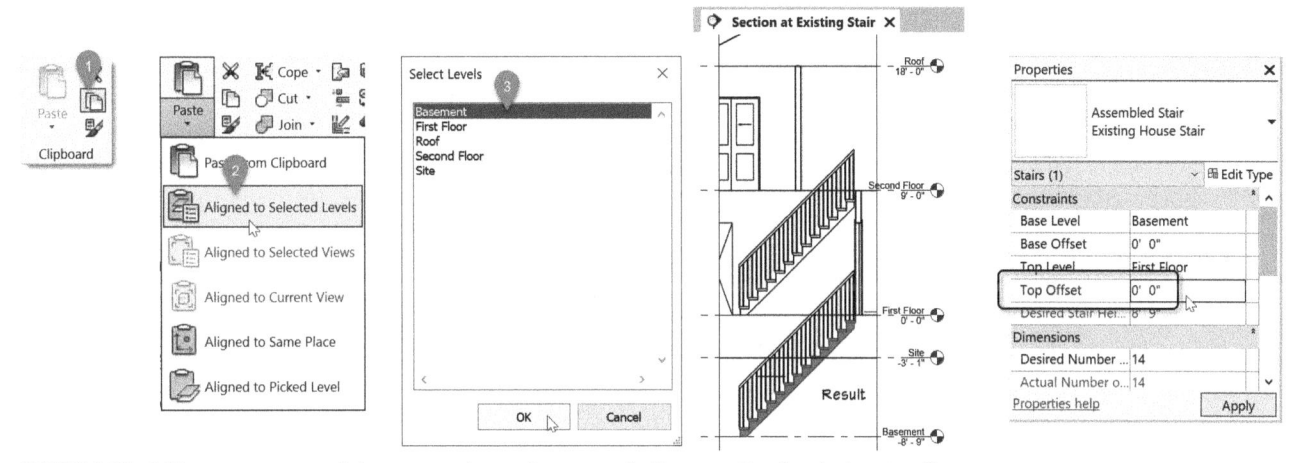

FIGURE 8.18 *Add a section view and then copy and paste the stair to the Basement Level and adjust its offset properties*

With the new stair still selected, on the Properties palette verify that the "Base Level" is: **Basement** and that the "Top Level" is: **First Floor**.

When you paste a wall, stair, or column to a different level like this, Revit will adjust the base and top offsets to the new levels, but will try to maintain the original height of the element by adding a Top Offset. In this case, the height between the Basement and First Floor is 3" [100] shorter than the height between the First and Second floors.

3. On the Properties palette, remove the "Top Offset" by typing a value of: **0** (zero) (see the right side of Figure 8.18).

EDIT STAIR DISPLAY

In the *First Floor Existing Conditions* plan view it is tough to tell that there are two stairs here.

1. Select the stair, then press the TAB key and select again.

Notice that both stairs are directly on top of each other. Not only does this make it difficult to select each stair, the display might be a bit misleading as well. Since we have two stairs here, what we want to see is the basement Stair above the break line and the first floor stair below. Let's look at our visibility/graphics settings.

2. On the View tab, on the Graphics panel, click the Visibility/Graphics button (or press VG).
    ⇨ Expand the Stairs category.
    ⇨ Uncheck all <Above> subcategories (see Figure 8.19).
3. Expand the Railings category and uncheck the <Above> categories there too and then click OK.

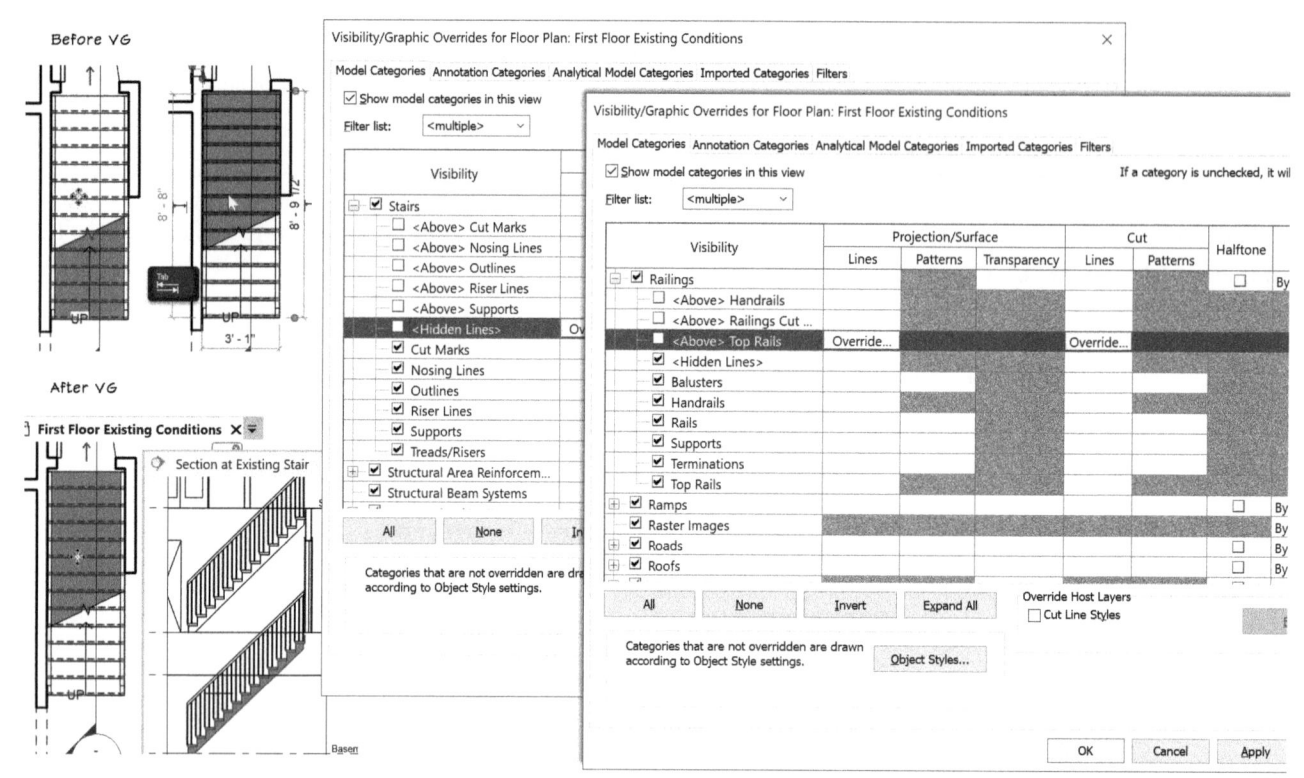

FIGURE 8.19 *Turn off the above subcategories for stairs*

When you pre-highlight and select the stairs now, the upper one should be the basement stair and the lower one the first floor stair. You can see this clearly if you have the section tiled next to the plan as you select.

EDIT THE ASSEMBLED STAIR

In both examples so far we have used the "Run" option to automatically create very simple stair layouts based upon our riser and tread dimensions. You can edit these simple shapes to add architectural detailing to your stairs if required. You can also completely create your own custom sketch to create very complex stair configurations as well. In this example, we will widen the lower portion of the interior stair and add a bull nose to the bottom two treads. To do this, we convert the stair run to a sketch and then modify the sketch.

1. Click on the tab of the *First Floor Existing Conditions* plan view to make it the active window.

    Select the first floor stair (not the one going down to the basement—use the section or Properties palette to verify that you selected the correct one).

    ⇨ On the Modify | Stairs tab, click the Edit Stairs button.

This returns you to creation mode and reveals the components created when we added the stair. Before we can add a custom bullnose condition at the base of the stair, we must convert it to a sketch-based component.

2. Select the stair run.

    ⇨ On the Modify | Create Stair tab, click the Convert button.

A warning will appear indicating that converting to a custom sketch is irreversible. This means that you will lose the ability to use any of the component-based stair editing features on this particular component, but you will be able to edit the sketch, which is what we will do here.

   ⇨ In the "Stair – Convert to Custom" dialog, click Close.

   ⇨ With the Run still selected, on the ribbon, click the Edit Sketch button (see Figure 8.20).

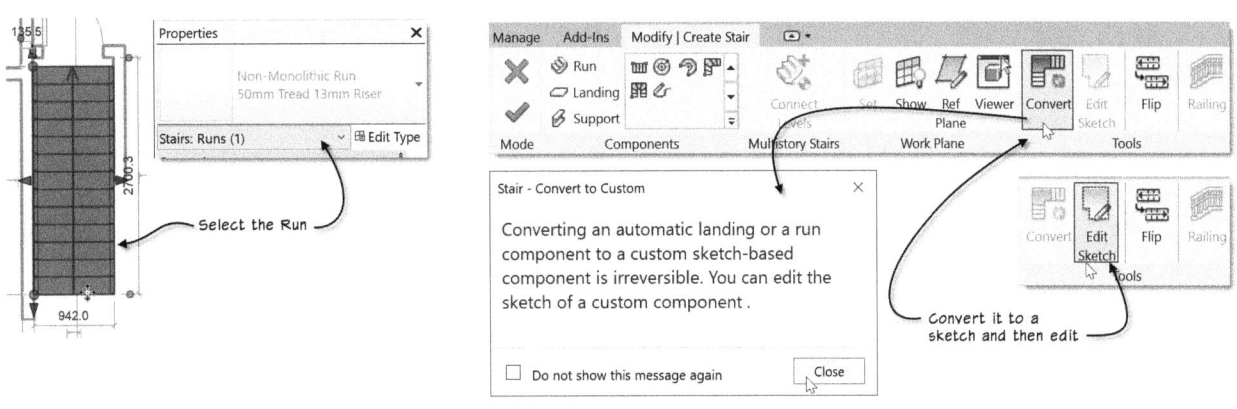

FIGURE 8.20 *Convert the run component to a sketch-based component*

By adjusting these sketch lines, we can change the shape of the stair. The stair sketch uses three colors on screen to indicate the function of each line. Green indicates a boundary line. There must be two boundary edges. The blue line at the center indicates the stair path. Editing this line influences the overall stair, so be careful when modifying it. The black lines are the individual risers. A gray text note will also appear near the sketch indicating how many risers are created and required.

On the ribbon you'll see three draw modes: Boundary, Riser, and Stair Path. We can use these to draw new lines of each type. You can also use any of the modify tools like Move, Copy, Rotate, and Trim to edit the lines already in the sketch.

3. On the Modify | Create Stair > Sketch Run tab, on the Draw panel, click the Boundary tool (see item 1 in Figure 8.21).

⇨ On the Options Bar, make sure that the "Chain" check box is checked.

4. Click the first point of the new boundary Line at the intersection of the right-hand Boundary Line and the bottom of the existing wall.

   Make sure you are snapping to the endpoint of the wall. Use the TAB as necessary to aid in getting the right point (item 2).

⇨ Click the next point at the other side of the wall's width (item 3).

⇨ Place the last point aligned with the third riser line and the wall's right face (item 4).

⇨ On the ribbon, click the Modify tool or press the ESC key twice.

5. Use the Trim/Extend to Corner tool to remove the unneeded segment (item 5)

   Remember to click the part you want to keep.

318 | Chapter 8

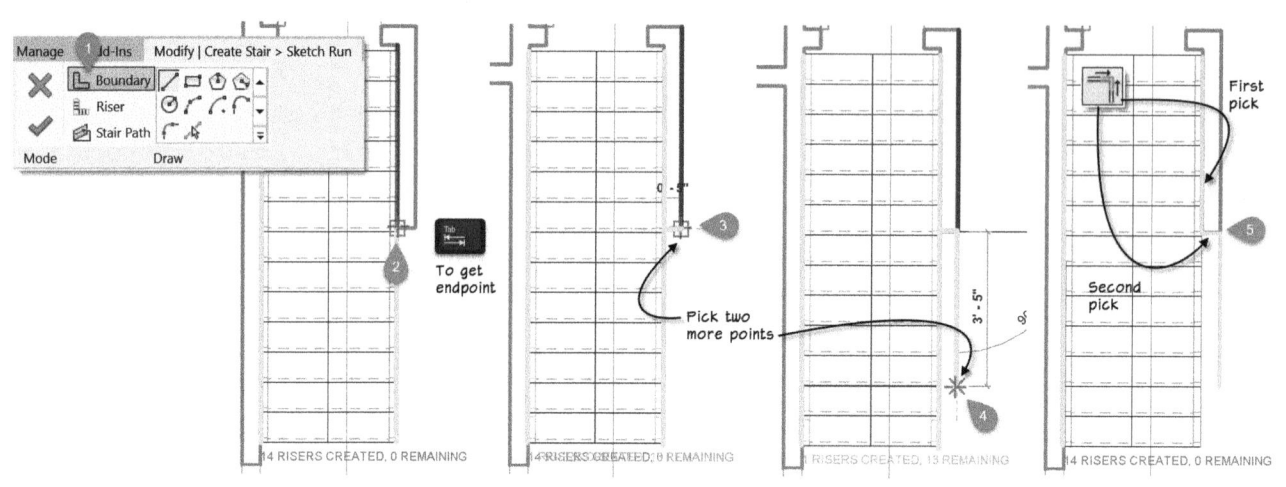

FIGURE 8.21 *Sketch two new boundary lines snapping to the existing wall for reference (sketch lines enhanced for clarity)*

6. On the Modify panel, click the Trim/Extend Multiple Elements tool.

⇨ For the Trim/Extend boundary, click the newly drawn green boundary Line (vertical one on the right).

7. Click each of the riser Lines to extend them to this boundary (see Figure 8.22).

Click them one at a time or drag a crossing window selection through them.

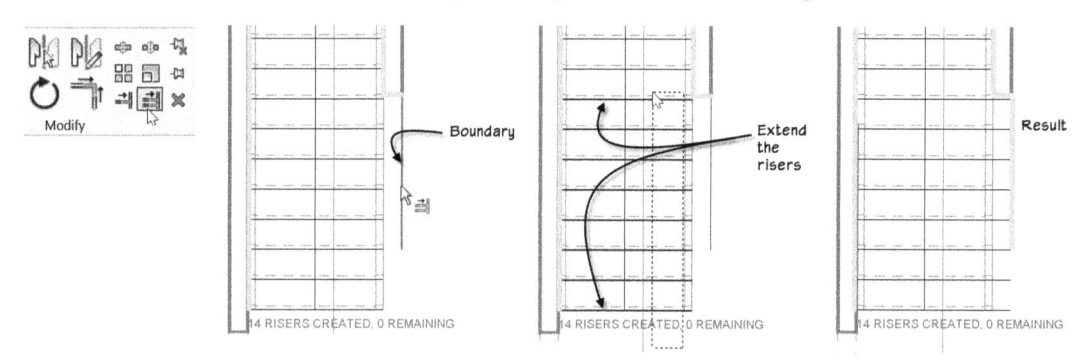

FIGURE 8.22 *Extend the riser lines to the new boundary line*

⇨ Click the Modify tool or press the ESC key twice.

On the lower portion of the stair, the risers will now come out flush with the wall. Next, we'll add the bull nose to the lower two steps.

ADD A BULL NOSE RISER

To add the bull nose riser, we simply sketch them in using the riser sketch tool on the ribbon.

1. On the Draw panel, click the Riser tool.

⇨ On the Options Bar, clear the "Chain" check box.

2. On the Draw panel, click the "Tangent End Arc" icon.

⇨ Snap to the right-hand endpoint of the second riser line from the bottom (see item 1 in Figure 8.23).

⇨ Move straight up and snap to the endpoint of the green boundary line (item 2).

3. Snap to the right-hand endpoint of the lowest riser line (item 3).

⇨ Snap the second point to the endpoint of the green boundary line again (item 4).

• The Aubin Academy •

Vertical Circulation | 319

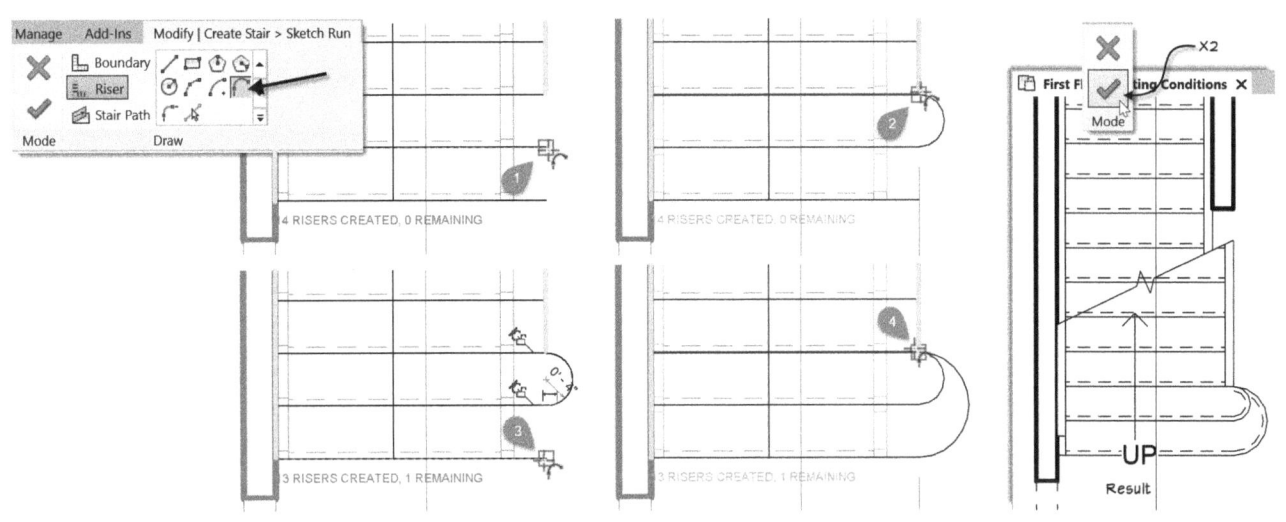

FIGURE 8.23 *Add arcs to the lower risers*

⇨ On the ribbon, click the Finish Edit Mode button.

This returns us to the Modify | Create Stair ribbon. To complete editing, we need to click Finish Edit Mode a second time.

4. On the ribbon, click the Finish Edit Mode button.

If a railing warning appears, we can simply ignore it for now.

VIEW THE STAIR IN 3D

Let's look at our progress in 3D. We have used the "Default 3D View" icon several times already which shows us a complete three-dimensional view of the entire model. This works well to see the exterior of the building, but not the inside. There are a few ways that we quickly view just the stairs in 3D. Let's look at one such way.

1. If your views are tiled, use the Tab Views button (or press TW) to group all tabs into a single window (see item 1 in Figure 8.24).

2. Make sure the *First Floor Existing Conditions* tab is active and then use the Close Inactive Views tool to close any other windows (item 2).

3. On the View tab, on the Create panel, click the Default 3D View tool (also on the QAT) (item 3).

⇨ On the View tab, on the Windows panel, click the Tile Views button (item 4).

Adjust the zoom as necessary.

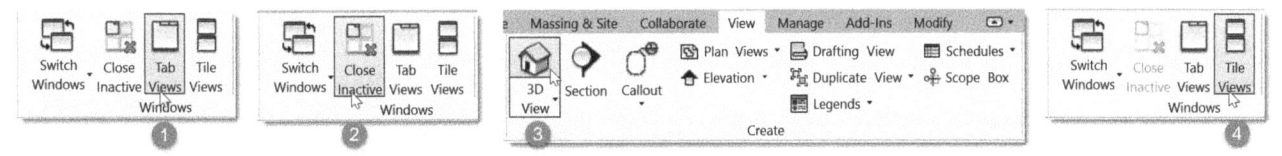

FIGURE 8.24 *Trim the existing boundary line to join it to the new sketch*

4. Click the tab of the *First Floor Existing Conditions* view tab to make it active.

⇨ Select the lower stair, its two railings, and their immediately adjacent walls (see the left side of Figure 8.25).

> **TIP:** Use the CTRL key to click on each object that you wish to add to the selection. Try to avoid selecting the basement stair or basement stair railings. Use the TAB key as necessary to assist in selection. You can hold down the SHIFT key and click an item to remove it if necessary.

• Revit Essentials for Architecture •

320 | Chapter 8

5. Click the tab of the 3D view window to make it active.

Clicking the tab changes views without accidentally deselecting the elements. If you do loose your selection, immediately right-click and choose: **Select Previous**.

⇨ In the *{3D}* view window, from the Temporary Hide/Isolate pop-up, choose: **Isolate Element** (see the right side of Figure 8.25).

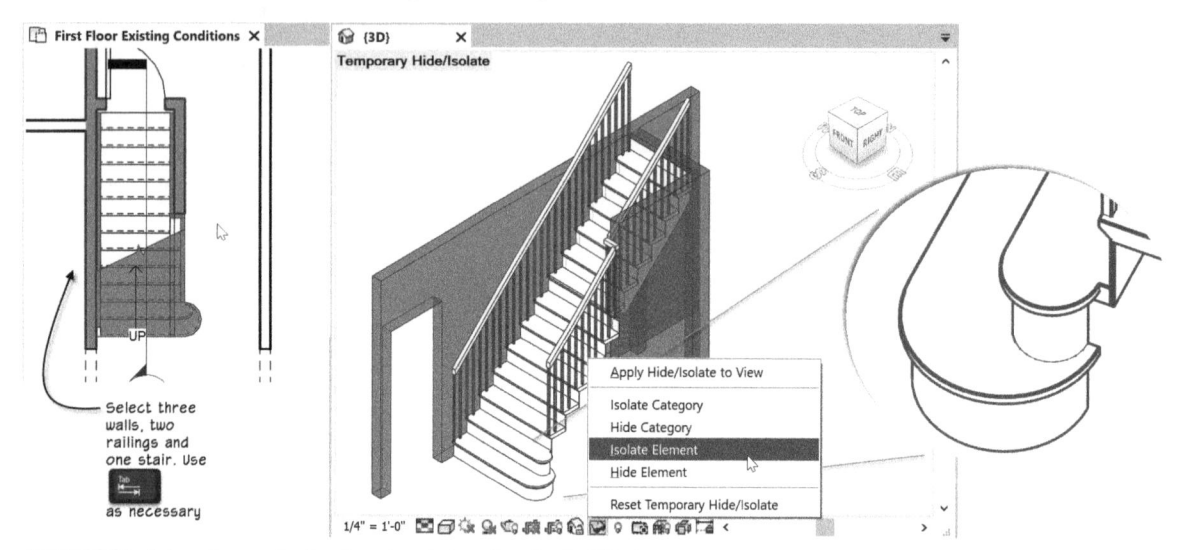

FIGURE 8.25 *Select elements in the plan view, isolate them in the 3D view*

> **TIP:** If you ended up with basement stairs in the 3D view, you could select them separately in the 3D view and then use the Temporary Hide/Isolate pop-up again and choose: **Hide Elements**.

Feel free to use the ViewCube or the Steering Wheel controls to spin the isolated selection around to an alternative viewing angle. With the stairs thus isolated, you should be able to see the two treads at the bottom of the stair and their bull nose quite clearly.

ADD A PLAN REGION

The cut line that you see in the plan view is controlled by the settings of the floor plan; specifically, the floor plan's "View Range." By default, floor plans are cut at 4'-0" [1,200]. This height works well for most items like walls, windows, doors and furnishings. But it ends up cutting the stair element a little low in most cases. This is particularly evident in this plan where we might like the stair cut line to occur above the location where we edited the sketch. We have two options for how to address this. First, you can edit the View Range settings of this floor plan and input a value for the Cut Plane that is higher than we have now. The trouble with this approach is that would apply across the entire floor plan. So, while it might solve the stair issue, it might create new issues on other items that were not present before. Instead, our second option is to create a plan region. This is a sketched region that allows you to adjust the view range in just a portion of the plan rather than the whole thing.

1. Click the *First Floor Existing Conditions* tab to make the plan active.

2. On the View tab, on the Create panel, click the Plan Views drop down and choose: **Plan Region** (see item 1 in Figure 8.26).

⇨ On the Modify | Create Plan Region Boundary tab, click the rectangle icon (item 2).

⇨ Drag a rectangle around the stair a little wider than the walls (item 3).

⇨ On the ribbon, click the Finish Edit Mode button (item 4).

• The Aubin Academy •

Vertical Circulation | 321

3. With the Plan Region still selected, on the Modify | Plan Region tab, click the View Range button (item 5).

⇨ In the "View Range" dialog that appears, in the Cut plane Offset field, input: **6'-0"** [**1,800**] and then click OK (item 6).

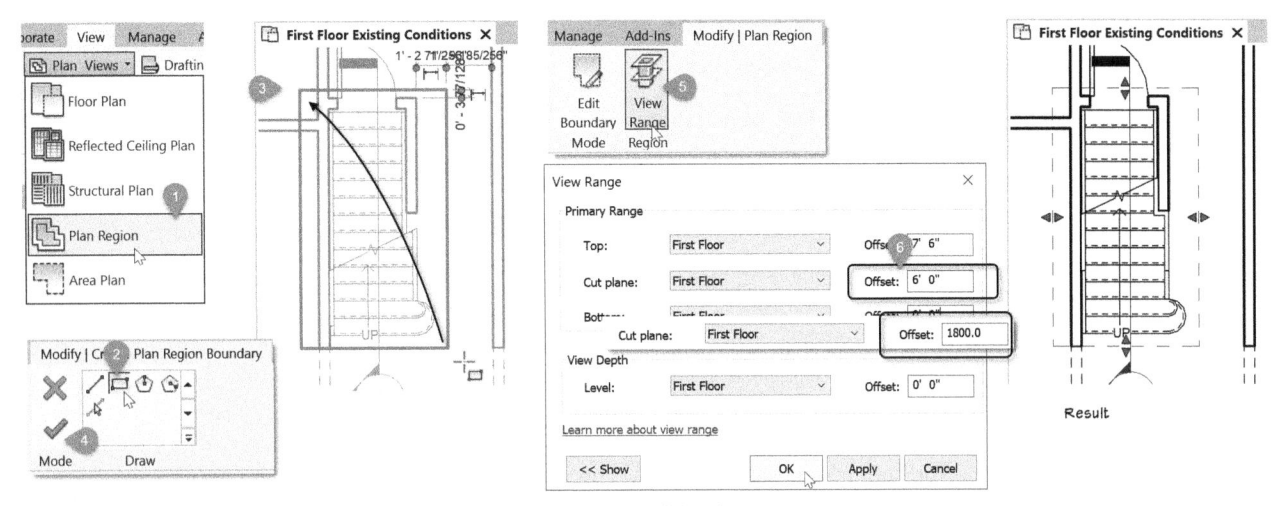

FIGURE 8.26 *Use a plan region to adjust the view range in a small area of the plan view*

The cut line for the stair will now appear higher in the plan view.

MODIFY THE RAILINGS

Having completed the edit of the stair above and especially after raising the cut plane on the stairs, it is now apparent that the railing could use a bit of adjustment as well. You can edit a railing by editing its sketch.

1. In the plan view, zoom in on the railing on the right side.

As you can see, this railing has matched the shape of the boundary line that we sketched above and makes a slight jog as it goes up the run of stairs. Let's eliminate the portion of the railing above the jog (adjacent to the wall).

2. Select the railing on the right side.

⇨ On the Modify | Railings tab, click the Edit Path button.

If your Modify tab says: Modify | Top Rails, deselect and try selecting again. Top rail is a subcomponent of railings. We want the parent railing here, not the top rail.

⇨ Delete the top two sketch lines, (the vertical one and the short horizontal one that are adjacent to the wall).

3. On the ribbon, click Finish Edit Mode (see Figure 8.27).

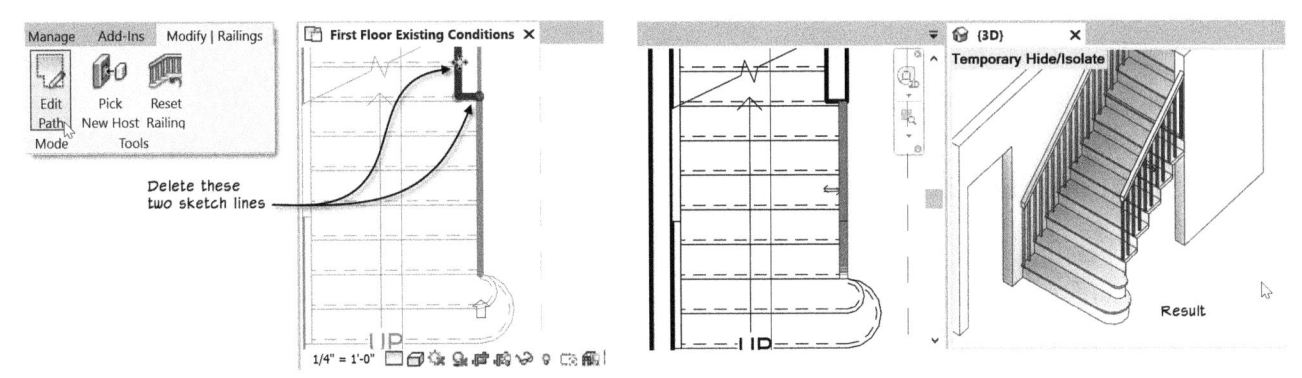

FIGURE 8.27 *Edit the railing sketch and remove the unnecessary lines*

• Revit Essentials for Architecture •

CREATE A SIMPLE RAILING TYPE

The railing on the other side of the stair does not need balusters or posts. It is attached to the wall. To represent this correctly, let's duplicate the existing railing type and then modify it.

1. Select the long railing on the left side of the stair.

    ⇨ On the Properties palette, click the Edit Type button.

2. In the "Type Properties" dialog click the Duplicate button (or press ALT + D) (see item 1 in Figure 8.28).

    ⇨ In the "Name" dialog, type: **Existing House Railing – No Balusters** and then click OK.

3. In the "Type Properties" dialog, beneath the "Construction" grouping, click the Edit button next to "Baluster Placement" (item 2)

    ⇨ In the "Edit Baluster Placement" dialog, in the "Main Pattern" area (at the top), for element 2, from the Baluster family list choose: **None** and change the Top setting to: **Host** (item 3)

4. Make sure that the "Use Baluster Per Tread On Stairs" check box is not checked (item 4).

5. In the "Posts" area (at the bottom), for Baluster Family, choose: **None** and for Top, choose: **Host** for all three components (item 5).

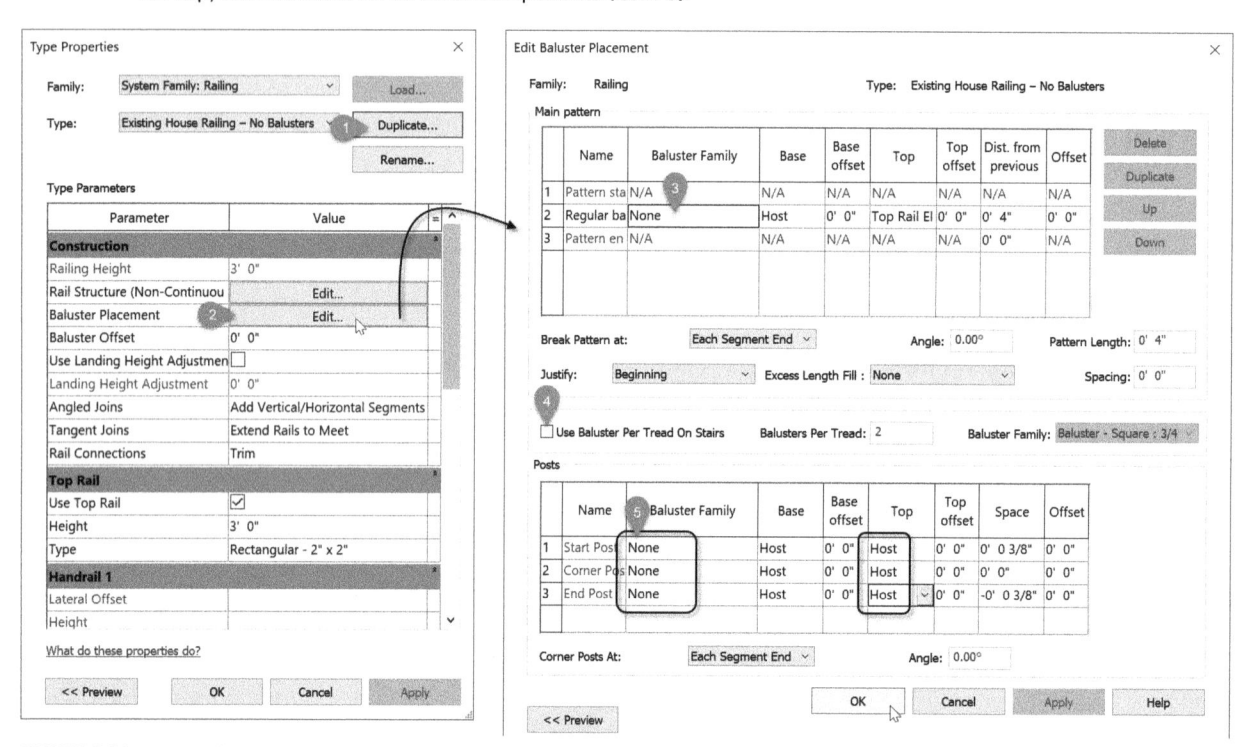

FIGURE 8.28 *Remove balusters and posts from the new railing type*

⇨ Click OK to return to the "Type Properties" dialog.

UNDERSTANDING HANDRAIL COMPONENTS

Railings can include Top Rails, Handrails and non-continuous rails. In the "Type Properties" dialog you will see the Rail Structure (Non-Continuous) parameter near Baluster Placement at the top. Some railing designs call for several parallel rails. Non-continuous rails would be used for this purpose and can be edited with the button located here. For handrails, we have three options: Top Rail, Handrail 1 and Handrail 2. These settings appear further down on the "Type Properties" dialog. A Top Rail Occurs at the top of the railing and remains in-plane with rest of the railing and can run continuously along the entire stair. Handrail 1 and 2 are also continuous and can be offset from the plane of the railing to the left or right. Continuous rails can also use automatic returns at both the top and bottom of the run. There are many options here, in this exercise, we'll explore a quick example to add a basic handrail return to give you an idea of how the tool works.

If you closed the "Type Properties" dialog for the railing, reopen it now.

1. Scroll down and take note of the Top Rail and Handrail settings (don't change them yet).

This railing (copied above from the default one) has a top rail that is rectangular in profile. There are no handrails currently assigned. Each kind of rail can be assigned a profile (which determines its shape across its section) and a height. The handrails can also have lateral offset and be positioned on either side of the railing plane (options include Left, Right, and Both). We'll remove the top rail and, in its place, add a handrail. This way we can take advantage of the wall return features below. (Top rails cannot use the wall return option, only handrails can).

2. In the Handrail 1 Grouping, click in the Type field. A small browse button will appear (see item 1 in Figure 8.29).

   ⇨ Click this browse button and then in the new "Type Properties" dialog that appears, from the Type list at the top choose: **Pipe – Wall Mount** and then click OK once.

   This returns you to the original "Type Properties" dialog (for the railing itself).

   ⇨ Still in the Handrail 1 grouping, right above Type, for Position, choose: **Left** (item 2)

3. Beneath the Top Rail grouping, uncheck the "Use Top Rail" check box and then click OK (item 3).

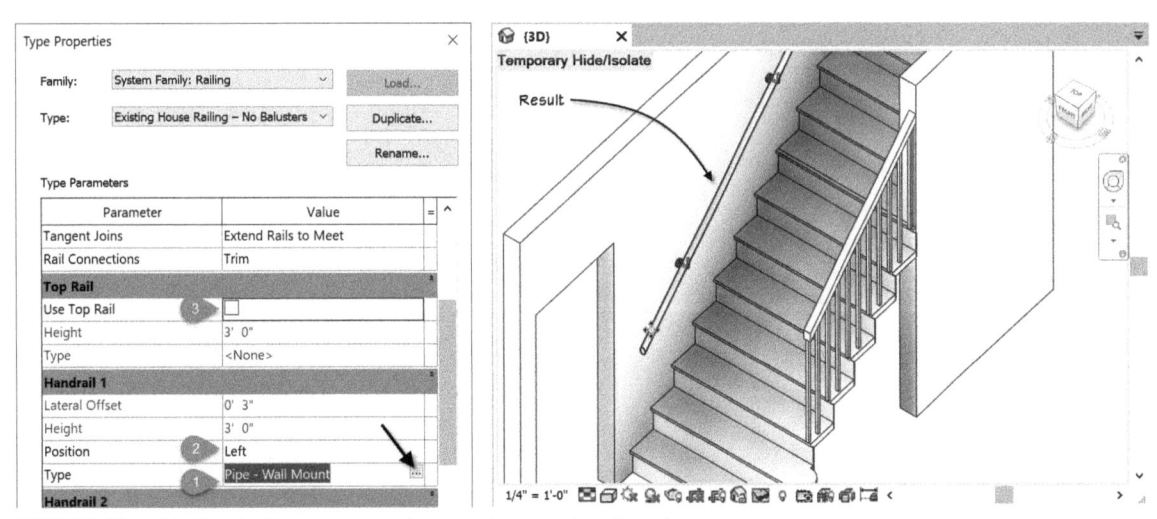

FIGURE 8.29 *Add a handrail component and remove the top rail in the railing type*

The new handrail does not yet terminate into the wall. This can be accomplished by selecting the handrail directly, instead of its host railing. In other words, the railing is the main host element, but it *contains* the handrail component nested within it. The stairs are the same way. To see this, you need to use the TAB key to toggle your selections. It might be easier to practice on the other railing first.

4. Place your mouse over the top edge of the railing (do not click) to make it pre-highlight.

   The entire railing will highlight and the tooltip and Status bar will read: *Railings: Railing: Handrail – Rectangular* [*Railings: Railing: 900mm*].

   ⇨ Press the TAB key. This time the Top Rail of the railing will highlight.

5. Press the TAB key again.

   The Top Rail will highlight this time and the Status Bar will read: *Top Rails: Top Rail Type: Rectangular - 2" x 2"* [*Top Rails: Top Rail Type: Rectangular - 50x50mm*] (see Figure 8.30).

   ⇨ Click to select the top rail.

• Revit Essentials for Architecture •

324 | Chapter 8

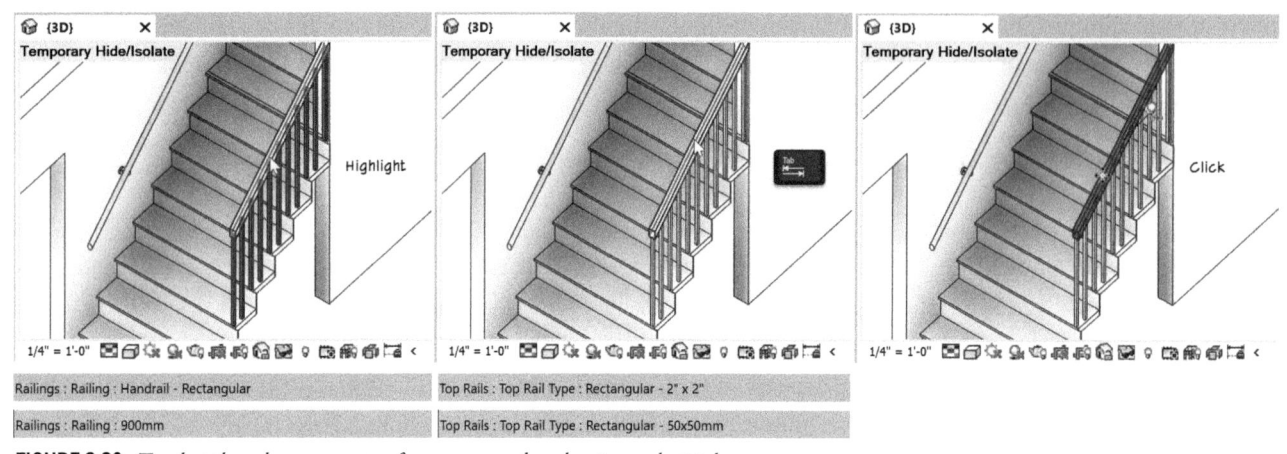

FIGURE 8.30 *To select the sub-components of a component-based stair use the* TAB *key*

We did this railing first just for practice. The railing at the wall is a little trickier because there are no balusters and so the pre-highlighting onscreen will be the same when you TAB. The only difference is the tooltip. You can see the tooltips onscreen directly at the cursor and also at the Status Bar at the bottom of the screen (shown at the bottom of the figure; see the "Status Bar" topic on page 76 in Chapter 3 for more information).

6. Place your mouse over the edge of the other railing (do not click) to make it pre-highlight.

    The railing will highlight and the tooltip and Status bar will read: *Railings: Railing: Existing House Railing – No Balusters*.

    ⇨ Press the TAB key.

    The pre-highlighting is unchanged, but this time the tooltip and Status Bar reads: *Handrails: Handrail Type: Circular - 1 1/2"* [*Handrails: Handrail Type: Pipe – Wall Mount*] (see Figure 8.31).

7. Click to select the Handrail.

FIGURE 8.31 *To select the sub-components of a component-based railing, also use the* TAB *key*

You can select the stair or its nested components in the same way. As always when using TAB to aid in selection, when the item you want to select is highlighted, click the mouse to select it. Therefore, using the tooltips onscreen or on the Status Bar is so important to ensure you make the correct selection.

8. With the handrail selected, on the Properties palette, click the Edit Type button.

    ⇨ In the Extension (Beginning/Bottom) grouping, for Extension Style, choose: **Wall** and set the Length to: **2"** [**50**].

If your building code requires it, you can add a tread depth to the extension using the check box here. Do not check it for this example. We'll use this check box in an example later in the chapter.

9. In the Extension (End/Top) grouping, for Extension Style, choose: **Wall** and set the Length to: **6"** [**150**] (see Figure 8.32).

• The Aubin Academy •

Vertical Circulation | 325

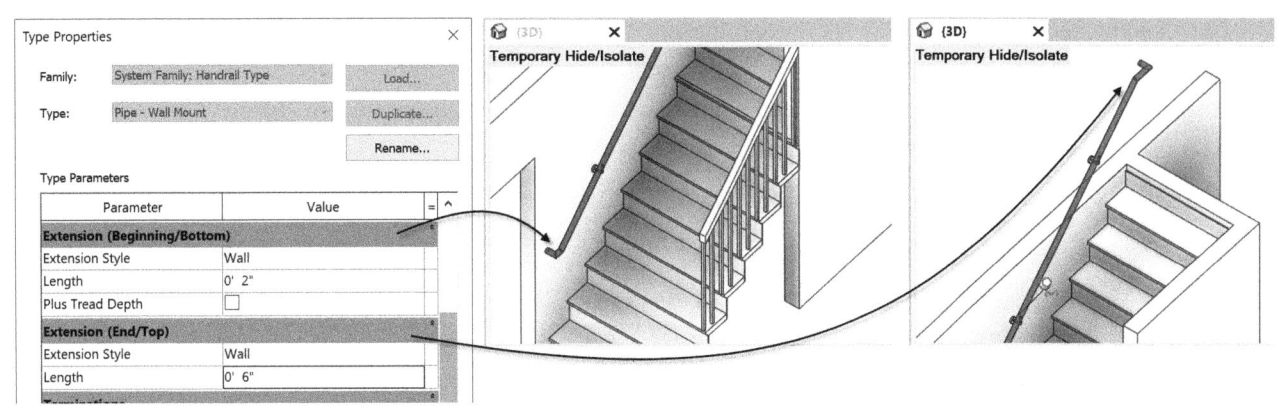

FIGURE 8.32 *Add extensions and wall returns to the railing*

Before you close the dialog, you can study the parameters in the Construction grouping. There you can change the clearance, height and shape (Profile) of the handrail. We won't change any of these settings here, but feel free to experiment on your own if you like. Take note of the position of the railing relative to the wall in the plan view. Notice that there is a small gap between it and the wall. We can easily adjust this.

10. Deselect the handrail and then select the railing itself.

    You will click away from the rail (to deselect) and then click on it again (to select) without TAB this time.

11. On the Properties palette, change the Offset from Path to: **0** (zero).

> **NOTE:** It is important to understand that the change we made here is a type-level change. This means that it affects all instances of the handrail type. In this case, we only have one instance of this handrail type in use, so it is inconsequential. Later in the "Add a Railing Extension" topic on page 351 below we will cover the steps required to duplicate the handrail type first before making edits. In general that procedure would be considered a "best practice" approach and should typically be followed in most new construction projects.

CREATE A COMPLEX RAILING TYPE

In the previous topics, we created a very simple new railing type by duplicating the original and removing all the balusters. In this example we will make a more complex custom railing and this will allow us to look a little more carefully at the "Edit Baluster Placement" dialog.

The first thing we need to understand is that railings (like stairs, walls, floors, and roofs) are system families. System families are so called because they are "built in" to the system. This means that the parameters, behavior and overall geometric characteristics of system families are predefined in the software and not editable by the user. Each system family can, however, have multiple types. A type is a collection of parameters that are applied to all elements assigned to the type. If a type parameter is modified, it affects all instances of that type in the entire project. The item we just created: *Existing House Railing – No Balusters*, is a type that belongs to the system family called: *Railing*. (The handrail we modified was also a type; we just did not duplicate it first). In this example, we will also duplicate the existing type and create a new one for the railing on the right side of the stair. However, this railing will use some nested components for the posts and balusters and even the shape of the top rail. Balusters, posts and the profile that we will use to shape the railing are all component (loadable) families. This means they can be loaded from external RFA files just like we did r 4 for the doors, windows and fixtures.

• Revit Essentials for Architecture •

The fact that the railing element itself is a system family, it's top and handrails are nested system families and that its posts and balusters can be nested component families make it the most complex object we have worked with so far. However, despite this, the process to create a complex railing type that uses custom families for the posts and balusters is manageable. Let's start by loading in the families we need.

Work in the *{3D}* view. You can keep it tiled with the *First Floor Existing Conditions* as before if you like.

1. On the Insert tab, click the Load Family button.

   ⇨ In your library folder, browse to the *Railings\Balusters* folder.

   ⇨ Select *Baluster - Custom1* [*M_Baluster - Custom1*], hold down the CTRL key and select *Post – Newel* [*M_Post – Newel*] and then click Open.

2. Click Load Family again and browse to the *Profiles\Railings* folder this time.

   ⇨ Select the *Decorate Rail* [*M_Decorate Rail*] file and then click Open.

   All three of these families have been included in the *Chapter08* folder for your convenience should your version of Revit not include these files. The families are now loaded into our project and can be used to make a railing type.

3. Select the railing on the right (open) side of the stair. (The one with balusters).

   ⇨ On the Properties palette click the Edit Type button.

   ⇨ In the "Type Properties" dialog, click the Duplicate button (or ALT + D) and name the new type: **Existing House Railing – w Balusters and Posts**.

4. Click the Edit button next to Baluster Placement.

   To make this dialog easier to read, you can drag the edge to make it wider.

5. At the top of the dialog, next to Regular baluster (line 2), choose: **Baluster - Custom1 : 3/4"** [**M_Baluster - Custom1 : 25mm**] from the Baluster Family list.

> **NOTE:** Values in the Name column can be edited. This is simply a description of the item you assign here. So if you build a more complex railing type with lots of items in the Main pattern, you can type in a custom name for each item. In our case, the name already assigned here is suitable, but you are welcome to change it if you prefer.

This is the only change we need to make in the Main pattern. However, here is a brief list of the other settings and what they do.

Base—This is where the bottom of the baluster should be placed. Each rail in the railing type will appear on the list. You can also choose: Host, which would be the stair object in this case.

Base offset—A numerical value that shifts the bottom of the baluster relative to its Base setting. Positive numbers move it up, negative numbers move it down.

Top—This is where the top of the baluster should end. Each rail in the railing can be used to set the height of balusters. Choose: Host to set a fixed height for the balusters using the Top offset setting.

Top offset—A numerical value that shifts the top of the baluster relative to its Top setting. Positive numbers move it up, negative numbers move it down.

Dist. From previous—This sets the spacing of balusters in your pattern. It is measured from the previous baluster on the list.

Offset—This shifts the balusters parallel to the railing.

The pattern here uses a single element. So, it is the simplest kind of pattern. Repeat the same element over and over. However, your pattern can contain multiple elements. So, you could for example create an A B B pattern. This would use baluster A, then B twice, then repeat the whole pattern. The buttons on the right are available to add (use Duplicate), Delete, and move them up and down in the pattern. Remember that distance from previous is measured from the previous element. So, the value input for A would be the spacing for the pattern repeat while the first B would measure from A and the second B from the first B.

Settings for Posts are basically the same. The only difference is that the post conditions are fixed. You can assign a post at each end of the railing and have posts appear automatically at any corners.

Some settings in the middle of the dialog control special cases. For example, you can use the Break Pattern at setting to control if the pattern should start over at each segment of the railing (Each Segment End) or run continuous along the railing length (Never). The "Use Baluster Per Tread on Stairs" setting is the one we use here to set the pattern repeat based on the stair treads instead of the values defined in the Main pattern.

6. In the middle of the dialog, check the "Use Baluster Per Tread on Stairs" check box.

⇨ For the Balusters Per Tread, leave it set to: **2**.

⇨ For Baluster Family, choose: **Baluster - Custom1 : 3/4"** [**M_Baluster - Custom1 : 25mm**] again.

7. Finally, at the bottom, for the Start Post choose: **Post — Newel : 4 1/4"** [**M_Post — Newel : 100mm**].

⇨ For the Corner and End Posts, choose: **None** and then click OK (see Figure 8.33).

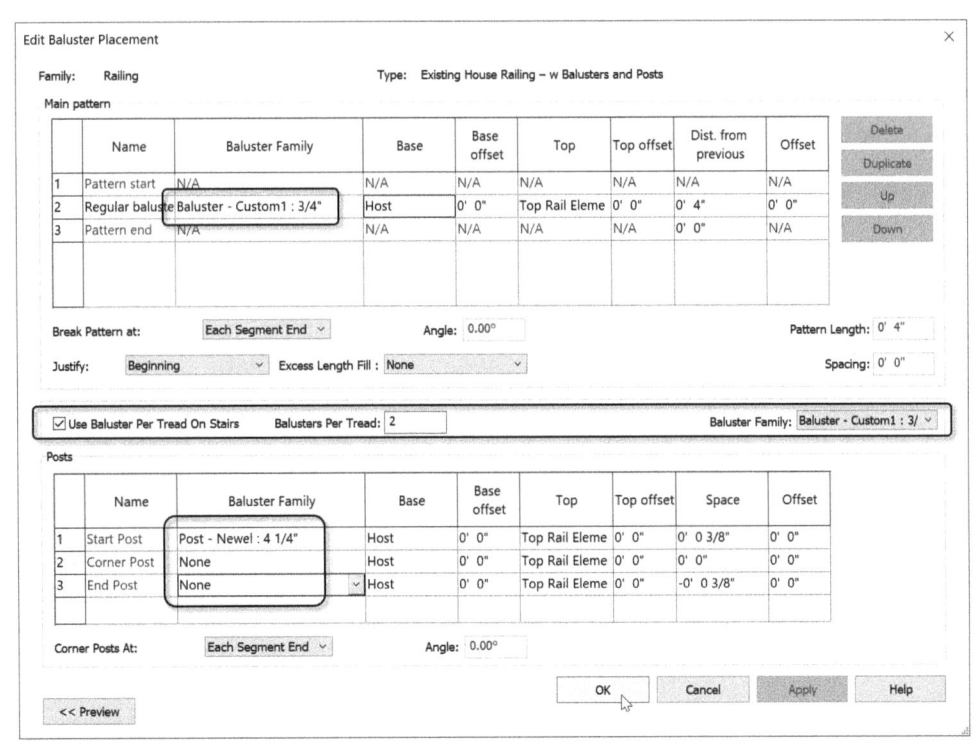

FIGURE 8.33 *Add balusters and posts to the new railing type*

You will be back in the "Type Properties" dialog. Next, we need to adjust the top rail.

8. Beneath the "Top Rail" grouping, click in the Type field.

⇨ A small browse button will appear. Click it to display another "Type Properties" dialog (see item 1 in Figure 8.34).

328 | Chapter 8

9. Click the Duplicate button (or ALT + D) and name the new type: **Existing House Top Rail** (item 2).

   ⇨ Beneath the "Construction" grouping, change the Profile to: **Decorate Rail : 2 5/8" x 2 3/8"** [**M_Decorate Rail : 65 x 60mm**] and then click OK twice (item 3).

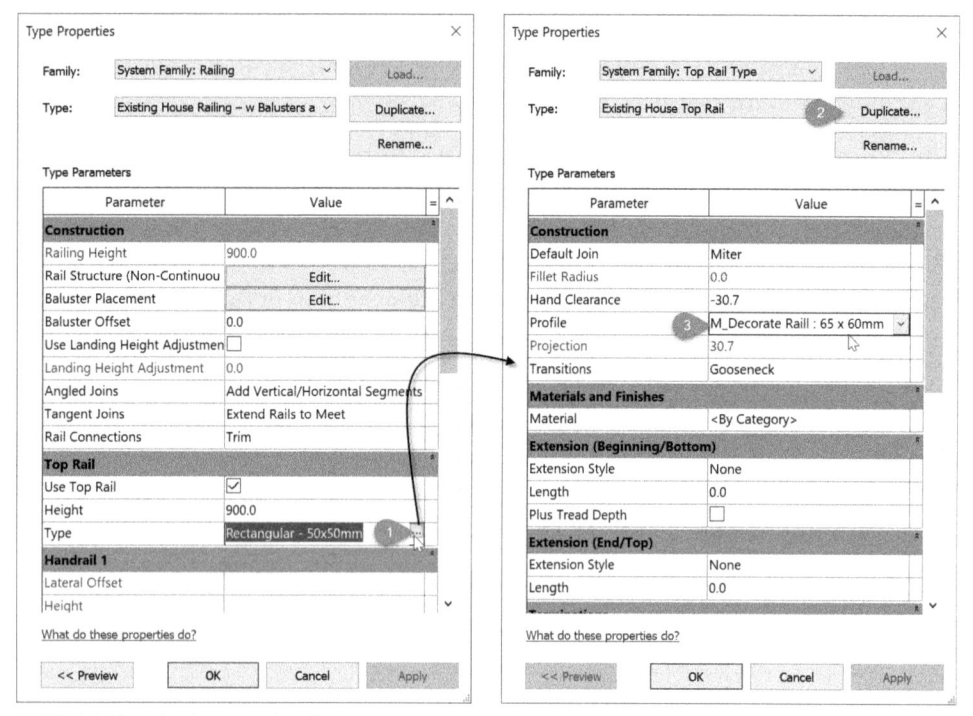

FIGURE 8.34 *Edit the top rail and create a new type*

The railing is a little too close to the edge, but that is easy to adjust.

10. On the Properties palette, change the Offset from Path to: **2"** [**50**].

To make the end post sit on a tread all by itself, click the Edit Path button and drag the control at the end of the sketch line down slightly (see Figure 8.35). This is easiest to do in plan view.

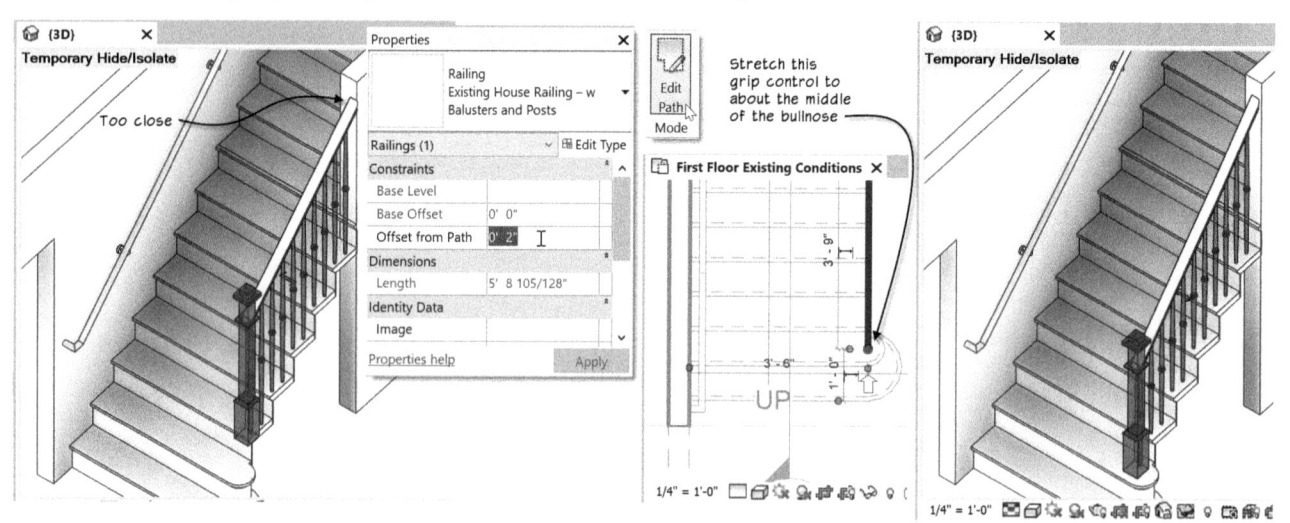

FIGURE 8.35 *After pasting in the new railing type, apply it to the railing, remove the top post and make other adjustments*

Examine the railing in both 3D and plan after you finish. Feel free to experiment with it further.

• The Aubin Academy •

> **BIM Manager Note:** As already noted, stairs and railings are system families. So, they cannot be saved and loaded as RFA files like component families can. In order to reuse custom types that you create for system families (like the railing types created here), you can use the Transfer Project Standards command on the Manage tab, or you can copy and paste. It is common best practice to create library files that contain all your firm's custom types to facilitate easy copying and pasting between projects. You can find a few examples of these in the installed Revit libraries. There is one for general system families that contains wall, floor, roof and ceiling types. It is called: *System Family Library.rvt*. The other contains many sample stairs and railings and is called: *Stair and Railing System Family Library.rvt*. These files are project files and can be found in the installed libraries in a subfolder called: *System Families*. Feel free to open these files and have a look around. Some of the types in these files are bit older and don't always use the latest features, but there is still quite a bit that can be learned from reverse engineering them. You are encouraged to look at railings to see a nice variety of examples of what you can do with customizing both railings and stairs. Copies of the files are included in the *OTB System Families* folder for your perusal. If you find a type in the file that you like, you can select it onscreen, copy it to the clipboard and then paste it into your project file. The copy/paste process will automatically import the railing type into your project.

MAKING TEMPORARY HIDE/ISOLATE PERMANENT

This 3D view we have open shows the results of our efforts nicely. But note that the view window is still surrounded by a cyan border. This indicates that we are in temporary hide/isolate mode. When we close Revit, the mode will be reset automatically, and all the building geometry will redisplay in this view. You can also choose the reset option from the pop-up on the View Control Bar to reset it manually any time. However, if you like, we can also make this display permanent in this view. Let's do that now.

1. From the Temporary Hide/Isolate pop-up, choose: **Apply Hide/Isolate to View**.
2. Right-click the ViewCube and choose: **Save View**.
   - In the "Enter name for new 3D View" dialog, type: **3D Existing Stairway Hall** and then click OK.
   - On the Properties palette, set the Phase Filter to: **Show Complete**.
3. From the View Control Bar click the Visual Style pop-up and choose: **Graphic Display Options** (or press GD).
   - Experiment with the various options.

     Figure 8.36 shows Hidden Line, anti-aliasing, Show ambient shadows and Sketchy Lines enabled. Feel free to try other combinations.

330 | Chapter 8

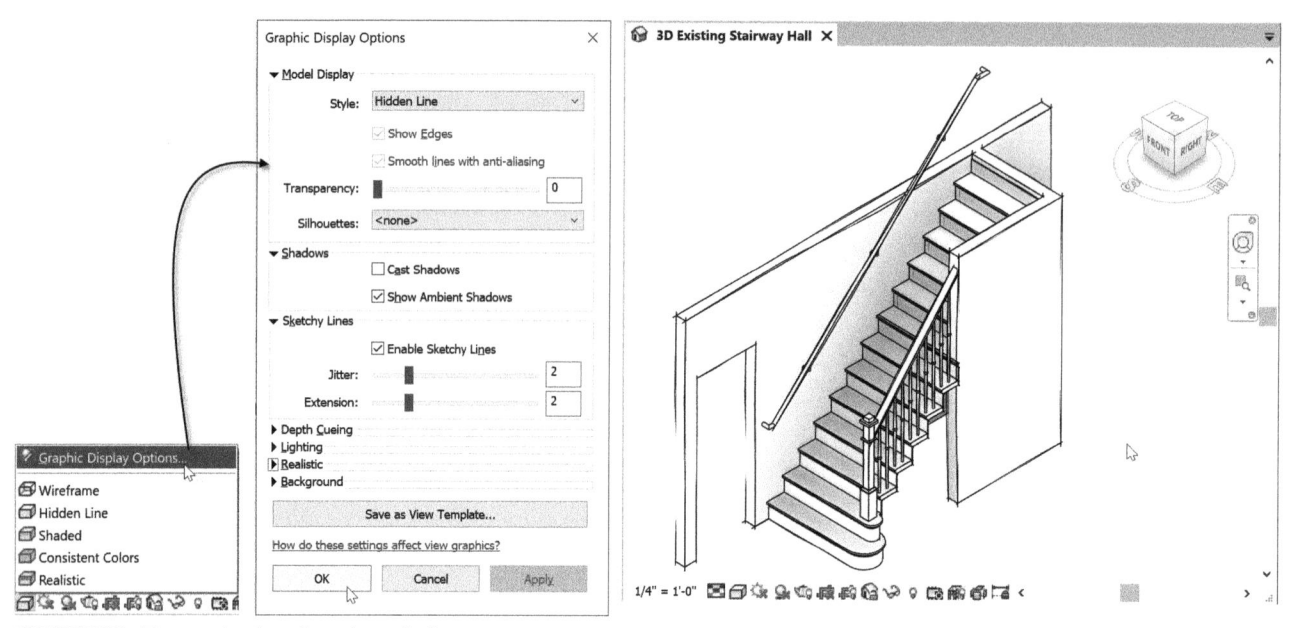

FIGURE 8.36 *The completed residential stair hallway*

We now have a permanent 3D view of the stair hallway. This completes our work in the residential project. We have plenty more vertical circulation explorations to make. We will now switch to the commercial project to continue those explorations.

4. From the File menu, **Save** and **Close** the Residential project.

COMMERCIAL CORE LAYOUT

While we have done much with the stair tools in the residential project, there is still more we can explore. To continue our exploration of vertical circulation, we will switch to the Commercial project. In this project, we will add a multi-story stair and some elevators in the building core and we will add ramps to the front entrance of the building.

PERFORM A COORDINATION REVIEW

We need to adjust a few issues with our linked structural file first. So, we'll start by opening that file. This feature is not available in Revit LT. If you are using Revit LT, please skip this topic.

Be sure that the Residential Project is saved and closed.

1. On the QAT, click the Open icon (or press CTRL + O).
2. In the "Open" dialog box, browse to the *Chapter08* folder.

⇨ Double-click *08 Commercial-Structure.rvt* if you wish to work in Imperial units.

⇨ Double-click *08 Commercial-Structure_M.rvt* if you wish to work in Metric units.

> **NOTE:** Please start with the file provided for Chapter 8 rather than attempting to continue from your own saved version from the previous chapter. A few changes have been included here that were not detailed in the previous chapter.

A warning dialog will appear on screen alerting you that your file requires coordination review. This warning is informational and can be ignored.

• The Aubin Academy •

3. Click OK to dismiss the warning dialog (see Figure 8.37).

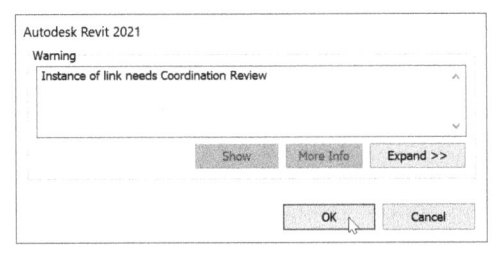

FIGURE 8.37 *An alert displays about the need for a coordination review*

4. On the Project Browser, double-click to open the *Level 2* structural plan view.
   ⇨ Right-click in the workspace and choose: **Zoom In Region** (or press ZR).
   ⇨ Drag a box around the core to zoom in on it (see Figure 8.38).

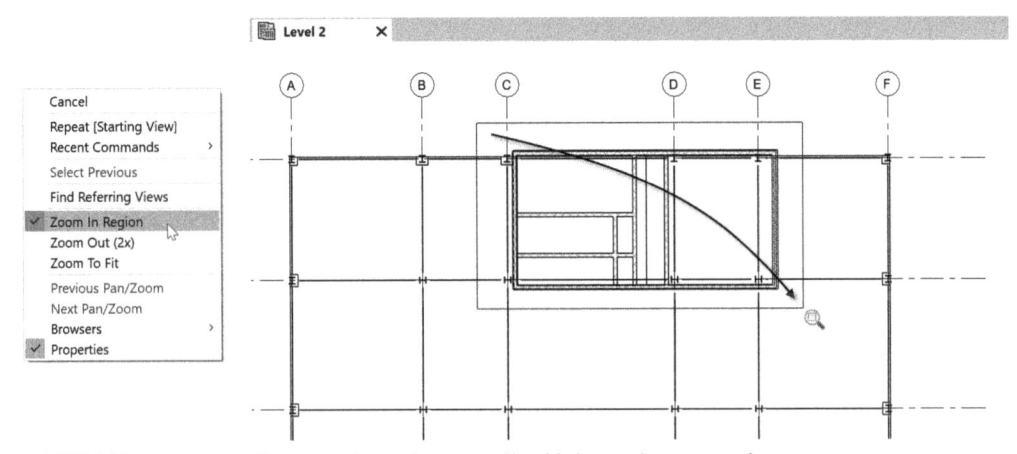

FIGURE 8.38 *Zoom in on the core and note the new walls added since the previous chapter*

In the previous chapter, we established links between the structural model and the commercial project. We used Copy/Monitor to create monitored copies of the geometry from the commercial project that is pertinent to the structural file. As you can see, some additional geometry has been added to the building core area in the linked commercial project since we established the Copy/Monitor link. In addition, there may be other less obvious changes that require coordination. This is what the warning during file open was telling us. To address these issues, we can perform a coordination review and reconcile the differences between the two files.

> **NOTE:** An additional exercise has been provided in the Appendix covering the creation of the walls provided here in the core. Feel free to do that exercise before continuing if you like.

5. On the Collaborate tab, click the Coordination Review tool and then choose the: **Select Link** option from the pop-up.
   ⇨ Click on the commercial project link file on screen to select it (it is easiest to click on one of the core walls).

In the "Coordination Review" dialog, various messages will appear in a column on the left. You can choose an action for how you wish to deal with the differences and, if desired, add a comment. Here are some of the actions you will typically see on the list:

Postpone—this option simply puts off your decision until next time.

Reject—option keeps your element as is and flags the change from the linked file as rejected.

Accept Difference—you are allowing your file and the linked file to be out of sync. This is like "agreeing to disagree."

332 | Chapter 8

The last option on the list describes what action you must take to make your model match the linked file. This could be "Modify," "Delete," "Move," etc. In this case, we have three overall issues, each with its own sub entries. The first one is not visible in this floor plan. The door in the north wall of the core moved in the architectural file. To see it, the {3D} view would work best. But let's skip it for now. Next is an entry about Structural Columns. The ones in the linked parent file have been deleted. At this point in the project, the team has decided that the structural columns should exist only in the structural model. Since this model is linked back to the architectural file, the architectural team will still see structural columns in their file. You can review this warning and its sub-warnings here, but we will deal with the issue outside of this dialog, so please do not select any action for it at this time.

The final entry is regarding the walls. Some have moved and some have new openings. We will deal with these items here. (This was not part of the lessons in Chapter 7, so be sure you are using the provided files for Chapter 8.) Within the "Coordination Review" dialog, we can update the walls and copy these openings to the structural model.

6. Expand Walls, then Maintain wall position.

   There are four sub entries. You must expand each one.

   ⇨ Select the first "Wall centerlines are different" entry.

If you can see the plan in background, both the wall from the host model and the link will highlight when this item is selected. If you expand it further, you will see each wall; the host file and link file versions, and you can select each one individually to see the difference a bit more clearly. We are working from a plan here, but you can do this in any view that shows the items you have selected.

   ⇨ Select the first "Wall centerlines are different" entry again, hold down the SHIFT key and click the last one (4 total, you do not need to expand them to do this).

   ⇨ In the Action column, click the drop down and choose: **Modify Wall** (see Figure 8.39).

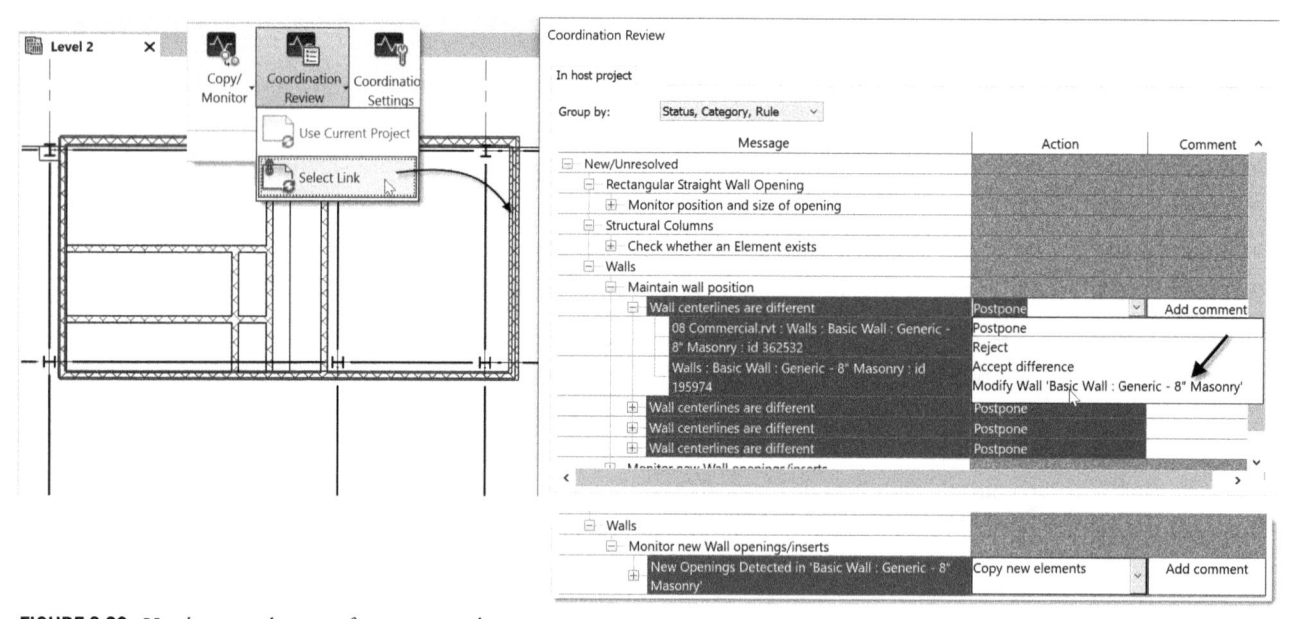

FIGURE 8.39 *Use the action list to perform your coordination review*

   This will apply to all four entries.

   ⇨ Click the Apply button to see the change in the plan beyond.

7. Expand Monitor new wall openings/inserts.

   ⇨ From the Action list, choose: **Copy new elements** (see the bottom of Figure 8.39).

8. Back at the top of the dialog, expand the first issue (Monitor position and

• The Aubin Academy •

size of opening) and set the Action to: **Move opening**.

The "Elements" button at the bottom right expands each item to show each individual element affected by the message. The Show button will attempt to zoom to the affected element in the model. Revit may need to open other views to do this. The Create Report button will generate an HTML file detailing the results of the coordination review. Feel free to experiment in this dialog if you wish.

⇨ Click OK to dismiss the "Coordination Review" dialog.

To deal with the missing columns, we will simply stop monitoring them. They are deleted in the architectural file, but we want them to remain here in the structural file.

9. Select one steel column, (use TAB as necessary) right-click and then choose: **Select All Instances > In Entire Project**.

⇨ On the ribbon, click the Stop Monitoring button (see Figure 8.40).

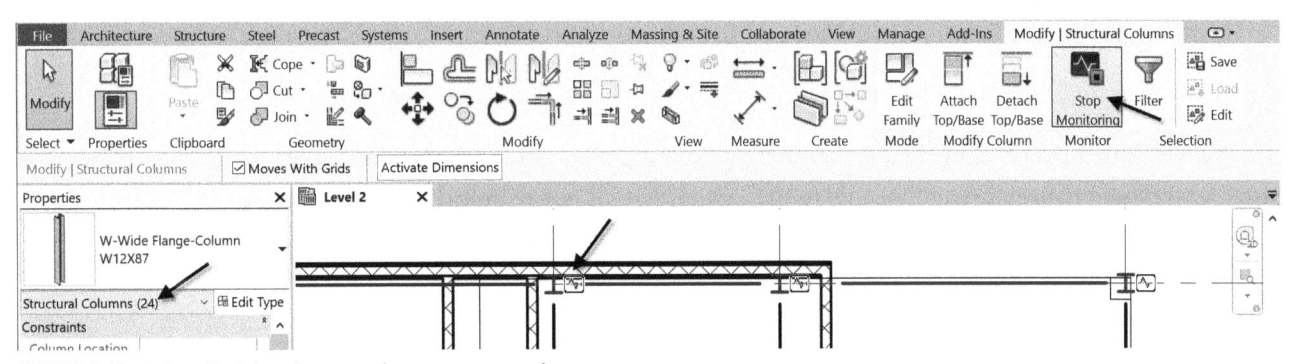

FIGURE 8.40 *Select all of the columns and stop monitoring them*

If you return to the "Coordination Review" dialog, you will see that the message about the columns no longer appears. There may still be a message about the openings, but since we copied them over, it is safe to ignore this.

10. Save and close the *08 Commercial-Structure.rvt* [*08 Commercial-Structure Metric.rvt*] file.

ADD A NEW STAIR TO THE COMMERCIAL PLAN CORE

Now that we have resolved any coordination issues in the core area, let's open the commercial project and begin adding some stairs. We will add a U-shaped egress stair to the space in the upper left corner of the core between grids 1 and 2 and C and D.

1. From the Home screen, click the Open button (or press CTRL + O) and then browse to the *Chapter08* folder.

⇨ Double-click *08 Commercial.rvt* if you wish to work in Imperial units.

⇨ Double-click *08 Commercial_M.rvt* if you wish to work in Metric units.

2. On the Project Browser, double-click to open the *Level 1* floor plan view.

⇨ Zoom in to the same area of the plan as we did above.

Some of the walls or columns might appear double in the core area. This is the linked structural file. We can adjust the visibility settings of the view to address this.

> **NOTE:** For purposes of this tutorial, the link in the dataset has been repathed to the Links folder of the dataset files instead of the structural file that you just edited. The linked file is a copy of the file opened here.

3. On the View tab, click the Visibility/Graphics button (or type VG)

334 | Chapter 8

The possibilities in the "Visibility/Graphic Overrides" dialog are nearly limitless. On Model Categories, we can turn on or off individual categories of model elements. We can also override their line styles, patterns, halftone settings, and adjust transparency. Several other tabs also appear with similar options for annotation elements, analytical elements, imported categories, etc. In this example, you have probably noticed all the trees that show in this view. We will hide those on the Model Categories tab and we will make changes on the Revit Links tab to deal with the core area display issues; we want to turn off certain redundant elements currently displaying from the linked structural model. Let's start with the trees.

4. On the Model Categories tab, uncheck Planting.

5. Click on the Revit Links tab. Two files will be listed (see item 1 in Figure 8.41).

   ⇨ Select *08 Commercial-Structure.rvt* [*08 Commercial-Structure_M.rvt*] and then in the Display Settings column, click the By Host View button (item 2).

6. In the "RVT Link Display Settings" dialog, on the Basics tab, click the Custom radio button at the top (item 3).

   ⇨ Remaining in the "RVT Link Display Settings" dialog, click on the Model Categories tab (item 4).

7. At the top, from the Model Categories drop down list, choose: **<Custom>** (item 5).

This allows us to edit the individual model categories just like we could for the host model itself. The difference is that the choices we make here apply only to the *Commercial-Structure* linked file.

   ⇨ In the Visibility column, uncheck Walls and then click OK twice (item 6).

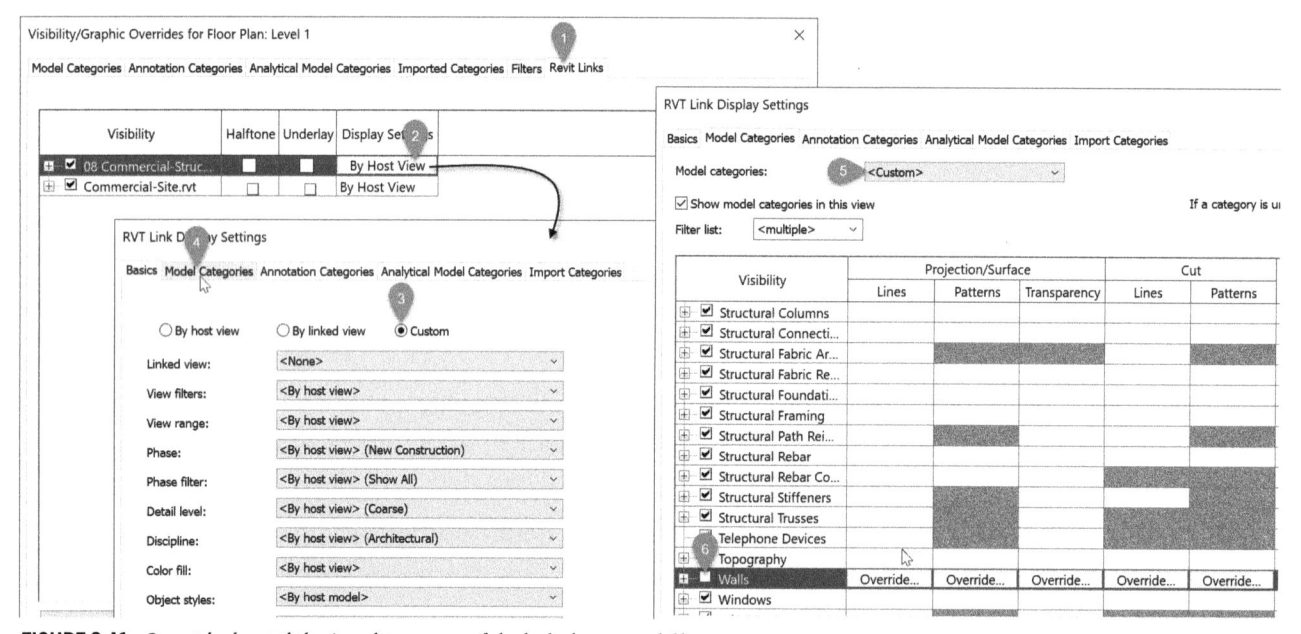

FIGURE 8.41 *Override the visibility/graphic settings of the linked structural file*

The redundant walls should no longer be displayed in this view. When you make a change like this, you likely want similar results to apply on the other floor plans. Visibility/Graphic Overrides are view-specific. This means that they apply only to the view where you apply them. However, we can save the changes we made here to a View Template and then apply this View Template to other views. This is more efficient than repeating the changes several times.

CREATE AND APPLY A VIEW TEMPLATE

View Templates offer as much power and flexibility as Visibility/Graphic Overrides. In this example, we will create a view template containing only the customizations to our linked structural file's display.

• The Aubin Academy •

1. On the View tab, on the Graphics panel, click the View Templates drop down and choose: **Create Template from Current View**.

   ⇨ Name the new template: **Typ Plan w Link Overrides** and then click OK (see the left side of Figure 8.42).

The "View Templates" dialog will appear next. Here you can verify the settings being captured in the view template, modify them or even exclude certain settings by unchecking in the "Include" column.

   ⇨ Make no changes and click OK.

2. On the Project Browser, select *Level 2*, hold down the SHIFT key and then click *Level 4*.

   This selects Levels 2 through 4.

3. Right-click any one of the selected views and choose: **Apply View Template** (see the right side of Figure 8.42).

   ⇨ In the dialog that appears, choose: **Typ Plan w Link Overrides** and then click the Apply Properties button.

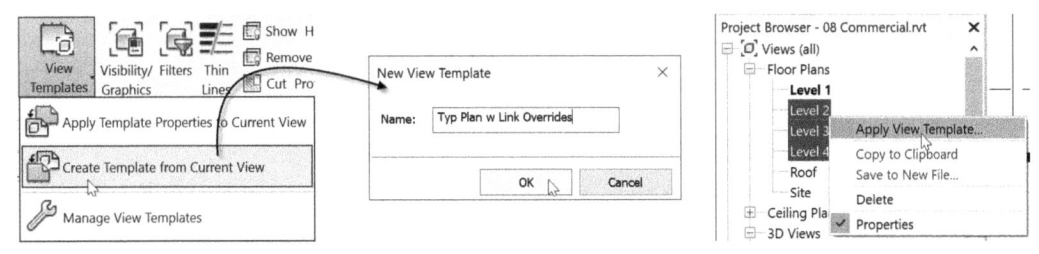

FIGURE 8.42 *Create and apply a view template to the plans*

The other plans now hide the walls from the structural file as well. If necessary, this View Template can be applied to other types of views as well. For now, we will stick to just the plans and move on to creating the core stairs.

4. Click OK to dismiss the dialog and then Save the file.

CREATE A U-SHAPED EGRESS STAIR

Previously, in the "Create a Straight Interior Stair" topic on page 310, we used the Run tool to create a straight stair for the residential project. To create a stair with a landing, you start the same way but create more than one run within the same stair. To do so, simply click short of the complete run. This leaves some of the risers unplaced. You then start another run nearby. When you do this, a landing will be created automatically. We will use this approach to create a U-shaped stair. For this example, we'll start on the second floor.

1. On the Project Browser, double-click to open the *Level 2* floor plan view.

2. On the Architecture tab, on the Circulation panel, click the Stair tool.

3. On the Properties palette, verify that the type is: **7" max riser 11" tread [190mm max riser 250mm going]**.

   ⇨ In the "Constraints" grouping, verify that Base Level is: **Level 2** and the Top Level is: **Level 3**.

   ⇨ In the "Dimensions" grouping, set the Desired Number of Risers to: **21**.

4. On the Options Bar, change the Location Line to: **Exterior Support: Left**.

   ⇨ Also on the Options Bar, for the Actual Run Width, input: **3'-8" [1100]**, make sure Automatic Landing is checked.

5. Locate the first point at the endpoint of the lower right corner of the stair core.

   ⇨ Drag the mouse horizontally to the left. When the message reads "11 Risers Created, 10 Remaining" click the mouse to set the next point along the bottom wall (see Figure 8.43).

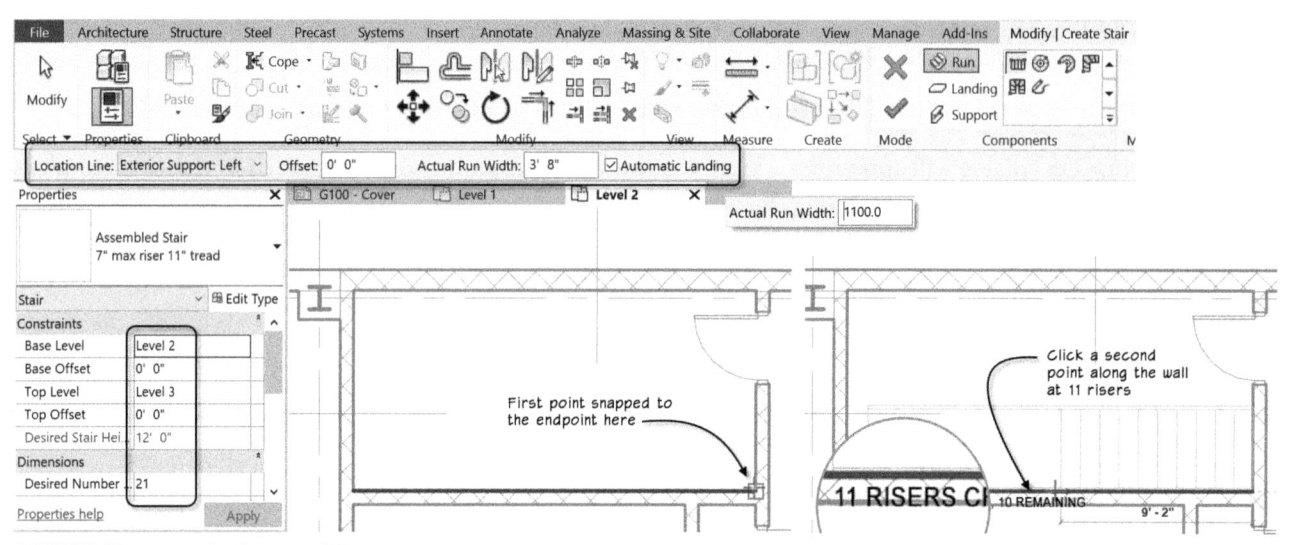

FIGURE 8.43 *Layout the first run of the stair*

6. Move the pointer above and aligned with the point just clicked and find the intersection with the opposite wall. Click to set the first point of the second run (see the left side of Figure 8.44).

   ⇨ Drag horizontally to the right along the wall and click to place all of the remaining risers (see the middle of Figure 8.44).

A U-shaped stair will appear (see the right side of the figure). The size is not exactly correct and it is not in the right spot. We can adjust both issues easily.

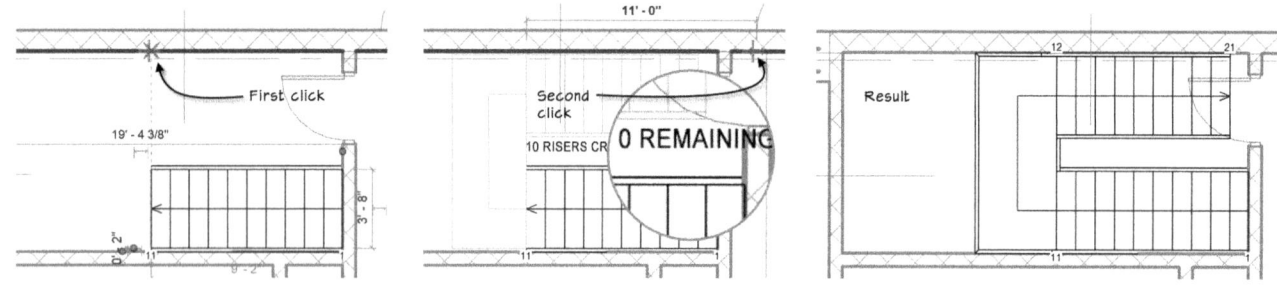

FIGURE 8.44 *Layout the second run of the stair*

7. Click the Modify tool, or press ESC twice.
8. Select the Landing component.

   Click in the middle of the landing near the path line.

9. On the Modify panel, click the Move tool.

   ⇨ Move to the left: **5'-6"** [**1875**] (see the left side of Figure 8.45).

Notice that the other stair components remain attached and move with the landing. If you move the Run components, they will adjust the size and shape of the landing instead. Therefore, we selected only the landing before moving. Try it if you like, but undo before continuing.

10. With the landing still selected, edit the temporary dimension to: **4'-6"** [**1350**].

    You can also drag the shape handle on the left edge and snap it to the face of the wall (see the right side of Figure 8.45).

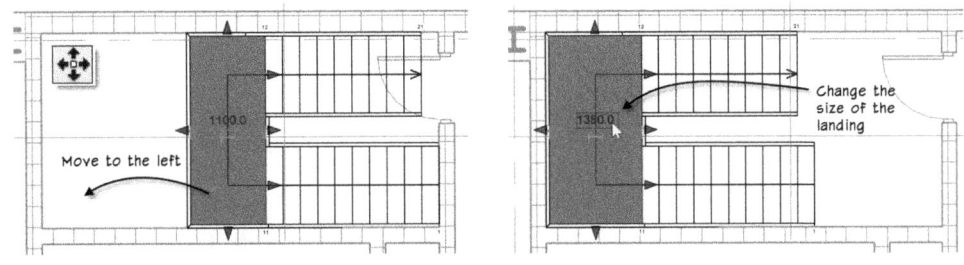

FIGURE 8.45 *Adjust the location and width of the landing*

Remember that when you create a stair, you also get a railing automatically. Let's verify the railing settings. (In cases where you prefer not to create the railing as you build the stair, choose the "None" option from the list).

11. On the Modify | Create Stair tab, click the railing button.

    ⇨ In the "Railing" dialog, choose: **Handrail – Pipe** [**900mm Pipe**].

    ⇨ For the Position, choose the **Stringer** radio button and then click OK (see Figure 8.46).

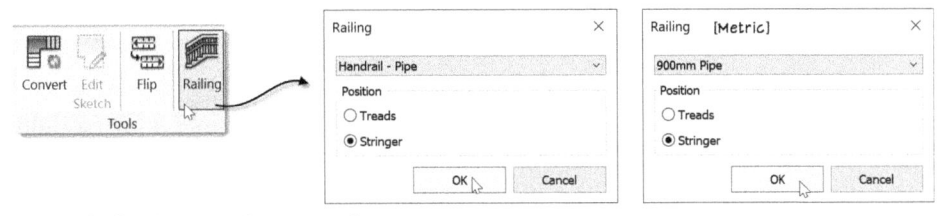

FIGURE 8.46 *Choose a railing type and its stringer position*

12. On the Mode panel of the ribbon, click the Finish Edit Mode button.

If you get a warning about the railing, you can ignore it for now. Study the result. Notice that the railing is shifted with respect to the stair. We saw the setting that controls this above. By default, railings have an Offset from Path applied. Let's remove that.

13. Using the CTRL key, select both railings.

    ⇨ On the Properties palette, change the Offset from Path setting to: **0** (zero).

14. Save the project.

CREATE A MULTISTORY STAIR

Let's look at our stair in a section view.

1. A section line runs horizontally through the stair. Double-click the blue section head to go to the: *Section at Building Core* view.

As you can see, the stair that we built only occupies the second floor. We can edit the stair to make it apply to multiple stories. In this case, we will make it go to the roof.

2. Select the stair element in the current Section view.

    Be sure to select the stair and not the railing for this step.

    ⇨ On the Modify | Stairs tab, on the Multistory Stairs panel, click the Select Levels button (see Figure 8.47).

    The geometry in the view window will gray out, including Levels 2 and 3 (which are already assigned to this stair). You can now select any additional levels that you wish to add to the stair.

3. Holding down the CTRL key, select Level 4 and Roof.

    ⇨ On the ribbon, click the Finish Edit Mode button.

• Revit Essentials for Architecture •

338 | Chapter 8

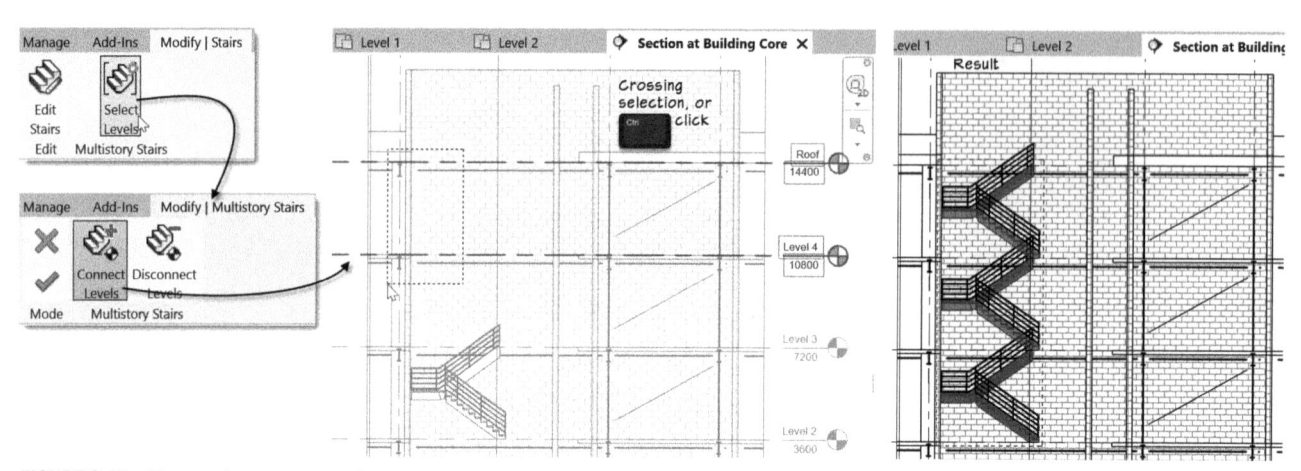

FIGURE 8.47 *Change the stair to a multistory stair*

EDITING A MULTISTORY STAIR

Multistory Stairs support levels of unequal height. Simply add the levels you need to the stair, and Revit will adjust the configuration of the stair to match the heights between the levels you select. To demonstrate, let's consider Level 1 and Street Level. Level 1 is the same floor to floor height as the other levels above, but Street Level is only a short distance below Level 1. Let's see how the stair reacts when adding these levels.

1. Select the stair.

    ⇨ On the Modify | Stairs tab, on the Multistory Stairs panel, click the Connect/Disconnect Levels button.

    This will again gray out the geometry and on the ribbon, we will have the Connect Level and Disconnect Levels buttons.

2. Click the Connect Levels button to activate it.

    ⇨ Select Street Level onscreen and then click the Finish Edit Mode button (see the left side of Figure 8.48).

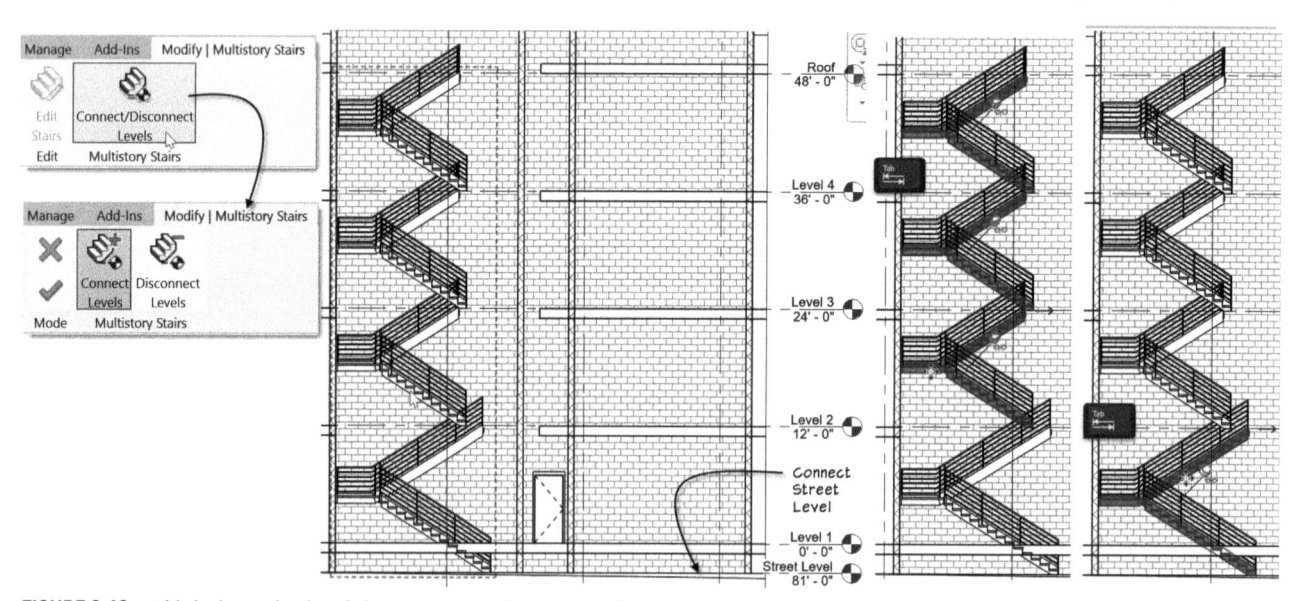

FIGURE 8.48 *Add the lowest level and then* TAB *in to see the various subgroups*

The resulting stair will now include a lower stair run that spans from Street Level to Level 2 (skipping Level 1). If you highlight the stair, a dashed box (like a group) will appear around the whole stair. If you press TAB, the top three stairs will highlight as a subgroup, while tabbing into the bottom only highlights the lower stair. In other words, each

• The Aubin Academy •

time Revit needs to adjust the stair configuration to accommodate the variance in level heights, it will spawn a new subgroup in your multistory stair (see the right side of Figure 8.48).

3. Select the multistory stair again (if you tabbed in, deselect and select it again with tabbing).

⇨ On the Modify | Stairs tab, on the Multistory Stairs panel, click the Connect/Disconnect Levels button.

⇨ Click the Connect Levels button, select Level 1 and then click the Finish Edit Mode button (see Figure 8.49).

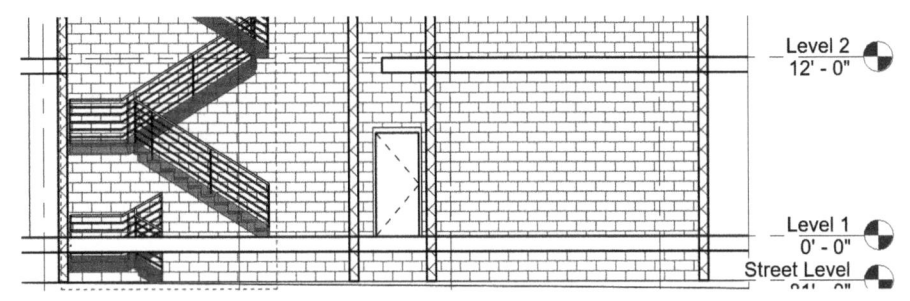

FIGURE 8.49 *Adding level 1 gives a very small stair at the bottom*

When you finish this time, you will end up with a very small stair at the bottom and another between Level 1 and 2. Furthermore, if you TAB in now, you will find that all four upper runs are part of the same subgroup and the small stair at the bottom is its own subgroup. Let's modify that lowermost stair. The floor slab on Level 1 is obscuring our view. Let's hide it temporarily.

4. Select the slab at Level 1, then on the View Control Bar, click the Temporary Hide icon (sunglasses) and choose: **Hide Element**.

5. Use the TAB key to highlight and then select the small stair at the bottom.

⇨ A small pushpin icon will appear on this item. Unpin it.

You can now edit this stair independently from the rest. If you don't unpin it first, Revit will attempt to apply any modifications you make to the stair in this subgroup to the other subgroups when you are finished. In this case, that would not yield desirable results. So be sure to unpin it first.

6. On the Modify | Stairs tab, on the Edit panel, click the Edit Stairs button.

⇨ Select the small landing to the left and the lower run and delete them.

⇨ Click the Finish Edit Mode button (see the left side of Figure 8.50).

7. TAB back in again and select the unpinned stair.

⇨ On the Properties palette, set the Base Offset to: **0** (zero).

The Desired Number of Risers should automatically adjust and the stair run should now span from Street Level to Level 1 (see the right side of Figure 8.50).

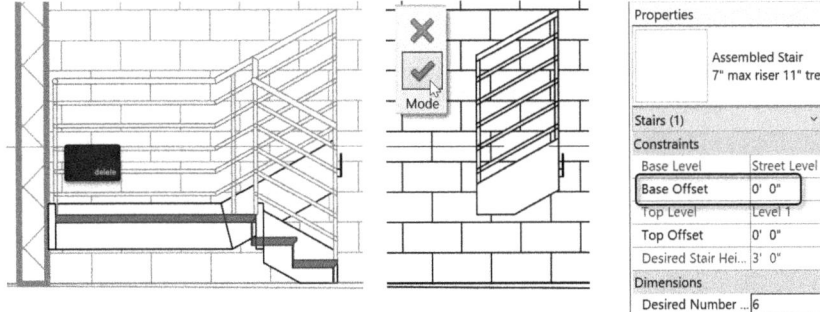

FIGURE 8.50 *Reconfigure the bottom stair*

• Revit Essentials for Architecture •

Let's adjust the lateral position of this stair relative to the others using the Align tool.

8. On the Modify tab, click the Align tool (or press AL).

⇨ For the alignment reference, click the third riser from the right on the stair above (see the left side of Figure 8.51).

⇨ Then click the edge of the riser on the small bottom stair (see the middle of Figure 8.51).

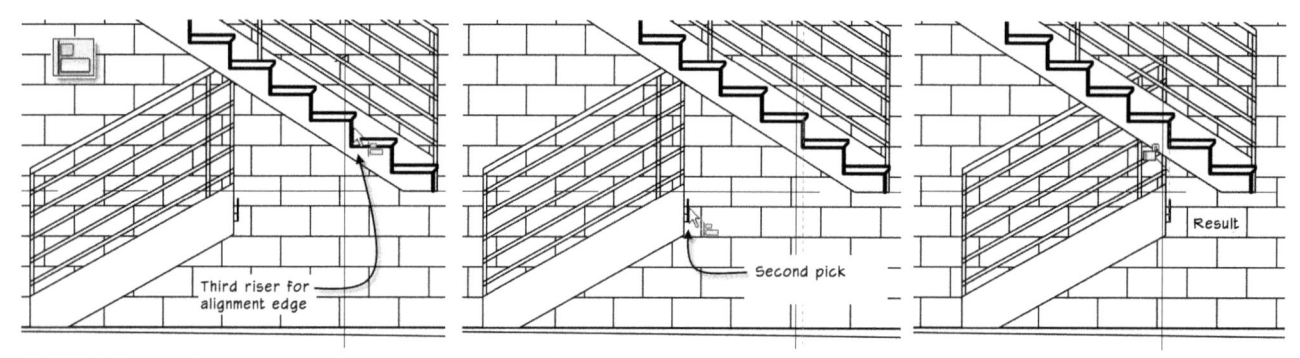

FIGURE 8.51 *Use align to position the new stair run*

You can see the result on the right-hand side of the figure. This completes the modification to the bottom stair. Notice that we can easily create this unique condition simply by unpinning the nested stair first. We will deal with landings on the right of the stair tower below.

ADJUSTING STAIR DISPLAY AND ADDING ANNOTATION

Stairs and railings have separate display components for both above and below the cut plane. (We first saw these in the "Edit Stair Display" topic on page 315 above.) We also have separate stair path annotation. In this sequence, we'll look at both features.

1. Switch back to the *Level 1* floor plan view tab (or open it if necessary).

The stair display here is a little busy and hard to understand. This is because we are seeing more than one stair run on top of each other. You can see this if you use your TAB key to highlight the various subcomponents of the multistory stair.

2. Highlight the upper run of the stair near the right side.

It will highlight with a dashed box around the entire multistory stair (see the left side of Figure 8.52).

⇨ Press TAB.

It will highlight just the subgroup stair this time. Pressing TAB again will go back to the overall (see the middle of Figure 8.52).

⇨ Move your cursor slightly to the left (about one tread) and then TAB again.

This time it will highlight the small stair at the bottom that we edited in the previous sequence (see the right side of Figure 8.52).

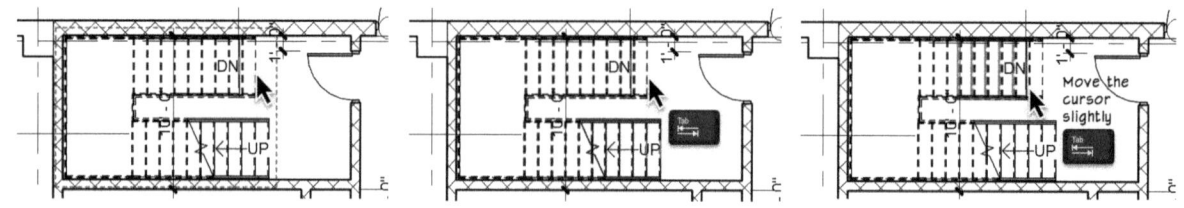

FIGURE 8.52 *Use TAB to see the various stairs visible within the view*

Vertical Circulation | 341

If you study what we are seeing a little more carefully, you can see that we have a stair starting on Level 1 and going up to Level 2. It shows this up to the cut plane and then dashes in beyond that to indicate the part of the stair above the cut plane. Like we saw in the "Edit Stair Display" topic on page 315 above, it can be nice to see the dashed portion of the stair above, but sometimes this makes the display a bit busy. And additionally, in this case that portion of the stair is concealing the small stair going down that we ought to see. Let's make a few adjustments.

3. On the View tab, on the Graphics panel, click the Visibility/Graphics button (or press VG).

   In the "Edit Stair Display" topic on page 315 above we turned off all of the above components. In this case, we'll leave the outline displayed.

   ⇨ Expand stairs, and then uncheck all Above components except <Above> Outlines.

   ⇨ Expand railings, and then uncheck all Above components and then click OK (see the left side of Figure 8.53).

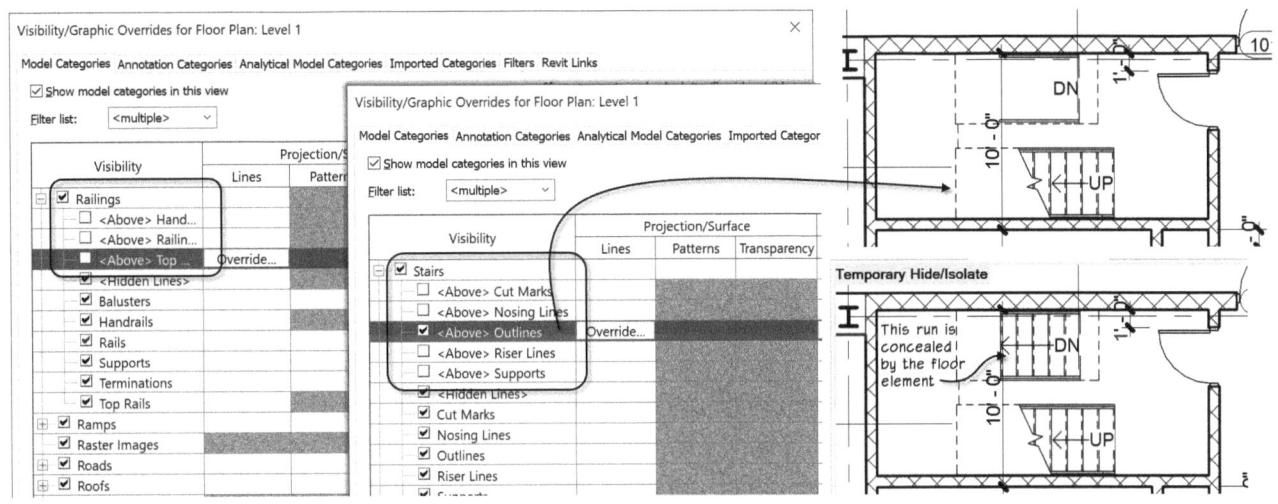

FIGURE 8.53 *Edit the display of the stair and railing "above" components*

The above portion of the stair should now display as a simple dashed outline (top-right of Figure 8.53). But notice that the lowermost run (the one we edited above), looks a little odd. We are only seeing its edges. These are the railings and the reason we don't see the stair, is because the floor slab is in the way. We will address this a little later.

> **TIP:** If you wish to verify that the slab is in the way, you can use temporary hide to hide the slab. To do this, first select the floor element, then on the View Control Bar, click the Temporary Hide/Isolate pop-up (sunglasses) and choose: **Hide Element**. To select the floor, you can place your cursor near the edge of an exterior wall and use the TAB key until it highlights. You can also turn on Select element by face. This is on the drop down directly beneath the Modify tool. Or you can even select it in the section view, then switch back to floor plan to hide. When you wish to restore the view, choose: **Reset Temporary Hide/Isolate** from the pop-up.

For now, let's add some annotation to indicate the direction of travel. There are also some default stair path annotations already applied to the stair. If you don't like the default one, you can modify it.

4. Select the "Up" annotation and on the Properties palette, from the Type Selector, choose: **Automatic Up/Down Direction : Standard** if it is not already chosen.

   ⇨ Repeat this in the other plan views including the *Roof* plan.

5. If you find a view that does not have the annotation, you can add one. On the Annotate tab, on the Symbol panel, click the Stair Path button. Then select the stair.

• Revit Essentials for Architecture •

This annotation shows direction relative to the current plan. Therefore, on the intermediate levels like Levels 2, 3 and 4, it shows both UP and DN labels. In Level 1, we see UP only and at the top of the run in the Roof level, we see DN only (see Figure 8.54).

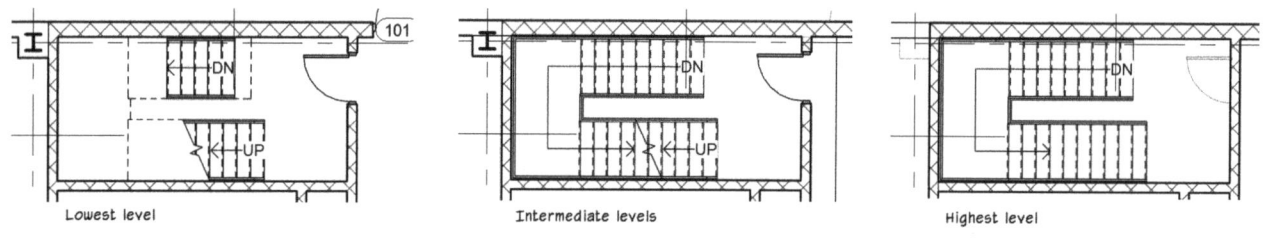

FIGURE 8.54 *Annotation applied to stairs shows the direction of travel relative to the current plan*

> **TIP:** The UP and DN annotations can be moved. Select the annotation and a blue control dot appears next to the text. Click and drag the text to a better location. The double arrow control allows you to move the arrow.

If you prefer, there is an alternative annotation that shows the direction of UP travel only for both stairs on each view. Feel free to use this one if you prefer.

6. Save the project.

FLOORS, LANDINGS AND SHAFTS

In the previous chapter, we created some simple floors and a roof for the project. We used a shaft opening element to cut these horizontal surfaces through all floors at the stair and elevator shafts. Another glance at the section in our current model will reveal that there are no landings on the entrance side (right) of the stairs and that our shaft is not deep enough (contributing to the display issue with the floor element cited above). For each floor, we have a single continuous floor element across the entire floor plate with a single shaft cutting out both the stair and elevator spaces.

At this point, to accommodate the stair elements that we have added, and add landings on the entrance side to meet the stairs, we need to adjust the shape of our existing shaft. We have a few options: we can edit this shape to reveal more of the slabs in the area of these landings, or we can remove the shaft, edit each of the floor sketches, and/or build the landings as separate elements. The exact approach that we take is really a matter of personal preference. If the shape of the void is the same on all levels, the shaft approach is easier because we only need one sketch. If the shape of each landing varies floor to floor, it is better to edit the sketch of each floor element instead. If the thickness of the landing is different than the thickness of the floors, creating separate landings might be best. If we edit the stairs, we also have the option to create landings as part of the stair. Let's look at two of the approaches mentioned. For the upper floors, we will do the simplest solution and edit the shaft. For the lowest level, we will edit the stair and make a custom landing. If you wish to try making floors as landings for the upper stairs, you are welcome to try that on your own.

EDIT THE SHAFT

Regardless of the approach we choose, the shaft we have here will require editing. So, we'll start with it. Editing the shaft is easy. We simply select it and then edit its sketch.

1. Return to the *Section at Building Core* section view. (If you closed it, open it from Project Browser).

   ⇨ Move the pointer near the edge of the shaft (you should be able to see where it cuts and place your cursor there).

   Use the TAB key to cycle through the different elements to find the shaft if necessary.

Vertical Circulation | 343

- ⇨ When the screen tip reads "Shaft Opening: Opening Cut" and the shaft pre-highlights, click the mouse to select it. The Shaft will turn semi-opaque while it is selected.

2. On the Properties palette, change the Base Constraint to: **Level 2**.

- ⇨ Set the Base Offset to: `-1'-0"` [`-300`].

3. On the Modify | Shaft Openings tab, click the Edit Sketch button.

- ⇨ In the "Go To View" dialog, choose: *Floor Plan: Level 3* and then click the Open View button (see Figure 8.55).

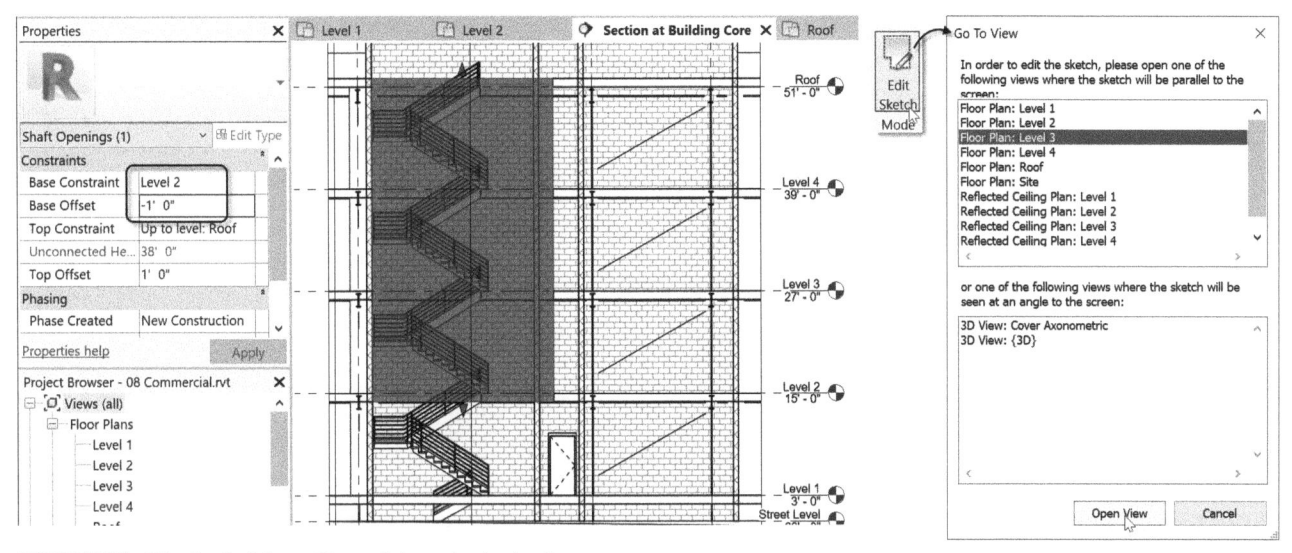

FIGURE 8.55 *Edit the shaft base offset and then edit the sketch*

4. Move the top horizontal sketch line up to the outside of the top exterior wall (at the stair).

- ⇨ Move the bottom line up to the outside bottom edge of the elevator shaft.

- ⇨ Move the right line to the outside right edge of the elevator shaft and the left line to the outside edge of the core wall.

You can drag the lines; use the Move tool or the Align tool for this (see Figure 8.56).

> **TIP:** You can make your sketch lines appear bolder on screen as you work by editing their line-weight in the Line Styles dialog (Manage tab, Additional Settings drop down).

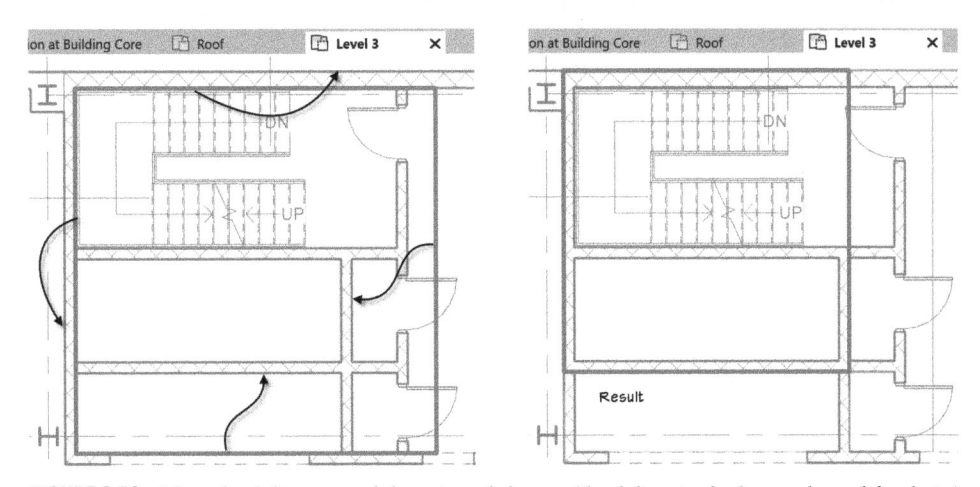

FIGURE 8.56 *Adjust sketch lines around the stair and elevator (sketch lines in the figure enhanced for clarity)*

5. Remain in sketch mode. On the Draw panel, click the Pick Lines icon.

• Revit Essentials for Architecture •

344 | Chapter 8

⇨ At the top of the stair, click the top right tread line near the DN label.

⇨ Also click the lower inside face of the wall in the stair core (see the left side of Figure 8.57).

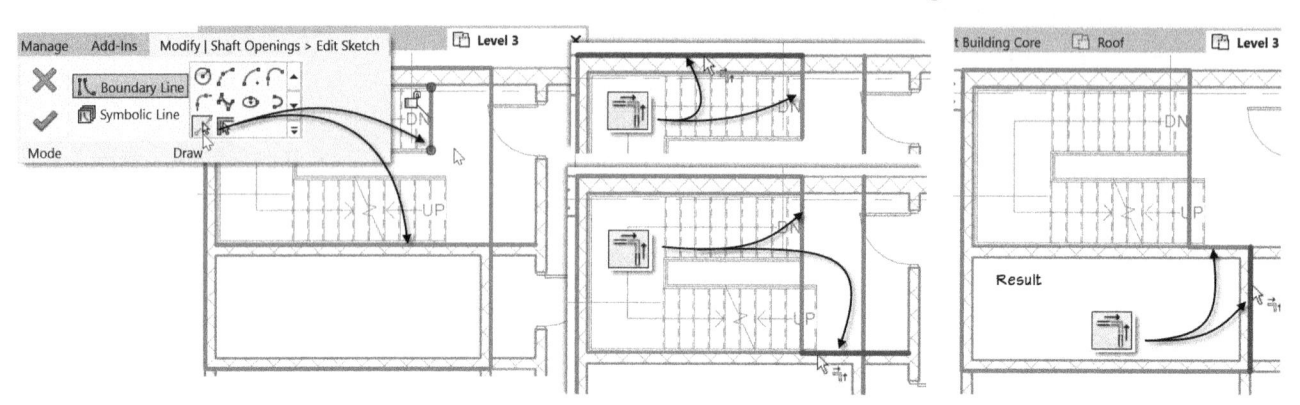

FIGURE 8.57 *Use the Pick Lines option to create sketch lines from existing wall edges. Trim/Extend to complete the sketch*

6. On the Modify panel, click the Trim/Extend to Corner button (or press TR).

⇨ Using the right side of Figure 8.57 as a guide, trim/extend the three corners indicated. (Remember, click the side of the line you wish to keep.)

7. On the Modify | Shaft Openings > Edit Sketch tab, click the Finish Edit Mode button.

⇨ Deselect the Shaft.

The result of this change in plan is noticeable at the middle of the stair between the two runs. The section will show the results much more clearly (see Figure 8.58).

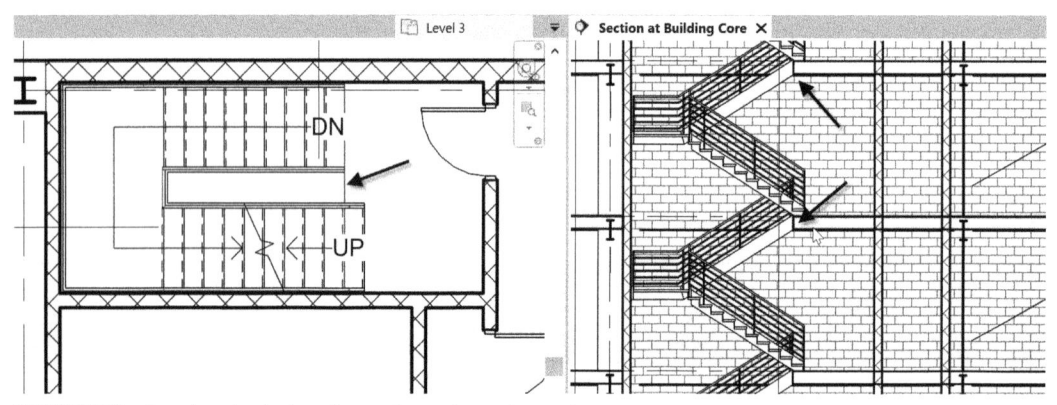

FIGURE 8.58 *Complete the shaft and view the results in plan and section*

JOIN GEOMETRY IN SECTION

When you study this edit in section view, you will notice that the floor slabs now extend to the stairs providing a nice landing at the right side. However, we also notice that the walls in the core area pass right through the floor slab. We can make these intersections clean up nicer by using the Join Geometry command.

(If it is not already open) on the Project Browser, double-click to open the *Section at Building Core* view.

1. On the Modify tab of the ribbon, on the Geometry panel, click the Join Geometry button.

⇨ On the Options Bar, check the Multiple Join check box.

2. Click the floor slab at Level 2 and then click each of the walls that intersect it (see Figure 8.59).

• The Aubin Academy •

Vertical Circulation | 345

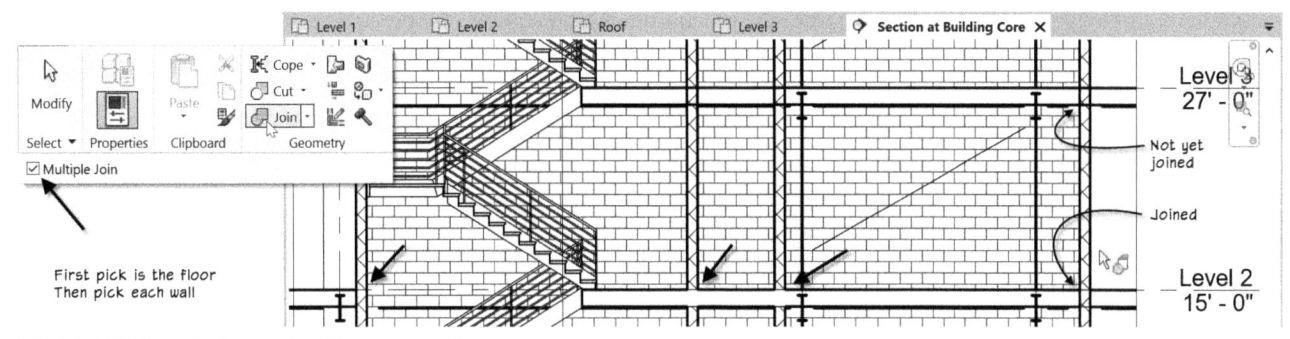

FIGURE 8.59 *Join the floor and wall geometry in the section*

3. Click the Modify tool or press the ESC key twice.
4. Repeat the process for each of the other floor slabs in the section.

    Remember to click the Modify tool after you complete each floor. Otherwise you will get an error.

The floors will now clean up much nicer with the core walls. Multiple Join is handy and reduces the number of clicks required to complete the task, but you must remember to cancel out before moving on to the next floor.

5. Save the project.

DUPLICATE AND MODIFY A SHAFT

Earlier we noted that the lowest level of our multistory stair was not displaying correctly because the floor element was concealing it. Let's address that now with an adjustment to the shaft opening element. However, since the shape of the shaft on the lowest level is not the same as the upper levels, we will need to make a new shaft instead.

(If it is not already open) on the Project Browser, double-click to open the *Section at Building Core* view.

1. Select the shaft.
2. On the Modify | Stairs ribbon, on the Clipboard panel, click the Copy to Clipboard button (or press CTRL + C).
   ⇨ On the Clipboard panel, click the drop down on the Paste button and choose: **Aligned to Selected Levels**.
   ⇨ In the "Select Levels" dialog, choose **Street Level** and then click OK.

The new shaft will remain selected. Notice that it is still three stories tall. Copy and Paste typically maintains the height of the pasted elements. We only need this new shaft to be one story tall, so let's adjust that next.

3. On the Properties palette, verify that the Base Constraint is: **Street Level**.
   ⇨ Change the Base Offset to: **0** (zero).
   ⇨ From the Top Constraint list, choose: **Up to level: Level 2**.
   ⇨ Change the Top Offset to: **-2'-0"** [**-600**] (see Figure 8.60).

346 | Chapter 8

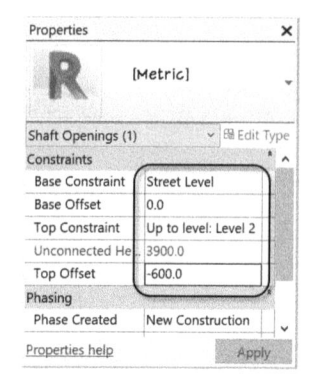

FIGURE 8.60 *Copy and paste the shaft to the Street Level and adjust its height settings*

4. On the ribbon, click the Edit Sketch button.

⇨ In the "Go To View" dialog, choose: *Floor Plan: Level 1* and then click Open View.

5. Using the Align tool, move the vertical sketch line running through the right side of the stairs to the inside face of the core wall on the right (see Figure 8.61).

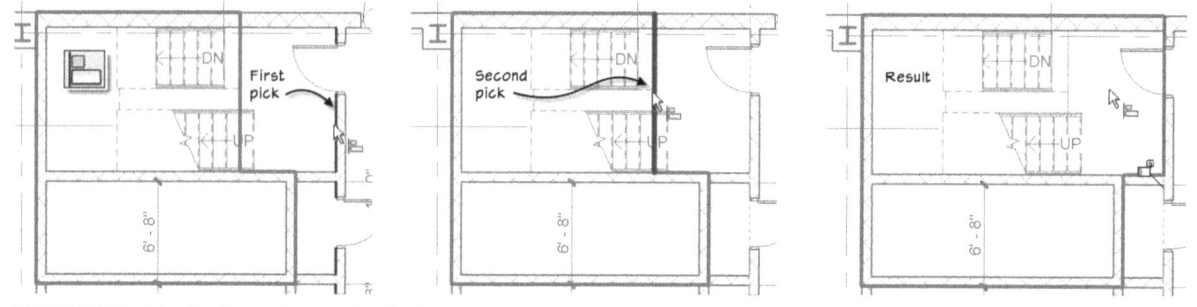

FIGURE 8.61 *Edit the shape of the shaft at level 1*

⇨ On the ribbon, click the Finish Edit Mode button.

Notice that following this change, we can now see the small stair run at the lowest level clearly without needing to hide the floor element.

We are modifying the shaft this way so that we can allow room for a custom landing on the right side of the stair. This was noted as one of our options above. Alternatively, you can approach the landing on the right the same as how we did for the other levels. If you choose to do that, you will want to align the sketch line noted about to the next riser over on the left *instead* of the core wall on the right. And then you can skip the next topic. The choice is up to you.

CREATE A CUSTOM STAIR LANDING

As we have already seen, a stair is made up one or more runs and can also contain supports and landings. Move your mouse around onscreen and you can highlight these individual components and select them (you will often need to use the TAB key to assist you in this). In this sequence, we'll edit the lowest stair element in our multistory stair and add a custom landing to it.

1. In the *Level 1* plan view, use the TAB key to assist and select the small lowermost stair element (the one we edited previously at the bottom of the multistory stair).

⇨ On the ribbon click the Edit Stairs button.

TIP: For this sequence, you might find it easier to close all view tabs except the *Level 1* floor plan and the *Section at Building Core* and then tile them (WT).

• The Aubin Academy •

2. On the Modify | Create Stair ribbon, on the Components panel, click the Landing tool.

⇨ For the creation mode, click the Create Sketch icon (see the left side of Figure 8.62).

When making a landing, the default mode is to pick two runs. A landing will be created automatically between them. In this case, we only have one run. Therefore, we need to use the Create Sketch option instead. This will allow us to sketch a custom shape for the landing.

A Modify | Create Stair > Sketch Landing tab will now appear on the ribbon.

3. In the Draw panel, click the Pick Lines tool.

⇨ Pick the three inside faces of the core walls; right, top and bottom.

⇨ On the lower run of stairs, click the second riser line from the right. On the upper run, click the rightmost riser line and the bottom edge of the run (see the middle of Figure 8.62).

⇨ Use Trim/Extend to Corner (TR) to close all the corners (see the right side of Figure 8.62).

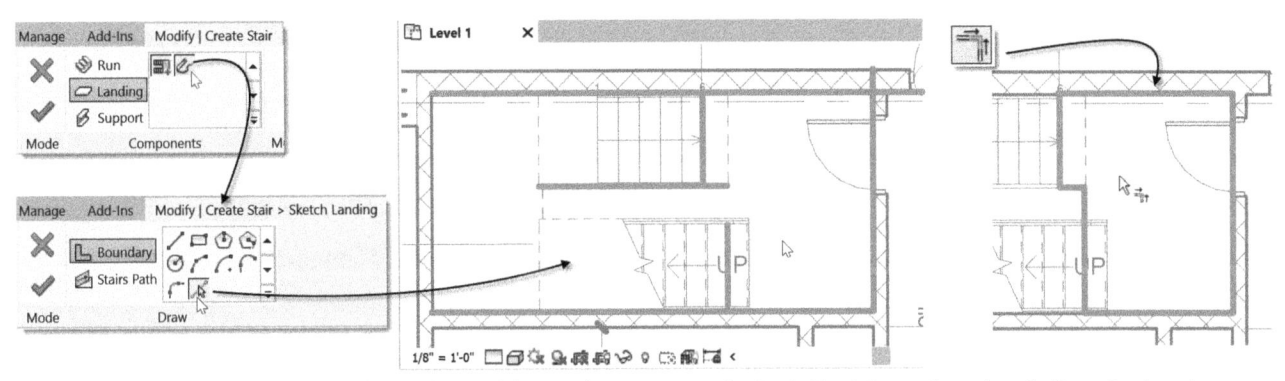

FIGURE 8.62 *Create a sketch-based landing and use pick lines and trim to create the sketch (sketch lines enhanced in the figure for clarity)*

4. Click the Finish Edit Mode button.

Unfortunately, that is not quite right. Notice how a border has been added all the way around the landing edge we sketched. These are the supports that Revit adds automatically to the landing. We can easily allow for this, but to do so, we must edit the sketch again.

5. If necessary, reselect the landing. On the Tools panel of the ribbon, click the Edit Sketch button.

⇨ On the Modify panel, click the Offset tool (or press OF).

⇨ On the Options Bar, set the Offset to: **2"** [**50**], and then uncheck the Copy check box.

⇨ Click in white space in the model view to shift focus away from the Options Bar.

⇨ Highlight one of the green lines, press TAB, then when offset to the inside, click (see Figure 8.63).

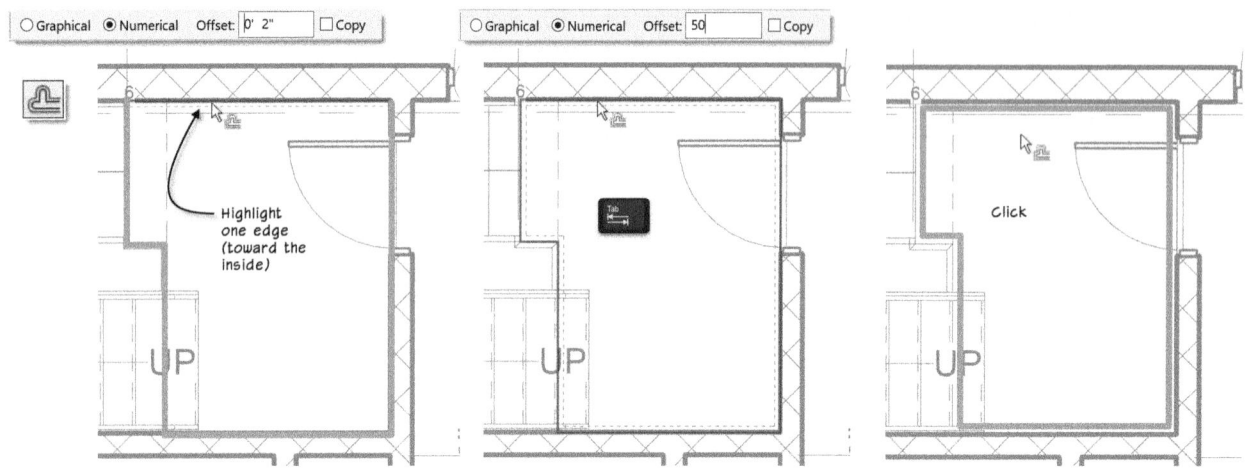

FIGURE 8.63 *Offset the edge of the landing sketch to the inside*

This offsets the entire shape inside by the offset value you input. However, two of these lines should remain where they were. So, we can simply offset them back without the TAB this time.

6. Remaining in the Offset command with the same options on the Options Bar, offset the vertical line at the top-left (adjacent to the short run of stairs) back towards the stair.

⇨ Offset the vertical line on the right back toward the core wall (see the left side of Figure 8.64).

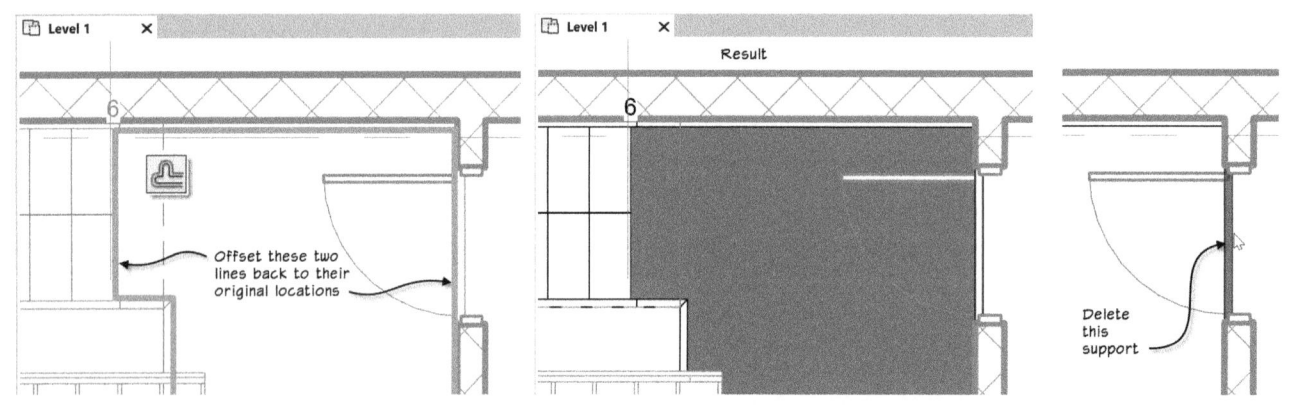

FIGURE 8.64 *Offset two sketch lines back to their original locations*

7. On the ribbon, click the Finish Edit Mode button.

This is much better, but we still have one support we don't need. The one on the right by the door. We can simply delete this.

8. Select the support at the doorway. Use TAB if necessary and then delete it (see the right side of Figure 8.64).

⇨ On the ribbon, click the Finish Edit Mode button.

The landing is now complete but notice that something else does not look quite right. When you create this landing, Revit tries to be helpful and adds a railing all the way around it. We saw this behavior back in the "Add a Stair" topic on page 23 in Chapter 1. As we saw then and earlier in this chapter, we can simply edit the sketch of the railing to fix this.

EDIT RAILINGS

We have a little more work to do the railings. We might want a different type of railing at the walls. And the railing at the landing we just built also needs to be adjusted.

1. On the Project Browser, double-click to open the *Level 2* floor plan view.
2. Select the inside railing.

    Make sure you select the railing and not the stair; use the TAB key if necessary.

    ⇨ On the ribbon, click the Edit Path button.

3. Draw the two segments indicated in Figure 8.65.

    Make sure you don't let the last segment snap closed. Leave a small gap. Zoom in as necessary to ensure this.

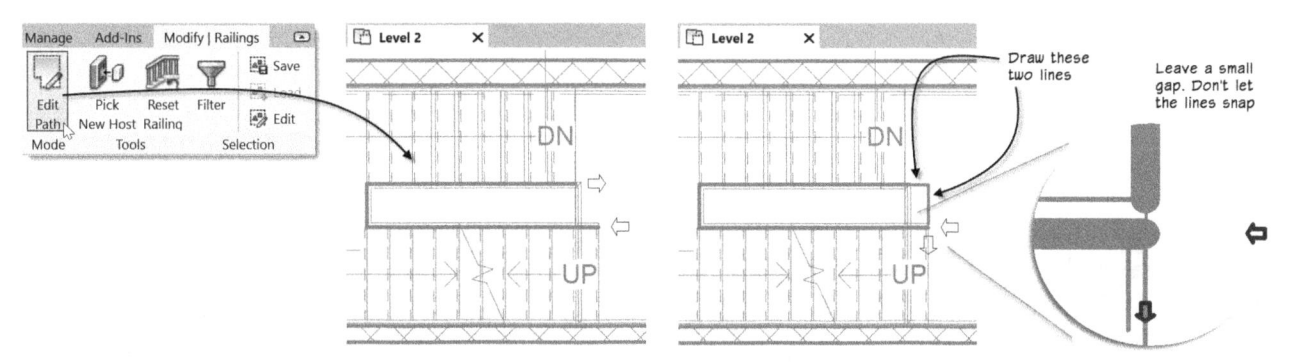

FIGURE 8.65 *Draw two segments in the railing sketch*

    ⇨ On the ribbon, click the Finish Edit Mode button.

The best way to view the result is in a 3D view. If we use the default *{3D}* view, we will have to isolate the stair (as we did above in the residential project) to see the railing. Another option is to create a new 3D view of just the stairs. In this case, creating a 3D view from the *Section at Building Core* view would be the best choice. It will give use a three-dimensional section view in which to study the stairs and railings.

4. On the Project Browser, right-click the *{3D}* view and choose: **Duplicate View > Duplicate**.

    ⇨ Right-click the *Copy of {3D}* view and choose: **Rename**.

    ⇨ In the "Rename View" dialog change the name to: **3D Stair Section** and then click OK.

5. In the view window, right-click the ViewCube and choose: **Orient to View > Sections > Section at Building Core** (see item 1 in Figure 8.66).

    Hold your SHIFT key down and drag with the wheel on your mouse to orbit the model around and see the effect.

> **TIP:** If you prefer, you can drag the ViewCube or use the Steering Wheel instead (see item 2 in Figure 8.66).

    Zoom in on the second floor at the point where we edited the railing. Pan to other floors as well (see item 3 in Figure 8.66).

• Revit Essentials for Architecture •

350 | Chapter 8

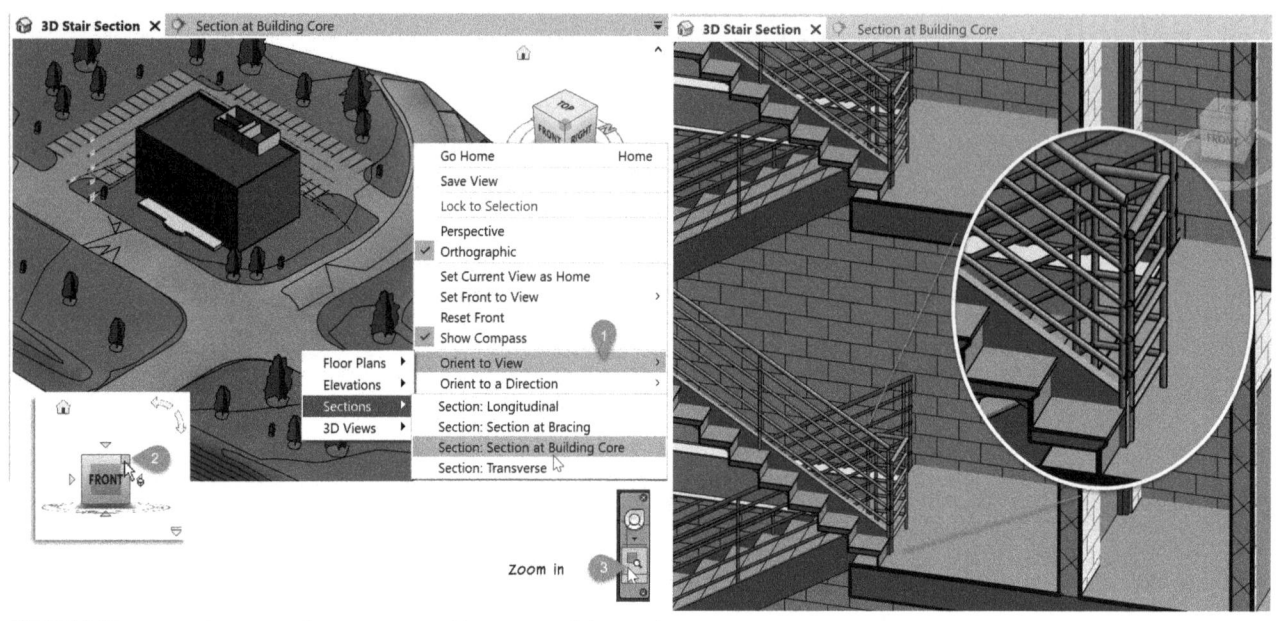

FIGURE 8.66 *Orient the view to the Section at Building Core and then study it in 3D*

> **TIP:** If you witness a strange artifact for the balusters in the 3D view, you can edit your sketch and pull the vertical sketch line back slightly from the horizontal segment, so they don't join. Leave the vertical segment about an inch [few millimeters] short.

Notice that the railing now wraps around the gap between the two runs and this change has occurred on the upper levels as well (see the right side of Figure 8.66). The railing we have on Level 1 needs a little attention as well.

6. Return to the *Level 1* floor plan view.

7. Select the railing on the bottommost stair.

   Notice that it is a single railing that wraps all the way around the landing and down each side of the stair.

8. On the Modify tab, click the Split Element tool (or press SL).

   ⇨ Click at the point just before where this railing overlaps the one for the other stair (see the middle of Figure 8.67).

   ⇨ Click the Modify tool or press the ESC key twice.

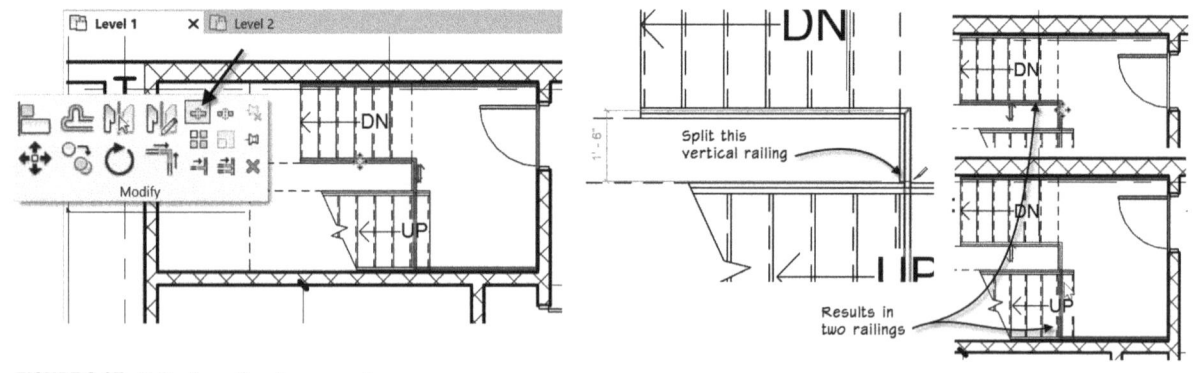

FIGURE 8.67 *Split the railing into two pieces*

This results in two railings. One that is on the inside of the stairs and has an "L" shape. The other on the outside of the stair and wrapping around the landing. The "L" shaped piece is all set. Let's edit the wrap around piece.

9. Select the railing on the outside of the stair that continues around the landing.

• The Aubin Academy •

⇨ On the ribbon click Edit Path.

⇨ Delete the two vertical sketch lines and the horizontal one along the bottom edge of the landing. (Leave only the two sketch lines along the top).

⇨ On the ribbon, click the Finish Edit Mode button.

ADD A RAILING EXTENSION

At the very bottom of the stair we can use the railing extension feature to add an automatic extension to the railing. We'll duplicate the railing type first so that it will apply only to the railing at the bottom of the stair.

1. Select the inside "L" shaped railing at the bottom stair.

    ⇨ On the Properties palette, click the Edit Type button and then click the Duplicate button (or press ALT + D) (see item 1 in Figure 8.68).

    ⇨ For the name, input: **Handrail – Pipe – Bottom Extension** (item 2).

2. Beneath the Top Rail grouping, click in the Type field, then click the small browse button that appears (item 3).

3. In the second "Type Properties" dialog that appears, click Duplicate (or press ALT + D) and name it: **Circular w Extension** (item 4).

    ⇨ Beneath the Extension (Beginning/Bottom) grouping, for Extension Style, choose: **Post**.

    ⇨ Set the Length to: **1'-0"** [**300**] and check the "Plus Tread Depth" check box.

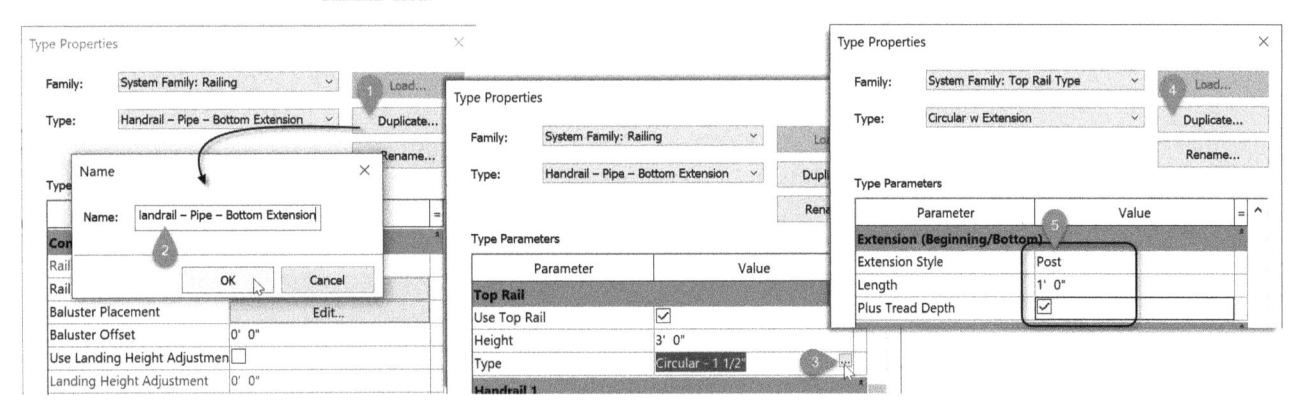

FIGURE 8.68 *Duplicate and rename the railing type and its nested top rail type*

4. Click OK twice to see the results.

5. In the *Level 1* floor plan, move door 101 to the left of this stair.

    ⇨ On the Properties palette, with the door selected, change the Level to: Street Level.

    In the *3D Stair Section* view, zoom in on the lower stair and orbit around so you can see the lower inside railing clearly (see Figure 8.69). If the door you just moved does not seem to be cutting the wall, repeat the steps from above in the "Add a New Stair to the Commercial Plan Core" topic on page 333 to hide the walls from the structural model in this view.

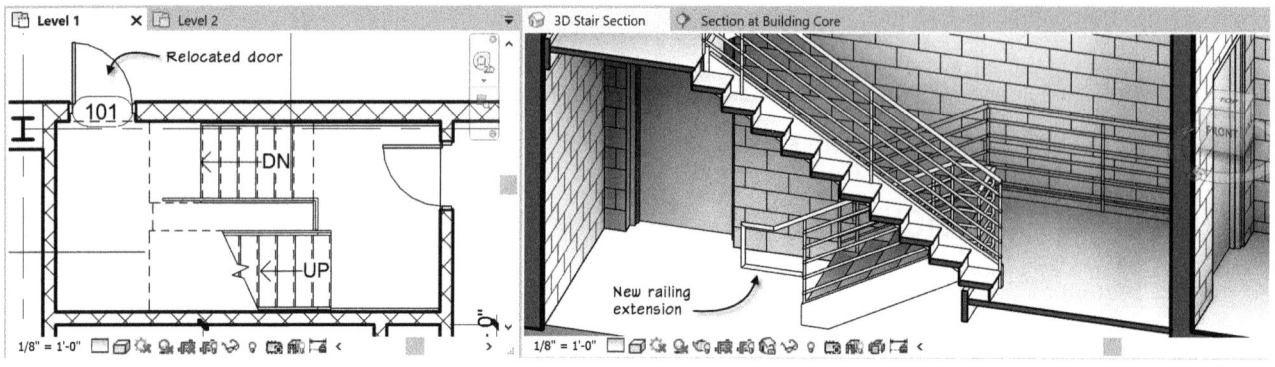

FIGURE 8.69 *Study the results of the new railing type and moving the door*

ADJUST THE OUTSIDE RAILINGS

The outside railing needs only a single handrail. Previously in the "Create a Simple Railing Type" topic on page 322 of the residential project, we created a new railing type that did not have any balusters. To save time, a similarly configured type is already provided in this file. However, if you wish, feel free to create your own following similar steps to those laid out above for the residential project.

> Continue in the *3D Stair Section* view.

1. Select both outside railings (the ones adjacent to the core walls, not the one between the stair runs).

   ⇨ From the Type Selector on the Properties palette, choose: **Handrail – Pipe – Wall**.

The railing will change to a single Handrail. If you edit the type of this railing, the settings resemble the one that built above in the "Create a Simple Railing Type" topic on page 322. Railing extensions have already been added to this railing type. You will notice that the lowermost rail is now a bit too long and goes past the wall into the hallway. You can edit its sketch to correct that.

2. Select the lowermost outside railing only.

   ⇨ Click the Edit Path button.

   ⇨ Stretch the sketch line back into the stairwell space and then click Finish Edit Mode (see the left side of Figure 8.70).

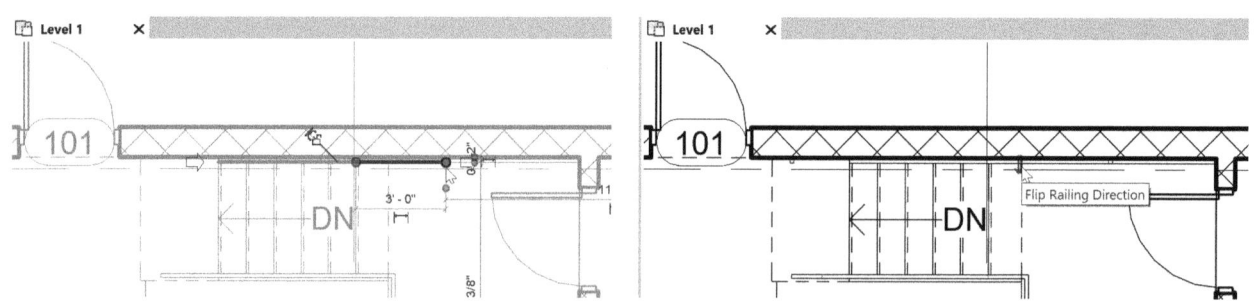

FIGURE 8.70 *Assign a new handrail type*

> Notice that the railing at the bottom is flipped.

3. Select the railing and then click the small Flip Railing Direction control (see the right side of Figure 8.70).

You might also notice that the railing seems to float away from the wall a little. If this is the case, you can input a new value into the Offset from Path parameter on the Properties palette. This value can be negative. Try a value of: **-2"** [**-50**] (see Figure 8.71).

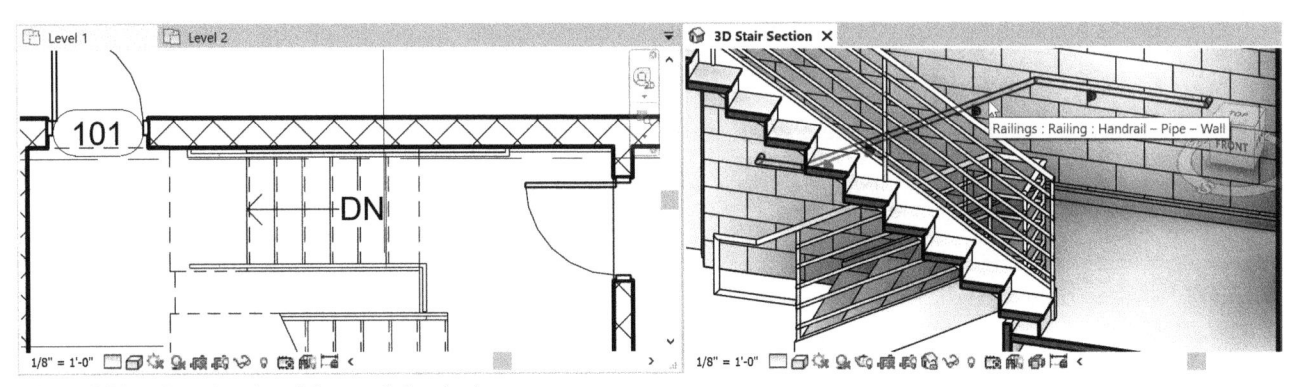

FIGURE 8.71 *Adjust the offset of the outside handrails*

4. Save the project.

RAMPS AND ELEVATORS

In this topic, we will add some ramps and elevators. Ramps and elevators are grouped here to round out our look at vertical circulation, but the approach to working with each one is quite different. Creating a ramp in Revit is like adding a stair. Elevators on the other hand are simply component families that we insert in our models like other components.

CREATE AN ENLARGED PLAN VIEW

Let's create an enlarged floor plan view showing just the front portion of the building.

 If it is not already open, on the Project Browser, double-click to open the *Level 1* plan view.

1. On the View tab of the ribbon, on the Create panel click the Callout tool.
2. Drag a box around the patio slab at the front of the building.
 ⇨ Right-click the callout boundary and choose: **Go To View** (see Figure 8.72).

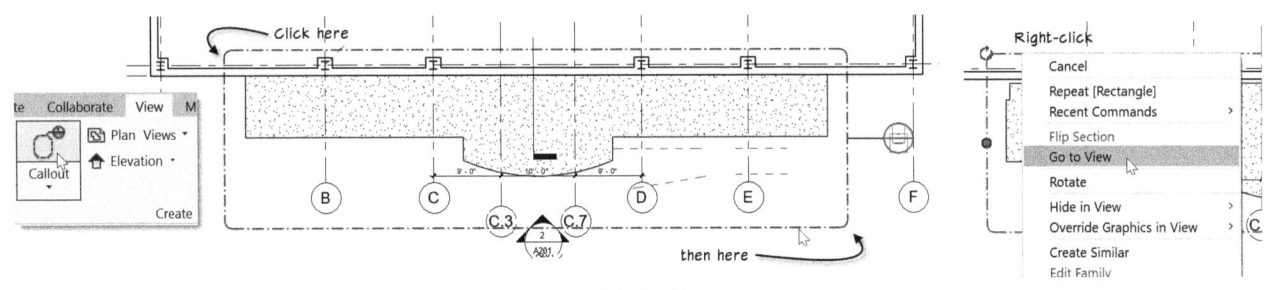

FIGURE 8.72 *Create the callout view of the patio slab at the front of the building*

3. On the Project Browser, right-click *Level 1 - Callout 1* and choose: **Rename**.
 ⇨ Name the view: **Entrance Plan** and then click OK.

ADD A RAMP

The Ramp tool is on the Architecture tab, on the Circulation panel. They are sketch-based elements but share some similarities with stairs. To save a bit of time and effort, the dataset includes a floor slab at the front of the building as an entrance patio. Some reference planes have been included here as well. These reference planes are provided to make it easy for us to the sketch the ramp in the following example.

1. Zoom in on the lower right corner at the front of the building where the dashed green reference planes are.

354 | Chapter 8

2. On the Architecture tab, on the Circulation panel, click the Ramp tool.

⇨ On the Properties palette, beneath the "Dimensions" grouping set the Width to: **3'-0"** [**900**].

⇨ Change the "Base Level" to: **Street Level** and the "Top Level" to: **Level 1**.

3. Starting at the lower left endpoint of the inclined reference plane, click on each reference plane endpoint moving first left to right, then up, then right to left (see top-left corner of Figure 8.73).

> **NOTE:** You only click the start and end of the runs. The landings fill in automatically.

Also, note in the figure, that the first click in the run will show a tooltip for the Endpoint, but not highlight the point with the customary square snap indicator. The square snap indicator does appear on the second click. This anomaly should not prove detrimental to completing the exercise.

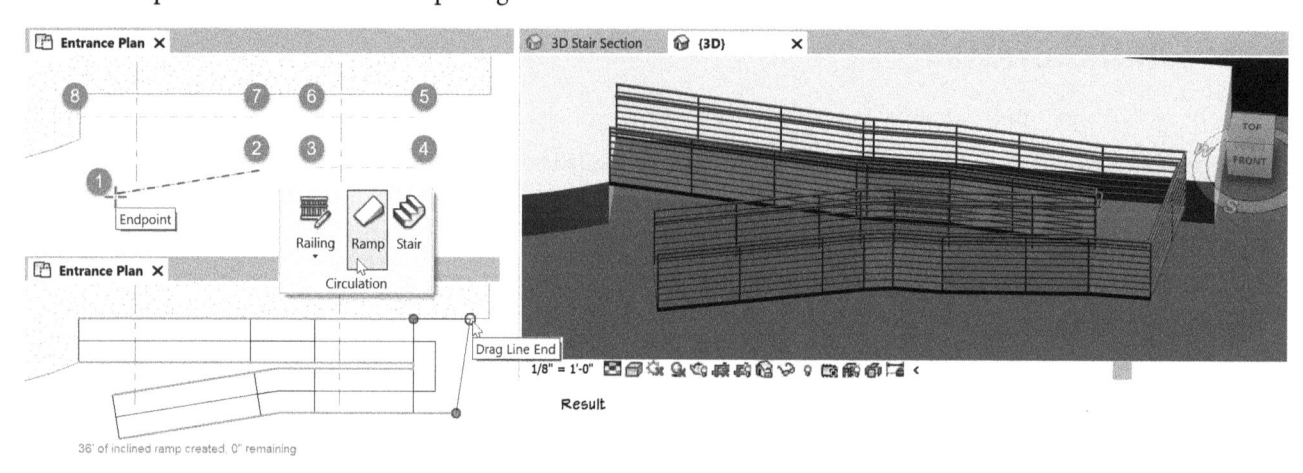

FIGURE 8.73 *Sketch the ramp using the provided reference planes and then study it in other views*

If you wish, you can edit the shape of the green outline on the right side at the landing to match the figure. Try moving the vertical green boundary line to the right about 1'-0" [300] to widen the landing, or even change the shape to angle or curve it if you like.

> **NOTE:** While we have provided the reference planes in this exercise to make the process of sketching the ramp go smoothly, you do not need reference planes when adding ramps in your own projects. Remember that you can sketch the run, or edit the risers or boundaries directly with the appropriate tools on the Draw panel. Boundaries are the green lines, risers are black and the path is blue.

4. On the Modify | Create Ramp Sketch tab, on the Tools panel, click the Railing button.

⇨ In the "Railing" dialog, choose: **Guardrail – Pipe** from the list and then click OK.

5. On the Modify | Create Ramp Sketch tab, click the Finish Edit Mode button.

If you get an error message about the railing, try flipping the railings using the control handle in plan. The guardrails come in on the wrong side sometimes. This should correct it.

View the ramp in various views to see the results (shown in 3D on the right side of see Figure 8.73).

6. Return to the Entrance Plan view and then Mirror the ramp and its railings to the other side.

7. On the Modify | Multi-Select tab, click the Mirror – Draw Axis tool (or press DM).

⇨ Use the midpoint of the patio curve to draw the mirror line.

Be sure that "Copy" is selected on the Options Bar so that you maintain the original when mirroring.

• The Aubin Academy •

8. Save the project.

ADD A CUSTOM SHAPED STAIR

We can add a few steps up to the patio leading to the main building entrance. To do this, we simply add another stair. However, since we want the risers to match the shape of the patio, we'll sketch it instead.

1. On the Architecture tab, click the Stair tool.
2. On the Properties palette, from the Type Selector, choose: **Monolithic Stair**.
    ⇨ Set the Base Level to: **Street Level** and the Top Level to: **Level 1**.
3. On the Draw panel, click the Create Sketch tool.
4. On the Options Bar, clear the "Chain" check box and then in the Offset field type: **6'-0"** [**1800**].
    ⇨ Click the first point at the midpoint of the curved edge of the patio (see Figure 8.74).

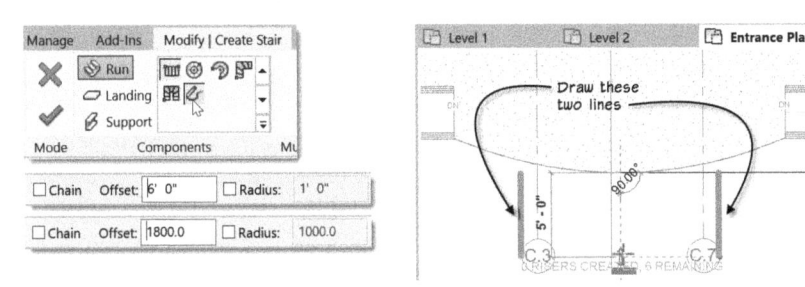

FIGURE 8.74 *Add two boundary lines drawn with the offset option*

   ⇨ Draw straight down and click below the bottom edge of the Ramps about: 5'-0" [1500].

   If you forgot to clear "Chain" above, press ESC once.

5. Repeat the process using the same settings and start at the same midpoint. Before you click the other end, tap the SPACEBAR to flip the sketch to the other side, then click.

You should have two vertical green lines centered on the patio and spaced: 12'-0" [3600] apart. These are the Boundaries of the stair (this is a monolithic stair, but in other stairs, these lines would become the stringers).

6. On the ribbon, click the Riser tool.
    ⇨ On the Draw panel, click the Pick Lines icon.
    ⇨ On the Options Bar, set the Offset to: **5'-0"** [**1500**].
7. Highlight the curved edge of the patio. Move the mouse slightly to make a dashed guideline appear below, and then click to create the Riser line (see top left panel of Figure 8.75).
8. Change the Offset to: **1'-0"** [**300**].
    ⇨ Highlight the Riser line you just added and offset a new line up from it. Repeat until you have created 5 more (6 total) (see top right panel of Figure 8.75). The last one will be right on top of the patio edge.

356 | Chapter 8

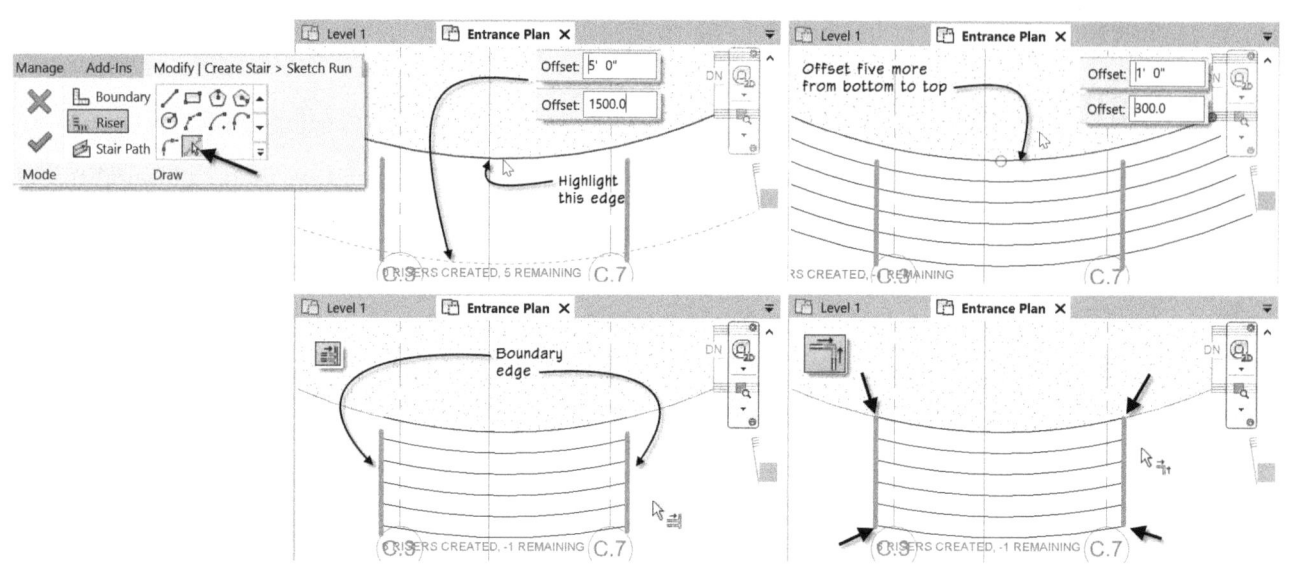

FIGURE 8.75 *Create the riser lines by offsetting from the curved patio edge and then trim to complete sketch*

9. Use the Trim and Extend tools to clean up the sketch.

   ⇨ Use the Trim/Extend Multiple Elements to trim the curved lines back to the green Boundary lines (see bottom left panel of Figure 8.75). Remember to click the green Boundary line as the trimming edge first, and then pick the side of the curve you wish to keep when trimming. You can also use a crossing selection to trim them all at once.

   ⇨ Use the Trim/Extend to Corner option to trim and extend the green Boundary lines to the curved black Riser lines at the top and bottom on all four corners.

10. On the ribbon, click the Finish Edit Mode button.

    This completes the sketch, but we are still in Edit stairs.

11. Click Finish Edit Mode a second time.

An ignorable warning will likely appear. (Warnings that appear in the lower right corner of the screen can sometimes be ignored, either because they are benign, or as in this case when to resolve them would sacrifice design intent.) You should always read the warnings however, and address them when you can, as many unresolved warnings can seriously degrade model performance. You can check for any unresolved warnings on the Manage ribbon's inquiry panel by clicking the Warnings tool. If this tool is grayed out, it merely means that you have no unresolved warnings in the model; which would be very good indeed! In this case, the warning tells us that we do not have the desired number of risers. Normally you would include the landing at the top of the stair flight as part of the stair and therefore include one more Riser. In this case, we have the patio slab instead and will be fine ignoring this message for now.

One problem not indicated by the warning or obvious from the plan view is that the stair direction is wrong. The highest tread is at the bottom of the screen and lowest by the patio. We can fix this with the flip control like we did for the residential stair at the start of the chapter.

12. Select the stair and click the Flip Stair's Up Direction control (refer back to Figure 8.6 above for an example).

TIP: If your stair disappears after clicking the flip control, undo and then edit the stair sketch. Zoom in closely on the stair. Select the green Boundary on one side of the stair and nudge it slightly. (Press the left or right arrow keys on the keyboard one time). Finish the sketch and try again.

13. Study the stair in section or 3D views before continuing.

• The Aubin Academy •

ADD RAILINGS TO THE ENTRY STAIR

If you want to add railing extensions to the railings, we can use the railing type created above.

   Return to the *Entrance Plan* view.

1. Select one of the railings on the new custom stair.
   ⇨ On the Properties palette, from the Type Selector, choose: **Handrail – Pipe – Bottom Extension**.
2. On the Modify | Railings tab, click the Edit Path button.

   A single sketch line appears.

3. On the Modify | Railings > Edit Path tab, on the Draw panel, click the Pick Lines icon.
   ⇨ Click the curved edge of the patio.
   ⇨ Use Trim/Extend to Corner to clean up.
4. On the ribbon, choose Finish Edit Mode (see Figure 8.76). If you get a warning, you can ignore it.

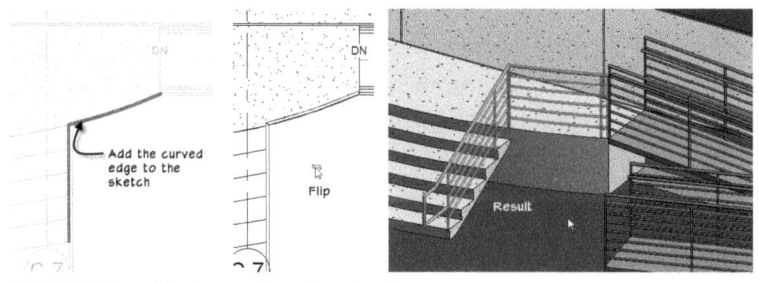

FIGURE 8.76 *Add a line to the railing sketch*

   Return to the *Entrance Plan* view.

5. Edit the other railing and repeat the process. (Or you can delete the other railing and mirror the one we just edited.)

If you wish, you can add a center railing on the stairs. To do this, click the Railing tool on the Architecture tab. Sketch a line down the center of the stairs (snapping to midpoints). Click the Pick New Host tool on the Tools panel, and then select the stair as the host. Finish the sketch. Use the Handrail – Pipe – Bottom Extension type to get the extension at the end.

ADD RAILINGS TO THE PATIO

Let's add guardrails to the Patio.

   Remain in the *Entrance Plan* floor plan view.

1. On the Architecture tab, on the Circulation panel, click the Railing tool.
   ⇨ On the Draw panel, click the Pick Lines icon.
   ⇨ On the Options Bar, set the "Offset" value to: **4"[100]**.
2. Pick the two edges of the patio on the right to place sketch lines (see the left side of Figure 8.77).
   ⇨ On the ribbon, click the Pick New Host tool and then click the patio slab.
3. Finish the sketch.

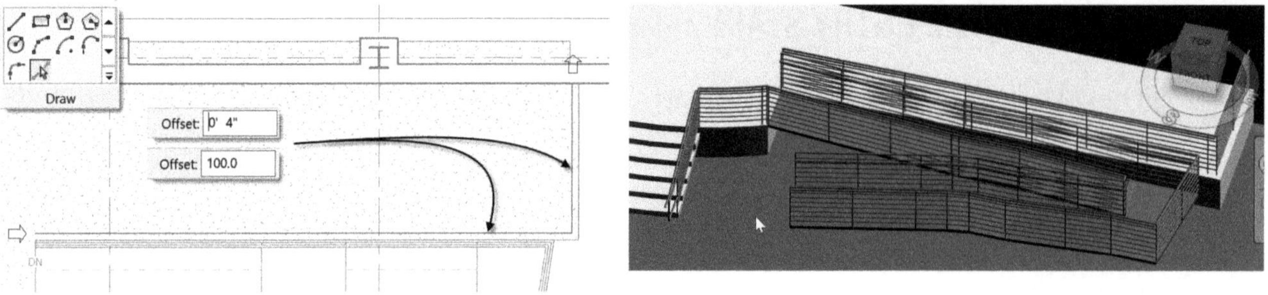

FIGURE 8.77 *Create railings from the patio slab (sketch lines in the figure enhanced for clarity)*

4. Mirror the patio railing to the other side.
5. Save the project when finished.

When finished with these railings, your model should look something like the right side of Figure 8.77.

ADD ELEVATORS

Unlike ramps and stairs, we do not have a dedicated tool or element category for elevators in Revit. Elevators are like other component families and we use the Component tool to add them in the same way that we added plumbing fixtures in Chapter 4. Elevator families can be created from scratch or derived from manufacturers drawing files. For this exercise, we will use families provided in the *Chapter08* folder.

1. On the Project Browser, double-click to open the *Level 1* floor plan view.
2. On the Insert tab, on the Load from Library panel, click Load Family.
   ⇨ Browse to the location where you saved the book's dataset files and then open the *Chapter08* folder.
   ⇨ Hold down the CTRL key, select: *Elevator Door-Center.rfa* and *Elevator-Hydraulic.rfa* and then click Open.

This will load these two families and make them available using the Component tool.

3. On the Architecture tab, on the Build panel, click the Component tool.
   ⇨ From the Type Selector, choose: **Elevator – Hydraulic – 2000 lbs**.
4. Place the elevator within the core space provided for it.
   ⇨ It should snap nicely into place, but if necessary, use Move or Align to position it in elevator core space. Repeat for a second one or make a copy.
5. Return to the Component tool, from the Type Selector choose: **Elevator Door-Center : 36" x 84"**.
   ⇨ Place a door at each elevator.

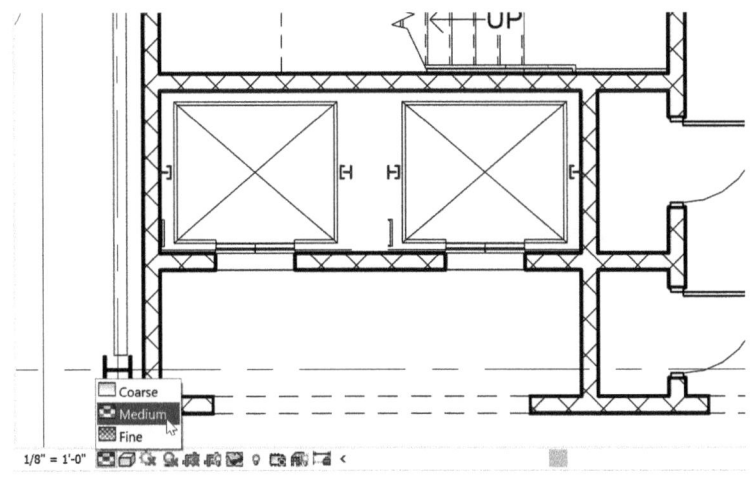

FIGURE 8.78 *Place two elevators and elevator doors in the core*

If you change the level of detail in the view to: Medium, you will see more detail displayed in the elevator family. This will make it easier to position the doors (see Figure 8.78). You will need to copy the doors to each floor of the building, (use Paste > Aligned to Selected Levels) but don't copy the elevators. They span multiple floors. However, there is a Height parameter on the Properties palette. So, select both elevators and then on the Properties palette, change the Height to: **51'-0"** [**14400**]. (Please note that the Height for this family is at the bottom, beneath Other).

6. Click the Modify tool or press the ESC key twice.

That completes the vertical circulation elements needed for the commercial project. Feel free to experiment further before closing.

7. Save and close the project.

SUMMARY

- ☑ Stairs and railings offer flexible configuration with type-based parameters and element-based variations.

- ☑ Stairs are assembled from one or more run elements and can also include supports and landing elements.

- ☑ Each component in a stair is a system family with its own types. You can also manipulate many instance settings as well.

- ☑ Components can be converted to sketch-based elements when design needs require customization.

- ☑ Like other Revit elements, stairs and railings can be demolished or added to any phase.

- ☑ Edit a stair type to apply changes to all stair elements sharing that type.

- ☑ Convert a stair element to a sketch to make customizations such as bull nosed treads.

- ☑ Edit the railing sketch to modify the extent of the railing.

- ☑ Create stairs with integral landings by drawing short runs in the sketch. Revit automatically fills in the landing in between runs.

- ☑ Creating a multistory stair is as easy as selecting the levels that the stair should span.

- ☑ You can use floor elements to model landings where necessary.

- ☑ You can create landing elements in a stair by selecting two runs you want connected or creating a custom sketch.

- ☑ Ramps are like stairs, but they are sketch-based.

- ☑ Custom shaped stairs can be created as a sketch and using the boundary and riser tools within the sketch mode.

- ☑ Railings are added automatically to newly drawn stairs. However, you can use the Set Host tool to sketch a custom railing and apply it to an existing stair, slab, or ramp.

- ☑ To add railing extensions, create a customized top rail type that includes the extension settings.

- ☑ Pre-made elevator component families can be loaded into the project and placed in the model.

CHAPTER 9
Floors and Roofs

INTRODUCTION

In this chapter we will focus on floors and roofs in both our residential and commercial projects. Roofs and floors in Autodesk® Revit® are "sketch-based" objects. This means that a simple two-dimensional sketch is utilized to indicate the shape and form of the floor or roof you create. From this 2D shape, Revit creates the 3D form. We will begin in the residential project with gable roofs and some floor elements. We will understand how to make walls attach to roofs, edit roof structure, and how to apply edge conditions and gutters. The commercial project will give us the opportunity to explore flat roofs and extrusion roofs.

OBJECTIVES

We have already seen simple examples of floors and roofs in previous chapters. You can construct roofs in a variety of ways. The simplest method is like floors. Roofs can interact with the walls of the building and we can apply custom treatment to their edges. After completing this chapter, you will know how to do the following:

- Build roofs
- Create a custom roof type
- Add and modify floors
- Work with roof edges and gutters
- Attach walls and join roofs

CREATING ROOFS

Since we are working concurrently on two different projects in this book, we will get an opportunity to look at both traditional sloped residential roofs and "flat" commercial roofs. The only real difference between the two in Revit is the slope parameters that we assign and the way that we treat the edges. To get started, we'll begin with the residential project.

OPEN A PROJECT

The lessons that follow require the dataset files included for download with this book. Refer to the "Download the Book Dataset" topic on page xi in the Preface for instructions on downloading and installing the book's dataset files.

1. Launch Autodesk® Revit®.
2. If you are on the Home screen, you can click the Open button beneath Models. Otherwise, from the File menu, choose **Open** > **Project**. In the "Open" dialog box, browse to the *Chapter09* folder.

   ⇨ Double-click *09 Residential.rvt* if you wish to work in Imperial units.

   ⇨ Double-click *09 Residential_M.rvt* if you wish to work in Metric units.

   You can also select it and then click the Open button.

CREATE AN EXISTING ROOF PLAN

In Chapter 8, we introduced the concept of creating a separate view for the existing construction and setting its parameters accordingly. Let's use the same technique now to create an "Existing Conditions Roof Plan" view.

1. On the Project Browser, right-click the *Roof* plan view and choose: **Duplicate View** > **Duplicate**.
2. On the Project Browser, select *Roof Copy 1* and then on the Properties palette, change View Name to: **Roof Existing Conditions**.
3. Scroll back up to the top and for the Underlay setting choose: **Second Floor**.

   ⇨ Scroll to the bottom and for the Phase, choose: **Existing**.

The new construction will disappear. The existing second floor will show in gray since, we set it as the underlay to the current view. The underlay is useful in helping us build the roof. We will turn it off when we are finished.

> **NOTE:** There is a selection toggle that controls if elements in an underlay can be selected onscreen or not. Refer to the "Selection Toggles" topic on page 81 in Chapter 3 for more information. We won't need to directly select the underlay elements here, so it does not matter if you have this toggled on or off. Regardless of the setting, you can still snap to the elements.

ADD THE EXISTING ROOF

While there is already a roof in this file, there is valuable experience to be gained in creating the roof from scratch. Therefore, we'll delete this roof and create it anew. We will begin with a simple gable roof on the existing house and then add a slightly more complex double gable on the new addition. The roof existing in the file is only partially displayed. This is because of the current view range settings. We will learn how to adjust the ow in the Modify the Roof Plan View topic. For now, we will work mostly in other views so there is no need to worry about the plan too much yet.

1. Select the roof onscreen and then press the DELETE key.
2. On the Architecture tab, on the Build panel, click the Roof tool.

   The Roof tool's default is Roof by Footprint. You can also choose this from the drop down. The Modify | Create Roof Footprint tab will become active and the Boundary Line and Pick Walls tools on the Draw panel should be active by default.

   ⇨ On the Options Bar, check the "Defines slope" check box.

   ⇨ In the Overhang field, type: **6"** [**150**].

   Verify that "Extend to wall core" is not selected.

3. Click in empty space (not on any model geometry).

This shifts the focus from the Offset text field to the model canvas. Using the middle button for this can be useful as well.

4. Move the pointer over the topmost horizontal wall and when the dashed line appears above and to the outside, click the mouse (see Figure 9.1).

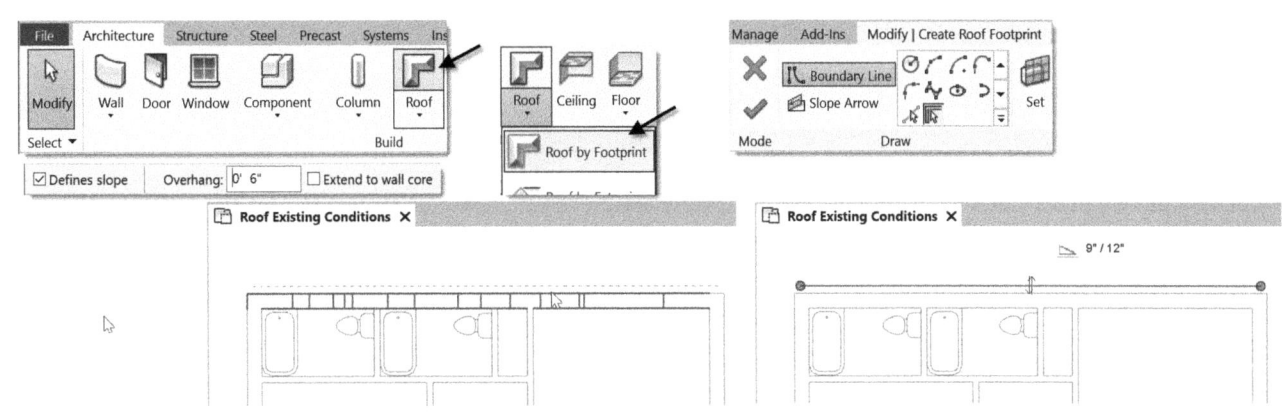

FIGURE 9.1 *Set the parameters for the first edge of the roof on the Options Bar*

⇨ Repeat this on the lower horizontal wall to create another sketch line below and to the outside of that wall.

Near both sketch lines, a triangular slope icon will appear.

5. On the Options Bar, clear the "Defines slope" check box and then click the outside vertical wall on the left.

⇨ Also click to the outside of vertical walls on the right (above and below the chimney) as shown in Figure 9.2.

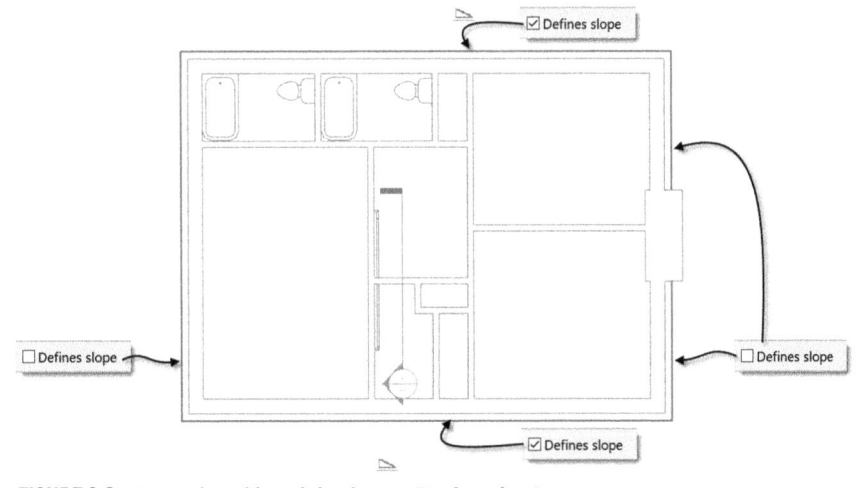

FIGURE 9.2 *Create the gable ends by clearing "Defines slope"*

Clearing the "Defines Slope" check box will make these ends of the roof gable ends. Since we have the chimney on the right side, we need to make the roof cut around it. We can accomplish this by drawing the remaining sketch lines relative to the chimney.

6. On the Draw panel, click the Line tool.

⇨ On the Options Bar, make sure that the "Chain" check box is selected and that there is no offset (set to zero).

7. Using Figure 9.3 as a guide, draw the remaining three sketch lines.

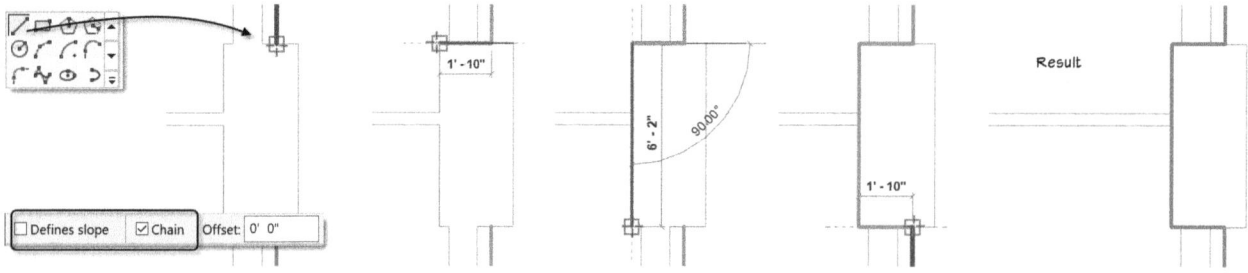

FIGURE 9.3 *Sketch around the chimney*

⇨ On the ribbon, click the Modify tool or press the ESC key twice.

Before we complete the sketch, let's adjust the slope of the roof.

8. Click on the top horizontal sketch line, hold down the CTRL key and then click the bottom horizontal line as well.

   On the Properties palette, beneath the "Dimensions" grouping, change the roof slope.

9. If you are working in Imperial units, for the Slope parameter type: **6"**. If you are working in Metric, set the Slope Angle to: **26.57**.

> **TIP:** As an alternative, you can select the sketch line and then edit the slope directly with the temporary dimension that appears next to the slope indicator of the slope defining line. However, you must do it one sketch line at a time if you do it this way.

⇨ On the ribbon, click the Finish Edit Mode button.

10. On the View tab of the ribbon, on the Create panel, click the Default 3D View button (this is also on the QAT).

Notice that the two roof edges that we designated as "Defines slope" have a pitch sloping up to a single gable ridge down the middle of the existing house. Feel free to orbit the model around and see it from different angles.

ADJUST THE CHIMNEY

Notice also that the roof has a cutout for the space of the chimney. (However, currently the chimney is too short). We can adjust the height of the chimney by simply dragging the control handles. You may recall that the chimney was constructed in Chapter 4 from an in-place family (or a loadable family if you are using Revit LT). To edit its height with a bit more accuracy, we can edit this in-place family.

   Remain in the default {3D} view.

1. Click on the chimney onscreen to select it.
2. On the ribbon click the Edit In-Place button.

⇨ Click again on the form of the chimney.

   This time you are selecting the extrusion element within the family.

3. On the Properties palette, change the Extrusion End to: **26'-6"** [**8100**] (see Figure 9.4).

   If you are working in Revit LT, you can replace the fireplace included here with the family in the *Chapter09* folder called: *09 Fireplace for LT.rfa* [*09 Fireplace for LT_M.rfa*].

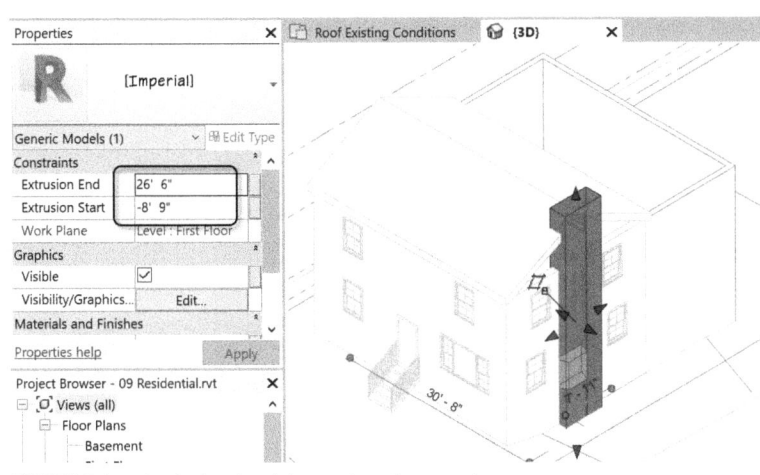

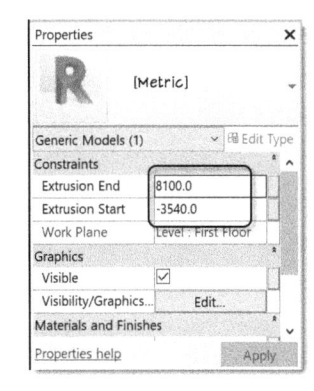

FIGURE 9.4 *Edit the height of the in-place chimney element*

4. On the ribbon click the Finish Model button.
5. Save the project.

ATTACH WALLS TO THE ROOF

Another issue that is evident here in the {3D} view is that the walls do not project all the way to the roof. In some cases when you draw a roof, you will be prompted to automatically attach the walls to the roof. Usually for this to occur, the walls must intersect the roof level. In this case, the walls stopped just beneath the roof so we were not prompted. However, we can still manually attach them to the roof. It is a good idea to get in the habit of checking for this condition.

The default {3D} view is set to the New Construction phase. We do have another 3D view that is set to Existing that will make selection of the walls easier. Let's open it now.

1. On the Project Browser, double-click to open the *Rear Existing French Door* 3D view.
2. Pre-highlight one of the exterior walls of the existing house.
   ⇨ Press the TAB key to highlight a chain of connected walls.
   ⇨ With the existing house exterior walls pre-highlighted, click the mouse to select them (see Figure 9.5).

NOTE: If you have trouble chain-selecting the existing walls, try selecting in another view, like a floor plan.

FIGURE 9.5 *Select a chain of walls*

• Revit Essentials for Architecture •

366 | Chapter 9

3. On the Modify | Walls tab, on the Modify Wall panel, click the Attach Top/Base button.

⇨ On the Options Bar, verify that "Top" is selected, and then click the edge of the roof (see Figure 9.6).

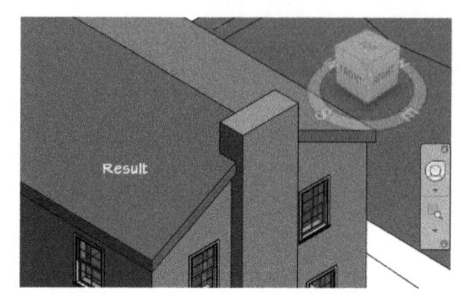

FIGURE 9.6 *Attach the walls to the roof*

4. Deselect the walls.

EDIT THE SECOND FLOOR WALL LAYOUT

There are many other roof options to explore. The best place to do so in this project is on the new construction of the addition. The second floor of the addition will extend the two existing bathrooms and have an outdoor patio on the left side of the plan. On the north and west sides of the patio, we will have low-height, parapet-type walls. The roof will cover the other portions of the addition, but the patio will be uncovered. Before we add the roof, we need to modify the walls a bit to reflect these design features.

1. On the Project Browser, double-click to open the *Second Floor* plan view.

2. Select one of the new construction walls, and then on the ribbon click the Create Similar tool (or press CS).

⇨ Start the first point on the vertical wall to the left, move horizontally across the plan and click approximately in the middle of the space.

⇨ Move straight up and draw a second segment by snapping to the exterior horizontal wall.

⇨ Click the Modify tool or press ESC twice.

3. Select each wall and using the temporary dimensions, edit their positions as show in Figure 9.7

> **TIP:** to control the positions of the witness lines on the temporary dimensions, try zooming in closer, or drag the controls on the witness lines to more favorable edges on the surrounding walls. Alternatively, you can add permanent dimensions (DI), and then edit them the same as temporaries while the walls are selected.

Floors and Roofs | 367

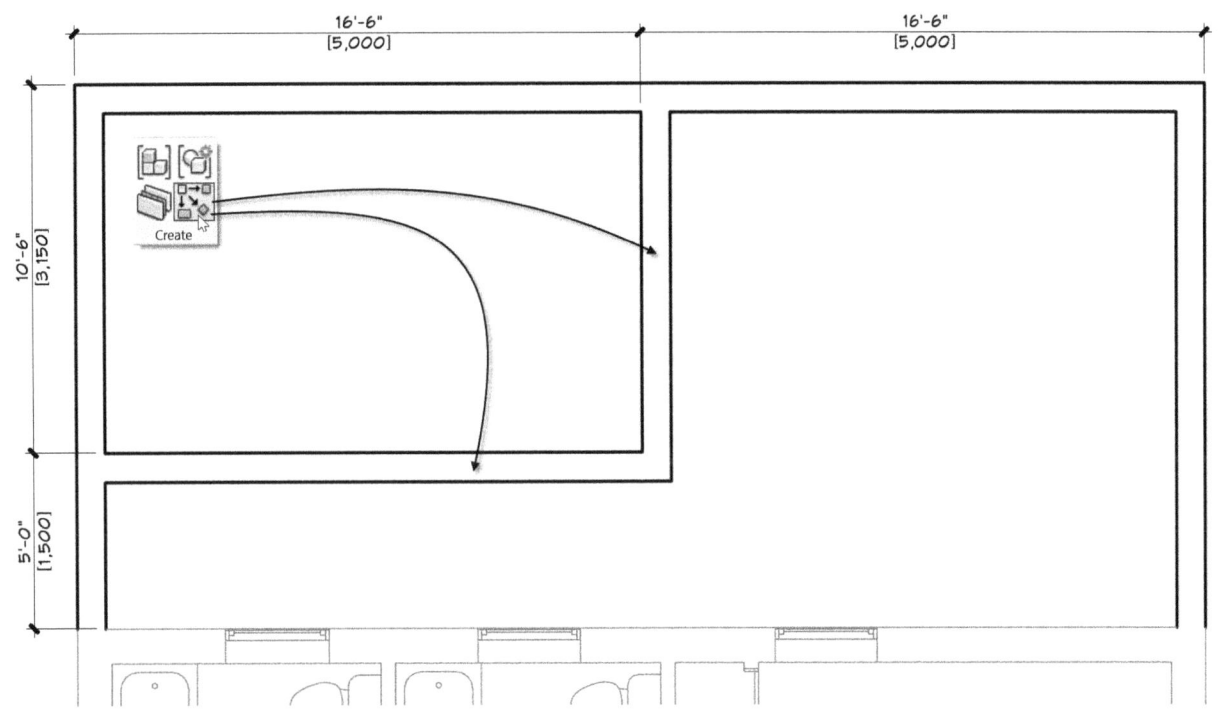

FIGURE 9.7 *Add two new walls to the Second Floor*

The space that we have just described in the top left corner is the outdoor patio. As noted previously, it will have low-height walls on two sides. Now let's edit the original exterior walls to reflect this condition. To do this, we are going to edit the Profile of the walls.

    4.   Select the top horizontal wall.

    ⇨   On the Modify | Walls panel, click the Edit Profile button. The "Go To View" dialog will appear.

    ⇨   In the "Go To View" dialog, choose: *Elevation: North* and then click Open View (see Figure 9.8).

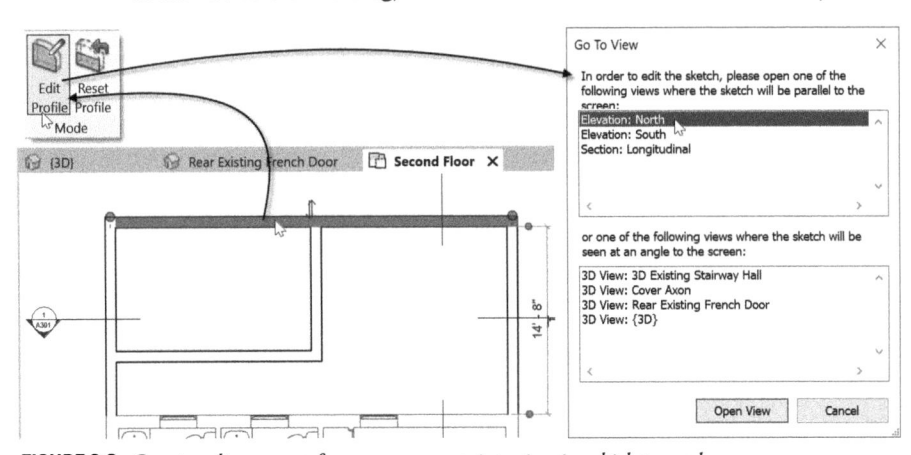

FIGURE 9.8 *Certain edits prompt for a more appropriate view in which to work*

When you begin an operation that cannot easily be performed in the current view, Revit will prompt you to open a more appropriate view. The "Go To View" dialog suggests all appropriate views in the current project in which to perform the operation. You should now be looking at the back of the house with the selected wall in sketch mode. In this mode we can edit the shape of the wall to "sculpt" it to meet the needs of the design.

    5.   On the Modify | Walls > Edit Profile tab, on the Draw panel, click the Pick Lines tool.

    ⇨   Click on the right vertical edge of the intersecting wall in the middle of the second floor (see the left side of Figure 9.9).

• Revit Essentials for Architecture •

> **NOTE:** This is the outside edge of the wall we drew earlier.

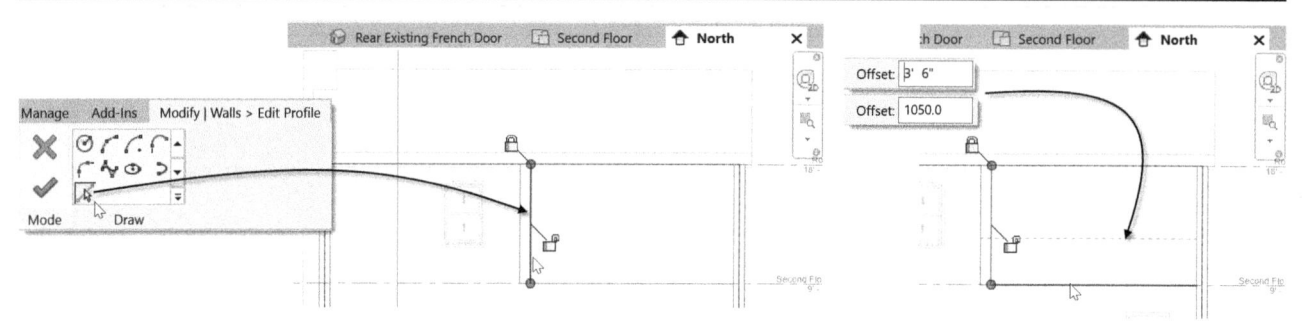

FIGURE 9.9 *Add sketch lines using pick lines*

6. On the Options Bar, type: **3'-6"** [**1050**] in the "Offset" field.

   ⇨ Highlight the Second Floor level line and when the guide line appears above the Level line, click to create the sketch line (see the right side of Figure 9.9).

7. Use the Trim/Extend to Corner tool (TR) to clean up the sketch and close all of the corners (see the left side of Figure 9.10).

> **NOTE:** Remember to click the side of the line that you wish to keep.

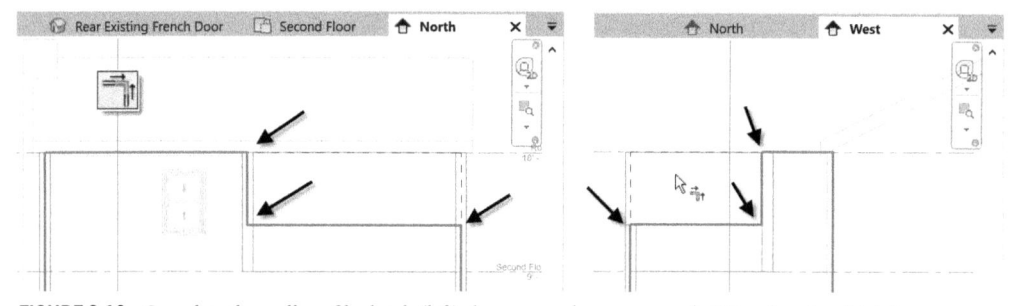

FIGURE 9.10 *Complete the wall profile sketch (left) then repeat the process on the West elevation (right)*

   ⇨ On the ribbon, click the Finish Edit Mode button.

8. Select the other wall (the vertical one on the right in the current view— on the left in the plan view) and repeat the process.

   ⇨ When prompted, open the: *Elevation: West* view.

9. Again, use the outside edge of the wall we drew above to create the vertical sketch line and then offset a line up from the Second Floor level line as before.

   ⇨ Trim/Extend to complete the sketch (see the right side of Figure 9.10).

   ⇨ On the ribbon, click the Finish Edit Mode button.

The new addition will be brick veneer on a stud wall backup. We can apply a wall type that represents this type of construction to our new construction walls.

10. Open the *Second Floor* plan view.

11. Select all the walls in the addition (the three original ones and the two new ones we just added).

    ⇨ On the Properties palette, from the Type Selector, choose: **Exterior Brick on Mtl. Stud**.

12. Open the *{3D}* view.

    ⇨ Hold down the SHIFT key and drag the wheel on your mouse to spin the model around and see the edits to the walls (see Figure 9.11).

> **TIP:** Remember: You can drag the ViewCube or use the Steering Wheel to orbit instead.

> **NOTE:** If the {3D} view does not show the new construction, change the Phase to: **New Construction** on the Properties palette.

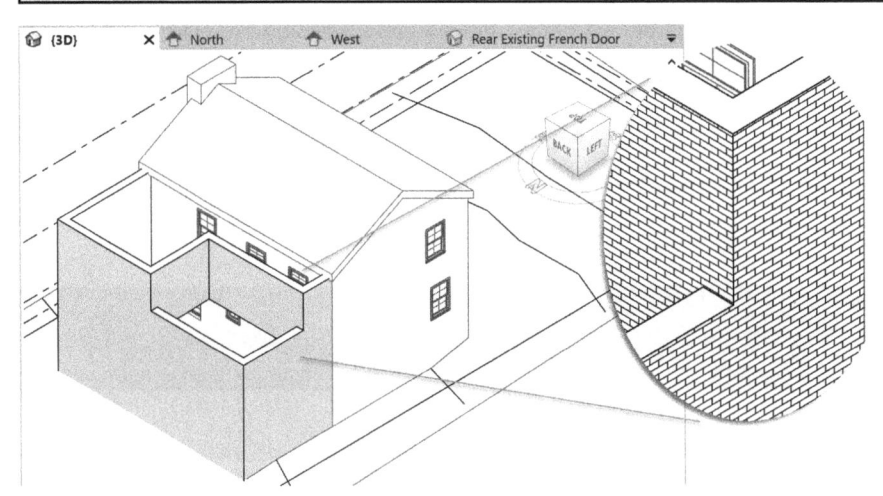

FIGURE 9.11 *View the model in 3D to see the completed wall edits*

13. On the Project Browser, right-click the {3D} view and choose: **Duplicate View > Duplicate**.
    ⇨ Name the new view: **New Addition Axon**.
14. Save the project.

ADD THE NEW ROOF

Now that we have prepared the second floor wall layout, we are ready to begin roofing the addition.

1. On the Project Browser, double-click to open the *Roof* plan view.

> **NOTE:** Be sure to open "Roof" this time, not "Existing Roof."

2. On the Properties palette, for Underlay, choose: **Second Floor**.
3. On the Architecture tab, on the Build panel, click the Roof tool.

    The tools on the Draw panel should default to Boundary Line and Pick Walls.

    ⇨ On the Options Bar, check the Defines slope check box and in the Overhang field, type: **6"** [**150**]
4. Click the two walls to place the two sketch lines indicated in Figure 9.12.

370 | Chapter 9

FIGURE 9.12 *Create the sloped sketch lines*

⇨ On the ribbon, click the Modify tool or press the ESC key twice.

5. Select both sketch lines.

⇨ On the Properties palette, beneath the "Dimensions" grouping, change the roof slope to: **6" / 12"** [**26.57°**].

⇨ Deselect the sketch lines.

> **TIP:** As an alternative, you can select the sketch line and then edit the slope directly with the temporary dimension that appears next to the slope indicator.

6. On the Draw panel, click the Line tool.

⇨ Clear both the "Defines slope" and "Chain" check boxes.

7. Draw a horizontal line aligned to the edge of the existing house roof and the width of the two sketch lines we already have (see the left side of Figure 9.13).

⇨ Use the Pick Walls option without slope and a: **6"** [**150**] offset to create the top sketch line (see the middle of Figure 9.13).

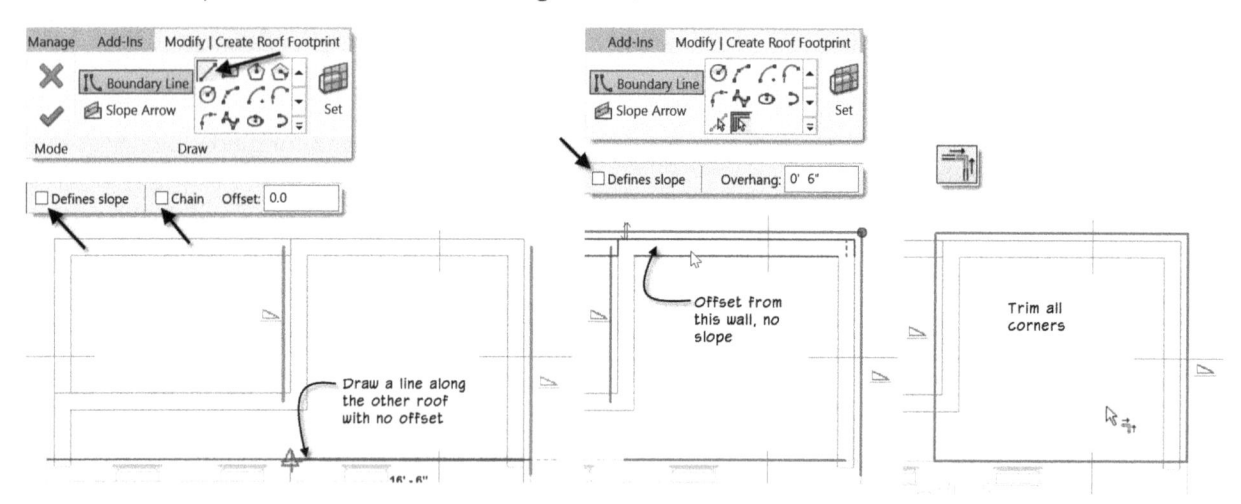

FIGURE 9.13 *Create two horizontal sketch lines that do not define slope*

8. Using the Trim tool, clean up the rectangular sketch shape (see the right side of Figure 9.13).

⇨ On the ribbon, click the Finish Edit Mode button.

9. Switch to the *New Addition Axon* 3D view tab.

⇨ Orbit the model to see the interaction of the two roofs clearly (shown on the left side of Figure 9.14 below).

JOIN ROOFS

As you can see in the 3D view, the new roof does not intersect with the existing one. This is easily corrected.

1. On the Modify tab, on the Geometry panel, click the Join/Unjoin Roof button.

Look at the Status Bar (lower left corner of the screen) and notice the message. You are prompted to: "Select an edge at the end of the roof that you wish to join or unjoin." We want to select one of the edges of the new construction roof. The next prompt will ask us to select a face to which to join. In that case, we will select the face of the existing roof.

2. Click on the edge of the new construction roof adjacent to the existing roof (see the left side of Figure 9.14).

    ⇨ Click on the face of the existing construction roof (see the middle of Figure 9.14).

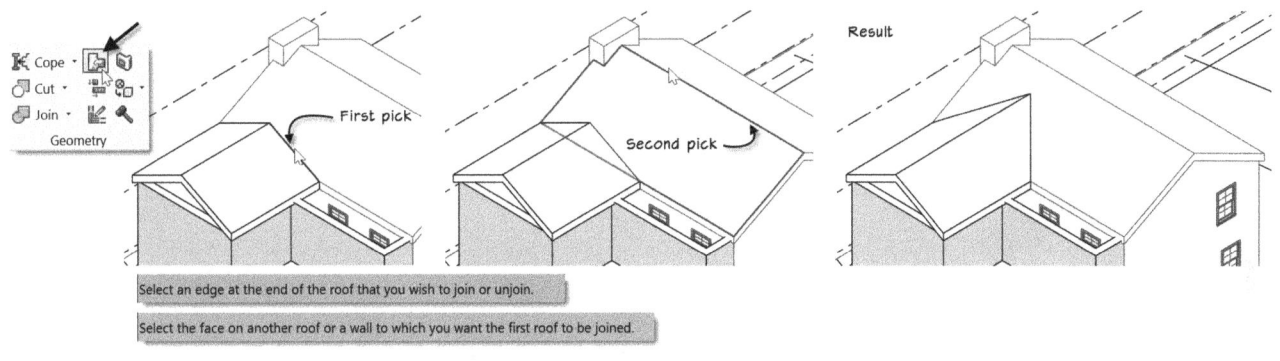

FIGURE 9.14 *Select an edge of the roof to join to the face of the other roof*

The new construction roof will now extend over the existing roof and form nicely mitered intersections (see the right side of the figure). The same tool can be used in reverse if you ever need to unjoin a roof.

3. Repeat the entire process to create the shorter new roof on the other side of the addition (see Figure 9.15).

TIP: Don't forget to change the slope. You can set it in the sketch as we have done so far or wait till you finish the sketch and then change the Slope on the Properties palette. This will apply to all sloped edges in the roof.

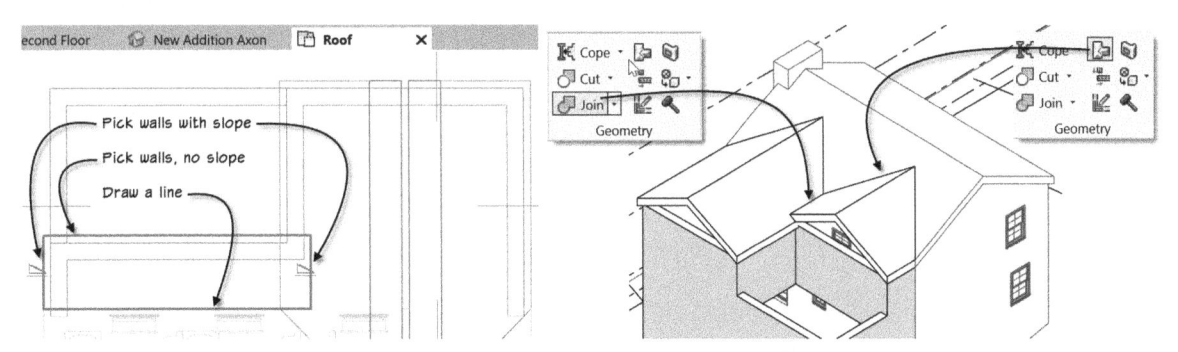

FIGURE 9.15 *Create the roof on the other side of the addition and join it to the other roofs*

Join roofs works when the two roofs meet perpendicular to one another. We will use a different technique to join the two new roofs together at the small valley between them. For that we will use the more generic Join Geometry tool.

4. On the Modify tab, on the Geometry panel, click the Join button.

    This is a split button. The default is Join Geometry. The drop down button on the lower half gives access to unjoin geometry and switch join order.

    Again, watch the Status Bar prompts.

    ⇨ Click on the first new construction roof, and then click the other to join them.

• Revit Essentials for Architecture •

⇨   On the ribbon, click the Modify tool or press the ESC key twice.

5. Using the technique covered above in the "Attach Walls to the Roof" topic on page 365, attach the five walls of the addition to the new roofs (see Figure 9.16).

> **TIP:** If you have trouble attaching the tall wall on the East side of the house to the new roof, attach it first to the existing construction roof and then attach it to the new construction roof.

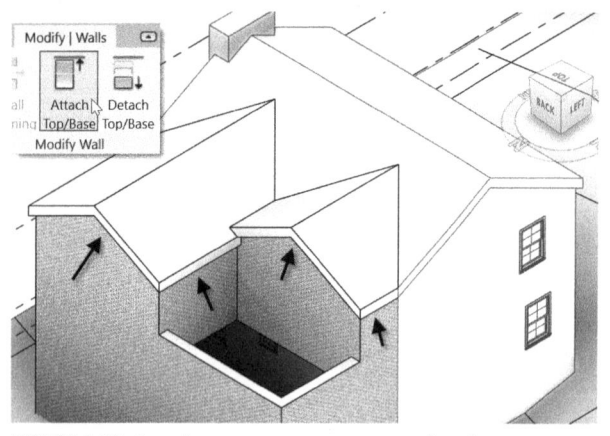

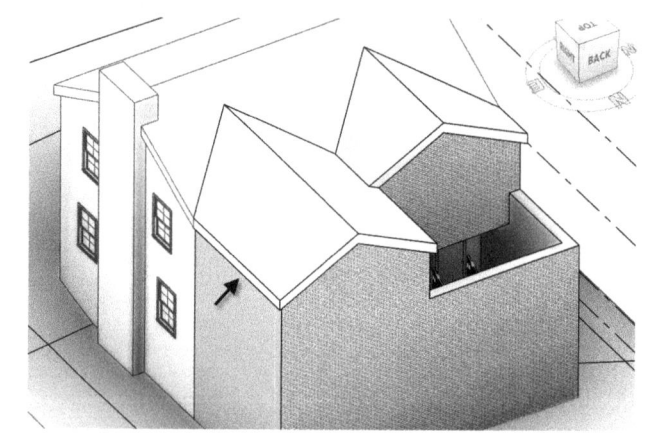

FIGURE 9.16 *Join the two new construction roofs with join geometry*

6. Save the project.

EDITING ROOFS

Now that we have created the roofs for the residential project, let's turn our attention to roofs editing techniques. In your own projects, you will work with roofs in much the same way as other Revit elements—start by laying them out with simple generic parameters and then over the course of the project, layer in additional details and parameters as design and project needs dictate. In this sequence, we will explore some of the possibilities available for editing roof elements.

MODIFY THE ROOF PLAN VIEW

You may have noticed that the *Roof* plan view looks a bit odd. The roof elements are being cut in plan which shows us only part of the sloped surface. While appropriate for an attic space, this kind of display is not how we would represent a typical roof plan. To show the roof correctly, we want to see the entire roof element uncut. To achieve this, we need to modify the view range of the *Roof* plan view.

Continuing in the Residential project.

1. On the Project Browser, double-click to open the *Roof* plan view.
2. Make sure you have nothing selected, then on the Properties palette, beneath the "Extents" grouping, click the Edit button next to "View Range" (or press VR).
⇨   In the "Primary Range" area, change both the "Cut Plane" and "Top" Offset to: **15'-0"** [**4500**] (see Figure 9.17).

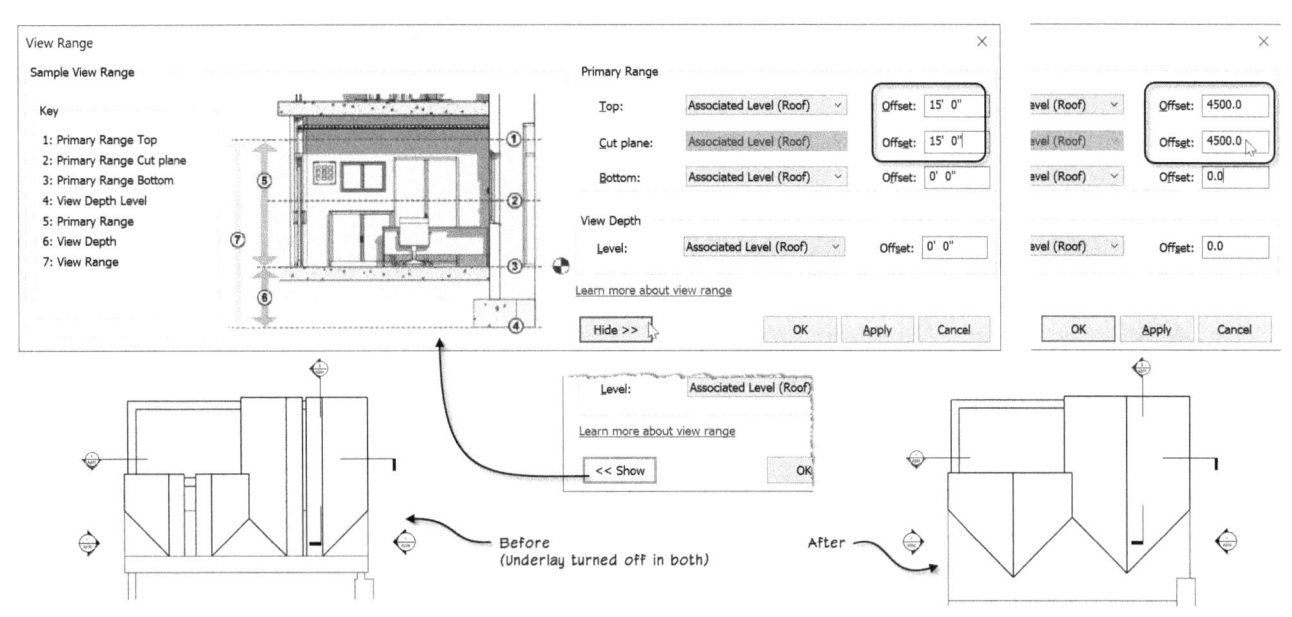

FIGURE 9.17 *Adjust the view range of the roof plan view*

    3.   Click OK to return to the Properties palette.

    4.   Beneath the "Graphics" grouping, for the "Underlay" choose: **None** and click Apply to see the results (see the lower right of Figure 9.17).

The figure also shows the Show/Hide button at the lower corner of the "View Range" dialog. This button expands the dialog to reveal an image that explains each of the view range settings graphically. There is also a help link right above this button to open the online help and learn more about view range. Feel free to explore this before continuing. (To learn more about View Range, check out the **Revit: View Range** course at **LinkedIn Learning**†).

> **BIM MANAGER NOTE:** Roof plans provide an excellent case for View Templates. We learned how to apply a View Template to a view in the "Apply a View Template" topic on page 161 in Chapter 5 and again in the "Create and Apply a View Template" topic on page 334 in Chapter 8. Once you have established the settings for a standard roof plan, consider creating a "Roof Plan" view template from it. You can do this on the View tab. On the Graphics panel, click the View Templates drop down button and choose: **Create Template from Current View**. If you want to use the view template in other projects, or add it to your office standard project template (RTE) file, use the Transfer Project Standards tool on the Manage tab.
>
> When you use a view template, you can apply its properties as we did in previous chapters, or you assign a view template to a view and it will maintain a direct connection to the view template. If the view template is changed in any way, the new settings will immediately become visible in the view(s) to which it is assigned. You connect a view template to the view on the Properties palette.

UNDERSTAND ROOF OPTIONS

The roof element has several options that we have not yet explored. Let's look at some of them now.

    1.   On the Project Browser, double-click to open the *Longitudinal* section view.

    ⇨   Zoom in Region around the eave at the left side of the section (see Figure 9.18).

        Notice the way the roof intersects the attached wall.

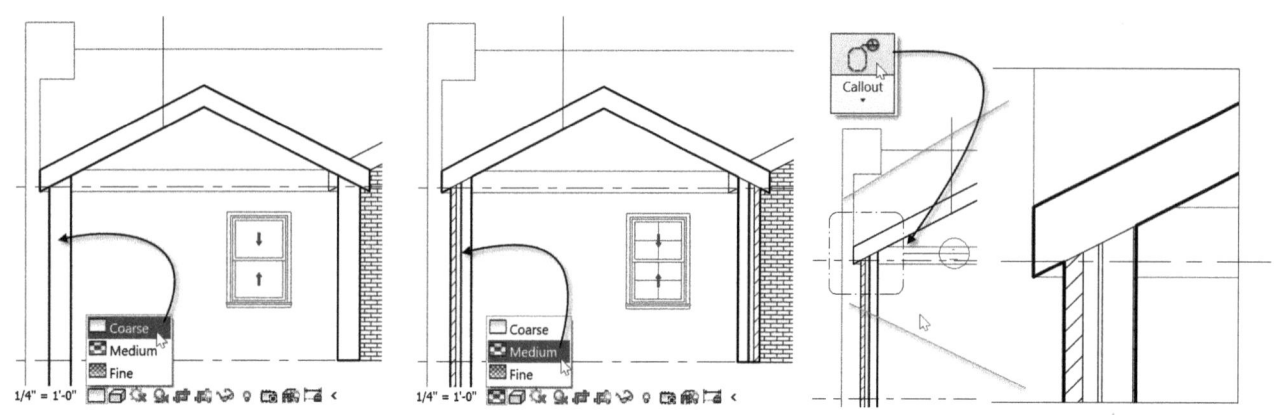

FIGURE 9.18 *Zoom in on the eave condition and then change the detail level*

Previously we swapped in a more detailed wall type for these walls. However, since we are currently viewing the model in "Coarse" display mode, we do not see any difference in the wall structure. To see the more detailed wall structure, we need to adjust the detail display level of the current view.

    2.   On the View Control Bar, click the Detail Level icon and choose: **Medium** (see the middle of Figure 9.18).

    ⇨   On the View tab, click the Callout tool and then make a callout around just the eave area on the left.

    ⇨   Open this view (see the right side of Figure 9.18).

The layers that make up the wall type's structure will appear including brick, a stud layer and air gap. This detail Level will make it a little easier to understand the various roof options that we are about to explore.

    3.   Select the roof (the one sectioned in this view).

    ⇨   On the Properties palette, beneath the "Construction" grouping, change the "Rafter Cut" to: **Two Cut – Plumb**.

            The results will probably not be satisfactory.

    ⇨   On the Properties palette, set the "Fascia Depth" to: **6"** [**150**]

Repeat the process and change the "Rafter Cut" to: **Two Cut – Square** (see Figure 9.19).

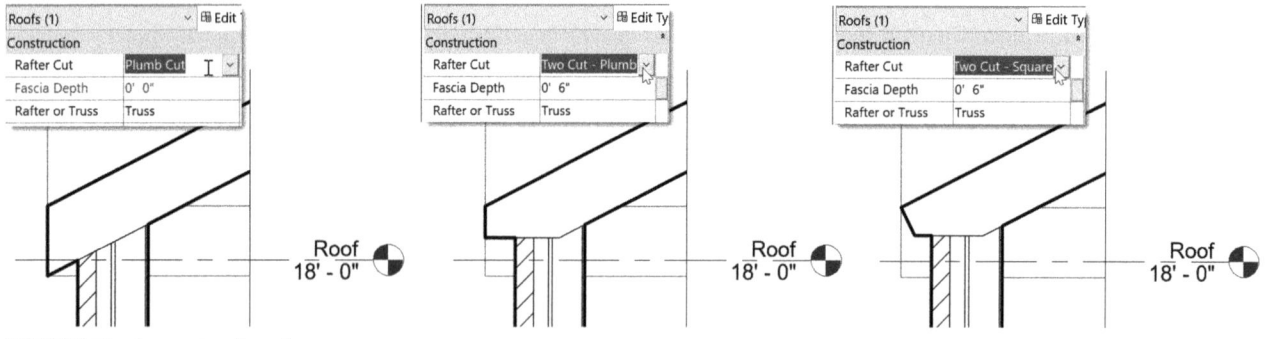

FIGURE 9.19 *Comparing the rafter cut options*

If any warnings appear, just click OK to ignore them.

    4.   Return to the Properties palette once more and change the "Rafter Cut" to: **Two Cut – Plumb** with a "Fascia Depth" of: **1'-0"** [**300**].

When we were adding the roof above, you may have noticed the "Extend to wall core" check box on the Options Bar. (We did not use this option when creating the roof.) When you choose this option, the Overhang setting will be measured relative to face of the core layer rather than the finish face of the wall. Figure 9.20 shows this option used with and without attaching the walls to the roof. If you wish, you can experiment with these options. Remember, if you choose to edit the roof while the section view is open, you will be prompted to open a more appropriate view—choose: *Floor Plan: Roof*. Cancel or undo any edits made if you do experiment with this setting.

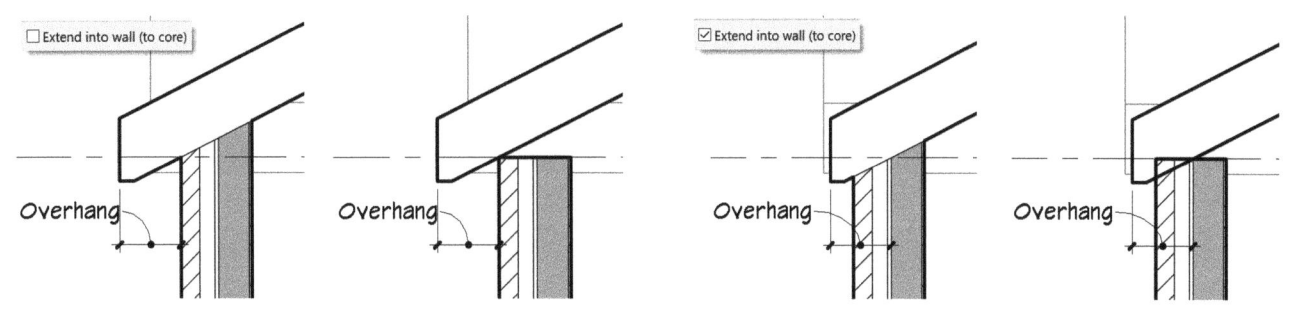

FIGURE 9.20 *Understanding the effect of the "extend to wall core" and attach options (Core layer shaded gray in the figure for clarity)*

There is one other setting worth exploring at this point. When you create your roof, Revit offers two modes of construction: Rafter or Truss. The difference between these two settings is simply the point that is used as the spring point for the roof.

   5.   Select the roof.

   ⇨   On the Properties palette, beneath the "Construction" grouping, change the "Rafter or Truss" to: **Rafter** then back to: **Truss**.

Notice how the entire roof appears to move down. Rafter measures the plate of the roof from the inside edge of the wall or core. Truss measures from the outside edge of the wall or core. This option is only available for roofs created using the "Pick Walls" option (see Figure 9.21). Look carefully at the intersection of the level and the wall. When "Extend into wall (to core)" is checked, the core face and level intersection is where the roof springs. When this is unchecked, it is the intersection of the level and the wall face instead.

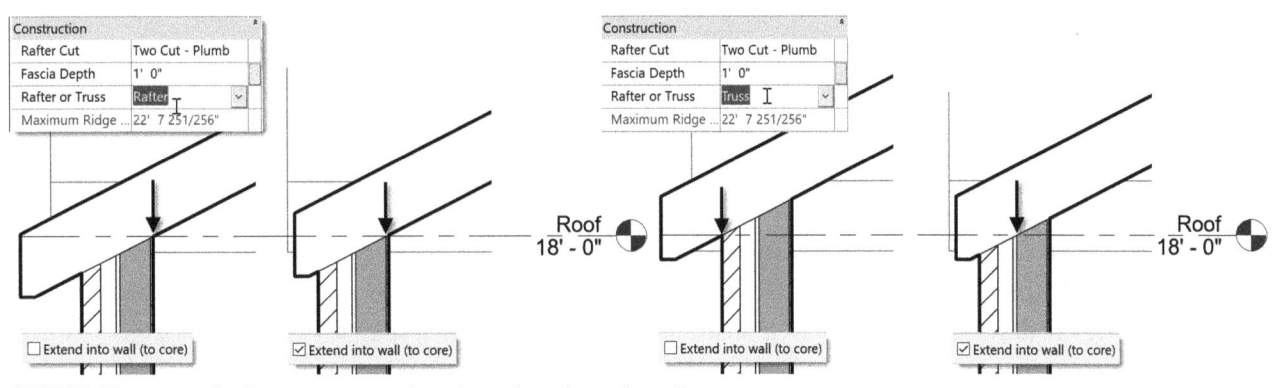

FIGURE 9.21 *Truss and rafter settings impact how the roof attaches to the wall*

Now that we've experimented with and understood the various settings, let's set the final settings for the roofs in this project.

   6.   Select all roofs (two new construction, one existing).

   ⇨   On the Properties palette, change the "Rafter Cut" to: **Two Cut – Plumb** with a "Fascia Depth" of: **6"** [**150**]

   ⇨   Set "Rafter or Truss" to: **Rafter** and then click Apply.

        If a warning dialog appears, click the Unjoin Elements button. Because of the change in the relationship between the roof and the wall on the left, Revit is "confused" and cannot maintain the join condition—we will fix this next.

   7.   Finally, select the wall on the left and use the Attach Top/Base tool to re-attach it to the roof.

        Attach it first to the existing roof, then repeat for the roof on the addition (see Figure 9.22). Repeat on the right side as well if needed.

• Revit Essentials for Architecture •

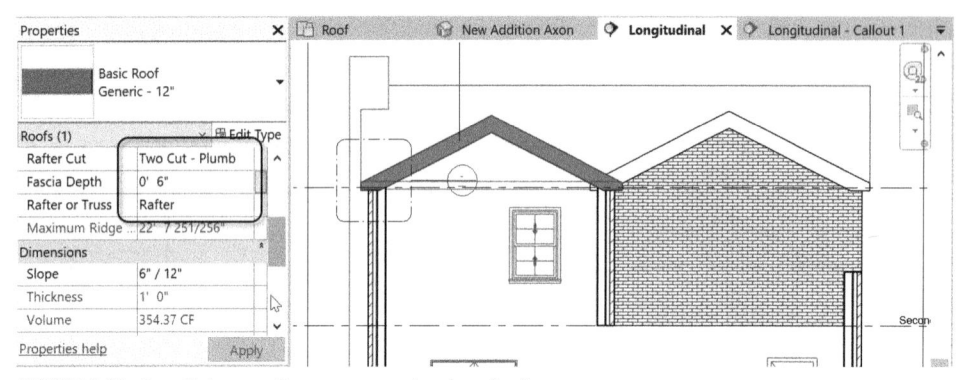

FIGURE 9.22 *Set all three roofs to two cut – plumb and rafter*

8. Save the project.

CREATE A LAYERED ROOF TYPE

Much like walls, roof structure can be composed of several layers. You can create your own roof type that contains the structure you need or transfer an appropriate type from another project using the Transfer Project Standards feature. In this example, we will build a new roof type from scratch.

1. Select all the roofs.
2. On the Properties palette click the Edit Type button.

   In the "Type Properties" dialog that appears, next to the type list, click the Duplicate button (or press ALT + D).

   ⇨ Change the name to: **Wood Rafters with Asphalt Shingles** and then click OK.

3. In the "Type Properties" dialog, next to the "Structure" click the edit button.

In the "Edit Assembly" dialog, you can see that the roof type currently contains only a single generic layer. You can add, edit, and delete layers to the roof structure in this dialog. When you build a new type in Revit, there are several things to consider. We can add as much or as little detail to the structure of the roof type as we wish. As a rule of thumb, you should seek to build your models as accurately as possible while remembering that any architectural drawing includes a certain degree of abstraction as a matter of industry convention and to facilitate clarity. All these points hold true in other areas of Revit as well, such as creating and editing wall types. We will see more on this in coming chapters. With these issues in mind, we will abstract our roof construction to just the three layers. We need a structure layer, which will be wood rafters, a plywood substrate, and asphalt shingles for the finish layer. We will exclude building paper, insulation, and interior finish in this example. These items can be added to the roof type later (which will automatically apply to all roof elements that reference the type) or we can apply these items graphically as drafting embellishment in a detail view (see Chapter 12 for more information on detail views). This model does not have a separate structural file. But in the case where there is one, if the rafters and sheathing later become part of that file, you can edit this type and remove them here.

The "Edit Assembly" dialog lists each layer of the roof type in a list with a numeric index number next to each one. There are four columns next to each item.

> **Function**—Click in this field for a list of predefined functions. The functions include "Structure," "Substrate," "Thermal/Air Layer," "Finish 1," "Finish 2" and "Membrane." The number next to the function name indicates the priority of the layer regarding material joins. These are in the order of construction. In this way, the Structure layer of one wall or roof will attempt to join with the Structure layer of another. One [1] is therefore the highest priority, while five [5] is the lowest. "Membrane Layers" have zero thickness and thus do not have priority nor do they join.

Floors and Roofs | 377

Material—Materials designate what the layer is made from. Material properties include patterns, render material, shading, and even structural and thermal characteristics to represent real-life materials.

Thickness—This is the dimensional thickness of the layer.

Wraps—Controls if the layer wraps around corners at the ends or at openings. If this is not selected, the layer simply cuts perpendicular at the ends and openings.

Variable—When the type is applied to a flat roof, one component on the list can be given a variable thickness. Editing tools for manipulating flat roofs (and floors) provide a means to add high and low points to the surface of the roof element. When the variable box is selected, such height variations are applied only to the variable component. (This is used to represent tapered insulation on flat roofs for example—see below.) When no layers use the variable option, thickness variations are applied uniformly to the roof essentially warping the surface.

4. In the "Edit Assembly" dialog click in the Material cell for the Structure layer (layer number 2).

   A small browse icon will appear at the right side of the cell.

   ⇨ Click the small browse icon to open the "Material Browser" dialog.

5. In the "Material Browser," at the top in the Search field, type: **structure**.

This will filter the list of materials to show only those that include the search word in their name or properties.

   ⇨ Select: **Structure, Wood Joist/Rafter Layer** [**Structure -Timber Joist/Rafter Layer**] and then click OK once (see Figure 9.23).

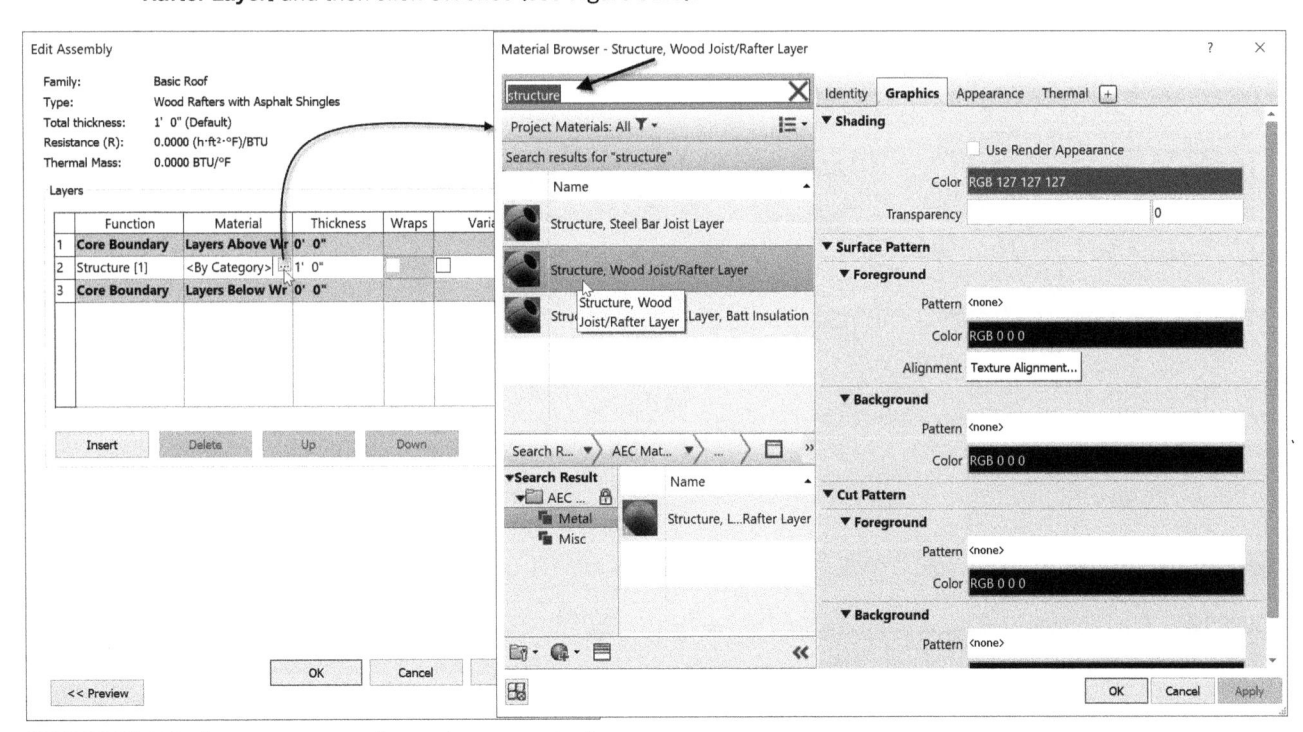

FIGURE 9.23 *Edit the existing structure layer to become wood rafters*

6. In the Thickness field, type: **7 1/4"** [**190**] and then press ENTER.

7. Beneath the list of layers, click the Insert button.

   A new zero thickness Structure layer will appear.

Notice that the new layer appears within the "Core Boundary." Roofs, walls, and floors have a core that contains the structural layers. You can have additional layers on either or both sides of the core. If a new layer that you insert

• Revit Essentials for Architecture •

378 | Chapter 9

does not appear in the desired location, select it and then use the Up and Down buttons to adjust its position in the overall structure of the roof.

8. With the new layer highlighted, click the Up button to place it above the Core Boundary.

    ⇨ Change the Function of the new layer to: **Substrate [2]**.

    ⇨ Change the Material to: **Plywood, Sheathing** and set the Thickness to: **5/8"** [**16**].

> **TIP:** Simply type: **plywood** in the search field to go directly to the material.

9. Click the Insert button again. (It should come in above the plywood, if it did not, move it there).

    ⇨ Change the Function of the new layer to: **Finish 1 [4]**.

    ⇨ Click the browse button in the Material filed, in the Search box type: **roofing** and then from the list select: **Asphalt Shingle** and click OK.

    ⇨ Set the Thickness to: **1/4"** [**6**]

If you wish to see how the type looks so far, click the Preview button at the bottom left corner of the dialog (see Figure 9.24).

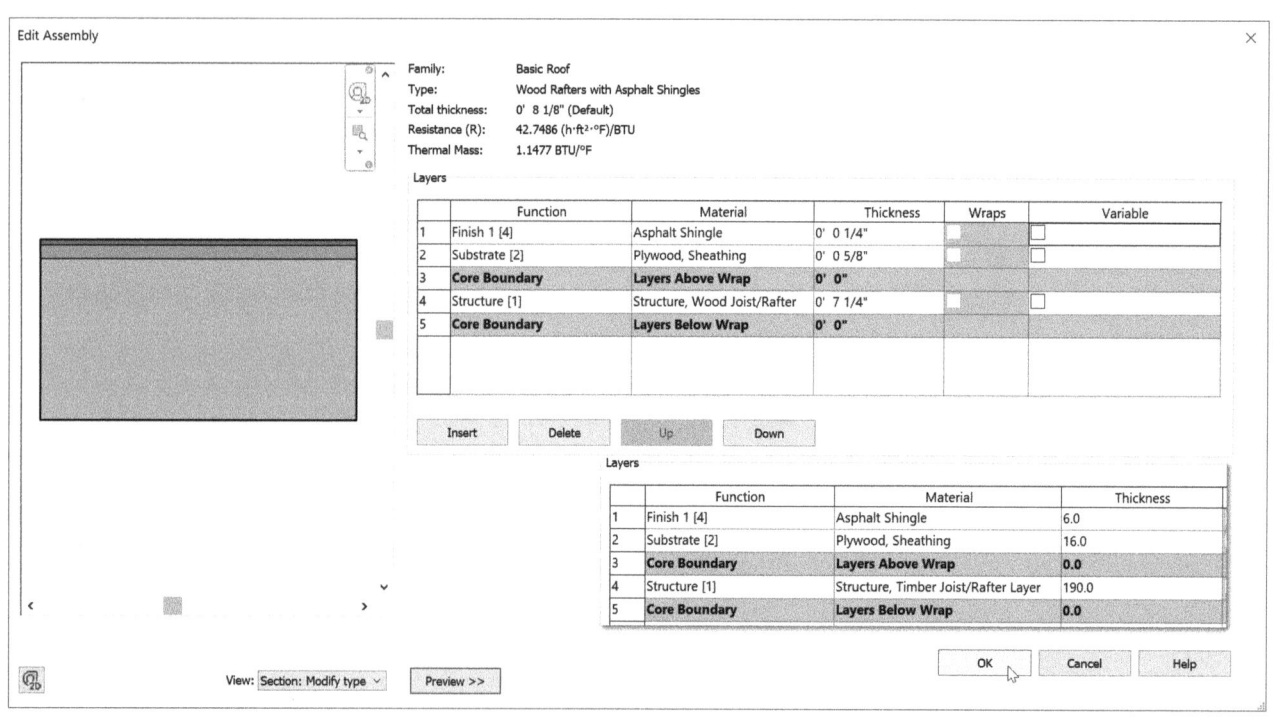

FIGURE 9.24 *Open the preview window to see the completed structure graphically*

10. Click OK twice to return to the view window.

Notice that the new roof layers appear in the section view—if you switched to a different view, please return to the *Longitudinal* section view now. Also note that the new layers will only appear if you left the section view in the Medium visual style from above. If you set it back to coarse, the graphics will simplify to show the outer edge of the roof only. If you have difficulty seeing the sheathing and asphalt shingle layers, try reopening the callout view we created above instead (see Figure 9.25).

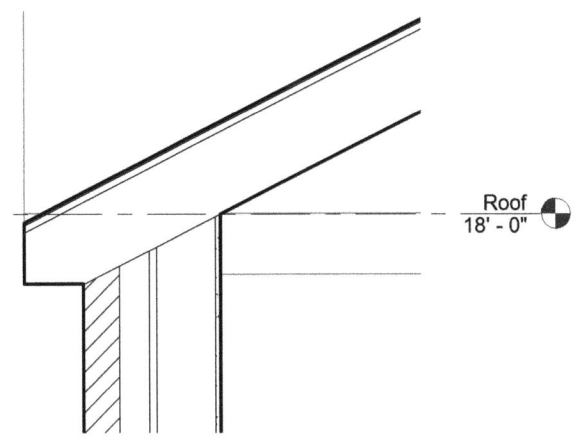

FIGURE 9.25 *Completed roof structure (shown at 1" = 1'-0" [1:10])*

APPLY A FASCIA TO ROOF EDGES

Creating the new type and editing its structure provides a satisfactory representation of the overall roof construction. However, the edges of the roof could use some further embellishment. A fascia allows us to apply a detailed profile condition to the edges of a roof. In this example, we will explore the application of both fascia boards and gutters to our roofs.

1. On the Project Browser, double-click to open the *New Addition Axon* view.
2. On the Architecture tab, click the drop down button on the Roof tool and choose the: **Roof: Fascia** tool.

There are some fascia types already in the project. However, as with the roof type above, we will create our own. A fascia is a simple element whose primary parameter is the assignment of a profile shape. The roof here has a 6" [150] roof edge as defined earlier so we will want a profile close to this depth.

3. On the Properties palette, click the Edit Type button.
   ⇨ Next to the type list, click the Duplicate button and for the Name, input: **Simple Fascia** and then click OK.
   ⇨ From the "Profile" list, choose: **Fascia-Flat : 1x6 [M_Fascia-Flat : 19 x 140mm]**.

   If you like you can assign a material such as: Clad – White (search for paint).

   ⇨ Click OK (see Figure 9.26).

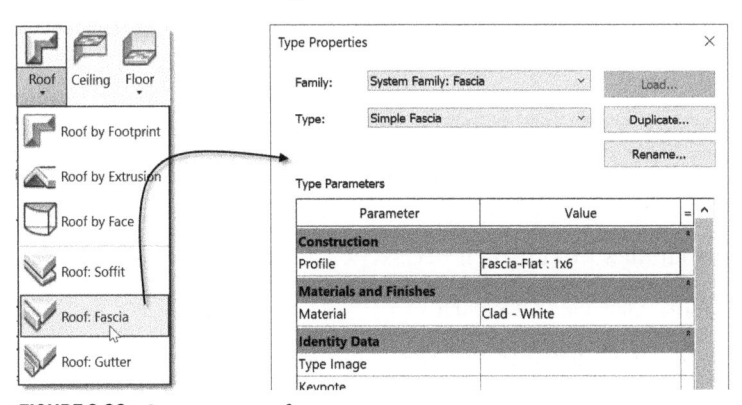

FIGURE 9.26 *Create a custom fascia type*

A glance at the Status Bar will reveal the following prompt: "Click on edge of Roof, Soffit, Fascia, or Model Line to add. Click again to remove." With the New Addition Axon view open, it is easy to accomplish this.

4. Move the pointer over the various edges of the roof elements on screen.

380 | Chapter 9

Notice that both the top and bottom edges of any given edge will pre-highlight (see Figure 9.27).

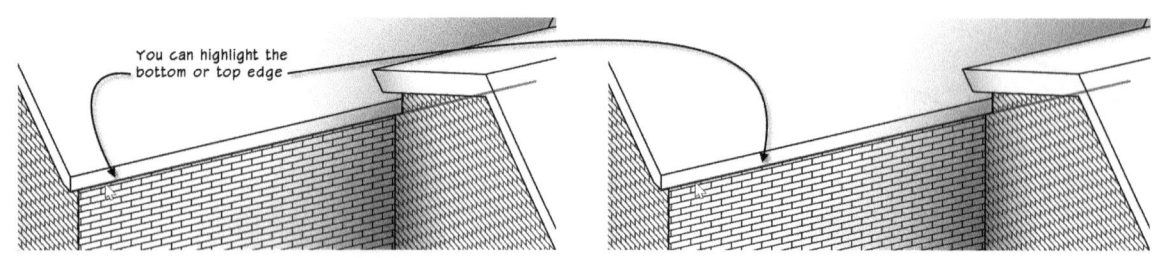

FIGURE 9.27 *When placing the fascia, you can pre-highlight either the top or bottom edge to place it*

➪ Click on a top edge to apply the Fascia.

Place Fascia boards on the top edges of all of the horizontal (fascia) edges of the new roof and all edges of the existing roof as shown in Figure 9.28.

> **NOTE:** Be sure to click the top edge of each roof edge, not the bottom.

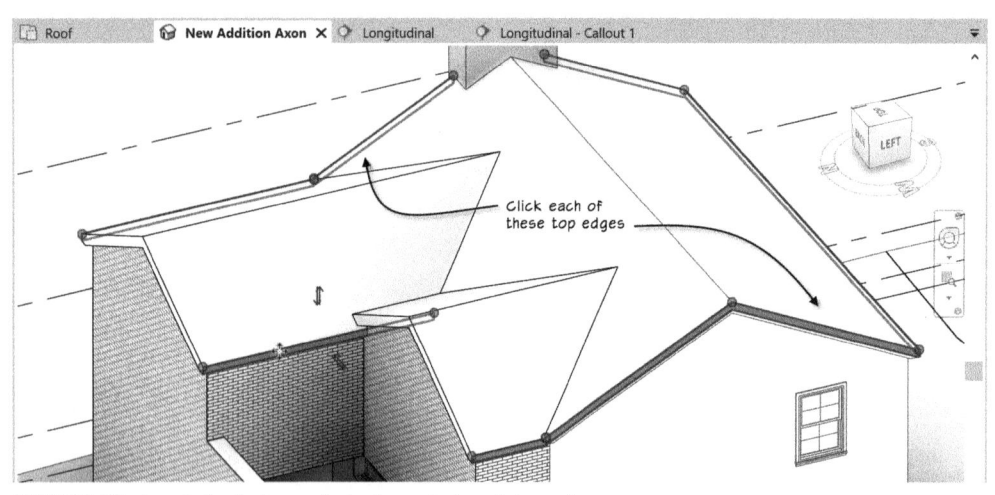

FIGURE 9.28 *Attach the fasciae to the horizontal edges of the roofs*

➪ On the ribbon, click the Modify tool or press the esc key twice.

We did not apply a fascia to the sloped (rake) edges of the new construction roof yet because we are going to use a different type for these. However, before we create the type, we need a more complex profile family from the library.

5. On the Insert tab, click the Load Family button.

Revit will open to a folder containing your default library installed with the software. If this has not occurred, you may have shortcut icons on the left side of the dialog to jump to library locations. If you do not have these icons, the appropriate files (without the subfolders) have been provided with the dataset files in the *Chapter09* folder. You can navigate manually to that location and access the families from there if necessary.

➪ Double-click on the *Profiles* folder and then double-click the *Roofs* folder.

➪ Select the *Fascia-Built-Up.rfa* [*M_Fascia-Built-Up.rfa*] file and then click Open.

This loads the new profile family into the current project. We now need to repeat the previous steps above to create a new fascia type using this profile.

6. On the Architecture tab, from the Roof tool, choose the: **Roof: Fascia** tool.

➪ On the Properties palette, click the Edit Type button.

• The Aubin Academy •

⇨ Duplicate the type, name it: **Built-up Fascia** and then click OK.

7. From the "Profile" list, choose: **Fascia-Built-Up : 1x8 w 1x6 [M_Fascia-Built-Up : 38 x 140mm x 38 x 89mm]** and then click OK.

8. Click each of the remaining roof edges (remember to click the top edge).

   There are four total along the gable ends of the new roofs.

   ⇨ On the ribbon, click the Modify tool or press the ESC key twice.

Zoom in on one of the intersections between the rake and fascia conditions. If you select one of the fascia boards, you will notice a drag control at the ends. You can stretch this control to modify the way the two fascia boards intersect. Also, with one of the fascia or rake boards selected, you will notice that all the boards select as a single element. To remove or add segments to this element, use the Add/Remove Segments tool on the Modify | Fascias tab. There is also a Modify Mitering tool. The options are "Horizontal," "Vertical," and "Perpendicular." Try them out if you wish to see how each option behaves. You can also use Join Geometry at the valley condition.

9. Save the project.

ADD GUTTERS

We also have a Gutter tool that we can add to our roofs. These are conceptually the same as fascia boards. They use a profile to determine the cross-section shape and sweep it along the path edges we select.

1. Zoom out to see just the new roofs.

2. On the Architecture tab, from the Roof tool, choose the: **Roof: Gutter** tool.

   ⇨ Click one of the top horizontal edges of the newly placed Fascia of the new construction roof.

   Be sure to pick the edge at the outside face.

If the gutter is not visible, it needs to be flipped. There are flip controls on the selected Gutter.

   Click the Flip control if necessary to flip the gutter to the outside.

3. Before clicking the next segment, click the Restart Gutter button on the Modify | Place Gutter tab.

When you create fascia, gutters, and other kinds of sweeps, multiple segments can be added to a single sweep. If you later click to select it, you will notice that they all select as one element. In this case, we will have more flexibility to select and flip our gutters if we start each segment as a new sweep.

4. Add Gutters (and flip as required) to the remaining horizontal new construction roof edges (see Figure 9.29).

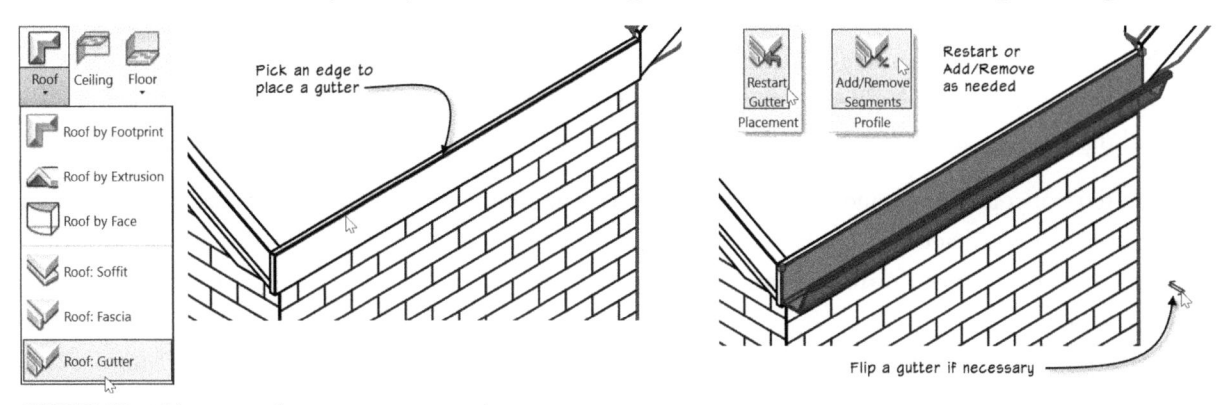

FIGURE 9.29 *Add gutters to the new construction roof*

If after you place the gutters, you pre-highlight the one in the valley between the two new roofs and notice it is too long. You can use the drag control on the fascia board (and the gutter if necessary) to shorten it.

5. On the Project Browser, double-click to open the *Longitudinal* section view.

6. Zoom in on one of the Gutters.

⇨ On the View tab, on the Graphics panel, click the Thin Lines button (or press TL).

Depending on which line you clicked (the roof edge or the fascia edge) when adding the gutters, you may notice that the gutter overlaps the fascia board. We can delete the gutter and re-add it, or we can apply an offset to the Gutter equal to the thickness of the fascia profile to compensate for this.

7. Select any of the Gutters that require adjustment.

⇨ On the Properties palette, change the "Horizontal Profile Offset" to: **3/4"** [**19**] and then click OK (see Figure 9.30).

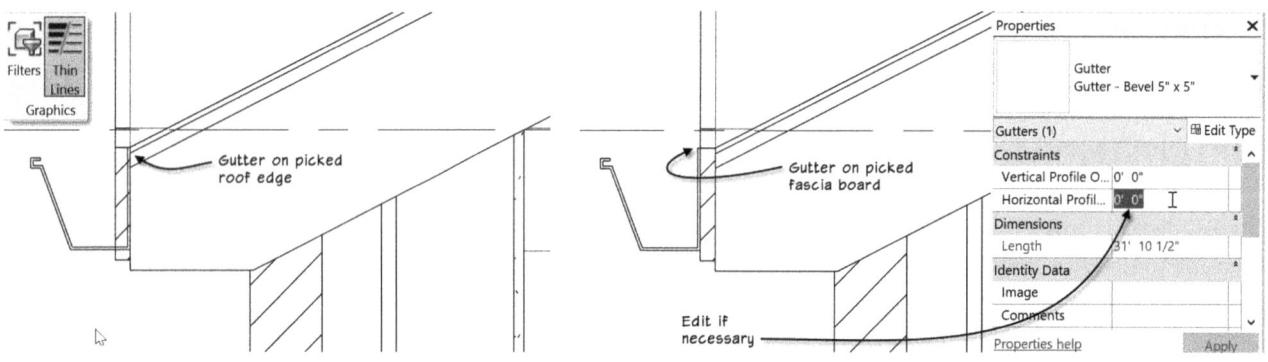

FIGURE 9.30 *Adjust gutter horizontal offset as required*

8. Click Thin Lines again to turn it off.

UNDERSTANDING LINE WEIGHT SETTINGS

The line weight currently used for the fascia boards and gutters in the section view is the same as that used for the walls. Since both items have a very small thickness, we have two very bold lines right next to each other and the result is not very legible. This can often tempt users into working permanently with Thin Lines turned on. Don't do it! Thin lines is just onscreen display and does not change the way that your views will output to print or PDF. Instead, you can override the line weight (and other display characteristics) of elements directly in the view. Overrides can be applied to most elements at the category or element level. If you wish to try this, simply select one of the gutters or one of the fascia boards. Right-click and choose: **Override Graphics in View > By Category**. (This command is also on the View panel of the ribbon.) In the "View-Specific Category Graphics" dialog that appears, expand the Cut item. Next click the Weight drop down and choose a thinner line like: 1 or 2 and then click OK to return to the view window and see the results. Repeat as necessary on other elements. You can also override projection lines (those beyond that are not cut) and other graphics like fill patterns in the same way.

A good way to test out your settings and see if you like them is to zoom the view to sheet size. When you finish your line weight edit, make sure that thin lines is off (making sure that you can see line weights displayed onscreen). Then from the Navigation Bar, choose **Zoom to Sheet Size** from the pop-up menu, or just type: ZS. This will give you a nice onscreen approximation of what the view will look like when printed to scale. Try adjusting the scale of the view as well and note the impact to the line weight display. In Revit, line weights and all annotation adjust automatically based on the scale of the view. Spend some time getting comfortable with this. Once you understand how easy it is to work directly in what is essentially a live plot preview; using scale settings, appropriate levels of detail and zoom to sheet size, you will hopefully relegate the use of thin lines to what it was designed for: a diagnostic tool to help you solve graphical display issues and use it accordingly. Turn thin lines on to assess a problem and once you solve it, turn it back off again returning to an onscreen display that closely resembles final output.

You can perform such edits to nearly any element. You can also right-click and choose: **Override Graphics in View > By Element**. In general, a category-level edit should be attempted first. It will apply to all similar elements in the current view. If you want to override just a specific element(s), use the "By Element" option instead. But use sparingly as it is sometimes difficult to identify and modify the element-level edit later.

> **BIM Manager Note:** It is important to get the overall defaults and global settings to your liking first. For example, if you find yourself applying the same override repeatedly, consider making the change "globally" in the "Object Styles" dialog. Object Styles establish the default graphical settings for all elements in all views throughout the project. Overrides, both category and element, modify the global settings only in current view. In some cases, what you may need is to edit the global setting making overrides unnecessary. To edit Object Styles, click the Manage tab, and click the Object Styles button. Remember, after applying category overrides, you can reuse them in other similar views by creating and applying a custom view template.

SKYLIGHTS

As a finishing touch to the residential roof, let's add a skylight in one of the new roofs. To do this, we must load another family into the project.

1. Return to the *Roof* plan view tab.
2. On the Insert tab, click the Load Family tool.
   ⇨ Double-click on the *Windows* folder.
   ⇨ Select the *Skylight-Flat.rfa* [*M_Skylight-Flat.rfa*] file and then click Open.
   ⇨ In the "Specify Types" dialog that appears, choose: 32" x 36" [800 x 900mm] and then click OK.
3. On the Architecture tab, click the Window tool. Turn off Tag on Placement.
   ⇨ From the Type Selector, choose: **Skylight-Flat : 32" x 36" [M_Skylight-Flat : 800 x 900mm]**.
   ⇨ Place it approximately as indicated in Figure 9.31.

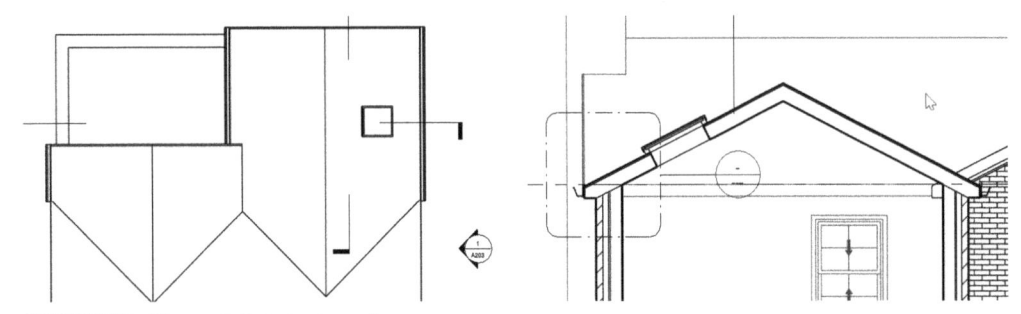

FIGURE 9.31 *Place a skylight in the roof*

4. Click the Modify tool to cancel and then select the window.

The skylight should appear cutting through the roof. If the section does not intersect the roof window, you can move the section line slightly in plan.

5. Save the project.

FINE-TUNING

More work could be done on the roofs, to refine them further. Feel free to experiment further and make your own modifications if you wish. You can edit the sketches of the roofs to modify their shapes, adjust the gutters and fascia and create additional types if you like. If you want to modify fascia and gutter items remember the Add/Remove Segments button on the ribbon. You can also adjust the position of the roof window and even add others if you like. Another thing to check is if your roof plan is not displaying both low height walls bounding the patio on the second floor. If this is the case, you can adjust the view range to fix it. In the Roof plan view, edit the View Range and then lower the View Depth to about: -10'-0" [-3000].

Finally, if you look carefully at the two new roofs on the back of the house, you will notice that their ridge lines do not line up. The small one over the bathrooms is too high. This is caused by the wall in the middle that we used to sketch both roofs. If you open the *North* elevation or the *Longitudinal* section, you should be able to assess this. An easy way to perform your analysis is to select just the two new roofs and then use Temporary Hide/Isolate (the sunglasses) to Isolate Elements. This will hide everything except the two roofs. Then you can easily take some measurements and even draw some reference planes to help understand the relationships. The reference plane tool is on the Architecture tab, on the Work Plane panel (or press RP). Draw them by clicking two points. You can snap from one ridge and then draw horizontally across to the other to see the issue (see the left side of Figure 9.32).

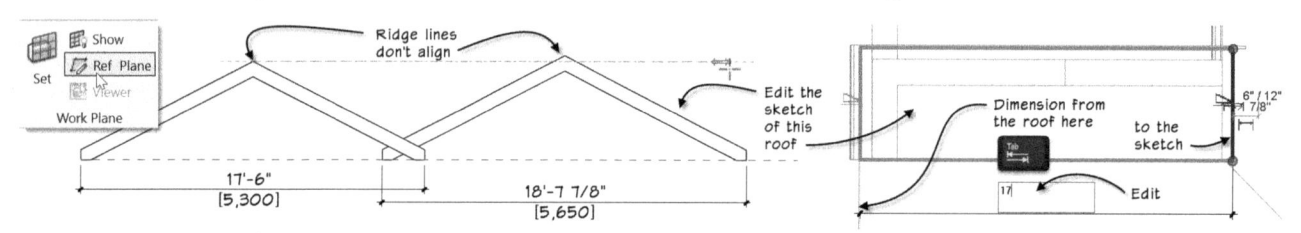

FIGURE 9.32 *Use reference planes and dimensions to identify the issue. Edit the sketch to fix*

You can also take some measurements. The width of the larger roof is what we want to match. The space it sits on is 16'-6" [5000] wide. With the 6" [150] overhand on each side that makes the roof a total of 17'-6" [5300] wide. However, referring back to Figure 9.20 and Figure 9.21 above, the overhang is applied below the slope line (the level line), so if our aim is to ensure that the two roofs match and end up with symmetry between our ridge lines, then we want to remove the distance of one overhang when performing our modification. This results in a value of 17'-0" [5150] wide for the smaller roof. To make this change, simply edit the sketch of the small roof. In the sketch, you can add a dimension from the existing roof on the left to the sketch line on the right. Be sure to use the TAB key to ensure that you are picking the existing roof; not the fascia, not the sketch of the new roof. Then select the sketch line on the right and this will activate the dimension you just placed. Input the value of: **17'-0"** [**5150**] to complete the edit and then finish the sketch (see the right side of Figure 9.32).

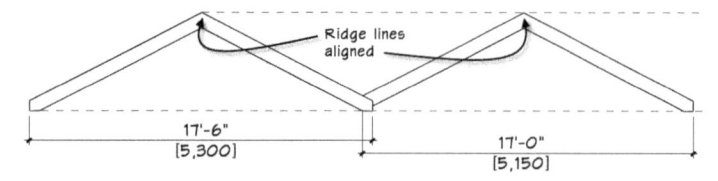

FIGURE 9.33 *After editing the sketch, the ridge lines should align*

After the edit is complete, the two ridge lines should align. You might need to stretch the endpoints of the fascia after this edit to fine tune it.

CREATING FLOORS

Use floor elements to model the floor platforms or slabs in your projects. Most often, the floor element is a simple horizontal structure that you create via a closed sketch of its plan boundary. In some cases, the floor may slope like in parking garages or theaters. We created floors in the commercial project in the "Adding Floors" topic on page 233 in Chapter 6. However, you have probably noticed that our residential project currently has no floors. So, in this topic, we will follow similar procedures to add and modify some floor elements here in the residential project.

1. On the Project Browser, double-click to open the *First Floor* plan view.
    - ⇨ On the View tab (or the QAT), click the Close Inactive Views button.
2. On the Architecture tab, click the Floor tool. (If you use the drop down, it is: **Floor :Architectural**).

    On the Draw panel, the Boundary Line and Pick Walls tools should be active by default.
    - ⇨ On the Options Bar, place a checkmark in the "Extend into wall (to core)" check box if it is not already checked.
3. Click on the vertical wall of the addition on the left (see item 1 in Figure 9.34).
    - ⇨ Click on each of the other two exterior walls of the new addition (items 2 and 3).
    - ⇨ Click the existing wall between the house and the addition last (item 4).
4. On the ribbon, click the Modify tool or press the ESC key twice.

Sketch lines will appear at all four walls. The one for the existing wall at the bottom (item 4) might be on the inside edge, if it is, drag the horizontal sketch line between the existing house and the addition to the other side of the existing wall (see Figure 9.34).

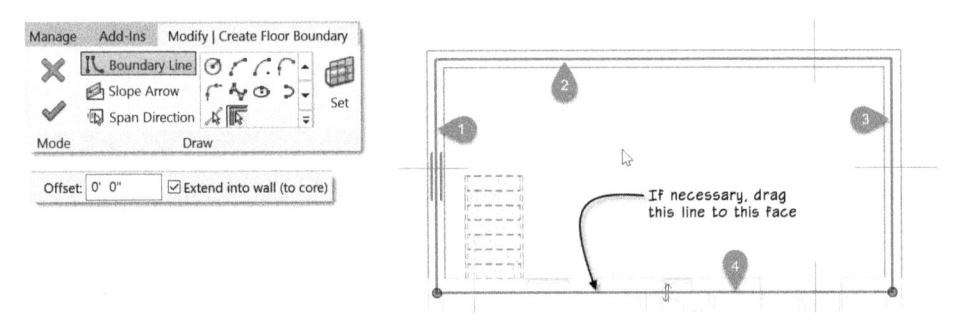

FIGURE 9.34 *Create the floor sketch for the first floor*

In this case, we cannot use the flip control as it would flip all four lines. Therefore, we are dragging only the one line manually. It will snap to the inside face.

- ⇨ Deselect the line and then on the Properties palette, from the Type Selector choose: **Wood Joist 10" - Wood Finish [Standard Timber-Wood Finish]**.

The structure of the floor is like the structure of the roof that we explored earlier. Feel free to edit the type parameters to study the structure but be sure to not make any changes currently.

5. On the ribbon, click the Finish Edit Mode button.
    - ⇨ In the dialog that appears, click Yes to join the geometry (see Figure 9.35).

386 | Chapter 9

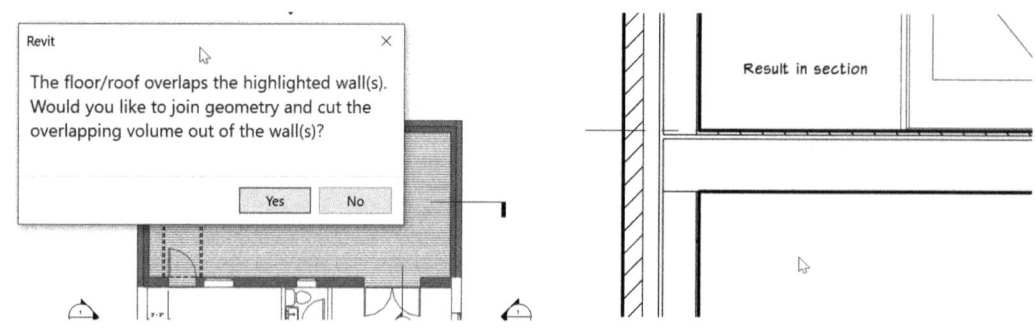

FIGURE 9.35 *Allow Revit to join the floor to the neighboring walls*

You can see the result of answering yes in section view in the figure on the right. The floor will interact with the wall geometry and cut into its volume. Notice how the individual layers also interact between wall and floor.

6. Repeat the entire process on the second floor.

    Create the sketch the same way initially, however, modify the sketch to conform to the "L" shape (excluding the outdoor patio) of the interior space of the addition. Use the Trim/Extend tool to do this (see Figure 9.36). Remember to edit the floor Properties and choose the same type as the first floor.

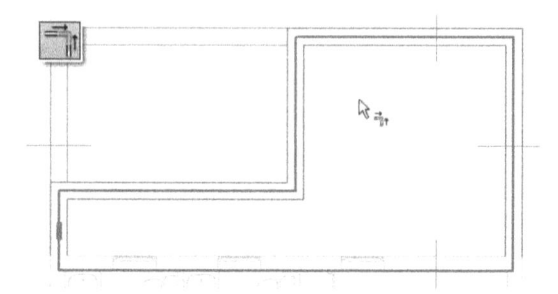

FIGURE 9.36 *Create the sketch for the second floor*

If a message asking you to attach walls that go up to this floor's level appears, click the Don't Attach button. In this case, the walls it is referring to are the walls in the existing part of the house. We don't want these attached to the new construction floor. When the Join Geometry message appears again, do click Yes as we did on the first floor.

CREATE A FLOOR TYPE

The last floor that we need to make is the one for the patio space on the second floor. The process is like the above. We are creating it separately because it will use a different type.

1. Click the Floor tool and use the same options.

2. Create sketch lines for each of the four walls that make up the patio and use the Trim/Extend tool to complete the shape (see Figure 9.37).

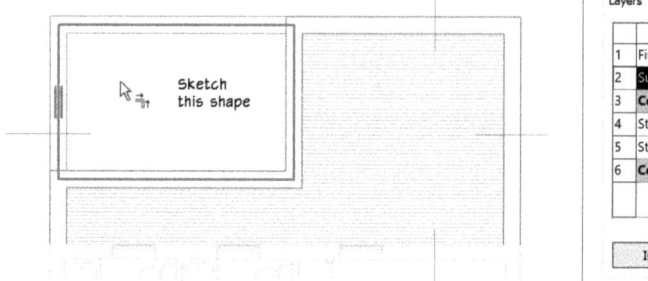

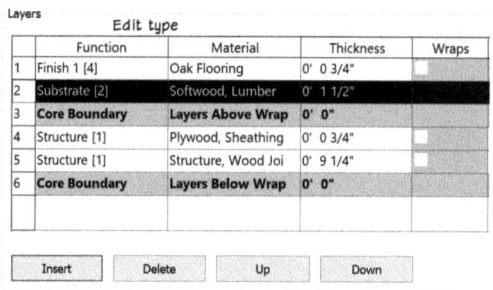

FIGURE 9.37 *Create the sketch for the patio floor*

3. On the Properties palette, click the Edit Type button.

• The Aubin Academy •

The Type chosen should already be: **Wood Joist 10" - Wood Finish** [**Standard Timber-Wood Finish**]. If it isn't, then choose it now.

⇨ Click the Duplicate button (or press ALT + D), name the new type: **Patio Floor** and then click OK.

The patio will have a wood deck built up on top of sleepers to provide drainage below. Therefore, we can use nearly the same layer makeup as the other floor system and simply insert the sleeper layer. While this floor type would have a membrane layer and flashing, we will not include those in the model but rather save those components for later in details (see Chapter 12 for more information on detailing).

4. Click the Edit button next to Structure, select layer 2 (Core Boundary), and then click the Insert button to add a new layer.

5. Set the new layer Function to: **Substrate [2]**.

⇨ Change the thickness of the new layer to: **1 1/2" [40]** and set the Material to: **Softwood, Lumber**.

⇨ Click OK to return to the "Type Properties" dialog.

6. Change the Function to: **Exterior**, and then click OK.

7. On the ribbon, click the Finish Edit Mode button.

⇨ In the dialog that appears, click Yes to accept joining with the walls.

ADJUST FLOOR POSITION AND JOINS

A couple of issues remain with the two floors on the second floor. First, the walls that highlighted automatically for join did not include the two walls we added at the start of the chapter. Second, the patio floor is too low relative to the other one. We can see these issues best in section.

1. On the Project Browser, double-click to open the *Longitudinal* section view.

   Examine the section to see both conditions noted here.

2. Select the patio floor (it is on the right in the section and may still be selected).

⇨ On the Properties palette, for the "Height Offset From Level" value, type: **1 1/2" [40]**.

This is the same amount as the thickness of the sleepers. By default, the entire thickness of floors is set below the associated level. Therefore, we need to shift the floor to properly represent that the sleepers are built up on top of the floor structure.

3. On the Modify tab of the ribbon, click the Join Geometry tool.

⇨ For the first pick, click the patio floor.

⇨ For the second pick, click the vertical wall.

The Join command will remain active. You can perform several Join operations in a row.

4. Join the same wall to the other floor if needed.

⇨ Join the two floors to one another (see Figure 9.38).

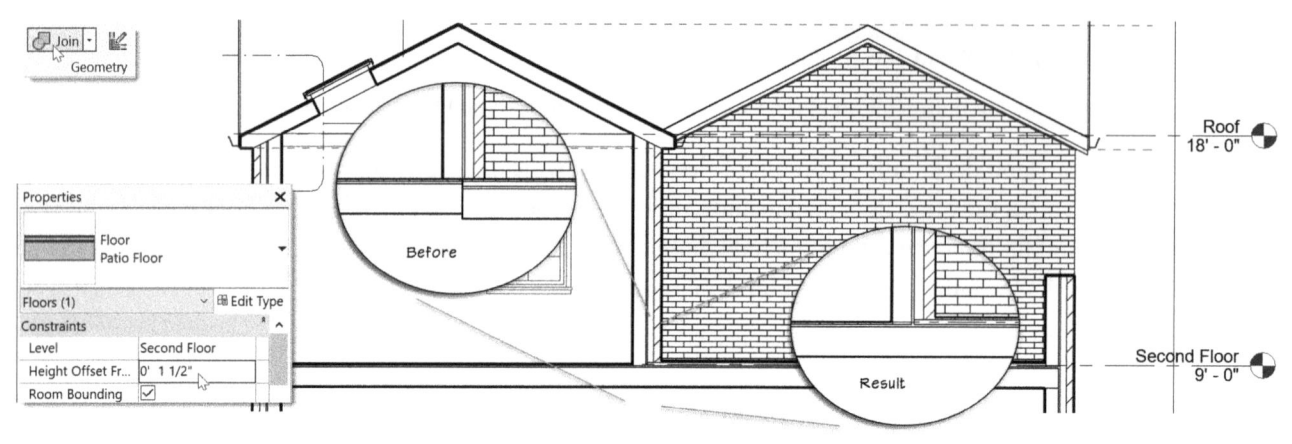

FIGURE 9.38 *Join the floors to the wall*

> **TIP:** Note the "Multiple Join" option on the Options Bar. Place a checkmark in this box to join several elements in one operation. To reset the tool, click in empty space and then start again.

5. On the Project Browser, double-click to open the *Second Floor* plan view.
6. Create a section cutting vertically (parallel to Transverse) through the patio.
   ⇨ Rename it: **Patio Section**.
7. Open this section view, change the Detail Level to: **Medium** and then repeat the join process here on the floors and wall.
   ⇨ Optionally you can adjust the crop region to crop just below the second floor and enlarge the scale.

> **NOTE:** Some joins may already be complete requiring no further action. Simply complete the joins that are necessary.

⇨ On the ribbon, click the Modify tool or press the ESC key twice.

Previously we mentioned the priorities of the layers within the roof (also wall and floor) structure. In these two sections, you can see this interaction very clearly. Notice the way that the structural layer of the floor cuts into the core of the walls. This is followed by substrate and then finishes.

8. Save and close the project.

COMMERCIAL PROJECT ROOF

Our commercial project already has a roof. However, it is currently just a flat slab. Also, the stair tower does not yet have a roof. Our aim in this section will be to refine the roof element already in the commercial project and to add additional required roof elements. We will also begin work on our commercial project's *Roof* plan view.

LOAD THE COMMERCIAL PROJECT

Be sure that the residential project has been saved and closed.

1. On the Home screen, click the Open button.

> **TIP:** The keyboard shortcut for Open is CTRL + O. Open is also located on the File menu.

2. In the "Open" dialog box, browse to the *Chapter09* folder.

⇨ Double-click *09 Commercial.rvt* if you wish to work in Imperial units.

⇨ Double-click *09 Commercial_M.rvt* if you wish to work in Metric units.

You can also select it and then click the Open button.

> **NOTE:** Some minor modifications have been made to the model since the last chapter. The layout of walls on the Roof level is slightly different than it was in the previous chapter. As such, the core walls were shortened to the level below and a new set of walls added on the roof. For this reason, please be sure to use the dataset provided with this chapter rather than attempting to continue in your previous files.

CREATE A ROOF BY EXTRUSION

Until now we have created our roofs with the footprint option. It is also possible to create a roof by sketching the profile of it in section and extruding this profile to form the roof. In Chapter 1 we looked briefly at creating a roof this way. Let's revisit that process in more detail for the roof at the top of our stair tower.

1. On the Project Browser, double-click to open the *South* elevation view.

To assist us in placing the roof, we will add some new levels. You may from Chapter 5 that a level can be created with automatically associated plan views, or it can be created without them and simply used for reference. We do not need a separate plan for the roof of the stair tower, so the levels we add here will not have associated plan views.

2. Select the Roof level line.

3. On the Modify | Levels tab, click the Copy tool.

⇨ Click anywhere to set the start point.

⇨ Move the mouse straight up, type: **8'-0"** [**2400**] and then press ENTER.

4. Repeat the process and create another copy: **4'-0"** [**1200**] above the previous copy (or **12'-0"** [**3600**] above the original Roof level).

Notice that when you deselect the levels, both copies have black-colored level heads. A level head will be blue if it has an associated floor plan view (or ceiling plan), and black if it has none. Look at the *Floor Plans* branch on the Project Browser to confirm that no new floor plan views have been created. (If you wish to create a level using the level tool instead, it defaults to adding plan views: however, you can turn this option off on the Options Bar before drawing the level.) You can also add plans later using the Plan Views drop down on the View tab of the ribbon.

5. Click on the blue text of the new level heads and rename the lower one to: **Stair Roof Low** and the upper one to: **Stair Roof High** (see Figure 9.39).

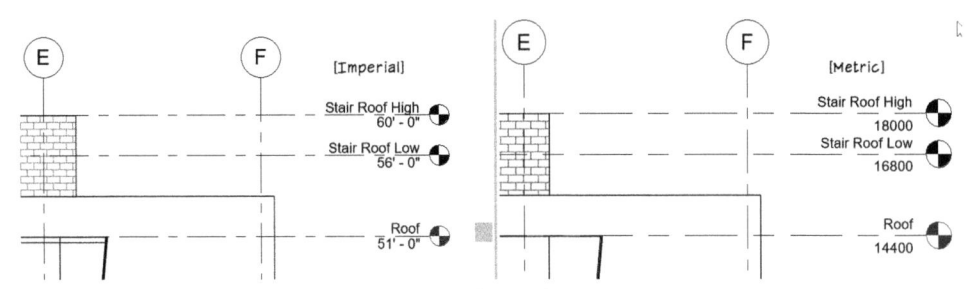

FIGURE 9.39 *Copy two new levels without associated floor plan views*

6. On the Architecture tab, click the drop down button on the Roof tool and then choose the: **Roof by Extrusion** tool (see item 1 in Figure 9.40).

390 | Chapter 9

A "Work Plane" dialog will appear. The work plane is the plane in which we will sketch. In this case, because we are making a roof by extrusion, an effective work plane will be perpendicular to the roof levels. Any of our numbered grid lines can serve this purpose—the numbered grid lines form planes parallel to the screen in the current elevation view. Once we have chosen a plane, we will be able to sketch the shape of our roof. When we finish the sketch, it will extrude perpendicular to the selected plane.

⇨ In the roof "Work Plane" dialog, choose: **Grid 4** (from the "Name" list) and then click OK (item 2).

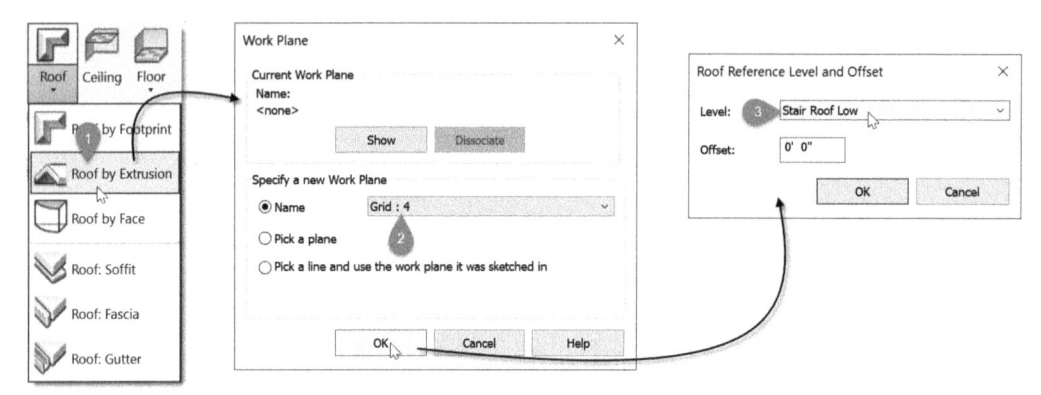

FIGURE 9.40 *Choose a column grid Line as the work plane*

As you can see in the figure, it is also possible to pick the face of some geometry such as a wall in the model to set the work plane. (We took this approach in 1.) In this case the named plane associated with the grid line works best. It is also common practice to create a reference plane to use as the work plane for the roof. Feel free to use any of these methods in your own work.

7. In the "Roof Reference Level and Offset" dialog that appears, select: **Stair Roof Low** and then click OK (item 3).

The roof must be associated with a Level. As you can see in the dialog, you can choose to create the roof at any level in the project and add an offset above or below the level if appropriate. In this case, we specifically created Stair Roof Low for the task at hand, so no offset is required.

8. On the Modify | Create Extrusion Roof Profile, on the Draw panel, click the "Start-End-Radius Arc" icon.

⇨ For the Arc start point, click the intersection of the Stair Roof Low Level and the left edge of the core wall (see item 1 in Figure 9.41).

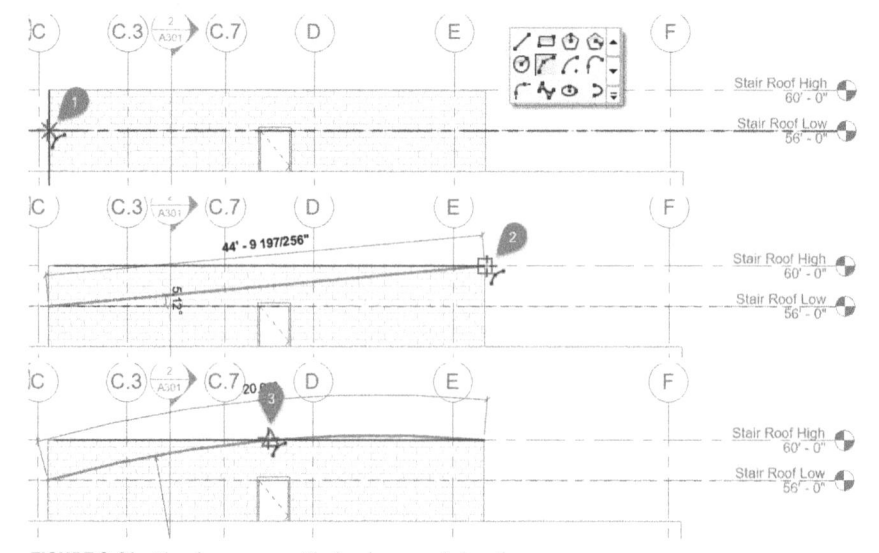

FIGURE 9.41 *Sketch an arc profile for the extruded roof*

⇨ For the arc endpoint, click the endpoint of the right edge of the core wall at the Stair Roof High level (item 2).

• The Aubin Academy •

Floors and Roofs | 391

- For the arc intermediate point, click at the midpoint of the top edge of the core wall (item 3).
- On the ribbon, click the Modify tool or press the ESC key twice.

When you draw a roof by extrusion, you create an open shape, not a closed shape. The thickness of the roof material will be determined by the roof properties and the type assigned to it just like the other roofs; therefore, we do not need to sketch the thickness of the roof.

9. On the Properties palette from the Type Selector, choose: **Steel Truss - Insulation on Metal Deck - EPDM** [**Steel Bar Joist -Steel Deck -EPDM Membrane**].

- Beneath Constraints, for the "Extrusion Start" type: **-2'-0"** [**-600**].
- For the "Extrusion End" type: **22'-0"** [**6600**].

> **TIP:** An alternate way to set the extrusion distance is to wait until after you have finished creating the roof. It will be extruded an arbitrary distance initially. You can then move to a plan view and use the shape handles to adjust the extrusion depth graphically. This technique was used in 1.

You probably noticed that there were no overhang parameters on the Properties palette or on the Options Bar. To create an overhang, you simply edit the sketch line or add additional segments. In 1 we simply dragged the endpoints to make the arc larger. Here we will add some extra line segments.

10. On the Draw panel, click the Line tool.

- Add a **1'-6"** [**450**] long horizontal line at each end of the Arc (see Figure 9.42).

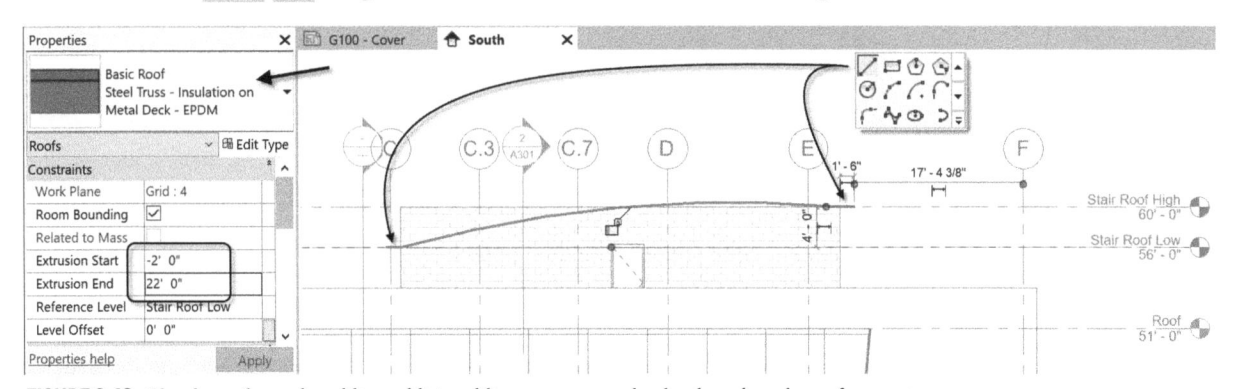

FIGURE 9.42 *Sketch overhangs by adding additional line segments to the sketch and set the roof properties*

11. On the ribbon, click the Finish Edit Mode button.

    The roof should appear with its thickness determined by the roof type that we chose.

12. On the QAT, click the Default 3D View icon to open the *{3D}* view (see Figure 9.43).

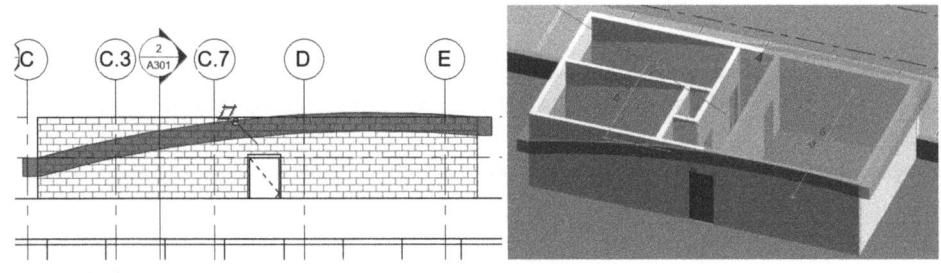

FIGURE 9.43 *The new roof intersects the core walls*

ATTACH WALLS TO THE ROOF

It appears our walls could use some adjustment. We already learned how to deal with this above.

1. On the Project Browser, double-click to open the *Roof* plan view.
2. Dragging from left to right, surround the entire core.

    Walls, stairs, and other objects will be selected by this action.

    ⇨ On the Modify | Multi-Select tab of the ribbon, click the Filter tool.

    ⇨ In the "Filter" dialog, click the Check None button, click the check box next to walls, and then click OK.

This will remove all other elements from the selection leaving only the core walls on the roof level selected.

3. On the Project Browser, double-click to open the *{3D}* view.

If you prefer, you can tile the two windows. The selection of walls will remain active. If the selection does not remain active, right-click in the view window and choose: **Select Previous**.

⇨ On the Modify | Walls tab, on the Modify Wall panel, click the Attach Top/Base button.

4. Verify that Top is selected on the Options Bar and then click on the edge of the roof (see Figure 9.44).

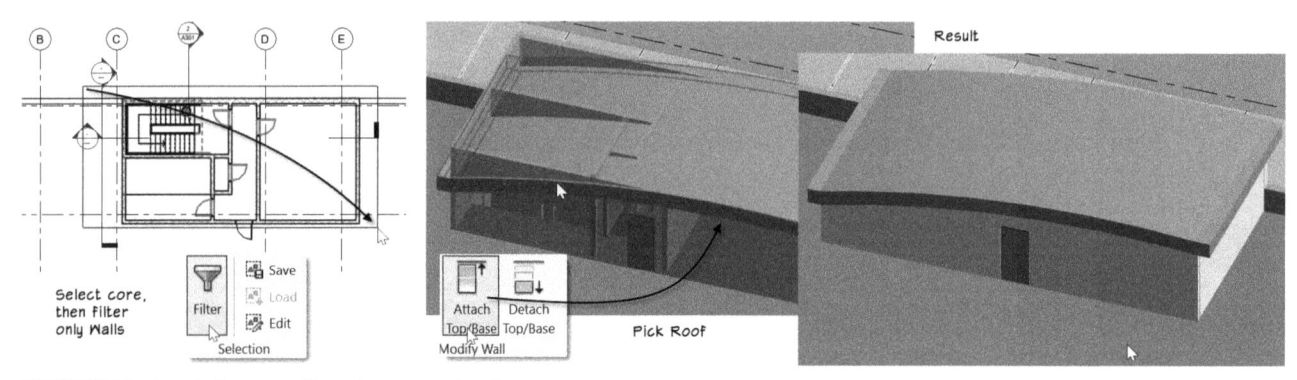

FIGURE 9.44 *Attach the core walls to the imported roof*

5. Deselect the walls to see the result and then save the file.

You can study this change in other views as well if you like.

Structural Core Walls

You may recall that in previous chapters we copied the walls to the Structural model using the Copy/Monitor tool. In the last chapter, the walls from the Structural model were hidden using Visibility/ Graphic Overrides (VG) and a custom View Template (see the "Create and Apply a View Template" topic on page 334 in Chapter 8, and the additional exercise for Chapter 9 in the Appendix — included as a PDF). This means that we are not seeing the redundant walls that would otherwise appear here from the Structural file. You can choose to return to the Structural model later and update the Copy/Monitor walls if you wish to make them match this new shape. Refer to the "Perform a Coordination Review" topic on page 330 in Chapter 8 for more details on the process.

DESIGN OPTIONS

Often when working on a design, you are interested in exploring more than one solution. Perhaps the client wants to see another idea, or maybe you are not satisfied with the current scheme. Either way, traditionally you would perform a Save As and make a copy of the file to work out your alternate scheme(s). This approach is fine, but once you have saved your alternate file, they are separate projects and switching from one to the other is not very convenient. As an alternative to the Save As approach, Revit offers Design Options. In this sequence, we look at a very simple example of the Design Options functionality and use it to consider an alternate design for the tower roof. If you are using Revit LT, design options are hidden in the user interface by default. To unhide them, from the File menu, choose: **Options**, click the User Interface tab and then check the Enable Design Options setting (see the right side of Figure 9.45).

1. On the Status Bar at the bottom of the screen (or on the Manage tab), click the Design Options icon (see the left side of Figure 9.45).

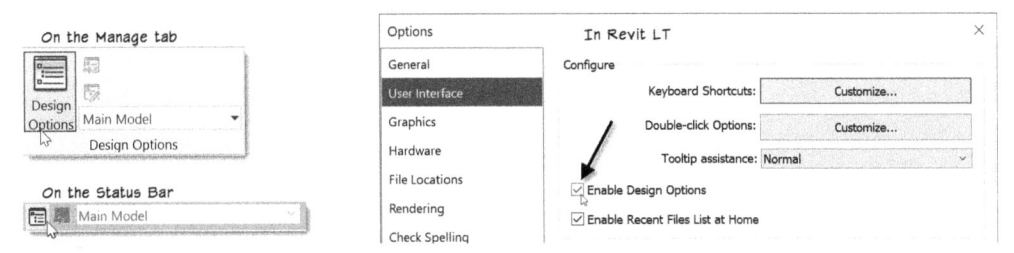

FIGURE 9.45 *Access design options*

The concept behind design options is simple: we have "Option Sets" and "Options." An option set is an area of work where you are considering more than one design scheme. Each scheme is an option. So, option sets *contain* options. You can have several options sets in a project, and each can contain several options. While Revit allows an option set to contain a single option, to be meaningful, an option set should have two or more options. You can only display and work on one option at a time in any view. One option in each option set will also be the "Primary" option. The primary option is what Revit will display if no overrides are applied to the view. Think of it as simply the option most likely to be accepted or the one that you favor over the others. Anything that is not part of an option is said to be part of the "Main Model". The main model displays all the time and forms the context for all option sets.

We are going to consider an alternate roof design for the tower. To do this, we will create an option set and two options. We will add the current design to one of these options and then build a second design scheme in the other. The rest of the building will remain "main model."

2. In the "Design Options" dialog, in the "Option Set" area, click the New button (see item 1 in Figure 9.46).

    Option Set 1 will appear and it will contain a single option called: Option 1.

    ⇨ Select Option Set 1 on the left, (item 2) and then in the "Option Set" area on the right, click the Rename button (item 3).

3. In the "Rename" dialog, type: **Tower Roof** for the new name and then click OK (item 4).

4. In the "Option" area, click the New button (item 5).

    ⇨ Select Option 1, in the "Option" area, click the Rename button and name it: **Curved Extrusion Roof** and then click OK.

    ⇨ Select Option 2, (item 6) in the "Option" area, click the Rename button (item 7) and name it: **Diagonal Slope Arrow Roof** and then click OK (item 8).

394 | Chapter 9

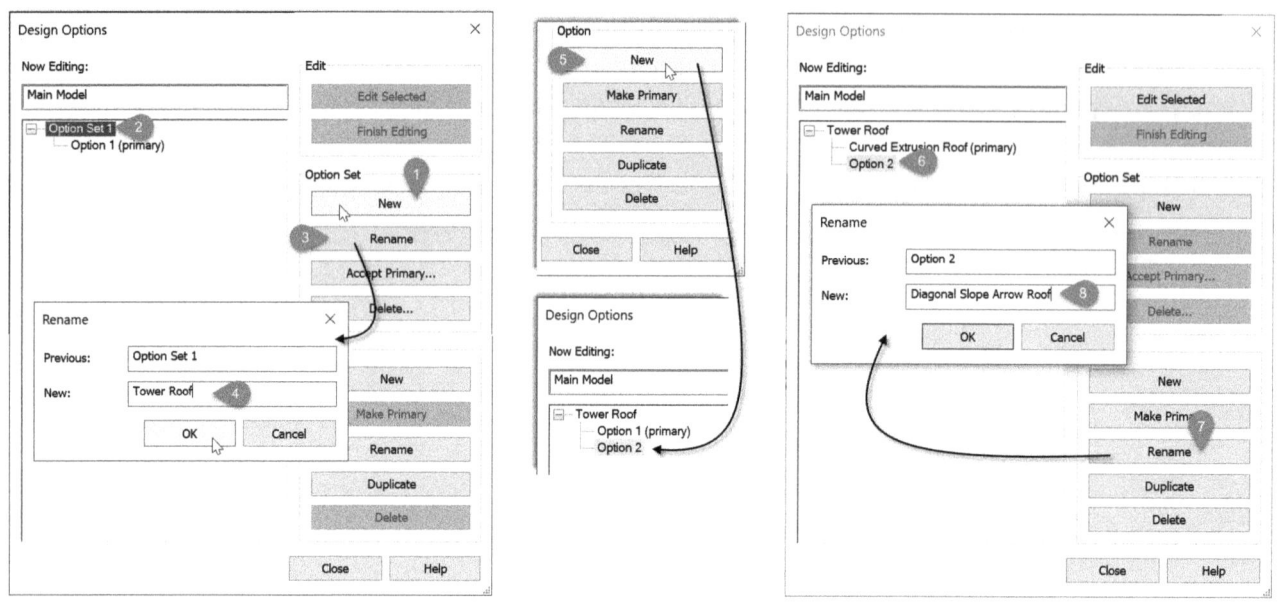

FIGURE 9.46 *Create and rename two options*

Now that we have two options, we need to add elements to each of them. Currently all our model elements are part of the main model. You can move existing elements from main model to one or more options and you can edit an option and add new elements directly to it.

5. Close the "Design Options" dialog.

6. In the *South* elevation view, make a window selection by clicking between grid B and C above the roof and drag a box around the tower beyond grid E and below the Roof level.

⇨ On the ribbon, click the Filter button.

⇨ Check only doors, roofs and walls. Click OK to complete the selection.

7. On the Status Bar, on the Design Options toolbar, (or on the Manage tab) click the Add to Set button.

⇨ In the "Add to Design Option Set" dialog that appears, make sure both Options are checked and then click OK (see Figure 9.47).

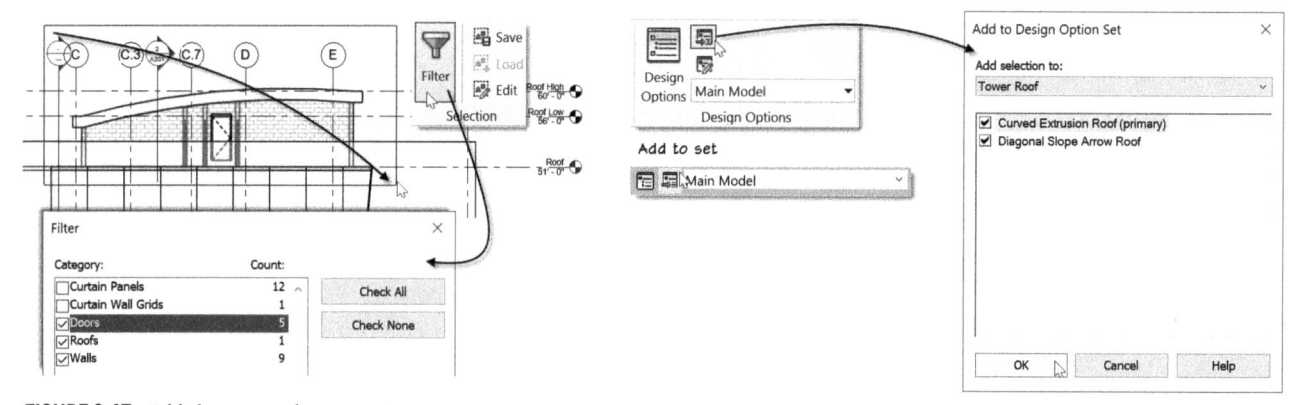

FIGURE 9.47 *Add elements to the two options*

This action copies the curved roof, the core walls and doors to both options. We can now modify the copy stored in the second option to create our second scheme.

8. On the Design Options toolbar on the Status Bar, click on the pop-up menu (currently reading: Main Model) and choose: **Diagonal Slope Arrow Roof**.

• The Aubin Academy •

Floors and Roofs | 395

This grays out the screen except those elements that we copied to this option. We are now editing the option and the elements in the Main Model are visible for reference. (The items in the other option(s) are not visible by default).

9. Select the curved roof onscreen and delete it.

   Keep in mind that this is only deleting the copy in this option. The one in the other design option is still there, but just not visible currently because we are editing the Diagonal Slope Arrow Roof option.

USING SLOPE ARROWS

For this roof we will return to a footprint roof. Slope Arrows offer an alternative to the "defines slope" check box. With defines slope, your slope is always perpendicular to the roof edge. With slope arrows, you can make the slope follow any angle you like.

1. On the Project Browser, double-click to open the *Roof* plan view.

> **NOTE:** Notice that the Main Model is still grayed out in this view. When you change the edit mode for options, it applies across the whole model. Therefore, all views can be used to edit this option (unless they have an override applied to them that prevents it – see below).

2. On the Architecture tab, click the Roof by Footprint button.

   Accept the defaults of Boundary Line and Pick Walls.

   ⇨ On the Options Bar, uncheck Defines slope and add a: **1'-0"** [**300**] overhang.

   ⇨ Pick each of the four exterior walls of the tower to create the sketch. Make sure the overhand goes outward.

3. On the Draw panel, click the Slope Arrow button.

   ⇨ Draw a Slope Arrow diagonally across the sketch. Be sure to snap it at both corners (see Figure 9.48).

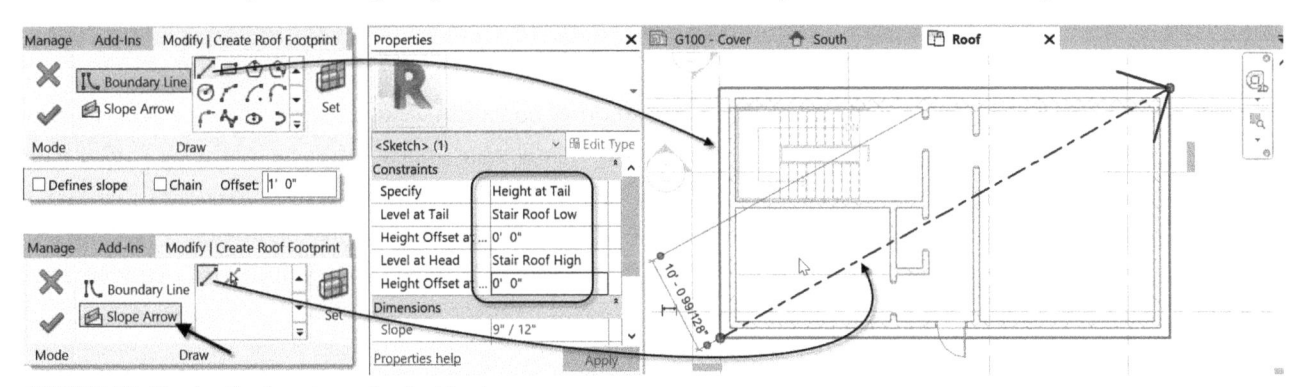

FIGURE 9.48 *Sketch a flat footprint roof and add a slope arrow*

A slope arrow can be drawn in any direction that you want the slope to follow. You can draw one or more slope arrows in the same roof sketch. The tail end of the arrow *must* touch the sketch lines. The head (arrow) end can be anywhere. In this case we have both tail and head touching the sketch, which works just fine.

4. With the slope arrow still selected, on the Properties palette, change the Level at Tail to: **Stair Roof Low** and the Level at Head to: **Stair Roof High**.

   ⇨ Change the Height Offset at Head to: **0** (zero).

5. On the ribbon, click Finish Edit Mode.

In the current *Roof* plan view, the new roof will not appear as based on the settings we just configured it is above the cut plane. We can view it in other views like the *South* elevation and the *{3D}* view.

• Revit Essentials for Architecture •

396 | Chapter 9

6. Repeat the procedure from the "Attach Walls to the Roof" topic on page 392 above to attach all the walls to the new roof.

7. Open the *South* elevation and/or *{3D}* view to complete the task and check the results (see Figure 9.49).

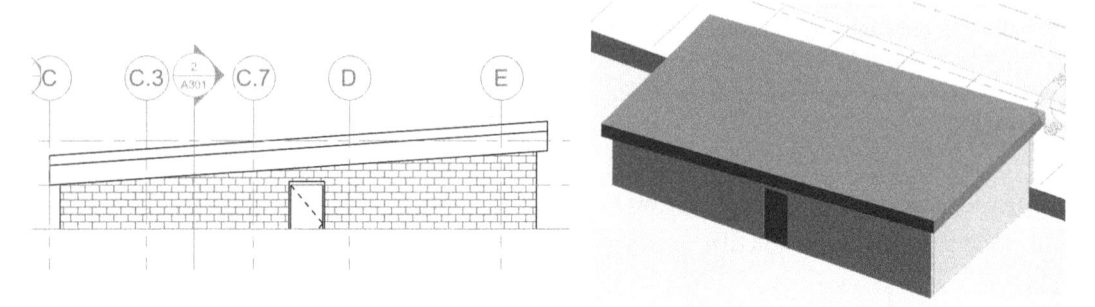

FIGURE 9.49 *Attach the walls to the new roof*

As you can see, the slope for this roof follows the direction of the slope arrow instead of the edges of the roof sketch. This is a very simple example. Feel free to experiment further with additional slope arrows and roofs. For now, we'll return to the main model and stick with just the two options until the next client meeting.

PRESENTING DESIGN OPTIONS

When you have design options, the assumption is that at some point in the design process, you will decide on one of the options and make it permanent. Doing so removes all the other options and returns all the geometry of the primary option to the main model. However, you can postpone this if necessary and keep multiple options well into the later phases of a project. The only caution is that having many design options in a project can have an impact on performance. So if the team has made a decision on a particular scheme, it is a good idea to return to the "Design Options" dialog, make the preferred option the Primary one and then "Accept" it. This does delete the other options, so you will want to keep a backup copy of your original file as an archive for safe keeping just in case.

Display behavior for options is controlled in Visibility/Graphics. The default is set to "automatic." This means that the primary option will be displayed, except while editing another non-primary option. So, the view will dynamically adjust between the primary and the actively edited option. If you want a particular view to display an alternate option permanently (for a client meeting for example), you can duplicate any view in your project, edit that view's Visibility/Graphics and on the Design Options tab, choose one of your options to display permanently in that view (see Figure 9.50). Just be aware that when you do this, the option you choose will always display in that view *even* when you are editing a different option. So, it is always best to maintain at least one view that is set to "Automatic" and use that for editing.

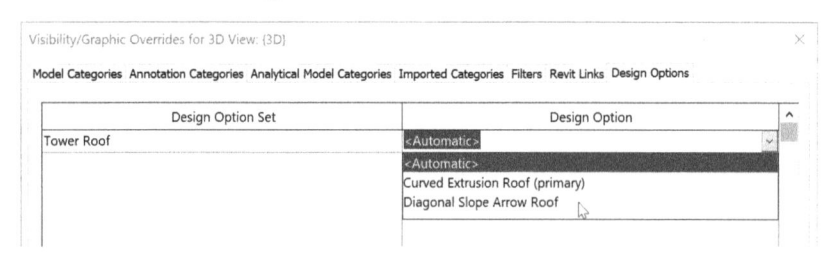

FIGURE 9.50 *You can override a view to display any option permanently in visibility/graphics*

Feel free to add additional option sets and options to explore the feature further if you like.

1. On the Project Browser, right-click the *{3D}* view and choose: **Duplicate View** > **Duplicate**.

    ⇨ Rename the new view: **Diagonal Slope Arrow Roof 3D**.

Floors and Roofs | 397

⇨   Edit the visibility/graphics (type VG), click the Design Options tab, and then choose: **Diagonal Slope Arrow Roof**.

If you like, you can repeat the process to create another 3D view that permanently shows the primary option. However, when not editing another option, the primary will show by default in all views that do not have an override like the one established here. So, the choice is yours.

2. On the Design Options toolbar on the Status Bar, click on the pop-up menu and return to: **Main Model**.

You should still have the various 3D views open. Click through each tab. The default *{3D}* view is set to Automatic. So, it will show the curved roof one you go back to editing Main Model, since this is the primary option. The other 3D view(s) have an override applied. So regardless of what you choose for the editing mode on the Design Options toolbar, the new *Diagonal Slope Arrow Rood 3D* (and the other copy if you made one) will continue to show the option that you assigned in VG regardless. (To learn more about Design Options, check out the **Revit: Phasing and Design Options** course at **LinkedIn Learning**†).

EDIT A ROOF SKETCH

Currently the main roof of this model covers the whole building including the area inside the stair core, part of which is cut away by the shaft element built in the previous chapter. At this point, it will make a little more sense to edit this roof and make it go around the core, and then add a new floor element in place of the roof that we removed.

1. Select the flat roof element. (Use the TAB key as necessary.)

> **TIP:** You can select a roof or floor in plan views by placing the Modify tool along its edge and using the TAB key to cycle to it. As an alternative, you will often find it easier to select in a section view first and then change views as necessary to edit. Another alternative is to enable the Select elements by face option from the drop down panel beneath the Modify tool.

You can see how it highlights within the stair core as well as around it.

2. On the ribbon, click the Edit Footprint button.

⇨   Using the Pick Walls Boundary Line option (with Defines slope unchecked and a 0 (zero) overhand, click the three exterior walls of the stair tower.

This should automatically trim one side of the horizontal wall at the top.

⇨   Click the opposite side to add a new sketch line. Click the Finish Edit Mode button (see Figure 9.51).

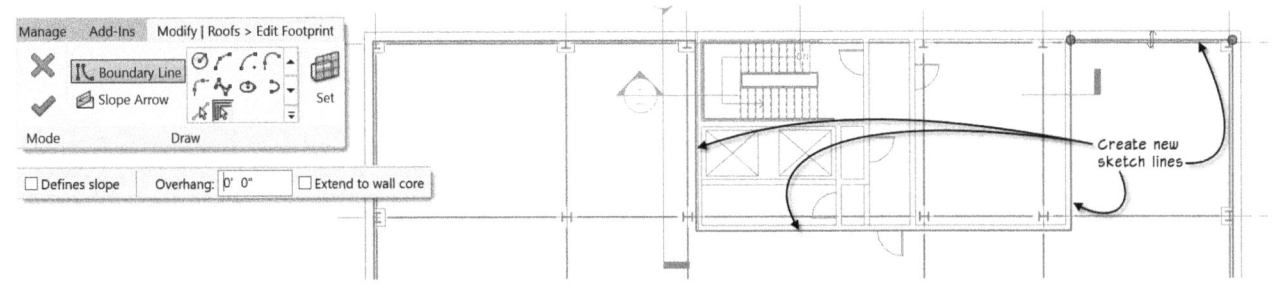

FIGURE 9.51 *Edit the sketch of the roof element*

Now let's create a floor in the same location to replace the part of the roof we removed.

3. On the Architecture tab, click the Floor tool and then using Pick Walls, click the inside edges of the stair core walls.

The same three that we clicked above, and the horizontal exterior wall at the top of the plan. But make sure the sketch lines are on the inside faces of the walls this time.

⇨ Click the Finish Edit Mode button.

⇨ When prompted to attach walls, choose Don't Attach.

Notice that we don't have to worry about the stair core, as the existing shaft opening will intersect this new floor and cut it for us. Therefore, we could do a simple rectangular sketch. Notice also that the doors that previously appeared oddly in this view are now displaying correctly. The issue was the height of the roof. The thickness of roof elements is measured above their host level by default (which concealed many of the doors in this plan). Floors extrude down from their level.

EDIT VIEW RANGE

Before we complete the stair tower roof, let's adjust the roof plan a little. The primary view range only displays elements at the Roof level to the cut plane. This is the default behavior. And as we noted previously, the new roof does not display in the *Roof* plan currently because it is above the cut plane.

1. On the Project Browser, double-click to open the *Roof* plan view (or just click its tab if you left it open).

⇨ Make sure that you have no objects selected, then on the Properties palette, edit the View Range (or press VR).

2. Change offsets of both the Primary Range Bottom and the View Depth to: **-1'-0"** [**-300**].

⇨ Change the Offset of the Cut Plane and the Top to: **20'-0"** [**6000**] and then click OK.

These adjustments give a generous range for the geometry on the roof and allow some flexibility in future edits. Notice that the core roof now displays in the plan view.

> **NOTE:** With the settings this way, we do not have a plan that shows the upper level of the stair tower. If you wish to create such a plan, make a duplicate of your *Roof* plan before making the previous edit.

USING SHAPE EDITING TOOLS

The final exercise in this chapter will be to add drainage sloping to the commercial project flat roof. To accomplish this, we will look at the third and final way that you can apply slope to a Roof: Shape Editing tools. When you have a flat roof or floor element in your model (no edges sloped and no slope arrows), you will see the Shape Editing panel on the Modify | Roofs tab of the ribbon when the roof or floor is selected. If even one edge of the roof or floor is set to slope defining, the tools will not appear (see Figure 9.52).

Please note that if you are using Revit LT, you will not have access to the shape editing tools. Please skip this topic.

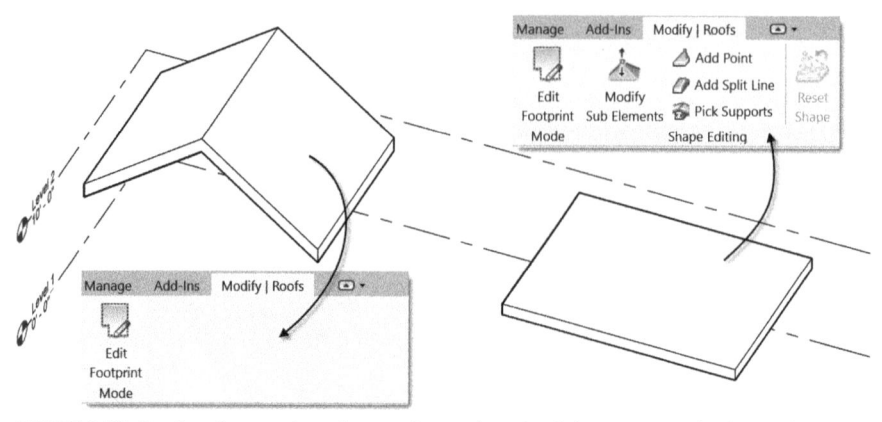

FIGURE 9.52 *Roofs or floors with no sloping edges in their sketch have access to the shape editing tools*

Continue in the *Roof* plan view.

1. Select the flat roof element. (Use the TAB key as necessary.)

    Notice the collection of Shape Editing tools appears on the ribbon as shown on the left side of Figure 9.52.

Moving left to right, the tools are as follows:

Modify Sub-Elements—This tool can be used to adjust the height of any points or edges of the shape edited element.

Add Point—Use this tool to add points to the surface of the roof or floor. Each point has a height that you can adjust to either a negative or positive offset from the roof or floor level. The roof form will conform to the shape of the edited points.

Add Split Line—This tool adds elevation changes using lines instead of points. Like the Draw Point tool, each line has a height that you can adjust to either a negative or positive offset from the roof or floor level. You can also edit the height of the line's endpoints independently.

Pick Supports—If you have structural supports set at accurate levels, you can use them to indicate the level changes of the roof or floor.

Reset Shape—The button (grayed out in Figure 9.52) is used to remove all edits and return the shape of the roof or floor to flat with no slopes.

We'll perform a simple edit to our roof's surface using a few split lines and points.

2. On the Shape Editing panel, click the Add Split Line tool.

This enables a special shape editing mode which is like other sketch modes but has some unique features as well. The main difference is that there is no finish edit mode and cancel buttons. To exit this mode, simply click the Modify tool as you would any other command. The existing edge of the roof outlines in a dashed green line. New points or lines you add will be blue. Gray lines appear when required. They are auto-calculated from the other lines and points. These turn out to be trickiest part of using these tools. If you want to avoid many unnecessary gray lines that make the shape of the roof overly complex, you need to be strategic with your use of split lines and points.

3. Click a point at the intersection of Grid 2 and the vertical green line on the left.

    ⇨ Draw straight across along Grid 2 and snap to the opposite green line on the right (see the left side of Figure 9.53).

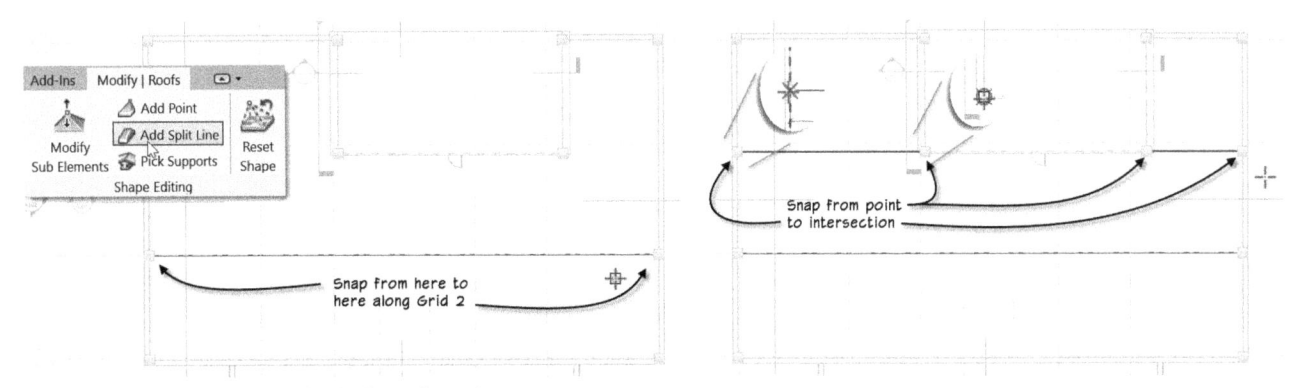

FIGURE 9.53 *Add split lines to divide the roof into three zones*

4. Remaining in the Split Line tool, click the green corner point at the lower left side of the stair tower area.

    ⇨ Draw horizontally to the left and snap at the intersection of the vertical green line.

    ⇨ Repeat on the other side (see the right side of Figure 9.53).

400 | Chapter 9

This divides the roof into three horizontal bands, with the top band being separated into two sections by the stair core in the middle. Let's slope each of these areas.

5. On the Shape Editing panel, click the Modify Sub Elements tool.

⇨ Select the horizontal dashed green line at the bottom of the plan (along Grid 1).

A temporary dimension will appear at the midpoint.

⇨ Click in this temporary dimension and input: **6" [150]** and the press ENTER (see the left side of Figure 9.54).

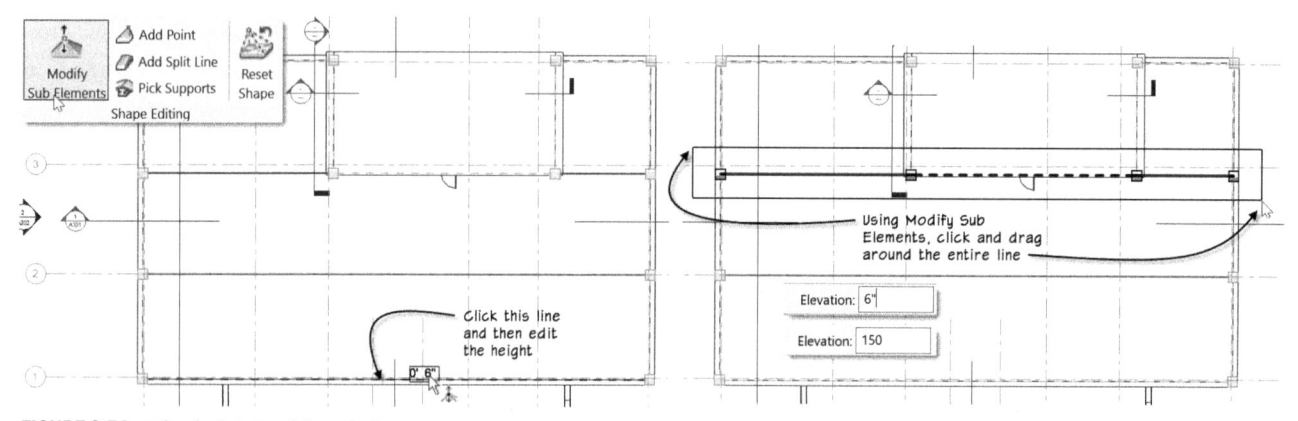

FIGURE 9.54 *Edit the height of the split lines*

6. Remaining in the Modify Sub Elements tool, drag a selection window around all three lines near Grid 3 (two blue and one green).

⇨ On the Options bar, change the Elevation to: **6" [150]** and then press ENTER.

Alternatively you can do the two blues lines one at a time. The green will end up in the same spot once you change both blue ones.

If you want to see the results of this change, you can create a section running vertically cutting through all three zones. When you do, you will see the roof has a slight zig-zag shape to it now (see Figure 9.55).

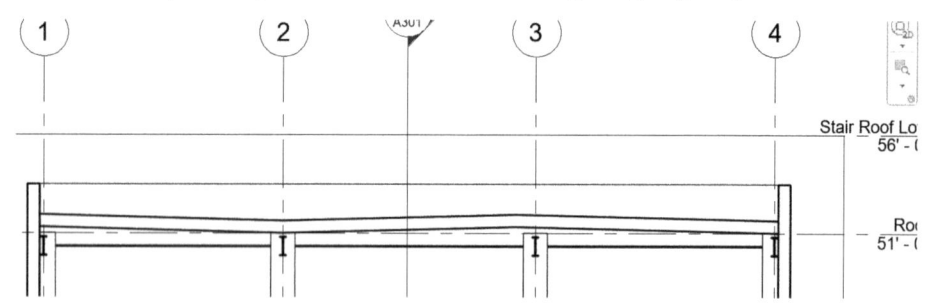

FIGURE 9.55 *View the results of the Modify Sub Elements edits in a new section*

To Ensure we have proper drainage, let's add some crickets to the roof. This can be done by adding and editing additional points and split lines.

Continue in the *Roof* plan view.

7. On the Architecture tab, on the Work Plane panel, click the Reference Plane button (or press RP).

⇨ On the Draw panel, click the Pick Lines tool. On the Options Bar, set the Offset to: **7'-0" [2100]**.

⇨ Offset two reference planes from Grid 2, one above it and one below and then click the Modify tool or press ESC twice to finish.

8. Select the roof again. (Clicking on the split line is the easiest way to select it).

⇨ On the Shape Editing panel, click the Add Split Line button.

• The Aubin Academy •

⇨ Snap to the intersection of Grid C and the reference plane and draw to the intersection of the other reference plane.

⇨ Repeat at Grid E (see Figure 9.56).

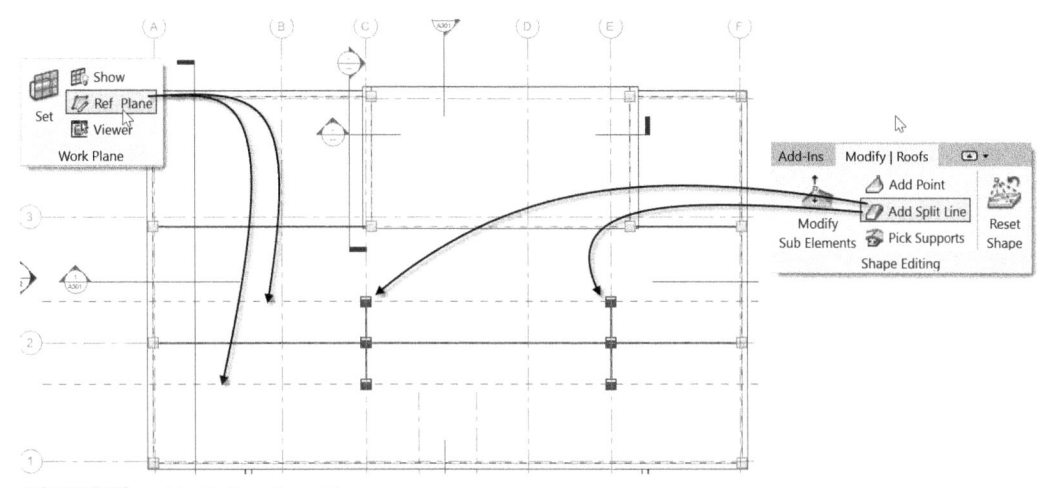

FIGURE 9.56 *Add split lines for crickets*

9. On the Shape Editing panel, click the Add Point button.

⇨ Snap to the midpoints of each of the three blue segments along Grid 2.

⇨ Repeat at each location shown on the left side of Figure 9.57. Snap to midpoints at all locations.

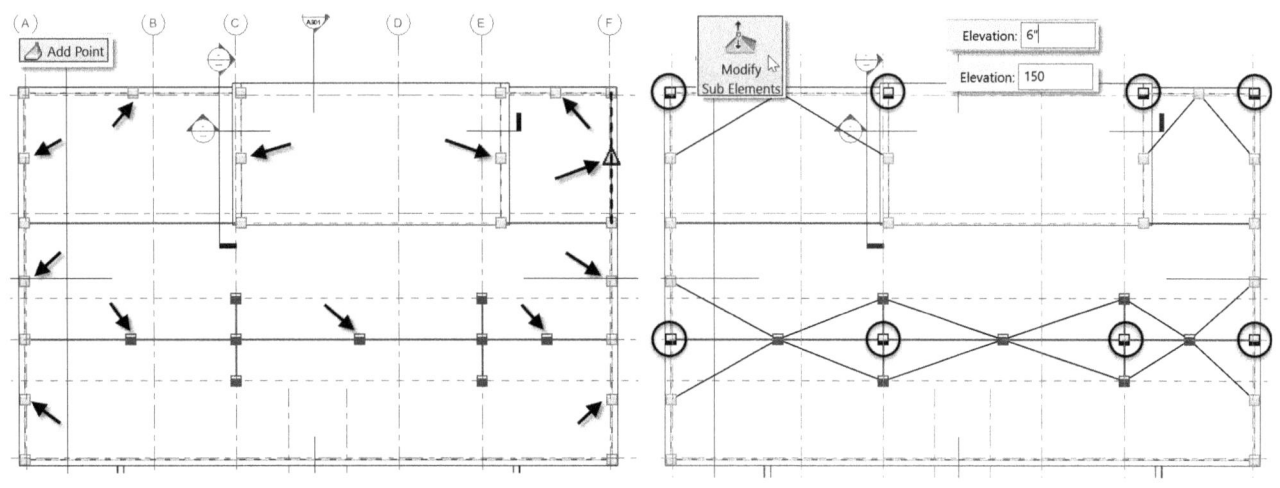

FIGURE 9.57 *Add points at several midpoints*

10. On the Shape Editing panel, click the Modify Sub-Elements button.

⇨ Select each point circled on the right side of Figure 9.57 and edit the Elevation to: **6"** [**150**].

As you make these edits, you will see gray lines appearing automatically as the shape of the roof adjusts.

Changing views will terminate the sub-element editing mode. You can also click the Modify tool first if you prefer. Notice that the roof now displays the edges of the ridges and valleys for the sloping planes (see Figure 9.58).

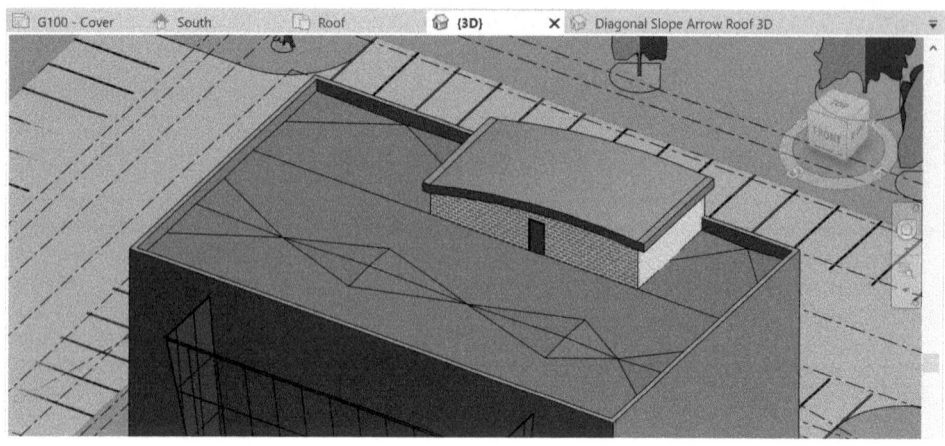

FIGURE 9.58 *Study the results in 3D*

ADJUSTING SLOPE

When designing a flat roof, there is often a minimum slope required by code for drainage. While we cannot input this directly in the shape editing tools, we can use a simple technique to measure the slope that results from our edits and then make appropriate adjustments.

1. Return to the *Roof* plan.
2. On the Annotate tab, on the Dimension panel, click the Spot Slope tool.
   ⇨ Move your mouse around the various surfaces of the roof.

The spot slope annotation symbol will appear on your cursor and will read the slope of each surface as you mouse over them. Use this moussing technique for quick measurements or click to place the permanent annotations in the view.

3. Click to place one or more spot slope symbols.
   ⇨ On the ribbon, click the Modify tool or press the ESC key twice.

If you discover a slope that is too shallow, simply select the roof, click the Modify Sub Elements button and then adjust the height of some of the points or lines to adjust the slope. You will get immediate feedback from the annotation as you make changes to the heights of the lines or points. In some cases, you may need to add new points or lines to achieve positive drainage at all points on the roof.

USING VARIABLE THICKNESS LAYERS

The default behavior in the sub-element editing mode is for the entire roof slab to be affected by the slope. If you prefer, you can edit the structure of the roof type applied to the roof element and make one of its material layer thicknesses variable. When doing so, the bottom surface of the roof will remain flat, while the top surface slopes according to the split lines and elevation points added above. This is an effective way to represent tapered rigid insulation in the construction (see the next few steps). The best way to see these sometimes subtle variations is in a section view. Let's use the one we created earlier.

1. On the Project Browser, locate Section 1.
   ⇨ Right-click it and choose: **Rename**. Call it: **Section at Roof**. Stretch the bottom of the crop region up so that it only shows us the roof, cropping out the levels below.

Take a close look at the roof element. Notice that both the top and bottom surfaces are sloped (maintaining a uniform thickness). We can designate one of the layers in the roof type structure as a variable thickness. When doing so, the bottom layers will remain flat, the variable layer will have a flat bottom and sloping top surface, and any layers on top of the variable one will follow the slope (with uniform thickness).

2. Select the roof.

⇨ On the Properties palette, click the Edit Type button.

3. Click the Edit button next to Structure.

⇨ Place a checkmark in the "Variable" column next to layer 2 and then click OK two times (see Figure 9.59).

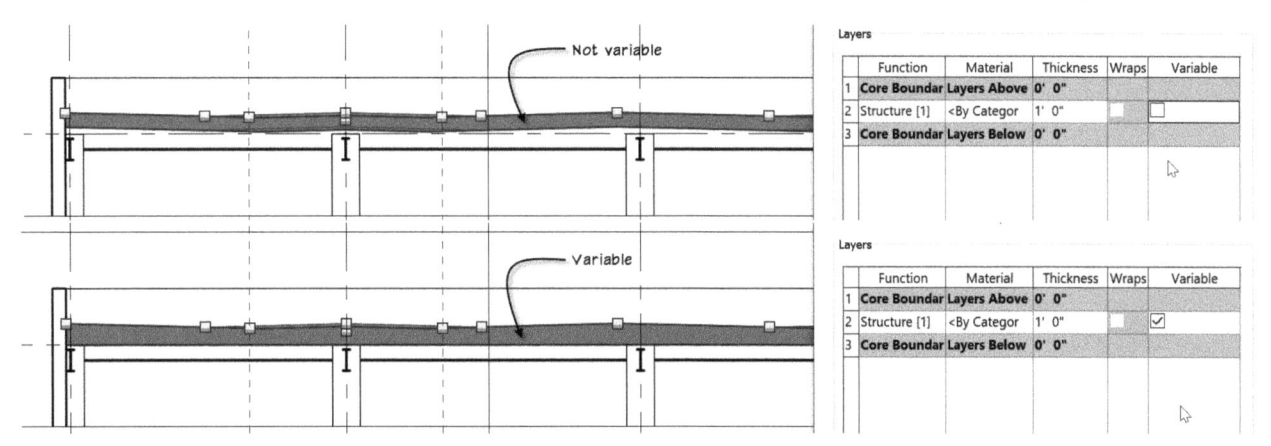

FIGURE 9.59 *Comparing the roof with and without a variable thickness layer*

Currently we are using a Generic type with only a single layer. To appreciate fully the effect of a variable component, we should assign a complex roof type.

4. With the roof still selected, from the Type Selector, choose: **Steel Truss - Insulation on Metal Deck - EPDM [Steel Bar Joist -Steel Deck -EPDM Membrane]**.

5. Edit the "Type Properties" again and then click the Edit button next to Structure.

⇨ Place a checkmark in the "Variable" column next to layer 2 (the insulation this time) and then click OK two times.

Now that we have a more detailed structure in place you can see that we have effectively represented tapered insulation and the support structure beneath it remains level. However, this roof type's lowest layer is meant to represent the steel bar joists. This means that the entire roof structure sits too high in the model.

6. Select the roof, and on the Properties palette, in the "Base Offset From Level" field, type: **-1'-4"** [**-400**] (see Figure 9.60).

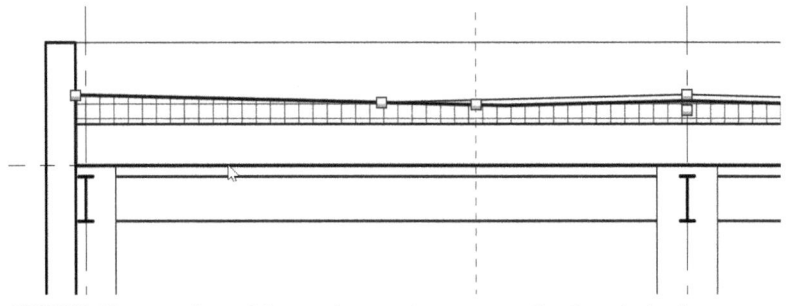

FIGURE 9.60 *Move the roof element down with a negative offset from the level*

Feel free to study the model in other views and experiment further with the roofs and floor slabs.

7. Save and Close the commercial project file.

SUMMARY

- ☑ Roofs are sketch-based elements that can be generated from existing walls or manually drawn sketch lines. A single roof can use a combination of each.

- ☑ Walls can be attached to roofs and remain attached as the model is modified.

- ☑ Join roofs together to resolve the intersection of complex roof planes.

- ☑ Roofs have many options for their construction and how they interact with neighboring elements.

- ☑ You can apply edge conditions to each roof fascia and rake.

- ☑ Gutters and other sweep profiles can be applied to roof edges.

- ☑ Skylights interact with and cut holes in roofs in the same way windows interact with walls.

- ☑ Create complex roof types that include layers of structure that share many features with complex wall types.

- ☑ Floors are added and modified via sketch mode like roofs.

- ☑ Floors may also have complex structure like roofs and walls.

- ☑ Edit a roof footprint or extrusion at any time by editing the sketch of the roof.

- ☑ Roofs can be created with a plan sketch like floors or via an extruded profile shape, usually drawn in elevation or section views.

- ☑ Slope arrows are another more complex way to add slope to footprint roofs. The slope follows the direction of the slope arrow.

- ☑ You can draw a slope arrow in any direction, but the tail must touch the sketch lines.

- ☑ Use design options to create alternate schemes within the same model.

- ☑ You can edit various design options and display them in custom views using Visibility/Graphic overrides.

- ☑ Flat roofs can accurately represent subtle drainage slope using the sub-element editing tools.

- ☑ You can represent variable thickness materials (such as tapered rigid insulation) by enabling variable thickness for the layer in the "Roof Type Properties" dialog.

CHAPTER 10
Developing the Exterior Skin

INTRODUCTION

In this chapter, we will enclose our commercial project with a building skin. The skin will be comprised of a masonry enclosure on three sides, with various curtain wall elements on the front and sides of the building. The front façade curtain wall begins on the second floor and spans the height of the third and fourth floors. In Chapter 5, we created a rough version to suggest this design element. In this chapter we will replace this with a more refined curtain wall. And create the other required curtain wall elements.

OBJECTIVES

To complete the shell of the commercial project we will apply a detailed wall type to the exterior walls already in the project. We will also build curtain walls for the front and side façades. Upon completion of this chapter, you will be able to:

- ◢ Create and swap wall types
- ◢ Add curtain walls to the model
- ◢ Modify a curtain wall
- ◢ Build a curtain wall type
- ◢ Build and add a stacked wall

CREATING THE MASONRY SHELL

Much of the skin of the commercial building is comprised of masonry walls. We will perforate portions of this masonry skin with curtain walls later in the chapter, but we will begin by swapping out the simple generic wall types used in early chapters with a more detailed wall type appropriate to the design at this stage.

OPEN A PROJECT

The lessons that follow require the dataset files included for download with this book. Refer to the "Download the Book Dataset" topic on page xi in the Preface for instructions on downloading and installing the book's dataset files.

1. Launch Autodesk® Revit®.

406 | Chapter 10

2. If you are on the Home screen, you can click the Open button beneath Models. Otherwise, from the File menu, choose **Open** > **Project**. In the "Open" dialog box, browse to the *Chapter10* folder.

⇨ Double-click *10 Commercial.rvt* if you wish to work in Imperial units.

⇨ Double-click *10 Commercial_M.rvt* if you wish to work in Metric units.

You can also select it and then click the Open button.

CREATING A BASIC WALL TYPE

As you can see, the project is largely unchanged from the previous chapter. We still have the very simple generic wall type used for the building skin. The first thing we'll do is refine that a bit.

1. On the Project Browser, double-click to open the *Level 1* floor plan view.

2. Pre-highlight (hover, do not click) one of the exterior walls (try the vertical one on the left).

⇨ Press the TAB key once to pre-highlight a chain of walls. All the exterior walls should pre-highlight including the one at the core.

> **NOTE:** If your cursor is closer to the outside edge when you press the TAB key, all of the outer walls will pre-highlight. However, if you move slightly to the inside edge of the initial wall, the chain selection will shift to go around the inside walls of the core. Be sure that you are highlighting the outside walls before you click to make the chain selection. You can try moving your mouse slightly from inside to outside edge to see the chain adjust.

⇨ Be sure the outer walls are highlighted and then click the mouse to select the chain of exterior walls.

3. Hold down the SHIFT key and then click to remove the masonry wall(s) at the core from the selection.

All of the exterior walls except the masonry wall at the core (the horizontal one at the top middle of the plan) should now be selected (see the left side of Figure 10.1).

> **NOTE:** The Modify | Walls tab should appear on the ribbon and the Type Selector should read: **Generic – 12"** [**Generic - 300mm**]. Beneath this, on the filter drop down you should see: **Walls (5)**. If your Properties palette does not appear this way, then you still have a core wall selected. Use SHIFT click to remove it.

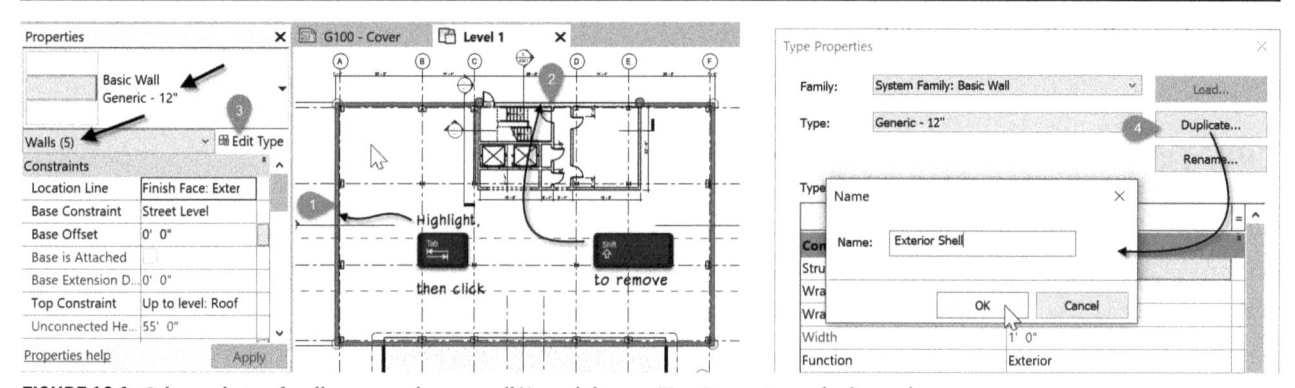

FIGURE 10.1 *Select a chain of walls, remove the core wall(s), and then use Type Properties to duplicate the type*

4. On the Properties palette, click the Edit Type button.

⇨ Click the Duplicate button (or press ALT + D).

⇨ For the name type: **Exterior Shell** and then press OK (see the right side of Figure 9.1).

• The Aubin Academy •

EDIT WALL TYPE STRUCTURE

We now have a new wall type. But right now it is just a copy of the original Generic type. Our next step is to modify the type to build the configuration we require. This will be a simple example of the process. Wall types can be much more complex when appropriate.

1. In the "Type Properties" dialog next to "Structure," click the Edit button.

> **TIP:** When working in the "Edit Assembly" dialog (and many similar dialogs) you can drag at the edge of the dialog frame to enlarge the window and make the contents of the columns easier to read.

If you completed the previous chapter and worked through the roof tutorials, you saw a very similar dialog there. Also, b Chapter 1, we did a very simple custom wall type example. So, by now you are likely becoming familiar with this process and the composition of these dialogs. The structure of wall and roof types do have much in common. Both allow you to configure the individual layers and assign materials. You will see other layered hosts sharing this feature as well such as floors, ceilings, etc. Wall types also have some additional parameters beyond this as well which we will see later. But let's adjust the layer structure first.

2. Select layer 2 (Structure [1]).

⇨ In the Thickness column, input: **7 5/8"** [**190**].

> **TIP:** To type a value of inches and fractions in Imperial units, you need to type a zero placeholder for feet first. Type the value as: 0 7 5/8. That is zero space, seven space, five forward-slash eight. As an alternative, you can type just 7 5/8" (including the inch " symbol) or the decimal equivalent: 7.625" (including the inch " symbol).

3. Click in the Material column, (where it says <By Category>) and then click the small browse icon that appears to open the "Material Browser" dialog (see the left side of Figure 10.2).

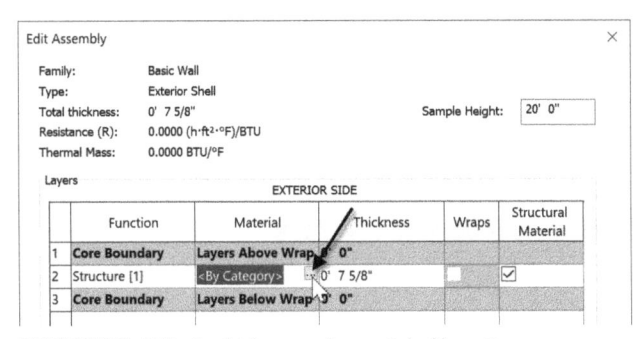

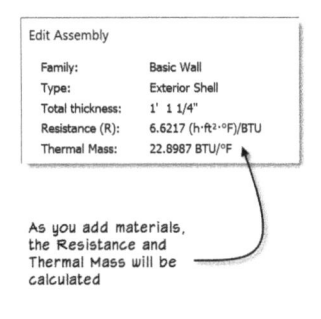

FIGURE 10.2 *Edit the thickness and material of layer 2*

4. In the "Material Browser" dialog, in the search field at the top, type: **Concrete**.

This will filter the list of materials to only those containing concrete in their names, descriptions or keywords.

⇨ Select: **Concrete Masonry Units** and then click OK.

5. Beneath the layers list, click the Insert button.

⇨ Click the Up button to move the new layer up above the Core Boundary.

⇨ From the Function list for the new layer, choose: **Thermal/Air Layer [3]**.

Functions determine the way that walls join with other walls, floors, ceilings, and roofs. A predefined list of functions is built into Revit. Structure layers will clean up with other Structure layers and interrupt layers of other functions.

Substrate layers have the next highest priority and will clean up with other Substrate layers, will be interrupted by Structure layers, and will interrupt layers of all lower priorities, and so on. Materials also play a role in cleanup behavior. For example, you may still see a line between the Structure layers in a wall join if they have different materials. To get a clean joint, the layers in both elements need the same function *and* material.

6. Change the Material to: **Air Infiltration Barrier**.

⇨ Change the Thickness to: **2"** [**50**].

> **TIP:** Remember when browsing the material list, you can filter first by searching for "Air". When typing the thickness, if you are working in Imperial, remember the inch " symbol or you can type: zero space two.

Notice that as you select materials for each layer, Revit will calculate the total R value of the assembly at the top of the dialog. For this to work, thermal properties must be assigned to the materials that you choose. All of the materials included in the original template we used to build this project contain the requisite thermal properties (see the right side of Figure 10.2).

7. Insert one more layer above the air layer.

⇨ Set its Function to: **Finish 1 [4]**.

⇨ Set its Material to: **Brick, Common**. (Remember typing: "Brick" at the top first will make it easy to find).

⇨ And set its Thickness to: **3 5/8"** [**90**].

> **TIP:** Remember, zero space three space five forward-slash eight if you are working in Imperial.

8. At the bottom of the "Edit Assembly" dialog, click the << Preview button (see Figure 10.3).

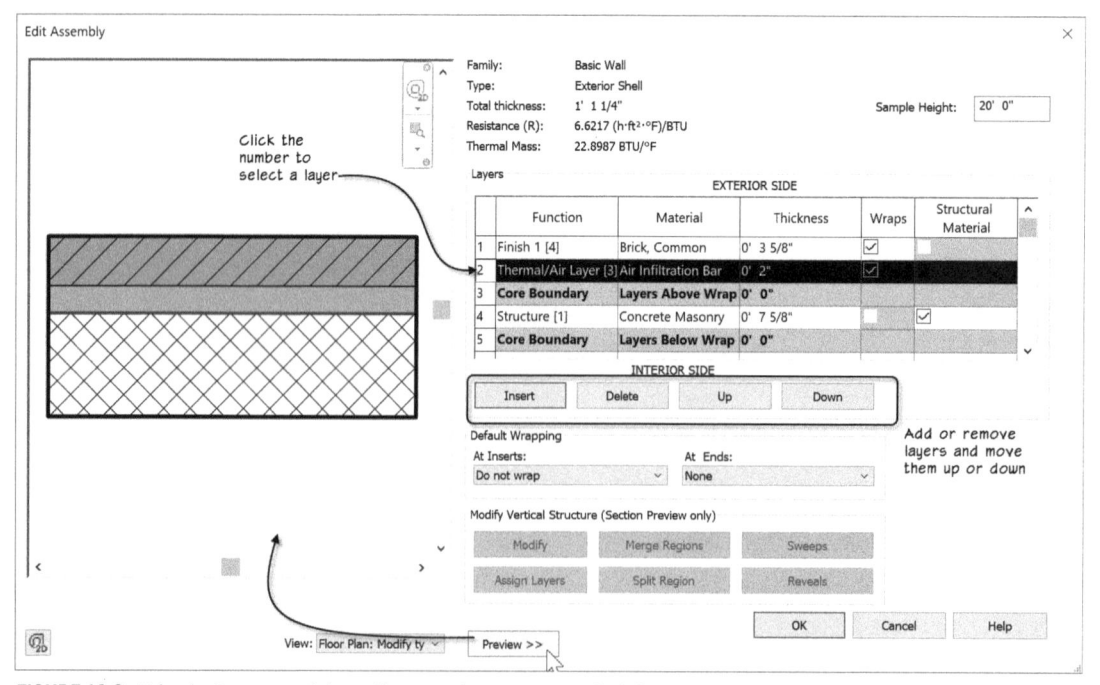

FIGURE 10.3 *Edit the Structure of the wall type and preview it on the left*

In the "Structural Material" column, you can select one layer in the assembly that should be considered structural. This must be a layer in the core.

9. Click OK twice to return to the view window.
10. On the View Control Bar (bottom left corner), change the Detail Level to: **Medium**.

    Study the results in the floor plan view.

11. Open the *{3D}* view and study the results there as well (see Figure 10.4).

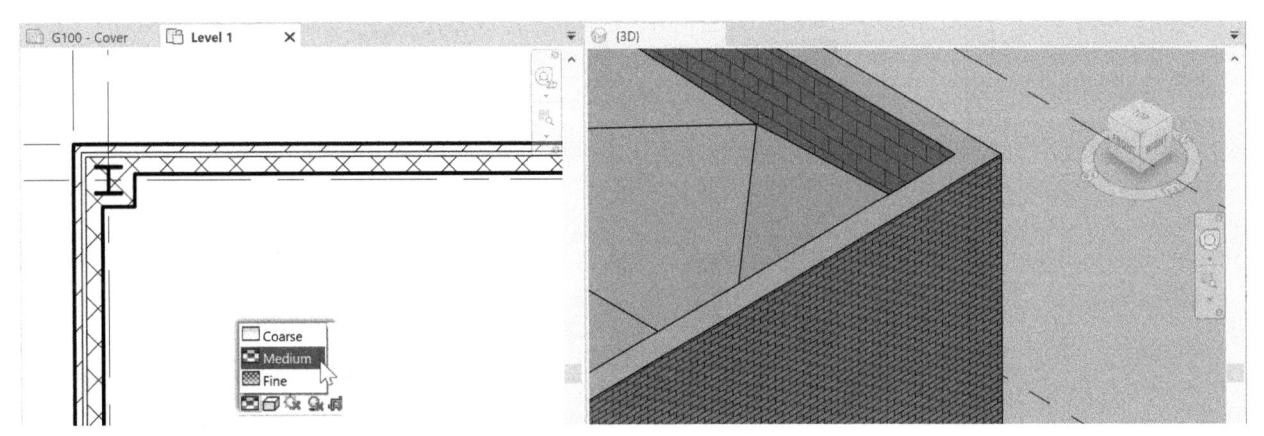

FIGURE 10.4 *Study the completed wall type in plan and 3D*

> **BIM Manager Note:** We could add more components to this wall type such as rigid insulation, membranes, and interior furring. Wall types with this level of detail are provided in the out-of-the-box template used to create this project file. You can simply choose one from the Type Selector to compare it to the simpler wall created here. Deciding how many material layers to represent within the structure of the wall (and therefore "build in" to the model) is a topic occupying many a CAD/BIM Standards committee. The exact choice upon which you and your firm ultimately settle will be influenced by a variety of factors, including preference for graphical display, estimating and quantity take-off needs, Green Building analysis, and potentially several other factors. Ultimately when making any such decisions, consider all factors and decide what approach gives the firm and the project team the best balance between effort expended and benefits gained throughout the life of the project. From a purely educational perspective, the wall we have constructed here is sufficient to convey the process of creating custom wall types, without necessarily addressing some of those admittedly important factors noted above that will undoubtedly come up in real projects.

⇨ Zoom and pan around the two views to study the results. As you zoom in closer in the 3D view, you will see the brick pattern appear when you are close enough for it to display legibly.

ASSIGN MATERIALS

When you assign a material to an element (such as the layers of the wall type above) you are presented the "Material Browser" dialog. Above we only searched and selected materials from the list. Materials will be discussed in more detail in Chapter 18, but let's take a moment here to look briefly at the "Material Browser" dialog.

1. On the Manage tab, click the Materials button.

The dialog is divided into a left and right pane. The left side allows us to search at the top (see item 1 in Figure 10.5) and browse through a list of materials in the current project (item 2). This left-hand pane can also be divided into two areas; the top is the materials in the current file (item 2), a list of materials contained in external library files is at the bottom (item 3). If you do not see the library pane, click the double chevron icon beneath the material list (item 4). The right side of the dialog is the material editor. If you do not see this pane and its many tabs, click the small reveal icon (double chevron pointing left or right) at the bottom (see item 5). You can also open the editor by hovering over a material in the list, and then clicking the small edit icon that appears to the right (looks like a pencil).

410 | Chapter 10

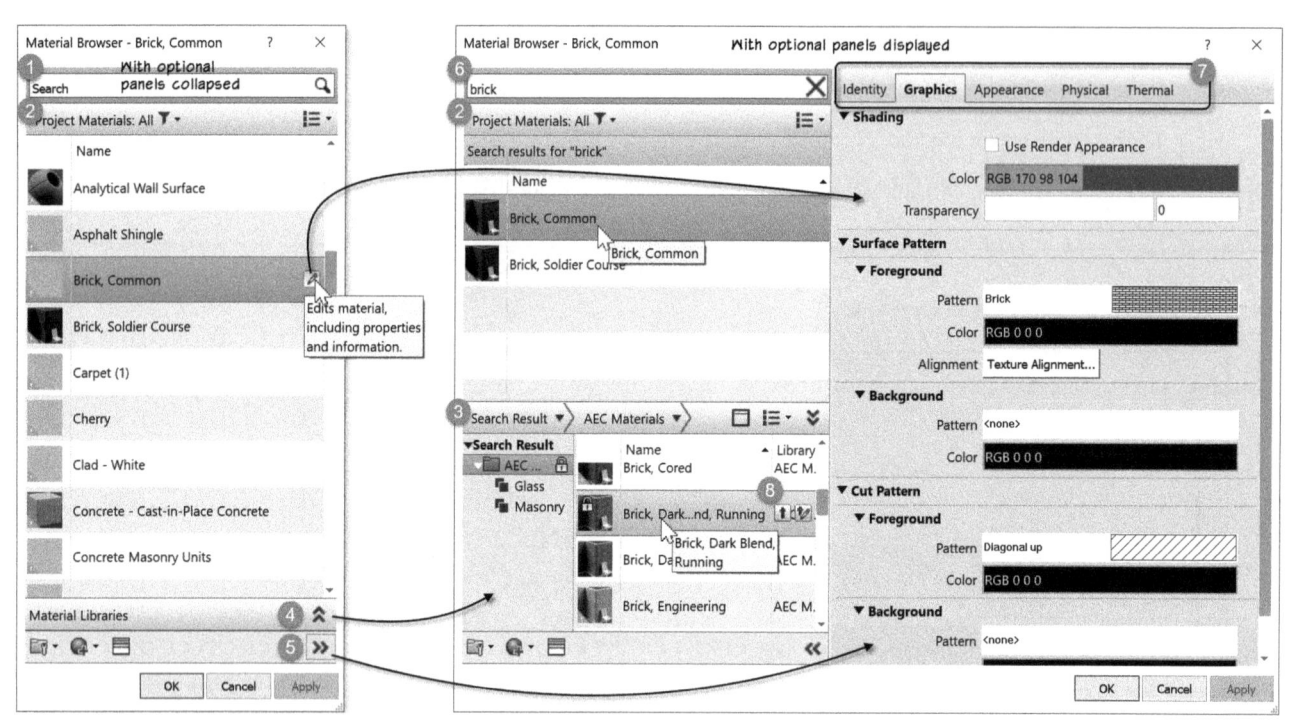

FIGURE 10.5 *Exploring the Material browser and editor*

2. If the library and editor panes are not displayed, click the appropriate icons (items 4 and 5) in the figure to open them now.

3. At the top of the "Material Browser" click in the Search field, type: **brick** (item 6).

   ⇨ Select **Brick, Common** from the list.

As we saw before, this will filter the material list to just those materials containing "brick" in their name, description or keywords. Notice also that the library list at the bottom also filters to show materials related to the search. So, while there are only two brick materials in the current project, several more are available in the library list. Five tabs will appear in the editor pane at the right (item 7). This will be the case for most materials that you select. (However, some materials will not have the Physical and/or Thermal tabs). These tabs each contain different aspects of the material that we can modify. If you import a material from the library, it will not always have all five tabs. The library pane contains materials stored in ADSKLIB files. These materials are shared by all Autodesk products including Revit, AutoCAD, Navisworks and more.

4. In the library list at the bottom, select the: **Brick, Dark Blend, Running** material.

Notice that the editor changes to show the properties of this material, but that this time the Graphics tab is missing. The Graphics tab controls settings that are unique to Revit and not shared by most other Autodesk products. Therefore, most of the library materials do not include this tab. However, it is required by Revit, so if you import one of these materials, the Graphics tab will be created automatically, but it will not have the correct properties assigned.

5. Hover over **Brick, Dark Blend, Running** and then click the small up arrow icon to add it to the project (item 8).

Notice that a graphics tab is added, but none of the settings are configured. You can manually assign the various hatch patterns and colors, or you can start with the existing brick material and duplicate it instead.

   ⇨ Right-click **Brick, Dark Blend, Running** in the list at the top and choose: **Delete**.

Notice that this only removes it from the top list, not the library.

6. In the top list pane, right-click on **Brick, Common** and choose: **Duplicate**.

• The Aubin Academy •

It will be in rename mode.

⇨ For the name input: **Brick, Dark Blend, Running** and then press ENTER.

Notice that by duplicating the existing brick material, this new copy already has appropriate hatch patterns assigned for both surface and cut patterns. Surface patterns are seen when viewing the material such as in elevation and the cut pattern is used when slicing through the material in plans or sections.

7. On the right side, click the Appearance tab.

The Appearance tab contains the settings for how this material will appear in rendered views. This can be in the canvas with realistic shading or when performing a rendering as we will see in Chapter 18. The specific settings on this tab can vary quite a bit from one material to the next. There are templates that control each class of material and there are many available. Since we have a masonry material here, the two primary settings are the image used to represent the bricks and its texture. The images are PNG files that are a photograph of bricks. This image is repeated along the surface to represent actual bricks. The default image here has a burgundy color. We can replace this with any image we want to adjust the look of the brick.

It is very important that you do not begin editing the settings on this tab without first replacing or duplicating the asset that controls them. Each of the tabs in the editor is controlled by an "Asset." In this case, we will replace the asset used here with the Dark Blend, Running one that we imported and then deleted above. Look at item 1 in Figure 10.6. There is a small hand icon with a number one superimposed over it. This means that the current appearance asset is used by this and one other material. Therefore, if you were to make any changes, they would apply to both materials. We can make this one unique using the Replace or Duplicate icons on the right.

8. At the top-right corner of the "Material Browser," click the Replace this asset icon (item 2).

The "Asset Browser" will appear.

The "Asset browser" is a library of assets that we can browse, import and assign to our materials. It also has a search field at the top.

⇨ In the Search field, type: **brick** (item 3).

⇨ Locate Brick – Running – Dark Blend, and then click the small replace icon on the right side (item 4).

412 | Chapter 10

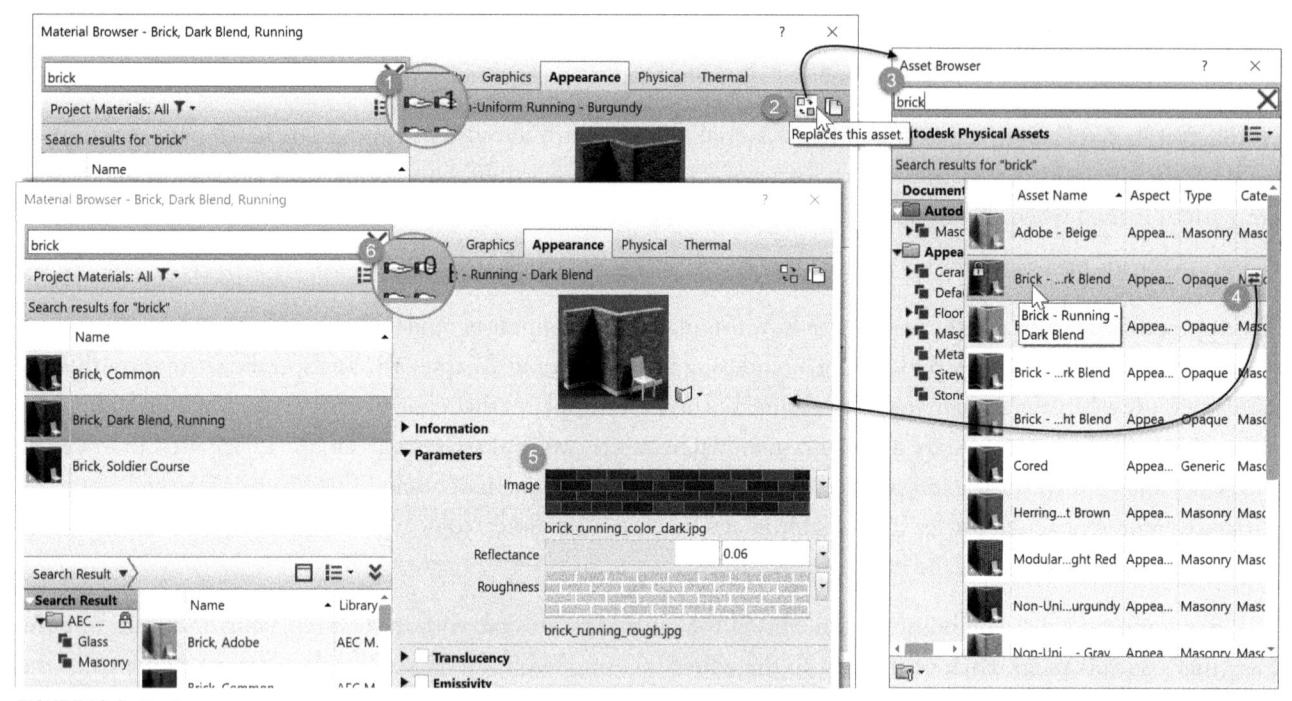

FIGURE 10.6 *Replace an asset*

Notice that the image used for the masonry settings is now the brown blend brick instead of the burgundy (item 5). The "Asset Browser" contains assets for Appearance, Physical and Thermal assets. You can use the same basic procedure on any of these tabs. You can also edit the various settings on each tab, but keep in mind that due to the modular nature of materials, you might be editing more than one material (as noted above). Notice the small hand icon (pointed out above) now reads: 0 (item 6). This means that the current material's appearance asset is used by zero (no) other materials. So if this icon does not indicate 0, it is usually safer to either replace the asset(s) as we have done here, or use the small duplicate icon right next to the replace icon to make a copy of the asset first before editing. When you copy an asset, you can rename it in the Information area and then edit the settings as required.

9. Click back to the Graphics tab.

    ⇨ In the Shading area, check the "Use Render Appearance" check box.

This will change the shading color to match the average color used in the image file on the Appearance tab.

10. In the "Material Browser," click OK to close it (this will also close the "Asset Browser").
11. Select any one of the exterior walls.

    ⇨ On the Properties palette, click the Edit Type button.

    ⇨ Edit the Structure and then assign the new **Brick, Dark Blend, Running** material to layer 1 and then click OK twice.

There is plenty more that we can do in the "Material Browser" but for now we continue refining the exterior shell of the building. Materials will be covered in more detail in coming chapters and topics.

ADDING WALL RETURNS AND WRAPS

When studying the 3D view, you will note that we still have the simple "stand-in" curtain wall feature on the front of the building. (This was created in Chapter 5.) We are going to re-design this façade below. However, it should be clear from looking at the current state of the façade that we need to modify the wall at the front of the building to at

Developing the Exterior Skin | 413

least allow for an entry lobby to the building. To do this, we'll simply split the front wall and add a few wing walls to add some depth to the main façade.

1. On the Project Browser, double-click to open the *Entrance Plan* floor plan view.
2. On the Modify tab, on the Edit panel, click the Split Element tool (or press SL).
   ⇨ On the Options Bar, place a checkmark in the "Delete Inner Segment" check box.

   We'll split the middle portion of the wall out from one edge of the patio to the other.
3. Click the first point of the split on the left side of the plan (use the edge of the patio as a guide).

   It does not have to be exact, we'll adjust below (see the top portion of Figure 10.7).

   ⇨ Click the second point of the split on the right side of the plan (again using the edge of the patio as a guide).
   ⇨ On the ribbon, click the Modify tool or press the ESC key twice.

Recall that the exterior walls use a Finish Face: Exterior Location Line. If you click to select one of the exterior walls (there are now two after the split), you will notice that the control handle (small round blue dot) is on the outside edge of the wall.

4. On the View Control Bar, from the Level of Detail pop-up, choose: **Medium**.
5. Select the wall on the left side of the plan.
   ⇨ Drag the control handle to snap at the intersection formed in the notch of the patio (see the bottom left side of Figure 10.7).
6. Right-click the wall and choose: **Create Similar** (or click the tool on the ribbon).
   ⇨ Draw a new wall as shown along the bottom of Figure 10.7 be sure to flip it as necessary.

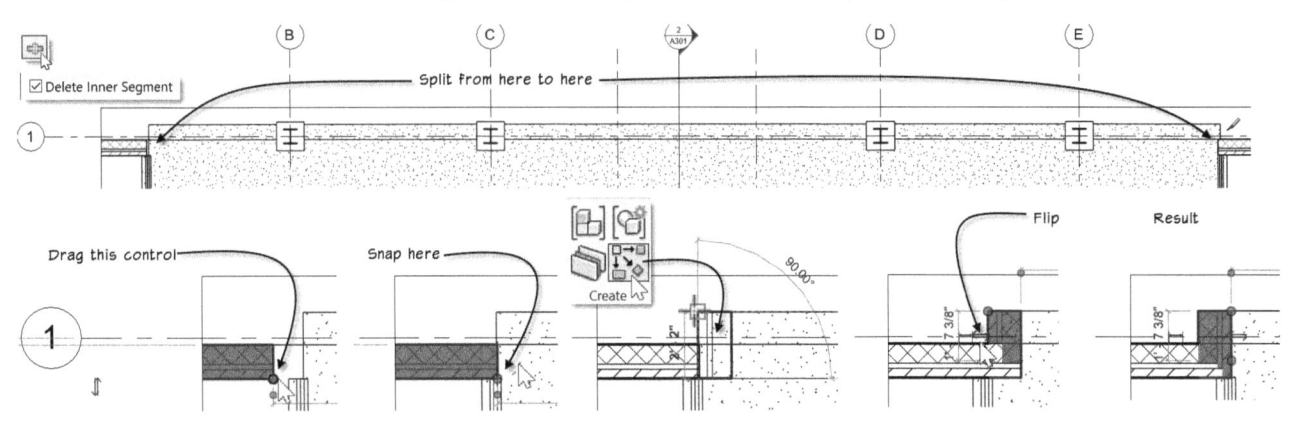

FIGURE 10.7 *Edit the end of the split wall and add a new short segment*

TIP: If you draw from top to bottom you won't have to flip. If you draw from bottom to top, you will need to flip the wall after you finish it. Or you can flip the wall after the first click by pressing the SPACEBAR on the keyboard. Then click the second point to finish the wall.

7. Repeat the process on the other side of the plan.

   When drawing the second wall, reverse the order of the first and second clicks. Click from bottom to top (or flip as indicated).
8. Open the *{3D}* view and study the results there as well.

Make sure that the height of the new walls matches the height of the original walls.

• Revit Essentials for Architecture •

414 | Chapter 10

If they do not, select the two new (short perpendicular) walls and on the Properties palette change the Base Constraint to: **Street Level** and the Top Constraint to: **Up to level: Roof** with a: **4'-0"** [**1200**] Top Offset.

9. On the Project Browser, double-click to open the *Entrance Plan* floor plan view again.

Notice the way that the wall layers terminate at the freestanding end of the wall. The air gap is exposed on the end of the wall. We can wrap the ends of the materials to close such gaps. We could do this both at the ends of wall and at openings created by doors and windows (inserts).

10. Select one of the exterior walls.

You do not need to select them all. The following will be a type-level edit, and type-level edits will apply to all elements of that type automatically.

⇨ On the Properties palette (or the Modify tab), click the Edit Type button.

⇨ Next to Structure, click the Edit button.

11. In the Default Wrapping area, from the At Ends drop down, choose: **Exterior**.

This does not fully solve the problem. If you open the preview, the brick now wraps over the end of the wall, but so too does the air gap.

12. In the layers list at the top, remove the checkmark from the "Wraps" column next to layer 2 (Thermal/Air Layer [3]).

You should now see that only the brick wraps and the air gap is covered over by the wrapping brick layer (see Figure 10.8).

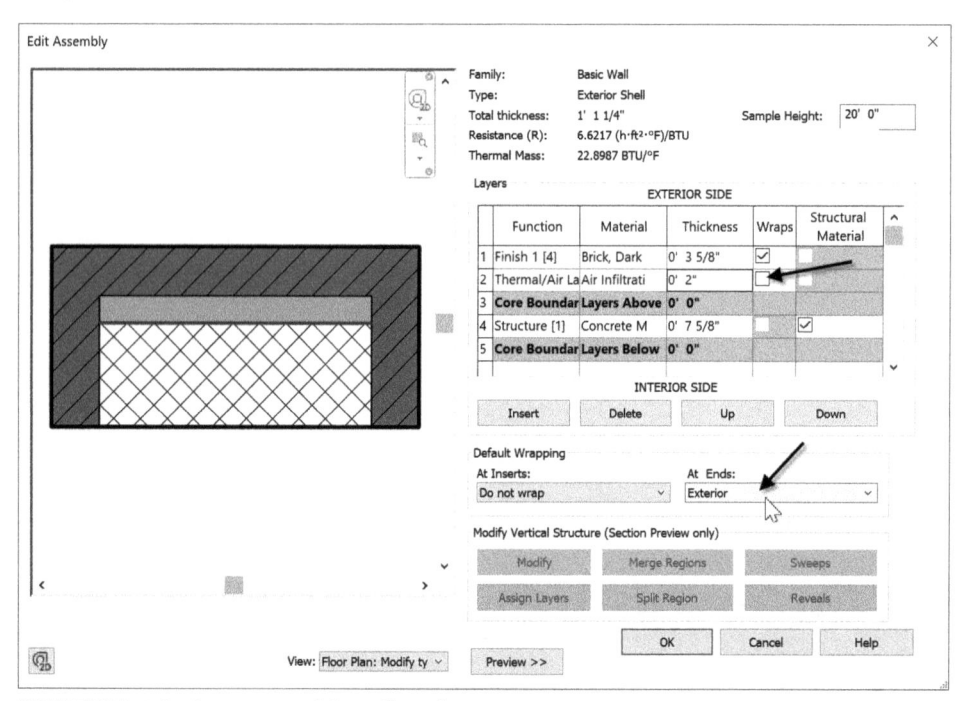

FIGURE 10.8 *Edit the wrapping of the wall type layers*

13. Click OK twice to return to the view window and study the results.
14. Save the Project.

WALL SYSTEM FAMILIES

A system family is a family that is built-in to the Revit system. They are predefined and cannot be modified at the family level. To manipulate a system family, we edit one or more of their types. Walls are system families. And there

• The Aubin Academy •

are three of them: Basic Wall, Curtain Wall, and Stacked Wall. All the walls that we have created so far in this book are basic walls. Basic walls can have one or more layers in their type's structure (as seen in the previous exercise). "Basic" does not necessarily mean simple or generic. A basic wall is defined by having a single continuous set of material layers (as seen when cut either horizontally or vertically). The "Generic" type walls we used in the early chapters are the simplest wall types available. But even though the wall type we just created above with its three layers is more complex, it is still a basic wall. This is because all the layers run the full length and height of the wall. A curtain wall, as we'll see next, defines a panel system along the length and/or height of the wall. A stacked wall "stacks" two or more basic wall types on top of one another. We will look at stacked walls later in this chapter. The major focus of this chapter will be on curtain walls.

WORKING WITH CURTAIN WALLS

Curtain walls in Revit are panelized wall systems. They come in a few varieties: Curtain Walls, Curtain Systems and Sloped Glazing. Curtain walls are drawn the same way as walls and using the same Wall tool. To create a curtain wall, you simply choose the appropriate type from the Type Selector as you draw the wall. A curtain system looks like a curtain wall but is typically created from (and on) the faces of other geometry such as a mass. Curtain systems allow for more complex geometry and can follow nearly any freeform shape. Sloped glazing is a roof family and you use the Roof tool to draw them. To get started, you simply draw a roof, change its type to sloped glazing and then follow the procedures covered in this chapter to panelize it. We will not do examples of curtain systems or sloped glazing in this chapter, but everything we do cover (like grids, mullions and panels) would apply to them as well. So, at the completion of the chapter, feel free to experiment.

A curtain wall type sets up a panel modulation along the length and/or height of the wall. Each panel can be assigned specific family elements such as glass or stone panels or even other wall types; for example, brick or metal panel exterior with CMU, metal stud or metal frame backup. The edges between the panels are mullions. You can decide which edges should receive mullion elements and which type of mullion each edge should use. You can even control the way that the mullions intersect with one another.

DRAW A CURTAIN WALL

The simplest way to create a curtain wall is to draw it using the Wall tool. Let's create a simple curtain wall at the front entrance to the building on the first floor. We'll draw it in the place where the wall we split out used to be.

1. Return to the *Entrance Plan* floor plan view.
2. On the Architecture tab, click the Wall tool.
   - From the Type Selector, choose: **Curtain Wall 1 [Curtain Wall]**.
   - On the Properties palette, verify that the Top Constraint is set to: **Up to level: Level 2**.
   - Change the "Top Offset" to: **0** (zero).

> **IMPORTANT:** Remember to always check the settings, in this case, the Top Offset "remembers" the height we used to establish the parapet height when drawing the exterior walls previously.

3. Click the first point of the curtain wall at the intersection of column grid 1 and the small wing wall on the left that we drew above (see the left side of Figure 10.9).

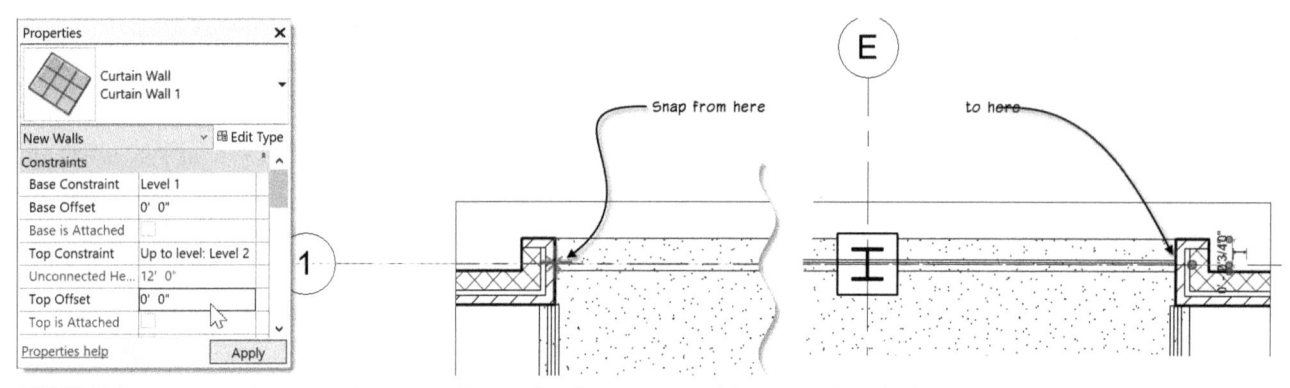

FIGURE 10.9 *Draw a single segment of curtain wall snapped to the intersection of the wing walls and column line 1*

        Use the TAB key if necessary to find the intersection. You can also use the keyboard shortcut SI to find it.

4. Pan to the right and then snap the endpoint of the curtain wall at the intersection of grid 1 and the other small wing wall (see the right side of Figure 10.9).

⇨ On the ribbon, click the Modify tool or press the ESC key twice.

The new curtain wall will appear as a thin plane of glass slightly offset from the column grid line and passing through the columns.

5. Select the new curtain wall.

    Locate the temporary dimension that appears (it should be at the right side).

⇨ Change the value of the upper temporary dimension to: **4"** [**100**] (see the left side of Figure 10.10).

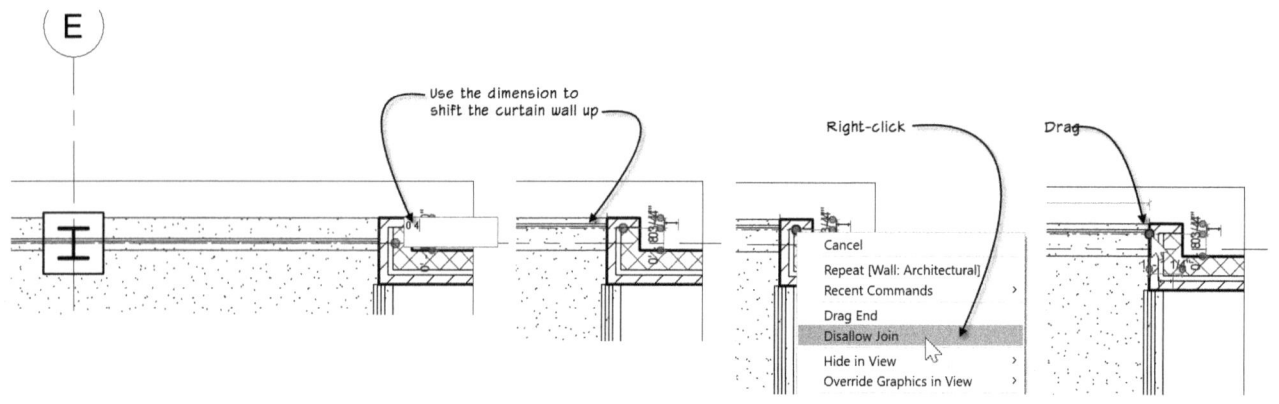

FIGURE 10.10 *Adjust the location of the curtain wall with the temporary dimension*

When you draw walls (including curtain walls), Revit attempts to join them automatically to other walls. This is often advantageous. In this case, however, we'll be subdividing the curtain wall into bays and the automatic join might cause us issues as we proceed. When you select this curtain wall, notice that the control grip at the ends is within the thickness of the neighboring wall. We can use the "Disallow Join" command to turn off the automatic joining behavior for a single intersection.

6. With the new curtain wall still selected, right-click directly on the control handle grip at the end (the small blue dot).

⇨ From the menu that appears, choose: **Disallow Join**.

⇨ Drag the grip handle until it snaps to the face of the wall (see the right side of Figure 10.10).

7. Repeat the process on the other end of the curtain wall.

8. Click the flip control at the middle of the curtain wall (or tap the SPACEBAR).

⇨ On the ribbon, click the Modify tool or press the ESC key twice.

HIDE IN VIEW

We will be working on this curtain wall from the vantage point of a few views. Let's look at what we have so far in 3D.

1. From the Project Browser, open the *{3D}* view.

   If necessary, orbit the model around to the front so that you can see the new curtain wall. You may also want to choose: **Shaded** or **Consistent Colors** from the View Control Bar.

The new curtain wall will appear at Level 1 as a continuous pane of blue glass. The slanted walls created in Chapter 5 are also visible here and partially obscuring our clear view of the new curtain wall. Let's hide these to make the view easier to read. The use of the Temporary Hide/Isolate method discussed in the "View the Stair in 3D" topic on page 319 in Chapter 8 would be appropriate here since we are going to later redisplay and unhide the curtain system. However, as you may recall, the Temporary Hide/Isolate mode applies only during the current work session. If you decide to leave the tutorial and return later, you will have to reapply the hide later. For this reason, let's use this opportunity to discuss permanent hide instead. Permanent hide allows us to hide selected elements in the current view permanently until we decide to unhide them.

2. Select the three slanted curtain walls modeled in Chapter 5 (use the CTRL key, and wait for the dashed edge to appear while pre-highlighting before clicking).

   ⇨ On the Modify | Walls tab, on the View panel, click the Hide in View drop down button and choose: **Hide Elements**.

The curtain system disappears and the curtain wall drawn above should now be clearly visible and easy to select (see Figure 10.11).

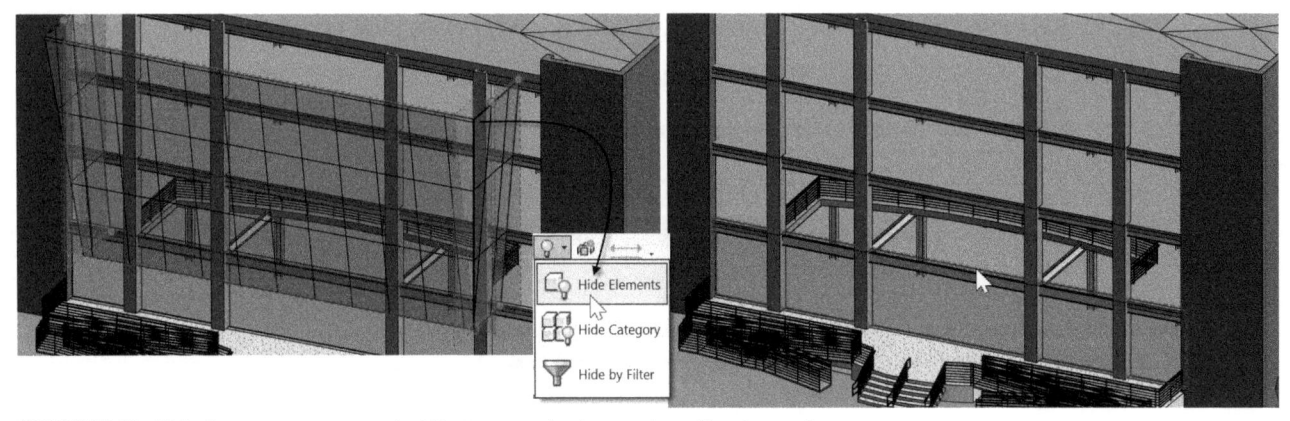

FIGURE 10.11 *Hide the curtain system in the 3D view to make the curtain wall easier to select*

UNDERSTANDING A CURTAIN WALL

A curtain wall is comprised of a curtain grid pattern in both the horizontal and vertical directions. Within each of the cells defined by these grids, is a panel. Panel families can be made to represent anything from glass to stone panels to louvers to doors. The number of grid divisions in the pattern is either a parameter of the curtain wall type or can be defined on the curtain wall instance directly. You can select the curtain grids and panels independently. By default, the curtain wall itself pre-highlights first. To select the internal elements like grid edges, mullions, and panels, you can use the TAB key. Each time you TAB, a different portion of the curtain wall will pre-highlight. With curtain walls, you can also select a single element and then right-click to get additional selection options such as selecting all panels or mullions along a continuous line horizontally or vertically. We'll try all these techniques below. Currently this curtain wall is one large panel of glazing because we haven't superimposed a curtain grid pattern on it yet. Therefore, tabbing (to experiment with selection options) will not yield very interesting results. Naturally, it

418 | Chapter 10

would be unlikely to have a single continuous panel of glass across the entire front of the building. Therefore, we will sub-divide the curtain wall next.

CREATE A WORKING VIEW

We can sub-divide the curtain wall in any view using the curtain grid tool. However, it will be easiest to create a new view to see and work on the curtain wall isolated from the rest of the model.

1. Return to the *Entrance Plan* floor plan view.
2. On the View tab, on the Create panel, click the Section tool.
   - Draw a Section line in front of (below in plan) and parallel to the curtain wall just a little wider both left and right.
   - Using the Control Handle, drag the "Far Clip Offset" of the Section back to just the inside of the curtain wall behind the Columns.
3. Deselect the Section line and then double-click the blue section head to open the section view.
   - Drag the top of the crop box down to just above the top edge of the curtain wall (slightly above Level 2).
   - Adjust the bottom of the crop region to just below the curtain wall.

The curtain system that we hid above will be visible here again because settings for hidden elements are view specific.

4. Make a crossing window selection of everything in the view.
   - On the ribbon, click the Filter button
   - Click the Check None button, and then check only RVT Links and Floors and then click OK.
   - On the ribbon, choose the: **Hide in View > Hide Elements** command again. (The shortcut is EH).
   - Select the Section line that appears in this view and hide it too (see Figure 10.12).

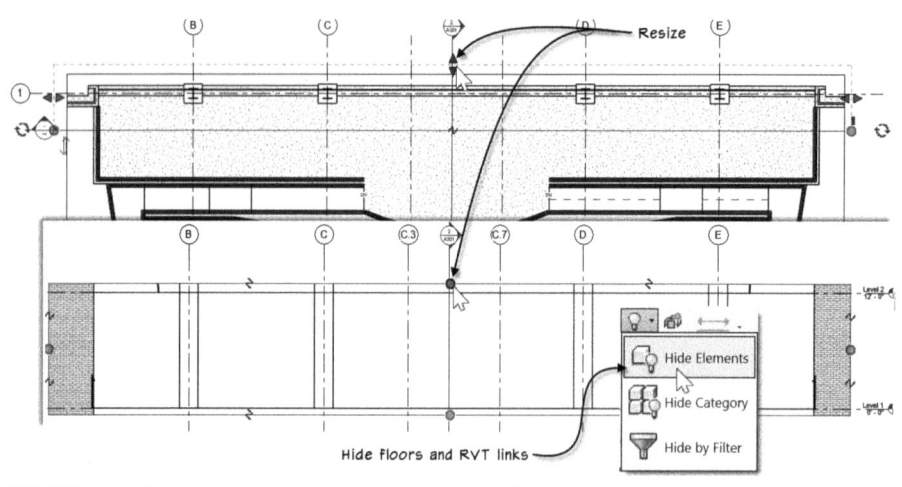

FIGURE 10.12 *Create a section around just the curtain wall*

5. On the Project Browser, right-click *Section 1* and choose: **Rename**.
   - Change the name to: **Entry Curtain Wall Section** and then click OK.
6. On the Project Browser, right-click the {3D} view and choose: **Duplicate View > Duplicate**.
   - Right-click *{3D} Copy 1* and choose: **Rename**.
   - Change the name to: **Entry Curtain Wall 3D** and then click OK.

As you can see, this view currently shows the entire extent of the model, but the upper slanted curtain wall is hidden in this view. This is because we copied the view from the view where it was already hidden. This copies the view and its view-specific edits. We can orient and simultaneously crop the view to match any other view on the Project Browser list, such as the section view we just created.

7. In the 3D view window, right-click on the ViewCube.

    ⇨ Choose: **Orient to View** > **Sections** > **Section: Entry Curtain Wall Section** (see Figure 10.13).

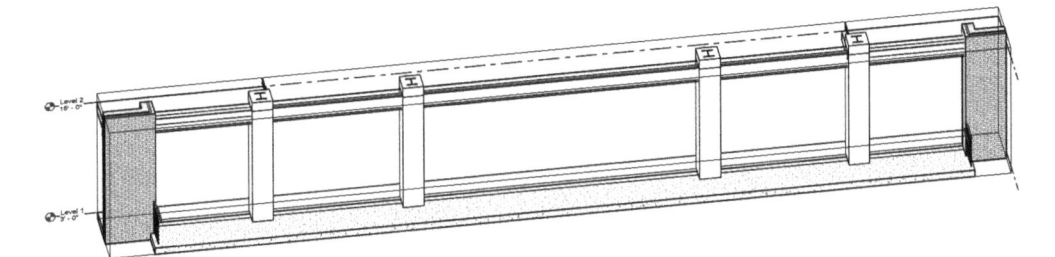

FIGURE 10.13 *Orient the copied 3D view to the section at curtain wall and view it as hidden line*

8. On the View Control Bar, change the Model Graphics Style to: **Hidden Line**.

    ⇨ Using the ViewCube, or SHIFT and drag with the wheel, adjust the angle and zoom level of the view.

9. Save the project.

We now have a section and a 3D view that are cropped to show only the curtain wall across the front entrance. In the 3D view, you will notice that the view is cropped to match the section in all directions, including the depth. To return to the head-on (elevation) viewpoint, click on Front on the ViewCube. The 3D view is good for checking your progress, but you will get some additional editing functionality in the section view. We will use both views below as we work.

ADD CURTAIN GRIDS

Now that we can see the curtain wall clearly without the rest of the model cluttering our view, let's sub-divide the curtain wall with curtain grids.

1. Make the *Entry Curtain Wall Section* view active.
2. On the Architecture tab, on the Build panel, click the Curtain Grid tool.

    Move the pointer near the top edge of the curtain wall. A grid line and temporary dimensions will appear.

TIP: So you don't get confused about where the top of the curtain wall is in the hidden line display, click the Hide Crop Region toggle icon on the View Control Bar.

⇨ Click to create a grid line in the middle bay between column C and C.3.

⇨ Click to create another in the bay between column C.7 and D (see Figure 10.14).

420 | Chapter 10

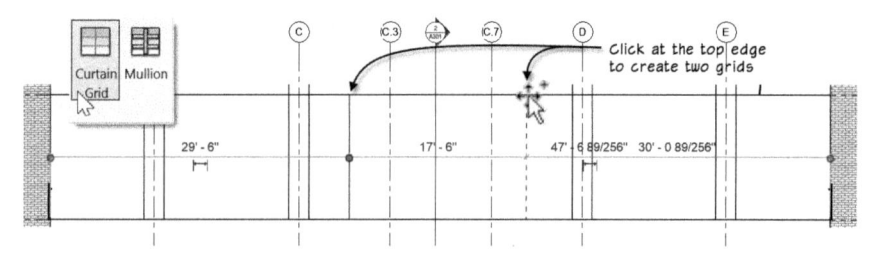

FIGURE 10.14 *Add two grid lines near the middle columns*

> On the ribbon, click the Modify tool or press the ESC key twice.

3. On the Annotate tab (or the QAT) click the Aligned Dimension tool (or press DI).

4. For the first witness line location, click the right face of the column at column line C (see the left side of Figure 10.15).

> Continue adding witness lines by clicking each of the two new curtain grids you added above and the left edge of the column on grid line D (see the right side of Figure 10.15).

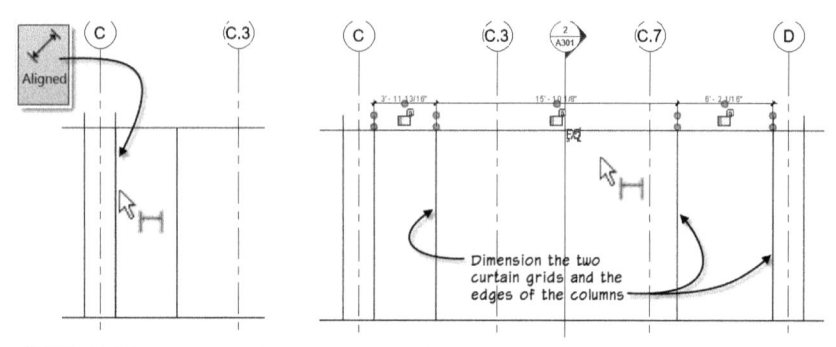

FIGURE 10.15 *Dimension the new curtain grids to the surrounding columns*

5. Click the Modify tool or press the ESC key twice.

6. Select one of the curtain grids.

Notice how the dimension values on either side of the selected grid line activate. This is called activating the dimension. We can now edit the value of this dimension (just like we can with temporary dimensions) to place the grid lines precisely relative to the columns.

> Click on the dimension value (between the selected curtain grid and the column) for the activated permanent dimension and then input a value of: **1'-0" [345]**. Press ENTER to complete.

7. Repeat on the other side.

Don't forget to change selection. If you go right to the dimension value, it will move the same grid line again.

You should now have a middle bay that has a grid line 1'-0" [345] away from the columns on each side. The distance between the grid lines should be 24'-0" [7200]. If this is not the case, make any required adjustments (see Figure 10.16).

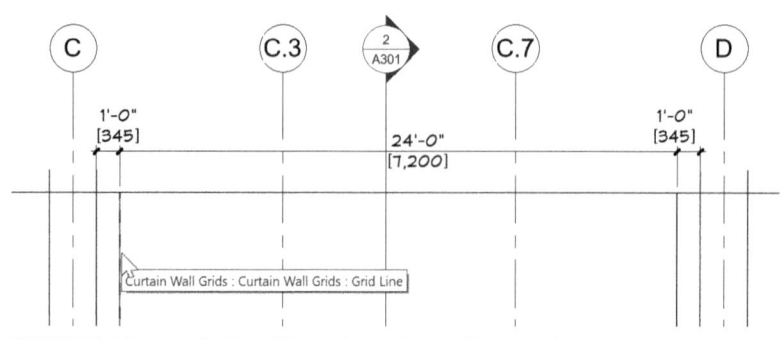

FIGURE 10.16 *Move both grid lines relative the neighboring columns*

• The Aubin Academy •

> **TIP:** Alternatively, you can select a curtain grid, drag the witness line control grips to locate them where you need them, and then click the small icon beneath the dimension to make it permanent.

We can add additional curtain grid lines by sketching them like the ones above, or we can copy them from the existing ones. Let's copy the ones we must create three wide bays and two small bays for the entrance to our building.

   8. Select the grid line on the left.
   9. On the Modify | Curtain Wall Grids tab, click the Copy tool.
   ⇨ On the Options Bar, place a checkmark in the "Multiple" check box.
   10. Pick any start point and then drag to the right.
   ⇨ Type: **6'-0" [1800]** and then press ENTER to create the first copy. Continue copying to the right.
   11. For the next copy, type: **3'-0" [900]** and then press ENTER.
   ⇨ Create another one at an offset of: **6'-0" [1800]** and then one more at: **3'-0" [900]**.
   ⇨ On the ribbon, click the Modify tool or press the ESC key twice (see Figure 10.19).

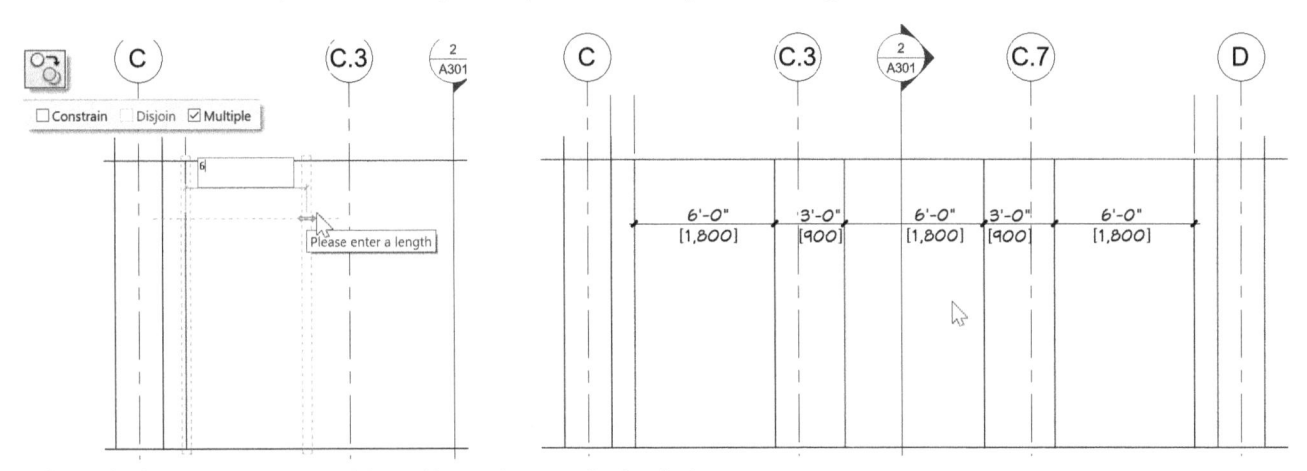

FIGURE 10.17 *Create several copies of the grid line making an a b a b a rhythm*

   12. Zoom out so you can see the entire curtain wall.
   13. On the Architecture tab, click the Curtain Grid tool.

   Move the pointer near the left edge of the curtain wall (left of column grid B). A grid line and temporary dimensions will appear.

   14. Click to create a horizontal grid line 4'-0" [1200] from the top (use the temporary dimensions to position it if necessary) (see Figure 10.18).

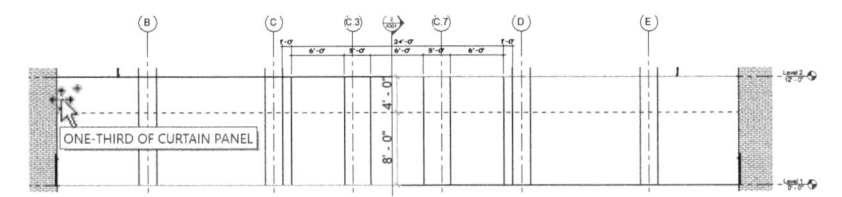

FIGURE 10.18 *Add a horizontal grid one third from the top*

   ⇨ On the ribbon, click the Modify tool or press the ESC key twice.
   15. Save your project.

ASSIGN CURTAIN PANEL TYPES

Now that we have several curtain grid lines dividing our curtain wall into individual panels, let's assign some panel types to these bays. Our building needs an entrance. The three bays that we have roughed out in the front need some doors. A curtain wall door is not a regular door family. It is a panel family that looks like and schedules like a door. To assign them, we can use the tabbing technique mentioned above.

1. Zoom in on the bay between column line C and D.
2. Place your Modify tool (mouse pointer) over the edge of one of the wider bays created above.
    ⇨ Press TAB and repeat as necessary until the panel in this bay pre-highlights—when it does, click to select it (see Figure 10.19).

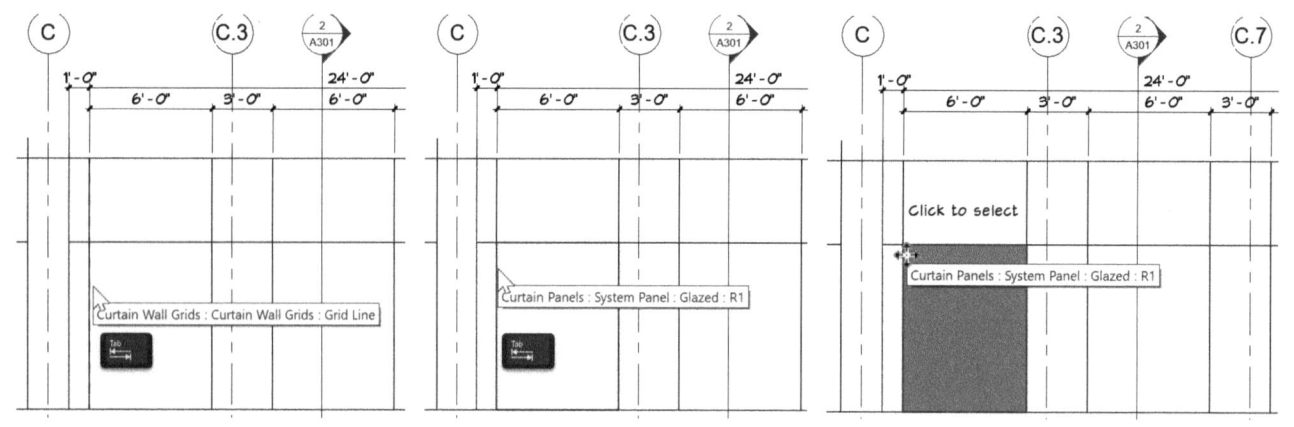

FIGURE 10.19 *Select one of the larger bays at the entrance*

3. Pre-highlight the next wide panel using the same technique.
    ⇨ Hold down the CTRL key and click to select it. You should have two wide panels selected after this action.
4. Repeat once more to select the remaining wide panel.
5. With the three panels selected, on the Properties palette click the Edit Type button.
    ⇨ In the "Type Properties" dialog, click the Load button.
    ⇨ In the "Open" dialog, double-click the *Doors* folder.

If you do not see a *Doors* folder, the families that are referenced have been provided with the dataset files in the *Chapter10* folder. You can load the file from there instead if you wish.

6. Select the *Door-Curtain-Wall-Double-Storefront.rfa* [*M_Door-Curtain-Wall-Double-Storefront.rfa*] file and then click Open and then click OK (see Figure 10.20).

> **BIM MANAGER NOTE:** Please note that even though the files referenced above are stored in a *Doors* folder, they are curtain panel families and not door families. Normal doors cannot be placed in a curtain wall. So, if you create your own custom curtain wall doors, be sure to choose the dedicated family template (*Door -Curtain Wall.rft* [*Metric Door -Curtain Wall.rft*]) for that purpose. Family templates and family creation techniques are covered in the next chapter.

Developing the Exterior Skin | 423

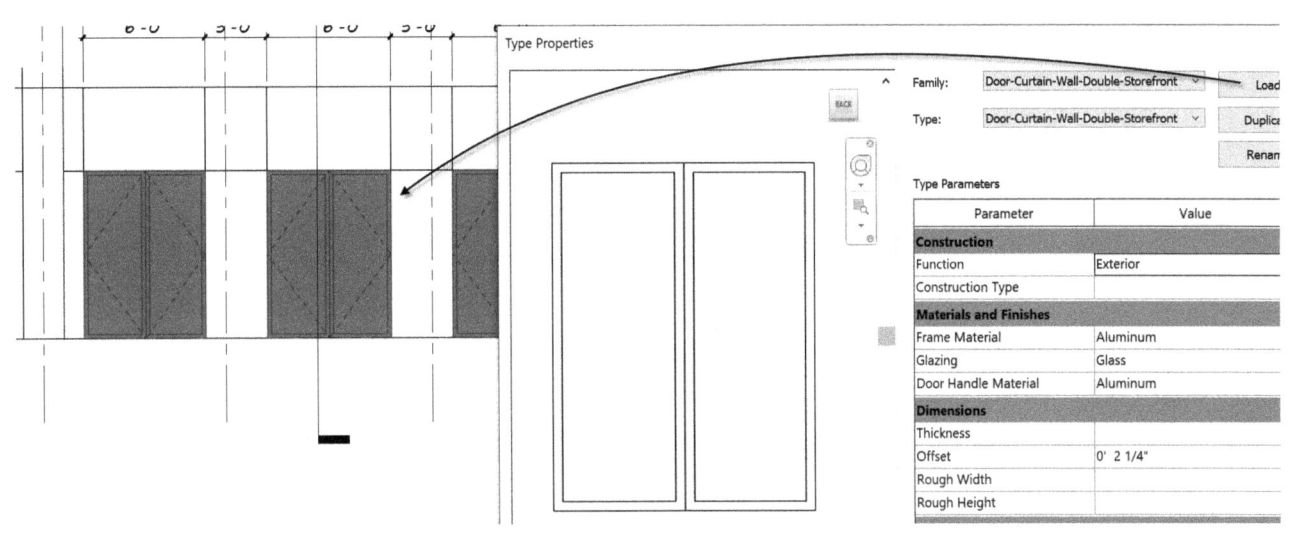

FIGURE 10.20 *Swap in storefront doors for the three wide bays*

ASSIGN MULLIONS

Our next task is to apply some mullions to the curtain grid lines.

1. On the Architecture tab, on the Build panel, click the Mullion tool.

   From the Type Selector, verify that: **2.5" x 5" rectangular** [**50 x 150mm**] is selected.

On the Modify | Place Mullion tab of the ribbon, on the Placement panel, there are three methods to create mullions: Grid Line, Grid Line Segment, or All Grid Lines. Grid Line is the default choice.

2. With the "Grid Line" button selected, click on the horizontal grid line at the top of the doors.

If you are zoomed in close enough, you should notice that the doors adjust in size to accommodate the mullion.

⇨ Try the "Grid Line Segment" option next on any grid segment.

3. Use the "All Grid Lines" option and then click to complete the process of adding mullions (see Figure 10.21).

⇨ On the ribbon, click the Modify tool or press the ESC key twice.

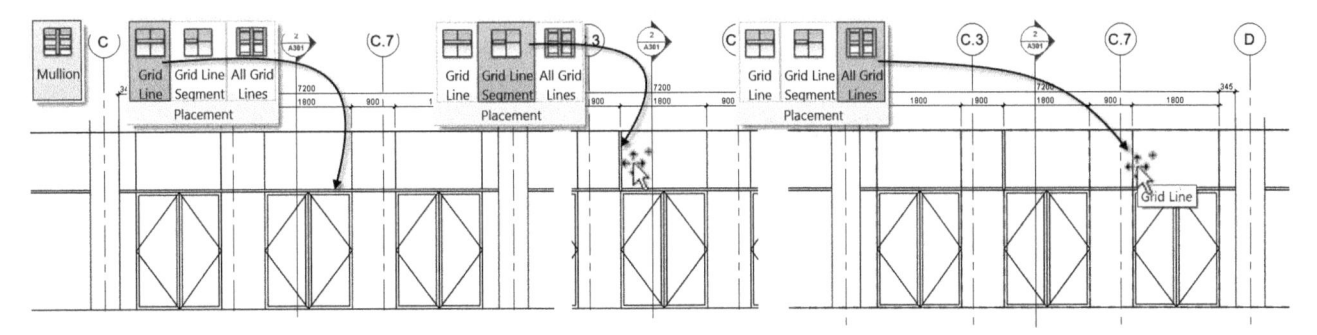

FIGURE 10.21 *Add mullions to the curtain grid lines*

Looking closely at the door panels, note that mullions were added at the sills. We can delete these individual mullion segments to finalize the door panels.

4. Using the TAB and CTRL keys, select the mullion segments indicated in Figure 10.22 and delete them.

• Revit Essentials for Architecture •

424 | Chapter 10

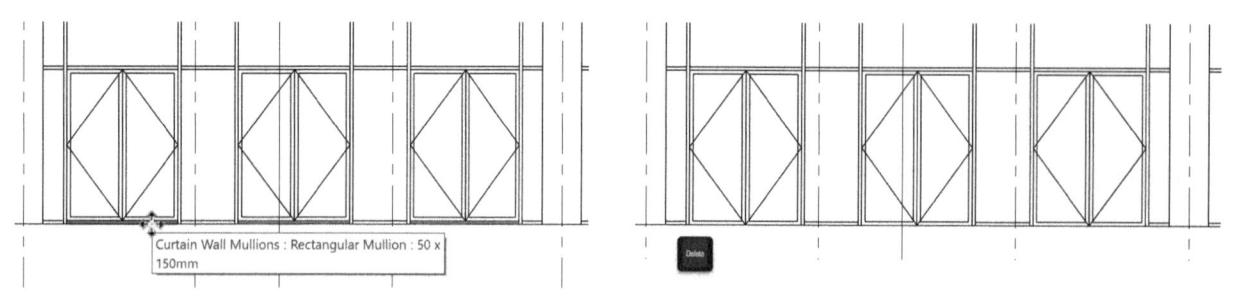

FIGURE 10.22 *Delete the mullions under the door panels*

EDIT MULLION JOINS

You will notice that the vertical mullions' joins have been given priority over the horizontal ones. If you prefer to have the horizontal mullions continuous and have the verticals stop and start at each intersection, you can toggle the mullion join behavior for each join.

1. Select one of the vertical mullions at the doors.

   Notice the Join icons that appear at each end of the mullion and also on the right-click menu (see Figure 10.23).

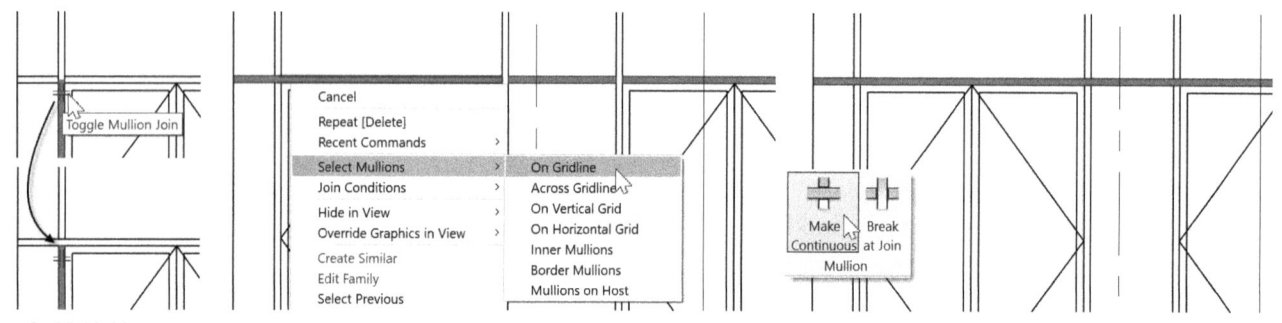

FIGURE 10.23 *Edit mullion joins using the onscreen control or the right-click menu and ribbon*

2. Toggle the mullion joins to your liking.

In addition to the control icons, you can right-click to access the same options. To use the right-click options effectively, select a single mullion, right-click on the selected mullion, and choose: **Select Mullions > On Gridline**. Once the entire gridline is selected, right-click again and choose: **Join Conditions > Make Continuous**. This would be the same as clicking the join icon on several separate mullions.

CREATE ADDITIONAL GRID LINES AND MULLIONS

The middle entrance bay is complete, but the other bays need attention.

1. Create a new curtain grid line 1'-0" [345] from the edges of the columns at grids B and E and on the left side of C and right side of D.

2. Add Mullions to each of these new grid lines Figure 10.24.

Developing the Exterior Skin | 425

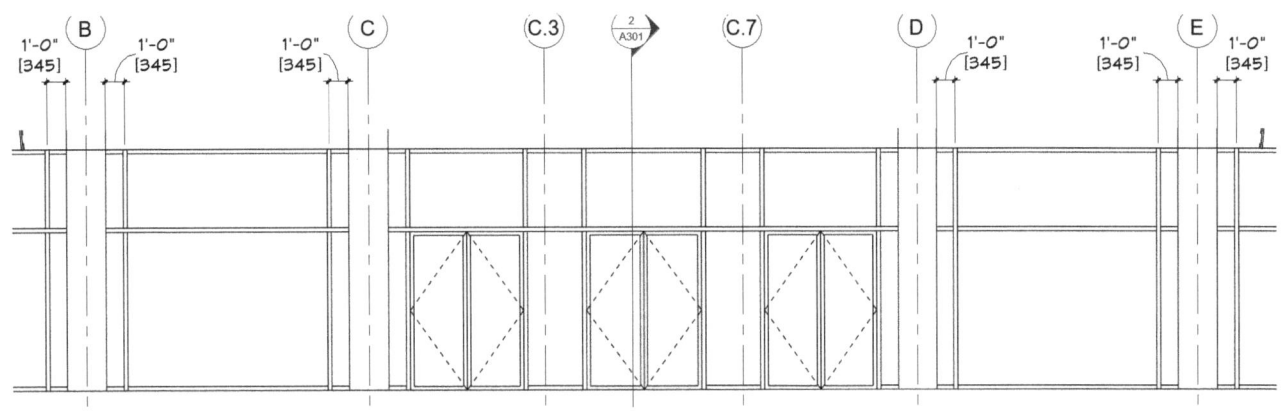

FIGURE 10.24 *Add more grid lines and mullions*

3. Toggle the Mullion Joins as appropriate.

USING A WALL TYPE FOR A PANEL

At each of the columns, we want to remove the horizontal mullions and swap out the glazing for a solid wall panel.

1. Zoom in on the column at grid B.

2. Using the CTRL key, select all three of the horizontal mullions crossing through the Column (one at the top, one at the door head height, and one at the bottom).

> **TIP:** If you have trouble with the selection, remember your TAB key. Also remember that they pass behind the Columns.

⇨ Delete the three selected Mullions (press the DELETE key) (see item 1 in Figure 10.25).

3. Select the horizontal curtain grid line.

⇨ On the Modify | Curtain Wall Grids tab, click the Add / Remove Segments button.

4. Click on the grid line in-between the two vertical mullions at the column (item 2).

The grid line will turn dashed between these mullions to indicate that a portion of it has been removed.

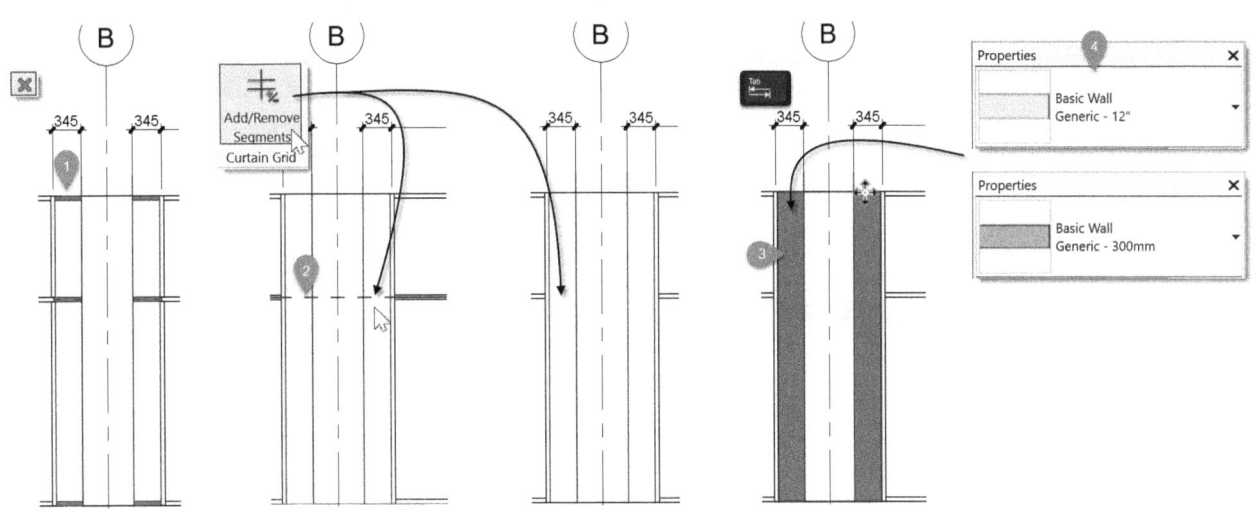

FIGURE 10.25 *Delete mullions, remove a grid line and swap out panels with a wall type*

426 | Chapter 10

You will now have a continuous vertical panel at the column as shown in the right panel of Figure 10.25. You may need to use the TAB key to pre-highlight it to see this. When you select it, remember that the column is in front of it.

5. Using the TAB key, pre-highlight and then select the new full height panel at column B (item 3).

⇨ From the Type Selector, choose: **Generic - 12" [Generic - 300mm]** (item 4).

6. Repeat the entire process for the other three Columns on the front façade.

7. On the Project Browser, double-click to open the *Entrance Plan* floor plan view.

⇨ Zoom in on the Columns at the front of the façade to see the result (see Figure 10.26).

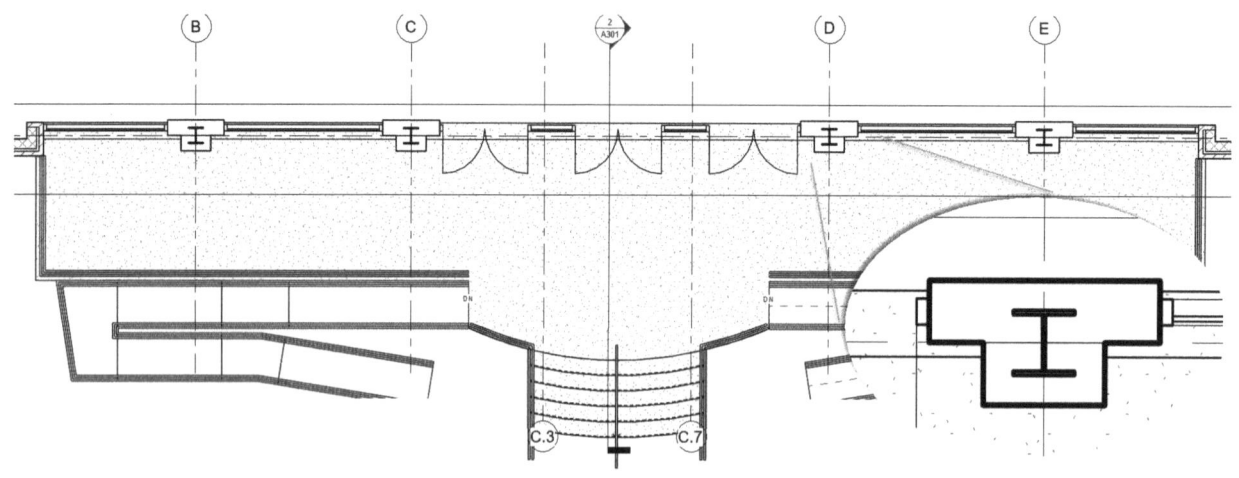

FIGURE 10.26 *Swap in a wall type in place of the curtain panels*

This procedure illustrates that you can use basic wall types as panels within a curtain wall. This adds a whole range of possibilities to your design potential with this tool. Notice also how nicely these infill wall "panels" interact with and merge with the columns.

8. On the Project Browser, double-click to return to the *Entry Curtain Wall Section* view.

9. Using the TAB and CTRL keys, select each of the four lower panels (two to the right of the entrance, two to the left).

⇨ From the Type Selector, choose: **Curtain Wall : Storefront** (see Figure 10.27).

TIP: Another option is to change one bay first and then use the Match Type tool (MA) to match this type to other panels.

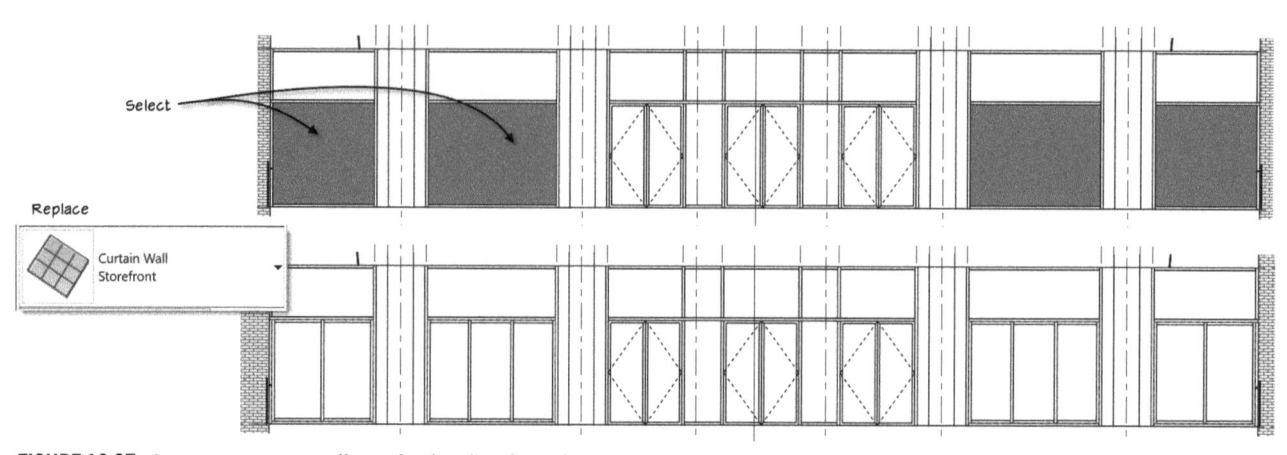

FIGURE 10.27 *Swap in a curtain wall type for the selected panels*

There are two interesting points worth mentioning on this step: first, we can use one curtain wall type as a panel within another. Second, the Storefront curtain wall type has built-in subdivisions of curtain grid lines and mullions preassigned to it. We will explore this kind of type-driven curtain wall further in the remainder of the chapter.

   10. Make one last substitution by selecting the two square panels between and above the doors.
   ⇨ From the Type Selector, choose: **System Panel: Solid**.
   11. On the Project Browser, double-click to open the *Entry Curtain Wall 3D* view.
   ⇨ Drag the ViewCube to orbit the model and study the results (see Figure 10.28).

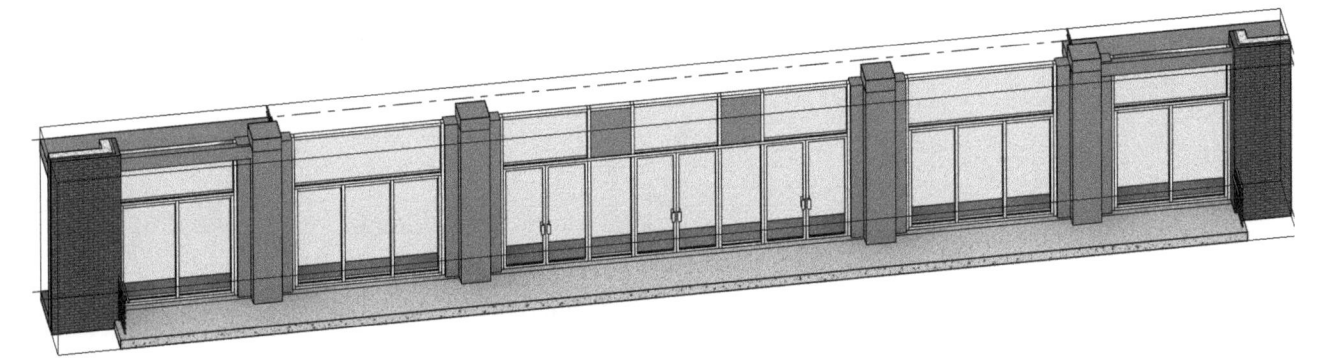

FIGURE 10.28 *Orbit the model to study the results (image shown shaded at fine level of detail)*

If you wish to see the curtain wall in the context of the rest of the building, you can also open the *{3D}* view and study it there. If you look closely, you will notice that the "Storefront" curtain walls that were used as panels include additional mullions around their perimeters. For purposes of our exercise, we won't worry about this; however, if you wanted to remove them, you could do so. These objects are "pinned" however, which in the case of a curtain wall, indicates that the element is defined at the type level. If you choose to delete them you will first have to click the blue pin icon that will appear to unpin them. This essentially adds an override to the curtain wall allowing you to remove the type driven mullions. We will learn more about curtain wall type properties in the coming exercises.

   12. Save the project.

CREATING HOSTED CURTAIN WALLS

The curtain wall we created above filled a space that had no previous enclosure. We drew it just like any other wall and then edited it. You can also create curtain walls from existing walls or even embed them within existing walls. In this way the wall will "host" the curtain wall. In this sequence we will use one of the types already provided in the current file and draw a curtain wall hosted in the exterior shell walls of the building.

DRAW A CURTAIN WALL

The first part of this exercise is like the previous one. We will draw a curtain wall using an existing type.

   1. On the Project Browser, double-click to open the *Level 2* floor plan view.
   ⇨ Close inactive windows.
   ⇨ On the View Control Bar, click the Detail level pop-up and choose: **Medium**.
   2. On the Architecture tab, click the Wall tool.
   ⇨ From the Type Selector, choose: **Curtain Wall : Storefront**.
   ⇨ On the Options Bar, from the "Height" list, choose: **Up to level: Level 4**.

428 | Chapter 10

3. On the Properties palette, verify that the "Top Offset" is set to: **0** (zero).

We will add the curtain wall directly over the vertical wall on the left side of the plan.

4. Click the first point of the curtain wall halfway between column lines 1 and 2 on the centerline of the vertical masonry wall (see the left side of Figure 10.29).

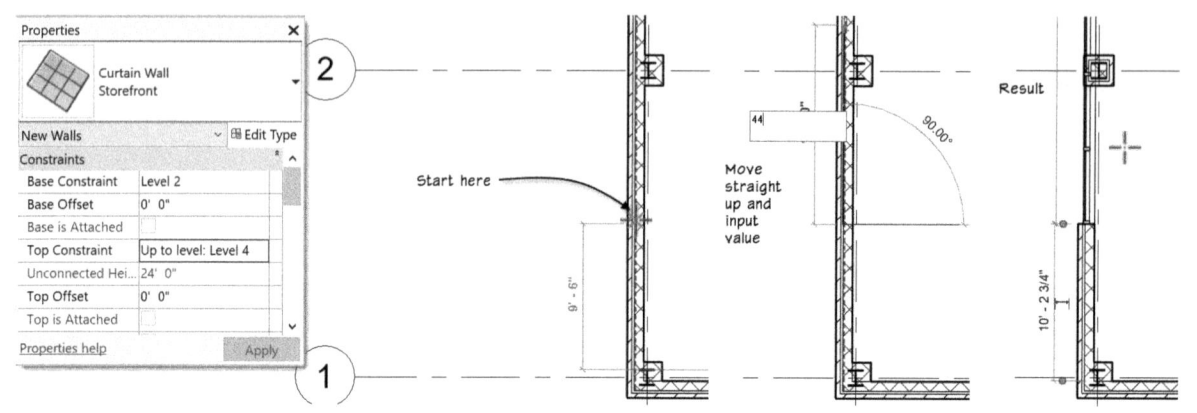

FIGURE 10.29 *Draw a new curtain wall on the second floor directly on top of the existing wall on the face of the brick*

⇨ Move the pointer vertically along the wall, type: **44'-0"** [**13500**] and then press ENTER (see the right side of Figure 10.29).

⇨ On the ribbon, click the Modify tool or press the ESC key twice.

The curtain wall should cut the host wall automatically. This is a setting within the curtain wall type. In some cases it will not (for example when using the Curtain Wall 1 type). If it does not cut automatically, we can use the Cut tool on the Modify tab to cut the wall manually with the curtain wall.

5. Zoom in on the column at column line 2.

Because we chose the *Storefront* curtain wall type above, this curtain wall already has curtain grid lines and mullions assigned to it. However, as you can see, the curtain wall is too close and the mullions intersect the columns.

6. Zoom out and then select the curtain wall. (Be sure to select the curtain wall itself, not the Mullions or glazing panels).

The glazing should appear on the outside of the curtain wall. If it does not, click the "Flip Wall Orientation" control.

Edit the temporary dimension in the thickness of the wall (it may be up near the top) to move the curtain wall out (away from the interior).

7. In the temporary dimension on the left, input: **3"**[**75**] and then press ENTER.

8. On the Project Browser, double-click to open the *{3D}* view (or click the Default 3D View button).

⇨ Orbit the model as needed to gain a clear view of the new curtain wall (see Figure 10.30).

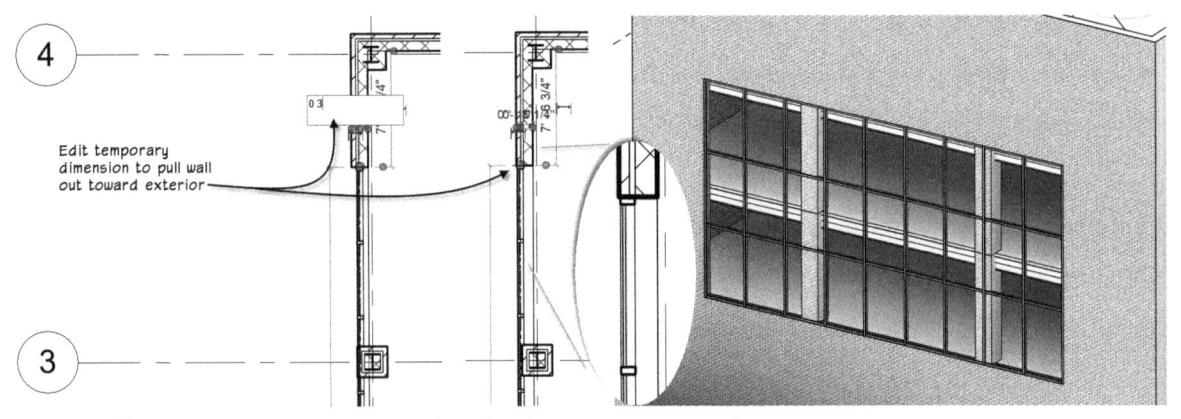

FIGURE 10.30 *Move the curtain wall out away from the columns using temporary dimensions*

If you look closely, you will see that the columns still intersect the mullions a bit. We can duplicate the affected columns and make them a little smaller.

9. In the *{3D}* view, using the CTRL key, select the four columns (The architectural columns).
   - On the Properties palette, click the Edit Type button and then click Duplicate (or ALT + D).
   - Name the new type: **20" x 24"** [**500 x 610mm**] and then click OK.
   - Edit the Depth to: **20"** [**500**] and then click OK.
10. Keep the four columns selected and switch back to the *Level 2* plan tab.
    - Move them to the right **2"** [**50**]. Return to the *{3D}* view to check the results (see Figure 10.31).

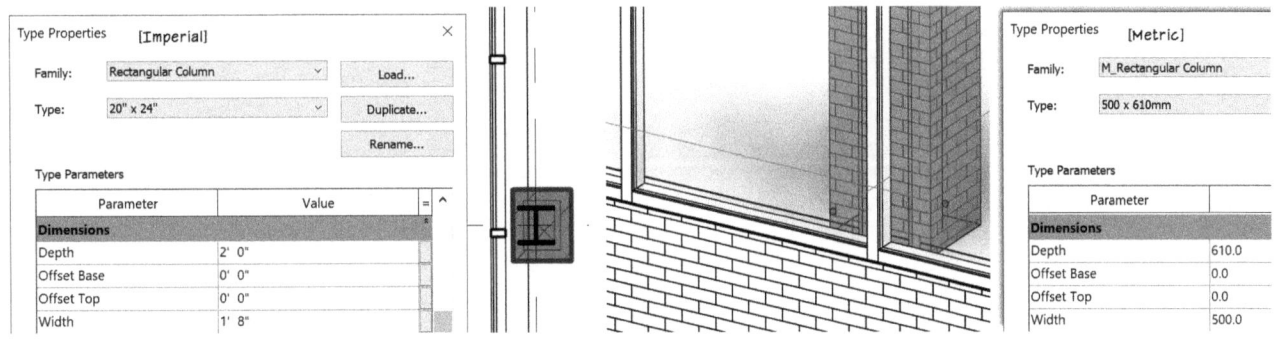

FIGURE 10.31 *Adjust the size of the columns at the curtain wall to accommodate the mullions*

11. Save the project.

ADJUST THE CURTAIN GRID SPACING

As you can see, this curtain wall type defines the spacing of grid bays automatically. In addition, the floor element between the second and third floors is clearly visible. We can make a few adjustments to the curtain wall type to match the building better.

1. Select the curtain wall. (Make sure the dashed outline is highlighting, not the panels or mullions before you click).
2. On the Properties palette, click the Edit Type button.
   - In the "Type Properties" dialog, click the Duplicate button (or ALT + D).
   - Name the new type: **Storefront - Levels 2 to 3** and then click OK.

Below, in the "Explore Curtain Wall Type Properties" topic on page 434, we will explore many of the settings in this dialog in detail. For now, we'll focus on just a few settings required by the current task.

430 | Chapter 10

3. Beneath the "Horizontal Grid" grouping, change the Spacing to: **4'-0"** [**1200**] and then click OK.

Notice the change in the overall grid spacing. Keep the curtain wall selected.

4. In the center of the curtain wall, click the Configure Grid Layout control.

Two dimension lines appear through the middle of the grid: one vertical and the other horizontal. To shift the horizontal grid lines up or down, edit the dimension on the horizontal origin line.

⇨ On the left side of the curtain wall, click the Horizontal Curtain Grid Origin temporary dimension.

There is also one for the angle, so pause your mouse over the dimensions for a tooltip to help you select the correct one.

⇨ Type a new value of: **2'-0"** [**600**] and then press ENTER (see Figure 10.32)

TIP: There are two temporary dimensions, both the horizontal and vertical origin lines. One moves the grid, the other rotates it. Be sure to use the tooltip to find the correct one before editing. If you want to experiment with the rotation as well, feel free to do so, but undo before continuing.

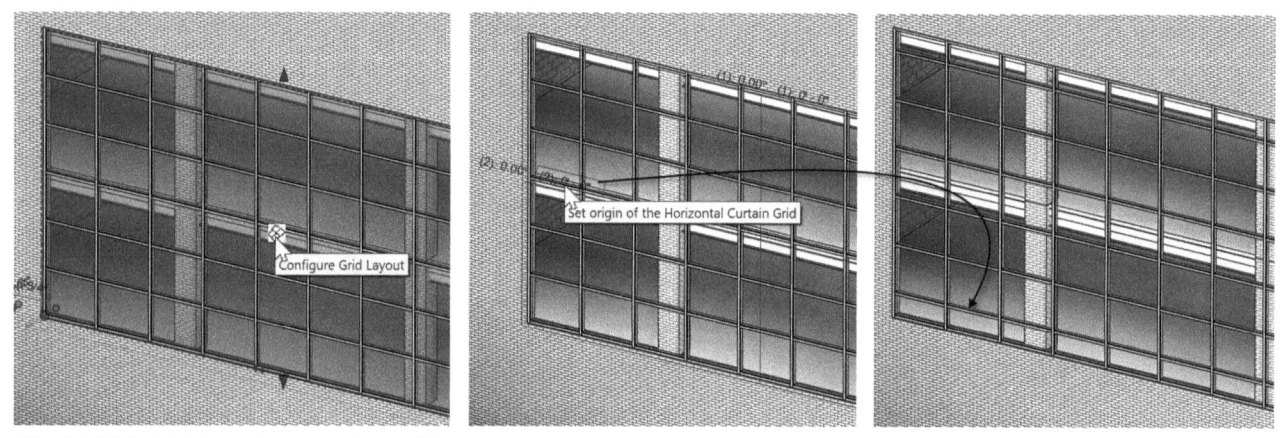

FIGURE 10.32 *Shift the grid pattern origin by half a bay*

We now have a short bay at the top and the bottom of the overall curtain wall and a full grid centered at the floor line between second and third floors. Let's replace those panels in the center with spandrel glass.

5. Select one of the panels in the middle of the curtain wall height (one that occurs at the floor line).

TIP: Place your mouse near the edge of the panel you want to select and then press TAB until it pre-highlights, then click.

⇨ Right-click and choose: **Select Panels > Along Horizontal Grid**.

Notice the small pushpin icons attached to each Panel—you may need to zoom to see them all. As with the Storefront curtain walls that were embedded into the larger curtain wall at the entry, the curtain wall type that we used here assigned the curtain grids, panels, and mullions automatically. These panel definitions are driven by the type and the pin icon (with a small link icon beneath it) indicates this. If you look at the Type Selector, you will notice that you cannot change the type (it is grayed out). To change a pinned item, you must unpin it first. You can simply click the pin icon on each one to unpin it, but since there are many selected, this would not be the most efficient approach. Instead we'll use the unpin tool.

6. On the Modify | Curtain Panels tab, click the Unpin tool (or press UP).

Developing the Exterior Skin | 431

⇨ Keeping the same selection of panels, from the Type Selector choose: **System Panel: Solid**.

⇨ Deselect the Panels to see that the entire row is now solid.

⇨ Repeat for the top and bottom (short height) rows (see Figure 10.33).

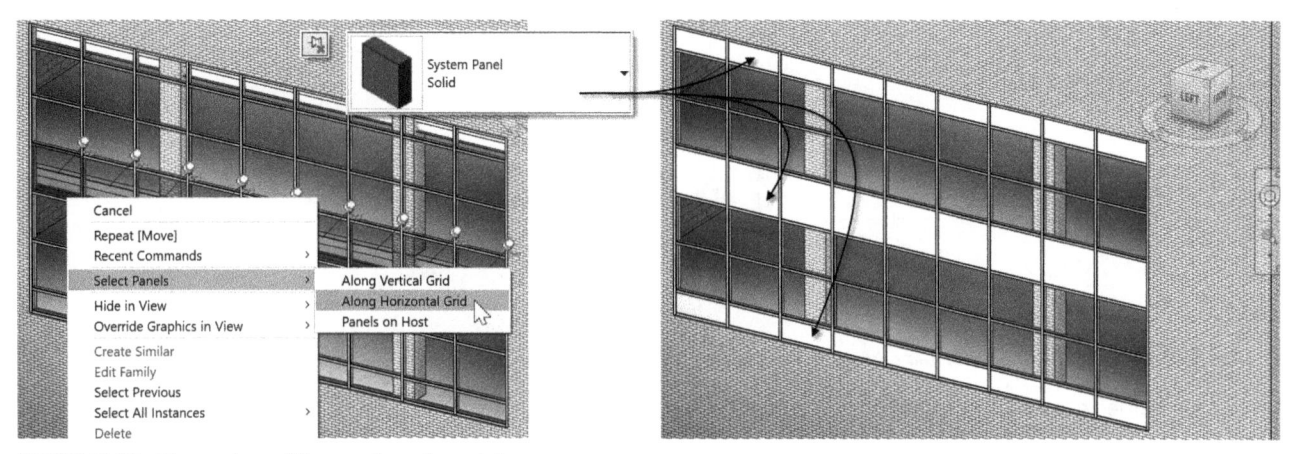

FIGURE 10.33 *Change the middle row of panels to solid*

MIRROR THE CURTAIN WALL

The other side of the building needs the same curtain wall.

1. Return to the *Level 2* floor plan view.

2. Delete the architectural columns on grids 2F and 3F.

3. On the Project Browser, double-click to open the *Level 3* plan view.

⇨ Delete the same two columns.

⇨ Return to the *Level 2* floor plan view.

4. Select the curtain wall and the architectural columns at grids 2A and 3A.

Keep in mind that the curtain wall segment is made up of many subparts. The whole curtain wall is represented by a blue dashed that will appear when you select it or pre-highlight it. Make sure you select this and not the individual internal components like the mullions or panels.

⇨ On the Modify | Walls tab, click the Mirror – Draw Axis tool.

On the Options Bar, verify that the "Copy" check box is selected.

5. Snap to the midpoint of the floor slab curve (in the center of the plan) and then drag straight up and click again (see the left side of Figure 10.34).

• Revit Essentials for Architecture •

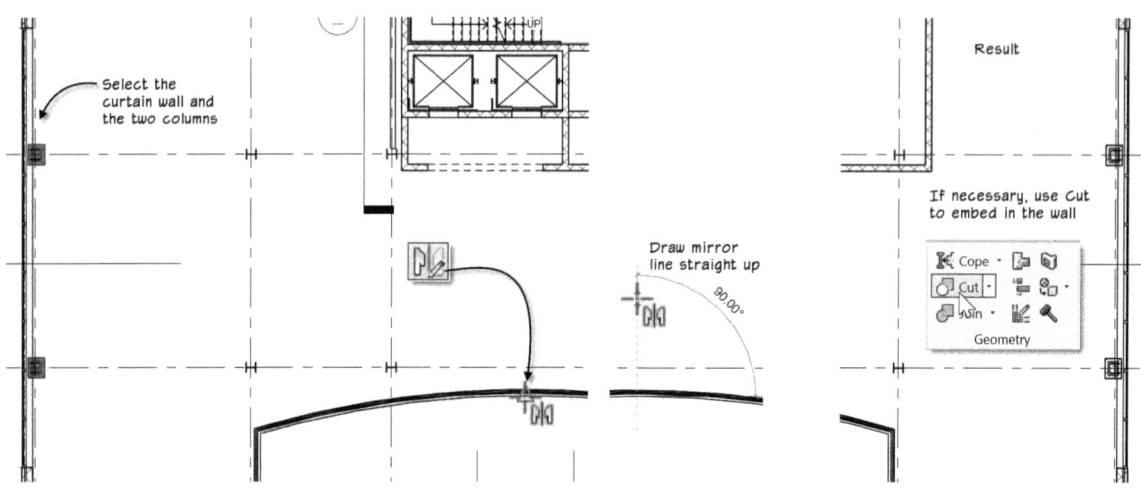

FIGURE 10.34 *Mirror the curtain wall and columns to the other side of the model*

6. In the *Level 3* floor plan, mirror the two columns.

The curtain wall will mirror over to the other side of the plan. If it automatically cuts the wall, then skip the next steps; otherwise continue.

USING CUT GEOMETRY

You can perform the next action in either a plan or 3D view. If you mirrored directly at the midpoint, this procedure should not be necessary.

1. With the new (mirrored) curtain wall still selected, on the Modify | Walls tab, click the Cut tool.
2. At the "First Pick" prompt, click the vertical wall on the right.
    ⇨ At the "Second Pick" prompt, click the mirrored curtain wall.
3. On the Project Browser, double-click to open the *{3D}* view.
    ⇨ Orbit the model and study the results.

ADD WINDOWS

Some basic punched windows will help complete the masonry portions of the façade. We will add ordinary punched windows to the masonry walls on the first and fourth floors on all four sides of the building. On the second and third floors, we will add windows to the north and south walls only (the ones without curtain walls).

1. Open the *Level 1* floor plan.
2. Add some windows on east and west walls.

    There are only a casement and double-hung families currently loaded. Load in the family named: *Window-Fixed.rfa* [*M_ Window-Fixed.rfa*] instead. Choose a few of the larger sizes. The file is provided in the *Chapter10* folder if you do not have it in your copy of Revit.

    ⇨ Add windows to one side and then mirror them to the other side.

3. Add one window to each of the short walls on the front of the building (south wall) and about three on the rear (north wall).

As we have done with other layout tasks, place the windows in general locations first, and then use dimensions to fine-tune their placement. The easiest way to do this is to create a continuous string of dimensions. This will make moving individual windows quick and easy.

Developing the Exterior Skin | 433

4. On the QAT, click the Aligned Dimension tool.

   ⇨ On the Options Bar, from the Pick list, choose: **Entire Walls** and then click the Options button next to it.

   ⇨ In the "Auto Dimension Options" dialog, check Openings and choose Widths and then click OK.

5. Select one of the exterior walls to dimension it and click a point outside the building to place the dimension.

   ⇨ Select a window, on the Options Bar, click the Activate Dimensions button and then edit the dimension values that activate to move the window (see Figure 10.35).

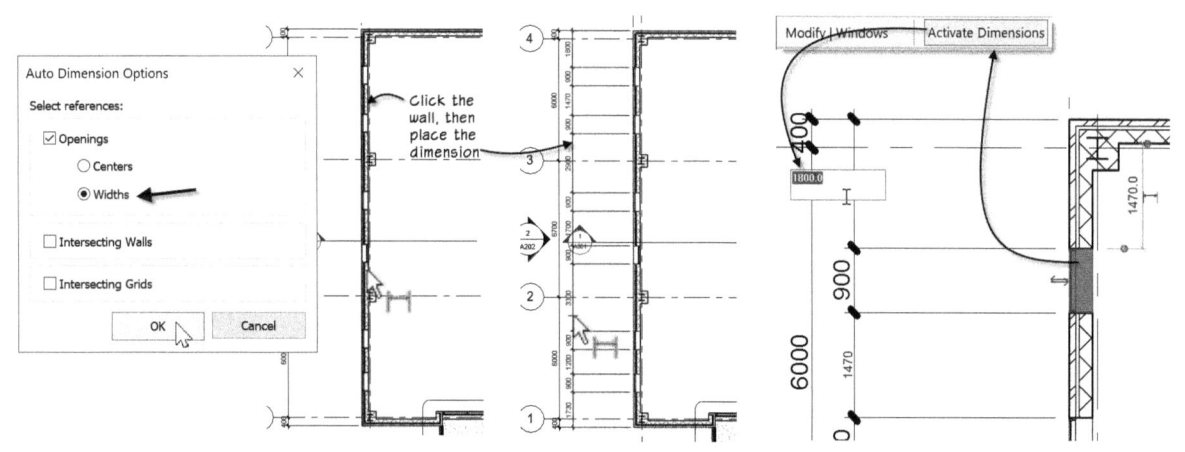

FIGURE 10.35 *Add a string of dimensions including the window openings and use it to move the windows*

6. Repeat for the other exterior walls.

7. Check your progress in the elevation views as you work and adjust as needed.

The exact number and location of windows is left to the reader as an exercise. If you would like them to fall on brick modules, open an elevation views such as *West*. Use the Align tool to shift the brick patterns to align with the major geometry. To do this, use the edge of geometry as the alignment reference and then click any line in the pattern to shift it. In this way, the brick coursing will be more logical, and you can use it to help you position the windows. You can add, dimension and move windows in elevation as appropriate. You can also fine-tune the position of the embedded curtain wall with dimensions and the align tool as well.

8. Back in the *Level 1* plan, select all the windows you added.

9. Keep all the windows selected and then copy them to the clipboard.

   ⇨ Open the *Level 4* plan and from the Paste drop down, choose: **Aligned to Current View**.

10. Select only the windows in the north and south walls.

    ⇨ Copy them to clipboard again, but this time, **Paste > Aligned to Selected Levels**.

    ⇨ Choose Levels 2 and 3 and then click OK.

MASONRY WINDOW SETTINGS

The window families included with Revit can be used in masonry or stud construction. When using them in masonry walls, there are some settings on the Properties palette that we can configure to make them coordinate with the brick wall better. The Window Inset parameter shifts the window within the thickness of the all. The Wall Closure settings work together with the wrapping features explored above in the "Adding Wall Returns and Wraps" topic on page 412. Finally, we can control if trim should display on the interior and exterior.

1. Right-click on any window and choose: **Select All Instances > In Entire Project**.

This command selects all elements of the same type either in the current view or the entire project. We chose the entire project option here since we want all windows; including those on the upper floors that we copied. If you changed the types of some of your windows, you could instead select all elements in 3D, then use the filter tool to select only the windows.

- For the Window Inset, input: **3 1/2"** [**80**] and then under Graphics
- Uncheck Exterior Trim Visibility.
- For Exterior Wall Closure, input: **5 1/2"** [**140**].

   To see the effect of wall closure, you must also edit the wall type.

2. Select any exterior wall and then click the Edit Type button.

- Under Construction, for Wrapping at Inserts, choose: **Exterior** and then click OK.

3. Study the results of all these changes in the {3D} view (see Figure 10.36).

FIGURE 10.36 *Add windows to the other floors*

4. Save the project.

EXPLORE CURTAIN WALL TYPE PROPERTIES

There are three curtain wall types provided in the out-of-the-box templates. The simplest one we used above and is named: **Curtain Wall 1** [**Curtain Wall**]. It has no built-in divisions and defaults to a single continuous panel of glass. We used this one in the first exercise at the start of the chapter and were able to add curtain grid lines and mullions manually. The next type is slightly more complex including a default grid spacing in both the horizontal and vertical dimensions. This type is named: **Exterior Glazing**. We used this one in Chapter 5 to create the front façade feature. Finally, we have the type used in the previous sequence: **Storefront**. As we have seen, not only does this one include predefined grid spacing but also adds mullions on all edges automatically (see Figure 10.37).

Developing the Exterior Skin | 435

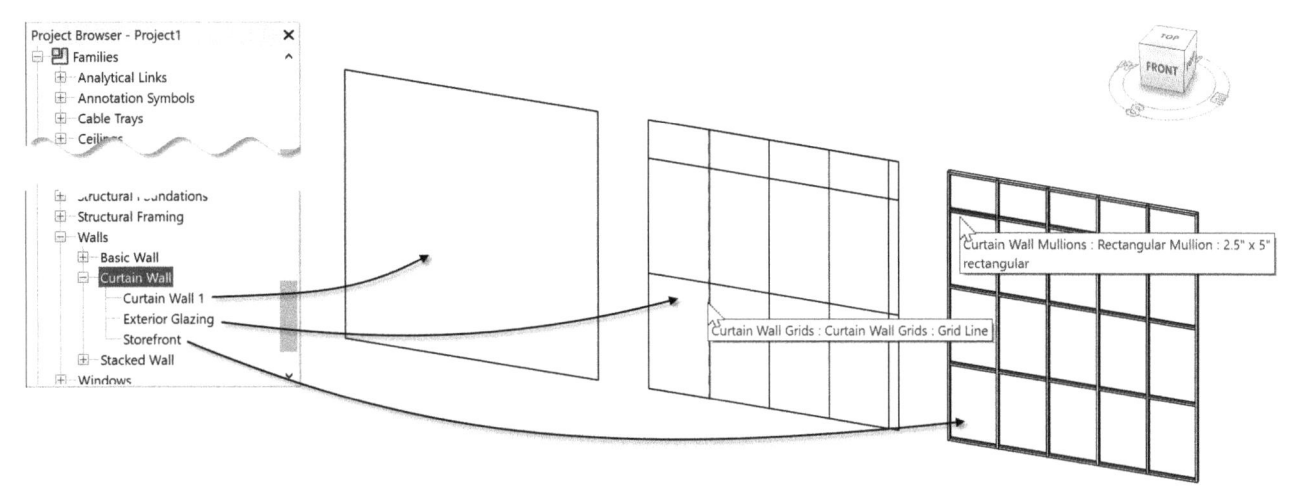

FIGURE 10.37 *Three curtain wall types are included in the out-of-the-box template files*

1. On the Project Browser, locate the *Families* branch and click the plus (+) sign icon next to it to expand it.

⇨ Click to expand *Walls* next, then *Curtain Wall* (see the left side of Figure 10.37).

Each of the types currently resident in the existing project will appear in the tree listing. Note that in addition to the three shown in the figure there is the one we created in the previous exercise. You can use the steps that we followed in the "Adjust the Curtain Grid Spacing" topic on page 429 above to modify and duplicate a type. Or you can duplicate and modify types directly from the Project Browser instead. You can also add an instance of a type to the model directly from here as well by dragging and dropping or using the right-click options.

2. Right-click on Storefront and choose: **Type Properties**.

This takes you directly to the "Type Properties" dialog for this type. This dialog is like any other "Type Properties" dialog. Following is a brief description of some of the important parameters seen here.

Under the "Construction" grouping are the following parameters:

Function—Since curtain walls are a wall family, they have the same list of "Functions" as other walls. We can create curtain wall types that are either "Exterior" or "Interior." (Most of the other Functions like "Foundation" or "Retaining Wall" would typically not be used for curtain walls.)

Automatically Embed—When this check box is selected, the curtain wall will attempt to embed itself automatically within another wall like the one that we created in the previous exercise. When this function is off you can still use the Cut tool to embed a curtain wall within another wall manually.

Curtain Panel—This parameter gives a list of all possible panel types that are loaded into the project. Choose the default to be used for the curtain wall here. All panels in a curtain wall will use this type initially and they will appear pinned (as we saw above) when selected. You can always unpin them and override the panel type used for one or more panels in the specific instance of the curtain wall element in the model (we also did this above).

Join Condition—Earlier in the "Edit Mullion Joins" topic on page 424, we edited the default join condition used by mullions. You assign the default condition to a curtain wall type here. Several options appear. You can make the horizontal or the vertical continuous, make the border continuous, or choose combinations of these.

Beneath the "Vertical Grid Pattern" and the "Horizontal Grid Pattern" groupings are three parameters each:

Layout and Spacing—Layout choices include "None," "Fixed Distance," "Fixed Number," "Maximum Distance" and "Minimum Spacing." When None is chosen the curtain wall will include a single panel across the entire horizontal or vertical dimension as appropriate (this is like **Curtain Wall 1 [Curtain Wall]**). Fixed distance will create curtain

• Revit Essentials for Architecture •

grid lines using the spacing indicated by the "Spacing" parameter. There may be panel space left over when using this option. Maximum Distance is similar in that it specifies the largest that the spacing can become but will size all bays equally up to the size indicated. In this case, there will not be any left over. Minimum spacing is the same except that it controls the smallest that the spacing can become. Choosing the "Fixed Number" option will disable the "Spacing" parameter. The number of bays is an instance parameter. This means that when you choose the "Fixed Number" option, you must then assign the number of bays individually to each instance of the curtain wall. You cannot do it globally in the "Type Properties" dialog, nor can you set a default here.

Adjust for Mullion Size—This parameter adjusts the location of curtain grid lines to maintain equal sized panels even when mullion sizes vary. When not checked, Spacing is measured from curtain grids.

Beneath the "Vertical Mullions" and "Horizontal Mullions" groupings, you can choose from a list of available mullion families to use for the Borders and the Interior Mullions. These mullions will be created automatically and will be pinned to the curtain wall as it is created (see above). You can unpin any mullion, as we did in the exercise above, and assign an alternate type as design needs dictate.

The remaining parameters are the standard identity data properties that we have seen in other object types. These are mostly used when doing quantities, schedules, and takeoffs.

3. Click Cancel to dismiss the dialog without making changes.

CREATE A NEW CURTAIN WALL TYPE

If your design calls for it, you can create your own custom curtain wall type. The type can control the spacing horizontally and vertically and which mullions and panels are used. For more customization potential, combine techniques of both type and instance approaches.

PREPARING FOR CURTAIN WALL CUSTOMIZATION

Earlier we hide the temporary front façade design while we worked on other aspects of the exterior building shell. We are now ready to revisit that design and build a custom curtain wall type for the front façade. So, let's restore the visibility of the hidden elements in the 3D view.

1. Switch to or open the default 3D view ({3D}).

⇨ Close inactive views.

2. On the View Control Bar, click the small lightbulb icon to enter Reveal Hidden Elements mode.

⇨ Select the three hidden curtain walls on the front of the building (use CTRL key or chain select) and then on the ribbon, click the Unhide Element button (or press EU) (see Figure 10.38).

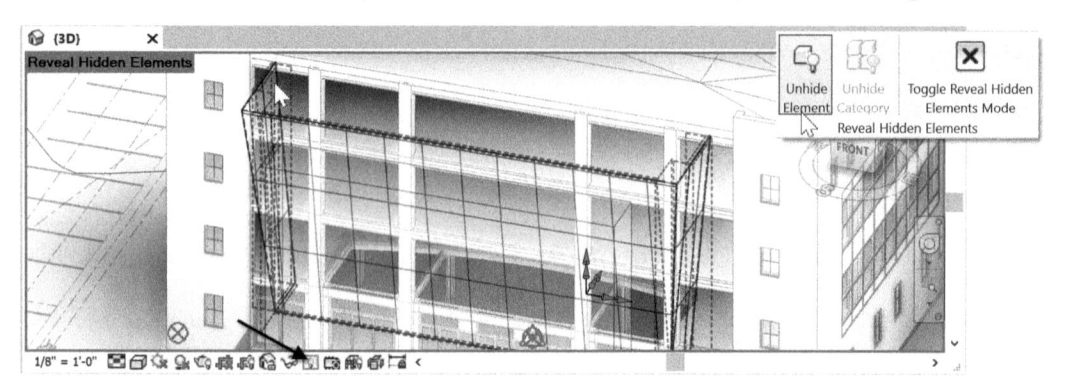

FIGURE 10.38 *Unhide the front façade curtain walls*

Developing the Exterior Skin | 437

⇨ On the ribbon, click the Toggle Reveal Hidden Elements Mode button
(or click the same button on the View Control Bar again).

Let's start with some basic modifications to these walls. The slope is a little too steep and the walls project out far from the main building. Let's adjust these things.

3. Select the three curtain walls again.

⇨ On the Properties palette, change the Angle from Vertical setting to: **3°**.

4. From the Project Browser, open the *Level 2* plan view.

Let's use the straight edge of the patio, just above the ramps, as the extreme point of the slope of this façade feature. Currently, it starts near this location and slopes out much further as it rises up the building. The easiest way to use this line is to add a reference plane.

5. On the Architecture tab, on the Work Plane panel, click the Reference Plane button (or press RP).

⇨ Draw a reference plane along the straight edge of the patio (see the left side of Figure 10.39).

You can draw it nearby first, and then use align to snap it back to the patio edge.

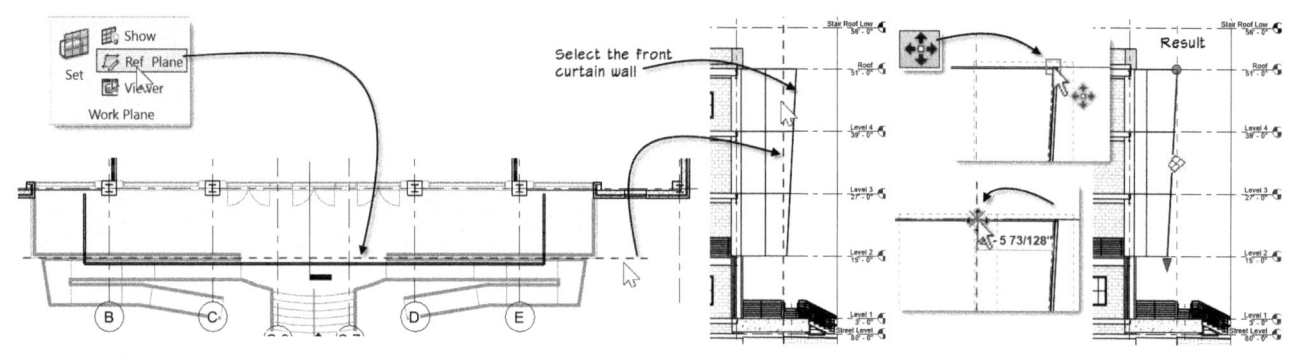

FIGURE 10.39 *Add a reference plane along the edge of the patio*

6. From the Project Browser, open the *Transverse* section view.

Notice how the reference plane appears here running vertically through the sloping façade (see the middle of Figure 10.39).

7. Use the move tool (MV) to move the sloping curtain wall in the section view from its topmost endpoint to the intersection with the new reference plane (see the right side of Figure 10.39).

8. Return to the *Level 2* plan.

⇨ Select the short slanted curtain walls parallel to Grid B.

⇨ Snap its endpoint to the face of the column at Grid B.

⇨ Repeat for the slanted curtain wall at Grid E (see Figure 10.40).

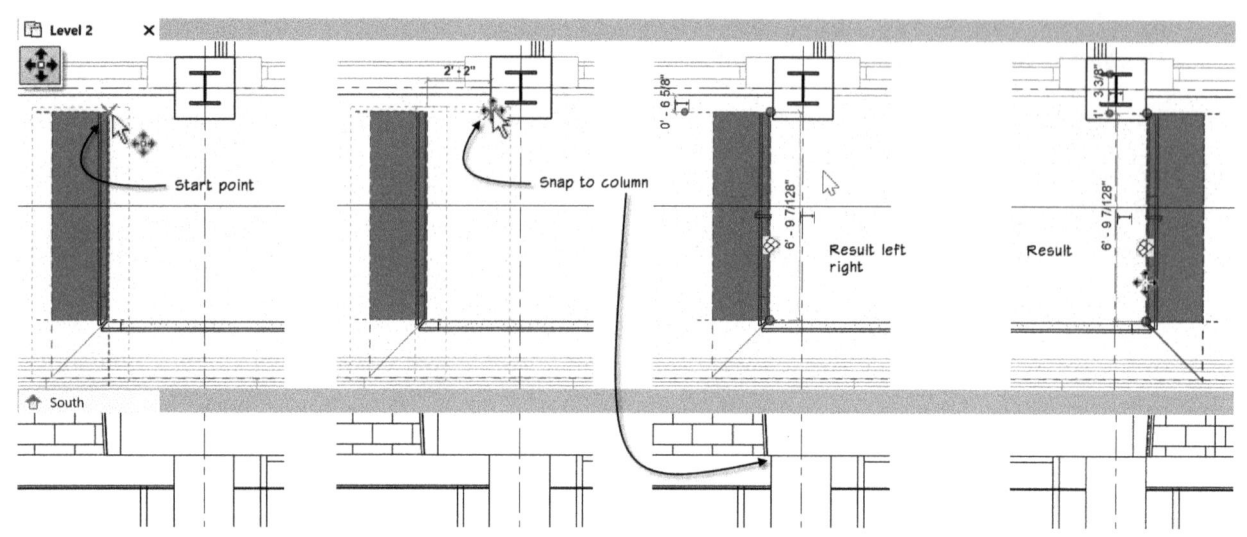

FIGURE 10.40 *Move the bottom edge of the slanted curtain walls to the columns*

9. On the Project Browser, double-click to open the *South* elevation view.

⇨ Tile just the *South* elevation and the *Transverse* section and close all other view tabs.

CONFIGURE BASIC TYPE SETTINGS

1. Select the three slanted curtain walls onscreen and on the Properties palette, click the Edit Type button.

⇨ Click the Duplicate button and name the new type: **Front Façade**.

2. Beneath the "Construction" grouping, choose: **System Panel: Glazed** for the Curtain Panel.

⇨ Change the "Join Condition" to: **Horizontal Grid Continuous**.

3. For the "Vertical Grid" pattern, verify that the "Layout" type is set to: **Fixed Distance**.

⇨ Set the "Spacing" to: **11'-0"** [**3300**].

4. For the "Horizontal Grid" pattern, verify that the "Layout" type is set to: **Fixed Distance**. And that the "Spacing" is set to: **12'-0"** [**3600**] (see Figure 10.41)

Developing the Exterior Skin | 439

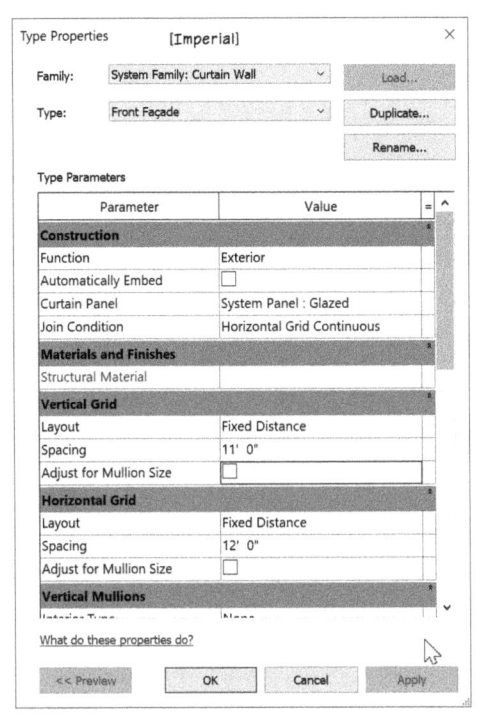

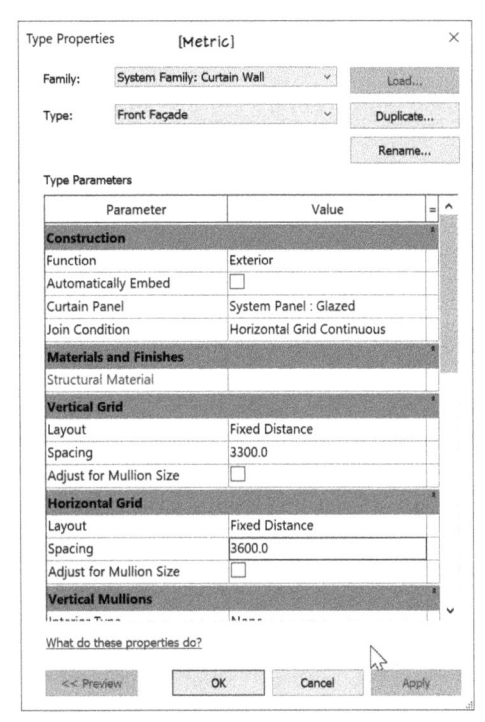

FIGURE 10.41 *Configure the grid pattern parameters for the new curtain system type*

5. Click OK to accept and apply the changes.

As we can see, the new spacing has been applied to the curtain wall in both directions. It may be easier to see the pattern clearly if we hide the column grid lines and section marks.

6. Select one column grid line, hold the CTRL key and select one section.
   ⇨ On the Modify tab, on the View panel, click the Hide in View button and then choose: **Hide Category**.

You should now be able to see the pattern clearly in the elevation view.

7. Save the project.

ADD HORIZONTAL MULLIONS

We now have the overall horizontal and vertical spacing established. Next, we'll address the shape and size of the mullions. In this sequence, we will edit the horizontal mullions to represent spandrels and the vertical Mullions to represent pilasters. We need to define a few new mullion types and then apply them to the horizontal and vertical orientations of the curtain wall. An easy way to define these types is on the Project Browser.

> **NOTE:** Curtain walls, curtain systems, and sloped glazing all use the same mullion definitions.

1. On the Project Browser, locate the *Families* branch, and click the plus (+) sign icon next to it to expand it.
   ⇨ Click to expand *Curtain Wall Mullions*, then *Rectangular Mullion*.
2. Right-click on: **2.5" x 5" rectangular [50 x 150mm]** and choose: **Duplicate**.
   ⇨ For the name, type: **Spandrel** and then press ENTER.
3. Right-click on: **Spandrel** and then choose: **Type Properties** (see Figure 10.42).

• Revit Essentials for Architecture •

440 | Chapter 10

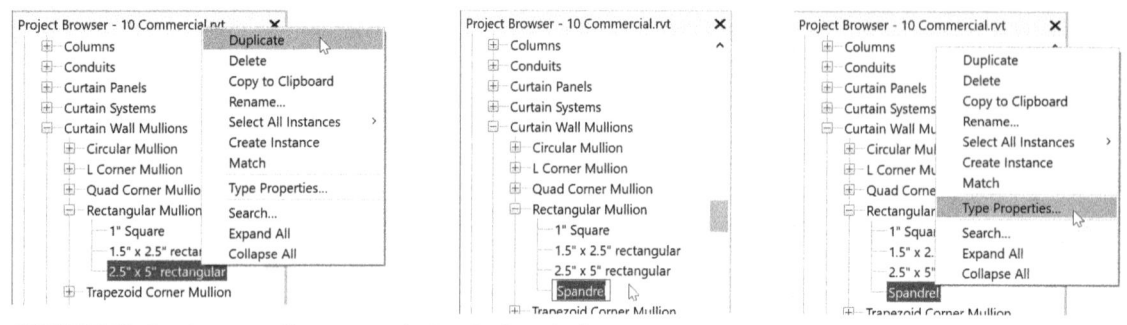

FIGURE 10.42 *Duplicate a mullion type on the Families branch of Project Browser*

There are several parameters in the "Type Properties" dialog for mullions. Let's take a look at several of them (see Figure 10.43).

Angle—Use this constraint to rotate the mullion relative to the curtain wall.

Offset—Input a positive or negative value here to shift the position of the Mullion in or out relative to the curtain wall.

Profile—The default shape for mullions is rectangular. Circular is also an option and you can create custom profile families that can be loaded into your project and then will appear in the list here.

Position—Similar to the Angle setting and used when Cross-Section is not vertical. The default option: **Perpendicular to Face** sets the mullion profile orientation parallel to the curtain wall and is useful in conditions where the surface is sloped, and you want the mullions to follow the slope. **Parallel to Ground** keeps the mullion horizontal regardless of the slope of the curtain wall.

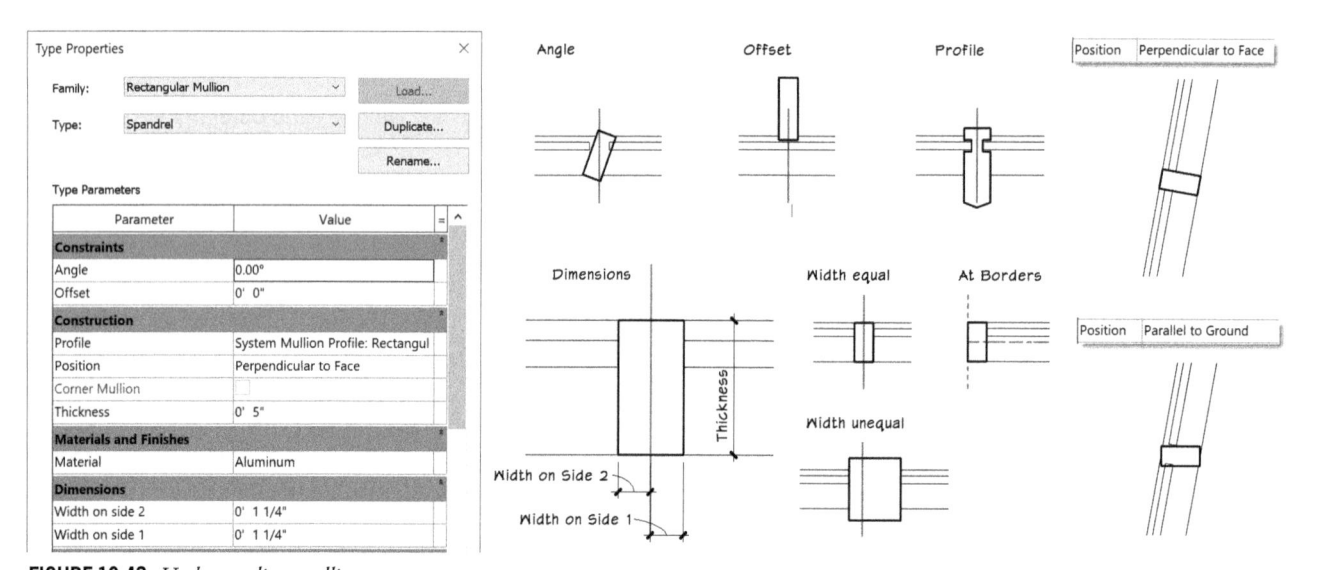

FIGURE 10.43 *Understanding mullion type parameters*

Corner Mullion—This check box indicates if the mullion defines a corner condition. This setting is read-only. You cannot make custom corner mullions (Not shown).

Thickness—This is the depth of the mullion as measured along its axis perpendicular to the curtain wall.

Material—You can choose a material for the mullion from the list of materials available in the project (Not shown).

Width on side 1 and Width on side 2—Unlike the "Thickness" parameter listed above, width is divided into two separate width parameters. If you set both parameters to the same value, then your mullion will be centered on the

• The Aubin Academy •

Developing the Exterior Skin | 441

curtain grid line. If you specify different settings, you will shift the mullion relative to the grid line making it off-center. In either case, the overall width will be the total of both settings.

At the borders, the total width is offset to the inside of the curtain wall regardless of the width on side 1 or 2 setting.

4. In the "Type Properties" dialog, for "Thickness" input: **1'-0"** [**300**].

⇨ For the "Width on side 1" and "Width on side 2" parameters, input: **1'-0"** [**300**].

Remember that the total width is the sum of both the "Width on side 1" and "Width on side 2" parameters, so in this case, this makes the mullion 2'-0" [600] wide.

⇨ Click OK to dismiss the "Type Properties" dialog and return to the model.

The mullion you just created will not appear in the model yet. All we did was create a new mullion type. We have not used it in the actual model yet.

5. Select the curtain wall facing us onscreen in elevation (be sure to select the curtain wall and not the mullions or grid lines—use the TAB if necessary). Choose Edit Type from the Properties palette.

6. Beneath the "Horizontal Mullions" grouping, choose: **Rectangular Mullion : Spandrel** for each of the Mullion conditions: "Interior Type, "Border 1 Type," and "Border 2 Type."

⇨ Click OK to see the result.

⇨ If a warning appears, click OK to dismiss it (see Figure 10.44).

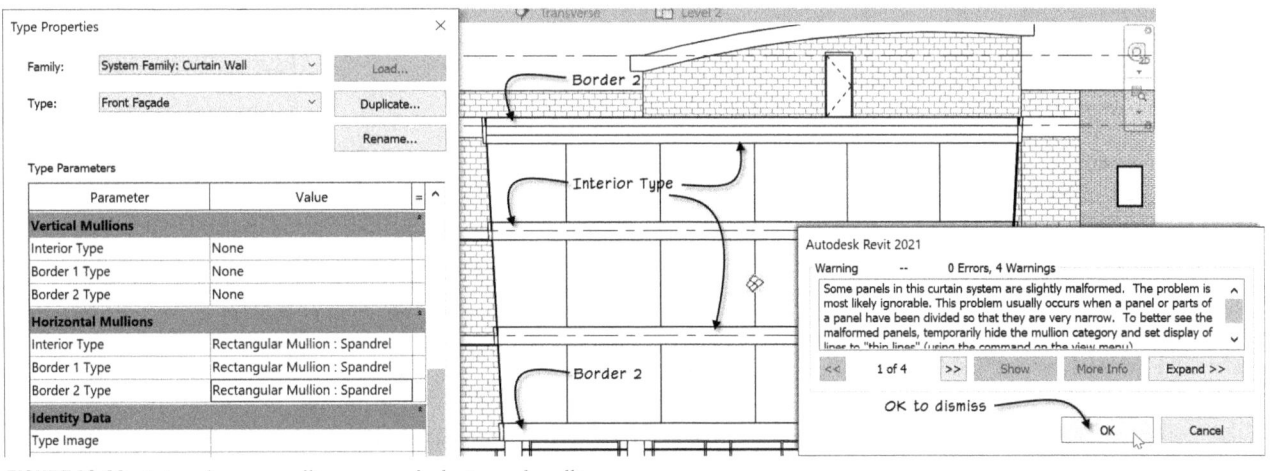

FIGURE 10.44 *Assign the new mullion type to the horizontal mullions*

The warning indicates that panels that are very narrow can be the cause. Since our curtain wall is slanted 3°, this likely has caused some very small panels at the edges. You'll also note that we have two mullions near the top; the border partially overlaps the highest interior mullion. We'll address this below.

ADD VERTICAL MULLIONS

Repeating nearly the same process, we can edit the vertical mullions. We also need a new type here.

1. On the Project Browser, return to the *Families > Curtain Wall Mullions > Rectangular Mullion* branch again.

2. Right-click on **2.5" x 5" rectangular** [**50 x 150mm**] and choose: **Duplicate**.

⇨ For the name type: **Pilaster** and then press ENTER.

3. Right-click on **Pilaster** and then choose: **Type Properties**.

⇨ Set the "Thickness" to: **10"** [**250**].

• Revit Essentials for Architecture •

442 | Chapter 10

⇨ Set both "Width" parameters to: **5" [125]** and then click OK.

This will make a 10" [250] square pilaster mullion.

4. Return to the "Type Properties" dialog for the: **Front Façade** type again.

5. Beneath the "Vertical Mullions" grouping, for "Interior Type," choose: **Rectangular Mullion : Pilaster**.

⇨ Leave "Border 1 Type" and "Border 2 Type" set to: **None**.

⇨ Click Apply to see the changes.

Notice that the spandrels in the middle of the curtain system are continuous horizontally. This is because we configured horizontal grid as continuous in the type parameters above. However, you can see that the bottom (and possibly the top) border mullions are not continuous.

6. In the "Type Properties" dialog for the: **Front Façade** change the "Join Condition" to: **Border and Horizontal Grid Continuous**.

⇨ Click OK to see the result (see Figure 10.45).

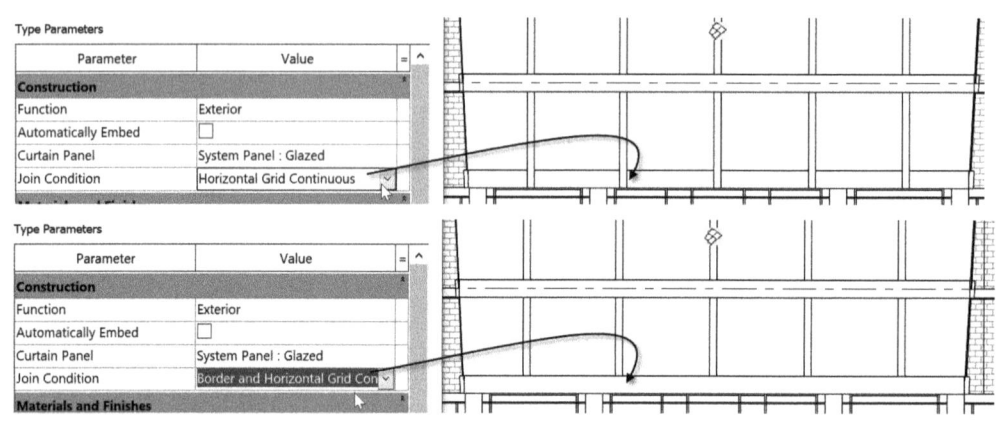

FIGURE 10.45 *Edit the join condition in type properties*

7. Save the model.

ADJUST MULLION POSITION

Take a close look at the curtain wall in the *Transverse* section view and you will note that the size of the horizontal bays is not equal. Notice that the level lines for Level 3 and Level 4 pass through the middle of the Spandrel mullions, but at Level 2 and the Roof they do not. Add some dimensions to double check things if you like. However, before you become concerned by how random the dimension values will seem, remember that our curtain walls are slanted 3° so this will affect our dimension values.

If you want to visualize this better, select the front curtain wall in the section view and change its Angle From Vertical to: 20°. You might get an error about malformed panels, click OK. Notice how the Spacing parameter for the horizontal grid lines (which locate the mullions) is measured along the angle, *not* vertically. This means that if we want the mullions to fall precisely relative to the level lines, we must perform a calculation. Fortunately for us, we can input many formulas directly into Revit. This includes many trigonometry functions which will be useful in this case. So, in this example, we know the vertical distance (this is our level to level height) and the angle (the slope of the wall). The trig function that can solve for this is the cosine.

Developing the Exterior Skin | 443

> **How do we know it is Cosine?**
>
> Many formulas can be input into input fields in Revit. This includes simple arithmetic to more advanced operations like logarithms, exponentiation and trigonometry functions. You can learn more about formulas and their syntax in the online help. Another resource is a popular post at the Revit Forum: **revitforum.org/showthread.php/1046-Revit-Formulas-for-quot-everyday-quot-usage**. A summary of the trigonometry functions is provided in the Appendix.

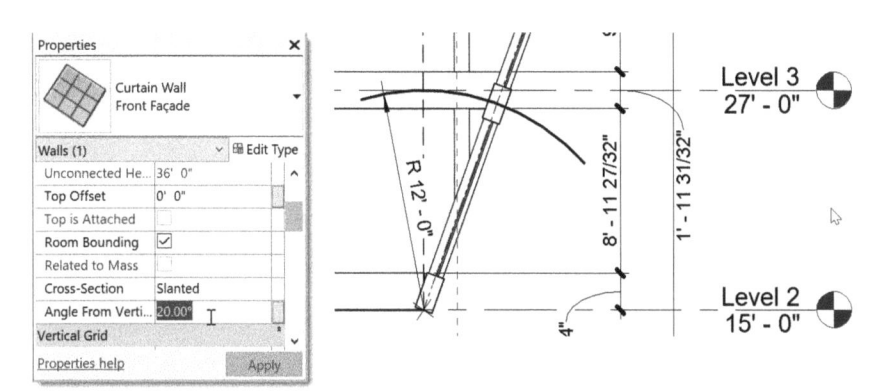

FIGURE 10.46 *To understand how the spacing values are applied, temporarily use a larger angle*

If you changed the angle of the curtain wall, set it back to 3° before continuing. In addition to calculating the distance required for the spacing of the horizontal bays, we will calculate and add top and bottom offsets to the curtain wall to compensate for the overlapping mullions at the border.

1. On the Project Browser, double-click to open the *South* elevation view.
2. Switch to the *South* View tab.
   ⇨ Highlight one curtain wall, press TAB and the click to chain select all three.
3. On the Properties palette, beneath Constraints, for Base Offset input: **=−1'-0"/cos(3)** [**=−300/cos(3)**].

You must include the equals (=) sign and the negative (−) sign. The equals sign is how we indicate that this is a formula that Revit should calculate. When you ENTER it, Revit will perform the calculation and input the value. Notice that the value will be only slightly larger than our input of **1'-0"** [**300**].

4. Use the same formula for the Top Offset, without the minus (make it a positive value) (see the left side of Figure 10.47).

This adjusts the curtain wall to the correct height, but now we have an extra Mullion occurring at the top and the Mullions at the middle floors are not centered on the Level lines anymore (see the middle panel of Figure 10.47). To correct this and get each of the Spandrel mullions centered on a level line, we need to shift the grid offset as we d id above in the "Adjust the Curtain Grid Spacing" topic on page 429. In the above referenced topic, we used the onscreen temporary dimensions. This time let's try the Properties palette.

5. Select all three curtain walls again (TAB as necessary).
   ⇨ On the Properties palette, beneath the "Horizontal Grid" grouping, input the same formula in the Offset: **=1'-0"/cos(3)** [**=300/cos(3)**] (see the right side of Figure 10.47).
   ⇨ In the warning that appears, click OK.

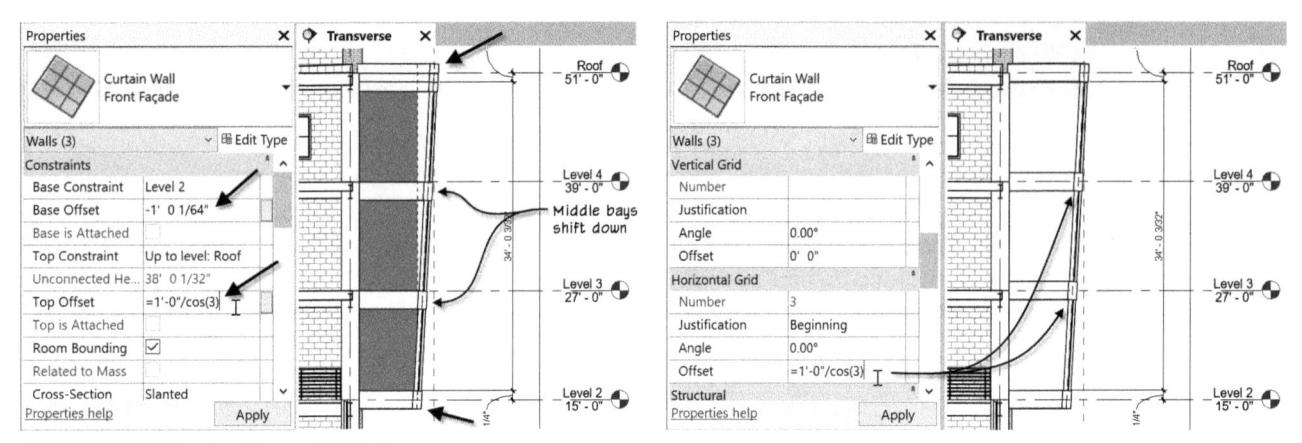

FIGURE 10.47 *Edit the offsets to shift the bays*

We still need to adjust the horizontal grid spacing (in the Type Properties) with one more formula.

6. Select any one of the three slanted curtain walls and then click Edit Type.

⇨ Beneath the Horizontal Grid grouping, for Spacing, input: =12' 0"/cos(3) [=300/cos(3)] and then click OK.

Let's make one small adjustment to the Spandrel mullion type.

7. Select any Spandrel mullion and then click Edit Type.

⇨ In the "Type Properties" dialog, beneath Construction, change the Position setting to: **Parallel to Ground** and then click OK (see Figure 10.48).

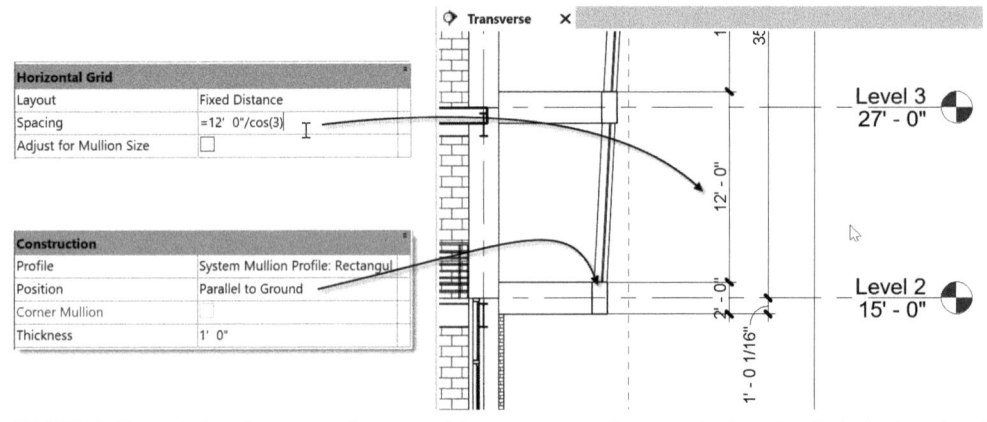

FIGURE 10.48 *Calculate the precise value required for spacing to get the spandrels aligned with the levels and make them parallel to the ground*

Looking at the *South* elevation, it appears that we now have a correctly sized and spaced Spandrel mullion at each level. However, if we were to investigate carefully (using a small crossing selection and the filter command), we would discover that there are two mullions at each location along the top and bottom edges. The reason for this has to do with the difference in how the border mullions are applied vs. the interior ones. Refer back to Figure 10.43 above and look at the "At Borders" item compared to the "With Equal" item. Interior mullions will their two width parameters applied to either side of the grid line. Border mullions will apply their entire width inside the edges of the curtain wall. So, while the top and bottom offsets have compensated for this we have ended up with two extra grid lines that are not needed.

8. Edit the Type Properties of the: **Front Façade** curtain wall type again.

⇨ Beneath Horizontal Grid, change the Layout to: **None** and then click OK.

A Revit warning will appear. The message indicates that type generated gridlines have become "non-associated." This means that the horizontal curtain grids currently in the model are no longer being controlled by the curtain wall type. You have two choices. If you simply click OK, the curtain grids will remain in the model but will no longer be pinned. The other option is to click the Delete Gridline button and remove them. This would also remove the mullions attached to those gridlines. We do not want to lose the two horizontal grids in the middle (at levels 2 and 3), so we'll click OK to dismiss the warning and not delete anything.

⇨ In the Revit Warning dialog, click the OK button (see Figure 10.49).

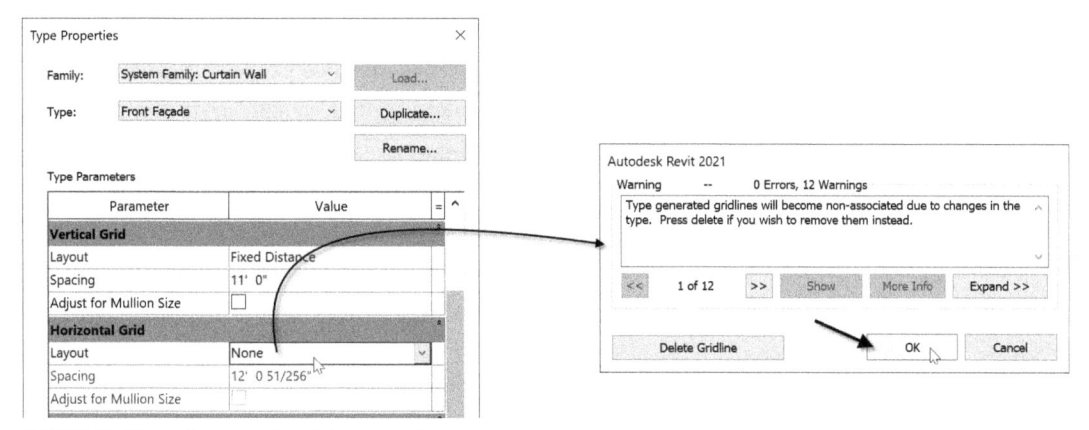

FIGURE 10.49 *Set horizontal grid layout to None*

The result of this change was to decouple the horizontal grids from the type. This means we can now individually select them and modify or delete them.

9. Click above the roof between column grid B and C and drag down and to the left slightly to just below the first the horizontal mullion at the Roof level (crossing selection) (see the left side of Figure 10.50).

   Be sure to only select the horizontal mullion and its underlying curtain grid, not any vertical ones.

   ⇨ On the ribbon, click the Filter button.

   Verify that the Curtain Wall Grids category is included and shows a Count of *only* 1. If it doesn't, try the selection again.

10. Click the Check None button, check only the Curtain Wall Grids check box and then click OK.

    ⇨ Press the DELETE key to delete this curtain grid and its mullions.

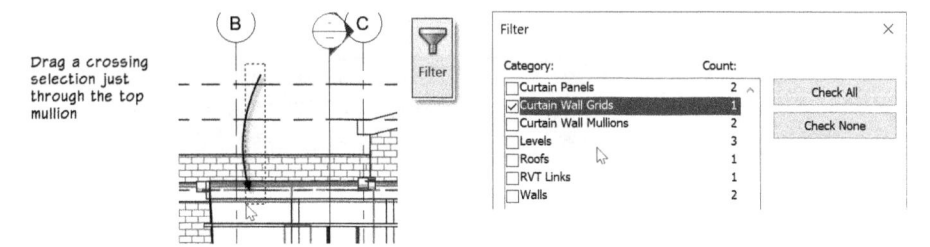

FIGURE 10.50 *Select just the top curtain grid and then delete*

If you would like to test that you no longer have double mullions, select one of the mullions and hide it with Temporary Hide/Isolate. When you are satisfied that there is only one mullion in each location, you can reset the Temporary Hide/Isolate.

11. Repeat this process to delete the curtain grid line at the two side walls (open another elevation or the 3D view to assist) and also the ones at bottom of the curtain wall at Level 2 on all three walls as well.

446 | Chapter 10

SUB-DIVIDE CURTAIN WALL BAYS

We can use virtually any of the techniques that we have covered so far to sub-divide the curtain wall that we have into smaller bays.

1. Continue in the *South* elevation view.

Our design currently has six bays—four equal ones in the center and two slightly smaller ones (that taper) at the ends. Remember the fact that the centered pattern is a function of the element's instance properties (as configured back in Chapter 5 in the "Slanted Walls" topic on page 168), and not something that we can set in the type. The spacing of the vertical bays was determined by the type (above in the "Configure Basic Type Settings" topic on page 438) and is at this point rather large. There are a few ways we can sub-divide these panels into smaller ones. We could return to the type, but you can only have one spacing for the entire curtain wall. So, if you want to vary the spacing, you must use another option. The next possibility will be by manually adding grid lines as we did with the curtain wall entrance at the start of the chapter. Finally, we can build custom panels that contain their own divisions. We'll see an example below.

2. On the Architecture tab, on the Build panel, click the Curtain Grid tool.

    ⇨ Move the pointer near the left edge of the curtain wall.

    A grid line and temporary dimensions will appear.

    ⇨ Using the temporary dimensions, click to create a horizontal grid line one-third from the top (see Figure 10.51).

    A tooltip may appear onscreen at your cursor, but you can also watch the Statues Bar as shown in the figure for a message indicating that you are at one third.

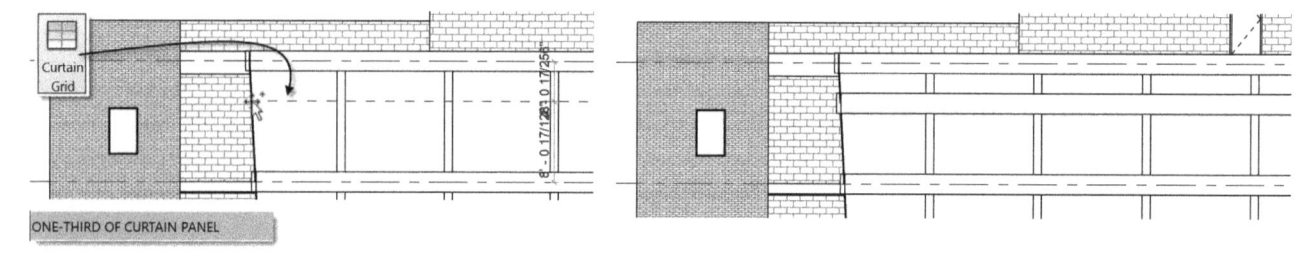

FIGURE 10.51 *Create a grid line that divides the bay at the top third mark*

> **TIP:** To get the tooltips to show onscreen at the cursor, you must have Tooltip Assistance set to at least Normal in the Options dialog. To open Options, choose it from the File menu.

Notice that the new grid line automatically creates mullions in the Spandrel type. It would be better to use something a little less "heavy" for these intermediate mullions. In fact, let's make a new mullion type for these horizontal bands.

3. On the Project Browser, expand the *Families > Curtain Wall Mullions > Rectangular Mullion* branch (as we did above).

    ⇨ Right-click on **2.5" x 5" rectangular [50 x 150mm]** and choose: **Duplicate**.

    ⇨ For the name, type: **Horizontal Band** and then press ENTER.

4. Right-click on **Horizontal Band** and then choose: **Type Properties**.

    ⇨ Set the "Thickness" to: **1'-6" [450]**.

    ⇨ Set both the "Width" parameters to: **2" [50]** and then click OK.

    ⇨ Set the Position to: **Parallel to Ground**.

• The Aubin Academy •

Developing the Exterior Skin | 447

        This will make a 4" x 18" [100 × 450] band mullion.

5. Pre-highlight one of the new Mullions (added automatically above to the new grid line), right-click, and choose: **Select Mullions** > **On Gridline**.

This is a handy way to select an entire row of mullions very quickly. Notice that when these mullions highlight, that they are all pinned to the curtain wall. Before we can assign the new **Horizontal Band** type to them, we must unpin them. You can click each of the pushpin icons individually, but this would be very tedious. Instead, use the tool on the ribbon.

⇨   On the Modify | Curtain Wall Mullions tab, click the Unpin tool (or press UP).

6. From the Type Selector, choose: **Horizontal Band**.

7. Repeat this process to add horizontal grid lines and band mullions to the other two floors as well.

8. Using the TAB key to carefully select, or open the {3D} view and repeat the process to add Horizontal Band mullions on the other two (small) faces of the curtain walls. You can do the entire process in 3D. Orbit the model as required.

Check the results in the section too. If you like, you can shift the new mullions relative to the plane of the curtain wall. This is the Offset parameter in the mullion type, and it takes either a positive or negative number. A value of 3" [75] gives a nice result. You only need to select one Horizontal Band mullion to make this change. Since it is a type parameter, it will apply to all of them.

9. Save the project.

SWAP PANEL TYPES

An alternative way that we can subdivide bays is to insert a panel type that is already subdivided. We saw one way to do this above in the "Using a Wall Type for a Panel" topic on page 425 where we embedded a curtain wall type (with its own type-based division spacing) in as a panel. For this example, we'll use a custom panel family included with the dataset for this chapter. In the next chapter, we'll learn how this custom panel family was built.

        Continue in the {3D} view or the *South* elevation.

1. On the Insert tab, on the Load from Library, click the Load Family button.

⇨   Browse to the *Chapter10* folder, select the *Curtain Panel.rfa* [*Curtain Panel_M.rfa*] file and then click Open.

2. Pre-highlight one of the larger panels along the bottom row of the curtain wall (see item 1 in Figure 10.52).

⇨   Right-click and choose: **Select Panels** > **Along Horizontal Grid** (item 2).

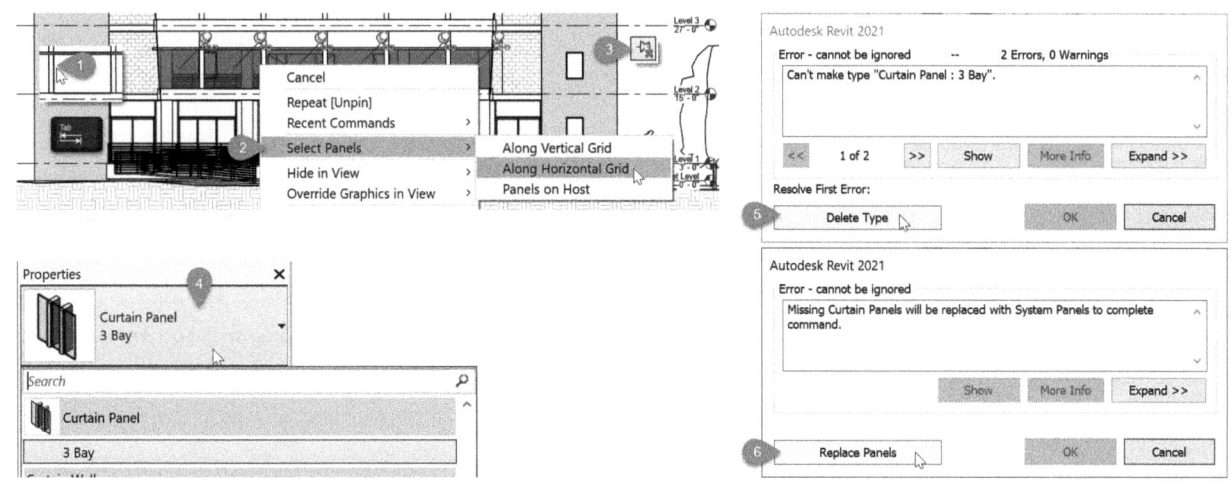

FIGURE 10.52 *Select one panel then right-click to select the entire row. Substitute the loaded panel type*

• Revit Essentials for Architecture •

⇨ On the Modify | Curtain Wall Mullions tab, click the Unpin tool (or press UP) (item 3).

3. From the Type Selector, choose: **Curtain Panel : 3 Bay [Curtain Panel_M : 3 Bay]** (item 4).

This will generate two warnings in succession. The first indicates that some panels cannot be made. If you look in your view window while this warning appears, you will see it is the two end bays. This is because the custom curtain panel we loaded can only be rectangular in shape. So, Revit will not allow it to be used in these locations.

⇨ Click the Delete Type button (item 5).

The wording of this button is a little misleading. We are not deleting the type, but rather the two instances that cannot be created. Upon clicking this, a new warning will appear. This one indicates that the two panels just deleted will be replaced with the default. This is required since you cannot have bays without a panel.

⇨ Click the Replace Panels button (item 6).

> **NOTE:** It is possible to have curtain panel families that are non-rectangular. But they must be created from the "adaptive" curtain panel template. The family loaded and used here did not use this template. Adaptive components are discussed in Chapter 17.

You should now have three equal divisions in each of the selected bays. The loaded family subdivides the bay equally. This is a simple illustration of what is possible. As stated above, we'll learn how to build this family in the next chapter. There are many other possibilities. A quick Google search will yield many examples that you can explore and even some you can download.

To repeat the process on the other two floors, you could repeat the same process but if you want to avoid the errors, you can select just the middle four bays (the rectangular ones) on each floor instead. You can use any selection technique to assist in this, but the fastest is just select the entire row as indicated above, and then using the SHIFT key, remove the two end bays from the selection. Unpin and then swap the type. Repeat for the final floor.

4. Replace the same four bays on each of the other floors and swap in the: **Curtain Panel: 3 Bay** type.

CORNER CONDITIONS AND MULLIONS

If you study the results in the 3D view (see Figure 10.53), you will see that the joints are not ideal. Revit does include several corner mullion families in common shapes. But experience shows that these do not work very well on slanted curtain walls. And even on vertical curtain walls, they have limited customization potential. You are welcome to try them (use the Mullion tool), but if you don't like the results, there are only a few user-definable settings. This is because corner mullions are system families and all their parameters and features are built-in to the system.

An alternative is to build something custom in the family editor. Doing so would be advanced, and while the subject of the family editor is the topic of the next chapter, time and space will not permit us from exploring such an example. For now, what we have is suitable for construction documents and basic visualization of design intent. We can always add view-specific detailing of the kind we will explore later in Chapter 12 to help convey proper intent and complete a documentation package. If after learning about the family editor (next chapter) and exploring the massing environment (in Chapter 17) you wish to try your hand at building a custom corner condition, you can return to the front façade and give it a try. But for now, our work on the front façade is complete.

FIGURE 10.53 *The completed front façade curtain system*

1. Save the model.

EDIT WALL PROFILES

A few more refinements remain to finalize the front façade of our commercial building. The most obvious one is closing in the building behind the front façade curtain wall.

1. On the Project Browser, double-click to open the *Level 2* floor plan.

2. On the Architecture tab, click the Wall tool.

    ⇨ On the Properties palette, change the Type to: **Exterior - EIFS on Mtl. Stud**.

    ⇨ Set the Location Line to: **Finish Face: Exterior**.

    Make sure that Base Constraint is set to: **Level 2**.

    ⇨ Change the Top Constraint to: Up to Level: **Roof**.

    ⇨ Change the Top Offset to: **4'-0"** [**1200**] and then click OK.

3. Start on the left side of the plan and click the first point at the intersection of the small vertical brick wall and column grid 1 (see Figure 10.54).

TIP: To force snapping to an intersection, type: SI.

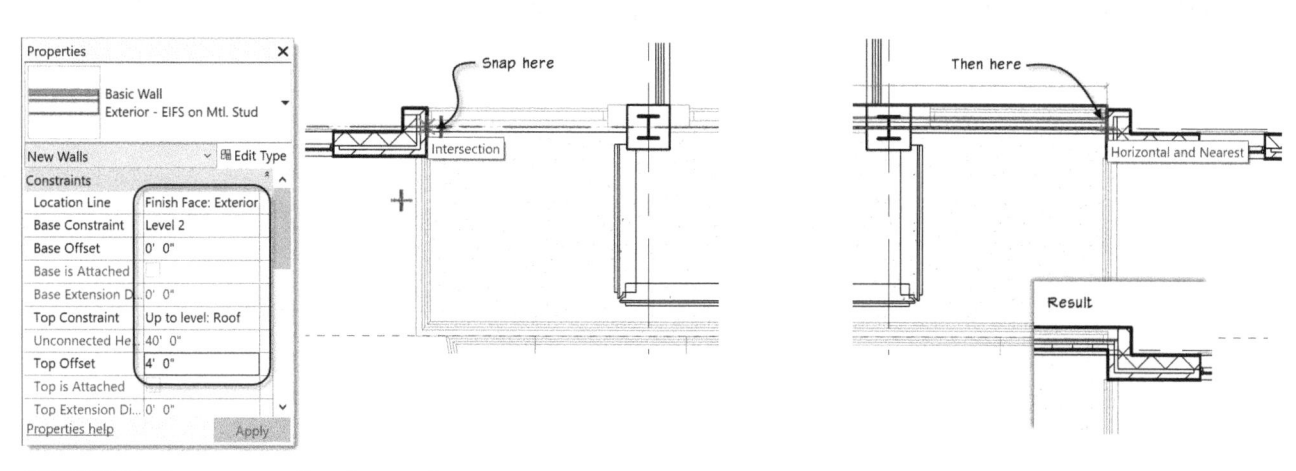

FIGURE 10.54 *Draw a new wall on the upper floors*

• Revit Essentials for Architecture •

450 | Chapter 10

> Make sure the wall thickness goes up (toward the building interior) and the exterior finish face is down. If the wall is oriented the other way, tap the SPACEBAR to flip it before clicking the second point.

⇨ Click the second point on the opposite side snapping to the intersection of the other short brick wall and the grid line.

You should now have a wall filling in the space that was previously open on the upper floors. However, it fills in the space behind our curtain system as well. To fix this, we'll use Edit Profile.

4. Return to the *South* elevation view.

5. Select the new wall and on the Modify | Walls tab, click the Edit Profile button (see item 1 in Figure 10.55).

⇨ On the Modify | Walls > Edit Profile tab, on the Draw panel, click the Pick Lines tool (item 2).

⇨ On the Options Bar, set the Offset to: **1'-6" [450]** (item 3). Highlight the Roof level line and move the mouse slightly as required to get the offset to occur below the line and then click to create a sketch line.

6. Remain in the Pick Lines tool and on the Options Bar, change the Offset to: **9" [225]** (item 4).

⇨ Highlight one of the sloping lines on side of the curtain wall. Click when it offsets to the inside. Repeat on the other side (item 5).

The figure shows the completed sketch, but your lines will not be trimmed yet.

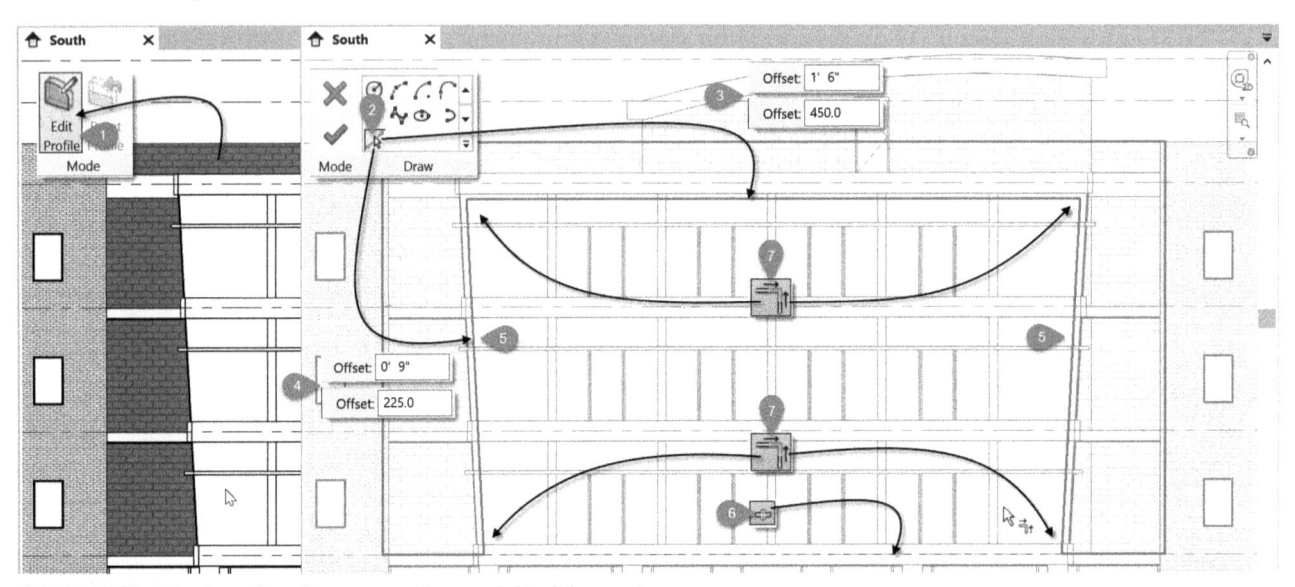

FIGURE 10.55 *Edit the wall profile to cut out the space behind the curtain system*

This will allow you to see the columns and roof to help create your sketch.

7. Using the Split Element tool (SL), split the bottom sketch line into two segments (item 6) (the figure shows the result after trimming; next step).

⇨ Split out the unnecessary segments at all corners to match the figure (item 7).

8. Click the Finish Edit Mode button to complete the sketch.

9. Add some punched windows to the new wall.

10. Edit the floor sketches on each level to make them conform to the new front façade shape (see Figure 10.56).

To edit a floor, select it and then click the Edit Boundary button. Modify the sketch at the front of the building to match the new shape of the front façade. It is easiest to select floors in a section view. When you do so and click Edit Boundary, you will be prompted to open a floor plan where you can edit the sketch.

> **IMPORTANT:** If Revit asks you if you want to attach walls to floor bottoms, answer: No. This would work well for interior partitions but not exterior shell walls. However, if you are prompted to join with the exterior walls and cut them, you can answer: Yes to this.

On the second floor, you can make a new floor for the small portion that sits under the Front Façade curtain wall or you can make it part of the existing floor sketch. Just be sure to leave the middle part open for a double volume space in the lobby below (You will end up with an inner loop inside the larger sketch). The roof is shown completed in Figure 10.56, but you should wait to edit it until we are done with the exterior shell and the stacked wall example below. Otherwise, you will likely have to redo it.

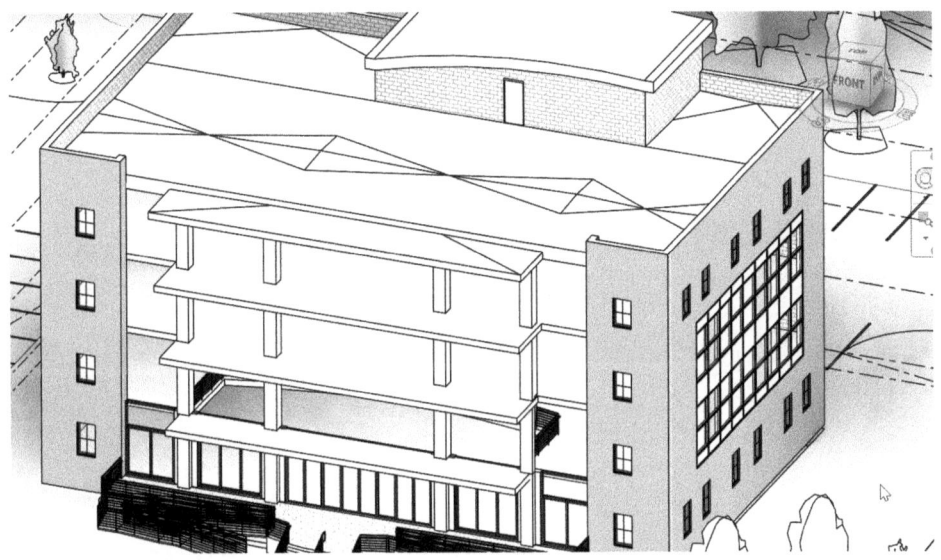

FIGURE 10.56 *Edit the sketch of the floors and roof to conform to the shape of the exterior shell (front façade hidden for clarity)*

11. Save the model.

If you wish to perform additional curtain wall explorations in this dataset, feel free to experiment now. For example, remember that since we have built all of our custom components in the curtain wall design as types, you can reuse them in other curtain walls and systems and any edits you make at the type level will apply throughout the model. For example, try varying the sizes of some of the mullions and see the effect on the façade. Perhaps even experiment with the Offset and Angle settings.

WORKING WITH STACKED WALLS

At the start of the chapter, we built a custom wall type and applied it to the exterior walls. We can take this further and create another kind of wall called a "Stacked Wall." A stacked wall simply uses two or more basic wall types stacked on top of one another to form a more complex design. Stacked walls are the third kind of wall system family.

In the simple example that follows, we will create a stacked wall that combines the wall type we created at the start of the chapter with two others provided with the Chapter 10 dataset files. This will give more articulation to the exterior shell wall forming a base condition at the first floor and a parapet condition at the roof.

IMPORT WALL TYPES FROM ANOTHER FILE

If you have types in one project file and you wish to use them in other project files, you can easily copy and paste them. That is what we will do here to import the types we need to build a custom stacked wall type.

1. On the Project Browser, open the *Level 1* floor plan.
   ⇨ On the QAT, click the Close Inactive Views icon.
2. From the File menu, choose: **Open > Project**.
3. Browse to the *Chapter10* folder, select the *CH10 Wall Types.rvt* [*CH10 Wall Types_M.rvt*] file and then click Open.

Three walls will appear onscreen in this file. The one in the middle matches the one built above in the "Creating a Basic Wall Type" topic on page 406. The other two are variations of this same basic wall. The one called **Exterior Base** has split-face concrete block on the exterior face and is a little thicker than the others. The **Exterior Parapet** type has brick on both sides. If you like, you can click on each one and then on Properties, click the Edit Type button then the Edit button next to Structure to study the layers and configuration (see Figure 10.57).

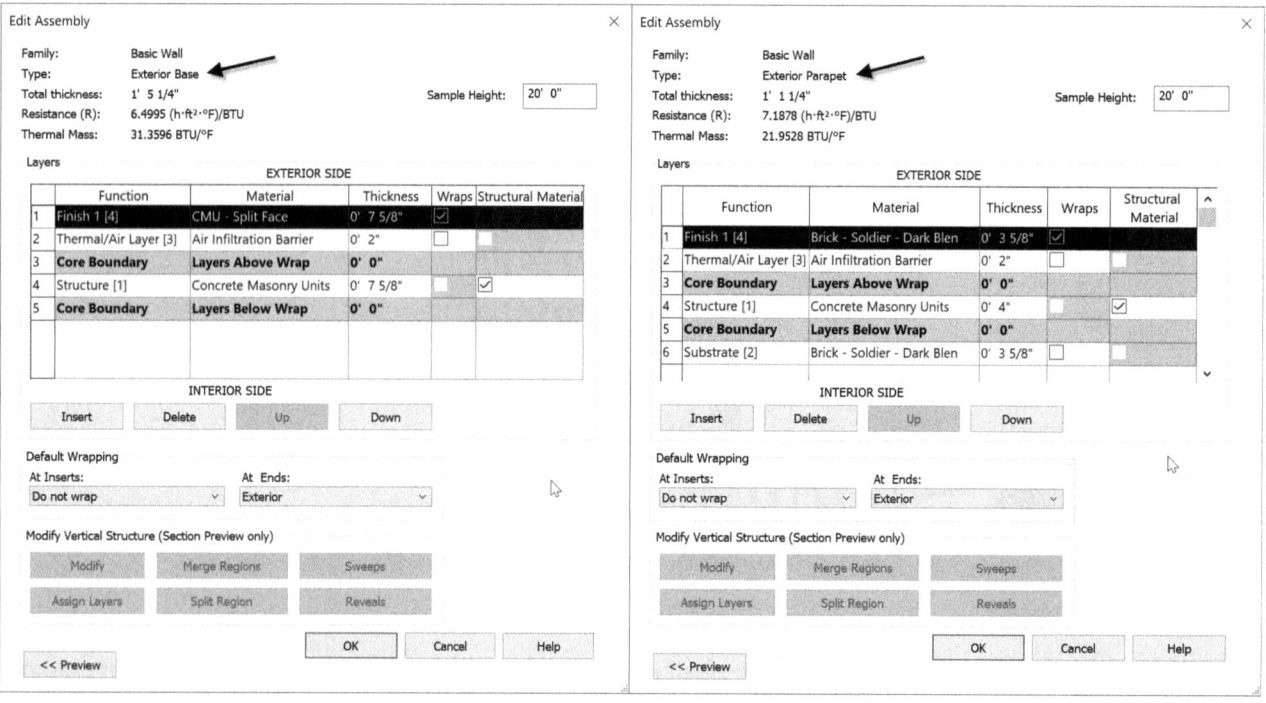

FIGURE 10.57 *Composition of the two custom wall types*

4. Select the Exterior Base and Exterior Parapet walls onscreen.
   ⇨ On the Modify | Walls tab, on the Clipboard panel, click the Copy to Clipboard button (or press CTRL + C).
   ⇨ Click the *Level 1* floor plan tab to switch back to the project.
5. On the Modify tab, click the Paste from Clipboard button (or press CTRL + V).
   ⇨ Click OK in the dialog that appears.
   ⇨ Click a point off to the side of the plan and then on the ribbon, click the Finish button (green checkmark).

This not only pastes the two small walls, but it also imports the wall types assigned to them. This means that these wall types are now part of this project and can be used to create elements in the model.

6. Select the two pasted walls and delete them.

Deleting the pasted walls only deletes these two instances. It does not delete the types from the project.

CREATE A STACKED WALL TYPE

In the simple example that follows, we will create a stacked wall that combines the wall type we created at the start of the chapter with the two we just pasted.

1. On the Project Browser, expand the *Families > Walls > Stacked Wall* branch.
2. Right-click on **Exterior – Brick Over CMU w Metal Stud** [**Exterior – Brick Over Block w Metal Stud**] and choose: **Type Properties**.
⇨ In the "Type Properties" dialog, click the Duplicate button and name it: **Brick Exterior with CMU Base** and then click OK.

Previously, we duplicated and renamed directly on the browser first, then edited the properties. This is simply an alternative way to achieve the same result. Notice that the new type name already appears in the *Sacked Wall* branch of the Project Browser. Unlike basic walls, with a stacked wall, there is only a structure parameter with an Edit button in the "Type Parameters" dialog.

3. Next to "Structure," click the Edit button.

The Structure of a stacked wall is very simple. You designate one or more wall types that you want to "stack" and how tall each should be. You can insert additional types by clicking the Insert button. Use the Up and Down buttons to move the various wall types relative to one another. Each type will be assigned an explicit height except for one. Only one can be variable and it will adjust to the actual height of the individual wall instance in the model. Use the "Variable" button to choose which one is variable.

You might want to drag at the edge of the dialog to widen it. This makes reading the type names easier.

4. Click in the Name field next to Type 1. From the pop-up menu, choose: **Exterior Shell** (this is the type we created at the start of the chapter).

Leave the Height set to Variable.

5. For Type 2, choose: **Exterior Base**.
⇨ Change the Height of Exterior Base to: **8'-0"** [**2400**].
⇨ At the bottom of the dialog, click the Preview button.
6. In the Offset field next to each type, input: **4"** [**100**].

Be sure to offset both. This shifts the wall type overall to compensate for the additional thickness that the base material adds. In this way, the wall will remain in the same relative position when we swap it into the model.

7. Select Type 1, and then click the Insert button.

This shifts the other two types down and inserts a copy of Exterior Shell above the original.

⇨ Change the type to Exterior Parapet.
⇨ Change the height to: **4'-0"** [**1200**].

Notice how the parapet type does not line up with the others. Also notice that at the top of the dialog is a drop down for Offset. It is currently set to Core Centerline. The core of the Exterior Parapet wall is not as thick as the others, so its core centerline does not line up. We can change this.

8. From the "Offset" list at the top, choose: **Core Face: Exterior** (see Figure 10.58).

454 | Chapter 10

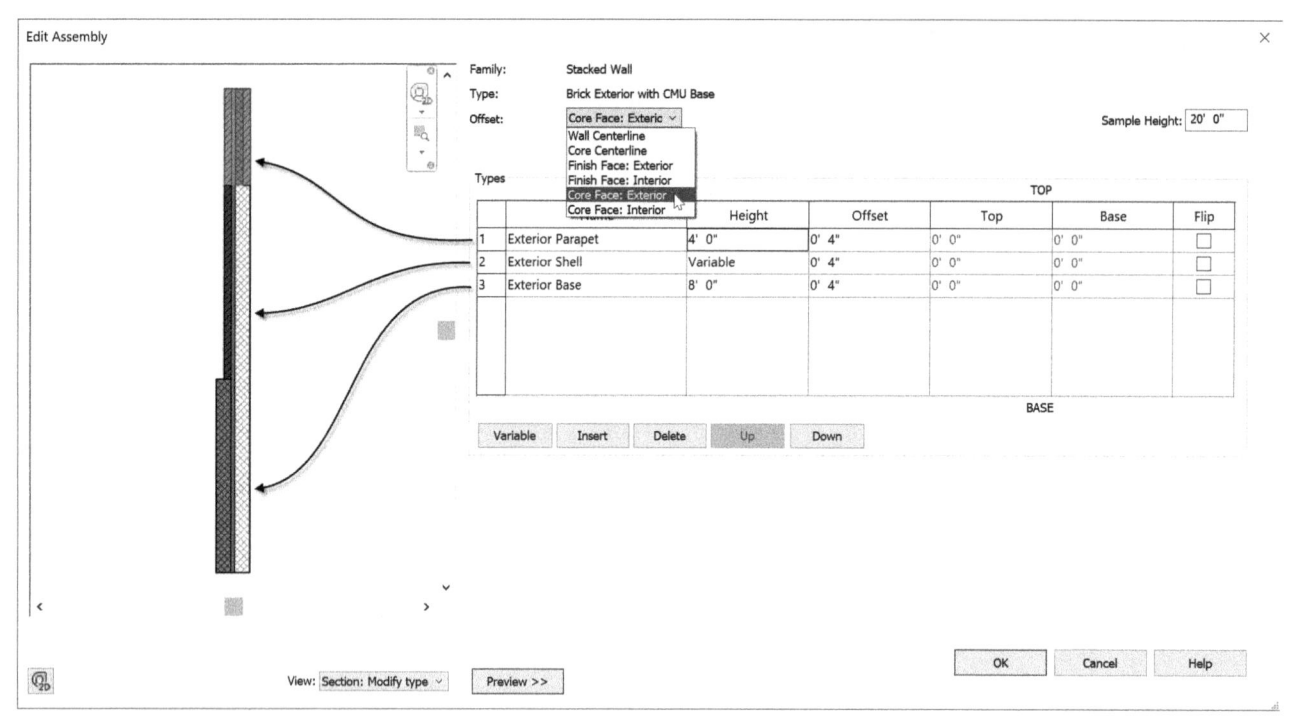

FIGURE 10.58 *Configure the stacked wall type*

9. When you are done studying the settings, click OK twice to dismiss the dialogs.

10. Back in the *Level 1* floor plan view, select one of the **Exterior Shell** walls in the model.

    ⇨ Right-click and choose: **Select All Instances** > **Visible in View**.

    ⇨ Use the CTRL key and add the exterior masonry wall at the stair core to the selection as well.

11. From the Type Selector, choose: **Stacked Wall: Brick Exterior with CMU Base** and change the Base Constraint to: **-1'-0"** [**-300**] (see Figure 10.59).

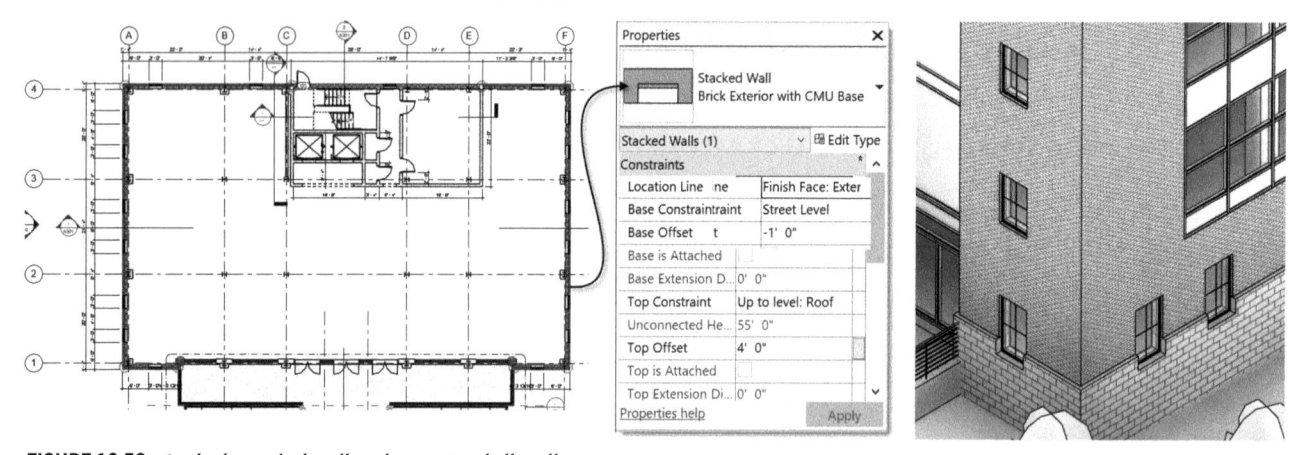

FIGURE 10.59 *Apply the stacked wall to the exterior shell walls*

DEALING WITH REVIT WARNING MESSAGES

You might get warnings. The first is likely about the dimensions we have been adding. Some of the witness lines are no longer valid. To examine the warning further, click the Expand button on the right side of the warning (see the right side of Figure 10.60). Note that in the resulting dialog box, you can expand the warnings to see specifically which elements are involved. Additionally you can see their element IDs (handy for selecting them if necessary—use the Select by ID tool on the Manage tab for this) and there is a Show button that will take you to a view that shows the condition.

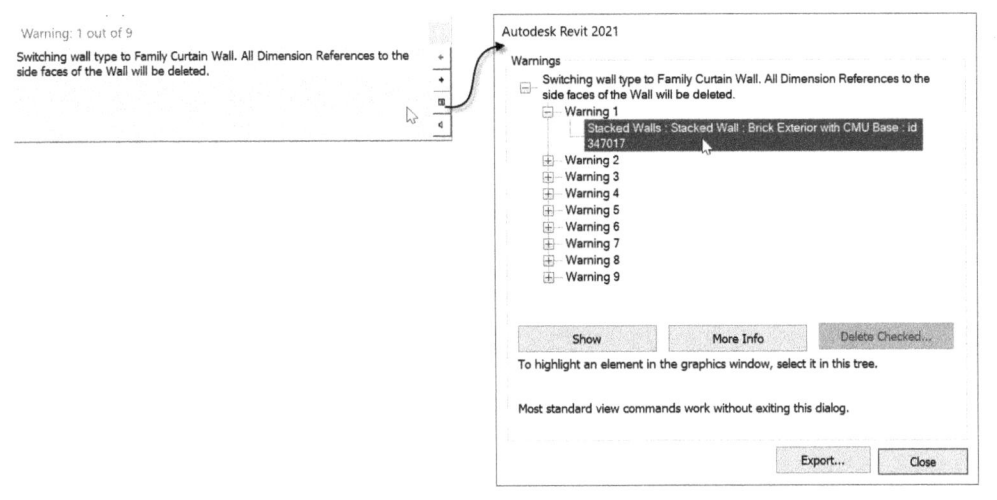

FIGURE 10.60 *Examine the warnings*

> **BIM MANAGER NOTE:** Some warnings are easy to miss since they disappear as soon as another object or item is picked, or they can be ignored deferring action till later. In the press of a deadline, it is easy to forget to review such warnings. For this reason, it is good practice to periodically review warnings that have built up in the model over time. This can be done on the Manage tab, on the Inquiry panel using the Warnings tool. Any unresolved warnings will show up there. As these conditions are resolved they will drop out of the dialog box. While it is extremely rare to have a model with no unresolved warnings whatsoever, it is desirable to keep them to an absolute minimum. As an example, after closing the dialog above, if you were to review any remaining warnings you would find a warning related to the number of risers in a monolithic stair and one about the railings. These would prove tricky to eliminate given the design needs of the project. However, it is still important to try to address and resolve as many ongoing warnings as possible. Nothing can kill the performance of a Revit project like hundreds of unresolved warnings. Prioritize warnings that affect live area calculations, quality issues like identical instances since that will affect counts, and duplicate values because that will affect documentation integrity.

1. Select one of the dimensions that lost a reference.

    ⇨ On the ribbon, click the Edit Witness Lines button.

    ⇨ Click on the elements required to add back the missing witness lines and then click in an empty space to finish (see Figure 10.61).

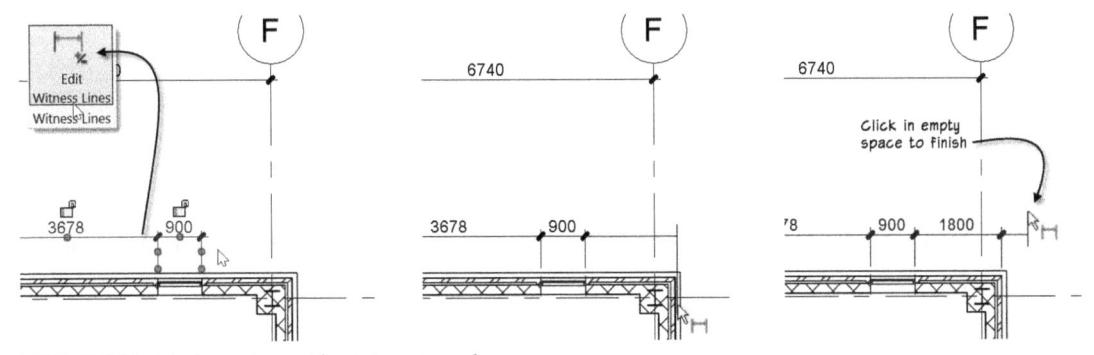

FIGURE 10.61 *Fix dimensions with missing witness lines*

You can use the Edit Witness Lines tool to add or remove witness lines from existing dimensions. When you click a new reference, it will be added. If you click on an existing reference, it will be removed. You must click in empty white space to finish. Do not press ENTER.

2. Repeat as needed on other floor plans.
3. Open the *Level 2* floor plan view.

Verify that the curtain walls on the sides of the building are still cutting the walls. If they are not, on the Modify tab, click the Cut tool. Select the exterior wall first and then click the curtain wall. Repeat on the other side.

4. Save the project.

> **HINT:** Stacked walls can be helpful in combining several different types of walls into a single assembly, but they can sometimes prove difficult to maintain. At any time you can right-click on a stacked wall and choose: Break Up. This will replace the stacked wall with a collection of basic walls from which it is composed.

EDIT THE ROOF

As we did above, you can edit the roof to make it match the changes to the building geometry. The basic process includes the following: you will likely need to reset the shape editing and redo the slope of the roof and its crickets. Refer back to the "Using Shape Editing Tools" topic on page 398 in Chapter 9 to perform the shape editing steps again. Some additional guidance on the best way to do this is provided in the Appendix. For the portion of roof over the slanted curtain walls, create a new roof. The existing roof will be a little too thick for this area, so you can duplicate the type and reduce the thickness of the structural layer. This is a small roof and you can use shallower structure.

ADD A WALL TYPE SWEEP

To complete the design of our shell wall, we need to add a parapet cap at the top of the parapet walls and a cap on the CMU base as a transition between it and the brick. It might be nice to add a soldier course as well. For these items we'll use wall sweeps and the vertical wall structure editing features. You can add a wall sweep in two ways. They can be added to the wall type parameters so that they automatically show on all instances of the wall type throughout the model or you can use the Wall Sweep tool which allows you to add Sweeps to the model manually at whatever location you designate. Let's look at an example of each.

1. On the Project Browser, expand the *Families > Walls > Basic Wall* branch.
2. Right-click the **Exterior Base** type and choose: **Type Properties**.
3. Next to Structure, click the Edit button.

    Make sure that the preview is showing. If it is not, click the Preview button at the bottom to open it (see item 1 in Figure 10.62).

    ⇨ From the View pop-up at the bottom, choose: **Section: Modify type attributes** (item 2).

    ⇨ In the Sample Height field at the top-right, input: **8'-0"** [**2400**] and then press ENTER (item 3).

This will shorten the height of the preview image to match the height we used in the stacked wall type. You can use normal zoom commands in the preview to zoom in and pan as necessary.

4. In the Preview, zoom in on the wall.
5. At the bottom of the dialog, click the Sweeps button (item 4).

    Please note that this button is only available if you are viewing the section preview. Position the "Wall Sweeps" dialog so you can see the preview window behind it.

Developing the Exterior Skin | 457

A sweep uses a profile family to create a form along the length of the wall. The profile family contains a two-dimensional closed shape. These can be simple rectangles or more detailed shapes. There are several families loaded in this file already, but the one that we will use must be loaded and has been provided in the *Chapter10* folder.

6. At the bottom of the dialog, click the Load Profile button (item 5).

⇨ Browse to the *Chapter10* folder, select the *Sill Cap.rfa* [*Sill Cap_M.rfa*] file and then click OK.

7. In the "Wall Sweeps" dialog, click the Add button.

⇨ From the Profile list, choose: **Sill Cap: 4" High** [**Sill Cap_M: 100mm High**].

⇨ For the Material Choose: **Concrete -Cast-in-Place Concrete**. Click the Apply button.

Notice that it is positioned on the outside of the wall at the bottom.

⇨ From the "From" list, choose: **Top**. For Offset, input: **-4"** [**-100**] (item 6) and then click the Apply button (item 7).

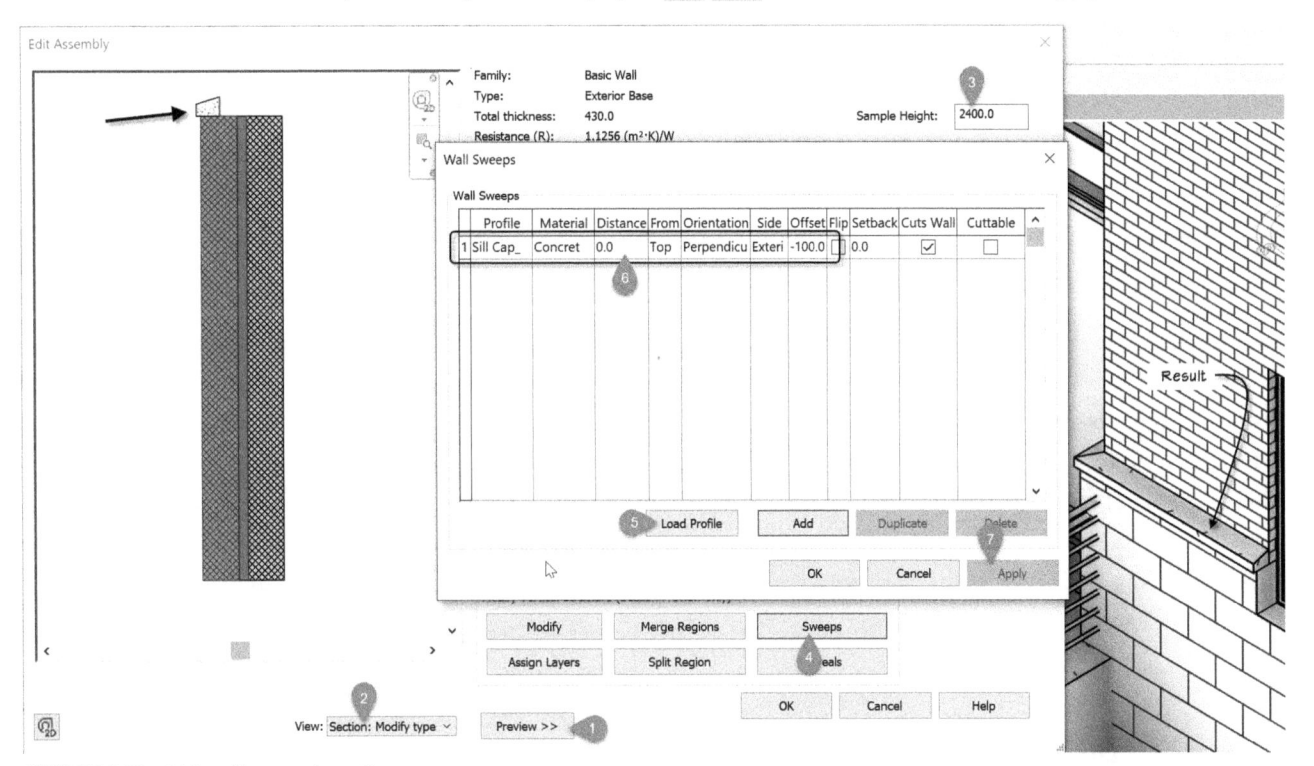

FIGURE 10.62 *Add a sill cap to the wall type*

8. Click OK three times to complete the Sweep.

9. On the Project Browser, open the {3D} view to see the results.

ADD A WALL INSTANCE SWEEP

The preceding process applies the same sweep condition on all instances of a wall type. Alternatively, you can use the Wall Sweep tool to place sweeps only to the walls you select.

Continue in the {3D} view.

1. On the Architecture tab click the drop down button on the Wall tool and choose the: **Wall: Sweep** tool.

2. On the Properties palette, click the Edit Type button.

⇨ Click Duplicate. Name the new type: **Parapet Cap**.

⇨ From the Profile list, choose: **Parapet Cap-Precast: 16" Wide** [**M_Parapet Cap-Precast: 350mm Wide**].

• Revit Essentials for Architecture •

⇨ For the Material, choose: **Concrete - Cast-in-Place Concrete** and then click OK to exit.

3. Following the prompt on the Status Bar, mouse over the exterior brick wall and click to place a parapet cap at the top of the wall. (Click on the outside edge of the wall to orient it the correct way).

⇨ Continue clicking parapet walls (including the EIFS wall we added behind the front façade (see Figure 10.63). You will need to orbit the view as you work to select all the walls.

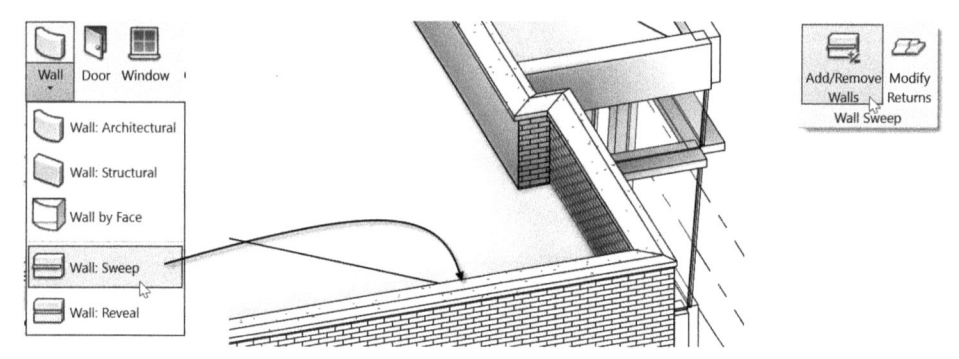

FIGURE 10.63 *Add a sweep parapet cap to the exterior walls*

If you miss a wall, you can select the sweep after it is created and use the Add/Remove Walls tool on the ribbon to modify it. Just be sure to use the TAB to highlight the nested parapet wall inside the stacked wall. If you click the stacked wall directly, it will generate a warning.

⇨ On the ribbon, click the Modify tool or press the ESC key twice.

You can edit the sweeps with the control handles that appear when you select them. So, if you don't want the sweep to go the entire length of the wall, just drag one of these control handles. You can add reveals the same way. They also use profiles but they cut away from the wall volume instead of adding to it (an example is provided in the "Add a Brick Shelf" topic on page 550 in Chapter 12). Sweeps integral to wall types cannot appear in schedules. Wall sweeps added at the instance level can appear in schedules. Wall sweeps added at the instance level *can* appear in schedules. Instance-level sweeps can also be assigned to different subcategories making it possible to hide them independently from their host walls. Both features make a compelling case for the use of instance sweeps even though you must click each wall to place them.

4. Save the model.

ADD A SOLDIER COURSE

Let's add one more detail to our exterior wall. We could make this modification with a sweep as well, but let's try an alternative approach.

1. On the Project Browser, expand the *Families > Walls > Basic Wall* branch.

2. Right-click the **Exterior Shell** type and choose: **Type Properties**.

3. Next to Structure, click the Edit button.

   Make sure that the preview is showing. If it is not, click the Preview button at the bottom to open it. Also make sure that a section preview is showing, if it is not, then from the View pop-up at the bottom, choose: **Section: Modify type attributes**.

4. Make sure that Layer 1 (the brick) is selected and then click the Insert button.

⇨ For the Function, choose: **Finish 1 [4]**.

⇨ For the Material, choose: **Brick - Soldier - Dark Blend**.

   Do not set a thickness (leave it a zero).

If you do not see this material, use the procedure covered above in the "Edit Wall Type Structure" topic on page 407 and the "Assign Materials" topic on page 409 to import it from the material library. Remember to check the "Use Render Appearance" check box to set the color on the graphics tab, and also on the Graphics tab, for the Foreground Surface Pattern, choose: Model pattern: **Brick Soldier Course [75mm vertical]**. You can assign a cut pattern too if you like.

5. In the Modify Vertical Structure area, click the Split Region button (see item 1 in Figure 10.64).

6. In the preview area, move the mouse point near the outside edge of the brick layer and click twice to create two splits in the material (item 2).

    This can be a little tricky. You can zoom in the preview to make it easier. There is no undo here and pressing ESC will cancel the dialog and you will lose all changes made to the wall so far. You can use the Merge Regions tool to join two splits back together.

Depending on how you are zoomed in, you may get a dimension to the top or bottom of the wall. The second split might measure from the previous one or from the opposite end of the wall. We want both to reference the bottom of the wall. To control this, you can use the Modify tool in the Modify Vertical Structure area. After selecting the small horizontal line that split the brick layer, you will see a small arrow control. Click this to flip and shift the dimension.

7. Click the Modify tool. Select one of the small split lines separating the brick layer (item 3).

    Temporary dimensions will appear in the preview window.

8. Edit the lower one to **15'-4" [4800]** and the one above that to **8" [225]** (item 4).

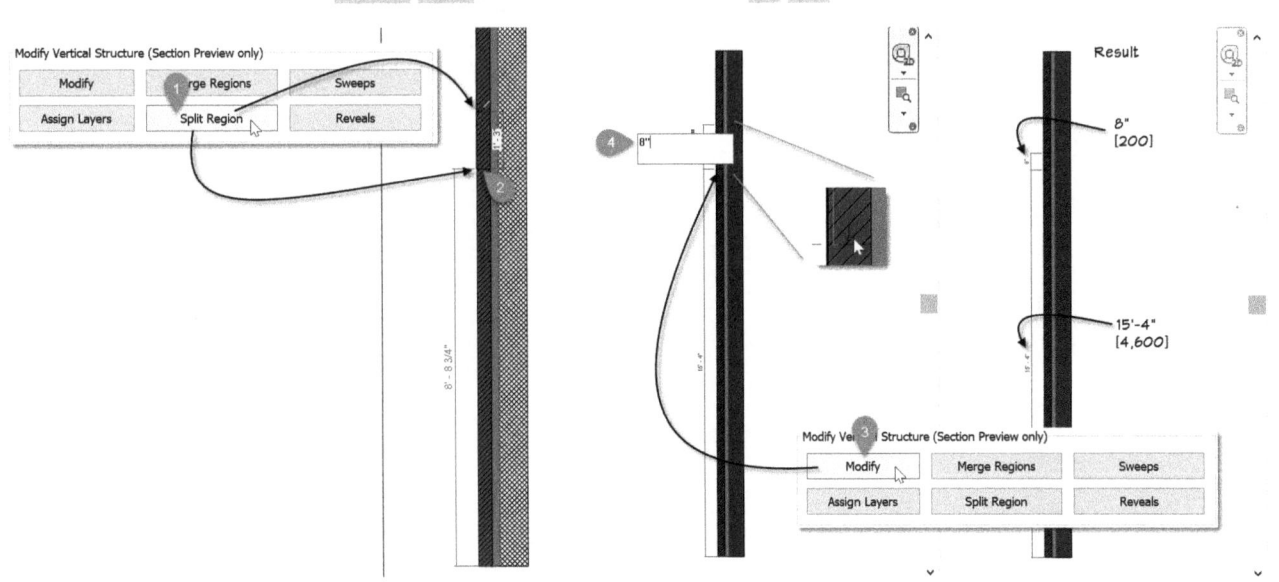

FIGURE 10.64 *Add a sweep parapet cap to the exterior walls*

It takes a little practice to get used to the interface here. You can't move one of these lines past the other. So, you might need to edit them more than once to get the result. Remember you can flip them to move the temporary dimensions. The final step is to assign the layer we created above to this split region.

9. In the Layers area, click on the number 1 in the left column. This will select the whole layer (see item 1 in Figure 10.65).

10. In the Modify Vertical Structure area, click the Assign Layers button (item 2).

11. In the preview window, zoom as required and then click on the split region (the 8" [200] tall one) (item 3).

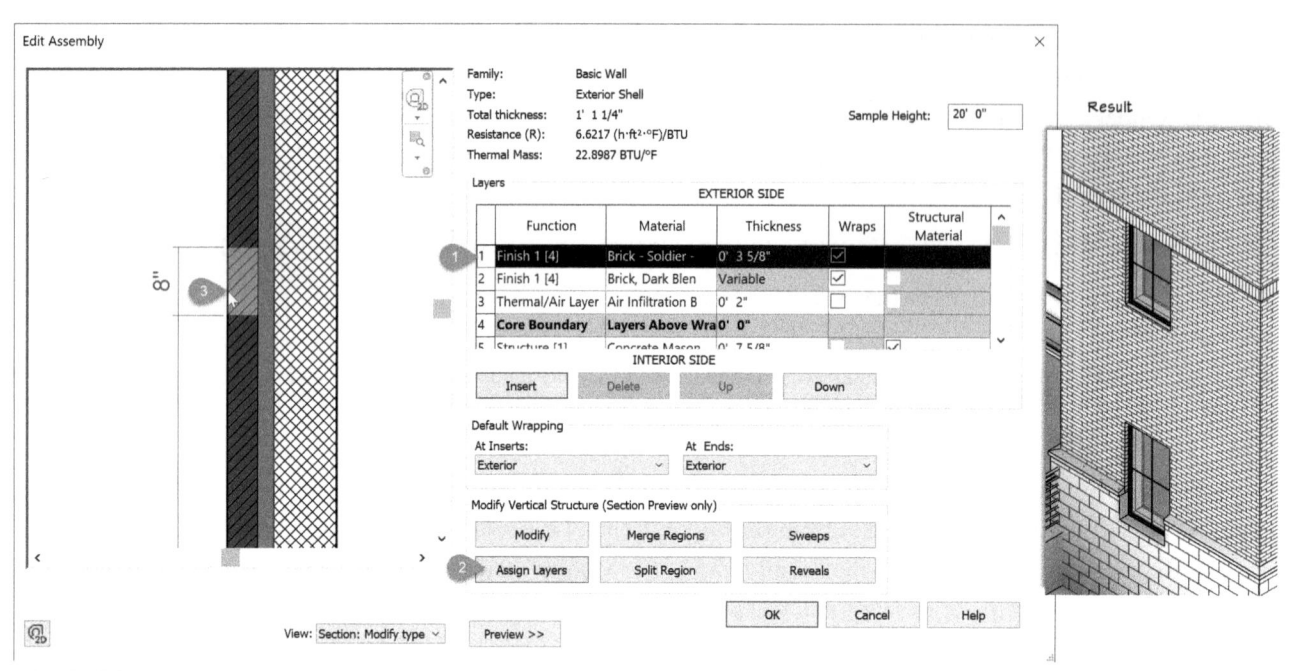

FIGURE 10.65 *Add a sweep parapet cap to the exterior walls*

12. Click OK twice to see the results (see the right side of Figure 10.65).

    If you wish, you can repeat the entire procedure to create additional soldier courses at other locations on the wall. Continue to make any other refinements or experimentations that you wish. When you are finished, close and save your project file and any other open files.

SUMMARY

- ☑ Walls are system families. There are three: Basic Wall, Curtain Wall, and Stacked Wall.
- ☑ You can create a custom wall type and edit it to add and delete layers (Components) in the Basic Wall family.
- ☑ Curtain walls can be drawn like walls and even embedded within other walls.
- ☑ Use Cut Geometry to manually embed the curtain wall (or other kind of wall) within the thickness of a wall.
- ☑ Curtain wall grids can be sketched manually or defined within the curtain wall type.
- ☑ Mullions can be added to curtain grid lines.
- ☑ Mullion joins can be toggled to horizontal or vertical to suit your preferences.
- ☑ Default joins can be assigned in the type or manually edited per mullion.
- ☑ Walls can be used as panels for curtain walls.
- ☑ A curtain wall type can contain a predefined pattern of horizontal and vertical grid lines.
- ☑ Custom curtain panel families can be used to create more complex curtain wall designs.
- ☑ A stacked wall contains one or more basic walls stacked on top of each other.
- ☑ If you wish to convert a stacked wall to individual basic walls, right-click and choose Break Up.
- ☑ Wall sweeps can be added to wall types or added per instance and used to represent bands, moldings, parapets, cornices, etc.
- ☑ Reveals work the same as sweeps but are voids.
- ☑ You can add detailing in the vertical structure of a wall such a soldier courses or other banding using the modify vertical structure tools in the wall type.

CHAPTER 11
Families and the Family Editor

INTRODUCTION

All elements that you create and use in an Autodesk® Revit® project belong to a family. As noted in Chapter 2, a family is an element that has a specific collection of parameters and behaviors. Within the limits established by the family and its parameters, a collection of "Types" can be generated. Understanding families and how to manipulate them is an important part of learning Revit. Families are the cornerstone of the Revit parametric change engine and their use and customization is the topic of this chapter.

OBJECTIVES

While there are several kinds of families in Revit, the primary focus of this chapter will be "Component Model Families." Component families (also referred to as "loadable families") are simply families that describe some physical component in the model. Conceptually however, topics discussed in this chapter apply to any kind of Revit family, including annotation families such as tags and title blocks. To illustrate this point, and as noted in the "Loading Custom Elevation Tags" topic on page 173 in Chapter 5, we will also explore a brief tutorial on creating a custom elevation tag. After completing this chapter, you will know how to:

- Explore the families contained in the current project
- Insert instances of families in your model
- Manipulate family types
- Create custom static (non-parametric) families
- Create custom parametric model families

KINDS OF FAMILIES

In the "Revit Elements" topic on page 41 in Chapter 2, a detailed discussion of the various kinds of elements available in Revit is presented. To review, Revit elements include primarily model elements and view-specific elements. Model elements include both hosts and components. View-specific elements include detail items and annotations. Figure 2.1 in Chapter 2 presents a summary of these items graphically.

Both model and annotation families include system families and non-system families. System families are families that are "built into" the software, i.e., "hardwired," and cannot be manipulated by the user in the interface. This can include built-in-place construction like walls and floors, but also includes items like views, project data, and levels. System families cannot be created or deleted. Their properties are predefined in the software. However, most system families like walls, floors, and roofs can have more than one type. A type is a saved and named variation of a family with preassigned values. Types can always be customized. A family must have at least one but can contain more types; each with its own unique user-editable settings. While we cannot, for example, create or delete wall families, we can add, delete, and edit the types associated with each of the provided wall families as we saw in the previous chapter.

System families vary considerably in their specific composition and features, but at the conceptual level, they share the same basic characteristics—the overall behavior of the element is defined by the system and cannot be changed; however, the specific object-level parameters can be manipulated via the creation and application of type and/or instance variations.

Any system family that is also a model element is also referred to as a "Host." A host is an element that can receive, support, or provide structure for other model elements. A "rule of thumb" to help you identify which model families are system or host families is to think of those parts of the building that are typically assembled on site from a collection of raw or basic materials—the so called "built in place" items. Examples include walls, floors, roofs, stairs, etc. Of course, there are exceptions to this "rule of thumb," such as columns. In Revit, columns are component families, not system families. Columns in the real world can be made off-site and then erected (like steel columns), or they can be made on-site (like cast-in-place concrete). So, the analogy is not perfect, but it is illustrative nonetheless.

Component families include all model elements that are not system families. Other "loadable" families include families that are not model elements like annotation, detail components, and title block families. Component families can be "Host-based" (require a host), or they can be freestanding (not requiring a host). Unlike system families, we can create, delete, and modify component families. This is accomplished in the Family Editor interface, and each family thus created can also be saved to its own unique file (with an RFA extension). System families cannot be stored as RFA files. Like system families, component families can contain multiple types. Unlike system families, component families are completely customizable. You can create nearly unlimited parameters and behaviors for such a family. Since they are created outside of the project editor context, component families can be loaded into any project. Therefore, they are also referred to as "loadable." The inverse of our system/host family rule of thumb described above is the component family rule of thumb. To identify typical component families, the guideline is "the parts of a building that are typically built in a shop or factory and then installed in the building." Examples include furniture, windows, doors, curtain wall panels, electrical and plumbing fixtures, etc. There are exceptions to this rule of thumb as well. The other parts of the curtain wall, including the wall itself, the curtain grids, and corner mullions are system families. So once again the analogy is meant only to illustrate the concept.

There is another type of family in Revit called the "In-Place Family." In-place families are like the component families in terms of creation and editing. However, an in-place family is created directly within a project (not in a separate family file as component families are), and it cannot be saved or exported to other projects. In-place families have the unique feature of being able to use many system family categories like walls and roofs. The only time you should consider creating an in-place family is for an element that is unique to a particular project with no possibility that you will ever want to reuse it elsewhere in the project or in future projects. This could be effective for unique "one-off" existing conditions in projects or very specialized design scenarios. In-place families are not intended for cases where they need to be used multiple times, copied, rotated, or mirrored, etc.; even within the same project. If your needs require this, you should create the item as a component family in the Family Editor instead and then load it into your project(s). If there is any doubt about whether a family should be a component family or an in-place family, it is probably safer to create it as a component family. Should you decide to copy an in-place family, you will find that Revit creates a completely new and unique family that is not connected in any way to the original. This means that unlike other families, a change to original will not affect the copy and vice-versa. In addition, duplicating in-place families often has a detrimental effect on project performance and size.

As has already been noted, many of the concepts covered in this chapter might apply equally to system families, component families, annotation families, detail item families, and even in-place families. However, for the purposes of the following discussions and tutorials, we will limit our discussion mostly to the use and manipulation of component (model) families. For techniques on manipulating editable variables of system families, refer to the previous chapter where several examples of manipulating and/or creating wall types were presented. The basic procedure for creating or editing a type (whether belonging to a system or component family) is nearly identical in all cases. A title block family was created in the "Create a Custom Title Block Family" topic on page 193 in Chapter 5. In this chapter, we will explore one annotation family example in the "Creating Custom Elevation Tags" topic on page 485 below. For an example of an in-place family, look back to the "Create A Unique Element" topic on page 136 in Chapter 4. Finally, Revit also includes a special kind of family called a "conceptual mass" or "adaptive component" family. Chapter 17 is devoted to this and other topics related to working in the conceptual massing environment.

> **NOTE:** Since the rest of this chapter will focus mainly on component/loadable families, for simplicity's sake, we will refer to component/loadable families as simply "Families" for the remainder of this chapter.

FAMILY LIBRARIES

A well-conceived template project is a critical component in successful Revit implementation (refer to Chapter 5 for more information). A well-stocked library of commonly used families is equally important. A "Library" is nothing more than a series of folders on your hard drive or network server that contain Revit content. Revit ships with a large library of ready-to-use items. These include component families, annotation symbols, and detail items. Some of these items are included in sample template files (see Chapter 5) and therefore automatically become part of each newly created project, and others are provided in family files (RFA) stored in the library folders.

The default United States installation creates the "Imperial Library" that is located in the *C:\ProgramData\Autodesk\ RVT 2021\Libraries\English-Imperial* folder (see Figure 11.1). Please note that the "Program Data" folder is hidden in Windows™ the search field. On the View tab, show hidden files.

466 | Chapter 11

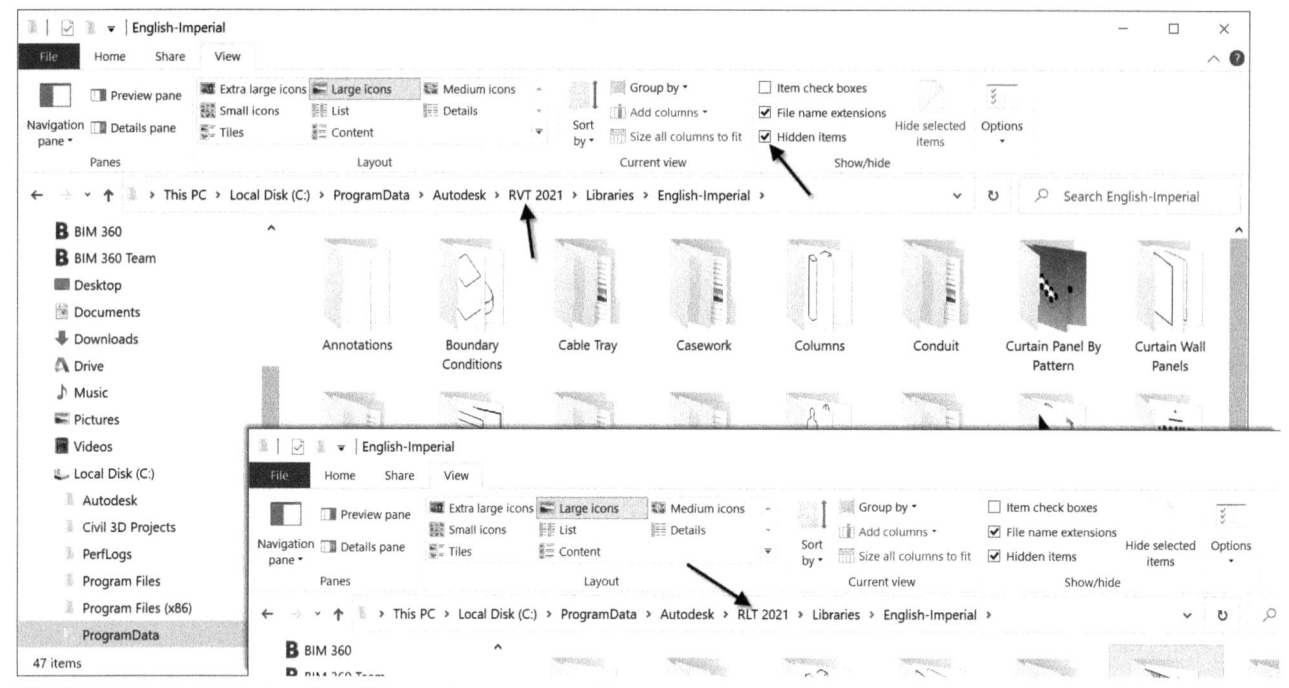

FIGURE 11.1 *An example of one of the folders in the Revit Imperial library*

> **NOTE:** The specific location of your library files will vary with your locality and particular version of Revit. Note that the figure shows an inset for Revit LT as an example. Check the documentation that came with your product for the specific location.

There are many items in the library. For example, the *US Imperial* library contains over 3,400 family files. As we have seen in previous chapters and as we will discuss in more detail below, a family can contain one or several "types." Therefore, the 3,400 imperial family files represent potentially several thousand readily available component elements that can be added to our projects. It is a good idea to become as familiar as you can with the provided content. The reason is simple; it is always easier to use or modify something that already exists than it is to create it from scratch. You may also find it useful to explore the libraries for other countries' components and unit systems as well since the items in imperial and metric libraries are not always identical. When you install Revit, several language packs are available. Try installing some of the others and explore the content they contain. You can browse through the library in Windows Explorer or directly from Revit. If you don't have the libraries indicated, there is a button on the Insert tab: on the Load from Library panel, click the Get Autodesk Content button. This will load your default browser to a page where you can download the content libraries.

There are a few ways to access family libraries from within Revit. If you are in a project, simply click the Insert tab and, on the Load from Library panel, click the Load Family button. As an alternative, for component families, a Load Family button is presented on the ribbon when you click the corresponding tool. A Load button is also available within the "Type Properties" dialog for any component family. Click any of these buttons to open a dialog and browse to an appropriate library folder and family file. This should take you directly to your default library. In other open dialogs, you can click the shortcut icon on the left (i.e., Imperial Library or Metric Library) to open your library. (These shortcuts are referred to as "Places.") Double-click a subfolder to view its contents. You can select a file (single-click) to see a preview on the right, or if you wish, you can use the Views icon at the top of the dialog to browse by Thumbnails (see Figure 11.2).

Families and the Family Editor | 467

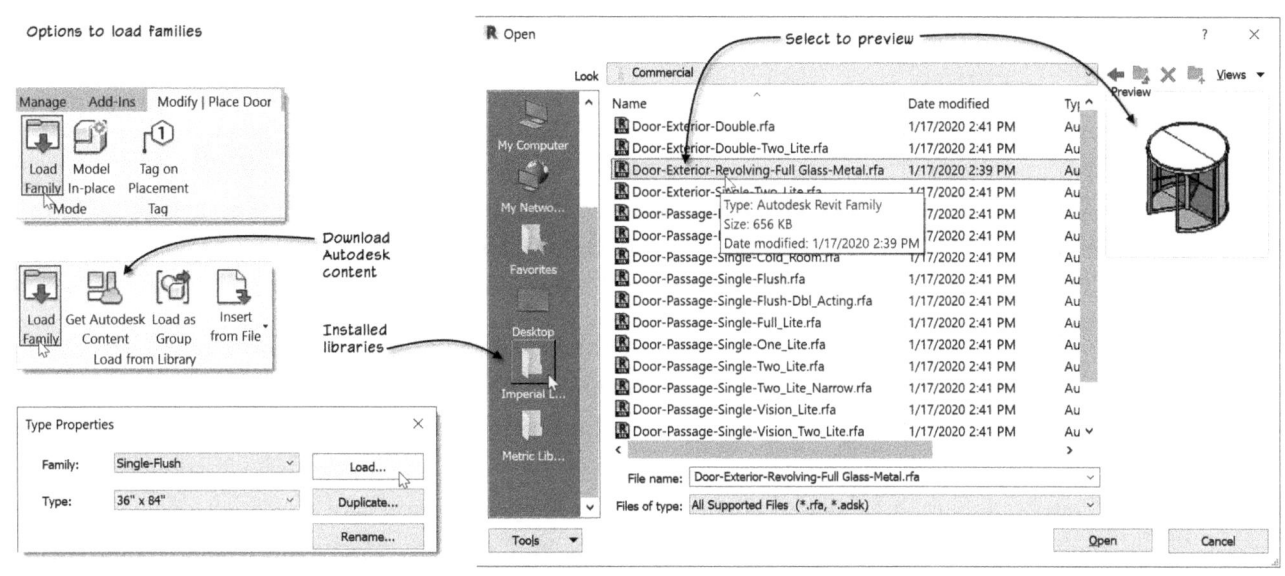

FIGURE 11.2 *Access a Library from within Revit from any load or open dialog*

No matter what method you use to browse your library, you can always open a family file directly into the Revit interface. From the File menu you can choose: **Open > Family**. The interface when a family file is loaded is slightly different than when a project file is loaded. In this state, the interface is referred to as the "Family Editor." While in the Family Editor, the ribbon will show family-specific tabs and tools. Some of the other functions will appear differently as well. You will still have a Project Browser, but it typically includes only a few views that have been developed for editing the current family. These views are only seen while in the Family Editor and do not appear in projects to which the family is loaded (see Figure 11.3).

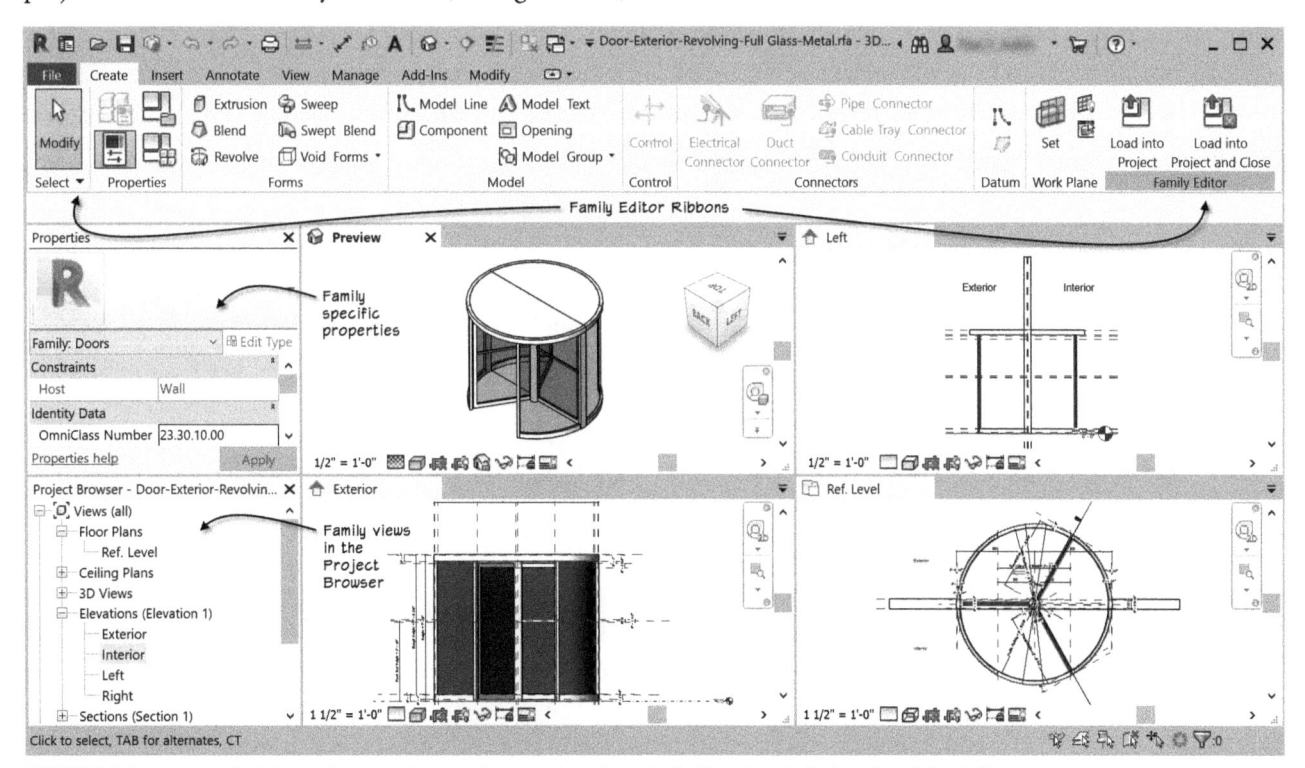

FIGURE 11.3 *The Family Editor (shown with Door-Exterior-Revolving-Full Glass-Metal.rfa door family loaded)*

If you are following along in this passage within Revit, feel free to view and open as many family files as you wish. However, please do not make any edits or save any changes to the out-of-the-box family files. Treat this as an exploratory exercise. In the lessons that follow later in this chapter, we will have the opportunity to load, edit, build and

• Revit Essentials for Architecture •

save our own families. The purpose of the current discussion is to give you familiarity with what has been provided with your software.

If you want to edit your library locations, you can do so by choosing: **Options** from the File menu. In the "Options" dialog, click the File Locations tab. There you can change your default template file and the location of the family template files and access your "Places" which are the icons that appear on the left side of the open dialogs. In the "Places" dialog, you can add a path, edit a path, delete a path, and change the order in which they appear. You can also edit your places directly from any open dialog using the Tools pop-up in the lower left corner.

In addition to any libraries that have been installed with your product on your local system, you may also have access to other libraries maintained by your firm's BIM support personnel. Libraries of this type are typically stored on the company network and accessible via your local or wide area network. Furthermore, several other online libraries can be found through a quick web search. Many third-party websites provide large libraries of Revit content that you can explore and download. Some are free and others charge a fee. You are encouraged to run a Google search for "Revit," "Revit families," and "Revit Content" to find some examples. Just be sure to carefully test out whatever you download. The quality of content can vary considerably.

FAMILY STRATEGIES

Do take the time to explore your family library. As you analyze each of the library items, many of the items will seem useful. You will also find those that you will deem not useful. Still others will prove useful after they have been modified in some fashion. If you take the time to perform this analysis of the included library content before committing any time and resources to customizing existing items and/or building new items from scratch, you can save yourself a great deal of effort and time. Perform the same analysis on any content you download from content websites. The other benefit to this process is that you will undoubtedly discover ways of performing certain tasks or representing certain items that you had not considered on your own. In other words, reverse engineering existing families can prove to be a tremendous learning experience. Just remember not to save changes to existing files. Always make a copy or "Save As" first; then save your changes to the copied file.

Nearly everything you do in Revit involves the use or manipulation of a family. We have already seen several examples of this in the previous chapters. We "used" families whenever we added something to our model. We manipulated families whenever we edited the type and/or clicked the "Duplicate" button in the "Type Properties" dialog. Whenever you wish to add an element to your model, the element you add will be part of a family. Always try to locate and use a family that already exists and is available to you before you modify or create custom families. The basic strategy of family usage is to maintain the following priorities:

> **1st, Use Existing**—See if what you want already exists somewhere (in the current project or in a library or on the web) and simply use it.
>
> **2nd, Modify Existing**—If the precise family (or type) you want does not exist, find a family (or type) that is close to what you need, duplicate, and modify it.
>
> **3rd, Create New**—If necessary, create a new family to represent what you need.

This basic approach is somewhat obvious and logical. However, it is surprising how often users will either resort immediately to building custom components without first checking the libraries or do the opposite and settle for some less than ideal component in their models. Follow this simple three-step guideline, and you will always have the right family for the job. The remainder of this chapter is devoted to tutorials that will illustrate this basic three-step approach.

ACCESSING FAMILIES IN A PROJECT

If you wish to use an existing family in your project, the first step is to explore what is available. The first place you should look is the current project. You can quickly see all the families available in the current project in the Project Browser. We did this in the previous chapter, but let's review the process now.

OPEN A PROJECT

The lessons that follow require the dataset files included for download with this book. Refer to the "Download the Book Dataset" topic on page xi in the Preface for instructions on downloading and installing the book's dataset files.

1. Launch Autodesk® Revit®.
2. If you are on the Home screen, you can click the Open button beneath Models. Otherwise, from the File menu, choose **Open** > **Project**. In the "Open" dialog box, browse to the *Chapter11* folder.
   - ⇨ Double-click *11 Commercial.rvt* if you wish to work in Imperial units.
   - ⇨ Double-click *11 Commercial M.rvt* if you wish to work in Metric units.

   You can also select it and then click the Open button.

Many interior walls have been added on several of the floors of this project since the last chapter. A few other modifications have been made as well. If you would like to try your hand at making these modifications yourself, please visit the Appendix for instructions on how to do so. Feel free to do this before continuing.

ACCESSING FAMILIES FROM PROJECT BROWSER

There are a few ways to see which families are already loaded into a project. Whenever you choose a tool from the ribbon, the list of family/type combinations will appear in the Type Selector. The family will be listed first with a small preview and gray header and the types will be listed beneath this. We have seen this already in several earlier chapters. While this method is effective for a category of element such as a door, or a window, the easiest way to see a more complete list of loaded families is via the Project Browser. The Project Browser has several major branches. The first branch is the *Views* branch. We have spent nearly all our time in previous chapters on this branch. Beneath this one are specialized view types such as *Legends*, *Schedules*, and *Sheets*. The *Families*, *Groups*, and *Revit Links* branches are at the bottom. (In the previous chapter, we used the *Families* branch to provide quick access to the curtain wall items we were editing.) If you expand the *Families* branch, you will see each element category currently loaded in the project. Expand any category, such as *Doors*, and you will see each family of that category. Finally, expanding one step further reveals all the types for any individual family.

1. On the Project Browser, double-click to open the *Level 3* floor plan view.
   - ⇨ Select any door element on screen.
   - ⇨ Open the Type Selector and study its contents (see the left side of Figure 11.4).
2. On the Project Browser, expand the *Families* branch, and then expand *Doors*.
3. Expand: *Door-Passage-Single-Full_Lite* [*M_Door-Passage-Single-Full_Lite*] (see the middle of Figure 11.4).

470 | Chapter 11

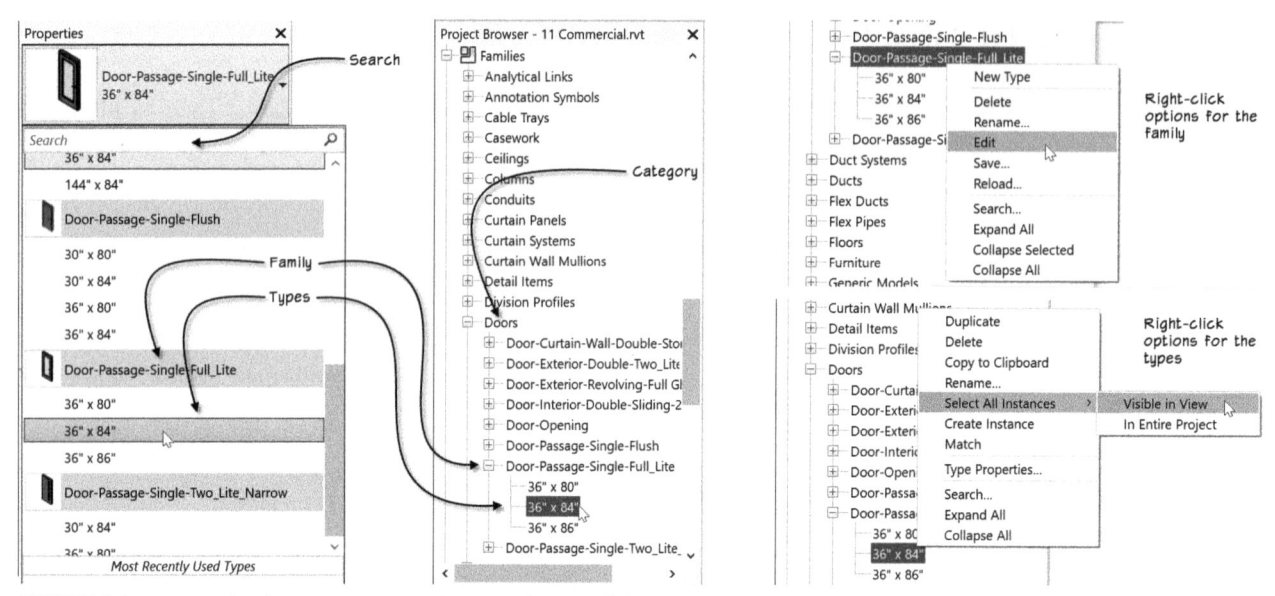

FIGURE 11.4 *Accessing families in a project via the Type Selector and the Project Browser*

4. On the ribbon, click the Modify tool or press the ESC key twice.

As you can see, all the door family/type combinations will be listed in the Type Selector and the Project Browser. In addition to simply taking inventory of families and types in the project, you can also use the list on Project Browser to manipulate and interact with families. Use the right-click menu to do this. You can right-click on the family and type branches of the Project Browser tree. (Right-clicking the Category branch will show only the Search and options to expand or collapse the list.) Recall that we used this technique to edit mullion families in the previous chapter.

> **BIM MANAGER NOTE:** When you right-click on the family name, you will only get a menu with editing options on component (loadable) families. If you right-click a system family, the menu will contain only Search, expand and collapse. A menu will always appear when you right-click types—either component family types or system family types. This is one way you can tell if an item is a component family or a system family. If an edit menu appears, it is a component family. If only Search appears, then it is a system family.

You can save all component families in a project to separate family files (RFA) by right-clicking on the *Families* branch and choosing the **Save** command. This command will create RFA files for all component families in the current project. You can also find the command on the File menu: **Save As > Library > Family**.

5. Right-click on the *Door-Passage-Single-Full_Lite* [*M_Door-Passage-Single-Full_Lite*] family and take note of the menu that appears.

⇨ Right-click on the type: 36" x 84" [900 x 2100mm] and choose: **Select All Instances > Visible in View** (see the left side of Figure 11.4).

Only one will be selected at the entrance to the suite. If you look at the Properties palette, the filter list will read Doors (1) indicating that one door is selected. There are two options of this command, all instances visible in view and all instances in entire project. The "Visible in View" option is often a little safer in most cases as you will only be selecting elements that you can see in the current view. When using the "In Entire Project" option, it selects all instances in the model, not just those visible in the current view. Depending on what you do with the selection, this could be a little risky. This door is not used anywhere else. Let's try a different one.

⇨ Expand the *Door-Passage-Single-Flush* [*M_Door-Passage-Single-Flush*] family, right-click on the type: 36" x 84" [900 x 2100mm] and choose: **Select All Instances > Visible in View**.

The Properties palette will read: Doors(6) this time (in the core area).

Families and the Family Editor | 471

⇨ Right-click the same type again and choose: **Select All Instances** > **In Entire Project**.

This time we get 32! So naturally, depending on the edit you did next, this could be riskier.

There are many other commands available on the right-click menu as well. You can Duplicate the current type, rename it, or edit its Type Properties. You can also create an instance directly from this menu, rather than first clicking the tool on the ribbon and choosing the type from the Type Selector. In some cases, this can be quicker; the result is the same, it is simply a matter of personal preference.

6. On the ribbon, click the Modify tool or press the ESC key to deselect the doors.

Let's add some furniture to this plan using the right-click option on the *Families* branch.

7. On the Project Browser, beneath *Families*, expand the *Furniture* branch and then the *Desk [M_Desk]* family.

⇨ Right-click on: *72" x 36"* [*1830 x 915mm*] and choose: **Create Instance** (see the left side of Figure 11.5).

In the Imperial file, the insertion point of this desk is on the privacy panel side. So, to place it in the offices at the bottom of the plan, tap the SPACEBAR twice to rotate it 180°. The orientation is correct in the metric file, but you will still need to rotate 90° for the offices on the side.

8. Place the new Desk in the corner office (see the middle of Figure 11.5).

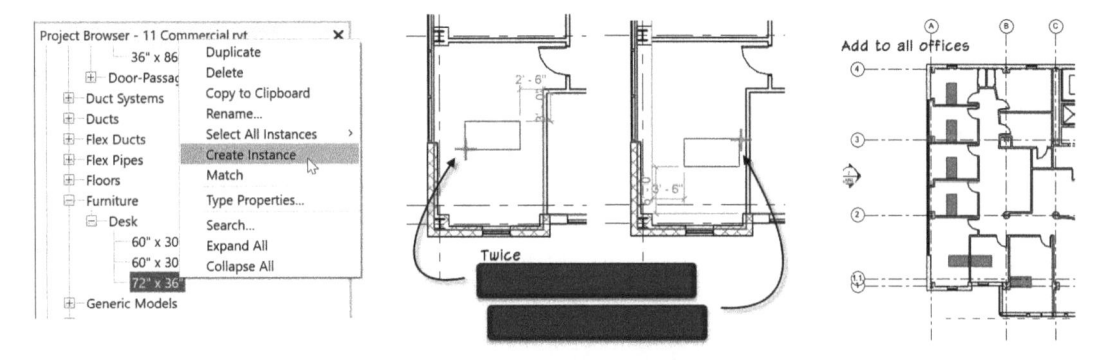

FIGURE 11.5 *Use the family tree right-click menu to add desks to the plan*

9. Repeat in other offices. Press the SPACEBAR to rotate the Desk before placement as required (see the right side of Figure 11.5).

TIP: With items like furniture, it can be easier to place them approximately first, then select the item and use the arrow keys on your keyboard to "nudge" them. Each press of the arrow will nudge a small amount. If you hold down the SHIFT key as you press the arrow, it goes 10x that amount. The amount of the nudge is controlled by how closely you are zoomed in. So, zoom in to make it finer and zoom out to make it coarser. You can also use Copy, Mirror, or Rotate commands on the Modify tab as needed.

10. On the ribbon, click the Modify tool or press the ESC key twice.

MATCH TYPE PROPERTIES

One of the useful functions on the type's right-click menu is "Match." With this command, you can apply the type parameters of the item highlighted in Project Browser to an element already in the model. This is a quick way to "paint" a type's properties onto existing element. We can try this out on the entrance to the suite on Level 3. Currently there is a single door. Let's make it a double glass door.

1. On the Project Browser, beneath *Families*, expand *Doors* then *Door-Exterior-Double-Two_Lite* [*M_Door-Exterior-Double-Two_Lite*].

⇨ Right-click on: *72" x 84"* [*1800 x 2050mm*] and choose: **Match**.

• Revit Essentials for Architecture •

472 | Chapter 11

When the cursor is moved into the plan view window, it adds a paint brush shape.

2. Click on the door at the entrance to the suite (see Figure 11.6).

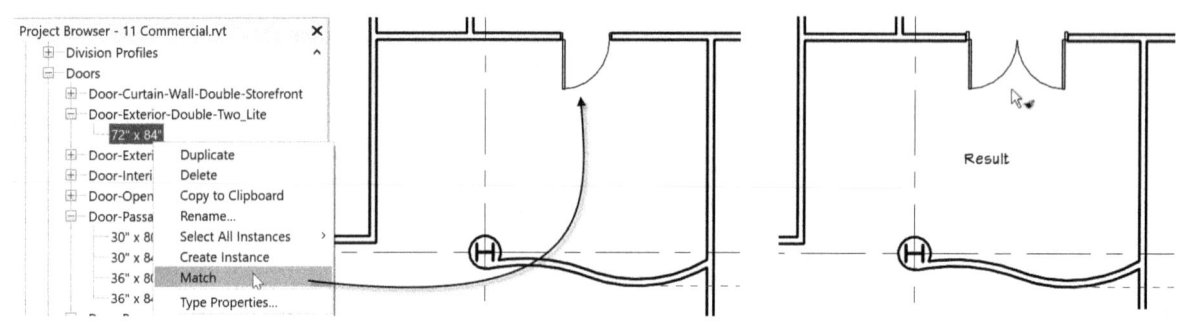

FIGURE 11.6 *Match a type from Project Browser to an element in the model*

The door will change to a double glass door. The frame will appear shifted a bit.

3. On the ribbon, click the Modify tool or press the ESC key twice.

⇨ Select the double door, on the Properties palette, uncheck the Masonry Frame check box.

⇨ Save the model.

There is also a Match Type button on the Modify ribbon. To use it, you must first select an existing element in the model, and then you can match the selected element's properties to other element(s) in the model. However, the nice thing about the right-click option shown here is that you can match from an item on the browser that is not necessarily already inserted in the project.

ACCESSING LIBRARIES

So far, we have limited our exploration to families that are already part of our current project. The process of accessing families from a library is nearly identical. Remember, a library is nothing more than a collection of files and folders stored on your local system or a remote server. To access and place a family in a project, you must first load it into your project. We have already discussed several ways to do this in the "Family Libraries" topic on page 465 above.

LOAD FAMILIES FROM "PREFERRED" LIBRARIES (PLACES)

We will continue in the same file and view (*Level 3*) as the previous topic.

1. On the Insert tab, on the Load from Library panel, click the Load Family button (see Figure 11.7).

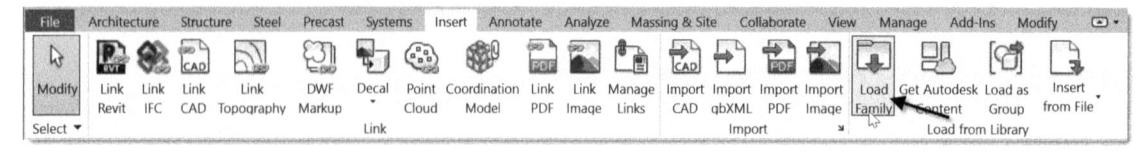

FIGURE 11.7 *Load a family from a library*

The "Load Family" dialog will appear starting in the last folder you accessed. Depending on the options you choose during installation, there may be additional libraries available to you. Each library that you have installed or added will appear as a shortcut on the left of the dialog.

2. On the left side, click the Imperial Library [Metric Library] shortcut icon if necessary.

If your preferred library did not open automatically, use the shortcut icons on the left or the drop down menu at the top to locate your desired library folder. The library folder will typically contain several subfolders. Each folder can contain additional folders or Revit family (RFA) files. Your CAD or BIM Manager may have installed the default libraries in alternate locations than those mentioned here. Please check with them to find the correct location.

> **TIP:** If you access a folder that is not among your shortcuts, you can add it to Places by drag and drop.

3. Double-click the *Furniture* folder then double-click the *Storage* folder, select the *Credenza.rfa* [*M_Credenza.rfa*] file, and then click Open.

> **NOTE:** If your version of Revit does not include either of the libraries mentioned herein, both family files have been provided in the *Chapter11* folder.

⇨ On the Project Browser, beneath *Families*, expand *Furniture* to see the newly loaded Credenza family in the list (see Figure 11.8).

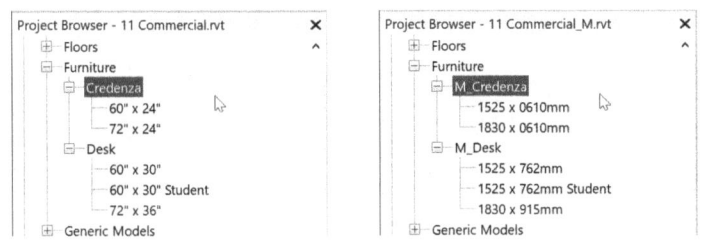

FIGURE 11.8 *The newly loaded family will appear among the others in Project Browser*

4. Click on 72" x 24" [1830 × 0610mm] and drag it to the model window.

   This is an alternative to the right-click approach above that achieves the same end. Use whichever method you prefer.

⇨ Place a Credenza in each office. When you drag it in, the bottom edge is the front. So, remember to tap the SPACEBAR to rotate them as required.

> **TIP:** If you want to rotate to align with an angled or curved edge, place the mouse over the item you want to match and then tap the SPACEBAR. The Credenza will align to the angle (or curve) of the item under your cursor. Each time you press the SPACEBAR, it will rotate again. You may need to repeat a few times to get the correct angle. To reset, move to empty space and tap the SPACEBAR again.

5. Repeat the entire process to load and place the family: *Chair-Executive.rfa* [*M_Chair-Executive.rfa*] in each office (see Figure 11.9).

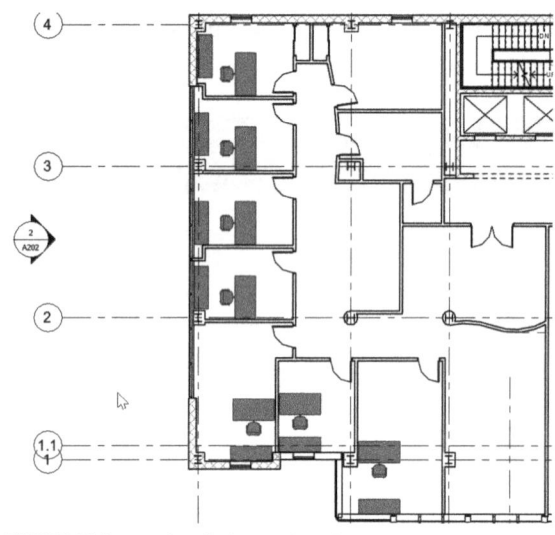

FIGURE 11.9 *Load and place a chair family in each office*

> **TIP:** To make sure that the desks and credenzas are oriented correctly, you can cut some sections, elevations or create a third floor 3D view. To do this, copy the {3D} view, rename and orient it as instructed in the "Create a Working View" topic on page 418 in Chapter 10. Mirror or rotate items as necessary.

6. Save the model.

We focused on the out-of-the-box libraries here. But there are many websites devoted to the distribution of Revit families, general tech support and discussions. A quick web search will yield many.

EDIT AND CREATE FAMILY TYPES

Until now, we have only worked with existing families and types. This was the first strategy outlined in the "Family Strategies" topic on page 468 above. In many cases, you will need to edit existing types and create your own types within existing families. This is our second strategy from that topic. You should try both approaches before resorting to creating a completely new family. There will certainly be situations where it is appropriate to create new families. (We will look at examples in detail below). For now, let's look at what we can do with existing types first.

VIEW OR EDIT TYPE PROPERTIES

In some cases, you will want to understand more about the family or type you are selecting before you place it in the model. You can view the Type Properties or edit the family directly from Project Browser. This is also accomplished via the right-click menu.

1. On the Project Browser, beneath *Families*, expand *Furniture* then *Desk [M_Desk]*.
⇨   Right-click on: 72" x 36" [1830 × 915mm] and choose: **Type Properties**.

We have seen enough examples of this dialog in previous chapters to know that if we make any edits here, they will apply to all Desks currently in the model (since they all currently share this type).

2. In the "Type Properties" dialog box, click on the "<< Preview" button at the bottom left corner of the dialog.

    This will expand the width of the dialog to include an interactive viewing pane on the left side.

If necessary, at the bottom of the viewing pane, click the "View" pop-up menu and choose: **3D View: View 1** (see Figure 11.10).

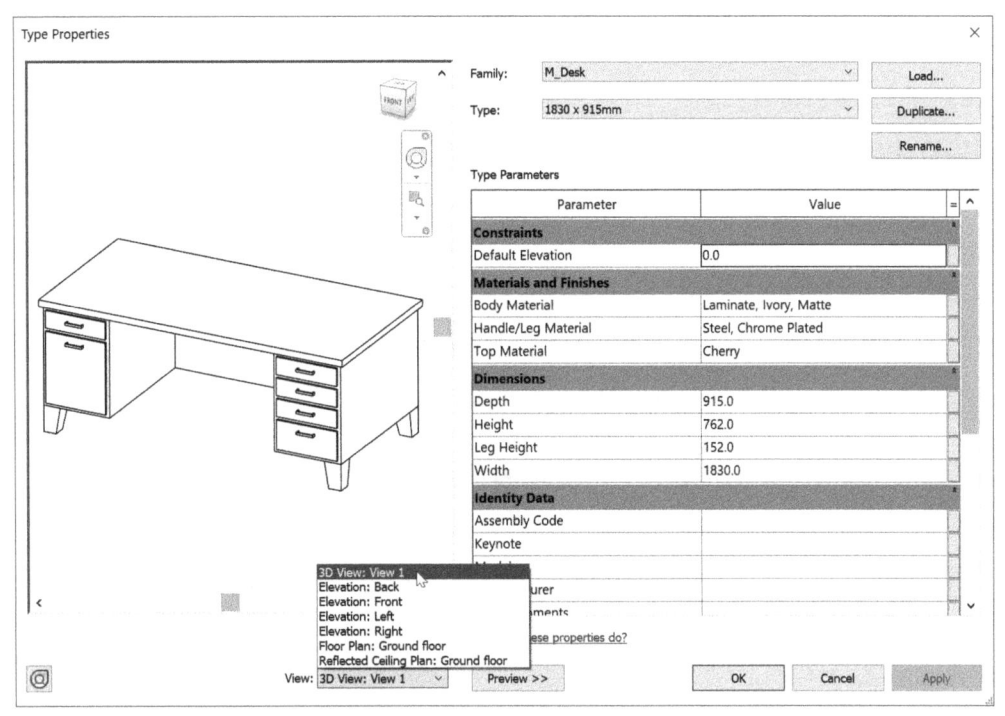

FIGURE 11.10 *Open the view pane and choose a 3D viewpoint*

There are several other view options, such as plan, elevation, and ceiling views. Try them all out if you wish and then return to the 3D view when finished. If you need to get a better look in any view, you can use standard navigation techniques. Right-click in the viewer to get a menu of standard zoom and scroll commands. There is also a "Steering Wheels" icon and the ViewCube.

   3.   Try zooming, panning and orbiting in the preview.

Take a close look at the parameters available at the right of the dialog. First, you can switch the family you are viewing by choosing another from the family list at the top. Likewise, you can choose any type from the type list beneath it. Changing either the family or the type will be reflected immediately in the viewer. Leave the family set to Desk but try choosing each of the other two types one at a time to see the viewer react. Return to the type: 72" x 36" [1830 × 915mm] when finished. Notice that all three types look essentially the same. This is critically important to understand. Study the various parameters listed in the tables below the family and type lists. These are the "Type Parameters." The shape of this desk with its two pedestals, four legs, closed back and top are all characteristics of the family called: "Desk [M_Desk]." The overall width, height, and even the height of the legs on the other hand are parameters of each type. As you choose a different type from the list, one or more of these values will change accordingly. It is like choosing between several models of a certain make car. A Honda Civic comes in several trim models, some have higher quality wheels, or better sound systems, but they are all Civics. In this analogy, "Civic" is the family and "LX" or "EX" is the type. Returning to our Desk on screen, go slowly through each of the three types again and study the viewer and especially the change in dimensions as you do. What this means is that if you simply want a different width or height desk, or perhaps wanted brass hardware rather than the default chrome, you will simply choose or create a new type. If, however, you wanted a different "make" of desk, with only a right or left pedestal for instance, you would need to choose or create a new family.

   4.   Click Cancel in the "Type Properties" dialog to dismiss it without making any changes.

CREATE A NEW TYPE FROM PROJECT BROWSER

For the group of offices running vertically along the left, let's create a new type for this Desk [M_Desk] family that is a slightly smaller size, yet a bit larger than the other types currently available.

1. On the Project Browser, right-click on: 72" x 36" [1830 × 915mm] and choose: **Duplicate**.

This will create a new type named: 72" x 36" 2 [1830 × 915mm 2] with the name highlighted and ready to be renamed. (Alternately, if you prefer, you can right-click the family name and choose: **New Type**, rename it, and the result will be the same.)

⇨ Name the new type: **66" x 30"** [**1650 × 762mm**] and then press ENTER.

You can give the type any name you want, but usually it is helpful to include in the name what makes this type different from others; in this case the size. This is standard approach taken in all the provided Revit content and a good practice to follow.

2. Right-click on: 66" x 30" [1650 × 762mm] and choose: **Type Properties** (or double-click it).

⇨ In the "Type Properties" dialog, change the Depth to: **2'-6"** [**762**].

Notice that when you click in this field, a temporary dimension appears in the viewer to indicate how this parameter will apply (see Figure 11.11).

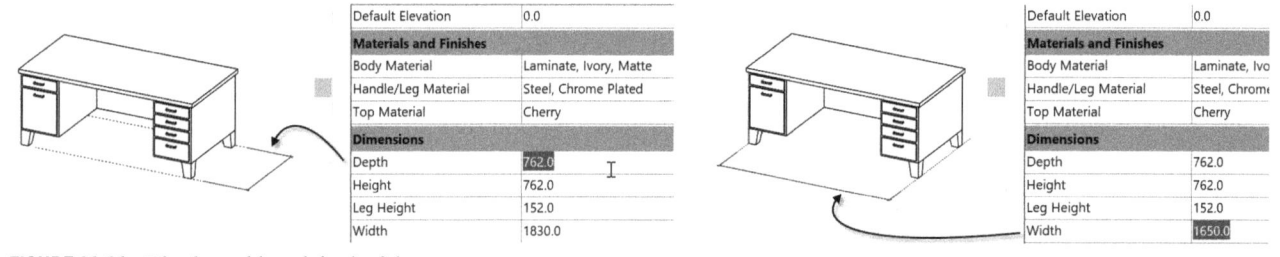

FIGURE 11.11 *Edit the width and depth of the new type*

⇨ In the "Type Properties" dialog, change the Width to: **5'-6"** [**1650**] and then click OK.

3. Right-click on the new type and choose: **Match**.

⇨ Click on each of the Desks in the offices along the left side of the plan (4 total) to change them to the new type.

Move the Desks if necessary, to align better with the walls.

> **TIP:** You can use the Align tool here to snap the edge of the desk to a wall. But remember if you want a little space between the desk and wall, select it, and then use the arrow keys on the keyboard to "nudge" it slightly. Zoom in to make the nudge increment finer, zoom out to make it coarser.

4. Save the model.

Because we can see that there is more than one type in this family, with different names, we have a good indication that this family is parametric, and new types with different parameters, sizes or materials, can be created. If there is only one type, and it has the same name as the family, it typically means that family is not parametric. While you could make additional types from such a family, you would be limited to editing identity data and materials. For an example, edit the properties of the *Chair-Executive*. The only editable parameters are the materials of the chair's components and the standard identity data information. Changing the width, height, and depth is not possible the way this family is built. Another way to say this is that to edit the dimensions of the executive chair, you would be required to open and edit the geometry of the family file directly.

Families and the Family Editor | 477

CUSTOMIZING FAMILIES

Even with the various libraries available, we often need components in our projects for which a suitable family is not readily available. In these situations, we can create our own custom family. Custom families can be simple or complex. In this topic, we will look at various examples of creating and using custom families in our projects.

DUPLICATE AN EXISTING FAMILY

When you decide to build your own family, it can be useful to start with an existing family that is close to the family you wish to create. Doing so will only require you to save as and edit the existing family which can be more expedient than starting from scratch. For example, flanking the corridor in the middle of our tenant suite is a secretarial space with room for two workstations. Perhaps the client would like desks in this area that have a CPU cubby rather than the two drawer pedestals occurring in the family we currently have loaded. We can save a version of the existing family, and then modify it to make this change. This is much more efficient than modeling the entire desk over again.

1. On the Project Browser, beneath *Families*, expand *Furniture* and then right-click on: *Desk* [*M_Desk*].

    ⇨ Choose: **Edit** from the right-click menu (see Figure 11.12).

> **TIP:** As an alternative, select one of the desks in the model, right-click and choose: **Edit Family** (or click the Edit Family button on the ribbon with the element selected).

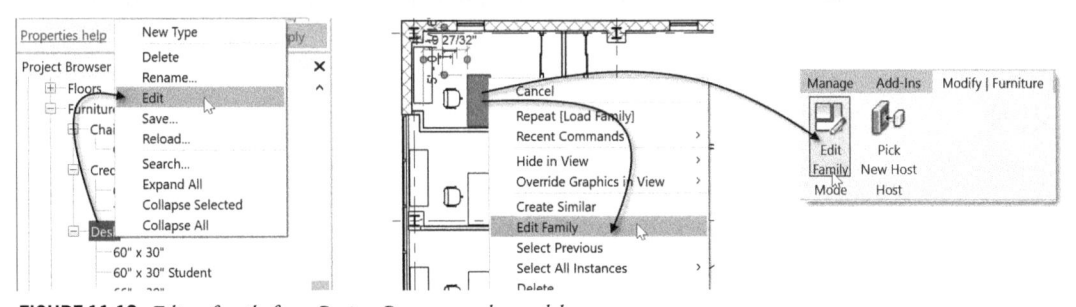

FIGURE 11.12 *Edit a family from Project Browser or the model*

The *Desk* [*M_Desk*] family will open into the Family Editor with a 3D view active. (You are no longer in the commercial building project file. You are now in the *Desk* family file where you can edit it directly.)

2. Move your Modify tool over each part of the desk and pause for the tool tip to appear (see Figure 11.13).

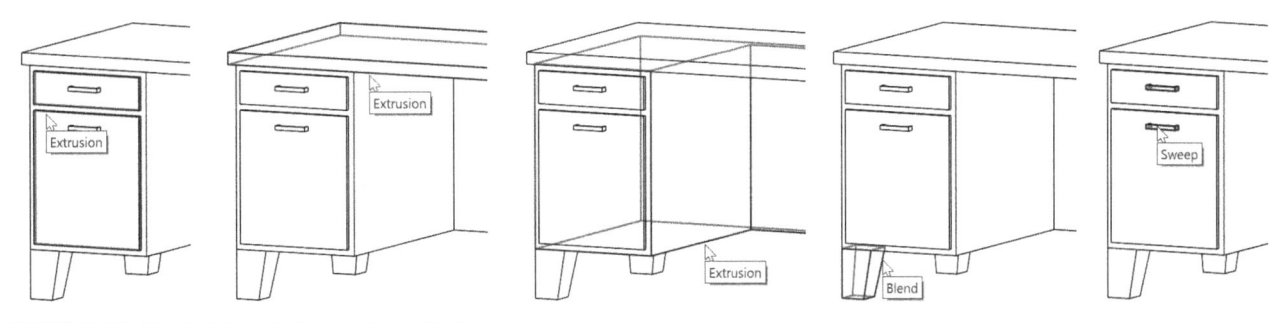

FIGURE 11.13 *The desk is made from various solid forms*

• Revit Essentials for Architecture •

KINDS OF FORMS IN THE FAMILY EDITOR

The desk is made from a collection of solid extrusions, sweeps, and blends. An extrusion is a 3D form created by a closed 2D shape that is "pushed" along a perpendicular path. A sweep is like an extrusion except that it follows a path, which can be any shape. A blend is form that starts with one closed shape and then "morphs" into a second closed shape. The transformation from the bottom shape to the top shape occurs along a perpendicular path. In addition to the three solid forms used in this family, we also have revolve and swept blend. A revolve is a shape derived from rotating a closed 2D shape about an axis. A swept blend is basically a blend that can have a non-perpendicular or curved path. The path is limited to one segment, but it can be any shape you wish—even a spline.

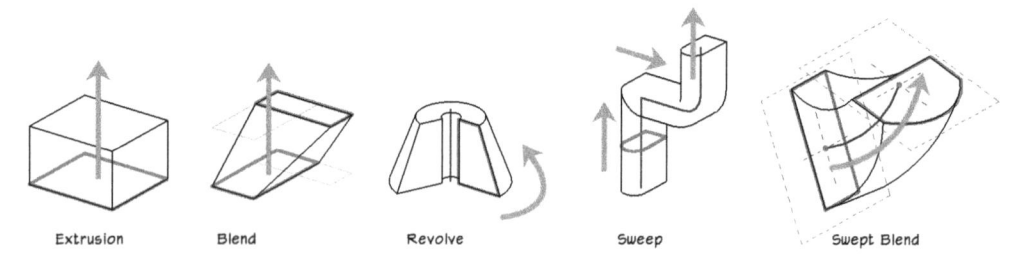

FIGURE 11.14 *The five forms available in the family editor*

Each of these five basic shapes can be made as solids or voids. Solids create physical material in the model, while voids carve away from the solid form to achieve more complex forms. In addition to this "raw material," a family can also contain other families. These "nested" families are added using the Component tool within the Family Editor. (We will see an example of a nested family below).

EDIT AN EXTRUSION

Let's make a simple modification to the one of the extrusion forms in this family. Like a project, you can edit in any view. Navigating the views in the Family Editor is nearly the same as within a project, except the names of the views are more generic and the quantity of views is typically much fewer.

1. On the Project Browser, expand *Views (All)* and then expand *Elevations*.
⇨ Double-click to open the: *Front* elevation view.
2. Select the extrusion on the left (that represents the drawer fronts) and then hold down the CTRL key and select the handles (a sweep) as well (see Figure 11.15).

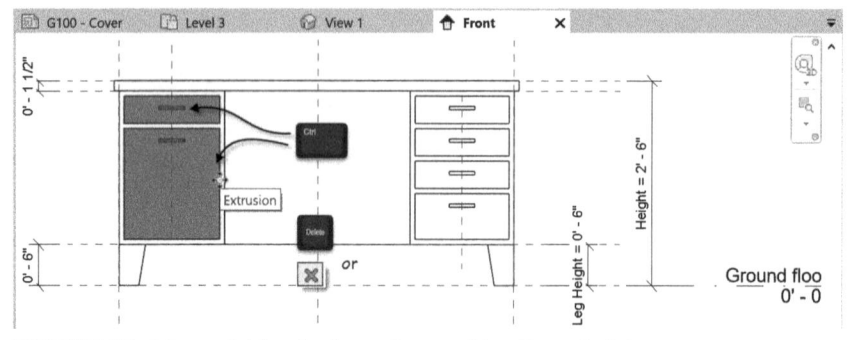

FIGURE 11.15 *Select and delete the drawer fronts and handles on the left*

⇨ Press the DELETE key to erase both elements.

Families and the Family Editor | 479

> **NOTE:** The author of this family chose to create a single extrusion that contained two shapes—one for the top drawer and another for the bottom. While this is a perfectly valid approach, it forces us to edit both drawers together. In your own families think about such issues carefully. You may ultimately like this approach best, but in some cases, you may decide to instead model each drawer separately as its own extrusion.

The pedestal on the left will become a cubby. Therefore, we have deleted the drawer fronts. We now need to make the cubby a bit narrower and then cut a void from in it to complete the cubby.

3. Click on the extrusion that comprises the major form of the desk.

    Notice all the shape handles that appear. We can simply drag one of these to make the cubby narrower.

    ⇨ Drag the shape handle (indicated in Figure 11.16) to the left and snap it to the reference plane (dashed vertical line in the middle of the pedestal).

    ⇨ Click the small open padlock icon that appears to apply a constraint to this reference plane.

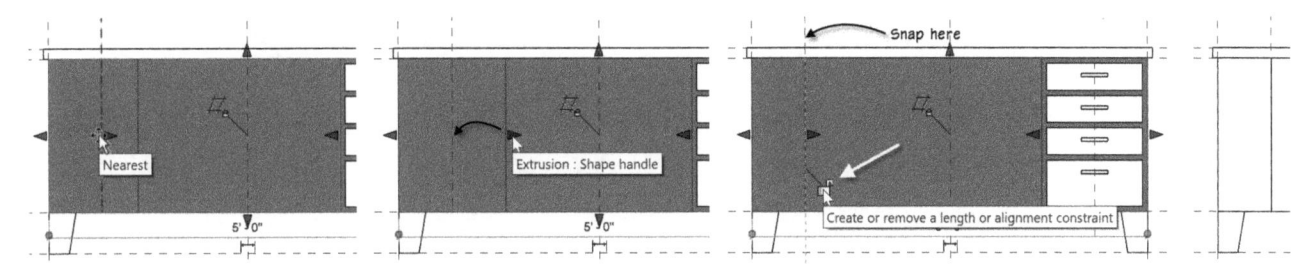

FIGURE 11.16 *Use the shape handles to resize the cubby pedestal*

This action "locks" this side of the extrusion to this reference plane. If the reference plane later moves, the edge of the extrusion will move accordingly. Let's try it out.

> **NOTE:** If you are working in metric units, before performing the next step, open the *Ground Floor* plan view, select the reference plane (that we just snapped the extrusion to) and then unlock the 203mm dimension that appears at the top of the plan. Return to the *Front* view to continue.

4. Deselect the extrusion and then select the reference plane.

    ⇨ Edit the temporary dimension that appears to: **1'-8"** [**500**] (see Figure 11.17).

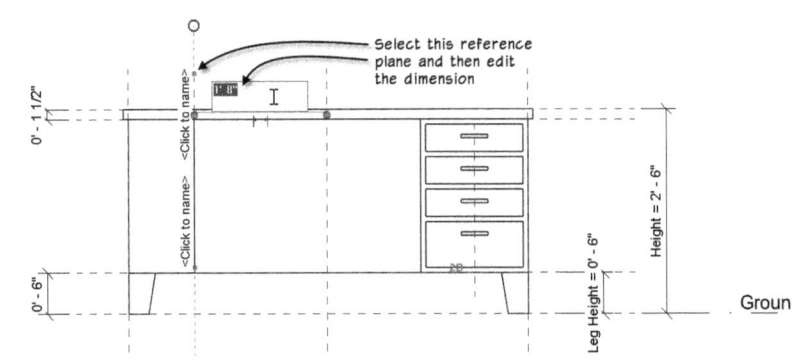

FIGURE 11.17 *Move the reference plane to move the constrained extrusion edge*

Notice that the reference plane moved and pulled the shape of the geometry with it. (In the metric file, you may need to move the legs back to the reference plane on the left).

5. On the ribbon, click the Modify tool or press the ESC key twice.

• Revit Essentials for Architecture •

480 | Chapter 11

ADDING A VOID FORM

Let's add the void next.

1. On the Create tab of the ribbon, on the Forms panel, click the Void Forms tool and then choose: **Void Extrusion** from the drop down.

Since we are working with solids and voids that are 3D forms, we need to indicate to Revit our preferred working plane. A working plane establishes a 2D surface in the model in which we can sketch our 2D shapes. In this case, since we are working on the *Front* elevation, a work plane parallel to front makes the most sense.

⇨ In the "Work Plane" dialog, from the "Name" list choose: **Reference Plane : Front** [**Reference Plane : Bottom**] and then click OK (see Figure 11.18).

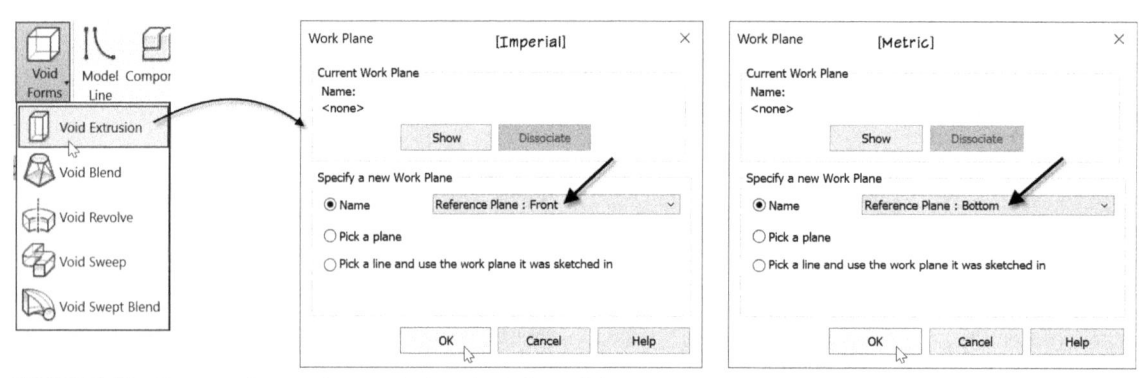

FIGURE 11.18 *Choose a reference plane in which to sketch the void shape*

2. On the Create Void Extrusion tab, on the Draw panel, click the Rectangle icon.
⇨ On the Options Bar, in the "Offset" field, type: **3/4"** [**19**].
3. Using Figure 11.19 as a guide, snap to one corner of the CPU pedestal.
⇨ Tap the SPACEBAR to flip the sketch to the inside (if necessary) and then snap to the opposite corner as shown.

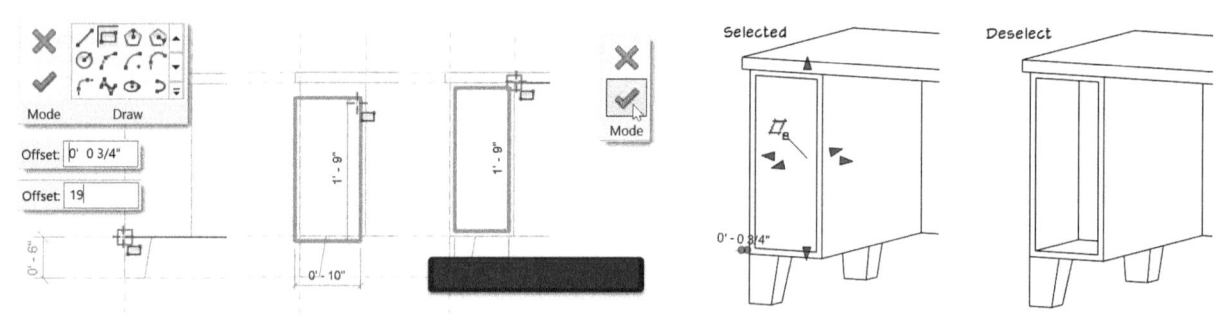

FIGURE 11.19 *Sketch the cut extrusion shape*

4. On the ribbon, click the Finish Edit Mode button (green checkmark).
⇨ On the Project Browser, beneath *3D Views*, double-click to open: *View 1*.
⇨ Deselect the Void.

From this view you can see that the Void is cutting away from the overall form of the desk. However, you can also see that it does not project back very far into the desk's depth. We can easily adjust this. (To see the cut extrusion more clearly, pass the Modify tool over the cubby to pre-highlight it.) The floor plan view might be a good location to work for this edit.

5. On the Project Browser, double-click to open the *Ground Floor* plan view.
⇨ Click the void extrusion in plan.

• The Aubin Academy •

It will be in the upper right in plan view in imperial, it will be in the lower left in the metric file.

⇨ Use the Shape Handle to stretch the Void back to the rear plane of the desk (it should snap automatically) then lock it (see Figure 11.20).

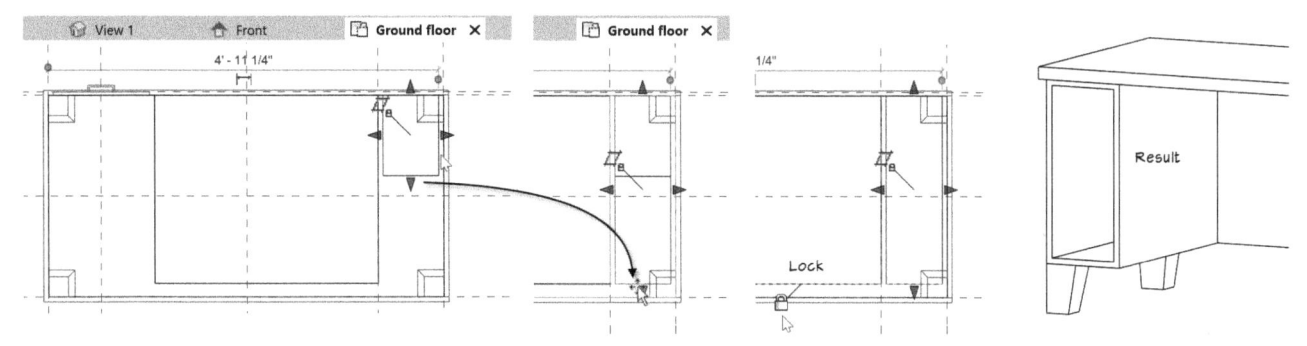

FIGURE 11.20 *Stretch the depth of the void using shape handles*

With the cut extrusion still selected note the Depth field on the Options bar shows the current dimension. The Depth can also be edited here as well. Also note that when the Void is selected, it will not appear to cut the solid. When you deselect the Void, it will resume cutting.

6. Deselect the void and return to the *View 1* 3D view to see the results.

SAVE A NEW FAMILY

We are ready to save the results and load our new family into the project.

1. From the File menu, choose: **Save As > Family**.

> **CAUTION:** It is very important to use Save As rather than Save. If you simply save the family, it will overwrite the existing *Desk [M_Desk]* family from which we started (in the library).

Revit imposes no limitations on where you can save family files, however, the location where you save family files is a very important consideration particularly in team environments. Check with your IT support personnel regarding the preferred location for saving family files. Sometimes firms have a "check-in" process for newly created content. It is also common to have prescribed naming procedures. Follow whatever guidelines or practices are in place in your company. For this exercise, we will simply save the family file (RFA) to our *Chapter11* folder. If you decide later that you wish to use this family in real projects, you can copy (and optionally rename) it from this location to a suitable location on your company network.

2. In the "Save As" dialog, browse to the *Chapter11* folder.

⇨ In the "File name" field, type: **Desk-Secretary.rfa** for the name and then click Save.

Before we load this family back into the project, let's edit its types. Remember, the family controls the available parameters and physical form of the element. However, the type(s) can have specific values for the established family parameters. Following the lead of the family from which we created this one, our types will have predefined values for the sizes.

3. On the Create tab, on the Properties panel, click the Family Types button.

The "Family Types" dialog will appear. At the top is a drop down list showing each of the existing types inherited from the *Desk [M_Desk]* family. Some of these are no longer necessary.

⇨ From the "Name" list, choose: **60" x 30" Student [1525 × 762mm Student]**

• Revit Essentials for Architecture •

482 | Chapter 11

and then click the Delete button (see Figure 11.21).

⇨ Repeat for the **72" x 36"** [**1830 × 915mm**] type.

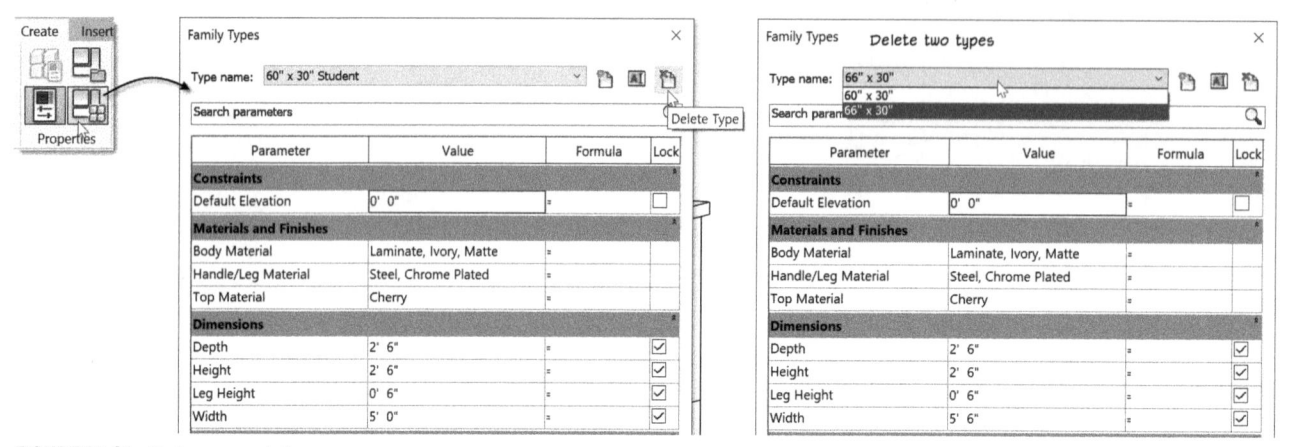

FIGURE 11.21 *Delete unneeded types*

The remaining type can stay for this family.

4. Click OK to dismiss the dialog.

5. On the QAT click the Save icon (or choose Save from the File menu).

NOTE: Since we have already saved this file as *Desk-Secretary.rfa*, we can simply choose Save this time to update the file. Save As would create a second copy of the file, which would be unnecessary.

LOAD THE FAMILY INTO THE PROJECT

On the ribbon, notice that there is a blue-gray tinted panel named: "Family Editor." This panel appears on all tabs of the ribbon. Go ahead and click through some of the tabs to see for yourself. Therefore, you will always have access to the buttons on this panel regardless of the ribbon tab you have active. This also serves to remind you that you are working in the family editor.

1. On the ribbon, click the Load into Project and Close button.

If a "Load into Projects" dialog appears, check the commercial project only and click OK. This will bring the project to the front, add this family to the project and run the Component tool so you can place an instance in the model.

2. Add two of the new desks (of the larger size) to the model in the secretarial spaces as shown in Figure 11.22.

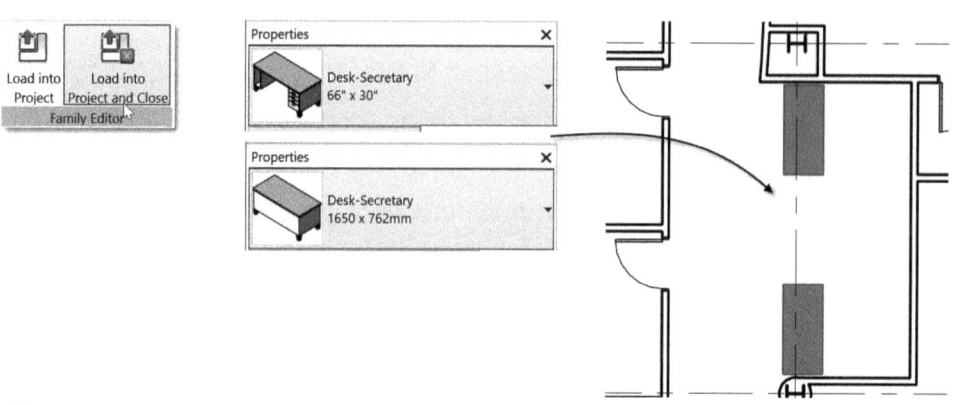

FIGURE 11.22 *Add two new desks to the model*

• The Aubin Academy •

Families and the Family Editor | 483

From the floor plan view, we cannot really see any of the edits we made. Let's add a Camera view to the project so we can get a look at our new component family.

3. On the View tab, click the drop down on the 3D View button and then choose: **Camera**.

⇨ Click a point behind the desks and then drag toward one of the desks.

⇨ Click again beyond the wall at the opposite side of the corridor (see the left side of Figure 11.23).

You will likely be too close to the desk to see it. You can adjust the camera to widen and lower the viewing angle.

4. On the Navigation Bar, click the Steering Wheel (or press F8).

⇨ In the lower corner of the Steering Wheel, click the small drop down arrow menu, then choose: **Increase/Decrease Focal Length**.

⇨ Drag the mouse down to widen the camera angle until you can most of the desk and the door to the right beyond.

⇨ Press ESC once to exit this mode.

⇨ Remaining in the Steering Wheel, click and hold down on the Up/Down region and drag down until the entire desk comes into view (see the right side of Figure 11.23).

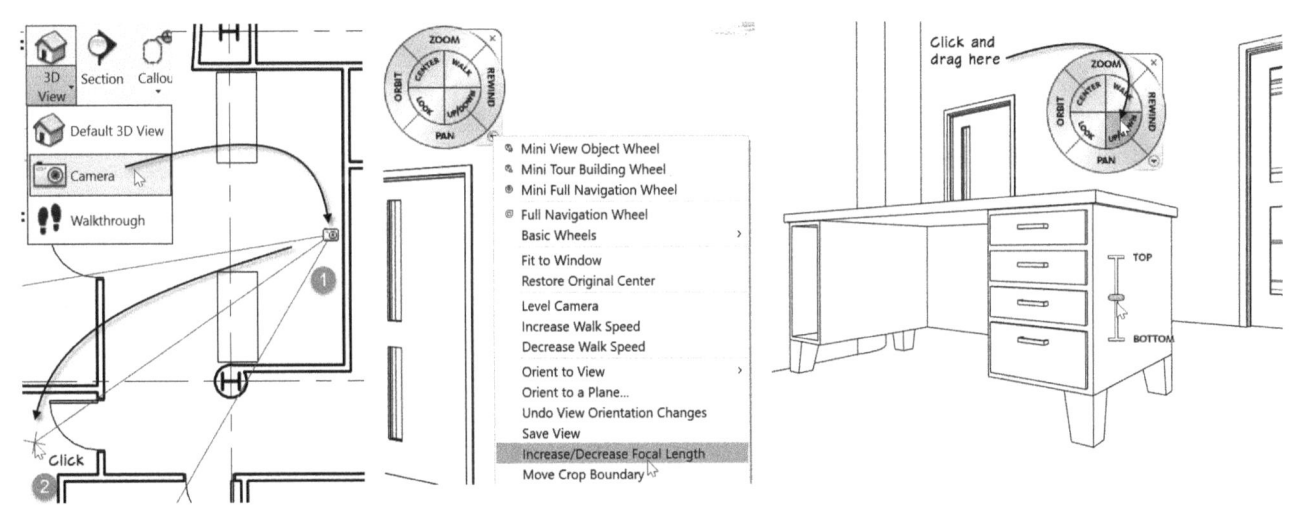

FIGURE 11.23 *Add a camera view from the plan*

⇨ Press ESC to cancel the steering wheel.

TIP: If your desk is facing the wrong way, select the desk, and then tap the SPACEBAR a couple times to rotate it. Drag it to adjust position if necessary. You can do this in the camera view or back in the plan.

5. On the Project Browser, right-click the 3D View 1 and rename it to: **Camera at Secretarial Desk**.

6. Save the project.

EDIT A FAMILY

Since this desk is now a computer-type desk, we should probably add a keyboard shelf in the middle. To do this, we simply repeat the process above and return to the Family Editor. We can model the shelf with a simple solid extrusion.

1. In the camera view, select the Secretary Desk and then on the Modify | Furniture tab, click the Edit Family button.

2. On the Project Browser, double-click to open the *Ground floor* plan view.

3. On the Create tab, on the Forms panel, click the Extrusion button.

• Revit Essentials for Architecture •

484 | Chapter 11

⇨ Using the rectangle option on the Draw panel, sketch a rectangular shape for the keyboard shelf in plan (see Figure 11.24).

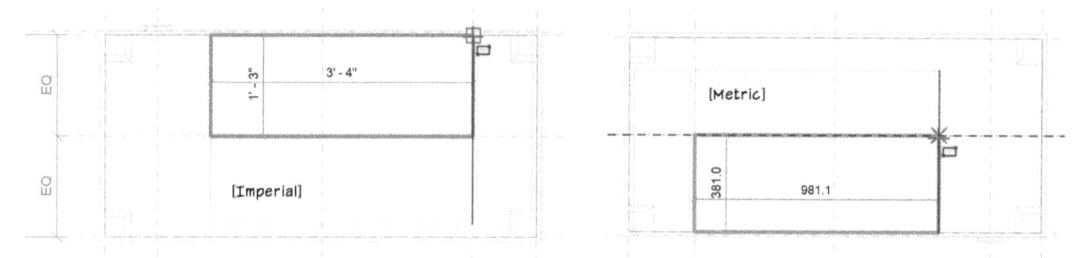

FIGURE 11.24 *Sketch the keyboard shelf*

Note the different locations in imperial and metric files. You do not need to close the lock icons.

4. On the Properties palette, beneath Constraints, set the "Extrusion Start" to: **2'-1"** [**625**] and the "Extrusion End" to: **2'-1 3/4"** [**644**].

5. On the ribbon, on the Mode panel, click the Finish Edit Mode button.

⇨ Return to the *View 1* 3D view (see Figure 11.25).

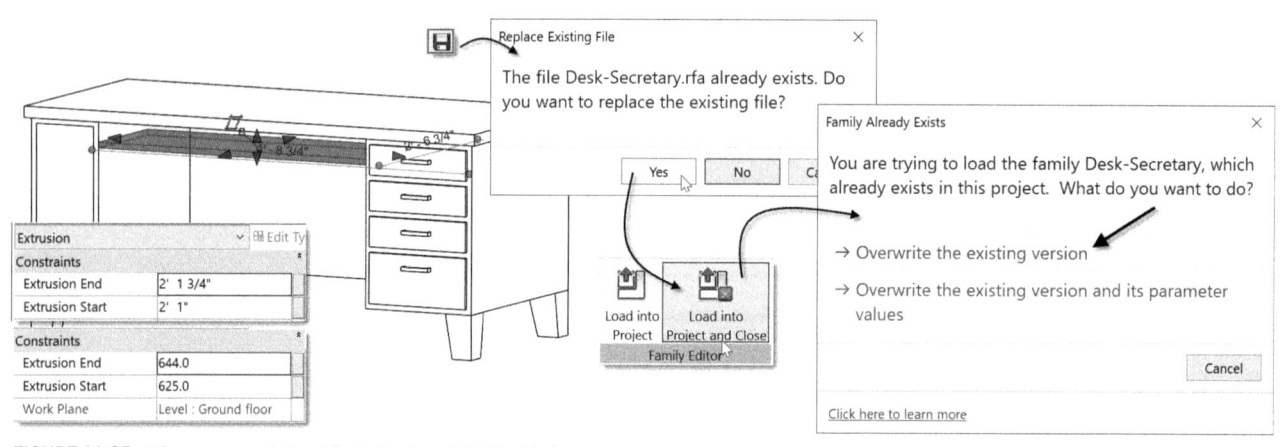

FIGURE 11.25 *The secretary desk with the keyboard shelf added*

6. Save the family, click Yes to overwrite the existing family if prompted, and then click the Load into Project and Close button.

7. In the "Family Already Exists" dialog, choose the "Overwrite the existing version" option.

Notice how the update to the desk now appears in the project in the camera view. If you move the camera to look at the other one, you will see it has changed as well. More importantly, if you choose the other size from the Type Selector, you will see that both have a keyboard tray. This is because a change to family geometry is applied to all instances of the family across all its types.

8. Save the project.

Congratulations. You have completed your first custom family. This was a very simple example and we took some shortcuts. But in many cases, the kind of edits we made here are all you will need to keep your project moving along and populate it with the content you need. However, there is plenty to learn about the Family Editor and its best practices. In the coming topics, we'll create a new family from scratch and get into more advanced family creation techniques as well.

• The Aubin Academy •

Families and the Family Editor | 485

BUILDING CUSTOM FAMILIES

In many cases, the preceding process will enable you to produce the family you need by leveraging your existing library content. However, sometimes it will be necessary (or easier) to start from scratch. In this case, you will simply create a new family file and begin modeling the item you require. All new families are created from predefined family templates. Revit ships with a large collection of pre-made family templates from which to choose. It is important to select the family template which best corresponds to the kind of family you wish to create. This is because the template you choose determines the category of the family and whether it requires a host. While possible to modify the category later, you cannot change the hosting behavior of a family once it has been created. There are also other less obvious behaviors that families inherit from their templates as well, so choose your template carefully.

CREATING CUSTOM ELEVATION TAGS

If you completed Chapter 5, one of the steps we conducted in the process of setting up the commercial project, in the "Loading Custom Elevation Tags" topic on page 173, was to import a custom elevation tag. In this passage, we will revisit that topic and go through the process of creating the elevation tags from scratch. Creating annotation families like the elevation tag is straightforward. These are simple 2D families, but many of the broader concepts also apply to more complex 3D families, so this is a good "warm-up" exercise.

Close the current project.

1. From the File menu, choose: **Close**. If prompted to save, choose Yes.

   If any other files are open, close them too. Once you have closed all open files the Home screen should display in response.

2. On the Home Screen, beneath Families, click the **New** button.

   ⇨ Browse to: *English-Imperial\Annotations* [*English\Annotations*].

This will display all the available annotation family templates. To create a custom elevation tag, we need to build two separate elevation mark families: Elevation Mark Pointer and Elevation Mark Body. We will start with the pointer.

⇨ From the list of available templates, choose the: *Elevation Mark Pointer.rft* [*Metric Elevation Mark Pointer.rft*] template file and then click Open (see Figure 11.26).

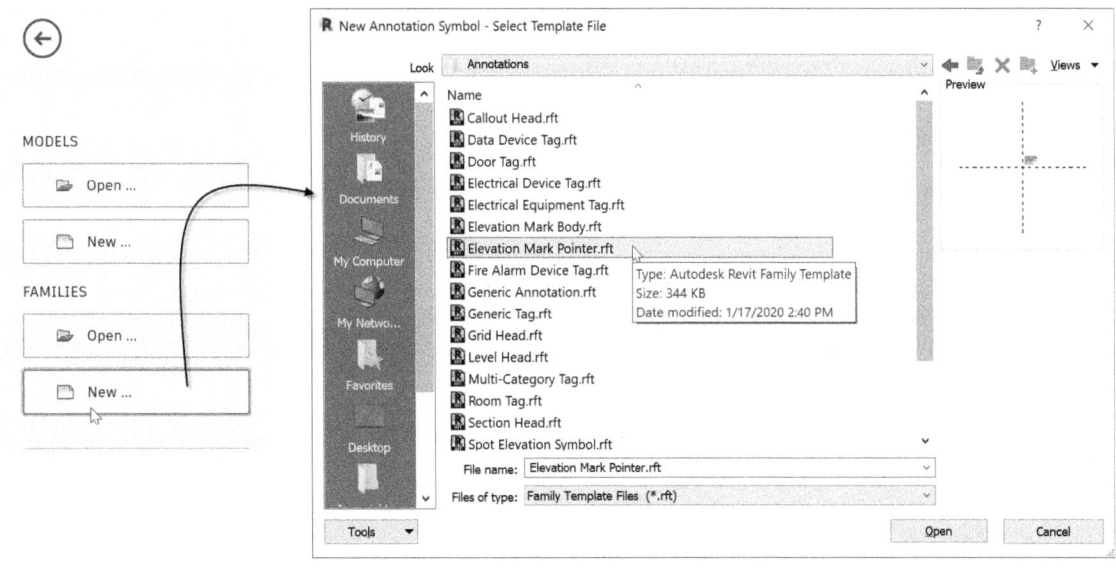

FIGURE 11.26 *Create a new annotation family and choose an appropriate template*

486 | Chapter 11

Most annotation family templates contain two reference planes marking the insertion point of the family and a descriptive note with some instructions. In this case, the note reads:

"Place elements/labels to represent the pointer element of an elevation mark.
The direction of the pointer is vertical from the intersection of the ref planes.
Insertion point is at intersection of ref planes.
Delete this note before using."

Pay close attention to these instructions as they will help us build our elevation tag successfully. We will build our tag to match the guidelines in the US National CAD Standard. The result can be seen in the tag we used in commercial project. We'll start with a filled region. A Filled Region is simply a two-dimensional shape with an outline and filled in with a pattern. The NCS elevation tag calls for a triangular shaped solid filled pointer surrounding a round tag.

3. On the Create tab, click the Filled Region tool.
4. On the Draw panel, click the Center-ends Arc tool.
   ⇨ Click to place the center of the arc at the intersection of the two reference planes.
   The radius is a "listening dimension."
   ⇨ Drag to the left along the horizontal reference plane, type: **5/16"** [8] for the radius and then press ENTER.
   ⇨ Move to the right to indicate a 180° arc pointing up and then click to set the arc (see Figure 11.27).

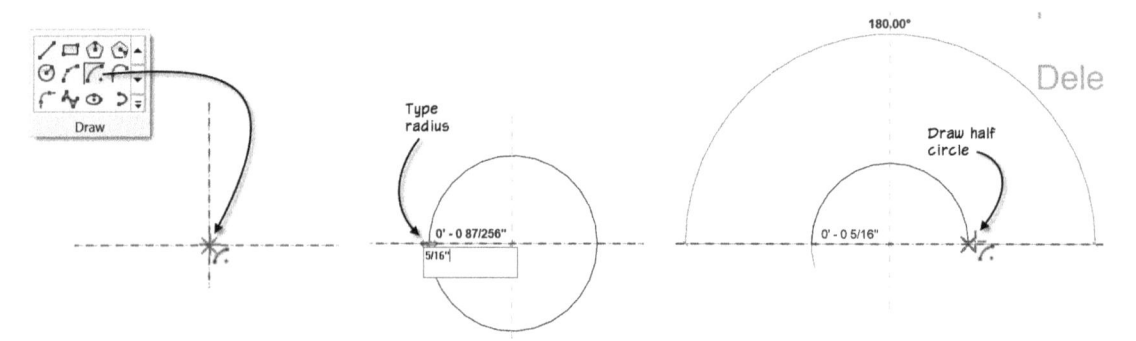

FIGURE 11.27 *Begin the outline of the filled region with an arc*

5. On the Draw panel, click the Circumscribed Polygon tool.
   ⇨ On the Options Bar, change the number of sides to: **4**.
6. Snap the center point to the intersection of the reference planes again.
   ⇨ Draw out the radius at a 45° angle and snap it to the arc (see the left side of Figure 11.28).

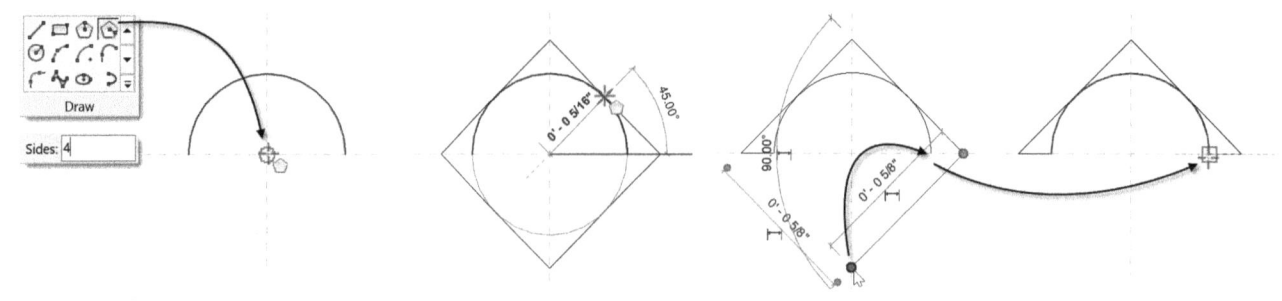

FIGURE 11.28 *Draw the triangular shape starting with a 4-sided polygon*

7. On the ribbon, click the Modify tool or press the ESC key twice.
8. Select the lower diagonal line on the left.

⇨ Click and drag the small blue shape handle up and snap it up to the end of the arc on the same side.

9. Repeat on the other side (see the right side of Figure 11.28).

This gives us the basic shape required, but we must fine-tune it just a little. Revit will not allow us to complete the shape as is, because the diagonal lines intersect the arc. We have two options to deal with this. We can either create three separate shapes by breaking the sketch at the point of intersection (along the 45°) or we can slightly nudge the sketch lines to form a small gap. Let's do the latter method here.

10. Select the two diagonal lines (select one, then hold down the CTRL key and select the other).

⇨ Zoom in close to the shape and then on the keyboard; press the up arrow key one time.

This will "nudge" the lines up slightly. The amount of the nudge depends on the zoom level. So, if you are unhappy with the result, undo, zoom in or out, and try again.

11. Select all the lines and the arc (the easiest way to do this is to pre-highlight one, press TAB, and then click to select the chain).

⇨ On the Line Subcategory panel of the ribbon, form the drop down list, choose: <**Invisible Lines**>.

12. On the ribbon, click the Finish Edit Mode button.

⇨ Verify that: **Filled Region: Solid Black** is chosen on the Type Selector and then deselect the element (see Figure 11.29).

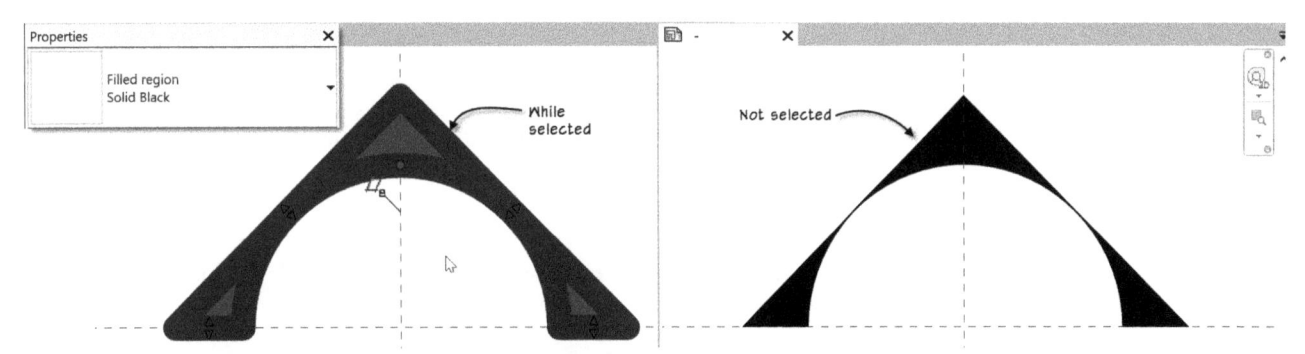

FIGURE 11.29 *The completed filled region shape for the elevation tag*

13. Delete the red text note.

⇨ Save the file to the *Chapter11* folder and name it: **NCS Elevation Tag Arrow**.

That completes the arrow. We will leave the file open for now and create the elevation body next.

14. From the File menu, choose: **New > Annotation Symbol**.

⇨ From the list of available templates, choose the *Elevation Mark Body.rft* template file and then click Open.

This template appears nearly the same as the other. However, this time the text note reads:

"Place elements/labels to represent the body of the elevation mark.
Load a pointer family and place instances where you wish arrows to be available in the project.
Insertion point is at intersection of ref planes.
Delete this note before using."

15. Delete the red note.

16. On the Create tab, click the Line tool and then choose the circle icon from the Draw panel.

⇨ Click to place the center of the arc at the intersection of the two reference planes.

488 | Chapter 11

- For the radius, type: **5/16" [8]** and then press ENTER.

17. On the Draw panel, click the Line icon and draw a horizontal line across the diameter of the circle (snap to the quadrant on either side).

18. On the Create tab, click the Label tool and then click a point on the vertical reference plane in the upper part of the circle to place it.

- In the "Edit Label" dialog, click Detail Number and then click the Add parameter(s) to label icon in the middle and then click OK (see Figure 11.30).

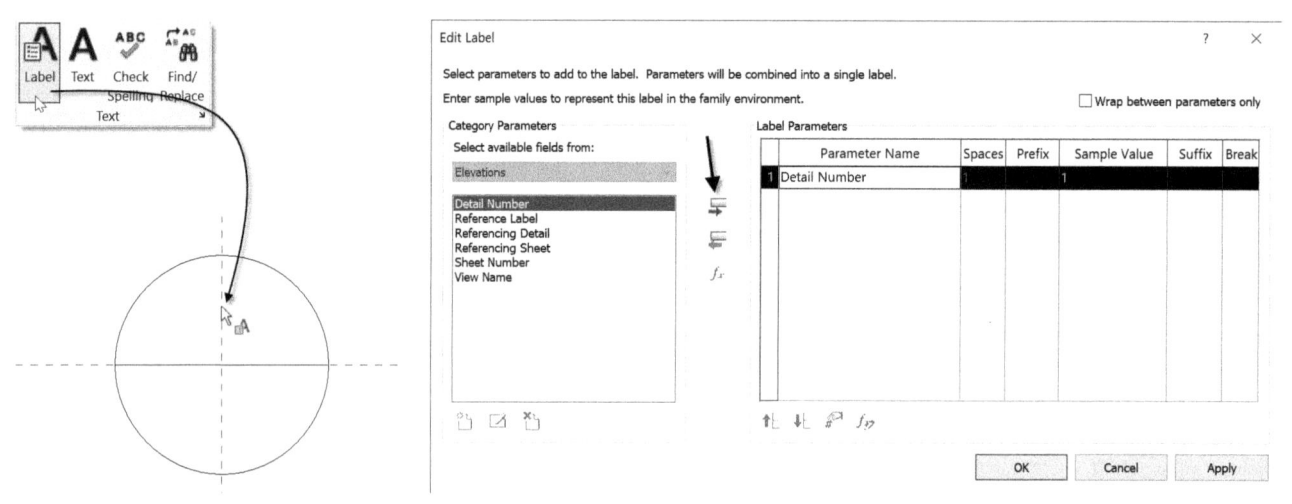

FIGURE 11.30 *Add a label to the tag*

19. Create a second Label in the lower portion of the circle for the Sheet Number parameter.

- On the ribbon, click the Modify tool or press the ESC key twice, and then fine-tune placement of both parameters as necessary.

A Label is special text that will report one or more parameters in the tag. We saw an example of this in the "Create a Custom Title Block Family" topic on page 193 in Chapter 5.

20. On the QAT, click the Save icon. You will be prompted to name the file.

- Save it to the *Chapter11* folder and name it: **NCS Elevation Tag**.

21. You should still see a view tab open for the *NCS Elevation Tag Arrow* family. Click it to switch to that file. (Optionally you can press CTRL + TAB to cycle to the other open file).

- On the ribbon, click the Load into Project and Close button.

You should only have one other file open; the new *NCS Elevation Tag* family file and therefore should not be prompted to choose a file. However, if you are prompted to select a project, be sure to choose: *NCS Elevation Tag*.

The Place Symbol command should run automatically; if it does not, on the Annotate tab, click the Symbol button.

22. Place an instance of NCS Elevation Tag Arrow anywhere onscreen and the click the Modify tool or press the ESC key twice.

23. Move it so that it is positioned properly with the center of the circle. (The Align tool works well for this.)

24. Select the arrow, copy it to the clipboard (CTRL + C) and then from the Paste drop down, choose: **Aligned to Same Place**. Tap the SPACEBAR to rotate it (see Figure 11.31).

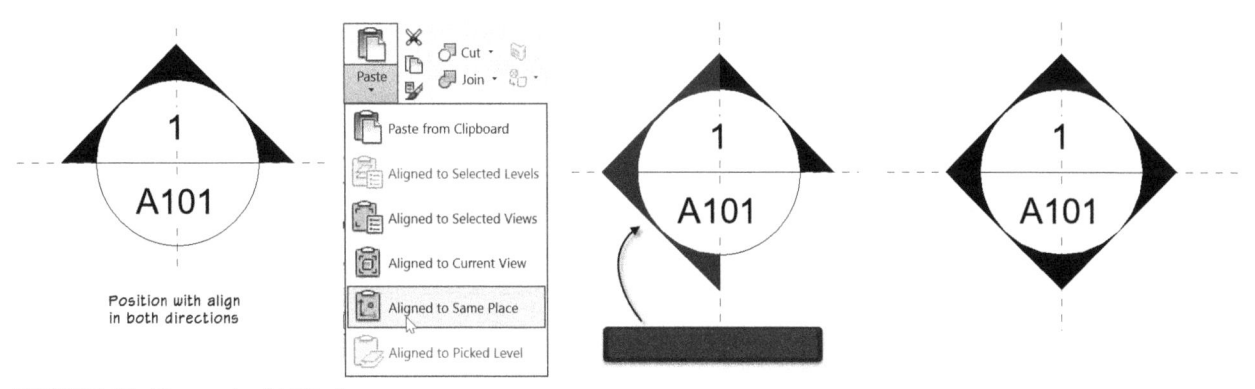

FIGURE 11.31 *The completed NCS elevation tag*

> ⇨ Paste Aligned to Same Place again, and then press the SPACEBAR twice this time.
>
> ⇨ Repeat the past once more, and then SPACEBAR three times.

That completes our custom elevation tag. Since the custom tag is already a part of our Commercial project, to test it out you can create a new project file. Simply create a new project from the default template and then follow the steps in the "Loading Custom Elevation Tags" topic on page 173 in Chapter 5 to load your tag and apply it to the default elevation tags.

25. Close and save all files before continuing to the next topic. (The Home screen should reappear.)

CREATE A NEW FAMILY FILE

Let's turn our attention back to model families. Keeping with the furniture layout on the third floor of the commercial project a little longer, let's create a custom reception desk for the lobby to the office suite. This will be the first of several model families we will build. This one is *not* parametric. We will build it in the size and configuration we need. The focus of this exercise is to expose you to the modeling tools in the Family Editor.

> **TIP:** It may be tempting to make your first family a door or window or some other more common element. However, this is not recommended. Furniture is chosen here because such elements tend to be free-standing (not hosted), many have simple straightforward geometry (like desks, shelves and storage units), and their parametric requirements are often limited as well to overall dimensions like width and height. Doors and Windows are much more complex than they first appear, with many complex relationships and parameters, making them a challenging place from which to begin your family editing explorations. Start simple with items like those showcased here and then work your way up to more complex objects.

1. Make sure all projects and families are closed, on the Home Screen, beneath Families, click the New button.

   Browse to your Templates (language and units preference) folder if necessary.

This will open the "New Family" dialog box to the folder that contains all the available family templates. Familiarize yourself with this list—there are many from which to choose. Remember the choice of template is important, so take the time to make a good choice.

Notice that some categories have more than one template. For example, in the list you can see that there is: *Electrical Fixture.rft*, *Electrical Fixture ceiling based.rft*, and *Electrical Fixture Wall based.rft*. All three create families of the electrical fixture category, but the ceiling based one requires a ceiling host object and the wall based requires a wall host. *Electrical Fixture.rft* requires no host and can be placed freestanding in a project. Any of the templates whose name ends in "based" require a host. In our case, the category we need for our reception desk is: furniture. Therefore, we

490 | Chapter 11

will select the *Furniture.rft* template. As you can see, unlike electrical fixtures, there is only one furniture template and it does not require a host. (Be sure to pick furniture and not furniture system).

⇨   Select *Furniture.rft* [*Metric Furniture.rft*] and then click Open.

> **NOTE:** If your version of Revit does not contain either of these templates, they have been provided in the *Chapter11* folder.

As with the previous exercise, we are now in the Family Editor. The difference here is that the current view contains only the two reference planes and no note. If you look at the view tabs that opened, you will notice that this family loads with four open views. This is common practice for working in model families, and it is often more convenient to work if we tile the windows. (If you see more than the four windows from the new family on the Switch Windows drop down, please close them first.)

2. On the View tab, on the Windows panel, click the Tile tool (or press WT).

⇨   From the Navigation Bar, from the Zoom fly out choose: **Zoom All to Fit** (or press ZA) (see Figure 11.32).

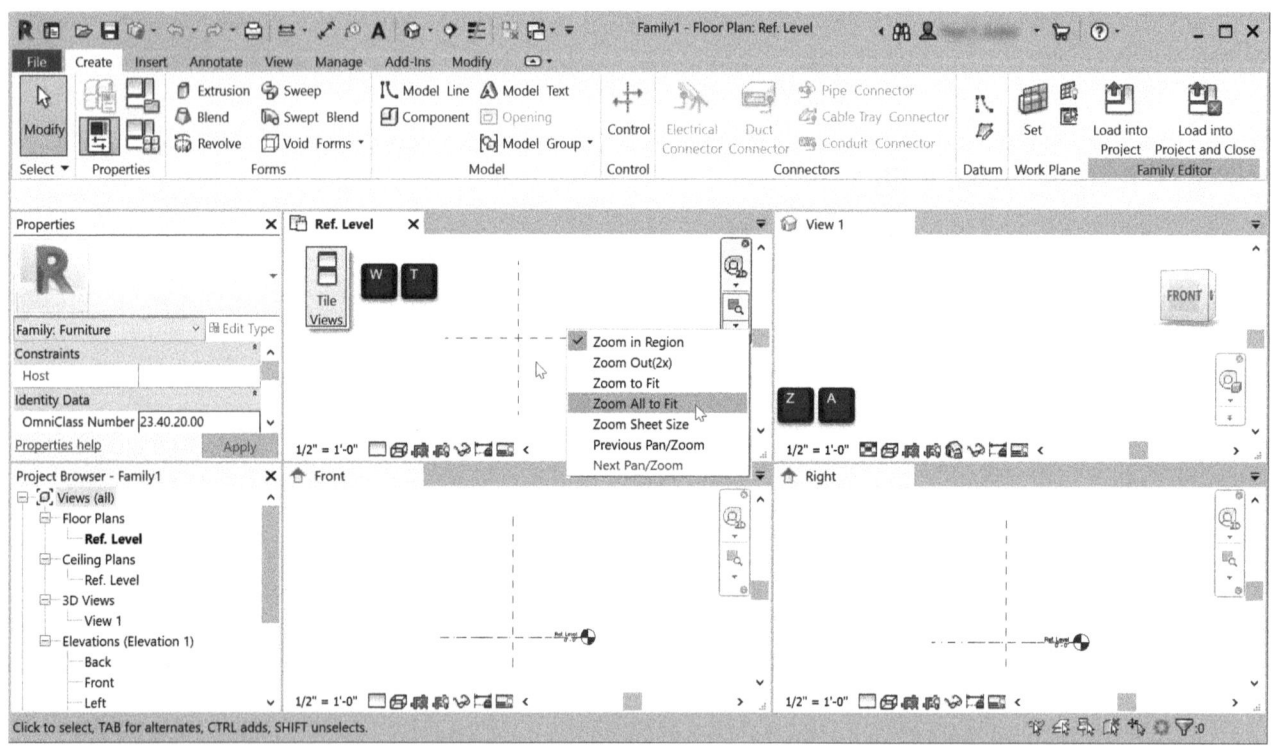

FIGURE 11.32 *Close other projects and families so that only the current family file's views show in the window menu, then tile and zoom all windows*

While it is not necessary to close the other projects and tile the views, it will be easier to work on the family in this environment. As we make changes in any view, we will see the results immediately in the others. Since we will be making many three-dimensional edits, this will be very helpful.

3. On the QAT, click the Save icon (or press CTRL + S).

⇨   In the "Save as" dialog, be sure you are in the *Chapter11* folder, type:
    Reception Desk for the Name and then click Save.

• The Aubin Academy •

BUILD FAMILY GEOMETRY

As we have already seen, there are two methods to create objects in our family: adding solid forms and adding void forms. Solid forms represent the actual physical materials from which our family object is created. Void forms carve away from solid forms to help us create more complex shapes. Both solid and void forms can be sculpted in five ways—Extrusion, Blend, Revolve, Sweep, and Swept Blend. (Refer back to the "Kinds of Forms in the Family Editor" topic on page 478 above for a more detailed description of each). We will see examples of each of these in this exercise.

> **NOTE:** Typically, the first step in building a custom family is to lay out a series of reference planes. The reference planes provide structure and form to the family's geometry. All geometry added to the family is typically constrained to one or more reference planes in some way. In this way, the reference planes can be moved (flexed) by a change in parameters, and they will in turn affect the shape of the geometry. This is how parametric families are created. You may recall seeing some examples of this in the desk family that we modified earlier. While we will build a parametric family below that fully utilizes this best practice approach, the following family example will focus on the various solid geometry forms available and will not be flexible. Given this focus, reference planes will only be used minimally in this example.

CREATE A SOLID EXTRUSION

The first form we will build is a simple extrusion for the work surface.

> Make sure that the Floor Plan : Ref. Level view is active. (The title bar and its name on Project Browser will appear bold—click the title bar to make it active.)

1. On the Create tab, on the Forms panel, click the Extrusion button.

In the center of the plan view are two reference planes that were part of the original Furniture template. Like the annotation family, these mark the insertion point and we will use them to center our geometry.

2. On the Modify | Create Extrusion tab, on the Draw panel, click on the Rectangle icon.
   ⇨ On the Options Bar, type: **3/4"** [**19**] in the "Depth" field.
3. Draw a rectangle next to the two reference planes at any size.
   ⇨ Edit the temporary dimensions to make the rectangle: **6'-0"** [**1800**] x **2'-6"** [**750**] (see Figure 11.33).

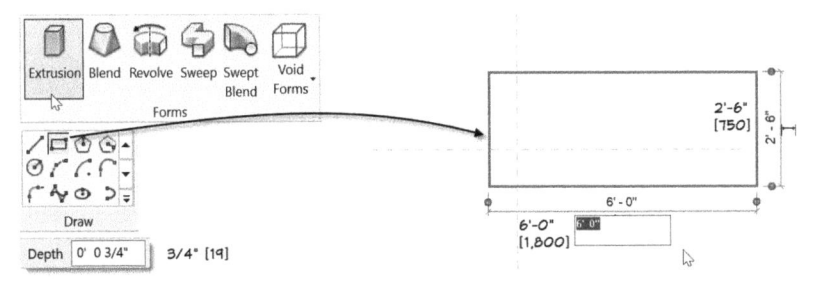

FIGURE 11.33 *Sketch a rectangle near the center of the plan and edit the temporary dimensions*

4. On the ribbon, click the Modify tool.
   ⇨ Select all four of the sketch lines.
5. On the Modify panel, click the Move tool.
   ⇨ For the Move Start Point, click the Midpoint of one of the edges.
   ⇨ For the Move End Point, snap to one of the reference planes (see Figure 11.34).

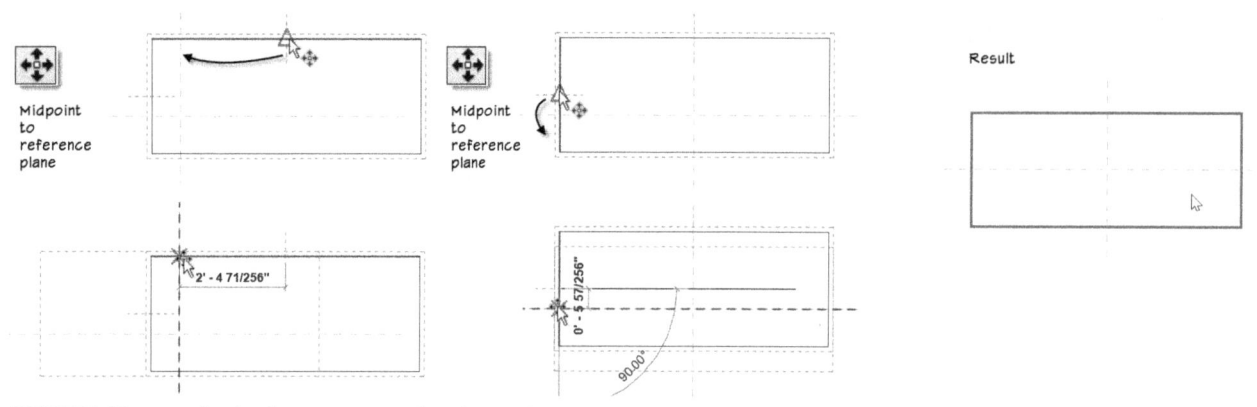

FIGURE 11.34 *Move the sketch to center it on the reference planes*

6. Repeat the Move operation in the other direction.

The rectangular sketch should now be centered on the reference planes. You can use the Measure tool on the QAT to verify if necessary.

7. On the Mode panel, click the Finish Edit Mode button (big green checkmark).

ADJUST THE VIEW WINDOWS

Now that we have some geometry built, we can adjust our view windows to show it better.

1. From the Navigation Bar, Zoom All to Fit (or type ZA).

> **NOTE:** The Zoom tool on the Navigation Bar should "remember" the previous mode used, so Zoom All to Fit should already be active, and simply clicking the Zoom tool should be enough. However, if you change the mode, you may need to click it a second time to actually execute the command.

Notice that the 3D view shows the model from the side.

2. Click in the 3D View (*View 1*) tab and then orbit the model (Click the corner of the ViewCube or hold down the SHIFT key and drag the middle wheel button on the mouse or use the steering wheel).

⇨ Zoom or otherwise fine-tune the view in each window to your liking.

On the View Control Bar (for the 3D View), change the graphic style to: **Shaded** (see Figure 11.35).

Families and the Family Editor | 493

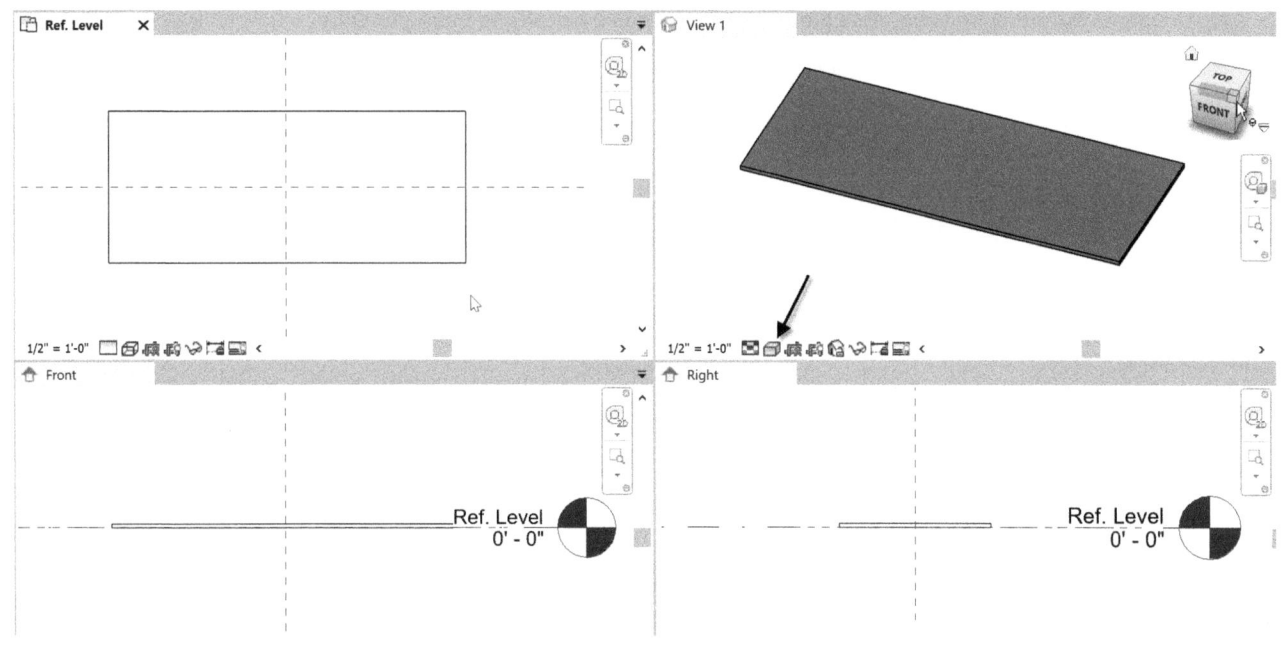

FIGURE 11.35 *Adjust all of the view windows to show the new geometry clearly*

3. Save the family.

CREATE A REFERENCE PLANE

If you study the model, you will notice that the desktop surface is sitting on the floor. While it is possible to edit the parameters of the extrusion to set it at the correct height (we did this above for the keyboard shelf), we will get more control if we create a new reference plane and designate it as the Work Plane for the solid extrusion.

1. Click on *Front* view tab to make it active.
2. On the Architecture tab, on the Datum panel, click the Reference Plane tool (or press RP).
    - ⇨ Clicking from right to left, click two points horizontally above the Ref. Level.
    - ⇨ Edit the temporary dimension that appears to: **2'-6"** [**750**].
    - ⇨ Click on the "Click to Name" control, input: **Work Surface Height** and then press ENTER (see Figure 11.36).

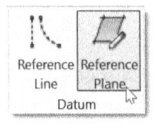

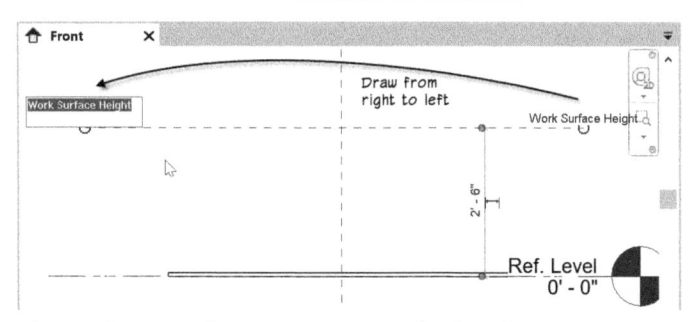

FIGURE 11.36 *Add a reference plane in elevation and set it to an appropriate height and name it*

You will see the name near the end of the reference plane while it is selected.

3. On the ribbon, click the Modify tool or press the ESC key.

This will give you a reference plane that marks the height of the top of our work surface.

4. Select the work surface extrusion element.
    - ⇨ On the Modify | Extrusion tab, on the Work Plane panel, click the Edit Work Plane button.

• Revit Essentials for Architecture •

494 | Chapter 11

⇨ In the "Work Plane" dialog, click the "Pick a Plane" radio button and then click OK.

⇨ In the viewport, select the reference plane (see Figure 11.37).

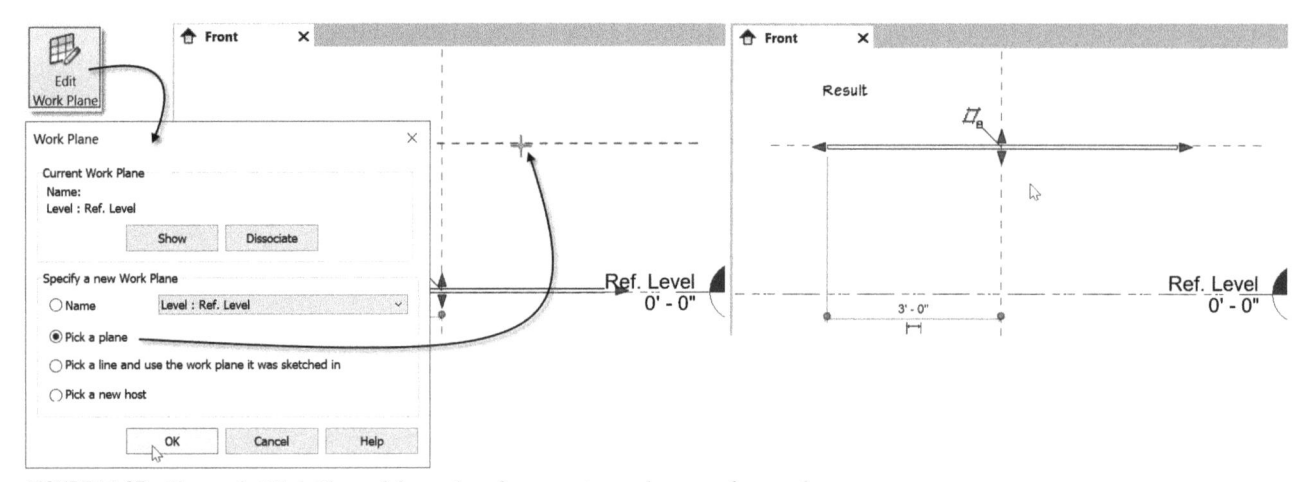

FIGURE 11.37 *Change the Work Plane of the work surface extrusion to the new reference plane*

Notice the work surface extrusion will shift up to the new height in the elevation and 3D Views. If you move the reference plane, the work surface will move with it. Try it out, but be sure to undo when done experimenting. You should also notice that the thickness of the work surface is now going down form the reference plane instead of up like it was when it was on the floor line. This is due to the way we drew the reference plane; right to left. If yours is pointing the opposite way, you have two options: reverse the reference plane, or set the thickness of the extrusion to negative. To reverse the reference plane, select it, click and drag one of its endpoints all the way past the opposite end. This will reverse it and the extrusion will flip. Alternatively, you can select the extrusion and on the Properties palette, set the value in Extrusion End to negative.

5. Adjust the zoom in all Viewports and Save the family.

CREATE A SOLID BLEND

Now that we have our desktop surface and it is located at the desired height, let's add some legs. For the main part of the leg, we will use a solid blend to give them a bit of a taper. We will square them off at the top later using a simple extrusion.

Make the plan view window active.

1. From the Navigation Bar (or right-click), use **Zoom In Region** and zoom in on the top left corner of the work surface.

2. On the Create tab, on the Forms panel, click the Blend button.

⇨ On the Options Bar, type: **1'-10"** [**550**] in the "Depth" field and then click the Rectangle icon.

⇨ Sketch a simple square near the corner of the desk.

3. Using the temporary dimensions and the left side of Figure 11.38 as a guide, make the shape **2"** [**50**] square set **2"** [**50**] away from the corner as shown.

> **TIP:** If you have trouble with the temporary dimensions, remember to select the sketch line you want to move *before* editing the dimension value. As an alternative, add some permanent dimensions. They will become editable when the sketch lines are selected. You can delete them after you complete the shape, or simply leave them. They will get absorbed into the completed form. The best part is that if you later edit the form, the dimensions will reappear inside the sketch.

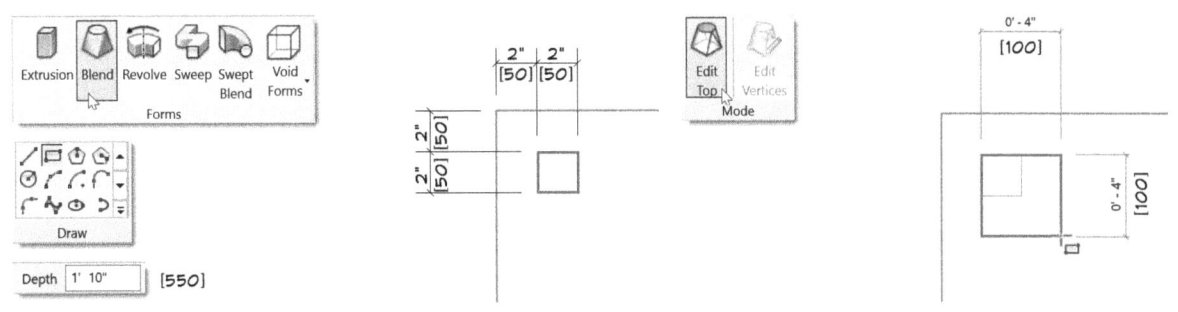

FIGURE 11.38 *Sketch the Base (Left) and Top (Right) of the Solid Blend*

A solid blend is basically an extrusion that transforms from one shape to another along the depth of the extrusion. In this case, we will use two squares of varying sizes that share a common offset from the desktop corner. This will give a tapered shape to the final leg form. When you build a Blend, you first sketch the shape of the bottom, then the shape of the top.

4. On the ribbon, click the Edit Top button.

   ⇨ Using the Rectangle option again, sketch a **4"** [**100**] square with the top left corner aligned to the square at the base (see the right side of Figure 11.33).

> **TIP:** You should be able to snap to the upper left corner and use the temporary dimensions to draw the other corner accurately. Or you can also add dimensions in this sketch as well if you prefer.

5. On the ribbon, click the Finish Edit Mode button (see Figure 11.39).

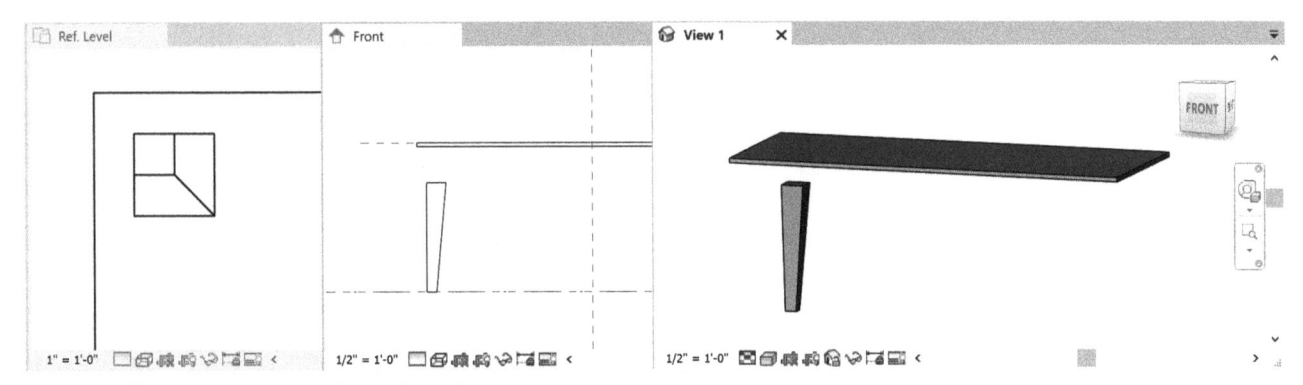

FIGURE 11.39 *Finish the blend and view the results*

There is a noticeable gap between the top of the leg and the work surface (orbit the 3D view as necessary to see this). We will fill this in with an extrusion.

Make the *View 1* tab active and deselect the blend.

6. Zoom in at the top of the blend. Orbit so you can see the top surface clearly.
7. On the Create tab, on the Work Plane panel, click the Set button.

   ⇨ In the "Work Plane" dialog, choose the "Pick a Plane" radio button and then click OK.

   ⇨ In the 3D view, click on the top of the Solid Blend leg (see the left side of Figure 11.40).

While it is most common to use reference planes and levels as work planes, you can also use the surfaces in the geometry of your model as a work plane. In this case, we will use the top of the blend. This creates a relationship between the two forms. Later if the blend moves, it will move the extrusion with it.

• Revit Essentials for Architecture •

496 | Chapter 11

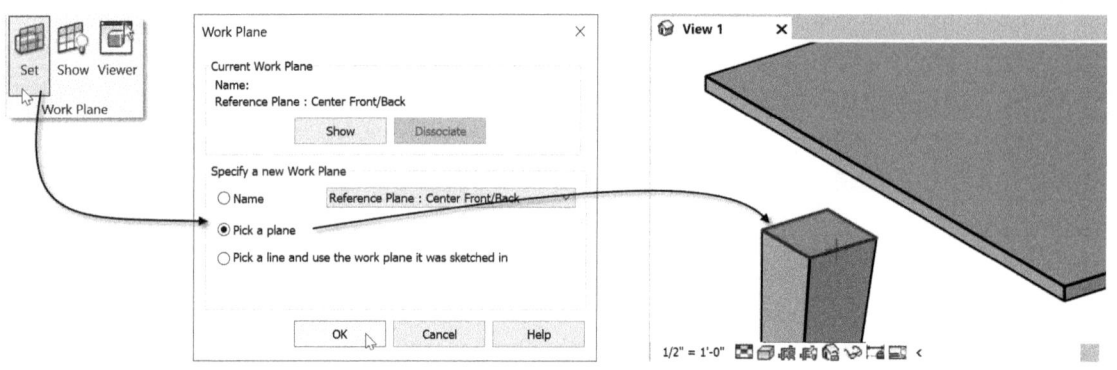

FIGURE 11.40 *The work plane icon allows you to choose the plane where you sketch the next solid form*

After you click the plane, you can click the Show button on the Work Plane panel. This will highlight the current Work Plane by tinting it blue. This gives you a good visual cue that the Work Plane has been set satisfactorily. You can also click the Viewer button. This will display a small floating window that looks directly at the new work plane. This viewer can sometimes be helpful particularly when the work plane is at an angle to the view. In this case, we don't need the viewer, but feel free use it if you like.

8. On the Create tab, on the Forms panel, click the Extrusion button.

⇨ On the Modify | Create Extrusion tab, on the Draw panel, click on the Rectangle icon.

9. In the 3D view, sketch a rectangle on the top of the leg (blend) snapping endpoint to endpoint (see Figure 11.41).

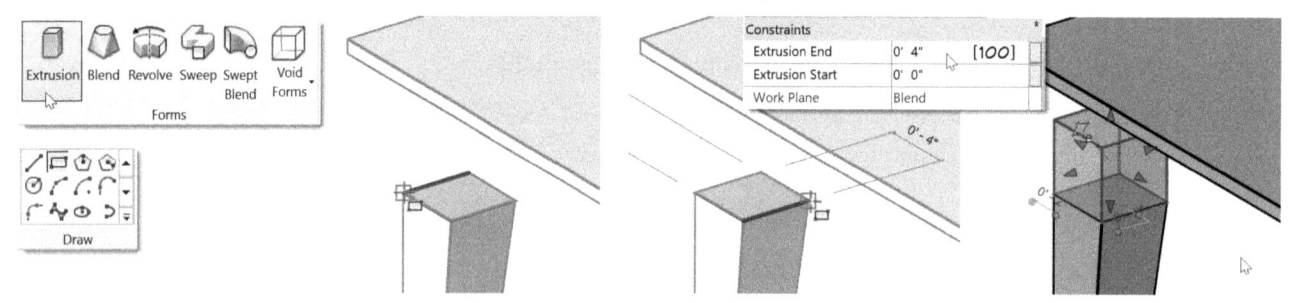

FIGURE 11.41 *Draw the extrusion sketch on the work plane at the top of the blend*

After sketching this shape, a lock icon will appear on each edge. You can close these locks to constrain the shape of the solid extrusion to the top shape of the Blend. This can be handy if you anticipate making edits to the Blend. This would keep the extrusion at the top of the leg coordinated with these changes. However, in some cases, such a constraint can have adverse effects. This could occur for example if you changed the shape of the Blend top to something other than rectangular. In this case, Revit might have trouble maintaining the constraints. If this were to occur, a warning dialog would appear at the time of edit. For the purposes of this tutorial, the decision is not critical. We'll see some examples of constraints in later tutorials.

10. On the Properties palette, set the "Extrusion End" to: **4"** [**100**] and then on the Mode panel, click the Finish Edit Mode button.

> **NOTE:** There are two ways to set the height of the extrusion; we can use the Depth field as we did earlier, or you can set the Extrusion Start and the Extrusion End on the Properties palette which will calculate the Depth for you. The end result is the same.

The extrusion will appear at the top of the leg but will be too short to reach the work surface. The number we used here was just an estimate.

11. Make the *Front* elevation tab active. The extrusion should still be selected; if it isn't, select the extrusion.

Families and the Family Editor | 497

⇨ Using the Shape Handle at the top, stretch it up to the bottom edge of the work surface.

You can also use the Align tool if you prefer.

MIRROR THE LEG

Now that we have one completed leg, we can mirror it to create the one on the other side.

1. Make the *Right* elevation tab active.

⇨ Select both the blend and the extrusion.

2. On the Modify | Multi-Select tab, on the Modify panel, click the Mirror -Pick Axis tool.

Click the reference plane running vertically in the view (Center Front/Back) as the Axis of Reflection (see Figure 11.42).

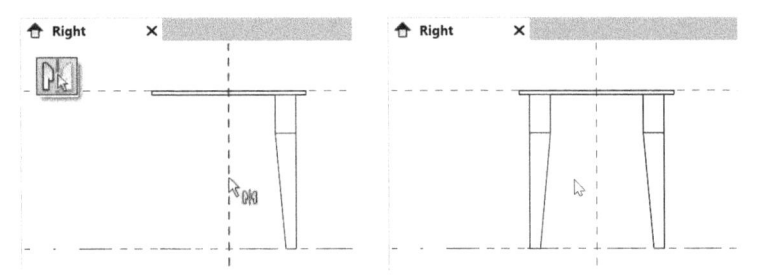

FIGURE 11.42 *Mirror the leg to create one on the other side*

CREATE A WORK PLANE AND ORIENT THE VIEW

We could simply mirror both legs again to the other side. But before we mirror them, let's vary the Blend of one of the legs to make a slightly "fancier" design. To help us with this, let's establish a new work plane.

1. Deselect the leg and make the *Ref. level* plan tab active.

⇨ Zoom in on the top left corner of the work surface.

2. On the Create tab, on the Datum panel, click the Reference Plane tool (or press RP).

⇨ Draw a 45° reference plane through the middle of the leg as shown on the left in Figure 11.43.

⇨ Click on the "Click to Name" control input: **Leg Path** and then press ENTER.

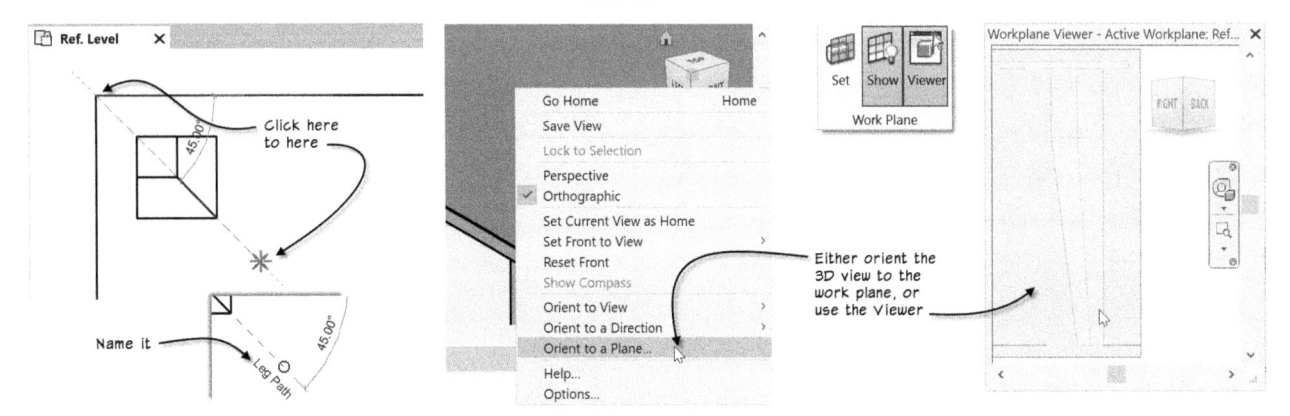

FIGURE 11.43 *Draw a 45° reference plane through the middle of the leg and name it*

Click on the title bar of the *3D View: View 1* window to make it active.

We are going to draw a path on the new reference plane that we just created. We can do this directly in the 3D view by orienting the view to look at the work plane or we can use the Viewer tool mentioned above. If you want to

• Revit Essentials for Architecture •

498 | Chapter 11

work directly in the 3D view, right-click directly on the ViewCube and choose: Orient to a Plane (see the middle of Figure 11.43). In the dialog that appears, choose the Leg Path reference plane and click OK. In the next few steps, we'll try the Viewer option instead.

3. On the Create tab, on the Work Plane panel, click the Set button.

⇨ In the "Work Plane" dialog, from the Name list, choose: **Leg Path** and then click OK.

If you still have the Show button enabled, you will see the change immediately in all views.

4. On the Create tab, on the Work Plane panel, click the Viewer button.

If you clicked the Show option above, it will still be active. You can leave it on if you like or turn it off by clicking the Show button again.

5. Drag at the edge of the viewer to make it larger. Right-click and choose: Zoom to Fit, and then zoom in on the right leg (see the right side of Figure 11.43).

CREATE A SOLID SWEPT BLEND

A swept blend is nearly identical to a blend. It also has two sketched shapes, one at the top and the other at the bottom. However, instead of connecting these two shapes along a perpendicular path whose height we specify, we instead draw the path using either a straight line of any angle or a curve. In this case, we'll draw a gentle curve. The only limitation of the Swept Blend is that the Path can only be a single segment. To work around this, we'll use a spline curve in this example.

1. On the Create tab, on the Forms panel, click the Swept Blend button.

2. On the Modify | Swept Blend tab, on the Mode panel, click the Sketch Path tool.

⇨ On the Modify | Swept Blend > Sketch Path tab, on the Draw panel, click the Spline icon.

3. Click the start point at the bottom of the existing leg (item 1 in Figure 11.44).

⇨ Click the next point straight up along the leg slightly above the first (item 2).

⇨ Click the third point up and slightly to the right of the existing leg about halfway up (item 3).

⇨ Click the last two points on the existing leg near the top of the existing blend (items 4 and 5). Press ESC to finish sketching.

⇨ To complete the path sketch, on the Mode panel, click the Finish Edit Mode button.

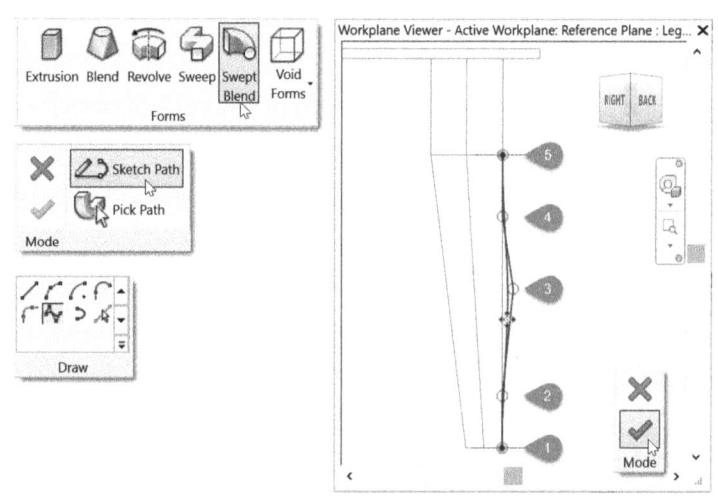

FIGURE 11.44 *Sketch the path for the swept blend*

Close the Viewer window and then make the plan view tab active.

Families and the Family Editor | 499

4. On the Swept Blend panel, click the Select Profile 1 button.

This allows us to edit the sketch of Profile 1. Like a blend, a swept blend, has two profiles. When you finish the path, the Modify | Swept Blend tab will reappear on the ribbon. On the Swept Blend panel, <By Sketch> will appear for the Profile choice. Two options are available for the profiles. You can sketch them, or you can use a profile family. A profile family is simply a family that contains a predefined profile shape. This can be useful for more advanced families or if you use the same profile shape frequently like moldings or any shape that you want to reuse in multiple families or projects. The Profile list will show any profile families loaded in the current family. You can use the Load Profile button to load external profile families into the current family. Refer to the "Build or Load a Mullion Profile Family" topic on page 526 below for an example. In this case, we will simply sketch the profile like we did for the blend above. Therefore, we will leave the Profile set to: **<By Sketch>**.

5. Click Edit Profile button (see the left side of Figure 11.45).
   ⇨ With the rectangle tool, trace the small square (of the existing blend). Do not close the lock icons.
   ⇨ Click the Finish Edit Mode button.

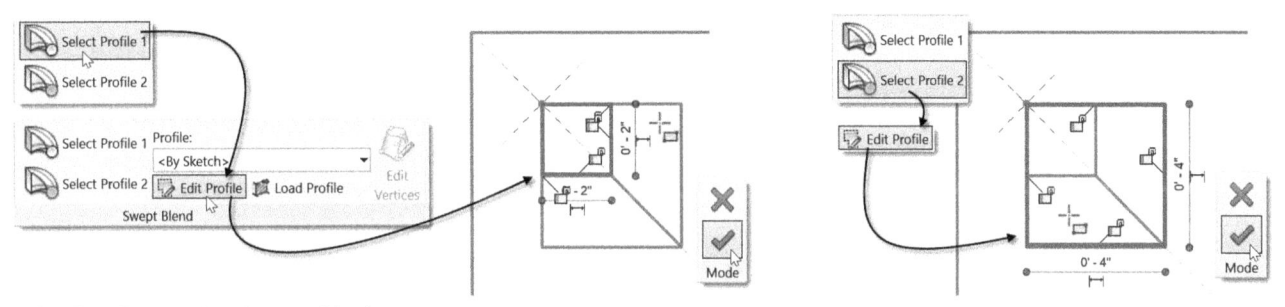

FIGURE 11.45 *Complete the swept blend*

Now we need to define Profile 2.

6. On the Swept Blend panel, click the Select Profile 2 button and then click the Edit Profile button.
   ⇨ Using the rectangle shape, trace the large square on the existing leg. Do not lock it.
   ⇨ Click the Finish Edit Mode button (see the right side of Figure 11.45).
7. Click the Finish Edit Mode button again to complete the Swept Blend.
   ⇨ Delete the original Blend.

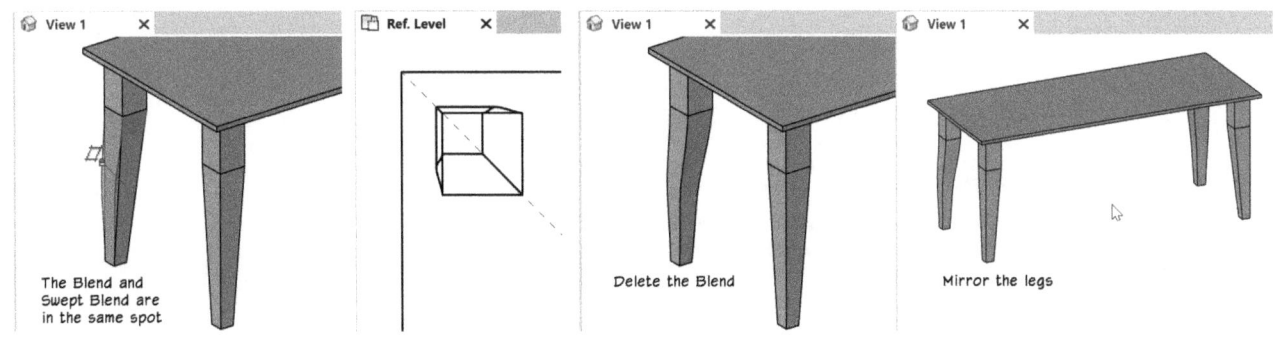

FIGURE 11.46 *Complete the swept blend*

8. In the plan view, using a window selection box, select both legs (4 elements total) and mirror about the (Center Left/Right) reference plane (see Figure 11.46).
9. Save the family file.

• Revit Essentials for Architecture •

CREATE APRONS AND A PENCIL DRAWER

Using another extrusion, we can add some geometry to represent the aprons around the work surface and a pencil drawer.

Make the *Ref. Level* floor plan tab active. Zoom as required to see the whole desktop.

1. On the Create tab, on the Work Plane panel, use the Set tool to set the Work Plane to: **Level : Ref. Level**.
2. On the Create tab, click the Extrusion Tool.
   - On the Draw panel, click the Rectangle icon.
   - On the Properties palette, for the "Extrusion Start" type: **1'-11 1/4"** [**581**]. For the "Extrusion End" type: **2'-5 1/4"** [**731**].
3. On the Options Bar, in the "Offset" field type: **3"** [**75**].
   - Snap the first point at one corner of the desktop.
   - Tap the SPACEBAR to flip the sketch to the inside the desktop shape and then click on the opposite corner of the desktop to finish the rectangle (see Figure 11.47).

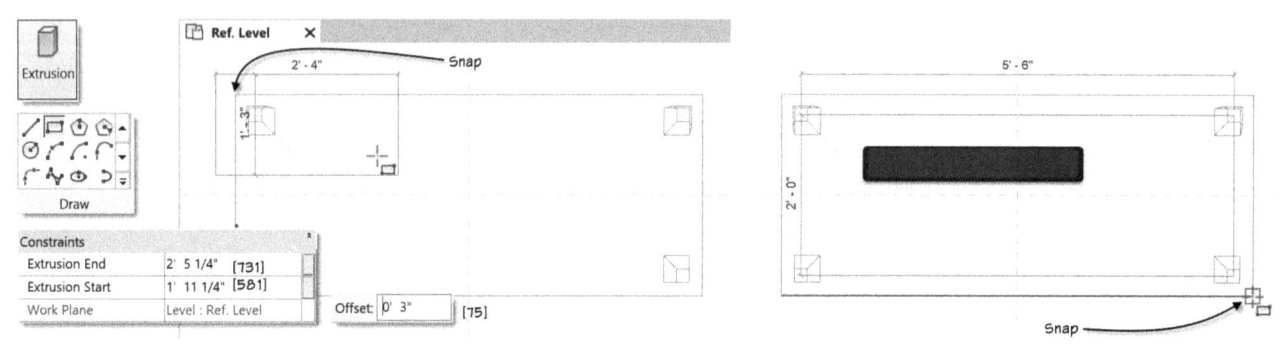

FIGURE 11.47 *Sketch a rectangle offset from the corners of the desktop*

4. On the Mode panel, click the Finish Edit Mode button.
5. Working in the *Front* tab create a: **1/2"** [**12**] deep extrusion for a pencil drawer using the face of the extrusion just drawn as a Work Plane (see Figure 11.48).

The exact size and position on the drawer are not important.

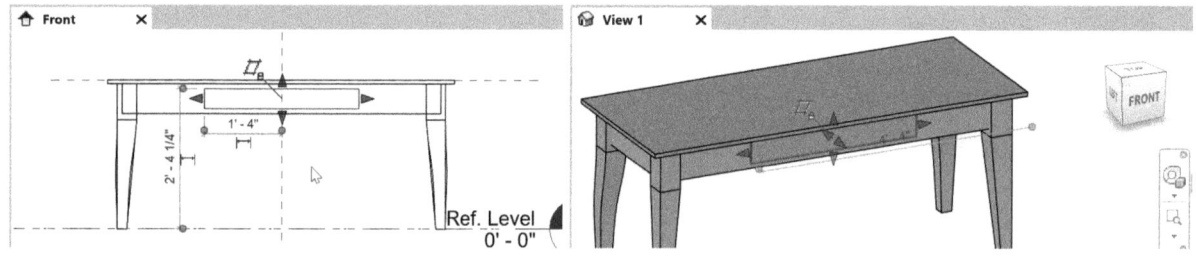

FIGURE 11.48 *Create an extrusion in the front elevation for a pencil drawer*

CREATE A SOLID REVOLVE

To add a drawer pull to the pencil drawer, we will use a solid revolve. A solid revolve is a form in which you sketch the profile of the form and then spin the profile around an axis. To create a simple drawer pull, you draw half of the cross section of the pull, and then place the revolution axis at the center of the pull.

Return to the plan *Ref. Level* tab to make it active.

1. Zoom in on the pencil drawer in the plan view.

2. On the Create tab, click the Revolve tool.

   On the Draw panel, verify that the Boundary Lines tool is active and, on the Options Bar, verify that "Chain" is selected.

   ⇨ Starting at the midpoint of the pencil drawer, sketch the form shown in the middle of Figure 11.49. The exact dimensions and shape are not critical, but some overall sizes are shown.

   Lines and arcs were used in the figure. Some suggested tools are indicated on the right side.

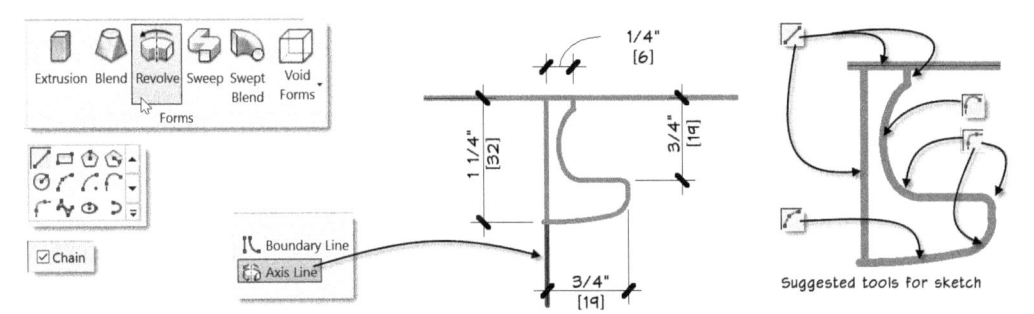

FIGURE 11.49 *Sketch the shape of the drawer pull*

3. On the Modify | Create Revolve tab, on the Draw panel, click the Axis Line button.

   ⇨ Draw a vertical line (any length) immediately below the sketch. Make sure it is directly on the reference plane (see the middle of Figure 11.49).

4. On the Mode panel, click the Finish Edit Mode button.

The axis line controls where the profile will rotate. You could draw it directly on top of the left edge of the sketch, but then Revit will warn you about double lines. It is much easier to draw it away from the sketch. The resulting Revolve form is the same either way. If you study the result in all views, you will notice that the drawer pull is on the floor. This is because Revit remembers the last work plane we used which was the Ref. Level. As a result, you cannot move the drawer pull to the correct height—try it in the *Front* view to see for yourself. If we wanted, we could create a new reference plane at the correct height and associate the revolve element to it instead. In this case, we will simply disassociate the work plane from the revolve which will allow us to move it freely.

   Make the *Front* tab active.

5. Select the drawer pull.

   A small Work Plane icon appears attached to the element.

   ⇨ Click the Work Plane icon to dissociate the work plane.

6. Move the drawer pull to center it on the height of the drawer (see Figure 11.50).

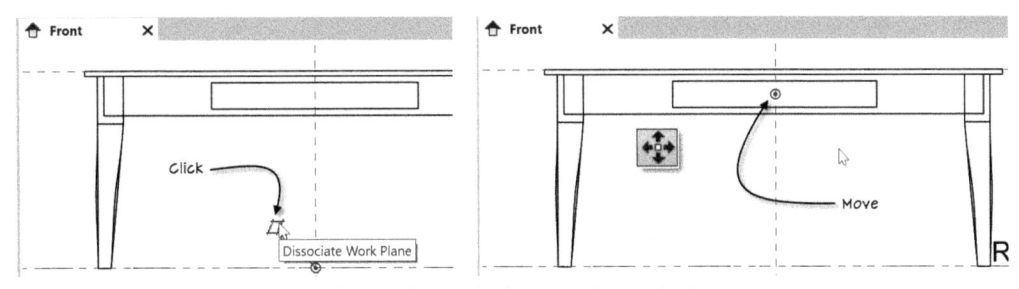

FIGURE 11.50 *Dissociate the work plane and move the drawer pull up to the drawer*

502 | Chapter 11

CREATE A SOLID SWEEP

There is one last solid form to try. Let's create a privacy screen using the solid sweep command.

Make the *Ref. Level* floor plan active.

1. Zoom out enough to see the whole desk.

Creating this form requires a few steps (like the swept blend). For a sweep, we need a path and a profile. When you begin the command, the Modify | Sweep tab will appear on the ribbon. The first step is to designate the path. You can do this by sketching or you can use the pick option to set the path from existing geometry.

Our work plane is still set to the floor level. Let's move it to the work surface.

2. On the Create tab, on the Work Plane panel, click the Set tool.
   ⇨ In the "Work Plane" dialog, from the Name list, choose: **Reference Plane : Work Surface Height** and then click OK.
3. On the Create tab, click the Sweep tool.
   ⇨ On the Modify | Sweep tab, on the Sweep panel, click the Sketch Path tool.
   ⇨ On the Modify | Sweep > Sketch Path tab, on the Draw panel, click the "Pick Lines" icon.
   ⇨ On the Options Bar, in the "Offset" field, type: **2"** [**50**].

As with the "Offset" option in other commands, as you hover over a line in the model, a green dashed line will appear temporarily indicating the side to which the sketch line will offset. As you create sketch lines here, be sure to offset to the inside of the desk surface.

4. Offset the three outside edges of the desk (not the one with the pencil drawer) to create a "U" shaped sketch (see Figure 11.51).

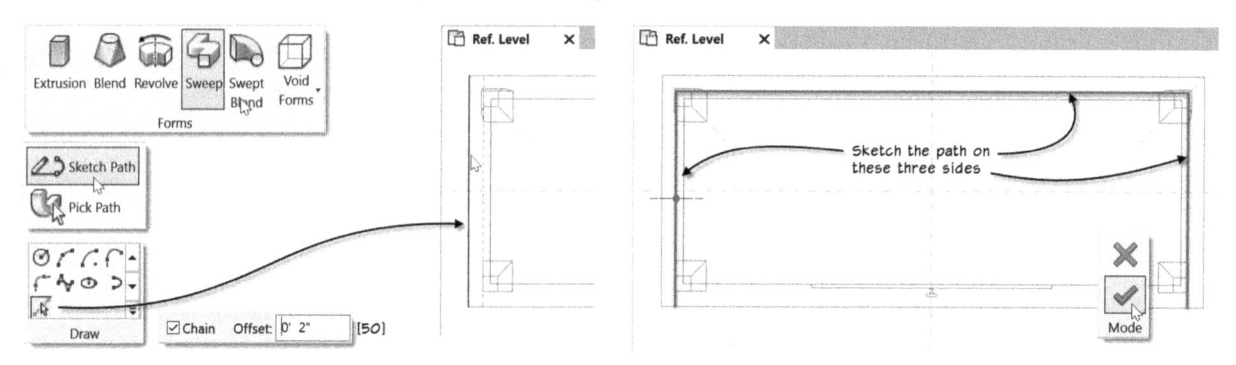

FIGURE 11.51 *Create sketch lines by picking the edges of the desktop*

5. On the Mode panel, click the Finish Edit Mode button.

These three lines will be the "path" of the sweep. We have seen sweeps in other chapters. A sweep "pushes" a profile along a path. It is like an extrusion except that the path does not have to be a simple straight line as it does in an extrusion and unlike both extrusions and swept blends, the path of a sweep can contain multiple segments. As we saw above with the swept blend, when you finish the path, the Modify | Sweep tab will appear automatically. The profile of a sweep can be either a sketch or a loaded profile. If you want to use a profile, it is possible to load an existing profile directly from the ribbon. This is a nice feature as you can store profile families in your library so that you can quickly create sweeps from your most common profiles. However, in this example, we will sketch the profile as a custom shape just for this desk.

6. On the Sweep panel, click the Edit Profile tool.

• The Aubin Academy •

Families and the Family Editor | 503

The profile travels perpendicular to and along the path. This means that since we sketched the path in plan, we must sketch the profile in elevation. When you click the Edit button, Revit will prompt us to select an appropriate view in which to sketch the profile.

⇨ In the "Go To View" dialog, choose: **Elevation: Front** and then click Open View.

Zoom the Front elevation view as necessary to center the red dot on screen.

The red dot indicates the start point of the profile. It appears automatically on the first segment of the path. If you are not satisfied with the default location of the profile, you can move it by dragging it back in the plan; but be sure to move it before you start sketching the profile.

7. Using the Line and Arc tools and the "Chain" option, create a profile similar to the one shown in Figure 11.52.

TIP: The exact shape of the profile is not critical. Just make sure to make a closed shape. Remember that you can zoom in to make sketch lines automatically snap to a smaller increment. The profile in the figure has a thickness of: 1/2" [12] and is about 8" [250] tall.

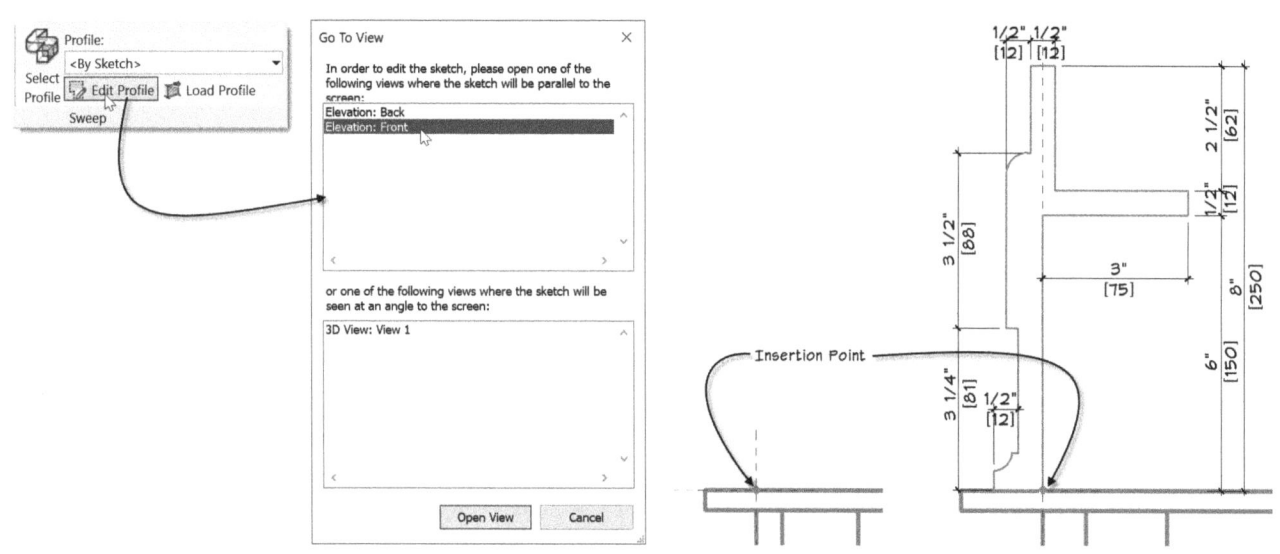

FIGURE 11.52 *Sketch the profile of the sweep*

8. On the Mode panel, click the Finish Edit Mode button. This returns you to the Modify | Sweep tab.

⇨ On the Mode panel, click the Finish Edit Mode button again to complete the sweep.

9. Zoom All Viewports to Fit (see Figure 11.53).

TIP: Try setting the Viewports to hidden line display to see the final product more clearly in plan and elevation. You can also use the Join Geometry tool to merge solid forms together.

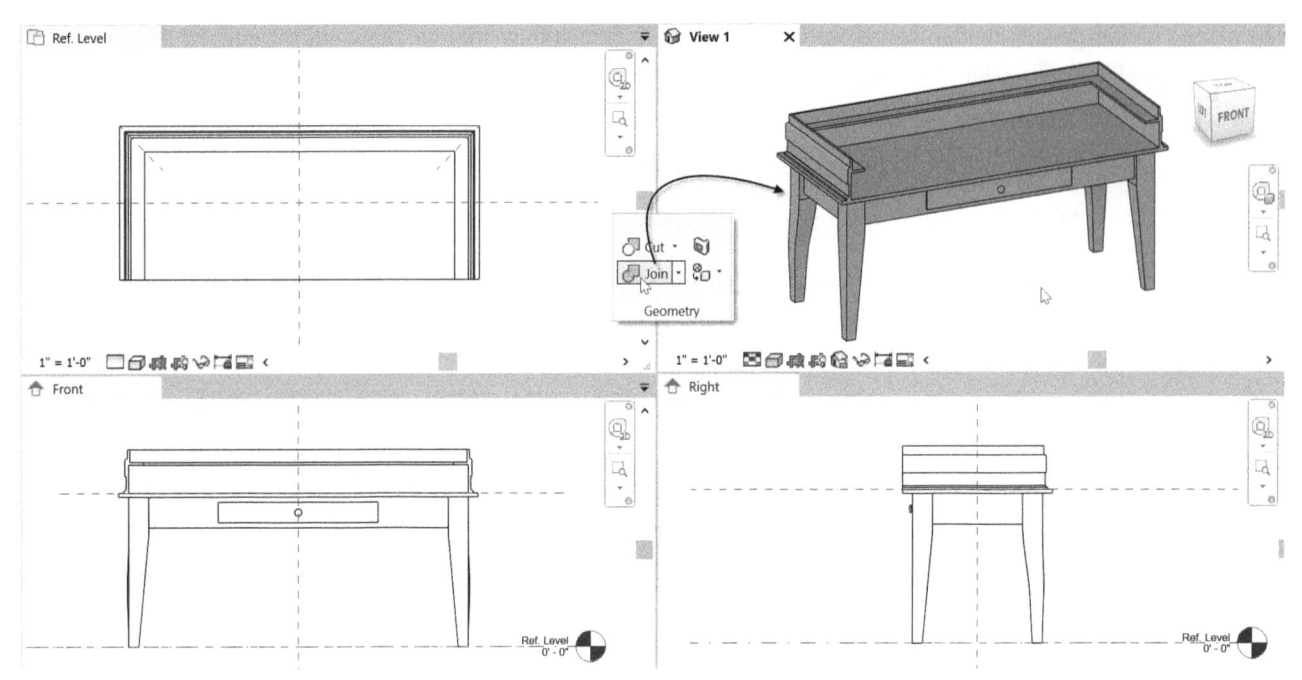

FIGURE 11.53 *Completed reception desk with privacy screen*

10. Save the Family file.

LOAD THE CUSTOM FAMILY INTO A PROJECT

At this point, we have completed the geometry of our custom family and are ready to load it into our commercial project. The process has been covered before. Let's review it now. We closed the project above to make it easier to tile the windows in the Family Editor. We now need to reopen our commercial project.

1. Reopen the *11 Commercial* project file.

    It will open as a tab in one of your tiled viewports.

2. On the Project Browser, double-click to open the *Level 3* floor plan view.

    This will also open as a tab in the same tile.

    ⇨ Zoom in on the reception space (in the middle of the plan).

    ⇨ Move your mouse over the G100 – Cover tab and then click the small X to close it.

We could also use the Load Family tool on the Insert tab, but since the family file is still open, it is easier to load from there.

3. Click on any visible tab that shows the reception desk family.
4. On the Family Editor tab, click the Load into Project and Close button.

The screen will switch back to the commercial project. The Modify | Place Component tab should become active as Revit puts you directly in placement mode. If this is not the case for you, switch to the Architecture tab and click the Component tool. The Reception desk should appear on the Type Selector.

5. Add an Instance of the Family to the reception space (see Figure 11.54).

TIP: Place the mouse over the curved wall and then tap the SPACEBAR. This will allow you to rotate it and match the curve as you place it.

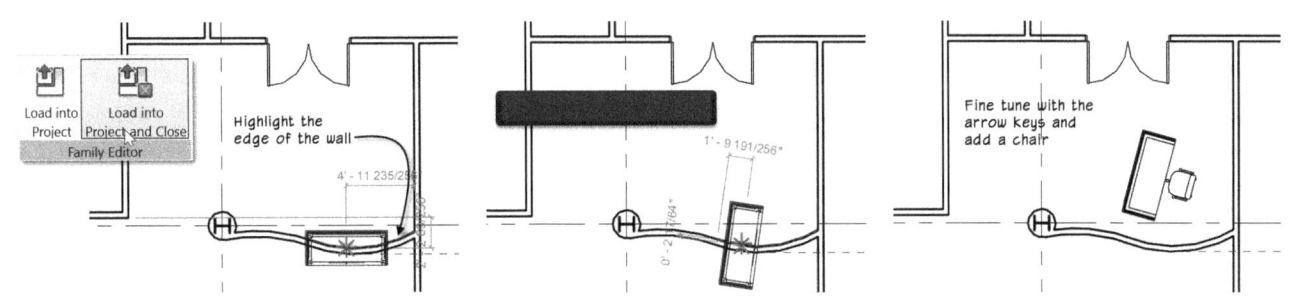

FIGURE 11.54 *Load the family and then add an Instance to the commercial project*

6. From the Type Selector, choose the Executive Chair.
   ⇨ Highlight the edge of the reception desk, tap the SPACEBAR to match the rotation, and then place one with the reception desk.
7. On the ribbon, click the Modify tool or press the ESC key twice.
   ⇨ Select both elements and use the arrow keys on the keyboard to fine-tune placement.
8. Save the project.

If you look on the Project Browser, beneath *Families* and *Furniture*, you will see that the *Reception Desk* family is now loaded. Notice also that its only type shares the same name as the family. Even though we did not create any types for this family, all families *must* have at least one type. Revit simply makes one for us using the same name if we do not create one of our own.

BUILDING PARAMETRIC FAMILIES

The reception desk tutorial was designed to introduce you to the basics of the modeling forms available in the Family Editor. All five forms were explored, and even though we did not create any void forms for the reception desk, we saw an example above in the "Adding a Void Form" topic on page 480. Voids can be made in any of the five forms just like solids. The reception desk family is a simple non-parametric family that cannot be edited in the project at all. If you select it and then click the Edit Type button, you see that it has no user-editable parameters other than basic identity data. To make even simple edits like changing the width, height, or depth, we would need to return to the Family Editor.

Families can be very simple or very complex. When you are first learning their scope and potential, it is helpful to start with simple examples and work your way up to more complex ones. This is exactly the approach this chapter has been following. As such, we have yet to cover one of the most powerful and useful aspects of families. That is their ability to be "parametric." Like much terminology that is associated with Building Information Modeling, the term parametric can sometimes be misused or misunderstood. Since it is nearly impossible to avoid hearing reference to the term in nearly any document, seminar, or training session on Revit, it will be helpful to take a moment to properly define the term. Parametric is the adjective form of the noun "Parameter." Browsing Merriam-Webster Online Dictionary" we find the following definition for the term:

Parameter—any of a set of physical properties whose values determine the characteristics or behavior of something.

This definition of parameter was selected from a few available variations because it is the most appropriate in the context of its use in describing the behavior of elements in Revit. When we describe something in software such as Revit as being parametric we are simply saying that the thing in question is characterized by its associated set of "properties," each of which hold "values determining characteristics of the element's behavior." In the specific case of

Revit, each element has one to several available parameters. We input values into these parameters to determine the specific characteristics of the element (wall, door, roof, furniture, etc.) which we are editing. Not specifically mentioned in the Webster's definition but implied using the term parametric in software is the ability to modify parameters at any time. Therefore, the ability for a parameter's value to determine the characteristics of behavior is not limited to the point of creation, but rather is a "living" parameter with ongoing influence over the element. This behavior is what makes the notion of parametric so significant in software like Revit. This dynamic interaction across the whole system (not just with model and annotation elements, but views and schedules as well) is often referred to in Revit as the "Parametric Change Engine."

Having outlined our definition of the term parametric, a parametric family is simply a family that has editable parameters. Typically, such a family will also have types—though it is not required. Therefore, as we will see, family parameters can be type-or instance-based. We could certainly continue in our Reception Desk family file and add parameters to the desk, but for simplicity, we will explore these topics by building a new family file from scratch.

CREATE A NEW PARAMETRIC FAMILY

As we did above, we will create a new family file based on one of the provided Revit family templates. We are going to create a simple binder bin to hang on the wall behind the reception desk. This object will be geometrically simpler than the reception desk, so we can focus on adding and working with parameters and flexible behavior. Before continuing, you should have closed the Reception Desk family, but if you still have it open, close it now.

1. Close the Commercial Project (and any other projects or families you have open) and answer yes to save if prompted to do so.

    This returns you to the Home Screen.

> **NOTE:** When closing families, avoid clicking the close box in the corner of each view window. When you do so, you are closing only that view. You would need to close each view this way and then when closing the last open view, you would also actually be closing the family file as well. However, the next time you open the family, only one view (the last one you closed) would open automatically. If you close from the File menu (or like we did above with Load into Project and Close button) instead, all of the open windows will be reopened the next time the family is opened in the Family Editor. However this is true *only* if the views are tiled. When views are tabbed, only the active view is remembered when you close.

2. Make sure all projects and families are closed, on the Home Screen, beneath Families, click the New button.

    Browse to your *Templates* folder if necessary.

    ⇨ Select the *Specialty Equipment wall based.rft* [*Metric Specialty Equipment wall based.rft*] template and then click Open.

> **NOTE:** If your version of Revit does not contain this template, a copy is included in the *Chapter11* folder.

   ⇨ On the View tab, click the Tile button (or press WT), and on the Navigation Bar, choose Zoom All to Fit (or press ZA).

3. On the QAT, click the Save icon (or press CTRL + S).

   ⇨ In the "Save as" dialog, browse to the *Chapter11* folder, name the file: **Binder Bin** and then click Save.

THE IMPORTANCE OF THE FAMILY TEMPLATE CHOICE

Like the furniture family template used above, this family opens with four view windows and some existing reference planes on screen. In addition, a temporary wall element is included in this template. This wall is provided since this is a "wall-based" (hosted) family and is used for reference while working in the Family Editor and will not be included with the binder bin when it is loaded into a project. We have chosen the "Specialty Equipment" template in this exercise primarily to utilize its wall hosted behavior. Recall that at the start of this chapter, we mentioned the importance of family templates. It was noted that category and hosting behavior were the two major features established by each template. It was also noted that of these two, the category could be changed later while the hosting behavior could not. Ultimately, we will change the category of this family to furniture to allow it to be grouped and scheduled with the other furniture items. Since there is not a wall-hosted furniture template provided, starting with this one and changing the category later will achieve our goals. In some cases, the choice of template is simply a judgment call, and a clear understanding of what the design/usage intentions for the family are that will help you make the final decision. Remember: when you build your own families, study the list of provided templates carefully before making your choice.

> **BIM MANAGER NOTE:** An argument could be made for using the *Casework wall based* [*Metric Casework wall based*] template here instead. A binder bin could be easily thought of as casework instead of furniture. The main reason to use furniture comes from how we want to list and schedule the elements in our model. If we want the binder bins to appear on the furniture schedule, then they must be part of that category. However, if you open the casework templates, you will note that they already include reference planes, parameters and dimensions. These items could certainly save time. So even if you intend to change the category as we do, starting with casework might be more advantageous than specialty equipment. However, in this exercise, we want to learn how to create these elements, so the choice of the simpler specialty equipment template gives us that opportunity.
>
> The choice of template determines many features of your family. So, in addition to its hosting behavior and category, templates also determine what sub-categories are available, line styles, built-in parameters and other behaviors as well. This includes whether the element is "cuttable." When model elements are cuttable, they interact with the cut plane in plan and section views. The graphics displayed will be a literal slice through the model at that location. Cuttable elements can also use a different line weight (often bolder) when such an element intersects the cut plane. If an element is not cuttable, the object will not be sliced, even if it intersects the cut plane, instead showing the entire object as it would appear in elevation. Furthermore, only its projection line weight setting will be available. Projection line weight is the setting used when the element (or a portion of the element) is seen beyond the cut plane. The easiest way to tell if an element is cuttable is to look in the "Object Styles" dialog (on the Manage tab, click the Object Styles button). Cuttable elements have a line weight setting in the Cut column, and non-cuttable elements do not have this field available (see Figure 11.55). If you are serious about becoming a proficient Family author, take the time required to become familiar with as many of the Family templates and their built-in behaviors as possible.

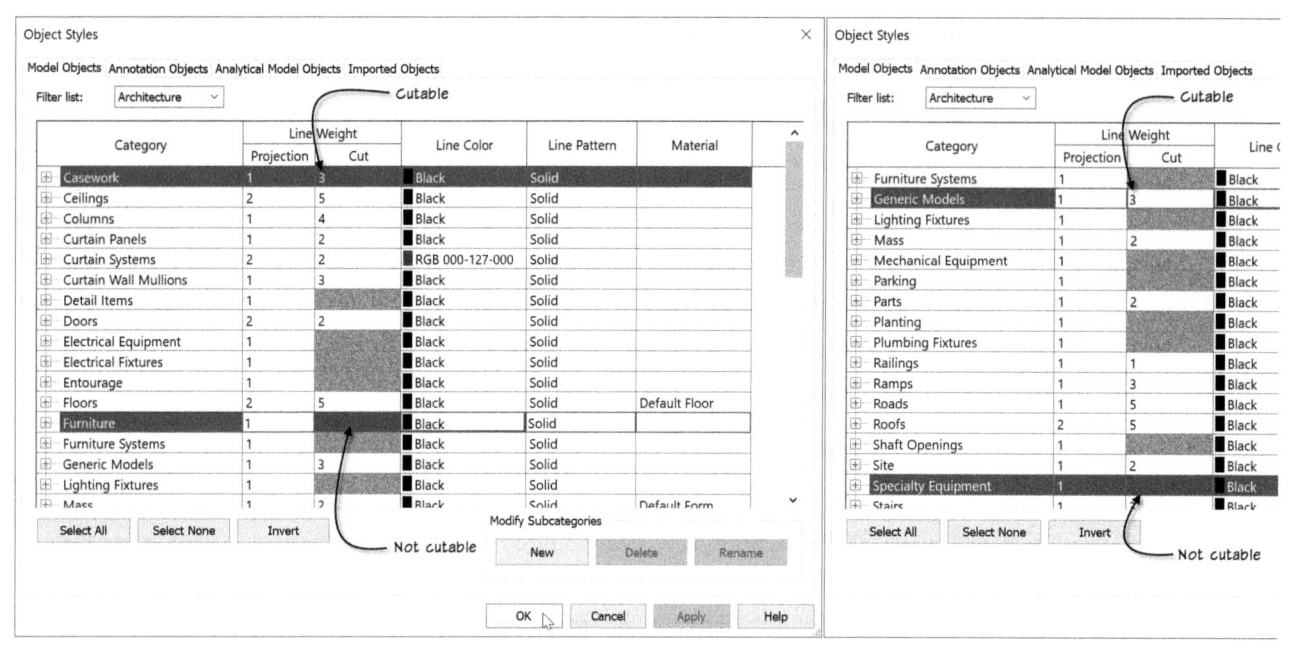

FIGURE 11.55 *Determining cuttable elements in the "Object Styles" dialog (filtered to show Architectural categories only in the figure)*

CREATE REFERENCE PLANES

Reference planes in families serve a vital purpose. If we wish to create a family with flexible dimensions, the procedure is to associate the parameters with various reference planes and then lock the geometry to these reference planes. In this way, we can vary the dimensions that control the locations of various reference planes, which in turn manipulate the geometry constrained to them. This makes the family's geometry parametric! So, let's start by adding some reference planes to our family.

1. Make the *Placement Side* elevation tab active.

> **NOTE:** View names in the various family templates are deliberately generic. For example, the plan view is often called "Ref. Level" because the Level included in most family templates is there for reference only. In the furniture template, we had elevation names like "Left" and "Front." Here we have "Placement Side" and "Back Side" instead of "Front" and "Back." This is typical of a wall-based template and helps you orient yourself relative to how the family will later insert within projects.

2. On the Create tab, on the Datum panel, click the Reference Plane button (or press RP).

   ⇨ Create four reference planes, two vertically on either side of the existing one, and two horizontally above the level as shown on the left side of Figure 11.56.

   Do not be concerned with the precise locations. Simply sketch the reference planes in the approximate locations indicated in the figure. We will adjust the temporary dimensions later.

   ⇨ Click the Modify tool to complete the command.

3. Name each reference plane as " indicated.

Families and the Family Editor | 509

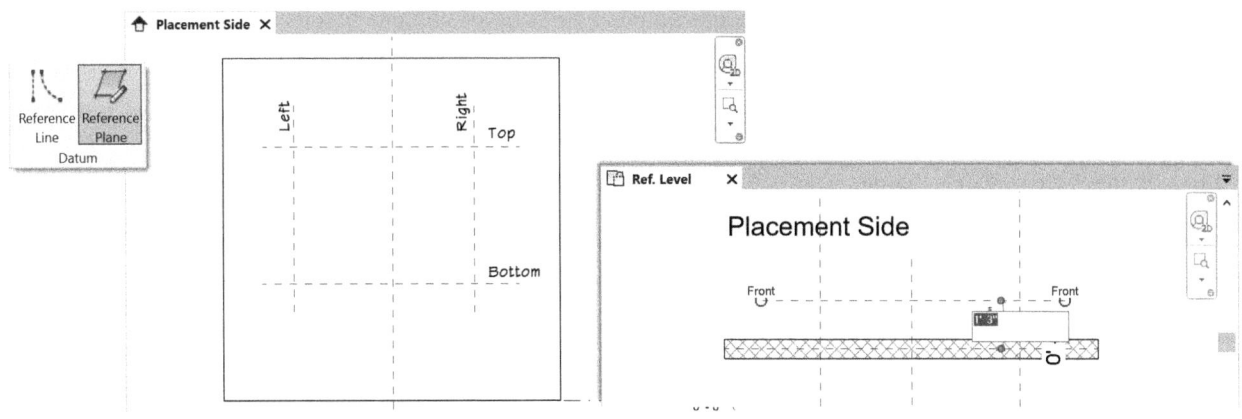

FIGURE 11.56 *Create and name four reference planes in elevation and one in plan*

> **BIM MANAGER NOTE:** On the Properties palette, you can assign the "Is Reference" parameter. Choices include the six cardinal directions (Left, Right, Front, Back, Top, and Bottom). When you use one of these options you establish the reference plane as that absolute edge of the family. For example, if you set the reference plane to Right, then that becomes the right edge of the family. If you later swap in a different family, it can automatically align properly if the new family also has a "right" reference plane. There are many interesting and powerful features of reference planes that time and space will not permit us to explore in this chapter. For a good explanation of reference planes, visit: **https://revitoped.blogspot.com/2006/03/once-upon-reference-plane.html** at the Revit OpEd blog by Steve Stafford. The article was published quite a while ago but remains relevant. You can find a vast collection of useful articles, tips, and musings on all things Revit at Steve's blog as well.

4. Make the *Ref. Level* floor plan tab active.

5. Start the reference plane command again.

   ⇨ Click the points from right to left to create a reference plane parallel to and above the wall (on the placement side).

   ⇨ Edit the temporary dimension that appears to: **1'-3"** [**375**] and name it: **Front** (see the right side of Figure 11.56).

6. Return to the *Placement Side* elevation tab.

7. On the Create tab, click the Extrusion tool.

   ⇨ On the Options Bar, set the "Depth" to: **1'-0"** [**300**] and then click the Rectangle icon.

8. On the Work Plane panel click the Set button. Choose: **Reference Plane : Front** from the Name list and then click OK.

   ⇨ Snap the first corner to the intersection of the Top and Left reference planes.

   ⇨ Snap the other corner to the intersection of the Bottom and Right reference planes (see Figure 11.57).

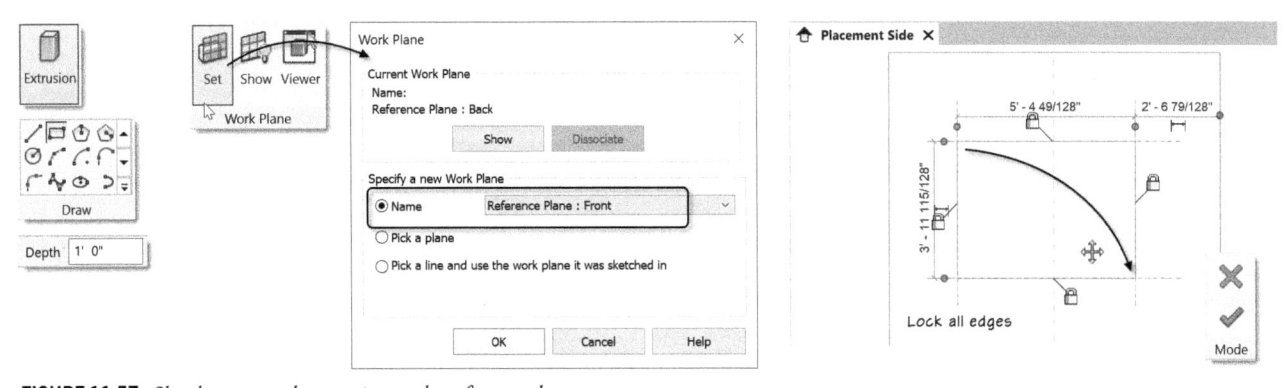

FIGURE 11.57 *Sketch a rectangle snapping to the reference planes*

9. Four open padlock icons will appear—one on each edge of the rectangle. Close each of the padlock icons to constrain the rectangle shape to the reference planes.

• Revit Essentials for Architecture •

510 | Chapter 11

- On the Mode panel, click the Finish Edit Mode button.

Take note of the extrusion in each view window.

10. In the *View 1* 3D view tab, change the display to: **Shaded**.

11. In the *Placement Side* view tab, drag one of the reference planes.

The exact amount of the move is not important. What is important is that the shape of the solid extrusion will adjust when you move the reference plane. This is because we locked the edges of the sketch to the reference planes.

- Undo the Move to return the reference plane to its previous position.

12. Save the Family file.

CREATE DIMENSION PARAMETERS

The first step in creating our parametric family is complete—we created some geometry that is constrained to our reference planes. The next task is to create dimension label elements and associate them with parameters that flex the reference planes.

Make the *Placement Side* tab active.

When adding labeled dimensions to a parametric family, it is very important to dimension to datum elements—like levels and reference planes—wherever possible. Try not to dimension directly to the geometry. There are certainly exceptions, but your general rule of thumb should be to always try to dimension to reference planes, levels, or reference lines. We could be careful when clicking points, using the TAB key to make sure, or we can temporarily hide the geometry instead. This will make it much easier to ensure we dimension the correct elements.

1. Select the extrusion onscreen.

- On the View Control Bar, click the Temporary Hide/Isolate icon (sunglasses) and choose: **Hide Element**.

2. On the Modify tab, on the Measure panel, click the Aligned Dimension tool (or press DI).

- Highlight and then click the Ref. Level line for the first witness line.

- Highlight and then click the Bottom reference plane.

3. Click in a blank space between the two references to place the Dimension (see Figure 11.58).

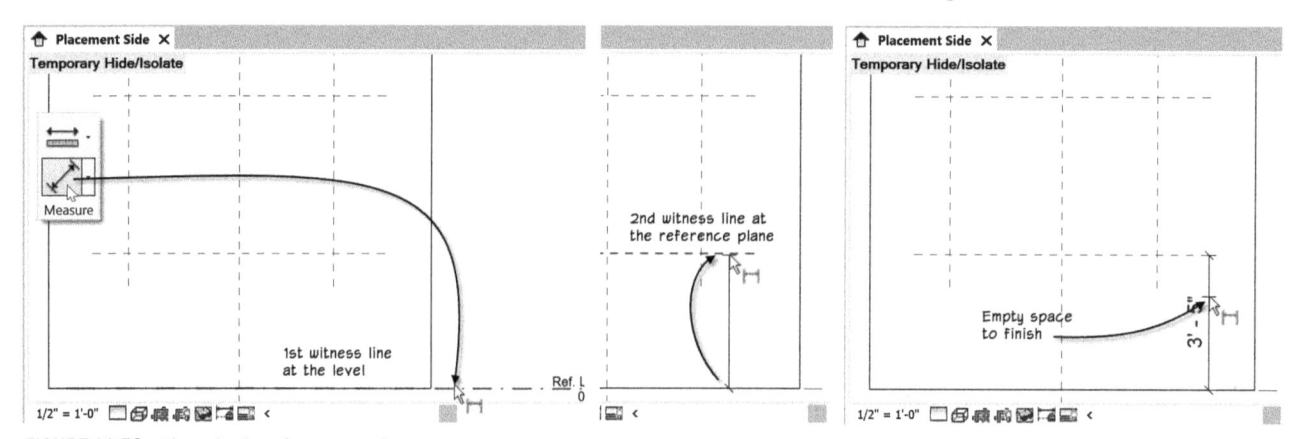

FIGURE 11.58 *Place the first dimension element*

Families and the Family Editor | 511

> **NOTE:** It is important to make sure you do not highlight any objects on your last click, or the dimension will assume you want to add any item you click to the dimension chain. Click in empty space to complete a dimension. Also, be sure to dimension the reference plane and not the bottom of the extrusion. If you did not hide the extrusion, doing so now will make it easier to dimension the reference planes.

   4. Repeat the process to add another dimension between just the Top and the Bottom reference planes (see the left side of Figure 11.59).

We want two separate dimension elements running vertically, not one continuous one. For the first horizontal dimension however, we will create a continuous string including the Left, Center and Right reference planes.

   5. Click the Left reference plane, then click the Center (Left/Right) one, and finally click the Right one.
   ⇨ Click in empty space to place the dimension above where the bin extrusion is.
   ⇨ Click the small EQ toggle on the dimension to toggle on equality (see the middle of Figure 11.59).

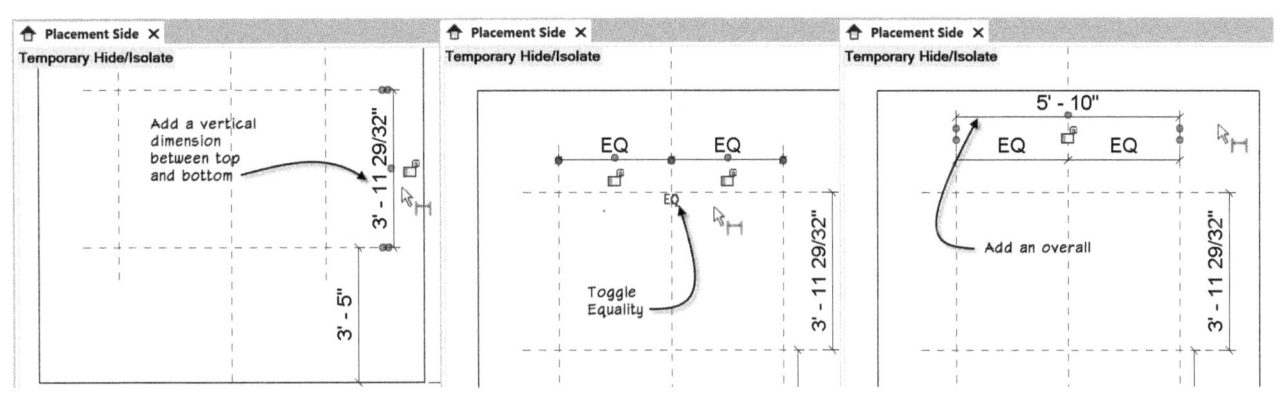

FIGURE 11.59 *Place the three more dimensions*

   6. Add one final Dimension horizontally between the Left and Right reference planes only—do not include the Center one in this string. Place it above the equality one (see the right side of Figure 11.59).
   ⇨ On the ribbon, click the Modify tool or press the ESC key twice.

Now that we have created several dimensions, we will create parameters that will control them. Recall that you can manipulate model geometry in Revit by editing the values of permanent dimensions and temporary dimensions. When you apply parameters to dimensions in a family file, you are doing the same thing. Let's take a look.

   7. Select the overall horizontal Dimension element (the one between left and right, not the EQ one).

Take note of the "Label" item on the ribbon (and the Properties palette). We use this drop down list to assign parameters to the selected dimension. You can also right-click and choose: **Label** if you prefer.

   ⇨ On the Modify | Dimensions tab, on the Label Dimension panel, next to "Label" (currently <none>) click the Create Parameter icon.

   The "Parameter Properties" dialog will appear; verify that the "Family Parameter" radio button is selected at the top.

   ⇨ In the "Parameter Data" area, in the "Name" field type: **Width** (see the middle of Figure 11.60).

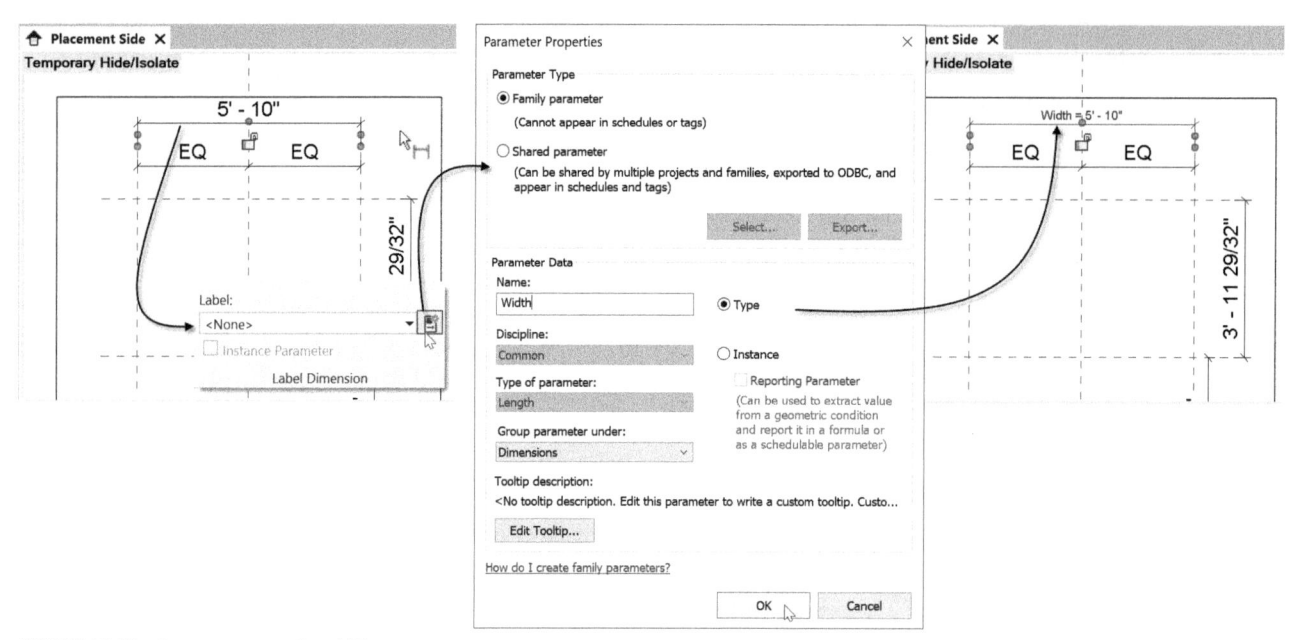

FIGURE 11.60 *Create a custom "Width" parameter*

Parameter type determines the "scope" of the parameter. Family parameters exist only in the family file in which they are created, and shared parameters can be used in more than one family or in project files. You can name a parameter anything you like, but keep in mind that Revit is case-sensitive where parameters are concerned: "width" and "Width" are not the same parameter. Discipline and type of parameter are determined automatically because we started the command by selecting a linear dimension. The "Group parameter under" value is assigned automatically based on the type of parameter. So, in this example, Revit automatically assigned this parameter to the Dimensions grouping. You can always modify this if you wish, but in most cases the default will be suitable.

On the right we can choose between "Type" and "Instance." Type parameters will appear in the "Type Properties" dialog (in projects) and changing the value will affect all instances of the current type. Instance parameters can vary object by object (and show in projects on the Properties palette). We have seen several examples of type and instance properties in the previous chapters. This parameter will be a type parameter and we will create an instance parameter below. Finally, at the bottom of the dialog is an Edit Tooltip button. A parameter named: "Width" is self-explanatory, but if you like, you can edit the tooltip. The tooltip will appear when you hover over the parameter name on the properties palette and can be helpful to give your end users some additional descriptive information on the parameter and its intended use.

8. Click OK to complete the parameter.

    Notice that the Label "Width" now appears in front of the Dimension text. This tells us that this Dimension is controlled by this parameter (see the right side of Figure 11.60).

9. Repeat the process on the vertical Dimension between the Top and Bottom reference planes.

    ⇨ Name the parameter: **Height**, and accept the other defaults as well.

10. Select the vertical Dimension between the Ref. Level and the Bottom reference plane and repeat the process once more.

    ⇨ Name the parameter: **Mounting Height**.

    ⇨ Click the Instance radio button (do not check Reporting Parameter) and then click OK (see Figure 11.61).

Families and the Family Editor | 513

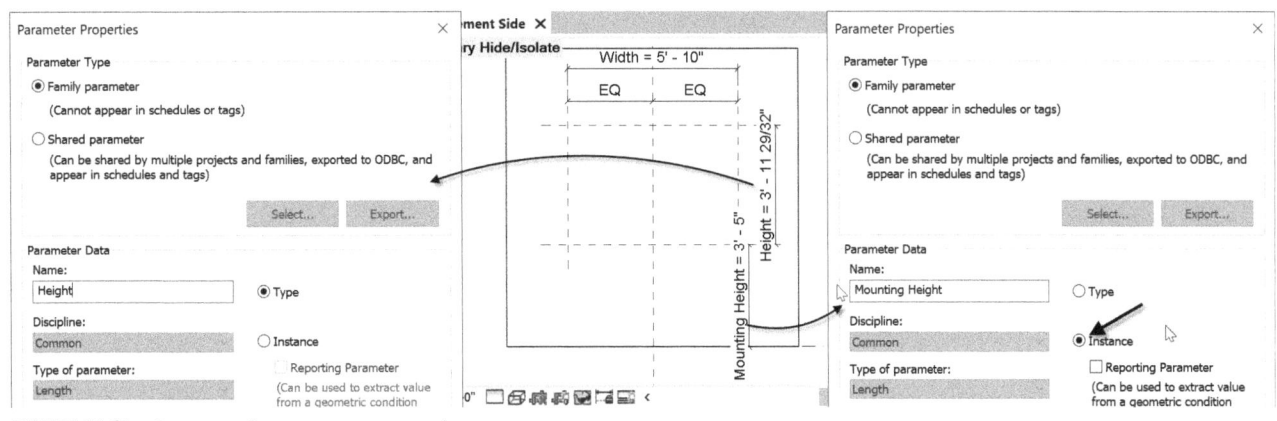

FIGURE 11.61 *Create another type parameter and one instance parameter*

11. On the View Control Bar, click the Temporary Hide/Isolate pop-up and choose: **Reset**.
12. Save the Family.

ADD FAMILY TYPES AND FLEX THE FAMILY

All that remains now is for us to test our family parameters. In Revit, this is typically referred to as "flexing" the family. When you flex the values of the parameters, you can see if the reference planes and geometry are moving as expected. We do this with the Family Types command. This command allows us to not only test to see if our parameters are behaving properly, but to also create some actual types that will load into projects when we load the family; thus the name of the dialog. Remember, just like the out-of-the-box families that we have used so far, users will be able to add new types to our custom family later. But it is still a good idea to stock it with a few preferred variations ahead of time.

1. On the Create tab, on the Properties panel, click the Family Types button.

Notice that the three parameters are listed at the top of the dialog beneath a "Dimensions" grouping exactly as we specified when creating them. To flex the parameters, move the dialog to the side so you can see the view windows in the background. Type numbers into the "Value" field next to each parameter and then click the Apply button. The dimensions in the view window will adjust to the new sizes you input.

2. Change the Width to: **4'-0"** [**1200**].
⇨ Change the Mounting Height to: **4'-6"** [**1350**].
⇨ Change the Height to: **2'-0"** [**600**]
3. Click the Apply button to see the change (see Figure 11.62).

TIP: In this exercise, we have waited until after adding several parameters to "flex" them. It is a very good practice, however, to perform this procedure immediately following the creation of each parameter. In this way, you can catch mistakes or issues before they become potentially compounded by other parameters and/or geometry. Some families can get very complex. Making sure that you test it thoroughly as you build will help you avoid potentially hours of frustration.

• Revit Essentials for Architecture •

514 | Chapter 11

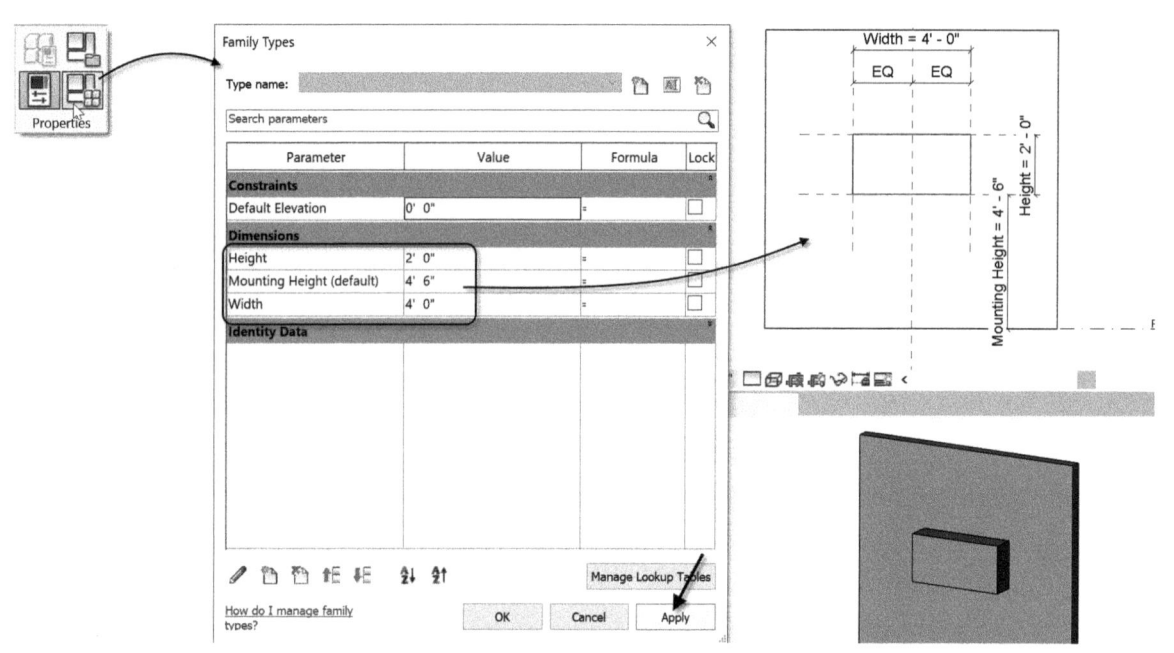

FIGURE 11.62 *View the custom parameters in the family types dialog and edit the values to flex the model*

> **NOTE:** If something did not work correctly, close the dialog and go back through the previous steps to find your error and then try again.

In the "Family Types" dialog, you can add types and add or edit parameters. Let's add some types.

4. At the top of the dialog, click the "New" icon (third from the right).

⇨ In the "Name" dialog, type: **48 wide 24 high** [**1200 wide 600 high**] and then click OK.

The new name will appear in a list at the top.

5. Click New again to create: **48 wide 18 high** [**1200 wide 450 high**].

⇨ Set the Height to: **1'-6"** [**450**]; leave the other dimensions the same and then click Apply.

Create additional types if you wish. Click Apply after each one to test them.

6. After you have created two or more types, choose each one off the list, and then click Apply one at a time as a final test.

Notice that creating types serves two important functions. First, you will likely wish to have some typical types available to your project team when this family is loaded, so adding them in the Family Editor allows you to pre-stock the family with types. Second, having a few types with different values makes your subsequent testing go more quickly. To flex the family, you just choose a different type from the list at the top and then click Apply.

Families and the Family Editor | 515

> **BIM MANAGER NOTE:** If your family requires fewer than half a dozen types, follow the procedures outlined here to add them to your family. However, if you need more than this, you should consider the use of a Type Catalog instead. A type catalog is a TXT file saved in the same folder as the family RFA file. When you load a family with an associated type catalog, a dialog will appear presenting a list of all available types. From this list, you can choose just the types you wish to load into your project. (We saw examples of this in previous chapters when loading doors, windows and structural columns). This can be very helpful in cases where the family contains dozens or even hundreds of variations. Loading such a quantity of types can inhibit performance and workflow. So, a type catalog makes working with such families much more manageable. Furthermore, type catalogs make managing and creating types much easier for the family author. Since they are just text files, they can be edited outside of Revit in a program like Excel where creating multiple types with similar values can be achieved much more efficiently. We will not build a type catalog in this book. If you wish to learn more about creating a type catalog, please search the online help.

7. Click OK when finished.

ADD HARDWARE

We are almost ready to load our family into our project. Before we do, our bin could use some finishing touches. Let's start with some hardware.

1. In the *Placement Side* elevation tab, create a reference plane **2"** [**50**] above the Bottom reference plane and name it: **Hardware Height**.

2. Add a Dimension between the Bottom reference plane and the new one. (Be sure to dimension the reference planes and not the extrusion).

    ⇨ Click to close the padlock control on the dimension (see Figure 11.63).

When you toggle the dimension equality control or close the padlock control, you are applying a constraint to your family rather than a parameter.

> **TIP:** Remember it this way: both parameters and constraints are rules in your family. A parameter is a value that a user can manipulate in the project without editing the family. A constraint "built-in" to the family can only be changed by editing the family within the Family Editor.

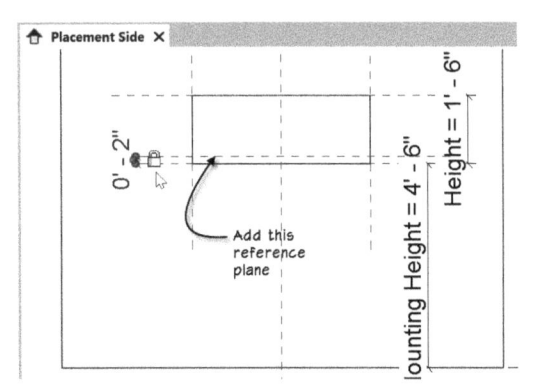

FIGURE 11.63 *Add a new reference plane, dimension it, and lock the dimension to constrain it*

The specifics of creating the hardware will be left to you as a practice exercise. You can make a knob using a solid revolve like the one we created for the reception desk above, or you can make a wire pull from a solid sweep. Just remember to use the new reference plane as the work plane to ensure that it remains in the proper location when the family flexes. For example, if you create a sweep, start in the plan view, edit the work plane, and choose the Hardware Height reference plane from the list. (If you get a warning when drawing the path, it is because of the cut plane in the plan view. You can temporarily lower the Mounting Height parameter while creating the form). Sketch the path centered on the bin in plan; then switch to the elevation and create the profile. A simple square profile is sufficient (see Figure 11.64).

> **TIP:** For a quick way to create the profile, sketch a 4-sided circumscribed polygon. This will make it easy to center and draw quickly.

If you opt for the revolve, you can build it nearly identically to the way we built the one for the reception desk above, except that you will want to set the Work Place to the Hardware Height reference plane first.

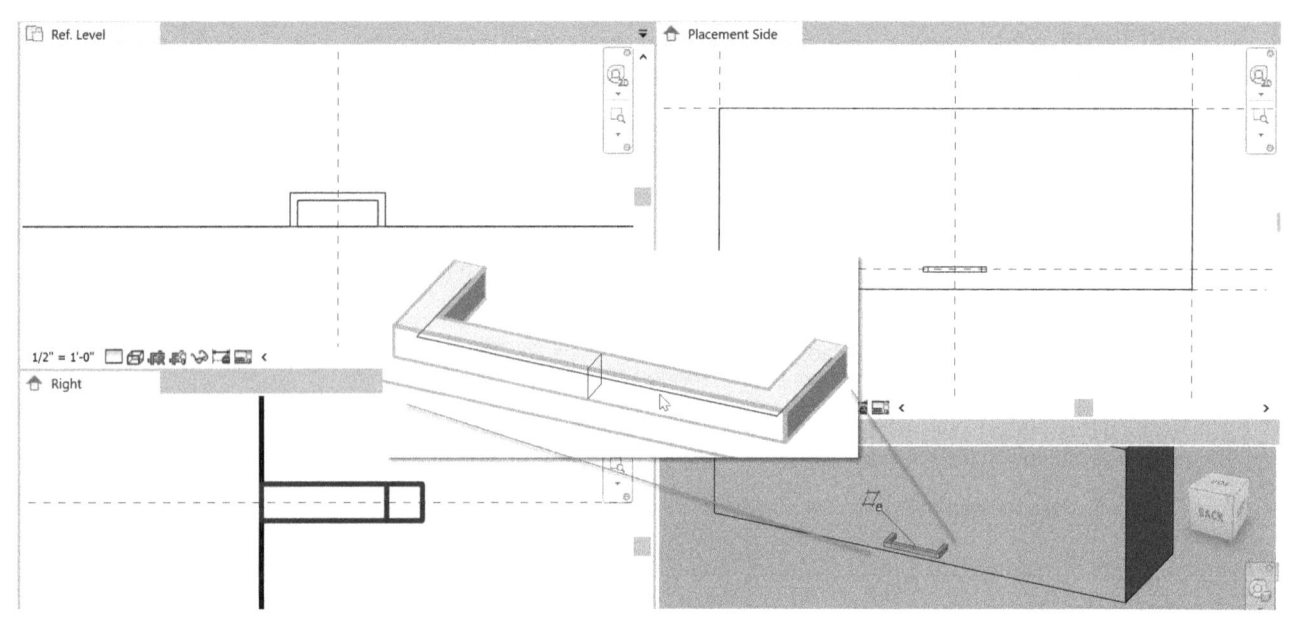

FIGURE 11.64 *Add a solid sweep wire pull for a handle*

When you have finished the solid, open the "Family Types" dialog and choose each of your predefined types in succession from the list and then apply to flex the model. The hardware should remain 2" [50] from the bottom edge and centered on the bin as you flex the model.

3. Zoom all Views to Fit when finished and save the Family.

CHANGING THE FAMILY CATEGORY

While it is maintained that the best practice approach is to choose a proper category at the start of the family creation process and not change it wherever possible, there are those times when it will become necessary or desirable to change the category of a family. At the start of the process building the current family, we used the *Specialty Equipment wall based.rft* [*Metric Specialty Equipment wall based.rft*] template file. This template was chosen more for the wall-based behavior than the Specialty Equipment category. But it would be preferable for it to use the Furniture category instead. Revit does not include a wall based furniture template, so the solution employed here was to build the family using another wall based template and then change the category to Furniture. Doing so will maintain the wall-based behavior but change the category as desired.

Changing the category is a simple process but does come with some warnings. Any custom subcategories (see the next topic) already added to the family will not be preserved. Further, some categories cannot (or should not) be changed. We cannot change Mass families to other categories and vice-versa. Doors and windows and Curtain Panels should not be changed and typically will not behave properly if you do. Changing from Specialty Equipment to Furniture can be done without detriment, but in general it is best to exercise caution; save a backup copy of your family and pin down the category as early in the family authoring process as possible. So, before we go any further with this family, let's change its category.

1. On the Create tab, on the Properties panel, click the Family Category and Parameters button.
2. In the "Family Category and Parameters" dialog, choose Furniture from the Family Category list (see Figure 11.65).

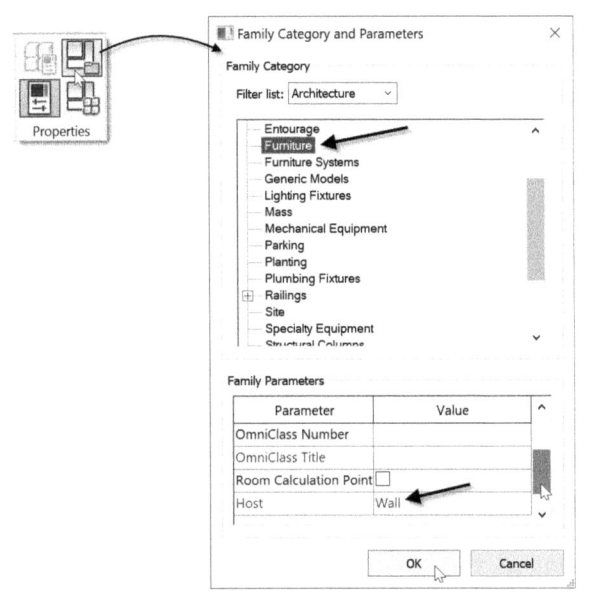

FIGURE 11.65 *Change the category of the current family*

If you look down at the bottom of the dialog, you will notice that the Host parameter is listed as: Wall. This is grayed out, which means that we cannot change it. The hosting behavior is built in and assigned by the template. Furniture would typically not need to be hosted. Therefore, Revit does not provide a hosted furniture template. But the method shown here can effectively overcome this slight limitation.

3. Click OK to complete the change.
4. Save the Family.

CREATING SUBCATEGORIES

Categories are the broadest classification of elements in Revit. Each family belongs to a category and with each family we built, our choice of template (Elevation symbol, Furniture and Specialty Equipment, then Furniture) determined the family's category. The list of categories available is predetermined by Revit—we cannot rename, add, or delete categories. However, we can add and delete "subcategories." A subcategory gives us more detailed control over the visibility of model and annotation elements by allowing parts of an element to appear differently from the whole. For example, the "Doors" Category includes subcategories for "Elevation Swing," "Frame/Mullion," and "Panel" (among others). Each of these subcategories gives us visibility control over these common sub-components globally for all door elements (across various families). When you build or modify a family, you can assign the various components within the family to any of the available subcategories. You can see a list of available categories and subcategories in the "Object Styles" dialog.

1. On the Manage tab, on the Settings panel, click the Object Styles button (see Figure 11.66).

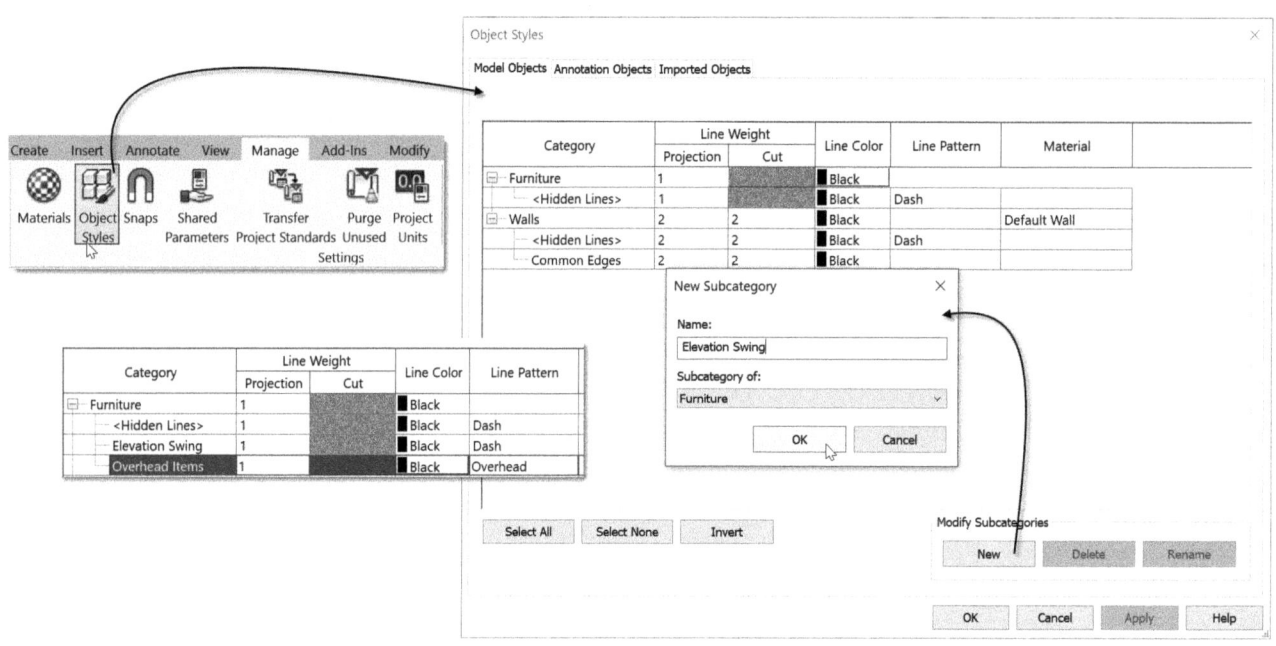

FIGURE 11.66 *Object styles shows the available categories and subcategories; new subcategories can be added*

Since we are currently in a family file, the list of available categories includes only those relating to the family we are editing—in this case Furniture. (If you wish to see a more complete list, you will need to repeat this command later in a project file.) Furniture contains one subcategory called, "Hidden Lines" by default. You should consider adding subcategories for overall conditions that would apply to most elements of this category. For example, if you were to edit a door family, you would notice that there is a subcategory for "Plan Swing" and another for "Elevation Swing." Since most drawings need to represent the swing of the doors regardless of the kind of door, the swing subcategories provide a useful way to control all door swings universally throughout the project without needing to edit several families individually. If you study most of the subcategories provided with the software, you will find they share this kind "global edit" strategy. While most of the subcategories you will likely require are already included in the provided family templates, there will be situations when you decide to create new ones. In the case of our binder bin family, it might be useful to have a subcategory to indicate the door swing much like the door families have. This is a somewhat gray area as not all families that belong to Furniture need this subcategory. For example, chairs and tables would not have need for an Elevation Swing. You will have to exercise some judgment here. The best advice that can be given is to add subcategories sparingly and after some careful consideration. Having subcategories is not bad, but having too many and ones that are too specific to a family can be undesirable to the rest of the project team; including the extended team and consultants.

2. Make sure Furniture is selected, and then at the bottom of the dialog, in the "Modify Subcategories" grouping, click the "New" button.
⇨ Name this new subcategory: **Elevation Swing** and then click OK.
⇨ Change the Line Pattern to: **Dash**.
3. Create another new subcategory named: **Overhead Items**.
⇨ Make its Line Pattern: **Overhead** and then click OK.

To use the new subcategory, you edit the element on the Properties palette and choose the subcategory you wish. If you do not assign a subcategory to an element, it simply associates with the parent category. In this case, everything we have added to the current family belongs to the main Furniture category and has no subcategory. In the next topic, we'll discuss Symbolic Lines and assign them to our new subcategories.

ADD SYMBOLIC LINES

Symbolic Lines are special Revit elements that can be added to families to embellish the 2D views. In projects, we have model elements and annotation elements. Model elements appear in all views, and annotation (including detail) elements appear only in the view to which they were added. In families, model elements behave exactly as they do in projects. However, the views that we see in the Family Editor are not transferred over to the project when we load the family. Therefore, drafting lines would not be transferred either. Instead, we use symbolic lines in the Family Editor. Symbolic lines will appear in all views parallel to the view in which they are created. So, if you add a symbolic line to a front elevation, it will appear in all sections or elevations that face the same direction, but not in any other views. The use of symbolic lines allows us to add detailing and embellishment that is view-specific like how we would use detail lines in a project. In this example, we will use symbolic lines to indicate the swing direction of the binder bin when it opens in the front facing elevation.

Don't confuse these with model lines. These are available too, but model lines are treated like model geometry and show in all views, not just the one they are drawn in. In other words, the symbolic lines that we will draw will show *only* when viewing the binder bin head on. If we used model lines instead, they would also show in 3D views or skewed elevations as well. We'll use symbolic lines for the swing indications here, but in some firms, these are created with model lines instead. Check with your CAD or BIM Manager to see how it is done in your firm.

Make the *Placement Side* elevation tab active and zoom in on the bin.

1. On the Create tab, on the Work Plane panel, click the Set tool.

   ⇨ Verify that the work plane is still set to: **Reference Plane : Front**. If not set it now and then click OK.

   If you wish, on the Work Plane panel, click the Show button (to display the Work Plane).

2. Select the extrusion and then on the View Control Bar, from the Temporary Hide/Isolate pop-up, choose: **Hide Element**.

3. On the Annotate tab, click on the Symbolic Line tool.

   ⇨ On the Subcategory panel, from the Subcategory list, choose: **Elevation Swing**.

Notice how the new subcategory added in the previous topic now appears here. If you forget to choose it while you are adding the element, you can edit the properties of the lines later the Properties palette.

On the Options Bar, verify that "Chain" is checked.

4. Sketch two lines as indicated (see the left side of Figure 11.67).

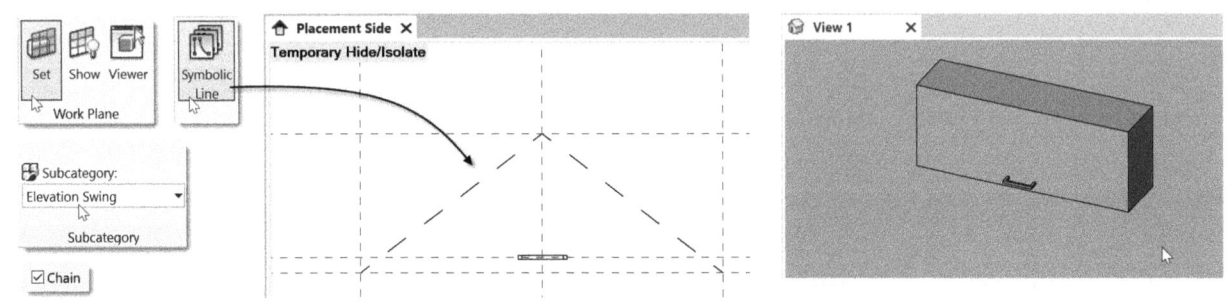

FIGURE 11.67 *Add symbolic lines to the front elevation using the new elevation swing subcategory*

Notice that the symbolic lines do not display in the 3D view (see the right side of Figure 11.67). This is by design. Symbolic lines only display in views parallel to the view in which they are created.

5. Click the Modify tool, or press ESC twice to finish.

520 | Chapter 11

If you recall, the default Mounting Height that we assigned above was 4'-6" [1350] for each type. While we did make these instance parameters (which means that each bin we add to our model can have its own Mounting Height), initially when we place them, they will fail to show in most plan views. This is because the default cut height in plan is 4'-0" [1200], which is below the lowest point of our bin's geometry. (You may have run into this when drawing the hardware above.) Assuming that you want to see the bins displayed in plan views even though they are mounted above the cut plane, you can add additional symbolic lines in the plan view that show an outline of our bin in a dashed line style to indicate that it is mounted above.

Make the *Ref. Level* floor plan tab active.

6. Hide the extrusion with Temporary hide.

7. On the Annotate tab, click on the Symbolic Line tool.

8. Check the Placement Plane drop down on the Options Bar.

It probably remembers the Hardware Height plane since we have switched back to a floor plan. Each view remembers the work plane that was active for that view until or unless you change it.

⇨ From the Placement Plane drop down list, choose: **Level: Ref. Level**.

9. On the Modify | Place Symbolic Lines tab, from the Subcategory drop down, choose: **Overhead Items**.

⇨ On the Draw panel, click the Rectangle icon and then snap to opposite corners of the reference planes.

⇨ Close all four padlock icons (see Figure 11.68).

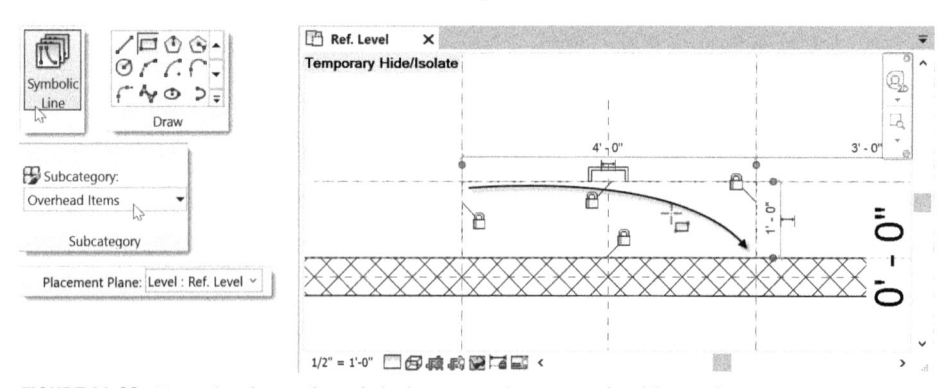

FIGURE 11.68 *Trace the plan with symbolic lines using the new overhead lines subcategory*

10. On the ribbon, click the Modify tool or press the ESC key twice.

At this stage it would be a good idea to flex.

11. Open the "Family Types," dialog, choose a different type and then click Apply.

Check that your Symbolic Lines are behaving as expected. If they do not follow the 3D geometry, you can use the Align tool and lock to fix it in the offending views. With the diagonal lines, you can Align the endpoints. Use TAB to highlight the endpoint, the click and lock it. Remember to align and lock to the reference planes wherever possible.

MAKING FAMILIES ABOVE THE CUT PLANE DISPLAY IN PLAN

We now have the symbolic lines that we need in plan, but there is one other important criterion determining whether they will display in projects. Since none of the model geometry of the bins intersects the cut plane, Revit simply will not show any geometry in plan views. This is despite the presence of our symbolic lines. In other words, the interaction with the cut plane is the first criterion that Revit considers. Once it is determined which objects are within the view range (and therefore should be displayed), Revit then considers how to display them. In our current family,

• The Aubin Academy •

all model geometry is above the cut plane. To trigger the family to display our symbolic lines, we need some part of the family to occur below or at least intersect the cut plane. To achieve this, we can draw an invisible line element passing through the Cut Plane. In this way, Revit will recognize that we wish to display this family in plan. It is an effective work-around, conveying our intent to the system. The "invisible line" will be visible in the Family Editor, but not in the Project Editor.

> **BIM MANAGER NOTE:** Earlier when discussing the choice of family template and categories, the issue of view range and cut plane was not mentioned. It should be noted that there are three Revit categories that will display above the cut plane without need for the work-around covered here. Those include: windows, casework, and generic models. If cutting behavior is your primary concern, Casework might be a viable option for this family. If you wish to explore this, you can change the category of the family as we did above. However, realize that this would delete the subcategories that we have already added. So once again, it is best to make such a decision early in the process of building your family. The longer you wait to make such a change, the more likely it is that you will need to redo some aspects of your family. Please note that our binder bin could really be thought of as Specialty Equipment, Furniture, or Casework. So, there is no right or wrong category to choose here. Discuss the issues with your team and try to build some standard guidelines for all family authors to follow. The most important issue is consistency. If everyone on the team is building things the same way, it goes a long way toward making your overall workflow much more predictable. Regardless of the ultimate choice you make regarding category, the following workaround for trigging overhead display will be useful in many of your families. It has applications like the one illustrated here, to display light fixtures like wall sconces, light switches in reflected ceiling plans, etc.

Make the *Placement Side* elevation tab active.

1. Change the Work Plane to: Reference Plane: **Back**.
2. On the Create tab, on the Model panel, click the Model Line tool.
⇨ From the Subcategory drop down, choose: <**Invisible lines**>.
3. Draw a Model Line from the Ref. Level to the reference plane at the bottom of the bin (see Figure 11.69).

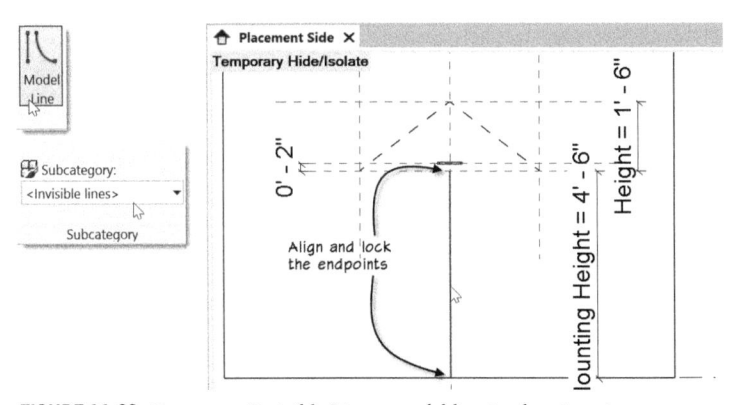

FIGURE 11.69 *Draw an <Invisible Lines> model line in elevation view*

4. On the ribbon, click the Modify tool or press the ESC key twice.

With the placement of this model line, Revit will "see" this object when it is above the default cut of: 4'-0" [1200]. Once the display of the object is triggered by interaction with the view range and cut, the family will display in plan. One final step remains. Recall the discussion above in the "Create a New Family File" topic on page 489 regarding cuttable families. The Furniture category is not cuttable. This means that interaction with the cut plane for a Furniture element simply determines if the element should display or not. Now that we have added the invisible line, we have established that the family should display in plans. However, since it is not a cuttable family, it will display all the family's geometry indiscriminately—not just the dashed symbolic lines as we would prefer. To make sure that only the symbolic lines display in plan and not the bin geometry we can use the visibility settings in the family to instruct

522 | Chapter 11

the bin and hardware geometry not to display in plan views. The symbolic lines, on the other hand, require no further intervention since they will display only in plan views automatically (having been created in plan).

5. In the *View 1* 3D view, select the bin extrusion and the hardware.

⇨ On the Properties palette, click the Visibility/Graphics Overrides button.

⇨ In the "Family Element Visibility Settings" dialog, clear the checkmark from the "Plan/RCP" box and then click OK (see Figure 11.70).

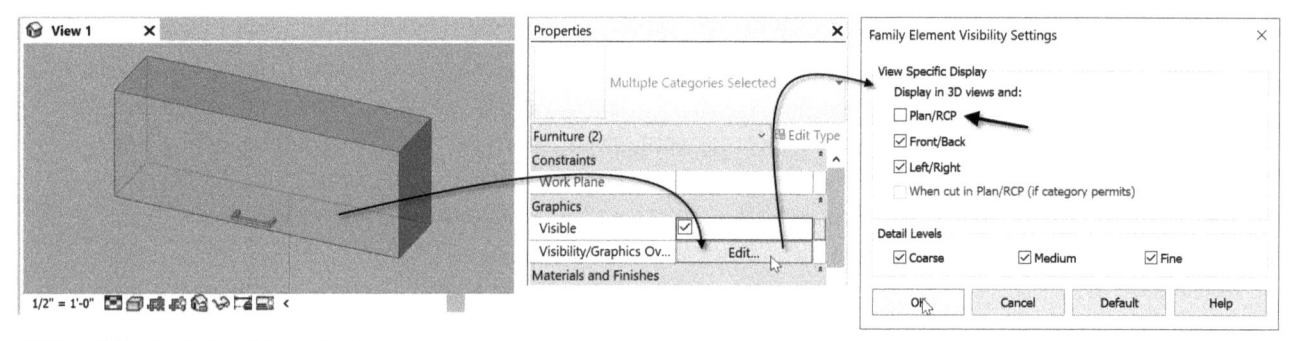

FIGURE 11.70 *Hide the solids in Plan/RCP*

6. Zoom all Views to fit, reset all temporary hide/isolate settings and save the Family file.

Congratulations, you have just created a parametric family from scratch! For the final test, let's load it into the project.

LOAD INTO PROJECT TO TEST

Make sure you are satisfied with the geometry and have tested the various types. Be sure to save the family before you continue.

1. Reopen the *11 Commercial* project, open the *Level 3* floor plan and zoom in on the reception area.

⇨ Close the G100 – Cover sheet tab.

2. Switch back to one of the views of the binder bin family and then on the ribbon, click the Load into Project button.

This will switch to the *Level 3* view of the Commercial project. The Modify | Place Component tab will be active allowing you to place the new family immediately.

> **NOTE:** In the previous exercises, we have favored the "Load into Project and Close" button. If you are certain that done editing the family, this is the preferred tool as it will both load the family into the project and them close the RFA file for you. If you think you might need to continue modifying the family, choose "Load into Project" instead. This will load the family, but leave the RFA file open in the background. When you have finished testing, you can switch windows and close it manually with the **Close** command on the File menu (or press CTRL + W).

Since this is a wall-based component family, you will need to click on a wall to place it.

3. Click on the wall behind the reception desk to place two instances—one of each type (see Figure 11.71).

At this point, we can test several of the behaviors of this new family. The first test is requiring the wall host. Next is verifying that it displays correctly in plan. It should appear as a dashed rectangle. Add a camera view to the reception area to look at the binder bin in 3D. (If you need a refresher on creating a camera view, refer to the "Load the Family into the Project" topic on page 482 and Figure 11.2 above.) The 3D view will give you an overall look at the space.

• The Aubin Academy •

Check the *Families* branch of the Project Browser under *Furniture* to see the newly loaded family. Return to the plan and cut a section through or place an interior elevation in the reception space looking at the binder bin. Open the new view(s). You should see the symbolic elevation swing lines in that view. Notice that, by default, both binder bins share the same mounting height. The Mounting Height parameter is an instance parameter, so try adding more than one bin to the project, and then edit the properties of one of them (on the Properties palette) to set the Mounting Height differently. Open the "Object Styles" dialog and beneath Furniture, experiment with changing the settings—turn off the Elevation Swing and/or change line styles. You can also edit these settings per view by clicking the Visibility/Graphics tool on the View tab (or just type VG). Finally, you can add, edit, or delete family types on the Project Browser as we did above.

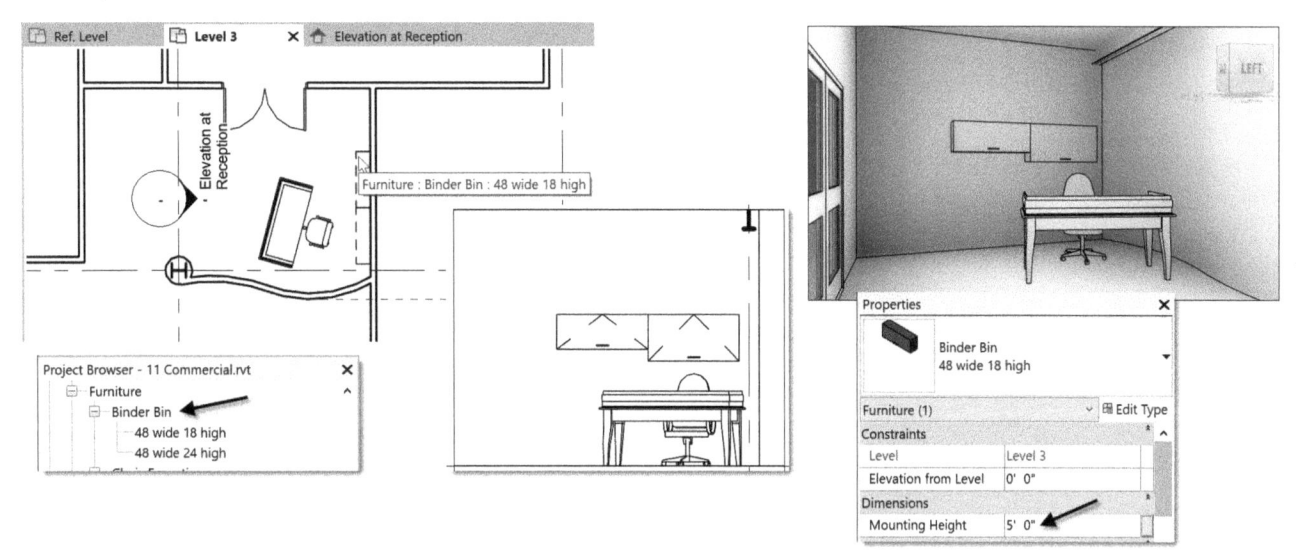

FIGURE 11.71 *Add some binder bins to the commercial project third floor reception space*

4. When you have finished experimenting with the binder bin, close the family file.
5. Save the commercial project.

CREATE A CURTAIN PANEL FAMILY

In the previous chapter, in the "Swap Panel Types" topic on page 447, we loaded a custom curtain panel family into the commercial project and used it in the curtain wall design at the front of the building. In the short exercise that follows, we will walk through the process used to create the custom curtain panel family loaded there. The process begins the same as any other new family. The only difference is the template we'll choose.

1. From the File menu, choose: **New > Family**.

Browse to the folder for your preference of units. There are four Curtain Panel templates:

Curtain Wall Panel.rft [*Metric Curtain Wall Panel.rft*]

Door – Curtain Wall.rft [*Metric Door – Curtain Wall.rft*]

Window – Curtain Wall.rft [*Metric Window – Curtain Wall.rft*]

Curtain Panel Pattern Based.rft [*Metric Curtain Panel Pattern Based.rft*]

The first three will create a curtain panel that will appear on the Type Selector when working with curtain walls, sloped glazing and curtain systems. The fourth is a special kind of curtain panel used in the conceptual modeling

524 | Chapter 11

environment. You can learn more about the conceptual modeling environment in Chapter 17. The door and window templates are a little more specific and share characteristics of both curtain panels and doors or windows, respectively.

- ⇨ Choose the *Window – Curtain Wall.rft* [*Metric Window – Curtain Wall.rft*] template and then click Open.

    This template opens only the *Ref. Level* plan view by default.

2. Open the *Exterior* elevation view.

- ⇨ Click and hold down the Exterior view tab and drag it away from the frame to "tear it off."

    It should now be a separate floating window.

3. If you have two monitors, you can drag it to your second monitor. Otherwise, drag it to the right vertical edge of the Revit application frame.

- ⇨ Blue highlighting will appear indicating how it will dock. When it highlights the right half of the window, release the mouse to dock the tab in a new tile.

- ⇨ Zoom All to Fit (ZA) (see Figure 11.72).

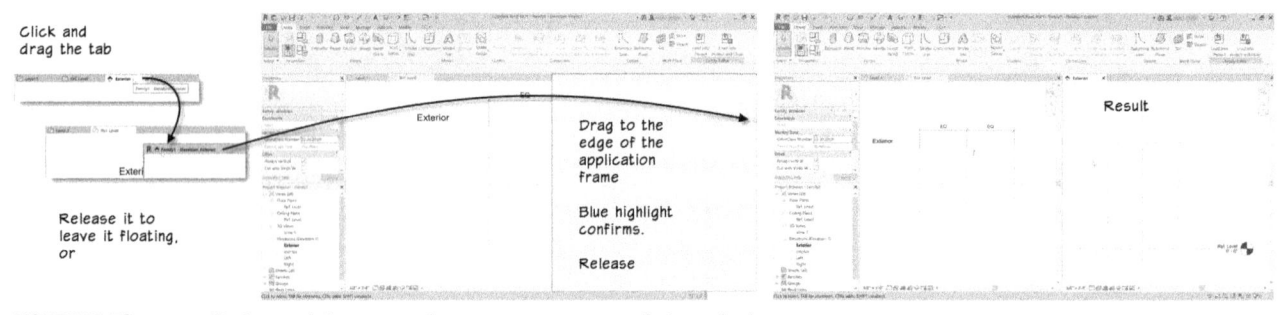

FIGURE 11.72 *Manually drag and drop view tabs to create a custom set of tiles and tabs*

Look at both the plan and exterior elevation views and notice that several reference planes are already present as well as an EQ dimension. There is not, however, an overall width dimension. This is because curtain panels behave differently than other families. The width and height are determined not by parameters, but instead by the curtain grids of the curtain wall to which they are assigned in a project. If you look at the exterior elevation, the panel size is the space defined by the left and right reference planes horizontally, the top reference plane, and the Ref. Level vertically. Therefore, we simply need to draw our panel geometry within this space. This behavior is unique to curtain panel families.

4. On the Manage tab, click the Object Styles button.

In the topic above, we learned about creating subcategories. Notice that this family belongs to the Windows category and as such has all the default window subcategories. The *Door – Curtain Panel* template would likewise be categorized as a door sharing its subcategories, and the *Curtain Wall Panel* template is assigned to the Curtain Panels category with only simple curtain wall subcategories.

- ⇨ Click Cancel to exit the "Object Styles" dialog.

ESTABLISH REFERENCE PLANES, CONSTRAINTS, AND PARAMETERS

Since this will be a flexible family, it begins like the previous example with reference planes, dimensions and parameters to drive them.

1. In the *Floor Plan: Ref. Level* view, draw two vertical reference planes in the middle of the panel—one on each side of the center reference plane.

    We'll establish the spacing next.

Families and the Family Editor | 525

2. Add a dimension including all reference planes *except* the center one.

⇨ Toggle the equality on (see Figure 11.73).

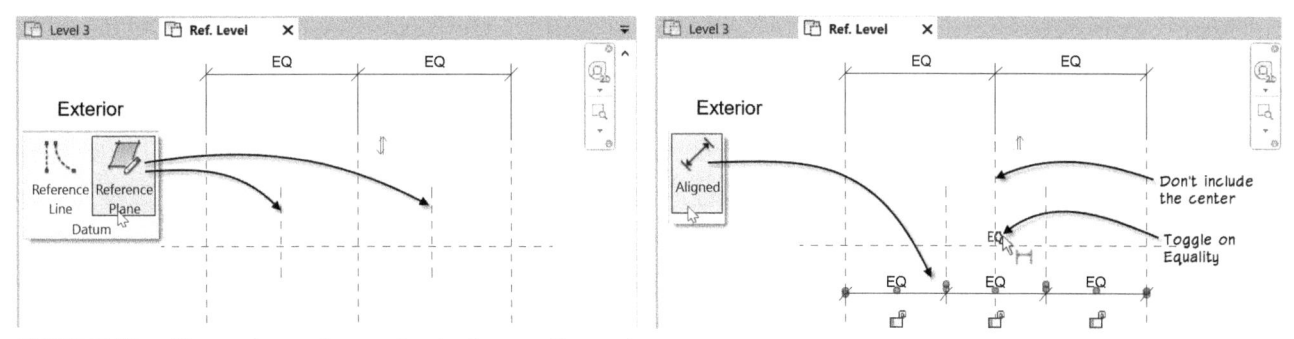

FIGURE 11.73 *Add two reference planes and make them equally spaced*

The next several steps are illustrated in Figure 11.74.

3. Click the Reference Plane tool, and then on the Draw panel, click the Pick Lines tool.

⇨ On the Options Bar set the Offset to: **1"** [**25**].

4. Offset a reference plane on each side of the two just created (four total).

⇨ Dimension the vertical reference planes and lock them.

5. Change the Offset to: **1 1/4"** [**31**] and Offset the Center (Front/Back) reference plane (running horizontally) to create a new horizontal one above it.

⇨ Name this new horizontal reference plane: **Panel Offset**.

6. Create a dimension between the Center (Front/Back) reference plane and the Panel Offset reference plane.

⇨ Label this dimension with a new Parameter also named: **Panel Offset**.

⇨ Leave it a type parameter and grouped under Dimensions.

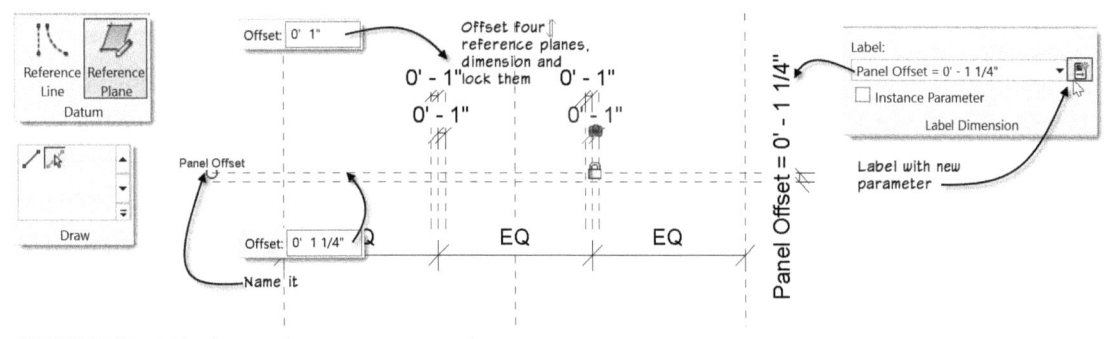

FIGURE 11.74 *Add reference planes, constraints, and parameters*

You can flex Panel Offset just like we did the other custom parameters above. Open the "Family Types" dialog and try a new value in the field and click Apply. Set it back to: **1 1/4"** [**31**] before closing the dialog. To flex the width and the equality dimensions, simply drag the left or right reference plane a little. You will see all the others adjust accordingly. Undo before continuing.

7. Save the family as: **Front Façade Window Panel**.

BUILD PANEL GEOMETRY

Now that we have reference plane framework in place, it is time to create some geometry.

1. In the *Exterior* view tab, set the work plane to: **Reference Plane: Panel Offset** (see item 1 in Figure 11.75).

• Revit Essentials for Architecture •

2. From the Create tab, add an extrusion (item 2).

⇨ Sketch three rectangles that snap to the reference planes and lock the sketch lines (item 3).

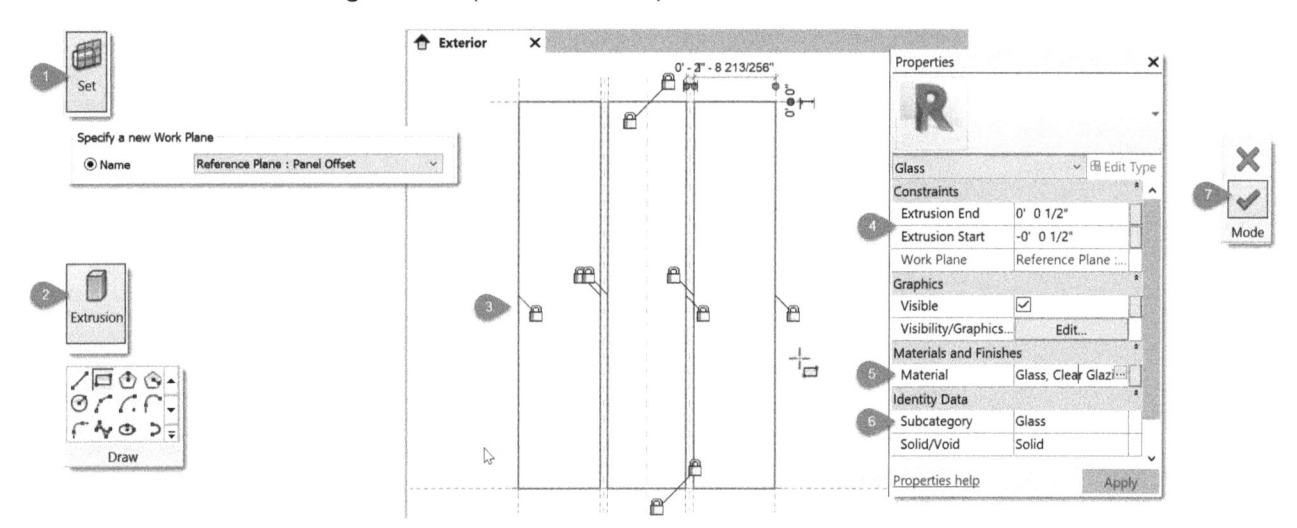

FIGURE 11.75 *Snap the sketch lines to the reference planes and lock them*

3. On the Properties palette, set the Extrusion End to: **1/2"** [**12**].

⇨ Set the Extrusion Start to: **-1/2"** [**-12**] (negative) (item 4).

Notice that the Depth field on the Options Bar will now read: 1" [24]. Revit simply calculates the resulting Depth from the two offsets.

4. Also on Properties, next to Material, click on <By Category> and then click the small browse icon that appears.

⇨ In the "Material Browser" dialog, choose: **Glass** and then click OK (item 5).

⇨ Beneath the identity Data grouping, change the Subcategory to: **Glass** (item 6).

5. On the Mode panel, click the Finish Edit Mode button (item 7).

You can best see the results back in the plan view. The extrusion appears like three panes of glass. If you open the 3D view and turn on shading, the glass will be transparent. To complete the panel family, we need to add some mullions between the panes of glass. You may also want to lighten the weight of the glass in plan. We could repeat the symbolic line procedure covered above. However, since we have assigned the extrusion to the Glass subcategory, we will have the ability to lighten all glass in plan view once it is loaded into the project. The nice thing about waiting to do it this way is that the change will apply to the glass of all windows, not just within this family. Furthermore, since these curtain panels will be at an angle to the work plane of the floor plan in the project (since we are applying them to slanted walls), the symbolic lines would not appear anyway. Remember that symbolic lines only appear when they are parallel to the view in which they are created in the family.

BUILD OR LOAD A MULLION PROFILE FAMILY

Profile families are simple 2D families that contain a closed profile shape. The shape can be drawn using any of the standard line and arc tools. Profile families give us a convenient way to save commonly used shapes. Profile families can be loaded into other families and used to create sweeps and swept blends. Unfortunately, we cannot use profiles in extrusions, revolves or blends.

1. On the Insert tab, on the Load from Library panel, click the Load Family button.

⇨ Browse to the *English-Imperial\Profiles\Curtain Wall* [*English\Profiles\Curtain Wall*] folder.

2. Choose: *Curtain Wall Mullion-Rectangular-Center.rfa* [*M_Curtain Wall Mullion-Rectangular-Center.rfa*] and then click Open.

If you prefer, you can build your own mullion profile. To do so, start a new family from the *Profile-Mullion.rft* [*Metric Profile-Mullion.rft*] template. In the family, sketch a closed 2D shape and save the family. Then use Load into Projects to load it into the panel family. You can also find another pre-made example in the *Chapter11* folder called *Mullion Shape.rfa*.

⇨ Continue in the *Exterior* elevation view tab with the work plane set to: **Reference Plane: Panel Offset**.

CREATE A MULLION USING A SOLID SWEEP.

To create the mullion from this loaded profile, we will use a sweep. It only needs a single line segment for the path.

1. On the Create tab, click the Sweep button (see item 1 in Figure 11.76).

⇨ Sketch the Path in elevation along the reference plane centered in the gap between glass panels. (Zoom as required).

⇨ Go ahead and lock the path to the reference plane. Use the Align tool if the lock does not automatically appear (item 2).

2. Finish the Path (item 3).

3. On the Sweep panel, from the Profile list (currently set to: <By Sketch>), choose one of the three sizes for the profile family loaded in the previous topic (item 4).

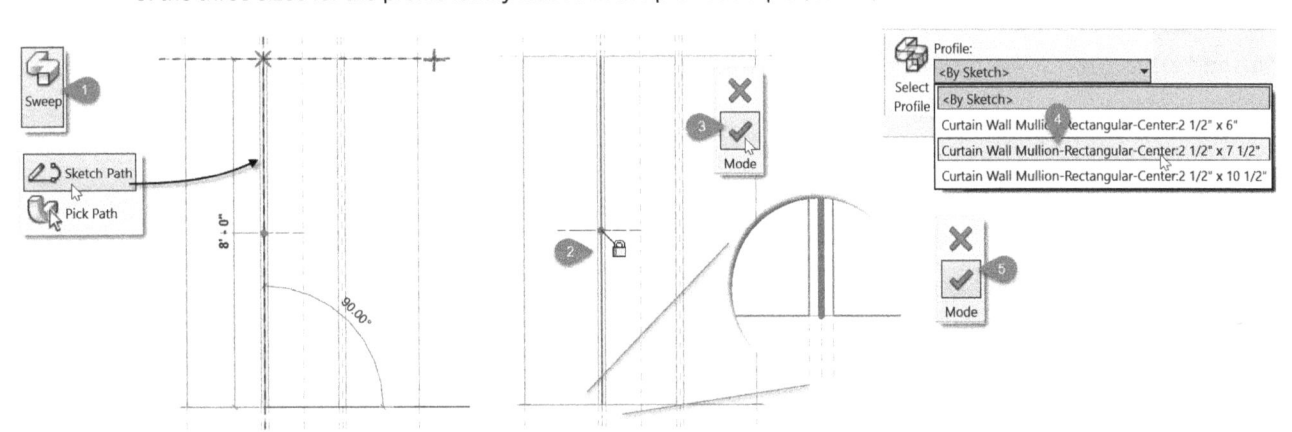

FIGURE 11.76 *Create a sweep using a loaded profile for the mullion*

There are other options. Notice that if you select the Profile, you can move it using both the X and Y offset fields on the Options Bar, or interactively in the view. It can also be flipped or rotated if necessary.

4. Finish the Sweep (item 5).

5. Repeat for the process for the other mullion.

6. Edit the Properties of both sweeps and set the subcategory to: **Frame/Mullion**.

7. Save the Family (see Figure 11.77).

> **NOTE:** You can copy the first sweep to the new location instead of building it over again. However, any locks you applied will be lost. So remember to edit the newly copied sweep and use the Align (AL) tool to align and re-lock the path sketch. Furthermore, you may also need to lock the endpoints at each end of the path to ensure that everything flexes properly.

528 | Chapter 11

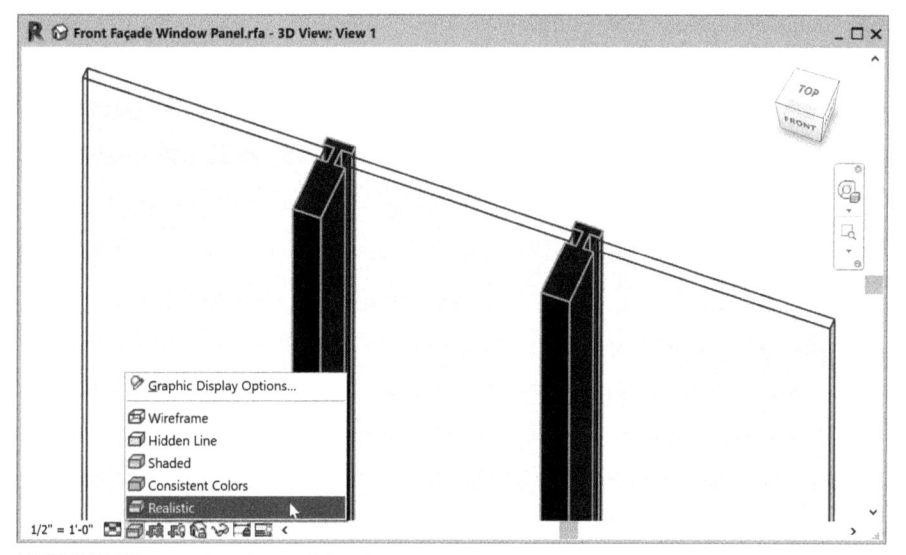

FIGURE 11.77 *Complete the panel family*

8. Load the family into the commercial project and swap it in for some of the panels in the curtain walls to test it out.

To see the panel flex, you must edit the size of your curtain wall bays. You can use any of the techniques from the previous chapter for this. Feel free to experiment if you like. Perform any further experiments you wish in the commercial project before continuing. Try editing the curtain grid spacing and see how the mullions in the panel family stay equally spaced. If you want to reduce the line weight of the glass in plan views, open Object Styles (Manage tab) and expand the Windows category. For the Glass subcategory, change the Cut line weight to something smaller such as pen 1 or 2.

9. Close the Panel Family.
10. Save and close the commercial project.

ADVANCED PARAMETERS AND FEATURES

In the binder bin example above, we made a basic parametric family by adding labels to dimension strings that in turn controlled the size of the object. Dimensional parameters are the most common parameters used in families and are the most straightforward to define. However, the potential of parameters goes well beyond the controlling of dimensions. In this topic, we will explore several additional features that are a bit more advanced. We will explore nested families, visibility parameters, array parameters, and the use of formulas in parameters.

CREATE A COAT HOOK FAMILY

For use in this exercise, a family file has been provided with the *Chapter11* files. The file contains a wall-based coat rack. It was built from scratch starting with the specialty equipment template as we did above for the binder bin. The category has been changed to Furniture and an Overhead Items subcategory was added. Similar geometry, reference planes, and dimension parameters have already been set up in the file. In this exercise, we will create a new family for an individual coat hook. We will then open the provided wall coat rack family file and load our coat hook family into it. From there we will explore several parameters and features mentioned in the previous paragraph.

You should have closed all files at the completion of the previous exercise, and the Recent Files window should now be displayed in Revit.

1. From the Home screen, in the Families area, click the "New" button to create a New Family.

⇨ Browse to your *Templates* folder if necessary, select *Generic Model*.

Families and the Family Editor | 529

rft [*Metric Generic Model.rft*] and then click Open.

2. Tile the windows (WT) and zoom all to fit. (ZA)

Since the coat hook does not need to be inserted on its own in a project and will only be nested into another family, Generic Model is fine here. There are several Generic Model templates. For this example, be sure to choose the non-hosted one.

> **NOTE:** If your version of Revit does not contain this template, a copy is provided in the *Chapter11* folder.

3. Save the Family and name it: **Coat Hook**.

   Make the *Ref. Level* floor plan window active.

4. Select the two reference planes onscreen.

Notice that they are pinned. This prevents us from moving them accidentally. We will unpin them, scale them down in size and then re-pin them. Since the size of our hook will be much smaller than the template setup, this will make it more convenient to work on it.

- On the Modify tab, click the Unpin tool (or press UP).
- On the Modify tab, click the Scale tool (or press RE), on the Options Bar, select the Numerical option and then type: **0.1** in the Scale field.
- Onscreen, click the intersection of the two reference planes to complete the scaling.
- On the Modify tab, click the Pin tool (or press PN).

5. Zoom in on the newly scaled reference planes.
6. On the Create tab, click the Revolve tool.

- Accept all the defaults and draw a vertical line starting at the insertion point (the intersection of the two reference planes) (see item 1 in Figure 11.78).
- Move straight up, type: **4"** [**100**], and then press ENTER.
- Zoom in more if necessary and draw a horizontal line to the right: **1/2"** [**12**] (item 2).

7. On the Draw panel, click the Start-End-Radius Arc tool (item 3).

- Move straight down vertically to the reference plane and click. Then for the radius type: **11"** [**275**]).
- Close the shape with a small: **1/2"** [**12**] long horizontal line.

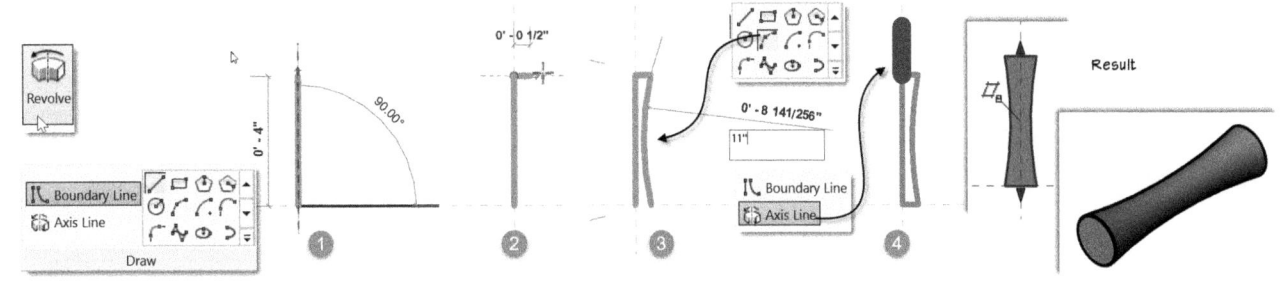

FIGURE 11.78 *Sketch the profile of the coat hook and axis and then finish the revolve*

8. On the Draw panel, click the Axis Line tool.

- Draw a short Axis line along the reference plane above the sketch (item 4).

9. On the ribbon, click the Finish Edit Mode button.

• Revit Essentials for Architecture •

530 | Chapter 11

> **NOTE:** It will be necessary to zoom the other view windows to study the results.

10. Save the family file.

WORKING WITH NESTED FAMILIES

Now let's open the provided *Wall Coat Rack* family and load the new *Coat Hook* family that we just built into it. When you load an instance of one family into another family, it is referred to as a "nested family."

1. From the *1* folder, open the *Wall Coat Rack.rfa* [*Wall Coat Rack_M.rfa*] family file.

   Work in the *Placement Side* view.

The parameters in this family are very similar to the binder bin family completed in the earlier exercise. We have a Width parameter centered on the Center (Left/ Right) reference plane with an EQ dimension. We also have a Height parameter and a Mounting Height. In addition to these familiar parameters, two 4" [100] locked dimensions appear on each end. These keep the shelf brackets at a fixed distance from each end. Finally, at the top of the shelf are two dimensions reading: 5" [125]. We need to create a new dimension parameter for these. We will create one parameter named: "Hook Inset" and apply it to both dimensions.

2. Select one of the 5" [125] dimensions at the top, hold down the CTRL key and select the other one.

3. Using the procedure in the previous lesson, create a new parameter named: **Hook Inset**. Include it in the Dimensions grouping and make it a type parameter.

   ⇨ Open the "Family Types" dialog and flex the Hook Inset parameter—set the value to: **6"** [**150**] and then click OK.

   Both reference planes should move a little closer to the center.

   Open the *Ref. Level* floor plan view.

4. The other tiles onscreen should still be showing the Coat Hook family. Click into any one of these open view tabs.

   ⇨ Click the Load into Project and Close button.

5. If prompted to save, answer yes and then back in the *Wall Coat Rack* family, place an instance of the hook anywhere on the Placement side of the wall in the plan view.

   Place it randomly; do not snap it to anything currently.

   ⇨ Click the Modify tool to cancel.

6. On the Modify tab, on the Modify panel, click the Align button (or press AL).

   ⇨ Align the hook to the back plate of the Coat Rack in plan. Lock the padlock to constrain it.

   ⇨ Align the center of the hook to the "First Hook" reference plane (on the right side of the rack) and lock it (see Figure 11.79).

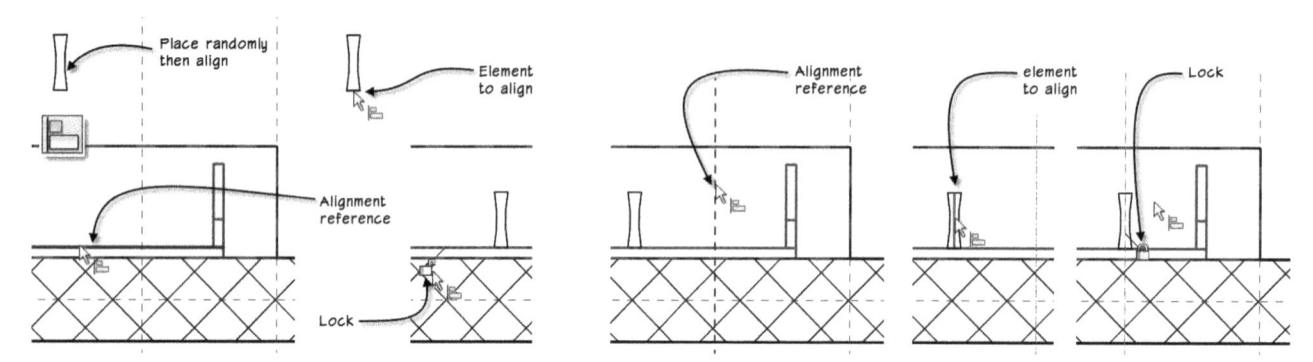

FIGURE 11.79 *Align the hook to the back board of the coat rack and to the first hook reference plane*

• The Aubin Academy •

When you align, be sure to click the reference plane first and then the middle of the hook. You may need to zoom in on the hook to highlight its centerline. Do not use align for the height of the hook (in elevation). We will achieve the correct vertical location with a new formula parameter.

7. On the ribbon, click the Modify tool or press the ESC key twice.

USE A FORMULA TO DRIVE A PARAMETER

If you were to study the elevation and open the "Family Types" dialog, you would notice that the height of the back plate of the coat rack is controlled by a "Height" parameter. We can create a formula based upon this variable height that keeps our hooks centered vertically on the back plate.

Switch to the *Placement Side* elevation tab.

1. On the Create or Modify tab, on the Properties panel, click the Family Types button.

   Move the "Family Types" dialog on screen so that you can see the *Placement Side* elevation in the background.

2. At the bottom of the "Family Types" dialog, click the New Parameter icon.

Until now, we have added all our parameters directly onscreen by first selecting a dimension. Using the "Family Types" dialog is an alternative approach and gives you access to all parameter types.

⇨ Name the new parameter: **Hook Height** and change the "Group parameter under" to: **Constraints**.

Verify that the "Type of Parameter" is: **Length** and leave it a type parameter.

In the previous method, when labeling a dimension, the type of parameter was automatically set to a Length parameter; but when adding it this way, we can make the type of parameter anything we like because it is not yet applied to anything in the model.

⇨ Click OK to complete the parameter (see the left side of Figure 11.80).

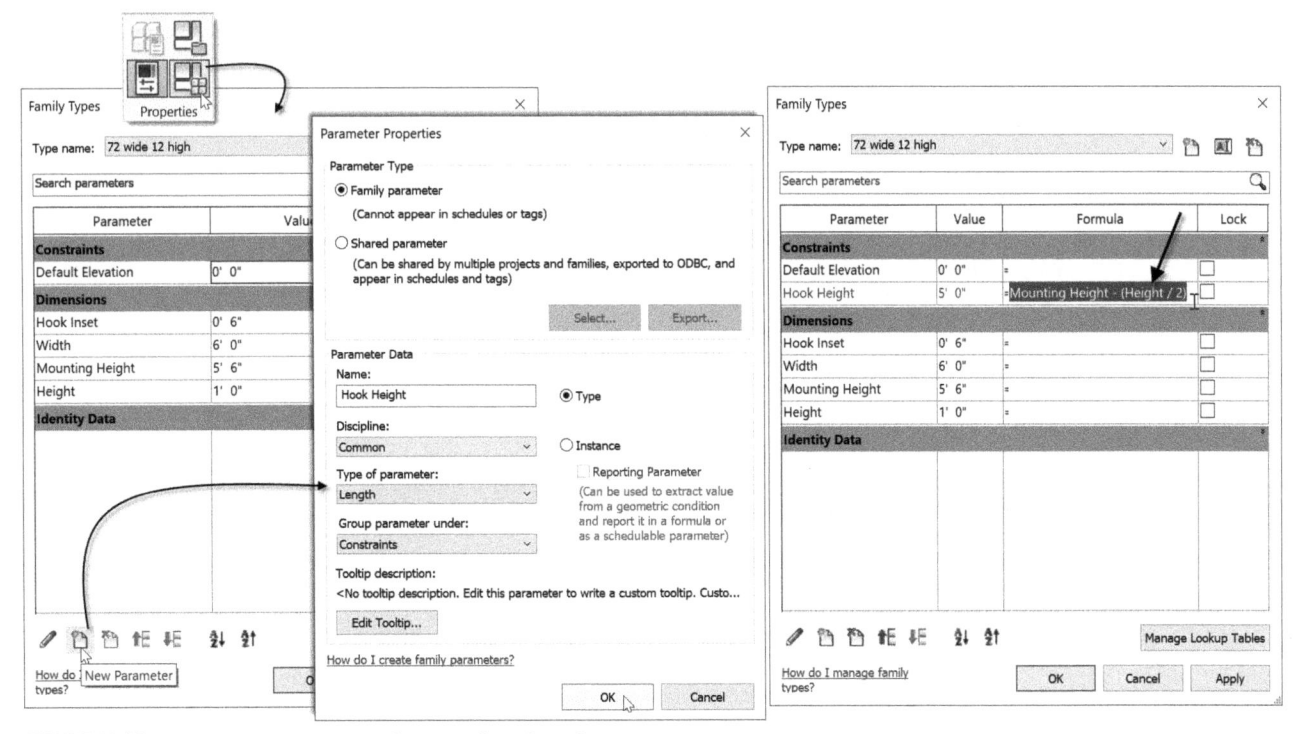

FIGURE 11.80 *create a new parameter and assign a formula to drive it*

3. Back in the "Family Types" dialog, click in the formula field to the right of the

532 | Chapter 11

⇨ new Hook Height parameter (see the right side of Figure 11.80).

⇨ For the formula, type: **Mounting Height - (Height / 2)**

> **NOTE:** Parameter names input into formulas are case-sensitive.

You will notice that once you click Apply, the result of the formula will be input as "read only" in the Value field (it grays out). Study the formula we just typed. We are asking Revit to start with the Mounting Height, which you can see from the elevation view goes from the floor to the shelf of the coat rack. From this we subtract half of the coat rack height. This means that no matter what values the Mounting Height and Height parameters assume, the value of this new Hook Height parameter when measured from the floor will place the hooks centered on the back board of the coat rack.

4. At the top of the "Family Types" dialog, choose: **72 wide 8 high [1800 wide 200 high]** from the Name list to flex the family and then click Apply.

Two types are predefined in this family, each with different Heights. Note the change in the Hook Height's automatically calculated value when flexing between the two types.

5. Click OK to dismiss the dialog.

6. Select the hook element onscreen (it is probably down at the floor).

⇨ On the Properties palette, in the Constraints grouping, locate the small associate family parameter button next to the Elevation from Level parameter and click it.

In this very narrow column on the Properties palette are small buttons that allow us to associate parameters to the values shown instead of setting them manually (see Figure 11.81).

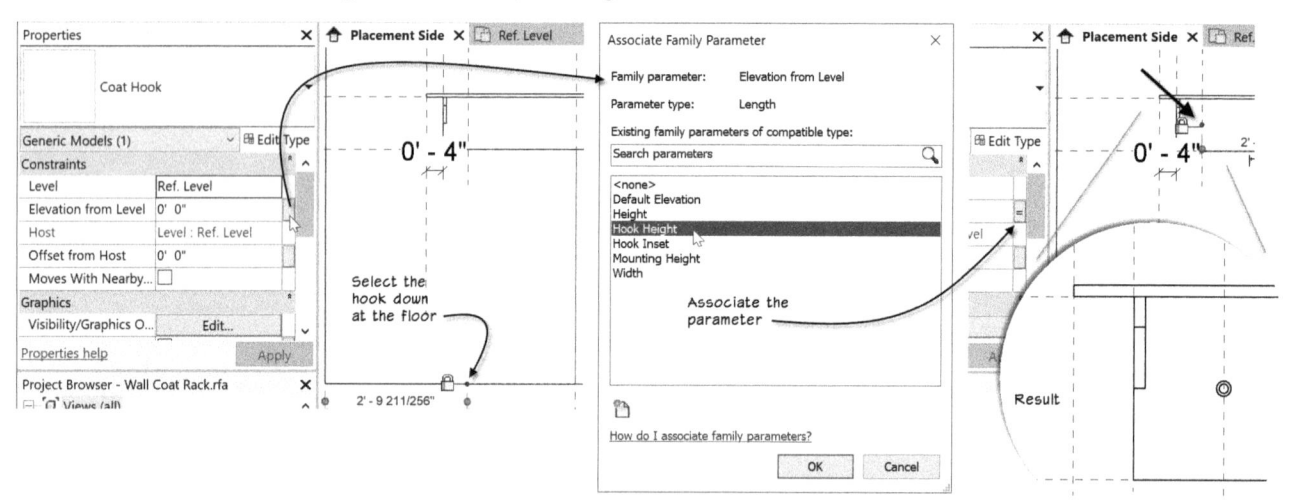

FIGURE 11.81 *A parameter button appears in the formula column next to the offset field*

7. Click this parameter button, and in the "Associate Family Parameter" dialog, select the "Hook Height" parameter and then click OK.

   Again, notice that the read only value of the resolved formula fills in automatically. Notice also the small equal (=) sign that now appears on the button (see the right side of Figure 11.81).

⇨ Click Apply or shift focus away from the Properties palette to complete the operation.

The hook will move to the center of the back plate height. You can re-open the "Family Types" dialog and test the formula by changing types and then clicking apply. If you wish, you can create additional types with varying Mounting Heights and back plate Heights to fully flex the new parameter.

• The Aubin Academy •

8. Save the Family file.

ADD A VISIBILITY PARAMETER

Sometimes you add details to a family that you don't always want to display. We can create a visibility parameter that will allow us to control the display of components in each type within the family. In this case, we will make it possible to turn the hooks on and off in each family type.

1. Select the Hook component and look to the Properties palette again.
   ⇨ Beneath the "Graphics" grouping click the associate family parameter button (in the same far right column) next to the "Visible" (checkmark) parameter (not the Edit button next to "Visibility").
2. In the "Associate Family Parameter" dialog, click the "New Parameter" icon.

Here is another alternative way to create parameters. Again, the method of creation is a matter of preference with the results being nearly the same in each case.

   ⇨ Name the parameter: **Show Hook**, group it under Graphics, leave it a "Type" parameter.

Notice that this time the "Type of Parameter" is assigned for us as a Yes/No type. Since we started from a Boolean value (a value that has two options only, like yes and no, true and false, or up and down). In other words, the Visible check box can only be checked or not checked; yes or no.

3. Click OK twice.

   Notice that an equals (=) sign appears on the button next to Visible and that the checkmark is now grayed out.

While you are working on the family in the Family Editor, invisible items will turn gray to indicate that it is invisible by default. However, there is a temporary display mode that will preview in the family editor viewport.

4. On the View Control Bar, click the Preview Visibility icon and choose: **Preview Visibility On**.

A yellow border labeled Preview Visibility will appear around the viewport. This setting, like other temporary display modes, is applied per view. So, you need to turn it on in each view where you want to use it.

5. Return to the "Family Types" dialog and create a new type. Name it: **60 wide 8 high (Shelf only no hooks)** [**1800 wide 200 high (Shelf only no hooks)**].
   ⇨ Edit the Width and Height to match the sizes in the name.
   ⇨ Uncheck the Show Hook check box for this type and then click Apply (see Figure 11.82).

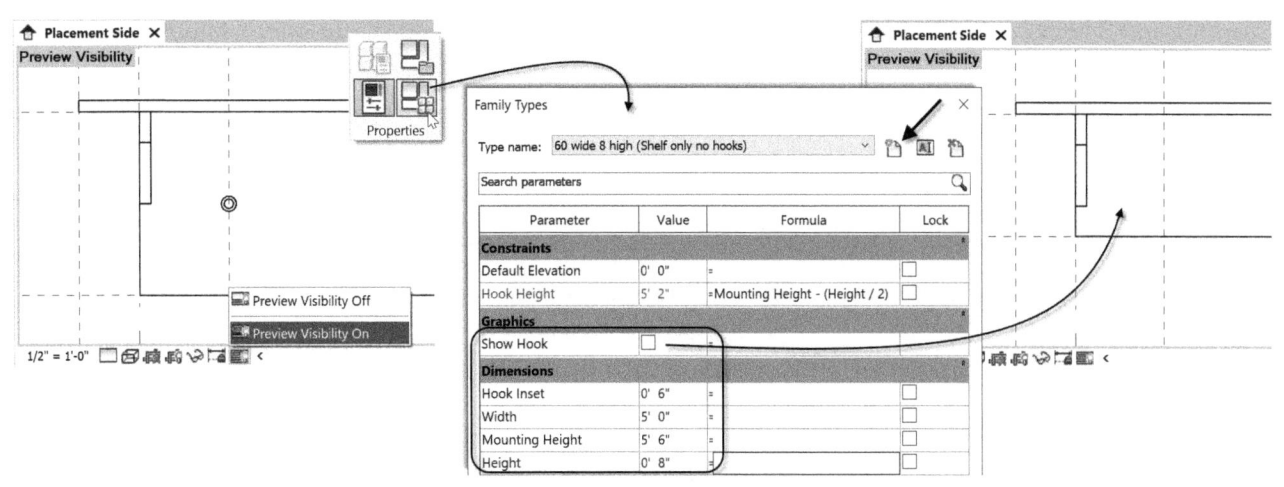

FIGURE 11.82 *Create a type that hides the hooks by unchecking the show hook parameter*

534 | Chapter 11

6. Click OK to exit the dialog.

CREATE AN ARRAY OF HOOKS

By default, when you use the Array command in Revit, it groups the arrayed elements and maintains some of the parameters used to create the array. We can utilize this feature to make a parametric array of hooks in our family.

Continue in the *Placement Side* elevation view tab. If Preview Visibility is still on, turn it off.

1. Select the hook and then on the Modify | Generic Models tab, click the Array button.

⇨ On the Options Bar, be certain that "Group and Associate" is checked.

⇨ Leave the Number set to 2 and for the "Move To" option, choose the: "**Last**" radio button.

Following the prompts at the Status Bar (bottom left corner of the Revit screen), we must indicate the start point and then the end point of the Array. We will use the reference planes for these.

2. For the First Point, click the "First Hook" (left side) reference plane.

⇨ For the End Point, click the "Last Hook" (right side) reference plane (see the left side of Figure 11.83).

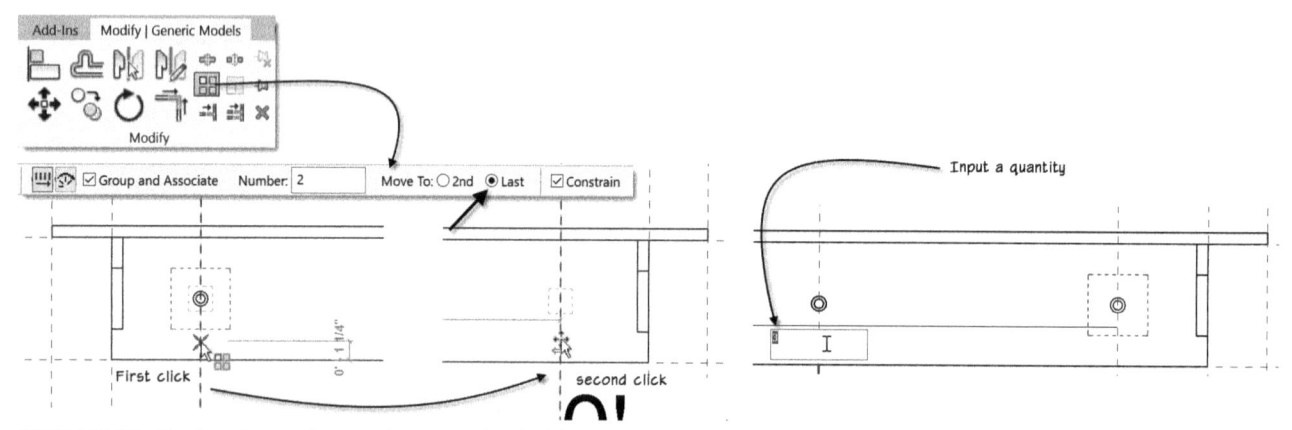

FIGURE 11.83 *Use the reference planes as the start and end of the array*

A temporary dimension will appear with the Array prompting you for the quantity of items.

3. Input: **3** for the "Array Count" and then press ENTER (see the right side of Figure 11.83).

⇨ On the ribbon, click the Modify tool or press the ESC key twice.

There are now 3 hooks on the back plate of the coat rack. Click on any hook to edit the array count or to gain additional options on the ribbon. Earlier, we constrained the hook on the left to the "First Hook" reference plane using the Align command. We need to also constrain the last hook (the one on the right) to the "Last Hook" reference plane. Otherwise, if you choose a different family type that changes the width of the coat rack, the last hook will no longer line up properly.

4. Return to plan view. On the Modify tab, click the Align tool (or press AL).

⇨ Following the process (illustrated in Figure 11.79 above), align the hook on the left to the "Last Hook" reference plane and lock it.

Zoom in on the hook on the left as required. Do *not* align the third hook in the middle.

5. On the Properties panel, click the Family Types button.

⇨ Create a new type named: **84 wide 12 high** [**2100 wide 300 high**].

⇨ Edit the Width and Height parameters accordingly, turn on Show Hook, move the

• The Aubin Academy •

dialog out of the way, and then click the Apply button to see the change.

If everything has flexed properly, the coat rack will have gotten larger but the hooks should still be positioned properly with their fixed offset at the ends and their height in the middle of the back board. The three hooks should remain equally spaced. If anything did not flex properly, investigate before continuing.

6. Click OK to close the dialog and then Save the Family file.

MAKING THE ARRAY COUNT PARAMETRIC

At this point, we have a coat rack that keeps our three hooks equally spaced even as we change its dimension parameters. As a finishing touch, let's change the array count into a parameter so that each type can have a different quantity of hooks.

1. Select one of the hooks.

Like before, a temporary dimension indicating the current array count will appear. This dimension includes a horizontal line and a text field in which we can edit the count. If you select the horizontal dimension line, rather than the text field, you expose the dimension options on the Options Bar.

2. Click on the Array dimension line to select it.

⇨ On the Options Bar, next to "Label" choose: **<Add parameter>** from the drop down list (see the left side of Figure 11.84).

3. In the "Parameter Properties" dialog, name the parameter: **Number of Hooks** and group under: **Graphics**.

⇨ Leave "Type" selected and then click OK.

Notice the label that now appears on the array dimension. You will only see this with a hook selected (see the right side of Figure 11.84).

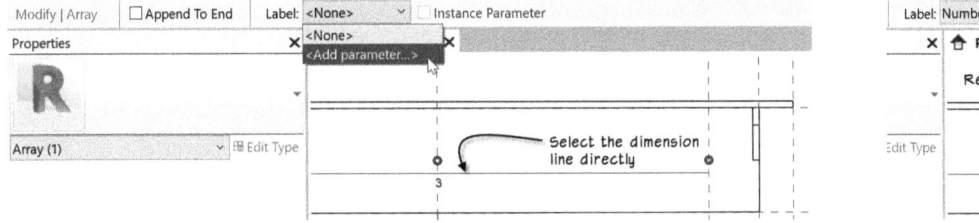

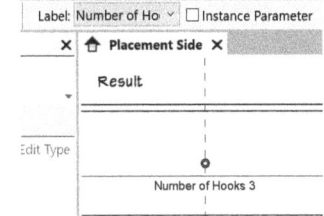

FIGURE 11.84 *Add a new parameter to drive the quantity of hooks in the array*

4. Re-open the "Family Types," dialog and change the "Number of Hooks" value a few times.

⇨ Click Apply after each change and watch the hooks appear and re-space automatically.

5. This parameter can be different for each type. Edit each type to give them appropriate values.

Don't worry about changing the quantity on the "Shelf only no hooks" type. Even though they show here in the Family Editor (when Preview Visibility is off), they will not appear when used in a project.

USE A FORMULA TO SET THE ARRAY COUNT

Finally, we can make the Number of Hooks a formula determined from the Width of the coat rack.

1. If you closed "Family Types," re-open it now.

2. In the formula field next to the "Number of Hooks" parameter, type: **(Width - (Hook Inset * 2)) / 10"** [**(Width - (Hook Inset * 2)) / 250 mm**] (see the top of Figure 11.85).

536 | Chapter 11

This formula uses parenthesis to group the operations. The Hook Inset is multiplied by two since it occurs at each end. This is subtracted from the Width to give the overall length of the array. This is then divided by the desired spacing of hooks. Keep in mind that since the array takes an integer value, the result will be rounded to the nearest whole number value. So, the spacing value used in the formula amounts to the "minimum" spacing.

If you'd like to tidy things up a bit in the "Family Types" dialog, you can use the icons at the bottom to reorder the parameters.

⇨ For example, under Dimensions put Height first, then Width, then Mounting Height and Hook Inset (see the bottom of Figure 11.85).

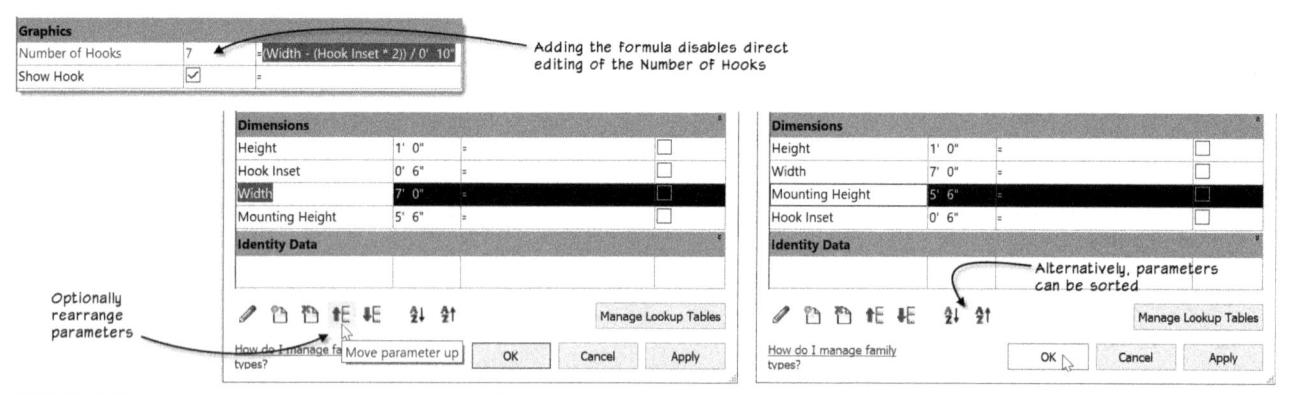

FIGURE 11.85 *Use a formula to calculate the number of hooks based on the width and reorder the list of parameters*

You can test the formula in the "Family Types" dialog by flexing to types with different widths.

LOAD THE RESIDENTIAL PROJECT

The family file is complete and ready to load into a project. Let's load it into our residential project.

1. Open the Residential project for your choice of units:

Like the commercial project, many interior walls have been added on several of the floors of this project since the last chapter. If you would like to try your hand at adding those walls yourself, please visit the Appendix for instructions on how to do so. In the meantime, please use the file provided in the *Chapter11* folder for this exercise.

2. In the residential project, on the Project Browser, double-click to open the *First Floor* plan view.

⇨ Switch to the *Wall Coat Rack* family and then click the Load into Project and Close button.

3. Place an Instance in the room on the left on the interior vertical wall.

⇨ On the ribbon, click the Modify tool or press the ESC key twice.

⇨ On the Project Browser, double-click to open the *Entertainment Room Camera* 3D view (see Figure 11.86).

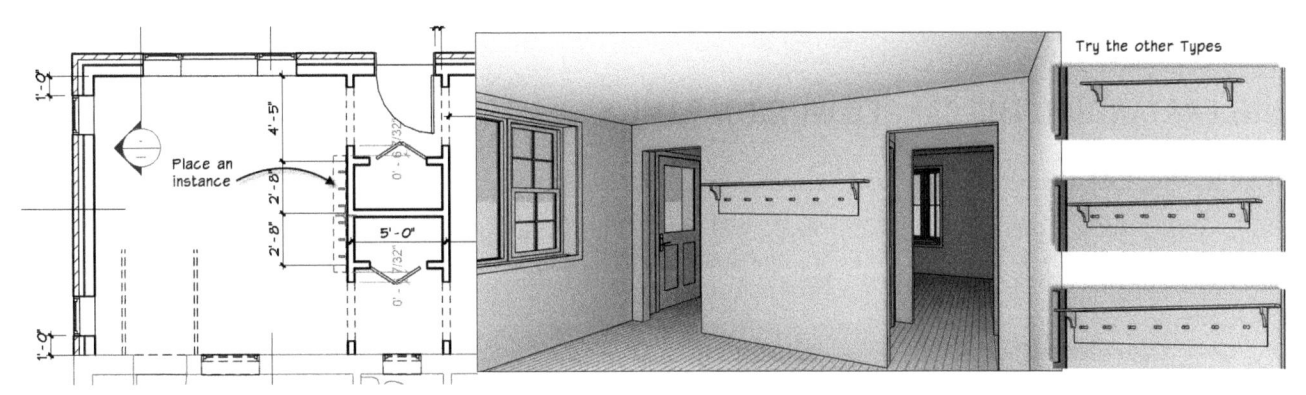

FIGURE 11.86 *Place an instance and then view the family in a 3D perspective view*

From the Type Selector on the Properties palette, try the different types to see them in the project. Note that the "No Hooks" type now displays without hooks without a special display mode active. The final test of any family is to flex it in a project. Remember to double-check each parameter and type. Thorough testing will prevent frustration later in your project cycle.

APPLYING CONDITIONAL DISPLAY WITHIN A FAMILY

While undergoing this process, perhaps you have noticed that the hooks are displaying in the floor plan view. If you don't want this to occur, we can edit the family and make a simple change.

1. Select the Coat Rack family onscreen and then on the ribbon, click the Edit Family button.

    This will reopen the family in the Family Editor.

2. Select any one of the hooks.

    A dashed box will appear around it. This is the array group that contains it.

    ⇨ On the Modify | Model Groups tab, click the Edit Group button.

    This places you in group edit mode.

3. Select the hook geometry again. (The same one whose group you edited).

    ⇨ On the Modify | Generic Models tab, click the Visibility Settings button.

    ⇨ Uncheck Plan/RCP and then click OK (see an example of this in Figure 11.93 below).

This dialog allows you set conditions under which the selected element will display. Model geometry will always appear in 3D views, but with the check boxes in this dialog, you can restrict its display in various orthographic views. The "Detail Levels" area at bottom of the dialog applies to all views; 2D and 3D. There you can restrict the selected element to display only under the detail level conditions indicated. For example, if you only wanted to see the hook in views set to Medium or Fine, you could uncheck Coarse. Give it a try if you like.

   ⇨ On the Edit Group floating toolbar, click the Finish button.

4. Click the Load into Project and Close button.

You will first be prompted to save. Answer Yes to this. Next you will be prompted to replace the existing file, answer Yes again. Finally, you will be prompted to overwrite the existing version of the family in the project file already. The first option applies *only* family level modifications to the project but leaves any customizations you made to the types in the project untouched. The second option overwrites both the family changes *and* the types. In this case, since we did not modify the types in the project, either option is fine and will yield the same results.

   ⇨ Overwrite the family and check the plan for the result of the changes.

• Revit Essentials for Architecture •

538 | Chapter 11

5. Save the project.

UNDERSTANDING THE GANGED WINDOW FAMILY

Back in , we loaded and added a custom family to the residential project. This family was for the existing window in the front of the house. This window was created by simply merging two out-of-the-box window families in a single new family. A few formulas are used to help calculate the combined width of the three nested windows into the width of the overall host family.

1. On the Project Browser, open the *{3D}* view.

⇨ At the front of the house, locate the ganged window and select it. The family is named: *Existing Living Room Front Window*.

2. On the Modify | Windows tab, click the Edit Family button (see Figure 11.87).

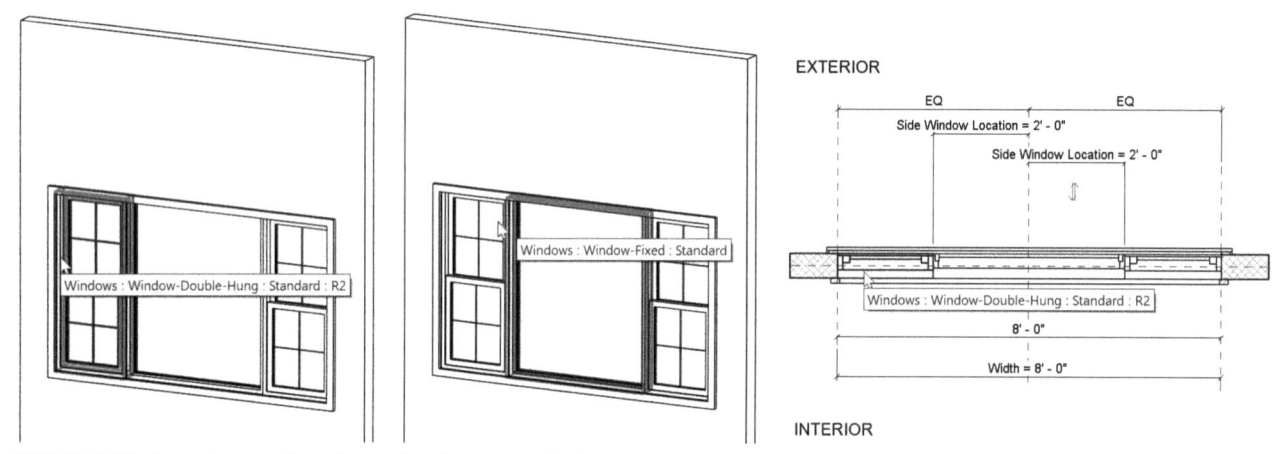

FIGURE 11.87 *Open the ganged window and explore it in multiple views*

The window will open in the Family Editor. You can open a few views and study how it is constructed. This family was created using the window template. This template starts with a wall, an opening in the wall and some basic dimensions. Since the nested windows also have the opening, the first step was to delete the opening element. The next step is to use the Load Family button to locate the various windows nested in here (both are out-of-the-box window families) and load them in. A third type is also preloaded that we will use below. Normally in a project, you would use the window tool to place them. In the Family Editor, you will use the Component tool. Place each nested window in the wall. Use Move and Align to position them correctly. Save the family.

Naturally, it is easy to create a simple static family this way for existing conditions. If you wish to create a parametric version of this family, it is a bit more involved. First you need to become familiar with the parameters in the nested window families. (You can use Edit Family on them to open them and look around as well). Next, in the host family you need to create "driving" parameters. A driving parameter is a parameter that will control or "drive" the parameter of the nested family. This can be things like Width and Height. These steps have already been performed on this family, so let's open Family Types and take a look.

3. Open the *Ref. Level* plan view.

Notice that there are two dimensions labeled with the Side Window Location parameter. The witness lines for these are attached to the Center (Left/Right) reference plane on one end and the edge of the side window on the other. When this dimension flexes, it moves the side windows. As you can see, the side windows touch the middle window. So, in Family Types a formula calculates half of the middle window width and uses this for the Side Window Location parameter.

• The Aubin Academy •

4. Open the "Family Types" dialog.

Scroll down to see the Side Window Location parameter and note the formula that makes it half the Middle Window Width. The overall Width parameter is also derived by a formula. This one simply adds the Middle Window Width and two times the Side Window Width (see Figure 11.88).

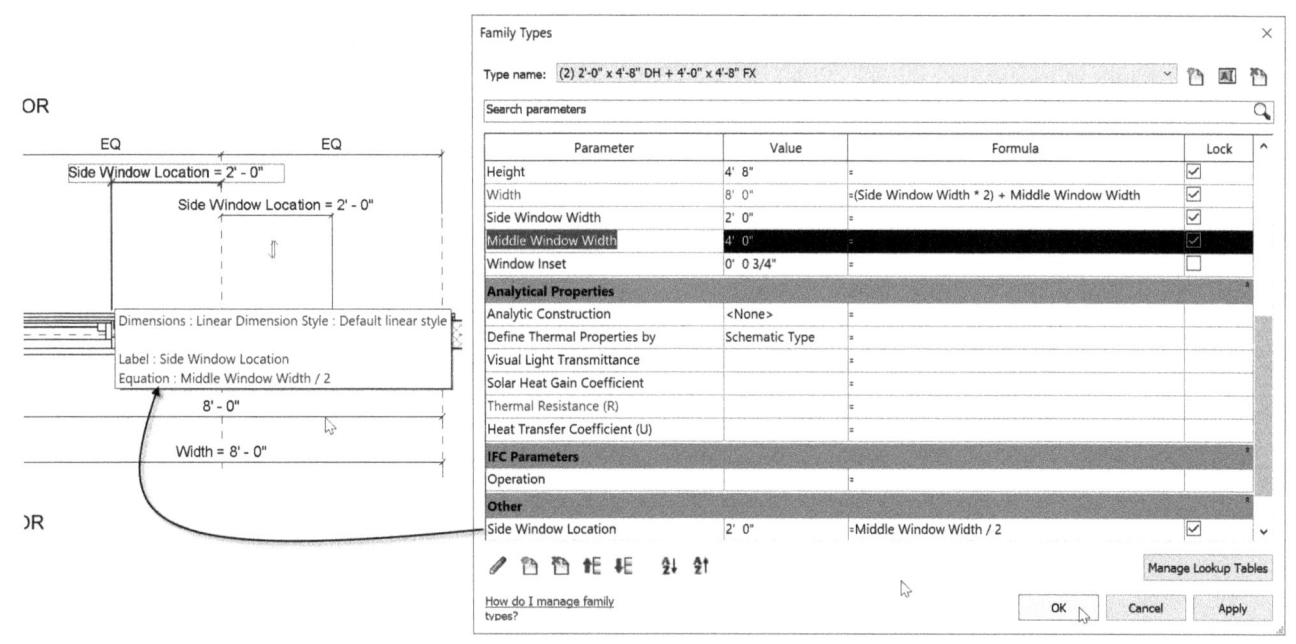

FIGURE 11.88 *Formulas driven by the widths of the middle and side windows*

⇨ Cancel the dialog without making any changes.

5. On the Project Browser, beneath *Families*, Expand *Windows > Window-Double-Hung*, right-click *Standard* and choose: **Type Properties**.

Scroll down to the Dimensions. Notice that many parameters including Width and Height are driven by parameters in the host family (as seen by the display of an equals sign).

⇨ Click the small Associate Family Parameter button (with the equals sign) next to Width (see Figure 11.89).

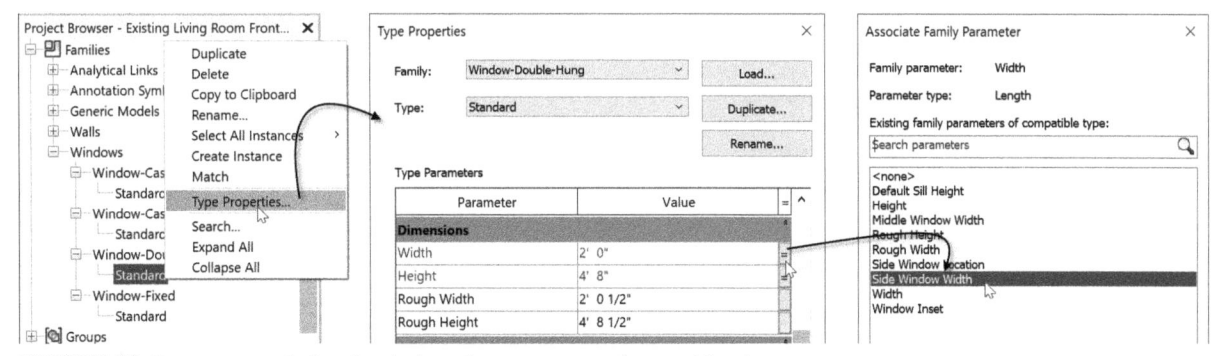

FIGURE 11.89 *Parameters in the host family drive the parameters in the nested families*

This shows us that the Width of the double hung window is being driven by the parameter called Side Window Width. This association allows the parent family to control the size of the nested components. This is also why the name of the nested family type is simply called: "Standard." Since the parameters can vary at the parent family level, it would be confusing to use sizes for the names in the nested types. But ultimately the naming convention used is really a matter of personal preference and/or office standards.

6. Cancel both dialogs without making any changes.

VISIBILITY AND FAMILY TYPES PARAMETERS

So now that we understand how this family works, let's make it a little more interesting. What if we wanted to be able to swap out a different type of window on the sides? If you look at Project Browser, you will note that there are two Casement window families already loaded in this family. Using a special kind of parameter called <Family Types> we can make the type of window flexible from the parent (host) family. Before we set that up, we have a preliminary step to complete. In addition to the type properties, these nested windows have instance properties too.

1. Open the *Exterior* elevation view.
2. Select the two side windows onscreen.

Look at the Graphics area on the Properties palette. There are several check boxes. Notice that the Exterior and Interior Trim Visibility check boxes are currently toggled off. These window families have a separate nested family to display their trim conditions. These can be toggled off if not needed. We will want these parameters controlled by the parent family as well to ensure consistency when we swap the side windows.

- Click the small associate family parameter button next to Exterior Trim Visibility.
- In the "Associated Family Parameter" dialog that appears, click the New Parameter icon.
- Name the new parameter: **Side Window Nested Trim Visibility** and then click OK twice.
- Repeat for the Interior Trim Visibility parameter and this time assign it to the same parameter.

3. Select only the side window on the left.

    A Label option will appear on the Options Bar.

- On the Options Bar, click the Label drop down and choose: **<Add Parameter>**.

Notice in the "Parameter Properties" dialog, that the Type of Parameter is: **Family Types: Windows**. This kind of parameter gives us access to a list of all the families and their types for the category selected. In this case, the list will show all the window families and types.

4. For the name, input: **Left Side Window Type**.

- For the Group Parameter under, choose: **Construction** and then click OK (see Figure 11.90).

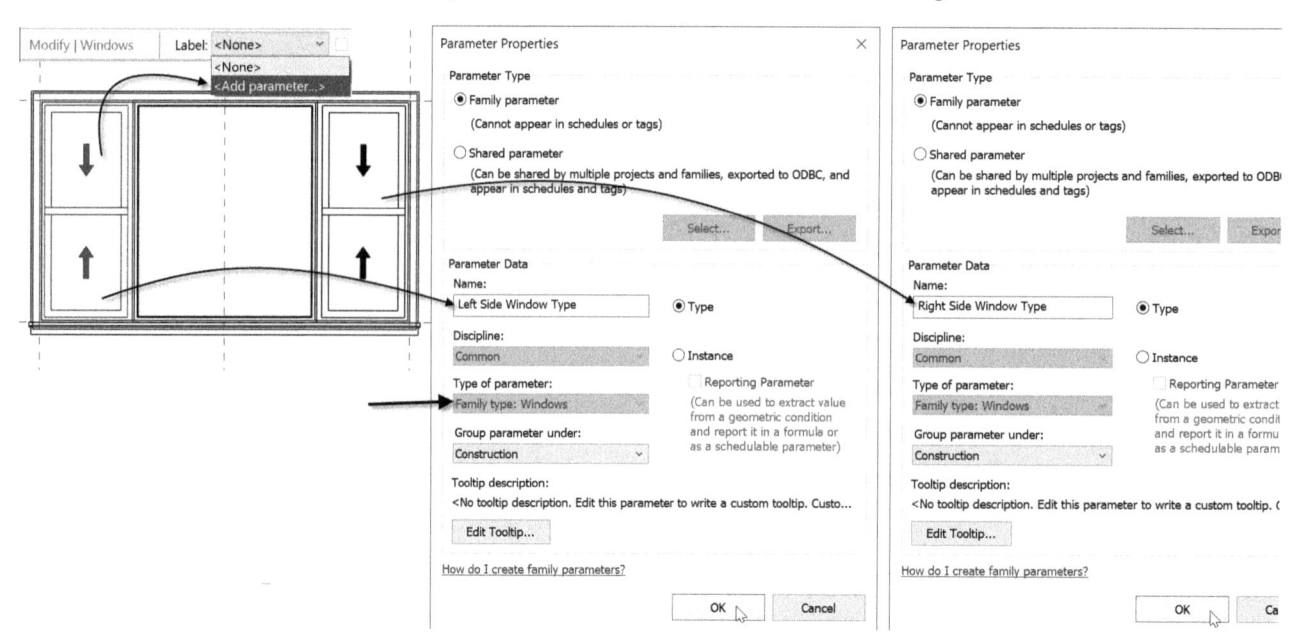

FIGURE 11.90 *Assign family types parameters to the side windows to make the kinds of windows used on the sides flexible*

5. Repeat the process for the right window and name its new parameter: **Right Side Window Type** (see the right side of the figure).

ASSOCIATE TYPE PARAMETERS

One last step remains. While the casement window family was preloaded, its type parameters have not yet been linked up with the host parameters.

1. On the Project Browser, beneath *Families*, Expand *Windows > Window-Casement-Single_Left*, right-click *Standard* and choose: **Type Properties**.

   ⇨ Click the small Associate Family Parameter button next to Height (this was shown above in Figure 11.89).

   ⇨ In the "Associate Family Parameter" dialog, choose **Height** and then click OK.

2. Repeat for the Width parameter. Assign it to: **Side Window Width**.

3. Repeat for each of the parameters in the Materials grouping and then click OK.

Material parameters allow you to make the materials assigned to family geometry flexible just like dimension and visibility parameters. In this case, by linking up the material parameters, we ensure that materials will be applied consistently to both the parent family and the nested windows.

4. Repeat the process for the *Window-Casement-Single_Right* family.

We are ready to test it out.

5. Open the "Family Types" dialog.

   ⇨ Beneath Construction, for the Left Side Window Type parameter, choose: **Window-Casement-Single_Left : Standard**.

   ⇨ For the Right Side Window Type parameter, choose: **Window-Casement-Single_Right : Standard**.

6. Click Apply to see the result (see Figure 11.91).

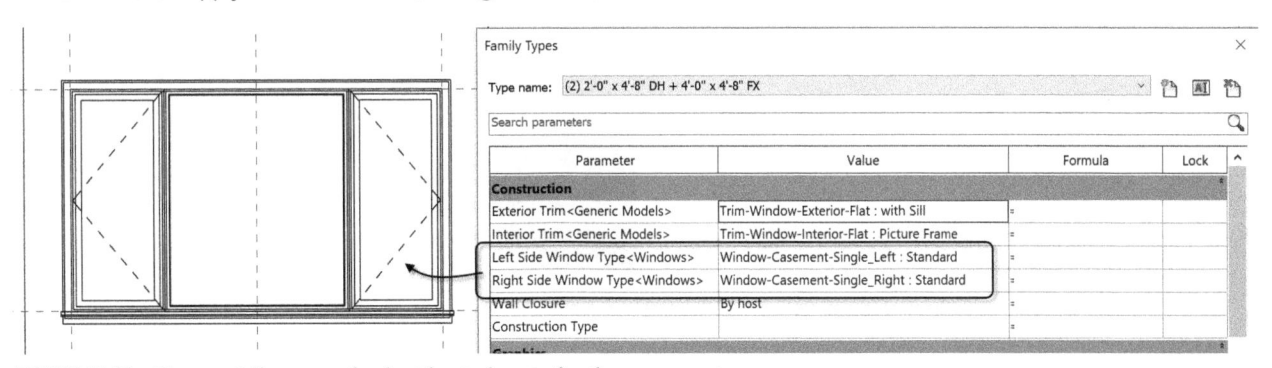

FIGURE 11.91 *Choose a different type for the side windows in family types to test it out*

The two double-hung windows are replaced by casements. This is a simple example of this very powerful feature. Feel free to experiment further. For example, instead of changing the setting in the current type, remember that best practice is to create a new type instead. At the top-right corner of the dialog, click the new icon and give it a descriptive name. Try other variations if you wish and click OK when you are finished. You can load it into the project if you wish and add it to the north wall of *First Floor* plan.

7. Save and close the window family file.

542 | Chapter 11

FAMILIES FROM MANUFACTURER'S CONTENT

As the final exercise for this chapter, let's remain in the residential project and create a custom family for a new whirlpool tub on the second floor. Rather than build this family from scratch, we will use drawing files (DWG) downloaded from a manufacturer's website. (In this exercise, the hypothetical manufacturer's files have been provided w Chapter 11 files, but the procedure would be the same if you visit and download from actual manufacturer's websites).

> **NOTE:** If any changes are required to the DWG files, you will need a copy of AutoCAD to open and edit them. Contact your Autodesk reseller for more information.

1. Keep the residential project open. Open the *Second Floor* plan view and close all other windows. Then minimize the plan view.

2. Create a new family and choose the *Plumbing Fixture.rft* [*Metric Plumbing Fixture.rft*] family template.

   ⇨ Tile the windows and zoom all to fit.

We are going to import two CAD files: one to represent the plan symbol. We only want this one to display in plan views. The other is a 3D version that will show in all other views.

   Make sure that the *Ref. Level* plan view is active.

3. On the Insert tab, click the Import CAD button.

   ⇨ Browse to the *Chapter11* folder and select the *Whirlpool_Tub_Plan.dwg* [*Whirlpool_Tub_Plan_M.dwg*] file (do not double-click).

   ⇨ At the bottom of the dialog, from the Colors list, choose: **Black and White**.

   ⇨ Check the Current view only check box.

   Verify that Positioning is set to: **Auto -Origin to Internal Origin** and then click Open (see the left side of Figure 11.92).

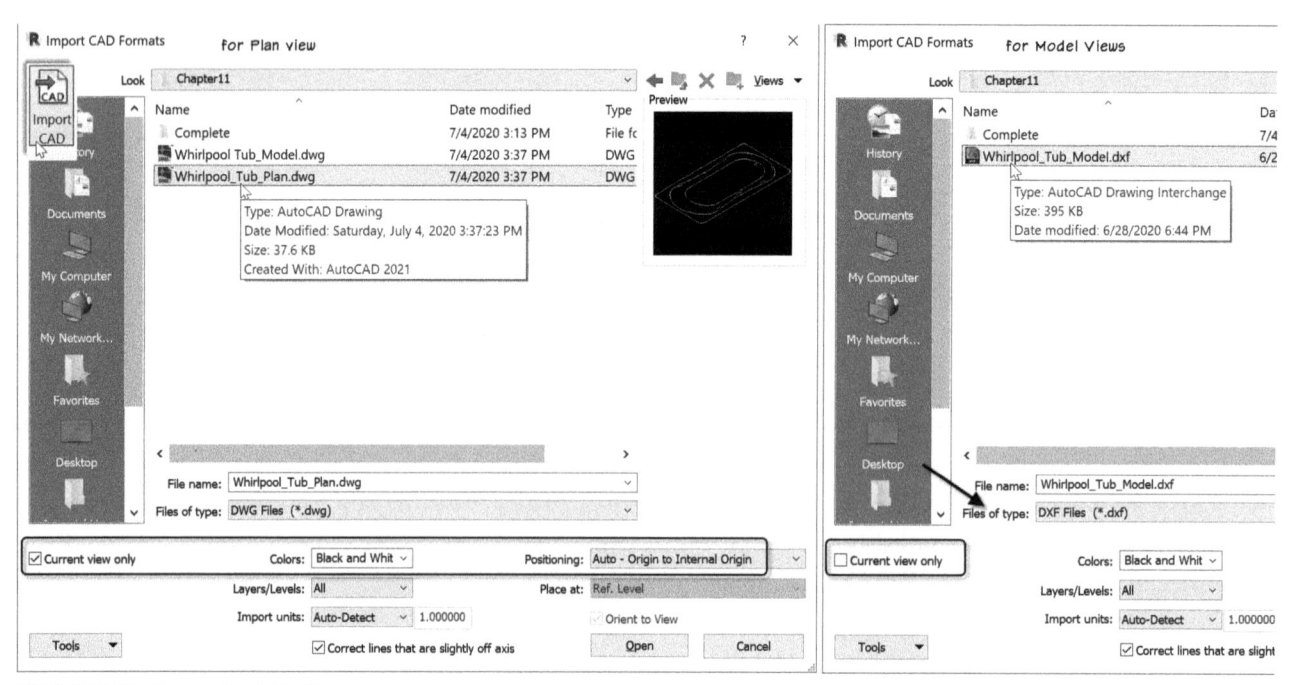

FIGURE 11.92 *Import the CAD files*

• The Aubin Academy •

Families and the Family Editor | 543

A 2D drawing of the plan symbol will appear in the plan view. You can import any AutoCAD or MicroStation drawing or even a SketchUp file this way. When you do, characteristics of the imported drawing, such as layers will be maintained. This file has only one layer, but if you import other drawing files, you can access their layers. Select the file and then on the ribbon click Query button or open the "Visibility/Graphics" dialog. If you zoom all views to fit, you will notice that since we checked "Current view only" this symbol only appears in the plan view.

   4.   Repeat the process to import another file.

Two versions of the file are provided for the model. There is a DWG version and a DXF version. The DXF version is recommended as it has many of the 3D facets hidden which makes for nicer hidden line displays in Revit.

- From the Files of type drop down, choose: **DXF Files**.
- Choose: *Whirlpool_Tub_Model.dxf* [*Whirlpool_Tub_Model_M.dxf*] this time.
- Use the same color and positioning options, but this time **uncheck** Current view only (see the right side of Figure 11.92).

This time the imported drawing contains a 3D model. Since we have a separate version for plans, we need to hide it in the plan view.

   5.   Zoom all windows to fit.

- Switch to the 3D view and then select the imported 3D drawing.

Note the pushpin icon. This appears since we chose the Origin to Internal Origin option. When you use this positioning option, Revit pins the import so that the position is maintained. Think of it as "locking" the position relative to the origin of the host file. You can, of course, unpin it if you decide to move it. In this case we will leave it pinned. If you are unable to select the element, you have Select pinned elements disabled. Click the Select drop down beneath the Modify tool and check: **Select pinned elements**.

Notice that both imports uses the corner of the object as the insertion point. This has lined up with the center reference planes in this new family. In most cases this won't cause any issues, but if you wish, you can unpin both elements and then move them to center the imports on the reference planes instead.

   6.   On the Modify | Imports in Families tab, on the Import Instance panel, click the Visibility Settings button.

- In the "Family Element Visibility Settings" dialog, clear the checkmark from the "Plan/RCP" box and then click OK (see Figure 11.93).

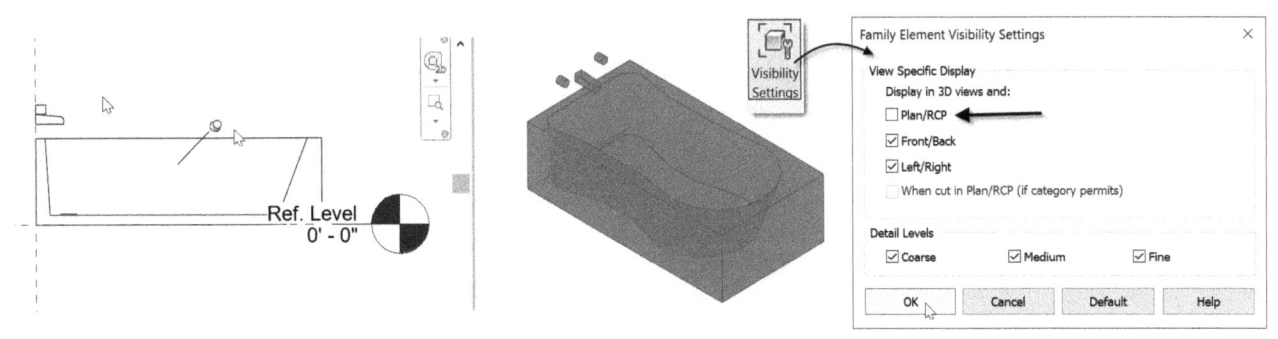

FIGURE 11.93 *Turn off visibility of the 3D element in plan views*

   7.   Save the family as: **Whirlpool Tub**.
   8.   Click the Load into Project and Close button.

We want the new family to insert on the second floor. If the *Second Floor* plan did not open, on the Project Browser, double-click to open the *Second Floor* plan view.

544 | Chapter 11

9. Demolish the bathtub at the top left of the plan. (On the Modify tab, click the Demolish tool, and then click the tub.)

10. On the Architecture tab, click the Component tool and place the Whirlpool Tub family in the same room (Use the SPACEBAR if necessary to rotate it as you place it).

There is a demolished wall in the bathroom space that is covering the new tub. You can apply element-level overrides to any object.

11. Select the demolished wall; on the Modify | Walls tab, on the View panel, click the Override Graphics in View drop down and choose: **Override By Element**.

   ⇨ In the "View-Specific Element Graphics" dialog, expand the Surface Transparency item, drag the slider to: 100% and then click OK (see Figure 11.94).

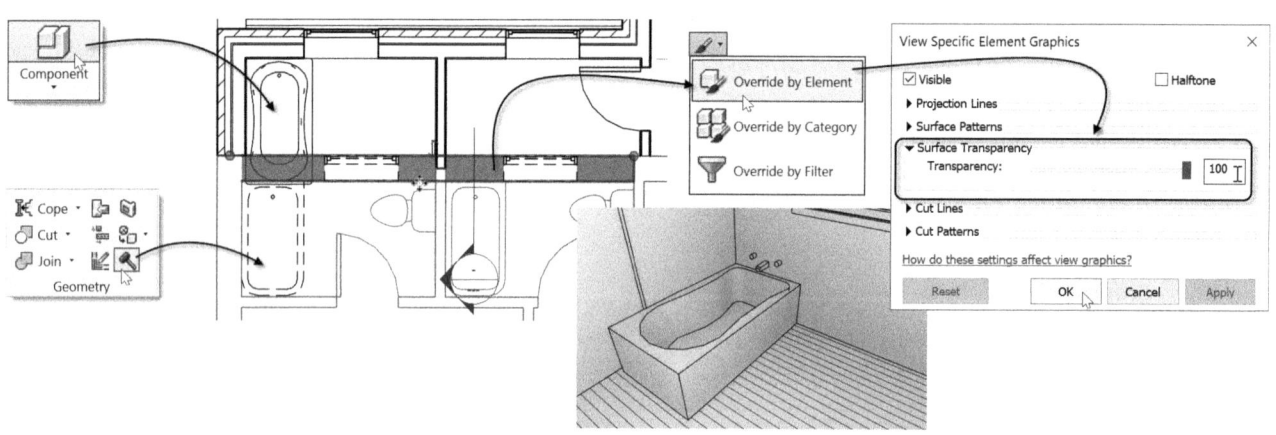

FIGURE 11.94 *Add the new family to the project and make the demolished wall transparent*

12. Cut a section, elevation or create a camera to look at the new tub in views other than plan.

    Notice that the 3D CAD file shows in these views.

This exercise shows how to quickly use imported geometry in your families. However, it is considered best practice to recreate such geometry using native Revit solid and void forms and then delete and purge the imported geometry. If you would like to try that out here, the specifics are left to you as an exercise.

One final family exercise dealing with angular parameters (in a door swing) is presented in the Appendix. If you wish you can skip to that exercise now or save it for later. Also, Chapter 17 is devoted to the conceptual massing environment. While this is not the same as the standard Family Editor, the conceptual massing environment is a modified and enhanced Family Editor environment. Feel free to explore that chapter now if you wish.

13. Save and Close the project and any open family files.

MORE FAMILY EDITOR RESOURCES

If you want to learn more about the family editor and creating Revit families, visit: **linkedin-learning.pxf.io/Aubin** and look for Paul's video training courses on the family editor titled: **Revit Architecture: Family Editor (Imperial and Metric)** and **Revit: Parametric Curvature in the Family Editor**[†].

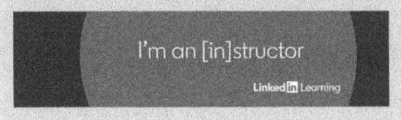

If you want a "deep dive" into the family editor, check out Paul's other book:

Renaissance Revit: Creating classical architecture with modern software—in this book, join Paul as he goes deep into building complex families in both the traditional and conceptual massing environments. This is done by following a series of tutorials on the creation of fully parametric classical column families. However, the concepts covered apply to a broad range of family content creation. The book is available in both black and white and full color editions.

Visit: **paulaubin.com/books** to learn more.

SUMMARY

We have covered quite a bit of ground in this chapter. By now, you should have a good grasp of the power and flexibility of families and the Revit Family Editor. Despite the lengthiness of this chapter, we have only scratched the surface of the potential inherent in families. Continue to explore and customize your own families. You are encouraged to practice and try other tutorials and try building your own custom families. The more examples you work through, the more comfort and confidence you will gain with this critical and powerful part of the Revit software package.

- ☑ An extensive library of family content has been included with your Revit software.

- ☑ Familiarize yourself with the provided library before embarking upon any customization.

- ☑ In addition to the included libraries, extensive libraries and resources are available on the Internet.

- ☑ The simplest way to customize families is to add or edit their types.

- ☑ Before building a custom family from scratch, determine if you can save a copy and modify an existing one first.

- ☑ Editing an existing family is accomplished by opening it in the Family Editor and making modifications and then saving a copy of the family file.

- ☑ You can build a completely custom family from one of the many provided family template files.

- ☑ Family templates establish the basic framework, category, and behaviors of the families you create—choose your template carefully.

- ☑ You can create a "singular" family—a non-parametric Family with only one type, or a "parametric" family—which has parameters allowing for interaction and multiple types.

- ☑ Add dimension parameters to your families to allow for various "sizes" or variations of the same basic family geometry.

- ☑ Advanced parameters such as visibility controls, formulas, and parametric arrays enable you to make very complex and robust families.

- ☑ You can use manufacturer's drawing files directly in families to create symbols and other items in your projects quickly.

- ☑ We have only scratched the surface—play, research, and explore!

SECTION III

Construction Documents

INTRODUCTION

Building Information Modeling describes an architectural design and delivery process that aims to put all members of the extended team in direct contact with a single digital model. While this may seem an ambitious goal, even if you are not yet collaborating with the extended team using BIM, there is much value to be gained in implementing BIM strategies within the internal design team. This is because using BIM helps you create better coordinated and higher quality design decisions. This leads to fewer errors, higher quality projects and often time and cost savings. These benefits can be achieved project both large and small and even if the Building Information Model is not shared outside the four walls of your architectural firm.

If your extended design team is also using Autodesk® Revit® and the BIM paradigm, so much the better for everyone involved. However, you will often find yourself working with professionals at different stages of BIM implementation. Some will be using Revit and BIM to its fullest potential, while others will continue to use traditional methods without use of Revit or BIM at all. This means that even though we may one day achieve "paperless" delivery and sharing of information, most firms and projects still rely on and produce traditional deliverables even as they look toward the future. Further, the creation of Construction Documents (typically in the form of printed or PDF drawings) remains an important part of the accurate conveyance of design intent and further is almost always still contractually required. Therefore, Contract Documents (CDs) will remain relevant and necessary for some time to come whether they are delivered digitally or in paper form. With these issues in mind, this section explores the tools that help us produce these deliverables in Revit and ends with an exploration of the Worksharing (Team Collaboration) features.

SECTION III is organized as follows:

Chapter 12 : Detailing and Annotation
Chapter 13: Working with Schedules, Tags
Chapter 14: Ceiling Plans and Interior Elevations
Chapter 15: Printing and
Chapter 16: Worksharing

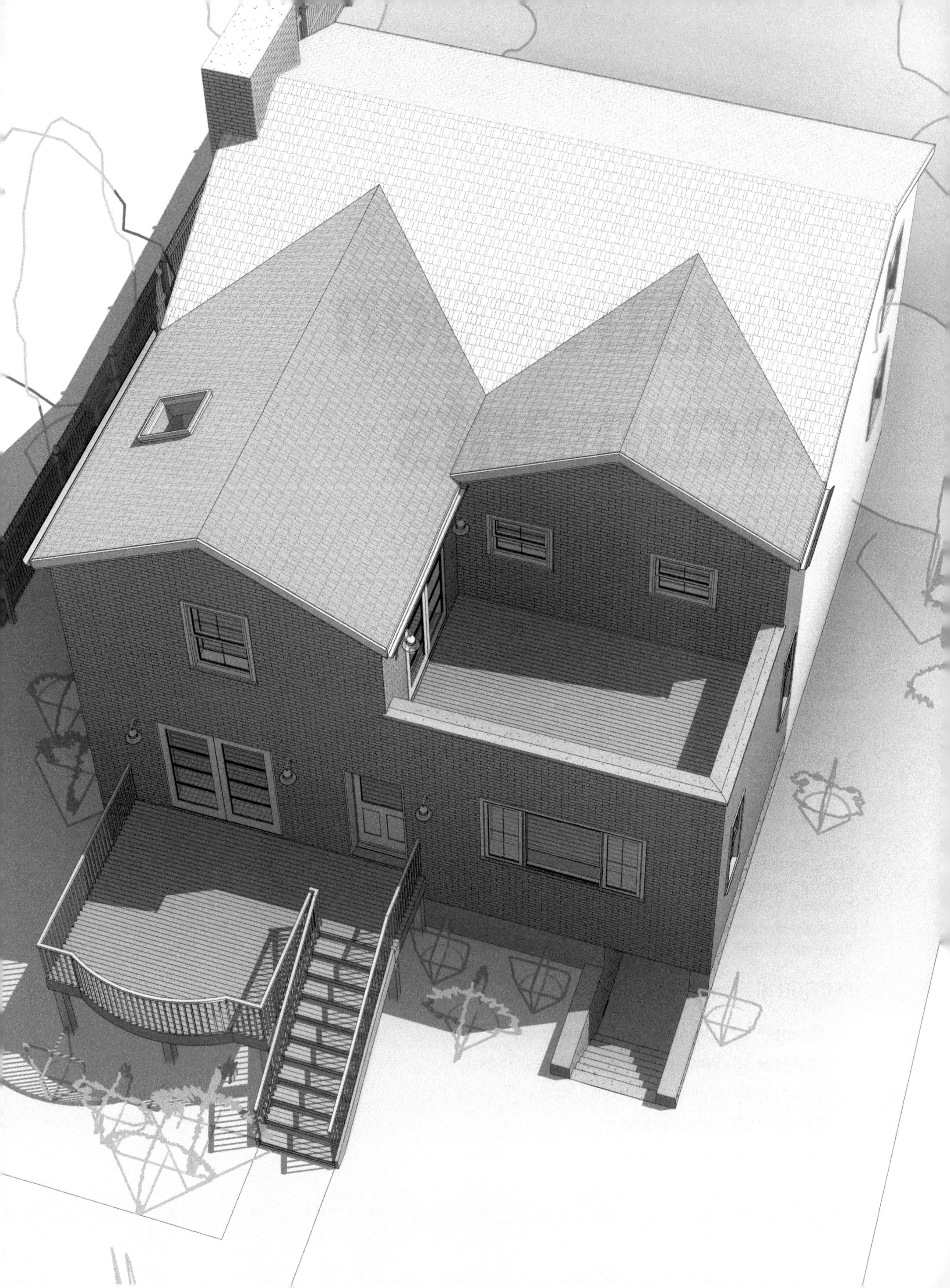

CHAPTER 12
Detailing and Annotation

INTRODUCTION

In this chapter, we will explore the process for creating construction details in Autodesk® Revit®. As the design development phase gives way to construction documentation, details are created to clarify basic plan, section, and elevation views of a project and assist in conveying overall design and construction intent. Before Revit, such details had been drafted independently of the overall drawings with perhaps some tracing to help minimize redundant effort. In Revit, much of the detailing can begin within a fully coordinated model view. You will then add detail information on top of this live Revit view.

The process is simple—first create a callout or section view of the model at an enlarged scale and then add additional drafted components, text, dimensions and other embellishments necessary to craft the detail and convey design intent. In most cases, such embellishments are at minimum drawn relative to an underlying building model view and can even remain automatically constrained or linked to the underlying model geometry shown in the view. It is important to understand, however, that unlike the other Revit views, all drafting components (just like annotation elements) appear *only* in the view to which they are added.

OBJECTIVES

In this chapter, we will create detail drawings using several techniques. Working first from the Revit model, we add additional information to create a wall-floor-foundation section detail. A variety of tools will be explored to assist in this process. We will also create a detail in our project using a detail originally created in AutoCAD. This process allows you to utilize detail libraries that you may already have directly within Revit. Our exploration will include coverage of detail lines, detail components, repeating details, filled and masking regions, and various annotations. After completing this chapter, you will know how to:

- Modify crop regions and add view breaks
- Add and modify detail lines
- Add and modify detail items and repeating details
- Add and modify text and leaders
- Add and modify filled regions, masking regions, and break lines
- Work with drafting views
- Import legacy details into a Revit drafting view

MODIFY WALL TYPES

To prepare us for the detailing tutorial that follows, we will modify the wall types currently in use in the residential project for the exterior walls. We will unlock the outer two components (called layers) of the brick wall and add a brick ledge to the foundation wall. Doing so will allow us to create a brick shelf on the concrete wall and extend the brick down to sit on it. These steps will make the model more accurately represent the construction, as well as helping us get a head start on the detailing process.

OPEN A PROJECT

The lessons that follow require the dataset files included for download with this book. Refer to the "Download the Book Dataset" topic on page xi in the Preface for instructions on downloading and installing the book's dataset files.

1. Launch Autodesk® Revit®.
2. If you are on the Home screen, you can click the Open button beneath Models. Otherwise, from the File menu, choose **Open** > **Project**. In the "Open" dialog box, browse to the *Chapter12* folder.

⇨ Double-click *12 Residential.rvt* if you wish to work in Imperial units.

⇨ Double-click *12 Residential_M.rvt* if you wish to work in Metric units.

You can also select it and then click the Open button.

ADD A BRICK SHELF

Let's start with the foundation wall. By modifying the wall type, we can create a brick shelf to receive the bricks from the exterior wall above. This will be achieved by adding a reveal directly to the wall type. The process will be similar to the one we followed in the "Add a Wall Type Sweep" topic on page 456 in Chapter 10.

1. On the Project Browser, double-click to open the *Basement* floor plan view.

In the area of the new addition there are four foundation walls; three bounding the outside perimeter and another framing the right side of the passageway to the existing basement. We do not want to apply a brick shelf to the wall in the passageway. Since we are going to edit the wall type, the easiest way to prevent this is to create a new type for the walls needing the brick shelf.

2. Using the CTRL key, select the three exterior foundation walls (two vertical and one horizontal) (see Figure 12.1).

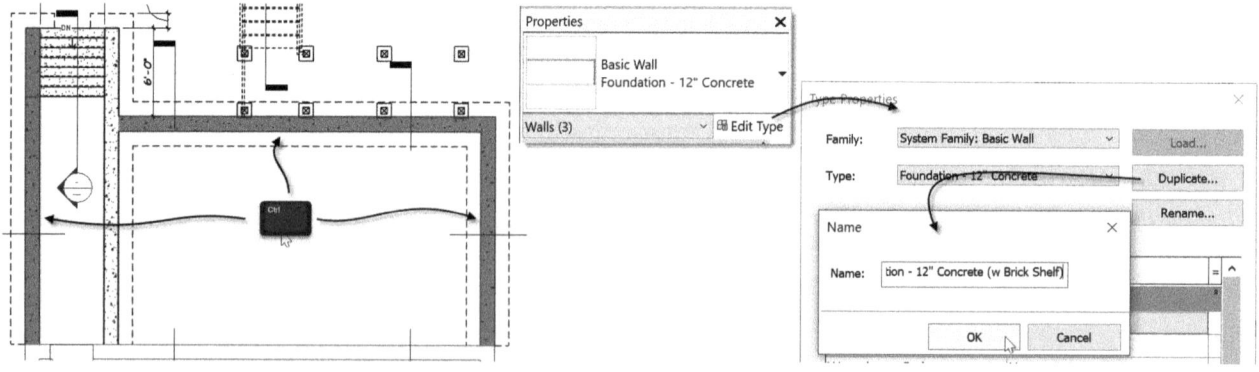

FIGURE 12.1 *Select the three exterior foundation walls*

⇨ On the Properties palette, click the Edit Type button. The "Type Properties" dialog will appear.

⇨ Next to the type list, click the Duplicate button (or press ALT + D).

A new "Name" dialog will appear. By default "2" has been appended to the existing name.

Detailing and Annotation | 551

3. Change the name to: **Foundation - 12" Concrete (w Brick Shelf)** [**Foundation - 300mm Concrete (w Brick Shelf)**] and then click OK.

4. Next to Structure, click the Edit button and then at the bottom of the dialog, click the << Preview button (see item 1 in Figure 12.2).

⇨ From the "View" list (bottom left), choose: **Section: Modify type attributes** (item 2).

⇨ In the viewer, Zoom in to the top of the wall. (You can use the mouse wheel, right-click or navigation bar) (item 3).

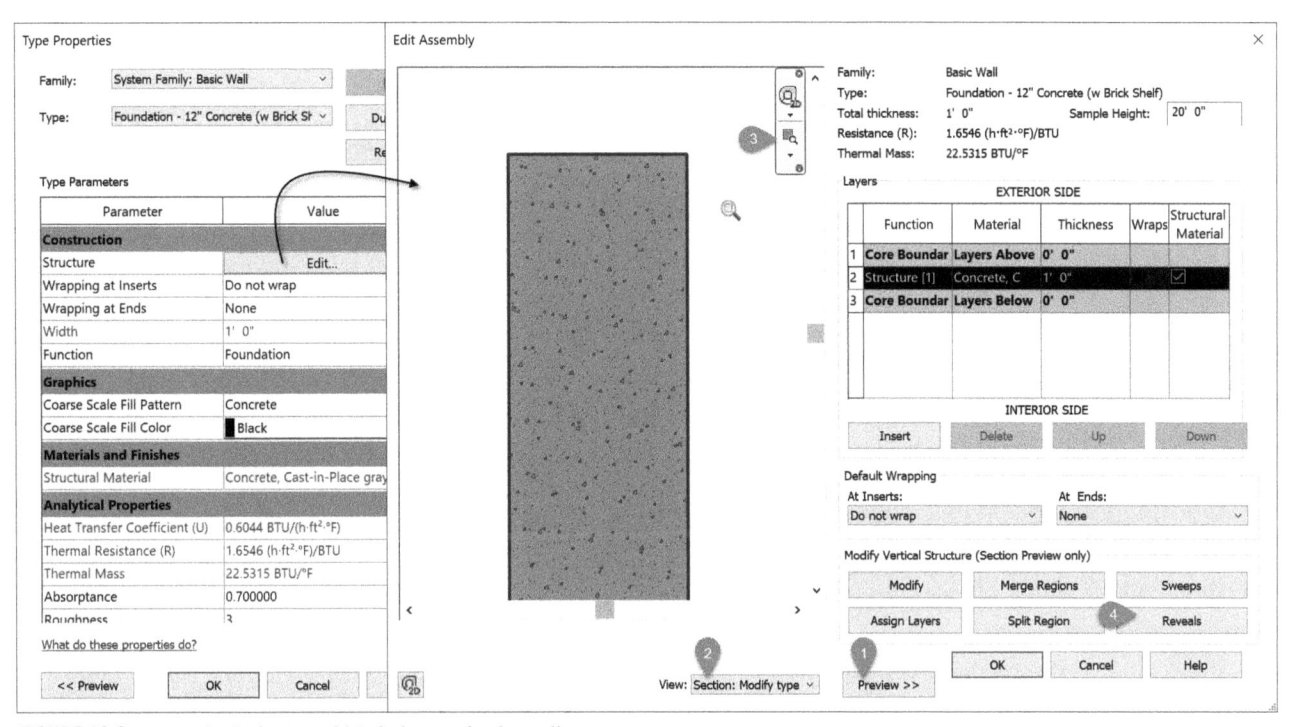

FIGURE 12.2 *Access the "Edit Assembly" dialog to edit the wall structure*

5. In the bottom right corner of the dialog, within the "Modify Vertical Structure" area, click the Reveals button (item 4).

> **NOTE:** The "Reveals" and other buttons in the "Modify Vertical Structure" area will not be available if you have not enabled the Section Preview as noted in the previous steps.

A reveal is a profile-based (void) extrusion that cuts away from the mass of the wall. Profile families were discussed in a few locations in the previous chapters.

⇨ In the "Reveals" dialog, click the Add button to add a Reveal.

Item "1" will appear using the default profile. None of the profile families currently loaded in this project meet our needs for the brick shelf. Fortunately, we can load one from an external file directly from this dialog. One has been provided in th *12* folder for this purpose.

6. From the "Reveals" Dialog click the "Load Profile" button (see item 1 in Figure 12.3).

⇨ Browse to th *12* folder, select the file named: *Brick Shelf Reveal.rfa* [*Brick Shelf Reveal-Metric.rfa*] and then click the Open button.

> **NOTE:** This is a simple reveal family built using the *Profile-Reveal.rft* [*Metric Profile-Reveal.rft*] template. Feel free to open the file directly and study it or try your hand at building it yourself.

• Revit Essentials for Architecture •

552 | Chapter 12

The Load Profile button is just a shortcut to loading the profile. You still need to assign it to the reveal. But the nice thing about this button is it allows us to load a profile without having to cancel all the way out and start over.

7. Click in the Profile field and then click again on the down arrow to display the Profile list.

⇨ Choose: **Brick Shelf Reveal : 12" d × 6" w** [**Brick Shelf Reveal-Metric: 300 d 3 140 w**] (item 2).

⇨ For the "From" setting, choose: **Top** (item 3) and then click the Apply button (item 4).

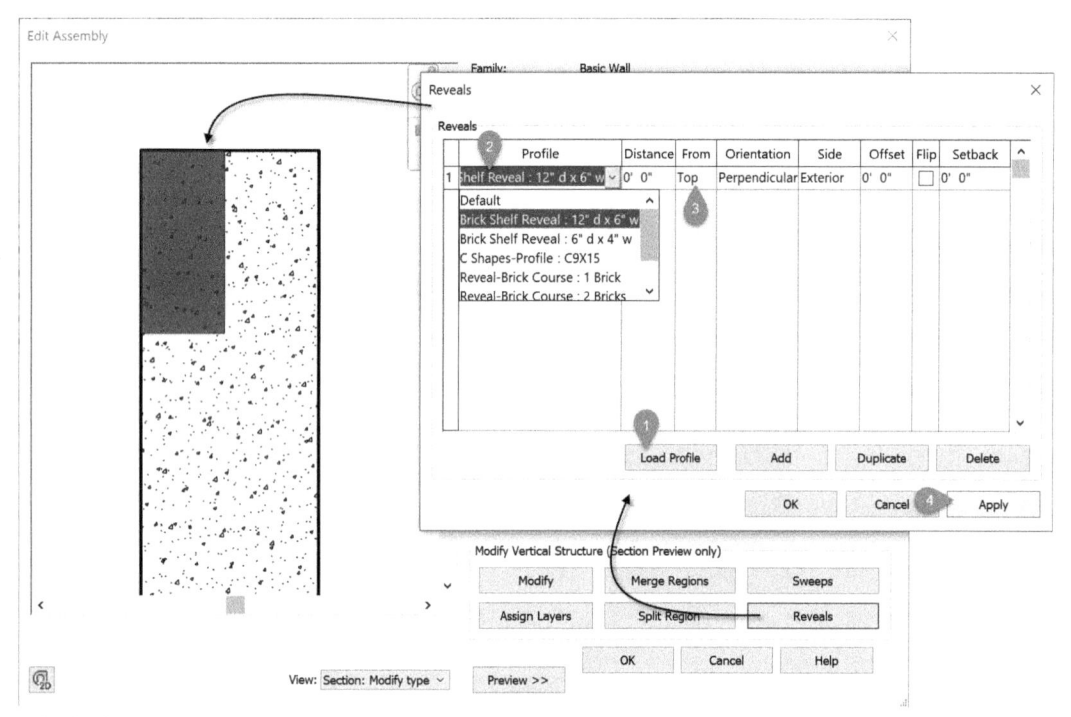

FIGURE 12.3 *Add a new profile, set it to top, and then click Apply to see the result*

In the "Edit Assembly" dialog in the background, you should see the reveal profile appear at the top left edge of the wall in the viewer. Move the "Reveals" dialog out of the way if necessary.

8. Click OK to return to the "Edit Assembly" dialog.

⇨ Click OK two more times to return to the *Basement* view window.

9. On the Project Browser, double-click to open the *Longitudinal* section view.

⇨ Zoom in on the left side to study the results (see Figure 12.4).

FIGURE 12.4 *Open the Longitudinal section view to see the results*

• The Aubin Academy •

UNLOCK WALL LAYERS

Now that we have a brick shelf in the foundation wall type, we should put some brick there. To do this, let's edit the brick wall type to unlock the outer material layers (to allow their top and/or bottom offsets to move freely from the wall's top and base offsets) and then project them down to sit on the foundation brick shelf.

1. In the section view, select the left exterior brick wall.

    ⇨ On the Properties palette, click the Edit Type button.

    The Preview window should already be open and set to a section preview. If it is not, open it again now and choose: **Section: Modify type attributes** from the "View" list.

2. Click the Edit button next to Structure.

    ⇨ Right-click in the viewer window and choose: **Zoom In Region**. Zoom in on the lower portion of the wall.

3. In the "Modify Vertical Structure" area, click the Modify button (see the left side of Figure 12.5).

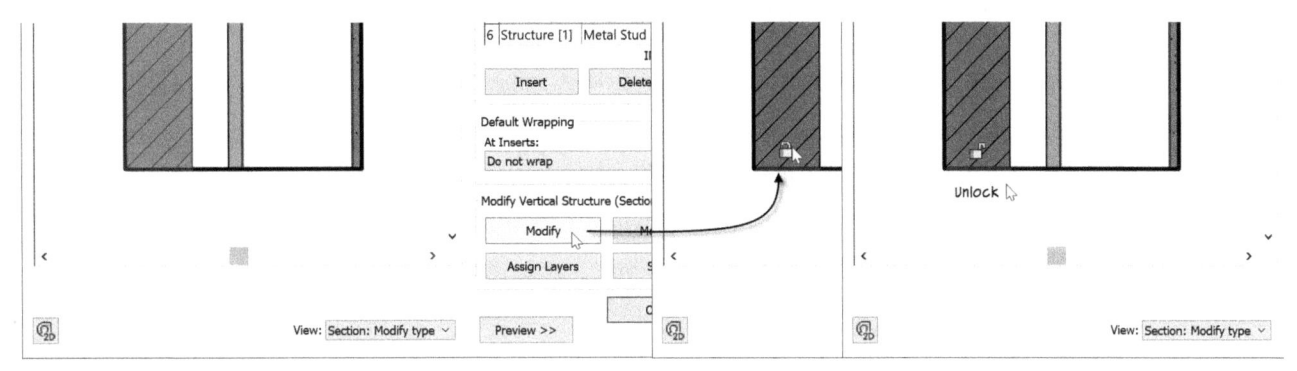

FIGURE 12.5 *Zoom in on the lower portion of the wall and then click the Modify button and unlock the bottom edge of the brick*

    ⇨ Click the bottom edge of the Brick layer.

The edge will highlight light blue to indicate that it is selected. A small padlock icon will appear on the edge. We can use this padlock icon to unlock the bottom edge of the layer, which will allow it to be moved independently from the wall in the model.

4. Click the padlock (to open it) and unlock the bottom edge of the layer (see the right side of Figure 12.5).

    ⇨ Repeat the process to unlock the bottom edge of the Thermal/Air Layer (next to brick).

5. Click OK twice to return to the model.

Upon returning to the model view window, you will note that the wall now has two shape handles at the bottom edge (see the left side of Figure 12.6). If you don't see the shape handles, deselect the wall, then select it again. You can use the second handle to modify the bottom edge of just the unlocked layers (called Base Extension on the Properties palette). The other handle will continue to modify the Base Constraint of the entire wall (see the right side of Figure 12.6).

554 | Chapter 12

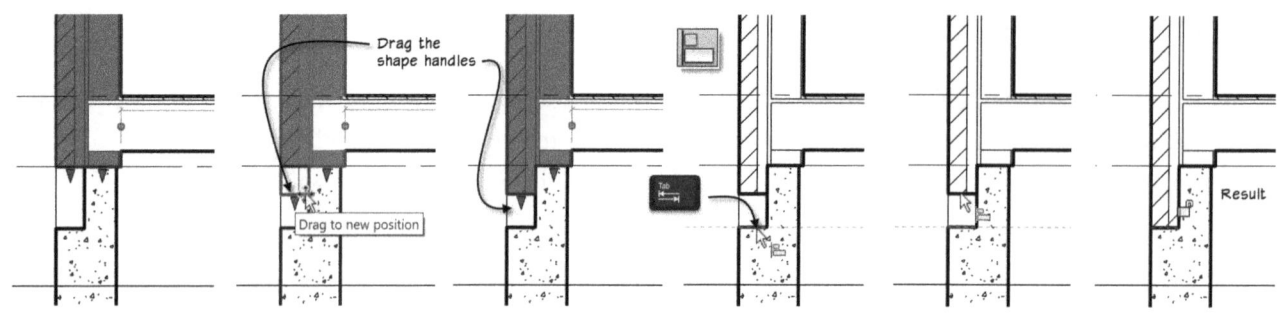

FIGURE 12.6 *Unlocking the layers makes a second shape handle appear. Use align to edit more precisely*

While the shape handle provides an easy way to edit the brick and air layers, the Align tool (AL) provides a nice alternative and tends to be more precise.

6. On the Modify | Walls tab, on the Modify panel, click the Align tool (or press AL).

    ⇨ For the reference line, click the bottom edge of the brick shelf on the foundation wall (use the TAB key as necessary to make the proper selection).

    ⇨ For the entity to align, click the bottom edge of the brick layer in the wall above (see the right side of Figure 12.6).

    ⇨ On the ribbon, click the Modify tool or press the ESC key twice.

    You can also edit the Base Extension setting on the Properties palette as an alternative. In this case, Base Extension should be set to: **-1'-0"** [**-300**].

So now the brick and concrete have the proper relationship, but there is still a bold line between them. This is because there are still two separate walls here. If you want the graphics to merge showing a thin line between all internal layers, use the Join Geometry tool.

7. On the Modify tab, on the Edit Geometry panel, click the Join tool.

    ⇨ Select the brick exterior wall first and then the foundation wall.

    ⇨ On the ribbon, click the Modify tool or press the ESC key twice (see Figure 12.7).

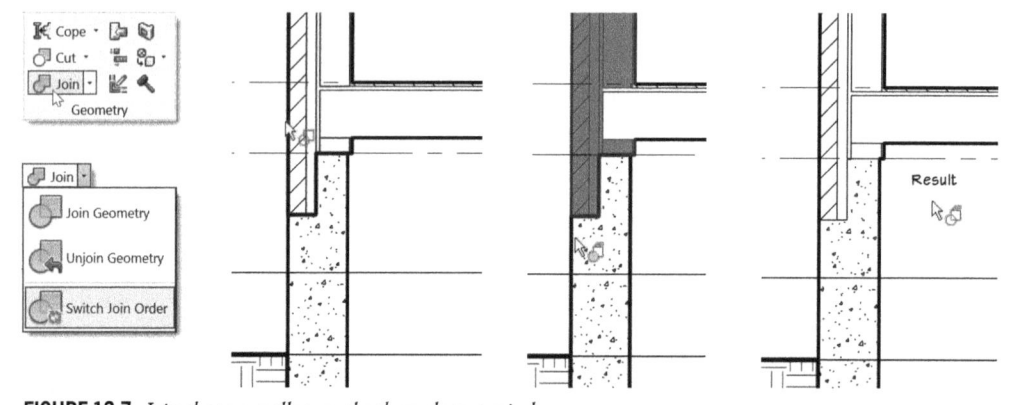

FIGURE 12.7 *Join the two walls to make them cleanup nicely*

> **TIP:** Be sure to click the brick wall first, and then join it to the foundation wall. Clicking in the opposite order will remove the customized bottom alignment. If this happens, you can use the Switch Join Order tool to fix it (pictured at the left of the figure).

You can repeat the procedure on the other two exterior walls if you like. However, it is not necessary currently, so feel free to postpone this to later.

8. Save the project.

• The Aubin Academy •

It should be noted that any two walls that overlap can be joined, yielding results like we have here. You can also join to many other elements like floors, roofs, ceilings and several others. The reveal procedure was shown with the unlocked brick layers, but the reveal is not required. You can simply unlock the brick layers, extend them down and then join to the foundation wall and the result in section will appear the same. Regardless of your specific choice in this exercise, reveals will prove a valuable modeling tool for you.

DETAILING IN REVIT

The typical Revit model includes enough data to generate most of the drawings that will be required in an architectural document set at an appropriate level of detail and accuracy. This is true for most plans, sections, and elevations. In the case of details, however, while it is theoretically possible to model all of the bricks, fasteners, joints, hooks, and other items that will actually occur in the building, the amount of effort (in man-hours) and the sheer size of the resultant model (in computer memory and hard drive requirements) would typically not yield a sufficient return on investment.

To keep the size of our models reasonable and to avoid spending additional and often unnecessary time modeling every bolt, screw, and piece of flashing, the strategy for most details in Revit is instead a "hybrid" approach. Often you will be able to start the process with a cut (callout) from the model. This live view of the model portrayed at the scale of the detail will give you a starting point upon which to add detail components and other view-specific two-dimensional elements and annotations. By separating a detail into both live model elements and view-specific embellishments, we achieve the best of both worlds: we have an underlay that remains live and changes automatically with the overall building model and we have all of the additional data required to convey design intent occurring only on the specific detail view, thus saving on overhead and unnecessary modeling effort. In the following exercises we will discuss the available tools and techniques using the wall and floor intersection from our residential project that we edited above.

ADDING A CALLOUT VIEW

Details are typically presented at larger (finer) scales than the drawings (coarser) from which they are referenced. The Callout tools in Revit will allow us to create a detailed view at a larger scale of any portion of the building model.

1. In the *Longitudinal* section view, be sure you can see the left exterior wall from the first floor down to the footing. (Zoom and Scroll as necessary).
2. On the View tab, on the Create panel, click the Callout tool (Rectangle callout).

For this example, all we need is a rectangular callout. However, if you click the drop down on the tool, you can also sketch a custom shaped callout as well.

⇨ From the Type Selector on the Properties palette, choose: **Section: Wall Section**.

3. Click a point outside the exterior wall on the left above the first floor and then drag a callout around the wall to beneath the foundation (see the left side of Figure 12.8).

556 | Chapter 12

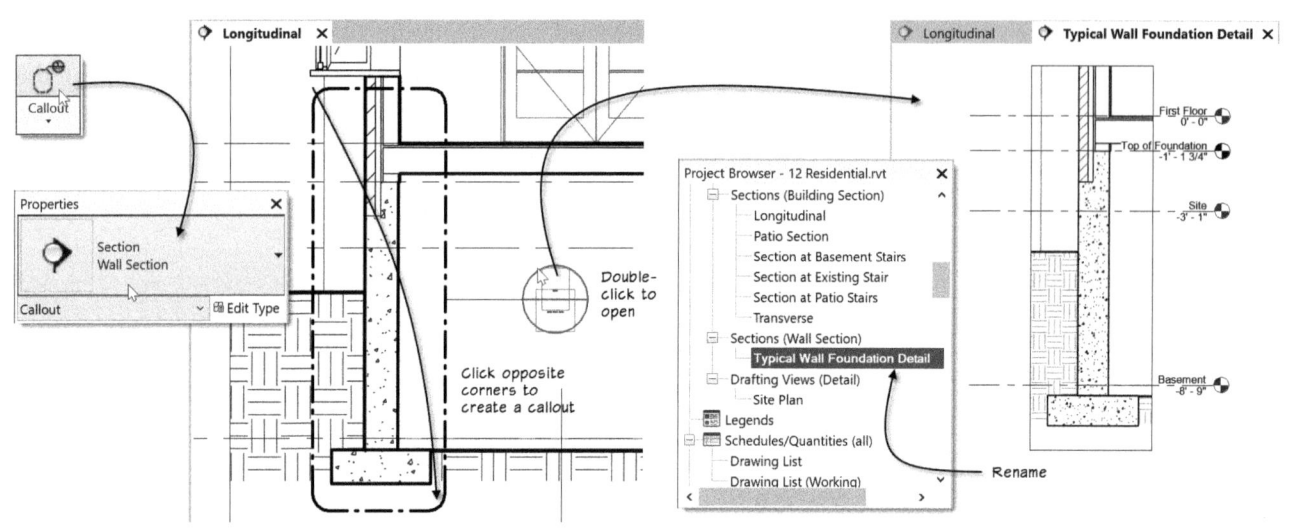

FIGURE 12.8 *Using the Callout tool, click two opposite corners to create the callout view and then rename and open it*

Revit will create a new branch on the Project Browser called: *Sections (Wall Section)* and a new view called: *Longitudinal – Callout 1*. Like section and elevation markers, a callout marker will appear. When you deselect all elements, this callout will remain blue. As with the others, this indicates that you can double-click it to jump to the referenced view. You can also open the view from the Project Browser.

4. On the Project Browser, beneath *Sections (Wall Section)* right-click on *Longitudinal – Callout 1* and choose: **Rename**.

   ⇨ Type: **Typical Wall Foundation Detail** and then click OK.

5. Open up the callout view (you can double-click its name on Project Browser or its Callout symbol) (see the right side of Figure 12.8).

Notice that the boundaries of the crop region in the *Typical Wall Section* view match the extents of the callout boundary that we sketched in the *Longitudinal* section view. If this boundary is adjusted in either view, the boundaries in the other view automatically adjust. If you wish to see this, try tiling the Longitudinal section view and the *Typical Wall Section* view side by side and test it out. Close any other windows first (see Figure 12.9).

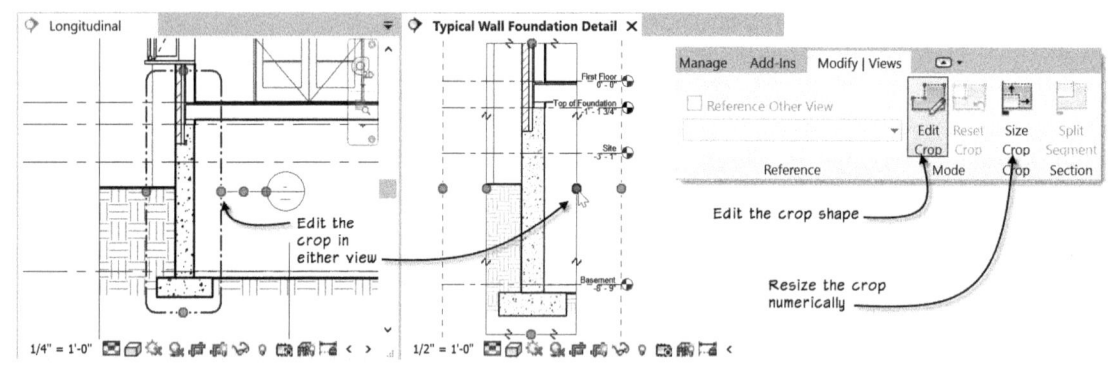

FIGURE 12.9 *Drag the Control Handles in either view to edit the extent of the Crop Region*

6. When you are finished experimenting, return the shape of the crop region to match approximately as shown in Figure 12.8 above.

   ⇨ Maximize the *Typical Wall Section* view and zoom to a comfortable size.

> **BIM Manager Note:** Like most categories, the line weight of the callout boundary can be adjusted. The figures show the Callout Boundary category set to a line weight of 6. To make this change, on the Manage tab, click Object Styles and then click the Annotation Objects tab. Set the line weight for Callout Boundary to match your preference. Note that the leader is a separate subcategory. So, you can make the boundary bold while leaving the leader much lighter.

ADJUST SCALE AND ANNOTATION VISIBILITY

Annotation is separate from the model geometry shown in a view. While the level of detail and graphical display characteristics of the model may vary from view to view, the model will display in all views unless you specifically override the display settings to hide it. Annotation, on the other hand, is applied on top of the model and occurs only in the specific view in which it is created. Model and annotation elements also differ from one another regarding scale. Annotation appears at a consistent height/size relative to its desired plot size, while the model geometry adjusts its size relative to the assigned scale. All this behavior occurs automatically.

1. In the *Typical Wall Foundation Detail* view, on the View Control Bar (bottom of the window) change the scale to: **3/4" = 1'-0"** [**1:20**] (see Figure 12.10).

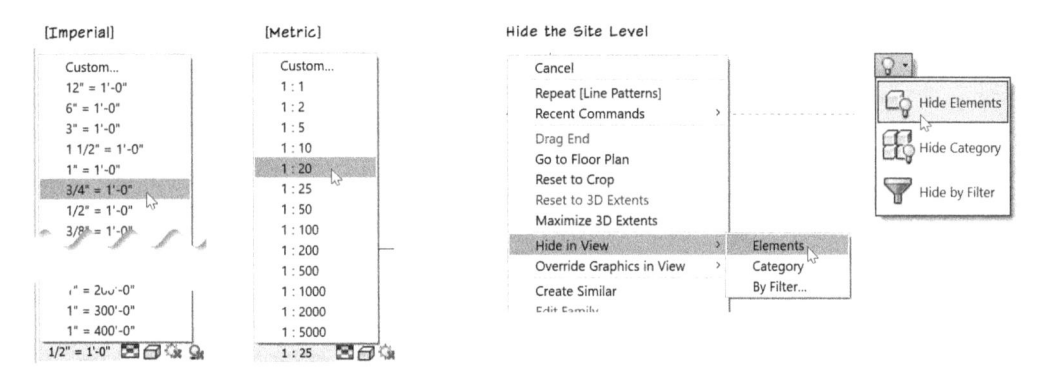

FIGURE 12.10 *Choose a larger scale for the detail view and hide the Site level*

2. Select the Site level line.

⇨ On the Modify | Levels tab, on the View panel, click the Hide in View icon and choose: **Hide Elements**. (Or you can right-click and choose: **Hide in View > Elements** from the menu that appears.)

This operation does not have any effect on any other view. We have hidden this level line in only the current view. The Site level is not relevant in the current callout view, so by hiding the level line, we eliminate potential clutter and confusion. In a similar fashion, we can adjust the location of the level heads and the length of the level lines as needed. Again, any such edits will be confined to only this view.

3. If necessary, adjust the length of the level lines using the control handle grips.
4. Save the project.

DETAIL LINES

We can draw a variety of view-specific elements directly on top of the section view of our model. We will start with detail lines. These are simple drafted elements much like the sketch lines with which you are already familiar. When you add a detail line, it appears only in the view to which you add it. If you wish to draft a line that appears in multiple views, use a model line instead. In this example, we will use detail lines to sketch in some flashing at the bottom of the wall cavity.

⇨ On the Annotate tab, on the Detail panel, click the Detail Line tool.

Notice the choices on the Modify | Place Detail Lines tab that appears are very familiar and match those that we have seen in many sketch-based objects so far.

⇨ From the Line Style list on the ribbon, choose: **<Wide Lines>**.

On the Options Bar, verify that there is a checkmark in the "Chain" check box.

1. Zoom into the bottom of the wall cavity (at the brick shelf).

⇨ Sketch the line segments shown in Figure 12.11.

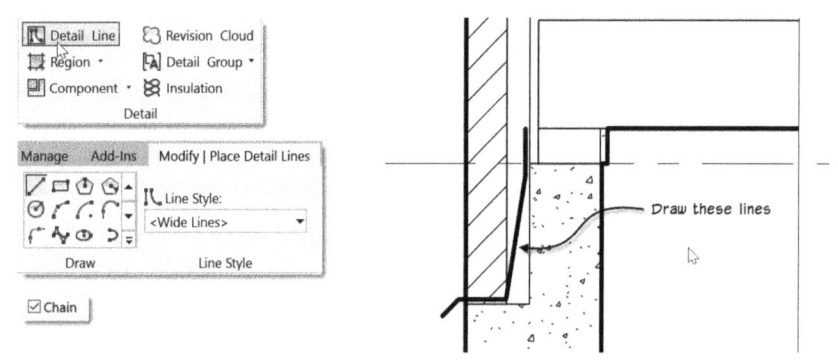

FIGURE 12.11 *Sketch detail lines to represent the flashing in the wall cavity*

To make it appear like flashing, it is best to avoid snapping these lines to the wall. You can nudge them with the arrow keys after drawing to fine-tune the results. Unlike the sketch lines that we drew in previous chapters, these lines are complete "as is." They do not describe the shape of a more complex element like a floor or a stair. These are simply drafted lines placed on top of a model view, much like drafting directly on top of a Mylar background in traditional hand drafting.

2. On the Project Browser, double-click to open the *Longitudinal* section view.

⇨ Zoom in to the same portion of the wall and notice that this linework does not appear in this (or any other) view.

3. Click back to the *Typical Wall Foundation Detail* tab.

> **TIP:** You can hold down the CTRL key and then press TAB to cycle through the open view tabs.

All the parts of the detail that we are going to create next could be created with detail lines following the same process. However, several other detailing tools are available to us. Let's look at each of them now.

DETAIL COMPONENTS

Detail components (also called detail items) are simply two-dimensional view-specific elements that (like detail lines) appear only within the view in which they are placed. They are more useful and more powerful than simple detail lines in that they are families and can be parametric. Like other families, a detail item family can have many types built into it. The parameters can be as simple as Length and/or Depth, or include dozens of parametric dimensions. For example, a "Wide Flange" family file included in the out-of-the-box *Detail Items* folder contains hundreds of types representing all the commonly available steel shape sizes. Another example that is a bit more pertinent to the detail that we are creating here is dimension lumber.

1. On the Annotate tab, on the Detail panel, click the Component drop down button.

⇨ Choose: **Detail Component** from the list.

Currently, there are no "Dimension Lumber" families loaded in our project. Like other components in Revit, we can simply load them from the library.

2. On the Modify | Place Detail Component tab, click the Load Family button.

⇨ In the "Load Family" dialog, from default library folder browse to:

Imperial: *Detail Items\Div 06-Wood and Plastic\061100-Wood Framing.*

Metric: *Detail Items\Div 06-Wood and Plastic\06100-Rough Carpentry\06110-Wood Framing.*

> **NOTE:** If you do not have access to either of these libraries, the family files mentioned in this tutorial have been provided in the *Chapter12* folder.

3. Double-click the file named *Nominal Cut Lumber-Section.rfa [M_Nominal Cut Lumber-Section.rfa]*.

The "Specify Types" dialog will appear.

Unlike most of the families we have seen so far, this family uses a "Type Catalog." A type catalog is used when families have dozens or even hundreds of types. We last saw an example of this back in Chapter 6 in the "Add Columns" topic on page 219. A type catalog is an external text file (TXT) with the same name and saved in the same folder as the family, that lists the parameter values of all the possible types. This method allows you to load just the types you need and not the entire list.

4. From the matrix of types listed at the right, hold down the CTRL key; click: **2×6 [50×150mm]** and then **2×10 [50×250mm]** to highlight them.

⇨ Click OK to load just these types into the project (see Figure 12.12).

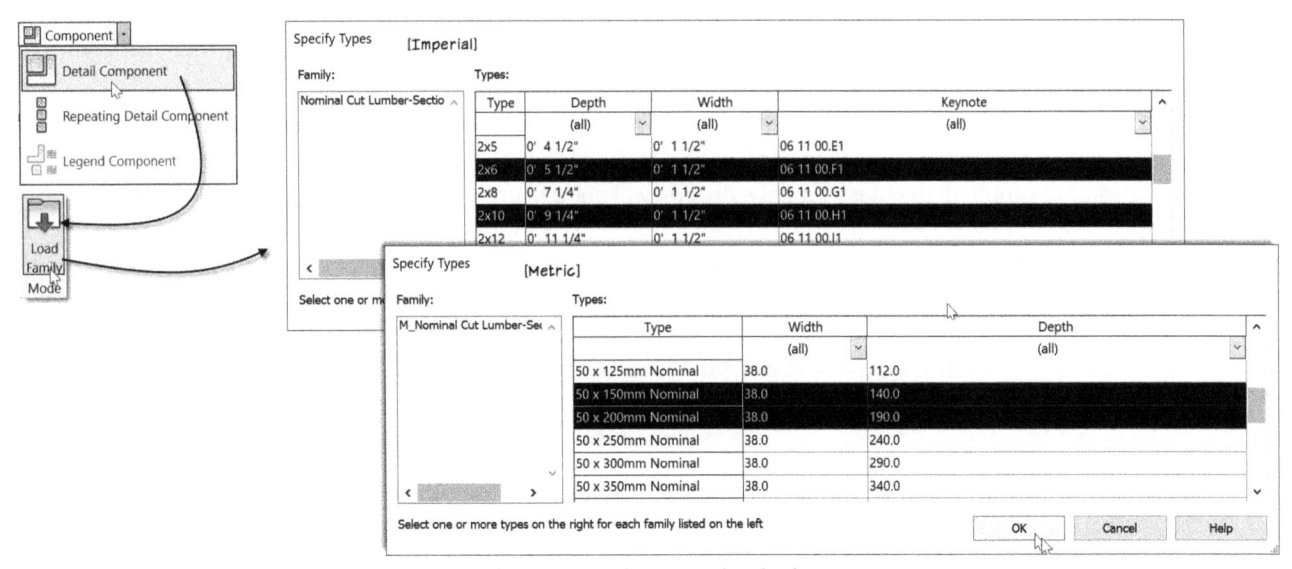

FIGURE 12.12 *Choose the detail component family and specific types that you wish to load*

5. From the Type Selector, choose: **Nominal Cut Lumber-Section: 2×6 [M_Nominal Cut Lumber-Section: 503150mm]**.

⇨ Press the SPACEBAR three times.

This will rotate it so the placement point is at the top left corner of the 2×6 [50×150mm].

6. Place two plates in the space between the floor joist and the foundation wall (see Figure 12.13).

> **TIP:** Use the Move or Align tools to assist in accurate placement.

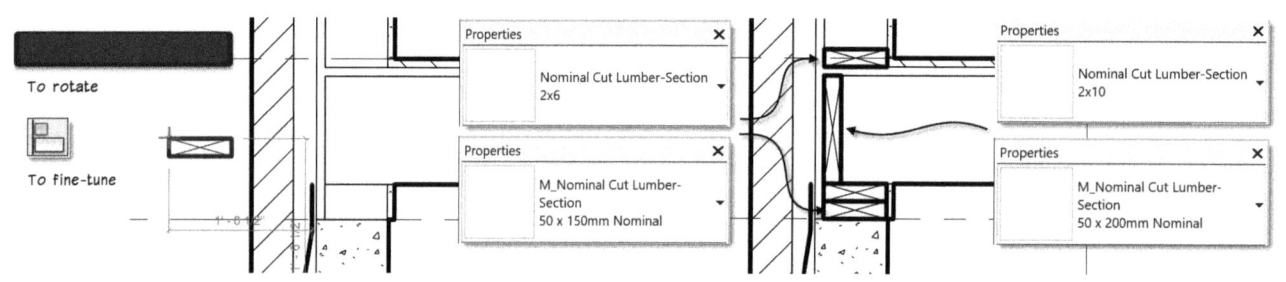

FIGURE 12.13 *Place a double top plate on the foundation wall, a base plate at the wall above and a rim joist*

⇨ Repeat the process (or copy) to add a sill plate above the joist at the first floor.

> **ADJUSTING THE LINE WEIGHT OF DETAIL COMPONENTS**
>
> Perhaps you have noticed how heavy the outline is around this component. In this family the subcomponent of the outline geometry is "Heavy Lines," which is set to a line weight of 5. If you wish to make this line weight less bold in your detail, you have three options: you can edit Object Styles in the current project and reduce the line weight assignment of the Heavy Lines subcomponent. This would apply the change globally in the project and all views that show a Heavy Lines component would reflect the change. If you prefer the change to apply to this view only, you can use Visibility/Graphics (VG) to edit the subcategory. Finally, if you want the change to apply to this and any future project, you can edit the family and modify the outline to use a different subcomponent. While editing the Object Styles in the current project is quicker and easier, it is not considered "best practice" for this sort of modification. While the desired line weight will be achieved, the effect will apply to all families that use the Heavy Lines subcategory and its name "Heavy Lines" will no longer be applicable. Edit the family for a more permanent solution. But you must have "write" access to your library folders to do this.
>
> To edit the family, select one of the *Nominal Cut Lumber- Section: 2×6 [M_Nominal Cut Lumber-Section: 50x150]* elements on screen. On the Modify Detail Items tab, click the Edit Family button (you can also right-click to find this command). This will open the family in the Family Editor. (The Family Editor was covered in detail in the previous chapter.) Select the outline. The outline element is a masking region, which is a polygon object with an outline and solid opaque fill. On the Modify Detail Items tab, click the Edit Boundary button to edit the sketch of the masking polygon. You will need to create the Medium Lines subcategory. To do this, click the Manage tab and then click Object Styles. Click the New button in the lower-right corner to add a new subcategory. Name the new subcategory Medium Lines and set its line weight to: 3. Click OK to finish. On the Modify Detail Items > Edit Boundary tab, chain select the entire outline (four lines) on screen and then choose: **Medium Lines** from the Type Selector. On the ribbon, click Finish Region and then save the family. Finally, click the Load into Project and Close button on the ribbon. Overwrite the existing family when prompted. If you don't have write access to the library, you can still edit the family. Just close without saving or save it to a different folder, and then overwrite the version in your project when prompted.
>
> A modified version of the family named: *Nominal Cut Lumber-Section_MED.rfa [M_Nominal Cut Lumber-Section_MED.rfa]* has been provided in *er 12/Complete* folder. You can make the edits listed here or load the provided family using the Load Family tool on the Insert tab.

7. On the Annotate tab, choose the Detail Component tool from the Component drop down button again.

⇨ Change the type to: **Nominal Cut Lumber-Section: 2×10 [M_Nominal Cut Lumber-Section : 50x250mm]**.

⇨ Use the SPACEBAR to rotate if necessary and place a rim joist (see the right side of Figure 12.13).

You use the same process to load and place any detail component. Revit ships with a very large collection of pre-made detail item families. As we discussed in the previous chapter, set aside some time to get acquainted with what is provided. You can use the components in the library, modify them, or build your own. It is usually best to start with those provided before endeavoring to create your own. Let's continue to add to our detail by repeating the load and add process to add an anchor bolt.

> **BIM MANAGER NOTE:** A frequent concern when creating these "hybrid" details is change management. What happens if, after placing detail components in several detail views, components in the model move? To help alleviate the problem of having to revisit all of those details to make sure that all of the affected detail components get updated, you can lock the detail components to the model geometry that they are aligned with. After using the Align tool to position a component, click the lock symbol that appears. This will cause the detail component to move with the associated model component. Conversely, you cannot accidentally move a detail component once it has been locked to model geometry, so you don't have to worry about accidentally modifying the model by inadvertently editing a detail component. Keep in mind that you can "over constrain" your models as well. Even though there is a potential benefit to locking the detail components to the underlying geometry, in some cases you may experience errors later in the design process when moving model components if such a move causing the locked relationship to become invalid. In such a case, the user performing the edit may not understand the error, nor know the impact of clicking the Remove Constraints button. As always in BIM, you must strike a balance between potential benefits of a chosen practice or procedure with the potential disadvantages.

8. On the Annotate tab, on the Detail panel, click the Component drop down button and choose the Detail Component tool from the list.

   ⇨ Click the Load Family button and browse to:

   Imperial: *Detail Items\Div 05-Metals\050500-Common Work Results for Metals\050523-Metal Fastenings.*

   Metric: *Detail Items\Div 05-Metals\05090-Metal Fastenings.*

9. Open the: *Anchor Bolts Hook-Side.rfa* [*M_Anchor Bolts Hook-Side.rfa*] file.

   ⇨ From the Type Selector, choose the: **1/2"** [**M16**] type.

10. Place the anchor at the midpoint of one of the lower studs. (It will overlap the studs).

    ⇨ On the ribbon, click the Modify tool or press the ESC key twice.

11. Select the bolt that you just placed.

    ⇨ On the Properties palette, change the "Length" parameter to: **1'-9"** [**525**].

    ⇨ Change the "Hook Length" to: **3"** [**76**] and then click OK.

12. With the bolt still selected, on the Modify | Detail Items tab, click the Mirror – Pick Axis tool, clear the Copy check box, and mirror the bolt about its center.

13. On the Modify | Detail Items tab, click the Align tool; use the top of the plate as reference and align the bottom of the bolt to it (see Figure 12.14).

    Fine-tune your placement as necessary to match the figure.

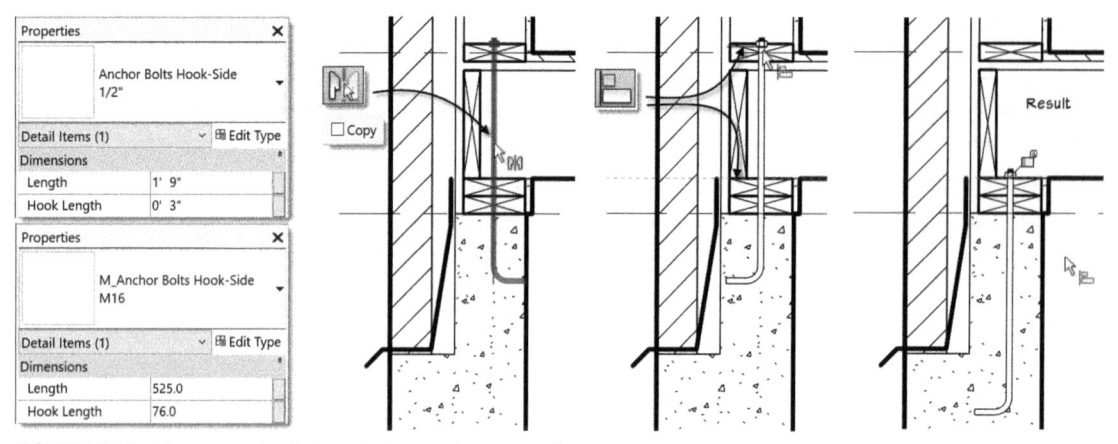

FIGURE 12.14 *Place an anchor bolt and adjust its location and parameters*

REPEATING DETAIL ELEMENTS

Repeating detail elements are detail components that automatically repeat about/along an invisible sketch line. This allows more rapid placement of detail components like studs, CMU, brick, etc. In the detail that we are constructing, we can see the brick layer of our wall with the heavy cut line on the exterior and the diagonal fill pattern. This rendition is fine for small scales and overall plans and sections. However, at the scale of this construction detail, adding mortar joints will better delineate the brick veneer and suggest the individual bricks. While we could place one mortar joint and then array or copy it, a repeating detail component is more expedient and the spacing can be edited later if necessary.

1. On the Insert tab, on the Load from Library panel, click the Load Family button.

2. Browse to the *Chapter12* folder, select the *Mortar Joint with concave joint.rfa* [*Mortar Joint with concave joint-Metric.rfa*] file and then click Open.

Now that we have loaded a mortar joint family, we will create a new repeating detail type that uses this detail component. If you wish, feel free to open this family in the Family Editor and study its composition.

3. On the Annotate tab, on the Detail panel, click the Component drop down button and choose the: **Repeating Detail Component** tool from the list.

Only one type is available on the Type Selector: **Repeating Detail: Brick**. We are going to use this as the basis for a new type. The procedure is the same as we have seen in many other instances.

4. On the Properties palette, click the Edit Type button.

    ⇨ In the "Type Properties" dialog, click the Duplicate button and then name the new type: **Mortar** and then click OK.

    ⇨ In the "Type Parameters" area, choose: **Mortar Joint with concave joint: Brick Joint** from the "Detail" list.

5. Leave all the other settings unchanged and then click OK to return to the view window.

6. Click at the bottom-left corner of the brick veneer and drag up past the top of the Crop Boundary and click again (see Figure 12.15).

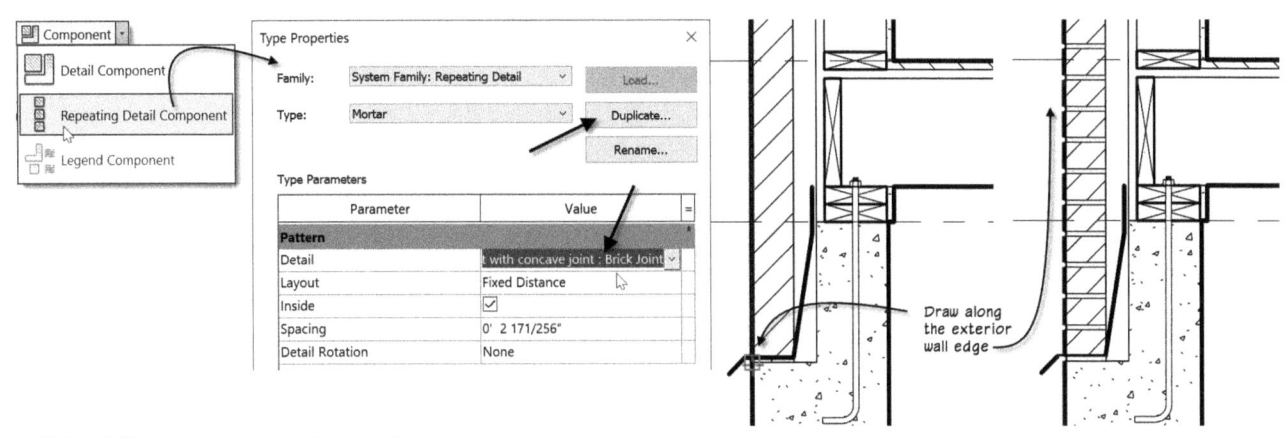

FIGURE 12.15 *Place a repeating detail for the mortar joints*

⇨ On the ribbon, click the Modify tool or press the ESC key twice.

7. Save the project.

FILLED REGIONS

Filled regions are two-dimensional shapes comprised of boundary lines and fill patterns. You can draw them any shape you like and use them to create, hatch, or cover up parts of the detail or other drawing. We will use a filled region here to illustrate the filled trench on the exterior side of the foundation wall.

1. On the Annotate tab, on the Detail panel, click the top part of the Region tool.

    The Modify | Create Filled Region Boundary tab will appear with familiar sketch tools.

    ⇨ From the Line Style panel on the ribbon, choose: **<Wide Lines>**.

    On the Draw panel, be sure that the Line icon is selected, and on the Options Bar that the "Chain" check box is selected.

2. Zoom into the bottom of the foundation wall near the footing.

    ⇨ Sketch the shape shown in Figure 12.16. The exact dimensions are not critical.

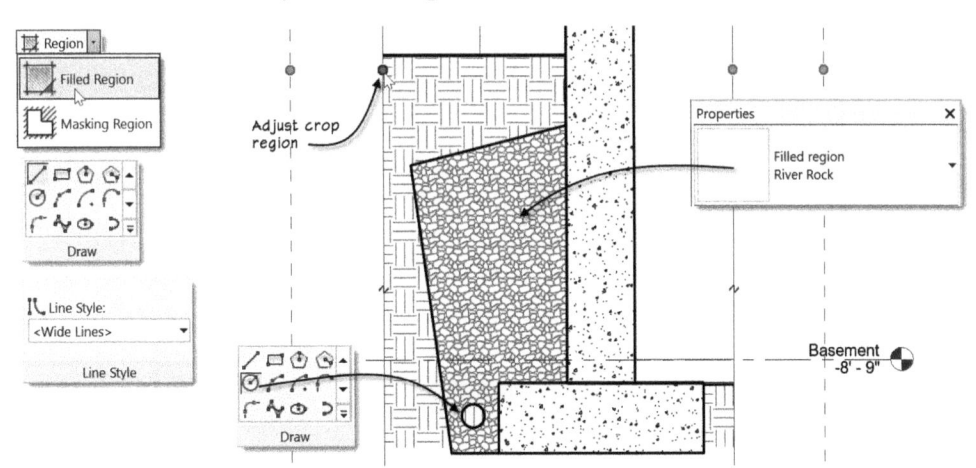

FIGURE 12.16 *Sketch a filled region boundary*

3. On the Draw panel, change the shape to Circle.

    ⇨ Add a sketched circle with a 2" [50] radius as shown at the bottom of the figure.

4. On the Properties palette, from the Type Selector choose: **River Rock**.

    ⇨ On the Mode panel, click the Finish Edit Mode button (see the right side of Figure 12.16).

• Revit Essentials for Architecture •

564 | Chapter 12

> **NOTE:** If necessary, you can widen the crop region to allow more room to draw the filled region.

CREATE A CUSTOM FILL PATTERN

The river rock fill pattern was not a default part of the out-of-the-box template. It was added to the provided file using a custom pattern file (PAT). It is easy to import custom PAT files and use them to create custom filled region types. For the next filled region, we'll also create a custom fill pattern and filled region type.

We need to create two custom items here: first we need to create a custom fill pattern. Next, we will use that fill pattern to make a custom filled region type. The PAT file we need has been provided in the *Chapter12* folder. We will not go over the process of building the PAT file here. You can search online for "creating custom PAT files in Revit" to learn more about how to do this if you are interested. PAT files can be used in both Revit and AutoCAD. There are also third-party add-ins available that simplify the process of creating PAT files. Such add-ins may incur licensing fees, so check with the provider's website to learn more.

1. On the Manage tab, click the Additional Settings drop down and choose: **Fill Patterns**.
2. In the "Fill Patterns" dialog, click the New button.

If you need a simple pattern, you can define patterns of parallel lines or crosshatch by simply specifying the spacing you need. In our case, we will use a modified version of the default earth hatch.

⇨ In the middle of the dialog, click the Custom radio button.

3. Beneath this, click the Browse button. In the *Chapter12* folder, choose: *Earth45.pat* and then click Open (see the left side of Figure 12.17).

⇨ Click OK twice to finish.

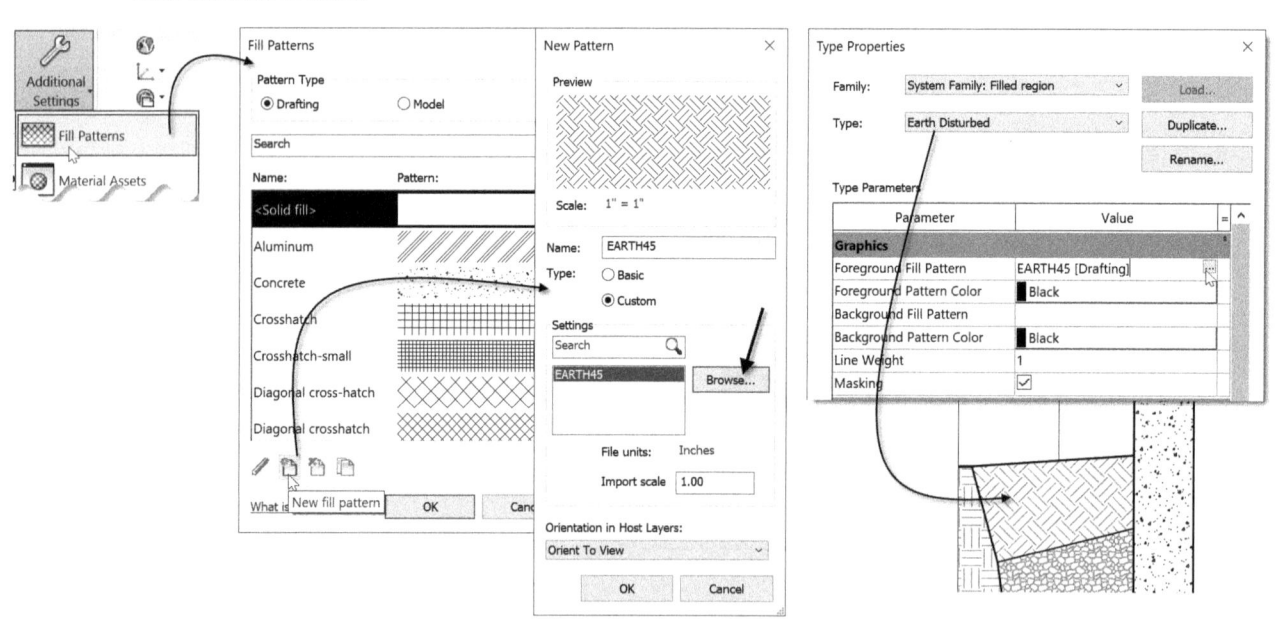

FIGURE 12.17 *Create a custom fill pattern and filled region type and add another filled region*

4. Add another filled region above the one we just drew to represent the finished grade above the gravel region. Again, precise dimensions are not required (see the right side of Figure 12.17).
5. On the Properties palette, click the Edit Type button.

⇨ Click the Duplicate button and name the new type: **Earth Disturbed**.

Detailing and Annotation | 565

⇨ Change the Fill Pattern to: **Earth45** and then click OK.

6. Click the Finish Edit Mode button.

ADDING BREAK LINES

Next let's drop in some break line components to hide part of the model. The break line family has instance parameters so we can individually adjust their size to fit the detail.

1. On the Annotate tab, on the Detail panel, click the Component drop down button and choose the: **Detail Component** tool from the list.

⇨ Click the Load Family button and browse to the *Detail Items\Div 01-General* folder.

⇨ Open the *Break Line.rfa* [*M_Break Line.rfa*] file.

2. Place a Break Line at the top of the detail to cover the top edge.

⇨ Press the SPACEBAR three times, and then place another Break Line covering part of the floor joist to the right (see Figure 12.18).

Break line components contain invisible masking regions that mask (cover up) the model objects beneath them. The concept of a mask is common in graphic design software and can be helpful in creating details.

⇨ Use the Shape Handles to adjust as necessary.

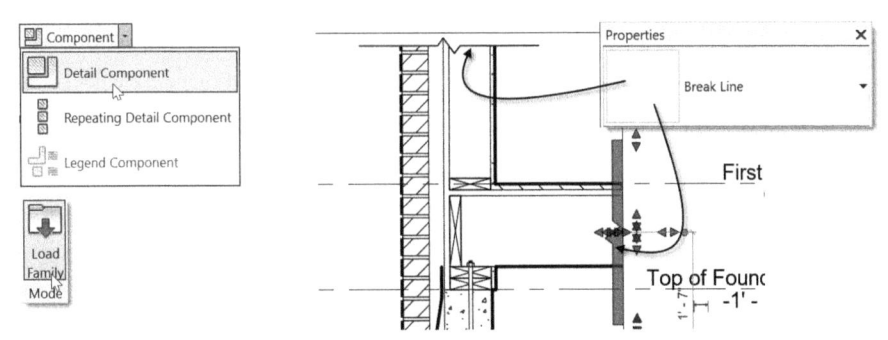

FIGURE 12.18 *Add break lines with integral masking regions*

Here we used a detail item family that contains a masking region, but if you like you can use the Region drop down tool and choose Masking Region. You draw them just like filled regions. The only difference is that there is only one type which contains the opaque mask.

BATT INSULATION

Next, we'll place some batt insulation in the wall and floor.

1. On the Annotate tab, on the Detail panel, click the Insulation tool.

⇨ On the Properties palette, set the Width to: **5" [130]**.

⇨ Set the Insulation Bulge to Width Ratio to: **3**.

2. Click the first point at the bottom midpoint of the stud space, move up vertically and then pick the second point above the Crop Region (see the left side of Figure 12.19).

• Revit Essentials for Architecture •

566 | Chapter 12

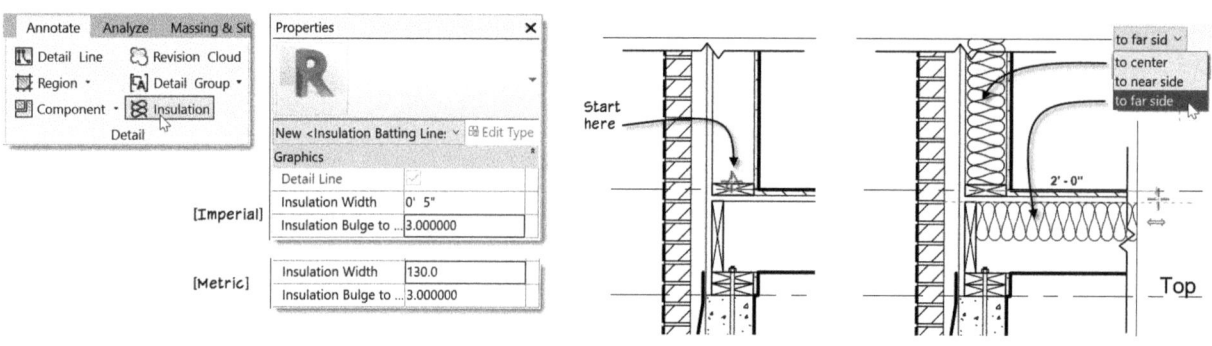

FIGURE 12.19 *Draw insulation in the stud cavity*

⇨ Press the ESC key *one time* (this deselects the previously drawn insulation but remains in the command).

3. On the Options Bar, choose "to far side" from the drop down list.

⇨ Click a point on the inside of the rim joist and drag to the right past the Crop Region (see the right side of Figure 12.19).

⇨ On the ribbon, click the Modify tool or press the ESC key twice.

ARRANGE DISPLAY ORDER

Notice that the insulation is not masked by the break lines. This is because there is an explicit display order for the view-specific detail items. The insulation is currently on top because it was added to the view after the break lines. We can shuffle the display order now.

1. Select the two break line components using the CTRL key.

⇨ On the Modify | Detail Items tab, click the Bring to Front button (see Figure 12.20).

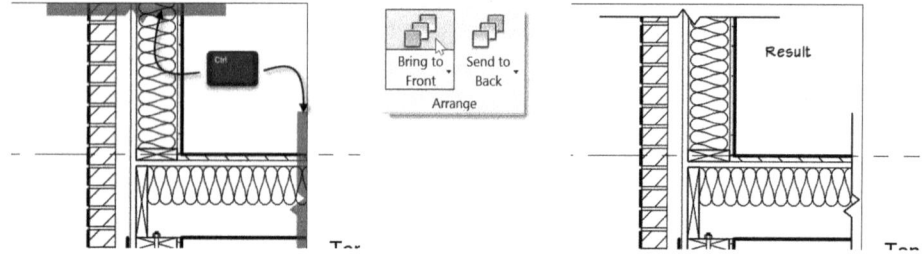

FIGURE 12.20 *Use the display order tools to shuffle the order of detail elements in the view*

2. Use the Send to Back button on the mortar joints repeating detail item to send it behind the flashing detail lines.

EDIT CUT PROFILE

Sometimes you encounter a situation where the automatically created graphics do not suit your specific needs in a view. One such example is the keyway locking the foundation wall to the footing. It is possible to modify the model geometry to rectify this situation, but as an alternative, Revit provides us with the Edit Cut Profile tool. This tool gives us the ability to edit the shape of the cut lines that Revit automatically generates. This type of edit is view-specific and two-dimensional. While it does not change the 3D shape of the model, it gives us a quick way to make the detail look the way we need without forcing us to model something that would have little or no benefit in other views. Since a key between the bottom of a foundation wall and the top of a footing would never be seen in any view other than a section or detail view, it would be difficult to justify the additional time or effort required to model it in 3D. Using the Edit Cut Profile tool, we can make the section or detail appear as required more quickly and without the extra modeling effort or overhead.

1. On the View tab, on the Graphics panel, click the Cut Profile tool.
   ⇨ On the Options Bar, select the "Boundary between Faces" option.

This option allows us to edit two boundaries—in this case the footing's boundary and the foundation wall's boundary—with one sketch. If we used the other option: Face, we would first need to edit the bottom face of the foundation and then go back, repeat the process and edit the top face of the footings.

2. Select the boundary line between the foundation wall and the footing (see Figure 12.21).

   The Create Cut Profile Sketch tab appears. The selected line changes to a tan color.

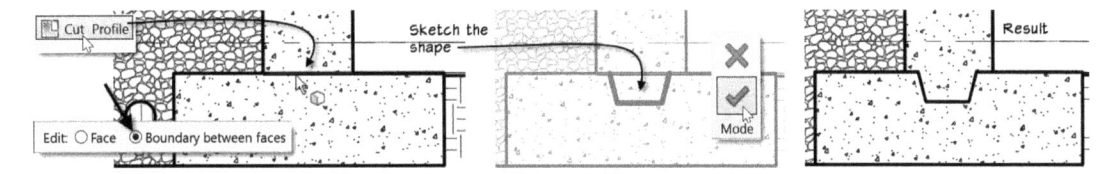

FIGURE 12.21 *Using the "Boundary between faces" option, select the face to edit and sketch out the shape*

3. From the Draw panel, using the Line shape, sketch the new path as indicated in the middle of Figure 12.21.

Be sure to start and end the chain of sketch lines on the tan edge. It should be an open shape.

⇨ On the Mode panel, click the Finish Edit Mode button.

In this case the fill pattern is the same on both sides of the Cut line, but if they were different you would notice that the fill pattern for the footing receded and the fill pattern for the foundation wall extended to fill in the key shape. There will be a thin element showing through here. This is a building pad used to cut the foundation from the toposurface. You can select it and then right-click and choose: **Hide in View > Category** (or press VH).

VIEW BREAKS

It is common that a detailed wall section will be too tall to fit on a sheet. So, it is typically broken into separate parts that crop away the areas not relevant to the current detail. The crop boundary for any view includes "View Break" controls and can be used to achieve this effect.

1. Select the crop boundary surrounding the section callout (it appears as a rectangle surrounding the drawing).

On each of the four edges of this crop region, a blue dot control handle appears at the midpoint and a "zig zag" break control appears on either side of it. The "zig zag" controls allow us to truncate the view into smaller parts facilitating placement on a sheet (see the left side of Figure 12.22).

568 | Chapter 12

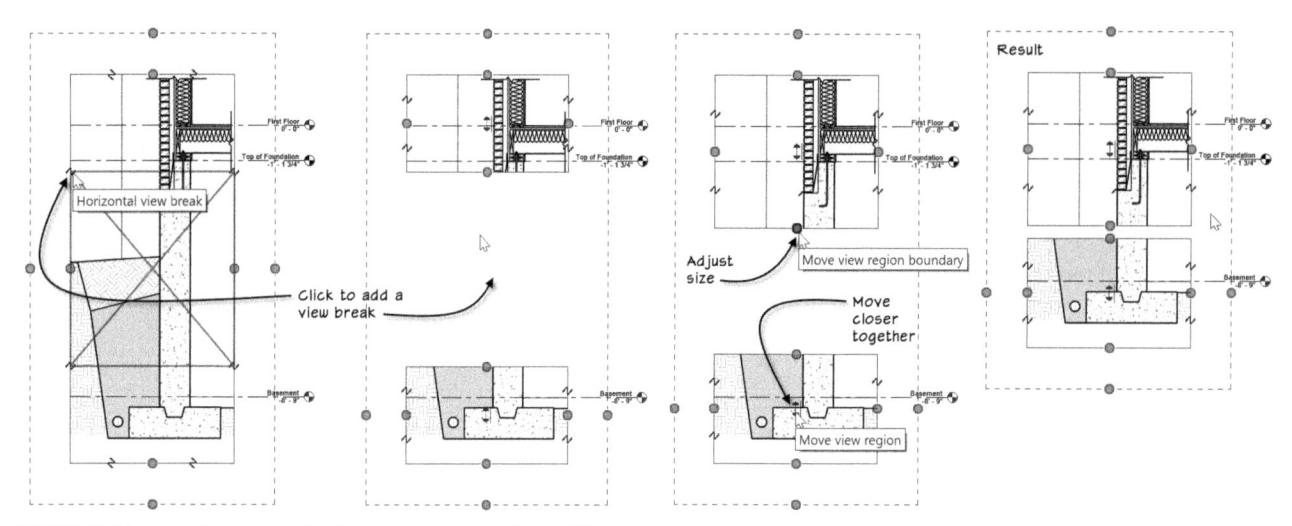

FIGURE 12.22 *View break controls allow you to crop out the middle portion of the section*

2. Click one of the view break controls on a vertical edge (there are four total; you can pick any one) of the crop boundary.

The view splits into two separate crop regions with a large gap in the middle. A blue arrow control handle appears in the middle of each view break region. We can use these to move the two portions closer together. Notice that along the vertical edges of each of the two new crop boundaries the same types of control handles appear. You can continue to break them into additional sub-views as necessary. But all breaks must be along the same direction as the first one—vertical in this case. In this example two is enough so we will not break it any further. However, we need to adjust the top view break so we can see the entire anchor bolt.

3. Using the blue dot control handle at the bottom of the upper view break, drag the edge down a bit to show all the anchor bolt.

⇨ Click on the view break control (in the middle) of the bottom view break and drag it up so the crop region is a little below the upper crop boundary (see the right side of Figure 12.22).

If you continue to drag so that you overlap the two view breaks, they will join back into one. This is how you "remove" the break.

> **CAUTION:** Be sure to move the portions of the view breaks with the control arrow in the middle. Do not drag the edge of the crop region. Doing so will move the area of the callout in both this view and the referring *Longitudinal* section view.

Although the sub-views are truncated and closer together, distances are dimensionally correct. Look at the level lines to the right of the views and note that the heights are unchanged. If we were to add a dimension from the *First Floor* to the *Basement*, it should read a distance of: 8'-9" [3540]. Let's try it out to see.

4. On the Annotate tab, on the Dimension panel, click the Aligned tool.

⇨ Add a dimension between the First Floor level and the Basement level.

⇨ Move to the left crop region boundary and click next to it (in the white space) to place the dimension string (see Figure 12.23).

• The Aubin Academy •

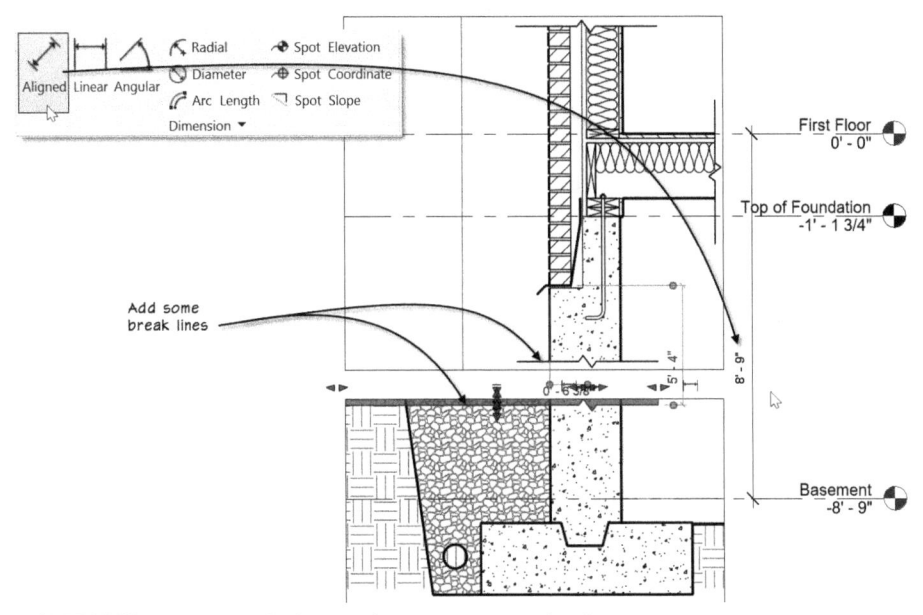

FIGURE 12.23 *Dimensions display true distances across view breaks*

As you can see, applying a view break is a graphical convention only and has no impact on the dimensional accuracy of the model being displayed in each portion of the crop boundary.

5. On the ribbon, click the Modify tool or press the ESC key twice.

6. Add Break Line detail components on the foundation wall at the break between the two halves of the detail.

7. Save the project.

ANNOTATION

Annotating a drawing with notes, dimensions, symbols, and tags is essential to communicating architectural design intent. Such annotations share common characteristics with other Revit elements such as having type and instance properties. As you would expect, type properties are shared by all instances of a text, dimension or tag type, while instance properties affect only the selected element(s). And like other detailing, annotation elements are view-specific elements and appear only in the view to which they are added. The exception to this is view tags and datum elements like section markers, elevation makers, level lines, grids, and callouts. These items are purpose-built to appear in all appropriate views and enhance the fully coordinated nature of a Revit project.

> **NOTE:** It is possible to create a view where annotation appears simultaneously in it and another "dependent" view. This feature is used to facilitate large drawings that require matchlines to fit on a standard sized sheet. If you would like to learn more, please look up "Dependent Views" in the online help.

Each view in Revit has a "View Scale" parameter and all annotations added to the view will respond to this scale and adjust size accordingly. View tags and datum elements are also included in this behavior. This means that no matter what the scale of the drawing, the annotation, view tags, and datum symbols (level heads and grid bubbles) will be the correct size required for output. This behavior also applies to line weights and drafting patterns. In addition, if the scale parameter of a view is changed, the text, line weights, and drafting patterns will automatically adjust. The line weights are controlled in a matrix based on common plot scales.

• Revit Essentials for Architecture •

> **NOTE:** Model patterns are like other model elements; they have an actual real-world size in the model. Drafting patterns adjust with the scale of the view like other annotation.

> **BIM Manager Note:** If desired, you can edit line weight settings on the Manage tab, from the Additional Settings drop down with the Line Weights command. However, try using the out-of-the-box settings as-is for a while before making any changes. Revit line weights behave quite differently from other CAD programs. So, before you embark on the task of changing all the settings to match existing (non-Revit) office standards, make sure you first fully understand how Revit manages line weights. You will likely find the out-of-the-box settings for scale and line weight to be adequate for most situations. If you do make changes, save these modified settings in a modified version of the standard Revit template file and make it your office standard. This is much more efficient than repeating your desired edits with each new project. A common practice is to keep a record of changes made in your projects that you want to later add to your standards. Periodically, you can use the Transfer Project Standards button on the Manage tab to migrate these settings into your project template.

CREATE A CUSTOM TEXT TYPE

A text type is simply a grouping of parameters that control the look and formatting of the text. There are several common parameters, that we can adjust such as font, bold, italic and size to name a few. Like other families and types, text types can be preconfigured and added to a project template. Create a new text type the same way you make other custom types; you simply duplicate an existing one, rename it, and modify its parameters. Let's do a quick example creating a text type that uses a different font and size.

> **NOTE:** Text height is the final plotted height—there is no need to calculate text size relative to the model or use multipliers.

1. On the Annotate tab, on the Text Panel, click the Text Types icon in the corner of the panel title bar (see the top half of Figure 12.24).
2. Next to the type list, click the Duplicate button (or press ALT + D).
   ⇨ For the name, input: **Standard Notes** and then click OK.

   For Text Font, you can use any font that is installed on your system.

Since the choice of fonts can vary widely from one computer to the next, your system may not have the same fonts as those indicated here. Feel free to choose a different font if you prefer.

   ⇨ In the "Text Size" field, type: **1/8"** [**3**] (see Figure 12.24).

Beneath this, you can choose to make the text bold, italic, or underline if desired. The "Width Factor" setting is used to compress or stretch the text horizontally. This is a multiplier. When set to: 1, the text draws in the way it was designed in the font. A value less than 1 will compress the text and a value greater than 1 will stretch it out. In the "Graphics" area, you can change the color of the text as well as assign an arrowhead to be used when you create text with a leader line attached.

3. From the "Leader Arrowhead" list, choose: **Arrow Filled 20 Degree**.

> **BIM Manager Note:** Arrowheads are system families. You can add additional types on the Manage tab from the Additional Settings drop down button, using the Arrowheads command. You cannot create a custom arrowhead family however, you can only duplicate and modify existing types.

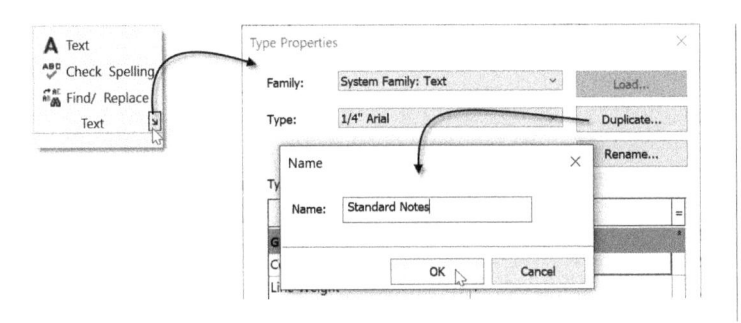

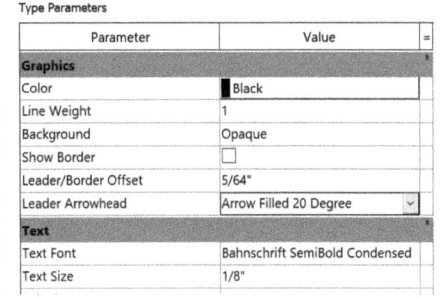

FIGURE 12.24 *Create a new text type*

⇨ Click OK to complete the new type.

PLACING TEXT

To place text in a view, simply click the location where you want the text to appear. If you choose one of the leader options on the ribbon, the first (and possibly second) click will be to place the arrow and elbow of the leader, then you click to place the text. If you click a single point, the text will flow in one continuous line without wrapping. If you click and drag two points, it will wrap to the width between the points. Regardless of your choice, you can always edit the wrapping of a text element later using the control handles on the text element. Pressing the ENTER key within a text element will insert a "hard" return. This will move the cursor to the next line regardless of the automatic wrapping. It is like pressing ENTER in a word processor.

1. On the Annotate tab, on the Text panel, click the Text tool.

   ⇨ On the Properties palette, from the Type Selector, choose: **Standard Notes**.

2. On the Format panel of the ribbon, choose the No Leader option and then on the left side of the detail, click and drag a text region near the top, close to the crop region edge.

   ⇨ Type: **Standard Face Brick Veneer - See Specifications for Color** (see the left side of Figure 12.25).

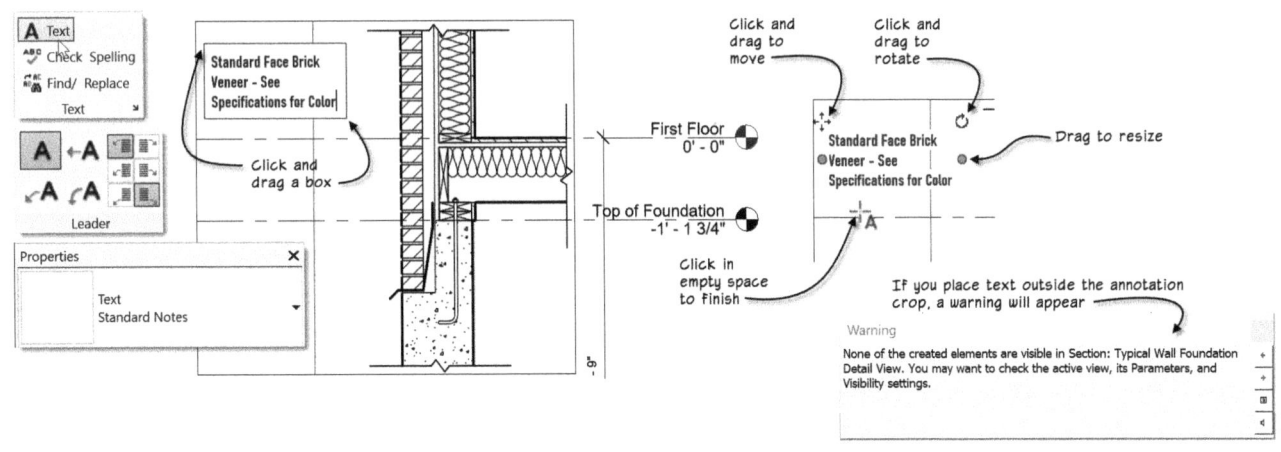

FIGURE 12.25 *Add a text element and type in the desired note*

3. Click next to the note (in the white space) to finish typing.

Some blue control handles will appear attached to the text element while selected. You can use the one on the left to move the element (while leaving any arrow heads in place), the one on the right to rotate it, and the two small round ones on either side to resize and reshape the element and its word wrapping (see the right side of Figure 12.25).

⇨ Use any of the control handles to fine-tune its placement.

⇨ Click the Modify button on the ribbon or press ESC.

• Revit Essentials for Architecture •

NOTE: If a warning message appears and a text element disappears, you have created the text outside the annotation crop region (see the bottom right corner of Figure 12.25). The annotation crop appears as a dashed boundary outside of the view crop region and hides any annotation that falls outside its boundaries. Review the next topic for a more thorough explanation of the annotation crop region.

ANNOTATION CROP REGION

In the exercises above, we adjusted the crop region of our detail callout views to fine-tune how much of the model's geometry was included in the view. In addition to the crop region, we also have the annotation crop region. This region falls outside the normal model crop region and affects only the annotation elements added to the view. When any portion of an annotation element intersects the annotation crop, the entire element disappears. So, if the note you created in the previous topic disappeared, then you created it on or outside of the annotation crop. While the annotation crop can be enabled in any plan, section, or elevation view, the most effective place to utilize it is in drawings that contain matchlines. In this way, if you have text or other annotation that occurs near the matchline, Revit can show a limited amount of the duplicate annotations on each matchline sheet. To see this feature in action, explore the dependent views feature. An example is shown in Figure 15.8 in Chapter 15. You can also look up dependent views and annotation crop regions in the online help.

There are two solutions to the problem: enlarge the annotation crop (select the crop region and use the controls on the dashed outer boundary to stretch it) or simply turn it off. In our current detail, we have no need to crop the annotation. Therefore, we will turn off the feature in the current view.

1. Select the crop region onscreen.

2. On the Properties palette, beneath the "Extents" grouping, clear the checkmark from the Annotation Crop setting and then click OK (see Figure 12.26).

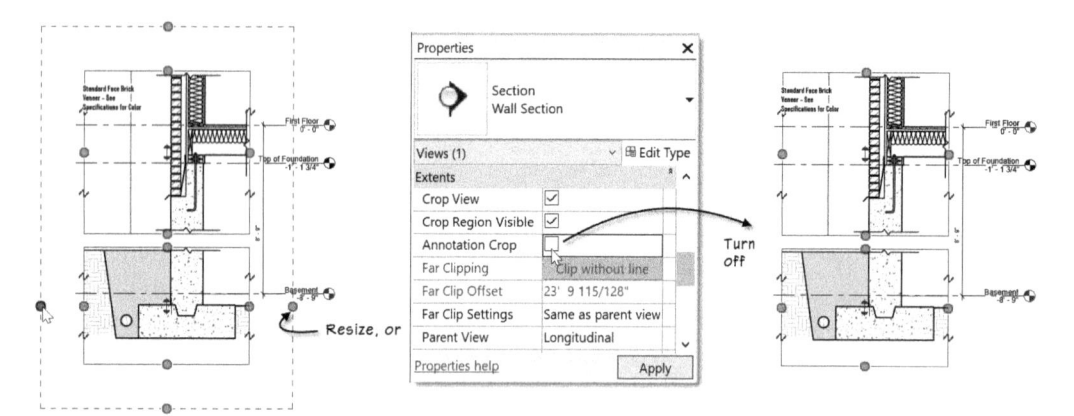

FIGURE 12.26 *Turn off the Annotation Crop*

If the notes you typed above were not showing, they should have now appeared.

NOTE: Another effective way to deal with the annotation crop in a detail view, such as the one we have here, would be to simply enlarge the annotation crop region using the control handles.

INCLUDING LEADERS WITH TEXT

To place a leader and arrowhead with a note, you can choose the appropriate option on the ribbon.

1. On the Annotate tab, click the Text tool again (or press TX).
   - On the Modify | Place Text tab, on the Format panel, click the One Segment button.
   - Click the Leader at Bottom Right button (if it is not already active).
2. In the view window, click near the middle of the double top plate on the foundation wall.

   This is the location of the arrowhead for the leader.
   - Drag to the left and click beneath the first note (a temporary guideline will appear to assist you).

   This is the end of the leader. A text object will appear. (If you selected the "Two Segments" icon instead, you would place two segments of the leader line before typing would begin).
3. Type the next note: **Double Top Plate – (2) 2x6** [**Double Top Plate – (2) 50x150**] and then click next to the note (in the white space) to finish typing (see Figure 12.27).

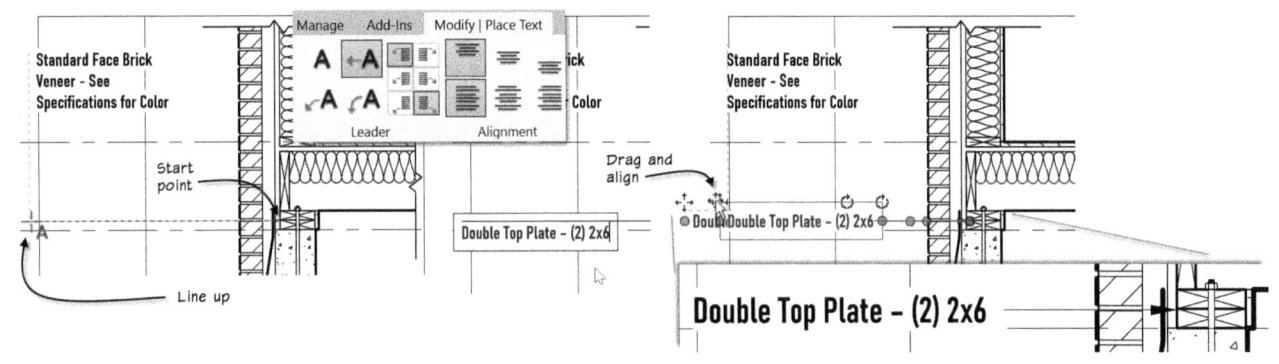

FIGURE 12.27 *Add a text element with a leader*

   - Using the Move handle, drag the text element to align it with the first one. A temporary guideline will appear to assist you.

When you drag a text element with a leader, be careful not to drag up or down as this will bend the leader line. This is because the leader's arrowhead stays attached to the element to which it points. If you want to move the entire thing (text and leader together), use the Move command (on the Modify tab of the ribbon) or the arrow keys on the keyboard (to nudge). Make any fine-tuning adjustments that you wish to the position of either text element.

   Use the grip on the right side of the text box to adjust the wrapping of the text if desired.
4. On the ribbon, click the Modify tool or press the ESC key twice.

You can determine the leader location for either the left or right side of the text on the format panel of the ribbon. In the process of adjusting the text box, the leader may now have shifted so that it is no longer horizontal. You can use the grip controls to adjust both the text box and the leader itself until it is to your liking.

The first text element we created does not have a leader attached to it. You can add leaders to existing text anytime.

5. Select the first text element (the brick veneer note).
   - On the Format panel, click the Add Right Straight Leader tool (see the left side of Figure 12.28).

A leader will appear attached to the text. You can then use the drag handles to modify its shape and adjust the location of the arrowhead.

   - Adjust with the drag controls as necessary to move the arrowhead to point at the brick.

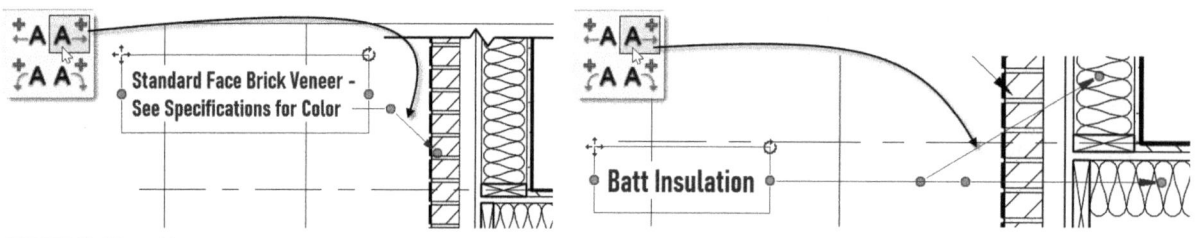

FIGURE 12.28 *Add a leader to an existing text element and add additional notes and leaders*

6. Using the Text tool with a leader option, add a note pointing to the batt insulation

⇨ Adjust the position of the note and leader as required (see the right side of Figure 12.28).

Sometimes you want to have the same note point to more than one location in the detail. You can add additional leaders to an existing text element. To do this, you simply select the text element and then click the appropriate icon on the ribbon. To remove a leader you no longer need, click the "Remove Leader" button.

7. With the Text selected, on the Modify Text Notes tab, on the Leader panel, click the Add Right Straight Leader button.

⇨ Position the leader and its arrowheads as necessary to point at the insulation in the floor (see the right side of Figure 12.28).

ADDING KEYNOTES

Adding text is not the only way to add notes to a view. We can also use keynotes. Keynoting allows you to annotate elements using a predefined list of notes. The notes are organized in an external keyed TXT file. If your firm uses a keynoting system, the tool provides a means to simplify the application of keyed notes and the compilation of all keys into a keynote legend for inclusion on title blocks.

However, it is not required that you utilize the keys to use the keynote functionality. Even if you do not currently use a keynoting system, you may still find the keynoting tools useful. This is because rather than being required to type out each note you add to a project, with keynoting you choose the note from a predefined list of standard notes. Furthermore, you can even preassign keynotes directly to your materials, family types, and your office standard templates and library files.

Revit includes a sample keynote file organized in CSI format (Construction Specifications Institute). You can use this list as-is, edit it, or create your own. Creating or editing your own file is easy. The keynote list is stored in a simple tab-delimited text file. If you wish to create your own file, search for "**About Editing the Keynote File**" in the online help for instructions and an example of the proper format. Of course using keynotes is optional, and to benefit fully from them, a certain amount of setup is required. You must decide if the benefits of doing so prove valuable enough to justify the initial configuration effort.

Before we begin adding keynotes to a project, you must choose a keynote file. You can use the same file for all projects in the office or have different files for each project.

1. On the Annotate tab, click on the Keynote drop down and then choose: the **Keynoting Settings** button (see Figure 12.29).

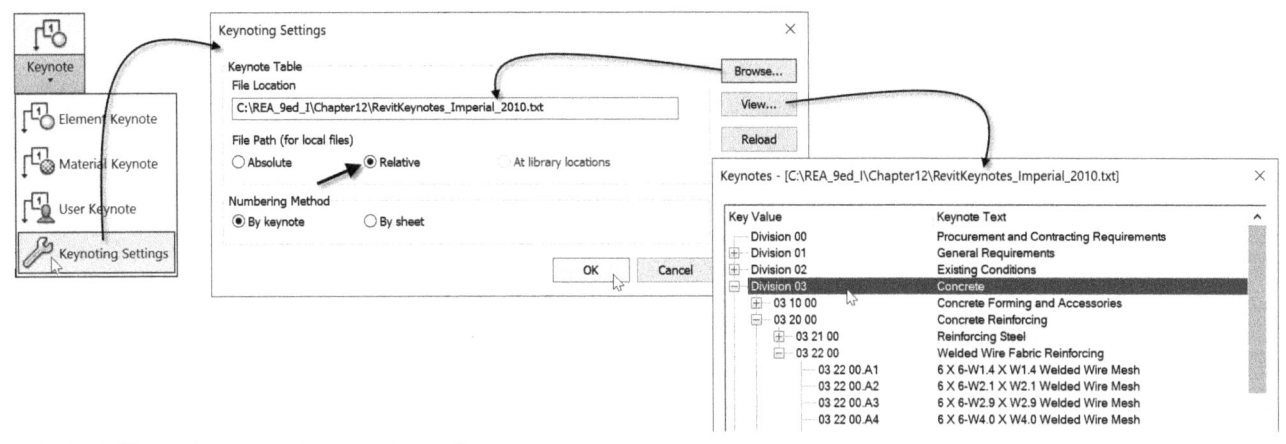

FIGURE 12.29 *Load a keynote file and configure other settings*

2. In the "Keynote Settings" dialog, use the Browse button to load the: *RevitKeynotes_Imperial_2010.txt* [*RevitKeynotes_Metric.txt*] file from *r 12* folder.

When assigning your chosen file to a project, the path to the file can be set to absolute, relative, or set by library location. An absolute path writes the complete path back to the drive letter. A relative path assumes that the keynote file is in the same location as the project file and therefore only writes the path relative to the location in which the project file is saved. Using the "At Library Locations" option writes the path relative to the locations defined on the "File Locations" tab of the "Options" dialog. The Options command is on the File menu.

Revit ships with a few sample files. The *RevitKeynotes_Imperial.txt* [*RevitKeynotes_Metric.txt*] file is based on the traditional 16 section CSI format and the *Revit Keynotes_Imperial_2010.txt* file (imperial only) is based on the newer CSI format and its 48 specification sections. These out-of-the-box keynote files are in the *C:\ProgramData\Autodesk\RVT 2021\Libraries\English-Imperial* [*C:\ProgramData\Autodesk\RVT 2021\Libraries\English*] folder. You can use one of the provided files instead or even create your own.

Keynotes can be numbered in your choice of two methods. The "By keynote" method will use a fixed and predefined key. The "By sheet" method will compile the numbering uniquely for each sheet of the set based on the notes used on that sheet.

⇨ Click the Relative radio button and leave the Numbering Method set to: **By keynote**.

If you wish to preview the file, click the View button. It will open in a separate window.

⇨ Click OK to dismiss the dialog.

3. On the Annotate tab, click the Keynote drop down button and then choose the: **Element Keynote** tool.

Move the cursor around on screen. Items that have a keynote assigned will appear as the mouse passes over them.

4. Move the mouse over the Anchor Bolt element on screen and then click it.

⇨ Click a point for the leader and then a point to place the keynote tag.

It requires two clicks. If you want a straight line leader, click twice along the same line.

A Keynote symbol will appear with the key for the associated note displayed.

5. Add a keynote for the plates and the rim joist if you wish (see the left side of Figure 12.30).

Most of the out-of-the-box detail components (like the anchor bolt and studs we used here) already have keynotes assigned to them from the provided keynote files. If you click an item that does not already have a keynote assigned (like the walls and floors) then the "Keynotes" dialog will appear. At the top of the dialog whatever keynote file you assigned above will appear in the title bar. A list of major categories will appear. Each contains additional sub-categories and notes. You can choose any appropriate note from the list for the item you are noting. You will only be prompted to select a note the first time you keynote an item. After assigning the note the first time, Revit will simply display that note on each subsequent instance you keynote.

UNDERSTANDING KEYNOTE TAGS

The default keynote tag has four types. Three of these types display the key and the fourth displays the text of the note. Using the text display option, you can use keynote tags to speed up data entry without being required to actually use "keyed" notes (see the right side of Figure 12.30).

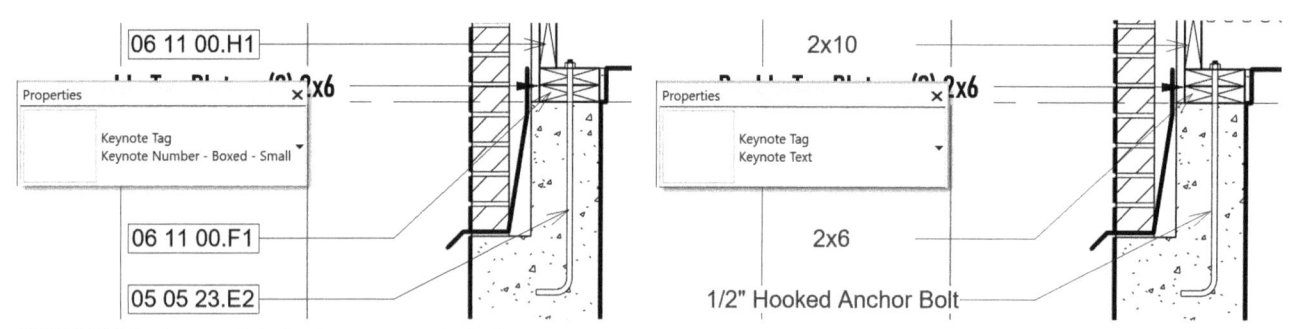

FIGURE 12.30 *The out-of-the-box keynote tag includes four variations*

1. Select one of the keynotes you have added.
2. From the Type Selector, choose: **Keynote Number** or **Keynote Text**.

A couple variations are shown in the figure. If you prefer a variation not shown, you can edit the keynote tag family.

> **TIP:** If you want the arrowhead of the keynote tags to match the text, select a keynote tag, click Edit Type and then choose the same arrowhead that your notes are using.

> **BIM Manager Note:** When you choose the Keynote Text option, you will notice that the text is center justified. To use right or left justified, edit the keynote family, select the appropriate label element and change its properties to your preferred justification. If you want to change anything else about the tag, such as the font that is used, this will also require that you edit the family.

Types of Keynotes—Keynotes have three modes: Element, Material, and User. The Element option reads the keynote assigned to the element in the model such as the keynote assigned to a wall, door, or detail item not the individual layers or subcomponents of the wall or door. To keynote the layers of a wall or components of a door, you would use the Material keynote option. This will read the keynote assigned to the Material of the selected subcomponent. So, with a wall, you would get a different material keynote for the brick or the studs or drywall. When you wish to override the predefined keynote setting, choose the User option. This option will display the "Keynotes" dialog and prompt you to choose a note even if there is one already assigned. Since this option is an override, it will not update if you edit the type or material of the selected element.

Keynotes offer some compelling features, but they are not as mature as other features in the software. For example, certain items cannot be keynoted, like drafting lines, repeating details, and batt insulation (all of which we have used in our detail here). Furthermore, keynotes have not been preassigned to all the out-of-the-box content. They have been assigned to the out-of-the-box detail component families as we have seen, but not to the out-of-the-box model families or materials. This means that to fully benefit from the power of key notes, a good deal of effort will be required to go through the library and assign key notes to both families and materials. While you might be tempted to abandon the keynote functionality altogether based on these limitations, remember that the alternative to keynotes is to manually type every note. Once set up, having keynotes assigned to elements will save a great deal of time in production and will help to standardize the verbiage and phrasing used on notes throughout the office. So, while not without their limitations they do remain worthy of your consideration.

Keynote Legend—If you want to compile a list of all the keynotes used on a sheet or throughout the entire project, you can create a keynote legend. A keynote legend lists all the keys and their corresponding notes. This can be a real time saver versus manually compiling such a list. You create a keynote Legend from the View tab. On the Create panel, click the Legends drop down button and choose: **Keynote Legend**. The rest of the steps would be like creating any other schedule. Schedules are covered in detail in the next chapter.

FINALIZING THE DETAIL

Our detail is nearly complete. With a few final edits, it will be ready to place on a sheet.

1. Using the process covered here, add additional notes and/or keynotes to the detail.
2. Using the Dimension tool, add dimensions to the footing and foundation walls.

> **TIP:** Remember to use your TAB key as needed to select the required edges to dimension.

The Crop Regions around the detail are becoming a bit distracting. We can turn off their display.

3. On the View Control Bar (at the bottom of the view window) click the Hide Crop Region icon or uncheck it on the Properties palette (see Figure 12.31).

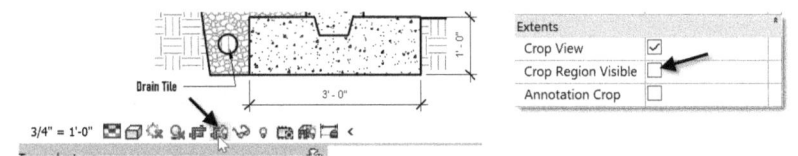

FIGURE 12.31 *Add additional notes, dimensions and hide the crop*

HIDING AN ELEMENT IN THE VIEW

On the left side of this detail we see a gray vertical line. This is the edge of the chimney beyond. In cases like this, where some piece of the model displays that we would rather not see, we can hide it in this view. We have two ways to approach this. Both are view-specific overrides leaving the chimney unchanged in all other views.

Method 1:

1. Select the Fireplace element.
   ⇨ On the ribbon, click the Hide in View drop down and choose: **By Element** (see the left side of Figure 12.32).

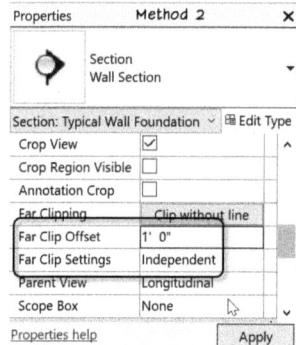

FIGURE 12.32 *Hide the fireplace in the current view only*

The fireplace will disappear. Should you need to make it reappear:

2. Click the small light bulb icon on the View Control Bar.

This will make all invisible elements reappear tinted in maroon.

- ⇨ You can then select the chimney (or any maroon element) and choose the appropriate unhide command on the ribbon (see the middle of Figure 12.32).
- ⇨ Click the lightbulb icon again to disable the mode.

Method 2:

Make sure you have no objects selected in the view window.

1. On the Properties palette, in the Extents grouping, for the "Far Clip Settings," change from: **Same as parent view** to: **Independent**.

This makes the Far Clip Offset field editable.

- ⇨ Change the Far Clip Offset to a small value like: **1'-0" [300]** and then click OK (see the right side of Figure 12.32).

This method will crop out everything in the view beyond 1'-0" [300] from the cut plane. Both methods are useful to have in your arsenal. In fact, you may find use for both in the same view. For example, even if using method 2 to reduce the far clip, you may still discover items that would be best hidden in the current view like the building pad near the foundation (noted above). Feel free to perform any additional finishing touches before continuing.

2. Save the project.

DETAIL THE REMAINDER OF THE WALL

To detail the rest of the wall section, you can follow the same procedures as outlined here. Start by returning to the *Longitudinal* section view and create a new callout of the top portion. Use the view break controls to crop the detail and remove the repetitive portions. Add masking break line detail components to each of the breaks. Hide the crop region of the view when finished. Begin adding detail components on top of the section cut as we did above, add drafting lines and edit the linework as required. Complete the detail with dimensions, notes and/or keynotes. Focus on the wall connection at the second floor and the overall studs, rafters, joists, and insulation. When you are finished, the detail should look something like Figure 12.33.

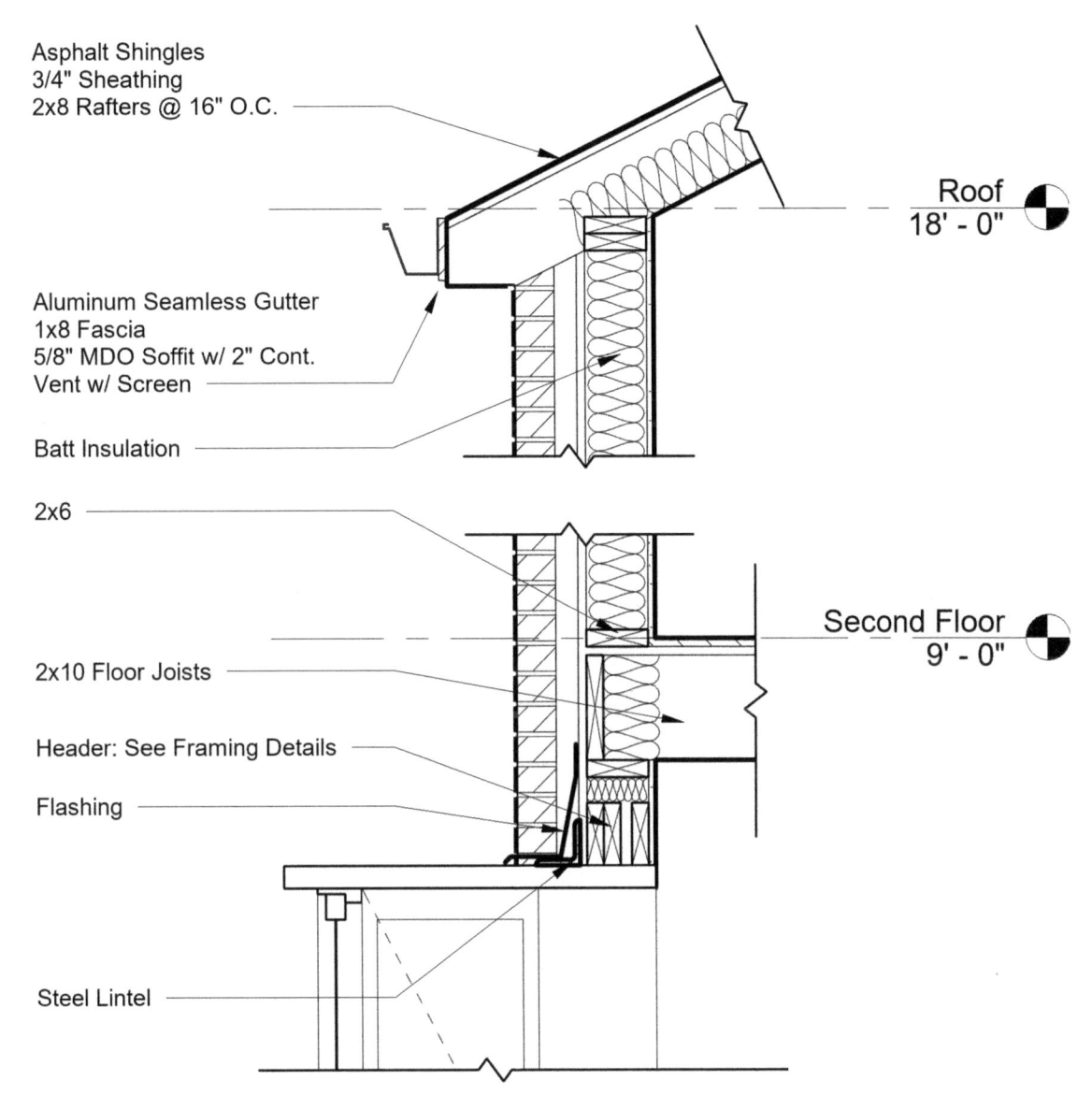

FIGURE 12.33 *Create additional details using the same process*

Most of the components that you will need are already loaded into this project; however, for items like the steel angle at the window lintel, you can simply load them in from the appropriate library. At the roof eave, you will need to rely more on filled regions, drafting lines, and edit cut profile. Let's take a look.

1. From the View tab, click the Callout tool.
   ⇨ On the Properties palette, choose: **Detail View: Detail** from the Type Selector.
   ⇨ Create a Callout bubble similar to the one shown in Figure 12.34.

580 | Chapter 12

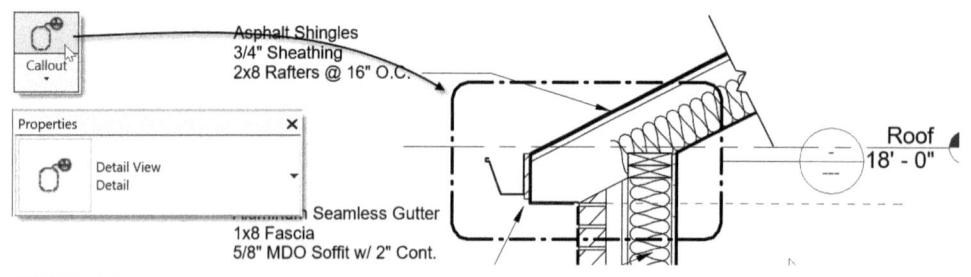

FIGURE 12.34 *Create a callout view for the eave condition*

2. On the Project Browser, expand the *Detail Views* branch.

⇨ Select the callout view, pause a moment and the click again to rename it (or press F2).

⇨ Input: **Typical Eave Condition** for the new name and then click OK.

3. With the *Typical Eave Condition* view still selected, on the Properties palette change the scale to: **1 1/2"=1'-0" [1:10]** and uncheck the Annotation Crop check box.

⇨ Double click on the *Typical Eave Condition* View to open it.

USING EDIT CUT PROFILE TO MODIFY WALL LAYERS

For almost any situation you can use the technique of first adding filled regions and/or masking regions to cover unwanted geometry and then sketching detail lines on top. Another approach is to revisit the Edit Cut Profile tool as we did above for the footing.

Work in the *Typical Eave Condition* view.

1. Select the Roof level marker; on the ribbon, click the Hide in View tool and choose: **Hide Category** from the pop-up.

2. On the View tab, on the Graphics panel, click the Cut Profile button.

⇨ Pass the cursor over the wall and when the stud layer pre-highlights, click the mouse.

The existing boundary of the stud layer will show as a tan outline.

3. On the Draw panel, click the Lines icon and draw the cut profile (see Figure 12.35).

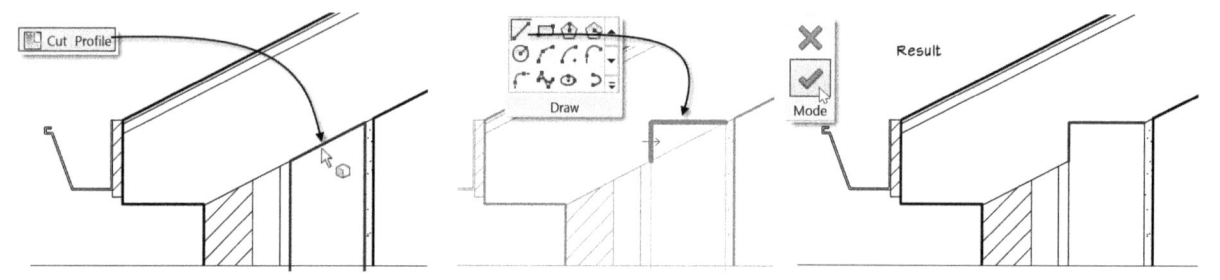

FIGURE 12.35 *Sketch the new edge of the cut boundary*

A small arrow handle will appear on the sketch line. It should be pointing to the inside of the stud to indicate that you wish to keep everything below the sketch line. If it points outside the stud, click it to reverse it. Be sure that the line touches the edges of the stud component on both sides.

⇨ On the Modify | Cut Profile panel, click the Finish Edit Mode button.

4. Use the Cut Profile tool again to edit the face of the brick, air gap, and sheathing layers so that your detail looks like Figure 12.36. (Zoom in and use Thin Lines if necessary, to see and snap to the edges required).

• The Aubin Academy •

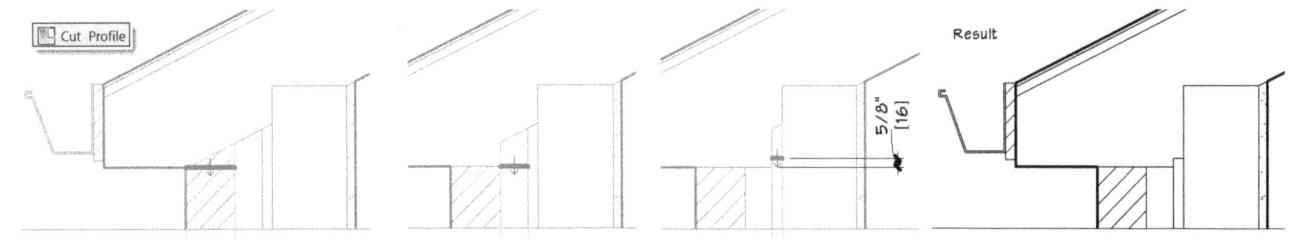

FIGURE 12.36 *Continue using cut profile to finish shaping the top of the wall layers*

The profile line for the Sheathing layer should be 5/8" [16] above the profile lines for the Air Gap and the Brick. You can add a dimension inside the sketch to help you position it correctly.

5. Use detail lines, masking regions, detail components, and repeating details to add embellishment to the detail (see Figure 12.37). (Suggestions appear in the figure).

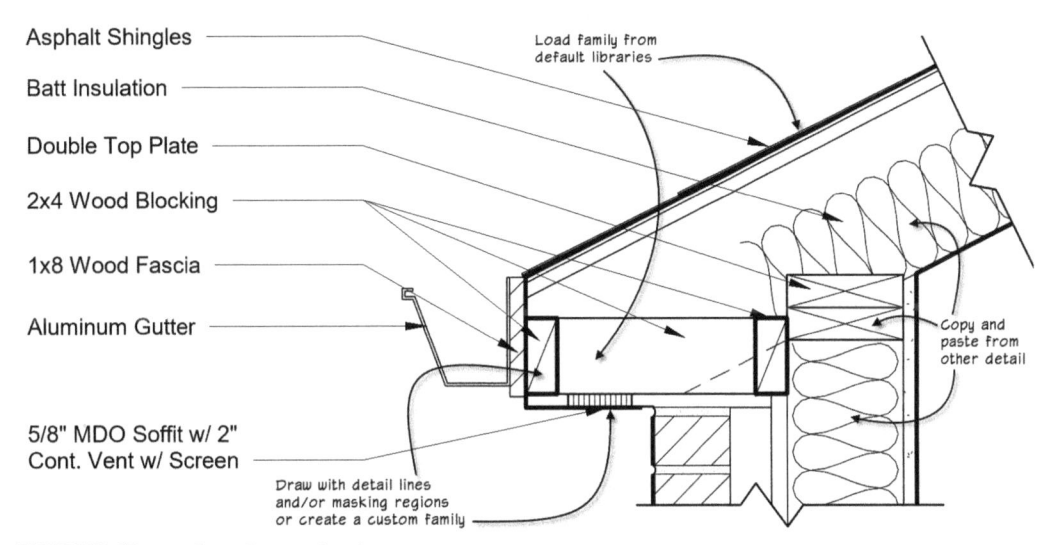

FIGURE 12.37 *Finishing the eave detail*

6. Make any additional edits and then save the project.

ADD A DETAIL SHEET

Once we have created one or more detail views, we can add them to sheets in the same fashion as other views. We explored this process back in Chapter 5. Let's review the steps here to create a new detail sheet where we can place our details.

1. On the Project Browser, right-click the *Sheets (all)* branch and choose: **New Sheet**.
   ⇨ In the "New Sheet" dialog, accept the default title block selected and then click OK.

This will create "G101 -Unnamed." This is because the last Sheet we created was Sheet G100.

2. On the Project Browser, right-click on *G101 – Unnamed* and choose: **Rename**.
   ⇨ In the Number field, type: **A601**.
   ⇨ In the Name field, type: **Details** and then click OK.

> **TIP:** You can also click directly on the (blue text) values in the title block and edit them directly on screen without right-clicking the sheet on Project Browser.

582 | Chapter 12

3. From the Project Browser, drag the *Typical Wall Foundation Detail* view and drop it on the sheet.

⇨ Click a point to place the detail. Move it around as desired to fine-tune placement.

4. On the Project Browser, double-click to open the *Longitudinal* section view (if you prefer, you can also open *A301 – Sections* sheet instead).

> **TIP:** The *A301 – Sections* sheet already contains the *Longitudinal* section view. If you are not sure which sheet contains a view, right-click it on Project browser and choose: **Open Sheet**.

Notice that the callout annotation has automatically filled in to indicate that the detail is number 1 on Sheet A601. This will also remain coordinated automatically (see Figure 12.38).

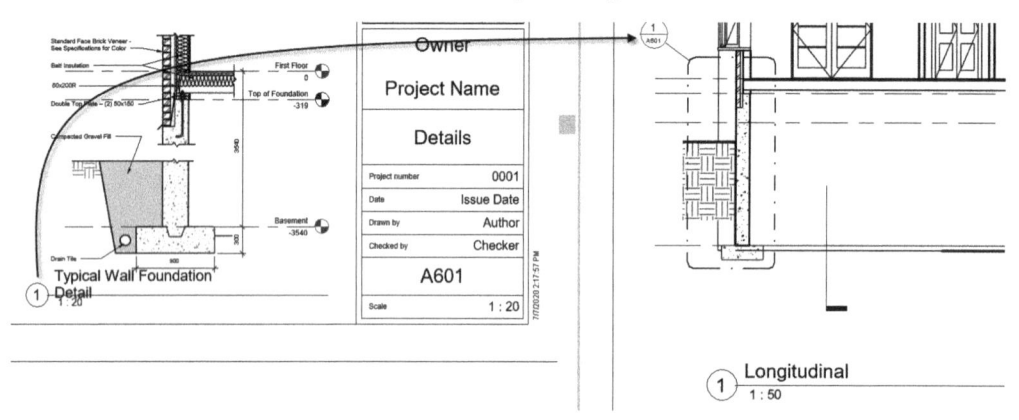

FIGURE 12.38 *Annotation will coordinate automatically after adding the detail view to a sheet*

5. Repeat the process to add the other two details to this sheet as well.

> **BIM Manager Note:** If your view titles are too long, you have a few options. You can certainly rename the view, but that is not ideal. There is also the "Title on Sheet" parameter on the Properties palette. When this is blank, the view name will be used on the view title. When you input a value in this field, the view titles will use that value instead. Alternatively, you can edit the view title family. Locate it on the Project Browser beneath the *Families > Annotation Symbols* branch. Right-click *View Title [M_ View Title]* and choose: **Edit**. Select the View Name label onscreen. On the Properties palette, click the Edit button next to Label. Check the "Wrap between parameters only" check box and then click OK. Load into Project and Close. When prompted, overwrite the existing version in the project to see the results. You can save the file when prompted if you wish, but you will need write access to its folder to do so. After this change, the title will no longer wrap to another line regardless of its length.

MANAGING VIEWS ON SHEETS

In some cases, you will add details to the sheet and then later wish to reorganize or renumber them. To do this, you select and edit the properties of the view in question. Edit the value of the "Detail Number" parameter. Be sure to type a value not yet in use—Revit will not allow you to duplicate an existing number or letter. To swap the numbers of two details, first edit one to a unique value, edit the other to the value originally used by the first, and then edit the first to the number or letter originally used by the second. If you make such a change, open the *Longitudinal* section view and note that the new numbers are reflected there as well. A change in one location is a change everywhere in Revit!

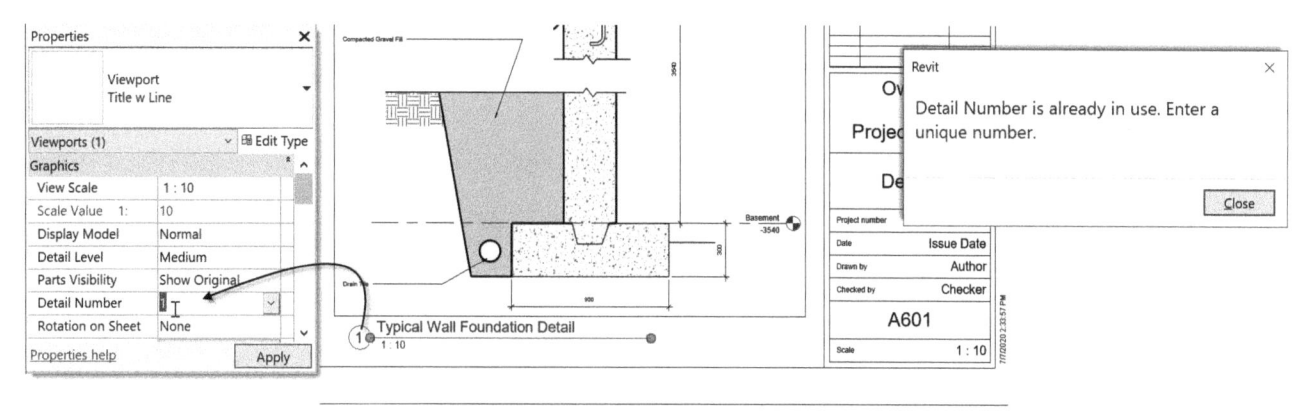

FIGURE 12.39 *The Detail Number can be edited on the Properties palette, but must be unique*

You can edit the view's properties directly from the sheet if you wish. Expand the sheet entry on the Project Browser to see a listing of all views already placed on a sheet. Click the name listed and the properties for the view will be listed on the Properties palette. You can also double-click the view from there to open it.

DRAFTED DETAILS (NOT LINKED TO THE MODEL)

In some cases, you will want to add a detail to a project that does not require a callout underlay from the model. There might be several situations where this is appropriate. Examples include typical details that are generic in nature such as a typical head, jamb, or sill detail. Other examples might include a flooring transition, typical blocking condition, wall type details or just a simple diagram of something related to the project but not specific to an area in the model. To create these kinds of details in Revit, we use a drafting view. A drafting view is like a simple blank sheet of paper. You can draw your detail on this blank page using any of the tools covered so far like detail components, filled regions, masking regions, drafting lines, and text. You can even add view references to other views if appropriate.

CREATING A DRAFTED DETAIL

In this example, we will create a drafting view and a simple carpet transition detail. This can be created either with or without a view reference callout in our floor plans. You can create it as a typical, unreferenced detail by creating a new drafting view on the View tab. If you want to reference the drafting view from a specific area of the plan, you can create a drafting view from the section and callout tools. To do this, you choose the "Reference other View" setting on the Options Bar before drawing the section or callout. For this example, we will create an unreferenced detail. In the next sequence, we will create a referenced one using the section.

1. On the View tab, on the Create panel, click the Drafting View tool.
    ⇨ In the dialog that appears, type: **Floor Transition Detail** for the name.
    ⇨ Choose: **3"=1'-0"** [**1:5**] for the scale and then click OK (see Figure 12.40).

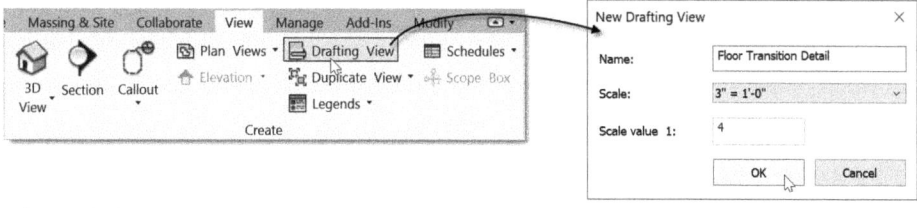

FIGURE 12.40 *Create a new drafting view*

A new drafting view will be created and opened. A drafting view is like a blank sheet of paper. There are no automatically generated graphics from the model.

584 | Chapter 12

2. On the Annotate tab, on the Detail panel, click the Component drop down button and choose the: **Detail Component** tool from the list.

3. Click the Load Family button and browse to:

   Imperial: *Detail Items\Div 06-Wood and Plastic\061600-Sheathing*.

   Metric: *Detail Items\Div 06-Wood and Plastic\06100-Rough Carpentry\06160-Sheathing*.

   ⇨ Open the *Plywood-Section.rfa* [*M_Plywood-Section.rfa*] file.

4. From the Type Selector, choose the: **3/4"** [**19mm**] type.

As before, you can find a copy of this file in *r 12* folder. Feel free to load the required detail components from there instead.

5. Click two points to create a horizontal length of plywood approximately 10" [250] long across the middle of the screen (see Figure 12.41).

   ⇨ Zoom in on the component after you draw it.

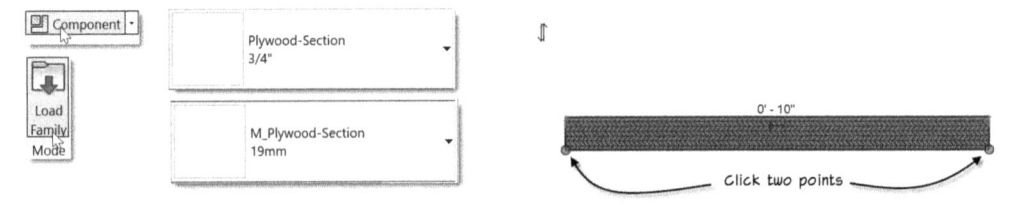

FIGURE 12.41 *Draw the plywood sub floor*

6. Click the Load Family button again and browse to:

   Imperial: *Detail Items\Div 09-Finishes\096000-Flooring\096400-Wood Flooring*.

   Metric: *Detail Items\Div 09-Finishes\09600-Flooring\09640-Wood Flooring*.

   ⇨ Open the *Wood Strip Flooring-Section.rfa* [*M_Wood Strip Flooring-Section.rfa*] file.

7. From the Type Selector, choose the: **1x3** [**19x76mm**] type.

   ⇨ Place the item on the top edge of the plywood.

Repeat the process to load four more Families from:

   Imperial: *Detail Items\Div 09-Finishes\096000-Flooring\096800-Carpeting*.

   Metric: *Detail Items\Div 09-Finishes\09600-Flooring\09680-Carpeting*.

   ⇨ *Carpeting-Section.rfa* [*M_Carpeting-Section.rfa*]

   ⇨ *Carpet Reducer at Flooring-Section.rfa* [*M_Carpet Reducer at Flooring-Section.rfa*]

   ⇨ *Carpeting Tack Strip-Section.rfa* [*M_Carpeting Tack Strip-Section.rfa*]

   ⇨ *Carpet Pad-Section.rfa* [*M_Carpet Pad-Section.rfa*]

With the first three, simply place them on screen in approximate locations for now. The *Carpet Pad-Section.rfa* [*M_Carpet Pad-Section.rfa*] family behaves like the *Plywood-Section.rfa* [*M_Plywood-Section.rfa*] family above did. You must click two points to place it.

8. You can click two points along the top edge of the plywood for this component.

9. Move and copy the carpet and wood flooring components on screen to match Figure 12.42.

• The Aubin Academy •

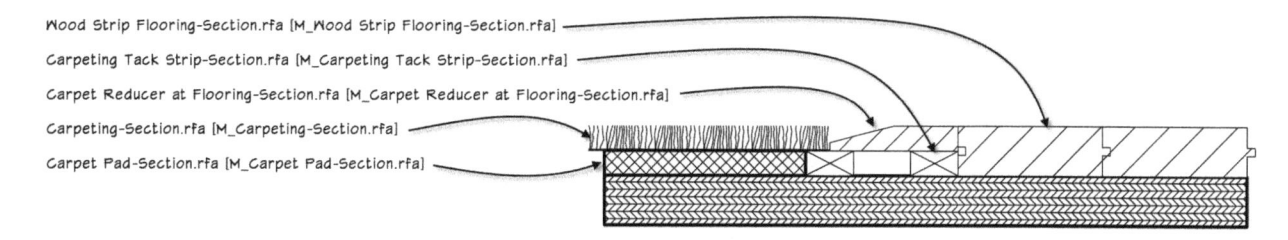

FIGURE 12.42 *Layout the detail components to create the basic detail*

10. Add a Break Line Detail Component to the end of the detail.

⇨ Edit the Element Properties of the Break Line and change the Dimensions parameters as indicated in Table 12.A.

TABLE 12.A *Sizes for the Break Mark*

Parameter	Setting
Jag Depth	1/4"[6]
Jag Width	3/8"[9]
Right	1"[25]
Left	1"[25]
Masking Depth	2"[50]

> **TIP:** Set the Jag Width and Jag Depth first and the Right and Left last. This will avoid the display of error messages.

11. Copy the Break Line to the other side, and then press the SPACEBAR twice to flip it.

12. Add notes or keynotes to complete the detail (see Figure 12.43).

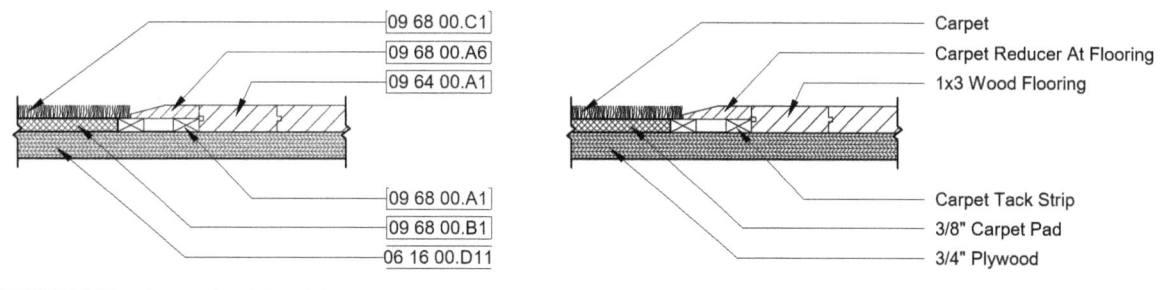

FIGURE 12.43 *The completed detail showing keynotes on the left and text notes on the right*

13. Add the detail to the *A601 – Details* sheet.

If you want this detail to be a typical detail, on the Properties palette, change the "Title on Sheet" parameter to **Typical Floor Transition Detail**. Otherwise, if you prefer to call it out from the plan, you can open the *First Floor* plan view, zoom in on an appropriate area and then click the Section tool. From the Type Selector, change the view type to: **Detail View: Detail**. Before you draw the section, check the "Reference other View" box on the ribbon and then choose: **Drafting View: Floor Transition Detail** from the list of views. Draw the section line. The callout will read detail 4 on sheet A601 (see Figure 12.44).

FIGURE 12.44 *You can optionally add a section callout that references the existing drafting view*

14. Save the file.

WORKING WITH LEGACY DETAILS

Often details are reused from one project to the next. These "standard" details are typically kept in libraries for easy reuse and retrieval. In the days before computer design and drafting software, such a library would be a three-ringed binder from which photocopies were made. With computers, these standard details are stored digitally. If your firm has been using CAD software for a while, you likely already have such a digital library of standard details. You can use these legacy files directly in your Revit projects. You simply import the DWG or DGN files into drafting views and then place them on sheets like other details.

CREATE A REFERENCED SECTION VIEW

In this tutorial we will assume that the handrail of the existing stair will be replaced with a new one. To show this, we will create a section marker callout of a handrail detail within a stair section view. However, instead of creating the actual section view in Revit or drawing an unreferenced drafting view as we did above, we'll make a referenced section that links to a drafting view and then add an AutoCAD file to it.

1. On the Project Browser, double-click to open the *First Floor* plan view.
   ⇨ Zoom in on the Stair in the middle of the plan.
2. On the View tab, click the Section tool.
   ⇨ From the Type Selector, choose: **Detail View: Detail**.
   ⇨ On the ribbon, check the "Reference other View" check box, and verify that the menu is set to: < **New Drafting View**> (see Figure 12.45).

These settings instruct Revit to create a new drafting view instead of the typical live section view of the model. The detail marker will point to this new drafting view.

3. Drag the section line through the railing as shown in Figure 12.45.

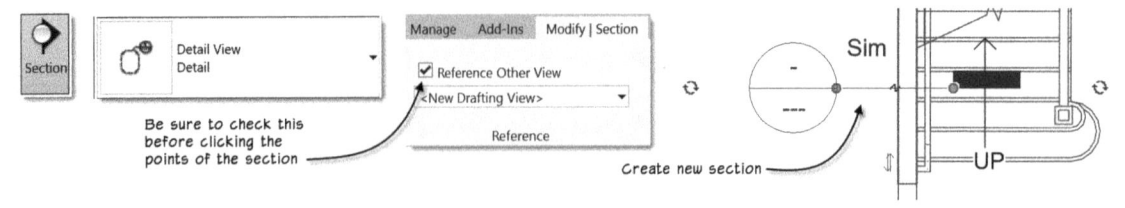

FIGURE 12.45 *Create a section that is set to reference a new drafting view*

Notice that on Project Browser, beneath *Drafting Views*, a new drafting view was created.

4. On the Project Browser, right-click the new drafting view called: *First Floor - Section 1* and choose: **Rename**.
   ⇨ Name the view: **New Railing Detail** and then click OK.
   ⇨ Double-click on the new view to open it.

We again have a blank page upon which to work. Drafting an image that makes sense relative to the detail cut location is up to you. The only reference back to the model is the callout.

LINK A CAD DRAWING

We have already seen how we can draft something from scratch. Now let's look at importing a legacy CAD file.

1. On the Insert tab, on the Import panel, click the Link CAD button.

    ⇨ In the "Link CAD Formats" dialog, browse to the *Chapter12* folder and select: *Typical Handrail Detail.dwg* [*Typical Handrail Detail-Metric.dwg*]. (Do not double-click it).

    ⇨ In the "Layer/Level Colors" area, choose: **Black and white**.

    ⇨ In the "Positioning" area, choose the: **Manual – Center** option (see Figure 12.46).

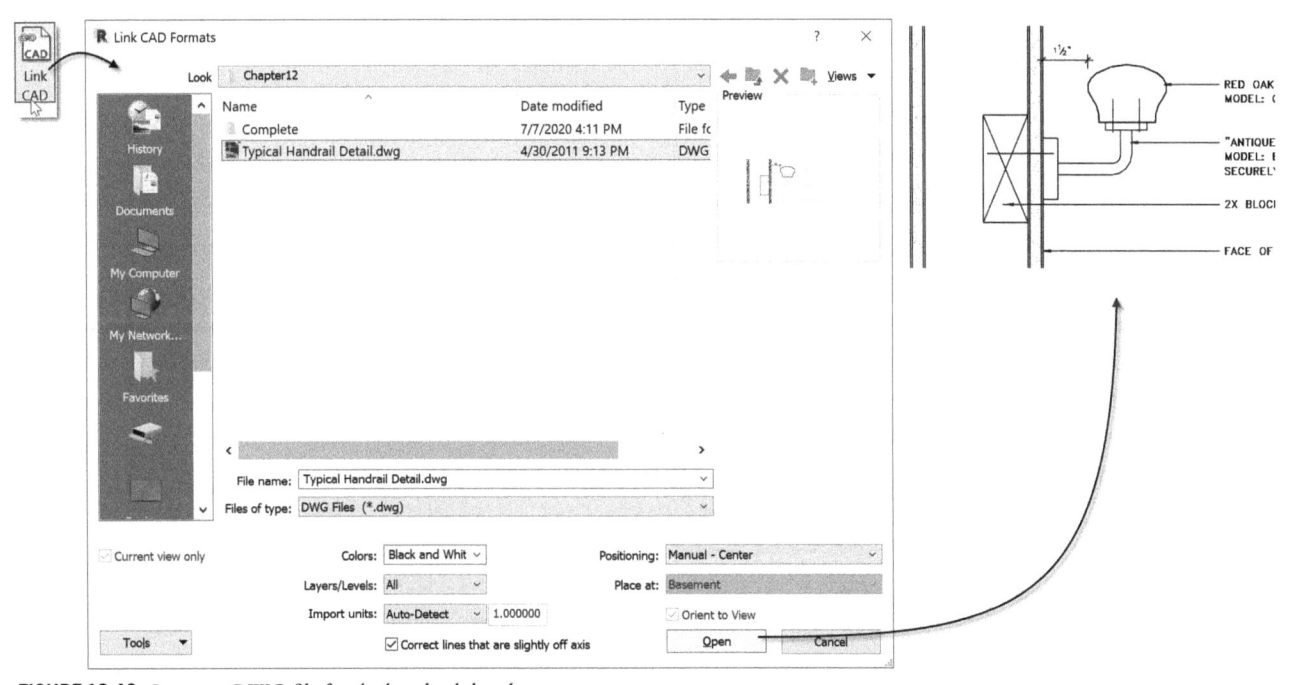

FIGURE 12.46 *Import a DWG file for the handrail detail*

2. Click Open to link the detail, and then click a point on screen to place the detail in the view.

With Link CAD, if the file were changed outside of Revit, you can simply reload the link to see the modified file. We also have the option to import the file which would embed it in the Revit project without maintaining the link. If you wish to import to the file instead, use the Import CAD tool on the Import panel instead. For a simple detail like this it makes little difference whether you choose link or import. However, most office standards will dictate using the link option. Check with your CAD/BIM Manager to be sure the best option.

3. Change the scale of the current view to: **6"=1'-0"** [**1:2**].

> **NOTE:** It is important to choose the same scale that the CAD file was created for, otherwise text and dimensions will be the wrong size when imported.

    ⇨ Zoom to fit. (Remember you can double-click your mouse wheel.)

Notice that if you change the scale, it has an impact on how the line weights of the imported view display. If you wish to experiment with the way that the line weights import, click the small dialog launcher icon on the Import panel title bar to open the "Import Line Weights" dialog (see Figure 12.47). Revit uses the line weights built into the

CAD file as is. If there are no line weights assigned to the CAD file's layers, then it looks to the colors of the layers and assigns line weights as listed in the "Import Line Weights" dialog for each color.

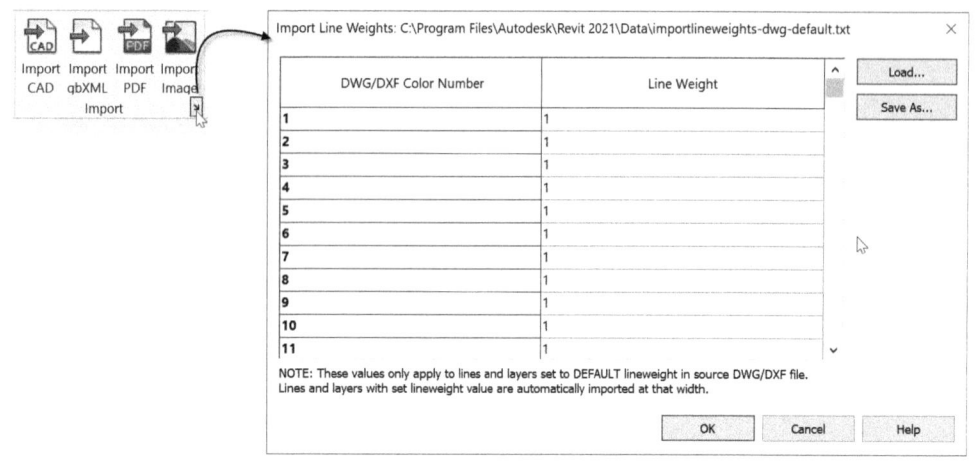

FIGURE 12.47 *Optionally set up a mapping table for layer colors and line weights*

This is a typical detail and there is no need for any changes. If we needed to make edits, we would need a copy of AutoCAD to open the file and make the required changes. After editing the file in AutoCAD, you return to Revit and use the Manage Links button on the Insert tab to reload the file. If you instead used the Insert option instead of link, you must delete the instance and re-import it to capture any changes.

> **BIM MANAGER NOTE:** If you choose to explode imported CAD files, you will discover that many element types are added to your file beyond what you see on screen or what you would otherwise expect. For example, you will likely end up with many line styles, text styles, and other elements bearing names reminiscent of the original CAD file's layers. In addition, regardless of whether you choose to explode the file, you will get materials bearing names like: Render Material 63-0-255 in your material list. In general, these items will not cause you difficulty, but they can increase the size of your files and cause confusion among team members.
> If you have decided to explode a CAD file, consider the following procedure. First, if you have access to the CAD program that created the file, open the file there first and clean up the geometry as much as possible. This includes deleting unneeded geometry and layers, purging the file, and re-saving it. Next, import the CAD file into a new empty Revit project. Explode the CAD file in this temporary project and perform additional cleanup. This will include reassigning linework to appropriate Revit line styles, changing text to Revit text types, etc. Please note that CAD dimensions and text leaders will not become Revit dimensions or leaders, so if you want actual leaders and dimensions, you will need to recreate these items. Once you have cleaned up the file to your satisfaction, you can select all the elements and copy and paste them back to a drafting view in your original project. In general, importing CAD files into Revit should not become a long-term practice. CAD files in a Revit project can unnecessarily bloat the file and cause performance problems. Over time, you will find it beneficial to recreate your standard CAD details in Revit format if you wish to continue using them in your Revit projects.

4. On the Project Browser, double-click to open the *A601 -Details* sheet view.
5. Drag the Drafting view and drop it on the Sheet.

This will become detail 5 on the sheet. If you return to the *First Floor* view, you will see that this number and sheet reference have appeared automatically in the callout (see Figure 12.48).

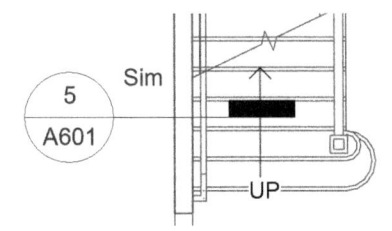

FIGURE 12.48 *Add the detail view to the Details Sheet*

    6.   Save the project.

ADDITIONAL DETAILING TECHNIQUES

Except for drafting (and legend) views, all views in the Revit project are generated directly from the building model. While Revit does a very good job of interpreting this model geometry into abstracted two-dimensional representations such as plans and elevations, there are often items that we wish to manipulate in order to create the Architectural drawings we are accustomed to producing. We have already seen all the techniques that are used to perform such edits. Until now we have used these techniques and tools only on detail views. However, you can add drafting embellishment on any Revit view including plans, sections, and elevations. All such edits, including those made with the Linework tool, filled regions, masking regions, detail components, edit cut profile, and drafting lines can be done on any view. More importantly, such edits apply only to the view in which they are applied.

EMBELLISHING MODEL VIEWS

Let's make a few enhancements to one of our elevation views.

    1.   On the Project Browser, double-click to open the *East* elevation view.

    ⇨   Close inactive views.

One common architectural drafting convention is to show the foundation in an elevation as dashed below grade. We can achieve this using a combination of the Linework tool and adding drafting lines. Let's start with the footing.

    2.   Select the Terrain element, and then on the View Control Bar, from the Temporary Hide/Isolate menu (sunglasses icon) choose: **Hide Element**.

A cyan colored boundary will appear around the viewport. Remember that this is the temporary hide/isolate command. The cyan boundary appears if some elements are temporarily hidden. Temporary hide/isolate is reset when the model is closed.

    3.   Select the Top of Foundation level, right-click and choose: **Hide in View > Elements**. (You can also use the ribbon tool.)

This is the permanent hide command. These elements will stay hidden even after closing and re-opening the model. Permanently hidden elements also do not print. To reveal hidden elements and unhide them, click the light bulb icon on the View Control Bar. If you try this now, a maroon colored border will surround the screen and the label in the corner will change to reflect the new mode. The hidden level line will appear maroon in color and the temporarily hidden terrain, which is still hidden, will appear cyan in color. You could unhide any element in this mode. Click the light bulb again to exit the mode.

    4.   On the Modify tab, on the View panel, click the Linework tool (or press LW).

    ⇨   On the ribbon, from the Line Style drop down list choose: **<Hidden>**.

    5.   Click on each of the edges of the footings to change them to <Hidden> lines.

590 | Chapter 12

Do not change any of the vertical foundation walls yet (see Figure 12.49).

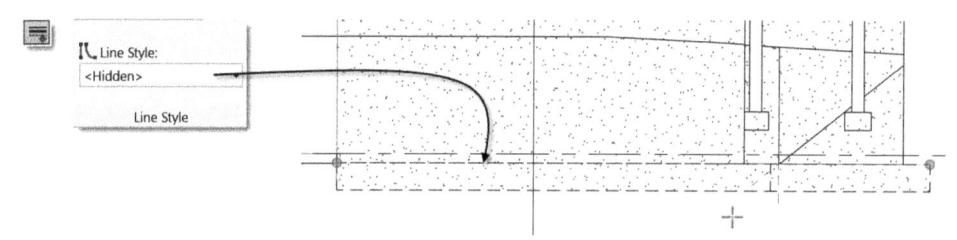

FIGURE 12.49 *Change the display of the footing lines to <Hidden> with the Linework tool*

You may need to pick more than once in the same general spot or a little to either side since there is more than one footing in the same spot in the elevation. If you are unhappy with the result, you can instead use the <Invisible lines> Type and then draw a continuous drafting line in on top. Be sure to lock the constraint padlock icon to keep the drafting line associated with the position of the footing if you take this approach.

6. On the View Control Bar, choose: **Reset Temporary Hide/Isolate**.

The terrain model will reappear. Notice that the footing still shows dashed through the terrain and is no longer hidden.

7. With the Linework tool still active, choose: **<Hidden>** from the Type Selector again.

⇨ Click on one of the vertical lines of the foundation walls.

With it still highlighted, a drag handle will appear at either end.

8. Drag the top handle down to the point where it intersects the terrain (see Figure 12.50).

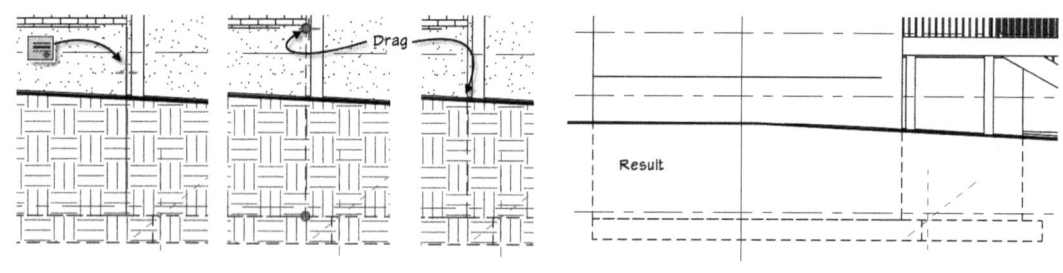

FIGURE 12.50 *Change the extent of the linework tool the drag handles (Result shown without hatching for clarity)*

9. Repeat for other vertical foundation wall edges.

Later if you wish to change the linework to a different line type or return it to its default setting, you can use the Linework tool again. To restore the default, use the <By Category> option from the drop down.

If you wish to modify the way that the terrain displays, you can use a Filled Region to trace over it. Draft additional linework as desired to complete the elevation. You can add notes, dimensions, and tags as required. If the linework tool is not working for an edge, you can try masking regions and drafting lines.

10. On the Annotate tab, on the Tag panel, click the Tag by Category tool.

⇨ On the Options Bar, clear the "Leader" check box.

11. Click on each of the Windows in the new addition. (Do not tag the windows of the existing house.)

Use Visibility/Graphics to override the color of the wall surface patterns to make the hatching a little lighter. Add some text or keynotes to the patio on the right or to indicate materials of the elevation such as brick veneer and roof shingles (see Figure 12.51).

> **NOTE:** Try the **Keynote > Material** option to keynote the materials inside the wall instead of the entire wall.

• The Aubin Academy •

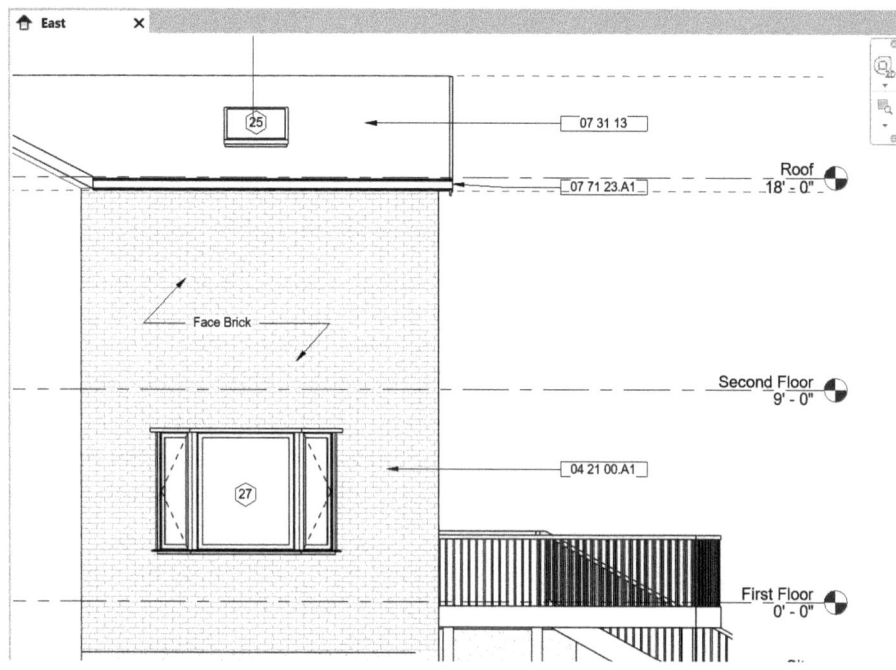

FIGURE 12.51 *Add tags and notes to complete the elevation*

Perform similar edits in other elevations if you wish.

12. Save the project.

CONTROLLING DISPLAY OF ITEMS BEYOND

To show depth in elevations, it is a common architectural convention to lighten the line weights of objects as they recede from view. We can use the Depth Cueing feature to assist with this. Like all graphical overrides, edits you make are view-specific. So, they will apply only to the view in which you make them. It may take you a little time and effort to fine-tune the elevations to display as desired, but you should be able to achieve acceptable results. We'll do a quick example here to illustrate the concept and process.

1. On the Project Browser, double-click to open the *North* elevation view.

    Feel free to repeat any of the previous edits (foundation display, notes, etc.) on this elevation before you proceed.

2. On the View Control Bar, click the Visual Style pop-up and choose: **Graphic Display Options** (or press GD).

    ⇨ In the "Graphic Display Options" dialog, expand Depth Cueing and check Show Depth.

    ⇨ Adjust the two sliders to your liking and click Apply after each change to see the results (see Figure 12.52).

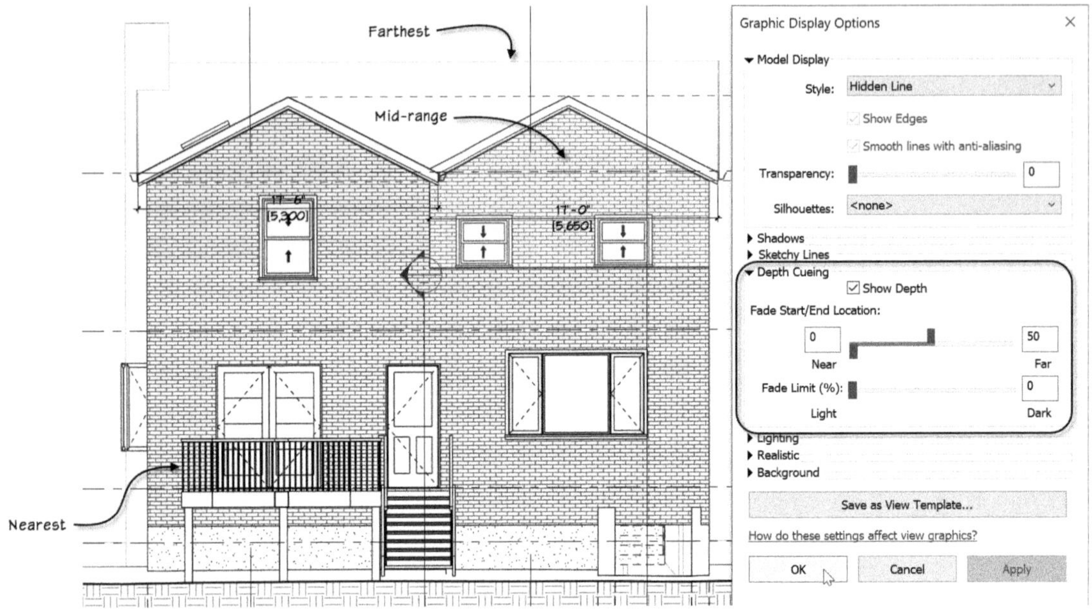

FIGURE 12.52 *Using Depth Cueing on an elevation*

This change may be hard to see without zooming in. The effect is subtle. If you want more direct control, you can override the elements in the view directly instead of using Depth Cueing. To do this, select the element(s) you want to modify, right-click and choose: **Override Graphics in View > By Element**. Make changes to the line settings and fill patterns.

3. Repeat any of these procedures on the remaining elevations and then save the project.

There is a feature called Silhouettes which will override the profile edges around your model in the current view. To access it, click the Visual Style pop-up on the View Control Bar (the tool that sets hidden line or shading) and choose: **Graphic Display Options**. In the "Graphic Display Options" dialog, you can choose a Line Style for Silhouettes. However, this feature lacks the capacity to control which edges receive the effect. Revit will determine which edges are silhouette edges and which are not. Give it a try and see if the results are satisfactory. If not, you can use the Linework tool to override the outline of elements in elevation the same way we dashed the footings.

LEGEND VIEWS

As our final exploration in this chapter, we will look at another type of two-dimensional view: The Legend view. This kind of view, as its name implies, is used to create symbol legends (or any kind of legend) in your project. When working in a legend view, you can add Legend Components. Legend components are symbolic versions of all families and types in your project, and as such are only graphical representations, not actual model elements.

1. On the View tab, on the Create panel, click the Legends drop down button and then choose the: **Legend** tool.

⇨ In the "New Legend View" dialog, input: **Door Types** for the name, choose: 1/4"=1'-0" [1:50] for the scale, and then click OK.

Like the drafting views we have created, a blank page will appear. There are two unique features of a legend view. The first is the availability of the legend component tool on the Annotate tab. The second is that a legend view is the only kind of view that can be placed on more than one sheet. We can use this tool to place a symbolic representation of any family in the project. In this case, we are building a door types legend, so we want to add elevation views of each kind of door, but do not want to add actual doors, which would throw off the count in the door schedule later. This is where the legend component comes into play.

2. On the Annotate tab, on the Detail panel, click the Component drop down button and choose the: **Legend Component** tool from the list.

⇨ On the Options Bar, from the Family list choose: **Doors: Single Flush: 36" x 80"** [**Doors: M_Single-Flush: 0915 x 2032mm**].

⇨ From the View list on the Options Bar choose: **Elevation: Front**.

3. Click a point on screen to place the symbol.

4. Repeat the process to place each of the following:

   Bifold-2 Panel: 30" x 80" [**Doors: M_Bifold-2 Panel: 0915 x 2032mm**]

   Door-Interior-Double-Sliding-2_Panel-Wood: 68" x 80" [**M_Door-Interior-Double-Sliding-2_Panel-Wood: 1800 x 2000mm**]

   Door-Exterior-Double-Full Glass-Wood_Clad: 68" x 80" [**M_Door-Exterior-Double-Full Glass-Wood_Clad: 1700 x 2100mm**]

5. Line them up next to one another. You cannot tag the symbols because they are not real doors, but you can add text and dimensions where appropriate.

⇨ Add labels, notes, and dimensions as appropriate (see Figure 12.53).

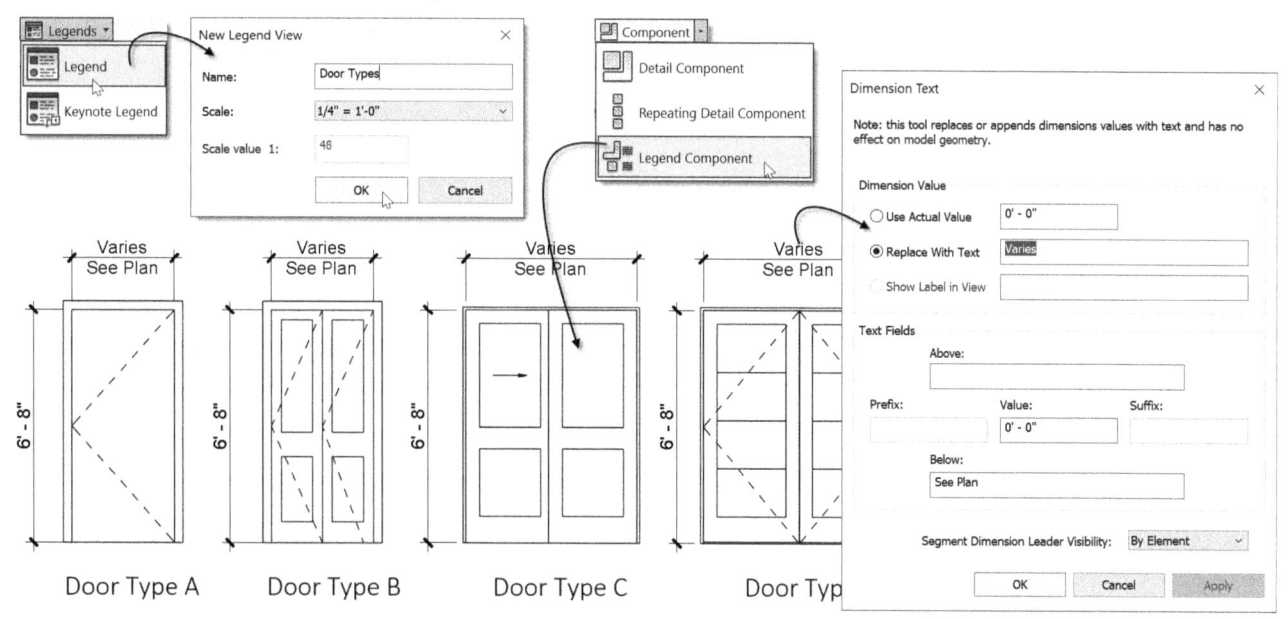

FIGURE 12.53 *Add a legend, legend components, notes and labels. Override dimension text as appropriate*

To edit the dimension values as shown in the figure, simply click on the dimension text and then edit the appropriate fields in the dialog that appears.

You can drag this legend view onto any sheet like the other views. Perhaps the most appropriate sheet for this legend would be the door schedule sheet. Since we have not created a door schedule yet, we will wait until the scheduling chapter for that task.

6. Save the project and close all files.

SUMMARY

Understanding the relationship between modeled elements and drafted elements is an important concept in Revit. Creating the basic model geometry can be accomplished in nearly any convenient view and as we have seen throughout this book and will remain coordinated as changes occur in all views. Drafting and annotation, on the other hand, occur in only the currently active view. This means that we can apply additional embellishments on top of an automatically generated model to explain and clarify design intent. We can modify the display of underlying model geometry in a variety of ways. We can also create drafting views, which contain only drafting elements and no model geometry. Using a combination of these techniques, we can fine-tune any Revit view for inclusion in our complete set of architectural construction documents.

- ☑ Detailing can occur as view-specific embellishment on top of the model and as completely independent drafting views.

- ☑ Create callout views of any overall view to create the starting point for a construction detail.

- ☑ Add view-specific detail component (2D) Families, drafting lines, repeating details, filled and masking regions to embellish the underlying model callout view.

- ☑ Each view has its own scale and visibility settings.

- ☑ Repeating detail components contain an array of detail components at a predefined spacing.

- ☑ Use masking regions in any view to hide unwanted portions of the model.

- ☑ Use filled regions to apply patterns to areas of a drawing.

- ☑ Annotate the detail with dimensions, text notes, and keynotes.

- ☑ Keynotes reference an external keynote file and help to maintain consistency in noting and reduce repetitive typing.

- ☑ Use cut profile to modify the automatically created profile of model elements within a view.

- ☑ Adding details to a sheet automatically numbers them and keeps the annotation coordinated.

- ☑ You can draw isolated two-dimensional details that do not link to the model. Use drafting views for this purpose.

- ☑ Link legacy CAD details to drafting views to leverage existing detail libraries.

- ☑ Edit any section or elevation view using similar techniques to those used to create and modify details.

- ☑ For elements that appear "beyond" in an elevation or section, use Depth Cueing to make them appear to recede.

- ☑ A legend view is a special kind of drafting view that allows symbolic representations of any project Family to be added and annotated.

CHAPTER 13
Working with Schedules, Tags and Data

INTRODUCTION

Schedules are an important part of any architectural document set. Generating schedules is often a laborious process of manually tabulating the hundreds—or sometimes thousands—of items in a project that require presentation in a schedule. For example, in firms that do not use BIM software, a door schedule involves the painstaking process of manually listing each door specified in a project and then typing in detailed information about each entry—such as size, hardware, etc. In Autodesk® Revit®, schedules are generated automatically from the building model data already in the project in real time. A schedule is simply another view of the project that differs from plans and elevations only in its presentation as tabular information rather than graphical information. You can create a schedule from nearly any meaningful information in the model and like all Revit views, you can edit in this view and see the change instantly in all views.

OBJECTIVES

In 5, we added some typical schedules to our commercial project. In this chapter, we will explore the workings of these schedules as well as create additional schedules not yet in our project. After completing this chapter, you will know how to:

- Add and modify a schedule view
- Edit model data from a schedule view
- Place a schedule on a sheet
- Work with tags
- Work with rooms and color schemes
- Add area plans and perform area calculations

CREATE AND MODIFY SCHEDULE VIEWS

In this chapter, we will return to our commercial project and look deeper into the scheduling tools in Revit. Back in 5 we simply imported schedules into the commercial project from an existing template project. We'll start with a quick review of those schedules and then take a detailed look at how to create a new schedule view from scratch. Even though we are exploring these tools in the commercial project, they would work equally well in the residential project. At the completion of this chapter, feel free to open the residential project and add some schedule views there as well.

OPEN A PROJECT

The lessons that follow require the dataset files included for download with this book. Refer to the "Download the Book Dataset" topic on page xi in the Preface for instructions on downloading and installing the book's dataset files.

1. Launch Autodesk® Revit®.
2. If you are on the Home screen, you can click the Open button beneath Models. Otherwise, from the File menu, choose **Open** > **Project**. In the "Open" dialog box, browse to the *Chapter13* folder.

   ⇨ Double-click *13 Commercial.rvt* if you wish to work in Imperial units.

   ⇨ Double-click *13 Commercial_M.rvt* if you wish to work in Metric units.

   You can also select it and then click the Open button.

VIEW AND EDIT IN EXISTING SCHEDULES

One of the most significant benefits of Revit schedules is that once you have added them to the project, they maintain themselves. In other words, even though we have not looked at the schedules since we added them back in 5, they have changed quite a bit. Let's have a look at how they have been shaping up.

1. On the Project Browser, beneath *Schedules/Quantities*, double-click to open the *Door Schedule* view.

Wow! Every door added to the project since 5 has been automatically added to the schedule. This is a live view of our project that is filtered to show only doors and present them in a list rather than a drawing. That's all there is to a schedule.

Let's focus on the Door Number column for the time being. Notice that the numbers are not sequential, and some are missing. Since a schedule is a live view, you can simply click in the door Mark field and edit the value. The results are the same as if you were editing the item from a plan or another view. You can work with a schedule and plan view tiled next to each other to assist in editing. You can also select a line item in the schedule and then click the Highlight in Model button on the Modify Schedule/Quantities tab. This highlights and zooms in on the selected item. If you do not have a suitable view window open, Revit will prompt you to allow it to search for and open alternate views. You can cycle through views to find the best one.

2. On the QAT, click the Close Inactive Views button.

   ⇨ Open the *Level 3* floor plan view, and then tile just the two windows (WT).

3. Select door 126 in the Schedule (see Figure 13.1).

   Notice how the door to the reception space highlights in the plan.

Working with Schedules, Tags and Data | 597

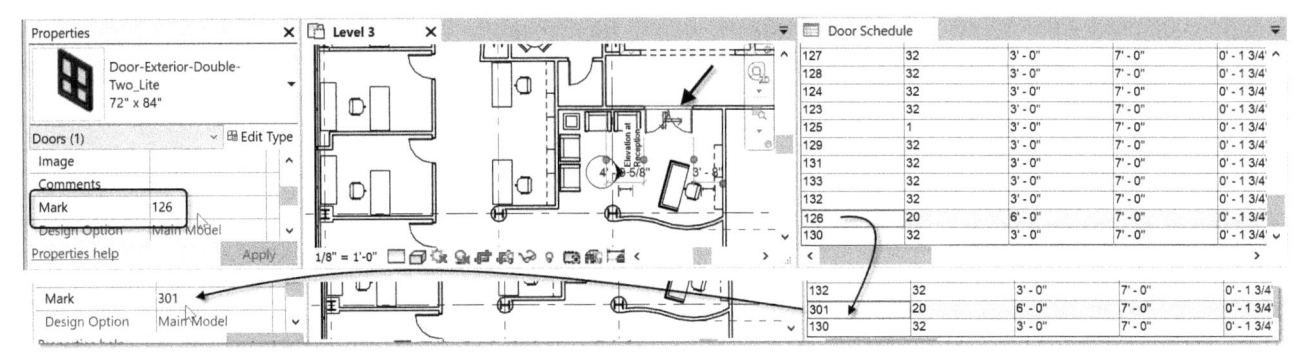

FIGURE 13.1 *Selecting an item in the schedule also highlights it in the open plan view. Changes made in the schedule can be seen on Properties*

4. In the schedule, change the number to: **301**.

No change will be evident in plan unless you click over to the plan view and then look at the Properties palette. Notice that the Mark field now displays the new number. Later we will add door tags to this plan as well. At that time you will see the new number displayed in the tag as well. We will renumber the rest of the doors later. For now, spend some time going back and forth between the plan and schedule views making selections. If you select a door in the schedule, and then click anywhere in the plan, it should stay selected. However, if you inadvertently click a second time, you will deselect the door in the plan (it will stay highlighted in the schedule however, even though it is no longer selected). To ensure that the selection is maintained, you can click the title bar of the plan view to switch views. This will ensure that you do not accidentally deselect the element(s). If you want to select more than one adjacent element on the schedule, you can click and drag through more than one element on the list. (Do not click first and then drag; click and drag in a single motion). Or you can click the first element, hold down the SHIFT key and the select another. All the items in-between the two selected elements will be highlighted on the schedule. Unfortunately, this only works for adjacent elements. If you start in the plan and select an element, it will not highlight in the schedule. So, it is usually good to start in the schedule, make the selection and then use the plan to edit.

As noted above, you have likely noticed that the doors in the schedule are not in numerical order. This is because the schedule is currently unsorted and is therefore showing items in the order that they were created. We can sort by any column in the schedule and even by more than one if appropriate. In this case, let's sort by door number.

Click on the title bar of the schedule view to make it active. Scroll down to an area where the numbers are out of order.

5. On the Properties palette, click the Edit button next to: Sorting/Grouping.

⇨ On the Sorting/Grouping tab, from the Sort by list choose: **Mark** and then click OK (see Figure 13.2).

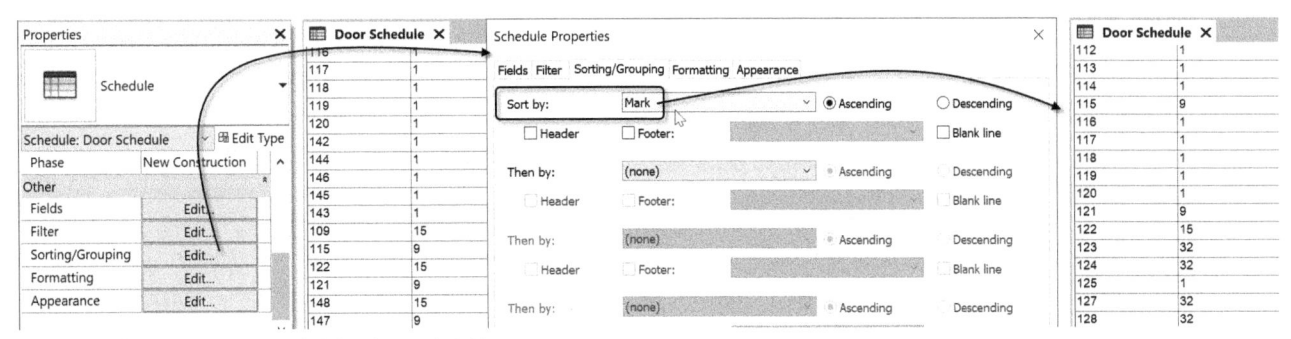

FIGURE 13.2 *Sort the door schedule by the Mark field*

The doors are now in numerical order in the schedule. They are still somewhat randomly placed in the plan, but the nice thing about the sorting is that when we later renumber the doors to more logically match the plan, they will automatically re-sort in the schedule as you renumber them. There are plenty of additional modifications that we

• Revit Essentials for Architecture •

598 | Chapter 13

could make to the *Door Schedule*. For now, however, we will leave them for later and instead create a new schedule. Before continuing, feel free to open any of the other existing schedules and study how they have come along since we set up the project.

6. Close the *Door Schedule* view.

CREATE A SCHEDULE VIEW

In Chapter 11, we added some furniture to this plan. In this topic, we will create a furniture schedule. To add a new schedule, look for the Schedules tool on the View tab of the ribbon, or we can also right-click on the *Schedule/Quantities* branch of the Project Browser.

Click the title bar of the *Level 3* floor plan view to make it active.

1. On the Project Browser, right-click the *Schedule/Quantities* branch and then choose: **New Schedule/Quantities**.

The "New Schedule" dialog will appear where we can select a category and give the schedule a name.

2. In the "New Schedule" dialog, select: **Furniture** from the Category list.

⇨ In the "Name" field, accept the default name of: **Furniture Schedule**.

3. Accept the remaining defaults and then click OK (see Figure 13.3).

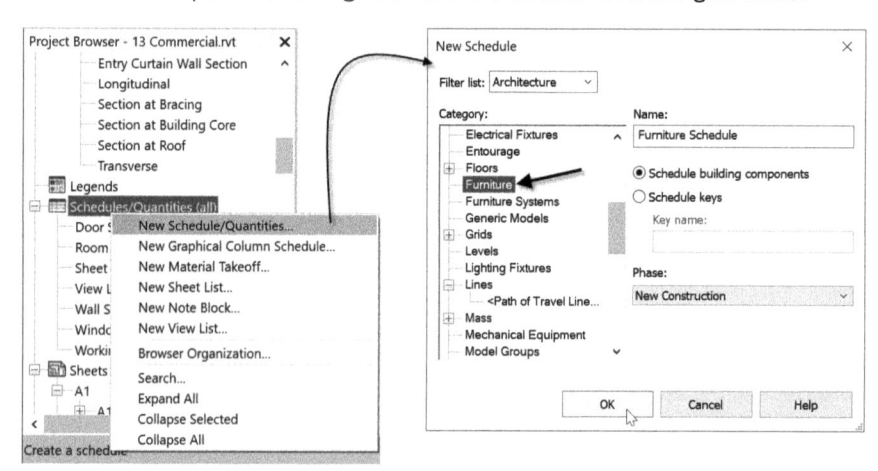

FIGURE 13.3 *Create a Furniture schedule*

The "Schedule Properties" dialog appears next. The first tab (Fields) presents a list of "Available Fields" on the left side and the fields appearing in the schedule on the right. This list includes all the parameters available for the items you are scheduling (furniture in this case). To add a field to a schedule, simply select it from the list and then click the Add parameter(s) icon to move it to the "Scheduled fields" list on the right (you can also double-click it). Once you add fields, you can adjust the display order on the right. Each field will become a column in the resultant schedule view.

4. In the "Available fields" list, choose: **Type Mark** and then click the Add button.

> **NOTE:** "Mark" is the term used for the "Number" or other unique designator of the items in the schedule. Most categories of elements include both a Mark, which is unique per instance, and a "Type Mark," which like other type parameters is common to all elements of the type.

⇨ Repeat for: **Manufacturer, Model, Cost, Count, Family and Type**, and **Comments**.

Be sure the order of fields is as listed in Figure 13.4. If you need to adjust the order, use the "Move Up" or "Move Down" buttons.

• The Aubin Academy •

Working with Schedules, Tags and Data | 599

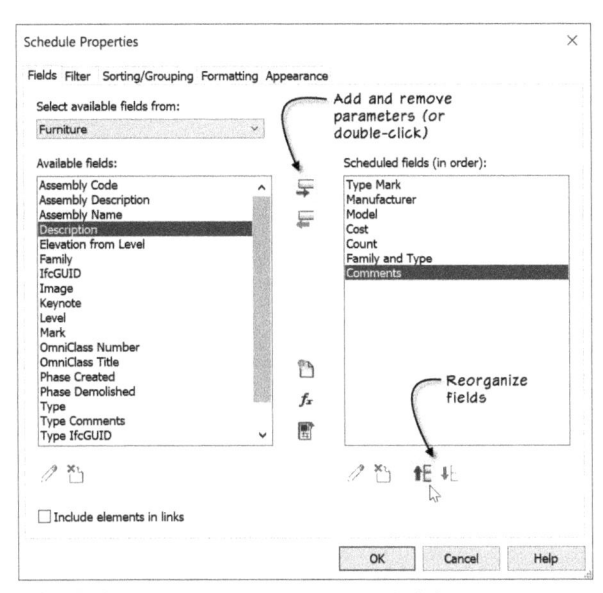

FIGURE 13.4 *Add fields to the Furniture schedule*

5. Click OK in the "Schedule Properties" dialog to create the schedule.

A *Furniture Schedule* view will appear beneath the *Schedules/Quantities* branch of the Project Browser and it will open on screen. The name of the schedule will appear at the top and directly beneath it; each field appears as a column header.

Make sure that you only have the *Furniture Schedule* and *Level 3* plan views open.

6. Switch to the *Level 3* floor plan view.

⇨ On the View tab, click the Tile button (or type: WT).

NOTE: If you use the keyboard shortcut to tile the windows, make sure that the floor plan is the active view before you type the shortcut. Shortcuts do *not* work while a schedule is active. This is because Revit will assume you are editing the data in the schedule. So if you type WT for example, and nothing happens, check your schedule and you will see the letters WT somewhere in whatever field was active in the schedule.

SCHEDULE APPEARANCE

If you scroll through the schedule you will see that there are several items listed, but as we scroll, we can lose track of where we are. There are a couple features we can enable in the schedule to make scrolling easier.

1. Switch to the *Furniture Schedule* tab.
2. Scroll through the schedule.

If your screen has low resolution, it is possible that you cannot see all lines of the schedule at once.

3. On the Modify Schedule/Quantities tab, click the Freeze Header button (see Figure 13.5).

⇨ Scroll again. Notice that the header will now remain at the top as you scroll.

• Revit Essentials for Architecture •

FIGURE 13.5 *Turn on the Freeze Headers option to keep headers from scrolling*

You can also zoom in the schedule view. To do this, you can either use the CTRL key with the + or – keys, or the CTRL key as you roll the wheel on your mouse. Give it a try.

We have one other option that can help with scrolling and viewing a large schedule. We can stripe the rows in alternating colors.

4. Make sure the schedule is the active view, and then on the Properties palette, click the Appearance Edit button.

   ⇨ In the "Schedule Properties" dialog, check the box next to: Stripe Rows.

   ⇨ Click the small color swatch icon next to First Row Stripe Color and choose your preferred color.

   ⇨ You can repeat for the Second Row Stripe Color if you wish.

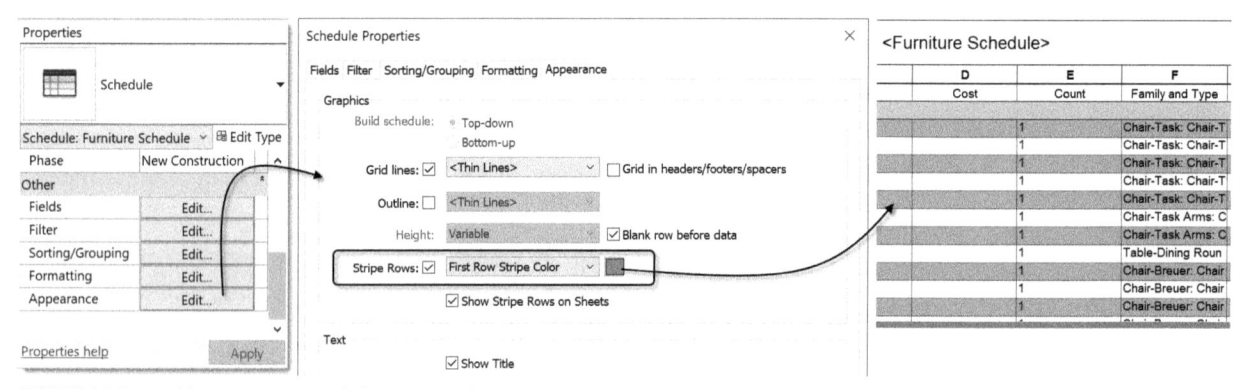

FIGURE 13.6 *Enable Stripe Rows and choose your colors*

5. Click OK to apply the result (see Figure 13.6).

EDIT MODEL ELEMENTS FROM THE SCHEDULE

Schedules can be a great way to edit your model.

1. Zoom in on the plan view to just the tenant suite on the left side (as close as you can while still seeing all furniture).

2. Click on any field in the schedule view. Repeat on as many elements as you wish.

As we saw with the door schedule, the corresponding furniture element highlights in the plan view.

3. Click in the "Type Mark" field for the first element in the list.

Notice that a standard text cursor appears in the field and you could begin typing a value.

   ⇨ Click in the "Manufacturer" column next.

   ⇨ Continue to click in each field in succession.

Working with Schedules, Tags and Data | 601

Notice that "Manufacturer" and "Model," however, appear with a drop down list icon. If you try to open the list, it will appear empty. The way these fields work is that you can type in any value, as in the plain text fields, but these values you type will begin populating a list that you can choose from in subsequent edits. Let's try it.

4. Widen the Family and Type column enough to read the values.

    To do this, click and drag the edge between the Family and Type and Comments headers.

5. Scroll as necessary and locate the first instance of Desk-Secretary and then click in the "Comments" field next to it.

    ⇨ Type: **Include Keyboard Tray and Footrest Option** and then press ENTER (see Figure 13.7).

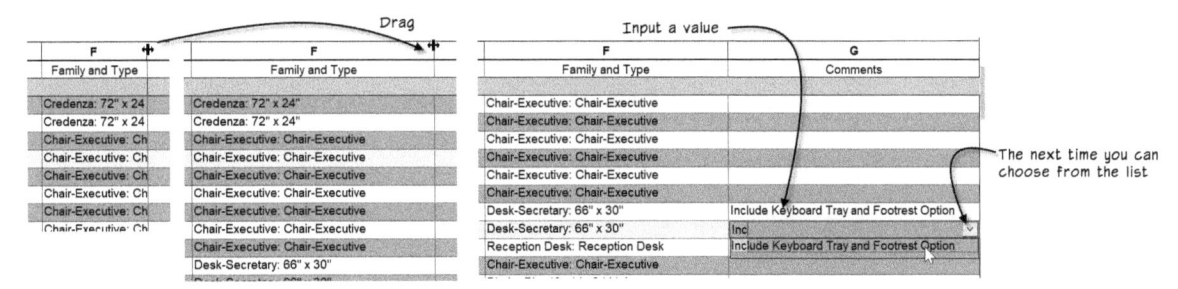

FIGURE 13.7 *Input a value in a list field*

There is a second secretarial desk beneath the one we just edited.

6. Click in the "Comments" field of the second secretarial desk and then click the drop down list icon.

Notice that the note typed above now appears in the list. Each new item you type will be added automatically to this list making it easier to input existing values—simply choose them from the list. You can also begin typing and an instant search will be performed which will make it easier to locate the item you want on long lists.

In a schedule you can include instance parameters like the one edited here, or type parameters. Instance parameters allow for a unique value for each instance of the item in the project as required. In this case, it would be possible to order a keyboard tray and footrest for one of the secretarial desks but not the other. With a type parameter, the value applies to *all* instances of the type in question. This is the case with "Manufacturer," "Model," and "Cost" fields. The assumption here being that the family and type in question represents an item that can be ordered from a catalog, purchased, and installed in the project. Therefore, the Manufacturer, Model, and Cost would be the same for all instances of that item. For our purposes, these behaviors are perfectly logical. However, in your own projects, if you wish to modify these behaviors, you must edit the families of the elements in question (refer to Chapter 11 for more information on editing families and for examples of both type and instance parameters). Let's edit a type parameter next.

7. Click in the "Manufacturer" field for one of the non-secretarial desks.

    ⇨ Type: **Acme Furniture** and then press ENTER.

8. A dialog will appear indicating that this change will apply to all instances of this type (see Figure 13.8). Click OK to accept this change.

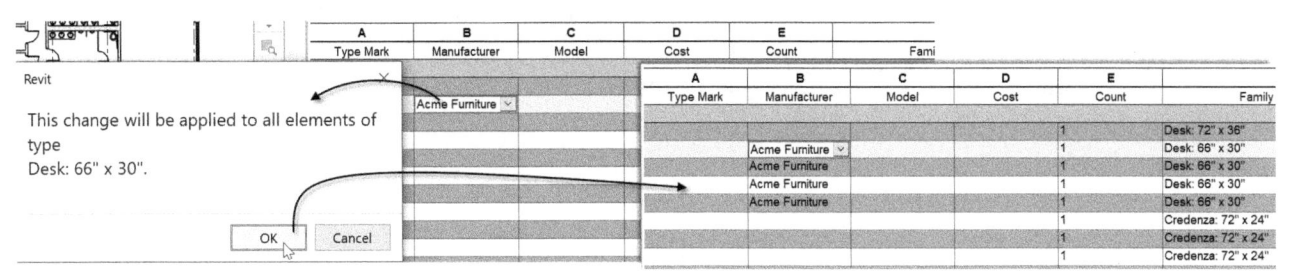

FIGURE 13.8 *Applying a change to a type parameter*

Scroll down in the Schedule and notice that the change has been applied to several desks.

• Revit Essentials for Architecture •

⇨ Repeat the process to add a Model designation and Cost to the same Desk. Use any values you like.

9. From the "Manufacturer" column next to: *Chair-Executive* [*M_Chair-Executive*] family, choose the **Acme Furniture** value.

⇨ Again, when you make this edit, it will apply at the type level. Click OK to confirm the change.

⇨ Add a Model and Cost to the Chair as well (see Figure 13.9).

10. Using the same process, assign a Manufacturer, Model, and Cost to the Corbu and Breuer chairs.

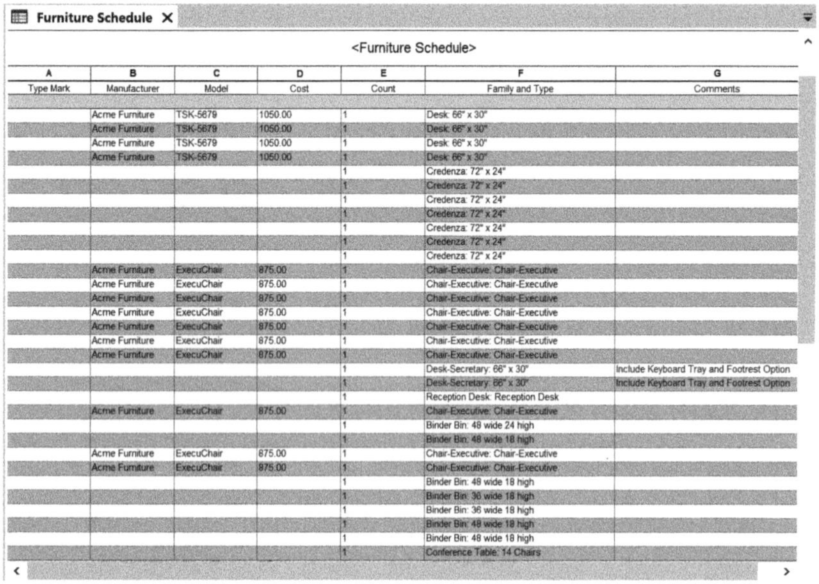

FIGURE 13.9 *Input several type parameters*

Be sure to click on the in-cell drop down and note how the list includes each new item you type in that field.

11. Save the project.

SORTING SCHEDULE ITEMS

Since many of the values in schedule are identical for several items, it might be nice to sort and group some of these values in the schedule instead of listing each element separately and showing so much repetition.

1. On the Properties palette, next to "Sorting/Grouping," click the Edit button (shown in Figure 13.2 above).

⇨ At the top of the dialog, from the "Sort by" list, choose: **Manufacturer** and then click OK.

Scroll to the bottom of the schedule to see the results.

All the blank fields (which are listed first in an alphabetic sort) are now at the top of the list, and the "Acme Furniture" items are next. The desks and chairs are still interspersed. If you wish, you can sort by more than one criterion.

2. On the Properties palette, click the Edit button next to Sorting/Grouping again.

⇨ At the top of the dialog, beneath "Sort by," from the "Then by" list choose: **Model** and then click OK (see Figure 13.10).

Working with Schedules, Tags and Data | 603

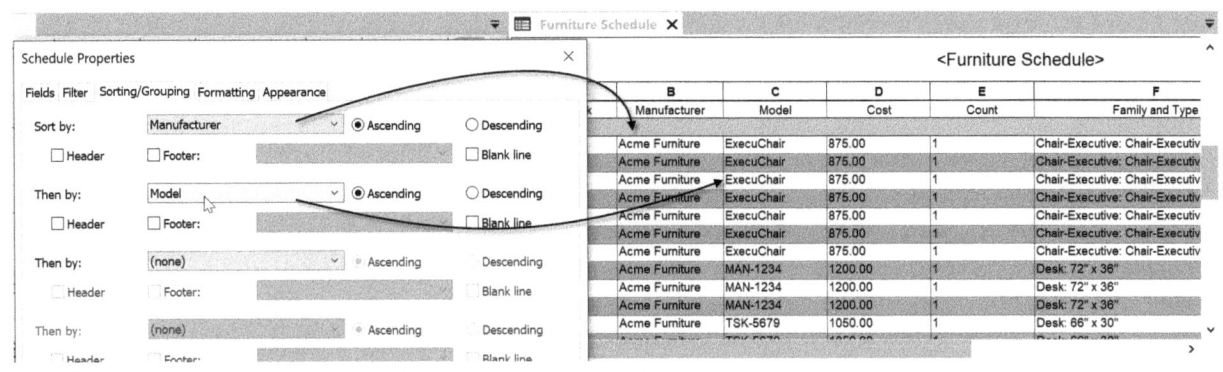

FIGURE 13.10 *Sorting the schedule first by Manufacturer, then by Model*

Several items in the schedule still do not have parameters assigned. Let's edit another item and see how the schedule responds with our current sort settings.

3. Locate an instance of the "Chair-Task" in the schedule and edit the "Manufacturer" to: **Furniture Concepts**.

⇨ Click OK in the dialog that appears.

Notice that the schedule immediately re-sorts to accommodate the new value.

4. Input a Model and Cost as well.

GROUPING SCHEDULE ITEMS

In addition to sorting the items in the schedule, we can also group them when all the values are the same. It would be easier to work with the schedule if we simply had one listing for each type of chair that reported how many there were instead of showing each as a separate line item. We need to make a simple change to display the schedule this way.

1. Return to the Sorting/Grouping tab of "Schedule Properties" dialog.

⇨ At the bottom of the dialog, clear the "Itemize every instance" check box.

2. Click the Fields tab.

⇨ Move the Count field to the bottom of the list and then click OK (see Figure 13.11).

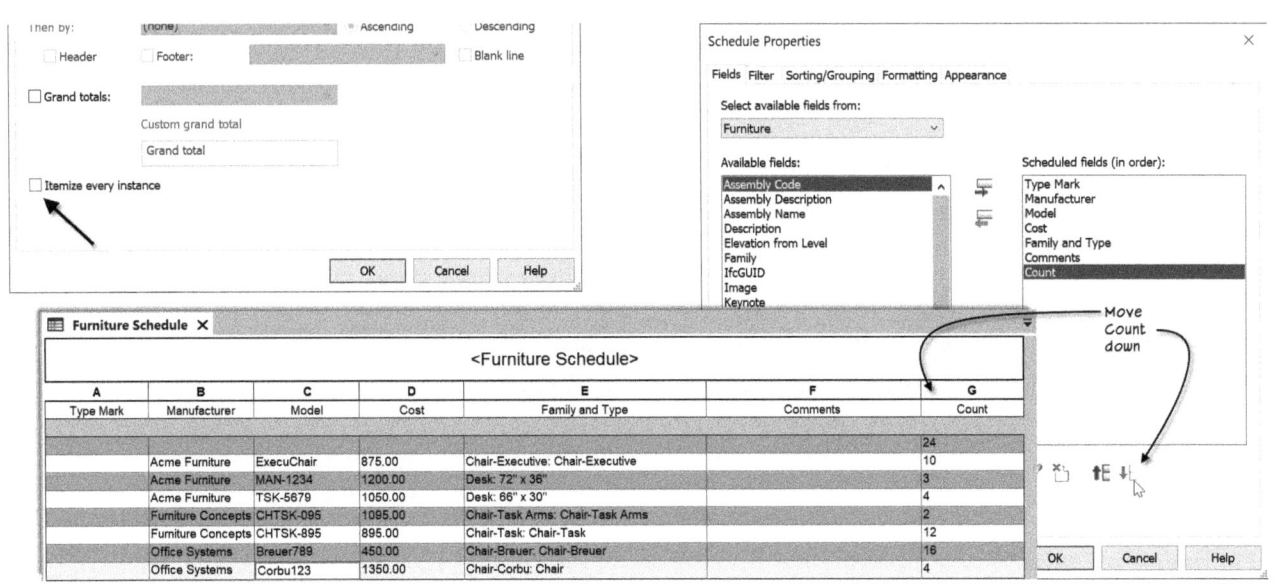

FIGURE 13.11 *Group items and show the count*

• Revit Essentials for Architecture •

There are nearly limitless ways that we can format and display the same data. Notice the way the blank fields at the top (Count 24 in the figure) show none of the values even though we have data (particularly family and type) for some of the values. This is because we are sorting on the Manufacturer and Model fields only and those fields are blank for those 24 items. If you edit the Schedule Properties and sort first by Family and Type instead, the result will change dramatically (see Figure 13.12).

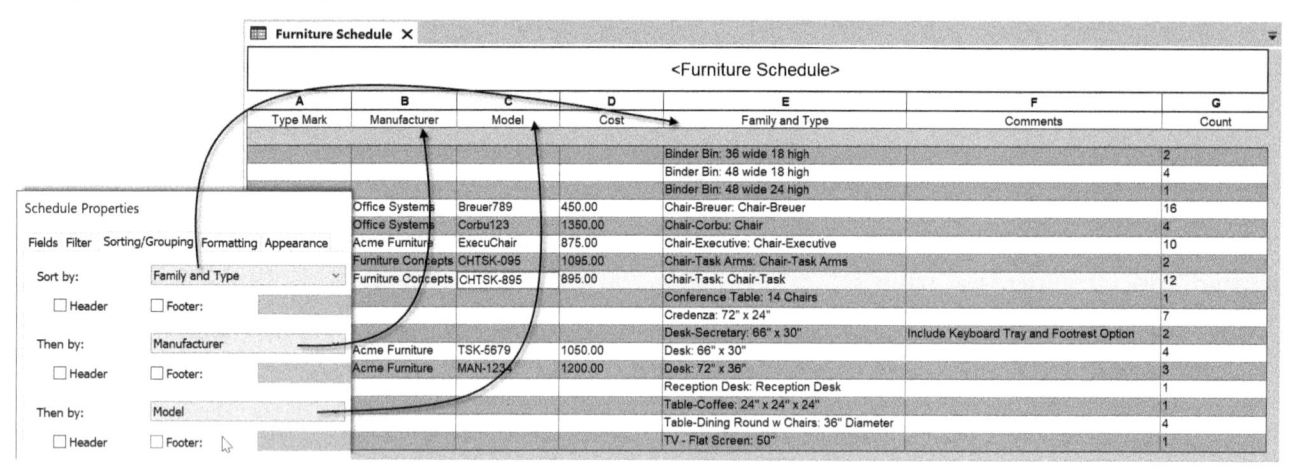

FIGURE 13.12 *Sort by Family and Type instead of Manufacturer*

Look at the Acme Furniture items. There are three separate entries because there are three separate families assigned to this manufacturer. Add up the items with blank Manufacturer, Model, and Cost and you will see that the total is still 24, only now can we continue to edit them because each family and type is listed separately.

DUPLICATING A SCHEDULE VIEW

The current format of our schedule view is useful for editing but is perhaps not ideal for reporting furniture and making budgetary and purchasing decisions. Sometimes you will find it useful to have two versions of the same view—one for working purposes, the other for presentation and printing. This is true of any kind of view, schedule, plan, or elevation, etc.

1. On the Project Browser, right-click *Furniture Schedule* and choose: **Duplicate View > Duplicate**.
2. Right-click *Furniture Schedule Copy 1* and choose: **Rename**.
   ⇨ In the "Rename View" dialog, type: **Working Furniture Schedule** and then click OK.

We'll use our working version of the schedule when we need to make quick edits. And below we will format the original differently for purposes of reporting the data in a more useful way. Regardless of where we make the edit, it will show in all views—both furniture schedules and the model. Before we edit the original schedule to format it more appropriately for printing, let's first complete the modifications to our furniture.

3. Edit the remaining items to add Manufacturers, Models, and Costs.
4. Add a code in the Type Mark column for each item. They can be any alpha numeric codes you like (see Figure 13.13).

Working with Schedules, Tags and Data | 605

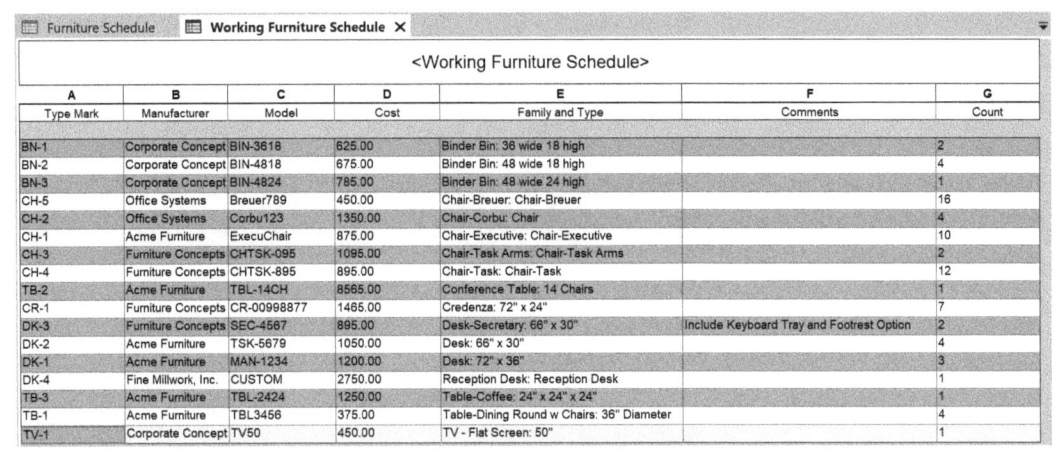

Type Mark	Manufacturer	Model	Cost	Family and Type	Comments	Count
				<Working Furniture Schedule>		
BN-1	Corporate Concept	BIN-3618	625.00	Binder Bin: 36 wide 18 high		2
BN-2	Corporate Concept	BIN-4818	675.00	Binder Bin: 48 wide 18 high		4
BN-3	Corporate Concept	BIN-4824	785.00	Binder Bin: 48 wide 24 high		1
CH-5	Office Systems	Breuer789	450.00	Chair-Breuer: Chair-Breuer		16
CH-2	Office Systems	Corbu123	1350.00	Chair-Corbu: Chair		4
CH-1	Acme Furniture	ExecuChair	875.00	Chair-Executive: Chair-Executive		10
CH-3	Furniture Concepts	CHTSK-095	1095.00	Chair-Task Arms: Chair-Task Arms		2
CH-4	Furniture Concepts	CHTSK-895	895.00	Chair-Task: Chair-Task		12
TB-2	Acme Furniture	TBL-14CH	8565.00	Conference Table: 14 Chairs		1
CR-1	Furniture Concepts	CR-00998877	1465.00	Credenza: 72" x 24"		7
DK-3	Furniture Concepts	SEC-4567	895.00	Desk-Secretary: 66" x 30"	Include Keyboard Tray and Footrest Option	2
DK-2	Acme Furniture	TSK-5679	1050.00	Desk: 66" x 30"		4
DK-1	Acme Furniture	MAN-1234	1200.00	Desk: 72" x 36"		3
DK-4	Fine Millwork, Inc.	CUSTOM	2750.00	Reception Desk: Reception Desk		1
TB-3	Acme Furniture	TBL-2424	1250.00	Table-Coffee: 24" x 24" x 24"		1
TB-1	Acme Furniture	TBL3456	375.00	Table-Dining Round w Chairs: 36" Diameter		4
TV-1	Corporate Concept	TV50	450.00	TV - Flat Screen: 50"		1

FIGURE 13.13 *Finish inputting values for all empty fields*

Notice that now when you click in a field and make an edit, all the corresponding elements now select in the plan. This is because you are selecting all these items consolidated in that row.

5. Save the project.

HEADERS, FOOTERS, AND GRAND TOTALS

The Count field is not the only way to have Revit tabulate the quantity of items. If you wish to show totals above or beneath the groupings, you can add Headers and Footers and Grand Totals to the schedule as well.

1. Close the *Working -Furniture Schedule* and return to the *Furniture Schedule*.

   ⇨ On the Properties palette, click the Edit button for Sorting/Grouping.

2. Change the first criterion back to: **Manufacturer**.

   ⇨ Beneath Manufacturer, place a checkmark in the "Header" check box and the "Footer" check box and accept the default of: **Title, count, and totals**.

3. Change the next criterion to: **Model**.

4. Change the third criterion to: **(none)**.

5. At the bottom of the dialog, check the "Grand totals" check box and accept the default of: **Title, count, and totals**.

   ⇨ If you wish you can input your own label for the grand total such as: **Total of all Furniture Items**.

   ⇨ Click OK to see the results (see Figure 13.14).

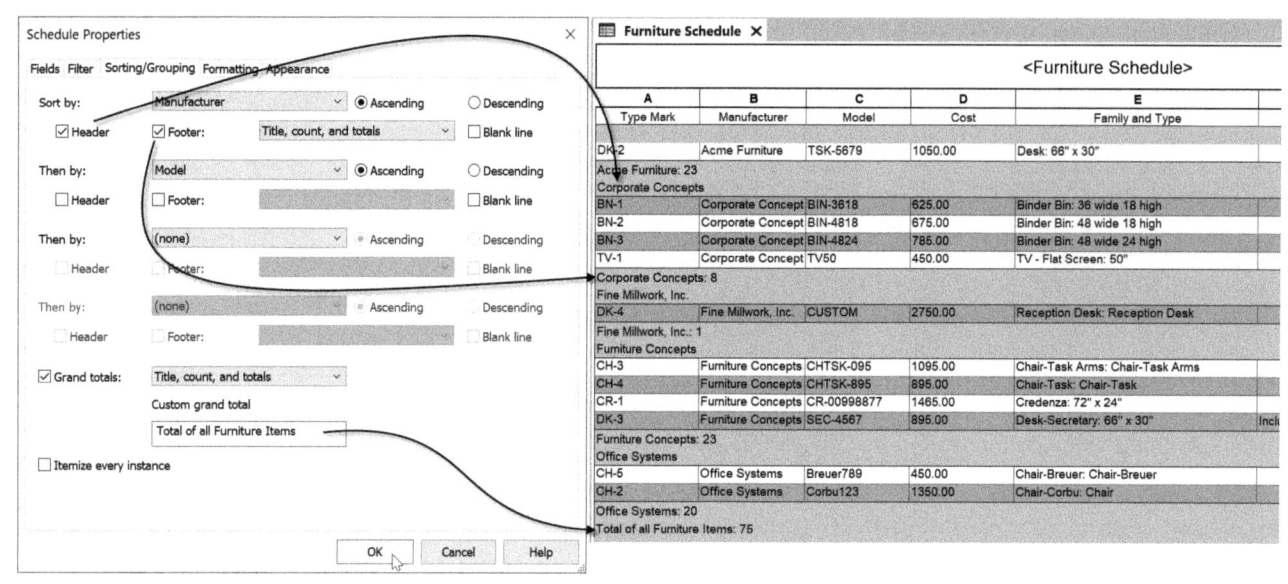

FIGURE 13.14 *Enable Headers, Footers, and Grand totals and study the results*

Several other combinations are possible. You have control over whether footers show totals, counts, and/or titles. Same for the grand total. If you wish to put a bit of space between each sort criterion, you can use the "Blank line" check box. In some cases, this will make your sub totals easier to read, particularly when there are many items in the schedule. If you would like to see for yourself, edit the properties once more and place a checkmark in the "Blank line" check box for the Manufacturer sort criterion only.

THE FILTER TAB

Sometimes you only need part of the information available. Suppose you were on the phone with your sales representative from Acme Furniture. You could create a version of your furniture schedule that listed only the items that you are specifying from this manufacturer.

1. Right-click the *Furniture Schedule* on Project Browser and choose: **Duplicate View > Duplicate**.

    ⇨ Rename it: **Furniture – Acme Furniture**.

2. On the Properties palette, click the Edit button next to "Filter."

3. From the "Filter by" list, choose: **Manufacturer**.

About a dozen operations are possible: equals, begins with, etc.

    Leave the next list set to: **equals**.

    ⇨ From the third list, choose: **Office Systems** and then click OK (see Figure 13.15).

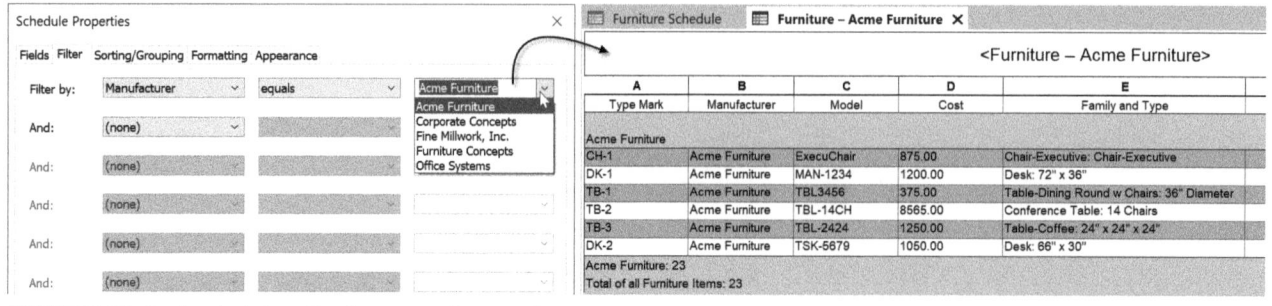

FIGURE 13.15 *Set the schedule to filter by a particular manufacturer*

Notice that the schedule now *only* shows the items from Office Systems. You can try other filters if you wish. Just be certain to always name such a schedule descriptively. You would not want someone to inadvertently think that the schedule they have open includes all the furniture. So, by making it clear that this is a filtered schedule, you can avoid such errors.

4. Close this schedule and return to the *Furniture Schedule*.

THE FORMATTING TAB

Let's take a brief look at the remaining two tabs. On the formatting tab you can configure the orientation and alignment of each individual field. On the appearance tab, you configure the look of the overall schedule as it will appear when printed from sheets. Many of the features in these two tabs can also be configured on the Modify Schedule/Quantities ribbon.

1. On the Properties palette, click the Edit button next to: Formatting.
2. Select the Cost field in the list at the left.
   ⇨ Change the "Alignment" to: **Right**.
   ⇨ From the list at the bottom choose: Calculate totals.

Since the Cost field is numerical (currency), right justification makes more sense. Adding the calculate totals will total up the cost of all items based on the quantities in the Count column. If you want to add a currency symbol to the numbers, you can click the Field Format button. In the "Format" dialog, uncheck "Use project settings" and then configure your preferred unit settings (see Figure 13.16). These settings will only apply in this schedule. If you want to change the project defaults instead, on the Manage tab, click the Project Units button. You can make similar edits there and they will apply throughout the project.

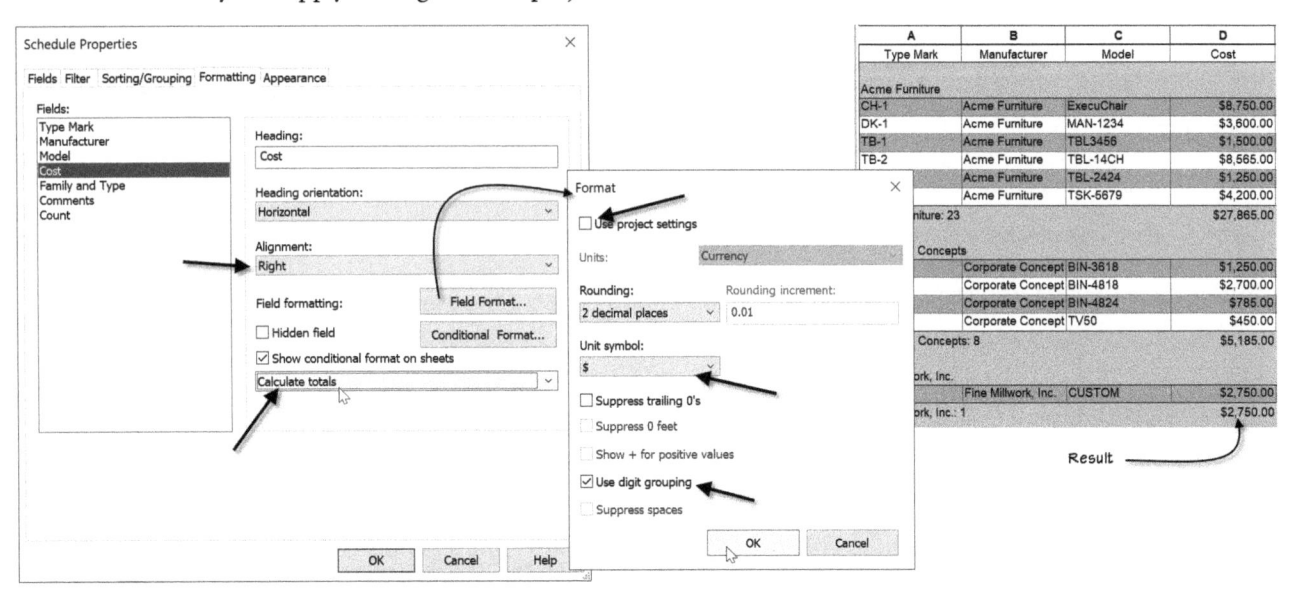

FIGURE 13.16 *Set the formatting options for the Cost field*

3. Click OK to see the results.

You should now have totals for the cost at each subtotaled grouping. The numbers should also justify to the right.

608 | Chapter 13

FORMATTING FROM THE RIBBON

Many of the formatting features are also available on the ribbon. Sometimes we add a field to help us in building the schedule, but later do not need the information anymore. One such field is the Family and Type field. Now that we have input all the other data, this column does not display very useful information for the final schedule.

1. At the top of the Family and Type click the column indicator (currently column "E").

If you look at the plan view, you should see that this action selects all furniture elements in the model.

⇨ On the ribbon, on the Columns panel, click the Hide button (see the left side of Figure 13.17).

The column will disappear. Column E is now the Comments column and it should now be selected.

2. Keep Comments selected and then click the Resize button (see the right side of Figure 13.17).

⇨ In the "Resize Column" dialog, input: **3"** [**75**] and then click OK.

This is the actual width of the column as it will appear when printed on a sheet. If you click and drag through more than one column, you can select multiple columns at once. Actions like Hide and Resize would then apply to all selected columns. If you resize this way, the value you input will be the total for all selected columns split evenly among them. Try it out if you like.

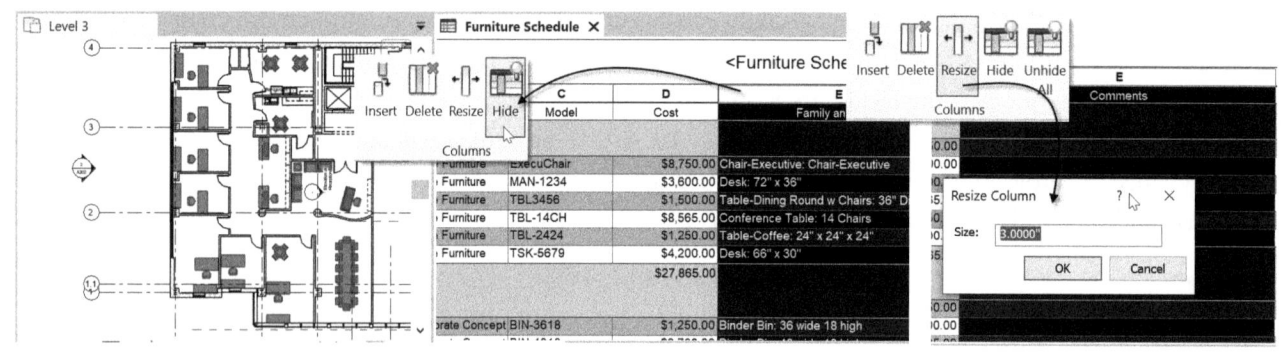

FIGURE 13.17 *Set the formatting options of several fields using the ribbon*

3. Click on the Count column (column F).

⇨ On the Appearance panel, click the Align Horizontal drop down and choose: **Right**.

Most of these changes display immediately in the view. Since we have the headers turned on for Manufacturer, we really don't need that column either. So, we can repeat the steps from above to hide it as well.

ADD A SCHEDULE TO A SHEET

There are several other options available on the ribbon. Some are visible in the schedule view, and for others we need to add the schedule to a sheet. You add a schedule view to a sheet the same way as any other view.

1. Create a new sheet from the default title block and name it: **A602 – Schedules**.

We have several schedules already on the other schedule sheets, so creating a new sheet will give us plenty of room to work.

2. From Project Browser, drag *Furniture Schedule* and drop it on the sheet.

⇨ Click a point near the top left corner of the sheet to place it.

Notice that with the Schedule still selected, there are control handles at the top of each column. You can use these to interactively change the width of each field however, notice that the Comments column that we sized above is already

• The Aubin Academy •

Working with Schedules, Tags and Data | 609

at the desired size. So, you can resize interactively with these control handles, or you can set the size of columns to exact values as we did above. The choice is up to you.

Since we created a new sheet and have plenty of room, let's resize each of the field widths to prevent the data from wrapping to a second line as it does by default. To do this, you simply drag the control handles to the right. Work from left to right across the schedule. Changes made here will be reflected in the view and vice/versa.

3. Resize each column as required to prevent wrapping (see Figure 13.18).

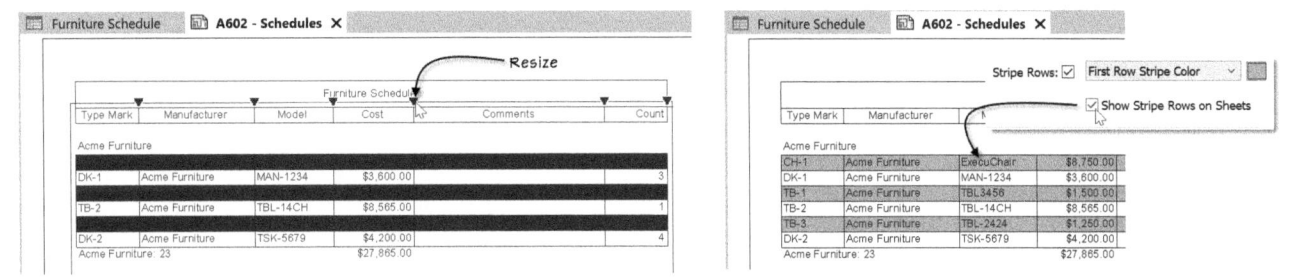

FIGURE 13.18 *Edit the width of the fields interactively on the sheet*

Notice that the striped rows show on the schedule. You can turn this off if you prefer. Return to the Appearance tab and uncheck "Show Stripe Rows on Sheets".

ADJUSTING SCHEDULE APPEARANCE

There are many other buttons on the ribbon that allow us to adjust the appearance of the schedule. These include: shading, borders and fonts.

1. Double-click the schedule on the sheet, (or right-click and choose: **Edit Schedule**).

This will reopen the schedule view.

2. In one smooth motion, click and drag through all the header text fields at the top.

    Start in Type Mark and drag to Count. Remember, click and drag. If you click first, it won't work.

3. Click the Font button.

    ⇨ Check the Bold box and make any other edits you choose.

4. Click the Borders button.

    ⇨ Click the None button. Select Wide Lines on the left and then click the Outside button.

    ⇨ Click OK to see the result (see Figure 13.19).

• Revit Essentials for Architecture •

610 | Chapter 13

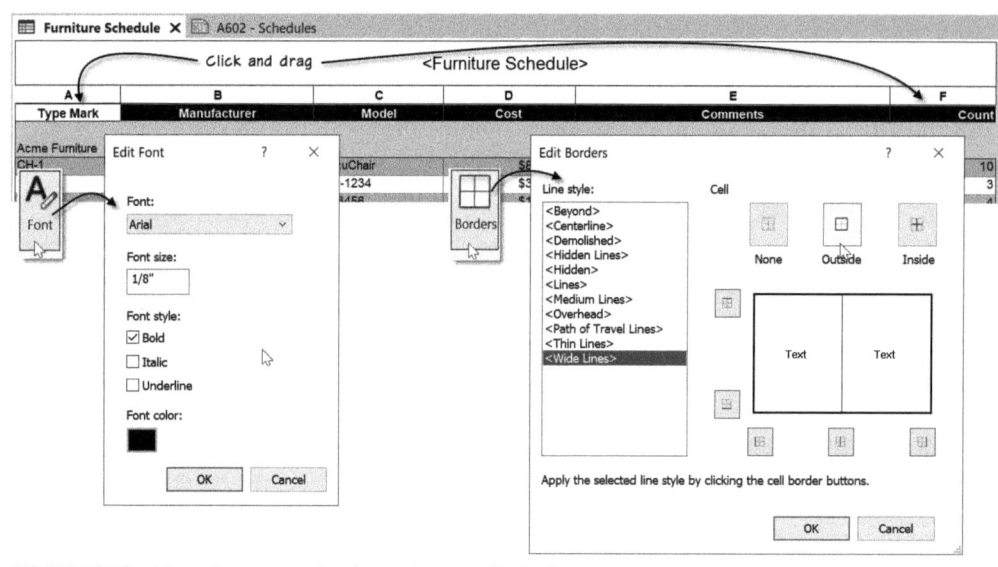

FIGURE 13.19 *Adjust font settings, borders and optionally shading*

Bold (and any shading) will show immediately, but to see the borders you need to open the sheet again.

5. Click back to the *A602 – Schedules* sheet tab to see the results.

If you ever need to remove your appearance customizations, you can click the Reset button on the ribbon. Many of the features explored here can also be achieved on the Appearance tab of the "Schedule Properties" dialog. The ribbon also includes several tools on the Titles & Headers panel. Here you can group columns under a common header by dragging through two or more column headers and then clicking the Group button. If you want to customize the title of the schedule, you can click in the title cell and use the Merge Unmerge button to customize it. By default, the title cell is simply all the columns merged into a single cell. If you unmerge, you can begin customizing it. You can even insert image files into the title. These explorations will be left to you as an exercise on your own. If you want to see the results of all your appearance modifications, return to the sheet.

> **NOTE:** Unlike graphical views, if you want to print a schedule, you must drag it to a sheet first and then print the sheet. If you don't want a title block, you can just delete it to print only the schedule.

SPLIT A LONG SCHEDULE

In some cases, the data in the schedule grows beyond the edge of the sheet. You can break the schedule into pieces to make it fit the sheet better. (An example occurs on the existing *A601 – Schedules* sheet).

1. On the Project Browser, double-click to open the A601 -Schedules Sheet view.

The schedules here have grown since they were placed and overrun the bottom of the sheet. We can split them to make the sheet legible.

2. Create another new sheet named: **A603 – Schedules**.
3. Select the *Window Schedule* and the *Wall Schedule* the sheet A601.
   ⇨ On the Clipboard panel, choose: Cut, (or press CTRL + X).
   ⇨ Return to *A603*, paste from the clipboard and position them on the sheet.

Working with Schedules, Tags and Data | 611

They are still too long for the new sheet. For the Window schedule, you should be able to widen the Type column to prevent its data from wrapping and solve the issue. The Wall Schedule we will split.

4. Select the *Window* schedule on the sheet.

5. Repeat the steps above in the "Add a Schedule to a Sheet" topic on page 608 to widen the columns required to stop them from wrapping.

6. Select the Wall schedule on the sheet and then on the right side is a small control handle (looks like a "Z"); click this control to split the schedule.

Using the other control handles that appear, you can make additional adjustments as necessary. The schedule can be split multiple times if required. To remove a split and put the two pieces back together, simply drag and drop one piece on top of another (see Figure 13.20).

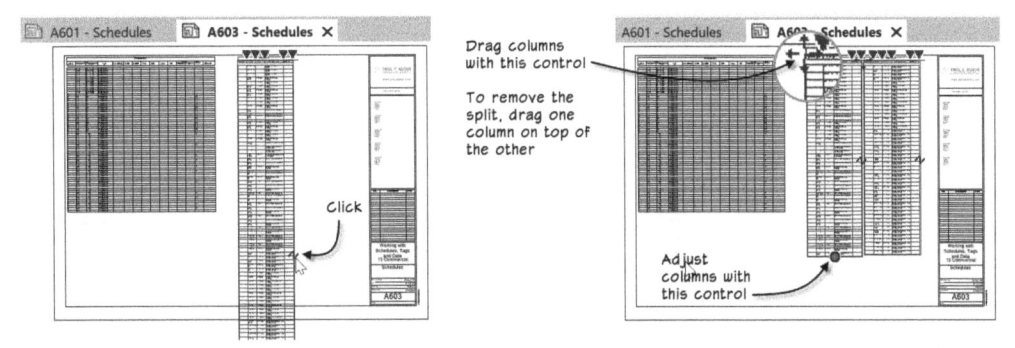

FIGURE 13.20 *Split the Schedule and make other adjustments if needed*

TIP: If after splitting a schedule it is still too long for the sheet, you can use the Filter tab to edit the schedule view. Filter by a number range or by floor level to shorten the overall schedule. Then duplicate this schedule view and Filter the new copy to include the rest. Drag the two (or more schedules) to different sheets. For example, in a 20-story building, you could create a schedule that included levels 1–10 and then duplicate it and change the filter to include levels 11–20. Then drag them to two different schedule sheets.

In the metric project, create another sheet and put the window and wall schedules on separate sheets to fit them better.

7. Save the project.

EDITING THE MODEL

Returning to our *Furniture Schedule*, let's see how it keeps up to date as we make modifications to the model.

1. Close all views except *Level 3* and the *Furniture Schedule*, and then tile them.

In the *Level 3* plan locate the conference room (bottom middle). The current table has 14 chairs around it. Perhaps you'd like to explore a different size and quantity. Let's take a minute to understand how the conference table family is constructed.

2. In the *Level 3* view, zoom in on the conference table.

⇨ Place your mouse over the conference table, note the way it pre-highlights, and note the name that appears in the Status Bar (or the onscreen tooltips).

The conference table is named: *Conference Table : 14 Chairs*.

3. Place your mouse over one of the Chairs.

The table will continue to pre-highlight.

• Revit Essentials for Architecture •

612 | Chapter 13

⇨ Press TAB.

Notice how the chair now pre-highlights independently (see the left side of 21).

In Chapter 11, we learned about nested families when building the coat rack with nested coat hooks. This conference table family and its chairs is another example of a nested family. The difference here is that the nested chairs are "Shared" families. When you make a nested family shared, it is part of the host family but can also be selected and scheduled independently. Another way to see this is to select the chairs in the schedule.

4. Locate the conference chairs in the Schedule (the quantity is 12) and click that row.

The 12 conference chairs should highlight in the plan (see the middle of Figure 13.21).

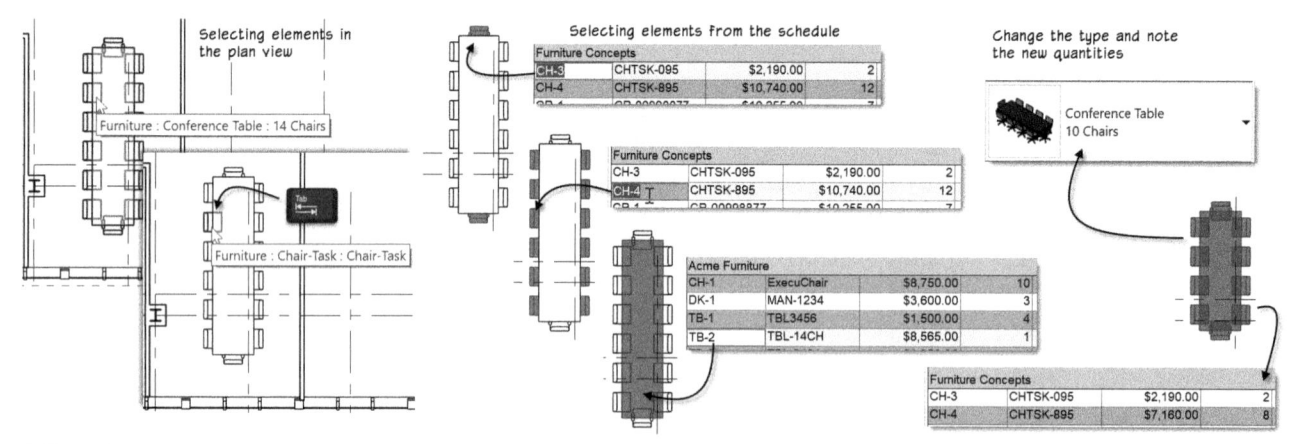

FIGURE 13.21 *Nested "Shared" families can be selected and scheduled independently. The chair count immediately updates when making an edit*

5. Click back into the plan view and then select the conference table (the table and chairs will highlight and select together).

⇨ From the Type Selector, choose a different size: **Conference Table : 10 Chairs**.

Notice the change in quantity of chairs both in plan and in schedule (see the right of Figure 13.21).

6. Try other sizes as well. Settle on the: **Conference Table : 12 Chairs** option and then adjust its position as required to fit comfortably in the space.

⇨ Add a credenza to one end of the room.

While the chairs took care of themselves, the conference table needs attention. The new type we selected does not have values for Manufacturer, Cost, and the other type-based fields. You can see this in schedule because an empty field appears at the top. We can certainly edit the values in the schedule as we did previously. However, we can also edit from the model.

EDITING SCHEDULE PARAMETERS FROM THE MODEL

We edited all the Manufacturer and other identity data from the schedule previously. While this is certainly an efficient way to make such edits, it is possible to edit these data fields using the same methods that we have employed when editing other types. Namely we can select an object and use the Edit Type button on the Properties palette, or we can right-click the item from the *Families* branch of the Project Browser.

1. Select the new conference table in the plan view.

⇨ On the Properties palette, click the Edit Type button.

2. Input values for the Manufacturer, Model, Cost and Type Mark (see Figure 13.22).

Working with Schedules, Tags and Data | 613

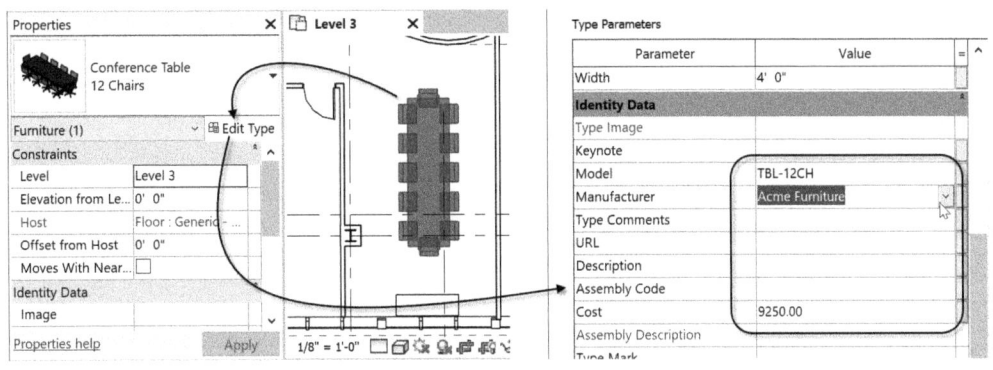

FIGURE 13.22 *Edit the type parameters of the new conference table*

3. Click OK to apply the change and update the model and schedule.

Notice that the change applies in the schedule immediately. Also notice that simply beginning to type in any field will run a search on the values you have previously input. When a previous value appears in the search, you can just select it from the list.

USING SCHEDULE KEYS TO SPEED INPUT

Schedule Keys allow you to define a named collection of instance parameter values that you can apply to an element in a schedule in a single step. They are very useful in door, window, and room schedules where there are many instance-based parameters. Let's return to our predefined *Door Schedule* for a brief demonstration of this powerful feature.

1. On the View tab, on the Create panel, click the Schedules drop down button and choose the: **Schedule/Quantities** tool.

2. In the "New Schedule" dialog, choose: **Doors** for the category and change the Name to: **Door Frame Style Schedule**.

3. Select the "**Schedule Keys**" radio button, change the Key Name to: **Frame Style** and then click OK (see Figure 13.23).

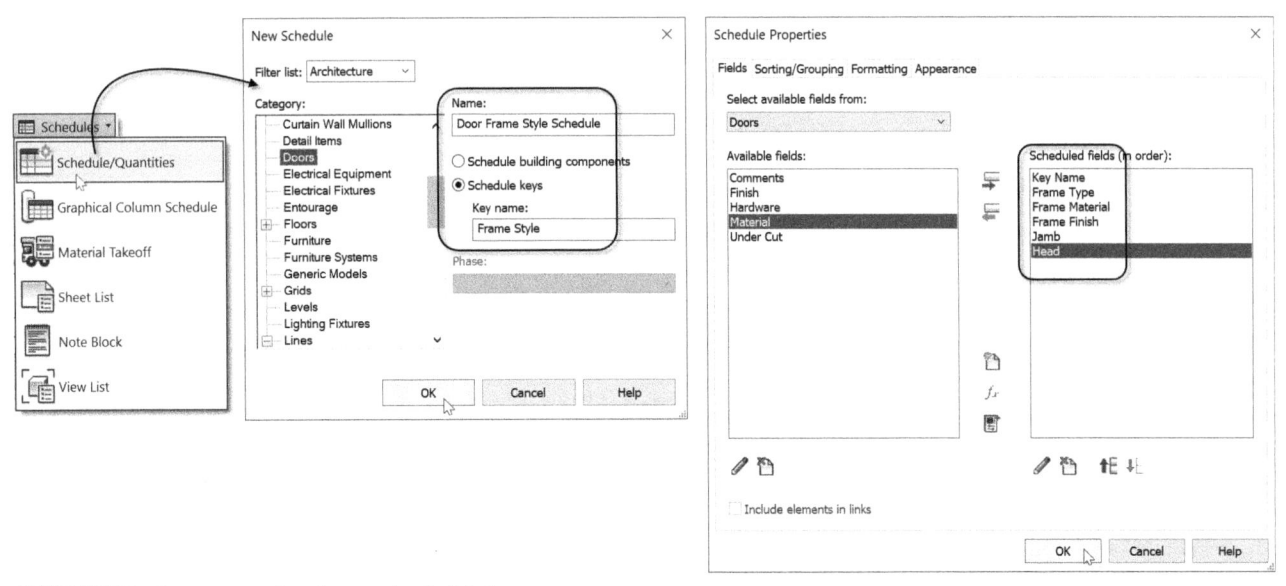

FIGURE 13.23 *Create a new door frame style schedule key*

Notice that the Available Fields list includes all the instance parameters for doors. Key Name is already added on the right. This field is required. This will be called: "Frame Style" based on our input in the previous dialog.

4. Add the five frame fields: "Frame Type," "Frame Material," "Frame Finish," "Jamb," and "Head."

• Revit Essentials for Architecture •

614 | Chapter 13

⇨ Click OK to finish.

Adjust the widths of the columns in the Schedule window if required.

5. On the Modify Schedule/Quantities ribbon tab, on the Rows panel, click the: Insert Data Row button.

⇨ Input appropriate values in the first three fields. Leave the Jamb and Head fields blank for now.

⇨ Add at least one additional Row. Add more if you like (see Figure 13.24).

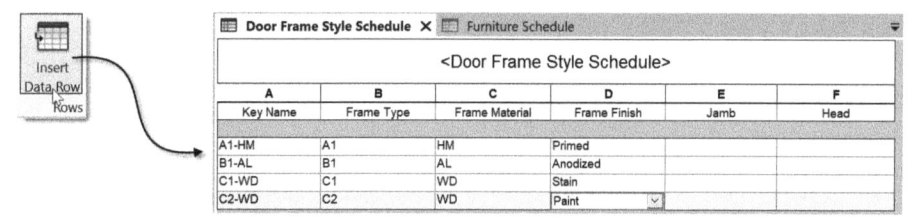

FIGURE 13.24 *Add rows and input standard values*

The Key Name is any unique identifier you like. In other schedules or when editing element properties, when you choose this key, the other five values will fill in automatically. We'll see this next.

6. On the Project Browser, right-click the *Door Schedule* and choose: **Duplicate View > Duplicate**.

⇨ Rename the duplicate: **Working Door Schedule**.

7. With *Working Door Schedule* active, on the Properties palette, click the Edit button for Fields.

8. Add the new "Frame Style" field and move it up to just before the existing Frame Type field on the list.

TIP: Select Hardware on the right before you click Add. The new field will insert below the selected one. You can always use the Move Up and Move Down buttons if necessary.

⇨ Click OK to finish.

Your duplicated door schedule should now have a Frame Style column. The value currently reads "(none)" for all rows. All the setup is now complete. To use the Frame Styles, we simply choose one of the values we created above from the pop-up list in the Frame Style field and all the corresponding values will fill in automatically.

9. Close, open, and tile views as desired to assist in editing the schedule.

10. Select any door and choose a Frame Style (see Figure 13.25).

FIGURE 13.25 *Choosing frame styles automatically fills in the preassigned values*

⇨ Repeat for as many doors as you wish.

Recall that our *Door Frame Style Schedule* is also controlling the Jamb and Head detail fields. However, at this time, we don't know which sheet will have those details. A wonderful benefit of this process is that you can return to the

• The Aubin Academy •

Working with Schedules, Tags and Data | 615

Door Frame Style Schedule at any time and fill in the detail designations. The change will be reflected immediately by all doors using that Frame Style and the schedule will update to reflect the change.

11. On the Project Browser, open the *Door Frame Style Schedule*. (If you still have it open, just click the tab).

   ⇨ Edit one or more Jamb and/or Head detail entries. Input something like: **1/A501** or **2/A501** (see the left side of Figure 13.26).

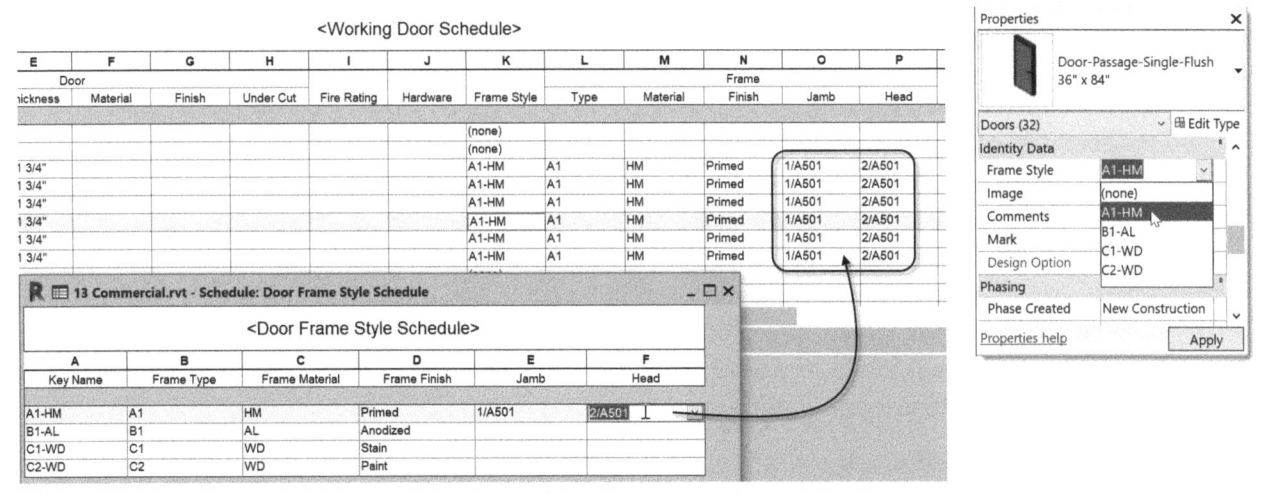

FIGURE 13.26 *Edit the key schedule later and the other schedules referencing it update immediately*

> **TIP:** To apply your Frame Styles even faster, drag through several items in the schedule to select the corresponding doors. Switch to the floor plan view, and then on the Properties palette you can choose a Frame Style that will in turn apply to all doors in the selection (see the right side of Figure 13.26). You can also start in the plan or other view, right-click and choose **Select All Instances** (either in view or in the entire project) and then edit on the Properties palette.

You can make another Schedule Key for the remaining door instance properties. While it is possible to make a single Schedule Key control all the properties, having two Keys gives more flexibility to mix and match door types and frame types. For example, a door of type: A-WD could in one instance use a frame type: A1-HM and in another use: C2-WD.

> **TIP:** Make your door schedule easier to read. Using the procedure covered in the "Headers, Footers, and Grand Totals" topic on page 605, edit Fields, add the Level field. In Sorting/Grouping, sort first by Level with a Header, and then by Mark (no header or footer for Mark). Finally, on the Formatting tab, (or on the ribbon) make the Level field a Hidden Field.

You can keep working in the *Door Schedule* if you wish. As noted, another Key Schedule will help you quickly fill in the "Door" columns. The Fire Rating column is a type-based parameter, so when you edit it, Revit will warn you that the value applies to all elements of the same type. Finally, if there are some doors on the schedule that should not be included, you can apply a filter to your schedule as we did in the "The Filter Tab" topic on page 606 above to exclude them (for example, if you did not want to include the openings or the curtain wall doors at the front facade).

To add the filter, simply edit each of the doors you want to exclude and add some identifiable value to one of its parameters. It can be as simple as some text in the Comments or Type Comments field. It can be anything, even "Don't Schedule." You could also create a custom Yes/No project parameter that you can check for items you don't want to include. The specifics are up to you. After adding this text or parameter, edit the Properties of the schedule; click the edit button for Filter, filter by Comments, Type Comments or your custom parameter, change to **does**

not equal, and then choose "**Don't Schedule**" (or not checked). Click OK twice to view the results. (Our current schedule does not include the Type Comments field, so if you use this field, you will need to add it to your schedule and optionally make it a hidden field). The filter value is case-sensitive, so type it the same each time. The only trouble with the method is that it is manual. You need to add the filtering comment to each door (or Type) you want to exclude. However, you can select one such door in a plan view, right-click and choose: **Select All Instances > In Entire Project**. With them all selected, add the comment on the Properties palette.

> **BIM MANAGER NOTE:** The need to occasionally apply a filter highlights one of the "dangers" of using online or manufacturer's content. You never know exactly what you will get, and you cannot assume that all families are created equally. Frankly, the same is true even with some of the out-of-the-box or even your own custom created content. In several places in this book you have been encouraged to explore content from various sources, but also to open it, edit it, and try to understand how it is built. Review the procedures covered in Chapter 11 for working with existing families and just remember that you should always analyze any outside content and perform the required "clean-up" steps on it before incorporating it into a project or your office standard. Your overall content strategy can anticipate issues like the one noted here with the door opening families and you can build the required properties that the schedule will filter on directly into the content in your library. Another option would be to change the category of the openings to Generic Models. This would eliminate them from the Door schedule, but then require you to use the Component tool (rather than the Door tool) to place them.
>
> One more consideration if you decide to input a value for the schedule filter. You will notice a small associate button next to many parameter values on the Properties palette like the ones we saw in Chapter 11 when associating family parameters to nested family parameters. In the project environment, you can do something similar using "Global Parameters." A global parameter is available project-wide and can drive the value of several elements or types. So, one way to speed up and/or centrally control the values that you place to use in your schedule filters would be to create and associate a global parameter to the values. For the door openings, edit the first type, click the associate global parameter icon next to the Type Comments (or another field you plan to use) and then create a new parameter in the dialog that appears. You can then switch to the next type and associate that same parameter to each of the other types. In this way, no matter what size door opening is chosen, it will not appear on the schedule. If you want to learn more about global parameters, you can download a conference paper on the subject from the **author's website**[‡].

12. Save the project.

WORKING WITH TAGS

Tags serve an important role in Architectural documentation. They provide a means of easily and uniquely locating and identifying elements in a project. All sorts of tags are needed in construction document sets: room tags, door tags, window tags, etc. Revit makes adding and managing tags simple. Furthermore, the data displayed in the tags comes directly from the host objects in the same way as the data that feeds schedules. Therefore, you need only add tags to a view and let Revit handle the rest.

ADDING DOOR TAGS

We have spent some time on our door schedule, but so far, we have not added any door tags. Adding tags to existing elements in the model is simple.

Continue in the *Level 3* floor plan.

1. On the Annotate tab, on the Tag panel, click the Tag by Category tool (or press TG).

   ⇨ Slowly move the pointer around the model pausing over different kinds of elements. Do not click yet (see Figure 13.27).

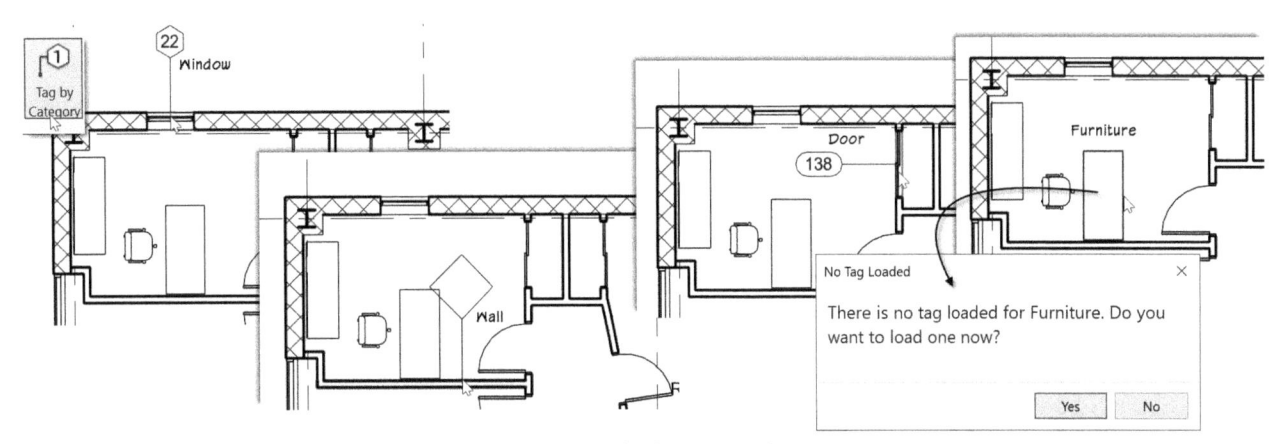

FIGURE 13.27 *Tag by category automatically uses the correct tag for the element you select*

Notice that the shape of the tag on your cursor changes with each element that you pre-highlight. Your project can have different tags loaded for nearly every category of element. Therefore, if you pre-highlight a wall, it will automatically place a wall tag—pre-highlight a door and you get a door tag and so on. You can place tags with or without a leader attached; the default (on the Options Bar) is with a leader. If an element pre-highlights but no tag appears, it means that this type of tag has not been loaded into your project yet. If you click such an object, you will be prompted to load an appropriate tag (shown on the right of the figure). Don't place any tags yet.

  2. On the Options Bar, clear the "Leader" check box.

  ⇨ Pre-highlight and then click on one of the doors to the offices at the left.

Notice that when the tag appears, it already has a number in it. The doors were numbered automatically when they were added to the model. In the "View and Edit in Existing Schedules" topic on page 596 above, we discussed the numbering of the doors already. The tag simply queries the element (the door in this case) for the instance mark value and then displays the value in the tag. (You can create custom tags that query and display nearly any parameter in an element.) You can continue placing tags manually using this tool just by clicking on them. However, there is a quicker method.

  ⇨ On the ribbon, click the Modify tool or press the ESC key twice.

  3. On the Annotate tab, on the Tag panel, click the Tag All tool.

  ⇨ In the "Tag All Not Tagged" dialog, check Door Tags at the top of the list

  Make sure that the "All objects" radio button is selected. (If you open this dialog with an element selected, it will default to "Only selected objects" instead).

  ⇨ Click the Apply button to add the tags (see Figure 13.28).

618 | Chapter 13

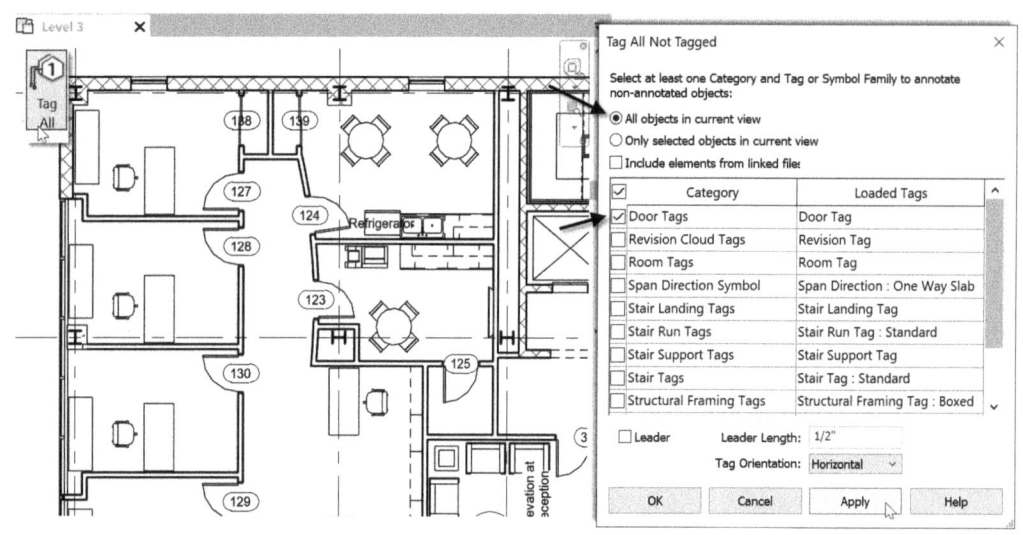

FIGURE 13.28 *Tag all doors that are not currently tagged*

Door tags will appear on all doors in the currently active view.

4. Remaining in the "Tag All Not Tagged" dialog, scroll down, check Window Tags and then click Apply.

5. Click OK to dismiss the dialog.

You should now have a tag on all doors and windows in the third floor. Notice that windows all use the same designation while the doors are all unique, a pretty common practice for identifying them. Door tags show the Mark property, while windows show the Type Mark.

RENUMBERING ELEMENTS

As we discussed previously, the current door numbering is not very logical. If you wish, you can renumber the doors so that they correspond better to the project. For example, you can renumber all the third floor doors starting with a prefix of 3 and incrementing sequentially from there. To renumber elements (like doors) you have three options:

a. Select the element onscreen and then edit the appropriate property on the Properties palette. Door tags use the "Mark" property. Windows and walls use the "Type Mark" so you would click the Edit Type button to modify it. The Type Mark like other type properties is shared by all instances of a type.

b. Edit the appropriate field in a schedule. Usually the Mark or Type Mark field will be the first field in the schedule.

c. Click directly on the door or tag and then edit the value directly in the tag. Be careful not to double-click here. You want to select the element, pause briefly, and then click again on the value in the tag. Make the edit and then press ENTER. The value will update on the Properties palette and the schedule as you would expect.

> **TIP:** If you do double-click and the tag opens in the family editor instead, you can adjust your settings to prevent this. From the File menu, choose: **Options**. On the User Interface tab, click the Customize button next to Double-click Options. For the Family entry, change it to: **Do Nothing**.

1. Using any of these three methods, try renumbering some of the doors (it is not necessary to do all of them).

2. Renumber one of the windows.

• The Aubin Academy •

Notice how the change applies to all windows in this view.

Even with the three methods listed here, the process of numbering can be tedious. As you have probably noticed, Revit simply numbers element sequentially from the previously created elements. This is true of doors, rooms, grids, sheets, etc. A common door numbering scheme is for the numbers of the door to match the room numbers. If a room has more than one door, then the room number plus a lettered suffix is used. This is the approach advocated by the United States National CAD Standard (NCS) and the preferred method for many an architectural firm. Unfortunately, there is no automated way to use this approach in Revit. If you wish to number doors this way, you are forced to number them manually to match this standard. However, there are many third party utilities out there for Revit that fill this void. To see what tools are available, perform a web search for "renumber tools for Revit" or something similar. You can also click the Autodesk App Store tool at the top-right corner of the application frame. This will open the Autodesk App Store in your web browser, and you can search there as well. Many tools are available. Some cost a fee, and some are free. CTC Software and Ideate software have many popular suites of tools that provide lots of added functionality to Revit. They both offer a renumbering tool. You can find more info at their websites or in the Autodesk App Store.

> **NOTE:** You are welcome to renumber any other elements, but doing so is not required in order to continue.

LOADING TAGS

Sometimes you want to tag elements in your model, but an appropriate tag is not loaded in your project. Like other families, you can simply load a tag from a library. Let's load a furniture tag and then tag some of our furniture. The tags panel on the ribbon is an expandable panel. This is indicated by the small drop down arrow on the panel title bar. Click here to access the loaded tags command.

1. Click on the Tags panel title bar. The panel will expand revealing an additional tool.
   ⇨ Click the Loaded Tags and Symbols tool.

Scroll through the list. All tag types are listed. Tags that are already loaded are listed next to their respective category. There is a "Filter list" drop down at the top of the dialog that you can use to limit the list to a discipline. Element categories with no tag loaded will be empty.

2. Click the Load Family button.
   ⇨ Browse to your library (Imperial or Metric) and open the *Annotations* folder.
   ⇨ Open the *Architectural* folder, select *Furniture Tag.rfa* [*M_Furniture Tag.rfa*], and then click Open.

> **NOTE:** As with other library content in this book, you can find a copy of the tag in the *Chapter13* folder.

3. Click OK to dismiss the "Loaded Tags" dialog (see Figure 13.29).

620 | Chapter 13

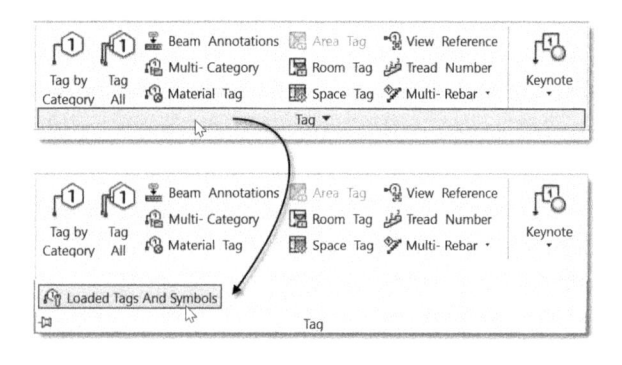

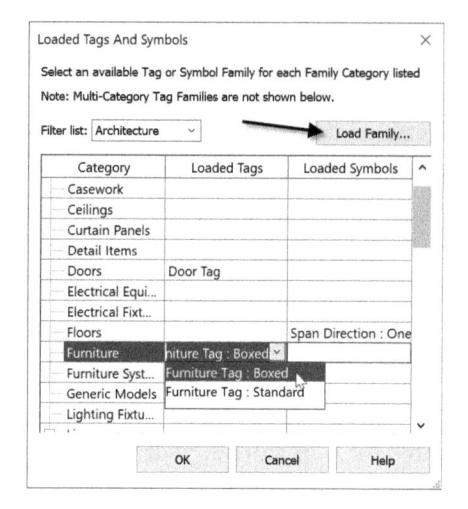

FIGURE 13.29 *Load a new tag for furniture*

4. On the Tags panel, click the Tag by Category tool (or press TG).

⇨ On the Options Bar, check the "Leader" check box.

⇨ In the text box, type: **3/8"** [**9**].

5. Tag some of the chairs on the right in the reception area (see the left side of Figure 13.30).

If your tag appears blank, you need to return to the "Duplicating a Schedule View" topic on page 604 above and add values to the Type Mark fields for each piece of furniture. If you did complete this step, your tag will appear with your Type Mark code already displayed.

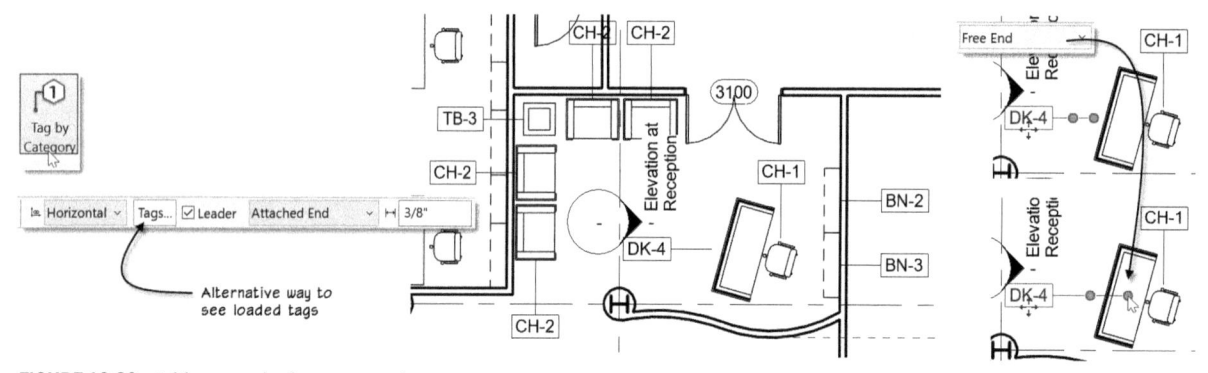

FIGURE 13.30 *Add tags to the furniture in the reception space*

After you place a tag, you can click on it and use the four-sided arrow control handle to move it and the round handles to add elbows to the leader. If you want complete control over the leader, select the tag and on the Options Bar, change the Leader type to: **Free End**. This gives you an additional control handle at the end of the leader allowing you to drag it freely (see the right side of Figure 13.30). You can also optionally add an arrowhead to the leaders. To do this, select one of the furniture tags, edit its type and then choose an arrowhead.

CREATE A FURNITURE PLAN VIEW

You do not have to tag all pieces of furniture in this view. In fact, this might be a good time to create a separate furniture plan for the third floor. At this point in the text, you should have the skills required to complete this task on your own. Therefore, we will review the overall steps only.

1. On Project Browser, right-click the *Level 3* plan and choose: **Duplicate View** > **Duplicate with Detailing**.

• The Aubin Academy •

This command creates a copy of the view including all the tags we have added so far. Duplicate would create a view of just the model geometry without any annotations.

   2. Rename this plan to: *Level 3 Furniture*.

   3. In the original *Level 3* plan, delete only the furniture tags added so far.

   4. In the *Level 3 Furniture Plan*, delete all the door and windows and tags.

> **TIP:** Make a window around all the tags added, click the Filter button, click Check None and then check only Door Tags and Window Tags and then click OK. Delete the tags. Do NOT hide them, be sure to delete them. The originals will still exist back in the **Level 3** plan.

   5. Tag all of the furniture in the view (Use TAB to tag nested chairs) (see Figure 13.31).

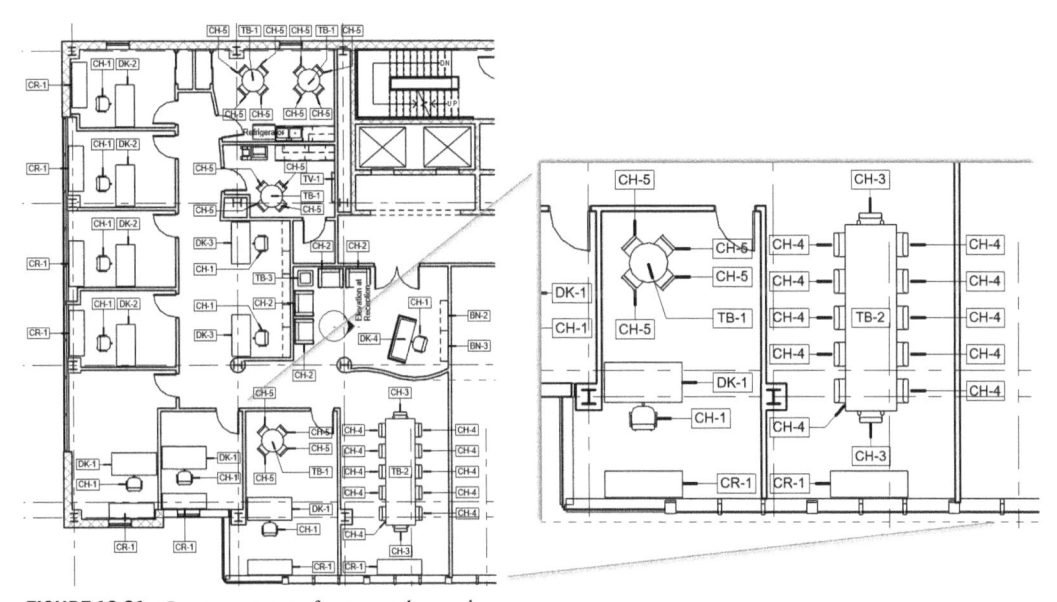

FIGURE 13.31 *Create a separate furniture plan and tags*

EDITING VIEW VISIBILITY GRAPHICS

Now that we have a separate furniture plan, we might not want to see the furniture in the *Level 3* plan anymore.

   1. On the Project Browser, double-click to open the *Level 3* floor plan view.

   2. On the keyboard, type VG. (You can also click the Visibility/Graphics tool on the Graphics panel of the View tab).

   ⇨ Uncheck the Furniture check box and click Apply (see Figure 13.32).

> **TIP:** For an alternative way to turn elements off: select an item, on the ribbon, click the Hide in View icon and from the pop-up, choose: **Hide Category**. You can also right-click and choose the: **Hide in view > By Category** command. These methods make the selected category invisible without a dialog. The keyboard shortcut to hide elements is: EH and to hide categories is: VH.

622 | Chapter 13

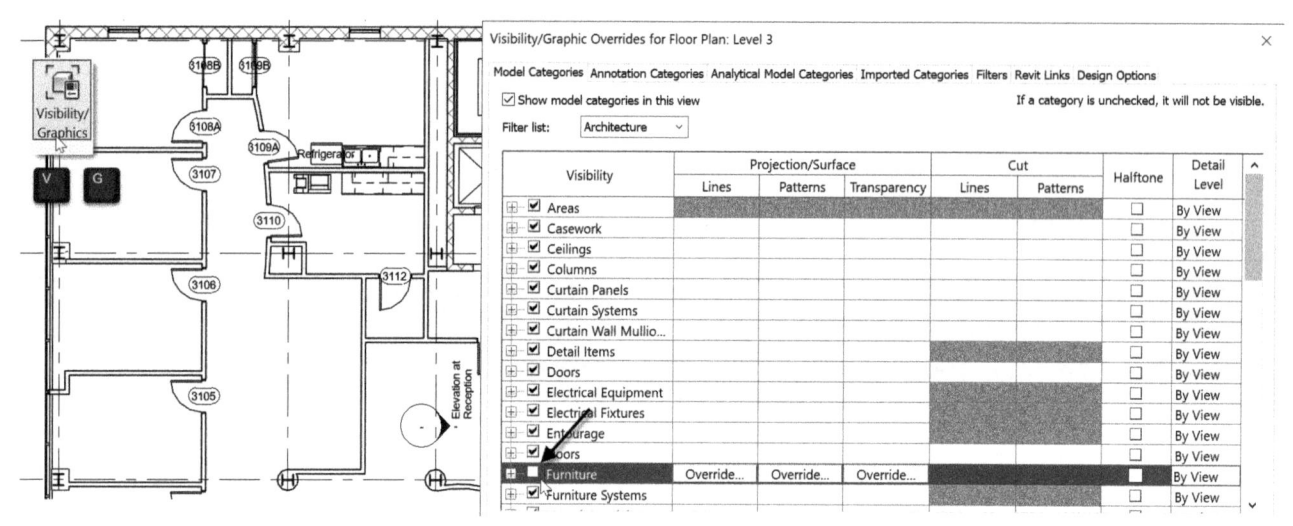

FIGURE 13.32 *Visibility/Graphic Overrides apply to the current view only*

Visibility/Graphic overrides apply to the current view only. This extensive dialog lists all Revit elements grouped into major categories shown on each of the tabs at the top of the dialog. Take note of the message at the bottom left corner of the dialog. This entire dialog is devoted to overriding the default graphical settings. Anything that is not overridden is drawn according to the settings in the "Object Styles" dialog. There is an Object Styles button here for direct access. Object Styles can also be accessed on the Manage tab. In most firms, you can typically expect that the settings in Object Styles have been thoroughly configured in the project template ahead of time to match office standards.

If you study just the Model Categories tab, you will see that in addition to being able to turn object categories on and off (using the check box) you can also override the line patterns and fills that each category uses. Furthermore, most categories have subcategories giving you even more fine control over visibility and graphic settings.

> Move the dialog out of the way so that you can see the result of the change. Notice that the furniture is now hidden in this view.

Perhaps you would like to see the furniture after all, but make it less prominent.

3. Check the box next to Furniture again to turn it back on and then check the Halftone column as well.

⇨ Click Apply to see the result (see Figure 13.33).

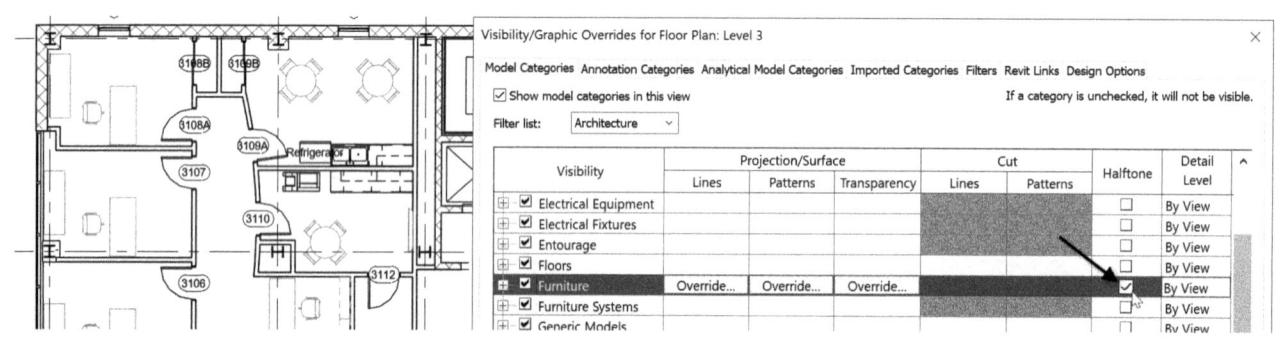

FIGURE 13.33 *Display the furniture as halftone*

While we will not go into detail on each item of the "Visibility/Graphic Overrides" dialog, a few additional tips are worth mentioning. If you wish to see all the categories and their subcategories, click the Expand All button. This will expand the entire list in one step. Any item can be overridden. For example, if you wanted to change the line weight, color, or pattern of the furniture, you select the Furniture item and then click one of the Override buttons that appear. A dialog will appear with additional override options. Let's look at an example in the furniture plan.

4. Click OK to dismiss the dialog.

Working with Schedules, Tags and Data | 623

5. Open the *Level 3 Furniture* view

⇨ Edit Visibility/Graphics in this view.

6. Click the Patterns Override button for Furniture.

⇨ Choose a Crosshatch pattern, pick a light gray color and then click OK and then Apply (see Figure 13.34).

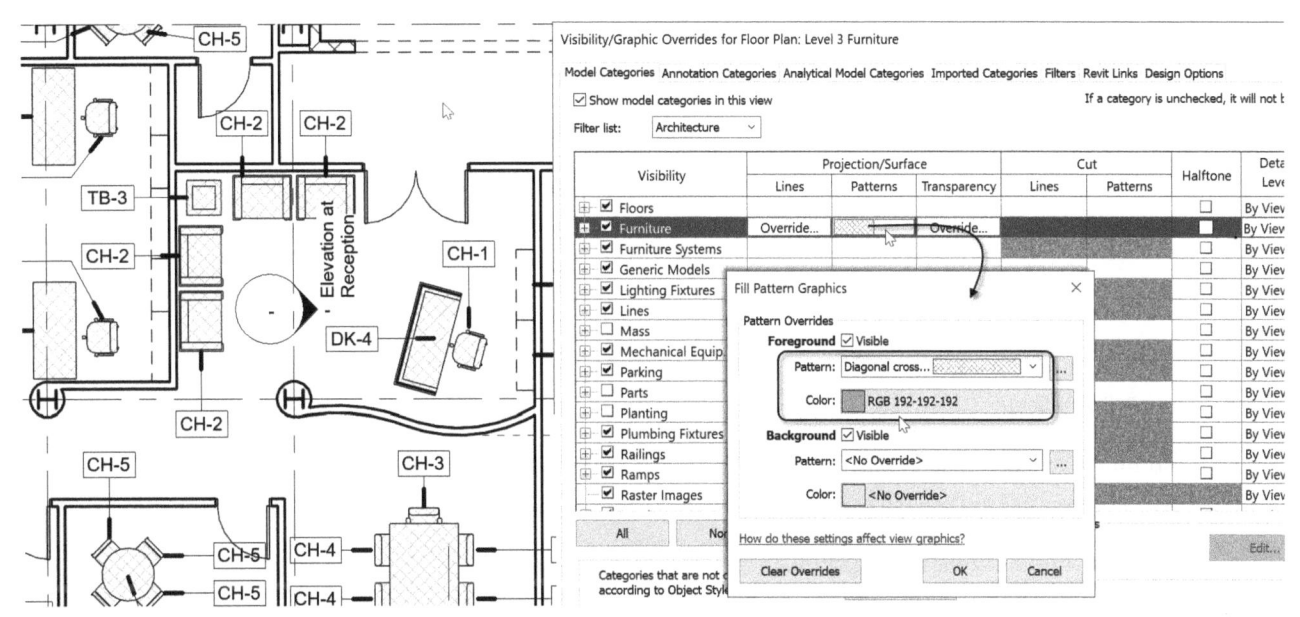

FIGURE 13.34 *Select an item and then click the Override button to change line pattern, color, weight, or fill patterns*

> **TIP:** For an alternative way to edit the visibility settings of elements: select an item, on the ribbon, click the Override Graphics in View icon and from the pop-up, choose: **Override by Category**. You can also right-click for this command.

You can make similar edits on the Annotation Categories tab. However, since annotation elements are simpler, there are fewer options to edit. The analytical Categories tab controls the structural analytical model. If you have imported DWG files, you will be able to turn on and off the layers in those files on the Imported Categories tab. The Revit Links tab gives extensive control over the visibility of a linked Revit file. Filters allows the same kinds of settings found on the Model Categories tab, but the effects are limited to elements that meet the user defined filter criteria. We will not look at the Filters tab in detail at this time. If you wish to learn more about any of the settings in this dialog and each of its tabs, please consult the online help.

7. Be sure that the settings for Furniture meet your preferences and then click OK.

OVERRIDE GRAPHICS BY ELEMENT

The "Visibility/Graphic Overrides" dialog allows us to manipulate the display at the category level. In some cases, you will wish to modify the display of individual elements independently of their category. For example er 11, we built a binder bin family for the reception area. You will notice that the fill pattern overrides did not apply to these elements. This is because they are above the cut plane. We can customize the linework however, so perhaps making the lines bolder might help them stand out in this view. We do not want to make all the furniture bold though, just these bins. So instead, we can use element-level overrides.

1. In the Reception area, select both binder bins.

⇨ On the ribbon, on the View tab, click the Override Graphics in View

• Revit Essentials for Architecture •

drop down button and choose: **Override by Element**.

2. Expand the Projection Lines item

⇨ From the Weight dropdown, choose a bolder line weight such as pen **3** and then click Apply (see Figure 13.35).

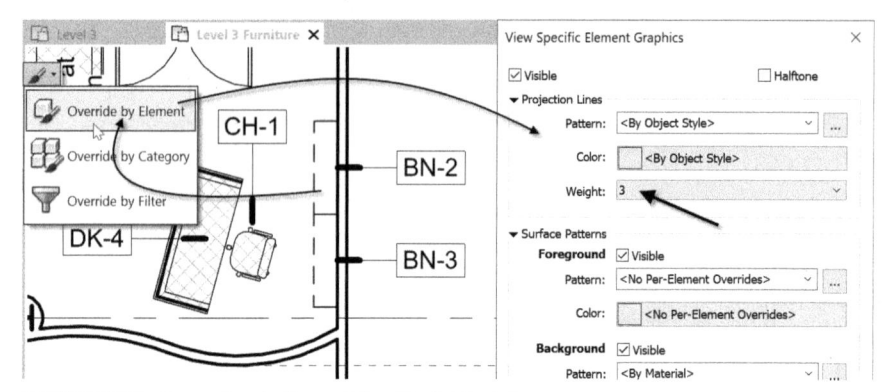

FIGURE 13.35 *Customize the line weight of individual elements*

3. Save the project.

You can also hide elements individually as well. This can be helpful in cases where hiding the category would be undesirable. For example, in the Level 3 Furniture Plan view, you may not want to see all the section and elevation indicators. You can certainly hide the category, but that would hide them all. So, if there are only certain ones that you want to hide, you can select the section(s), and then on the ribbon or right-click, choose: Hide in View > Elements.

In general, you should hide by element only in cases where hide by category would not give desirable results.

ROOMS AND ROOM TAGS

A Room element is a non-graphic selectable model element used to represent an actual room or other defined space in your project. Rooms are used for the obvious spaces that you would consider rooms like offices, kitchens, corridors, closets, and lobbies. However, you can define a room for any program space you wish to label or quantify. Rooms are model elements even though they do not display graphically by default. Rooms are useful to generate room schedules, reports, perform area calculations, volume calculations, finish schedules, and of course for room tags. Rooms are used for any occupied space. In most instances, rooms can be created automatically from the bounding walls and other elements already in your model. However, not all geometry can "bound" a room, and in some situations Revit will be unable to correctly determine the proper shape and boundary of the room without a little manual intervention. Consider situations where the shape of the room you wish to define has no walls or other "hard" boundaries. This may be the case in open plan layouts or outdoor spaces. In these cases, you can manually sketch Room Separations. We'll explore both techniques here.

Continue in the *Level 3* floor plan view. Close all other view tabs.

1. On the Architecture tab, on the Room & Area panel, click the Room tool (or press RM).

A few buttons appear on the ribbon.

By default, the Tag on Placement option is enabled (the button is highlighted). This means that as we add rooms, Revit will also create room tags. This will prevent the need to add the tags manually after the rooms are placed, so it is a good idea to leave this enabled.

There are two other buttons: Place Rooms Automatically and Highlight Boundaries. With Place Rooms Automatically, you can place a room in every enclosed space onscreen with a single click. Highlight Boundaries will show you where rooms can be placed automatically, before you click.

2. Click the Highlight Boundaries button.

   All room bounding elements will highlight in orange and a message will display.

   ⇨ Click Close on the message to finish.

3. Click the Place Rooms Automatically button.

   A message will display indicating how many rooms were created.

   ⇨ Click Close to dismiss the message.

While at first this may seem the quickest way to create rooms, the tool is flawed. First, we have no control over the order the rooms are placed in, so the numbering is very random. Also, it will create rooms in every possible enclosed space, including shafts and empty spaces like the unoccupied tenant space on the right of our plan. For these reasons, it is unlikely you find the results of this command useful.

4. Undo the previous command by pressing CTRL + Z.

5. On the Architecture tab, on the Room & Area panel, click the Room tool again.

   ⇨ Zoom In Region around the two spaces to the left of the Stair tower in the upper left corner of the plan.

6. Move the cursor outside the plan, but do not click.

   Notice that the shape of the room is just a generic rectangle and does not conform to any surrounding model geometry. To shape your rooms, you must create them within an enclosed space defined by bounding elements such as walls.

7. Move the cursor into the room at the corner of the plan (see Figure 13.36).

   Notice that this time it conforms to the shape of the space.

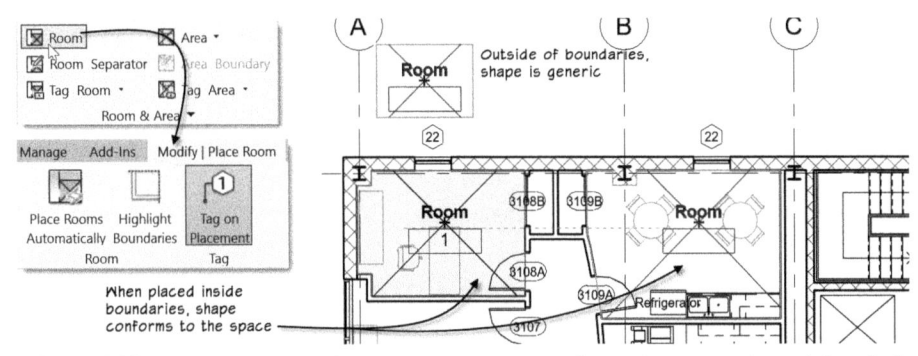

FIGURE 13.36 *A reference graphic (the "X") appears as you are placing the room. It shapes differently depending on nearby bounding elements*

   ⇨ Click within the space to create the room and its tag.

8. Move into the space across the hall to the right and then click again.

Notice that Revit attempts to align the tags as you place rooms. While the room tool remains active, the existing rooms will remain highlighted with blue shading on screen. This will make it easier to place the remaining ones while keeping track of the ones already placed. Also, note that the first room was automatically numbered as "1" and the next one sequentially numbered "2." The problem with this is that you would likely want the reception space to be the first number and then number sequentially from there. Not surprisingly, you can renumber the rooms at any time and their tags will automatically update. However, knowing that Revit will number sequentially and using a little strategy as we place rooms can save us the effort of renumbering in many situations. And this is again why we will typically avoid the "Place Rooms Automatically" tool.

9. Remaining in the room tool, zoom out and move the mouse into the reception space. Don't click yet.

626 | Chapter 13

> Notice how the corridor flows into the reception, secretarial spaces, and conference room. In this open plan configuration, we need to create some manual boundaries before we can add proper rooms.

⇨ On the ribbon, click the Modify tool or press the ESC key twice.

10. On the Room & Area panel, click the Room Separation Line tool.

11. Sketch a horizontal line segment above column line 2 to enclose the reception space (see item 1 in Figure 13.37).

⇨ Press ESC once, and then sketch a vertical line segment next to column line C to enclose the conference room (item 2).

Snap both to the endpoints to the existing walls and then to the intersection with the column.

12. To enclose the secretarial space, use a start-end-radius arc and sketch it as indicated (items 3 through 5).

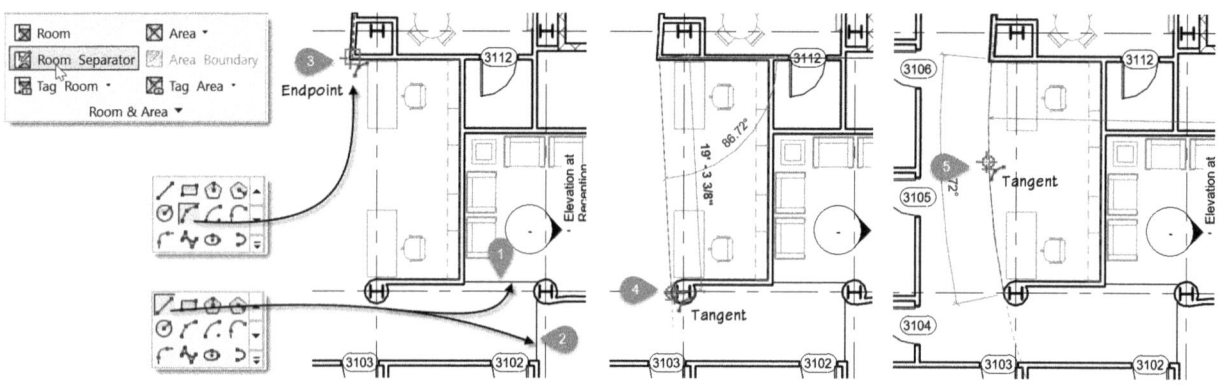

FIGURE 13.37 *Sketch room separation lines as indicated*

13. Test your room separation by returning to the Room tool and placing a room in the reception area.

It should now give the proper shape room. Revit automatically uses the next number in the sequence as you can see (3 in this case). If you want a different pattern to your numbering such as: 3101, 3102, etc., edit the first number to 3101 and then return to the Room tool. It will pick up at 3102 and continue sequencing from there.

⇨ On the ribbon, click the Modify tool or press the ESC key twice.

14. Click on the Room in the reception area (to find the room, move the mouse around and look for the "X" to highlight and then click it).

⇨ On the Properties palette, change the Number value to: **3101** and then press ENTER.

Notice that the room tag updates with the new number. Alternatively, you can edit the number directly from the tag.

15. On the Architecture tab, click the Room tool again (RM).

⇨ Add the remaining Rooms starting with the conference room and continuing clockwise around the tenant suite.

⇨ When you get to Room 1 and 2, click Modify or press ESC.

16. Renumber Room 1 and Room 2 to fit in sequence with the other Rooms.

17. Continue adding the remaining Rooms, but skip the two closets at the top of the plan (see Figure 13.38).

Working with Schedules, Tags and Data | 627

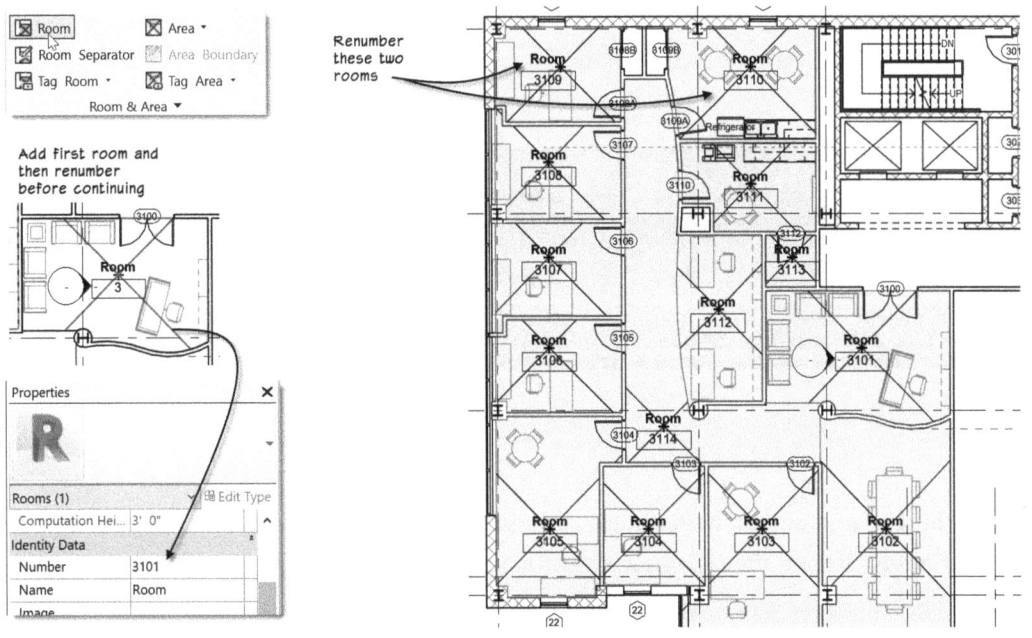

FIGURE 13.38 *After renumbering the reception space, add the remaining rooms*

⇨ On the ribbon, click the Modify tool or press the ESC key twice.

> **TIP:** If you want to hide the name on the elevation tag in the reception space, we can edit the type. Select the triangle portion of the tag and then click Edit Type. In the "Type Properties" dialog that appears, change the Elevation Tag setting to: **1/2" Circle [10mm Circle]** and the click OK.

We could add rooms to the two closets at the top of the plan if we wanted, but they do not really need to be treated as separate rooms. Let's incorporate their area into the rooms they are attached to.

18. Zoom in on Room 3109 (the break room to the left of the stair tower).

⇨ Select the small vertical wall between the room and the closet.

⇨ On the Properties palette, uncheck Room Bounding and then click Apply or simply shift focus back to the drawing window.

19. Move your cursor around in the middle of Room 3109 until the Reference indicator (the "X") pre-highlights and then click (see Figure 13.39).

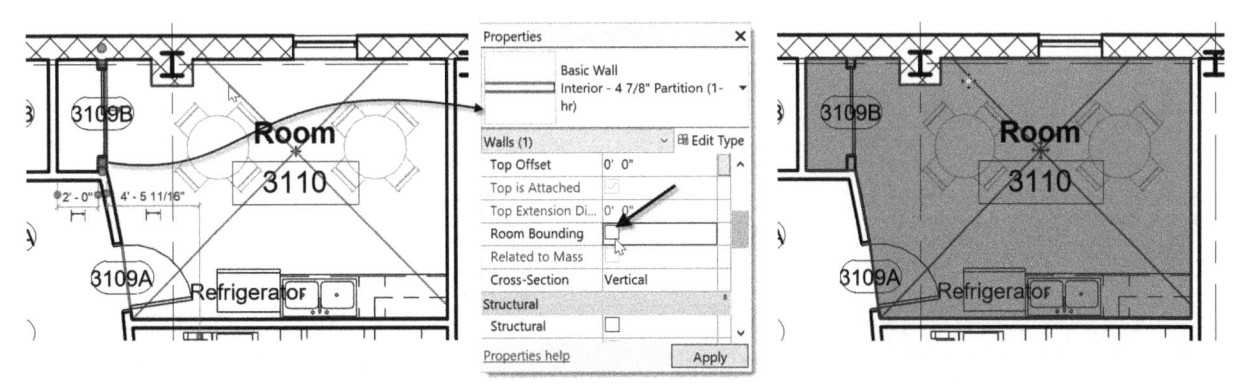

FIGURE 13.39 *Turn off room bounding for the closet spaces at the top of the plan*

Notice that the room now flows into the closet ignoring the closet wall. You can repeat this process on the other office. To do this you would first have to split the long vertical wall (use the Split tool on the Modify tab). Otherwise, the entire length of the wall would become non-bounding, adversely affecting all the offices below it. If you try toggle

• Revit Essentials for Architecture •

off Room Bounding for this wall before splitting it, Revit will generate a warning about "Multiple Rooms in the same enclosed region." If you get such a warning, read it carefully and then click Cancel and check your Room Boundaries again carefully.

> **TIP:** If you are doing a lot of work with rooms, you can turn on the Interior Fill and/or Reference (the "X") subcategories in the view to make them easier to see and select. These are both off by default and only display when pre-highlighting and selecting a room as we have seen. If you decide to do this, type VG to open the Visibility/Graphic Overrides dialog, expand rooms and check either or both items. When you are finished working with rooms, be sure to turn them back off or they will print that way. As an alternative, you can duplicate your floor plan and create a "Working Level 3" plan; then display the subcategories there only.

EDIT ROOM NAMES

We can edit the room names in the same way as the numbers. You can select the rooms and edit the name on the Properties palette, or you can simply click on the tag, click on the blue name value, and then type in the new value.

1. Click on the tag in the reception area. Pause for a moment and then click again on the blue name label.

    An editable text field should appear on screen. Be careful not to double-click or you might end up in the family editor for the tag family.

    ⇨ Type: **Reception** and then press ENTER.

2. Rename the: **Conference Room** next (it is directly below Reception).

You can continue to rename rooms this way, but in the case where several rooms have the same name, like the offices, there is a quicker way.

3. Move your mouse around inside one of the offices and near the tag.

    ⇨ When the reference indicator (the "X") pre-highlights click to select the room.

    ⇨ Using the CTRL key, select all the remaining offices (2 at the bottom, 1 in the bottom left corner, and 4 at the left).

4. On the Properties palette, for the Name type: **Office** and then click Apply (see Figure 13.40).

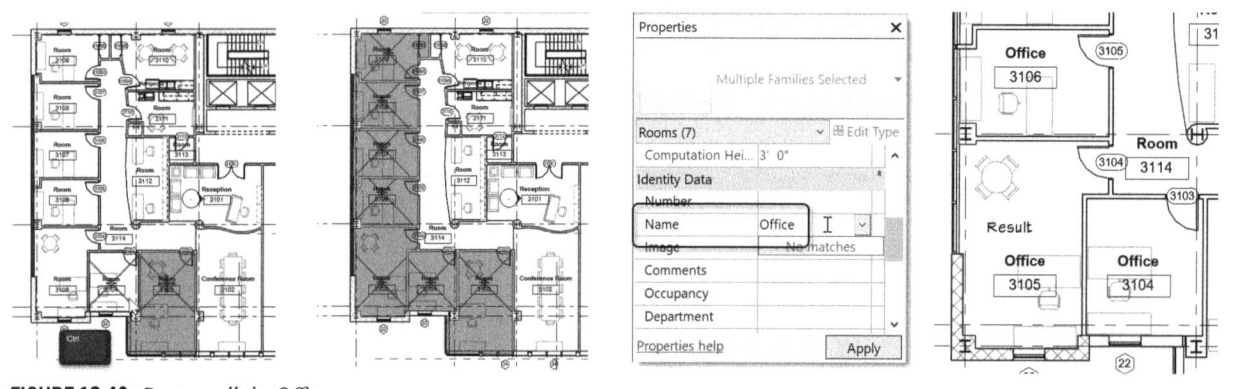

FIGURE 13.40 *Rename all the Offices*

> **TIP:** While this approach is effective, if you remember to edit the value on the Properties palette before you place the room, you can set the Room Name and then place one or more rooms with the desired name without the need to go back and rename.

VIEWING A ROOM SCHEDULE

Among the schedules we added to the project back in Chapter 5, was a Room Schedule. At the start of this chapter, that schedule was still empty. Let's look at that schedule now to see how it reflects the data that we just added to the model.

1. On the Project Browser, double-click to open the *A601 -Schedules* sheet view.
   ⇨ Zoom In Region on the Room Schedule.

Now that we have added rooms to our model, this schedule has been filled in to list these rooms. Notice that this is really a room finishes schedule and that currently there is no finish information listed. We can add finish data directly in the schedule as we did in the furniture schedule, or we can select a room and edit the Properties in the model. However, you cannot edit a view directly on a sheet. If it is a graphical view, right-click and choose: **Activate View**. For a schedule, right-click and choose: **Edit Schedule** (or just double-click it).

2. Select the schedule on the sheet, right-click, and choose: **Edit Schedule**.

> **NOTE:** You can, of course, go directly to the schedule on the Project Browser. It is not necessary to first open the sheet; this is simply an alternative method.

3. Close or minimize all views except the *Room Schedule* view and the *Level 3* floor plan.
   ⇨ Tile the windows.
4. Select one of the rooms whose name still reads: "Room" in the schedule.

   The room will highlight in the plan.

   ⇨ Type an appropriate name in the schedule.
   ⇨ Repeat until all rooms are named (see the left of Figure 13.41).

For the utility space just above Reception, we will need to move the tag outside the room to make it more legible. However, if you try to move a room tag outside of its room boundaries, a warning will appear. To do this, you must first enable the leader option on the Options Bar. Then you can safely move the tag outside the room.

5. Select the Utility Room tag.
   ⇨ On the Options Bar, check the Leader option, and then using the move control on the tag, drag the tag outside the space (see the bottom right corner of Figure 13.41).
6. With the tag still selected, on the Properties palette click the Edit Type button.
   ⇨ For the Leader Arrowhead option, select an arrowhead of your choice and then click OK.
7. Make the schedule view active, and then on the Properties palette, edit it to sort by: **Number**.

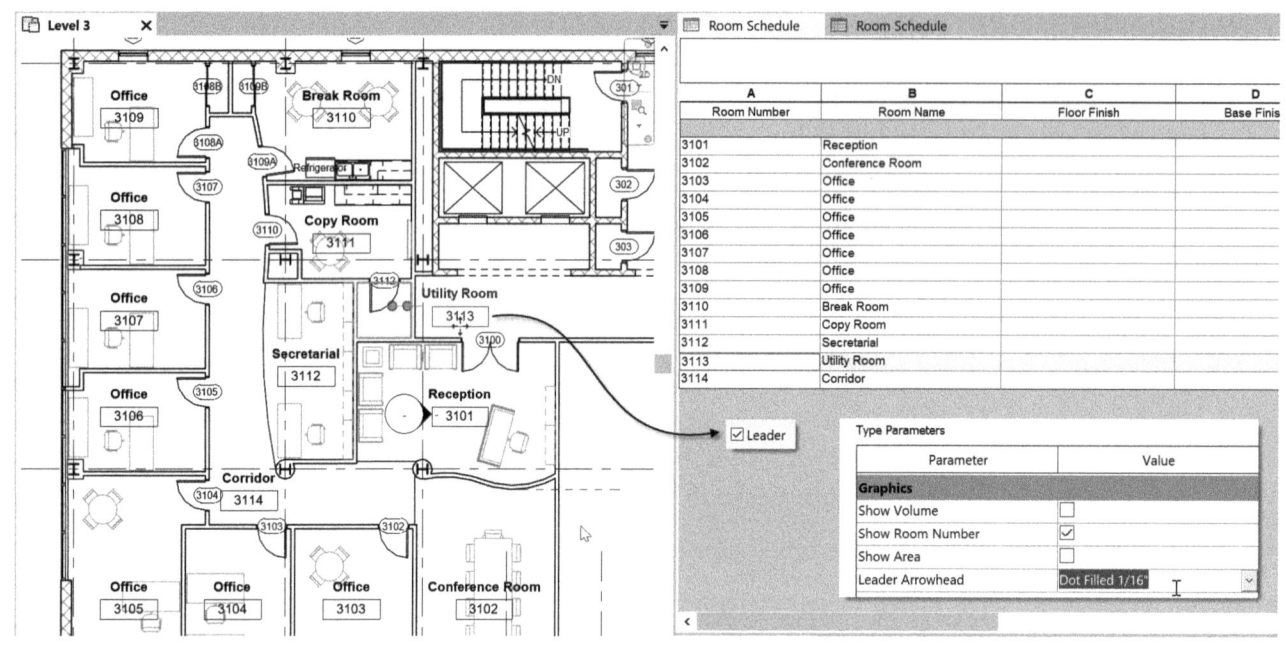

FIGURE 13.41 *Finish renaming, renumbering, and adjusting tag locations*

ADDING ROOM FINISH INFORMATION

Using the procedure covered in the "Using Schedule Keys to Speed Input" topic on page 613 above, create a **Room Style Key Schedule** that includes all of the finish fields: "Base Finish," "Ceiling Finish," "Ceiling Height," "Floor Finish," and "Wall Finish." Create a few key styles such as those shown in the top portion of Figure 13.42.

Once you have defined a few styles, you can add the Room Finish Style key field to your Room Schedule and use it to input the finishes quickly based on room type. For example, the two large offices at the bottom of the plan could be assigned the Executive Office key, while all the others get the Standard Office key. Define and assign as many keys as you wish. Remember, if you change a value in the schedule key later, the *Room Schedule* will automatically reflect the change. You can use any of the methods discussed so far to make the selections and edits. Also, remember that you can select many objects in the plan and then use the Filter tool to remove everything but rooms from the selection. This should make selection quicker for the rooms with common settings. When you are finished, your *Room Schedule* should look something like Figure 13.42. Please notice in the figure that you can manually edit custom values in the fields if you leave the Room Finish Style set to "none" (see the highlighted space in the figure). If you prefer, you can define another room style, but in spaces that are unique like the Utility Room, it is just as easy to not assign a room style and instead assign the values of each finish directly.

FIGURE 13.42 *Create a Room Finish Key Schedule and then use it to input values for the finishes of all of the rooms*

Working with Schedules, Tags and Data | 631

TAGGING OTHER VIEWS

If you return to the *Level 3 Furniture Plan*, you will note that it does not have room tags. At first this may seem strange, until we recall that annotation is *always* view-specific. This means that tags and other annotation will appear only in the view to which it is added. However, it is very easy to add the tags to any plan that needs them.

1. On the Annotate tab, click the Tag All tool.
   ⇨ Select the Room Tag item and then click OK.

That added all the room tags, but since there are already many furniture tags in this view, it might be useful to add leaders to the room tags so we can move them around and make things more legible.

2. Making a crossing selection, surround the entire plan.

   This will select everything.

   ⇨ On the ribbon, click the Filter button, click Check None, and then check only Room Tags and then click OK.

You should now have just the room tags selected.

3. On the Options Bar or Properties palette, check the Leader check box.
4. Move each room tag to a better location. In this plan, pulling them outside the rooms might be best.

You will need to move them around to make the plan legible but starting with the Tag All tool does save considerable time over manually tagging. In some cases, you might find copy and paste quicker. If you have two plans that can accommodate tags in the same location, select all the tags in the original plan (use Filter like we did here to select quickly), press CTRL + C, and then use Paste Aligned (Modify tab) in the other view with the **Current View** option. This will copy all the tags exactly as they appear in the first plan. You can then fine-tune placement by moving those that require it. Remember, if a room tag needs to move outside the boundary of its room, enable the Leader option first.

5. Save the project.

QUERYING DATA

You should now be getting comfortable with using schedules. We have explored many examples and you are no doubt beginning to see just how powerful schedules are. One of the biggest benefits to scheduling in Revit is all the robust data we can readily extract from our model. This data extraction is the "I" in BIM. While the potential data we can extract is virtually limitless, in this topic, we will focus on a couple of very simple queries.

REPORTING THE ROOM IN THE FURNITURE SCHEDULE

We have a detailed furniture schedule and a detailed room finish schedule. It might be useful to have Revit report in which room each piece of furniture is located directly in the furniture schedule.

1. On the Project Browser, right-click the *Working Furniture Schedule* view and choose: **Duplicate View > Duplicate**.
   ⇨ Rename the view: Furniture Location Schedule.
2. On the Modify Schedule/Quantities tab, on the Columns panel, click the Insert button.
   ⇨ In the "Select Fields: dialog that appears, at the top left corner, click the pop-up menu beneath "Select available fields from" and choose: **Room**.

Notice that all the Room fields are now available to add to the Schedule. All we need is Room Name and Number.

3. Add **Room: Name** and **Room: Number** to the right side.

• Revit Essentials for Architecture •

632 | Chapter 13

⇨ Use the Move Up and Move Down buttons to locate the fields where you want them and then click OK twice (see Figure 13.43).

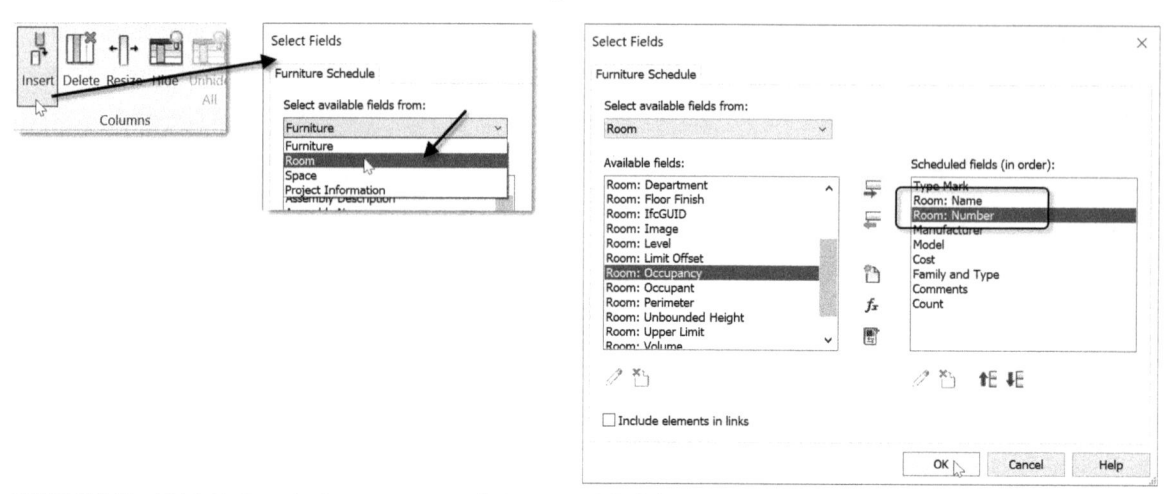

FIGURE 13.43 *Add fields from the Rooms category to the Furniture Schedule*

Room names and numbers now appear in the schedule, but because of the way that we are currently sorting and grouping, the data appears incomplete. A quick modification on the Sorting/Grouping tab will take care of this.

4. From the Properties palette, edit the Sorting/Grouping.

⇨ Change the first sort criterion to: **Room: Name**. Enable the Header option and the Blank Line option.

⇨ Change the second criterion to: **Room: Number**. Enable the Header option.

Make sure that the third criterion is set to: **Model**.

5. On the Formatting tab, make both the **Room: Name** and **Room: Number** fields hidden fields.

This removes the redundancy. When you use a field as a header, you can hide its column.

⇨ Click OK to see the result (see Figure 13.44).

We now have a schedule that shows all the furniture grouped by the room it occupies.

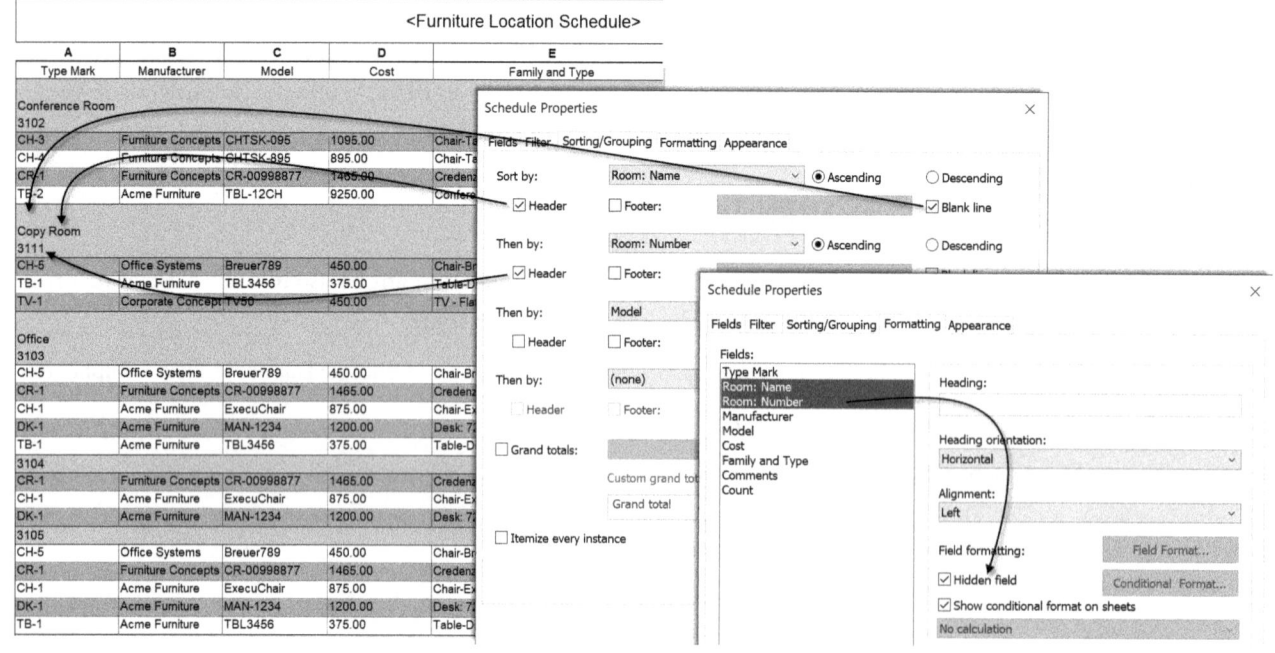

FIGURE 13.44 *Sort and group by room fields*

• The Aubin Academy •

Working with Schedules, Tags and Data | 633

There are many other ways that this schedule can be sorted, grouped, or formatted. Please feel free to experiment further. Remember, if you are uncertain how a combination of settings will look, make a duplicate of the schedule first.

CONDITIONAL FORMATTING

Another very useful way that you can highlight important data in a schedule is using conditional formatting. This allows you to shade cells in color that meet certain criteria that you designate.

1. On the Properties palette, click the Edit button next to Formatting.
2. Select the Cost field on the left and then on the right, click the Conditional Format button.
   - From the Test drop down list, choose: **Between**.
   - Type in a range of values such as: **250** and **850**.
3. Click the color swatch next to Background Color and choose any color.
4. Click OK twice to see the change.

Notice how cost values that fall within this range highlight in the color you indicated. You can try other conditions for additional fields if you wish. This can be a powerful way to quickly locate certain data in a detailed schedule.

MATERIAL TAKEOFFS

Most model elements have materials assigned to their components. These materials determine how the components render in various views. For example, a brick material controls the cross hatching in plan and the brick coursing pattern in elevation as well as the brick photo texture applied in rendering. In addition to the display characteristics, materials can also have identity data assigned to them. A Material Takeoff is a schedule that can query the material properties assigned to model elements. Using a material takeoff, we can ask Revit for the volume of concrete or the area of wood flooring used in our project. Like other schedules, we can limit the query to a single category like walls, or we can do a multi-category takeoff from many element categories at once.

1. On the View tab, on the Create panel, click the Schedules drop down button and choose the: **Material Takeoff** tool.
   - In the "New Material Takeoff" dialog, accept the <Multi-Category> choice on the left, name the takeoff: **Concrete Takeoff** and then click OK.

Scroll through the list of fields. Since we did a multi-category schedule, the fields listed will be those that are common to all element categories. Also, several material fields will be available. These will all be prefixed with the word "Material" in front of the field name.

2. Add the following fields: "Family and Type," "Material: Name," "Material: Description," and "Material: Volume."
   - Click OK to create the takeoff.
   - Widen all columns so that you can read all the data more comfortably.

The resultant takeoff is very long and includes far more than concrete. Scroll through the entire list. Notice that our best chance for isolating just the concrete is the Material: Name column. Any of the Concrete materials use the word "Concrete" in the name. We do have to be careful however as several materials have "Concrete Masonry Units," in their name, which we don't really want to include in the volume of concrete. Therefore, we need to be specific about the filter criterion we establish.

3. On the Properties palette, click the Edit button next to Filter.
   - For the first Filter by criterion, choose: **Material: Name**.

• Revit Essentials for Architecture •

634 | Chapter 13

⇨ Change the operator to: **contains**.

⇨ In the text field, type: **Concrete**.

4. For the next criterion, choose: **Material Name** again, **does not contain**, and type: **Masonry Units** (see Figure 13.45).

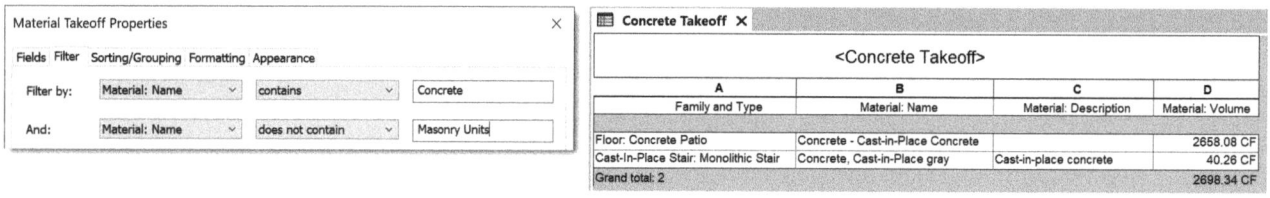

FIGURE 13.45 *Add filtering to limit the takeoff to just concrete materials*

Another approach that would yield the same result would be to filter by Material: Name containing: "Cast-in-Place." Please note that, in either case, filters are case-sensitive. To fine-tune the takeoff further, edit the Formatting options. Set the alignment of the volume column to right and select the Calculate totals option. On the Sorting/Grouping tab, turn on Grand totals for this to display (each of these enhancements is shown in the figure).

Filtering and totals work in any schedule. The only difference between a schedule and a material takeoff is the inclusion of the material fields in the material takeoff. You can get pretty good raw data from your model directly in Revit schedules. There is even the possibility of creating formula fields and custom parameters. Both are out of the scope of what we will cover here.

EXPORT SCHEDULE DATA

Even with the functionality we have seen here for schedules, you might find that you need to process the raw data in a way that is not easy to accomplish directly in Revit. In such cases, you can export any schedule to an Excel compatible file. This file is a static delimited text file (TXT) export, (not linked back to the model). However, you can open such a file in Excel or any program that can import delimited text files and process the data in nearly limitless ways. Also, there are third-party tools available that create bi-directional links between Excel files and your Revit model. Check the Autodesk App Store.

> **NOTE:** Another option is to use Dynamo. Dynamo is on the Manage tab and opens a separate program window. Here you can build a script that uses pre-made blocks of code. Dynamo gives direct access to the behind the scenes Revit application programming interface (or API) in a user friendly visual scripting environment. Among the many powerful nodes and features built into Dynamo are nodes for import and export of Excel data. So using these nodes you could build a script that provided round-trip functionality from and to Revit via Excel. There are many online resources for learning Dynamo. Visit: **dynamobim.org** to learn more. In addition to those resources the author has a free introduction to Dynamo workshop handout (and dataset). You can download it by visiting: **paulaubin.com/topics/dynamo**. The session is called: **Computational BIM Workshop – Dynamo for Revit for Beginners**[‡].

1. Open the *Door Schedule* (or any Schedule you wish to export).

2. From the File menu, choose: **Export > Reports > Schedule**.

⇨ If necessary, browse to the *Chapter13* folder.

⇨ Accept the default file name and then click Save.

3. In the "Export Schedule" dialog, accept all defaults and then click OK.

Working with Schedules, Tags and Data | 635

You can open the resultant file in Microsoft Excel or any other spreadsheet or database program. Please note that such exported reports do not remain linked to your Revit model. As your project progresses and changes are made, you will need to re- export the reports.

ADD IMAGES TO SCHEDULES

Sometimes you want to display images in a schedule instead of just text and data. Any model element can reference an external image file (BMP, JPG, PNG or TIF). The image will be visible in the "Manage Images" dialog and if you add it to a schedule, it will show in the schedule when it is placed on a sheet. Let's look at a quick example. Perhaps you would like to show a photograph or illustration of each piece of furniture on your furniture schedule.

1. Open the *Level 3 Furniture Plan*.
2. In the Reception space, right-click one of the Corbu chairs and choose: **Select All Instances** > **Visible in View**.
   ⇨ On the Properties palette, click in the Image field and then click the small browse button that appears.
   ⇨ In the dialog that appears, click the Add button at the bottom. In the *Chapter13* folder, select the *Corbu.png* file and then click Open.
   ⇨ Click OK to dismiss the "Manage Images" dialog.

This will only display the name of the image file on the Properties palette. To see the image, you must add this field to the schedule and then look at the schedule on a sheet. Since we already have our Furniture schedule on the A602 sheet, we only need to add the Image field to that schedule.

3. Open the *A602 – Schedules* sheet.
   ⇨ Double-click the schedule on the sheet (or right-click it and choose: **Edit Schedule**).
4. On the ribbon, on the Columns panel, click the Insert button.
   ⇨ Add the Image field to the schedule and then click OK.
   ⇨ Click back to the sheet *A602* tab.

   The image column and the *Corbu.png* image that we added should now appear in the schedule (see Figure 13.46).

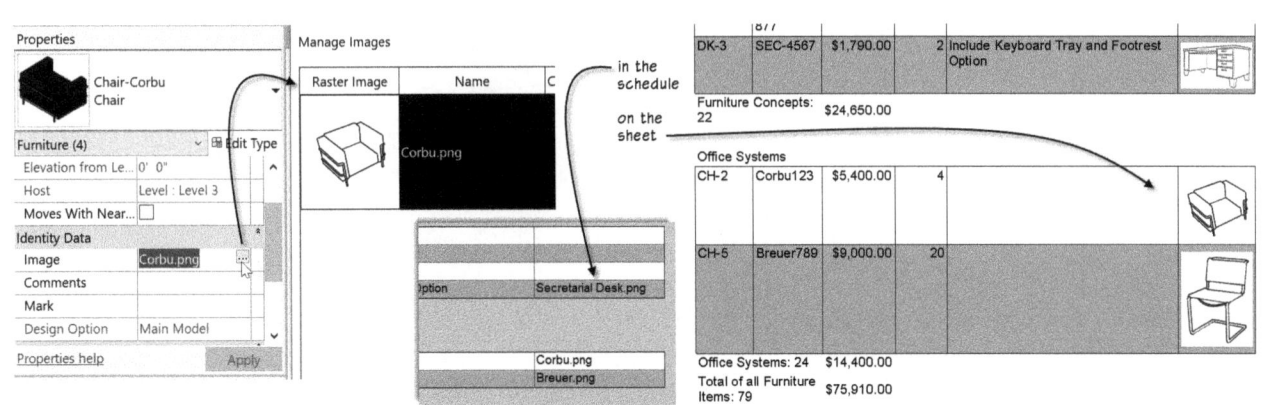

FIGURE 13.46 *Add the Image field to an existing schedule and preview it on a sheet*

This is a very simple example. If you wish you can experiment further. Several other image files have been provided in the dataset. There is also a Type Image property which would seem more appropriate in this example. However, it takes a little more effort to set it up. You must edit the family in the family editor and add the Type Image there. You then save and reload the family back into the project and replace the existing when prompted. You are left this approach as a challenge exercise if you so choose.

• Revit Essentials for Architecture •

ADD A COLOR SCHEME

When working with rooms (or areas—see next topic) we noted how they only display on screen during creation and selection. In many cases, this is appropriate particularly in printing construction documents. There are times however when graphical indication of rooms (or areas) can be valuable, for example, when creating a programmatic color-coded diagram. Revit gives us this ability with Color Schemes.

CREATE A NEW VIEW WITH ALTERNATE ROOM TAGS

Let's make a color-coded third floor plan.

1. On the Project Browser, right-click on *Level 3* and choose: **Duplicate View** > **Duplicate with Detailing**.
   ⇨ Rename the new view: **Level 3 Color Plan**.
   ⇨ Close inactive views.
2. Make a window selection around the entire plan.
   ⇨ On the ribbon, click the Filter button.
   ⇨ In the "Filter" dialog, click the Check None button and then check only the Door Tags and Window Tags boxes and then click OK.
3. Delete the selected tags.

Remember, each view's annotation is unique to that view. We have only deleted the door and window tags in the *Level 3 Color Plan*, not in the original *Level 3* plan.

4. Right-click one of the room tags and choose: **Select All Instances** > **Visible In View**.
   ⇨ From the Type Selector, choose: **Room Tag: Room Tag With Area [M_Room Tag: Room Tag With Area]**.

All of the room tags in this view will now display the area beneath the tag (see Figure 13.47).

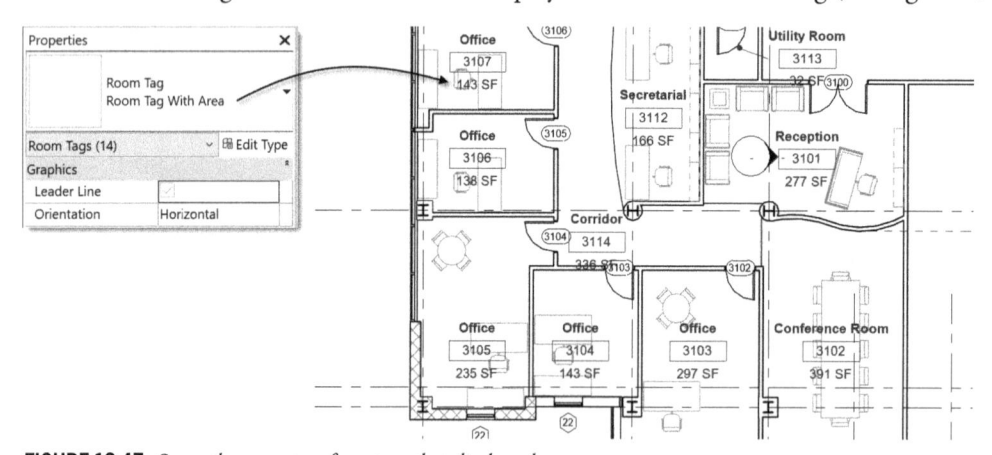

FIGURE 13.47 *Swap the room tags for a type that displays the area*

The room tag used here was part of the template from which the project was created.

5. Move around the plan and adjust the location of any tags to make them more legible as required.

If any of your tags used a leader, you will need to edit this new type and add your preferred arrowhead again. This is because the arrowhead setting is unique for each type.

> **BIM MANAGER NOTE:** You can create a room tag family (or any tag) that displays any of the parameters you wish. While we will not create one here, building a tag family is nearly identical to the process we used to create the custom elevation tag in Chapter 11. In fact, creating a custom tag family is also like creating a custom title block family like we did in the "Create a Custom Title Block Family" topic on page 193 in Chapter 5. If you wish to experiment on your own, select one of the tags in this project that is like the one you wish to create. On the ribbon, click the Edit Family button to launch the family editor and load the tag for editing. Save the file as a new name and manipulate it to suit your needs. The text values are special elements called "Labels." You can add or edit labels in the Family Editor and have them report any of the parameters available. If you wish to add a parameter that is not included on the list available, you must create a custom parameter. This must be done with a "Shared Parameter" (the Shared Parameters tool is on the Manage tab) if you want it to appear in a tag. Shared Parameters are created from a Shared Parameter file. A shared parameter file is simply a text file saved on a hard drive or network server. The advantage of this file is that you can store your custom parameters in this file, save it to a common network server location, and then all users in the firm can access and use these parameters in their projects, schedules, and tags.
>
> There should only be one shared parameter file for the entire firm. The file should be stored on a network drive accessible to all authorized users. These points are very important to guarantee that custom parameters work properly. Having more than one shared parameter file will almost certainly cause problems, annoyances, or even outright failures in the implementation of custom parameters in projects. The shared parameter file is merely the holding place for the parameter definition. It is not the parameter itself. A single shared parameter file can store hundreds of custom parameters for an unlimited number of projects and users. Therefore, please heed this recommendation and implement a single network-based shared parameter for your office. For more information on creating and working with shared parameters, see the online help.

ADDING A COLOR SCHEME

By adding a color scheme to a view, we can graphically represent any of the data fields in our room elements.

1. Deselect all objects and then direct your attention to the Properties palette.

At the top of the Properties palette, just below the Type Selector, you should see *Floor Plan: Level 3 Color Plan* on the filter drop down list.

2. Scroll down and locate the Color Scheme item and click the button (labeled <none>) next to it.

You can make a color scheme based on any of the room's data fields. There are two predefined schemes: Name and Department.

3. From the Category list at the top, choose: **Rooms**.
   ⇨ Select the Name scheme on the left and then click OK (see Figure 13.48).

638 | Chapter 13

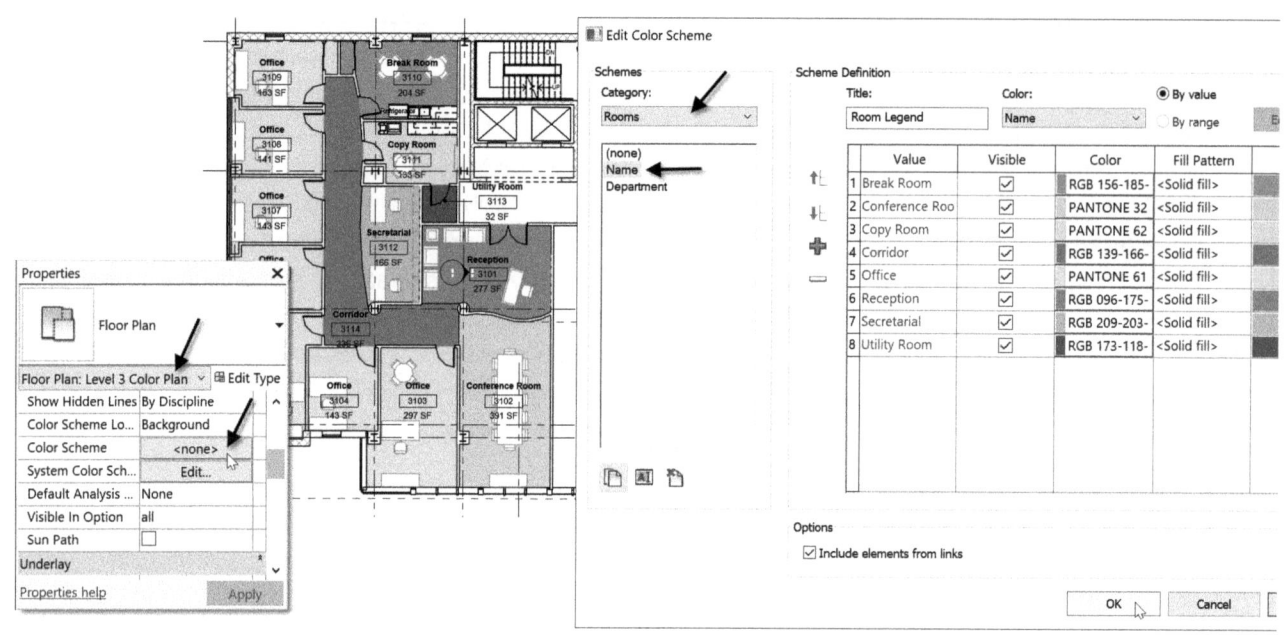

FIGURE 13.48 *Add a color scheme to the Level 3 Color Plan view*

As you can see, it is easy to add a color scheme. However, a scheme based on room names does not convey much useful information. We could try the Department scheme, but currently none of our rooms have a value set for the department property, so this would not yield useful results either. If you want to try the Department scheme, edit each room's properties and type in a value for the Department field. Then apply this color scheme to see the results. You can type in anything you like for the department values.

CREATE A CUSTOM COLOR SCHEME

Using the **Room Tag with Area** tag as we did above is a useful way to display the area of each room directly in the plan, but it might also be useful to show this data more graphically using color coded shading. Let's build a custom color scheme to convey this information.

1. On the Properties palette click the Color Scheme button again (it is now labeled "Name" instead of <None>).
2. At the bottom of the list area, click the Duplicate icon.
   ⇨ In the "New Color Scheme" dialog, type: **Area by Range** and then click OK.
3. At the top of the dialog, change the Title to: **Room Area Legend**.
   ⇨ From the Color drop down choose: **Area**.

Notice all the Room parameters are included on this list. You can make a color scheme from any parameter on this list.

⇨ In the warning that appears, click OK.

There are two ways to create an area scheme: by the actual values in the model (By value) and by ranges that you define (By range). By value is the default; but we'll build a "by range" scheme instead.

4. At the top right, click the By range radio button.

All existing values will be replaced by just two.

5. Click in the "At Least" column for the last item (currently 20.00 SF [20m2])
   ⇨ Change the value to: **50 [5]** and then press ENTER.

• The Aubin Academy •

Working with Schedules, Tags and Data | 639

6. Click the Add Value icon (large green plus sign).

A new 100.00 SF [10m2] value will appear.

7. Select the 100.00 SF [10m2] value, and then click the add value icon again.

> **IMPORTANT:** Make sure you select the last item in the list each time **before** you click the add value icon or the new value will be added in between the one you have selected and the one after it.

A new 150.00 SF [15m2] value will appear.

8. Keep selecting the last item and clicking the Add Value icon until you reach 300.00 SF [30m2] (see Figure 13.49).

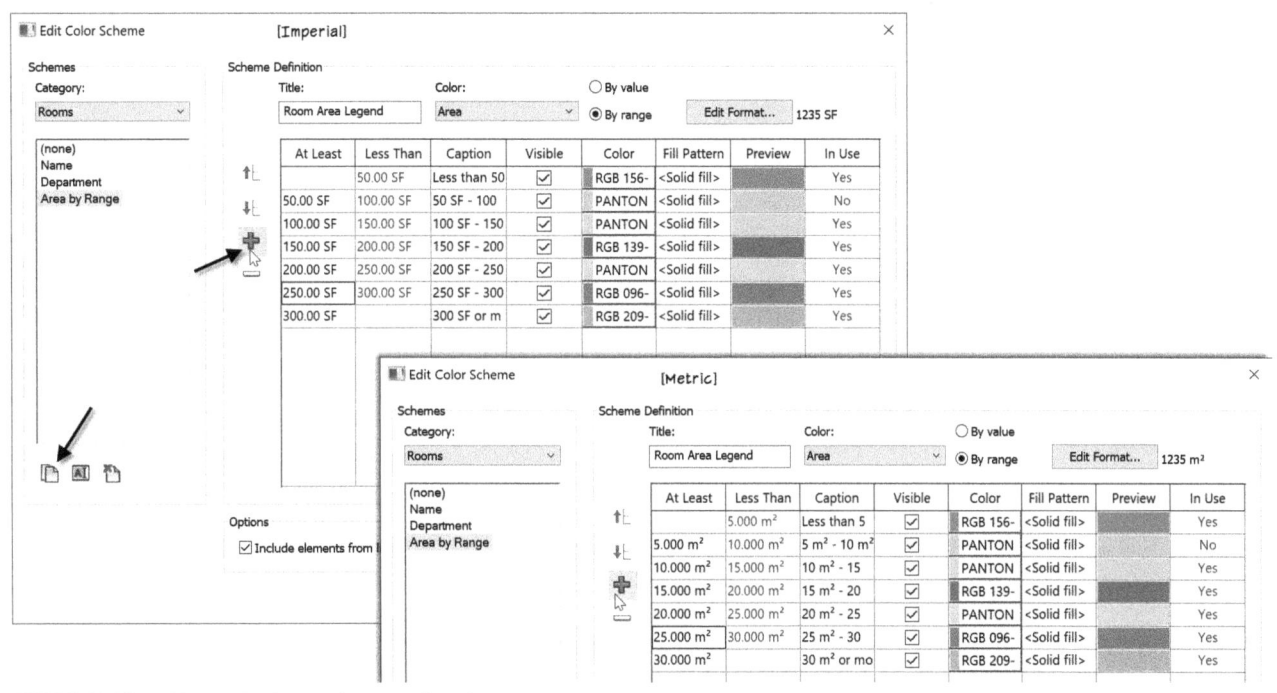

FIGURE 13.49 *Add several values to the area color scheme*

By default, the colors are assigned automatically. This is the easiest way to see immediate results. If you prefer to designate your own colors, you can click the color buttons next to each item. We will not do that for this exercise.

⇨ Click OK to accept the default color scheme and display it in the view.

Notice that the colors in the view change to reflect the new scheme. Since we defined several ranges, rooms are grouped by which range their area falls within.

ADD A COLOR SCHEME LEGEND

It may not always be obvious what the colors in a plan represent. So, to make it easier to understand the color scheme, we can add a legend.

1. On the Annotate tab, on the Color Fill panel, click the Color Fill Legend tool.

⇨ Zoom out a bit allowing room to the left side of the plan.

2. Click a point to the left of the plan to place the color fill legend (see Figure 13.50).

• Revit Essentials for Architecture •

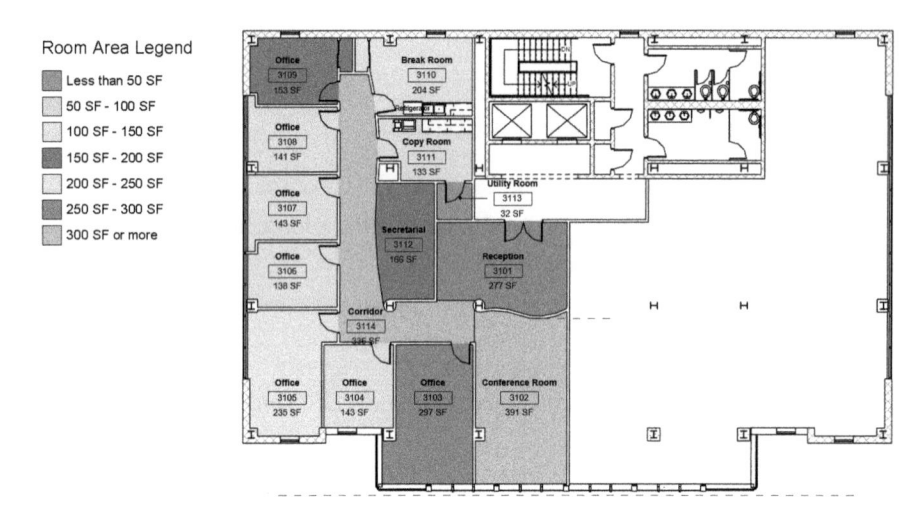

FIGURE 13.50 *Complete the color scheme and add a legend*

If you wish, you can fine-tune the graphical display and hide categories you don't wish to see in this view.

CREATE ANOTHER COLOR SCHEME

You can continue to experiment by creating new color schemes. Simply return to the Properties palette and click the color scheme button. There you can make new duplicates and configure them. Let's do one more. Now that we have a legend, there is also an alternate way to get to the "Edit Color Scheme" dialog.

1. Select the color scheme legend onscreen and then on the ribbon, click the Edit Scheme button.

2. Click the Duplicate icon and name the new scheme: **Floor Finish** and then click OK.

   ⇨ Change the Title to: **Floor Finish Legend** and then from the "Color" list choose: **Floor Finish**.

   ⇨ Click OK in the warning dialog.

3. Click OK again to return to the plan view and see the results.

In this case, the colors show where the floor finish varies based on the values we assigned earlier in the chapter. Feel free to create other schemes and vary the colors or other settings. If you want to make any of these permanent, duplicate the floor plan view first. After you complete the "Working With Area Plans" topic on page 641 below, you can make a color scheme for your area plan as well.

EXPORTING REPORTS

In some jurisdictions detailed area analysis with triangulated area proofs are required. You can generate such a report from Revit in HTML format. This tool will export the rooms in your model, so you can have any floor plan open for this procedure.

1. From the File menu, choose: **Export** > **Reports** > **Room/Area Report**.

   ⇨ In the dialog that appears browse to the *Chapter13* folder.

2. Click the Options button in the lower right corner. At the bottom of the "Area Report Settings" dialog, check the "Report window area as a percentage of room area" check box.

   If you wish, edit the fonts and/or colors to be used in the report and then click OK.

At the bottom of the dialog is a Range drop down. It defaults to Current view, which is fine for our example, but you can also choose the Select views option. So, in a project where you need to generate a report for every floor of your building, you can choose this option and select a view for each floor.

3. Accept the default file name and then click Save.
4. Launch your web browser and open the HTML file created to view the report.

The HTML file is accompanied by a folder that contains all the images. If you share the report with anyone, be sure to include this folder as well.

WORKING WITH AREA PLANS

Using the alternative room tag and color scheme shown in the previous topic is a quick way to see the area of each room. We can also see the area on the Properties palette when we select a room. And we can also add area as a field to our room schedule. So, there are lots of ways to see the area of rooms. This area is certainly useful information, but we have limited control over how the areas of rooms are calculated. For room area computation, you can use one of four methods: wall finish, wall centers, wall core, or core centers. However, this setting is global, and *all* rooms will be calculated the same way. To make your choice, expand the Room & Area panel on the Architecture tab and then click the Room and Volume Computations button.

If you need to calculate areas more precisely than is possible with rooms, or if you need to follow code requirements or leasing area standards such as BOMA, you need to use Areas and Area Plans instead of rooms. Areas are very much like Rooms, but they are not related or connected to each other in any way. They are placed like rooms and we can create schedules focused on them too. An Area Plan is a special type of floor plan that allows for much more control in documenting and calculating the areas of a plan. The process is as follows:

a. Create an Area Plan. (If required, create a new area scheme. Or you can use an existing one).

b. Generate Area Boundary Lines (like room separation Lines).

c. Add Area elements (like rooms).

d. Assign properties such as Area Type.

e. Generate schedules and/or color schemes.

The area plan feature is not available in Revit LT. If you are using Revit LT, please skip this topic.

CREATE AN AREA PLAN

Let's run through the process. Area plans are required before any of the other steps can be performed. Area plans are tied to "Area Schemes." There are two area schemes built into the software and you can copy them in the "Area and Volume Computations" dialog (Architecture tab, expanded Room & Area panel). In this example, we will use the built-in: **Rentable** area scheme.

1. On the Architecture tab, on the Room & Area panel, click the Area drop down button and choose: **Area Plan**.

    ⇨ In the "New Area Plan" dialog that appears, make sure the type is set to: **Rentable**, select Level 3, and then click OK.

    ⇨ In the dialog that appears, click Yes.

The Rentable area scheme has some rules built into it based on common rentable area requirements for commercial buildings. When you create the area plan, Revit will therefore offer to generate some of the area boundary lines you need automatically based on the exterior walls of your model. The lines thus generated will try to logically choose the most appropriate face of each wall, be it the centerline, exterior face, or face of glazing. It is not a bad idea to answer yes to this question and see what Revit determines. You can always delete the auto-generated lines later and draw them over again manually if necessary. Before we begin working with area boundaries and areas, let's adjust the cropping of this plan.

2. Check Crop Region Visible, and then zoom out to see the crop.

⇨ Using the control handles, reduce the size of the crop to crop out all of the site information in this view (see Figure 13.51).

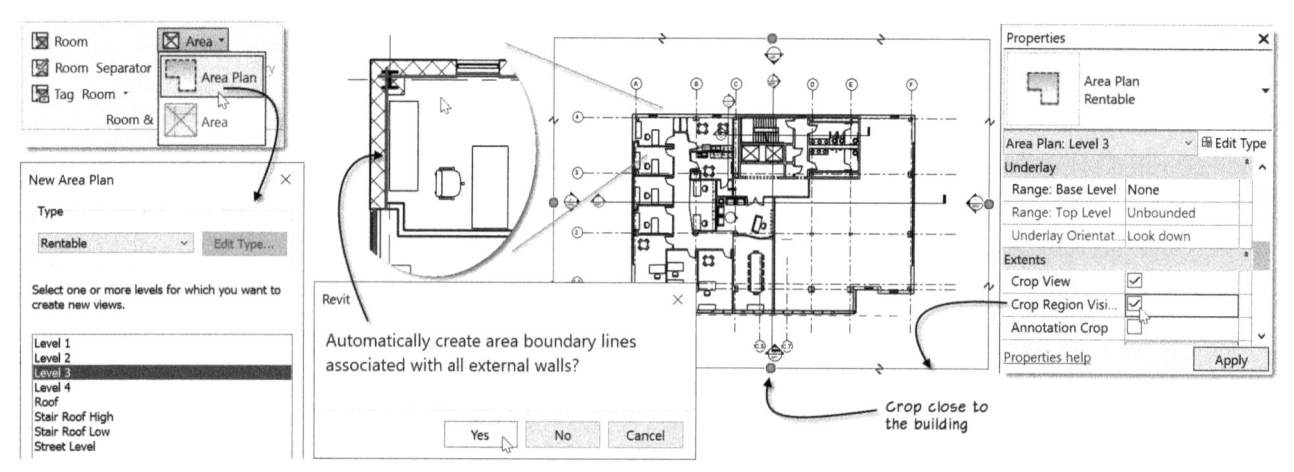

FIGURE 13.51 *Create a new area plan view and adjust its settings*

3. Hide the section line category. (Select any section, right-click and choose: **Hide in View** > **Category**).

ADDING AREA BOUNDARY LINES

Some purple lines will appear on the exterior walls. Some are at the face of the glazing on the curtain walls; others are at the faces of the walls. Area elements behave almost identically to rooms. They are added in similar fashion by clicking within an enclosed region bounded by area boundary lines (the purple lines we have here). The goal of our area plan is different from that of our rooms. Here we want to measure the area of each tenant. Therefore, we do not need boundaries at each room and office. Rather, we only need one overall area element to represent the entire tenant space on the left side of the third floor. Another can be placed in the vacant space to the right of the plan and two in the core: one for the vertical penetrations and the other for the floor common area. So, our next task is simply to draw the required boundary lines to separate these areas.

1. On the Room & Area panel, click the Area Boundary tool.

2. On the Modify | Place Area Boundary tab, click the Pick Lines tool.

⇨ Click each of the walls that separate the tenant space from the rest of the plan (the demising walls) and several walls in the core as well (see Figure 13.52)

Working with Schedules, Tags and Data | 643

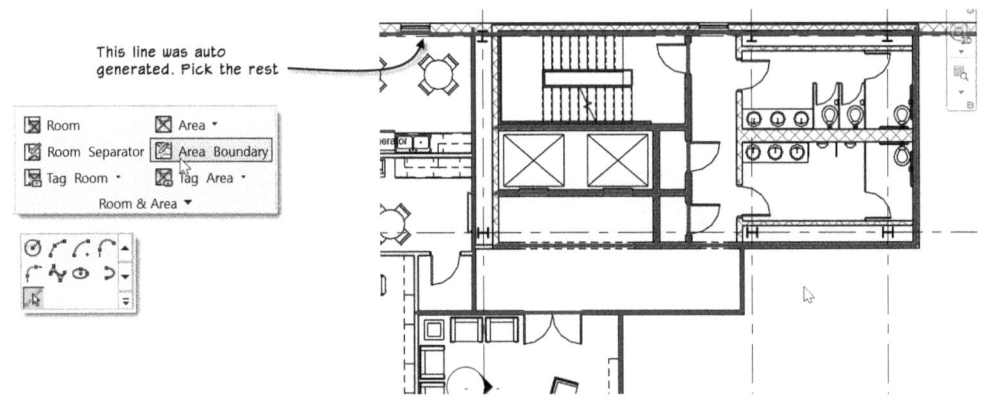

FIGURE 13.52 *Pick area boundary lines along the walls that separate the various areas required (Area lines enhanced in the figure for clarity)*

Area boundary lines don't always close like other sketch lines. We will perform some basic trimming, but it is not always necessary to trim every corner. Overlapping lines are acceptable with area boundaries. Do the overall trimming and wait till you add areas (below) and see if adjustments are needed. On the Options Bar there is an "Apply Area Rules" check box. With this selected for the Pick Lines icon, Revit will draw the line along the center of the picked wall when you first click it. In the core area, you might want the face of the wall. For now, do not worry about this. The "rules" are dynamic. So later when we add areas, and assign them to functions, the picked "rule-based" lines will know how to adjust automatically. So, for now leaving them at centers is perfectly fine.

3. Use Trim/Extend as required to complete the sketch (see Figure 13.53).

Use TAB as required. Be sure to only trim the area boundary lines and not the underlying walls.

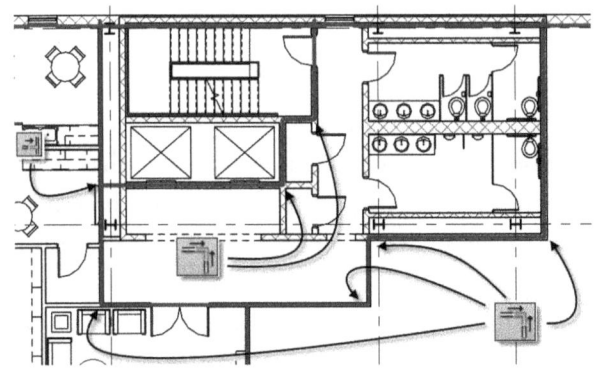

FIGURE 13.53 *Trim area boundary lines to separate the tenant space and the core areas (Area lines enhanced in the figure for clarity)*

ADD AREAS

We are now ready to add Areas.

1. On the Architecture tab, on the Room & Area panel, click the Area drop down button and choose: **Area**.

    Make sure that Tag on Placement is enabled.

Move the cursor around the screen and notice that the area behaves just like rooms. However, unlike rooms, areas do not see model elements like walls. They will only find regions defined by the area separation lines.

2. Place an area in each region (four total).

3. Click on the tag for the area in our office tenant space and edit the name to: **Tenant 3A**.

    ⇨ Name the tenant space on the right: **Unoccupied**, name the toilet/lobby space: **Level 3 Common** and the stair and elevator area as: **Vertical Penetration**.

• Revit Essentials for Architecture •

4. Select the Tenant 3A area element.

Just like rooms, you can look for the "X" that passes through the area element near where you placed the tag.

⇨ On the Properties palette, change the Area Type to: **Office Area**.

> **TIP:** You might find it difficult to select areas since the rooms are also visible. You can go to Visibility/Graphics (VG) and hide rooms to make selection of areas easier.

5. Repeat for the other Areas:

⇨ Set Unoccupied to: **Office Area**. Set Level 3 Common to: **Floor Area** and set Vertical Penetration to: **Major Vertical Penetration** (see Figure 13.54).

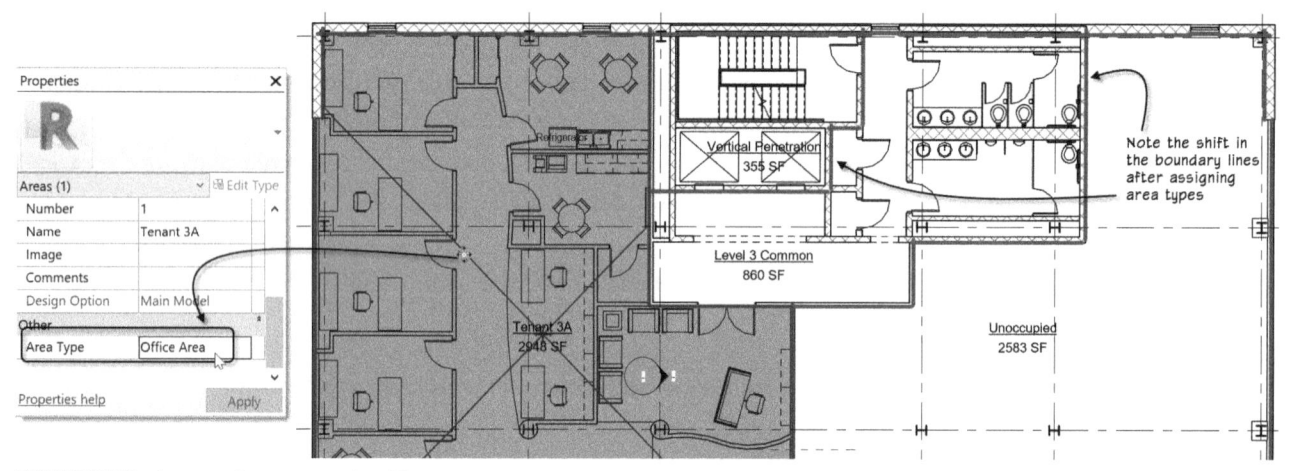

FIGURE 13.54 *Assign each area to an Area Type*

Notice the way that area boundary lines will adjust position after you are done assigning area types to all the area elements. This is because we checked the "Apply Area Rules" option on the Options Bar above. Now that Revit understands the function of each space as defined by its area, it can apply the rules correctly and move those boundary lines from their default centerline position to the correct location as determined by the rules. For example, in the core of the building, we have a major vertical penetration. This kind of space is measured to the outside face of the wall, while the two tenant spaces (both set to office space) continue to use a centerline boundary at their shared wall. This is because each tenant would be charged for half of the area of the shared wall between them.

PRESENTING AREA DATA

As a finishing touch, you can create a rentable area schedule and/or apply a color scheme to your area plan. Follow the procedures covered already in this chapter. You can see an example in Figure 13.55. Color schemes can apply to either rooms or areas. When you apply a color scheme to an area plan, you can color-code the Areas based on the Area Type or any other criteria of the area objects. A scheme based on area type is already included in the file. The simplest way to apply it is to add a color fill legend to this view. When you do, Revit will prompt you to apply the color scheme. Give it a try!

Working with Schedules, Tags and Data | 645

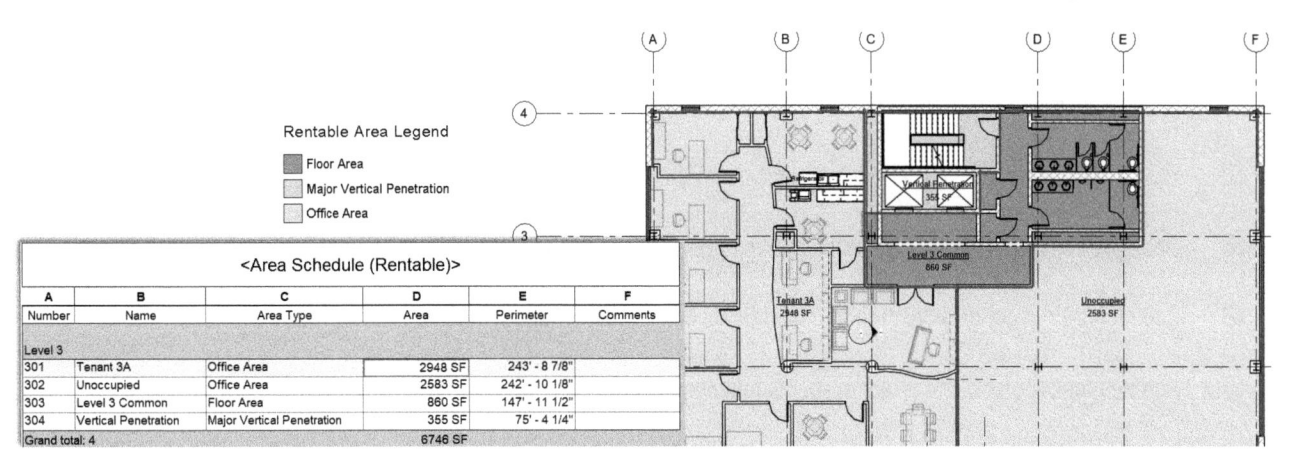

FIGURE 13.55 *Create an area schedule and color scheme (Furniture in the figure set to halftone and 70% transparent in VG)*

If you like you can continue with this file and create rooms on the other floors of the building and create area plans for the other floors as well. Also feel free to create or modify any other schedules that you like. (To learn more about Areas and Area Plans, check out the **Revit Area Calculations** course at **LinkedIn Learning**)[†].

1. When finished, close and save the file.

SUMMARY

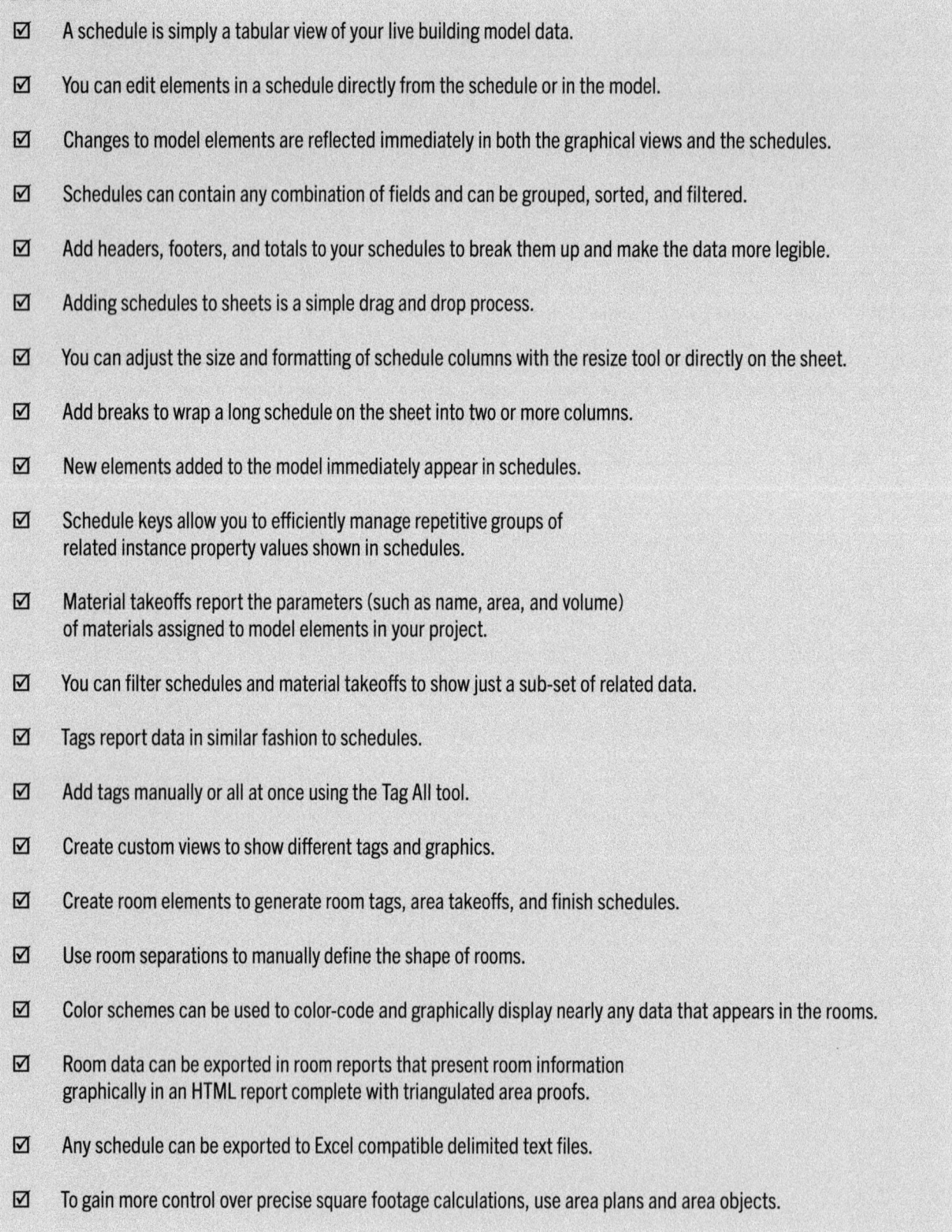

- ☑ A schedule is simply a tabular view of your live building model data.
- ☑ You can edit elements in a schedule directly from the schedule or in the model.
- ☑ Changes to model elements are reflected immediately in both the graphical views and the schedules.
- ☑ Schedules can contain any combination of fields and can be grouped, sorted, and filtered.
- ☑ Add headers, footers, and totals to your schedules to break them up and make the data more legible.
- ☑ Adding schedules to sheets is a simple drag and drop process.
- ☑ You can adjust the size and formatting of schedule columns with the resize tool or directly on the sheet.
- ☑ Add breaks to wrap a long schedule on the sheet into two or more columns.
- ☑ New elements added to the model immediately appear in schedules.
- ☑ Schedule keys allow you to efficiently manage repetitive groups of related instance property values shown in schedules.
- ☑ Material takeoffs report the parameters (such as name, area, and volume) of materials assigned to model elements in your project.
- ☑ You can filter schedules and material takeoffs to show just a sub-set of related data.
- ☑ Tags report data in similar fashion to schedules.
- ☑ Add tags manually or all at once using the Tag All tool.
- ☑ Create custom views to show different tags and graphics.
- ☑ Create room elements to generate room tags, area takeoffs, and finish schedules.
- ☑ Use room separations to manually define the shape of rooms.
- ☑ Color schemes can be used to color-code and graphically display nearly any data that appears in the rooms.
- ☑ Room data can be exported in room reports that present room information graphically in an HTML report complete with triangulated area proofs.
- ☑ Any schedule can be exported to Excel compatible delimited text files.
- ☑ To gain more control over precise square footage calculations, use area plans and area objects.

CHAPTER 14
Ceiling Plans and Interior Elevations

INTRODUCTION

Reflected ceiling plans will be the primary focus of the chapter with a brief exploration of interior elevations as well. Reflected ceiling plan views are included in the default project template file used to start both projects in this book. Therefore, we simply need to open these views and add appropriate model data and annotation. The default templates include only exterior elevations. Therefore, we will need to indicate which rooms we wish to elevate and create the required interior elevation views and any embellishments they require.

OBJECTIVES

Ceiling plans are very similar to other plans in many ways. The specific properties do vary. And of course, a ceiling plan looks at what is above the cut plane instead of what is below. We will add ceiling elements to the model and ceiling view specific annotation. After completing this chapter, you will know how to:

- Add and modify ceiling elements
- Understand ceiling types
- Add and modify ceiling component families
- Manipulate the view properties of the ceiling plan
- Create and articulate interior elevation views

CREATING CEILING ELEMENTS

Ceiling elements are used to convey the material of the ceiling plane—such as acoustical tile ceiling, gypsum board, or other ceiling treatment. They also have a height measured from the floor level and show in sections or ceiling plans. The default tool when creating ceilings allows you to pick a point within a closed space in the model (much like creating rooms, demonstrated in the previous chapter). However, they are sketch-based elements, and can utilize all the typical functions like the "Pick Walls" and other sketch methods on the ribbon during creation and editing.

OPEN A PROJECT

The lessons that follow require the dataset files included for download with this book. Refer to the "Download the Book Dataset" topic on page xi in the Preface for instructions on downloading and installing the book's dataset files.

1. Launch Autodesk® Revit®.
2. If you are on the Home screen, you can click the Open button beneath Models. Otherwise, from the File menu, choose **Open** > **Project**. In the "Open" dialog box, browse to the *Chapter14* folder.

⇨ Double-click *14 Commercial.rvt* if you wish to work in Imperial units.

⇨ Double-click *14 Commercial_M.rvt* if you wish to work in Metric units.

You can also select it and then click the Open button.

CREATING AN ACOUSTICAL TILE CEILING

Suspended acoustical tile ceilings in commercial office buildings are constructed in one of two ways. In the first method, walls are built past the height of the ceiling tiles (to a fixed height or all the way to the deck) and each room contains its own ceiling. In the second method, the walls are built only up to the height of the underside of the ceiling (underpinned) with the ceiling plane being continuous across the tops of the walls.

In Autodesk® Revit®, when each room contains its own ceiling and the walls continue past the ceiling plane height, ceiling elements can usually be created quickly with the "Automatic Ceiling" function of the ceiling tool. This is the default function of the ceiling tool. When you have an underpinned ceiling, you can instead use the Sketch Ceiling option to draw the shape of the overall ceiling plane using any of the available sketching tools. We will explore both creation methods as we continue to refine the third floor of our commercial project.

Revit usually creates both a floor plan and a ceiling plan view whenever you create a new level in a project. The template from which we originally created the commercial project includes such views. In this sequence, we will work in the ceiling plan views for the first time. Be sure that you work in a ceiling plan view when adding ceiling elements. If you do not, you will receive a warning like the one shown in Figure 14.1.

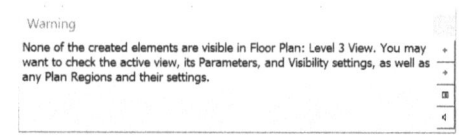

FIGURE 14.1 *Attempting to add ceilings in floor plan views yields a warning*

1. On the Project Browser, expand the *Ceiling Plans* branch.
2. Double-click to open the *Level 3* ceiling plan view.

> **NOTE:** Please be sure that you are opening the *Level 3* ceiling plan view and not the *Level 3* floor plan view.

3. On the Architecture tab, on the Build panel, click the Ceiling tool.

On the Modify | Place Ceiling tab, the Automatic Ceiling button is enabled by default. On the Status Bar, a message will appear "Click in an area bounded by walls to create ceiling."

⇨ From the Type Selector, if it is not already selected choose: **Compound Ceiling : 2' x 4' ACT System** [**Compound Ceiling : 600 × 1200mm Grid**].

⇨ Move the cursor around the screen pausing within various Rooms—do not click yet.

Ceiling Plans and Interior Elevations | 649

Notice that the behavior is like the room tool from the previous chapter. However, unlike the room tool, this tool does not have the "Room Separation" option, nor can it recognize those room separation lines already in the model. Therefore, if the auto-detecting routine does not automatically recognize the room you need, you can use the Sketch Ceiling tool on the ribbon instead. We will try the sketch option a little later. For now, we will add a ceiling in a room that is recognized by the auto-detection routine.

   4.   Move the cursor into the office above grid line 3 on the left side of the plan. The room boundary should highlight automatically.

   ⇨   Click in the room above grid line 3 to add a ceiling (see Figure 14.2).

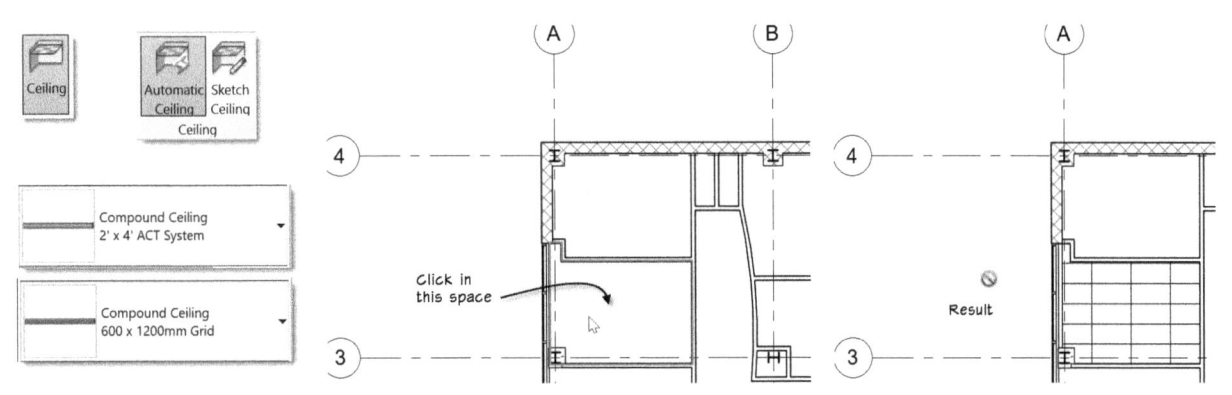

FIGURE 14.2 *Add a ceiling to an office*

   ⇨   On the ribbon, click the Modify tool or press the ESC key twice.

EXPLORE CEILING PROPERTIES

Before adding any more ceilings, let's take a few moments to explore the one we just created.

   1.   Click on one of the Ceiling grid lines.

Notice that each line is individually selectable. However, they behave together as a unit. The auto-creation routine will attempt to center the grid in the room left to right and top to bottom. You can move any grid line if you like, and the entire grid pattern will move with it. Use this technique to apply custom centering (see below).

        With a grid line selected, look to the Properties palette.

Even though we have only selected a grid line in the pattern, the ceiling's properties appear on the palette. Take note of the "Level" and "Height Offset From Level" parameters. Ceilings are measured from the level as you might expect. In this case, it defaulted to: 8'-0" [2600] above the associated level. Notice also that Revit calculates the area, perimeter, and volume of the ceiling. You cannot change these values directly; they are the result of the ceiling's shape and composition. But like other elements, if you move a bounding wall or edit the ceiling type to change its thickness, these numbers will adjust accordingly. Try it if you like, just be sure to undo before continuing.

   2.   Change the Height Offset from Level value to: **9'-0"** [**2700**] (see Figure 14.3).

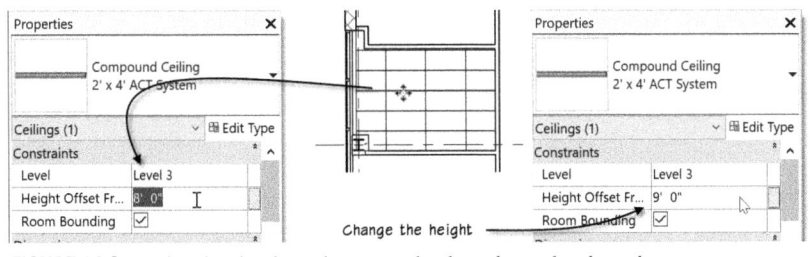

FIGURE 14.3 *Ceiling height above the current level can be easily adjusted*

• Revit Essentials for Architecture •

650 | Chapter 14

We won't see the effect of this change until we open a section view, which we will do below. While you are on the Properties palette, also take notice of the Room Bounding check box. Like many other elements, ceiling elements can be used as room boundaries and this is selected by default. Rooms and the room bounding setting were discussed in the "Rooms and Room Tags" topic on page 624 in Chapter 13. If you enable the calculate volumes setting for rooms, then ceilings can bound rooms. The only way to see this is in a section view. We will discuss this setting in more detail below, in the "Study a Ceiling in Section" topic on page 656.

   3.   On the Properties palette, click the Edit Type button.

Notice that a ceiling element's type has an Edit "Structure" button like many other "layered" hosts. If you were to edit this Structure, you would notice that it is comprised of a simple core element with a finish layer on the bottom. The grid pattern comes from the material assigned to this finish layer (see Figure 14.4).

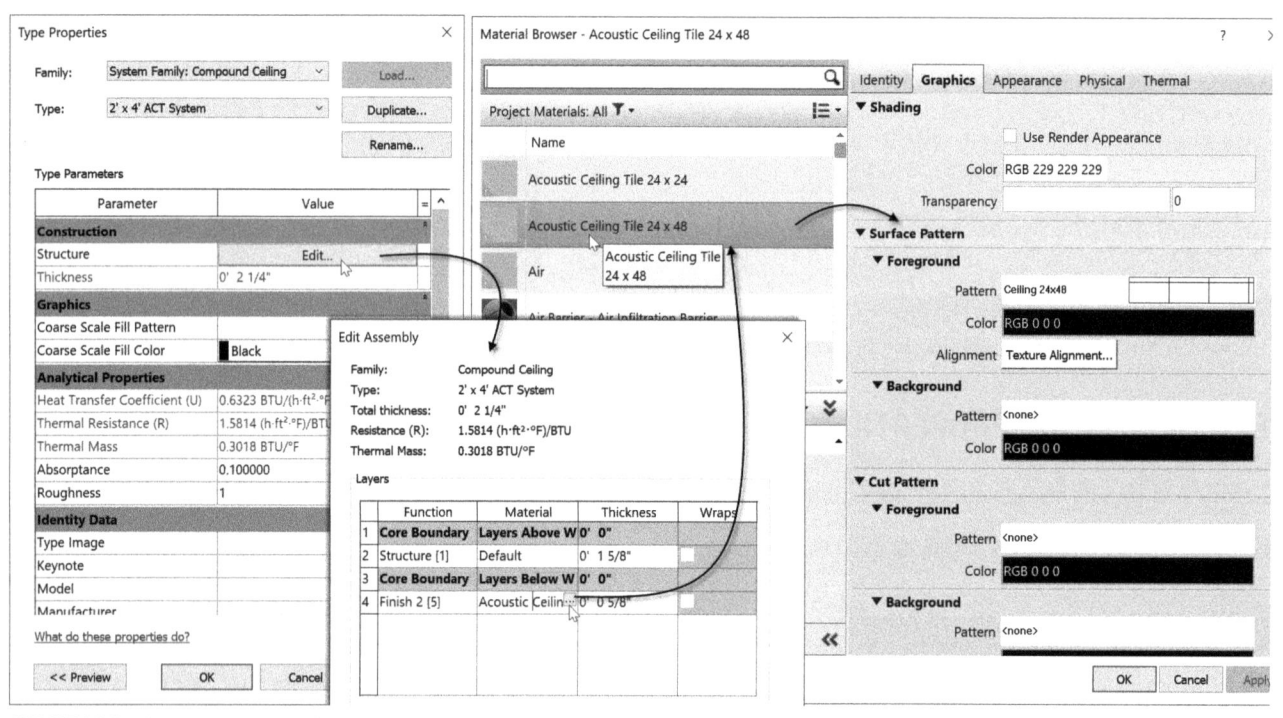

FIGURE 14.4 *The type properties of the ACT ceiling uses a "Ceiling Tile" material*

We do not need to make any changes to the material, structure, or type properties. However, such exploration is educational, particularly when you realize that editing a ceiling type is nearly identical to editing other layered element types such as a wall, floor, or roof type. Keep this in mind if you need to create custom ceiling types in your own projects.

   ⇨   Cancel all dialogs when you are finished exploring.

ADD ANOTHER CEILING

Now that we have a better understanding of the ceiling element, let's continue with adding ceilings to our model.

   1.   On the Architecture tab, click the Ceiling tool again.

You can easily change the height of the ceiling before you place it. Just make the edit on the Properties palette before you click to place the ceiling.

   ⇨   On the Properties palette, change its Height Offset to: **9'-0"** [**2700**].

   2.   Click a point within the space below grid line 3 to add another ceiling.

   ⇨   On the ribbon, click the Modify tool or press the ESC key twice.

• The Aubin Academy •

Ceiling Plans and Interior Elevations | 651

You can verify that is was created at the desired height by selecting one of the grid lines again and looking at the properties.

MOVE, ROTATE, AND ALIGN CEILING GRIDS

We could continue and add additional ceilings in the other rooms, but for now we will work with just these two.

1. Select one of the vertical grid lines of the ceiling you just added.

2. On the Modify Ceilings tab, click the Move tool (or press MV) and then move the grid line a small amount (see Figure 14.5).

   The exact amount of the move is not important.

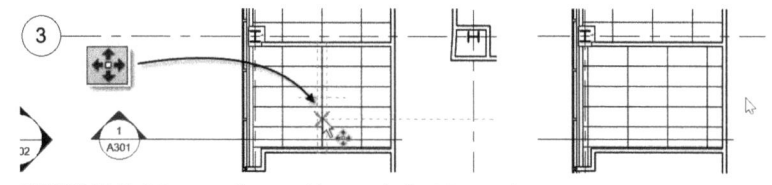

FIGURE 14.5 *Move a ceiling grid line with the Move tool*

As noted above, notice that the entire grid will reposition with this move, not just the selected grid line. Also, only the grid pattern is affected by this move, not the boundary of the ceiling element, which still conforms to the shape of the room. You can use other typical modification techniques as well, such as rotate. If you need your grid pattern at a different angle, simply click the Rotate tool and rotate the grid line. The rest of the grid will follow.

3. Using the Rotate tool (RO), rotate the grid (see Figure 14.6).

   The precise amount of the rotation is not important.

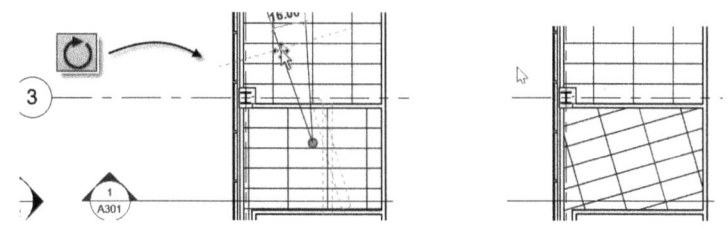

FIGURE 14.6 *Rotate a grid using the Rotate tool*

You can also use the Align command to create alignment between the grids in two different rooms.

> **NOTE:** It is not necessary to undo the rotation first. Align will rotate the grid back to horizontal for you. If you prefer, or find it easier to visualize, you can undo the rotation first.

4. On the Modify tab, click the Align tool (or press AL).

   ⇨ Select one of the vertical grid lines in upper office.

   ⇨ Click on one of the grid lines in the other room to align it (see Figure 14.7).

• Revit Essentials for Architecture •

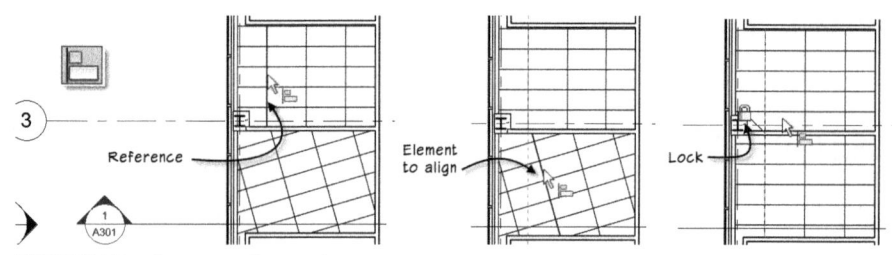

FIGURE 14.7 *Align two ceiling grids*

   5. Click the padlock icon that appears to constrain the alignment.
   6. Select one of the vertical grid lines and move it left or right. (Use the Move tool or simply nudge it with arrow keys).

Notice that the ceiling grids in both rooms now move together. When you move this way, you are simply moving the model pattern that is applied via a material to the ceiling, not the ceiling itself. Therefore, the pattern remains clipped to the shape of the room as you move or rotate it.

> **NOTE:** This behavior applies to any patterned material. For example you can use the same techniques to shift or align a brick pattern on wall. However, with wall surface patterns you will need to use TAB to highlight the pattern lines.

CREATE SEVERAL OFFICE CEILINGS

Some of the spaces that we have will prove problematic for the automatic ceiling creation option. The routine does not recognize columns. Also, the curtain walls can sometimes make finding closed boundaries difficult. To create the next several ceilings, we'll use the sketch option instead. In addition, we will sketch a single continuous underpinned ceiling for the non-office spaces in the suite.

   1. Zoom out to see the entire plan.
   2. On the Architecture tab, click the Ceiling tool again.

      Move your mouse around the screen and look for rooms where you can generate a ceiling boundary automatically.

Of the remaining spaces, you will only be able to auto-generate a few of them: the top-left corner office, the break room and the copy room at the top of the plan will work. You will notice however, that for the office and break room at the top that the ceiling will flow into the closets. This is because of the modification we made to the room bounding property back in Chapter 13. If we want separate ceilings in the closets, we will have to sketch these rooms instead. We'll create an auto-ceiling now and then modify them below.

   3. Create ceilings using the automatic method in the two rooms at the top of the plan that give a clean boundary (see the left side of Figure 14.8).

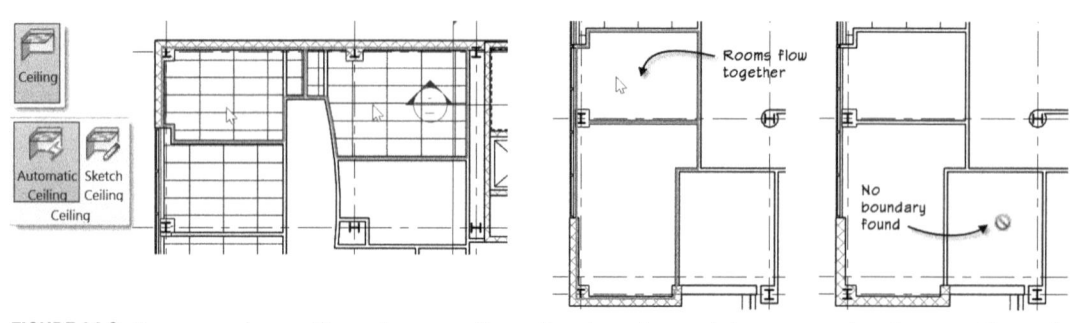

FIGURE 14.8 *Create several new ceilings using auto-ceiling, adjust the wall as needed to accommodate the auto-ceiling tool*

The two lower left offices at the corner will not work well with the automated option.

4. Place your mouse inside the enclosed space (don't click) and you will see the problem (see the middle of Figure 14.8).

⇨ Move the mouse into the other spaces nearby and no boundary will be found at all. The cursor will change the general prohibition sign (see the right side of Figure 14.8).

⇨ On the ribbon, click the Modify tool or press the ESC key twice.

For the offices on the left, you can stretch the length of the wall touching the column on grid line 2. This will allow automatic ceilings. But the graphics of the connection between this wall and column will no longer appear correct. However, unlike rooms, after an automatic ceiling is created it will not become invalid if its boundary walls change. So, we can edit the wall, create the ceiling, then edit the wall back to its original position.

5. Select the wall running parallel to grid line 2.

⇨ Using the shape handle at the end near grid line A, stretch the wall into the column. (You can also use the Trim/Extend to Single Element tool for this).

6. Run the Ceiling tool again and create ceilings in these two offices, which should now work with automatic ceiling.

7. Select the same wall and stretch back to the face of the column (see Figure 14.9).

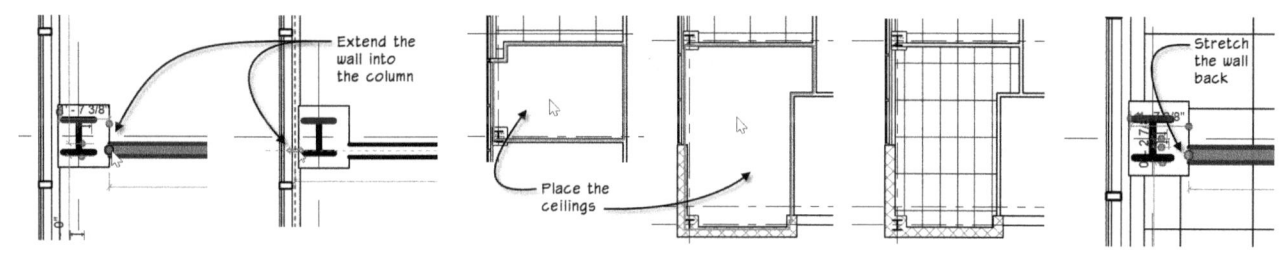

FIGURE 14.9 *Adjust the wall to enclose the space before creating an automatic ceiling*

Notice that we can adjust the wall without harming the ceiling. This same technique can be used in other locations, or we can use the sketch option for ceilings.

CREATE A CEILING VIA SKETCH

To create the next several ceilings, we'll use the sketch option instead to overcome some of the issues noted above. We will also sketch a single continuous underpinned ceiling for the non-office spaces in the suite.

1. Repeat the Ceiling tool.

2. On the Modify | Place Ceiling tab, click the Sketch Ceiling button.

The Create Ceiling Boundary tab appears with the normal compliment of sketch tools.

By now, the sketch tools in Revit should be very familiar to you. The basic steps are summarized here, but please feel free to use whatever techniques you prefer to sketch the inside shape of the room. On the Draw panel, there are two "mode" buttons: Boundary Line and Slope Arrow. Most of the time you will use the Boundary Line mode. This allows you simply to sketch the boundary of the ceiling element using the typical shape icons. The Slope Arrow mode allows you to create a sloped ceiling such as a cathedral ceiling. While we are not covering this method currently, feel free to open the residential project and try this mode out later.

3. On the Draw panel, click the Pick Walls icon.

⇨ Zoom in on the two offices at the bottom of the plan.

4. Pick the four walls in the middle office (see the top of Figure 14.10).

654 | Chapter 14

> Use the flip controls to change the side of the sketch lines if required.
>
> ⇨ Use Trim/Extend to clean up the sketch (see the right side of Figure 14.10).
>
> ⇨ On the ribbon, click the Finish Edit Mode button.
>
> A new Ceiling will appear in the office in the shape you sketched.

5. Repeat for the other office.

> ⇨ Use Pick Walls as indicated in the figure.
>
> ⇨ Use the Pick Lines tool to pick the bottom edge of the column and two edges of the curtain wall (see the bottom of Figure 14.10).

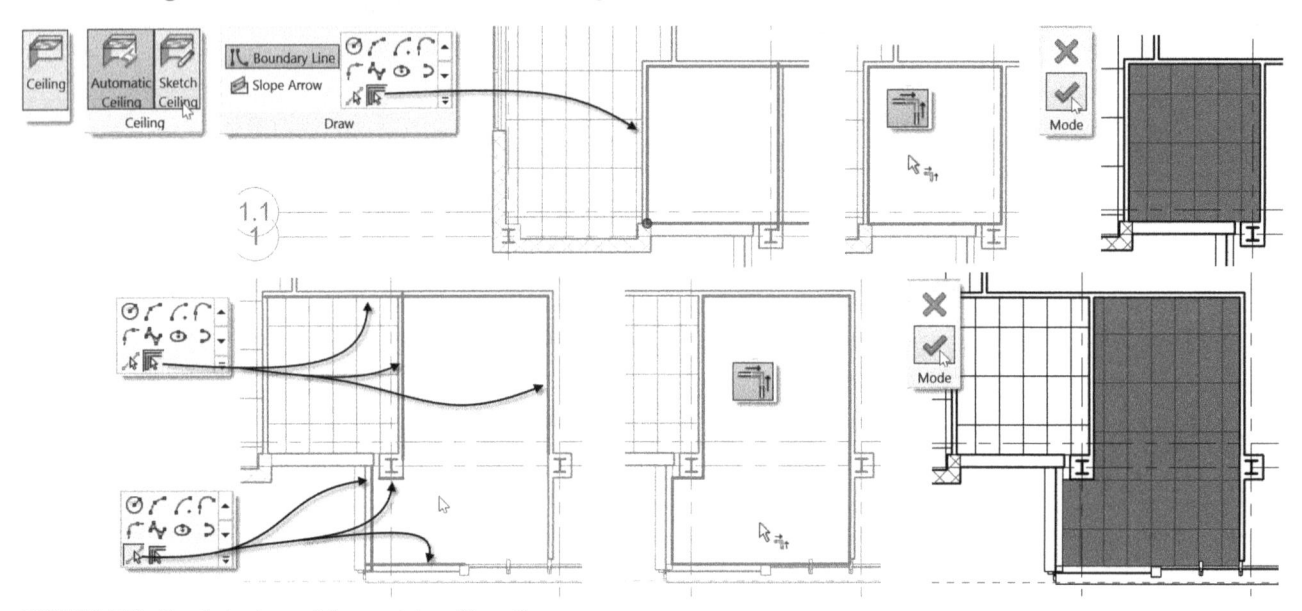

FIGURE 14.10 *Sketch the shape of the remaining office ceiling*

> ⇨ Use Trim/Extend to clean up the sketch and then click the Finish Edit Mode button.

> **TIP:** When sketching a complex shape like this office, use Pick Lines to get one edge on each side and then use Trim/Extend to cleanup. Do not select several edges along the curtain wall for example. One will do. Creating sketches with the fewest segments possible is a good habit to develop.

Notice that Revit will typically choose what it considers to be the best orientation for the ceiling grid. If you wish, you can rotate the grid 90° to orient the offices all the same. To do this, remember, simply select one of the grid lines, and then use the Rotate tool and rotate the line 90°. The remainder of the grid will match the new orientation.

6. Make a window selection of all the ceilings, use the Filter tool to filter everything except ceilings.

> ⇨ Edit the Properties of the selected ceilings; make sure that the Height Offset is set to: **9'-0"** [**2700**].

7. Save the project.

EDIT AN EXISTING CEILING

You can edit the shape of any ceiling element by editing its sketch. If the ceiling has a pattern like the ones we have, just select any line of the pattern. In cases where you don't have a pattern, place the cursor near the edge of the room and use the TAB key to pre-highlight and then select the ceiling element. Once you select the edge, the Modify | Ceiling tab will appear, and you can click the Edit Boundary tool to return to the sketch.

1. Select the ceiling in the upper left corner office (beneath grid line 4).
2. On the ribbon, click the Edit Boundary button.
   ⇨ Use Trim to exclude the closet from the sketch.
   ⇨ Delete the unnecessary sketch lines and then click the Finish Edit Mode (see Figure 14.11).

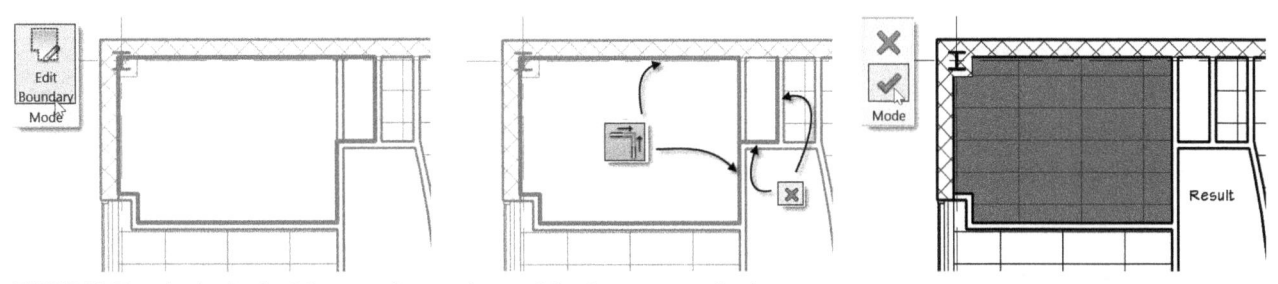

FIGURE 14.11 *Edit the sketch of the two ceilings at the top of the plan to remove the closets*

3. Repeat the process on the break room across the hallway. Here you can move the sketch line at the back of the closet to enclose the shape or draw a new line.

CREATE AN UNDERPINNED CEILING

The ceilings created so far were all contained wholly within single rooms. When you need a ceiling in a space that does not have clear boundary walls, or that must span across several spaces at once, you can sketch it directly. When you do this, you will have a single continuous ceiling grid that can represent an underpinned ceiling.

1. On the Architecture tab, click the Ceiling Tool.
2. On the Modify | Place Ceiling tab, click the Sketch Ceiling button.
   ⇨ Sketch the outline shown in Figure 14.12. Don't include the Conference Room. We will do this one later.

   You can create most of the required edges with the Pick Walls tool. Pay attention to the side of the wall for each sketch line and flip as required. At the round column use the Lines tool and the Pick Lines tool as indicated. Trim to clean up the shape.

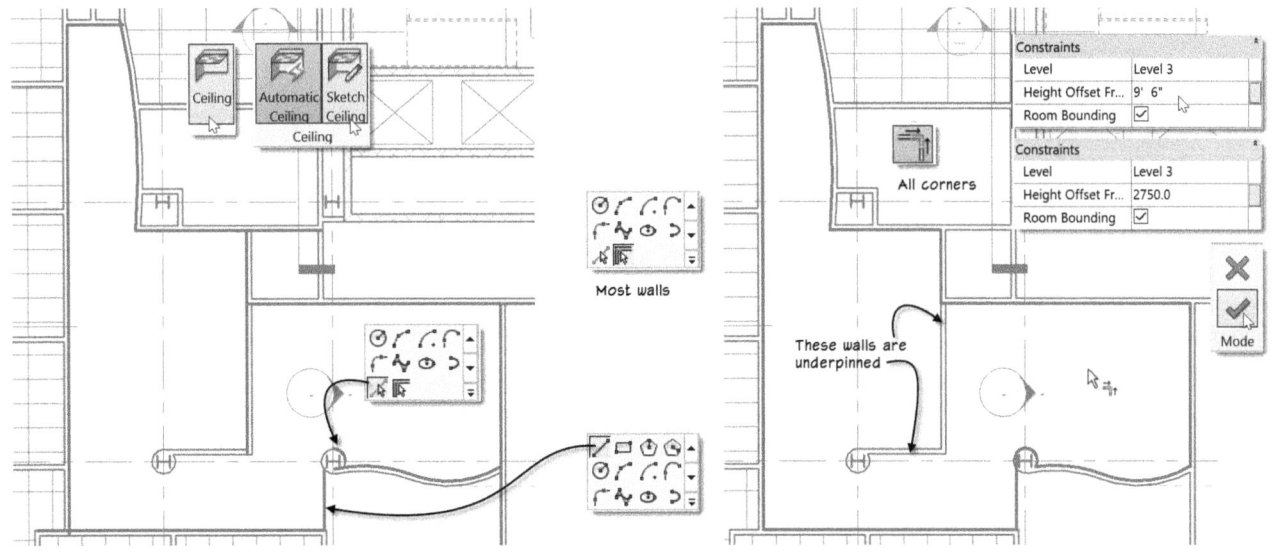

FIGURE 14.12 *Sketch an underpinned ceiling across several rooms*

3. On the Properties palette, change the "Height Offset From Level" to: **9'-6"** [2750].
   ⇨ On the Mode panel, click the Finish Edit Mode button.

• Revit Essentials for Architecture •

656 | Chapter 14

> **TIP:** If you try to complete the sketch and warning appears, it usually means you missed a trim somewhere. Simply click the Continue button in the warning and look for an untrimmed corner. Revit usually highlights the offending portion of the sketch with the orange alert color, look closely for it. It is a good habit to zoom to see all a sketch before attempting to finish it.

STUDY A CEILING IN SECTION

At this point we have several ceiling elements in our project. We have done all the work in the reflected ceiling plan view. Let's check out how things are looking in the section.

1. On the Project Browser, double-click to open the *Longitudinal* section view.

> **TIP:** If you prefer, double-click the Section Head in the plan instead.

⇨ Zoom in on the third floor at the left side of the section.

Notice that the ceiling in the offices at the left is a bit lower than the one in the public spaces. Also, notice that the walls currently go all the way to the floor deck above. Since we have made a single continuous underpinned ceiling in the public spaces, we might want to adjust the walls to stop at the ceiling height instead. The section view helps us spot the problem, but the edit is best accomplished in the ceiling plan view.

2. Return to the *Level 3* ceiling plan view tab.

3. On the Modify tab, click the Split tool (SL) and split the wall at the back of the secretarial area (see the top left side of Figure 14.13).

⇨ Select the two walls in the underpinned area (see the right side of Figure 14.13).

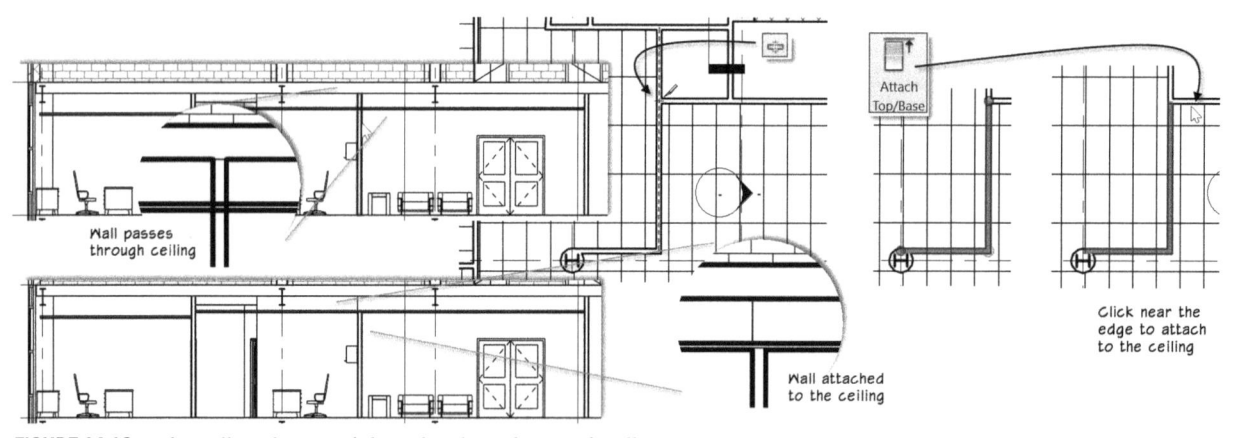

FIGURE 14.13 *Split walls as shown and then select the underpinned walls*

4. On the Modify | Walls tab, on the Modify Wall panel, click the Attach Top/Base button.

⇨ Move your mouse to the edge of the ceiling. The edge of the ceiling will pre-highlight.

⇨ Click when the ceiling pre-highlights to attach the selected walls to the ceiling (see the right of Figure 14.13).

> **NOTE:** You could also edit the properties of the walls and change their Top Constraint to Unconnected at a height of 9'-6" [2750]. However, if you anticipate that the ceiling height will change at some point, the Attach option is better as it will stay connected to the ceiling. Further, the graphics in the section will be nicer with Attach.

Ceiling Plans and Interior Elevations | 657

Now that we have adjusted the height of the walls, the model more accurately reflects our design intent. You can see this best by returning to the *Longitudinal* section view (see the lower portion of the figure for the result).

   5.   Return to the *Longitudinal* section view tab.

In the *Longitudinal* section view, move your mouse near the middle of the office space. When your mouse is over the room element, it will pre-highlight as it does in plans. Notice that its height ignores the ceiling element; even though the element is set to room bounding as noted in the "Creating an Acoustical Tile Ceiling" topic on page 648 above (see the left side of Figure 14.14).

   6.   On the Architecture tab, expand the Room & Area panel and click the Area and Volume Computations button.

   ⇨   In the "Area and Volume Computations" dialog, for Volume Computations,
          choose the: Areas and Volumes radio button and then click OK.

   Pre-highlight the Room again and notice that it now conforms to the height of
   the bounding ceiling element (see the right side of Figure 14.14).

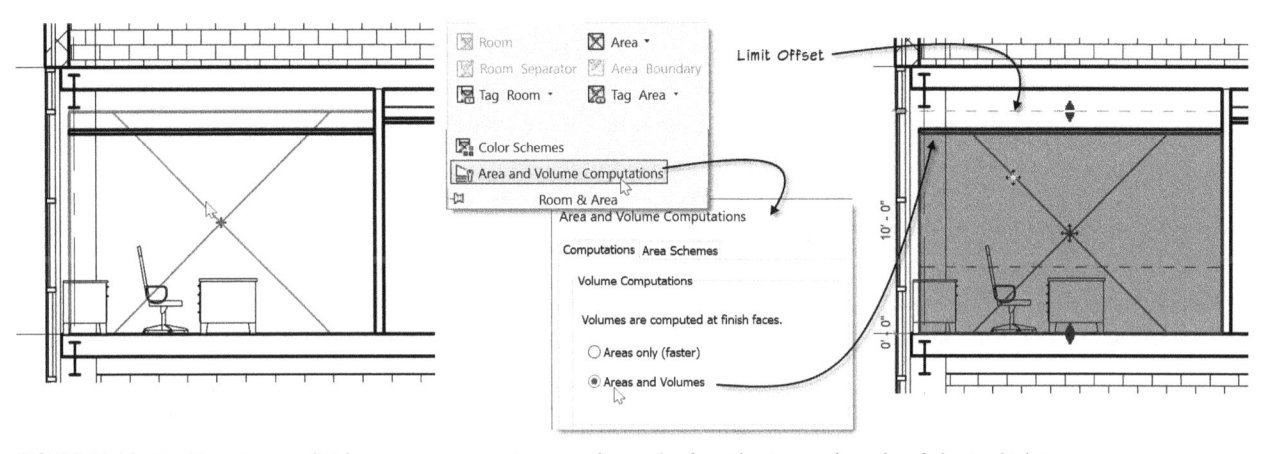

FIGURE 14.14 *Enabling Area and Volume computations is required to make the ceiling's room bounding behavior kick in*

Also note that for rooms with varying ceiling height boundaries the room object must be taller than the highest boundary for volume to be computed correctly. The "Limit Offset" property on the Properties palette controls this. Or you can stretch the control handle visible in the section.

   7.   On the Project Browser, double-click to open the *Level 3* ceiling plan view.

EDIT ELEMENT AND VIEW VISIBILITY

If you study the two underpinned walls in the secretarial area you will notice that even though the walls now sit beneath the height of the ceiling plane, they continue to hide the ceiling as if they were going all the way through. This is simply the default behavior of the graphics and there is an easy fix.

   1.   Select the same two walls again.

   ⇨   On the View panel, click the Override Graphics in View drop down button and choose: **Override by Element**.

> **TIP:**   You can also right-click and choose: **Override Graphics in View > By Element**.

   2.   Expand the Surface Transparency item. Drag the slider all the way to
            the right and then click Apply (see Figure 14.15).

   ⇨   If you like, you can also override the Cut Lines Weight to make it slightly lighter.

• Revit Essentials for Architecture •

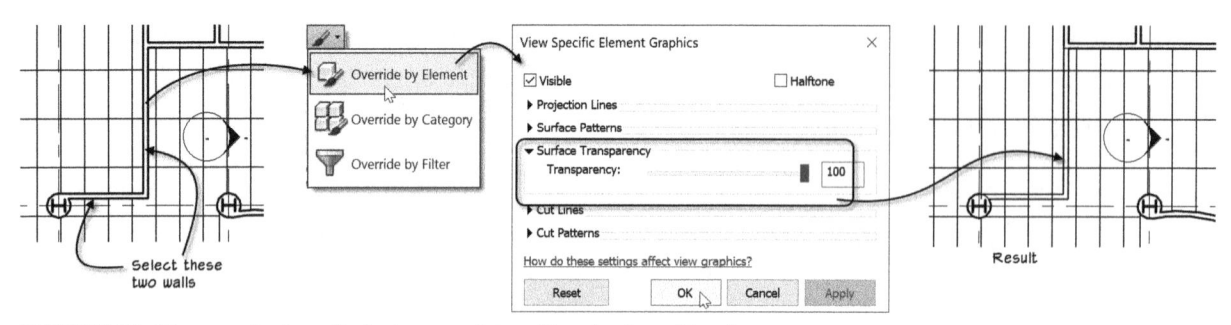

FIGURE 14.15 *We can make the walls display correctly in ceiling plan by making them transparent*

The transparency feature can also be useful in 3D views when you wish to display elements that would otherwise be obscured by elements in front of them. Another application would be to make items like furniture display without their white mask on shaded plans. For example, recall the "Add a Color Scheme" topic on page 636 in Chapter 13. Transparency was applied there to hide these masks in the color plan in this chapter's version of the file.

If you want to designate some of your walls as being a few inches above the ceiling plane, there is no need to modify the ceiling plan graphics, but you may want to consider selecting the walls in question and modifying their properties to represent this. To do this, select a wall and on the Properties palette, change the Top Constraint to: **Unconnected**. Set the Unconnected Height to: 6" [150] taller than the ceiling height.

> **IMPORTANT:** Be aware that if you previously attached the top of the wall to the floor or ceiling, you would need to Detach it before this change will become apparent. Attach takes precedence over the height settings of the wall.

If you go to all this trouble to make the wall heights correct, you probably would like to indicate the wall types in the drawing with a wall tag. Tags were covered in Chapter 13. You can find an additional exercise for adding the wall tags in follow-up to our exercises in this chapter in the Appendix.

ADDING A DRYWALL CEILING

For the Conference Room, we will use the same basic process as the other ceilings, but simply choose a different ceiling type.

1. On the Architecture tab, on the Build panel, click the Ceiling tool.
   ⇨ From the Type Selector choose: **Compound Ceiling : GWB on Mtl. Stud [Compound Ceiling : Plain]**.
2. On the Modify | Place Ceiling tab, click the Sketch Ceiling button.
   ⇨ Follow the process outlined above to create a ceiling sketch in the Conference Room.
   ⇨ Click Finish Ceiling to create the ceiling.

As you can see, except for choosing a different type, the process is the same as with ceiling grids.

3. Use the Automatic Ceiling tool to add a ceiling to the Copy Room.

SWITCH TO A DIFFERENT GRID SIZE

Like other elements in Revit, you can change the type used on an existing element at any time. Suppose you preferred a 2' x 2' [600 × 600mm] ceiling grid layout instead of the 2' x 4' [600 × 1200mm] one we used. With an existing ceiling selected, you can simply choose a different type from the Type Selector. As you would expect, you can also duplicate and modify an existing type, assign a different pattern, and achieve other ceiling designs not included in this project file. Feel free to experiment with this on your own later if you wish. The process is nearly the same as creating a new wall or floor type.

1. Select one of the grid lines on the large underpinned ceiling in the middle of the plan.
2. From the Type Selector, choose: Compound Ceiling: **2' x 2' ACT System [Compound Ceiling: 600 × 600mm grid]**.

    Adjust the centering of the ceiling grid in the public area if you like.
3. Save the project.

ADDING CEILING FIXTURES

Now that we have completed adding ceiling elements to our project, we can add some lights and other fixtures to the ceiling plan. To achieve the optimal lighting layout, you may need to adjust the location of your grid lines. You can use your move and rotate commands as noted above to this. If you rotate a grid and an error appears indicating that constraints are no longer satisfied, simply click the "Remove Constraints" button and then, if desired, use the align tool again to reapply constraints. This may occur if you previously used align and locked the grids in one room to another. Before we get started, it might be helpful to have some room tags in the plan. You can add them manually, use Tag All, or borrow them from another plan with copy and paste.

1. From the Project Browser, open the: *Level 3 Furniture*.
2. Right-click on any room tag in this view, and choose: **Select All Instances** > **Visible In View**.
   ⇨ Copy to the clipboard (or press CTRL + C).
3. Return to the *Level 3* reflected ceiling plan.
   ⇨ On the Modify tab, on the Clipboard panel, click the Paste drop down and choose: **Aligned to Current View**.
   ⇨ Close inactive views.

ADDING LIGHT FIXTURES

Let's start with a simple fluorescent lighting fixture in the offices.

1. Zoom in on the Break Room (3110).
2. On the Architecture tab, on the Create panel, click the Component tool (or press CM).
   ⇨ On the Place Component tab, click the Load Family button.
   ⇨ Browse to your library folder and open the *Lighting\Architectural\Internal* folder.
   ⇨ Select the: *Troffer × 2 × 4 Parabolic.rfa* [*M_Troffer -Parabolic Rectangular.rfa*] family file and then click Open.

> **NOTE:** As mentioned in previous chapters, if you do not have these families in your installed library, you can find copies of them in *Chapter14* folder.

3. Place a light fixture randomly in the break room. Do not try to snap it (see the left side of the Figure 14.16).
   ⇨ Use the Align command to align it to the grid lines (see the middle of the Figure 14.16).

You do not need to lock them when you align. Later if you move the grid, the lights will move too automatically. This is because the lights are hosted by the ceiling. If you use face-based fixtures, the fixtures will not stay aligned to the grid lines.

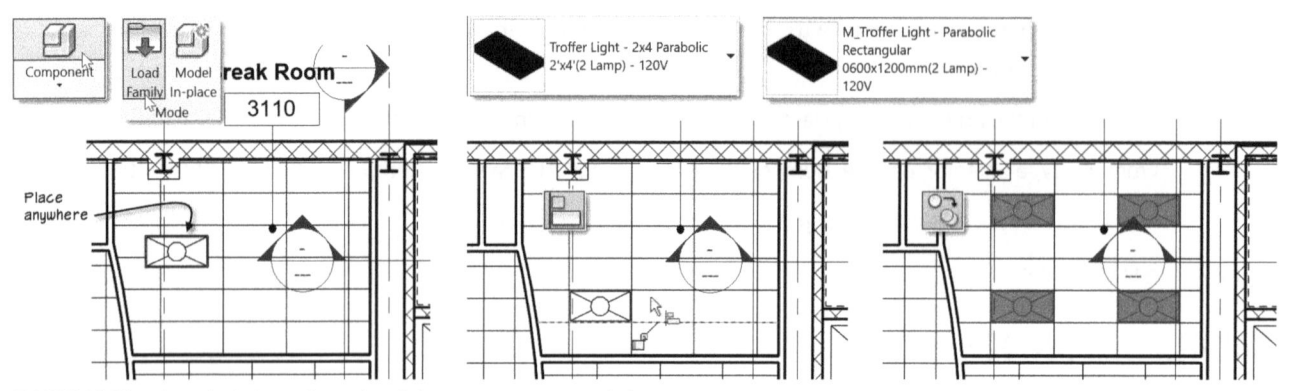

FIGURE 14.16 *Align the light to the grid and then copy it to create a lighting pattern*

4. Select and then copy the light as appropriate for the space (see the right side of the Figure 14.16).

If you are not satisfied with the position of your lights relative to the grid lines, you can move the grid line one-half a tile or one-quarter of a tile in either direction. The lights will move with them. Try it!

The light fixtures are families that use the Light Fixture family template. They contain two-dimensional graphics for the ceiling plan, three-dimensional graphics show in other views. Also, they contain illumination information that is used when you generate a rendering of your Revit model (refer to Chapter 18 for information on rendering in Revit). If you cut a section of the room and its light fixtures, you will see that the fixture is recessed and cuts the ceiling element.

5. Run the Component tool again and add a light to Office 3109.
   ⇨ Align it to the grid in both directions.

Let's say that we only needed two lights in this office. The best orientation for them might be rotated 90°.

6. Select one of the grid lines on the ceiling pattern.
   ⇨ Click the Rotate tool (or press RO), and then on the Options Bar, in the Angle field, type: **90** and then press ENTER (see the top of Figure 14.17).

Notice that the light rotates with the grid. This is very helpful. However, you will likely still need to fine-tune the position of the grid pattern to center it. You can use any move technique.

> **TIP:** To center a grid after you move or rotate it, you can draw a temporary detail line diagonally across the room. You can draw another one diagonally across one tile on the ceiling gird. Then move midpoint to midpoint. Delete the guidelines when you are done (see the bottom of Figure 14.17). If you only need to center in one direction, you can use a dimension with the equality constraint. Pick witness lines at two opposite walls, then a third witness line on any ceiling grid line. Toggle equality. That will shift the ceiling grid to the center of the room. If you want the tile centered instead of the gird, delete the dimension, remove the constraint when prompted and then move the grid half the distance of one tile.

Ceiling Plans and Interior Elevations | 661

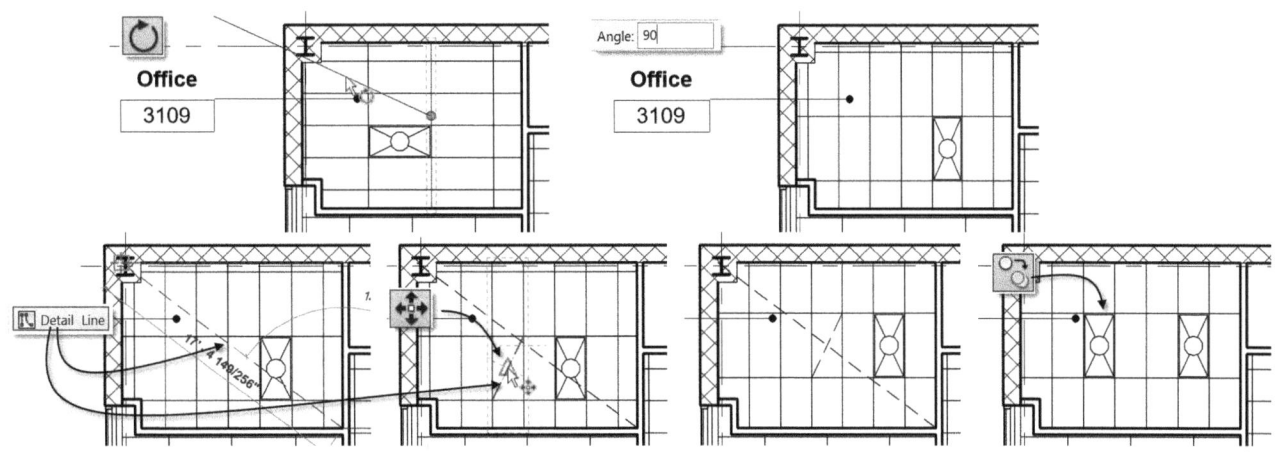

FIGURE 14.17 *Rotate and move the grid and the lights move with it. Use diagonal drafting lines to assist with centering*

7. Adjust the grids in the other similar size offices.

> **TIP:** You can rotate the grids in several offices at once. Simply hold down the CTRL key, select a grid line in two or more offices, and then go to rotate and input your angle on the Options Bar and then press ENTER.

⇨ Select the lights in the office and copy them to the other offices.

⇨ Fine-tune positions as required.

8. Either copy or use the Component tool to place additional lights and make adjustments to other grids (see Figure 14.18).

> **NOTE:** You can copy lights from room to room as long as the ceilings in both rooms are at the same height.

• Revit Essentials for Architecture •

662 | Chapter 14

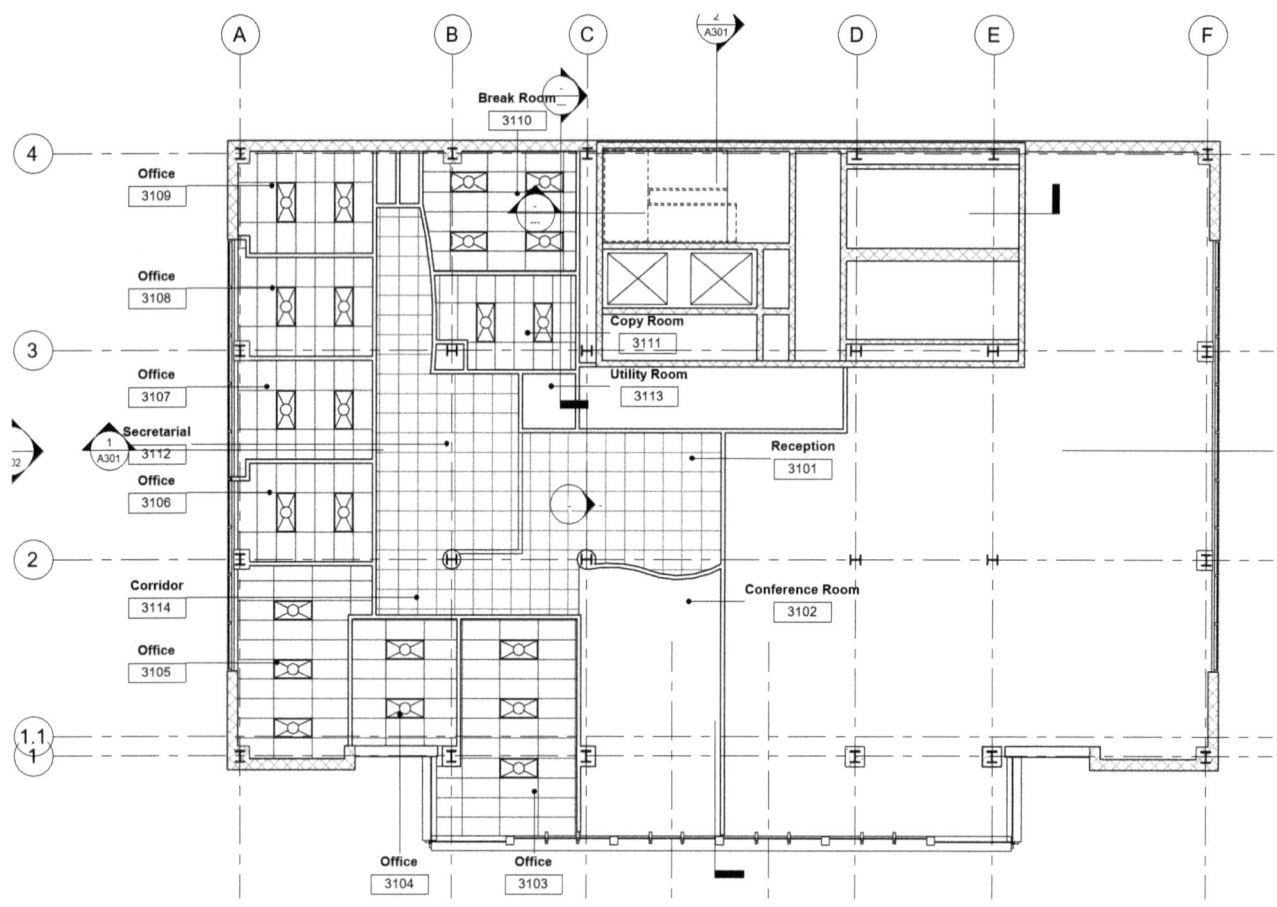

FIGURE 14.18 *Copy the lights to other offices and rooms*

DISPLAY DOORS IN REFLECTED CEILING

Some firms prefer for doors to show in RCP to make it easier to locate light switches, exit signs, and other RCP equipment relative to door swing. To do this, you need to adjust the cut plane of the ceiling plan view.

1. Deselect all elements so that the Properties palette shows the properties of the current view.
2. Beneath the Extents grouping, next to View Range click the Edit button (or press VR).

   ⇨ For the Cut Plane Offset, change the value to: **6'-6"** [**1950**] and then click OK (see Figure 14.19).

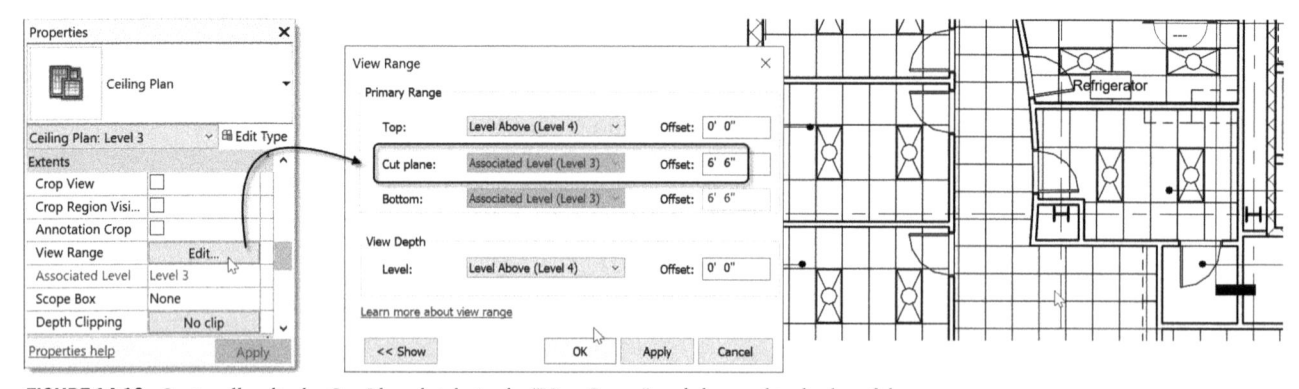

FIGURE 14.19 *Optionally edit the Cut Plane height in the "View Range" and the graphic display of doors*

This shows doors, but they display the same as they would for floor plans. You might also consider editing the door graphic defaults in the "Visibility/Graphics overrides" dialog to match your office standards.

• The Aubin Academy •

Ceiling Plans and Interior Elevations | 663

3. On the View tab, click the Visibility/Graphics tool (or type VG).

⇨ In the "Visibility/Graphic Overrides" dialog, expand Doors.

⇨ In the Cut column next to the Panel subcomponent, click the Override button. Choose a fine dashed line pattern such as: **Dash 1/16"** [**Dash**] and then click OK.

⇨ Repeat for the Plan Swing component, but override the Projection Lines this time (see Figure 14.20).

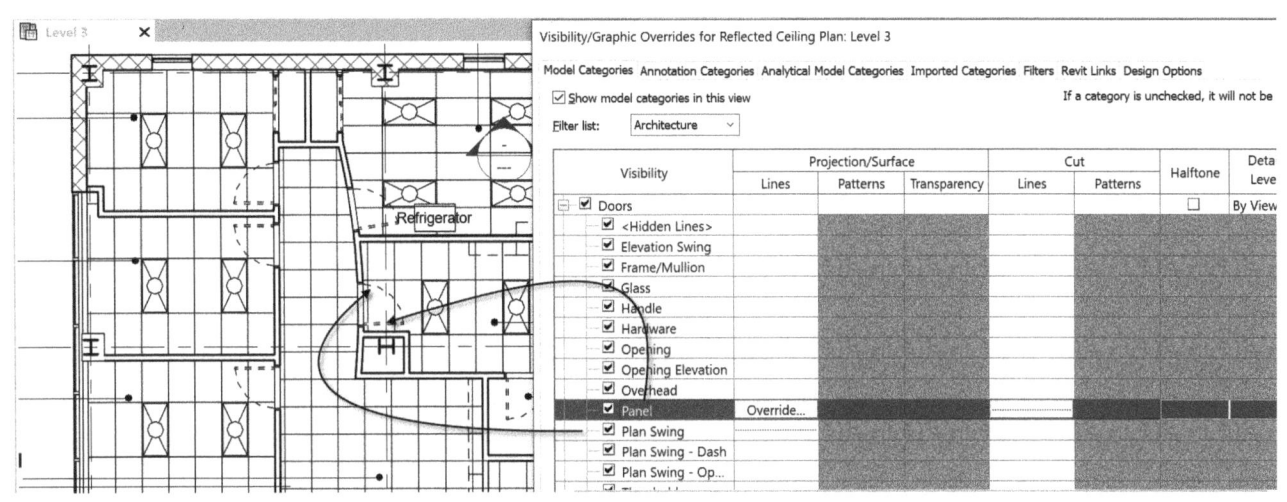

FIGURE 14.20 *Optionally edit the visibility/graphics of the doors category*

You can choose different line patterns if you prefer, and/or edit the color or line weight as well. You can also use the Halftone check box for Doors instead. The exact graphical settings are left to you and your company standards.

> **TIP:** If you make such an edit and wish to use it on other floors of the building, you can save a View Template. On the View tab, on the Graphics panel, click the View Templates drop down button and choose: **Create Template from Current View**. Give it a name and click OK twice. To use it on other ceiling plans, use the: **Apply Template to Current View** command. To apply to several views at once, select them with the CTRL key in the Project Browser, then right-click and choose: **Apply Template Properties**.

ADDING LIGHT SWITCHES

Sometimes it is nice to see light switches on the ceiling plans instead of floor plans. The out-of-the-box light switch families provided with Revit work better in floor plans. However, it is simple to modify them. A modified version is provided in the *Chapter14* folder. You add switches like any other component family.

1. On the Architecture tab, click the Component tool.

2. Click the Load Family button again, browse to the *Chapter14* folder and then open the *Switch-Single (rcp).rfa* [*Switch-Single (rcp)_M.rfa*] family file.

This family file is a modification of the standard Revit library symbol with modifications to allow it to display in reflected ceiling plan. We discussed symbolic lines and forcing overhead items to display in the "Making Families above the Cut Plane Display in Plan" topic on page 520 in Chapter 11. In summary, for any elements to display in a plan view (ceiling plan in this case), there must be some element that passes through the cut plane height that triggers Revit to display its 2D plan representation. The two ways to deal with the situation are to lower the cut plane of the ceiling plan view (currently set at: 6'-6" [1950] after the modification in the previous topic) or to add an element to the family file that passes through this default cut plane and provide dedicated plan graphics in the family. The family file provided in the *Chapter14* folder has a simple model line drawn vertically and set to the **<Invisible**

Lines> line style that passes through the reflected ceiling plan cut plane. This triggers Revit to display the graphics for this symbol in the RCP. Detailed steps were pro a similar family in Chapter 11.

> If you prefer, you can edit the Properties of the *Level 3* ceiling plan view again and lower the View Range further and then use the out-of-the-box family.

3. Place a light switch adjacent to the latch side of the door in one of the offices.

> **NOTE:** This is a wall-based family, so you must click on a wall to place it. Use temporary dimensions to assist in placement.

4. Place or copy additional switches in the other offices.

ADDING WIRING

The full version of Revit includes a wiring element. If you have Revit LT, then you don't have a wiring element. However, even if you do have the wiring element, to use it you need to use families that are connected to an electrical system and create the corresponding panels and elements. If you do not have these items, as an alternative you can show a simple representation of the wiring connection to the switches, using detail lines. As you may recall, detail Lines are view-specific and will show only in this reflected ceiling plan.

1. Zoom in on the Break Room.
2. Select the four lighting fixtures in this space.
   ⇨ On the Modify | Lighting Fixtures tab, on the Create Systems panel, click the Power button.

   This displays the Modify | Electrical Circuits panel.

   ⇨ Click the Arc Wire button (see the top left of Figure 14.21).

Several wires will appear. If you wish, you can customize their graphical display. To do so, select one of the wires, then on the ribbon click the Override in View button and choose: Override by Category. (You can right-click to get to this command if you prefer). In the "View Specific Category Graphics" dialog, choose a line pattern and line weight beneath the Project Lines item. Click OK to see the results (see the right side of Figure 14.21).

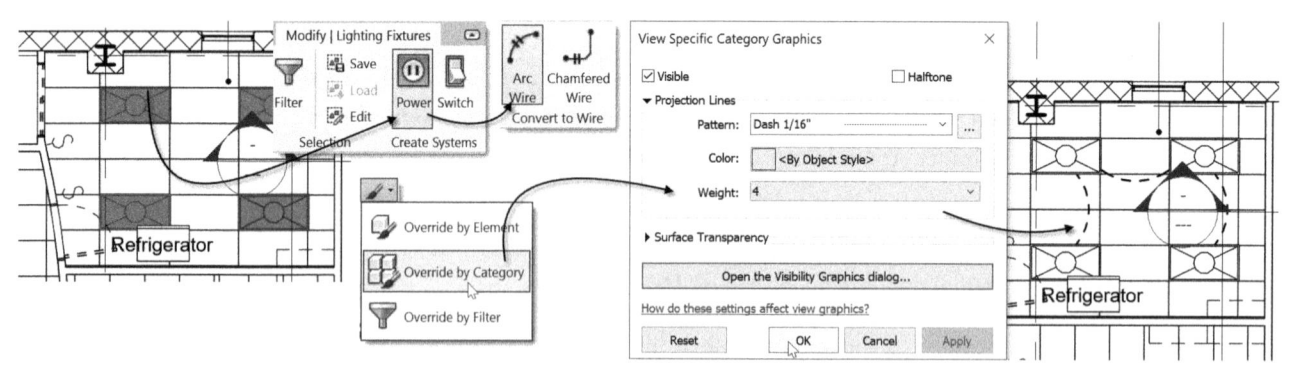

FIGURE 14.21 *Add circuits and wiring*

3. Repeat this process in the other rooms to add wiring in them as well.

If you do not have the MEP functionality or prefer to use detail lines, then you can use Detail Lines instead. On the Annotate tab, on the Detail panel, click the Detail Line tool. On the Line Style panel, from the Line Style list, choose: **<Hidden>**. On the Draw panel, click the Start-End-Radius Arc icon. Draw an arc from light to light in the space. Repeat for other fixtures and rooms.

Ceiling Plans and Interior Elevations | 665

At this point, you can continue adding elements to the reflected ceiling plan as needed. Following procedures covered in this and previous chapters, you can add text, dimensions, and tags as necessary. Feel free to add lighting in the other rooms that need them and be sure to browse the library for other ceiling mounted elements like exit signs and diffusers.

4. When you are finished adding elements to your reflected ceiling plan, save the project.

CREATING INTERIOR ELEVATIONS

No construction documents set would be complete without interior elevations. Adding such views in Revit is easy to do.

1. On the Project Browser, double-click to open the *Level 3* floor plan view.
2. On the View tab, on the Create panel, click the Elevation tool.
    ⇨ From the Type Selector, choose: **Elevation : Interior Elevation**.

    Move the cursor into the secretarial area—do not click yet.

Move the cursor around the space and watch the orientation of the elevation head change dynamically (see Figure 14.22).

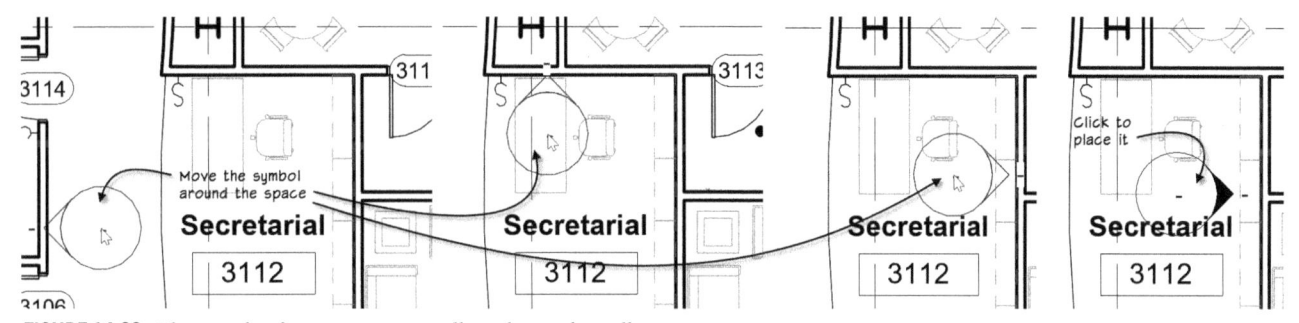

FIGURE 14.22 *Elevation heads orient automatically to the nearby walls*

The orientation of the elevation symbol automatically orients to a nearby wall. This makes creating single elevations easy, especially to angled or curving walls. Move slowly along the curved wall to see this clearly.

3. When the symbol is pointing right, click to place the elevation tag in the room.

    On the ribbon, click the Modify tool or press the ESC key.

You will notice that on the *Interior Elevations* branch of the Project Browser a new view appears.

⇨ Select the elevation symbol (the circle) and then drag it to a more convenient location as required (see Figure 14.23).

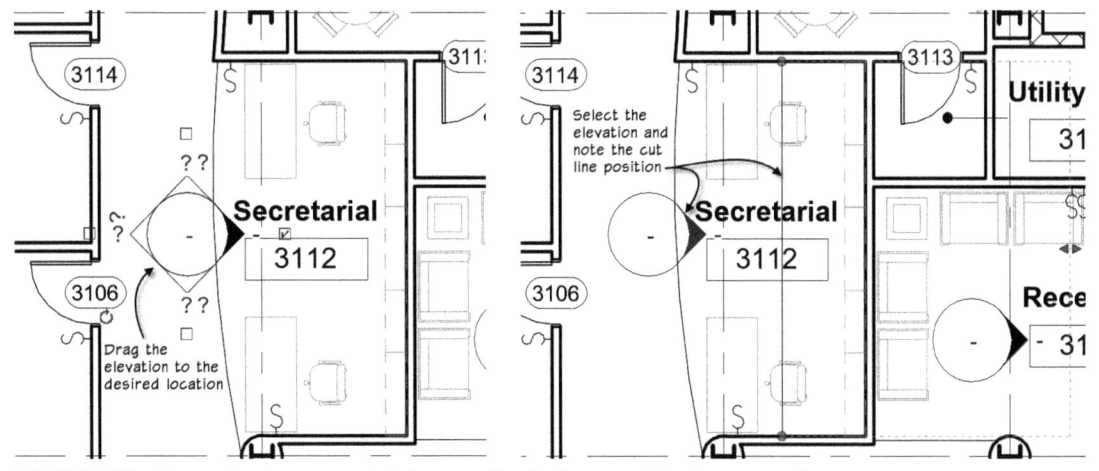

FIGURE 14.23 *Moving the elevation symbol does not affect the location of the elevation cut line*

• Revit Essentials for Architecture •

666 | Chapter 14

When you do this, the triangle view tag will move with it. But notice that the elevation line stays where it was cut. You can move it if necessary, but in this case, it should be in a useful location and not require movement. You can add up to four elevations to a single tag. However, make sure that they can all fit on a single sheet. The sheet reference can only report one sheet value.

With the tag selected, notice the three empty check boxes on the other four sides of the tag.

4. Check the box on the left and it will add a new elevation in that direction (see Figure 14.24).

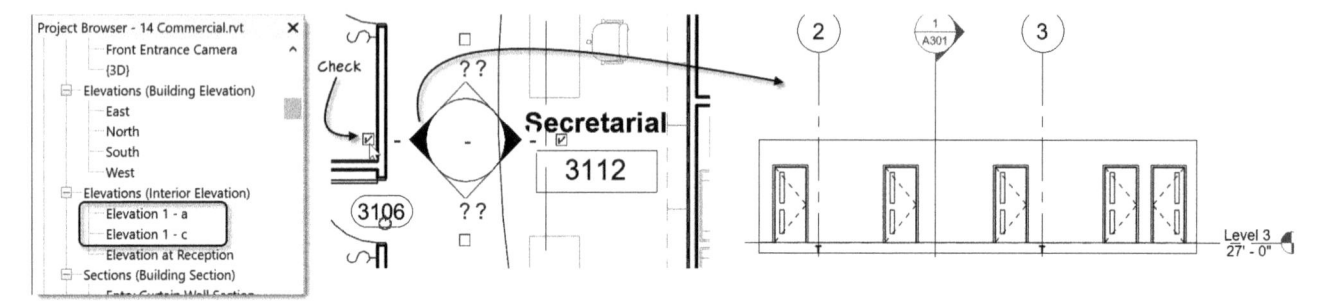

FIGURE 14.24 *Add a new elevation view to the secretarial space*

5. Double-click on triangle part of one of the elevations to open it.

Notice that the view is cropped nicely to the size of the room. You can adjust the cropping if you need to fine-tune it. If you don't want to see the section markers, right-click them and choose: **Hide in View > Category** (or use the tool on the ribbon). Depending on where you clicked the elevation marker, you may or may not be seeing the desks.

You can move the symbol in plan and adjust the location of the elevation cut line. It will appear as a long blue line when the triangular portion is selected.

6. Feel free to add other interior elevations and add them to a sheet (see Figure 14.25).

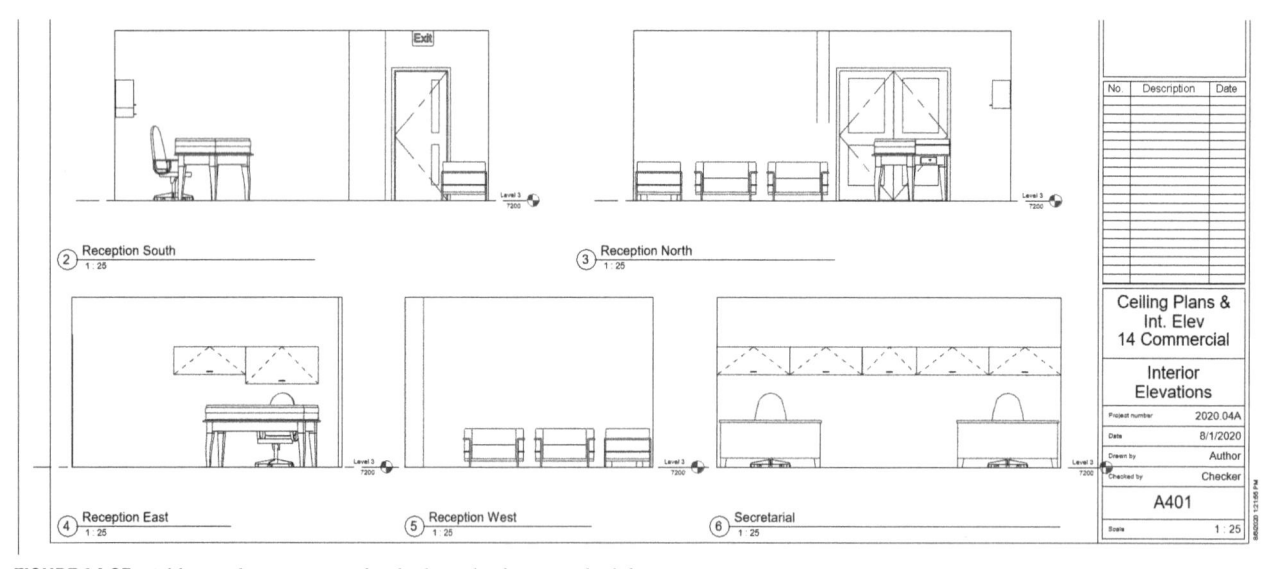

FIGURE 14.25 *Add new elevation views by checking the direction check boxes*

You can complete these views in any way you wish. Add notes, dimensions, or tags. Drop them onto a new Sheet to round out the set. When you drag them to a sheet, the numbers and sheet references will automatically fill in. If the ceiling height varies, you have two options. You can edit the crop region of the view and adjust its sketch, or you can use a masking region to cover up the portions of the elevation above the ceiling that you don't want to see.

> **TIP:** If you want the name of the elevations on the Project Browser to vary from the name shown on the title bar on the sheet, you can select the view on the Project Browser and then in the Properties palette, change the Title on Sheet parameter.

7. Continue to work in the project, making further enhancements if you wish.

8. When you are finished, save and close the project.

SUMMARY

Reflected ceiling plans and interior elevations are two important parts of a complete construction documentation set. In this chapter, we have taken a brief look at the steps to create both important document types.

- ☑ Ceiling elements are easily created from existing walls by picking points within a bounded space.

- ☑ If bounding walls are not available, or if you wish to create a custom ceiling shape, you can sketch the ceiling using standard sketch tools.

- ☑ Ceiling types control the structure of a ceiling element like other "layered" types.

- ☑ Acoustical tile ceilings are simply ceiling types that have a finish layer assigned to an appropriate material and surface pattern.

- ☑ The grid lines in the material use a model pattern. Moving or rotating the pattern does not change the ceiling element shape.

- ☑ To create an underpinned ceiling, use the sketch ceiling tool.

- ☑ Adjust the height of walls to coordinate with the underpinned ceiling after creation.

- ☑ Drywall ceilings are created with the same process and simply use a different type.

- ☑ You can change grid size by swapping the type.

- ☑ Light fixtures and switches are component families that you load and place in the ceiling plan.

- ☑ You can represent simple wiring using the Circuit and Wire tools. Alternatively, you can use detail lines.

- ☑ Add interior elevations using the elevation view tool.

- ☑ Check more than one box on the interior elevation tag to add additional elevations to the same symbol.

CHAPTER 15
Printing and Output

INTRODUCTION

After all the hard work you put into building and annotating your models, you may be ready to generate some output. Autodesk® Revit® can output data in a variety of forms. The most common method of output is, of course, printing (or plotting). We also can output our design digitally in a variety of formats. In this chapter, we will look at the various ways we can generate output from Revit.

OBJECTIVES

Creating output from Revit is simple. Several options are available on the File menu. After reading this chapter, you will know how to:

- Configure Print Setup options
- Print to a hard copy printer
- Create a multi-sheet PDF file
- Export your model in various formats

DATASET

For the purposes of the topics covered in this chapter, you can open any Revit project. A version of the commercial project has been provided in the *Chapter15* folder. You can practice printing and exporting from this project or if you wish, open the "Complete" version of the Residential project from the *Chapter12* folder instead. Feel free to open and print your own Revit projects as well.

THE FILE MENU

Output from Revit can be grouped into two overall categories: Printing and Exporting. Each of these items has a menu with sub-options on the File menu (see Figure 15.1).

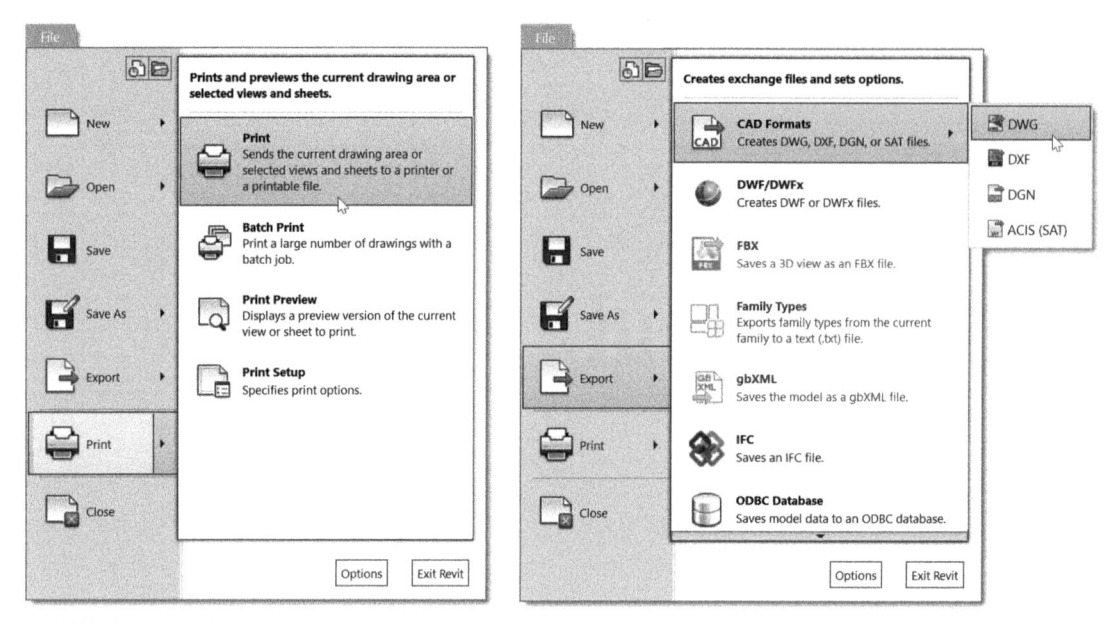

FIGURE 15.1 *The File menu includes sub-menus with many output options*

When you open the File menu, pause for a moment over any item with the small arrow next to it (such as Print or Export) and the submenu will appear on the right side. The Print sub-menu has commands for outputting to hard copy devices such as plotters and printers. You would also use print to output to "digital plotters" such as PDF. Under Export, you find many commands to export some or all of your project data in many popular design file formats such as AutoCAD (DWG), IFC (IFC), Image files (PNG, JPG, BMP) and a variety of others. Some options will be unavailable if you are not in a supported view when opening the menu. For example, to export to FBX, you must start from a 3D View.

PRINT SETUP

Printing (Plotting) is perhaps the most common output. To prepare for your print, you should typically start with Print Setup. The "Print Setup" dialog box has many settings that can be configured to enhance the quality of printed output. From the File menu, choose: **Print Setup** to access this dialog (see Figure 15.2).

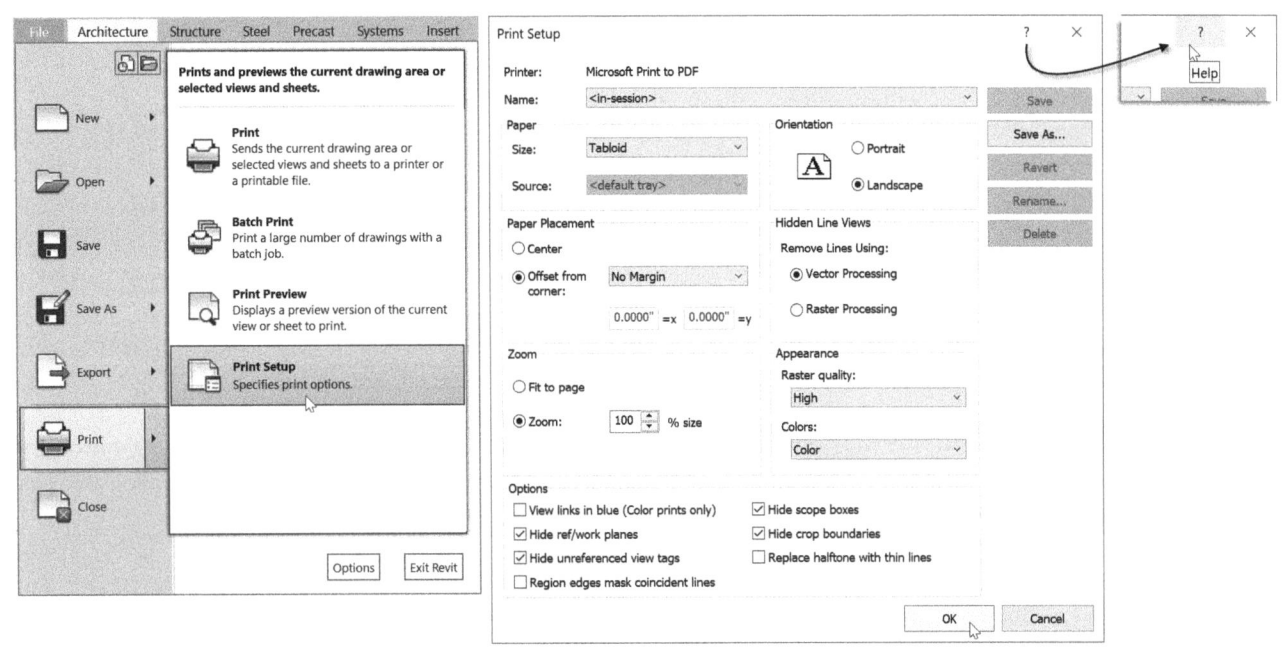

FIGURE 15.2 *The print setup dialog*

If you make changes to any of the default settings in this dialog, you can click the Save As button on the right and give the configuration a new name. The Print Setups are stored in the project. This custom configuration will then be available to you when you print the project in the future (the figure shows the setup as: <in-session>). This is not a saved setup and can be changed for each print. A brief description of each item is listed here. If you want to access the built-in help, click the question mark (?) icon at the top right of the dialog. A help window will appear with a detailed description of the item.

> **TIP:** If you create custom Page Setups, they can be shared with other projects using the Transfer Project Standards tool on the Manage tab of the ribbon.

Be certain that the printer you wish to use is listed at the top of the dialog before you configure the options in the dialog. If it is not listed, click Cancel and make sure the desired printer is properly installed first.

Name—When you make changes to the Print Setup settings, you can save and name them. Click the Save or Save As buttons at the right to do this. This is retained in the project for future use. You can also rename and delete existing named setups with the buttons on the right.

Paper—Set the correct paper size. Only sizes that the printer driver supports will be available.

Orientation—Set to Portrait (vertical) or Landscape (horizontal).

Paper Placement—Center will work for most printers. Otherwise, choose: Offset from corner and its associated options. You may need to experiment with your printer and driver to find the right combination for correct placement. If you make such adjustments, be sure to save the configuration with a descriptive name to preserve your efforts. (It is also not a bad idea to write the offsets down somewhere, just in case).

Hidden Line Views—Most construction document views in Revit are set to hidden line. For example, plan views, elevation views, sections views, and many 3D views default to hidden line. Printing times can vary when choosing between these options. So, you might want to experiment. In some cases, Revit will alert you that it will use Raster

Processing even though you selected Vector. It is fine to accept this when it occurs. It will only apply to the view in question, not the entire print job.

Zoom—To print to the view's current scale setting it must be set to: 100% of size. To print a half-sized set, change the value to: 50%. Keep in mind that everything will be smaller including all annotations. Fit to page will also potentially affect the actual size and scale of the printed output. Fit to page might be fine for check plots, but if you want your print to be "to scale," choose: 100%.

Appearance—If you are using raster processing, choose an appropriate raster quality. The higher the quality you choose, the longer it will take to print. If you are printing to a color printer and want black lines, remember to set the colors to black lines. This will result in all lines printing black—even ones that are colored on screen.

Setting the colors to grayscale will print any lines in the view that are black in solid black ink, and every other color will be a value of gray. If the gray printed output does not look exactly the way you want, try setting the colors to Color and then set the printer driver to black and white. This often gives slightly different grayscale results.

Options—This tells Revit to print or hide certain elements in the view. Hide reference/ work planes is very useful. You would not typically want these items to print; likewise for scope boxes and crop boundaries. The "Hide unreferenced view tags" option will hide any elevation, section, or callout tag view that has not yet been placed on a sheet. This is a very useful feature (see Figure 15.3). The figure shows the screen when you choose the Preview button in the "Print" dialog.

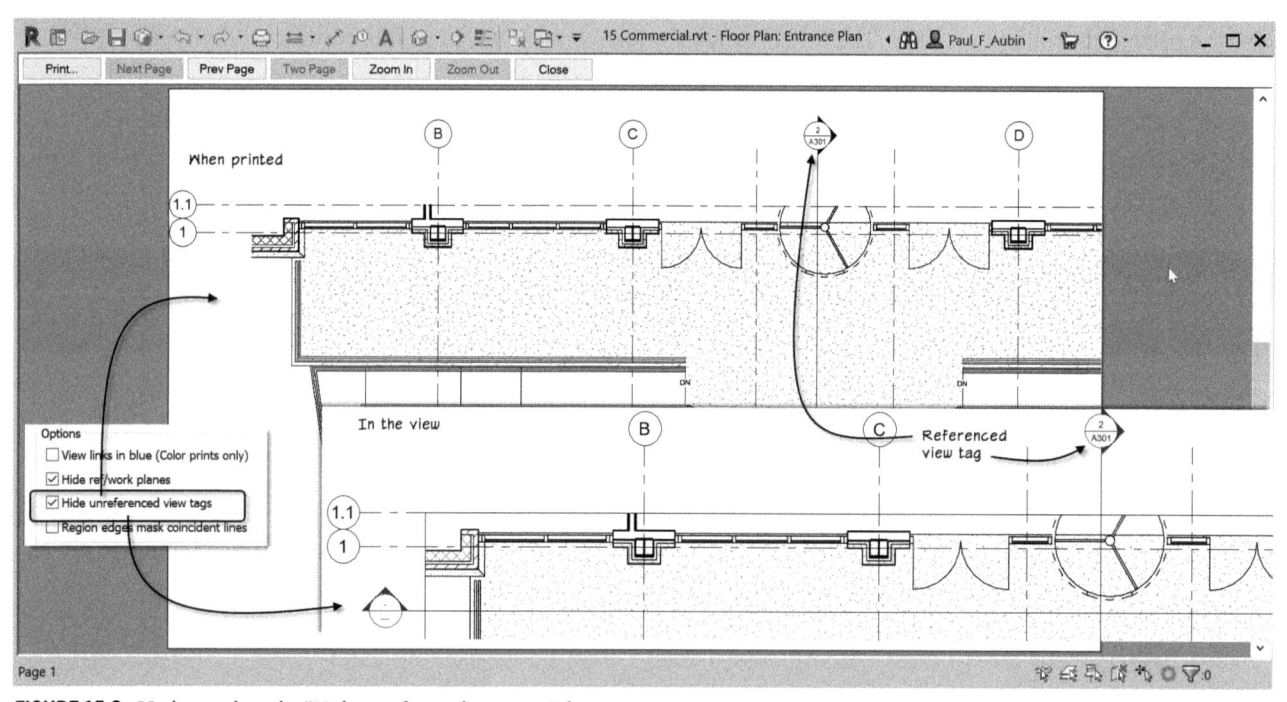

FIGURE 15.3 *Understanding the "Hide unreferenced view tags" feature*

PRINT

When you are ready to print, from the File menu choose: **Print > Print** (or press CTRL + P). Most often, you will want to print sheets because they are designed for this purpose and include title blocks and borders and make a more professional presentation. However, if you wish to print from another view you can do that as well.

Always choose your printer from the list at the top first. Click the Properties button if necessary and make any edits to the printer's unique properties (these properties vary by printer device, which is why you want to choose the printer first). For the "Print Range" you have the option of the "Current window," the "Visible portion of the current window" (for example, the zoomed-in area on screen), or "Selected views/sheets." If you choose the "Select views/sheets" option, the "Select" button will become available. Click on this button to choose a range of sheets or views to print (this is sometimes referred to as batch printing). In the "View/Sheet Set" dialog that appears, you can check or uncheck the views and/or sheets you want to print. At the bottom, you can filter the list. So for example, if you only want to print sheets, at the bottom, uncheck the Views box (see the left side of Figure 15.4). Check All and Check None buttons appear on the right to assist in selecting.

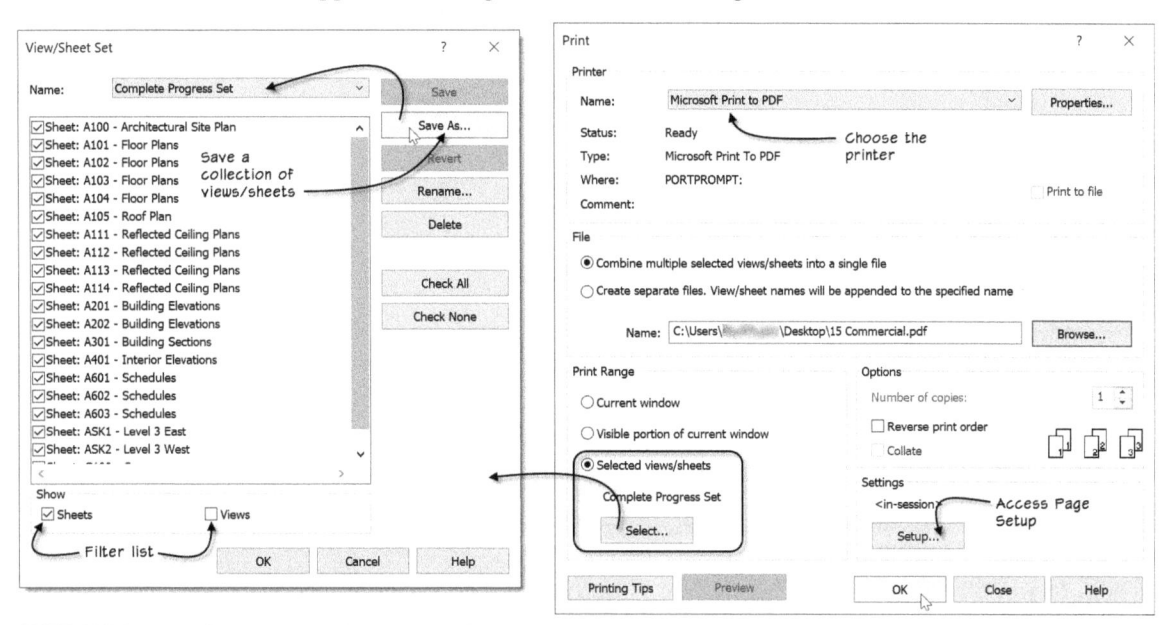

FIGURE 15.4 *Create lists of views and/or sheets to plot*

Back in the "Print" dialog, under Options choose "Reverse print order" if your printer prints pages face up. If a physical printer is used (as opposed to a PDF or other "digital" printer), you may also set the number of copies to be printed and whether they are collated. Click the Setup button to open the "Print Setup" dialog (shown above) and make additional edits. Click OK to print (see the right side of Figure 15.4). If you want to close the dialog without printing, just click the Close button.

If you use the "Visible portion of current window" option, it prints only the part of the view that is displayed within the current window onscreen. To set what you want to print, close the "Print" dialog, re-size, and zoom the view's window accordingly. The proportion of the window is also important and should be like the paper size and layout (portrait vs. landscape). If the window proportions do not match the paper proportions, the printed output may exclude part of the view or might include extra white space.

There are two more commands on the File menu Print sub-menu. The **Print Preview** command works exactly as you'd expect and generates a preview onscreen of what the print will look like with the current settings. If you wish, feel free to configure your choices in both the "Page Setup" and "Print" dialogs and go ahead and print. Depending on how many views or sheets you print, it should take a few minutes to generate your prints. If you wish to conserve paper, try printing a PDF instead. You will need a PDF print driver such as Adobe Acrobat or one of the many alternatives to create a PDF. Revit does not supply such a driver by default. The final command on the Print submenu is: **Batch Print**. This dialog has two tabs, the first for selection of the views and/or sheets that you wish to include in the print job. The Reorder tab allows you to shuffle the order of the printed views or sheets. This is useful if you are printing your whole set and want your general (G) sheets to come before your architectural (A) sheets. When you click Print, a message appears indicating that the print job will be performed by a second instance of Revit.

PRINTING A MULTI-SHEET PDF

If you have a PDF print driver, you can create PDF plots. Depending on the specific driver you have, you may even be able to print full size architectural drawing sizes such E1 or A1. When you choose your PDF plotter at the top, the "File" area of the dialog will become available. Here you can choose to combine all the sheets into a single PDF file. When you do this, Revit will create hyperlinks in the resulting PDF file allowing you to click on section and elevation markers and have it jump right to the sheet reference (see Figure 15.5).

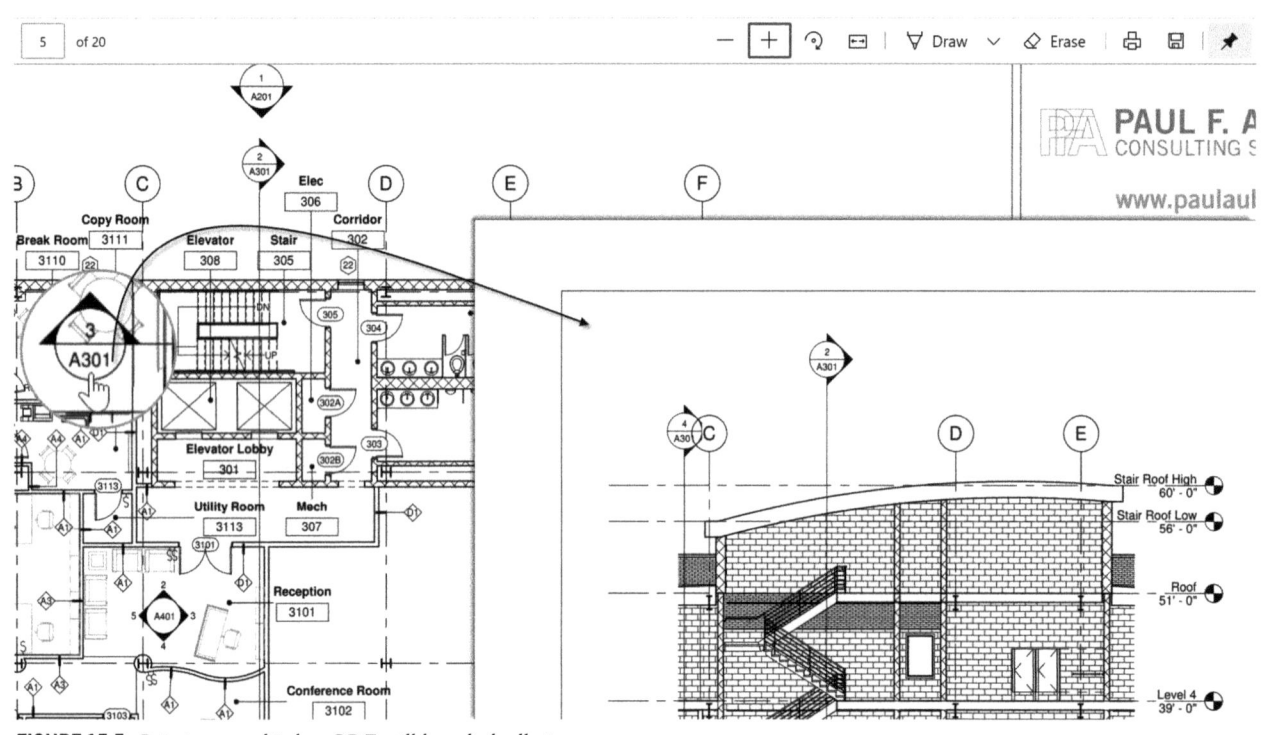

FIGURE 15.5 *Printing a multi-sheet PDF will hyperlink all views*

If you prefer, you can select the "Create separate files" option and it will make a separate PDF for each sheet. Please note that this option is the default, so make sure you change it if this is not what you want.

EXPORT TO CAD

Export is the most extensive menu of the output choices. You can export your Revit model to popular CAD file formats like DWG and DGN, gbXML, FBX, IFC, ODBC, and more. Time and space will not permit us to go into all formats in detail. Do take the time to look at the sub-menu on the File menu and look up any formats that interest you in the online help. For this discussion, we will focus on export to DWG. DWG is the industry standard for CAD data storage and transmission. It is likely that at least some of your consultants and partners on any given project work directly in this format using AutoCAD. Many existing CAD files persist in this format as well. When it comes time to share your design data with team members outside your firm, DWG may often be a requested, or even required. Fortunately, exporting Revit projects to DWG is simple. The basic steps are as follows:

> **Configure your output settings**—From the File menu, choose: **Export > Options > Export Setups DWG/DXF**. This opens the "Modify DWG/DXF Export Setup" dialog. You can configure the way Revit should treat layers, lines, patterns, text, and more. Several layer standards are included on the Layers tab such as the industry standard, AIA (part of the U.S. National CAD Standard (NCS) guidelines). You can edit any of the items in the dialog to match your company's or your recipient's company standard (see Figure 15.6). At the bottom left corner of the dialog, you can click the icons to create or duplicate setups and create new ones. Use the tabs across the top to change the various

settings. You can map Revit line styles to AutoCAD linetypes on the Lines tab. On the Patterns tab, map Revit fill patterns to AutoCAD hatch patterns. Establish font mapping on the Text & Fonts tab. On Colors, you can use either the AutoCAD color index or true RGB colors. If you export 3D views, the Solids tab controls if the export will create meshes or ACIS solids. Configure unit conversion options on the Units & Coordinates tab. Also on the Units & Coordinates tab, for Coordinate system basis, you will want to choose "Shared" if your project uses shared coordinates (see the "Survey Points, Project Base Points, and Shared Coordinates" topic on page 287 in Chapter 7). And finally, on General, you can edit a variety of settings such as the DWG file format used.

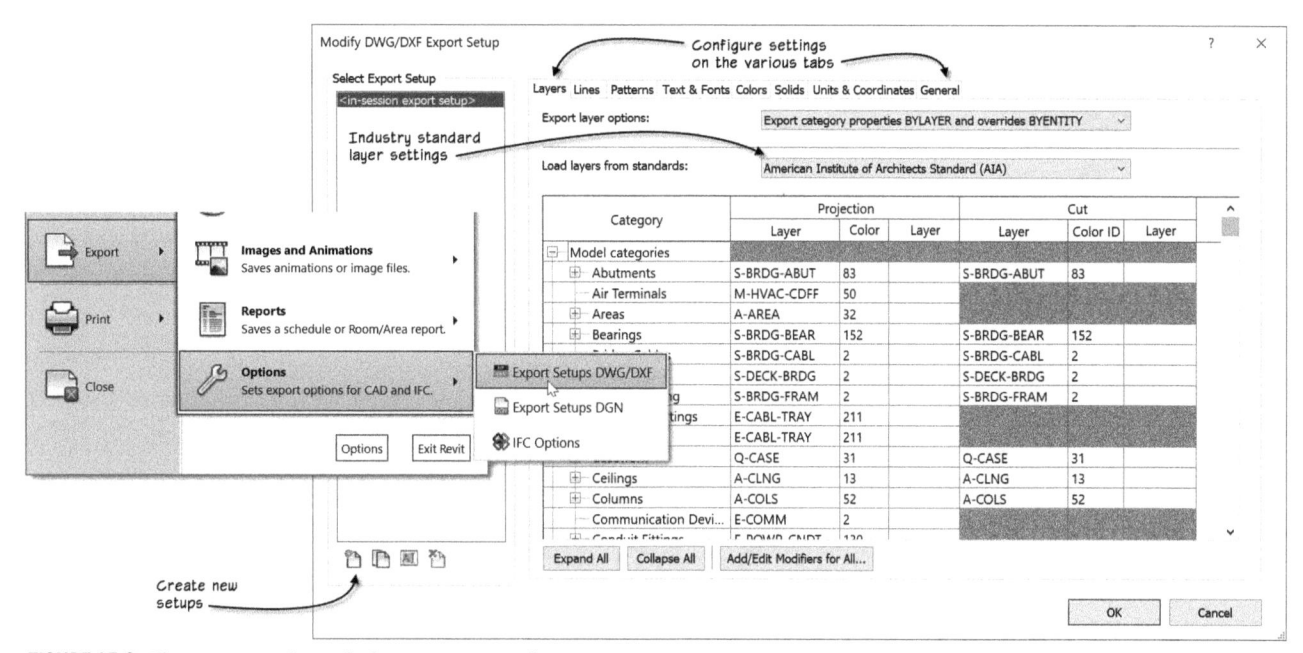

FIGURE 15.6 *If necessary, configure the layer mapping used to map Revit categories to DWG Layers*

Export to DWG—From the File menu, choose: **Export > CAD Formats > DWG**. If you created an Export Setup in the "Modify DWG/DXF Export Setup" dialog, it will be listed at the top left corner (see item 1 in Figure 15.7). You can also click the browse button to open the dialog and configure one directly from here (item 2). Any view list sets you created in Print Setup will appear in the drop down at the top right (item 3). Several options appear next to "Show in list" to help you filter the list of views and/or sheets to be exported (item 4). Select the check boxes for the views you want to export in the Include column (item 5). If you want to save the list for later, use the icons at the top of the list (item 6). Click Next to continue (item 7).

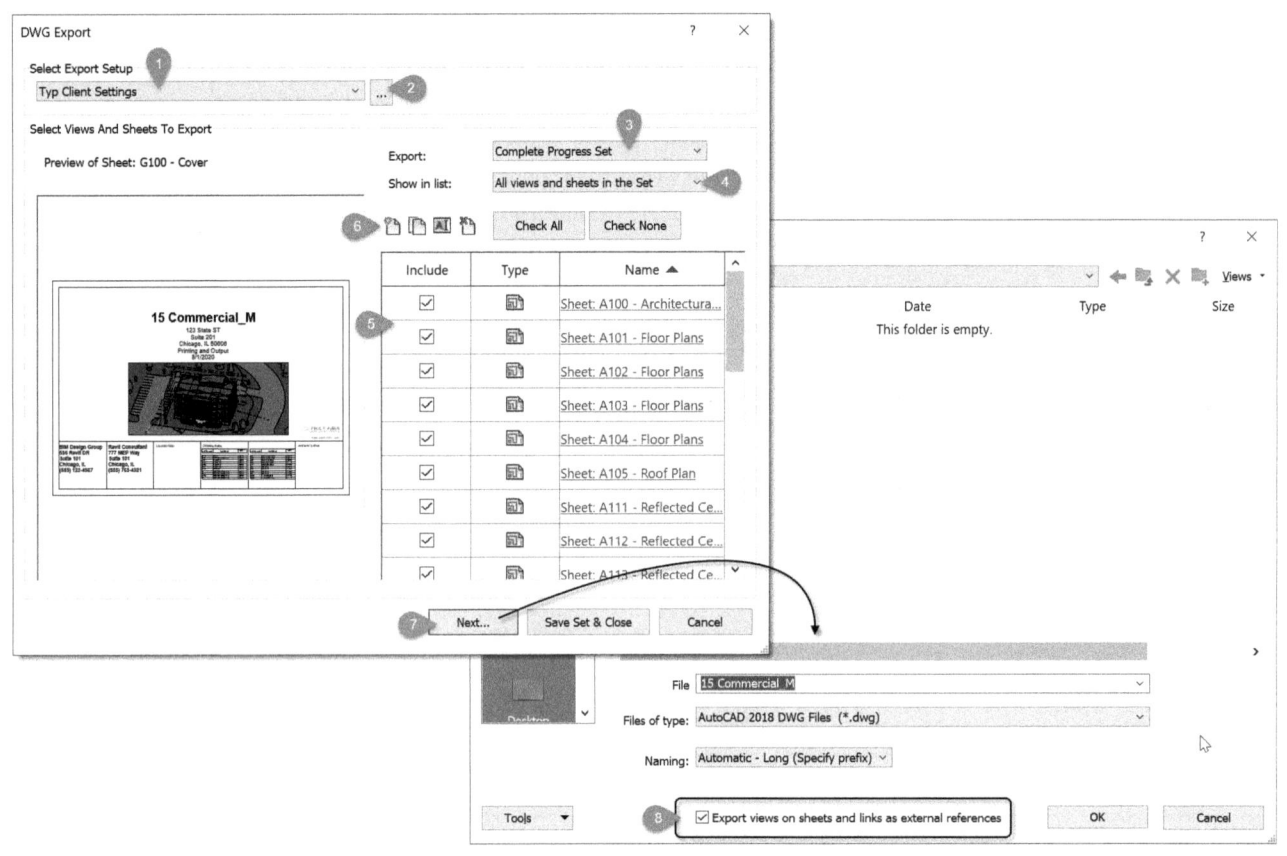

FIGURE 15.7 *Export one or more CAD files and configure their properties*

Choose name and location to save the file(s)—After you select your list of views to export, click Next at the bottom of the dialog. The "Export" dialog will appear where you can browse to a folder to save the files, choose your file naming options, and optionally have Revit XREF views onto sheets. This is a very handy feature as most AutoCAD users set up sheet files that include a title block in paper space with each drawing externally referenced onto the sheet. When Revit exports sheets, it can emulate this setup by creating DWG files of each Revit view and then a separate DWG for the sheet view with XREFs to the separate DWGs. This setting is recommended (item 8).

Open the file(s) in CAD—If you have AutoCAD or Microstation, go ahead and try exporting one of the book projects to DWG or DGN. Configure any settings you wish to experiment or match your office standards. Open the resulting files in CAD and study the results. Revit does a nice job of creating CAD files following industry standard best practices.

Naturally, any CAD files thus created will not maintain the "smarts" of the Revit project. Two-dimensional views like plans, sections and elevations will export as 2D only linework. 3D views will create 3D solids or surface geometry. Everything will be dimensionally accurate, but each view in Revit will become a separate (and disconnected) drawing in CAD. So, while the linework can be edited in AutoCAD, unlike the native Revit project, changes made to a plan view will not be reflected in elevation or section and vice/versa.

DEPENDENT VIEWS AND MATCHLINES

When a drawing is too large to fit on a sheet, it is customary for the drawing to be split into sections and a matchline to be employed. To accommodate this need, Revit provides the dependent view feature. You can duplicate a large view into several dependent views that can each be cropped down to partial plans. Unlike the standard duplicate options, dependent views share their annotation. Annotation added or editing in either the parent or child view is reflected in both. To set up dependent views, right-click the overall view and choose: **Duplicate View > Duplicate as a Dependent**.

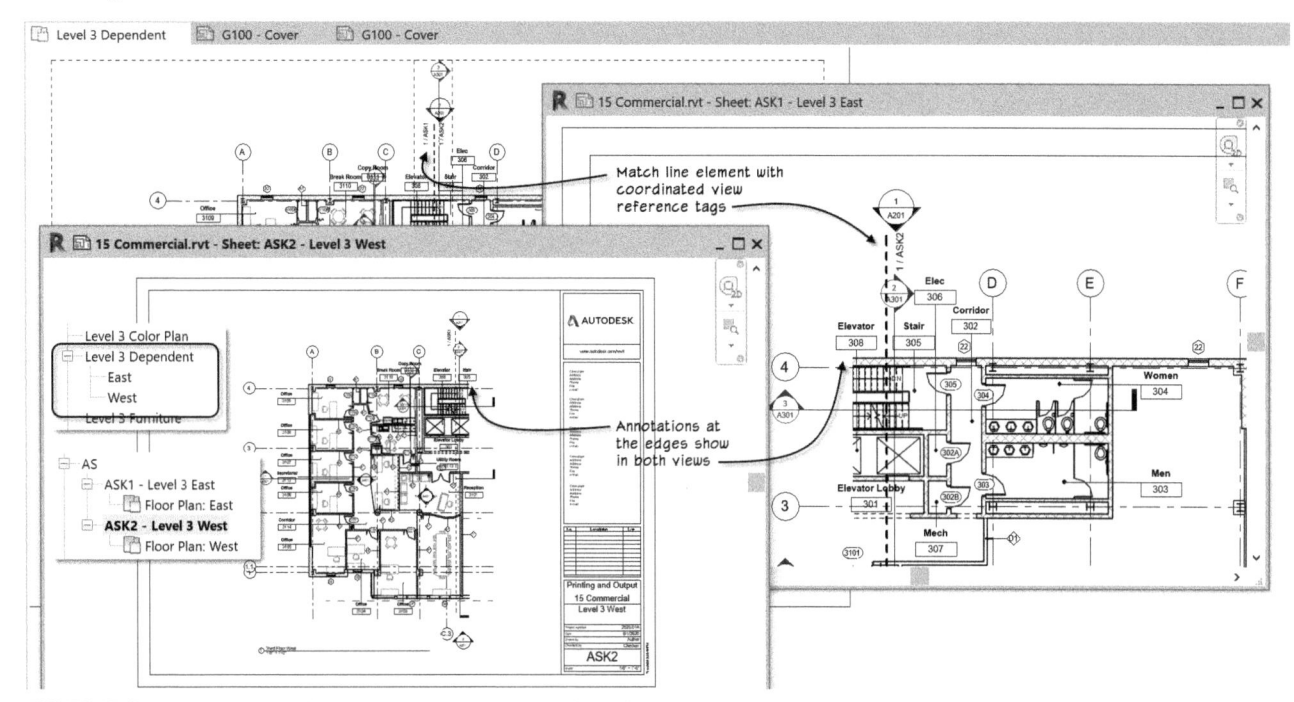

FIGURE 15.8 *Simple example of an overall plan split into two dependent views*

Repeat for as many sections as you need. For example, to create a plan with east and west sections and a matchline, you will have one overall view (referred to as the host view) and two dependent views. The dependent views are shown indented beneath their parent on the Project Browser. Adjust the crop regions as appropriate in each of the dependents (see Figure 15.8). The outer dashed line around the crop region is the annotation crop region. This controls which annotations will be repeated in each view. Near the edges, size the annotation crop to include only those tags and other annotation that you wish to repeat on both sides of the matchline. A Matchline tool and View Reference tool are available on the View tab.

SCOPE BOXES

In complex buildings, you may have multiple levels or grids in different sections of the building. By default, all datum elements show across the full extent of the building. While it is possible to stretch the handles and adjust them manually, this can become tedious on large projects. A scope box is a three-dimensional box that you sketch in plan. Use the handles to adjust its size. Give the scope box a unique name. You can then use this scope box to control the extents of datum elements and views. Look for the Scope Box property on the Properties palette. This will size the extent of the assigned elements to within the scope box. Views also can use scope boxes to control the extent of their crop region (or the section box for 3D views). Views or datum elements that do not use a scope box will show: **None** on the Properties palette (see Figure 15.9).

678 | Chapter 15

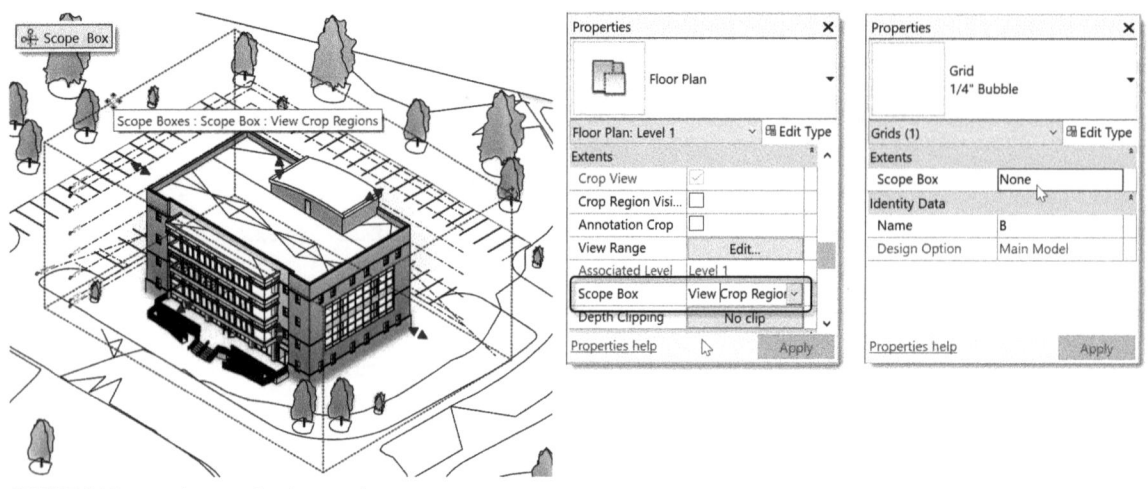

FIGURE 15.9 *Simple example of a scope box*

REVISION TRACKING

Despite every Architect's best efforts, revisions are a part of any document set. Once you have issued your drawings for bid and the inevitable revision packages must go out, use the revision cloud tool on the Annotate tab and the coordinated revision table available on the View tab; click the small icon on the Sheet Composition panel title bar to manage them (see Figure 15.10).

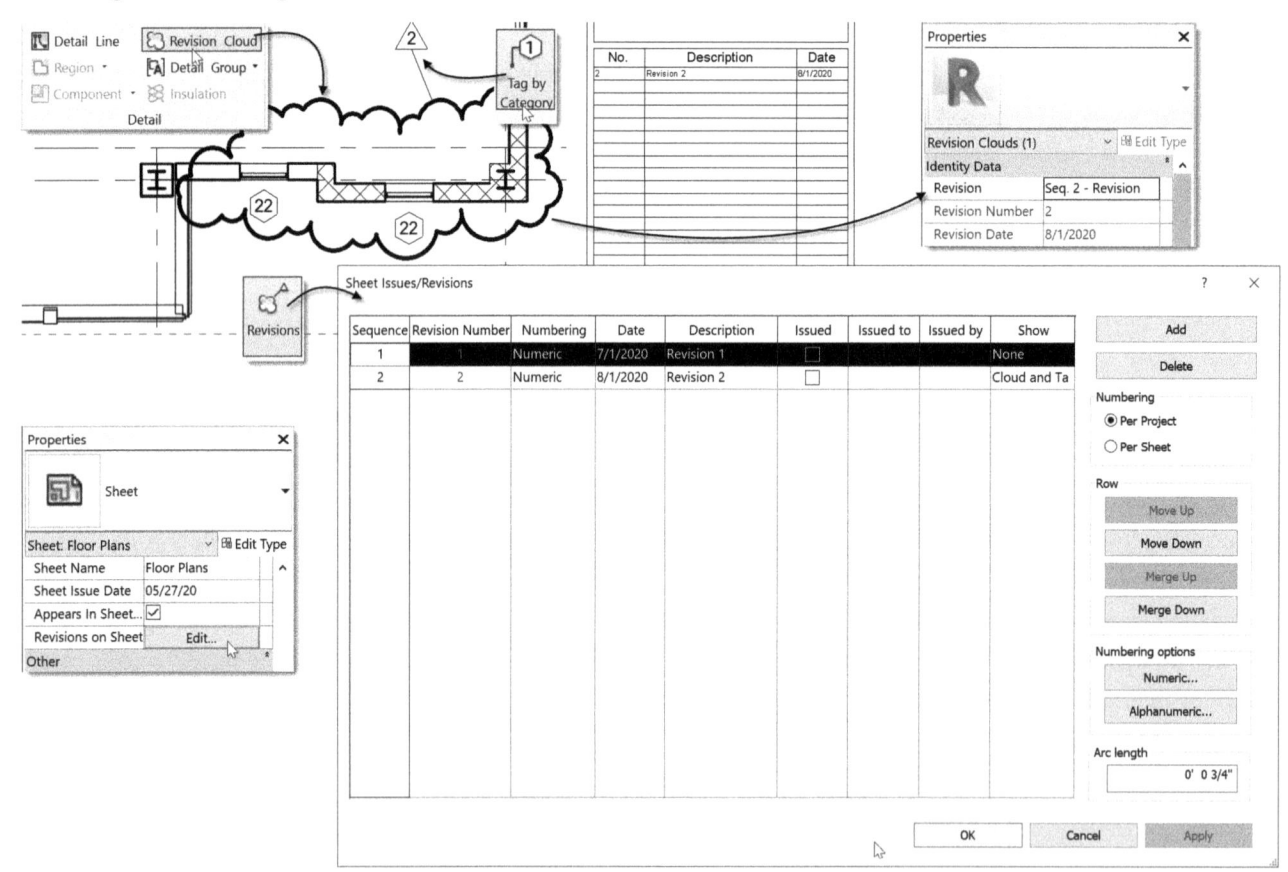

FIGURE 15.10 *Revision tracking coordinates, revision clouds, and tags with the table in the title block*

You add each new revision in the "Sheet Issues/Revisions" dialog (access it from the Sheet Composition panel as shown in the figure). When you add revision clouds (Annotate tab), they will appear automatically in the table on the sheet. For sheets without clouds, you can click the Revision on Sheet edit button on the Properties of the sheet to manually add any revision or issue to that sheet's title block.

SUMMARY

- ☑ Output from Revit includes many useful options. The overall process is simple and straightforward, regardless of the specific output desired.

- ☑ Like other Windows software, choose Print Setup to configure the Print options.

- ☑ Save your choices for future use in the project.

- ☑ Choose Print from the File menu to print to paper.

- ☑ Use Print to create PDF output as well. A PDF print driver is required.

- ☑ Choose: **Export** > **CAD** to create DWG output directly from Revit.

- ☑ Revit provides tools for matchlines and tools for revision tracking.

CHAPTER 16
Worksharing

INTRODUCTION

The term "Worksharing" applies collectively to the various techniques used in the Autodesk® Revit® platform to work in teams of multiple individuals and firms. Worksharing typically refers to the internal segmentation of a project using Worksets and Central and Local Files but can also include processes we have already seen in this book such as linked Revit (RVT) files and linked AutoCAD (DWG) files. Worksharing enables team members to work independently and simultaneously without impeding the work of others. Care must be taken when enabling worksets to ensure that a strategy appropriate to the team dynamics is established. In this chapter, we will introduce the concepts and key terminology used in worksharing as well as briefly discuss general worksharing issues and strategies. The only way to share work in Revit LT is using linked files. Coordination review and worksharing are not available in Revit LT. If you are using Revit LT, most of this chapter will not apply to you.

OBJECTIVES

This chapter will provide an overview of the salient concepts and suggestions for using worksharing. After completing this chapter, you will understand:

- ▲ Key worksharing tools available
- ▲ Workset terminology
- ▲ Where to find additional worksharing resources

WAYS TO SHARE WORK

Architectural projects usually involve teams of professionals either within the same firm (under the same roof) or dispersed among several companies and/or physical locations. Whether you simply need to load a CAD file as a background for your own design work or you need to manage a fully coordinated Revit model among several members of your firm, Revit has tools and capabilities suited to the task.

LINKING AND IMPORTING

In earlier chapters, we explored two forms of linking: linked RVT files and linked CAD files. If you need to simply keep track of work being done in another application such as AutoCAD or MicroStation, then file linking is the appropriate solution. DWG (AutoCAD) and DGN (MicroStation) files can be either linked or imported into your

Revit model. If you wish to maintain the ability to update the file periodically as the original author of the file makes changes, choose to link the file. In this scenario, you simply reload the linked file when you receive an updated version from your consultant or teammate. If you instead need to use the geometry in the CAD file to assist you in creating your Revit model and have no need to reload changes in the future, you can import instead. This places a static copy of the file within your Revit model. You can leave this imported file intact as a single element in the Revit model or even choose to explode it. If you explode it, Revit will convert the imported geometry into simple Revit drafting and model lines. You should not explode these files unless necessary, as it will increase overhead and memory demands on your system depending on how large and extensive the imported files are. A better approach when exploding is deemed necessary to create a temporary Revit file first. Import the CAD data to this file, explode it, and then clean it up. This might involve reassigning linework to office standard line types, deleting unnecessary items and other measures. Once the geometry is suitably cleaned up, you can copy and paste it to your project file. Examples of linking and importing DWG files can be found in Chapters 7, 8, 11 and 12.

While linking to CAD files does help bridge the gap between your firm and those not using Revit software, it is always better if you can get the entire project team working in the same software and file format. Therefore, wherever possible, having all team members using Revit is preferable. They can be on the full version of Revit which has all disciplines or even on Revit LT. However, it is critical that all team members use the same version (2021, for example). You can still work in separate models and utilize linking in this scenario as discussed in Chapter 7. In fact, this is often the preferred workflow for managing various disciplines. In the case of RVT files, you will typically link the file. Should you decide that it is desirable to "merge" two RVT files into a single file, it is possible to bind a link. This converts it to a group but breaks the link to the original file. You can then ungroup the group thus created to access the individual elements. You can also use copy and paste or Group Save and Group Load instead. Open one of the files, copy all the elements that you wish to merge, and then paste them into the other project. Group all the model, annotation, and datum elements you wish to merge, save the group file out to an RVT file and then load that RVT file into the other project. Remember, model and annotation elements will be stored in separate model and detail groups. Chapter 7 covers the process in more detail.

Revit also can import and export IFC files. The Industry Foundation Class (IFC) standard attempts to define a universal standard file format for the storage of building model data. IFC is currently the only bridge format that allows walls, doors, windows, roofs, floors, and other building components to be preserved when imported and exported to and from Revit and other BIM software. While the technology is promising, it still cannot preserve all the nuances that each software package introduces into its building models. If you absolutely must work in a team that uses Revit and other BIM packages together, then spend some time testing out the IFC import and export commands and settings found on the File menu. IFC files will be linked like other files and you manage those links in the Manage Links dialog as well.

COORDINATION MONITOR AND INTERFERENCE CHECK

When you link two Revit files together (such as an architectural file and a structural file), you can use the coordination tools to keep track of duplicate elements or elements that rely upon one another in each file. For example, if the structural columns are in the structural file and the partitions and the architectural columns are in the architectural file, these elements can get out of sync as users in each model make changes. Using the Copy/Monitor, Coordination Review, and Interference Check items on the Collaborate ribbon tab, you can copy elements between files, watch them for changes, and make updates to keep both linked projects synchronized. Look for more information about Copy/Monitor and Coordination Review in Chapter 7.

We have not looked at Interference Check yet, so let's take a quick look. To try this feature out, you can open a file from one of the earlier chapters. The most complete version of the commercial project is in the *Chapter15* folder. This will be suitable for exploring this feature.

An interference check searches the model for conditions where the 3D geometry of one object is interfering with (in the same space as) the geometry of another. An interactive report is generated when you run the command that allows you to select the elements in question to highlight them in the model. This allows you to assess the problem and work on solutions. To run an interference check, click the Collaborate tab, and then the Interference Check drop down button. Choose: **Run Interference Check** from the menu that appears. In the "Interference Check" dialog, two columns appear. You can run interferences between any combination of selected Categories in the same project or between the current project and a linked Revit file. Running the check between the current project and a linked project is the more common scenario, but in complex projects, running it between different elements in the current project can be very valuable as well.

Figure 16.1 shows an example comparing the curtain wall at the front facade in the current project with structural framing in the linked *Commercial-Structure.rvt* file. Start by running the interference check (item 1 in Figure 16.1). Next, in the right column, choose the structural project file link from the drop down at the top (item 2). In each column, check one or more categories that you wish to check against in the list beneath each file (item 3). When you click OK (item 4), Revit will analyze the elements in your model and look for clashes between the categories you selected .

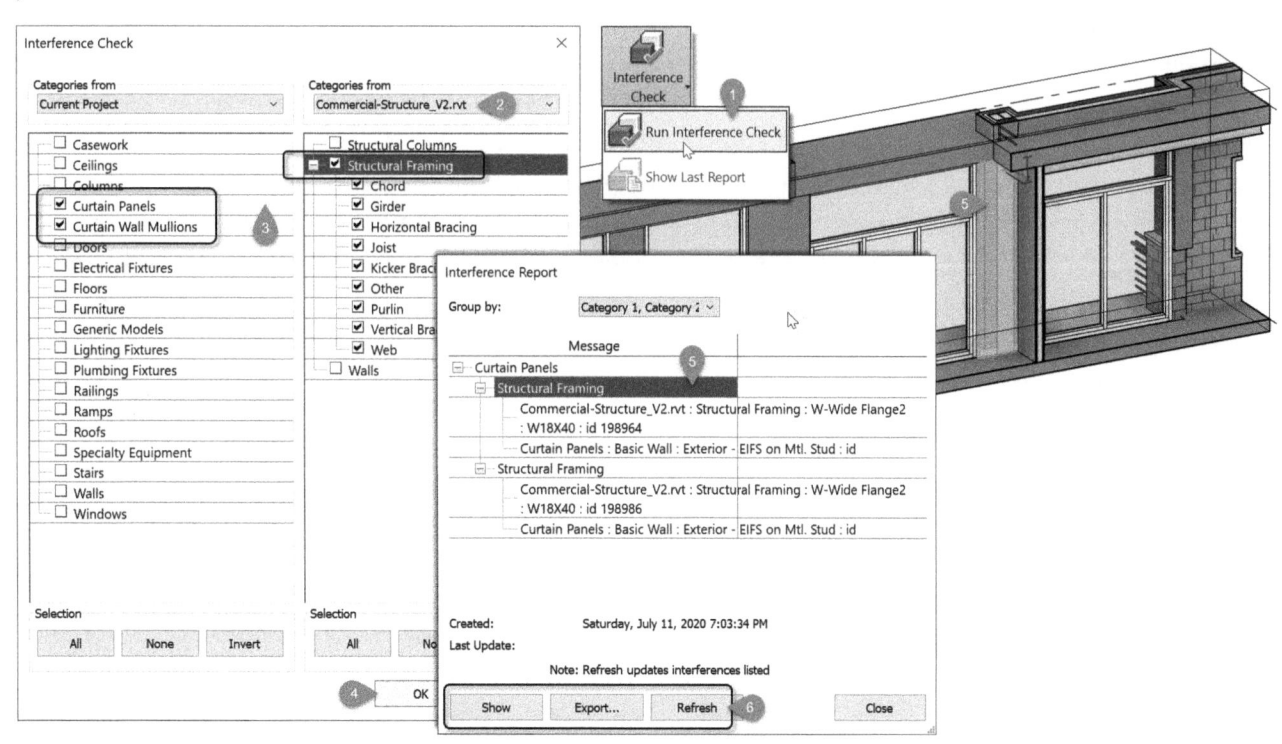

FIGURE 16.1 *Using the Interference Check Tool*

When the "Interference Report" dialog appears, you can expand any condition listed to see the elements that interfere. If you have an appropriate view open on screen, you can click on one of the items listed in the clash and see it highlight onscreen (item 5). If you do not have an appropriate view open, you can click the Show button to have Revit search for an appropriate view (item 6). If you click the Export button, you can generate an HTML report of the clashes found. An example of the report is provided in the *Chapter16* folder. You can use the element IDs in the report to select elements later if necessary. To select by element ID, on the Manage tab, click the Select by ID button. Type in the ID to select it.

As you fix the problems listed, you can click the Refresh button to run the report again. The interference check tool offers a nice way to spot potential problems before they go too far in the design process. It is most effective when we are surgical in our approach, comparing a single category against another instead of the whole of the model against the whole of another. For much more complete tools and functionality, consider evaluating Autodesk Navisworks. Revit models can be exported directly to Navisworks for robust interference checking, timeline simulation, and rendering functionality.

ENABLING WORKSHARING

It is typical that more than one member of your firm will need to access and work in the project at the same time. Enable "Worksharing" to allow different members of the project team to work simultaneously on the same project file. Each user saves their own "Local file," which remains connected back to a master "Central file" that keeps all changes and team interactions coordinated. While workset use is most common on a team project, it can be used in any Revit project and some sole practitioner firms find it useful as a tool for managing project data and visibility of elements. Whatever your specific situation, achieving success with worksets requires a clear understanding of each tool, careful pre-planning and ongoing management.

> **NOTE:** The following is a brief introduction to the concept of worksharing. It is intended to introduce the concepts, define the terminology, and suggest some common scenarios for their usage. A comprehensive tutorial-based exploration of the topic falls out of the scope of this text. Consider attending a formal training session at a local training provider or Autodesk reseller. To learn more about hands-on training opportunities, visit the author's web site at: **paulaubin.com**. While there, checkout the many conference papers posted there and available for free download from: **paulaubin.com/conferences**. On the right-hand side, click the link for Worksharing to find a PDF document and an accompanying ZIP file with a sample dataset for a session named: The **Autodesk Revit Worksets Workshop**[‡]. The paper includes a step-by-step tutorial showcasing the worksharing features. The tutorial works best if you can follow along with one or two other individuals. This document and its Revit files are now rather old, but most of the worksharing functionality it discusses is still applicable. The files will require upgrade to the latest version of Revit when you open them.

GETTING STARTED WITH WORKSETS

Before using worksets the feature must be enabled in a project. After it is turned on, some configuration will be required. Typically, this task should be performed by a single member of the project team knowledgeable in worksets and their nuances. This person is often referred to as the "Project Coordinator" or some similar title. They might be a CAD Manager, BIM Manager, or simply a project Architect on the project who has good knowledge of Revit and worksharing.

To enable worksets the first time, use the Collaborate or the Worksets buttons on the Collaborate tab. The Worksets button is also located on the Status Bar at the bottom of the Revit screen (see Figure 16.2).

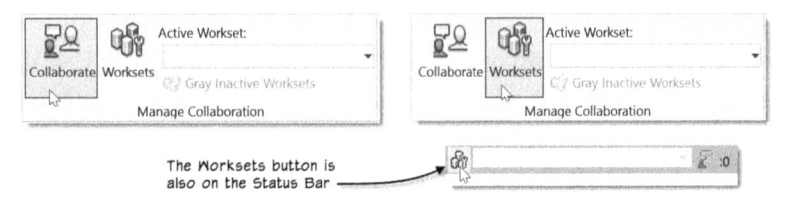

FIGURE 16.2 *Enable worksharing using the Collaborate or the Worksets buttons*

Every member working on the team should understand the basic concepts of a workset-enabled project. In addition, it is recommended that each member of the team reviews the help resources provided with the software and that multiple team members practice together on a sample workset project before working live for the first time.

UNDERSTANDING WORKSETS

The concept behind worksets is simple. Normally, in a computer environment, only one user at a time can access a file at the same time. Since by default, Revit places all project elements within a single file, this would naturally impede teamwork. Using worksets, there is still a single "Central" file that houses all project data, but from this central file, each team member must save a local copy (which maintains its association with the central file). In this way, when any team member saves work from their local copy back to the central, those changes are synchronized with the central file and become available to all members of the team. Simply having the central and local files is not always enough, however; the vast collection of potentially editable elements within the project files must be managed. Worksets are used for this purpose. A workset is basically a named group of elements that can be "checked out" by an individual user. Once checked out, a workset becomes "read-only" to other members of the team. This allows those members to view any part of the project that they wish, but only edit those parts that they have checked out. When saves back to central are made, users can choose to "relinquish" their elements and worksets and/or check out other ones. The concept is like a traditional public library. If you wish to check out a book or video, it must be available at the time of your visit. If someone else has already checked out the item, you must wait for them to return it before you can check it out.

The biggest challenge involved in a Revit workset-enabled project is deciding how to organize the worksets and which specific elements they will contain. You want to have enough worksets to meet the team's requirements, but don't want to have so many that management of them becomes problematic. Any worksets you or your team members create are referred to as "User-Created" worksets. There are other worksets that are created and maintained automatically by Revit. These include "Views," "Families," and "Project Standards" worksets.

> **View Worksets**—For each view, a dedicated view workset is created. It automatically contains the view's parameters (scale, visibility, graphics style, etc.) and any view-specific elements such as text notes, dimensions, detail elements, etc. associated with that view. View-specific elements cannot be moved to another workset. To move them, you would cut the elements in question from their current view and paste them into a new view.
>
> **Family Worksets**—One workset is created for the definition of each loaded family in the project. (This is not for the individual instances in the project, but rather their presence on the Project Browser tree). If you edit a family (in the family editor), and then reload it, you will be checking out that associated family workset on reload.
>
> **Project Standards Worksets**—One workset for each type of project setting, such as Materials, Line Styles, Text, Dimensions, etc.
>
> These three kinds of worksets are created and maintained automatically by Revit—no user initiation is required.
>
> **User-Created Worksets**—Elements that are part of your model will be associated with one or more "User Defined" worksets. These contain all the building model elements in a project. The quantity and composition of user defined worksets is completely user defined; thus the name. By default, Revit will create two such worksets when the feature is first enabled. They are called: "Shared Levels and Grids" and "Workset1." When you initialize worksharing, all the level and grid elements in your project are assigned automatically to the "Shared Levels and Grids" workset and all of the rest of the model geometry is assigned to "Workset1." However, from that point on, any new model element (including levels and grids) will go to the active workset at the time of creation. You can keep these two default worksets, rename them, add more or even delete them. However, at least one user defined workset must remain.

686 | Chapter 16

You can reassign a model element from one workset to another, but you cannot assign it to more than one at the same time. Therefore, careful planning is important. The project coordinator must therefore attempt to anticipate the needs of the project team and create worksets to house model elements in a way that supports these needs. While there are no set "rules" regarding this, there are common best practices. The factors to consider include:

- Project size
- Team size
- Team member roles
- Default workset visibility
- Project performance issues

Each of these factors may have an impact on the use and composition of each workset. Larger projects and larger project teams will typically have more worksets. This stands to reason. However, even small projects can benefit from worksets, so this is not the only factor. When you open a project that has worksets enabled, you can optionally choose which worksets to load before opening the file. Choosing to open only those worksets needed for a task can help files load more quickly and preserve valuable computer resources. You can also take advantage of workset visibility to hide entire worksets in one or more views as appropriate. Therefore, any or all these factors can play an important role in determining the ultimate composition of worksets in a project. Also, remember that each project is unique and while you may follow many common strategies from one project to the next, you must always be flexible enough to allow for specific circumstances that may arise in a particular project. The most common problem for beginners is creating too many worksets. Start off with as few as possible (usually the two default ones will be sufficient). Only add additional worksets when a clear need has been identified by the project team or they have valid prior experience to justify it.

INITIALIZE WORKSHARING

As was mentioned above, it is typically advisable for a single experienced member of the project team to take responsibility for workset management and setup. Worksets must be enabled before they can be used. This is a one-time task per project. The next step is to create a central file and save it in a location that all team members can readily access. This location is typically on a network server on the company LAN (Local Area Network). But if you subscribe to the Autodesk BIM 360 Design service, you can host your central models in the cloud and users can access the project from any location with Internet access. Cloud model collaboration has many benefits but does come with additional cost per user. Talk with your Autodesk Reseller to learn more.

> **NOTE:** If you want to follow along in the topics below, you can open the version of the Commercial project from Chapter 15 as a starting point and create a central model from it.

As noted above, there are two buttons on the Collaborate tab that allow you to initialize worksharing (see Figure 16.2 above). The Collaborate button is the simpler of the two. If you click the Collaborate button, you will be given the choice between a LAN-based (Within your network) or BIM 360 cloud-based central model. The remaining workset setup will use the defaults automatically (see the left side of Figure 16.3).

If you prefer to configure your workset setup right away, click the Worksets button instead. This will create a LAN-based central model (but you can later save to BIM 360 if you wish). The dialog that appears allows you configure the initial worksets you plan to use in the project (see the right side of Figure 16.3).

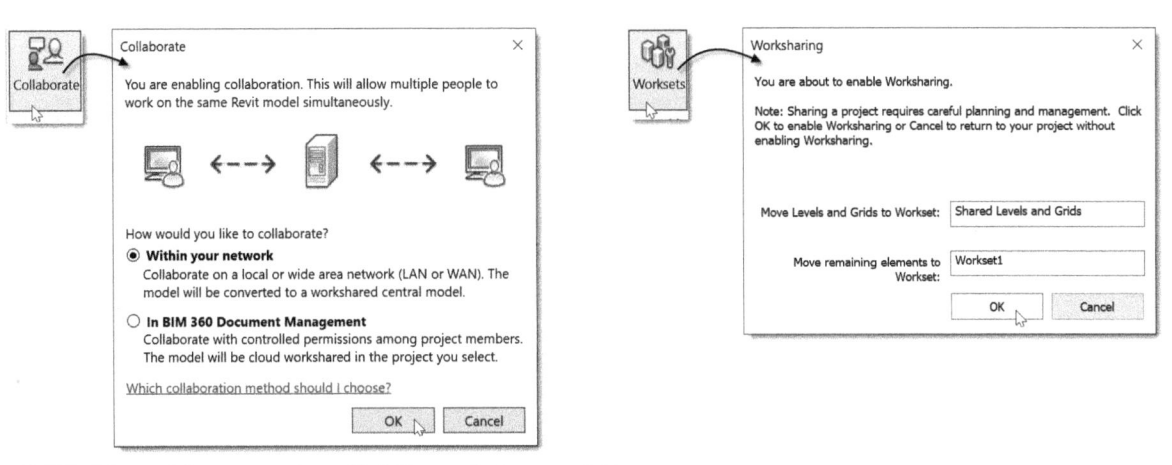

FIGURE 16.3 *Worksharing must be enabled. Two methods are available*

As noted above, two user-created worksets will be suggested by default. You can see these by clicking the Worksets button. If you initialized using the Worksets button (instead of Collaborate) the "Worksets" dialog will display when you click OK in the "Worksharing" dialog. You can always reopen it at any time by clicking Worksets again. You can accept the default names or type your own. You can also rename a workset later (provided that no users are accessing the project at the time you choose to rename). Additional user-created worksets can be added at any time. You can also use this dialog to list all the "Views," "Families," and "Project Standards" worksets.

CREATE A CENTRAL FILE

Before users can begin working in a workset-enabled project, there must be a central file. This file is the main "hub" of the project. It should be located on a network server accessible to all team members. After worksharing has been enabled, you use the: **Save As > Project** command on the File menu to save a central file. The first time that Save As is chosen after enabling worksets, the file saved automatically becomes a central file. So, make sure you point it to a network server location. After that, if you wish to create a new central file for any reason, you must choose: **Save As > Project** from the File menu, click the Options button, and then check the "Make this the central location after save" check box (see Figure 16.4).

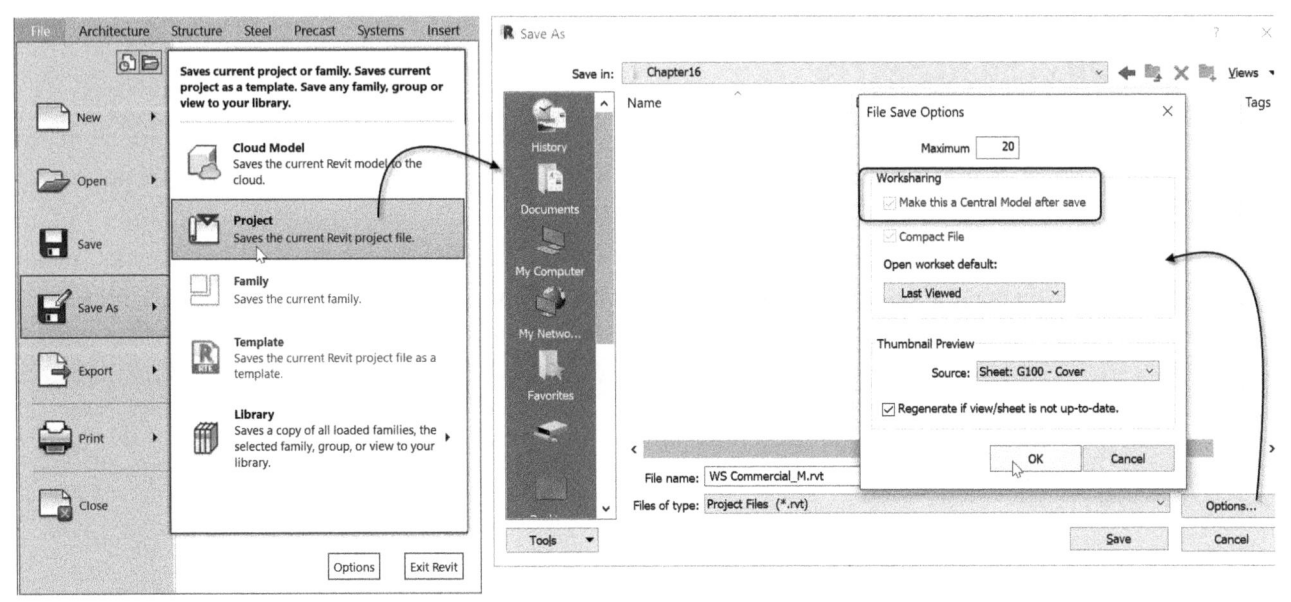

FIGURE 16.4 *Making a file the Central file*

• Revit Essentials for Architecture •

> **BIM Manager Note:** Naming your central file is an important consideration. Choose a clear and descriptive name. When Revit creates a Local file from your central it automatically appends your username as a suffix. For example, if the "Central" file is named: *ABC Office Towers.rvt*. When you create a local file, it will become *ABC Office Towers_User Name.rvt*. This should be clear enough to distinguish one from the other. Further, since the central file will always be on the network server and the Local file is typically in the *My Documents* folder (by default) or some other local folder like: *D:\Revit Projects*, this should also clarify the difference. Remember, whatever naming convention and procedure you adopt, make sure it is clearly communicated to all project team members and that all are required to follow it. Finally, if you are using BIM 360, one of the benefits is that Revit will manage the naming for you. So, you simply name your central model in the cloud any logical name you like (no suffixes or qualifiers required). This is because when accessing it, Revit will automatically create the local file and name it behind the scenes in a temporary folder. Meanwhile, what the user will see is the same user-friendly name that the central file had on BIM 360. But there is no chance that you can accidentally work in the central model when using BIM 360. This is a very nice perk for sure!

While it is possible to move or make a copy of the central file, it is highly recommended that you maintain only one central file to avoid confusion to project team members and potential loss of work. You can and should regularly back up the central file using whatever method is currently in place in your firm, but avoid simply making a separate copy to another location on the network as users may mistakenly open this file and create local files from it. The best way to make a backup of the central is with the "Detach from Central" option. Like it implies, this will disconnect the file from the central making it a stand-alone copy of the project. You should naturally use this with caution. This is because once you "detach" you cannot "reattach." This command is useful for a few situations. For example, if you want to open the project "read only," or to assist with archiving or troubleshooting. It is also a very effective way to plot document sets or create renderings. Project managers who are not regular Revit users can also find opening a detached copy gives them an "anxiety free" way to open a project and perform checking/querying activities.

It is really very important that users understand these issues. If user A creates work synchronized to central file A, and user B works in a detached file or synchronized to central file B, there is no way for these two to synchronize their work with one another. Such a situation would largely defeat the whole purpose of using worksharing. Please make sure that all team members understand this lest they decide to do a "save as" and work on a quick study off to the side. This may be acceptable practice in a CAD environment, but it will cause grief and rework in a Revit environment and should be avoided.

EDITABLE AND OPEN WORKSETS

The "Worksets" dialog has a column labeled "Editable" and another labeled "Open." Both will read either Yes or No next to each workset (you can see an example on the right side of Figure 16.3 above). Both designations are potentially confusing. When you make a workset "editable" you are making it editable only to yourself—in other words, you are "checking it out." This "locks" the workset to other users. They can still borrow from your workset if they submit an editing request and you grant it. So, if editable says: Yes, you have the workset checked out (and your name will be listed in the Owner column). If it says No, it is available for anyone to check out or borrow from.

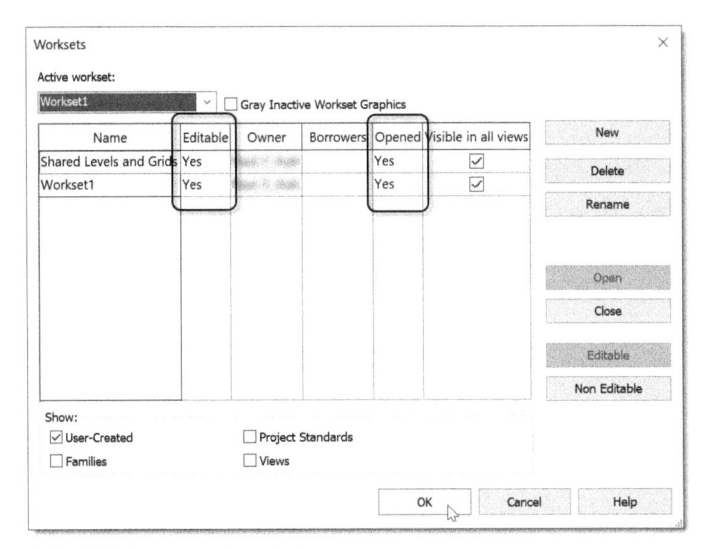

FIGURE 16.5 *The Worksets dialog*

When a workset is "Open" (Open reads: Yes) it will be visible on screen. If Open reads: No, then it is closed and the workset will not be visible. Choosing not to open certain worksets is a strategy frequently employed by firms working on large projects to help speed load times.

CREATING ADDITIONAL WORKSETS

After the central file has been saved, the next step in setting up your central file is to decide if you need any additional worksets, and if so, how many. Dedicated worksets give you broad control over a collection of elements belonging to that workset. For example, if you are personally responsible for geometry in the core of the building and wish to prevent anyone else from making edits to core elements, you can create a dedicated: Core workset and "check it out." This makes you the only user able to edit items associated with that workset even if you are not actively editing them. In the public library analogy above, instead of checking out just a copy of "*The Lord of the Rings*" this would be like checking out the entire fiction section!

If you prefer a less absolute approach, use "Element Borrowing." With or without dedicated worksets, any element not checked out by another user is available to edit—even if you don't have the workset checked out or current. Simply select an element and begin editing it. Revit will allow you to borrow the element (if it is available), leaving the rest of the elements in its workset available to other users. See the "Borrowing Elements" topic on page 698 below for more information.

It is recommended that you only create the worksets that you are *certain* your team will require. Rely instead on element borrowing for most editing and save dedicated worksets for those items that need the extra level of "locking" control or as a tool to manage visibility and/or performance. If you are not sure which worksets you need, try not creating any for the first project and leave all model elements on Workset 1. Doing so will have the team using element borrowing exclusively. If you run into limitations with this approach, consider adding additional worksets. This approach is considered "best practice" at many large architectural firms who find that additional worksets add complexity to the project but not always a commensurate level of value or benefit.

In the case where you have determined additional worksets are required by the project team, you return to the "Worksets" dialog to add them. On the Collaborate tab, click the Worksets button (or the button on the Status Bar) and then click the New button to add a workset. You can name each descriptively. An important consideration when creating new worksets is their default visibility. If you wish to have the workset automatically visible in all project views by default, then check the "Visible in all views" box when creating it. However, to help increase performance on large projects, you can opt to leave this setting disabled and allow users to control the visibility of each workset manually (see Figure 16.6). In the figure, "Structural Links" is off by default, while all others are on.

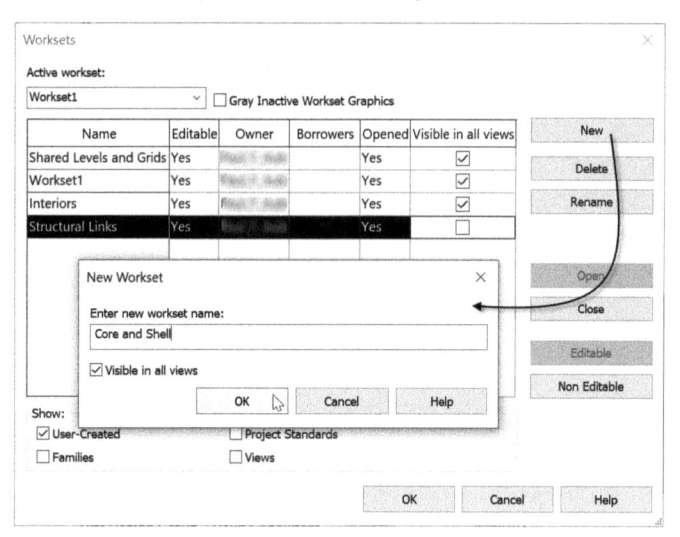

FIGURE 16.6 *You can disable visibility by default of a new workset if desired*

When setting up the initial worksets, try to divide building elements into logical groupings. These will often be "task-based" to support the work of the team member who will author its contents. For example, in a typical commercial office building like the project constructed in this book, you might create a workset for the exterior shell of the building, the core elements, the lobby, and one for interior elements. Furniture and equipment could also be separated but try not to make worksets for things that we can already manage using categories. So, since there is already a furniture category, having a furniture workset is redundant. However, if you intend to have furniture, equipment, casework and maybe even electrical fixtures on that workset, then it may make more sense.

You can add new worksets at any time in a project. However, it is a good idea to try to establish the basic workset organization as early as possible. This will make it easier for project team members to become comfortable with the project and its organization. As new worksets are added later in the project, be sure that these and their functions are clearly communicated to the project team. Also remember, that if you are uncertain on whether a workset is needed, leave it out initially and see how the project goes. If it becomes evident that the workset is required, you can add it later.

REASSIGNING WORKSETS

When you start a new project with a collection of typical worksets, there will be no model geometry, so creating the worksets will be the final step of setting up worksharing. However, if an existing project has worksets enabled after geometry has already been added (say after a schematic design phase), existing elements in the model may need to be moved to an appropriate workset(s). For instance, if a workset named "Interiors" has been created, then any interior elements such as partitions, doors, furniture, etc., should be assigned to this workset.

To reassign existing elements to a different workset, select one or more elements, on the Properties palette choose the desired workset from the "Workset" list (see the left side of Figure 16.7).

> **IMPORTANT:** Following your initial setup, it will be up to the team members to create new elements on the appropriate workset as they work. This includes Shared Levels and Grids. Revit only places Levels and Grids on this workset automatically the first time it is enabled. After that, *all* new model elements go to the active workset.

Worksharing | 691

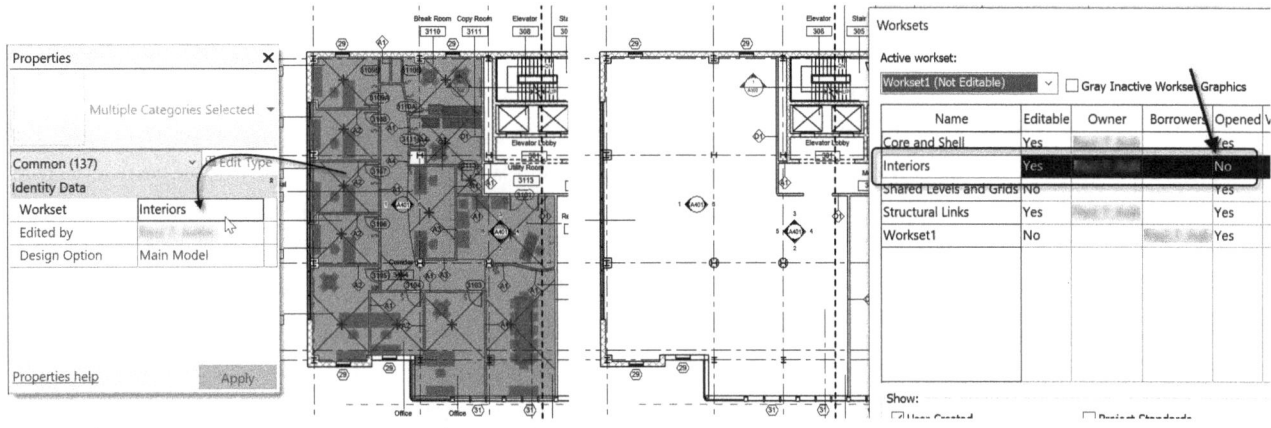

FIGURE 16.7 *Move a selection of elements to a different workset*

Once you have assigned some elements to another workset, you can try going back to the "Worksets" dialog and close the workset to see the effect (see the right side of Figure 16.7).

> **TIP:** If you select one or more elements and attempt to change their workset and the Workset option is grayed out, try the following: First, make sure that you only have model elements selected. (You can use the Filter tool to remove any tags, view tags, notes, or dimensions from the selection). You should be able to edit it now. If they remain grayed out, try to right-click in the drawing area and choose: **Make Elements Editable**. This will borrow the selection of elements and allow you to change the workset. See the "Borrowing Elements" topic on page 698 below for more information on element borrowing.

> **NOTE:** Another item to watch for is nested elements like curtain wall mullions, grids, and panels. These items cannot be added to worksets separately from their parent curtain wall or system. The same is true for stair and railing subcomponents. When you change the workset of the curtain wall, curtain system, stair or railing, it automatically changes all the girds, mullions, panels, rails, runs and supports as well.

WORKSET TOOLTIPS

When you work in a workset-enabled project, the tool tips that appear when elements are pre-highlighted will report the workset in front of the usual element Category : Family : Type designation (see Figure 16.8).

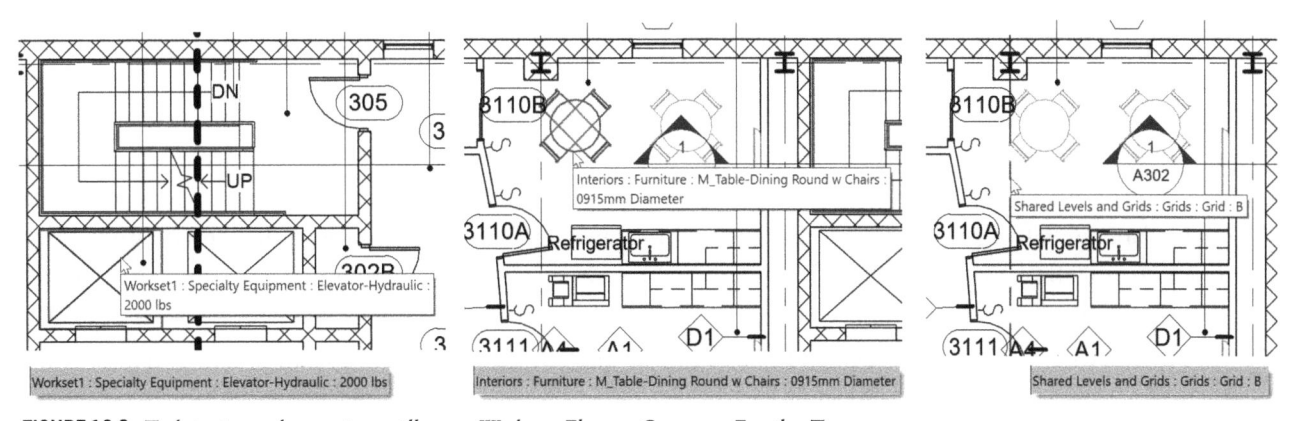

FIGURE 16.8 *Tool tips in workset projects will report Workset : Element Category : Family : Type*

• Revit Essentials for Architecture •

WORKSET VISIBILITY

Worksets offer an alternative way to control element visibility, but unlike most visibility settings in Revit, when you close a workset, its elements will be invisible in ALL views, not just the current view. This is what makes workset visibility so unique and powerful. In addition to this, there is another way to control the visibility of worksets. They can also be controlled on a per view basis like other visibility settings in Revit. When we discussed the creation of new worksets in the "Creating Additional Worksets" topic on page 689 above, this is what the default visibility setting was for. You can open the "Worksets" dialog anytime to see the defaults for each workset and you can change them too. To see which worksets are visible in a view, open the "Visibility/Graphics Overrides" dialog (VG). A Worksets tab will appear in the dialog. On this tab, you can override the default visibility state for each workset in the current view (see Figure 16.9). Next to each Workset listed will be three options: Show, Hide, and Use Global Settings. Use Global Settings is the default and will use whatever setting is enabled in the "Worksets" dialog. The Show and Hide settings override the global setting accordingly. Please note that if a workset is closed, it will not display even if the Visibility/Graphics is set to: Show.

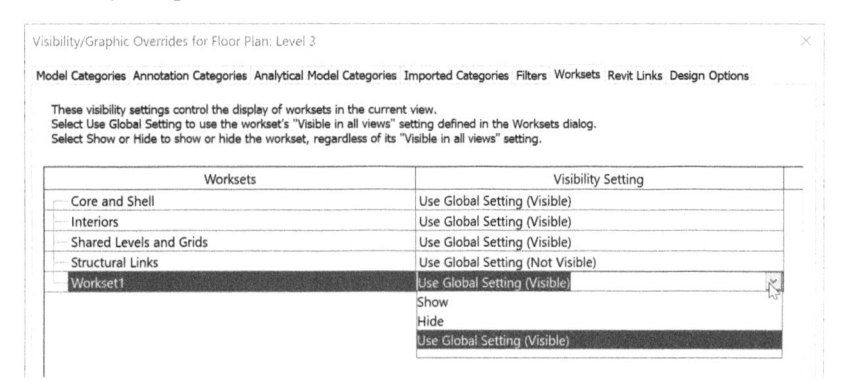

FIGURE 16.9 *Choose which Worksets you wish to display in a particular view in the Visibility/Graphics dialog*

This offers us a powerful way to manage the specific visibility of a collection of elements assigned to the same workset in a project. To fully realize its potential, take care in the planning stages to determine the default (global) visibility of each workset in the project. Users can change the settings later, but it is a good idea to establish effective defaults ahead of time.

Remember, anything you do in the "Visibility/Graphic Overrides" dialog is an override for the current view only. If you want to temporarily turn off a workset throughout the project, close it instead. See the next topic for more details.

CLOSE WORKSETS AND CLOSE THE CENTRAL FILE

Following your initial setup, you should relinquish all worksets. If you don't, team members will try to edit elements and be told that they are locked by you! As a final step in your central file creation, relinquish (check back in) all the worksets you created. Fortunately, this is easy to do while synchronizing with the central file. Close any open dialogs. On the Collaborate tab of the ribbon, on the Synchronize panel, click the Synchronize with Central button. This button is also available on the QAT. The "Synchronize with Central" dialog will appear. In the "After synchronizing, relinquish the following worksets and elements" area, check the "User-Created Worksets" check box. If any other check boxes in this area (like Borrowed Elements, View or Family Worksets) are available, be sure to check them too and then click OK (see the left side of Figure 16.10).

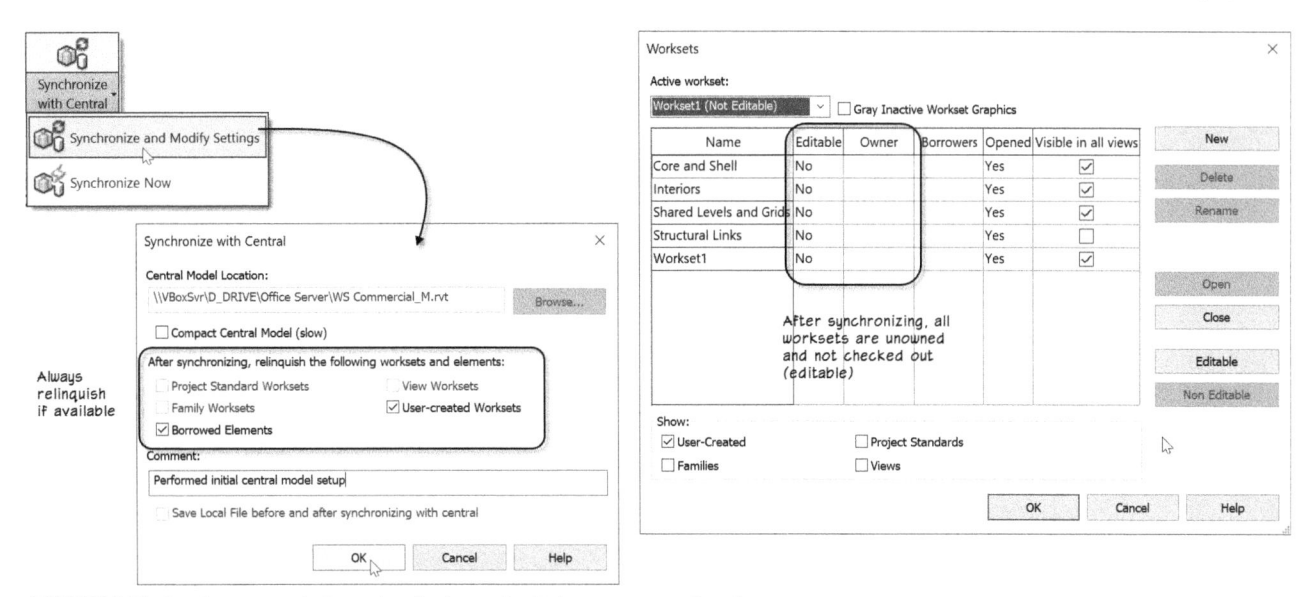

FIGURE 16.10 *Synchronize with Central and relinquish all elements to complete the setup*

Relinquishing the worksets will make them "non-editable" to you and available for editing to other team members. If you return to the "Worksets" dialog, you can confirm that "No" now appears in the Editable column for all Worksets and the Owner column is empty (see the right side of Figure 16.10).

The final step is to close the central file. In normal use and day-to-day project work, you and all the team members should avoid opening and working directly in the central file *at all costs*. Only under special circumstances (usually related to data recovery and/or routine maintenance) would you want to open the central file directly. The integrity of the central file is critical to your project's success. Please close the central and do not reopen it! All project work going forward will be performed in a Local file (see the next topic).

> **BIM Manager Note:** A notable exception to the "never work in the central file" rule is regularly scheduled model maintenance. Regular maintenance should be performed on the central file, including Audit, Compact, and recreating all Local files. These tasks are best performed by the project data coordinator or other person knowledgeable in Revit and Revit worksharing and only when all other users are not working in their local files.

JOINING A WORKSHARE TEAM

Each member of the project team must create and work in a local copy of the central file. From this local copy, users can check out the worksets in which they need to work, borrow elements, and work alongside other team members. When a user checks out a workset or borrows an element, the element is locked in the central file and becomes read-only to other team members until that user relinquishes it.

CREATING A LOCAL FILE

To participate in a workshare enabled project, you create first a local file. On the QAT, click the Open icon or on the Home screen click the Open button beneath Models. Browse to the central file on the server and select it. At the bottom of the "Open" dialog is a check box labeled: "Create New Local." This check box is selected by default. Verify that it is checked and then click Open (see the left side of Figure 16.11). Revit will create a local file from the selected central file. The local will be created in the default location indicated in the "Default path for user files" setting on the File Locations tab of the "Options" dialog. If you want to view or change this setting, choose the Options button from the File menu (see the top right side of Figure 16.11).

• Revit Essentials for Architecture •

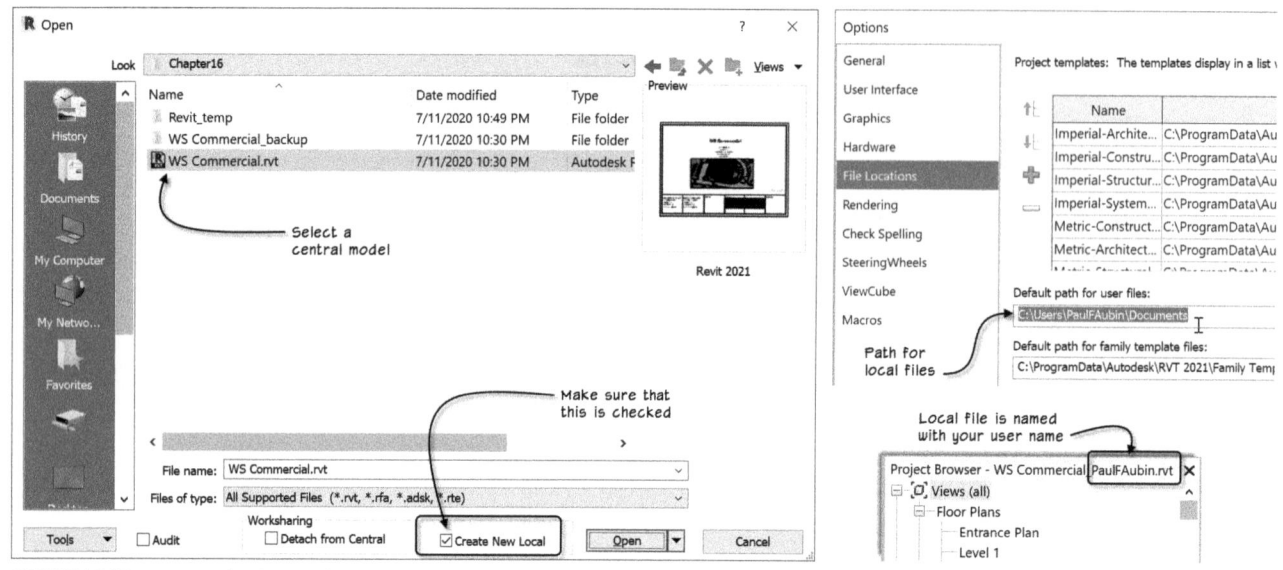

FIGURE 16.11 *Create a local copy of the central file in the default location*

You can verify that you are working in a local copy as the file name at the top of the Project Browser will be the name of the central model plus a suffix that is your login name (see the bottom right of Figure 16.11). It is very important that you do not uncheck the "Create New Local" check box. If you do so, you are opening the central file! Remember, rule number 1 of worksharing is that opening the central file should be avoided at all costs. If there is a rule number 2, it is to refer to rule number 1.

Feel free to open "Options" and change the path for local files if you wish. The exact location is a matter of personal preference, but it is a good idea to establish a standard location for everyone in the office. While you are in the "Options" dialog, take note of your username on the General tab. This is the username that Revit will use for all worksharing functions. If you are signed into your Autodesk account, then your worksharing username will be the same.

When you open your local file, you can choose which worksets you wish to open. In larger projects, this can make load times quicker. To do this, click the small drop down next to the Open button (see the left side of Figure 16.12). Editable loads the worksets you have checked out. Last Viewed opens the same ones that were open the last time you opened the file, and Specify allows you to select the ones you want to load. After choosing "Specify," click the Open button and an "Opening Worksets" dialog will appear next. Choose the worksets that you wish to open by using the SHIFT and CTRL keys to select multiple items, and the Open or Close buttons as desired (see the right side of Figure 16.12).

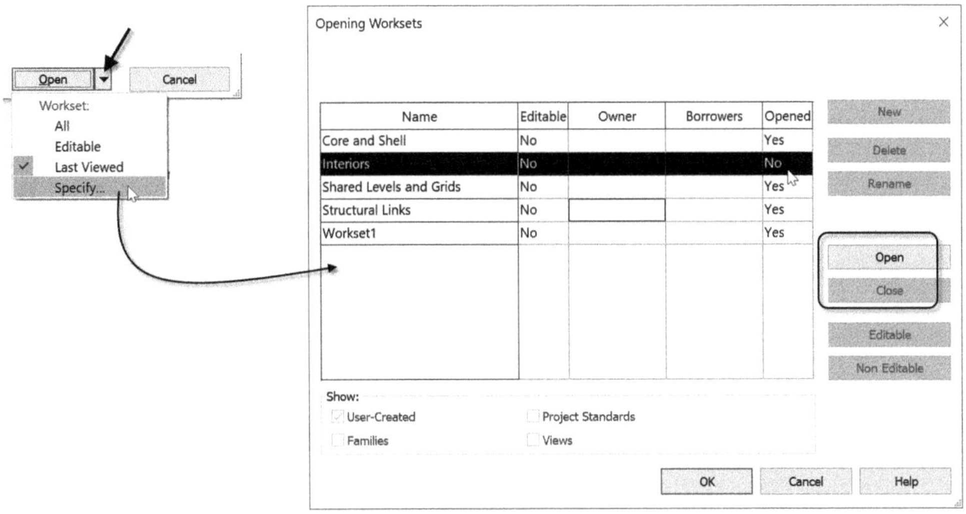

FIGURE 16.12 *Open and close worksets in the "Opening Worksets" dialog as you are opening the local file*

> **BIM MANAGER NOTE:** When you first create the central file, you can indicate an option for Open workset default to make Specify or another choice the default option. This default will apply to all users and their local files.

When you click OK on this dialog, the model will load with only those worksets that you specified. You can see this by opening views that show elements assigned to a workset that you did not load. The elements associated with that workset will not appear in that view. Should you realize that you need to open a workset that you did not choose to open initially; you can simply launch the "Worksets" dialog, and then select the workset you need and click the Open button. You can Close worksets that you no longer need in the same fashion. Opening and closing this way is project-wide (in all views). Closing unneeded worksets also reduces the load on the computer's resources, potentially increasing performance. This is different than we discussed above in the "Workset Visibility" topic on page 692. Hiding or showing worksets in the "Visibility/Graphic Overrides" dialog only applies to the individual view(s) whose properties you are editing.

The first time you have Revit automatically create a local file using the procedure covered here, it will save the file by appending your username (from the "Options" dialog) to the original file name. Subsequently, when you follow the same method again (select the central and let Revit create a new local), you will be prompted either to overwrite the existing file or create a new one with a date and time stamp (see Figure 16.13). You should re-create your local file on a regular basis to keep the file healthy. Using the date and time stamp option essentially gives you an additional backup copy. However, always work in the latest local file. Save the local file and synchronize with central frequently.

• Revit Essentials for Architecture •

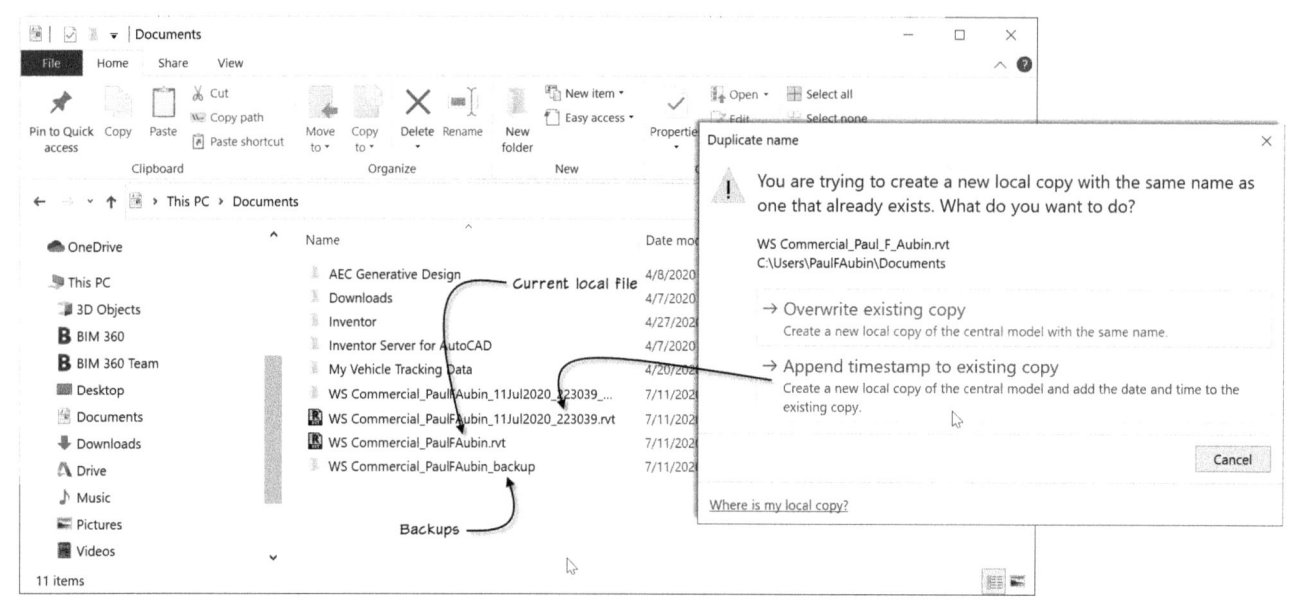

FIGURE 16.13 *Creating another new Local can overwrite the existing or append a date and time stamp*

OPENING FILES FROM THE HOME SCREEN

If you access your models from the Home Screen, the recent files area will have badges on the files displayed there. These badges indicate the type of file. If there is no badge, it is a non-workshare or stand alone project. This is the type of projects we have worked on throughout the book so far. Workshare enabled projects will appear with a small badge. If it is the workshare icon, this indicates a central or local file. If there is a small cloud icon superimposed on top of it, then it is a BIM 360 workshare model (see Figure 16.14).

The best part about opening files from the Home Screen is that Revit manages your local for you automatically. If you click on a central model on the Home Screen, an alert will appear indicating that a local copy will be created instead. This is exactly what we normally want to happen. If you are deliberately trying to open the central, you must browse to it directly using the normal open command. The message indicates this as well. But most of the time, you will want to open a local, so the default behavior of the Home Screen makes this easy to do (see the lower right corner of Figure 16.14).

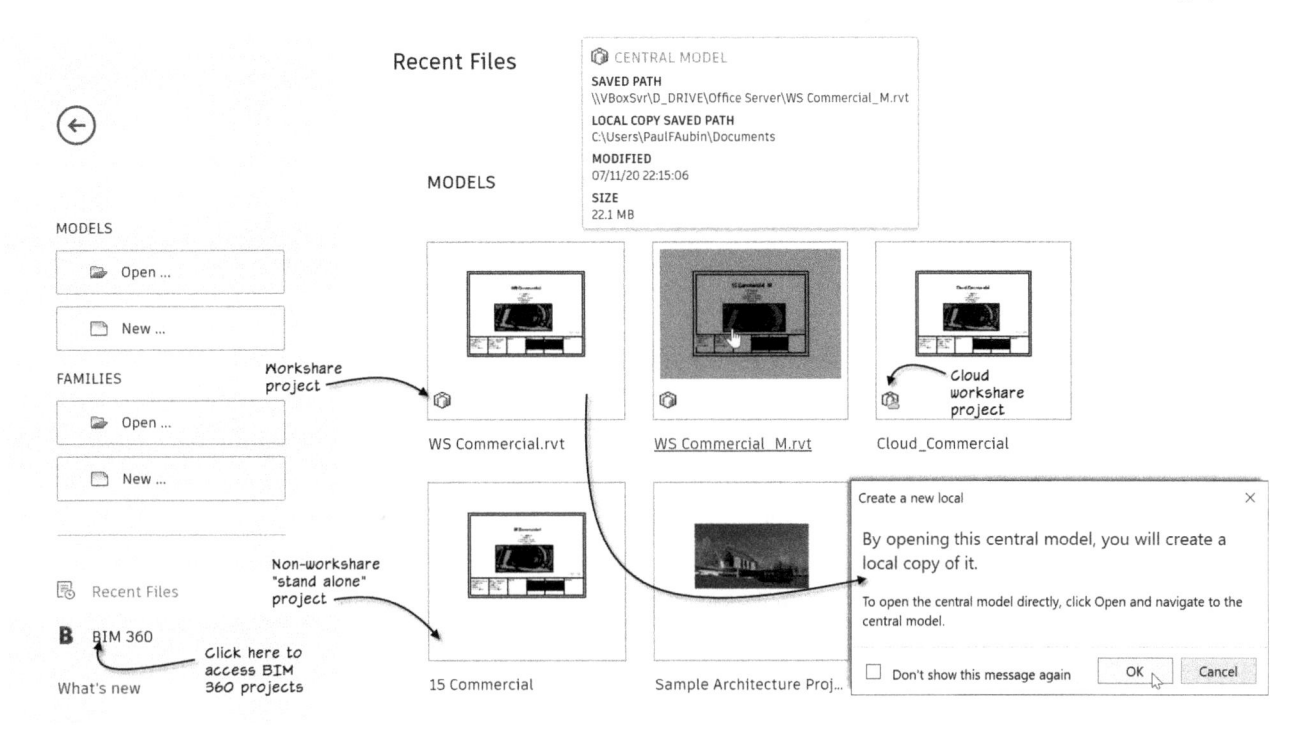

FIGURE 16.14 *Opening files from the Home Screen reveals the type of file and ensures that you open them correctly*

If you want to access a BIM 360 project, click the tab on the left side of the Home Screen. This will display your available BIM 360 projects. To access projects on BIM 360, you must have an account and the proper access rights to the project and files. If you have the required permissions, the folders and files will appear on the BIM 360 tab. Start at the top by choosing the correct account. Next select the project from the drop down list. You can then browse to and open a cloud-based workshare model. When accessing cloud-based workshare models, you will always be working in a local copy (even though the name will *not* include your user name as LAN-based ones do) and the file will be stored in a cache folder on your local system (see Figure 16.15).

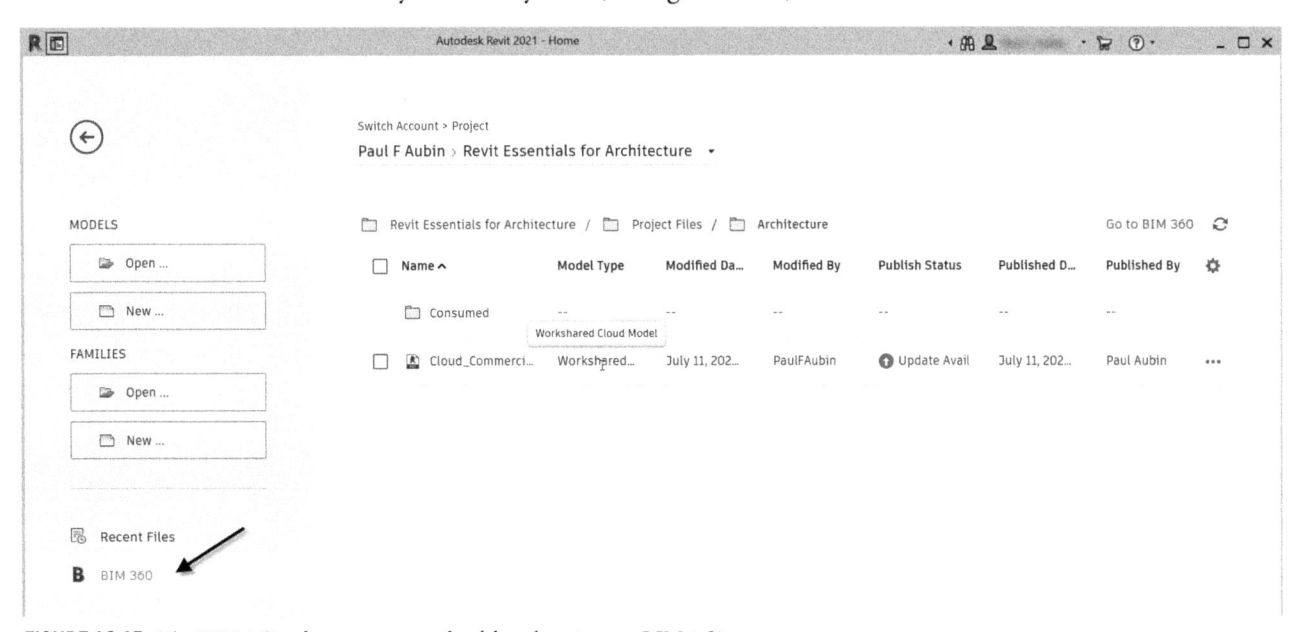

FIGURE 16.15 *The BIM 360 tab gives access to cloud-based projects on BIM 360*

EDITING WORKSET ELEMENTS

Perhaps the most confusing term in the worksharing paradigm is "Editable." When you make an element or workset editable, you are essentially checking the item out from the central file. However, when you look at the list of worksets, they will be listed as "editable" or "not editable." This implies that you must make the workset editable to edit items in it. This is **not** the case. Remember, if you make a workset editable, you are checking out the entire workset and *all* its geometry (checking out the entire fiction section in the library). Usually this is not what you want to do. There are a few approaches you can take to editing the model. In general, if an element that you wish to edit is not being edited by another user, Revit will allow you to edit it directly, even if you do not have the associated workset checked out (editable). As noted above, this is called "borrowing." It happens automatically and is completely transparent. If another user is actively editing the element, or has the workset checked out (set to Editable), you will need to check with that user or issue an "Editing Request" to that user. The other user can then choose to allow your edit or refuse your request. In any case, a good line of communication between you and your team is crucial. Also keep in mind that Open/Close is not the same as Editable/Not Editable. Opening a workset does not automatically make it editable (check it out). If you do need to make a workset editable, this action is achieved in the "Worksets" dialog.

EDITING REQUESTS

When you need an element that is checked out by someone else, you can contact the user to coordinate the edits. It is possible to use the "Editing Request" feature, but the experience is not ideal. With this feature, the owner of the element will be alerted by pop-up message on their screen. This will alert them that you wish to borrow an element that they own. You can grant requests directly from this alert.

> **TIP:** If you are an Autodesk Subscription customer, you have access to the Worksharing Monitor tool. Visit your Autodesk account for more information. The Worksharing Monitor is a separate application that provides tools to manage Worksharing in the background. It has a nicer alert mechanism than the built-in editing request feature.

The flow is as follows. If you try to edit an element that is already owned by someone else or is part of a workset that is checked out by someone else, you can click the "Place Request" button in the error that appears. An alert will appear on the other user's screen. They can respond to the request in the pop-up or click the Editing Request icon on the Status Bar to open the "Editing Requests" dialog. There they can grant or deny the request. The decision will appear on the requesting user's screen as a pop-up message.

Keep in mind that you can only grant requests for elements that you have not yet modified. If you have modified them, Revit will alert you that you first need to save the changes by synchronizing with central. There are limitations with the feature. Messages do not always appear right away and once you issue a request; you will be forced to wait for it before you can continue working in Revit. Usually it is better to simply contact the other user outside of Revit via phone, email, or text message and resolve the issue.

BORROWING ELEMENTS

While it is possible to check out (make editable) an entire workset, it is usually better to rely on borrowing. Borrowing occurs in real-time as you edit elements in the model and is completely transparent to the users. If no one else is editing the element already or if the workset to which it belongs is not locked for editing, Revit will "borrow" the element from the workset as soon as you try to modify it and allow you to make changes; no additional steps required. From that point on, no one else on the team will be able to edit that element until you relinquish it. When you Synchronize with Central, the element will be relinquished automatically (unless you specify otherwise) and the changes will be updated to the central file. You can also select an element and borrow it without making any changes. Do this with the small icon that appears with the element selected (see the top left of Figure 16.16). If you select more than one element, you can right-click instead and choose: **Make Elements Editable**. Be careful as choosing: **Make Workset Editable** will check out the workset instead of borrowing the selected elements. So typically you will want to use: **Make Elements Editable** only (see the bottom left of Figure 16.16).

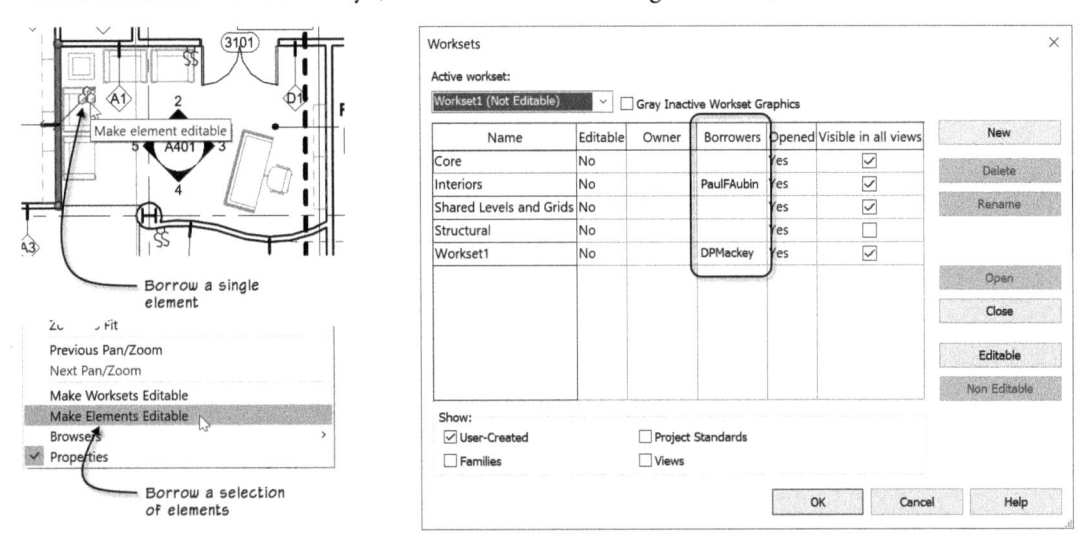

FIGURE 16.16 *Make a workset editable or borrow an element*

If you open the "Worksets" dialog, you can see any borrowers listed next to each workset in the list (see the right side of Figure 16.16).

ADDING NEW ELEMENTS

Any new elements that you add to a model will be added to the active workset. You can choose the active workset from the drop down list on the Collaborate tab, on the Status Bar (see Figure 16.17) or at the top left corner of the "Worksets" dialog (shown in Figure 16.16). As you can see in the figure, you can make a workset active even if it is not editable. In other words, you do *not* need to check out a workset to add new elements to it. However, you will want to pay attention to the active workset. This is very important since you don't want to add several objects to the wrong workset. If you do inadvertently add elements to the wrong workset, you can always select them and change their workset on Properties as noted above.

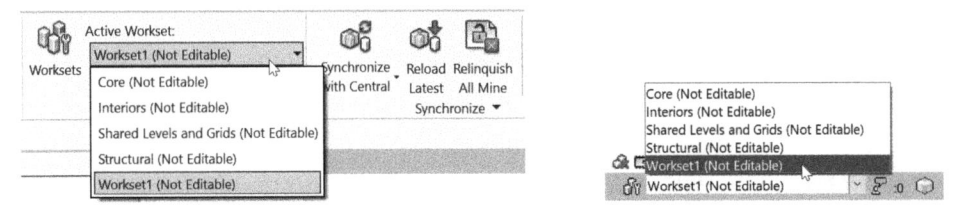

FIGURE 16.17 *Change the active workset on the Collaborate tab, the Status Bar, or in the "Worksets" dialog (shown in previous figure)*

SYNCHRONIZE WITH CENTRAL

You should save your work at regular intervals regardless of whether you are working in a workset-enabled project or not. When you work in a local file, there are two types of save: Save and Synchronize with Central. When you choose: **Save** from the File menu, the QAT, or press CTRL + S, you are only saving your local copy of the project file. This is very important to do, and it is a good idea to do this regularly; for example, every 15–30 minutes. Also, at regular intervals (but perhaps not quite as frequently), you should Synchronize with Central. You will find this tool on the QAT and the Synchronize panel of the Collaborate tab. It is a split-button with two options: the **Synchronize and Modify Settings** and the **Synchronize Now** tools. Synchronizing every 30 minutes or so would be a practical choice, or whenever you would like to publish your changes so your team members can get access to your additions and edits. Synchronize with Central updates the central file with all of the changes that you have made in your local file and also retrieves changes made to the central file by other team members since you opened your local copy, last synchronized, or last performed a Reload Latest. If you choose the Synchronize Now tool, default options are used without prompting. The Synchronize and Modify Settings tool opens the "Synchronize with Central" dialog. This dialog gives you the option to relinquish your worksets and borrowed elements (highly recommended). You can add comments to document your synchronization as well. These will be recorded in the log file maintained by the Central file and might be useful if there is ever a reason to roll back changes to a previous version (see Figure 16.18).

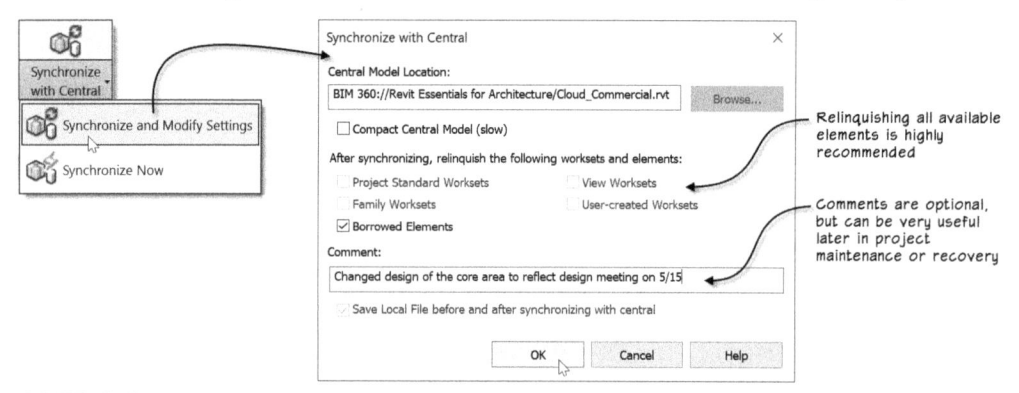

FIGURE 16.18 *The "Synchronize with Central" dialog offers options during the synchronize process*

As a rule of thumb, you should always check the "Save the Local File before and after synchronizing with central" check box. This will save your local copy before and after synchronizing with the central file. The local save before is a failsafe procedure that ensures your work is saved in case the synchronize fails and crashes Revit. (This is a rare occurrence, but still a good choice regardless). The local save after helps keep your file on disk up-to-date once all the additions and edits by your team members are merged into your local file during the synchronize with central process. As a rule of thumb, you should always relinquish your borrowed elements and any of the other items listed in the relinquish area like user-created worksets and other worksets. You may wish to keep your worksets checked out if you are still actively editing them. Otherwise, you should relinquish them. Comments are also a good idea as noted above.

The Synchronize with Central process involves three sub-processes: reloading the latest data in the current central file; merging the additions and edits in your local file with the latest data in the central file; and finally writing the combined data back to the central file. During this process, the central file is locked so no other team members can access it. The duration of the synchronize with central depends on the quantity of elements added and edited being merged in both the local and central files, their complexity, and the time it takes to read and write the data to the central file over your network. The process can take time, so plan accordingly.

RELOAD LATEST

Sometimes you may leave your Revit session inactive for a while with a workset enabled project loaded. You may also open a local file that has not been synchronized in a while. If you have not made any changes, but know that your team has continued to work, you can use the Reload Latest (RL) tool. This tool downloads the latest changes from the central file and updates your local file but does not push any changes from your local file to the server. If you have made changes, then it is better to simply synchronize with central which both uploads your changes and downloads your teammates changes.

RELINQUISH ALL MINE

Sometimes you make changes that you decide you don't want to keep. In such a case, your edits have still resulted in elements being borrowed from the central file. Therefore, unlike most other software where you could simply close the local file and choose not to save, in Revit, you must relinquish all your borrowed elements and discard your changes by not saving. If you simply close your file without saving, you will still be listed as a borrower and/or owner of one or more worksets and elements. Naturally, it is very important to be sure that you do not want to save the changes. Once you choose to close a file and not save, there is no undo. The changes are gone. So, make certain first. If you do this, make sure you relinquish all your worksets so that other team members can gain access to those elements.

DEFAULT 3D VIEWS IN WORKSET-ENABLED PROJECTS

When you click the Default 3D View tool, workset-enabled projects will create a new 3D view as usual, but the name will also include your username. This happens automatically when you click the tool (see the left side of Figure 16.19). Notice in the Project Browser the new 3D view named: *{3D PaulFAubin}* in the figure. Each user will get their own 3D view like this one when they first click the tool. Subsequently, clicking the tool will reopen the user-specific 3D view if it already exists. When you next synchronize, View Worksets will be checked in the relinquish area. This is because a new view was added and will occur anytime you create (or modify) a view in a workset-enabled project.

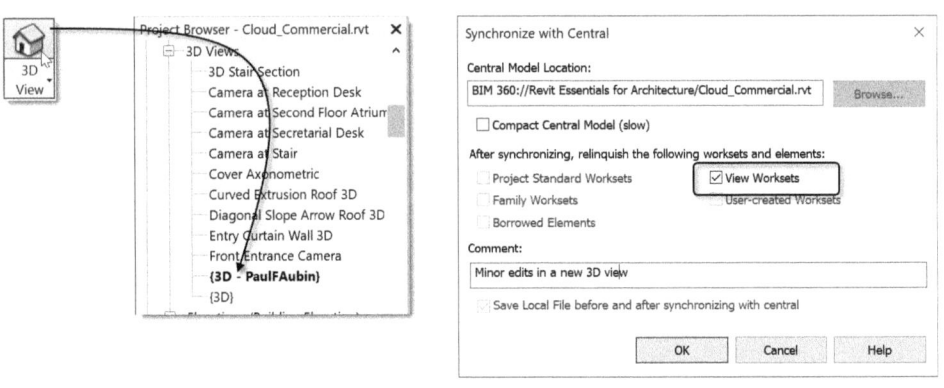

FIGURE 16.19 *Default 3D view names are appended with your user name in workshare projects*

WORKSHARING DISPLAY

With the Worksharing Display feature, you can color-code the onscreen display of elements to reflect their status in workshare-enabled projects. The worksharing display options icon will appear on the View Control Bar. Click it to configure the settings and choose a display mode (see Figure 16.20). There are four modes, and each can be customized in the "Worksharing Display Options" dialog.

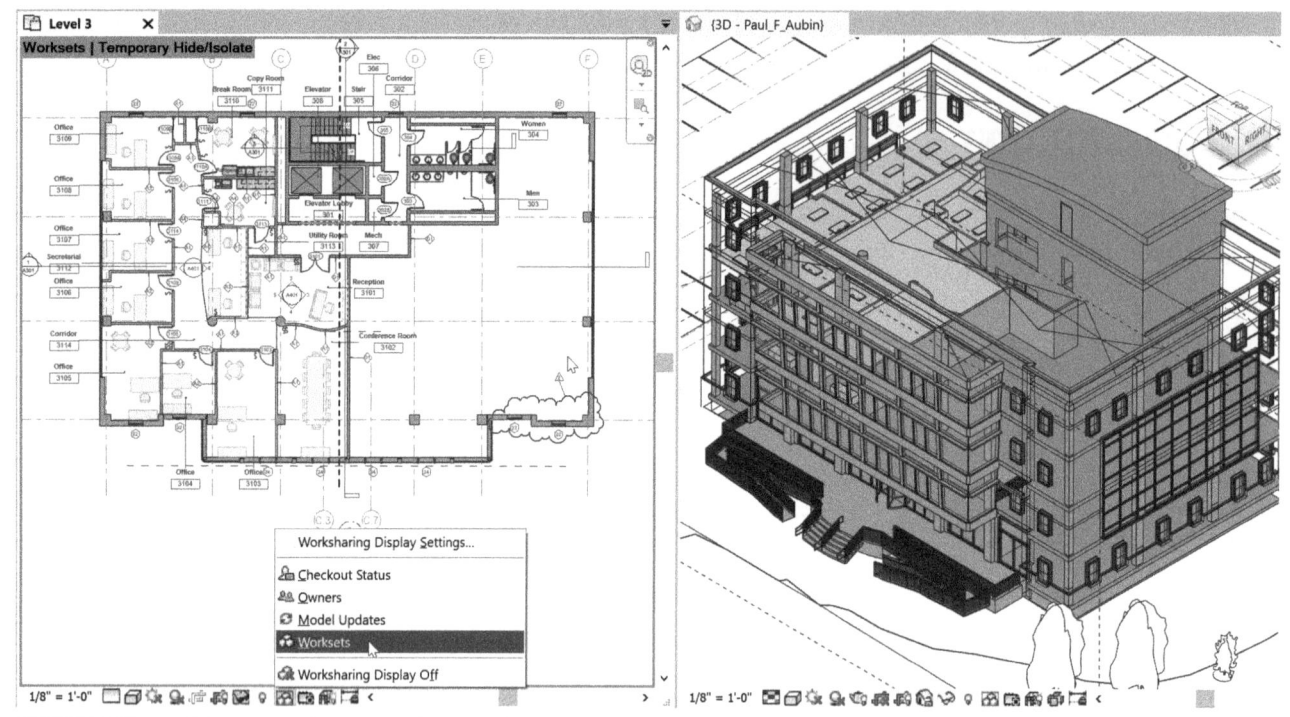

FIGURE 16.20 *Worksharing Display Options display useful worksharing information in color codes onscreen (some elements hidden in the figure)*

Checkout Status—This mode shades elements that are checked out (either as part of a workset or borrowed). Three colors are used: a color for elements you have checked out (green by default), one for other users (red by default), and a third for elements that are not owned by anyone (this color is not shown by default, but can be turned on using the Worksharing Display Settings command).

Owners—This mode shades elements based on the user who owns them. Each user who has edited the project is listed with their own unique color. Colors can be modified in the "Worksharing Display Settings" dialog.

Model Updates—This mode displays updated and deleted elements using different colors. By default, blue is used for any element that is changed and red for any element that is deleted. This can be helpful to determine how far out-of-date your local file is.

Worksets—It shades each dedicated workset in a unique color. This can be a useful way to identify if elements are on the wrong workset.

For each display mode, you can choose which conditions to show and change the color(s) used in the "Worksharing Display Options" dialog. This is a per-view temporary display mode. Unlike other features in worksharing, these display modes can update in near real-time.

MANAGING LINKED FILES

In a workshare-enabled project, linked files can be unloaded on a per-user basis. Traditionally, firms would create worksets to manage this. But this is unnecessary. Simply open the "Manage Links" dialog, select the Revit link you wish to unload and then click the "For me" button in the Unload area. This will unload the link only for you and other users will not be affected. You can also find this option on the right-click menu of the link on the Revit Links branch on Project Browser (see Figure 16.21).

FIGURE 16.21 *Linked Revit files in workshare-enabled projects can be loaded and unloaded on a per-user basis*

Despite this functionality, some firms will still prefer to create dedicated worksets for links. Check with your BIM Manger to see what the procedure is in your firm.

WORKSET TIPS

Keep the following tips in mind when working in workset projects.

- **Never work directly in the central file.** If you must open the central file for any reason, perform your required tasks quickly and get out quickly. Inform your team before opening the central file and have them synchronize with central and close their local files first. Any maintenance or other work performed directly in the central file ought to be performed by the Project Data Coordinator exclusively. And since no one can work in their local files while this maintenance takes place, it should typically be done during off-hours to minimize project disruptions.

- **Save and Sync often!** Save both your local copy and synchronize with central frequently. Doing so is the best way to ensure smooth team workflow and minimize data loss.

- Revit projects can get large. Central files can get even larger. While it is important to save often, synchronize with central times can be very long on big projects. **Plan your synchronizations to take advantage of down times.**

- **Always relinquish all borrowed elements and worksets** before leaving work for any extended period: going to lunch, attending a meeting, leaving at the end of the day, going on vacation, etc. Nothing makes a coworker crankier than trying to edit an element locked by someone who is out of the office and cannot relinquish it to them.

- If you have been away from your computer for a while and left a project file open (which is not recommended) reread the previous tip! After that, perform a **Reload Latest** (Collaborate tab, Synchronize panel). This command synchronizes your local copy with the latest saved changes of the central file without saving your additions and changes back to the central file.

- If you want to see how "out-of-date" your local file is before reloading latest, **use the Model Updates worksharing display mode.**

- **Check the "Review Warnings" dialog** (Manage tab, Inquiry panel) on a regular basis. Perhaps once a week. Excessive unresolved warnings can have a negative impact on performance and even in extreme cases can corrupt your central file.

• Revit Essentials for Architecture •

- **Recreate your local file on a regular schedule.** It is recommended that you do so every day or even each time you open the project. Remember, Revit will automatically offer to date and time stamp your previous local file for you (see the "Creating a Local File" topic on page 693 above). So, your old local files become extra backups. And consider this; unless you were the last person to leave the office yesterday, if you re-open an old local file, even one saved at the end of the day yesterday, you will be starting the day with an out-of-date file. Those folks that were in the office after you have since synchronized their changes making it necessary for you to start the day with a reload latest or synchronize just to get up-to-date. It is much better to simply create a new local at the start of each workday, or anytime you have been away from the office for any extended period.

- **You can never have too many backups** of your central file or local files. Hard drives are much cheaper than hours of recreating lost work.

- **Linked Revit files can be loaded and unloaded on a per-user basis.** Alternatively, use a workset to manage links, since each user can control which worksets are active and displayed in their own work session. Either way, you can control which Revit links appear in your local file without affecting your colleagues. You can even have a separate workset for each discipline or even each linked file if needed.

- **Be careful with using the Activate View feature on sheets.** While this is a handy command, sometimes annotation added in this mode can lose its association to the proper view workset and not display properly or disappear altogether. It is recommended that you expand the sheet on the Project Browser and then double-click the view you wish to edit to open it directly instead.

- **If you must share work with users in separate physical locations, seriously consider subscribing to the BIM 360 service.** Cloud worksharing eliminates many of the hassles inherent in other solutions and has excellent performance.

- **When archiving a central file, do not just copy it to an archive folder.** Copying the file makes it a local file which remains associated with the original central file. To make an archive copy, open the central file with the "Detach from Central" option. This will break the link to the central file. Then from the File menu choose: **Save As**. Click the Options button and choose the "Make this a Central file after save" option as shown in Figure 16.4 above. It is a good idea to save such archived central files to a location that is not easily accessible by the project team. This will help prevent a team member's inadvertently opening the archived central file rather than the current one. You can also simply zip up this folder after creating it and then delete the archived copy. There is also an ETransmit tool which helps automate this process.

- It is also popular for firms to create DWG exports and/or PDF files for archive purposes.

- If you or a team member wishes to open a project "read only" to take measurements, print, or perform other work that they do not wish to save, open the file with the "Detach from Central" box selected in the "Open" dialog. Use this option with caution, however. **There is no way to change your mind later and "re-connect" a detached file with the central.** Once you have detached it, it cannot be reattached!

- **Detach from central can be a great way to have a hard "pencils down" deadline for printing.** Inform the team that at a specified time, a detached copy of the project will be made, and all plots will be generated from this copy. Therefore, any work that the team needs to appear in the progress set MUST be synchronized before this deadline. After the plot, the detached copy can be discarded or archived. Plotting is usually quicker from a detached copy as well.

GOING FURTHER

This chapter explains the basic concepts of team collaboration, worksharing and worksets. The best way to learn and implement multiuser Revit projects is to practice with at least one other individual. This will give you a better sense of the nuances of working in a workset-enabled project. A copy of the commercial project has been provided with the dataset files in the *Chapter16* folder. *WS Commercial.rvt* is a central file. To use it, you must first open it and then go to: **Save As**. Save it on a server if you have access to a network. Otherwise, for practice purposes you can save it on your hard drive. Close the central and then make a local copy of this newly saved version and explore. If you want to try your hand at making a central file, the completed version from Chapter 15 instead (which is a stand-alone version) and walk through the procedures outlined at the start of this chapter to make it a central file.

Feel free to experiment in these files. If you have a colleague who can help you, each of you can create a local copy and work simultaneously. Each of you should make changes, synchronize with central, and then reload from the central file. Try borrowing elements, try to edit the same element as your colleague, and see what happens. Be sure to use the worksharing display modes as well for good visual feedback as you work. And remember to visit: **paulaubin.com/conferences** and look for the PDF called **AB3728-L, The Autodesk Revit Worksets Workshop** and the accompanying ZIP file with a sample dataset that has step-by-step instructions for up to three users to follow simultaneously. The document was created on a much older version of Revit but should still give you ample practice potential.

SUMMARY

- ☑ Working in teams is an important part of AEC production.

- ☑ Using linked files, element borrowing, and worksets, Revit provides the means to accomplish sharing of data and managing coordinated team projects.

- ☑ When implemented with care, worksets provide an invaluable toolset to the extended Revit project team.

- ☑ AutoCAD and Microstation files can be linked into Revit models.

- ☑ Import CAD files when you do not need them to update. Link them when you wish to be able to update them regularly in their native software.

- ☑ Worksets provide the means to sub-divide a project into parts to help manage workflow, performance and visibility.

- ☑ Enable worksets in the project and create user-created worksets as needed.

- ☑ Move existing elements to appropriate worksets if required by your project team.

- ☑ Try relying on element borrowing instead of creating extensive user worksets.

- ☑ Save the project file as a central file on a network server accessible to all users.

- ☑ Each user creates a local file from the central file in which to perform day-to-day work.

- ☑ Decide which worksets to open when opening the local file.

- ☑ You can edit elements that are not in an editable workset if they are not being edited by other users.

- ☑ Editing an element in a non-editable workset is called "borrowing."

- ☑ Borrowed elements and editable worksets can be relinquished during synchronize with central operations.

- ☑ Save your local file and synchronize with central often.

- ☑ Consider subscribing to Autodesk BIM 360 Design Collaboration for an enhanced cloud-based worksharing experience.

SECTION IV

Conceptual Massing and Rendering

INTRODUCTION

Conceptual modeling tools in Autodesk® Revit® offer exciting potential for the design phases of a project. This collection of tools allows you to explore design studies in a freeform three-dimensional environment. These can be explored and presented independently in the conceptual modeling environment, or such studies can be loaded into project to form the basis for a project's overall design. Rendering has long been a feature of the Revit software. Many of the underlying tools share a common platform and similar experience across the wide variety of Autodesk products. These include 3D navigation, materials, lighting, and rendering. Chapter 17 will introduce the conceptual massing tools, and Chapter 18 will take a look at rendering.

SECTION IV is organized as follows:

Chapter 17 : Conceptual Massing
Chapter 18: Rendering

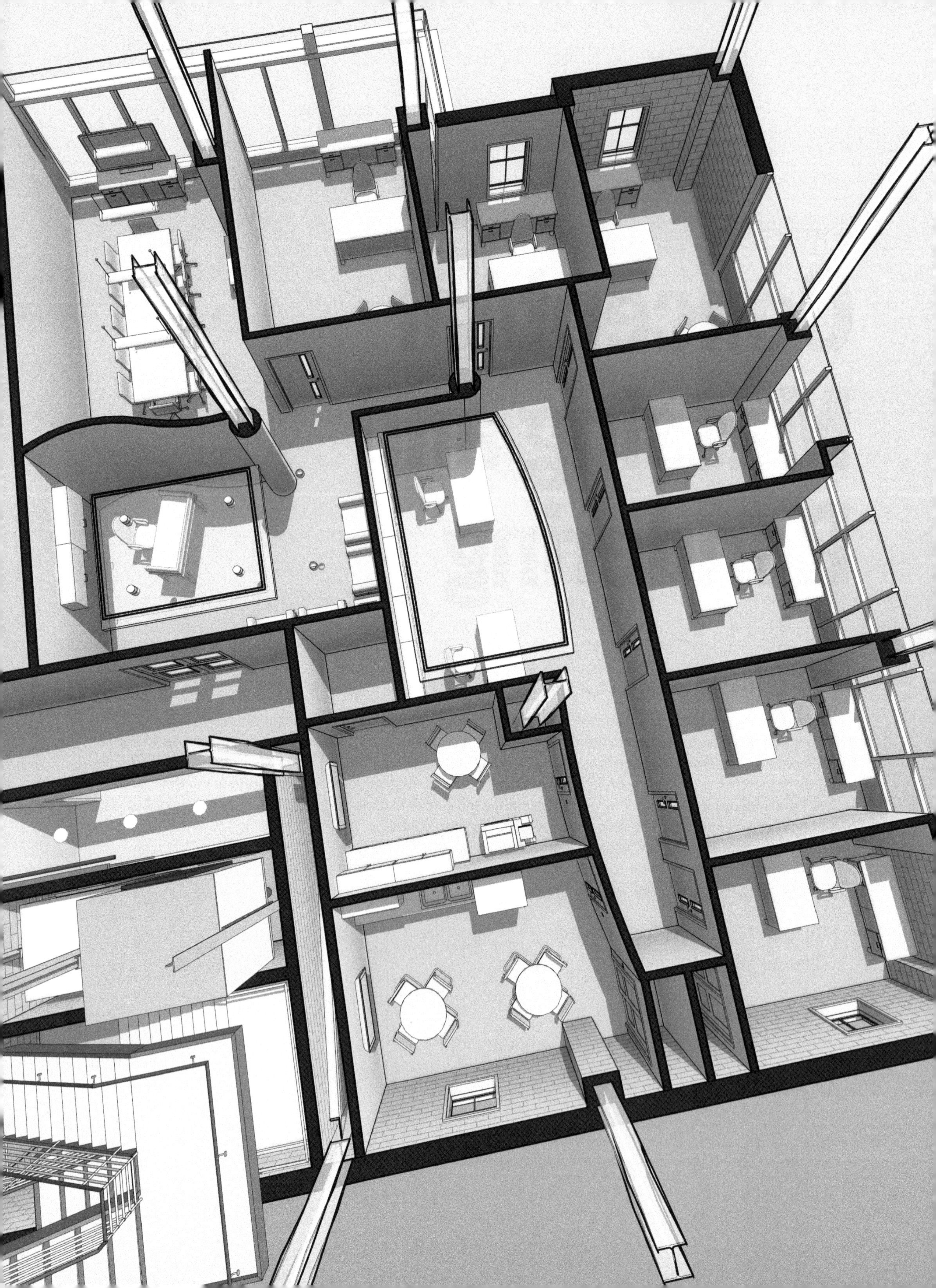

CHAPTER 17
Conceptual Massing

INTRODUCTION

The massing environment offers tools to explore conceptual design concepts in a free-form 3D environment. The massing environment is a variation of the family editor and, therefore, shares many of its traits with all other Autodesk® Revit® families. The environment allows you to easily create and edit forms, create complex parametric shapes and patterned surfaces, and apply adaptable sub-components to patterned surfaces. The conceptual massing environment is meant to facilitate working/designing/creating/experimenting all while remaining in a 3D view. Therefore, when you open the conceptual massing environment, the default three-dimensional view {3D} is active. This is just one of the many differences you will discover in this environment. It is possible to make all of the shapes and forms that are available in the standard family editor, but the tools and workflows are different and there is an enhanced ability to edit and manipulate the forms in real-time without sketch modes. Complex interactive and parametric form modeling and design rationalization is also possible. The features discussed in this chapter are not available in Revit LT. If you are using Revit LT, you can skip this chapter.

OBJECTIVES

Discussion of the mass modeling capabilities in Revit could fill an entire book on their own. Time and space here will therefore not permit complete coverage. The goal of this chapter is to introduce you to the basic workflow and features to get you started using this exciting toolset. In this chapter you will:

- Learn how to access the conceptual massing environment
- Learn how to create 3D forms
- Understand the difference between model and reference-based forms
- Create a conceptual mass loadable family
- Work with divided surfaces, patterns, and points
- Understand the difference between driving and driven points

IN-PLACE VS. LOADABLE FAMILIES

The conceptual massing environment is available both as an external environment in which you work in a specialized Family Editor (creating a "loadable" massing family) and in the in-place family mode where you work directly within the context of a project. Use the in-place mode if your massing depends on the context of other elements in your project file, or if you prefer to design your massing within the context of the project elements. As with any in-place modeling, the forms you make remain within the current project and cannot be saved out for use in other projects. There are a few limitations with the conceptual massing environment when working in in-place mode; you will not be able to view reference planes in 3D views (this is typical with Revit). However, you will be able to reference the levels and reference planes through the Set Work Plane tool, and you can also reference geometry that exists in the project (such as walls, floors, topography, etc.) by selecting the geometry and Creating Forms from the project geometry.

Use the external Family Editor environment when you want maximum flexibility in form manipulation, when you want to be able to load the conceptual mass you create into multiple projects, or when you want to iterate a design without necessarily loading it into a project environment.

ACCESSING THE CONCEPTUAL MASSING ENVIRONMENT

The massing environment is accessed a little differently depending on if you are creating a "loadable" mass or an in-place mass family. To create a "loadable" massing family, you must use the proper family template such as the: *Mass.rft* [*Metric Mass.rft*] family template. Family templates were discussed in Chapter 11. You can access this template directly from within the *Conceptual Mass* subfolder in your family templates folder, or by using the: **New > Conceptual Mass** command from the File menu. In either case, the "Select Template" dialog will open to the *Conceptual Mass* folder of your Revit templates folder (see Figure 17.1).

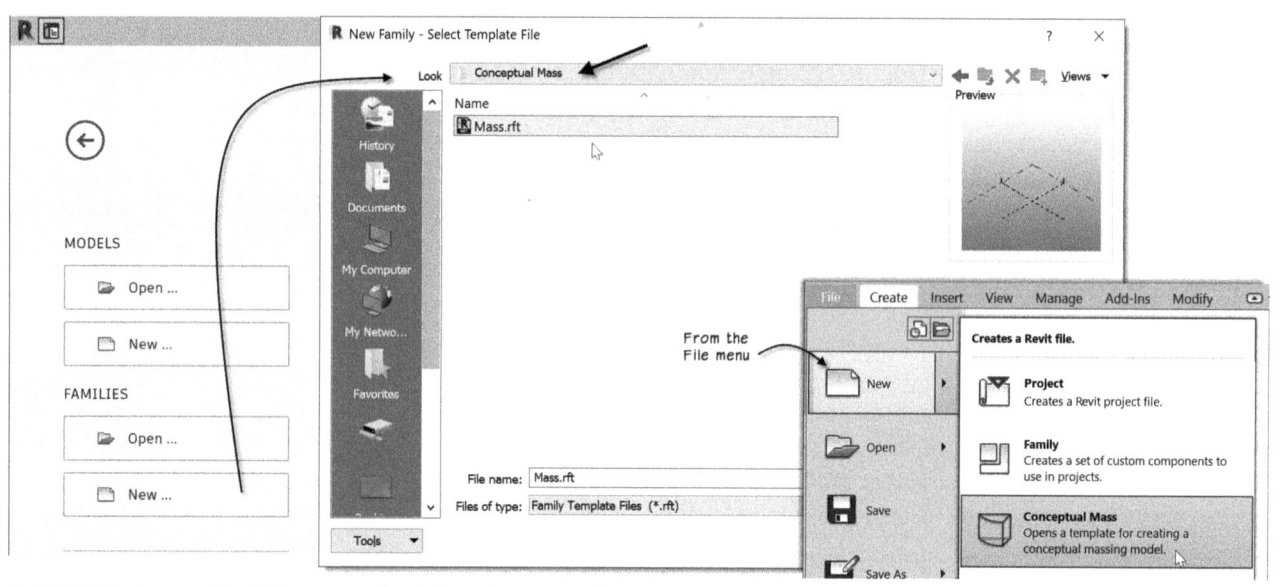

FIGURE 17.1 *Create a "loadable" massing family from the conceptual massing family template*

The *Mass.rft* [*Metric Mass.rft*] family template file will open in the conceptual mass family editor environment. There are a few other templates that also open to the conceptual massing environment: The *Generic Model Adaptive.rft* [*Metric Generic Model Adaptive.rft*] family template file creates a family that can adjust to the unique conditions in its context. (The potential of the Adaptive Component is vast and could fill several chapters on its own. We will explore a very simple kind of adaptive family below in the "Stitching Borders of the Divided Surface" topic on page 747). There are also the *Generic Model Pattern Based.rfa* [*Metric Generic Model Pattern Based.rfa*] and the *Curtain Panel Pattern Based.rfa* [*Metric Curtain Panel Pattern Based.rfa*]. These templates allow you to build a component that can be repeated on a divided surface in the massing environment. We will see an example of this below in the "Create a Pattern-Based Curtain Panel Family" topic on page 741.

If you are already working in a project and wish to create an in-place massing family instead, you can do so from the tool on the ribbon. On the Architecture tab, from the Component tool drop down button, choose the: **Model In-Place** tool. In the "Family Category and Parameters" dialog box, choose **Mass** and then click OK.

The second method for accessing the In-Place conceptual mass environment is from the Massing & Site tab on the ribbon. From this tab, click on the In-Place Mass button. Creating an in-place mass this way will automatically enable the "Show Mass" mode. A dialog will appear indicating that masses will be shown temporarily in the model. You can also click the Show Mass button to enable it without the dialog. The Show Mass tool is on the Massing & Site tab.

THE MASSING ENVIRONMENT INTERFACE

When you create a conceptual mass in the conceptual mass environment, you will default to an axonometric view. The environment includes one level and two vertical reference planes by default. Like other family templates, the two reference planes are pinned and the intersection of the two reference planes indicates the insertion point of the mass when it is loaded and placed in a project. Unlike other families, you can create additional levels in this environment. You can also create reference planes using the tools on the Create tab of the ribbon. Unique to the conceptual massing environment, you can create levels and reference planes directly in 3D.

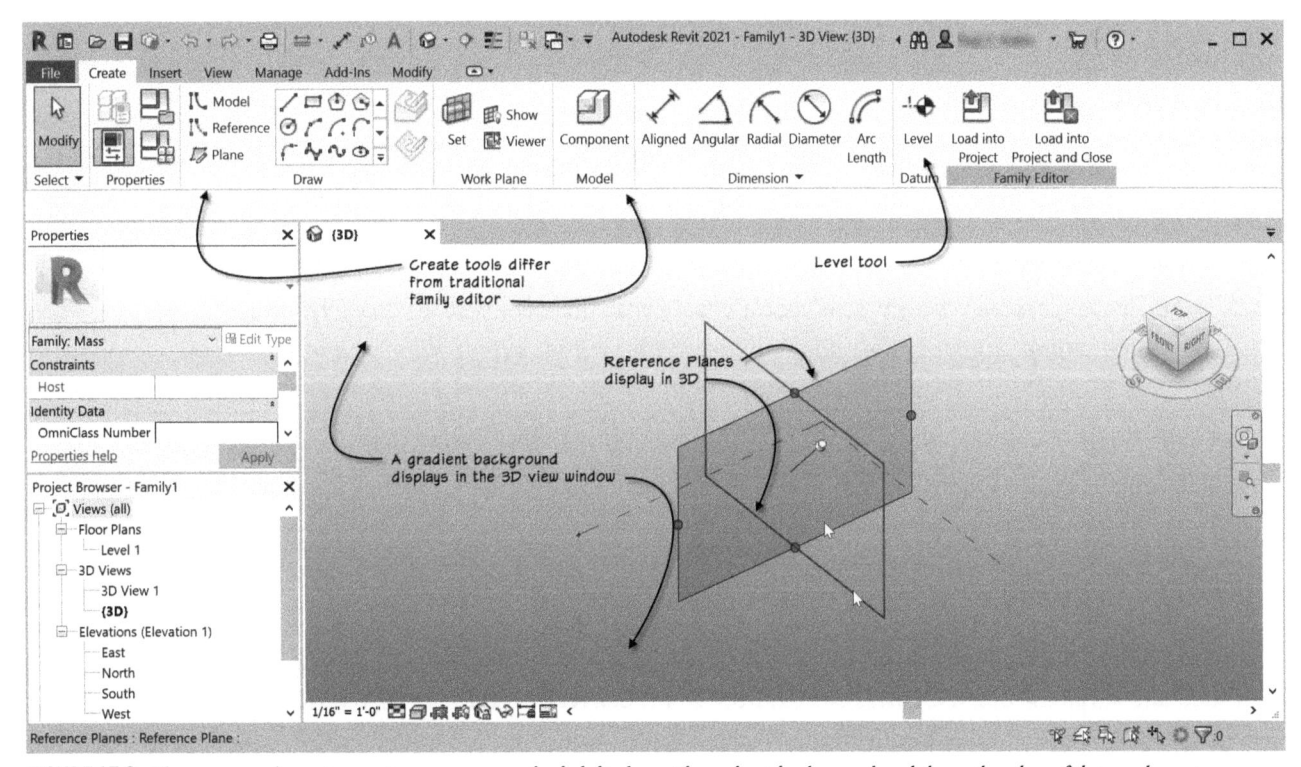

FIGURE 17.2 *The conceptual massing environment uses a shaded display with gradient background and shows the edges of datum elements*

The visual style is set to shaded by default. A gradient background is also enabled. You can adjust the colors of the gradient background in the "Graphic Display Options" dialog box accessed from the Visual Styles pop-up icon on the View Control Bar (or press GD).

The conceptual mass family is work plane-based by default, which means that when it is loaded into and placed in a project environment (or another mass family environment) it will look for host faces, rather than levels or reference planes as many families require. (Family hosting behaviors are discussed in Chapter 11.) This makes the family very flexible regarding placement. Another unique feature to the conceptual mass family environment is that project location is exposed; this allows you to perform still-frame sun and shadow studies from directly within the conceptual mass environment. Other kinds of families must first be loaded into a project environment before you can perform a sun and shadow study. The sun path feature is also available directly in the massing environment.

CREATING FORMS IN THE CONCEPTUAL MASS ENVIRONMENT

There are two form creation methods: model-based forms are drawn using model lines and reference-based forms are drawn using reference lines or other referenced geometry. You make the choice between creating a model-based or reference-based form when you create a new form. Each has advantages and limitations. You can find complete details in the "Model-Based and Reference-Based Forms" topic on page 725 below. For now, we will first look at building the basic kinds of forms before delving into the differences between model line and reference line creation methods.

Many forms are possible in the conceptual modeling environment. Like the standard family editor (Chapter 11), you can create extrusions, blends, sweeps, swept blends, and revolves. You can also create both solid and void forms. In the conceptual environment, you can also create lofts, surface (or mesh) models, and even patterned surfaces. Unlike the standard Family Editor, you don't need to choose a specific tool for the type of form you want to create before you create it; rather, you simply sketch the required shapes and use a single "Create Form" button to make any type of form. Revit will interpret your sketch geometry and give you an appropriate form. When more than one form is possible, you will be offered a choice. We'll look at several examples next.

OPEN A MASSING FAMILY

The lessons that follow require the dataset files included for download with this book. Refer to the "Download the Book Dataset" topic on page xi in the Preface for instructions on downloading and installing the book's dataset files.

1. Launch Autodesk® Revit® if you do not already have it running. Close any files you have open.
2. On the Home screen, beneath Families, click the Open button. Browse to the *Chapter17* folder.
⇨ Double-click *Form Examples-01.rfa*. You can also select it and then click the Open button.

> **NOTE:** Units are not a critical aspect of understanding the conceptual modeling environment. For this reason, only an Imperial units dataset is provided for this chapter.

CREATING FORMS

In the conceptual massing environment, you can make many types of forms. Three-dimensional forms can be both solid and surface geometry. Forms created from solids behave as if they are carved from a single piece of solid material like a block of wood or poured from concrete. If you were to section a solid model, it would show material all the way through. A surface model behaves as though it were constructed from thin material like an eggshell or cardboard box. Surface models can be either closed or open shapes. A closed shape would be like a cardboard box. If you sectioned it, it would be hollow inside. An open shape would appear more as if it were made from sheet metal not necessarily defining an enclosed form.

THE INTENT STACK

Whether you get a solid or surface form depends on the geometry you use to create it. We will see examples of both below. Many forms are possible, such as extrusions, lofts, sweeps, revolves, and swept blends. (Each of these will be covered in the next topic.) No matter what type of form you are making, the process is the same; select some lines and

Conceptual Massing | 713

click on the Create Form button. Depending on what lines and/or elements are selected, Revit will determine which type of form can be made from the selection set. If more than one form is possible from the selection set, Revit will provide a set of thumbnail sketches directly onscreen referred to as the "intent stack." Each will show one possible solution from the selection. You can choose from the forms presented by clicking the desired thumbnail. Let's start our exploration of the Create Form process with a look at the Intent Stack.

> You should have the *Form Examples-01.rfa* open. If not, please open it now.

The *Form Examples-01.rfa* file contains the two standard reference planes included in the *Mass.rft* template file and a total of three levels (the standard Level 1, plus Levels 2 and 3). The only geometry in this file is two model lines. Creating a form from these two simple lines can produce three separate results.

1. Select both the lines on screen. (Select only the lines, not the reference planes or levels.)
⇨ On the Modify | Lines tab of the ribbon, on the Form panel, click on the Create Form button.

Three sketches appear on the screen; each sketch represents a possible form-intent that can be created based on the selection set (in this case, two parallel lines).

> If you place your cursor over one of the sketches, the form in the main view will preview that form in wireframe.
> If you have trouble moving from one glyph to the next, move away first then back to the one you want.

2. Click on one of the sketches to create that form (see Figure 17.3).

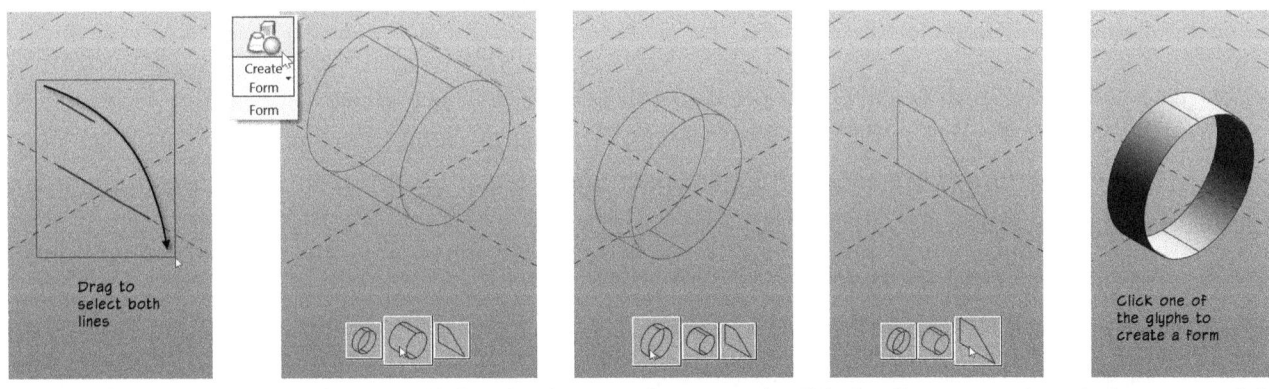

FIGURE 17.3 *When more than one form is possible from the selection set, the intent stack will display allowing you to choose the form you intended*

As noted above, Revit will determine if your selection will yield a solid or surface form. In this case, all three possible forms will yield surface models: a round hollow cylinder in the first two choices and a flat wedge-shaped plane in the third instance. If you wish to try more than one form, undo after creating and then repeat the process to choose a different intent.

CREATING EXTRUSIONS

If you select only one line, and then click the Create Form button, your result will be a simple rectangular shaped plane.

1. If you created a form from both lines, undo it now to return to the two original lines.
2. Select the long line (lower one), and then on the Create tab, click the Create Form button.

The Line will "extrude" to a flat plane running parallel to Level 1. When Revit determines the type of form that can be created this time, there is only one option: a single straight line will yield a flat plane. No intent stack will display since there is only one option.

3. Select the other line (the short one) and then click the Create Form button.

• Revit Essentials for Architecture •

714 | Chapter 17

This time, the plane will be created perpendicular to the levels. The reason that one line extrudes horizontally and the other vertically has to do with how they were drawn and, more specifically, which work plane was active at the time of creation (see Figure 17.4). You can see the Work Plane on the Properties palette with the line selected.

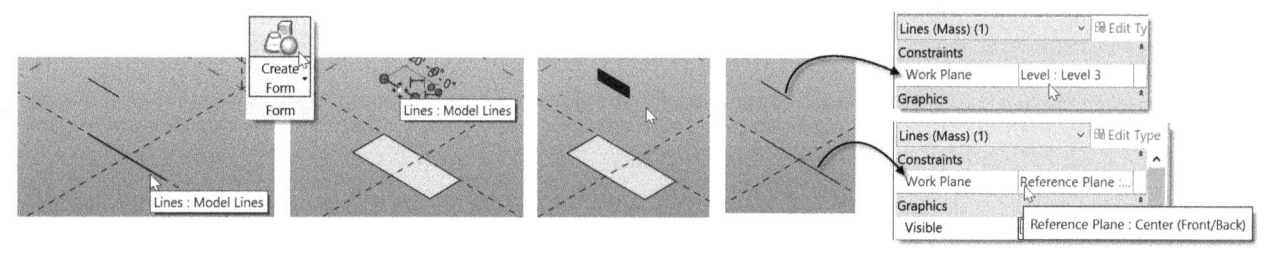

FIGURE 17.4 *The work plane in which a line is drawn determines the direction that it will extrude*

⇨   Undo the creation of both planes (return to the original lines).

4.   Select the long line.

On the Properties palette, notice that the Work Plane for this line is: **Reference Plane: Center (Front/Back)**.

5.   Select the other Line.

Notice that the Work Plane this time is: **Level: Level 3**.

When Create Form yields an extrusion, the direction of the extrusion will be perpendicular to the work plane.

⇨   Deselect all elements.

Unlike the standard family editor and project editor environments where you must use the Set (Work Plane) tool to designate the active work plane, in the conceptual massing environment, simply selecting a level or reference plane (or even the surface of any 3D form) makes it the current work plane.

6.   Select Level 1 onscreen.

7.   On the ribbon, on the Draw panel, click the polygon icon.

⇨   Accept all defaults and draw the shape any size.

Notice that the shape draws on the selected level.

⇨   Click the Modify tool and then select the shape you just drew.

Notice that the default selection behavior in the massing environment is chain selection. So, when you pre-highlight the polygon, it automatically highlights the whole shape. (You can still select just one edge if you like; use the TAB key to do so. This is discussed below.)

8.   With the polygon selected, click the Create Form tool (see Figure 17.5).

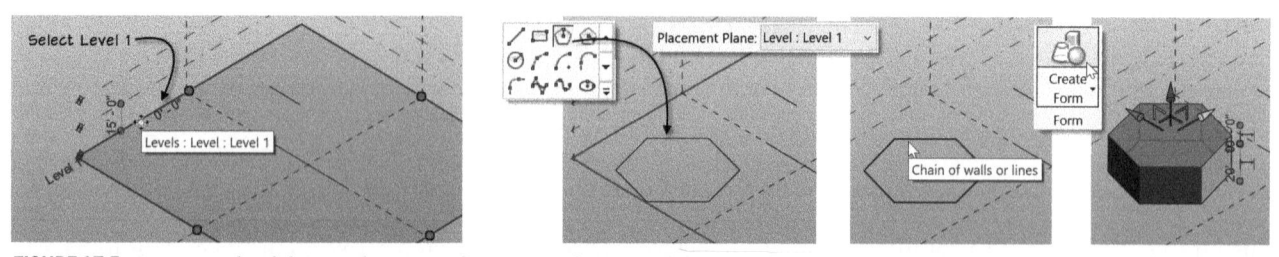

FIGURE 17.5 *Draw any closed shape and use create form to extrude it to a solid*

When you have a closed shape defined by multiple lines, your result will be an extruded solid. If you draw an open shape, the result will be surfaces as if each line had been extruded separately to a plane. Also, notice that since we made Level 1 the active work plane, the shape extruded "up" from Level 1. Select one of the reference planes to

• The Aubin Academy •

Conceptual Massing | 715

make it active and then repeat the process to create extrusions perpendicular to the one created here. Feel free to try a combination of open and closed shapes (see Figure 17.6).

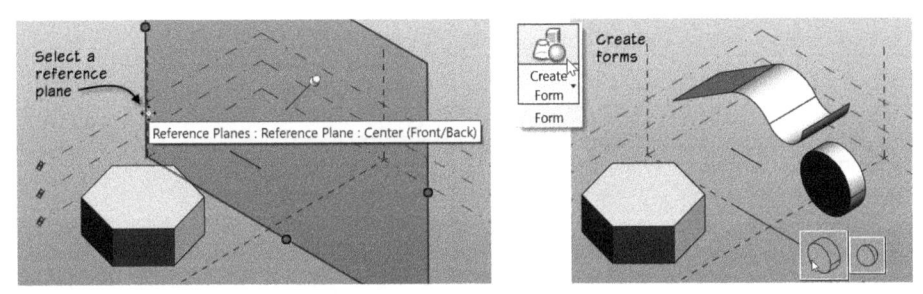

FIGURE 17.6 *Experiment with a series of open and closed shapes on different work planes*

9. Close the *Form Examples-01.rfa* file.

⇨ Saving this file is optional. If you created a form that you wish to use again, please save the file.

CREATING A LOFT FORM

A loft form is made by selecting two or more shapes and clicking on the Create Form button. The form will blend between the shapes selected. The profiles can be either open or closed or a combination of open and closed loops. Selecting two shapes will give you something like a blend from the traditional family editor. Selecting three or more shapes will give a lofted form that will morph from one shape to the next along a drawn o path.

1. From the *Chapter17* folder, open *Form Examples-02.rfa*.

Two sets of profiles are included in this file. On the left side, there are three closed shapes. If you select any of these three shapes and edit their properties, you will note that each has its work plane associated to one of the three levels in the file. The three open shapes on the right side are associated to the three corresponding reference planes (see the left side of Figure 17.7).

2. Pre-highlight one of the closed shapes on the left.

> **NOTE:** Chain select is the default behavior in the conceptual massing environment. To select just one segment of the chain, you would use the TAB key. This is opposite of the order in the project and traditional family environments.

⇨ Press the TAB key (see the right side of Figure 17.7).

Just one segment of the shape should now be pre-highlighted. Press TAB again to pre-highlight the chain.

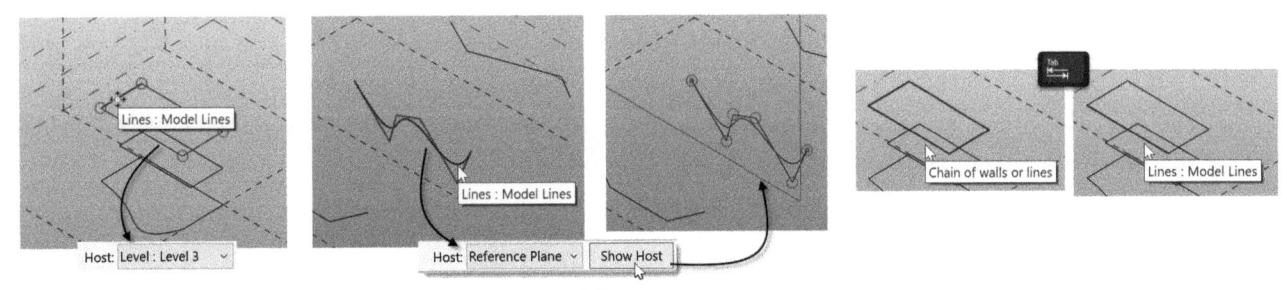

FIGURE 17.7 *A collection of shapes provided to experiment with lofting*

Select each shape and note the work plane. There is also a Show Host button on the Options Bar which will highlight the work plane onscreen (see the middle of the figure).

3. Select all three closed shapes on the left side (you can use a window selection box for this).

• Revit Essentials for Architecture •

⇨ On the Modify | Lines tab, click the Create Form button (see the left side of Figure 17.8).

You will get a very different result if you select only two of the three shapes. Try undoing and then selecting only the top and bottom shapes. The result is more like a blend and will have less curvature on the front face.

4. Select the three open shapes on the right and then click the Create Form button (see the right side of Figure 17.8).

You can use any selection method to select the shapes; remember your SHIFT, CTRL, and TAB keys as well as your window and crossing selection boxes.

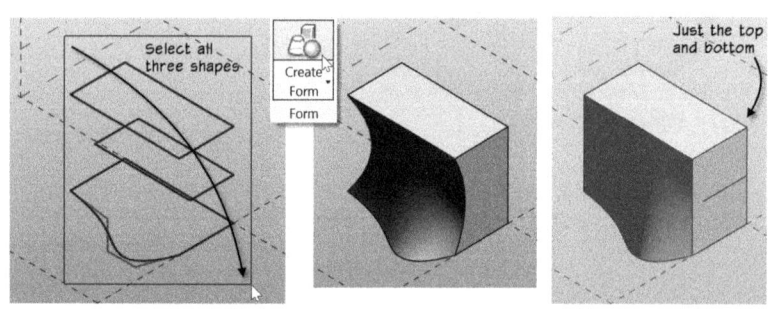

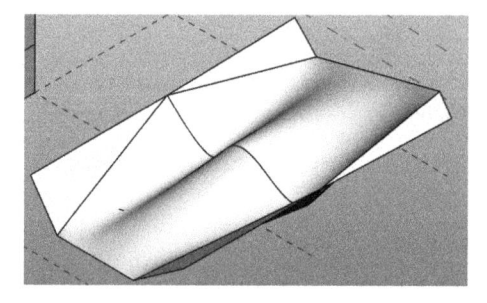

FIGURE 17.8 *Create a loft form from closed or open shapes*

Feel free to experiment further before continuing.

5. Close the *Form Examples-02.rfa* file.

⇨ Saving this file is optional. If you created a form that you wish to use again, please save the file.

CREATING A REVOLVE FORM

A revolve form is made by selecting a linear axis and another shape that is co-planar to the axis. The shape can be either a closed loop of lines (which will create a solid revolve) or an open loop of lines (which will create a surface revolve). The axis can be either a reference-based line or a model-based line. The revolve will default to a full 360 degrees, but this can be changed on the Properties palette.

> **NOTE:** You cannot use the Add Profile tool on revolve forms. See the "Adding Profiles" topic on page 724 below.

1. From the *Chapter17* folder, open *Form Examples-03.rfa*.

This file has a straight vertical line at the intersection of the two reference planes (which is also the insertion point of the family as noted above) and a simple closed shape next to it. You will also notice that the Center (Front/Back) reference plane is shaded in this file. On the Create tab of the ribbon, on the Work Plane panel, notice that the Show Work Plane tool is active. This makes the current work plane shaded and therefore visible in the view window. This tool is a simple toggle. You can try it now if you like. Toggling it off will make the reference plane invisible again (unless selected). The Show Work Plane tool is view specific. So, if you switch to other views on the Project Browser, the active work plane will not be shaded unless you toggle the Show Work Plane tool on.

2. Select both the closed shape and the vertical line (use any selection method).

⇨ Click the Create Form button (see the left side of Figure 17.9).

Conceptual Massing | 717

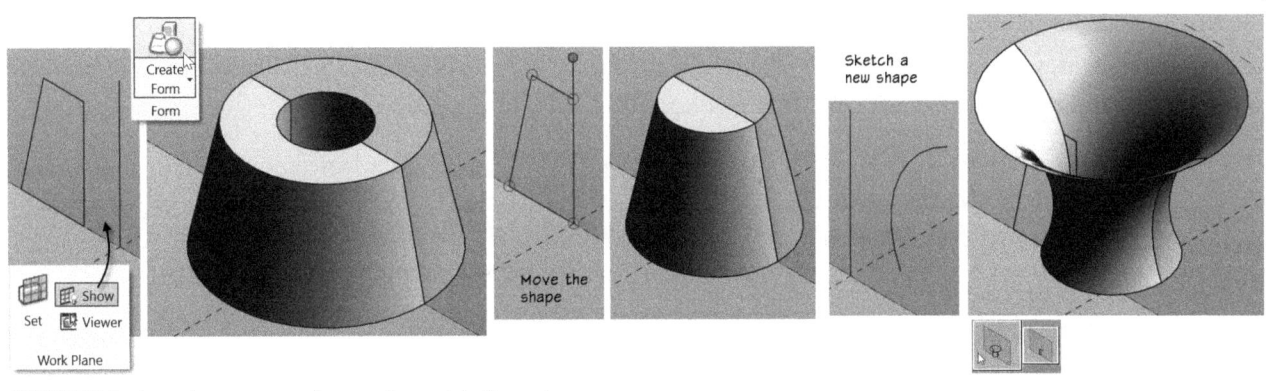

FIGURE 17.9 *A revolve requires a shape and a straight line axis*

This geometry produced a hollow form since the axis did not touch the shape. If you want to experiment, undo the form creation and try moving the closed shape toward the axis line. Revit gives you an ignorable warning about overlapping lines. This is fine. Try the Revolve again and note the new result is solid (see the middle of Figure 17.9).

If you want to try another variation, undo again and this time draw an open shape on the same plane as the axis line. (The work plane is already shaded, but if you want to be sure, simply select the Center, or Front/Back, reference plane.) Try drawing a simple arc. When you create a form this time, you should get an intent stack. Choose the Revolve option (see the right side of Figure 17.9).

Feel free to experiment further before continuing.

3. Close the Form *Examples-03.rfa* file.

⇨ Saving this file is optional. If you created a form that you wish to use again, please save the file.

CREATING A SWEEP FORM

A sweep form consists of an explicit user-drawn path and a profile (open or closed loop of lines) drawn perpendicular to the path. The sample file provides some geometry to get us started.

1. From t 17 folder, open *Form Examples-04.rfa*.

This file has two paths (the arcs drawn on Level 1) and two shapes: one closed and one open. As you can see, the current work plane is at the end of one of the arcs. You can use the Set Work Plane tool on the Create tab to set the work plane. If you pre-highlight the endpoint of one of the arcs, that point will become the active work plane (see below). Let's start by creating a solid sweep and then a surface sweep from the shapes already in this file.

2. Select the closed shape and the arc in the middle of the view window.

⇨ Click the Create Form button.

3. Repeat for the open shape and its arc (see Figure 17.10).

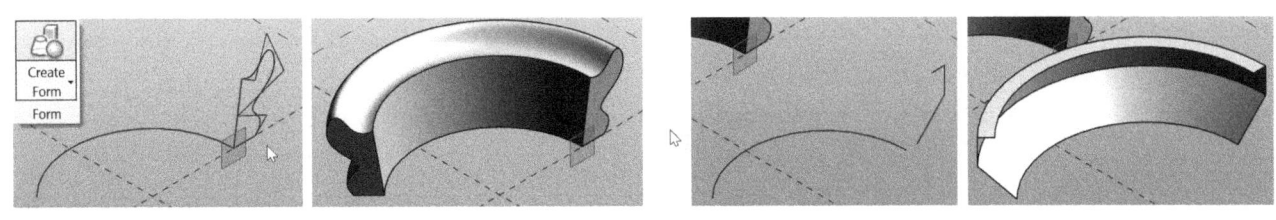

FIGURE 17.10 *Create sweeps from the provided shapes*

• Revit Essentials for Architecture •

718 | Chapter 17

Since there were already shapes provided in the file, we didn't need to worry about the work plane. However, if you undo the two forms, we can start again with the paths and draw new shapes to sweep. This will give us an opportunity to learn about the two methods to set the work plane perpendicular to the path.

> **Method 1:** Use the Set Work Plane tool to set the endpoint of the path to be the current work plane, and then draw your profile on that work plane.
>
> **Method 2:** Place a reference point on the path, and then set the active work plane to that point.

4. Undo the creation of the previous sweeps (or reopen the file without saving).

5. On the Create tab, on the Work Plane panel, click the Set Work Plane tool.

   ⇨ Click on one of the endpoints of the arc to set the plane of the endpoint to be the current work plane (see the left side of Figure 17.11).

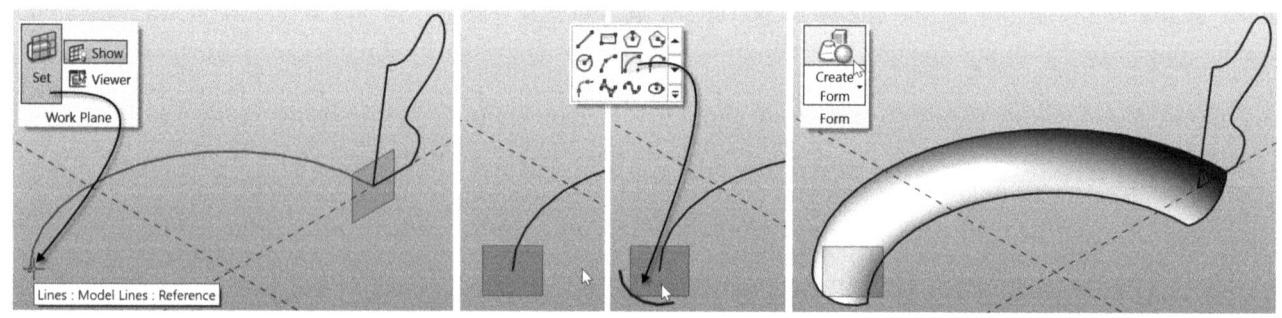

FIGURE 17.11 *Set the endpoint of the arc as the current work plane, draw a new shape at the endpoint of the path and create the swept form*

6. Draw a shape on this Work Plane. The exact shape is up to you. It can be closed or open.

   ⇨ Select the path and the new shape and then Create Form (see the right side of Figure 17.11).

Let's now try method 2. In method 2, you can place a point anywhere along the sweep path and use that point as a work plane. For this exercise, work on the second arc path or undo the previous form and work on that path if you prefer.

7. On the Create tab, on the Draw panel, click on the Point Element tool.

   ⇨ Move your cursor over the arc path.

   The path will highlight under your cursor.

8. Click anywhere along the arc path as it is highlighted to place the reference point.

> **NOTE:** Reference points are described in more detail in the "Divided Surfaces, Patterns, Components, Points" topic on page 736 below.

   ⇨ On the ribbon, click the Modify tool or press ESC.

9. Select the new Reference Point.

Like selecting levels or reference planes, selecting the new reference point will make it the active work plane. You can also use the Set Work Plane tool on the Create panel as we did for the other path as well (see the left side of Figure 17.12).

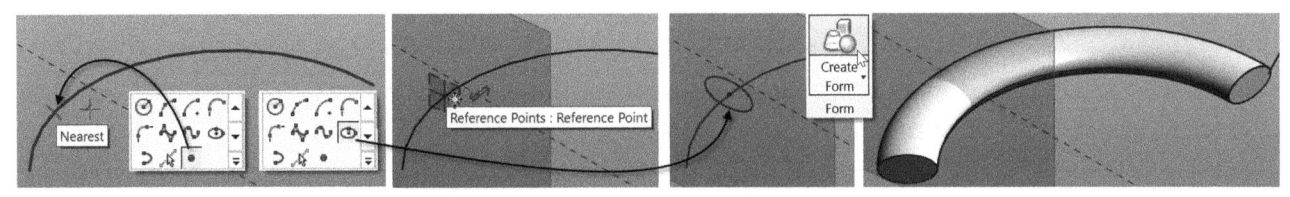

FIGURE 17.12 *Add a reference point and then select it to make it the current work plane*

> **NOTE:** When using the Set Work Plane tool, the plane that is perpendicular to the host path should be first in the selection order automatically. If it is not, you may have to cycle through the various work planes of the point using the TAB key to get the desired plane.

   10. Draw a shape on the new work plane. Select it and the path and then create form (see the right side of Figure 17.12).

The profile does not have to be connected to the path, but it does have to be drawn perpendicular to the path. Once the form is created, if it is a model-based form (see the "Model-Based and Reference-Based Forms" topic on page 725 below), selecting any face, edge, or vertex of the form will display on-screen arrow controls, which can be used to modify the shape of the form. See the "Global and Local Controls" topic on page 721 below for more information.

> **NOTE:** If the profile is large and the path has tight curves, you may see an error message about self-intersecting forms and the form will fail to be made. If this happens, try making your profile smaller.

   Feel free to experiment further before continuing.

   11. Close the *Form Examples-04.rfa* file.

   ⇨ Saving this file is optional. If you created a form that you wish to use again, please save the file.

CREATING A SWEPT BLEND FORM

A swept blend form is like the sweep form. However, instead of having just one profile, the swept blend has two or more profiles which blend while following along the explicitly drawn path.

   1. From the *Chapter17* folder, open *Form Examples-05.rfa*.
   2. Select all the elements on screen (two rectangles and an arc) and then click the Create Form button (see Figure 17.13).

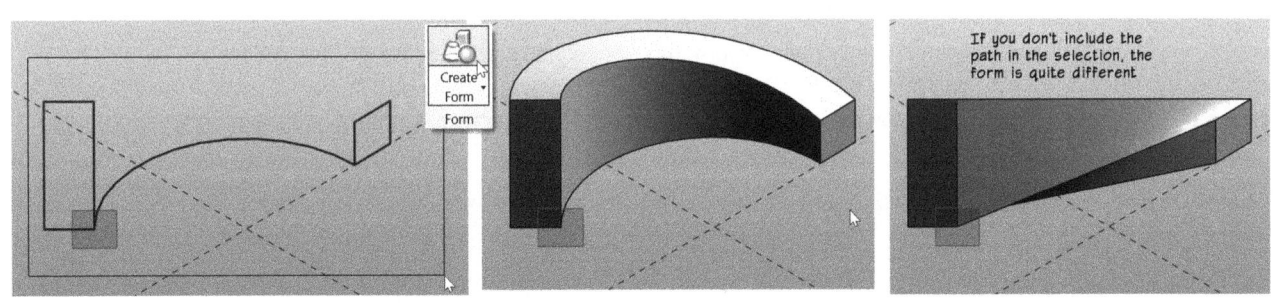

FIGURE 17.13 *A swept blend is made from two profiles and a path*

   ⇨ Undo and try creating the form again without selecting the arc and note the difference.

> **NOTE:** Both sweep forms and swept blend forms can have paths consisting of multiple line-segments. These are referred to as "multi-segment sweeps" or "multi-segment swept-blends." However, you cannot add a profile (see below) to a form made from a multi-segment path.

You can combine many of the techniques that we have explored so far. For example, undo the previous form and you can add a reference point to the path like we did for the sweep above. Once you have the reference point, we can make it active and draw another profile on that work plane.

   3.   Undo the previous form.

   ⇨   On the Create tab, click the Point tool and then add a reference point on the path.

   4.   Select the new reference point to make it the active work plane.

   ⇨   Draw a new rectangle on this work plane.

   5.   Select the three profiles (two original rectangles at each end and the one you drew) and the arc path.

   ⇨   Click the Create Form button.

   Try it both with and without the arc selected. The difference is subtle, but noticeable (see Figure 17.14).

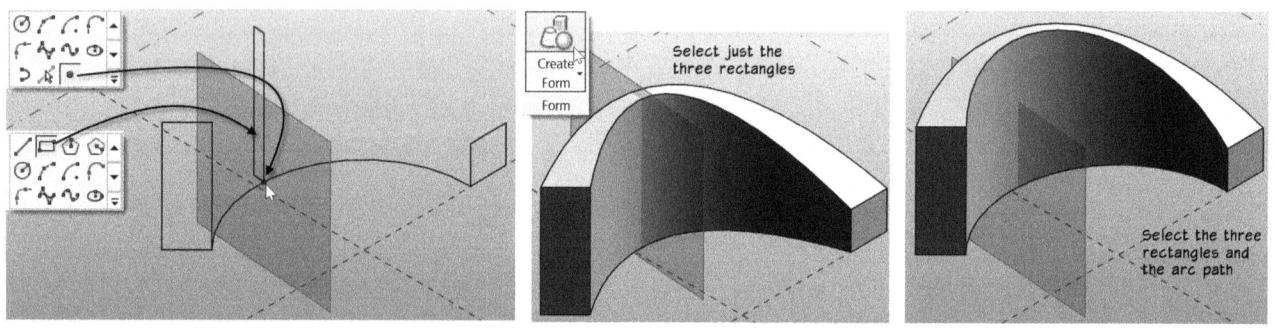

FIGURE 17.14 *Add an additional profile to the path and create a new form*

Technically there is little difference between the loft and the swept blend. In the examples that we explored here; the only difference was the path. In the case of the loft, we used an "implicit" path meaning that Revit interpolated the path based on the profiles we selected. In the case of the swept blend, we had an "explicit" path meaning that we drew the path using a model line (arc) element.

   Feel free to experiment further before continuing.

   6.   Close the *Form Examples-05.rfa* file.

   ⇨   Saving this file is optional. If you created a form that you wish to use again, please save the file.

EDITING FORMS IN THE CONCEPTUAL DESIGN ENVIRONMENT

When you select the whole or any part of a form, the Modify Form tab will appear on the ribbon with some additional editing tools. Selection of existing forms defaults to the sub-element level, meaning that as you move your mouse over a form, the edges, surfaces, and vertex points will pre-highlight under your cursor. If you wish to select the entire form, press TAB to cycle to Form Element selection. Selecting either a sub-element or the complete form gives you access to the same Modify | Form ribbon tab. If you select a sub-element, you will also get an onscreen drag handle for further direct manipulation. In this topic, we will look at the tools on the Form Element panel of the Modify | Form tab and explore the onscreen direct manipulation techniques.

USING X-RAY

Select any portion of a form, and the X-Ray button becomes available on the ribbon (it is also available on the right-click menu). X-Ray changes the visibility of the selected form. When X-Ray is toggled on for an element, the form becomes transparent and you see the underlying structure, or bones, of the form. The profile(s) of the form is shown in purple, and the path appears in black. Each vertex is also accentuated with a round filled vertex handle. All the faces, edges, and vertices of the form continue to be available for editing with the use of the arrow controls and temporary dimensions. Even if you deselect the element, X-Ray remains active although the contextual Modify | Form tab disappears. Reselect any part of the form to re-display the contextual tab and gain access to the X-Ray toggle on either the ribbon or right-click.

1. From the *Chapter17* folder, open *Form Examples-06.rfa*.

This file has a collection of the forms that we created in each of the other files above.

2. Select the revolve form in the upper left corner.
    ⇨ On the Modify Form tab, click the X-Ray button.

Take notice of the black line in the center of the form. This is the original path (axis) for this revolve. Paths display in black in X-Ray mode. Notice that this line is a continuous black line. Explicit paths (an actual path we create) like the one used for this revolve display as a continuous (solid) line.

3. Select the extrude (hexagon shaped) form on the right.
    ⇨ On the Modify Form tab, click the X-Ray button (see Figure 17.15).

Notice that enabling X-Ray for a new selection disables it for the previous selection. The X-Ray tool is an object-specific visibility mode; only one element can be in X-Ray mode at a time. When an object is in X-Ray mode, every view will display the object in this mode. Notice also that the path element (black line) this time is dashed. This indicates that the path is "implicit" (not an actual path that we sketched to create the form, one derived from the profiles used to create it).

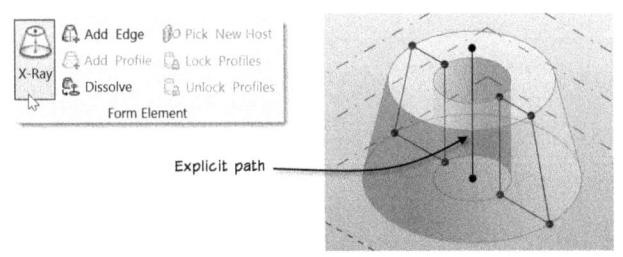

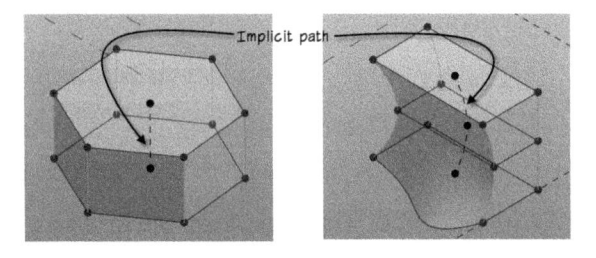

FIGURE 17.15 *Study the various forms in the dataset in X-Ray mode*

X-Ray mode is a useful mode in which to edit forms because you can see all of the faces of the form, manipulate its "skeleton," and still get a sense of the form's overall shape through the shaded faces. Feel free to experiment further. You can drag the vertices or edges directly onscreen while X-Ray is active. We'll do this in the next topic.

GLOBAL AND LOCAL CONTROLS

By now you have noticed the drag controls that appear when you select a sub-element of a form. These controls have two or three arrows for direct manipulation and sometimes some other specialized arrows as well. Red, green, and blue arrows allow you to drag the selected element while constraining movement along an absolute axis. Standard 3D modeling conventions use the labels X, Y, and Z for length, width, and height, respectively, with respect to the overall coordinate system (global) of the file. The labels U, V, and W are also used when the coordinates are localized

722 | Chapter 17

to an element (local). Revit allows you toggle between the global (X,Y,Z) coordinates and the local (U,V,W) coordinates using the SPACEBAR. When you toggle to the local coordinates, the arrows change color to orange. (Try this on the hexagon shape, for example.) Working in X-Ray mode and using the global and local controls, let's manipulate some of the forms.

1. Select the hexagon form and place it in X-Ray mode.

    ⇨ Try selecting an edge of the form

    ⇨ Select a corner vertex.

Notice that when you select a face, edge, or vertex, the same arrow controls appear indicating that you can drag the sub-element in any of the three directions indicated by the arrows (see Figure 17.16).

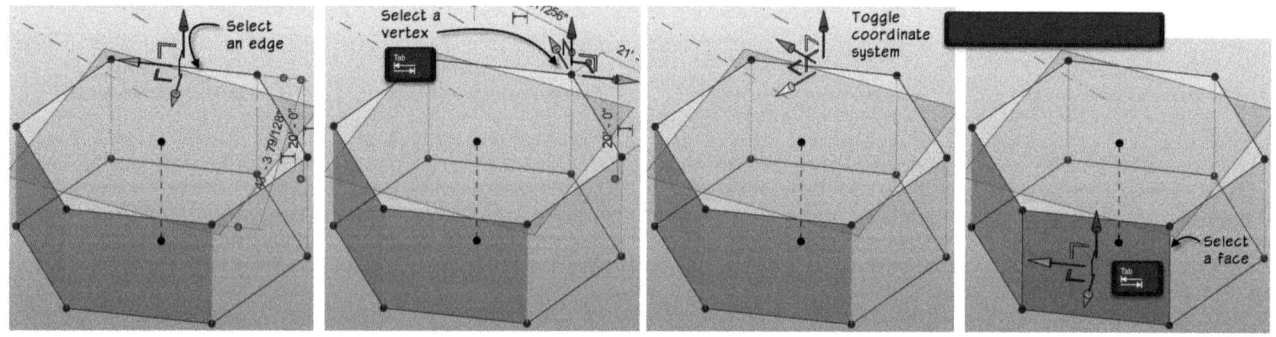

FIGURE 17.16 *Select sub-elements like edges and vertices to access sub-element modification controls*

2. Tap the SPACEBAR to toggle from local to absolute axis and back.

    You can drag these controls if you like, but undo before continuing. For now, we just want to focus on selection.

You can always select the whole form by placing your cursor over the form, press the TAB key once, and then click on the form. Once the whole form is selected, you won't have the local control icon anymore, but you will have access to common editing tools like Move, Copy, Rotate, and Mirror on the Modify Form contextual tab of the ribbon. You have access to these tools with a sub-element selected as well, but the transformation would apply to the selected sub-element only.

3. Select any part of the revolve form in the upper left corner.

    ⇨ On the Modify Form tab, click the X-Ray button.

4. Using the TAB key, select the outside vertex at the bottom.

    ⇨ Try some of the manipulations indicated in Figure 17.17.

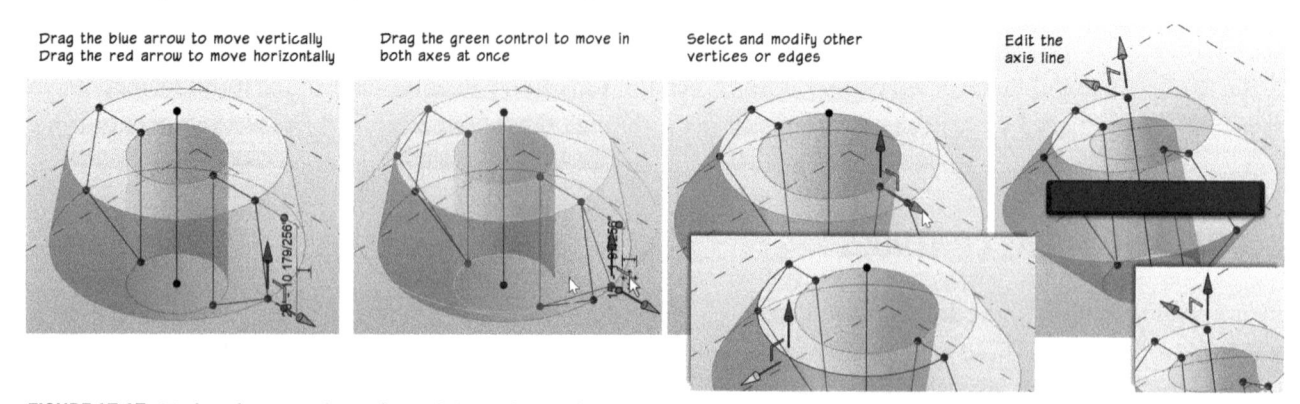

FIGURE 17.17 *To directly manipulate a form, click an edge, surface, or vertex point and then use the arrow controls to manipulate the shape*

The figure shows just a few possibilities. Don't forget to toggle the axis from global to local using the SPACEBAR and see the effect on your manipulations.

ADDING AND DELETING EDGES

The Add Edge tool allows you to add a vertical or angled edge to the face of a form. It does not work on the top or bottom faces of forms.

1. Select the extruded hexagon form again.
⇨ On the Modify | Form tab of the ribbon, click the Add Edge tool.

Hover the cursor over a vertical face of the form.

A preview of a single, vertical edge will appear. Move the mouse around to see the preview edge move around. Notice that if you move your mouse over the top surface, the preview edge will disappear.

2. When the preview edge is where you like it, click once to place the edge (see the top of Figure 17.18).

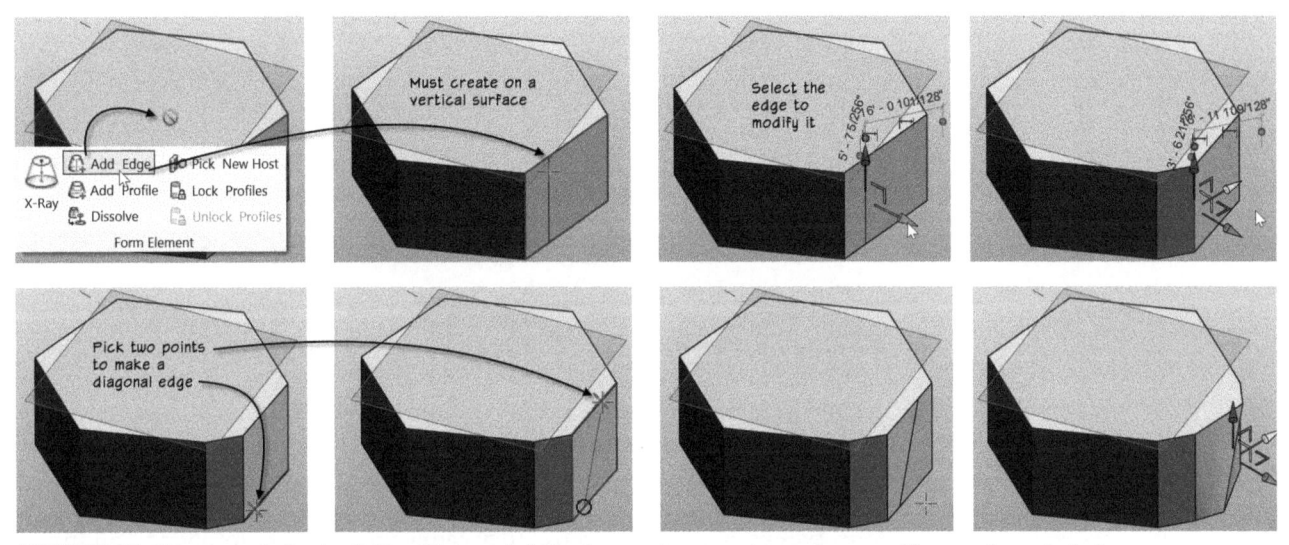

FIGURE 17.18 *Place vertical edges by clicking. Place angled edges by snapping two points at the top and bottom of a vertical edge*

If you want an angled edge, you can click two points instead. Start the Add Edge tool the same way. Instead of clicking once on the vertical face of the form, click on the bottom edge of the vertical face to place the first point. Click again on the top edge of the same face to place the second point. Use object snaps to gain more accuracy (see the bottom of Figure 17.18).

Edges can be added to most forms. You can also delete existing edges and user-created edges. To delete an edge, simply select the edge and then press the DELETE key.

3. Select the edge of any form.
⇨ Press the delete key (see Figure 17.19).

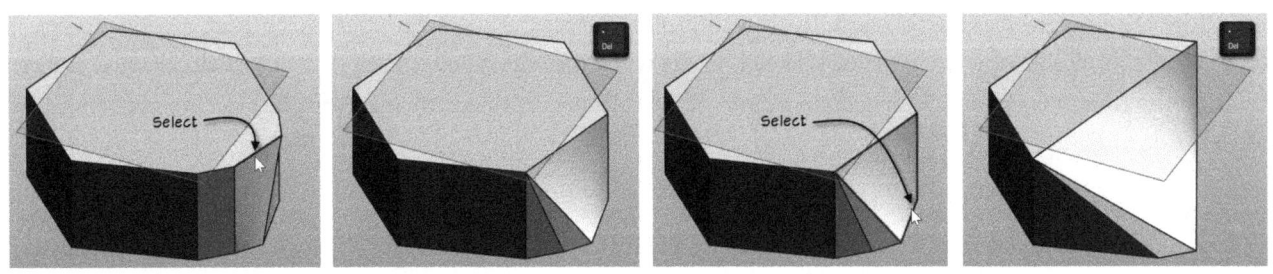

FIGURE 17.19 *You can delete an edge of a form*

This works with surfaces too. Give it a try.

ADDING PROFILES

You can add a new profile to an existing form using the Add Profile tool. Add profile will work for all form types except revolve and multi-segment path sweeps.

1. Select the curved swept form in the middle (remember you can select the face, edge, or vertex).
    ⇨ On the Modify | Form tab, click the X-Ray button.
2. On the Modify | Form tab, click the Add Profile tool.
    ⇨ Move your cursor over the form and click once to place the profile.

Once the Profile is placed, you can manipulate it using the arrow controls (see Figure 17.20).

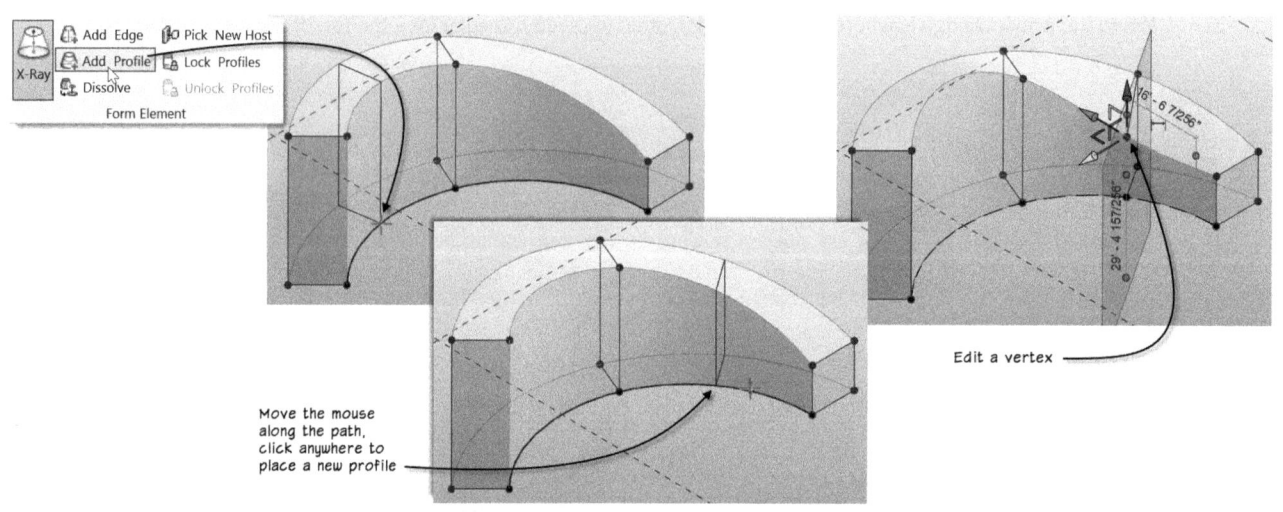

FIGURE 17.20 *Add a profile to a form and manipulate the resultant edges*

Profiles can be added to extrusions, lofts, sweeps, and swept blends. They cannot be added to revolves or multi-segment path sweeps.

Try additional manipulations. For example, notice the small right-angle symbol at the intersection of each pair of arrows on the arrow controls. Dragging a single arrow constrains movement along a single axis. Dragging the right-angle control instead will allow free movement in the plane defined by the two adjacent arrows. For example, to move within the X,Y plane, drag the right-angle symbol between the red and green arrows.

EDIT PROFILE

The Edit Profile method allows you to edit the profiles of a form using familiar sketch-based tools and techniques. To use the tool, select the edge of a form, and then on the Modify | Form tab, click the Edit Profile button. If you select the entire form before clicking this tool, Revit will display a select profile cursor. Simply click on an edge to begin editing. The form will gray out, and the selected profile will appear in sketch mode. Use any of the normal editing tools on the ribbon to edit the shape of the profile. When you are finished, click the Finish Edit Mode button (see the left side of Figure 17.21).

DISSOLVE FORMS

When a form is selected, you will find the Dissolve tool on the Form Element panel. Simply select a form, and then click the Dissolve tool. The form will be replaced with a collection of shapes and points that would be required to create the same form. This tool gives a fall back when X-Ray or Edit Profile proves insufficient to make the desired manipulations to a 3D form. You can use Dissolve to start over, while preserving your original shapes (see the right side of Figure 17.21). Note that each profile will be accompanied by a point. This point will define a work plane for each profile, making it easier to perform further manipulations.

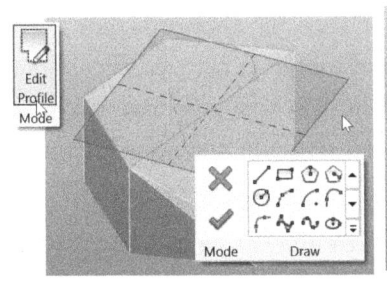

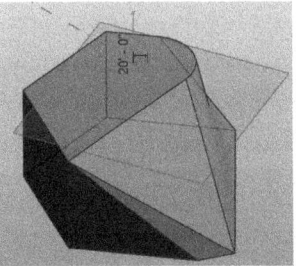

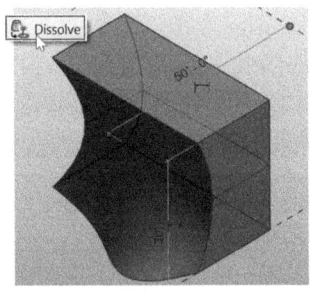

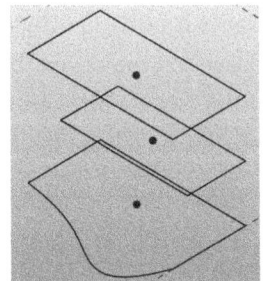

FIGURE 17.21 *Edit profiles using sketch mode tools and dissolve forms back to original model lines*

After manipulating the resultant shapes, you can create a new form from them.

OTHER MANIPULATIONS

Several other tools are available on the Modify Form tab. Lock Profiles will turn a freeform into an extrusion. The top and bottom profiles will be made the same and locked together so that editing one will affect the other. On the Modify panel, you can also use the standard move, copy, rotate mirror, and scale tools on most form and sub-element selections. Continue experimenting in the current file before continuing to the next topic.

1. Feel free to experiment further before continuing.
2. Close the *Form Examples-06.rfa* file.
⇨ Saving this file is optional. If you created a form that you wish to use again, please save the file.

MODEL-BASED AND REFERENCE-BASED FORMS

The conceptual massing environment can create two related, but unique, types of forms: model-based forms and reference-based forms. Model-based forms are drawn using model lines, and reference-based forms are drawn using reference lines or other referenced geometry. You make the choice between creating a model-based or reference-based form when you create a new form. On the Create tab, on the Draw panel, buttons are provided for each mode. Select the Model button to create a model-based form. Select the Reference button to create a reference-based form. Revit defaults to model-based forms, so if you want a reference-based form, be sure to select the Reference tool first (see Figure 17.22). The third button (also shown in the figure) is to create reference planes. These are just like the reference planes created in the traditional family editor. You can use them to make work planes for drawing either model or reference lines.

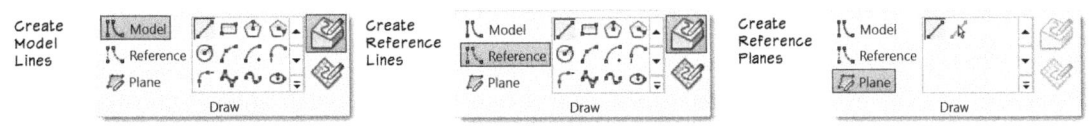

FIGURE 17.22 *Use the line and reference buttons to indicate the kind of shape to draw*

Model-based forms and Reference-based forms each have unique attributes. When you create a form using model lines (refer to the next topic), the model lines used to sketch the basic shape of the form will be absorbed into the form. From a conceptual point of view, the model lines are replaced with the solid or void form created from them. However, it is possible to access the profiles and shapes later using the X-Ray mode (see the "Using X-Ray" topic on page 721), the Edit Profile tool (see the "Edit Profile" topic on page 724), or Dissolve the form (see the "Dissolve

Forms" topic on page 724) as discussed previously. However, each of these techniques is one step removed from the form itself.

Model-based forms have the most real-time flexibility because you can select any vertex, edge, or face of the form and move it using the control arrows (refer to the "Global and Local Controls" topic on page 721 above). Model-based forms are "unlocked" by default, which means there are no constraints maintaining relationships between faces of the form (see the left side of Figure 17.23). If you delete a model-based form, the initial sketch(es) you made to create the form will also be deleted; if you want the original shapes back, be sure to dissolve the form first.

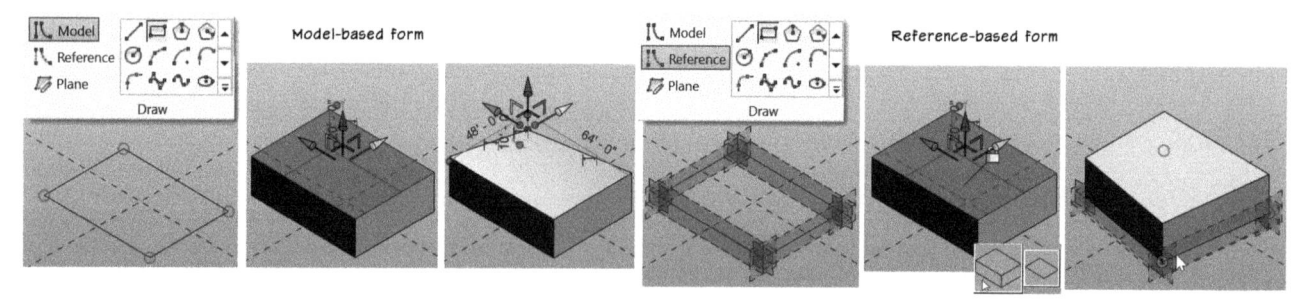

FIGURE 17.23 *Example of a model-based form on the left and reference-based form on the right*

When you create a form from reference lines or other reference geometry, the reference lines used to sketch the basic form will remain available and selectable after the form is created. The form continues to remain dependent on the reference lines (edges or faces) and, to edit the shape of the form, you must edit the reference lines or host forms and edges. Reference-based forms are "locked" by default, which means that all profiles that are parallel to the original reference lines will always remain parallel to—and exactly match the size of—the reference lines (see the right side of Figure 17.23). When you delete a reference-based form, the underlying reference lines will remain in the canvas and can then be edited and reused to create another form. Dissolve is not necessary.

If you try this and you select a vertex of this form, notice that you do not get arrow controls. This is because the profiles are locked for reference forms by default. Also, notice the on-screen lock icon which indicates that the profiles are locked. You can unlock the form by selecting the form and then either click on the on-screen lock icon or click the Unlock Profiles button on the Modify | Form tab of the Ribbon. If you unlock the profiles, the base of the form still follows changes made to the reference lines, but the rest of the form becomes free-form like model-based forms. In this state you could use the Edit Profile tool to edit the unlocked profiles except for the base. X-Ray will show locked forms as dashed like the way implicit paths were shown in the examples above. If you dissolve the form while its profiles are locked, only the reference lines will remain. If the profiles are unlocked, you will get model lines for the unlocked profiles.

The difference between a model-based and reference-based forms is most apparent when used to create Curtain Panels for a patterned surface (refer to the "Divided Surfaces, Patterns, Components, Points" topic on page 736 below), for example, if you are creating a panel that has a fixed thickness and you want to load this panel into a pattern across a non-planar face. The panel will conform to the shape of the non-planar face, but if it is reference-based, it will maintain its thickness. If it is model-based, the thickness and shape of the panel can vary from one side of the panel to the other and it will appear tapered (see Figure 17.24).

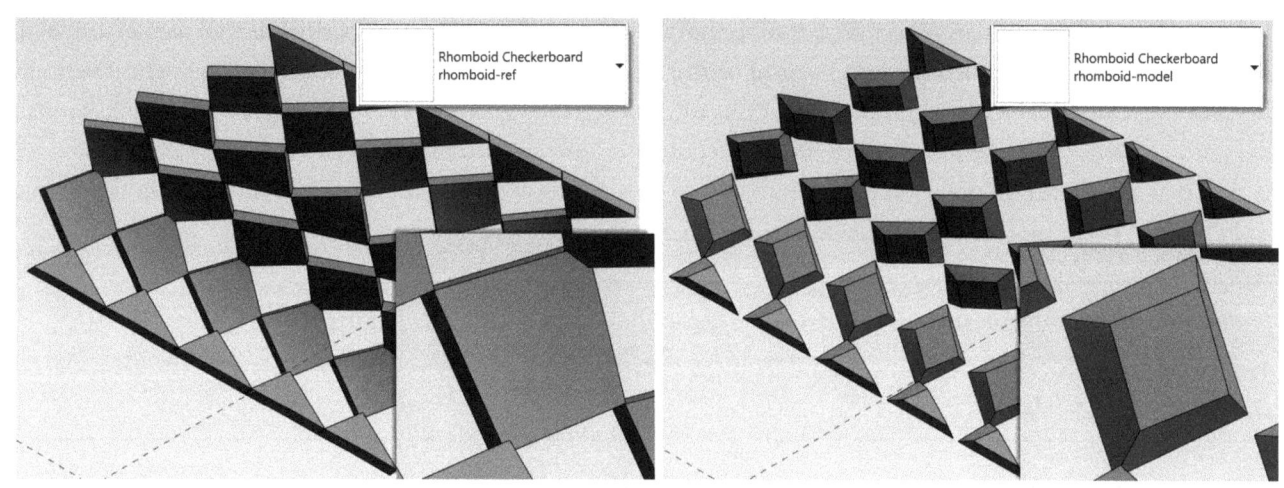

FIGURE 17.24 *Comparing a surface with model-based panel and a reference-based panel*

> **NOTE:** The model shown in Figure 17.24 is provided with th files in the *Chapter17* folder. The file is named: *Model or Reference.rfa*. If you open this file, you can select the surface, and then from the Type Selector you can switch between the **rhomboid-ref** and **rhomboid-model** panels provided in the file.

On the left side of the figure a reference-based panel is loaded. Notice that the top face and bottom face of the panel are the same size—this is a result of the reference-based form's having locked profiles. On the right side of the figure, a model-based panel is used. Notice that the panels appear to taper from one side of the face to the other. As the top face of the component adapts to the changing size of the contoured, patterned surface, the bottom face of the component also conforms.

In addition to forms created from reference lines, reference-based forms can also be created from the edges and faces of existing geometry. For example, if you select the top edge of one form and the top edge of another form and then click on the Create Form button, the result will be a surface spanning between the two edges that is a reference-based form. If you select the surface and delete it, the edges that were selected to create the form will not be deleted (see Figure 17.25).

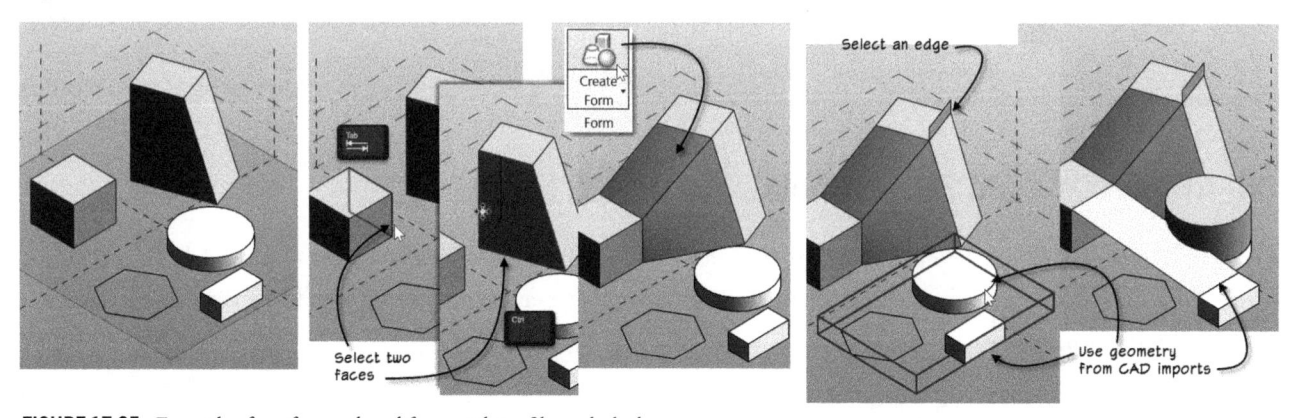

FIGURE 17.25 *Example of a reference-based form with profiles unlocked*

> **NOTE:** The model shown in Figure 17.25 is provided with dataset files in the *Chapter17* folder. The file is named: *Reference from 3D Forms.rfa*. If you open this file, you can try to create forms from both the Revit 3D forms and the imported AutoCAD 3D forms in the file. Use TAB to select surfaces and edges. Use CTRL to add to your selection.

Reference-based forms can also be created from imported geometry. You can import two-dimensional or three-dimensional geometry; select lines, edges, or faces of the imports; and then use the selected elements to create new forms in the conceptual mass environment. For this to work, the imported geometry must be in ACIS solid format and not polymesh. Also, the provided file includes a polyline. You will be unable to select this shape or its edges. So be sure that 2D shapes are individual lines and arcs, or you can explode the imported file. Just keep in mind that exploding imported files should usually be avoided wherever possible.

> **NOTE:** If any line in your selection set is a reference line, then your resulting form will be a reference-based form. In other words, if your selection set consists of both model lines and reference lines, then the resulting form will be a reference-based form.

MODEL AND REFERENCE FORM RULES OF THUMB

Here are some tips and considerations for when to use a model-based form and when to use a reference-based form:

- Create reference-based forms when you create a curtain panel using the *Curtain Panel Pattern Based.rft* [*Metric Curtain Panel Pattern Based.rft*] template file.

- If you expect to make frequent edits to profiles of a form, consider reference-based forms as you can edit them quickly by modifying the reference lines directly.

- You can use the Dissolve form functionality to restore the original components of a form. This offers more flexibility than X-Ray mode as you are essentially starting over with the original shapes.

- If you have a solid idea of what you want your final form to look like, create a reference-based form.

- If you are brainstorming design ideas for the massing of a new building and desire the most flexibility in free-form editing in real time on the screen, create a model-based form.

> **TIP:** Before creating a form from model lines, you always have the option of changing model lines into reference lines. To do so, select the model line(s), and on the Properties palette under Identity Data, check the box next to "Is Reference Line." This can be very helpful if you forget to select the Reference tool on the ribbon before you begin drawing. However, once you have created a form from the model lines, this option will no longer be available. In that case, you would need to dissolve the form, select the resulting model lines and convert them. Then recreate the form.

CREATE A NEW CONCEPTUAL MASS LOADABLE FAMILY

At the start of the book, in Chapter 1, we worked on a simple pavilion house model. Using that model as our concept, let's explore some options for the pavilion in our conceptual massing environment. This will be a very simple practical example to practice what we have covered here so far.

CREATE A NEW FILE AND ADD LEVELS

We will start with a new file and add some levels that we can use to help us build the model.

1. From the File menu, choose: **New > Conceptual Mass**.
   ⇨ Choose the *Mass.rft* [*Metric Mass.rft*] family template file and then click Open.
2. Save the Conceptual Mass family and name it: *Pavilion Concept.rfa*.

Conceptual Massing | 729

⇨ Close any other open files.

3. On the Create tab of the ribbon, click on the Level button.

Creating a new level in a 3D view in the conceptual mass editor is a one-click process. After clicking on the Level tool, move your cursor over the canvas area and you will notice a temporary dimension from the existing Level 1 to your cursor.

4. Use the temporary dimension to locate it 10'-0" [3000] above Level 1 and then click once to place the new level.

> **TIP:** If you prefer, you can simply type: **10 [3000]** and press the ENTER. The new level will automatically be placed at 10'-0" [3000] above Level 1.

5. Create another Level **10'-0" [3000]** above the level you just created (see Figure 17.26).

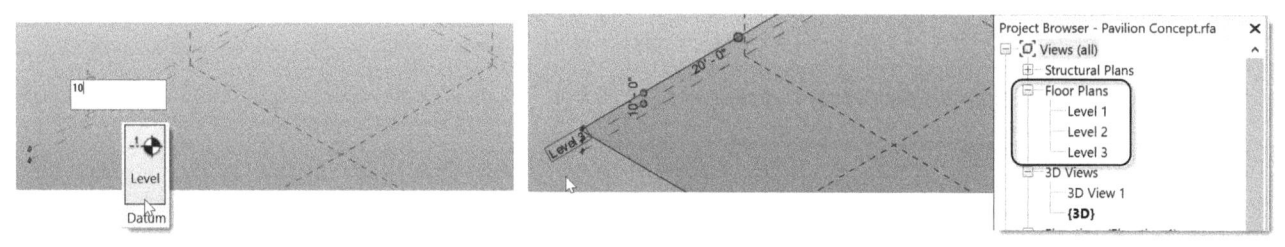

FIGURE 17.26 *Create two new levels*

⇨ On the ribbon, click the Modify tool or press the ESC key twice.

The two new levels will be named "Level 2" and "Level 3." Just as we saw in the "Working with Levels" topic on page 155 in Chapter 5, floor plan views for each new level will be added to the Project Browser. You can see the name of any level in the view window when you select it. You can also edit its properties to see and change the name.

CREATE A SOLID FORM

Now that we have a few levels; we will create the basic mass form of the pavilion.

1. Select the lowest level on screen.

Since we just drew levels, the last level that we drew is the active work plane. As we saw above, in the conceptual massing environment, you need only select a datum (level, reference plane, point or surface) element to make it the active work plane.

2. On the ribbon, on the Draw panel, click the Model tool, and then click on the Rectangle icon.

Recall from the "Model-Based and Reference-Based Forms" topic on page 725 above that the Model tool creates model lines, which will mean that forms created from them will be model-based forms. If you prefer reference-based forms, you will click the Reference tool instead. Check the tool frequently as well, as Revit defaults to model lines.

• Revit Essentials for Architecture •

730 | Chapter 17

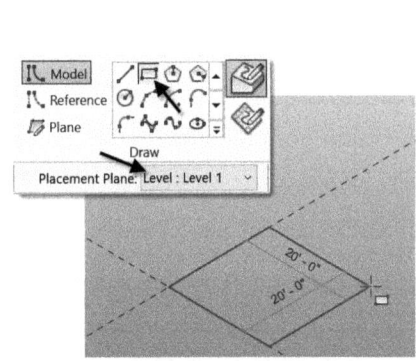

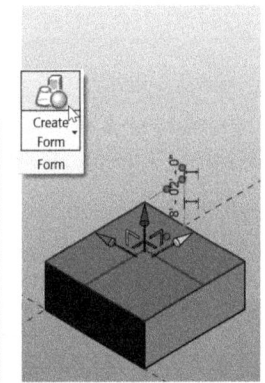

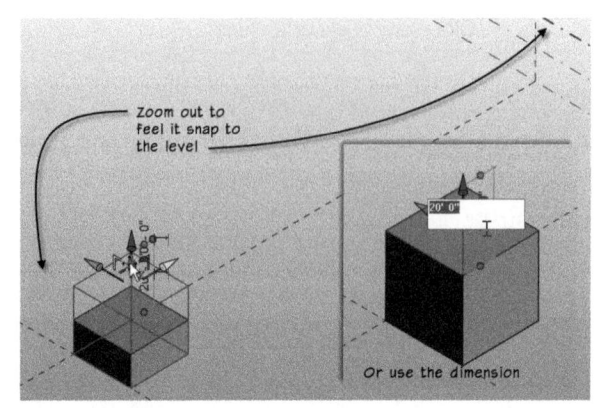

FIGURE 17.27 *Using the model drawing mode, draw a rectangle and then create form and stretch its height*

    3.   Draw a rectangle starting at the intersection point of the two reference planes.

    ⇨   Watching the temporary dimensions, make the rectangle: 20'-0" by 20'-0" [6000 by 6000] (see the left side of Figure 17.27).

    ⇨   On the ribbon, click the Modify tool or press ESC.

    4.   Select the rectangle and then click on the Create Form button.

This will create an extrusion of arbitrary height. We want to modify the height of the extrusion to be at Level 3. The top face of the solid extruded form should still be selected; if it is not, select it now.

    5.   Click and drag the blue arrow control up.

           This drags the height of the top face up. Notice that when you get close to one of the levels, the level line highlights, allowing you to snap to the height of the level.

    6.   You may also use the temporary dimensions to type in the desired height of: **20'-0"** [**6000**] (see the right side of Figure 17.27).

SCULPT THE TOP SURFACE

Let's edit the top face of our basic rectangular form to create a curved, asymmetrical barrel vault. There are several approaches we could take for such a form. For this example, we'll look at using a Void form to carve the shape we want from the existing cube form.

    1.   On the Create tab, on the Draw panel, click the Start-End-Radius Arc shape.

Next to the draw tools are two buttons: Face and Work Plane. These are two drawing modes for all the line drawing tools. Using the Face option, we can draw directly on the faces of our existing geometry.

    2.   If necessary, click the Draw on Face button.

    ⇨   Place your cursor over the vertical side face of the solid extrusion and notice that the outline of face highlights.

           This indicates that we will be drawing on this face.

    3.   Draw an arc on the side face (see Figure 17.28).

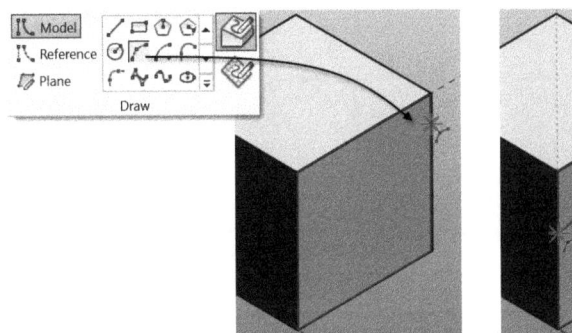

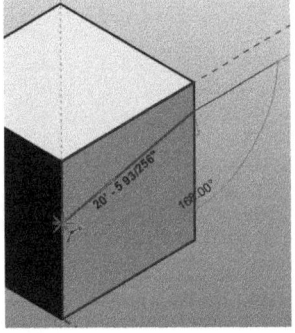

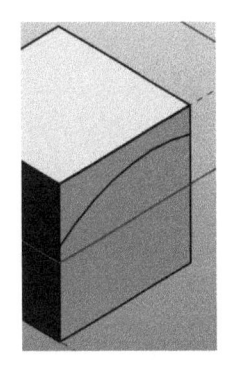

FIGURE 17.28 *Draw an arc for the bottom edge of the profile on the face of the box*

4. On the Draw panel, click the Line draw icon.

Look directly below the Draw panel and on the Options Bar, notice that the Placement Plane reads: **Level 1**. Even though we were able to draw the arc directly on the surface, this did not make the surface the active work plane. So before drawing the remaining lines, we need to set this surface as our work plane. To do this, we'll use the Set tool.

5. On the Work Plane panel, click the Set tool and then select the surface of the 3D form (see the left side of Figure 17.29).

   Notice the change to the Placement Plane setting on the Options Bar (see the middle of Figure 17.29).

   ⇨ Draw three straight lines to create a closed shape as shown in the figure.

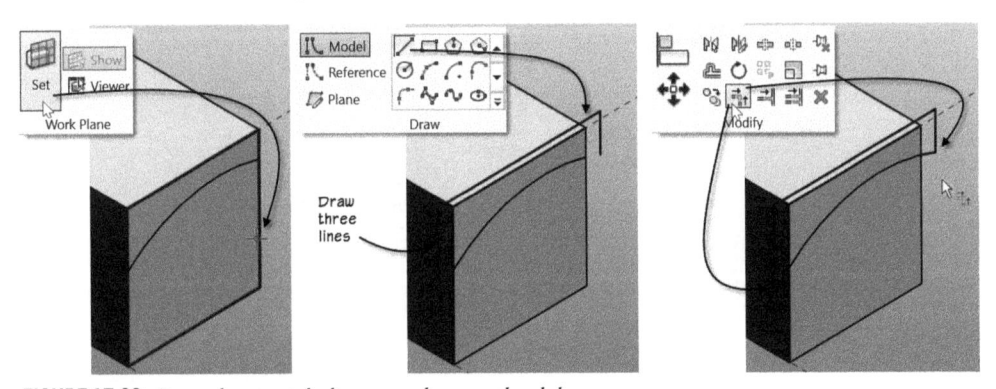

FIGURE 17.29 *Draw three straight lines to make an enclosed shape*

   ⇨ Use the Trim/Extend to Corner tool to clean up the corners.

Next, we want to create a similar profile on the opposite side of the box extrusion.

6. Orbit the model around to see the opposite face.

7. On the ribbon, on the Work Plane panel, click the Set Work Plane button and then click the back face of the box (now facing us).

8. Draw a similar profile on the current work plane with the arc sloped the other way.

You can draw this shape manually, or after you set the work plane, you can click the Pick Lines tool. You will need to use the TAB key to chain select in this instance. This will copy the shape to the new work plane. Next, use the Mirror Draw Axis tool with the "Copy" option turned off. Snap to the midpoint when drawing the mirror line. This will flip the shape in place (see Figure 17.30). You can use the ViewCube to orient the view of the model to one of the elevations to views the results.

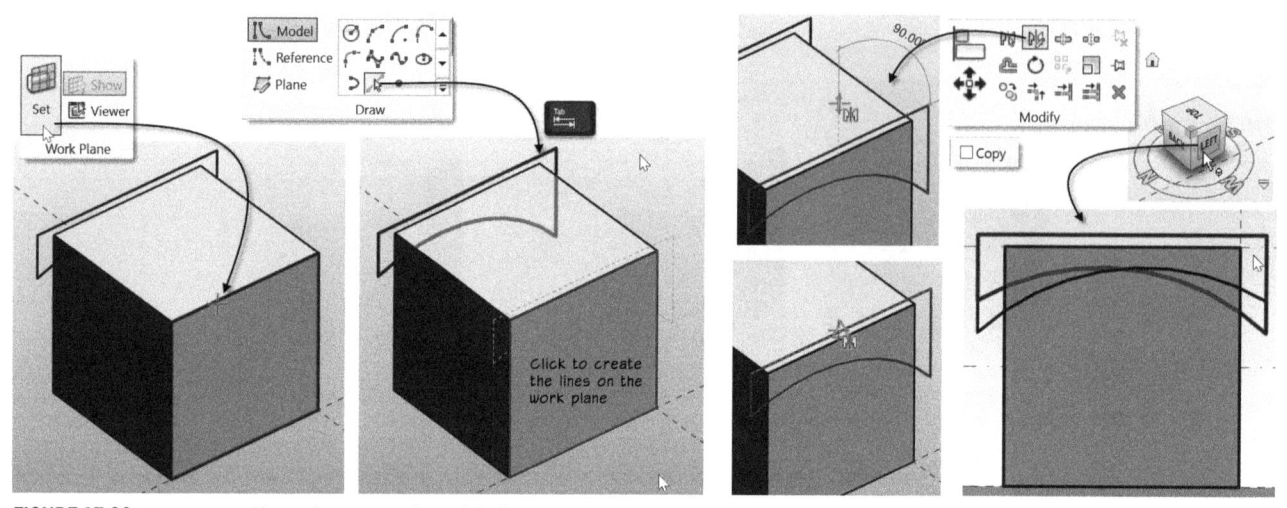

FIGURE 17.30 *Draw a profile on the opposite face of the box*

If you changed the orientation of the view with the ViewCube, click one of its corners to orbit back to an axonometric viewpoint.

9. Select both profiles.

⇨ Click the drop down button on the Create Form tool and choose: **Void Form** (see Figure 17.31).

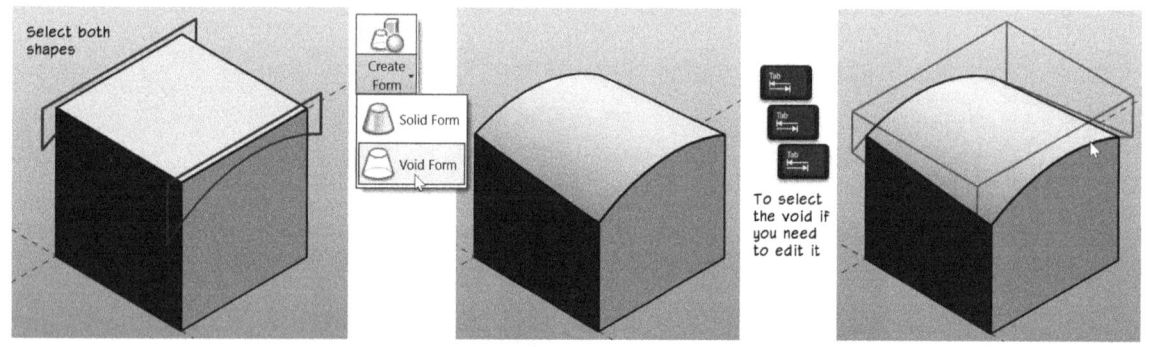

FIGURE 17.31 *Create a void form from the two profiles*

A lofted void form is made and automatically cuts the solid extrusion. If you need to modify the void form, you can still access it by putting your cursor over the area of the void form and pressing TAB to cycle through the selection options. When the void form pre-highlights, click to select it (see the right side of Figure 17.31). Once the void form is selected it will temporarily disengage from the solid form and you can select edges, faces, and vertices of the void form and drag to edit the shape of the void by using the arrow controls just like solids. You can even enable X-Ray mode or use Edit Profile for the selected void form. If necessary, you can even Dissolve it.

If you had clicked on the Create Form button and not specified a void form, then a solid loft form would have been created by default. Whether a form is a solid or a void is an instance property of the form and can easily be toggled on the Properties palette. Simply change the Solid/Void parameter under Identity data (see Figure 17.32). The exception to the ability to swap between Solid and Void is if a form is already participating in a geometry combination (meaning it is joined or cut by another form). If this is the case, then the Solid/Void parameter will not exist for that form on the Properties palette. In that case, you would have to first use the uncut tool.

TIP: Another option is to uncheck the "Cuts Geometry" setting on the Properties palette. This disables the cutting behavior of the void form. This setting can also be associated to a family parameter so that the cutting behavior can be controlled parametrically in the family.

Conceptual Massing | 733

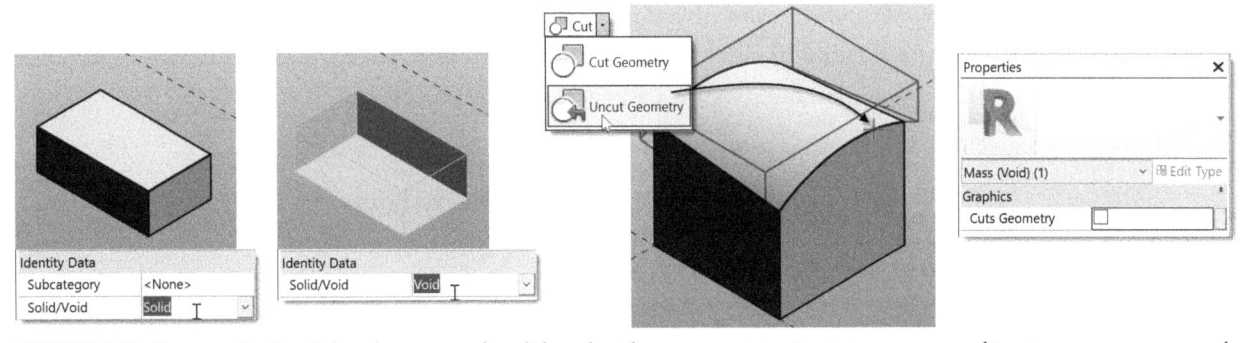

FIGURE 17.32 *You can edit the solid/void parameter for solids and voids not yet participating in a geometry combination, or you can uncut them*

10. Save the file.

ADD A BAY WINDOW

Continuing the same side of the model, let's add a contemporary bay window to the pavilion. Make sure that the active work plane is still the back face of the box. If it is not, use the Set Work Plane tool to set it now.

1. On the Draw panel, click the Pick Lines tool.

   ⇨ On the Options Bar, in the Offset field, type: **2'-0"** [**600**].

   ⇨ Offset the three straight edges inward (see the left side of Figure 17.33).

2. Change the Offset to: **4'-0"** [**1200**] and offset the curve downward.

   ⇨ On the Modify tab, use the Trim tool to clean up (see the right side of Figure 17.33).

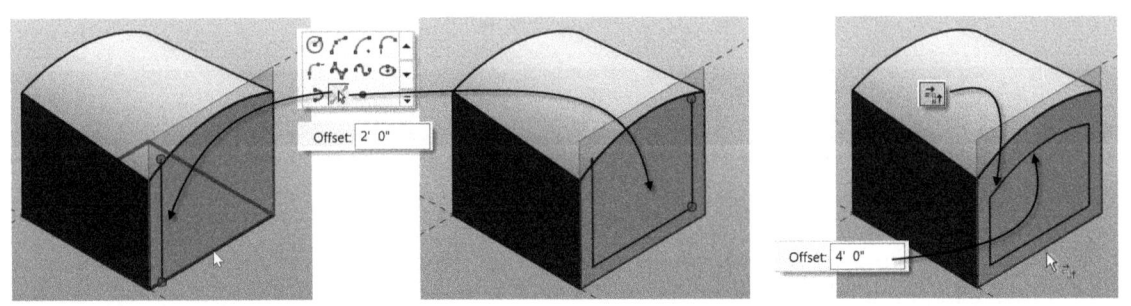

FIGURE 17.33 *Using pick lines with an offset, create a new shape within the work plane face*

3. Select the new profile shape and on the ribbon click Create Form.

   ⇨ Temporary dimensions will remain after the form is created. Edit the depth of the extrusion to: **4'-0"** [**1200**] (see the left side of Figure 17.34).

FIGURE 17.34 *Create an extruded form and edit the depth temporary dimension and then make several free-form manipulations to the bay form*

4. Deselect the form and then select the curved edge at the top of the bay extrusion. Use the TAB key as necessary.

You will get an arrow control and a second control with a round dot at the end rather than an arrowhead. This control allows you to interactively change the radius of the selected arc edge. The arrows will move the curve within its plane and closer or further away from the overall building (or perpendicular to its plane).

- ⇨ Using the arrow controls, move the curve in toward the building slightly about: **1'-0" [300]**.
- ⇨ Using the Change Radius control, drag slightly up (reducing the radius slightly).
- ⇨ Select the vertex on the left, and using the arrow control drag it away from the building slightly (see the right side of Figure 17.34).

You can continue to fine-tune the forms in this model if you like. Feel free to use any of the techniques covered so far. You can work in X-Ray mode, add edges, add profiles, and create additional forms. You can use Edit Profile or even Dissolve. If you use Edit Profile, note that profiles will be projected to the work plane. Sketching is always performed on a 2D plane. Free-form modifications will be reapplied when you finish editing the profile. When you are satisfied with your explorations, we'll load this family into a project and see how it fits on the site.

5. Save your Conceptual Mass family.

LOAD A CONCEPTUAL MASS FAMILY INTO A PROJECT

To test out our design, let's open the original Pavilion project from Chapter 1 and then load our conceptual massing family and test it out on the site.

1. From the *Chapter17* folder, open the *17 Pavilion.rvt* project file.

   There will be two open {3D} tabs now. One for the project we just opened, and the other for the family.

2. Click the tab for **Pavilion-Concept -3D View: {3D}** to switch back to the family.

> **TIP:** You can cycle through open view windows by holding down the CTRL key and pressing TAB.

- ⇨ On the ribbon, click on the Load into Project button.

Revit will load the family into the project environment and automatically turn on mass visibility in the project. A message will appear alerting us of this.

3. Read and then dismiss the message to continue.

The mass model will be attached to the cursor ready to place in the project. If you tap the SPACEBAR, it will rotate, but in 90° increments. It will probably be difficult to place it in the {3D} view, however. So, let's switch to the *Site* plan view instead.

4. On the Project Browser, double-click to open the *Site* plan view.

This will cancel the place mass command.

5. On the Massing & Site tab, on the Conceptual Mass panel, click the Place Mass tool.

We want the bay window to be oriented to the right.

- ⇨ Tap the SPACEBAR as many times as necessary to rotate the model and orient it correctly (with the bay to the right).
- ⇨ Click to place the model and then click the Modify tool or press ESC.

6. Fine-tune the placement using move, align and/or rotate as required (see Figure 17.35).

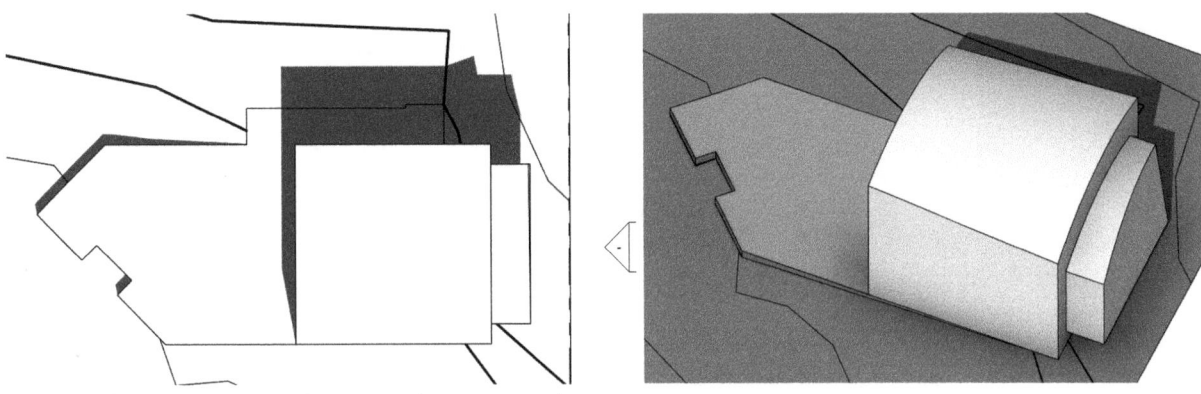

FIGURE 17.35 *Place the mass in the project and position it on the site*

CREATE MODEL ELEMENTS FROM THE MASS MODEL

You are now ready to begin applying walls, roofs, and curtain systems to the faces of the conceptual mass. The next several steps refer to Figure 17.36.

1. Back in the 3D view, select the mass model onscreen.
   - On the Modify | mass tab, click the Mass Floors button (item 1).
   - In the "Mass Floors" dialog that appears, check Level 1 and 2 and then click OK.

Notice the two red shaded mass floor elements that appear. You can select each one individually and on the Properties palette, you can see its perimeter, area and volume. It is also possible to create floors from these surfaces.

2. On the Massing & Site tab, on the Model by Face panel, click the Floor button (item 2).
   - Select both mass floors and then on the ribbon, click the Create Floor button.
3. On the Massing & Site tab, on the Model by Face panel, click the Wall tool (item 3).
   - From the Type Selector, choose: **Generic - 8" [Generic – 200mm]** and then for the Location Line, choose: **Wall Centerline**.
   - Pick each of the vertical surfaces around the model except the curved surface of the bay window (at the East) and the wall at the patio (to the West). Ignore any warnings. There are five total walls.
4. On the Model by Face panel, click the Roof tool (item 4).
   - On the Properties palette, for "Picked Faces Location" choose: **Faces at Bottom of the Roof**.
   - Pick the top surface of the model and then on the ribbon click the Create Roof button.
   - Pick the top of the bay window and then Create Roof.

   The roofs will stop at the edge of the surface and not look very natural.
   There will be grip controls at each edge, however.

5. Drag the controls slightly on all edges to make overhangs for the roofs.
6. On the Model by Face panel, click the Curtain System tool (item 5).
   - Pick the curved surface of the bay window (at the East) and then click the Create System button.

   Orbit the model so you can see the West side.

   - Pick the wall at the patio (at the West) and then click the Create System button.

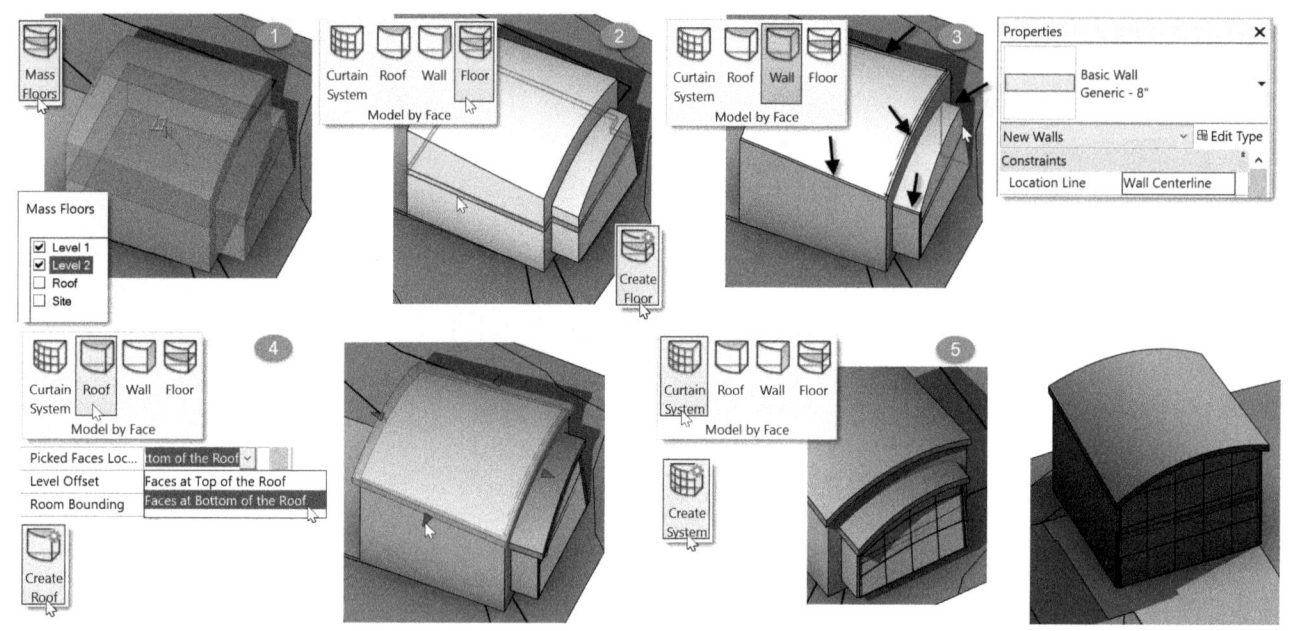

FIGURE 17.36 *Add walls, floors, curtain systems, and roofs to the faces of the mass model*

Some cleanup may be required after you apply the elements to the mass. When you have finished adding the elements, turn off the Show Mass tool (Massing & Site tab, Conceptual Mass panel). You can adjust the type assigned to any of the walls, roofs or floors. Apply materials, add doors and windows, and apply mullions and panels to the curtain system. Also feel free to duplicate the curtain system type and make a new type with different grid spacing. These are just suggestions. The specific steps are left to you as an additional exercise.

If you want to modify the massing form, return to the conceptual mass. It should still be open, but if you closed it, you could reopen it. Make whatever design modifications you wish. Load the modified version back into your project. When prompted overwrite the existing. If you turned the display of masses off, turn it back on. Then you can select the walls, roofs, floors, mass floors and curtain systems and on the ribbon, click the Update to Face button. In some cases, you may have to recreate one of the items, but most of the time, they will update to the match the modified form.

Feel free to experiment further before continuing.

7. Close all files.

⇨ Saving this file is optional. If you created a form that you wish to use again, please save the file.

DIVIDED SURFACES, PATTERNS, COMPONENTS, POINTS

Once a complex form has been created using the tools described above, it must be rationalized to create a buildable structure. The conceptual mass environment allows us to rationalize complex geometric surfaces through the Divided Surface and Patterning tools. It also provides a tool to apply adaptable components to the surface divisions for further parametric design studies and ease of transition to fabrication. By simplifying complex structures, we also potentially make them less expensive to build. We will study several iterations of a freeform roof structure, all while remaining in the conceptual massing environment.

BUILD A FREEFORM ROOF SURFACE

In this tutorial, we will create a freeform roof surface, divide the surface, apply a pattern, and then create and load a component onto the pat face.

1. In the *Chapter17* folder, open the file named: *Freeform Roof.rfa*.

The file was created from the default *Mass.rft* [*Metric Mass.rft*] template but contains an additional vertical reference plane named "End 1" parallel to the default "Center (Left/Right)" reference plane. The first profile we need has also been begun with a few model lines already in the file. To begin, we will finish the profile at reference plane: End 1 and then copy it to the center reference plane.

2. Select the reference plane named End 1.

    This is the one that has the three lines drawn on it already. Selecting it will make it the active work plane.

Remember, setting the work plane is very important before you begin to draw, or the element you create may be in the wrong location and built at the wrong orientation. The Show button is toggled on the file which will display the current work plane as a helpful reminder. If you like, on the Work Plane panel you can toggle this off if you prefer not to see the work plane highlighted.

3. On the Create tab, on the Draw panel, click the Spline Through Points tool.

    ⇨ Place the first point at the endpoint of the short vertical line.

    ⇨ Place a few points to create a curved shape and snap the last point at the endpoint of the tall vertical line (see Figure 17.37).

    ⇨ On the ribbon, click on the Modify tool or press ESC.

If you are unhappy with your shape, you can select any point and use the move control arrows to shift it. Limit movement within the same plane, so only drag the blue or green arrows. If you move the red arrow, you will shift the point out of plane and make a 3D spline. In some cases, that is desirable, but for this simple example, we will keep it flat on the End 1 reference plane. Notice how selecting points makes them the work plane, so be sure to press ESC when you are done and then reselect the End 1 reference plane to reset it as the work plane.

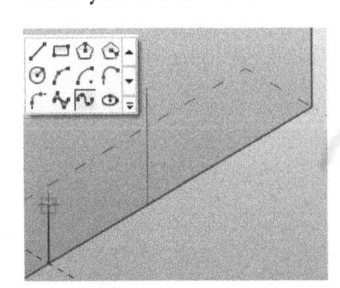

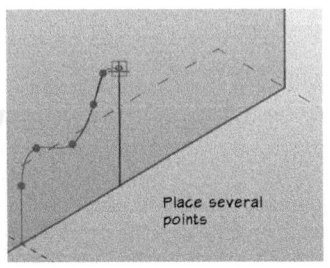

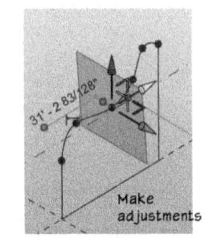

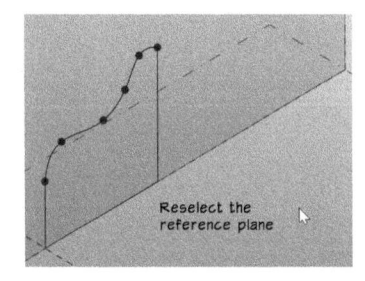

FIGURE 17.37 *Draw a spline through points to close the shape*

738 | Chapter 17

> **DRIVING POINTS:**
>
> The Spline Through Points tool allows you to place points in 3D space. The points then "drive" the shape of the resulting spline. The points you place are considered "Driving Points" because when you adjust their location using the arrow controls (or any other movement), the spline will conform to the modified point location. The points "drive" the shape of the spline. You can even delete some of the points if necessary. The spline will adjust accordingly. To add new points to the spline is a little trickier. If you want to add one to the ends, simply place a new reference point near either end, then select both the new point and the spline. On the Draw panel, click the Spline Through Points button. This will update the spline to pass through the new point. If you want the new point in the middle of the spline somewhere, you first need to dissolve the existing spline (select the spline, and then click the Dissolve button). Then add your new point(s) where you want them. Select all the points and click the Spline Through Points icon. A new spline will be passed through all the points.

4. Select the spline (only the curve, not the points) and then hold the CTRL key and add the three straight lines (4 total).

> **NOTE:** Notice that selecting the spline does not automatically chain select the other lines. This is because even though we had the reference plane End 1 as the active work plane, the spline through points is actually a 3D element. However, a spline through points is capable of chain selecting other splines that touch it end to end.

⇨ On the Properties palette, check the Is Reference Line check box.

5. Click to select the "Center (Left/Right)" reference plane to make it the active work plane.

⇨ On the Draw panel, click the Reference button and then the Pick Lines icon.

6. Click on the spline, and then on each of the three straight lines (see Figure 17.38).

As you click the lines, a copy of each line will appear on reference plane "Center (Right/Left)."

⇨ On the ribbon, click on the Modify tool or press ESC.

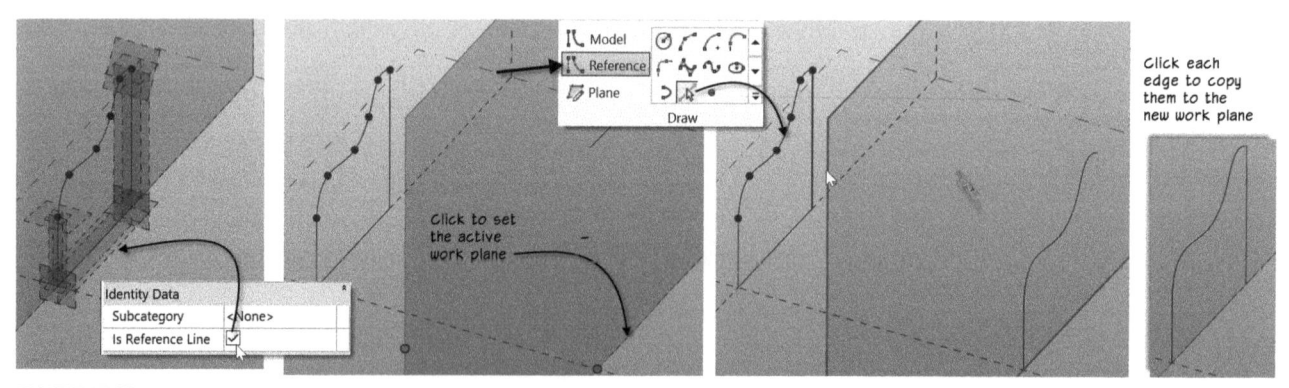

FIGURE 17.38 *Using the pick lines tool make copies of each of the lines*

7. Select all eight lines (two splines and six straight lines) and then click the Create Form button.

8. Select the form and then click the X-Ray button.

As we saw above, this will allow you to see the structure of the form, including the splines, points, and implicit path. Since we used reference lines to create this form, there are not many items revealed by X-Ray, but it is an effective way to halftone the form while we modify it. Let's modify the shape of the form a little.

9. Select the tall vertical reference line on the "Center (Right/Left)" reference plane (use TAB to assist) and with the CTRL key held down, select the spline as well.

⇨ The endpoint shared by these two lines will appear as an open circle. Drag it away from the form to create a slight taper (see Figure 17.39).

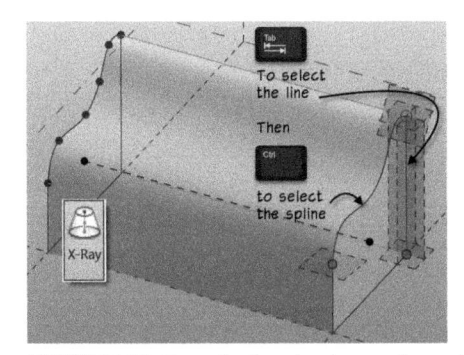

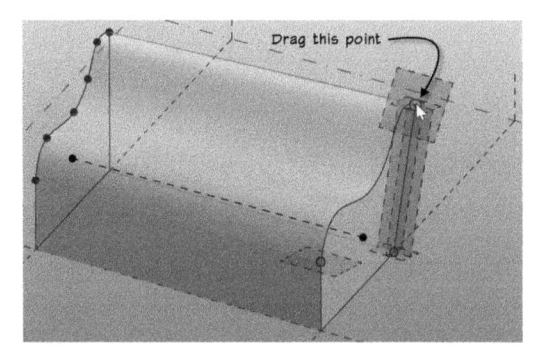

FIGURE 17.39 *Drag the shared endpoint of two edges to modify the form*

You can continue to make modifications to the form if you like. Just be certain that you do not inadvertently open the shape formed by the reference lines at either end. In other words, we started with two closed shapes. When you loft two closed shapes you get a solid form. If you only modify one edge and disjoin the endpoints from one another, it will create an open shape at one end and the 3D form will fail.

10. Select the 3D form and then toggle off the X-Ray mode.

> **NOTE:** We used reference lines here to present an alternative to the forms created previously in this chapter. The same form could have been created with model lines. It is a matter of preference.

APPLYING A DIVIDED SURFACE TO A FORM

Next, we will divide the top surface of the form, pattern it, create a component, and add the component to the panels.

1. Select the top (wavy) face of the form. Use TAB to assist in selection.
2. On the Modify | Form tab, on the Divide panel, click the Divide Surface tool.

This creates a default divided surface. The surface displays as a grid subdivided in the "U" and "V" directions. U and V are used to describe the width and depth of a local coordinate system, in this case, the local coordinate system of the top wavy face.

The spacing of the U and V coordinates can be adjusted in a few ways: on the Options Bar (item 1 in Figure 17.40), on the Properties palette, or by clicking on the coordinate icon located at the center of the divided surface (item 2). Additional modifications such as rotation angle, justification, layout orientation, and offset are accessible on the Properties palette as well (item 3).

740 | Chapter 17

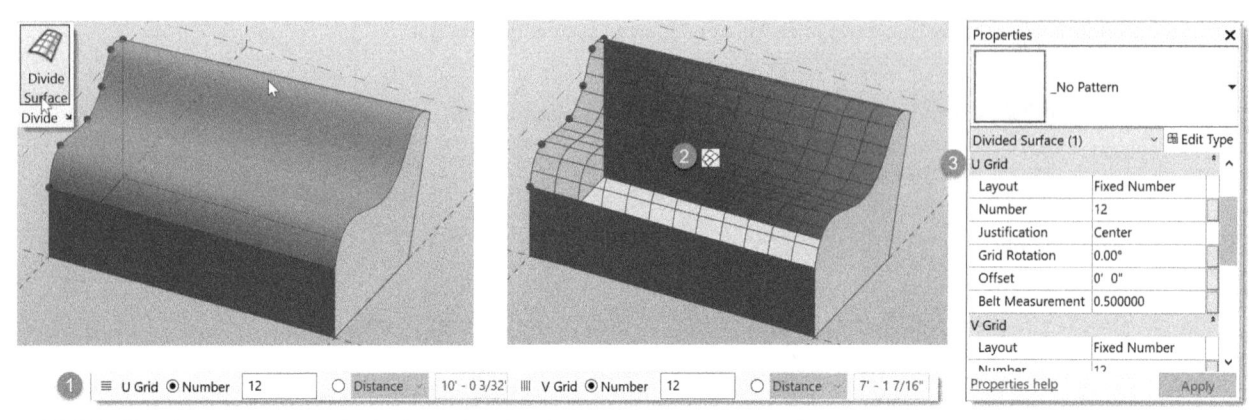

FIGURE 17.40 *Edit the parameters of a divided surface directly, on the Options Bar or on the Properties palette*

3. On the Options Bar or Properties palette, change the U-spacing to: **21** and the V-spacing to: **10**.

For a divided surface, the Type Selector on the Properties palette is used to choose a pattern. By default, no pattern is applied, and the Type Selector simply reads: **_No Pattern**. If you open the Type Selector, you will see several patterns to choose from.

4. From the Type Selector, choose the: **Rectangle Checkerboard** pattern (see the left side of Figure 17.41).

Patterns are system families, and it is not possible to make a new user-defined pattern. However, it is possible to edit an existing pattern. We will do this below. When you apply a pattern to a surface, the divided surface grid will automatically turn off. You can see this on the Modify | Divided Surface tab, on the Surface Representation panel. There are three tools there to control what is displayed for a divided surface. Currently it will show only Pattern. If you want to see the surface and pattern at the same time, click the Surface button. Similarly, if you toggle the Pattern button it will hide the pattern and display only the surface.

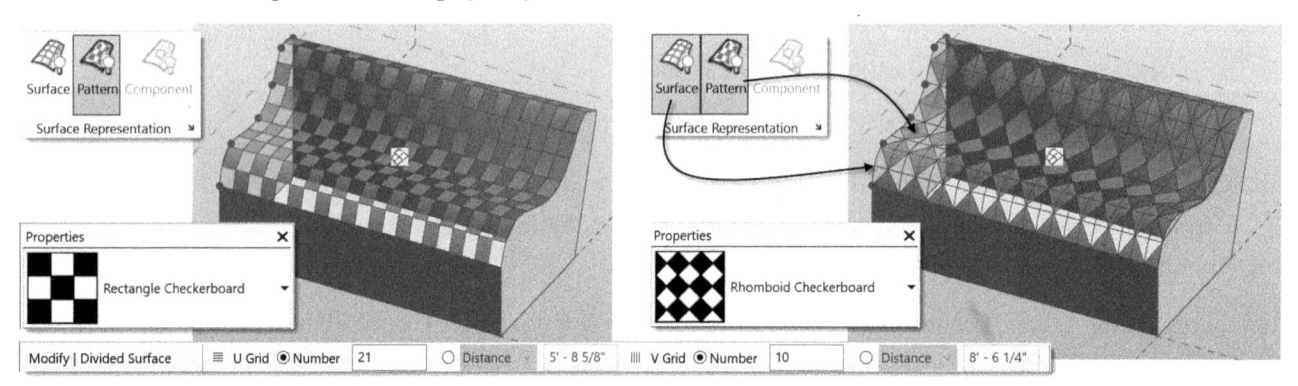

FIGURE 17.41 *Apply a pattern to the surface*

You will see little difference in turning both on with our current Rectangle Checkerboard pattern. This is because the surface lines match the pattern lines exactly. However, if you try a different pattern, it might be easier to understand the difference between surface and pattern. The surface is the actual face of the geometry that is divided with a UV grid. The pattern is applied to this and repeats within the UV grid. With a rectangular grid, you have one pattern per grid, so we see no difference. Let's try a rhomboid pattern instead.

5. From the Type Selector, choose the: **Rhomboid Checkerboard** pattern.

This seems to just rotate the pattern we started with. However, the underlying grid is still rectilinear. Let's turn on the surface display to see this.

⇨ On the Surface Representation panel, click the Surface toggle button (see the right side of Figure 17.41)

• The Aubin Academy •

A grid rectilinear grid will now be superimposed over the rhomboid pattern. Notice that one diamond of the rhomboid takes four squares of the grid.

6. From the Type Selector, choose the: **Rhomboid** pattern.

    ⇨ Toggle the Surface display option back off.

CREATE A PATTERN-BASED CURTAIN PANEL FAMILY

In this sequence, we will create a parameterized component using a predefined family template. This component will be applied to the patterned surface and conform to its shape and pattern.

1. From the File menu, choose: **New > Family**.

    ⇨ Select the *Curtain Panel Pattern Based.rft* [*Metric Curtain Panel Pattern Based.rft*] file and open it.

This family template is a special curtain panel template that has all the tools and capabilities of the conceptual mass environment; it is designed to be used with a patterned surface. We will use this environment to draw a single component that will then load into our surface pattern and it will automatically conform to each "cell" of the pattern. The template file consists of a grid (blue), several points, and reference lines connecting the points.

2. Click near the outer edge of the blue grid onscreen to select it.

    Notice that on Properties palette, you have access to all of the same patterns as you did in the conceptual mass file (see the left side of Figure 17.42).

3. From the Type Selector, choose the: **Rhomboid** pattern (see the left side of Figure 17.42).

    When building a pattern-based curtain panel, you will always want to choose the same pattern that you will be using in the conceptual mass family.

Notice as we saw above that the rhomboid shape is defined using four cells of the grid. This means that when the component is loaded into the conceptual mass model and placed on a patterned surface, a single component will span four cells of the divided surface. This will help you plan your U and V spacing back in your main massing file.

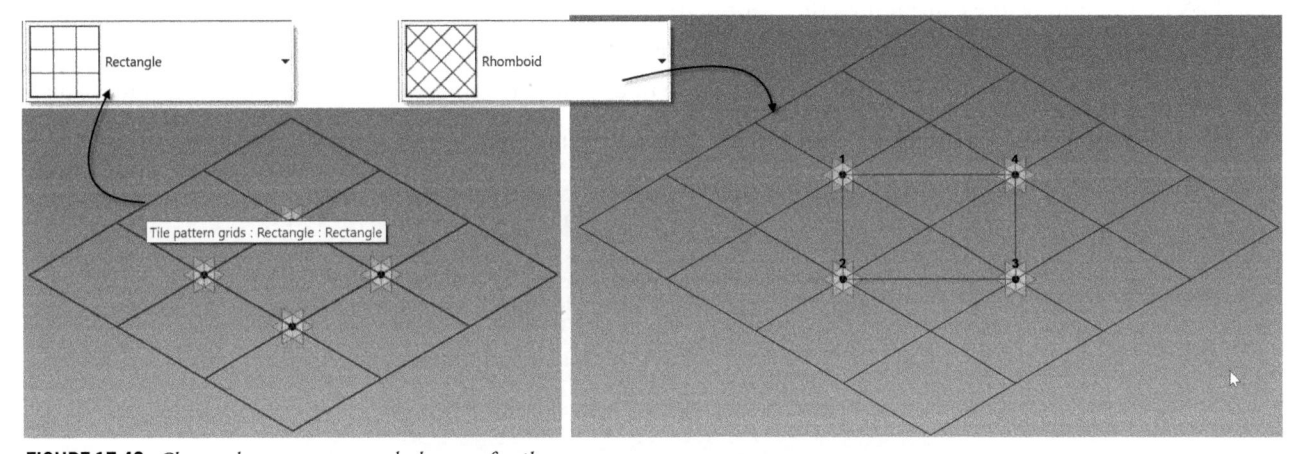

FIGURE 17.42 *Change the pattern to match the mass family*

The points and the green reference lines define how the component will lay out when it is applied to the patterned surface in the mass family file. When you build a pattern-based curtain panel, it is recommended that you create reference-based forms (refer to the "Model-Based and Reference-Based Forms" topic on page 725 above for more information). The reason for this is that as the cells of the pattern change shape in the massing family, the panels must conform to the new shapes. This works best if the panels are reference-based forms. The reference lines in the family template will get us started. But we can add more as needed.

742 | Chapter 17

4. On the ribbon, on the Draw panel, click the Point icon.

⇨ Pre-highlight one of the green reference lines onscreen and then click to place the point directly on the reference line.

⇨ On the ribbon, click on the Modify tool or press ESC.

Notice the relative size of the reference point. It is smaller than the others that were already in the file. Above we discussed "driving" points. The larger points are driving points. They "drive" the shape of attached geometry. The smaller points are "driven points." They are controlled by the geometry to which they are attached. The driven point is hosted by the line and can't be moved off the line.

> **Driven Points**
>
> A driven point is a point whose location is controlled (driven) by the line (or surface) upon which it is placed. If the line or surface moves, then the point will move along with the line. By default, placing a reference point along an existing line or reference line creates a Driven Point. This is like other hosting relationships utilized elsewhere in Revit.

5. Select one of the large (numbered) points and then drag it slightly.

Notice how the two attached reference lines will reshape with the point's new location and that the small hosted point will stay connected to the line.

⇨ Undo the movement of the large numbered point.

6. Select the small hosted reference point and try to drag it off the reference line.

Notice that it will move freely along the length of the reference line but will not move from it. With the reference point still selected look at the Properties palette. Beneath the Dimensions grouping, notice the "Driven by Host" parameter. This is a simple check box. You can easily convert a driven point to a non-driven (free to move) point by deselecting this check box. However, you once you uncheck this, you cannot check it again. So, if you do check it now, be sure to undo before continuing. The "Normalized Curve Parameter" determines where along the line (as a percentage of its total length) a driven point will be. For example, if we change the Normalized Curve Parameter to: 0.5 then the driven reference point will remain located at the midpoint of the line, even if the length of the line changes.

7. Change the "Normalized Curve Parameter" to: **0.5** (see Figure 17.43).

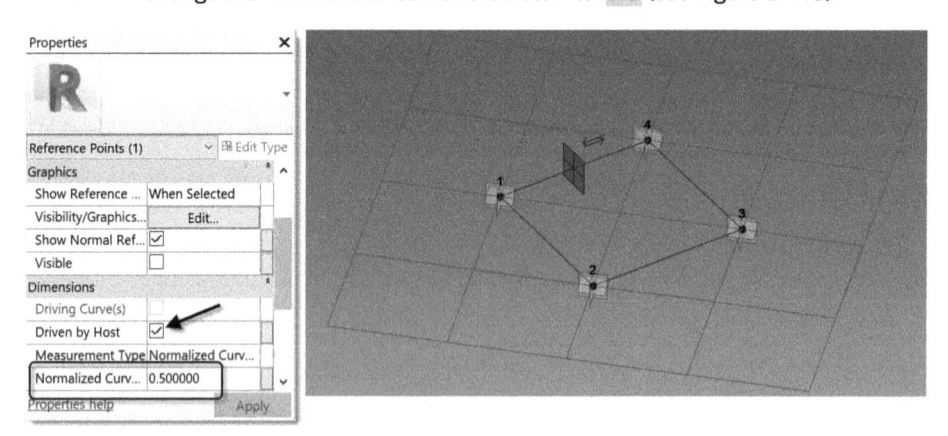

FIGURE 17.43 *On the Properties palette you can control the location of the driven point along the reference line*

⇨ Select one of the points at the corners of the green square and drag it.

Notice how, as the length of the reference line changes, and the driven reference point now remains at its midpoint.

Conceptual Massing | 743

⇨ Undo the change to return to the default diamond shape.

> **BIM Manager Note:** Remember that we are working in the Family Editor. As such, it is also possible to place a labeled dimension between the driven point and the end of the line. This sets up a parametric relationship like the many we explored in Chapter 11. We can also click the small "associate family parameter" buttons in the right column of the Properties palette to assign parameters to any of the values shown. When forms are hosted on one of the work planes of the driven point, the form will react when the parameter is flexed. We have the same potential for constraints and parameters in the conceptual massing environment as we do in the traditional Family Editor: more, in fact, since reference points give us even more opportunities to establish nested relationships.

For now, we will create a simple non-parametric example. If you want to try making a parametric panel family, you can apply the concepts discussed in Chapter 11 to any family you create in the conceptual massing environment.

8. Select the driven reference point (small one) onscreen to make it the active work plane.

9. On the Draw panel, click the Reference tool and then click the Rectangle shape icon.

    Make sure that the Draw on Work Plane button is also selected. If it is not, click it now.

The active work plane is currently the reference point. So, we can draw the rough shape anywhere and then move it into position. It can often be easier to draw off to the side and then move the final shape.

10. Without snapping to any existing geometry, draw a rectangle: **1'-0"** [**300**] tall by **4"** [**100**] wide (see the left side of Figure 17.44).

⇨ On the ribbon, click on the Modify tool or press ESC.

11. Select the rectangle onscreen. Using the open circle control at the top corner, drag the corner down: **5"** [**125**].

⇨ Repeat for the bottom corner dragging it up: **5"** [**125**] (see the middle of Figure 17.44).

12. Use the Move tool to center it on the reference point. Snap from the midpoint of the long edge to the reference point (see the right side of Figure 17.44).

If you ended up with model lines, remember that you can select them and check Is Reference Line on the Properties palette. No need to start over.

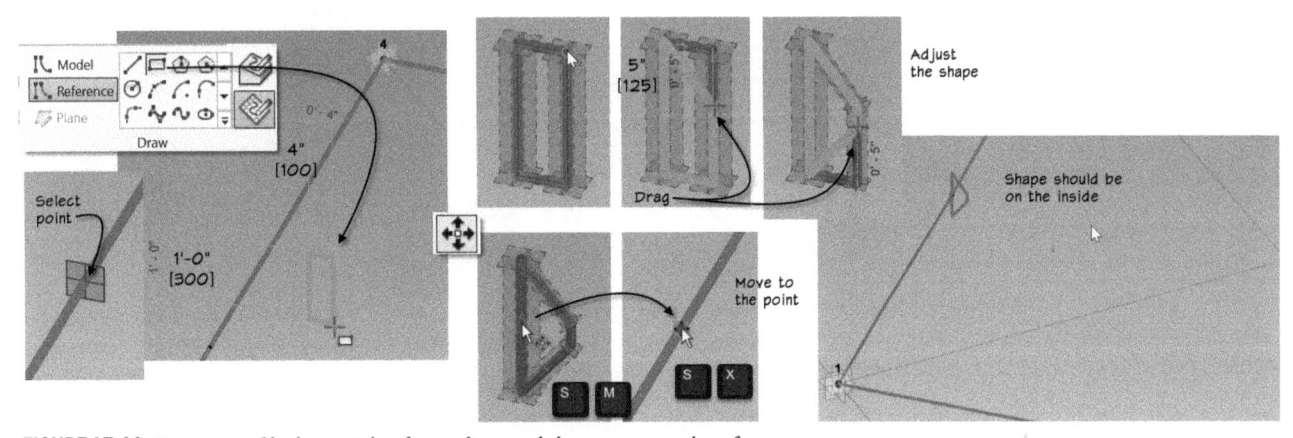

FIGURE 17.44 *Draw a profile shape with reference lines and then move it to the reference point*

13. Select all of the reference lines in the view and then click the Create Form button (see Figure 17.45).

• Revit Essentials for Architecture •

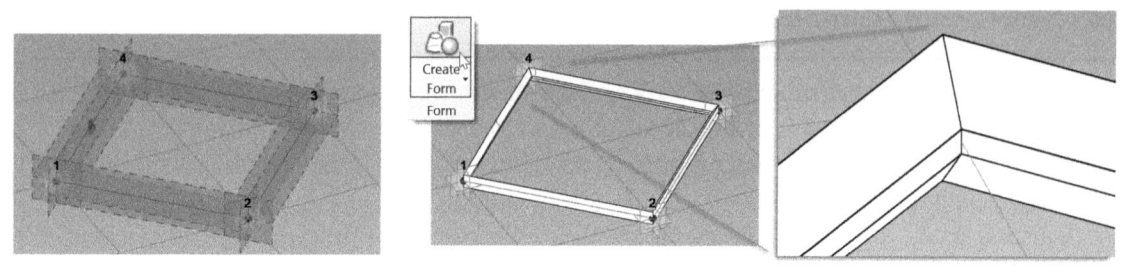

FIGURE 17.45 *Create a form from all of the reference lines; the result will be a sweep*

Once again, in this example we have created a reference-based form. When working in the *Curtain Panel Pattern Based.rft* file, you should always create reference-based forms. Reference-based forms will give you the most predictable and controllable outcome when the curtain panel is loaded into the mass family. Reference-based forms ensure that the panel will conform to (and remained locked to) the reference lines which in turn conform to the shape of the pattern along the UV pattern grid.

14. From the File menu, choose: **Save As** > **Family**.
    ⇨ If necessary, browse to the *Chapter17* folder, name the file: **Roof Panel** and then click Save.
    ⇨ On the ribbon, click the Load Into Project button.

The *Freeform Roof.rfa* conceptual mass family file will come to the front, and the new panel family will now be loaded in this file.

APPLY THE CUSTOM FAMILY PANEL

Unlike other families, loading a pattern-based curtain panel will not trigger the Component tool. We will add it to the surface on the Properties palette.

1. Select the patterned surface onscreen.
   ⇨ From the Type Selector, beneath Rhomboid, choose the: **Roof Panel** type (see Figure 17.46).

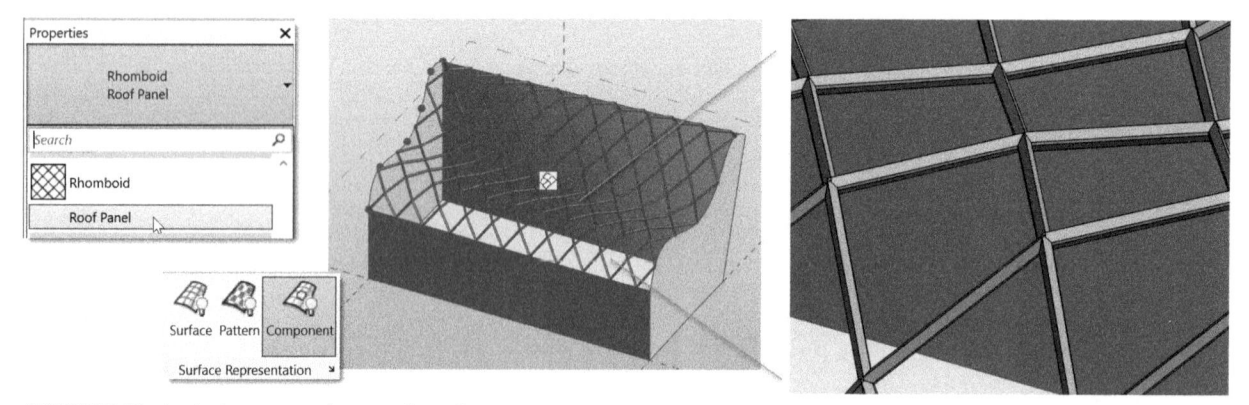

FIGURE 17.46 *Apply the new panel type to the surface pattern*

If you look on the ribbon, you will note that on the Surface Representation panel, the Component tool is the only one active now (see the right side of the figure). Now that we have a component applied to this surface, the pattern and surface representations are automatically hidden. However, the buttons are still available here and you can toggle them on and off as needed.

The loaded curtain panel component begins to define a structure for the glazed roof. You could repeat the procedure and create several panel variations and load them all into the conceptual mass to quickly evaluate several design iterations. You can also update the one we have here to refine the design a bit. For example, let's add some glazing to the panel family and then reload it back into our freeform roof file.

2. The family should still be open. Click its *{3D}* view tab to switch back to it.

3. Select the sweep solid form onscreen.

⇨ On the View Control Bar, click the Temporary Hide/Isolate icon and choose: **Hide Element** from the pop-up.

Notice that all the reference lines are still here without the need for X-Ray. This is one of the advantages of using reference lines instead of model lines.

4. Click to select the chain of reference lines (the original four that the file started with).

⇨ Click the Create Form button.

⇨ From the Intent Stack, choose the simple plane option.

This will give you a simple plane that we can assign to a glass material. If you prefer your glazing to have a thickness, choose the extrusion option from the Intent Stack and set it to a very thin thickness. This can be done easily with the Positive and Negative Offset fields on the Properties palette. If you decide to change from a plane to an extrusion later, you can click the plane and use the arrow controls to extrude it.

5. With the plane still selected, on the Properties palette click in the material field and choose the Glass material.

6. Back in the view window, Reset the Temporary Hide/Isolate.

7. Save the family and then choose: Load into Project again.

⇨ In the "Family Already Exists" dialog, choose the "Overwrite the existing version" option (see Figure 17.47).

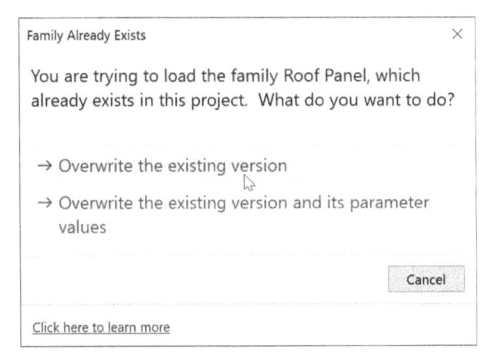

FIGURE 17.47 *Reload the modified panel family*

You can still modify the form using any of the form modification tools discussed in this chapter and the pattern and component will update to conform to the new surface. You can also change the properties of the divided surface including the U and V spacing, the rotation angle, and mirror, or flip the component on the Properties palette.

CREATE A PANEL FOR THE EDGE CONDITION

The edges of divided surfaces can sometimes be problematic. To help remedy this, we can use custom curtain panels to "stitch up" the borders of a divided surface. We will explore a very simple application of the feature to create a more acceptable edge condition.

1. Switch back to the *Roof Panel* family once again.

⇨ From the File menu, choose Save As > Family.

⇨ Name the new family: **Roof Panel - Edges**.

746 | Chapter 17

The process of stitching up the edges involves a few tricks. First, you must create a custom panel for use at the edges and corners. In our case, a triangular shape should do nicely. Next, we must eliminate all the partial panels that Revit added automatically at the edges. Revit does an admirable job of trying to adapt the panels to the irregular shaped portions of the pattern like the edges, but we'll still need to eliminate them and add a custom triangular panel manually. Finally, each of the points in the family template is numbered. If we drag the panel from the Project Browser into the canvas area, we can manually place the panel and "stitch" the points in numerical order to place them. In this way, we can apply a panel to each edge condition that requires it in the precise way that the design calls for. Before we can explore all of this, we need to build a new panel. Fortunately, we can reuse some of what we already have.

   2.   Select the blue grid by its edge.

   ⇨   From the Type Selector, choose the: **Triangle (Flat)** pattern.

A warning will appear alerting us that Revit is unable to create the form elements. There are only two options: cancel and delete elements. Normally we would not want to delete elements, but the good thing is that our carefully created reference planes will be preserved. So, recreating the geometry will be easy.

   ⇨   In the warning dialog, click the Delete Instance(s) button.

The grid, reference lines, and points will adjust accordingly. Our manually drawn reference lines will remain, but our hosted reference point has been deleted. Let's recreate it.

   3.   On the Draw panel, click the Reference Point icon and click on a reference line that runs perpendicular to the profile shape. (Parallel to the original edge that hosted a point) (see the left side of Figure 17.48).

        Make sure the point is hosted to the main reference lines in the file, not our profile shape.

   ⇨   On the ribbon, click on the Modify tool or press ESC.

   4.   Select the profile shape that we drew above. The whole chain should select with a single click.

   ⇨   On the Options Bar, click the Host drop down and choose: **Pick**.

        This lets us reestablish the host of these lines.

   ⇨   Select the point we just created (see the middle of Figure 17.48).

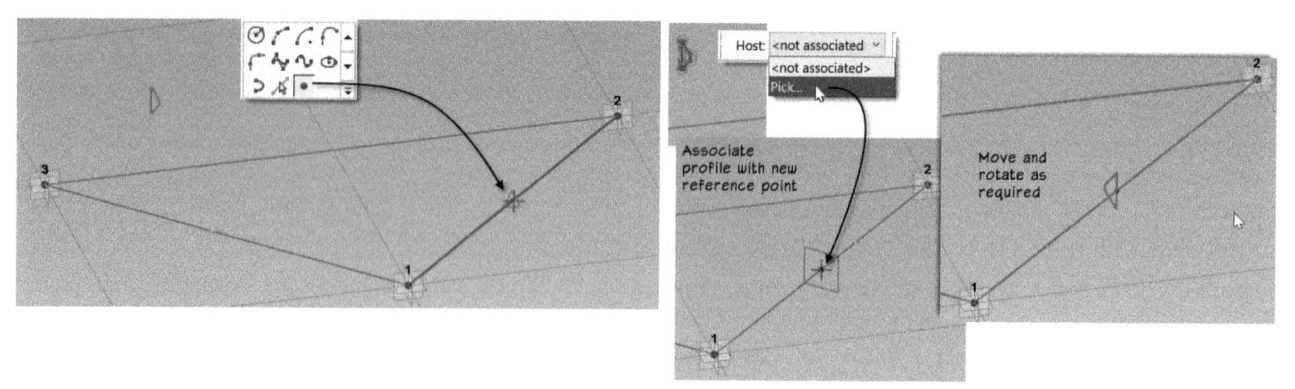

FIGURE 17.48 *Add a new hosted point and rehost profile to it*

   5.   Select the hosted reference point and then drag it along the reference line.

        Notice that the profile moves with it. This confirms that it is now correctly hosted.

   ⇨   On the Properties palette, change the Normalized Curve Parameter to: **0.5**.

   6.   Select the profile chain again and move it to the point as we did above. If necessary, rotate it so that it points to the inside of the triangle.

We have now reestablished all the proper hosting relationships and can recreate our geometry.

Before doing so, let's look a little closer at the main reference points in the file that came with the template. In this file we now have three. There were previously four. Notice, when you pre-highlight and select them, that they are referred to as: Adaptive Points. Notice also that they are numbered. This will be important below when we perform the stitching process. Keep this in mind and make a mental note of the sequence of the numbering.

> Repeat the procedure covered above to recreate the panel geometry.

7. Select the large triangle and the profile shape and create form for the frame geometry.

⇨ Select only the large triangle and create either a thin extrusion or a simple plane for the glass. Assign the glass material to it as we did above.

8. On the ribbon, click the Load into Project and Close button. Save when prompted.

STITCHING BORDERS OF THE DIVIDED SURFACE

You should now be back in the *Freeform Roof* file. We now have our custom panel for the edges and are ready to begin the "stitching" process. The first thing we want to do is remove the partial panels created by default. Then we add the new triangular panel manually to each location where it is required. We can adjust some display settings to make this process easier.

1. Select the divided surface onscreen.

⇨ On the Properties palette, set the Border Tile option to: **Empty**.

The default option was: Partial, which did a pretty nice job in this case, but in cases where you are not satisfied with the partial result, you cannot modify how Revit makes the partial tiles. Therefore, we are setting it to empty. Overhanging would create a full tile that extends past the edges and would almost never be desirable.

2. On the Project Browser, expand the *Families* branch and then expand the *Curtain Panels* branch.

⇨ Expand: *Roof Panel - Edges*.

Like other families, if you do not create any types in the family, Revit will automatically create a single type using the same name. Having both the family and type the same name might be confusing.

3. Right-click the type (indented beneath the *Roof Panel - Edge* family) and choose: **Rename**.

⇨ Name it: **Triangular Edge**.

4. Drag the newly renamed Triangular Edge type and drop it in the canvas area.

The panel will be attached to your cursor at point number 1. Recall that we took note of the numbers above. Using object snaps, click where you want point 1, then point 2, and finally point 3 (see Figure 17.49).

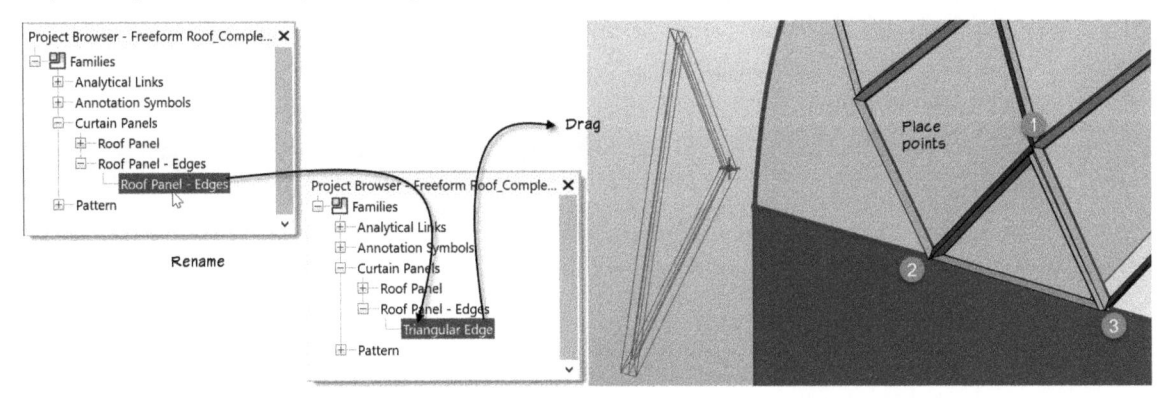

FIGURE 17.49 *When you drag a panel from Project Browser, you can place the points in order*

748 | Chapter 17

If you zoom in and look carefully, you will notice that it is difficult to get the points to snap to the precise locations required. To make it easier to place the edge panels, we can temporarily hide the other panels.

5. Delete the triangular panel you just placed.

6. Select the free-form surface.

⇨ On the ribbon, on the Surface Representation panel, click the Component toggle button (this turns off the components).

⇨ Then click both the Surface and Pattern toggle buttons (this toggles the surface and grid pattern back on).

7. On the Surface Representation panel itself, click the "Display Properties" dialog launcher icon.

⇨ On the Surface tab, check the Nodes check box and then click OK (see the left side of Figure 17.50).

8. Repeat the drag and drop process from the Project Browser and place a triangular panel at the edge.

   Revit will easily snap to the nodes now displayed.

9. Add a second panel right next to the first one and then cancel the command (see the right side of Figure 17.50).

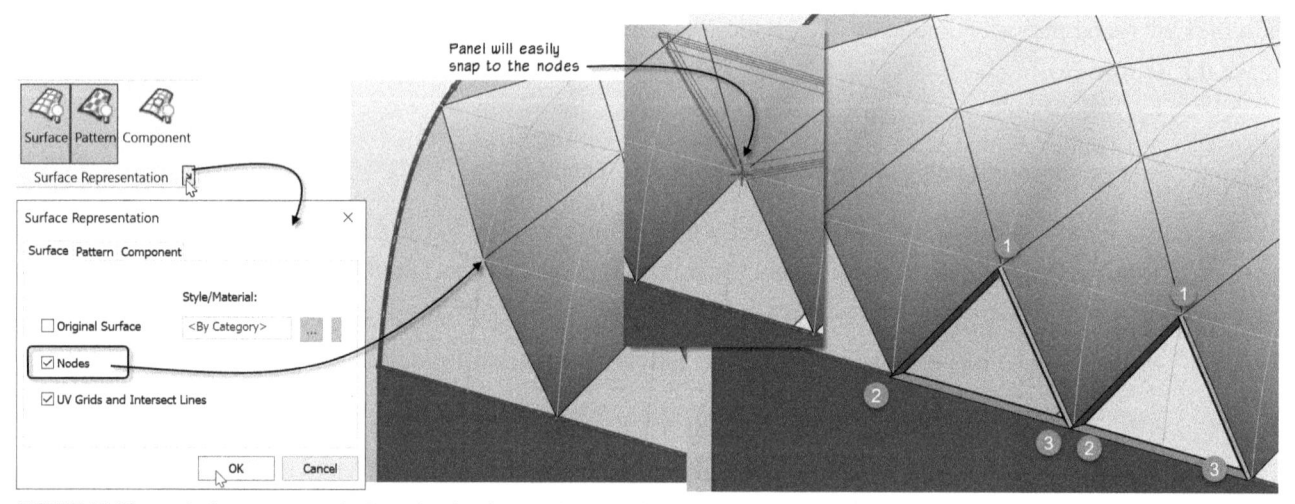

FIGURE 17.50 *With the component display off and nodes on, placement becomes much easier. Place two panels*

10. Using the CTRL key, select both panels.

⇨ On the Modify panel, click the Repeat icon (see Figure 17.51).

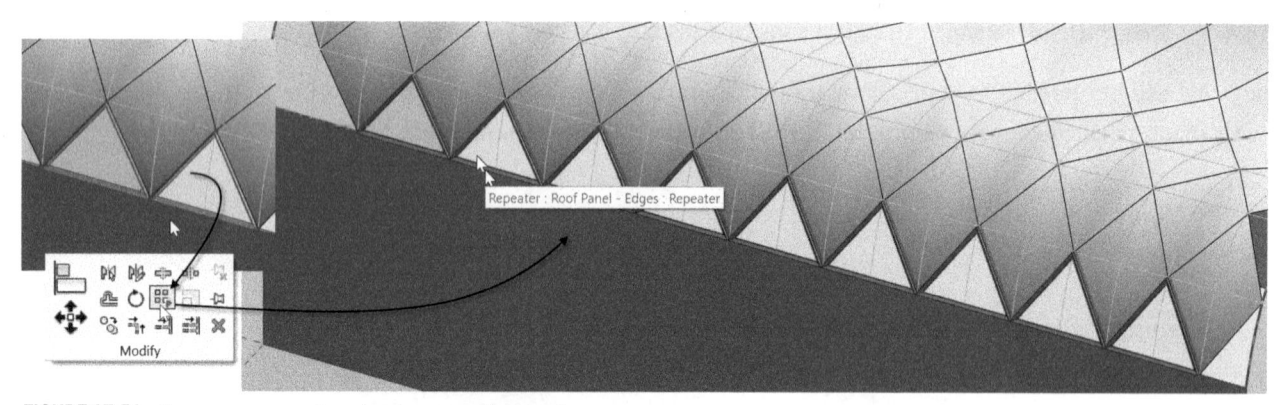

FIGURE 17.51 *Repeaters can speed up the placement of manual components*

You will have to do two manual panels on each of the four edges and then click repeat. But this is still much quicker than placing all the edge components manually. If you get unexpected results with the repeater, it probably means that you did not snap to the nodes when placing the components. Snapping all three points to the nodes is critical to having the repeater work successfully. An easy way to help ensure that you snap only to nodes is to select the surface and use the Temporary Hide/Isolate tool to isolate the element. Once you have applied repeaters on all four edges, you must also do the corners manually as well.

11. When you have added all the edge panels, toggle the Component display back on and the Surface and Pattern off to see the result.

USING INTERSECTS FOR DIVIDED SURFACES

When you divide a surface, Revit calculates the direction of the U and V grids. The automatic orientation is not always ideal. With the Intersects tool, we can have the grid lines coincide with Levels and reference planes.

1. Select the end wall at the Center (Left/Right) reference plane. (You will have to TAB a few times).

    ⇨ On the ribbon, click the Divide Surface tool.

    Notice that the gird is at an odd angle.

2. Following the process covered in the "Create a New File and Add Levels" topic on page 728 above, add four levels each: **12'-0"** [**3600**] apart (you will have five levels total when done).

3. Select the divided surface and then on the UV Grids and Intersects panel, click the Intersects List button.

    ⇨ Check all the Levels and then click OK.

4. On the ribbon, turn off the U Grid (see Figure 17.52).

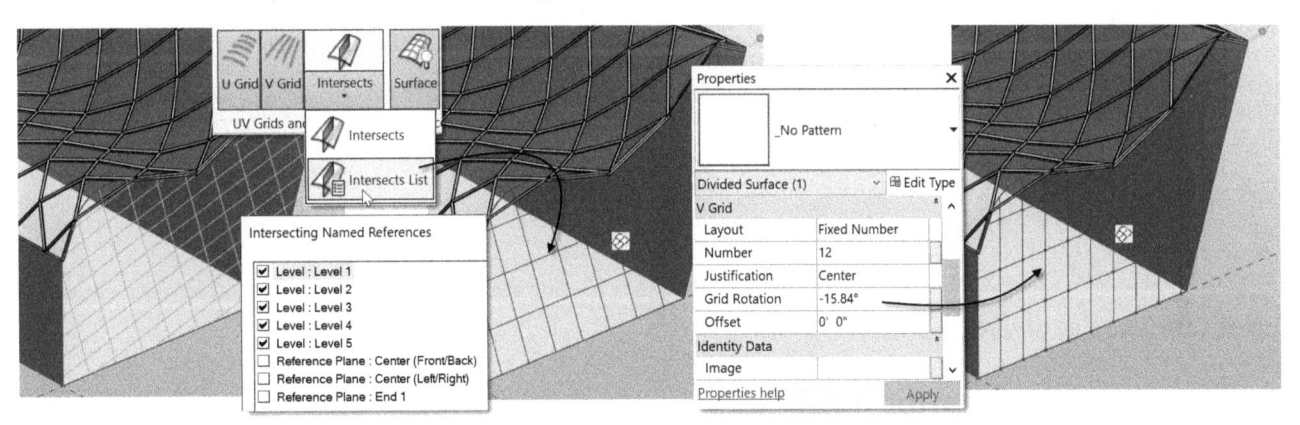

FIGURE 17.52 *Turn on intersects with levels and turn off the U Grid*

This solves the horizontal grids. But notice that the vertical ones (V Grid) are still rotated. You can add some reference planes and repeat the Intersects approach, or you can rotate the V Grid on the Properties palette. To figure out how much to rotate, open an elevation view like the *East* elevation. There you can measure the angle of the V Grid. Unfortunately, the dimension tool will not see the grid directly. So, repeat the procedure from above to turn on the nodes for this grid. Then draw a line that snaps to two node points along the V Grid. Then measure this angle with a dimension. Once you have the desired value, you can input it (or its negative value) into the Grid Rotation parameter on the Properties palette (see the right side of Figure 17.52).

There is much more to explore with divided surfaces. Feel free to continue experimenting in this or any of the other files used in this chapter. Try making more curtain panels and applying them to the new surface if you like. When you get a design to a point where you are ready to incorporate it into a project, you can simply load it into a project file like we did above in the "Load a Conceptual Mass family into a Project" topic on page 734. When you toggle off the Show Mass mode, any curtain panels you have in your massing study will continue to display in the project because they are categorized as curtain panels, not masses. Therefore, unlike walls, floors, or roofs, it is not necessary to apply geometry over the divided surface/curtain panel studies. They can be used directly in the project. However, if you wish to edit them, you will have to return to the massing environment and edit them there.

750 | Chapter 17

5. Close all files.

⇨ Saving these files is optional. If you created forms that you wish to use again, please save the file(s).

DIVIDE AND REPEAT

In the previous exercise, we used the repeat feature to repeat our curtain panel along the edges of our divided surface. Repeat can be used on linear paths as well with the equally powerful divide feature. The divide feature works similarly to divided surface except that it divides a line, edge or curve with a series of nodes. In addition to what we have already seen from repeat, the repeat feature allows us to attach a family to the nodes on the divided curve and repeat it at each node. In this short exercise, we'll perform a simple example.

1. Open the file named: *Divide and Repeat.rfa*.
2. Select the spline. On the Modify | Lines tab, click the Divide Path button.

Six small dots will appear equally spaced along the length of the spline. There will also be a small number near the middle. This is the quantity of nodes. You can click on it to edit it like other temporary dimensions.

3. Click in the quantity dimension and change the value to: **10**.

You can also change the quantity and other settings on the Properties palette. For example, you can change the measurement type to a distance instead of an equal quantity. You can add offsets at either end and turn on number labels for each node if you like.

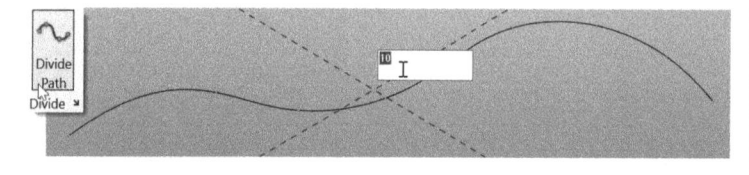

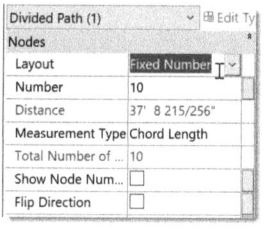

FIGURE 17.53 *Divide the spline into equal nodes*

CREATE A SIMPLE ADAPTIVE COMPONENT

Next, we need a component to repeat on these nodes. In the previous exercise, we used an adaptive family for stitching the edges. Adaptive families have many uses. In this example, we will create a very simple adaptive component family that will repeat along this path.

1. From the File menu, choose: **New > Family**.

⇨ In the "Select Template File" dialog, choose the *Generic Model Adaptive.rft* [*Metric Generic Model Adaptive.rft*] template and then click Open.

Let's create a simple streetlight.

2. On the Create tab, click the Point element tool and click onscreen to place it. The exact location is not important.

⇨ Cancel the command, select the new point, and on the ribbon, click the Make Adaptive button (see Figure 17.54).

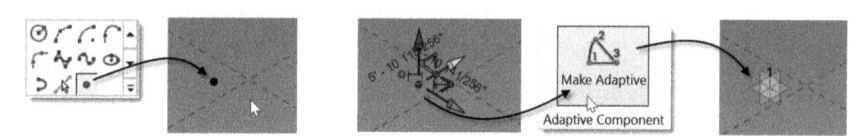

FIGURE 17.54 *Create a new point and make it adaptive*

• The Aubin Academy •

This point will both serve as the work plane for our geometry and be used later to attach this family along the nodes of the divided path.

3. Click the Circle tool.
   ⇨ On the Work Plane panel, click the Set button.
   ⇨ Click the vertical work plane on the adaptive point that runs parallel to the Center (Front/Back) reference plane.
4. Draw a small circle about: **4"** in radius (see Figure 17.55).

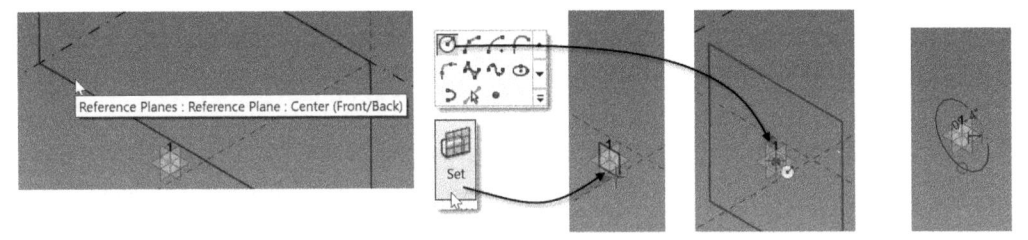

FIGURE 17.55 *Set the active work plane and draw a circle*

If you have trouble drawing the circle or if an error appears, zoom in closer and then try again. The circle will be oriented vertically, when we extrude it, the cylinder will be laying on the ground.

5. Select the circle and then click Create Form. Choose the cylinder option.
   ⇨ Set the length to: **25'-0"** [**7500**]. Make sure it extrudes up and to the right.
6. Set the opposite end of the tall cylinder as the active work plane and then draw a rectangle at the end.
   ⇨ Create form with it to create a box at the end (see Figure 17.56).

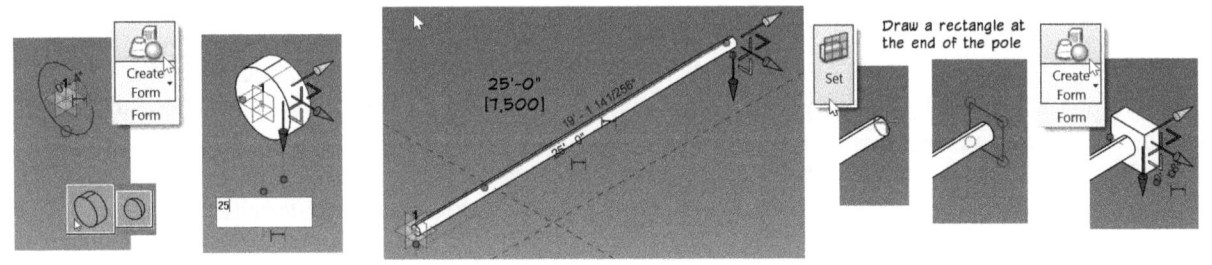

FIGURE 17.56 *Complete the light poll by adding a box to the end*

7. Save the family and give it name such as: **Light Pole**.
   ⇨ Click the Load into Project and Close button.
8. Place it by snapping directly to one of the nodes on the path and then cancel the command (see the left side of Figure 17.57)

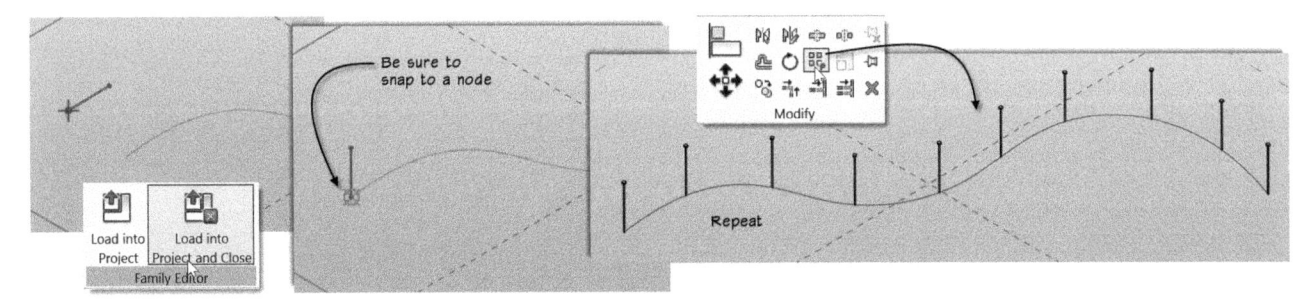

FIGURE 17.57 *Place the component and then repeat it*

   ⇨ Select the instance you just placed and then on the Modify panel, click the Repeat button (see the right side of Figure 17.57).

• Revit Essentials for Architecture •

You will now have an instance of the family at each Node. This is just a simple example. Since we only had one adaptive point, we had to get the orientation just right in the family file (This sometimes requires some trial and error). But in the earlier example above, where we had three points, it is much more flexible since we can determine the exact orientation of the family as we are placing its adaptive points. Also, as we saw above, if you place two or more of them, the repeat pattern will match. For example, if you undo here and place a second light pole on node 3, and then select both and repeat, it will skip every other node. You are encouraged to explore further in this file if you wish before closing.

GOING FURTHER

If you want a "deep dive" into the family editor, check out Paul's other book:

Renaissance Revit: Creating classical architecture with modern software—in this book, join Paul as he goes deep into building complex families in both the traditional and conceptual massing environments. This is done by following a series of tutorials on the creation of fully parametric classical column families. However, the concepts covered apply to a broad range of family content creation. The fully parametric Corinthian column is modeled entirely using the massing environment. The book is available in both black and white and full color editions.

Visit: **paulaubin.com/books** to learn more.

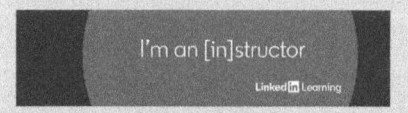

Paul has also authored many video training courses on the LinkedIn Learning platform. Visit: **linkedin-learning.pxf.io/Aubin** and look for: **Revit Architecture: Advanced Modeling** which includes coverage of the massing environment and **Revit: Parametric Curvature in the Family Editor**[†].

There are also several freely downloadable resources at: **paulaubin.com/conferences** as well[‡]. Links on the right-hand side direct you to various topics of past conference papers that are available for free download. As an alternative to the divide and repeat functionality showcased in the last exercise of this chapter, consider using Dynamo. You can find an example by visiting: **paulaubin.com/topics/dynamo** and downloading the session materials for: **Computational BIM Workshop — Dynamo for Revit for Beginners**. One of the examples in that paper illustrates the use of Dynamo to repeat elements along a freeform path. This gives a nice alternative to the approach demonstrated here.

SUMMARY

The lessons in this chapter merely scratch the surface of the possibilities in the Conceptual Massing Environment. The aim of this chapter has been to introduce you to the key concepts and get you acquainted with the possibilities. Please continue to explore and experiment in your own files.

- ☑ In the conceptual massing environment, you can create and edit forms freely while maintaining the level of accuracy needed ultimately to build the forms.

- ☑ The conceptual massing environment allows you to design directly in a 3D view, while making it easy to view and edit levels, reference planes, and work planes directly onscreen.

- ☑ Create forms that emulate extrusions, lofts, revolves, sweeps, blends, and swept blends, and interactively edit the forms in real time using the on-screen arrow controls.

- ☑ Forms can be modified using the add edge and the add profile tools.

- ☑ Forms can be viewed and edited in a new element-specific visual style called "X-Ray mode," which reveals the skeleton profiles and paths of the form, making them readily available for editing.

- ☑ Edit forms using edit profile which mimics sketch mode in many other Revit tools, or use dissolve to return to the original shapes, make modifications, and recreate the 3D forms.

- ☑ Conceptual mass elements can be loaded into a project and have walls, floors, roofs, and curtain systems applied to them using the "By Face" tools.

- ☑ Surfaces (whether planar or non-planar) can easily be rationalized using the divide surface tool, which creates a modifiable UV grid on the surface.

- ☑ Divided surfaces can be further rationalized by applying patterns and loading components onto the surface.

- ☑ Using provided curtain panel pattern based templates provide a guided environment for creating components that can then be loaded into the mass family and placed on the patterned surfaces.

- ☑ Curtain panels can be "stitched" to the edges of divided surfaces by dragging them from the Project Browser into the canvas and placing the points sequentially onscreen.

- ☑ Grids can be applied to divided surfaces using the levels and reference planes.

- ☑ Use the repeat tool to duplicate placed adaptive components in a pattern along surfaces or divided paths.

CHAPTER 18
Rendering and Presentation

INTRODUCTION

Whether you want to create a photorealistic rendering of your model or representational presentation with a freehand feel, there are tools built directly in the Revit software for nearly any kind presentation. You need only maintain a single model for both documentation and visualization purposes. This speeds the process of rendering and visualization because no exporting is required, and you do not have to build and maintain two models. Quick renderings can be created at any point in the design process to help make design decisions and verify that your design intent is being maintained. You can choose between shaded, shadowed and sketchy line presentations. Or you can generate a photorealistic rendering all from same model.

Autodesk® Revit® creates an accurate representation of the lighting conditions (both daylight and artificial) and materials applied to the objects in the 3D view you are rendering. Multiple renderings, presentations or even animated walkthroughs and solar studies can be created as presentation tools to show a client or to aid the design team in understanding the design. Revit LT does have many of the features discussed in this chapter, but it does not have in-product rendering capability. If you are using Revit LT, you will only be able to render in the cloud, but most of the other content in this chapter will apply to Revit LT.

OBJECTIVES

The aim of this chapter is to familiarize you with several visualization tools and the overall rendering process and capabilities native to Revit. We will explore working in 3D views, shading, graphic display options, lighting, materials, and generating renderings and output. At the completion of this chapter you will know how to:

- Set up camera views
- Understand graphical display options
- Configure daylight and artificial lighting
- Work with materials' rendering properties
- Launch the "Render" dialog and create a rendering
- Use cloud rendering

TO RENDER OR NOT TO RENDER

The first question to ask yourself is: "what kind of presentation are you interested in?" If you want a photorealistic rendering, there is a little more setup and a few important considerations. If you do not need or want a photorealistic rendering, you have more options for quick output but to get really good results, you should still be prepared to spend some time setting up the model to achieve the desired results. Most presentation options and settings are accessible from the "Graphic Display Options" dialog. We will also need to look at settings in the "Sun Settings" and "Location, Weather and Site" dialogs. If you are doing a photorealistic rendering, then the "Material Browser" and "Rendering" dialog will be quite important as well. If you want to do a shaded, hidden line or sketchy line display, then you can work from any view. If you want a photorealistic rendering, then you must work in a 3D view. The nice thing is that many of the settings and steps required can support both photorealistic and emotive type outputs.

USING THIRD PARTY TOOLS LIKE ENSCAPE

Another very popular option is the use of third-party tools like Enscape. Enscape is a plugin that works inside of Revit. You must purchase a copy of the software and they do offer a free trial. While we will not explore this tool here, it is a very popular plugin for Revit and allows for real-time photorealistic quality directly in a viewport. This offers a compelling alternative to generating separate standalone renderings and can save quite a bit of time by eliminating the need to click render. However, even if you are using Enscape you will still find value in many of the topics covered in this chapter, like materials and lighting, since Enscape works directly inside of Revit. Furthermore, the Realistic visual style (below) in Revit offers another alternative if you do not have access to Enscape.

OVERALL WORKFLOW FOR PHOTOREALISTIC RENDERINGS

Let's start with a high level overview of the basic steps required for each kind of visualization. First let's outline the steps required for a photorealistic rendering.

Define a 3D view—The "rendering" dialog is only available from three-dimensional views, therefore, creating a 3D view is the first step in the rendering process. Both Isometric and perspective views can be used. If you want to render an elevation, section or plan you can make an orthographic 3D view first, and then change the orientation to match the plan, elevation or section you want. The ViewCube is a handy way to do this. A well-composed 3D view is often the most critical step in creating a good presentation. A nicely composed image is often the difference between a good rendering and a great rendering!

> **NOTE:** Recall that you can right-click on the ViewCube to orient any 3D view to match an existing plan, section, or elevation. Refer to either the "Edit Railings" topic on page 349 in Chapter 8 or the "Create a Working View" topic on page 418 in Chapter 10 for more details.

Assign Materials—Materials are typically assigned to elements directly in the model as part of their family and type settings. Despite this, you may need to make modifications to these default materials or create new materials for use in your project. Materials give both color and texture to your renderings. A large library of predefined materials is included with Revit and many of the other Autodesk products.

Define Lighting—You can define both natural (day lighting) and artificial lighting for your rendering. To use natural light, you indicate the longitude/latitude position of your model and the time of day and time of year. Artificial lights will include information such as their intensity, color, etc. Artificial lighting families can even include/reference photometric IES files provided by the lighting manufacturer to add more realism to the effects created by the light. A photometric

IES file accurately represents the shape and pattern of the light, as well as its intensity and color. A background for the rendering can be included and defined when lighting is defined. The background settings do have impact on the natural lighting calculations done during the rendering process.

Define the Render Settings—The rendering settings include both the quality and size of the output. Both have a direct impact on the time it takes to render your final image. Understanding how the rendering will be used can help you make informed choices about both size and quality of renderings. Revit includes default quality presets to get you started and you can customize them as required. Use the "region" option to define a smaller portion of the view for Revit to render. This will allow you to quickly see a portion of the rendering to determine if your material, lighting and rendering selections are producing the desired results.

Render the Image—Grab a cup of coffee and render the image. Rendering can be a lengthy process depending on many factors. So, plan accordingly and make sure you are satisfied with all your settings before you start the final render. Render a file at night and, if all goes well, when you return to the office in the morning a high-quality rendering will be waiting for you!

Adjust Image—you can make minor adjustments to the rendering even after the rendering process has completed! You can adjust basic exposure of the image as well as shadow intensities and color values. Adjusting can save time because the entire view may not need to be re-rendered if the exposure controls can help you get the results you want.

Save/Export Rendering—Once complete, renderings can either be saved to the project or exported to an external file. Saving a rendering to a project will make it part of the project file. This makes them easy to find, but such renderings can't be modified further in Revit and might increase the size of your project file. Renderings exported to a file can be manipulated further in an image editor such as Photoshop. Furthermore, you can still use a saved image in Revit by inserting it into Revit using the Image tool.

OVERALL WORKFLOW FOR NON-PHOTOREALISTIC RENDERINGS

If you don't need or want a photorealistic rendering, you can generate many other kinds of visualizations. Tools like shading, shadows, ambient shadows, anti-aliasing, sketchy lines and realistic shading are among the many visualization tools that are available to us. Many of the previous steps are still required to some degree.

Define a view—While you are not limited to 3D view for any of the non-rendered outputs, you will still want to create a dedicated view for the purpose of outputting the presentation. This can be a plan, elevation, section, or it certainly can be a 3D view as well.

Materials—Depending on the type of output, materials may or may not be required. Materials determine the colors in shaded views so if you use realistic shading, then materials will also be important.

Lighting—Artificial lights are not considered in shaded views. They do appear in realistic shading if you turn them on. If you enable shadows, daylighting is considered. In non-rendered views we are less concerned with "accurate" photometry and more with conveying a mood and selling the image.

Output—When you are not rendering, you save the steps in the render dialog and more importantly the time waiting for the rendering to complete. This can be a big advantage in favor of opting to not do a photorealistic rendering. Output from such a view can be as simple as printing the view. We can place such views on sheets, and we can export them to image files and save them to the project.

So now that we understand the overall process and steps required, let's dig a little deeper into the procedures involved. We'll begin again with photorealistic rendering in the next several topics.

MODEL PREPARATION

It can sometimes be a challenge to create a single BIM suitable for design, documentation, and rendering. The needs of each of these tasks do have plenty of overlap, but there are unique considerations for each as well. Consider items like moldings and trim. For design and documentation, you might find it suitable to use linework in an elevation view. But such linework would not be available to rendering. If you decide to model these elements instead, it can add overhead to the model that would not always be beneficial to the other needs the model serves.

Despite this however, creating a model that will perform well when rendered typically involves the same considerations you want to make to optimize overall Revit performance. For example, it is important to remember that not everything needs to be modeled in 3D. Consider if the 3D geometry is serving a vital purpose. There may be items that do not need to be displayed in 3D to serve their intended function. Even if you plan to show, count, schedule, and dimension an element in multiple views, it does not necessarily need to contain detailed 3D geometry. A model family can be just as successful relying on symbolic lines in plan and elevation views as it would be using 3D geometry. Sometimes such an approach can offer a nice compromise between modeling and performance. Again, making such decisions when building your model will have a positive impact on the overall performance of your model, not just your renderings, so it is good to get in the habit of thinking this way. Just because something can be modeled in 3D, does not mean it should be modeled in 3D. On the other hand, sometimes to generate acceptable results in a rendered view, you must include it in your model and build it in 3D.

To help decide if something should be modeled in 3D you can ask the following questions:

- Will this item show in a rendering?
- Do you need to check interference or clashes (r 16) for the item in question?
- Will this item need to be shown in more than one view? (Floor plan and section for example).
- Will this item need to be seen large and up close, or is it more likely to appear in the distance?

If you answer yes to any of these questions, then you can probably make a case to model at least the overall form of the object. If you answer no to these questions, then you may want to consider using 2D drafting items to represent the object. Using 2D drafting items for objects when it makes sense can reduce the object and face count of your models, enhancing both rendering performance and overall model performance. In some cases, it can also cut down on the amount of view-specific graphical overrides you may need to apply.

Another model setup consideration to enhance rendering performance is to set up dedicated views specifically for rendering. Having dedicated rendering views offers many advantages. You can control the detail level of the view (Coarse, Medium, or Fine). If the families in the project have been created with multiple levels of detail, then setting to a lower detail level can reduce the geometry in the view even while higher levels of detail are used in other views not being rendered.

You can also turn off the visibility of model categories not needed in the rendering. View templates can be used to quickly apply changes to other rendering views. Refer to the "Editing View Visibility Graphics" topic on page 621 in Chapter 13 for more information on editing the Visibility/Graphics of a view, and refer to the "Create and Apply a View Template" topic on page 334 in Chapter 8 for information on using View Templates.

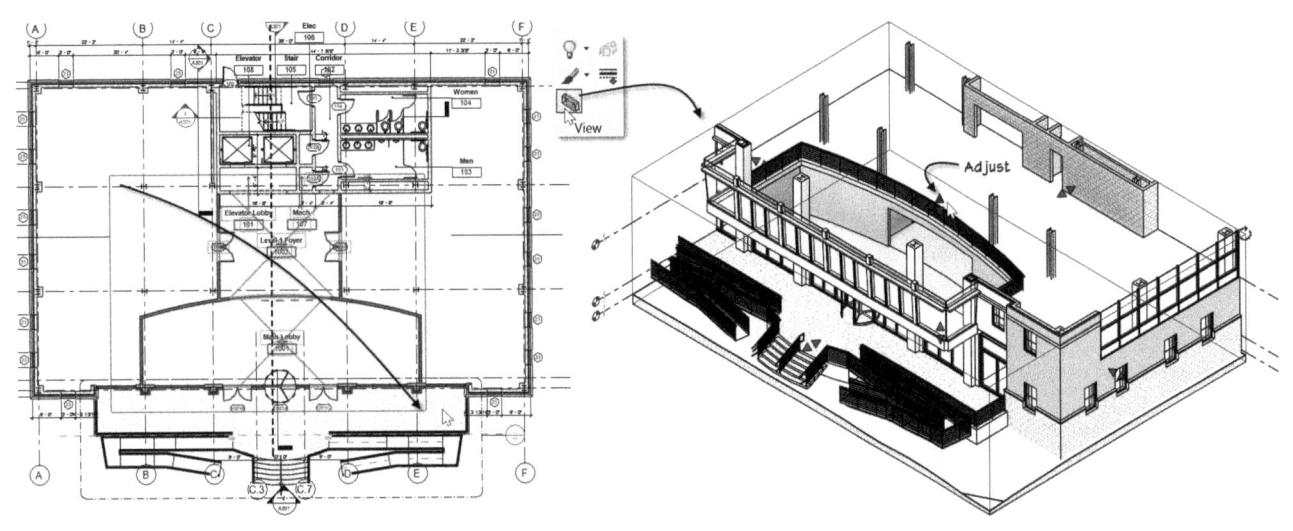

FIGURE 18.1 *Quickly create a section box from a selection*

Another tool you can use to limit geometry in a view is a section box (see Figure 18.1). A section box will limit the extents of the 3D view cropping off portions of the model not required for rendering. This can be especially useful when rendering interior views. The section box can be used to crop out the entire model except the interior space you are rendering. The easiest way to do this is to select the elements you want included in the view, and then on the Modify tab, on the View panel, click the Selection Box tool (BX). The default {3D} view will be cropped to the selection in 3D. You should rename the view descriptively. You can also use the right-click option on the ViewCube to make such a view. We looked at creating cropped 3D views using the ViewCube method in the "Create a Working View" topic on page 418 in Chapter 10. If you create a camera view, you can use the far clipping to crop out portions of the model not seen by the camera.

3D VIEWS AND CAMERAS

A 3D view can either be an isometric view or a camera view which generates a perspective view based on camera placement position and camera target position. We have created several 3D views elsewhere in this book. Refer to the "Viewing the Model in 3D" topic on page 129 in Chapter 4 for an example of creating an isometric view with the Default 3D tool and refer to the "Load the Custom Family Into a Project" topic on page 504 in Chapter 11 for an example of creating a Camera view.

Once you have a 3D view, you can adjust the viewing angle using any of the techniques already covered. Some topics to review include the "View The Model in 3D" topic on page 11 in Chapter 1 and the "View Navigation" topic on page 51 in Chapter 2. Once you have positioned a view the way you like, you can save the view to the Project Browser by right-clicking the Home icon on the ViewCube and choosing: **Save View**. Apply the View Template you made above to the new views. This will allow you to have multiple views of your model that can quickly be accessed and specifically set up and optimized for rendering.

You can create Camera views from any view, but it is easiest to place a camera while in a plan view. When placing a camera, the first click is where the camera will be positioned, or where you would be standing if you imagine yourself taking a picture. You can control the height of the camera position on the Options Bar before you click the point. The height of the target point can also be modified from the Options Bar. The default for both is at eye level (about 5'-6" [1650]), which makes a 2-point perspective. If you vary the height of the points, you can create a 3-point perspective. The positioning of a camera can be changed after it is placed. To do this, open any view but typically a plan works best. On the Project Browser, right-click the Camera view and choose: **Show Camera**. Edit the Camera using the settings on the Properties palette, or the controls on screen. The Steering Wheel on the Navigation Bar (see the "View Navigation" topic on page 51 in Chapter 2) offers many ways to interactively adjust a 3D view directly onscreen.

Isometric views have a scale parameter which determines how big they will be when dragged to a sheet or printed. Camera views use a Crop Size to determine their size. With the Camera view open, click the crop boundary onscreen. On the Modify | Cameras tab, click the Size Crop tool. You can either edit the field of view or maintain the current proportions. The size you indicate will be the size that the view will print (see Figure 18.2). If you use the "Field of view" option, it changes the proportion of the Camera, effectively changing the lens. The grip handles on the edge of the crop region do the same thing. Be careful not to stretch them too far as the view will become a distorted "fisheye" view.

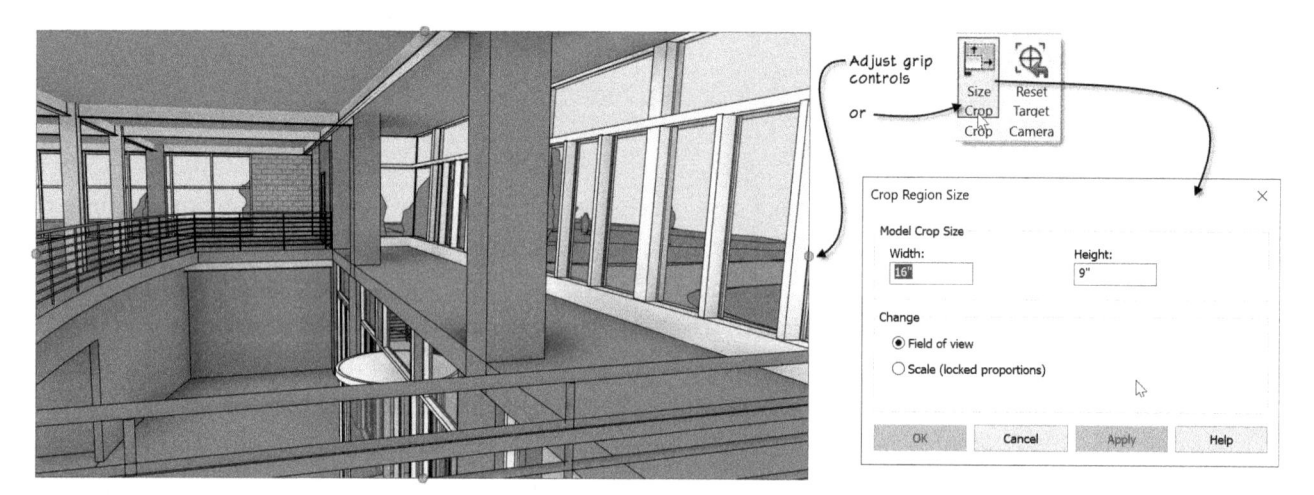

FIGURE 18.2 *Edit the size of the Camera crop*

You can also adjust the focal length onscreen using the Steering Wheel. To do so, open the steering wheel and then right-click or click the small menu icon. Choose: **Increase/Decrease Focal Length**. If you have a perspective/camera view, you can change it to an axonometric/parallel view and vice/versa. To do this, right-click the ViewCube and choose: **Toggle to Parallel-3D View**. This will be: Toggle to Perspective-3D View when starting from a parallel view. Please note that to toggle to a perspective view, you must first enable cropping and make the crop region visible in the parallel view. Finally, you can uncrop a perspective view. When you do this, it will fill the screen and give a more immersive 3D experience. When an uncropped 3D view is active, you can orbit, walk, and fly in the viewport. You can even use standard 3D navigation tools like the arrow keys or the w, a, s and d keys to navigate in fly mode.

MATERIALS

One of the key components to creating a good rendering is the application of convincing materials. Revit like most Autodesk products, ships with the Autodesk Materials library. Material libraries you use and create in one Autodesk product will be easily transferable to other products such as AutoCAD, Inventor and Navisworks. The default library includes a good basic set of architectural materials you can use right away in your projects. The material library can also be modified to create new materials to match your project's specific needs.

There are two types of materials in the "Material Browser" as distinguished by a small yellow triangle in the corner of their thumbnail. Those with the yellow triangle are "older" materials. Those without are "newer" physically based render (PBR) materials. Most modern render engines use physically based materials and they give higher quality results. Therefore, wherever possible, you should use a PBR material for the best result in renderings (see Figure 18.3). We will explore how to choose a PBR material below.

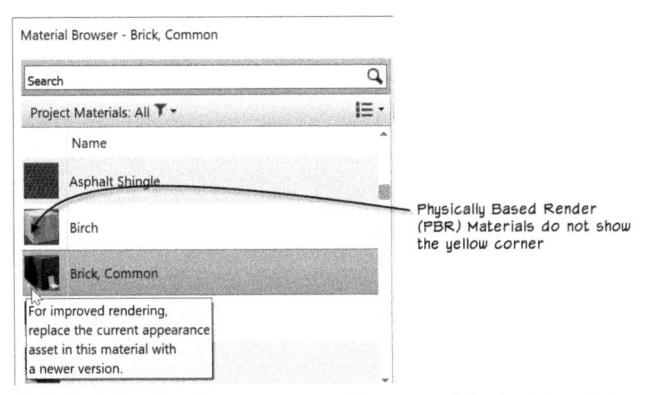

FIGURE 18.3 *Identifying newer and older materials in the Material Browser*

Regardless of the type of material, they are applied to elements in your model as either type or instance parameters. For layered system families such as walls, floors, ceilings, and floors, you apply materials to each individual layer in the assembly at the type level. Loadable component families such as doors, windows, furniture, and equipment can use material parameters either at the type or instance level (see Figure 18.4).

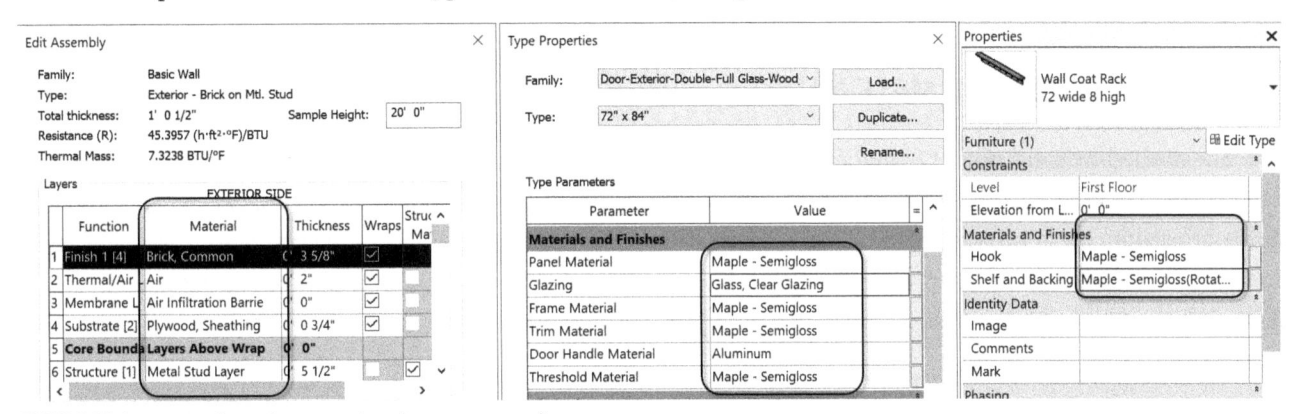

FIGURE 18.4 *Materials can be assigned to element types and/or instances*

Another way materials can be applied to objects is with the Paint tool. Found on the Modify tab, Geometry panel, the Paint tool will allow you to assign any material to a single face of an element. This simply applies an override to the assigned material for just the selected face. This can be useful if one side of a wall has one color of paint and the other side has a different color of paint. Or to apply materials to the edges of elements. In this way, only one wall type need be created, and the Paint (PT) tool used to get the render appearance correct. If the entire face is not the same material, you can first use the Split Face (SF) tool to sketch a shape on the surface and then paint another material (see Figure 18.5). There is also a Remove Paint tool to use when you want to remove the override.

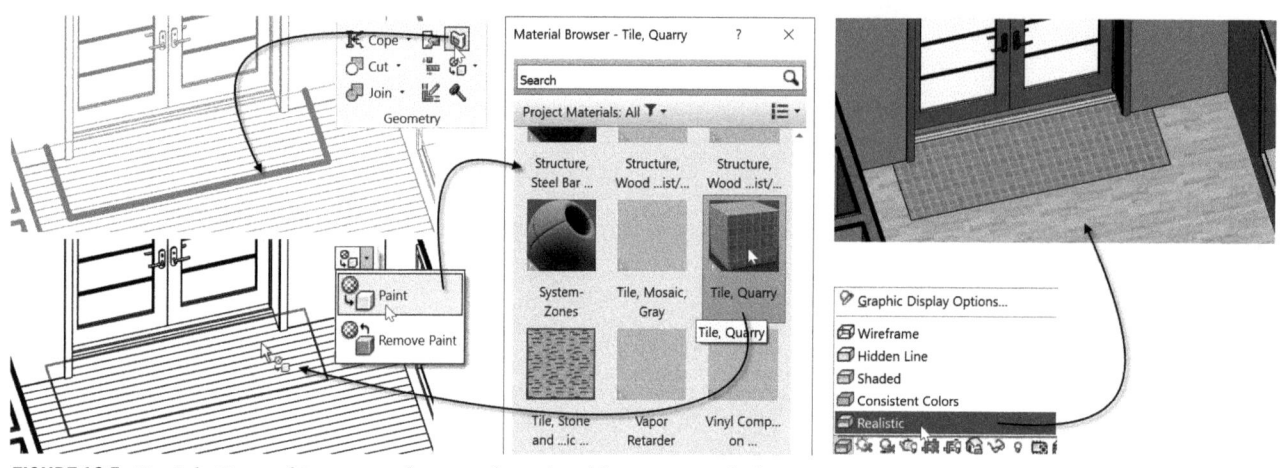

FIGURE 18.5 *Use Split Face and Paint to apply materials to selected faces or areas of a face*

The final way in which materials can be defined is at the category level. When the material assignment is: <By Category> the category level material will be used. This is a less common way to apply materials, but if you choose to do so, use Object Styles on the Manage tab to view and assign category level materials.

CREATING AND EDITING MATERIALS

The out-of-the-box collection of materials shipping with Revit offers a good starting point. However, at some point you will need to modify and/or create some of your own materials. To edit and/or create materials we use the "Material Browser" dialog. It can be accessed from the Manage tab, on the Settings panel. You will also access this dialog when assigning a material to an element. The dialog lists all materials defined in your current project, allows you to browse materials stored in external material library files and provides the interface to create new and edit existing materials.

The "Material Browser" dialog has three main areas. On the left we have the list of materials available in the current document at the top, and in any loaded libraries at the bottom. If you only see the document materials, you can click the small Show/Hide icon near the top middle of the dialog to display the library pane below. On the right side of the dialog is the multi-tabbed material editor. This side of the dialog can also be hidden with the small control at the bottom of the window. It is recommended that you open all the available panes and enlarge the dialog as large as your monitor will allow (see Figure 18.6). The figure calls out the major interface elements of the "Material Browser."

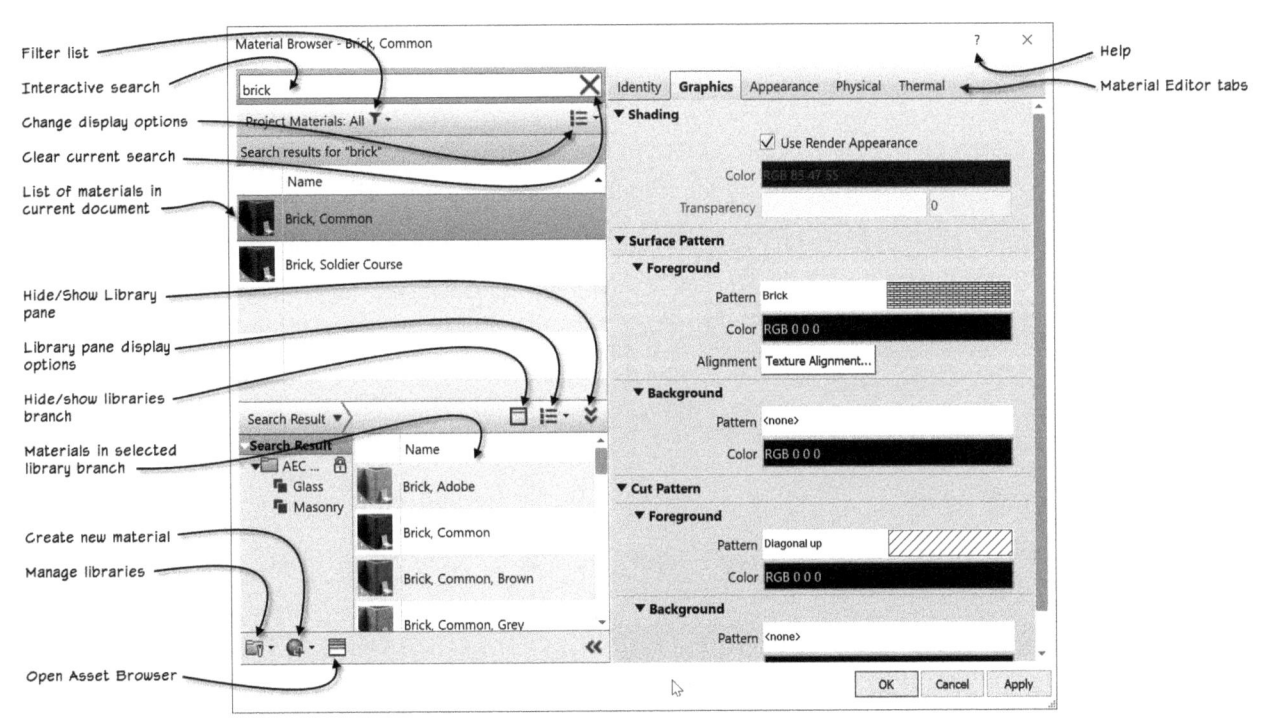

FIGURE 18.6 *The Material Browser and Material Editor*

A material is comprised of a collection of assets. At a minimum, a Revit material must contain Identity, Graphics and Appearance. Each of these occupies a tab in the material editor on the right side of the dialog. The other two tabs: Physical and Thermal are optional. As you explore your list of materials, you will no doubt discover some that do not have these tabs. In such case, a plus (+) icon appears instead where you could add this aspect to the materials. Each tab pertains to an aspect of a material. The identity tab contains information that is useful when tagging and scheduling materials such as model and manufacturer and keynote. Think of it as the "meta data" for materials (the "I" in BIM). The Graphics tab controls the most basic visual settings for non-rendered views like hidden line and shaded views. When you use the Shaded visual style in plans, sections, and 3D views, the shading settings control the color and transparency of the material. Surface patterns appear on the faces of the element when viewed directly in such views. When you cut through a material in plan or section and view it in hidden line or shaded at medium or fine level of detail, you will see the cut pattern.

When the Realistic visual style is used in the view window, or when you render the view, the settings on the Appearance tab will be used instead of graphics. Appearance usually includes a bitmap texture such as bricks or wood grain. There are often other settings specific to the kind of material. Textures can also be created directly in the material editor from "procedural" textures for some classes of materials. A procedural texture is an alternative to a bitmap image and is created mathematically from a series of settings. There are many choices like checker, noise, wood grain and tiles. Many materials will have a second bitmap for a relief or bump map (which can simulate surface texture and roughness) and some (like glass) have transparency, reflectivity and even self-illumination. You can click through several materials in the browser and compare settings to get a sense of what is possible.

The specific settings available on the Appearance tab will vary with the kind of material. If using the older style materials, there are dedicated asset types for masonry, paint, carpet, concrete, water, glass, etc. There is also a "Generic" appearance type which has most of the settings contained in the more specialized ones. If using a PBR material, choices include: Glazing, Layered, Metal, Opaque and Transparent. All types include at least one Image setting. The image most often references an external image file. Image files can be saved in PNG, JPG, TIF and many other standard formats. When image files are used for some part of the material, you can edit the image properties by choosing

764 | Chapter 18

Edit Image or clicking on its name. This includes seeing the path to the image file, (or changing it to a different file if required), offsets, scale, etc. (see Figure 18.7).

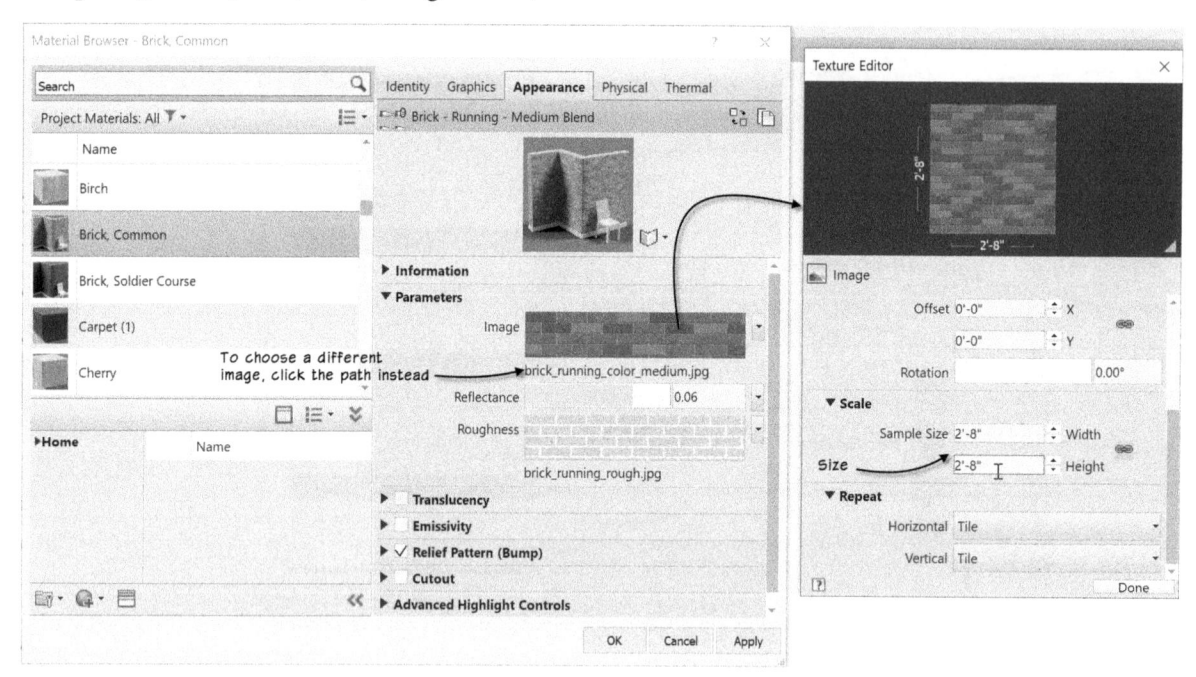

FIGURE 18.7 *Image properties like size, rotation and repeat can be accessed by clicking directly on the image*

Most materials will use image file. If you can obtain an image file of the material you are trying to create you can substitute your image file to get a custom look for the material. The image settings will also include sizing information. You can use this to match the image used for the material to a real world size. For example, if you are creating a custom brick material, and the image file you have is three bricks wide by nine bricks tall, you would set the size to: 2'-0" [600] (assuming a standard sized brick). Images may also be rotated, scaled or shifted with offsets if required.

While it is certainly possible to download custom images from online sources such as product manufacturers or even go out and photograph real materials and use them as images, it can be a lot of work to get image processed and enhanced correctly in order to get satisfactory results. Such work would take place outside of Revit in an image editing program such as Photoshop.

Before you embark on any such work, be sure you familiarize yourself with the vast library of material assets shipped with the product. Using another dialog called the "Asset Browser" we can locate hundreds of high quality appearance assets. There are materials in all categories like masonry, glass, plastic, metal, etc. To use one of the provided assets in your materials, click the small Replace Asset icon at the top right side of the material editor. This will open the "Asset Browser." There you can search for keywords to help you find the material you need. Once you locate one that you want to use, pause your mouse over it and a small replace icon will appear to the right. Click this icon to replace the asset of the currently selected material with the one you have chosen. Like the main Material Browser, the Asset Browser will show the small yellow corner triangle to indicate older style materials (see Figure 18.8). So, if you want to use the latest and highest quality PBR assets available, be sure to look for materials without the yellow corner to replace your appearance asset. Once replaced, the asset is part of your current file and you can edit it if necessary. Edits to the asset in the current file do *not* affect the library. For most common materials like brick, wood, concrete and paint you can find an asset in the Asset browser that is close to what you need and then adjust the color or other minor settings to make it work for your project.

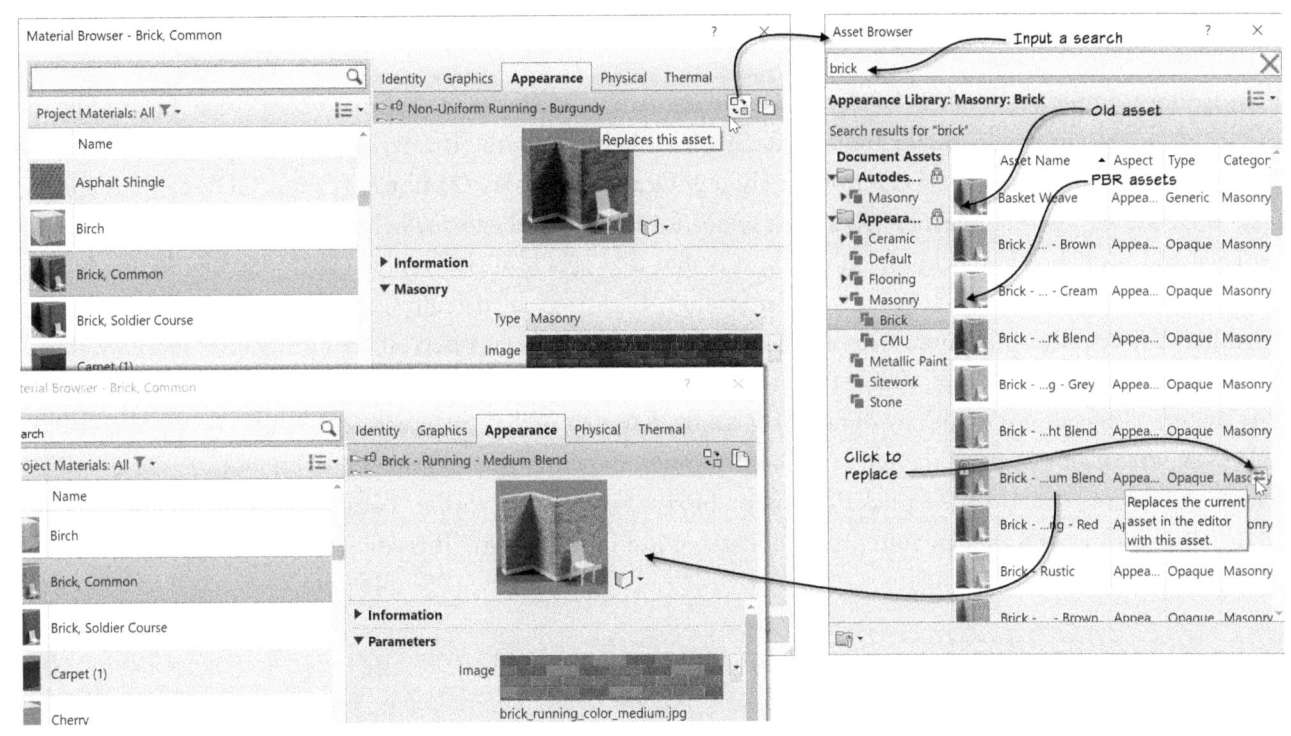

FIGURE 18.8 *Edit or replace assets*

If you are only concerned with how the material displays in your drawings and renderings, the graphics and appearance tabs will give you everything you need. However, we can add Thermal and Physical assets to our materials. Thermal aspects allow materials to report their actual performance values when performing green building analysis. Properties include light transmittance, permeability, reflectivity, and thermal conductivity to name a few. Physical assets can be used by your structural engineer to calculate actual load and strength characteristics of structural materials. If you wish to explore these properties, feel free to open the Asset Browser and explore. However, you might want to create a new material before you begin so that you do not inadvertently change one of your project materials. Starting with the provided library should get you going in most cases. Add custom materials only after you have ruled out the out-of-the-box offerings.

CREATE A PHYSICALLY BASED RENDER MATERIAL

There are two ways that you can ensure that you are using the latest PBR high quality materials. You can start with an existing material, edit it and use the Asset Browser to replace its appearance asset with a PBR material asset. Or you can create a PBR material from scratch. To do this, start with the New Material icon in the "Material Browser." On the Appearance tab, click the "Replace this Asset" icon at the top. In the "Asset Browser" expand the Appearance Library. Then expand: *Miscellaneous > Base Materials*. The five base material templates will appear there. Choose the one that you wish and replace the one currently used by your new materials. Finally, back in the "Material Browser," expand the Information item at the top of the Appearance tab. Rename the asset more descriptively. Proceed to make any changes required by your new material.

LIGHTING

Playing just as important a role in rendering as materials and modeling is the lighting of the scene. Depending on the scene, you might have natural light/daylight, artificial lights, or both. The daylight for a scene is easy to set up. In your 3D view, from the View Control Bar choose: **Graphic Display Options** (or press GD). In the Lighting area, there are six lighting schemes including options for interior and exterior lighting as well as combinations of artificial and sunlight. If you choose one of the schemes that uses sunlight, you can click the Sun Setting button to configure your sun settings. It is labeled: **<In-session, Lighting>** by default. Click it to configure daylight. The "Lighting" Solar Study option uses "over the shoulder" lighting and is not based on your geographic location. If you want to use accurate sun lighting, choose one of the other options such as "Still" (see item 1 see Figure 18.9). Beneath this you can also choose a single day or multi-day study. For each of these, you will set a range of times and will be able to export an animation of the sun as it travels through the times you indicate. Next, choose your geographical location, time, and date (item 2). Click the location browse button to access the "Location Weather and Site" dialog. In this dialog, you can search for your project address or just input the city. This will set your daylighting accurately for your location.

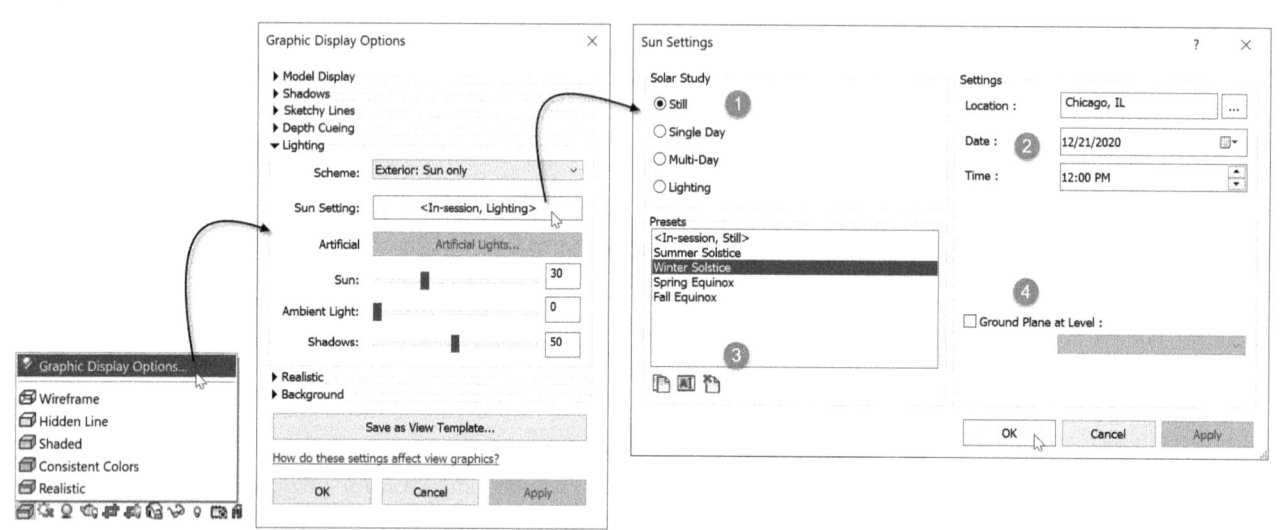

FIGURE 18.9 *Set the position of your project by city, date, and time and choose or create a lighting preset*

Beneath the solar study option, you can select a preset, or use the icons beneath them to duplicate and create new ones. A preset will remember the other settings in the dialog for future use. On the right side, you can uncheck "Ground Plane at Level" if your model has a toposurface. When this is checked, shadows will cast on the plane of the level you select. With it unchecked, they will cast on geometry like your topography instead.

Back in the "Graphic Display Options" dialog in the Shadows area, you can enable the "Cast Shadows" option and optionally the "Show Ambient Shadows" option. Shadows will appear directly in the 3D view and cast accurately based on your sun settings. Ambient Shadows apply a touch of realism to the shading by darkening the edges with a little bit of gradient shading. At the top of the "Graphic Display Options" dialog, the Style drop down list offers the same choices as the pop-up on the View Control Bar. To get a good preview of what the rendering will look like, set the style to: **Realistic**. Finally, at the lower portion of the Lighting area, you can adjust the intensity of the Sun, add Ambient Light and adjust the intensity of the shadows. Make small incremental changes to these settings and click Apply after each one to see the results. Small adjustments can have a big impact on the final result (see Figure 18.10).

Rendering and Presentation | 767

FIGURE 18.10 *Configure the lighting options and test them out with realistic shading in the viewport (Realistic shading with artificial lights shown)*

The final piece of the puzzle when it comes to daylighting is making sure that you have true north oriented correctly. This can be accomplished in any plan view. The *Site* plan is usually the most logical choice. So set true north, you must first use the Properties palette to set the *Site* plan's orientation to: **True North** (see item 1 in Figure 18.11). Then on the Manage tab, on the Project Location tab, choose: **Rotate True North** from the Position drop down button (item 2). This behaves much like the rotate command except that rotation appears to go opposite of what you expect (item 3). This is because north is always pointing up. So, when you finish rotating, it will look as if the building rotated instead of north. However, if you go back to Properties and choose: Project North again, the building will snap back to its previous orientation. And in fact, the shadows in any view (except those set to the "Lighting" scheme) will match the proper orientation of true north.

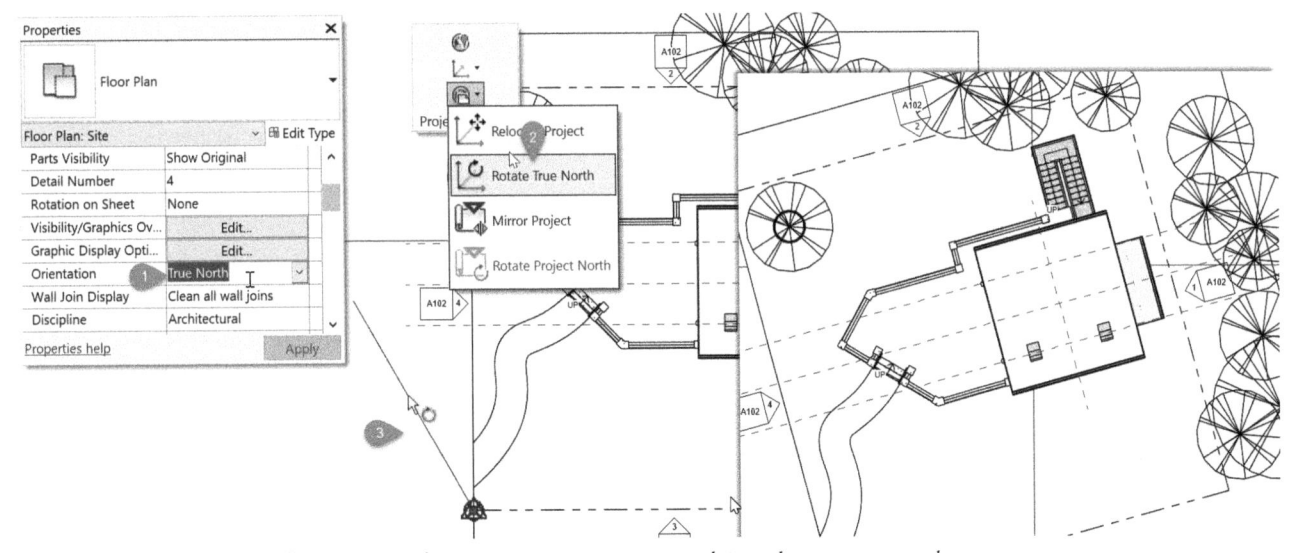

FIGURE 18.11 *If you need to change your north orientation, use rotate true north in a plan set to true north*

• Revit Essentials for Architecture •

SUN PATH

Revit includes a graphical representation of the Sun's position and path across the sky. It can be toggled on in most views using the Sun Path control on the View Control Bar. For a quick tutorial covering its use, refer back to the "Solar Studies" topic on page 34 in Chapter 1. Unfortunately, you cannot use the Sun Path to change the direction of north, so be sure to do that as discussed in the previous topic first. But it does offer an alternative to all the date and time settings the "Sun Settings" dialog. You can change the time and the date simply by dragging the sun icon (see Figure 18.12). If you have shadows turned on, they will update accordingly in real time.

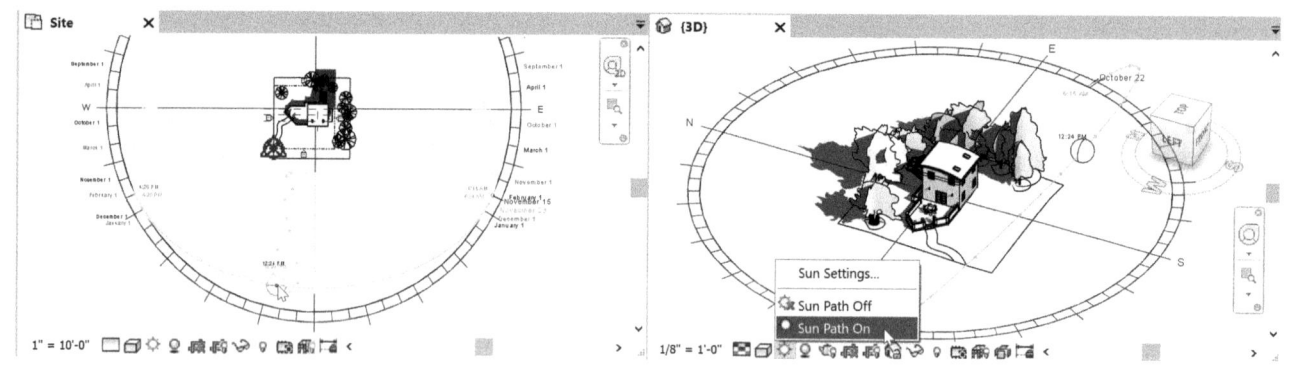

FIGURE 18.12 *Use the View Control Bar to turn on a graphical representation of the Sun Path directly in the view window*

ARTIFICIAL LIGHTING

Artificial lighting for a scene is established by lighting families placed into the project. Lighting families include both the actual geometry of the fixture itself, plus the lighting information required for it to cast light into the scene. There are many lighting families shipped with Revit. We added several from the out-of-the-box content to the third floor of our commercial project in Chapter 14. You can create or open a camera view from that project and render one of the third floor spaces. If it is an exterior space, it will use both the artificial light and sunlight shining in through the windows using the sunlight settings you define. Interior spaces without windows will use the artificial light only.

The out-of-the-box light fixtures have photometric information defined as type parameters of the fixture. This photometric information affects the intensity, color, and other properties of the artificial light source in the rendering. New types can be created, or existing types altered to create different lighting conditions or fixtures to match your needs. Remember that a light fixture family gives you two things: geometry that represents the actual fixture and the lighting information that casts light in the space during rendering or when using the Realistic display mode. Lighting manufacturers sometimes provide Revit families of their fixtures. If you are specifying a fixture, contact the manufacturer to see if they have Revit files available. In many cases, they will at least have IES files available. An IES file (sometimes referred to as a "photometric web file") describes the actual physical and geometric distribution of light from a fixture. Lights that have these files assigned to them can describe lighting conditions much more accurately and any light fixture family can have an IES file embedded within it. When you use such a family as the light source, the accurate geometric distribution of lighting will be generated automatically and used in the rendering. You do not need to perform any special steps to enable it. When using the Realistic shading mode, light fixtures with photometric web (IES) files tend to give better results than those without them. This is true even if you simply replace the light source in the family with a generic IES file. But naturally if you have access to the specific and correct IES file from the manufacturer, that is best.

> **BIM Manager Note:** If your manufacturer does not provide a Revit family, but does have an IES file, you can download it and build your own family file that uses this IES file to cast its light. To do this, choose one of the Lighting Fixture family templates from which to build your family. These templates contain a light source set to generic parameters. You can select this light source, edit its Light Source Definition properties and change it to a Photometric Web distribution. Finally, edit the family types and change the generic Photometric Web File to the IES file you downloaded. Use the techniques covered in Chapter 11 to build the geometric parts of the fixture. If you have a family already that is close to what you need, you can simply save a copy of it and then change its light source to the IES file.

IN-VIEW RENDERING

The Realistic visual style offers a close approximation to an actual rendering. Using Realistic allows you to preview the render materials and lighting quality directly in the viewport. This is nearly real-time and therefore much quicker than rendering. And if you take care in configuring the graphical display options discuss the "Lighting" topic on page 766 above, you might even find the result suitable for your needs and dispense with rendering entirely. Furthermore, you can export the results to an image file if you like. From the File menu, choose: **Export > Images and Animations > Image**. You can export to JPG or PNG and even specify the resolution to create high quality output.

The Realistic visual style can use both sunlight and artificial light. In the "Graphical Display Options" dialog be sure to choose one of the lighting schemes that include artificial lights if you wish to include them. Above in Figure 18.10 is an example using both sunlight and artificial lights. If you want to use artificial only, and if the scene shows the exterior through windows, you will see bright white off in the distance through the windows. If your intention is a nighttime scene, then to correct this, choose: **Gradient** from the Background options and set all three colors quite dark (see Figure 18.13).

FIGURE 18.13 *In a scene with only artificial light, consider darkening the sky with a gradient background*

770 | Chapter 18

RENDER

The model is ready to go, you have composed your view, materials have been applied, and lights have been defined in the model; it is now time to render. The "Render" dialog is available from the View Control Bar and on the View tab (or press RR). Click the "tea kettle" icon to open the "Rendering" dialog and create your first rendering (see Figure 18.14).

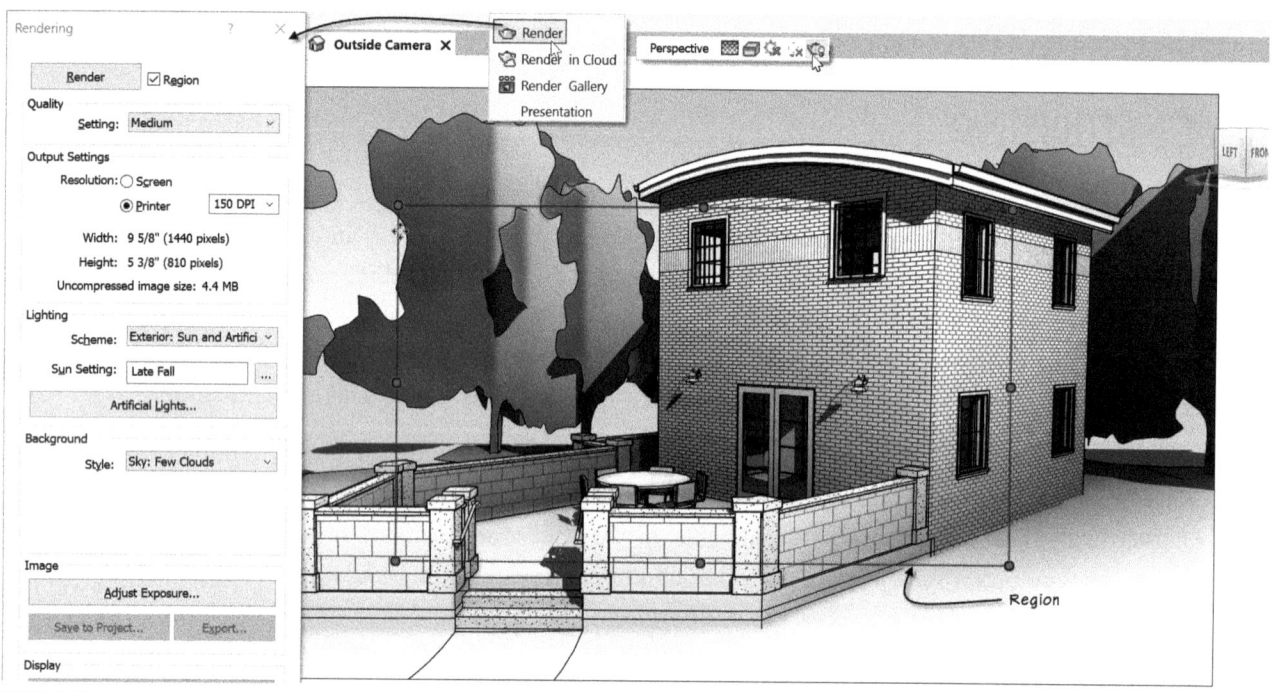

FIGURE 18.14 *Open the "Rendering" dialog, configure settings and render the scene*

Refer to Figure 18.14 for the next several items.

Render—The Render button is right at the top. However, you should configure all your settings first, and then come back and click this when you are ready. Next to Render is the "Region" check box. This is handy when you are doing test renders. You can use the onscreen controls that appear when you check this box to indicate a smaller area to render. With this unchecked, the entire view will render.

Quality—The Quality drop down lists four presets and the option to edit a custom one. The presets allow you to quickly choose a quality for the render without the need to configure the specific rendering settings. This makes achieving results very quick and easy. In general, the lower the quality, the faster the rendering will complete. If you want to run a quick test to see if you have your lights and materials right, choose: **Draft**. If you are ready for the high quality render and have time to wait, you can choose: **Best**. However, in most cases, acceptable results can be achieved with Medium or High in a significantly shorter period. So be sure to experiment and try each setting and compare. In many cases, Best takes significantly longer, but any difference in quality is only slightly noticeable.

Output Settings—Output Settings determine the size of the final rendering. Computer images like digital photos and renderings are measured in pixels. In general, the more pixels in an image, the higher the quality of that image. However, the trade off is increased file size of the rendering and increased time to render. When running test renders you can use Screen resolution for quick results. With the Printer resolution option, you can designate your preferred pixel resolution instead. The default settings range from very small 75 DPI to very large 600 DPI. However, you can type in a custom number in place of any of the default.

Understanding your intended final use of the rendering is important to make the right choice in output settings. If the image will only be seen on a screen such as in a PowerPoint presentation, then Screen resolution can be safely used. If

• The Aubin Academy •

you intend to print the image, then select the Printer option and your desired DPI setting. Remember from the "3D Views And Cameras" topic on page 759 above that the size (in printed units) of the camera view is determined with the Size Crop tool. The DPI setting will determine how many pixels are rendered for each unit in the final image. For example, in Figure 18.2 above, the view was set to 6" [150] wide by 4 1/2" [112] tall. (This size will appear in the "Render" dialog when you choose the Printer option.) If you choose 75 DPI, the final width of the image will be 450 pixels. If you choose 300 DPI it will be 1,800 pixels! (Slightly less for metric) Furthermore, when the height and width are considered, you will realize that doubling the resolution quadruples the total pixels.

At 75 DPI   Width 900 pixels   Height 675 pixels   Total size: 607,500 pixels

At 150 DPI   Width 1,800 pixels   Height 1,350 pixels   Total size: 2,430,000 pixels

In general, for printing, try 150 DPI first. If you are satisfied with the results, you need not render any higher. If you need to increase it, try typing in 200 or 250 next. Just remember that the higher you go, the longer it will take and the larger the file, and you may not be able to notice the difference in the final printed image anyhow. So, in general, use the lowest value you can safely get away with.

Lighting—the settings in this section are the same as we have already discussed above in the "Lighting" topic on page 766. You can configure the settings in the "Graphic Display Options" dialog as we have seen or wait till you get to the "Rendering" dialog and configure them here. Remember to choose one of the six schemes first before configuring other settings. The main difference between the interior and exterior schemes are a different default exposure setting. Despite the default however, the exposure can be adjusted both before and after the rendering is complete if you are not satisfied with the results. Do this with the Adjust Exposure button in the Image area.

If you select an option which includes sunlight, you will be able to modify the sun settings as we did above. Not discussed above was the Artificial Lights button. If artificial lights are part of the lighting selection, this button will be available. Click it to see a list of all the lights in your model. You can turn lights on or off in this dialog by checking or unchecking them. As you select them in the dialog, if they are visible in the current view, they will highlight onscreen. You can also dim lights here by typing in a value between 0 and 1. A value of 1 indicates the light is on and not dimmed; a value of 0 means the light is fully dimmed (off). A value of .5 would shine the light at half intensity.

If you have added many lights, the list could be quite long. To help you manage the list, lights can be grouped. Click the New button to create a new group. Name it descriptively. Next, using the SHIFT and/or CTRL keys, select one or more lights in the list and then click the Move to Group button. Groups can be disabled with a single click, so this makes it easier to manage your lights. For example, if you are rendering a single office space, you would not need to use the lights in the neighboring office spaces. Every light you leave on in the scene takes processing power. It makes no sense to calculate lights in another room. Therefore, you will want to turn off lights that are not in your current rendering whenever possible.

Background—allows you to determine what is seem in the background beyond your model. Choices include several preset sky and cloud options, a solid color , gradient, or even an image file. To do this, choose: **Image** from the Style drop down. In the "Background Image" dialog, click the Image button and locate a suitable image on your hard drive. Keep in mind the orientation of your 3D view, the vantage point, time of day, and lighting. For the image you select to be believable in your final rendering, the perspective and shadows need to match. For the scale settings, you can make the image stretch to fit your rendering size, or leave it set to its original size.

The final option is Transparent. Use this if you plan to composite the image in an image editing program like Photoshop afterwards. Save the image in a format that supports alpha channels like PNG if you use this option.

Image—Click the Adjust Exposure button to edit the overall exposure, highlights, mid tones, and shadows of the rendered image. Settings can be changed prior to rendering or after. If you render first, you can edit the exposure and using the Apply button get immediate feedback on screen. After generating a rendering, the Save to Project and Export buttons will become available. Saved renderings will occupy a new branch on the Project Browser. Export will save them out to the hard drive in your choice of file format.

GENERATE THE RENDERING

Once you have configured all the settings to your liking, click the Render button at the top of the dialog. This will begin processing the results, which, depending on your settings, can take minutes or hours. If you are not certain about the settings you have chosen, start with the Draft setting and remember you can use the Region option to limit the rendering as well.

During the rendering process Revit will display a rendering progress bar. You will see how long the render process has been running and the number of artificial lights in the rendering. Once the rendering has started, you cannot do other work in Revit. So, try to plan your longer render jobs to occur during off hours, such as in the evening after business hours. Or as an alternative, consider using Cloud Rendering instead (see below).

POST-RENDERING EXPOSURE ADJUSTMENT

When the rendered image is complete, if the results are not as expected you can use the Adjust Exposure button. Adjusting here can often get the results you are looking for without the long process of altering lighting and re-rendering the scene. The exposure adjustments can be immediately applied to the scene by pressing the Apply button in the dialog. You can also set your exposure adjustments choices before you render.

Exposure Value is like the F-Stop on a camera. You can make the overall scene darker or lighter by making changes to this setting. The pixels of an image fall into three broad categories: highlights, mid tones, and shadows. Highlights are the brighter sections of the scene. Mid tones are the middle range and shadows are the darkest areas of the image. Adjusting any one of these does not affect the others. This can give you finer control over the image than the exposure value alone would. The white point setting will shift the colors in the scene to a warmer or cooler end of the color spectrum. If images are orange or red in color, you can shift the white point values cooler to get a more balanced appearance. Saturation controls the color intensity of the image. A value of 0 will result in a grayscale image, while 1 is the default. Higher than 1 will make the colors much more intense.

Any changes made to the exposure values will be remembered by the camera for this view unless changes are made in the lighting section. When you are done with the rendered image you can click the Show Model button at the bottom of the dialog to return to normal model display. The button will toggle between Show Model and Show the Rendering. If changes occur in the model they will not be reflected in the rendering. You will have to render again to include them.

CLOUD RENDERING

As previously noted, rendering is often a balancing act between time to render and quality of output. To get high quality renderings, you often must tie up your computer for a great deal of time. This is where Cloud Rendering can be a big help. Cloud rendering is and online service. You can access it from the View tab by clicking the Render in Cloud button. This will prompt you to login into your Autodesk account if you are not already logged in. Then a dialog will display where you can configure your desired settings and generate the rendering (see Figure 18.15). Best of all, after a few moments, the render job will be uploaded to the Autodesk servers and you will be able to continue working in Revit while your rendering is completed in the cloud. You can opt for an email notification when the rendering is complete.

Rendering and Presentation | 773

> **NOTE:** Depending on the settings you choose, your rendering may not be free. Autodesk charges cloud credits to use paid services like Rendering. Higher size and quality typically incurs higher cloud credit costs. Check with your Autodesk reseller for more information on cloud credits and how to acquire them.

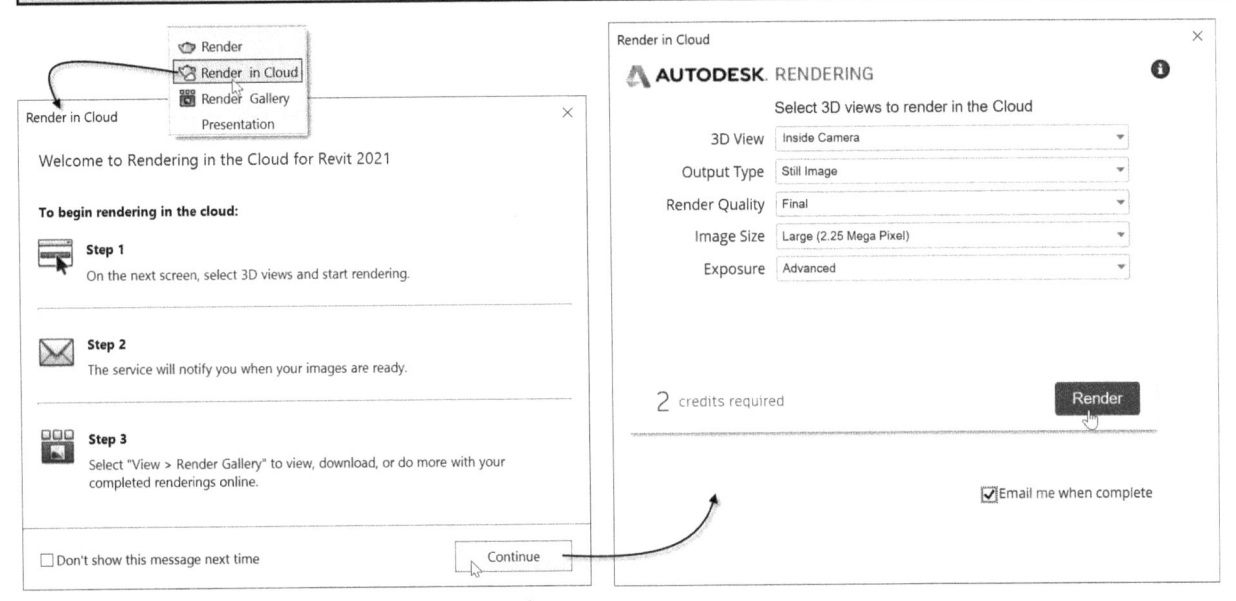

FIGURE 18.15 *Adjust exposure after the rendering is complete*

To view the completed rendering, click the link in the email that you received, or on the Presentation panel, click the Render Gallery button. This will launch your default web browser to the My Renderings page. There you will see all your renderings listed by project. You can see the status of each rendering, download completed renderings as image files and even choose to render the image again without having to upload the file again. In addition to the standard photorealistic rendering, you can create panoramas, solar studies and illuminance renders.

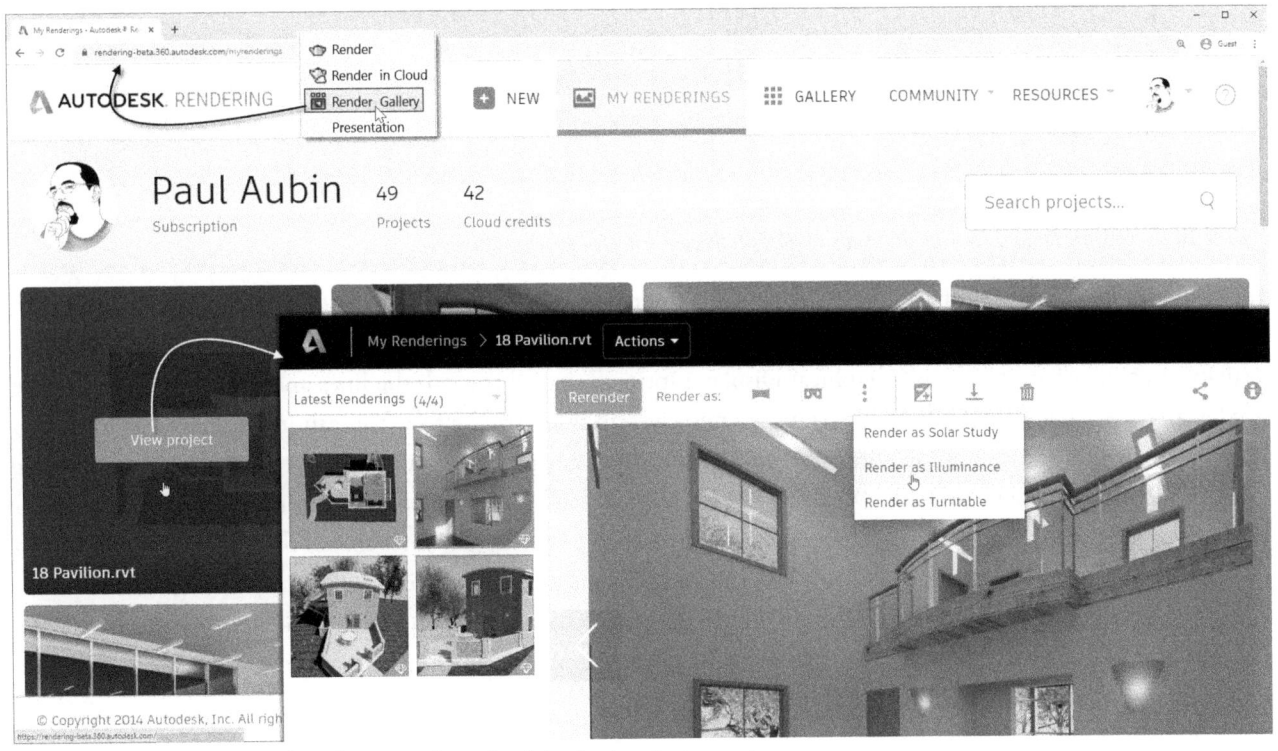

FIGURE 18.16 *Launch the render gallery to see the results of the cloud render in your browser*

• Revit Essentials for Architecture •

NON-RENDERED PRESENTATIONS

In the "Lighting" topic on page 766 above we explored many settings in the "Graphic Display Options" dialog. Many of these are visible directly in the viewport without the need to render! Best of all, these display options can often make very compelling presentations without the need for the time-consuming rendering process. Furthermore, the quality and mood that such presentations can convey gives many nice alternatives to the finality or a finished photorealistic rendering. To explore some of the possibilities, open the "Graphic Display Options" dialog again (GD).

For example, if you look back to Figure 18.10 and Figure 18.13, these images show the model in the Realistic visual style with anti-aliasing, shadows and ambient shadows all turned on. Edges is turned off. As previously noted, the first figure uses daylight and artificial, the second uses artificial only and a gradient background with dark grays for all three colors. If we take the same view and make a few adjustments, we can vary the image in quite a few ways. Figure 18.17 shows just a few examples all using Hidden Line and Consistent Colors.

FIGURE 18.17 *Graphic Display Options give many possibilities for non-rendered presentation views*

The "Smooth line with anti-aliasing" feature removes some of the jagged edges of angled and curved lines onscreen. This setting can be enabled globally in the "Options" dialog (File menu). If it is not enabled globally, then it will be available as a per-view setting in "Graphical Display Options." It will smooth the lines and makes it appear a little less hard edged; removing the "jaggies." Transparency gives an interesting effect. You can input any value from 0 to 100%., which applies to all surfaces in the view. Alternatively, transparency can be applied by category in Visibility/Graphics or even by object override. We discussed shadows already. Both cast shadows (controlled by your daylight settings) and ambient shadows (which applies shading to the view). Sketchy lines makes the edges look more hand drawn. Jitter controls the amount of variation in the lines. Extension is seen at corners making the edges overlap. You can set both values in a range of 1 to 10. Click Apply after each change to see the results and adjust. If you arrive at a collection of settings you like, you can click the Save as View Template button to preserve them in a View Template that can be applied to other views.

The silhouettes feature allows you to choose a line style to be applied at edges of geometry to emphasis them (see Figure 18.18). This is like how you would profile your edges in hand drawings. The effect is applied to system families like walls, floors and roofs. It does not always give exactly what you need on its own, but you can customize the effect using the linework tool. We looked at the linework tool in the "Embellishing Model Views" topic on page 589 in Chapter 12.

FIGURE 18.18 *Silhouettes profiles the edges of geometry in the view*

Like rendering, Graphical Display Options gives many background options as well. Gradient and Sky are similar, but with Sky the colors are automatic, whereas we can custom them with Gradient. For plan and section views, another nice option to consider is the coarse scale fill pattern. This setting must be configured for each wall, floor and roof type. Edit the type properties and then choose a fill pattern and color. This will show when the view is set to coarse. As you can see, there are nearly endless possibilities to explore. Several files are provided in the *Chapter18* folder for you to experiment with. Since units have little impact on any of the items discussed in this chapter, the files are provided in Imperial units only. If you prefer to work in Metric, you can open any of the complete versions from previous chapters instead.

OUTPUT

When you generate renderings, the onscreen rendering is not permanent. If you quit Revit, the rendering will be lost. You have two options for saving your rendering images. In the "Rendering" dialog, you can use the Save to Project button to create a raster image of the rendered output and add it to a branch on the Project Browser. Such views cannot be further modified, but they can be added to a sheet and printed with the project. To create an external image file, use the Export button. This will save the image to an image file on your hard drive. You can choose between popular formats like BMP, TIF, JPG, and PNG. Exporting renderings to a file is a more flexible alternative to saving the rendering to the project. This allows you to modify the image outside of Revit in any image editing program. If you need the rendering as part of the Revit document set, you can import the image file back into the project (Insert tab, Image button) and place on a sheet. For non-rendered presentation views, from the File menu, choose: **Export > Images and Animations > Image**. In the dialog that appears, you can set the size of the image in pixels horizontally or vertically. Figure between 200 and 300 pixels per printed inch for good printed output. If you are using the image onscreen in PowerPoint or similar, you can use a lower resolution.

ENTOURAGE

Before you finalize your output whether it is rendered, shaded or hidden line, it is a good idea to add some entourage to help give it a finishing touch. People and cars can help scene a sense of scale and trees and plants will go a long way toward softening up an image and making it appear less sterile. Plants are especially helpful in situations where you can see the edges of your site in an unnatural way. We often only have topography for the immediate site conditions, but when you generate a perspective, you will typically see well beyond these edges. Planting and Entourage families use RPC elements to represent people, shrubs, trees, cars and several other items. An RPC uses a collection of photographs that are applied to simple flat armatures. In hidden line and shaded view, they appear as simple freeform outlines. They also have 2D symbols for their plan representation. But when you use realistic shading or perform a rendering, the photographic content is swapped in. With a little strategic placement of these elements, you can really bring your rendering to life (see Figure 18.19).

FIGURE 18.19 *Entourage can make a huge difference in a presentation*

ANIMATIONS

Revit also can create simple walkthrough and solar study animations. We did a solar study back in Chapter 1. To create a walkthrough, start in a plan view, click the View tab and from the 3D View drop down button choose the Walkthrough tool. Click a point to start the walk and then continue clicking points to draw a path for the walkthrough. Click the Finish button to complete the path. A Walkthrough branch will appear on the project browser. Walkthrough views are animated camera views. They share many characteristics with other cameras and have additional controls to make them move along the walkthrough path. To play the walkthrough on screen, open the Walkthrough view from the Project Browser. Select the crop border on screen and then click the Edit Walkthrough button on the ribbon. On the Modify Cameras tab, you will have several video-style buttons to play, fast forward, and reverse the walkthrough. Finally, you can export the walkthrough to an AVI file using the: **Export > Images and Animations > Walkthrough** command on the File menu.

GOING FURTHER

Paul has also authored many video training courses on the LinkedIn Learning platform. Visit: **linkedin-learning.pxf.io/Aubin** and look for: **Revit: Rendering**†.

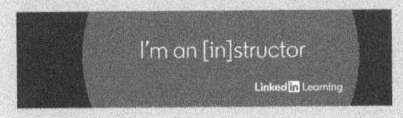

SUMMARY

- ☑ To generate renderings in Revit, continue working with a single model that you are already using for design and documentation.

- ☑ Consider the rendering process when building your model to help optimize it.

- ☑ Course level of detail, Visibility/Graphic overrides, Section boxes, and Worksets can all be effective ways to optimize model geometry before rendering.

- ☑ Rendering can be performed from any 3D view.

- ☑ Assign materials from the vast library provided with the software or create your own.

- ☑ Use daylight, artificial lighting, or both.

- ☑ Most lighting families include photometric lighting data giving renderings realistic lighting qualities.

- ☑ Render to one of several preset quality settings.

- ☑ Adjust exposure to fine-tune results.

- ☑ To create high quality renderings without tying up your computer, use Cloud Rendering!

- ☑ Photorealistic renderings are not the only way to create high quality presentations. Get familiar with the many graphical display options available such as anti-aliasing, shading, shadows, ambient shadows, sketchy lines, backgrounds and much more.

- ☑ Save an image file of your rendering for the greatest flexibility.

- ☑ Export presentation views from the File menu and even create animated solar studies and walkthroughs.

Appendix

The Appendix is provided as a PDF document and included with the dataset files. Refer to the "Download the Book Dataset" topic on page xi in the Preface for instructions on downloading and installing the book's dataset files and the accompanying Appendix.

The Appendix includes additional optional exercises to accompany many of the chapters throughout the book.

Endnotes

† Paul F Aubin has authored an extensive collection of Revit training videos available on the LinkedIn Learning platform. These are video courses that you can watch at your own pace. There are also exercise files included with each course so you can follow along. LinkedIn Learning is a subscription-based video training library with hundreds of courses available on a wide variety of topics. Your subscription gives you access to the entire library. Free trial memberships are available. Individual courses are also available for purchase "a la cart" if you prefer. To learn more about Paul's course offerings, visit: **https://linkedin-learning.pxf.io/Aubin**.

Disclosure: *The text in this book (including the link here) contains affiliate links and I will be compensated if you make a purchase after clicking on my links.*

‡ The author's website has many free resources available for download. These include many conference papers on various Revit and BIM topics. Visit: **paulaubin.com** and then click the Conferences link. There you will see several categories on the right-hand side of the page. Choose a category to see the papers and other downloads available. Many of the conference papers include accompanying datasets in downloadable zip files. You can use these sample files to follow along with the steps in the paper.

Index

Symbols

\<By Category\> 590
\<Hidden\> lines 589
\<Invisible lines\> 521
3D Model 39
   Considerations 758
3D View 11
   Default 241, 319, 364, 418

A

Activate Dimensions button 210, 212
Adjust Exposure 772
Align tool 17, 24, 285, 534, 554, 659
   to shift brick patterns 433
Ambient Light. See Lighting: Ambient
Ambient Shadows. See Shadows: Ambient
Annotation Crop Region 572
Anti-aliasing 329, 774
Appendix
   as PDF 779
Apply Area Rules 644
Arc
   Center-ends 486
   Start-End-Radius 21, 664
   Tangent End Arc 91
Area
   Create 643
Area and Volume Computations 657
Area Boundary Lines
   Create 642
Area Plan
   Create 641
   Understanding 641
Area Type
   Modify 644
Array 534
   Group and Associate 213, 534
   understanding 211
Array tool 209
Artificial Lighting 768
Artificial Lights button 771
Asset Browser 411, 764
Associate Family Parameter button 532, 539, 541
AutoCAD 410, 588, 674, 676, 681
Autodesk® Navisworks® 684
Autodesk® Revit® LT vii
Autodesk Materials library 760
Autodesk Subscription 698
Automatic Ceiling 648

B

Base Point 283
Batt Insulation 565
Beam
   Create 237
   Offsets 239
Beam System 239
BIM vii, viii, 1, 14, 39, 40, 41, 47, 68, 85, 547, 595, 631, 682
Book Dataset Files xi
Borrowing Elements. See Worksets:Element Borrowing
Brace
   Create 240
Brace tool 240
Break Line Components 565
Browser Organization 50, 198
   Custom 199
Building Information Modeling. See BIM
Building Pad
   Create 282

C

CAD vii, 201, 586, 587, 674, 682
   Explode 588
Camera
   Create 483
Cartoon Set
   Create 183
   Printing 201
Category 517
Ceiling 648, 650, 653
   by Sketch 653
   Create 648, 650, 652, 658
   Drywall 658
   Edit 654
   Edit Structure 650
   Edit type 658
   Fixtures 659
   Height Offset From Level 649, 655
   Move and Rotate Grids 651
   Properties 649
   Room Bounding 650
   Suspended Acoustical Tile 648
   Underpinned 655
   Understanding 647
   view in Section 656
Central File 684
   Create 687
   Detach 688, 704

782 | Index

Close Inactive Views 192, 596
Cloud Rendering 772
Color Fill Legend 57
Color Scheme
  Apply 636, 637, 644
  Custom 638, 640
Column 219, 220
  Architectural 219
    merging with walls 220
  Create 218
  Edit 223
  setting default height 221
  Structural 219
    Create 220
    place at Columns 221
    place on Grids 221
  Top Level 222, 224
Component 134, 544, 659, 661
  Create 134
Computer Aided Design. See CAD
Conceptual Massing Environment 709, 711, 725
  Add Edge 723
  Add Profile 724
  Add Split Line 399
  Chain Selection 714, 720
  Create Form 710, 712, 713, 727, 730, 732, 738, 745, 751
    Extrusion 713
    Loft 715
    Revolve 716
    Sweep 717
    Swept Blend 719
  Delete Edge 723
  Dissolve Form 724
  Edit Form 720
  Edit Profile 724

Sub-element controls 721
Constraint
  Top 15, 16
Constraints
  Reveal 122
Construction Specifications Institute (CSI) 137, 574
Coordinates
  Project 283
  Shared 283, 284, 287
Coordination Review 330, 331, 682
Copy and Paste 301
Copy/Monitor 295, 331, 682
  copy Grids and Levels 295
  copy Walls and Columns 297
Copy tool 97, 106, 209
Create New Local 693, 694
Create Similar tool 107
Crop Boundary. See Crop Region
Crop Region 174
  Adjust 231
  Annotation. See Annotation Crop Region
  hide/show 174
  resize 174
Crop Size 760
CSI format 574
ctrl key 73, 78
Curtain Grid
  Create 419, 446
Curtain Panel 726
  Assign 422
Curtain Panel Edge Conditions 745
Curtain System
  by face 735
Curtain Wall 415
  Corner Mullions 448
  Create 415

  Door panel 422
  Edit Mullion Joins 424
  Grid
    Add / Remove Segments 425
    Adjust curtain grid spacing 429
    Offset 443
  Mullion 423
    Create 423
    Custom Type 439, 441
    Understanding 439
  Pin and unpin elements 427
  Storefront 427
  Subdivide bays 446
  Type Properties 434
  Understanding 417
  using custom panels 447
  Walls as panels 425
Cut Plane 521, 662, 663
Cuttable 137
Cut tool 432

D

Datum 156
Defines slope 166, 362
delete key 121
Demolish tool 308
Design Options 392
  Create 393
  Main Model 393
  Option Set 393
  Presenting 396
  Primary 393
Detail
  Drafted 583
  Level of 60, 77
Detail Component 560
  Create 558

Index | 783

Detailing
    hybrid approach 555
Detail Level
    Medium 374, 388, 409
Detail Line 557, 664
Dimension
    Aligned 120
    Create 215, 568
    Edit 215
    Edit Witness Lines 455
    Label 511
    Lock 120
    make temporary dimension permanent 8
    Override Text Values 593
    Permanent 33, 119, 214
    Permanent, editing objects with 214
    Temporary 8, 82, 93, 99, 104, 115, 118, 125
    Toggle Equality 8
    Wall Faces 33
    Witness Line 95, 100
Disallow Join 416
Display Order 566
Dissolve 724, 725, 732, 734, 738
Divided Surface 736, 739
    apply custom panel 744, 747
    Create 739
    Pattern 740
    place by point (stitching) 747
Divide Path 750
Door 112, 116
    change size 118
    Create 9, 112, 182
    display in Reflected Ceiling 662
Door Tags
    Add 616
Drafting View 583

Draw
    Rectangle 24
Driven Point 742
Driving Point 738

E

Edit Assembly dialog 376
Edit Cut Profile 566, 580
Edit Family 483, 637
Edit Group button 268
Editing Request 698
Edit Label 488
Edit Profile 502, 724, 725, 734
Edit Type 75, 650
element IDs 454, 683
Elevation 665
    checkbox to add new 666
    Double-click to open 666
    elements beyond 591
    embellishments 589
Elevation Tag 171
    Load 173
Elevator
    Create 353, 358
Enable Worksharing 684
Enscape 756
Entourage 775
Equality Constraint 120
esc key 7, 78
Export 669
    Image 769, 775
    Setup 674
    to CAD 674
    XREF views onto sheets 676
Extend into wall (to core) 362, 385
Extrusion 139
    Create 483

Edit 478

F

Family 47
    access from Project Browser 469
    Annotation 49
    category 507
    Category
        Change 516
    Component 48, 463, 464
    Create Adaptive 750
    Create Conceptual Mass 728
    Create Elevation Tag 485
    Create model 489
    Create Type 474
    Curtain Panel 523
    Custom 477
    custom ganged window 538
    Duplicate 477
    Entourage 775
    flexing 513
    from DWG 542
    In-Place 113, 136, 464
    Load 11
    Loadable 49, 463, 709
    Load into project 734
    Massing Templates 710
    Nested 530
    New 481
    parametric 508
    Pattern-based Curtain Panel 741, 745
    Planting 775
    Profile 526, 551
    RPC 775
    Shared 612
    solid forms 491
    Strategy 468
    System 47, 49, 301, 414, 463

• Revit Essentials for Architecture •

Template 485, 660
Family Already Exists 221, 484, 745
Family Category and Parameters 711
Family Editor 467, 490, 709
   Preview Visibility 533
   Solid Form 478
   Void Form 478
Family Element Visibility Settings 543
Family Types 481, 513, 530, 531, 535, 538
Far Clip Offset 578
File
   ADSKLIB 410
   AutoCAD 586
   BMP 775
   CAD 588, 681
   DGN 67, 586, 681
   DWG 67, 542, 586, 681
   Export DWG 670
   Export FBX 670
   Export IFC 670
   Export Image 670
   HTML 641
   IES 768
   JPG 763, 775
   Keynote 574
   New 67
   Open 4, 67
   PAT 564
   PDF 183, 670, 673
   Photometric Web 768
   PNG 411, 763, 775
   RFA 67, 464, 481
   RTE 148
   RVT 681
   Save 9, 67
   Save a Group 272
   Save As 67
   Shared Parameter 637
   Template 94, 148, 465
   TIF 763, 775
File Format 682
File menu
   Close 155
Filled Region 486, 563, 590
   Custom 564
Finish Edit Mode 21, 24, 26
Flip Control 10, 18
Flip Wall Orientation 428
Floor
   Create 18, 233, 385, 735
   Create from walls 233
   Create new type 386
   from Mass 735
   Offset 387
Footing
   Create 243
Form
   Create 729
   Modify 738
   Solid 712
   Void 712, 730
Forms
   Model-based 725, 726, 728
   Modify with control handles 734
   Reference-based 725, 726, 727, 728, 741
   Solid 712
   Solid/Void parameter 732
   Surface 712
Formula 531
   Number of Hooks 535

G

Generic Models 137
Graded Region 306
Graphic Display Options 329, 592, 756, 766, 771, 774
Grid 205, 207
   adjust Extents 208
   Control Handles 207
   copy grids 209
   Create 206
   Numbering 208
   visible in other views 216
Group
   Add Attached Detail 262
   add Attached Detail to 271
   Add element 267
   Attached Detail 252, 254
   convert to Link 273, 294
   Create 249, 251, 260
   Create Attached Detail 262
   Create Instance 253, 270
   Detail 251
   drag Origin 253
   Duplicate 256
   Edit 213, 242, 255, 265, 267
   Excluded members 261
   in Project Browser 252
   insert 297
   Load 682
   Members
      Exclude 257
   Mirror 263
   Model 251
   Nested 269
   Restore All Excluded 265
   right-click in Project Browser 264
   Save 682
   Save to 295
   save to a file 272
   shown in schedules 261
Guide Grid 216

H

Create 216

Gutter 381

H

Halftone 622

Hide Column 608

Hide Crop Region 577

Hide in View 577, 589, 666

Hide reference/ work planes 672

Hide unreferenced view tags 672

Hiding Element

   in View 577

Highlight Boundaries 624

Highlight in Model 596

Home Screen 50, 64

Host element 464

Host parameter 517

I

Import CAD 542, 587

Import Line Weights dialog 587

Increase/Decrease Focal Length 760

In-Place

   Edit 364

Instance parameter 311, 601

Intent Stack 713

Interference Check 682, 683

Interference Report 683

Interior Elevation 665

Intersects tool 749

Isolated Foundation 243

Is Reference Line checkbox 738

Itemize every instance 603

J

Join Geometry 235, 344, 371, 387

Join tool 142, 554

Join/Unjoin Roof 371

K

Keyboard shortcuts 72

Key Name 614

Keynote 574

   Materials 590

Keynote Tag

   Understanding 576

Key Schedule

   Create 613

   Edit 614

L

Label 195, 488

   Create 195

   Edit 195

LAN 686

Layer

   Variable Thickness 402

Legend

   Color Fill 644

   Color Scheme 639

Legend Component 592

   Create 592

Legend View

   Create 592

Level 155

   Adjust 175

   and associated plan views 158

   Control handles 156

   Create 155, 269, 389, 729

   Create in 3D 711

   Edit 14

   Elevation Base 157

   Height 176

   Offsetting 159

   Renaming 160

Level of Detail 223

   Medium 27, 239

Level tool

   grayed out 155

Library 465

   Out-of-the-box 466

   Preferred 472

Lighting 756, 766, 771

   Ambient 766

   Groups 771

   photometric 768

Lighting Fixture

   Create 659

Lighting manufacturers 768

Lighting Schemes 766

Light Switches

   in Ceiling Plan 663

Lines

   Detail 46

   Model 46

Line weight 382, 560

Linework tool 589

Link

   Bind 274

   CAD 277, 278, 587

   CAD to current view only 278

   Convert to 295

   convert to group 274

   reload from 297

   Revit 283

   Understanding 276

LinkedIn Learning xii, 277, 373, 397, 645, 752, 777, 779

   Revit Templates 154

Link files 682

Links

   Manage 274

Index

Load Family 68, 113, 127, 220, 380, 447, 466, 472, 504, 561, 562, 584, 619, 659, 663

Load into Project 482, 522, 734, 744, 745

Load into Project and Close 196, 484, 488, 530, 536, 543, 747, 751

Load Profile button 552

Local Area Network. See LAN

Local File 684

   Create 693

     re-create regularly 695

Location 766

Location Line 6, 95

Location Weather and Site dialog 290, 293, 756

M

Make Elements Editable 699

Make this the central location after save 687

Make Workset Editable 699

Manage Images 635

Manage Links. See Links:Manage

Manage Links dialog 298

Mass Floors button 735

Match Type Properties 471

Material

   Assign 745

   Edit 377

Material asset

   Appearance 412

   Physical 412

   Thermal 412

Material Browser 409, 762

   Appearance tab 411

Materials 756, 760

   Appearance 763

   Assigning 761

   Create 762

   Graphics 763

   real world size 764

Material Takeoff

   Create 633

Measure tool 307

Microstation 676

Mirror 431, 497

Model Elements

   Annotation 557

Model Group

   Create 241

   Origin Control Handle 242

Model Line 725

Model Objects 43

Modify tool 7

Move 106, 285

Mullion tool 423

N

Navigation

   3D 55

Navigation Bar 12, 51, 483

Navisworks 410

NCS. See US National CAD Standard

New Type

   created from Project Browser 476

Nodes

   display 748

Normalized Curve Parameter 742

North

   Project 283, 292

   True 283, 292, 767

O

Object Selection 77

Object Styles 517, 622

Offset tool 96

Options Bar 6, 66, 76, 89, 113, 221

Options dialog 9, 68, 468, 694

Orbit 12, 130

Origin 283

Overhead Items 528

Override Graphics in View 382, 544, 623, 657

Overwrite the existing version 484

P

Padlock icon 479

Paint tool 761

Pan 12, 130

Parameter 505

   <Family Types> 540

   Create 510

   Custom 200, 637

   derived by formula 539

   Integer 535

   Number of Hooks 535

   Properties 511

   visibility 533

Parts

   Create 225

   Divide 226

   Intersecting References 226

   Show 227

   Understanding 225

Paste

   Aligned 227

     to Current View 659

     to Selected Levels 228, 234, 315

Pattern

   Custom 564

PBR Materials 760

   Base Materials. See PBR Materials:Templates

Replacing with 764
Templates 763
PDF
  multi-sheet 674
  plot to 203
Phase 362
  Assign Elements 108
  Created 108
  Demolish a stair 306
  Demolished 108
  Edit 305
Phase Filter 110, 111, 114, 329
  Show All 144
Phase Status 111
Phasing 108
  Properties 109
Photorealistic Rendering 756
Photoshop 764
Pick Lines 103, 140, 211, 230, 367, 502, 654, 733, 738
Pick Walls 233, 362, 385, 653, 655
Place Request 698
Place Rooms Automatically 624, 625
Place Symbol tool 488
Plot
  PDF 34
Point Element tool 718
Pre-highlight 54
Presentation Options 756
Printing 669
Print/Plot 672
  Selected views/sheets 673
Print Setup 670, 675
  Save 671
Processors
  multi-core x
Profile

<By Sketch> 499
Project
  Create 148
Project Base Point 287, 288
  clipped/unclipped 291
Project Browser 13, 32, 50, 66, 73, 170, 198, 252, 256, 270, 274, 469
  Interior Elevations branch 665
  Revit Links branch 274
  Sheets branch 199
Project Information
  Edit 197
Project Location 767
Project Units command 150
Properties palette 5, 15, 60, 74, 89, 99, 111, 113, 227

Q

QAT. See Quick Access Toolbar
Quick Access Toolbar 66, 68

R

Railing 302
  add Supports 352
  Baluster placement 325
  create by sketch 357
  create extension 351
  Create Type 322
  customize type 325
  Edit 321, 349
  edit Extension 324
  Edit Path 25
  Handrail 322
  non-continuous rail 322
  Posts 327
  Top Rail 322
RAM x
Ramp

Create 353
Ramp tool 353
Reference Line 726, 727
  draw on Reference Point 743
Reference other View 585, 586
Reference Plane 138, 479, 710
  Create 138, 493, 497, 508, 525
  Create in 3D 711
  Name 497, 508
Reference Point 718, 720, 742, 746, 750
  Hosted to Reference Line 742
Render 757, 770, 772
  Background 771
  Illuminance 773
  Output Settings 770
  Panorama 773
  Quality 770
Render Gallery button 773
Rendering dialog 770
Rendering Output 775
Rendering Settings 757
Renumbering 618
Repeating Detail Element 562
  Duplicate 562
Repeat tool 748, 750, 751
Report
  Export 640
Reset Temporary Hide/Isolate 590
Resize Column 608
Reveal
  Create 550
Reveal Constraints. See Constraints:Reveal
Reveal Hidden Elements 589
Revisions 678
Revit Elements 41

788 | Index

Annotation 44, 569
Component 42
Datum 44, 205, 216
Detail 45, 251
Host 42
Model 42, 47, 251, 463, 647
Views 45
View-specific 463
Revit implementation 465
Revit link 273
Revit LT 682. See Autodesk Revit LT
    enable Design Options 393
    Parts not available 225
    shared coordinates not available 287
Ribbon 68
    Contextual 69
    Panels 69
    Tools 71
    View State 70
Roof 166
    by Extrusion 20
    by face 735
    by Footprint 166, 369
    Create 20, 166, 362
    Create new type 376
    Edit 372
    Fascia 379
    Overhang 374
    Rafter Cut 374
    Shape Editing 398
Roof Plan View 372
Room 624, 625, 626
    Bounding 275, 627
    Create 625
    in Groups 275
    Reference 627
    Understanding 624

Room Names
    Edit 628
Room Separation Line tool 626
Room Tag
    Copy 659
    Leader 629
    outside of its room boundaries 629
Rotate 284, 660
    with copy option 307

S

Scale 58
Schedule
    Add fields 180
    Appearance 607, 609
    Area 645
    conditional formatting 633
    Count field 604
    Create 27, 180, 598
    display images in 635
    Duplicate 604
    Edit 596, 629
    edit parameters from the model 612
    Export Data 634
    Filter 606
    Footers 605
    Formatting 607
    from other projects 181
    Furniture reporting Rooms 631
    Grand Totals 605
    Grouping 603
    Headers 599, 605
    Modify Elements 28
    Open 596
    reflecting model changes 611
    Ribbon formatting 608
    Room 629
    Room Key 630

    select a category 598
    Sorting 597, 602
    Split 610
    Stripe Rows 599
    use for Selection 596
    use to edit the model 600
    using to query data 631
    Working view 604
Schedule Keys 613
Schedule Properties
    add Fields 598
Scope Box 176
    Create 677
Section 13, 151
    Create 177
    Open 179
    unreferenced 586
Select available fields from 631
Select by ID 683
Selection
    all Instances 224, 225, 239, 241, 470, 616, 636, 659
    Crossing 92
    Filter 79, 132, 241, 418
    pinned elements 543
    right-click 79
    Toggles 81
    Window 92
    with tab key 269
Selection Box 78
    Crossing 78
    Window 78
Select Profile 499
Set Work Plane 731
Shadows 766, 774
    Ambient 329, 766, 774
Shaft

• The Aubin Academy •

Edit 342
Shaft Opening
   Create 235
Shared Coordinates
   Acquire 290
   Exporting 675
   linking by 293
Shared Location
   Saving 289
Shared Parameters tool 637
Sharing work with others 681
Sheet
   Activate View 31
   add Drafting View 588
   add Elevations to 666
   add Schedule to 608
   Add View to 31
   Cover 196
   Create 30, 183, 581
   Create placeholder 188
Sheet Index. See Sheet List
Sheet Issues/Revisions 678
Sheet List
   Create 186
   Sort 200
Sheet view 30
shift key 73, 78
Show Mass 711
Show Work Plane 716
Silhouettes 592, 775
Sketch Ceiling button 653, 655
Sketch mode 18
Sketch Path 502
Sketchy Lines 329, 774
Skylight
   Create 383

Slab Foundation 243
Slope Arrows 395
Sloped Glazing 415
Snaps 83
   Endpoint 6
Solar Study 34
   analemma 35
Solid Form
   Create Blend 494
   Create Extrusion 491, 496, 509, 526
   Create Revolve 500, 529
   Create Sweep 502, 527
   Create Swept Blend 497
spacebar 63
   to flip 117
   to rotate 734
spacebar to rotate 471
Spline
   Create 750
Spline Through Points 737, 738
Split Element tool 105
Split Face tool 761
Spot Slope tool 402
Stacked Wall
   adding wall types to 453
   Create Type 453
   Understanding 451
Stair
   Add Railing automatically 304
   Adjust display 340
   component-based 301
   Components 302
   Create 23, 302, 310, 335
   Create U-shaped egress 333
   custom shape 355
   Cut plane 341
   Display properties 315

Edit 308, 346
Edit type 313
Landing 302, 336
Multistory 337
Multistory, Edit 338
New type 312
Number of Risers 313
Run 302, 336
Support 302
Support types 313
Starting View 198
Status Bar 76
Steel-shapes
   industry standard sizes 220
Steering Wheel 12, 51, 53, 55, 320
Steering Wheels 475
Step Footing
   Create 246
Structural Framing 237
Subcategory 517, 528
Sun Path 34, 768
Sun Settings 756, 766, 768
Surface Representation panel 744, 748
Surface Transparency 657
Survey Point 287, 288
   clipped/unclipped 291
Symbolic Line 519, 520
Synchronize with Central 68, 692, 695, 699, 700

T

tab key 77, 80
   Chain Selection 81
   Dimensioning 80
   Pre-highlight 80
Tag
   No tag Loaded 135

Index

on Placement 10
other Views 631
with Leader 590, 617
Tag All Not Tagged 617
Tag by Category tool 590
Tag on Placement 113, 624
Tags
   Loaded 619
   Understanding 616
Template
   Commercial 153
   Construction 152
   Create your own 154
   default 149
   None 154
   Residential 153
Temporary Hide/Isolate 77, 241, 246, 320, 417, 510, 589, 745
   Apply to view 329
Text
   Model 46
Text Notes 570
   Add Leaders 573
   Create 571
   Custom Type 570
   leader 570
Text tool 194
Text Type
   Duplicate 194
Tile Windows 596
Title bar
   Move 32
Title block 184
   Custom 193
Title on Sheet 185, 585
Tooltips 53, 72
Toposurface 163

Create 162
Create from CAD 281
display in elevation 170
Edit 305
Place Point tool 163
Transfer Project Standards 301, 376, 671
Transparency 774
Trim/Extend 102, 104, 107, 141, 368, 654
Type
   Duplicate 122
Type Catalog 220, 559
Type Parameter 601
Type Properties 173, 474
Type Selector 7, 75, 116, 173, 223, 257, 368, 415, 658
Typical design conditions
   create with groups 250

U

U and V coordinates 739
Underlay 5, 238
   Orientation 238
Units
   AutoCAD 150
   imperial ix, 63
   metric ix, 63
Unlock Profiles 726
Update to Face 736
Use Global Settings 692
US National CAD Standard 173, 486
UV grid 740

V

Versions
   New xi
View

3D 129, 756, 759
Activate 59
Activate View 198
add to sheet 582
Camera 759
Change Scale 557
Create a Callout 555
Create a working view 418
create Enlarged View 353
create existing conditions 309
Create Section 314
Deactivate 60
Default 3D 759
Dependent 676
Detail 60
Drafting 201, 583
Duplicate 57, 329, 362, 620, 636
Duplicate as Dependent 676
Elevation 170
Furniture Plan 620
Hide in 417
Interior Elevation 665
Legend 592
match line 676
Scale 569
Schedule 179
Section 177
Sheet 183
View Break 567
View Control Bar 27, 76, 223, 329
ViewCube 12, 51, 55, 320, 427, 475, 756, 759, 760
   Orient to View 419
   save view 329
View Navigation 12
View Range 244, 372, 398
Views
   aligning on sheets 190

• The Aubin Academy •

View/Sheet Set 673

Views on sheets

   aligning with guide grids 216

View Template 74, 334, 392, 758, 759

   Apply 161

View Title

   adjusting 191

Visibility/Graphic Overrides 245, 315, 334, 523, 621, 662, 692, 758

   Design Options in 396

Visibility Settings button 543

Visual Style 131

   Consistent Colors 27

   Realistic 27, 769, 774

   Shaded 27, 165

Void

   Create 480

   Cutting Solid 480

Void form 140

W

Walkthrough Animation 776

Wall

   Attach Top/Base 22, 656

   attach to Roof 365, 392

   Base Extension 553

   by face 735

   Constrain to levels 164

   convert to Structural 231

   create 6

   Create 89

   Create New Type 26

   Edit Profile 246, 367, 449

   Existing 108

   Height 167

   Opening 126

   Rectangular 92

   Return 412

   Slanted 168

   Structural 229

   Top Constraint 133

   Top Offset 167

   underpinned 657

   unlock layers 553

   Wrap 413

Wall Foundation 243

Wall Joins 232

   Edit 232

Wall Sweep 456, 457

   instance sweep 457

   integral to wall type 456

Wall tool 415

Wall Type

   Create 406

   Edit Structure 407

   Layer Functions 407

   Layers 407

   using Copy and Paste to import 452

Warning 243, 251, 258, 445, 454, 629, 648, 703, 746

   Review Warnings 259

Wide Area Network. See WAN

Window 124

   Create 10, 124, 432

   Modify 16

Window Tile 319

Wiring

   using circuits and wires 664

   using Detail Lines 664

Work Plane 20, 226, 390, 480, 493, 710, 714, 737, 751

   Edit 493

   on surface 730

   Set 495, 498

   Set tool 731

Worksets 684, 703

   Add new element 699

   and Default 3D View 701

   Borrowing 698

   Close 692

   Create 689

   Editable 688, 698

   Editable/Not Editable 698

   Enable 684, 686

   for Links 690, 704

   Open/Close 698

   Reassigning 690

   Relinquish 692, 701

   Reload Latest 700

   Specify on open 694

   Tooltips 691

   Understanding 684, 685

   User-Created 685

   username 694

   Visibility 692

   Visible in all views 689

Worksets dialog 688

Worksharing Display 701

Worksharing Monitor tool 698

Workstations x

X

X-Ray 721, 724, 725, 726, 734, 738, 745

Z

Zoom 12, 51, 130

   All to Fit 132, 490, 492

   In Region 15, 52, 553

   Shortcuts 52

   to Fit 52

   to Sheet Size 52, 382

Lightning Source UK Ltd.
Milton Keynes UK
UKHW051309220722
406233UK00009B/856